# MyVirtualChild

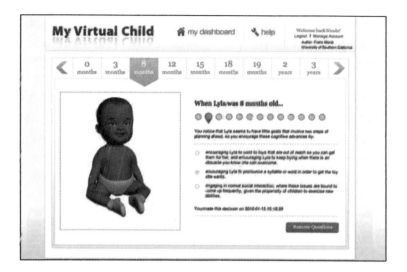

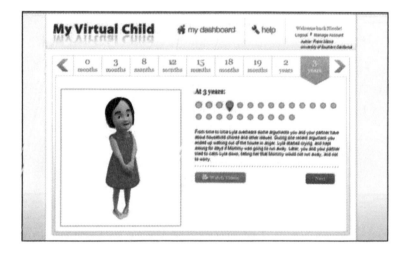

# Why Do You Need This New Edition?

- **New Chapter Self-Tests at the End of the Book.** New to this edition, for each chapter we have added a 25-question multiple-choice practice test that will help you prepare for class, quizzes, and exams. Answers to all questions can be found at the back of the book.

- **New *Technology and the Developing Child* Feature Boxes.** Each chapter includes a new boxed discussion exploring technology's impact on child development. An emphasis on exciting and pioneering research encourages you to think about both the potential negatives and positives associated with growing up in a digital age, from the rise of cyberbullying to advances in fetal-maternal medicine.

- **New Learning Objectives Tied to Feature Boxes.** Improving on the learning system that helps you ORGANIZE and RETAIN chapter material as you read, we have added Learning Objectives to feature boxes to help you connect feature content to the learning goals of each section and chapter. As with the rest of the Learning Objectives, you will find them in the margins and in the Summary of each chapter so that you can structure your review.

- **New In-Text References to MyDevelopmentLab Resources.** Icons integrated throughout the text direct you to expanded, Web-based topics, giving you access to extra information, videos, and simulations. The icons offer only a highlight of the materials available at MyDevelopmentLab; many more resources are available.

- **New Expanded Coverage.** In addition to hundreds of new research citations, there is a range of new and expanded topics in this edition, including an increased emphasis on the relationship between technology and child development, more examples of relevant cross-cultural studies, and increased coverage of how cultural factors and variations impact the developing child.

# THE
# DEVELOPING CHILD

## THIRTEENTH EDITION

**Denise Boyd**
*Houston Community College*

**Helen Bee**

**PEARSON**

Boston  Columbus  Indianapolis  New York  San Francisco  Upper Saddle River
Amsterdam  Cape Town  Dubai  London  Madrid  Milan  Munich  Paris  Montreal  Toronto
Delhi  Mexico City  Sao Paulo  Sydney  Hong Kong  Seoul  Singapore  Taipei  Tokyo

Editorial Director: Craig Campanella
Editor in Chief: Jessica Mosher
Executive Editor: Jeff Marshall
Editorial Assistant: Michael Rosen
Director of Development: Sharon Geary
Senior Development Editor: Jessica Carlisle
Director of Marketing: Brandy Dawson
Senior Marketing Manager: Nicole Kunzmann
Marketing Assistant: Jessica Warren
Senior Managing Editor: Maureen Richardson
Senior Project Manager/Liaison: Harriet Tellem
Operations Supervisor: Mary Fischer

Operations Specialist: Diane Peirano
Art Director, Cover: Leslie Osher
Text and Cover Designer: Jill Lehan Yutkowitz
Cover Art: © Dejan Ristovski/iStockphoto
Media Director: Brian Hyland
Media Editor, Editorial: Peter Sabatini
Media Editor, Production: Caitlin Smith
Full-Service Project Management: Chitra Ganesan/PreMediaGlobal
Composition: PreMediaGlobal
Printer/Binder: Quad Graphics
Cover Printer: Lehigh–Phoenix Color

*This book is dedicated to my two favorite growing children, Mackenzie and Madeleine.*

Credits and acknowledgments borrowed from other sources and reproduced, with permission, in this textbook appear on pages 546–548.

**Library of Congress Cataloging-in-Publication Data**
Bee, Helen L.,
    The developing child / Helen Bee, Denise Boyd. — 13th ed.
        p. cm.
    Includes bibliographical references and index.
    ISBN-13: 978-0-205-25602-0
    ISBN-10: 0-205-25602-3
    1. Child psychology—Textbooks. 2. Child development—Textbooks.
    I. Boyd, Denise Roberts. II. Title.
    BF721.B336 2013
    155.4—dc23

                                        2011042943

10 9 8 7 6 5 4 3 2 1

Student Edition:
ISBN 10: 0-205-25602-3
ISBN 13: 978-0-205-25602-0

Instructor's Review Edition:
ISBN 10: 0-205-25605-8
ISBN 13: 978-0-205-25605-1

Ála Carte
ISBN 10: 0-205-25635-X
ISBN 13: 978-0-205-25635-8

# BRIEF CONTENTS

# CONTENTS

# FEATURES

Hello, and welcome to the study of a fascinating subject—children and their development. Welcome, too, to the adventure of science. From the very first edition of this book, one of Helen Bee's goals has been to convey a sense of excitement about scientific inquiry. We hope that each of you gains some feeling for the way psychologists think, the kinds of questions they ask, and the ways they go about trying to answer those questions. We also want you to gain some sense of the theoretical and intellectual ferment that is part of any science. Think of psychology as a kind of detective story: Psychologists discover clues after hard, often painstaking work; they make guesses or hypotheses; and then they search for new clues to check on those hypotheses.

Of course, we also want you to come away from reading this book with a firm foundation of knowledge in the field. Although there is much that developmental psychologists do not yet know or understand, a great many facts and observations have accumulated. These facts and observations will be of help to you professionally if you are planning (or are already in) a career that involves working with children, such as teaching, nursing, social work, medicine, or psychology; the information will also be useful to you as a parent, now or in the future. We hope you enjoy the reading as much as we have enjoyed the writing.

## How to Work with This Textbook

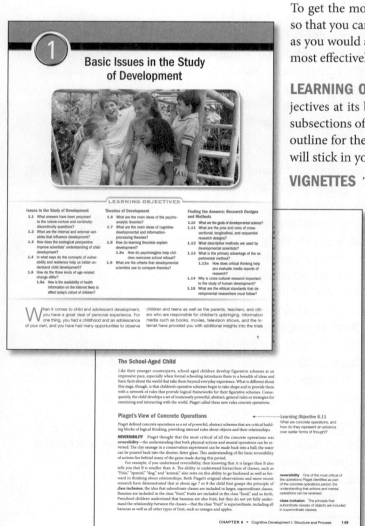

To get the most out of any textbook, you should think of yourself as working with it so that you can understand and remember the information in it, rather than reading it as you would a magazine, a newspaper article, or a novel. To work with your textbook most effectively, take advantage of its structural and pedagogical features.

**LEARNING OBJECTIVES** Before you read each chapter, read over the Learning Objectives at its beginning. Each of these Learning Objectives is paired with one of the subsections of the chapter, or with a chapter feature box, so these questions provide an outline for the material you should know by the end of the chapter. More information will stick in your mind if you have an idea of what to expect.

**VIGNETTES** The story at the beginning of each chapter will engage your interest in the major topics and themes.

**HEADINGS AND SUBHEADINGS** Think of the headings and their subheadings as a way of dividing the information that follows them into categories. The information in each major section and subsection is linked to the heading and subheading under which it is found. Each of the Learning Objectives listed at the beginning of the chapter is repeated next to its corresponding subheading, to help you keep in mind the big picture. Thinking of the material in this way creates a kind of information network in your mind that will make it easier to recall the material when you are tested. Structuring your notes to correspond to these headings and Learning Objectives will help even more. To have the best chance of creating the information network, stop reading between major sections, reflect back on what you have read, and review your written notes.

**MARGIN GLOSSARY** Key terms are defined in the margins. As you come to each boldfaced term in the text, stop and read its definition in the margin. Then go back and reread the sentence that introduced the key term. Reading over the key terms in the margins just before you take an exam can also be a helpful review strategy if you have thoroughly studied the material in which the terms are introduced.

**THINK CRITICALLY QUESTIONS** Think Critically questions encourage you to relate material in the book to your own experiences. They can also help you remember the text because linking new information to things you already know is a highly effective memory strategy.

**CONDUCT YOUR OWN RESEARCH** Each chapter ends with a feature that encourages you to replicate the findings of a developmental study in an informal way or find out more about a specific topic.

**SUMMARY** Looking over the chapter summary can also help you assess how much information you remember. The summaries are organized by the same Learning Objective questions presented at the beginning of the chapter.

**KEY TERMS** Key terms are listed alphabetically at the end of each chapter in addition to being defined in the margins. When you finish a chapter, try to recall the definition of each term. A page number is listed for each term, so you can easily look back if you can't remember a definition.

**SELF-TESTS** A 25-question multiple choice test for each chapter is at the end of the book. Use these chapter tests to assess your knowledge and prepare for quizzes and exams.

At this point, the task of understanding and remembering the information in a developmental psychology textbook may seem overwhelming. However, when you finish reading this book, you will have a better understanding of both yourself and other people. So, the benefit you will derive from all your hard work will be well worth it.

*Denise Boyd*

One of the greatest challenges in updating a text is being open to new theories and concepts and willing to rethink and reorganize whole chapters, rather than sticking reflexively (or defensively) to old rubrics. In addition, revising sometimes includes eliminating favorite examples that are out of date and searching for new metaphors that will speak to current students. Perhaps hardest of all, one must cut as well as add material. Over many editions, the changes accumulate; if you were to compare this edition to the first edition, published in 1975, you would find almost no common sentences, let alone common paragraphs. Still, my goal was to retain most of the threads running from the first through the eleventh editions that made Helen Bee's approach to development unique. In particular, four central goals have guided the writing of *The Developing Child*:

- To actively engage the student in as many ways as possible.
- To find that difficult but essential balance among theory, research, and practical application.
- To present the most current thinking and research.
- To maintain a strong emphasis on culture.

## New to the Thirteenth Edition

Following are some chapter highlights of the new edition.

### Chapter 1

- A new chapter-opening vignette on commonly held beliefs about development that introduces the idea of child development as a science
- A new *Technology and the Developing Child* topic, "Cohort Effects of Health Information on the Internet"

### Chapter 2

- A new chapter-opening vignette on culturally-specific birth preparations introduces the recent medical and technological advances that have made childbirth and infancy safer around the world
- Updated discussion on early studies that suggested that maternal cocaine use led to developmental problems in children
- Coverage of the HIV/AIDs epidemic and pregnancy in Africa
- A new *Technology and the Developing Child* topic, "High-Tech Monitoring for High-Risk Pregnancies"

### Chapter 3

- New topics include cross-cultural research on the incidence of cesarean sections, cultural differences in responding to infant sleep patterns, and cultural practices and motor development
- New figure detailing the Back to Sleep Campaign
- A new *Technology and the Developing Child* topic, "Helping Preterm Infants Learn to Suck"

### Chapter 4

- Topics on which coverage has been expanded and updated include left-handedness, a discussion of precocious puberty, rates of sexual activity for U.S. high school students, the variation of sexual experience across ethnic groups, cross-cultural perspectives on sexual activity in the teen years, and updates on accidents and accidental death among adolescents

- New figure summarizing teen sexual activity across cultures
- A new *Technology and the Developing Child* topic, "Repetitive Strain Injury (RSI) of the Hand in Children and Teens"

## Chapter 5

- A new *Technology and the Developing Child* topic, "Cochlear Implants and Speech Development"

## Chapter 6

- New discussion of egocentrism as a lifelong theme of cognitive development.
- A new *Technology and The Developing Child* topic, "What Infants Learn from Television"

## Chapter 7

- New chapter opening vignette about a highly gifted child who was thought to have autistic disorder in early childhood
- New topics covered include the relationship between ethnic groups and IQ scores
- A new *Technology and the Developing Child* topic, "The Digital Divide and Cognitive Test Scores"

## Chapter 8

- Updated topics include new studies on infant-directed speech as a tool that infants use in language development
- A new *Technology and the Developing Child* topic, "Handwriting and Brain Development"

## Chapter 9

- New chapter opening vignette about an infant who displays behavior that is associated with the development of an inhibited temperament in early childhood
- A new *Technology and the Developing Child* topic, "Facebook and the Big 5"

## Chapter 10

- A new *Technology and the Developing Child* topic, "Identity Play in Virtual Environments"
- New discussion of culture and self descriptions

## Chapter 11

- New coverage of attachment and adoption
- New discussion of sex differences in parenting across cultures
- New discussion of culture, personality, and social status
- Updated discussion of aggression within cliques
- New discussion of heterosexual and homosexual relationships across cultures
- New coverage of bullies and victims
- New *Thinking About Research* topic, "The Resource Dilution Hypothesis"
- New *Technology and the Developing Child* topic, "Cyberbullying"

## Chapter 12

- Updated vignette about Thomas Lickona's approach to character education
- New *Technology and the Developing Child* topic, "Cinema Therapy for Children"

## Chapter 13

- Updated discussion of parental employment.
- *New Technology and the Developing Child* topic, "Expanding the Microsystem with Digital Communication.
- New figure on two-parent families around the world

## Chapter 14

- Revised and updated sections include those on nonparental care, television, and video games
- New *Technology and the Developing Child* topic "Computers in the Preschool Classroom"
- New figure on homeschooling
- New figure on poverty and age

## Chapter 15

- A new chapter-opening vignette examines non-normative developmental paths and how they combine with expected developmental changes, including the resulting frustrations and challenges
- A new *Technology and the Developing Child* topic, "Suicide and Social Networking"
- Updated discussion of culture, age, gender, and ethnicity
- Revised and updated section on eating disorders

## Chapter Self-Tests

- 15 New Chapter Tests

# Pedagogy

The Thirteenth Edition of *The Developing Child* includes several important pedagogical features.

**Learning Objectives** Learning Objectives, each paired with one of the subsections of the chapter, are introduced on the first page of the chapter. The Learning Objectives reappear in the margin next to the corresponding chapter subsection and again in the end-of-chapter summary. New feature box learning objectives appear next to the corresponding feature, and are also covered in the chapter summary. The Learning Objectives help students organize and retain the material as they read the textbook by informing them of the key information they are expected to take away from that section of the chapter, and the feature-specific learning objectives encourage them to apply chapter themes and concepts to boxed content. The Learning Objectives help you, the instructor, assess student learning outcomes because they are tied to the test items in the accompanying *Test Bank*.

**Vignettes** Each chapter begins with a compelling vignette which engages readers' interest in the chapter topic.

**Margin Glossary** All boldfaced terms in the text are defined in the margin as well as in a glossary at the end of the book.

**Think Critically Questions** The critical thinking questions at the end of the chapter encourage students to relate information in the text to their personal experiences.

**Conduct Your Own Research** Each chapter ends with a feature that gives readers instructions for either informally replicating a developmental study's findings or for finding out more about a specific topic.

**Summary** Summaries are organized by major chapter headings and include bulleted entries summarizing the information that follows each subheading.

**Developmental Science in the Real World** Every chapter includes a boxed discussion of the application of scientific knowledge to a practical question. The intent of these discussions is to show students not only that it is possible to study applied questions with scientific methods but also that all the theory and research they are reading about has some relevance to their own lives. To facilitate this goal, each *Developmental Science in the Real World* box begins with a brief vignette about a parenting issue and ends with questions for reflection designed to encourage readers to apply ideas to issues.

**Thinking about Research** Every chapter includes a boxed discussion of a particularly important study or series of studies. Each *Thinking about Research* box ends with two questions for critical analysis that encourage readers to critically evaluate the findings presented in the box.

**Technology and the Developing Child** Today's developing child is growing up in a technologically infused world that is remarkably different from that of earlier generations. With an emphasis on emerging research, the new *Technology and the Developing Child* boxes examine the effect of this new environment on child development. Topics include the effects of well-established technologies such as television, as well as issues surrounding more recent developments like social networking. The discussion ends with two questions that encourage readers to use their Internet research skills to think more deeply about the topic.

**Chapter Self-Tests** Practice tests for each chapter appear at the end of the book. Each offers 25 multiple-choice practice test questions and their answers to help students evaluate their knowledge and prepare for exams and quizzes.

## Teaching and Learning Package

**Test Bank** Amy Malkus of East Tennessee State University has provided an extensively updated Test Bank containing over 1,800 thoroughly reviewed questions, including multiple choice, completion (fill in the blank), and critical essays. Test items have also been written to assess student comprehension of select videos, simulations, and other multimedia features within MyDevelopmentLab, for instructors who wish to make MyDevelopmentLab a central component of their course. Every test item is correlated with the Learning Objectives introduced in the textbook. All questions are accompanied by the correct answer, a page reference, a difficulty ranking, and a question-type designation. The *Test Bank* is also available in **Pearson MyTest**, a powerful assessment generation program that helps instructors easily create and print quizzes and exams. Questions and tests can be authored on-line, allowing instructors ultimate flexibility and the ability to efficiently manage assessments anytime, anywhere. For more information, go to www.PearsonMyTest.com.

**Instructor's Manual** The *Instructor's Manual*, prepared by Arthur McGovern of Nichols College, is a wonderful tool for classroom preparation and management. The easy-to-find format includes detailed cross-references to features in the *Instructor's Manual*, as well as to other print and media supplements and outside teaching resources. The *Instructor's Manual* is both comprehensive and extensive. Each chapter includes the following resources:

- An At-a-Glance Grid, with detailed pedagogical information, references to both print and media supplements for each concept, and a chapter overview.
- An Integrated Teaching Outline, with summaries of key concepts.
- List of key terms.
- Lecture material, including outlines and suggested discussion topics, with references to pertinent activities in the *Instructor's Manual* and videos from the Pearson video library.
- Updated classroom activities, demonstrations suggested readings, and out of class projects

- An updated list of video, media, print, and Web resources.
- The appendix includes a compilation of handouts and video offerings.

**PowerPoint™ Presentation**   Pauline Zeece of The University of Nebraska-Lincoln has prepared a dynamic PowerPoint presentation that is an exciting interactive tool for use in the classroom. Each chapter includes the following:

- Key points covered in the textbook.
- Images from the textbook, with demonstrations.
- Embedded videos

Video-embedded PowerPoint slides are available on DVD (ISBN: 0-205-85278-5) that allow instructors to seamlessly integrate videos into their lectures without the need for Internet access. Lecture-only PowerPoint slides are available on our Instructor's Resource Center for your convenience (www.pearsonhighered.com/IRC). Please contact your Pearson representative if you do not have access to the Instructor's Resource Center.

**Classroom Response System (CRS)**   Prepared by Pauline Zeece of the University of Nebraska-Lincoln, the Classroom Response System (CRS) facilitates class participation in lectures as well as a method of measurement of student comprehension. CRS also enables student polling and in-class quizzes. CRS is highly effective in engaging students with class lectures, in addition to adding an element of excitement to the classroom. Simply, CRS is a technology that allows professors to ask questions to their students through text-specific PowerPoints provided by Pearson. Students reply using handheld transmitters called clickers that capture and immediately display student responses. These responses are saved in the system grade book and/or can later be downloaded to either a Blackboard or WebCT grade book for assessment purposes. These are available for download on the Instructor's Resource Center at www.pearsonhighered.com.

**MyDevelopmentLab**   MyDevelopmentLab combines proven learning applications with powerful assessment to engage students, assess their learning, and help them succeed.

- **An individualized study plan for each student** based on performance on chapter pre-tests, this tool helps students focus on the specific topics where they need the most support. The personalized study plan arranges content from less complex thinking, such as remembering and understanding—to more complex critical thinking skills—such as applying and analyzing—based on Bloom's taxonomy. Every level of the study plan provides a formative assessment quiz.
- **MyVirtualChild** is an interactive simulation that allows students to play the role of a parent and rare their own virtual child. By making decisions about specific scenarios, students can raise their children from birth to age 18 and learn firsthand how their own decisions and other parenting actions affect their child over time.
- **Media Assignments for each chapter** —including videos with assignable questions—feed directly into the grade book, enabling instructors to track student progress automatically.
- **The Pearson eText** lets student access their textbook anytime and anywhere, and anyway they want, including listening online.
- **The MyDevelopmentLab Question Library** provides over 1,800 test items in the form of Pre-Tests, Post-Tests, and Chapter Exams. These questions are parallel forms of questions found in the instructor test bank, ensuring that students using MyDevelopmentLab for review and practice will find their tests to be of similar tone and difficulty, while protecting the integrity of the instructor test bank.
- **ClassPrep** is available for instructors within MyDevelopmentLab. This exciting new instructor resource makes lecture preparation easier and less time consuming. ClassPrep collects the very best class preparation resources—art and figures from our leading texts, videos, lecture activities, classroom activities, demonstrations, and much more—in one convenient on destination. Search through ClassPrep's extensive database of tools by content topic or by content type; select resources appropriate for your lecture, many of which can be downloaded directly; or build your own folder of resources and present from within ClassPrep.

**Pearson Video Resources** Quality videos make the text content come to life in class and engage students in the learning experience by helping them truly contextualize the material they are learning. We have been filming videos in the continental United States as well as around the world to help bring the science of development to life. Following are some of our video resources (please contact your Pearson representative to obtain these):

- **MyDevelopmentLab Cross-Cultural Videos** Filmed on location both in the United States and internationally, these videos show similarities and differences in development across cultures throughout the lifespan.
- **Observation Videos for Lifespan Development** (ISBN: 0-205-87909-8) This DVD contains videos for all stages of lifespan development, including: Infancy, Preschool, Middle Childhood, Adolescence, Early Adulthood, Middle Adulthood, and Late Adulthood

**Accessing All Resources** For a list of all student resources available with *The Developing Child, Thirteenth Edition,* go to www.mypearsonstore.com, enter the text ISBN (0-205-25602-3) and check out the "Everything that Goes With it" section under the book cover.

For access to all of the Instructor supplements for *The Developing Child, Thirteenth Edition,* go to www.pearsonhighered.com/irc and follow the directions to register (or log in if you already have a Pearson user name and password to access the catalog).

You can request hard copies of the supplements through the Pearson sales representative. If you do not know your sales representative, go to www.pearsonhighered.com/replocator and follow the directions. For technical support for any of your Pearson products, you and your students can contact http://247.pearsoned.com/

# ACKNOWLEDGMENTS

Thanks to the wonderful people at Pearson who participated in the development and completion of this project. In addition, I am grateful to all of the reviewers who took time to comment on this and previous editions of *The Developing Child*. The following people provided invaluable feedback through their reviews for the Thirteenth Edition:

Janet Arndt, *Gordon College*
Stephanie Babb, *University of Houston-Downtown*
Patricia Bellas, *Irvine Valley College*
Nicole Bragg, *Mt. Hood Community College*
Alaina Brenick, *University of Maryland*
Jennifer Brennom, *Kirkwood Community College*
Barbara Briscoe, *Leeward Community College*
Sharon Carter, *Davidson County Community College*
Elaine Cassel, *Lord Fairfax Community College*
Michelle Clark, *Christopher Newport University*
Wanda Clark, *South Plains College*
Carrie Dale, *Eastern Illinois University*
Gloria Daniels, *Hinds Community College*
Stephanie Ding, *Del Mar College*
William Elmhorst, *Marshfield High School*
Lisa Fozio-Thielk, *Waubonsee Community College*
James Guinee, *University of Central Arkansas*
Sharon Habermann, *Providence Theological Seminary*
Sandra Hellyer, *Ball State University*
Mary Hughes Stone, *San Francisco State University*
Annette Iskra, *Xavier University of Louisana*
Alisha Janowsky, *University of Central Florida*
Tara Johnson, *Indiana University of Pennsylvania*
Jennifer Kampmann, *South Dakota State University*
Dr. William Kimberlin, *Lorain County Community College*
Salvador Macias, *University of South Carolina Sumter*
Nicole Martin, *Kennesaw State University*
Donna Mesler, *Seton Hall University*
Nick Murray, *East Carolina University*
Lisa Newell, *Indiana University of Pennsylvania*
Linda Petroff, *Central Community College*
Laura Pirazzi, *San Jose State University*
Lakshmi Raman, *Oakland University*
Amy Resch, *Citrus College*
Robert Stennett, *Gainesville State College*
Jeffrey Turner, *Mitchell College*
Ruth Wallace, *Butler Community College*

# Basic Issues in the Study of Development

When it comes to child and adolescent development, you have a great deal of personal experience. For one thing, you had a childhood and an adolescence of your own, and you have had many opportunities to observe children and teens as well as the parents, teachers, and others who are responsible for children's upbringing. Information media such as books, movies, television shows, and the Internet have provided you with additional insights into the trials

**developmental science** The study of age-related changes in behavior, thinking, emotions, and social relationships.

and tribulations of development that go beyond your own personal experiences. As a result, you have probably formed several beliefs about development that you regard as absolutely true.

Think about what you believe to be true beyond dispute about sibling relationships. Here are a few ideas:

*Siblings always fight.*
*Siblings of the same gender fight more than opposite gender siblings do.*
*Sibling fights are usually sparked by jealousy—"Mom loves you best."*

You may be so sure that these propositions are true that you will find it shocking that, as the aptly named best-selling book *Nurture Shock* (Bronson & Merryman, 2009) pointed out, research does not support any of them. The truth is that the degree of conflict between siblings depends on a lot of factors and, consequently, varies considerably from one family to another. Moreover, brother-brother and sister-sister siblings don't fight any more or less than brother-sister pairs do. And competition for parental affection is rarely the cause of sibling conflict.

We have to apologize a bit for whetting your appetite to learn more about sibling relationships. You'll have to wait until you get to Chapter 13 to get more details about the issues we have just raised. Our purpose in drawing attention to them here is to spark your curiosity about how well so-called "common sense" thinking about developmental psychology corresponds to the science of developmental psychology.

As you work your way through the chapters of this text, you will no doubt encounter many research findings that will challenge your beliefs. But we want you to keep in mind that the goal of developmental psychologists isn't simply to cause people to question and alter their beliefs. Instead, developmentalists seek to understand the processes that underlie human development and to find ways to help parents, teachers, therapists, and others who work with children do so effectively. To that end, they develop theories and conduct research aimed at describing, explaining, predicting, and influencing development.

## Issues in the Study of Development

Centuries before researchers began to use scientific methods to study age-related changes, philosophers proposed explanations of development based on everyday observations. Many of their questions and assertions about the nature of human development continue to be central to modern-day **developmental science**. ◉ Watch at **MyDevelopmentLab**

◉ **Watch** the **Video** *So Much to Choose from* at **MyDevelopmentLab**

**Learning Objective 1.1** - - - - - - - - - - - → What answers have been proposed to the nature-nurture and continuity-discontinuity questions?

### Two Key Questions

Two important questions have shaped the scientific study of child development. First, philosophers and scientists alike have debated the degree to which inborn tendencies and environmental factors influence development. Second, there are differing opinions as to whether age-related change occurs in stages.

**THE NATURE-NURTURE DEBATE** The argument about nature versus nurture, also referred to as heredity versus environment or *nativism* versus *empiricism*, is one of the oldest and most central theoretical issues within both psychology and philosophy. For example, have you ever heard someone say that "baby talk" will interfere with a child's language development? If so, then you have heard an argument for the nurture side of the debate. Such a statement assumes that language development is mostly a matter of imitation: The child must hear language that is properly pronounced and grammatically correct in order to develop linguistic fluency. The nature side would counter that children possess some kind of internal mechanism to ensure that they develop fluent language, no matter how many "goo-goo-ga-gas" they hear from those around them. "Which side is right?" students invariably ask. If there were a simple answer to that question, the debate would have ceased long ago. Instead, the controversy continues today with regard to many developmental processes, including language development.

Philosophically, the nature side of the controversy was represented by the *idealists* and *rationalists*, principally Plato and René Descartes, both of whom believed that at least some knowledge is inborn. On the other side of the argument were a group of British philosophers called *empiricists*, including John Locke, who insisted that at birth the mind is a blank slate—in Latin, a *tabula rasa*. All knowledge, the empiricists argued, is created by experience. From this perspective, developmental change is the result of external, environmental factors acting on a child whose only relevant internal characteristic is the capacity to respond.

In contrast to both rationalists and empiricists, other philosophers believed that development involved an interaction between internal and external forces. For example, the Christian notion of *original sin* teaches that children are born with a selfish nature and must be spiritually reborn. After rebirth, children have access to the Holy Spirit, which helps them learn to behave morally through parental and church-based instruction in religious practice.

French philosopher Jean-Jacques Rousseau also believed in the idea of interaction between internal and external forces, but he claimed that all human beings are naturally good and seek out experiences that help them grow. For Rousseau, the goal of human development was to achieve one's inborn potential. "Good" developmental outcomes, such as a willingness to share one's possessions with others who are less fortunate, resulted from growing up in an environment that didn't interfere with the child's expression of his own innate characteristics. In contrast, "bad" outcomes, such as aggressive behavior, were learned from others or arose when a child experienced frustration in his efforts to follow the dictates of the innate goodness with which he was born.

The views of two of psychology's pioneers illustrate the way early psychologists approached the nature-nurture issue. G. Stanley Hall (1844–1924) believed that the milestones of childhood were dictated by an inborn developmental plan and were similar to those that had taken place in the evolution of the human species. He thought that developmentalists should identify **norms**, or average ages at which milestones happen. Norms, Hall said, could be used to learn about the evolution of the species as well as to track the development of individual children. So, for Hall, development was mostly about the nature side of the debate.

John Watson explained development in a way that was radically different from that of G. Stanley Hall. In fact, Watson coined a new term, behaviorism, to refer to his point of view (Watson, 1913). **Behaviorism** defines development in terms of behavior changes caused by environmental influences. Watson did not believe in an inborn developmental plan of any sort. Instead, he claimed that, through manipulation of the environment, children could be trained to be or do anything (Jones, 1924; Watson, 1930). As Watson put it,

> *Give me a dozen healthy infants, well-formed, and my own specified world to bring them up in and I'll guarantee to take any one at random and train him to become any type of specialist I might select—doctor, lawyer, merchant, chief, and yes, even beggar-man and thief, regardless of his talents, penchants, abilities, vocations, and the race of his ancestors. (1930, p. 104)*

In a famous study known as the "Little Albert" experiment, Watson conditioned a baby to fear white rats (Watson & Rayner, 1920). As the baby played with the rat, Watson made banging sounds that frightened the child. Over time, the baby came to associate the rat with the noises. He cried and tried to escape from the room whenever the rat was present. Based on the Little Albert study and several others, Watson claimed that all age-related changes are the result of learning (Watson, 1928). 👁—Watch at **MyDevelopmentLab**

**STAGES AND SEQUENCES** The nature-nurture controversy is not the only "big question" in developmental psychology. An equally central dispute concerns the *continuity-discontinuity issue*: Is a child's expanding ability just "more of the same," or does it reflect a new kind of activity? For example, a 2-year-old is likely to have no individual friends among her playmates, while an 8-year-old is likely to have several. We could think of this as a *quantitative* change (a change in amount) from zero friends to some friends, which suggests that the qualitative aspects of friendship are the same at every age—or,

**norms** Average ages at which developmental events happen.

**behaviorism** The theoretical view that defines development in terms of behavior changes caused by environmental influences.

👁—Watch the **Video** *Little Albert* at **MyDevelopmentLab**

*John Watson's pioneering research on emotional learning in infants helped psychologists better understand the role of classical conditioning in child development.*

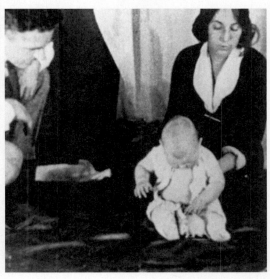

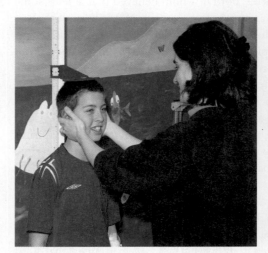

*Which photo represents* continuous *or* quantitative *change? Which illustrates* discontinuous *or* qualitative *change?*

as developmentalists would express it, changes in friendships are *continuous* in nature. Alternatively, we could think of the difference in friendships from one age to another as a *qualitative* change (a change in kind or type)—from disinterest in peers to interest, or from one sort of peer relationship to another. In other words, in this view, changes in friendships are *discontinuous*, in that each change represents a change in the quality of a child's relationships with peers. Thus, friendships at 2 are quite different from friendships at 8 and differ in ways that cannot be captured by describing them solely in terms of the number of friends a child has.

Of particular significance is the idea that, if development consists only of additions (quantitative change), then the concept of stages is not needed to explain it. However, if development involves reorganization, or the emergence of wholly new strategies, qualities, or skills (qualitative change), then the concept of stages may be useful. Certainly, we hear a lot of "stagelike" language in everyday conversation about children: "He's just in the terrible twos" or "It's only a stage she's going through." Although there is not always agreement on just what would constitute evidence for the existence of discrete stages, the usual description is that a stage shift involves not only a change in skills but some discontinuous change in underlying structure (Lerner, Theokas, & Bobek, 2005). The child in a new stage approaches tasks differently, sees the world differently, is preoccupied with different issues.

**Learning Objective 1.2** ------------>
What are the internal and external variables that influence development?

## Influences on Development

Most modern developmental psychologists agree that essentially every facet of a child's development is a product of some pattern of interaction of nature and nurture (Rutter, 2002). Further, most recognize that some aspects of development are continuous and others are more stagelike. Consequently, the discussions have become a bit more complex.

**MATURATION**    Nature shapes development most clearly through genetic programming that may determine whole sequences of development. Developmentalist Arnold Gesell (1880–1961) used the term **maturation** to describe genetically programmed sequential patterns of change, and this term is still uniformly used today (Gesell, 1925; Thelen & Adolph, 1992). Any maturational pattern is marked by three qualities: It is universal, appearing in all children, across cultural and historical boundaries; it is sequential, involving some pattern of unfolding skill or characteristics; and it is resistant to environmental influence. In its purest form, a maturationally determined developmental sequence occurs regardless of practice or training. You don't have to practice growing pubic hair; you don't

**maturation**    Sequential patterns of change that are governed by instructions contained in the genetic code and shared by all members of a species.

have to be taught how to walk. In fact, only extreme conditions, such as severe malnutrition, prevent such sequences from unfolding. Yet even confirmed maturational theorists agree that experience plays a role.

**THE TIMING OF EXPERIENCE** Research tells us that specific experience interacts with maturational patterns in intricate ways. For example, Greenough (1991) notes that one of the proteins required for the development of the visual system is controlled by a gene whose action is triggered only by visual experience. Moreover, experience is required to maintain the neural connections underlying vision (Briones, Klintsova, & Greenough, 2004). So some visual experience is needed for the genetic program to operate. The timing of specific experiences may matter as well. The impact of a particular visual experience may be quite different if it occurs at birth than if it occurs when a baby is older.

Developmentalists' thinking about the importance of timing was stimulated, in part, by research on other species that showed that specific experiences had different or stronger effects at some points in development than at others. The most famous example is that baby ducks will become imprinted on (become attached to and follow) any duck or any other quacking, moving object that happens to be around them 15 hours after they hatch. If nothing is moving or quacking at that critical point, they don't become imprinted at all (Hess, 1972). So the period just around 15 hours after hatching is a **critical period** for the duck's development of a proper following response.

In humans, we more often see *sensitive periods* than true critical periods. The difference is that a **sensitive period** is a time when a particular experience can be best incorporated into the maturational process, whereas a critical period is a time when an experience *must* happen or a particular developmental milestone will never occur. For example, infancy and early childhood are sensitive periods for language development. A child who is physically isolated from other humans by an abusive parent during these years will not develop normal language, but she will develop some language function once she is reintegrated into a normal social environment. 👁—|Watch at MyDevelopmentLab

**INBORN BIASES** Another kind of internal influence is described by the concepts of *inborn biases*. For instance, researchers such as Elizabeth Spelke (1991) have concluded that babies come into the world with certain preexisting conceptions about the behavior of objects. Very young babies already seem to understand that unsupported objects will move downward and that a moving object will continue to move in the same direction unless it encounters an obstacle. Theorists do not propose that these built-in response patterns are the end of the story; rather, they see them as the starting point. Development is a result of experience filtered through these initial biases, but those biases constrain the number of developmental pathways that are possible (Cole & Packer, 2011).

**BEHAVIOR GENETICS** The concept of maturation and the idea of inborn biases are both designed to account for patterns and sequences of development that are the same for all children. At the same time, nature contributes to variations from one individual to the next. The study of genetic contributions to individual behavior, called **behavior genetics**, uses two primary research techniques—the study of identical and fraternal twins and the study of adopted children. If identical twins are more like each other on some dimension than other kinds of siblings are, despite having grown up in different environments, this is rather compelling evidence of a genetic contribution for that trait. In the case of adopted children, the strategy is to compare the degree of similarity between the adopted child and his birth parents (with whom he shares genes but not environment) with the degree of similarity between the adopted child and his adoptive parents (with whom he shares environment but not genes). If the child turns out to be more similar to his birth parents than to his adoptive parents, or if his behavior or skills are better predicted by the characteristics of his birth parents than by characteristics of his adoptive parents, that evidence would again demonstrate the influence of heredity. Behavior geneticists have shown that heredity affects a remarkably broad range of behaviors (Netherlands Twin Register, 2010). These include intellectual as well as social and emotional functioning. Consequently, you will be reading about the results of twin and adoption studies in several future chapters.

**critical period** Any time period during development when an organism is especially responsive to and learns from a specific type of stimulation. The same stimulation at other points in development has little or no effect.

**sensitive period** A period during which particular experiences can best contribute to proper development. It is similar to a critical period, but the effects of deprivation during a sensitive period are not as severe as during a critical period.

**behavior genetics** The study of the genetic contributions to behavior or traits such as intelligence or personality.

👁—|Watch the **Video** *Windows of Opportunity for Childhood Development* at **MyDevelopmentLab**

The study of identical twins, like these two girls, is one of the classic methods of behavior genetics. Whenever pairs of identical twins are more like each other in some behavior or quality than are pairs of fraternal twins, a genetic influence is likely at work.

**internal models of experience**
A theoretical concept emphasizing that each child creates a set of core ideas or assumptions about the world, the self, and relationships with others through which all subsequent experience is filtered.

**GENE-ENVIRONMENT INTERACTION**    A child's genetic heritage may also affect his environment (Caspi & Moffitt, 2006), a phenomenon that could occur via two routes. First, the child inherits his genes from his parents, who also create the environment in which he is growing up. So a child's genetic heritage may predict something about his environment. For example, parents who themselves have higher IQ scores are not only likely to pass their "good IQ" genes on to their children, but also likely to create a richer, more stimulating environment for those children. Similarly, children who inherit a tendency toward aggression or hostility from their parents are likely to live in a family environment that is higher in criticism and negativity—because those are expressions of the parents' own genetic tendencies toward aggressiveness or hostility (Reiss, 1998).

Second, each child's unique pattern of inherited qualities affects the way she behaves with other people, which in turn affects the way adults and other children respond to her. A cranky or temperamentally difficult baby may receive fewer smiles and more scolding than a placid, even-tempered one; a genetically brighter child may demand more personal attention, ask more questions, or seek out more complex toys than would a less bright child (Saudino & Plomin, 1997). Furthermore, children's interpretations of their experiences are affected by all their inherited tendencies (Plomin, Reiss, Hetherington, & Howe, 1994).

**INTERNAL MODELS OF EXPERIENCE**    Although we often associate experience exclusively with external forces, it's just as important to consider each individual's view of his or her experiences—in other words, the internal aspect of experience. For instance, suppose a friend says to you, "Your new haircut looks great. I think it's a lot more becoming when it's short like that." Your friend intends it as a compliment, but what determines your reaction is how you hear the comment, not what is intended. If your internal model of your self includes the basic idea "I usually look okay," you will likely hear your friend's comment as a compliment; but if your internal model of self or relationships includes some more negative elements, such as "I usually do things wrong, so other people criticize me," then you may hear an implied criticism in your friend's comment ("Your hair used to look awful").

Theorists who emphasize the importance of such meaning systems argue that each child creates a set of **internal models of experience**—a set of core ideas or assumptions about the world, about himself, and about relationships with others—through which all subsequent experience is filtered (Epstein, 1991; Reiss, 1998). Such assumptions are certainly based in part on actual experiences, but once they are formed into an internal model, they generalize beyond the original experience and affect the way the child interprets future experiences. A child who expects adults to be reliable and affectionate will be more likely to interpret the behavior of new adults in this way and will create friendly and affectionate relationships with others outside of the family. A child's self-concept seems to operate in much the same way, as an internal working model of "who I am" (Bretherton, 1991). This self-model is based on experience, but it also shapes future experience.

**ASLIN'S MODEL OF ENVIRONMENTAL INFLUENCE**    Theoretical models are useful for organizing ideas about how all these factors interact to influence development. One particularly good example of a theoretical approach that attempts to explain environmental influences is a set of models summarized by Richard Aslin (1981), based on earlier work by Gottlieb (1976a, 1976b) and shown schematically in Figure 1.1. Aslin and his colleagues have used these models to study infants' perception of speech and objects (e.g., Aslin, 2011; Maye, Weiss, & Aslin, 2008). In each drawing the dashed line represents the path of development of some skill or behavior that would occur without a particular experience; the solid line represents the path of development if the experience were added.

For comparison purposes, the first of the five models shows a maturational pattern with no environmental effect. The second model, which Aslin calls *maintenance*, describes a pattern in which some environmental input is necessary to sustain a skill or behavior that has already developed maturationally. For example, kittens are born with full binocular vision, but if you cover one of their eyes for a period of time, their binocular skill declines.

The third model shows a *facilitation* effect of the environment, in which a skill or behavior develops earlier than it normally would because of some experience. For example, children whose parents talk to them more often in the first 18 to 24 months of life, using more complex sentences, appear to develop two-word sentences and other early grammatical forms somewhat earlier than do children who are talked to less. Yet less-talked-to children do eventually learn to create complex sentences and use most grammatical forms correctly, so the experience of being talked to more provides no permanent gain.

When a particular experience does lead to a permanent gain, or an enduringly higher level of performance, Aslin calls the model *attunement*. For example, children from poverty-level families who attend special enriched child care in infancy and early childhood have consistently higher IQ scores throughout childhood than do children from the same kinds of families who do not have such enriched experience (Ramey & Ramey, 2004). Aslin's final model, *induction*, describes a pure environmental effect: In the absence of some experience, a particular behavior does not develop at all. Giving a child tennis lessons or exposing him to a second language falls into this category of experience.

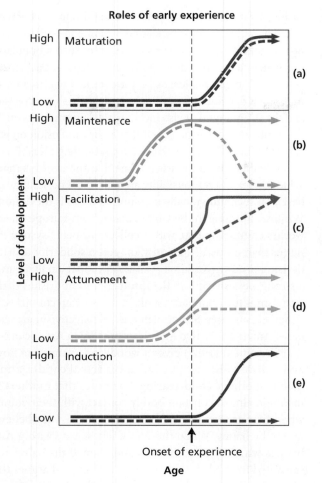

**Roles of early experience**

**FIGURE 1.1** Aslin's Models of Environmental Influence

Aslin proposed five models of possible relationships between maturation and environment. The top model shows a purely maturational effect; the bottom model (induction) shows a purely environmental effect. The other three show interactive combinations: maintenance, in which experience prevents the deterioration of a maturationally developed skill; facilitation, in which experience speeds up the development of some maturational process; and attunement, in which experience increases the ultimate level of some skill or behavior above the "normal" maturational level.

(*Source:* Aslin, Richard N. "Experiential Influences and Sensitive Periods in Perceptual Development," *Development of perception. Psychobiological perspectives: Vol. 2. The visual system* (1981), p. 50. Reprinted by permission of Elsevier Science and the author.)

## The Ecological Perspective and the Cultural Context of Development

◀-----------Learning Objective 1.3

How does the ecological perspective improve scientists' understanding of child development?

Until quite recently, most research on environmental influences focused on a child's family (frequently only the child's mother) and on the stimulation available in the child's home, such as the kinds of toys or books available to the child. If psychologists looked at a larger family context at all, it was usually only in terms of the family's economic status—its level of wealth or poverty. Since the early 1980s, however, there has been a strong push to widen the scope of research, to consider the *ecology*, or *context*, in which each child develops. The late Urie Bronfenbrenner (1917–2005), one of the key figures in this area of study (1979, 1989), emphasizes that each child grows up in a complex social environment (a social ecology) with a distinct cast of characters: siblings, parents, grandparents, baby-sitters, pets, teachers, friends. And this cast is itself embedded within a larger social system: The parents have jobs that they may like or dislike; they may or may not have close and supportive friends; they may be living in a safe neighborhood or one full of dangers; the local school may be excellent or poor; and the parents may have good or poor relationships with the school. Bronfenbrenner's argument is that researchers not only must include descriptions of these more extended aspects of the environment but must also consider the ways in which all the components of this complex system interact with one another to affect the development of an individual child. (We will look more closely at Bronfenbrenner's theory in Chapter 13.)

One aspect of such a larger ecology is the still broader concept of *culture*, a system of meanings and customs, including values, attitudes, goals, laws, beliefs, morals, and physical artifacts of various kinds, such as tools and forms of dwellings. For a system of meanings and customs to be called a culture, it must be shared by some identifiable group, whether that group is the entire population of a country or a subsection of such a population; it must then be transmitted from one generation of that group to the next (Cole & Packer, 2011). Families and children are clearly embedded in culture, just as they are located within an ecological niche within the culture. The majority U.S. culture, for example, is strongly shaped by the values expressed in the Constitution and the Bill of Rights; it also includes a strong emphasis on "can-do" attitudes and on competition.

Anthropologists point out that a key dimension on which cultures differ from one another is that of *individualism* versus *collectivism* (e.g., Kashima et al., 2005). People in cultures with an individualistic emphasis assume that the world is made up of independent persons whose achievement and responsibility are individual rather than collective. Most European cultures are based on such individualistic assumptions, as is the dominant U.S. culture, created primarily by Whites who came to the United States from Europe. In contrast, most of the remainder of the world's cultures operate with a collectivist belief system in which the emphasis is on collective rather than individual identity, on group solidarity, sharing, duties and obligations, and group decision making (Kashima et al., 2005). A person living in a collectivist system is integrated into a strong, cohesive group that protects and nourishes that individual throughout his life. Collectivism is the dominant theme in most Asian countries, as well as in many African and South American cultures. Strong elements of collectivism are also part of the African American, Hispanic American, Native American, and Asian American subcultures.

Greenfield (1995) gives a wonderful example of how the difference between collectivist and individualist cultures can affect actual child-rearing practices as well as people's judgments of others' child-rearing. She notes that mothers from the Zinacanteco Maya culture maintain almost constant bodily contact with their young babies and do not feel comfortable when they are separated from their infants. They believe that their babies require this contact to be happy. When these mothers saw a visiting American anthropologist put her own baby down, they were shocked and blamed the baby's regular crying on the fact that he was separated from his mother so often. Greenfield argues that the constant bodily contact of the Mayan mothers is a logical outgrowth of their collectivist approach, because their basic goal is interdependence rather than independence. The American anthropologist, in contrast, operates with a basic goal of independence for her child and so emphasizes more separation. Each group judges the other's form of child-rearing to be less optimal or even inadequate.

Such differences notwithstanding, researchers note that it is wrong to think of collectivism and individualism in either-or terms, because there are elements of both in every culture (Green, Deschamps, & Páez, 2005). Consequently, when researchers categorize a given culture as collectivist or individualist, they are referring to which of the two sets of values predominates. It is also true that there is a considerable amount of individual variation within cultures. Thus, people who live in individualistic societies may nevertheless, as individuals, develop a collectivist orientation. The same is true for their counterparts in collectivist societies.

Learning Objective 1.4 ------------→

## Vulnerability and Resilience

In what ways do the concepts of vulnerability and resilience help us better understand child development?

At this point, it should be clear to you the same environment may have quite different effects on children who are born with different characteristics. One influential research approach exploring such an interaction is long-term study of a group of children born in 1955 on the island of Kauai, Hawaii by Emmy Werner and Ruth Smith (Werner, 1993, 1995; Werner & Smith, 1992, 2001). Werner and Smith found that only about two-thirds of the children who grew up in poverty-level, chaotic families turned out to have serious problems themselves as adults. The other third, described as *resilient*, turned out to be "competent, confident, and caring adults" (Werner, 1995, p. 82). Thus, similar environments were linked to quite different outcomes.

Many theorists argue that the best way to make sense out of results like Werner and Smith's is to think of each child as born with certain *vulnerabilities*, such as a difficult temperament, a physical abnormality, allergies, or a genetic tendency toward alcoholism (Garmezy, 1993; Howard, Carothers, Smith, & Akai, 2007; Rutter, 1987, 2005b). Each child is also born with some *protective factors*, such as high intelligence, good coordination, an easy temperament, or a lovely smile, which tend to make her more resilient in the face of stress. These vulnerabilities and

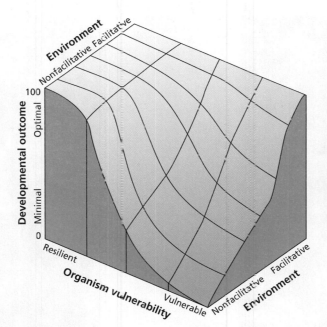

**FIGURE 1.2** Horowitz's Model of Vulnerability and Resilience
Horowitz's model describes one possible type of interaction between the vulnerability of the child and the quality of the environment. The height of the surface shows the "goodness" of the developmental outcome (such as IQ or skill in social relationships). In this model, only the combination of a vulnerable infant and a nonfacilitative environment will result in a really poor outcome.

(*Source: Exploring Developmental Theories: Toward a Structural/Behavioral Model of Development*, by Horowitz, F. D. Copyright 1987 by Taylor & Francis Group LLC-Books. Reproduced with permission of Taylor & Francis Group LLC.)

protective factors then interact with the child's environment, and thus the same environment can have quite different effects, depending on the qualities the child brings to the interaction.

A more general model describing the interaction between the qualities of the child and the environment comes from Fran Horowitz (1987, 2003), who proposes that the key ingredients are each child's vulnerability or resilience and the "facilitativeness" of the environment. A highly facilitative environment is one in which the child has loving and responsive parents and is provided with a rich array of stimulation. If the relationship between vulnerability and facilitativeness were merely additive, the best outcomes would occur for resilient infants reared in optimal environments, and the worst outcomes for vulnerable infants in poor environments, with the two mixed combinations falling halfway between. But that is not what Horowitz proposes, as you can see represented schematically in Figure 1.2 above. Instead, she is suggesting that a resilient child in a poor environment may do quite well, since such a child can take advantage of all the stimulation and opportunities available. Similarly, she suggests that a vulnerable child may do quite well in a highly facilitative environment. According to this model, it is only the "double whammy"—the vulnerable child in a poor environment—that leads to really poor outcomes.

In fact, as you will see throughout the book, a growing body of research shows precisely this pattern. For example, very low IQ scores are most common among children who were low-birth-weight babies and were reared in poverty-level families, while low-birth-weight children reared in middle-class families have essentially average IQs, as do normal-weight infants reared in poverty-level families (Werner, 1986). Further, among low-birth-weight children who are reared in poverty-level families, those whose families offer "protective" factors (such as greater residential stability, less crowded living conditions, and more acceptance, more stimulation, and more learning materials) achieve higher IQ scores than do equivalently low-birth-weight children reared in the least optimal poverty-level conditions (Bradley et al., 1994). The key point here is that the same environment can have quite different effects, depending on the qualities or capacities the child brings to the equation.

*Many children who grow up in poverty-stricken neighborhoods are high achievers who are well adjusted. Developmentalists use the term* resilient *to refer to children who demonstrate positive developmental outcomes despite being raised in high-risk environments.*

## Three Kinds of Change

Age-related changes are a part of our everyday lives, so much so that we often give them little thought. Yet, consider the difference between a human being's first step and his or her first date. Clearly, both are related to age, but they represent fundamentally different kinds of change. Generally, developmental scientists think of each age-related change as falling into one of three categories.

**Learning Objective 1.5**
How do the three kinds of age-related change differ?

*Walking and puberty are normative age-graded changes; they happen to every individual within fairly narrow age ranges. The precise ages within these ranges when these milestones occur in an individual's life are individual differences.*

**Normative age-graded changes** are universal; that is, they are common to every individual in a species and are linked to specific ages. Some universal changes, like a baby's first steps, happen because we are all biological organisms subject to a genetically programmed maturation process. The infant who shifts from crawling to walking and the older adult whose skin becomes progressively more wrinkled are both following a plan that is an intrinsic part of the physical body, most likely something in the genetic code itself. However, some changes are universal because of shared experiences. In each culture, the *social clock*, or a set of age norms, defines a sequence of normal life experiences, such as the common practice of beginning children's formal education sometime between the ages of 5 and 7.

Equally important as a source of variation in life experience are historical forces, which affect each generation somewhat differently. Such changes are called **normative history-graded changes**. Social scientists use the word **cohort** to describe a group of individuals who are born within some fairly narrow span of years and thus share the same historical experiences at the same times in their lives. For instance, ask anyone what distinguishes children who are growing up in the twenty-first century from their counterparts in earlier eras, and the word "technology" is likely to be included in the answer. Consequently, developmental scientists are interested in studying the impact of today's high-tech world on the development of children and adolescents (see *Technology and the Developing Child* on page 11).

Finally, **nonnormative changes**, or **individual differences**, result from unique, unshared events. One clearly unshared event in each person's life is conception; the combination of genes each individual receives at conception is unique. Thus, genetic differences—including physical characteristics such as body type and hair color as well as genetic disorders—represent one category of individual differences. Characteristics influenced by both heredity and environment, such as intelligence and personality, constitute another class of individual differences. Other individual differences are the result of the timing of a developmental event.

**normative age-graded changes**
Changes that are common to every member of a species.

**normative history-graded changes**
Changes that occur in most members of a cohort as a result of factors at work during a specific, well-defined historical period.

**cohort** A group of individuals who share the same historical experiences at the same times in their lives.

**nonnormative changes (individual differences)** Changes that result from unique, unshared events.

## Cohort Effects of Health Information on the Internet

Surveys show that more than 90% of parents search the Internet for information on children's health topics (Moseley, Freed, & Goold, 2011). Consequently, pediatricians have expressed concern about the prevalence of inaccurate health information online (Scullard, Peacock, & Davies, 2010). In response, the American Academy of Pediatrics (AAP) developed a website to which pediatricians can direct parents (http://www.healthychildren.org) who are looking for reliable information on children's health topics.

Studies suggest that parents appreciate receiving such "information prescriptions" from their pediatricians (D'Alessandro, Kreiter, Kinzer, & Peterson, 2004). Moreover, research shows that

children of parents who are knowledgeable about health tend to show better health outcomes than those of parents who are less knowledgeable (DeWalt & Hink, 2009). Thus, the efforts of professional organizations such as the AAP to provide parents with reliable sources of health knowledge may cause today's cohort of children to be healthier than their counterparts in previous eras.

### FIND OUT MORE

*Use your Internet search skills to answer these questions.*

1. Take a look at www.healthychildren.org. Use the website's search tool to find information on a parenting topic, such as

breastfeeding or punishment. What suggestions do you have for making the website more helpful?
2. Do a Google search on a disease, such as asthma or measles. You will find that many medicals journals nowadays publish research articles online. What are the pros and cons of making such information available to non-scientists via the Internet?

> **Learning Objective 1.5a**
> How is the availability of health information on the Internet likely to affect today's cohort of parents and children?

# Theories of Development

**Developmental theories** are sets of statements that propose general principles of development. Students often say that they dislike reading about theories; what they want are the facts. However, theories are important, because they help us look at facts from different perspectives. A brief introduction to several important theories will help you understand some of the more detailed information about them presented in later chapters. ◉⎯Watch at **MyDevelopmentLab**

◉⎯Watch the **Video** *Different Approaches to Psychology* at **MyDevelopmentLab**

## Psychoanalytic Theories

◄------------Learning Objective 1.6
What are the main ideas of the psychoanalytic theories?

The most distinctive and central assumption of the **psychoanalytic theories** is that behavior is governed by unconscious as well as conscious processes. Psychoanalytic theorists also see development as fundamentally stage-like, with each stage centered on a particular form of tension or a particular task. The child moves through these stages, resolving each task or reducing each tension as best he can. This emphasis on the formative role of early experience is a hallmark of psychoanalytic theories. In this view, the first 5 or 6 years of life constitute a kind of sensitive period for the creation of the individual personality. Sigmund Freud (1856–1939) is usually credited with originating the psychoanalytic approach (1905, 1920), and his terminology and many of his concepts have become part of our intellectual culture. Another theorist in this tradition, Erik Erikson (1902–1994), has also had a large impact on the way psychologists think about personality development.

*When parents divorce, boys are more likely to show disturbed behavior or poorer school performance than are girls. But why? Theories can help to explain facts like this.*

**FREUD'S THEORY** Freud proposed the existence of a basic, unconscious, instinctual sexual drive he called the **libido**. He argued that this energy is the motive force behind virtually all human behavior. Freud also proposed that unconscious material is created over time through the functioning of the various *defense mechanisms*, several of which are listed in Table 1.1 on page 12. We all use defense mechanisms every day, and Freud's ideas about them continue to be influential among psychologists (Cramer, 2000).

**developmental theories** Sets of statements that propose general principles of development.

**psychoanalytic theories** Developmental theories based on the assumption that age-related change results from maturationally determined conflicts between internal drives and society's demands.

**libido** The term used by Freud to describe the basic, unconscious, instinctual sexual energy in each individual.

## Table 1.1 — SOME COMMON DEFENSE MECHANISMS

| Mechanism | Definition | Example |
|---|---|---|
| Denial | Behaving as if a problem doesn't exist | A pregnant woman fails to get prenatal care because she convinces herself she can't possibly be pregnant even though she has all the symptoms. |
| Repression | Intentionally forgetting something unpleasant | A child "forgets" about a troublesome bully on the bus as soon as he gets safely home from school every day. |
| Projection | Seeing one's own behavior or beliefs in others whether they are actually present or not | A woman complains about her boss to a co-worker and comes away from the conversation believing that the co-worker shares her dislike of the boss, even though the co-worker made no comment on what she said. |
| Regression | Behaving in a way that is inappropriate for one's age | A toilet-trained 2-year-old starts wetting the bed every night after a new baby arrives. |
| Displacement | Directing emotion to an object or person other than the one provoking it | An elderly adult suffers a stroke, becomes physically impaired, and expresses her frustration through verbal abuse of the hospital staff. |
| Rationalization | Creating an explanation to justify an action or to deal with a disappointment | A man stealing money from his employer says to himself, "They won't give me a raise. So what if I took $50?" |

✱ Explore the Concept *Freud's Five Psychosexual Stages of Personality Development* at **MyDevelopmentLab**

**id** In Freudian theory, the inborn, primitive portion of the personality, the storehouse of libido, the basic energy that continually pushes for immediate gratification.

**ego** In Freudian theory, the portion of the personality that organizes, plans, and keeps the person in touch with reality. Language and thought are both ego functions.

**superego** In Freudian theory, the "conscience" part of personality, which contains parental and societal values and attitudes incorporated during childhood.

**psychosexual stages** The stages of personality development suggested by Freud: the oral, anal, phallic, latency, and genital stages.

**psychosocial stages** The stages of personality development suggested by Erikson, involving basic trust, autonomy, initiative, industry, identity, intimacy, generativity, and ego integrity.

A second basic assumption is that personality has a structure, which develops over time. Freud proposed three parts of the personality: the **id**, which is the source of the libido; the **ego**, a much more conscious element, the "executive" of the personality; and the **superego**, which is the center of conscience and morality, since it incorporates the norms and moral strictures of the family and society. In Freud's theory, these three parts are not all present at birth. The infant and toddler is all id—all instinct, all desire, without the restraining influence of the ego or the superego. The ego begins to develop in the years from age 2 to about 4 or 5, as the child learns to adapt her instant-gratification strategies. Finally, the superego begins to develop just before school age, as the child incorporates the parents' values and cultural mores.

Freud thought the stages of personality development were strongly influenced by maturation. In each of Freud's five **psychosexual stages**, the libido is centered in that part of the body that is most sensitive at that age. In a newborn, the mouth is the most sensitive part of the body, so libidinal energy is focused there. The stage is therefore called the *oral stage*. As neurological development progresses, the infant has more sensation in the anus (hence the *anal stage*) and later in the genitalia (the *phallic* and eventually the *genital stages*). ✱ Explore at **MyDevelopmentLab**

**ERIKSON'S THEORY** The stages Erikson proposed, called **psychosocial stages**, are influenced by common cultural demands for children of a particular age, such as the demand that a child become toilet trained at about age 2. In Erikson's view, each child moves through a fixed sequence of tasks, each centered on the development of a particular facet of identity. For example, the first task, central to the first 12 to 18 months of life, is to develop a sense of *basic trust*. If the child's caregivers are not responsive and loving, however, the child may develop a sense of basic mistrust, which will affect his responses at all the later stages.

In both Freud's and Erikson's theories, the critical point is that the degree of success a child experiences in meeting the demands of these various stages will depend very heavily on the interactions he has with the people and objects in his world. This interactive element in Freud's and all subsequent psychoanalytic theories is absolutely central. Basic trust cannot be developed unless the parents or other caregivers respond to the infant in a loving, consistent manner. The oral stage cannot be fully completed unless the infant's desire for oral stimulation is sufficiently gratified. And when a stage is not fully resolved, the old pattern or the unmet need is carried forward, affecting the individual's ability to handle later tasks or stages. So, for example, a young adult who developed a sense of mistrust in the first years of life may have a more difficult time establishing a secure intimate relationship with a partner or with friends. ✳ Explore at MyDevelopmentLab

✳ Explore the Concept *Erikson's First Four Stages of Psychosocial Development* at MyDevelopmentLab

## Cognitive Theories

◀----------- Learning Objective 1.7
What are the main ideas of cognitive-developmental and information-processing theories?

In psychoanalytic theories, the quality and character of a child's relationships with a few key people are seen as central to the child's whole development. **Cognitive-developmental theories**, which emphasize primarily cognitive development rather than personality, reverse this order of importance, emphasizing the centrality of the child's actions on the environment and her cognitive processing of experiences.

**PIAGET'S THEORY** The central figure in cognitive-developmental theory has been Jean Piaget (1896–1980), a Swiss psychologist whose theories (1952, 1970, 1977; Piaget & Inhelder, 1969) shaped the thinking of several generations of developmental psychologists. Piaget was struck by the great regularities in the development of children's thinking. He noticed that all children seem to go through the same kinds of sequential discoveries about their world, making the same sorts of mistakes and arriving at the same solutions. For example, all 3- and 4-year-olds seem to think that if you pour water from a short, fat glass into a tall, thin one, there is more water in the thin glass, since the water level is higher there than in the fat glass. In contrast, most 7-year-olds realize that the amount of water is the same in either glass.

Piaget's detailed observations of such systematic shifts in children's thinking led him to several assumptions, the most central of which is that it is the nature of the human organism to adapt to its environment. This is an active process. In contrast to many theorists, Piaget did not think that the environment shapes the child. Rather, the child (like the adult) actively seeks to understand his environment. In the process, he explores, manipulates, and examines the objects and people in his world.

The process of adaptation, in Piaget's view, is made up of several important subprocesses—*assimilation*, *accommodation*, and *equilibration*—all of which you will learn more about in Chapter 6. What is important to understand at this preliminary point is that Piaget thought that the child develops a series of fairly distinct "understandings," or "theories," about the way the world works, based on her active exploration of the environment. Each of these "theories" corresponds to a specific stage. Piaget thought that virtually all infants begin with the same skills and built-in strategies and since the environments children encounter are highly similar in important respects, he believed that the stages through which children's thinking moves are also similar. Piaget proposed a fixed sequence of four major stages, each growing out of the one that preceded it, and each consisting of a more or less complete system or organization of concepts, strategies, and assumptions.

**cognitive-developmental theories** Developmental theories that emphasize children's actions on the environment and suggest that age-related changes in reasoning precede and explain changes in other domains.

**scaffolding** The term used by Bruner to describe the process by which a teacher (or parent, older child, or other person in the role of teacher) structures a learning encounter with a child, so as to lead the child from step to step—a process consistent with Vygotsky's theory of cognitive development.

**zone of proximal development** In Vygotsky's theory, the range of tasks that are slightly too difficult for a child to do alone but that can be accomplished successfully with guidance from an adult or more experienced child.

◉ Watch the Video *Zone of Proximal Development* at MyDevelopmentLab

**VYGOTSKY'S THEORY** Like Piaget, Russian psychologist Lev Vygotsky (1896–1934) was primarily concerned with understanding the origins of the child's knowledge (1978\1930). Vygotsky differed from Piaget, however, in one key respect: He was convinced that complex forms of thinking have their origins in social interactions (Duncan, 1995). According to Vygotsky, a child's learning of new cognitive skills is guided by an adult (or a more skilled child, such as an older sibling), who models and structures the child's learning experience, a process Jerome Bruner later called **scaffolding** (Wood, Bruner, & Ross, 1976). Such new learning, Vygotsky suggested, is best achieved in what he called the **zone of proximal development**—that range of tasks which are too hard for the child to do alone but which she can manage with guidance. As the child becomes more skilled, the zone of proximal development steadily widens, including ever harder tasks. Vygotsky thought the key to this interactive process lay in the language the adult used to describe or frame the task. Later, the child could use this same language to guide her independent attempts to do the same kinds of tasks. ◉ Watch at MyDevelopmentLab

*Piaget based many of his ideas on naturalistic observation of children of different ages on playgrounds and in schools.*

**information-processing theories** A set of theories based on the idea that humans process information in ways that are similar to those used in computers.

👁— **Watch** the **Video** *The Penny Test* at **MyDevelopmentLab**

**INFORMATION-PROCESSING THEORY**  Although it is not truly a cognitive-developmental theory, many of the ideas and research studies associated with **information-processing theory** have increased psychologists' understanding of Piaget's stages and other age-related changes in thinking. The goal of information-processing theory is to explain how the mind manages information (Munakata, 2006). Information-processing theorists use the computer as a model of human thinking. Consequently, they often use computer terms such as *hardware* and *software* to talk about human cognitive processes.  👁— **Watch** at **MyDevelopmentLab**

Theorizing about and studying memory processes are central to information-processing theory (Birney, Citron-Pousty, Lutz, & Sternberg, 2005). Theorists usually break memory down into subprocesses of encoding, storage, and retrieval. *Encoding* is organizing information to be stored in memory. For example, you may be encoding the information in this chapter by relating it to your own childhood. *Storage* is keeping information, and *retrieval* is getting information out of memory.

Most memory research assumes that the memory system is made up of multiple components. The idea is that information moves through these components in an organized way (see Figure 1.3). The process of understanding a spoken word serves as a good example. First, you hear the word when the sounds enter your *sensory memory*. Your experiences with language allow you to recognize the pattern of sounds as a word. Next, the word moves into your *short-term memory*, the component of the memory system where all information is processed. Thus, short-term memory is often called *working memory*. Knowledge of the word's meaning is then called up out of *long-term memory*, the component of the system where information is permanently stored, and placed in short-term memory, where it is linked to the word's sounds to enable you to understand what you have just heard.

Each memory component manages information differently. Information flows through sensory memory as if in a stream. Bits of information that are not attended to drop out quickly. Short-term memory is extremely limited in capacity—an adult's short-term memory can hold about seven items at a time. However, information can be retained in short-term memory as long as it is processed in some way—for example, when you repeat your grocery list to yourself on the way to the store.

Long-term memory is unlimited in capacity, and information is often stored in terms of meaningful associations. For example, suppose you read a sentence such as "Bill wrote a letter to his brother." When you think about the sentence later, you might mistakenly recall that it contained the word *pen*. This happens because information about the process of writing and the tools used to do it are stored together in long-term memory.

There are both age-related and individual differences in information processing. As you will learn in Chapter 6, the number of items that can be retained in short-term memory at one time is far more limited in young children than in adults and older children. In addition, among children of the same age, some use more efficient strategies for remembering and solving problems. Looking at differences of both kinds and examining children's thinking from Piaget's and Vygotsky's perspectives provide a more complete picture of how children acquire the ability to reason logically.

**FIGURE 1.3** The Information-Processing System
Information-processing research on memory is based on the assumption that information moves into, out of, and through sensory, short-term, and long-term memories in an organized way.

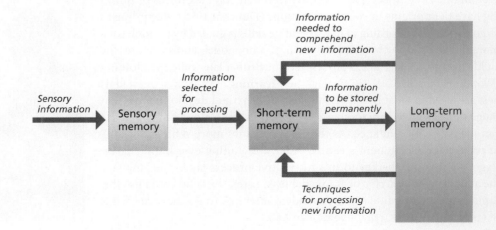

# Learning Theories

◄------------Learning Objective 1.8

How do learning theorists explain development?

**Learning theories** represent a theoretical tradition very different from that of either the psychoanalysts or the cognitive-developmentalists, one in which the emphasis is much more on the way the environment shapes the child than on how the child understands his experiences. Learning theorists do not argue that genetics or built-in biases are unimportant, but they see human behavior as enormously plastic, shaped by predictable processes of learning. Three of the most important learning theories are Pavlov's classical conditioning model, Skinner's operant conditioning model, and Bandura's social cognitive theory.

**learning theories** Psychological theories that explain development in terms of accumulated learning experiences.

**CLASSICAL CONDITIONING** **Classical conditioning**, made famous by Ivan Pavlov's (1849–1936) experiments with his salivating dog, involves the acquisition of new signals for existing responses. If you touch a baby on the cheek, she will turn toward the touch and begin to suck. In the technical terminology of classical conditioning, the touch on the cheek is the *unconditional stimulus*; the turning and sucking are *unconditioned responses*. The baby is already programmed to do all that; these are automatic reflexes. Learning occurs when some new stimulus is introduced to the system.

**classical conditioning** One of three major types of learning. An automatic, or unconditional response such as an emotion or a reflex comes to be triggered by a new cue called the conditional stimulus, after having been paired several times with that stimulus.

The general model is that other stimuli that are present just before or at the same time as the unconditional stimulus will eventually trigger the same responses. In the typical home situation, for example, a number of stimuli occur at about the same time as the touch on the baby's cheek before feeding: the sound of the mother's footsteps approaching, the kinesthetic cues of being picked up, and the tactile cues of being held in the mother's arms. All these stimuli may eventually become *conditional stimuli* and may trigger the infant's response of turning and sucking, even without any touch on the cheek. ◉ Watch at **MyDevelopmentLab**

**operant conditioning** The type of learning in which the probability of a person's performing some behavior is increased or decreased because of the consequences it produces.

Classical conditioning is of special interest in the study of child development because of the role it plays in the development of emotional responses, as Watson's Little Albert experiment so aptly demonstrated. For example, things or people present when you feel good will become conditional stimuli for that same sense of well-being; things or people previously associated with some uncomfortable feeling may become conditional stimuli for a sense of unease or anxiety. This is especially important in infancy, since a child's mother or father is present so often when nice things happen—when the child feels warm, comfortable, and cuddled. Thus, mother and father usually come to be conditional stimuli for pleasant feelings, a fact that makes it possible for the parents' mere presence to reinforce other behaviors as well. A tormenting older sibling might come to be a conditional stimulus for angry feelings, even after the sibling has long since stopped the tormenting. Such classically conditioned emotional responses are remarkably powerful. They begin to be formed very early in life, continue to be created throughout childhood and adulthood, and profoundly affect each individual's emotional experiences. Moreover, therapists can use the principles of classical conditioning to help children resolve a variety of emotional problems (see *Developmental Science in the Real World* on page 16). ◉ Watch at **MyDevelopmentLab**

**positive reinforcement** The process of strengthening a behavior by the presentation of some pleasurable or positive stimulus.

◉—Watch the **Video** *Three Stages of Classical Conditioning* at **MyDevelopmentLab**

◉—Watch the **Video** *Classical Conditioning: Rat Race* at **MyDevelopmentLab**

◉—Watch the **Video** *B.F. Skinner Biography* at **MyDevelopmentLab**

◉►—Simulate the **Experiment** *Learning* at **MyDevelopmentLab**

**OPERANT CONDITIONING** The second major type of learning is **operant conditioning,** the process through which the frequency of a behavior increases or decreases because of the consequences the behavior produces. When a behavior increases, it is said to have been *reinforced*; when it decreases, the behavior is said to have been *punished*. Psychologist B. F. Skinner (1904–1990) discovered the principles of operant conditioning in a series of animal studies. He believed that these principles strongly influence human development. ◉—Watch at **MyDevelopmentLab**

Reinforcement occurs when a consequence increases the frequency of a particular behavior. With **positive reinforcement**, an *added* stimulus or consequence increases a behavior. Certain kinds of pleasant stimuli—such as praise, a smile, food, a hug, or attention—serve as positive reinforcers for most people most of the time. But strictly speaking, a reinforcer is defined by its effect; we don't know that something is reinforcing unless we see that its presence increases the probability of some behavior. For example, if a parent gives a child dessert as a reward for good table manners, and the child's frequency of good table manners increases, then the dessert is a reinforcer. If the frequency does not increase, then the dessert is not a reinforcer. ◉►—Simulate at **MyDevelopmentLab**

*Computer-assisted instruction programs have built-in reinforcements such as cheering audiences that appear on the screen when a child answers a question correctly.*

### Helping Children Who Are Afraid to Go to School

Dr. Rawlins, a psychologist who works in a large urban school district often treats children with *school refusal*, a condition in which a child refuses to go to school. Psychologists believe that, unless a child is attempting to avoid a specific threat such as a bully, school refusal results from a pattern of associations that is similar to that shown by Watson's Little Albert experiment. That is, for some reason, the neutral stimulus of school has become associated with stimuli that naturally provoke anxious responses in children. Thus, psychologists reason that children's fear of school can be unlearned through the same stimulus-response mechanism that produced it—a type of therapy called *systematic desensitization* (Scheffer, 2011; Wolpe, 1958).

In a systematic desensitization intervention, the therapist teaches the child to control his respiration rate and muscular contractions to achieve a state of physical relaxation. Next, the therapist helps him learn to "switch on" his relaxation response with each step in the process of getting to and staying in school. For example, the child first learns to relax while getting dressed. Next, he practices relaxing while waiting for the bus. Once at school, the child initiates his relaxation response in front of the school entrance. The final step is to relax in the classroom and to initiate the relaxation response whenever he experiences feelings of anxiety during the day. After repeating these steps several times, most children with school refusal learn to associate going to school with relaxation responses rather than with anxiety.

**Learning Objective 1.8a**
How do psychologists help children overcome school refusal?

#### REFLECTION

1. How could systematic desensitization be used to help a child who was bitten by a dog overcome her subsequent fear of all dogs?
2. What actions on the part of parents, teachers, or peers might prevent a child with school refusal from benefiting from systematic desensitization?

**Negative reinforcement** increases a behavior because the reinforcement involves the termination or removal of an unpleasant stimulus. Suppose your little boy is whining and begging you to pick him up. At first you ignore him, but finally you do pick him up. What happens? He stops whining. So your picking-up behavior has been negatively reinforced by the cessation of his whining, and you will be more likely to pick him up the next time he whines. At the same time, his whining has probably been positively reinforced by your attention, so he will be more likely to whine on similar occasions.

In laboratory situations, experimenters can be sure to reinforce a behavior every time it occurs or to stop reinforcements completely so as to produce *extinction* of a response. In the real world, however, a pattern in which a behavior is reinforced on some occasions but not others, or *partial reinforcement*, is more common. Studies of partial reinforcement show that children and adults take longer to learn behaviors under partial reinforcement conditions, but once established, such behaviors are much more resistant to extinction. If you smile at your daughter only every fifth or sixth time she brings a picture to show you (and if she finds your smile reinforcing), she'll keep on bringing pictures for a very long stretch, even if you quit smiling altogether.

Both positive and negative reinforcements strengthen behavior. **Punishment**, in contrast, weakens behavior. Sometimes punishments involve eliminating nice things (for example, "grounding" a child, taking away TV privileges, or sending her to her room). Often they involve administering unpleasant things such as a scolding or a spanking. What is confusing about such consequences is that they don't always do what they are intended to do: They do not always suppress the undesired behavior. ✳ Explore at **MyDevelopmentLab**

Say, for example, a parent suspends a teenager's driving privileges for coming home after curfew in the hope that the penalty will stop the behavior of coming home late. For some teens, this approach will be effective. Others, though, may respond with defiance, by staying out later and later each time their driving privileges are restored. To these teens, the parent's "punishment" is a form of recognition for the defiant attitude they hope to project. For them, the "punishment" is actually a positive reinforcement. Thus, punishment, like reinforcement, must be defined in terms of its effect on behavior; if a consequence doesn't weaken or stop a behavior, it isn't a punishment.

**BANDURA'S SOCIAL COGNITIVE THEORY** Albert Bandura's variation of learning theory is by far the most influential among developmental psychologists today (1989, 2004, 2008). Bandura argues that learning does not always require direct reinforcement. Learning may also occur merely as a result of watching someone else perform some action. Learning of

✳ Explore the Concept *The Shaping Process* at **MyDevelopmentLab**

**negative reinforcement** The process of strengthening a behavior by the removal or cessation of an unpleasant stimulus.

**punishment** The removal of a desirable stimulus or the administration of an unpleasant consequence after some undesired behavior in order to stop the behavior.

this type, called *observational learning*, or *modeling*, is involved in a wide range of behaviors. Children learn how to hit from watching other people in real life and on television. They learn how to be generous by watching others donate money or share goods. Bandura also calls attention to *intrinsic reinforcements* such as the pride a child feels when she figures out how to draw a star or the sense of satisfaction you may experience after strenuous exercise.

Finally, and perhaps most importantly, Bandura has gone far toward bridging the gap between learning theory and cognitive-developmental theory by emphasizing important cognitive (mental) elements in observational learning. Indeed, he now calls his theory "social cognitive theory" rather than "social learning theory," as it was originally labeled (Bandura, 1986, 1989, 2008). For example, Bandura now stresses the fact that modeling can be the vehicle for learning abstract information as well as concrete skills. In abstract modeling, the observer extracts a rule that may be the basis of the model's behavior, then learns the rule as well as the specific behavior. A child who sees his parents volunteering one day a month at a food bank may extract a rule about the importance of "helping others," even if the parents never actually articulate this rule. Thus, through modeling, a child can acquire attitudes, values, ways of solving problems, even standards of self-evaluation.

Collectively, Bandura's additions to traditional learning theory make his theory far more flexible and powerful, although it is still not a strongly developmental theory. That is, Bandura has little to say about any changes that may occur with age in what or how a child may learn from modeling. In contrast, both psychoanalytic and cognitive-developmental theories are strongly developmental, emphasizing sequential, often stagelike qualitative change that occurs with age. ⊙ Watch at MyDevelopmentLab

If a dose of cough syrup suppresses this child's cough, his parent is likely to administer another next time the child starts coughing. This is an example of negative reinforcement: The parent's behavior of administering cough syrup makes the child's coughing (an unpleasant stimulus for both parent and child) go away. Therefore, the chances that the parent will reach for the cough syrup the next time the child starts coughing increase.

⊙ Watch the Video *Bandura's Bobo Doll Experiment* at MyDevelopmentLab

## Comparing Theories

After learning about theories of development, students usually want to know which one is right. However, developmentalists don't think of theories in terms of right or wrong but, instead, compare them on the basis of their assumptions and how useful they are to understanding human development.

**ASSUMPTIONS ABOUT DEVELOPMENT**   When we say that a theory assumes something to be true, we mean that it begins from a general perspective on development. We can think of a theory's assumptions in terms of its answers to three questions about development.

One question addresses the *active or passive issue*: Is a person active in shaping her own development, or is she a passive recipient of environmental influences? Theories that claim a person's actions on the environment are the most important determinants of her development are on the active side of this question. Cognitive-developmental theories, for example, typically view development this way. In contrast, theories on the passive side of the question, such as classical and operant conditioning, maintain that development results from the action of the environment on the individual.

As you learned earlier in the chapter, the *nature or nurture question* is one of the most important issues in developmental psychology. All developmental theories, while admitting that both nature and nurture are involved in development, make assumptions about their relative importance. Theories claiming that biology contributes more to development than environment are on the nature side of the question. Those that view environmental influences as most important are on the nurture side. Other theories assume that nature and nurture are equally important, and that it is impossible to say which contributes more to development. ((•─ Listen at MyDevelopmentLab

Developmental theories also disagree on the *stability versus change issue*. Theories that have no stages assert that development is a stable, continuous process. Stage theories, on the other hand, emphasize change more than stability. They claim that development happens in leaps from lower to higher steps.

◄─────────── Learning Objective 1.9

What are the criteria that developmental scientists use to compare theories?

((•─ Listen to *The Right Hand* at MyDevelopmentLab

Table 1.2 lists the theories you have read about in this chapter and the assumptions each makes regarding these issues. Because each theory is based on different assumptions, each takes a different approach to studying development. Consequently, research derived from each reveals something different about development.

A theory's assumptions also shape the way it is applied in the real world. For example, a teacher who approached instruction from the cognitive-developmental perspective would create a classroom in which children can experiment to some degree on their own. He would also believe that structuring the educational environment is important, but that what each student ultimately learns will be determined by his or her own actions on the environment. Alternatively, a teacher who adopted the learning theory perspective would guide and reinforce children's learning very carefully. Such a teacher would place little importance on ability differences among children. Instead, he would try to accomplish the same instructional goals for all children through proper manipulation of the environment.

**Table 1.2**

## COMPARING THEORIES

| | Theory | Main Ideas | Active or Passive? | Nature or Nurture? | Stages or No Stages? |
|---|---|---|---|---|---|
| Psychoanalytic Theories | Freud's Psychosexual Theory | Personality develops in five stages from birth to adolescence; in each stage, the need for physical pleasure is focused on a different part of the body. | Passive | Nature | Stages |
| | Erikson's Psychosocial Theory | Personality develops through eight life crises across the entire lifespan; a person finishes each crisis with either a good or a poor resolution. | Passive | Both | Stages |
| Cognitive Theories | Piaget's Cognitive-Developmental Theory | Reasoning develops in four universal stages from birth through adolescence; in each stage, the child builds a different kind of scheme. | Active | Both | Stages |
| | Vygotsky's Socio-Cultural Theory | Social interaction is critical to the development of thinking and problem-solving; stages in the development of reasoning reflect internalized language. | Active | Both | Stages |
| | Information-Processing Theory | The computer is used as a model for human cognitive functioning; encoding, storage, and retrieval processes change with age, causing changes in memory function. | Active | Both | Some theories have stages; others do not |
| Learning Theories | Classical Conditioning | Learning happens when neutral stimuli become so strongly associated with natural stimuli that they elicit the same responses. | Passive | Nurture | No stages |
| | Operant Conditioning | Development involves behavior changes that are shaped by reinforcement and punishment. | Passive | Nurture | No stages |
| | Bandura's Social Cognitive Theory | People learn from models; what they learn from a model depends on how they interpret the situation cognitively and emotionally. | Active | Nurture | No stages |

**USEFULNESS**   Developmentalists also compare theories with respect to their usefulness. Before reading this section, you should understand that there is a fair amount of disagreement among psychologists on exactly how useful each theory is. Nevertheless, there are a few general criteria most psychologists use to evaluate the usefulness of a theory.

One kind of usefulness has to do with a theory's ability to generate predictions that can be tested with scientific methods. For example, one criticism of Freud's theory is that many of his claims are difficult to test. In contrast, when Piaget claimed that most children can solve hypothetical problems by age 12 or so, he made an assertion that is easily tested. Thus, Piaget's theory is viewed by many developmentalists as more useful in this sense than Freud's. Vygotsky, the learning theorists, and the information-processing theorists have also proposed many testable ideas (Thomas, 2005).

Another criterion by which psychologists judge the usefulness of theories is their *heuristic value*, the degree to which they stimulate thinking and research. In terms of heuristic value, we would have to give Freud's and Piaget's theories equally high marks. Both are responsible for an enormous amount of theorizing and research on human development, often by psychologists who strongly disagree with them.

Yet another way of thinking about a theory's usefulness is in terms of practical value. In other words, a theory may be deemed useful if it provides solutions to real-life problems. On this criterion, the learning and information-processing theories seem to stand out because they provide tools that can be used to influence behavior. A person who suffers from anxiety attacks, for example, can learn to use biofeedback, a technique derived from classical conditioning theories, to manage them. Similarly, a student who needs to learn to study more effectively can get help from study-skills courses based on information-processing theories.

Ultimately, of course, no matter how many testable hypotheses or practical techniques a theory produces, it is of little or no value to developmentalists if it doesn't explain the basic facts of development. On this criterion, learning theories, especially those of classical and operant conditioning, are regarded by many developmentalists as somewhat less useful than other perspectives (Thomas, 2005). While they explain how specific behaviors may be learned, the complexity of human development can't be reduced to connections between stimuli and responses or behaviors and reinforcers.

**ECLECTICISM**   As you can see, the point of comparing theories is not to conclude which one is true. Instead, we compare them to understand the unique contribution each can make to a comprehensive understanding of human development. Consequently, today's developmental scientists try to avoid rigid adherence to a single theoretical perspective. Instead, most adopt an approach known as **eclecticism**, the use of multiple theoretical perspectives to explain and study human development (Parke, 2004).

To better understand the eclectic approach, think about how ideas drawn from several theories might help us better understand a child's disruptive behavior in school. Observations of the child's behavior and her classmates' reactions may suggest that her behavior is being rewarded by the other children's responses (a behavioral explanation). Deeper probing of the child's family situation may indicate that her acting-out behavior reflects an emotional reaction to a family event such as divorce (a psychoanalytic explanation). The emotional reaction may arise from her inability to understand why her parents are divorcing (a cognitive-developmental explanation). When appropriately applied, each of these perspectives can help us gain insight into developmental issues. Moreover, we can integrate all of them into a more complete explanation than any of the perspectives alone could provide us with.

## Finding the Answers: Research Designs and Methods

The easiest way to understand research methods is to look at a specific question and the alternative ways in which it can be answered. Suppose we wanted to answer the following question: "What causes children's attention spans to increase as they get older?" How might we go about answering this question?

**eclecticism**   The use of multiple theoretical perspectives to explain and study human development.

**Learning Objective 1.10** ----------➤
What are the goals of developmental science?

# The Goals of Developmental Science

Developmental psychology uses the scientific method to achieve four goals: to *describe*, to *explain*, to *predict*, and to *influence* human development from conception to death. To describe development is simply to state what happens. "Children's attention spans get longer as they get older" is an example of a statement that represents the description goal of developmental psychology. All we would have to do is measure how long children of various ages pay attention to something to meet this objective.

Explaining development involves telling why a particular event occurs. As you learned earlier in this chapter, developmentalists rely on theories to generate explanations. Useful theories produce predictions researchers can test, or **hypotheses**, such as "If changes in the brain cause children's attention spans to increase, then children whose brain development is ahead of that of their peers should also have longer attention spans." To test this biological hypothesis, we would have to measure some aspect of brain structure or function as well as attention span. Then we would have to find a way to relate one to the other.

We could instead test an experiential explanation of attention-span increase by comparing children of the same age who differ in the amount of practice they get in paying attention. For example, we might hypothesize that the experience of learning to play a musical instrument enhances children's ability to attend. If we compare instrument-playing and non–instrument-playing children of the same age and find that those who have musical training do better on tests of attention than their agemates who have not had musical training, the experiential perspective gains support.

If both the biological and the experiential hypotheses are supported by research, they provide far more insight into age-related attention-span change than would either hypothesis alone. In this way, theories add tremendous depth to psychologists' understanding of the facts of human development. They also provide hints about how to influence development.

**Learning Objective 1.11** ----------➤
What are the pros and cons of cross-sectional, longitudinal, and sequential research designs?

# Studying Age-Related Changes

When researchers set out to study age-related change, they have basically three choices: (1) study different groups of people of different ages, using what is called a **cross-sectional design**; (2) study the *same* people over a period of time, using a **longitudinal design**; or (3) combine cross-sectional and longitudinal designs in some fashion in a **sequential design**.

**CROSS-SECTIONAL DESIGNS**   To study attention cross-sectionally, we might select groups of participants at each of several ages, such as groups of 2-, 5-, 8-, and 11-year-olds. If we find that each group demonstrates a longer average attention span than all the groups that are younger, we may be tempted to conclude that attention span does increase with age, but we cannot say this conclusively with cross-sectional data, because these children differ not only in age, but in cohort. The differences in attention might reflect educational differences and not actually be linked to age or development. Furthermore, cross-sectional studies cannot tell us anything about sequences of change over age or about the consistency of individual behavior over time, because each child is tested only once. Still, cross-sectional research is very useful because it is relatively quick to do and can give indications of possible age differences or age changes.

**LONGITUDINAL DESIGNS**   Longitudinal designs seem to solve the problems that arise with cross-sectional designs, because they follow the same individuals over a period of time. For example, to examine our attention-span hypothesis, we could test a particular group of children first at age 2, then at age 5, next at age 8, and finally at age 11. Such studies look at sequences of change and at individual consistency or inconsistency over time. And because these studies compare the same people at different ages, they get around the cohort problems of cross-sectional designs. However, longitudinal designs have several major difficulties. One problem is that longitudinal designs typically involve giving each participant the same tests over and over again. Over time, people learn how to take the tests. Such practice effects may distort the measurement of any underlying developmental changes.

**hypothesis**   A testable prediction based on a theory.

**cross-sectional design**   A form of research study in which samples of participants from several different age groups are studied at the same time.

**longitudinal design**   A form of research study in which the same participants are observed or assessed repeatedly over a period of months or years.

**sequential design**   A form of research study that combines cross-sectional and longitudinal designs in some way.

*Only by studying the same children over time (that is, longitudinally), such as this boy Eddie at three ages, can developmentalists identify consistencies (or changes) in behavior across age.*

Another significant problem with longitudinal studies is that not everyone sticks with the program. Some participants drop out; others die or move away. As a general rule, the healthiest and best-educated participants are most likely to stick it out, and that fact biases the results, particularly if the study continues into adulthood.

Longitudinal studies also don't really get around the cohort problem. For example, one famous study, the Oakland Growth Study, followed individuals born between 1913 and 1928 into old age. Consequently, the study's participants experienced certain major historical events, such as the Great Depression and World War II, that probably influenced their development. So, we don't know whether the ways in which they changed across these years, when they were children and teenagers, were caused by developmental processes or by the unique historical period in which they were growing up.

**SEQUENTIAL DESIGNS**   One way to avoid the shortcomings of both cross-sectional and longitudinal designs is to use a sequential design. To study our attention-span question using a sequential design, we would begin with at least two age groups. One group might include 2- to 4-year-olds, and the other might have 5- to 7-year-olds. We would then test each group over a number of years, as illustrated in Figure 1.4. Each testing point beyond the initial one provides two types of comparisons. Age-group comparisons provide the same kind of information as a cross-sectional study would. Comparisons of the scores or behaviors of participants in each group to their own scores or behaviors at an earlier testing point provide longitudinal evidence at the same time.

Sequential designs also allow for comparisons of cohorts. Notice in Figure 1.4, for example, that those in Group A are 5 to 7 years old at testing point 1, and those in Group B are 5 to 7 years old at testing point 2. Likewise, Group A members are 8 to 10 at point 2, and their counterparts in Group B are this age at point 3. If same-age comparisons of the two groups reveal that their average attention spans are different, the researchers have evidence that, for some reason, the two cohorts differ. Conversely, if the groups perform similarly, the investigators can conclude that their respective performances represent developmental characteristics rather than cohort effects. Moreover, if both groups demonstrate similar age-related patterns of change over time, the researchers can conclude that the developmental pattern is not specific to any particular cohort. Finding the same developmental pattern in two cohorts

**FIGURE 1.4** A Hypothetical Sequential Study
A hypothetical sequential study of attention span across ages 2 to 13.

|  |  | Age at testing point 1 | Age at testing point 2 | Age at testing point 3 |
|---|---|---|---|---|
| Group | A | 5 to 7 | 8 to 10 | 11 to 13 |
|  | B | 2 to 4 | 5 to 7 | 8 to 10 |

provides psychologists with stronger evidence than either cross-sectional or longitudinal data alone.

Learning Objective 1.12 ----------➤

What descriptive methods are used by developmental scientists?

# Descriptive Methods

A researcher interested in studying the relationship between age and attention span must decide how to go about finding relationships between *variables*. Variables are characteristics that vary from person to person, such as height, intelligence, and personality. When two or more variables vary together, there is some kind of relationship between them. The hypothesis that attention span increases with age involves two variables—attention span and age—and suggests a relationship between them. There are several ways of identifying and describing such relationships.

**CASE STUDIES AND NATURALISTIC OBSERVATION**   **Case studies** are in-depth examinations of single individuals. To examine changes in attention span, a researcher could use a case study comparing an individual's scores on tests of attention at various ages in childhood. Such a study might tell a lot about the stability or instability of attention in the individual studied, but the researcher wouldn't know if the findings applied to others.

Still, case studies are extremely useful in making decisions about individuals. For example, to find out if a child has mental retardation, a psychologist can do an extensive case study involving tests, interviews of the child's parents, behavioral observations, and so on. Case studies are also frequently the basis of important hypotheses about unusual developmental events such as head injuries and strokes.

When psychologists use **naturalistic observation**, they observe people in their normal environments. For instance, to find out more about attention span in children of different ages, a researcher could observe them in their homes or child-care centers. Such studies provide developmentalists with information about psychological processes in everyday contexts.

The weakness of this method, however, is *observer bias*. For example, if a researcher observing 2-year-olds is convinced that most of them have very short attention spans, he is likely to ignore any behavior that goes against this view. Because of observer bias, naturalistic observation studies often use "blind" observers who don't know what the research is about. In most cases, such studies employ two or more observers for the sake of accuracy. This way, the observations of each observer can be checked against those of the other.

Like case studies, the results of naturalistic observation studies have limited generalizability. In addition, naturalistic observation studies are very time-consuming. They must be repeated in a variety of settings before researchers can be sure people's behavior reflects development and not the influences of a specific environment.

**CORRELATIONS**   A **correlation** is a number ranging from −1.00 to +1.00 that describes the strength of a relationship between two variables. A zero correlation indicates that there is no relationship between those variables. A positive correlation means that high scores on one variable are usually accompanied by high scores on the other. The closer a positive correlation is to +1.00, the stronger the relationship between the variables. Two variables that move in opposite directions result in a negative correlation, and the nearer the correlation is to −1.00, the more strongly the two are inversely related.   ◉ Watch at **MyDevelopmentLab**

To understand positive and negative correlations, think about the relationship between temperature and the use of air conditioners and heaters. Temperature and air conditioner use are positively correlated. As the temperature climbs, so does the number of air conditioners in use. Conversely, temperature and heater use are negatively correlated. As the temperature decreases, the number of heaters in use goes up.

If we want to test the hypothesis that greater attention span is related to increases in age, we can use a correlation. All we would need to do would be to administer attention-span tests to children of varying ages and to calculate the correlation between test scores and ages. If there was a positive correlation between the length of children's attention spans and age—if older children attended for longer periods of time—then we could say that our hypothesis had been supported. Conversely, if there was a negative correlation—if older children paid attention for shorter periods of time than younger children—then we would have to conclude that our hypothesis had not been supported.

◉ Watch the **Video** *Research Methods* at **MyDevelopmentLab**

**case studies**   In-depth studies of individuals.

**naturalistic observation**   A research method in which participants are observed in their normal environments.

**correlation**   A statistic used to describe the strength of a relationship between two variables. It can range from −1.00 to +1.00. The closer it is to +1.00 or −1.00, the stronger the relationship being described.

# Experimental Methods

◄ - - - - - - - - - - - -Learning Objective 1.13

What is the primary advantage of the experimental method?

As useful as they are, case studies, naturalistic observations, and correlations reveal little about *causal* relationships between variables. For instance, the amount of time that children spend watching television is correlated with excessive weight gain, but it's highly doubtful that watching television causes a child to gain too much weight. Instead, the television-watching and weight gain are correlated because both are related to the actual causes of weight gain: too many calories (eating snacks while watching television) and too little exercise.

When developmental scientists seek to identify the cause of an age-related change, they turn to experiments. An **experiment** is a research method that tests a causal hypothesis. Suppose, for example, that we think age differences in attention span are caused by younger children's failure to use attention-maintaining strategies, such as ignoring distractions. We could test this hypothesis by providing attention training to one group of children and no training to another group. If the trained children got higher scores on attention tests than they did before training, and the no-training group showed no change, we could claim that our hypothesis had been supported.

A key feature of an experiment is that participants are assigned *randomly* to participate in one of several groups. In other words, chance determines the group in which the researcher places each participant. When participants are randomly assigned to groups, the groups have equal averages and equal amounts of variation with respect to variables such as intelligence, personality traits, height, weight, health status, and so on. Consequently, none of these variables can affect the outcome of the experiment.

Participants in the **experimental group** receive the treatment the experimenter thinks will produce a particular effect, while those in the **control group** receive either no special treatment or a neutral treatment. The presumed causal element in the experiment is called the **independent variable**, and the behavior on which the independent variable is expected to show its effect is called a **dependent variable** (or the *outcome variable*). ◉► Simulate at **MyDevelopmentLab**

Applying these terms to the attention-training experiment may help you better understand them. The group that receives the attention training is the experimental group, while those who receive no instruction form the control group. Attention training is the variable that we, the experimenters, think will cause differences in attention span, so it is the independent variable. Performance on attention tests is the variable we are using to measure the effect of the attention training. Therefore, performance on attention tests is the dependent variable.

Experiments are essential for understanding many aspects of development. But two special problems in studying child development limit the use of experiments. First, many of the questions developmentalists want to answer have to do with the effects of unpleasant or stressful experiences—for example, abuse or prenatal exposure to alcohol or tobacco. For obvious ethical reasons, researchers cannot manipulate these variables. For example, they cannot ask one set of pregnant women to have two alcoholic drinks a day and others to have none. To study the effects of such experiences, developmentalists must rely on nonexperimental methods, like correlations.

Second, the independent variable developmentalists are often most interested in is age itself, and they cannot assign participants randomly to age groups. Researchers can compare the attention spans of 4-year-olds and 6-year-olds, but the children differ in a host of ways other than their ages. Older children have had more and different experiences. Thus, unlike psychologists studying other aspects of behavior, developmental psychologists *cannot* systematically manipulate many of the variables they are most interested in.

To get around this problem, developmentalists can use any of a number of strategies, sometimes called *quasi-experiments*, in which they compare groups without assigning the participants randomly. Cross-sectional comparisons are a form of quasi-experiment. So are studies in which researchers select naturally occurring groups that differ in some dimension of interest, such as children whose parents choose to place them in child-care programs compared with children whose parents keep them at home. Such comparisons have built-in problems, because groups that differ in one way are likely to be different in other ways as well. Families who place their children in child care are also likely to be poorer, more likely to have only a single parent, and may have different values or religious backgrounds than

◉► Simulate the **Experiment**
*Distinguishing Independent and Dependent Variables* at **MyDevelopmentLab**

**experiment** A research method for testing a causal hypothesis, in which participants are assigned randomly to experimental and control groups and the experimental group is then provided with a particular experience that is expected to alter behavior in some fashion.

**experimental group** A group of participants in an experiment who receive a particular treatment intended to produce some specific effect.

**control group** A group of participants in an experiment who receive either no special treatment or some neutral treatment.

**independent variable** A condition or event that an experimenter varies in some systematic way in order to observe the impact of that variation on participants' behavior.

**dependent variable** The variable in an experiment that is expected to show the impact of manipulations of the independent variable; also called the *outcome variable*.

## Responding to Media Reports of Research

Have you heard that developmental psychologists have proven that listening to classical music raises children's IQ scores? In today's information age, parents hear such claims nearly every day. How can they evaluate such them? The thinking strategies collectively known as *critical thinking* can help. These strategies include:

■ **Independent thinking.** When thinking critically, we do not automatically accept and believe what we read or hear.

■ **Suspension of judgment.** Critical thinking requires gathering relevant and up-to-date information on all sides of an issue before taking a position.

■ **Willingness to modify or abandon prior judgments.** Critical thinking involves evaluating new evidence, even when it contradicts pre-existing beliefs.

Applying the first of these three characteristics to the claim about classical music and children's IQs involves the understanding that research shouldn't be regarded as a source of fixed, immutable truth. In fact, learning to question accepted "truths" is important to the scientific method itself. So, judgments about the truth of any claim shouldn't be based on the authoritativeness of its source. That is, a

claim isn't necessarily true just because it's based on a study published in a prestigious journal.

Applying suspension of judgment and willingness to change often requires people to change some old habits. This is especially true of the common tendency to respond to research on the basis of personal experiences, or *anecdotal evidence*. A non-critical thinker might say, "I agree with that study because my uncle always has classical music on in his house, and all of his kids are really smart." In contrast, a critical thinker would investigate the methods used in the study on which the claim is based.

With regard to the music-IQ claim, a critical thinker who looked deeper into the study behind the claim critic would learn that it was an experiment (Rauscher, Shaw, & Ky, 1993). So, the claim that exposure to classical music *causes* differences in IQ scores might be justified. However, the study involved adults, not children. Moreover, classical music raised participants' scores on a spatial reasoning test, not an IQ test. The effect also turned out to be temporary. Nevertheless, soon after the study appeared in a scientific journal, the news media began intimating that classical CDs were as essential to the well-equipped

nursery as diapers and baby wipes. By contrast, developmental scientists whose critical thinking skills are highly developed responded to the Mozart mayhem with skepticism. Many carried out carefully designed experimental studies of their own with infants and young children. As a result, most developmentalists now believe that there is no such thing as the Mozart Effect (Pietschnig, Voracek, & Formann, 2010).

### CRITICAL ANALYSIS

1. What kind of studies would be needed to determine whether adults and children differ in their responses to different types of music?

2. Suppose a study found that the babies of parents who regularly play classical music in their homes progress more rapidly in motor development than their peers. What variables other than music might account for such a finding?

**Learning Objective 1.13a**
How does critical thinking help you evaluate media reports of research?

---

those who rear their children at home. If researchers find that the two groups of children differ in some fashion, is it because they have spent their daytime hours in different places or because of these other differences in their families? Such comparisons can be made a bit cleaner if the comparison groups are initially selected so that they are matched on those variables that researchers think might matter, such as income, marital status, or religion. But a quasi-experiment, by its very nature, will always yield more ambiguous results than will a fully controlled experiment. However, as noted in the *Thinking about Research* discussion, media reports of research often do not provide consumers with sufficient information about research methods. Such information is vital to determining the validity of a research finding. Likewise, it can help parents and others who work with children determine the relevance of the research to their own lives. ✳️ Explore at **MyDevelopmentLab**

✳️ Explore the Concept *How to Be a Critical Thinker* at **MyDevelopmentLab**

---

**Learning Objective 1.14** ----------▶ **Cross-Cultural Research**

Why is cross-cultural research important to the study of human development?

Can you imagine toilet training a newborn? Most people in Western cultures would consider such efforts unlikely to be successful. But in cultures where diapers are unheard of, toilet training begins in the first few days of life. Moreover, it is accomplished through far more careful observations of newborns' patterns of physical functioning than is common in industrialized societies (Rogers, 2007) Such examples illustrate why **cross-cultural research**, or research comparing cultures or contexts, is important to developmentalists. For one thing, developmentalists want to identify universal changes—that is, predictable events or processes that occur in the lives of individuals in all cultures. Developmentalists don't want to make a general statement about development—such as "Attention span increases with age"—if the phenomenon in question happens only in Western, industrialized cultures. Without cross-cultural

**cross-cultural research** Any study that involves comparisons of different cultures or contexts.

research, it is impossible to know whether studies involving North Americans and Europeans apply to people in other parts of the world.

Second, one of the goals of developmental psychology is to produce findings that can be used to improve people's lives. Cross-cultural research is critical to this goal as well. For example, developmentalists know that children in cultures that emphasize the community more than the individual are more cooperative than children in cultures that are more individualistic. However, to use this information to help all children learn to cooperate, developmentalists need to know exactly how adults in collectivist cultures teach their children to be cooperative. Cross-cultural research helps developmentalists identify specific variables that explain cultural differences.

All of the methods you have learned about, which are summarized in Table 1.3, are used in cross-cultural research. Cross-cultural researchers borrow methods from other disciplines as well. One such strategy, borrowed from the field of anthropology, is to compile an *ethnography*—a detailed description of a single culture or context based on extensive observation. Often the observer lives within the culture for a period of time, perhaps as long as several years. Each ethnography is intended to stand alone, although it is sometimes possible to compare several different studies to see whether similar developmental patterns exist in varying contexts.

Alternatively, investigators may attempt to compare two or more cultures directly, by testing children or adults in each of several cultures with the same or comparable measures. Sometimes this involves comparisons across different countries. Sometimes the comparisons are between subcultures within the same country, as in the increasingly common research that

Most of the studies in developmental science involve children in industrialized societies who attend school for several hours each day. By studying children, like this girl, whose cultures require them to spend much of their time working rather than going to school, developmentalists can determine which age-related changes in cognitive functioning are likely to be attributable to formal education and which arise from natural, presumably universal, developmental processes.

## Table 1.3

### RESEARCH METHODS AND DESIGNS

| Method | Description | Advantages | Limitations |
|---|---|---|---|
| Cross-Sectional Designs | Participants of different ages studied at one time | Provide quick access to data about age differences | Ignore individual differences; cohort effects |
| Longitudinal Designs | Participants in one group studied several times | Track developmental changes in individuals and groups | Time-consuming; findings may apply only to the group that is studied |
| Sequential Designs | Study that combines both longitudinal and cross-sectional components | Yield cross-sectional and longitudinal data relevant to the same hypothesis | Time-consuming; different attrition rates across groups |
| Case Studies | In-depth study of one or a few individuals using observation, interviews, or psychological testing | Provide in-depth information; important in the study of unusual events | Results may not generalize beyond the case that is studied; time-consuming; subject to misinterpretation |
| Naturalistic Observation | Observation of behavior in natural settings | Participants behave naturally | Researchers' expectations can influence results; little control over conditions |
| Correlation Studies | Determination of mathematical relationship between two variables | Assess strength and direction of relationships | Cannot demonstrate cause and effect |
| Experiments | Random assignment of participants to control or experimental group; manipulation of independent variable | Identify cause-effect relationships | Results may not generalize to nonresearch settings; many variables cannot be studied in experiments |
| Cross-Cultural Research | Research that either describes culture or includes culture as a variable | Provides information about universality and culture-specificity of age-related changes | Time consuming; difficult to construct tests and methods that are equally valid in different cultures |

compares children or adults from different ethnic groups or communities in the United States, such as African Americans, Hispanic Americans, Asian Americans, and European Americans.

**Learning Objective 1.15** - - - - - - - - - →
What are the ethical standards that developmental researchers must follow?

# Research Ethics

No matter which of the research strategies summarized in Table 1.3 a researcher chooses to use, she is ethically bound to conduct her research according to a well-established set of rules. *Research ethics* are the guidelines researchers follow to protect the rights of animals and humans who participate in studies. Ethical guidelines are published by professional organizations such as the American Psychological Association, the American Educational Research Association, and the Society for Research in Child Development. Universities, private foundations, and government agencies have review committees that make sure that all research these organizations sponsor is ethical. Guidelines for animal research include the requirement that animals be protected from unnecessary pain and suffering. Further, researchers must demonstrate that the potential benefits of their studies to either human or animal populations are greater than any potential harm to animal subjects. ◉▸ Simulate at **MyDevelopmentLab**

◉▸ Simulate the **Experiment**
*Ethics of Psychological Research* at
**MyDevelopmentLab**

Ethical standards for research involving human participants are based on the following major themes:

**PROTECTION FROM HARM**   It is unethical to do research that may cause permanent physical or psychological harm to participants. Moreover, if there is a possibility of temporary harm, researchers must provide participants with some way of repairing the damage. For example, if the study will remind participants of unpleasant experiences, like rape, researchers must provide them with counseling. ◉ Watch at **MyDevelopmentLab**

◉ Watch the **Video** *Human Cloning: The Ethics* at **MyDevelopmentLab**

**INFORMED CONSENT**   Researchers must inform participants of any possible harm and require them to sign a consent form stating that they are aware of the risks involved in participating. In order for children to participate in studies, their parents must give permission after the researcher has informed them of possible risks. If children are older than 7, they must also give consent themselves. If the research takes place in a school or child-care center, an administrator representing the institution must also consent. In addition, human participants, whether children or adults, have the right to discontinue participation in a study at any time. Researchers are obligated to explain this right to children in language they can understand. ◉ Watch at **MyDevelopmentLab**

◉ Watch the **Video** *Drapetomania: Robert Guthrie* at **MyDevelopmentLab**

**CONFIDENTIALITY**   Participants have the right to confidentiality. Researchers must keep the identities of participants confidential and must report data in such a way that no particular piece of information can be associated with any specific participant. The exception to confidentiality is when children reveal to researchers that they are being abused or have been abused in any way by an adult. In most states, all citizens are required to report suspected cases of child abuse.

**KNOWLEDGE OF RESULTS**   Participants, their parents (if they are children), and administrators of institutions in which research takes place have a right to a written summary of a study's results.

**PROTECTION FROM DECEPTION**   If deception has been a necessary part of a study, participants have the right to be informed about the deception as soon as the study is over.

## THINK CRITICALLY

- How have culture, religion, and science shaped your views of development?
- Researchers have found a positive correlation between a mother's age at the birth of her child and the child's later IQ: Very young mothers have children with lower IQs. How would an ecological approach help us understand this finding?

# CONDUCT YOUR OWN RESEARCH

Jenna is a 6-year-old who throws a temper tantrum every time she doesn't get her way. Describe her behavior to several people and ask them to explain it. Compare their explanations to those of the psychoanalytic, cognitive, and learning theorists.

## SUMMARY ✓ Study and Review at MyDevelopmentLab

### Issues in the Study of Development

**1.1** What answers have been proposed to the nature-nurture and continuity-discontinuity questions?

The question of the degree to which development is influenced by nature and by nurture has been central to the study of development for thousands of years. Theorists on the nature side of the debate favor biological explanations, while those on the nurture side endorse experiential explanations of age-related changes. Psychologists who favor continuity emphasize the quantitative aspects of development, while those who view development as discontinuous often propose stage models to explain developmental change.

**1.2** What are the internal and external variables that influence development?

Internal variables that influence development include factors such as maturation, critical and sensitive periods, inborn biases, individual genetic variations, and internal models of experience. External variables include parent behaviors and characteristics of the physical environment. Theoretical models try to explain how internal and external variables interact.

**1.3** How does the ecological perspective improve scientists' understanding of child development?

The ecological perspective attempts to explain how external factors such as family and culture influence development. Bronfenbrenner proposed a contextual model highlighting the more extended aspects of a child's environment. Cultural influences filter down to the child through social institutions and through her neighborhood and family. All the components of this complex system interact to affect development.

**1.4** In what ways do the concepts of vulnerability and resilience help us better understand child development?

Developmental psychologists often discuss development in terms of vulnerability and resilience. The idea is that certain risk factors, such as poverty, predispose children to develop in undesirable ways. However, protective factors, such as high IQ, prevent some children from being negatively influenced by risk factors.

**1.5** How do the three kinds of age-related change differ?

Normative age-graded changes are those that are experienced by all human beings. Normative history-graded changes are common to individuals who have similar cultural and historical experiences. Nonnormative changes, such as the timing of experiences, can lead to individual differences in development.

**1.5a** How is the availability of health information on the Internet likely to affect today's cohort of children and adolescents?

More than 90% of parents search the Internet for health information. Research shows that parents' knowledge and children's health are positively related. Therefore, the availability of health information may cause today's cohort of children to be healthier than children in earlier times.

### Theories of Development

**1.6** What are the main ideas of the psychoanalytic theories?

Psychoanalytic theories suggest that internal drives strongly influence development. Both Freud and Erikson proposed stages to explain the process of personality development as people age.

**1.7** What are the main ideas of cognitive-developmental and information-processing theories?

Cognitive-developmental theories propose that basic cognitive processes influence development in all other areas. Piaget's theory has been especially influential, but interest in Vygotsky's ideas has grown in recent years. Information-processing theory also explains development in terms of cognitive processes.

**1.8** How do learning theorists explain development?

Learning theories emphasize the influence of the environment on children's behavior. Classical and operant conditioning principles explain learning in terms of links between stimuli and responses. Bandura's social cognitive theory gives more weight to children's cognitive processing of learning experiences and attempts to explain how modeling influences development.

**1.8a** How do psychologists help children overcome school refusal?

Psychologists use a therapy based on classical conditioning principles, systematic desensitization, to help children who refuse to go to school. The therapy involves teaching the child to use techniques that help her physically relax and to associate these techniques with each step in the process of getting to and remaining in school.

**1.9** What are the criteria that developmental scientists use to compare theories?

Psychologists don't think of theories as "true" or "false." Instead, they compare theories on the bases of assumptions and usefulness.

## Finding the Answers: Research Designs and Methods

**1.10** What are the goals of developmental science?

The goals of developmental psychology are to describe, to explain, to predict, and to influence age-related change. Developmental psychologists use various methods to meet these goals.

**1.11** What are the pros and cons of cross-sectional, longitudinal, and sequential research designs?

Cross-sectional studies, in which separate age groups are each tested once, provide quick answers to questions about age differences but do not allow for observation of developmental processes. Longitudinal studies, which test the same individuals repeatedly over time, enable researchers to observe developmental processes at work, but researchers cannot determine whether the changes they observe can be generalized to individuals other than those who participate in the study. Sequential designs balance the pros and cons of cross-sectional and longitudinal studies by combining both approaches.

**1.12** What descriptive methods are used by developmental scientists?

Case studies and naturalistic observation provide a lot of important information, but it usually is not generalizable. Correlational studies measure relations between variables.

They can be done quickly and yield information that is more generalizable than information from case studies or naturalistic observation.

**1.13** What is the primary advantage of the experimental method?

To test causal hypotheses, it is necessary to use experimental designs in which participants are assigned randomly to experimental or control groups. An experimenter manipulates an independent variable in order to observe its effects on a dependent variable.

**1.13a** How does critical thinking help you evaluate media reports of research?

Critical thinkers display independent thinking, suspension of judgment, and willingness to modify or abandon prior judgments. These strategies help them resist the tendency to accept media reports of research on the basis of the authoritativeness of the sources (i.e., scientists, scientific journals). They investigate the methods used in the studies on which media reports are based and evaluate whether reporters' claims about them are supported.

**1.14** Why is cross-cultural research important to the study of human development?

Cross-cultural research helps developmentalists identify universal patterns and cultural variables that affect development.

**1.15** What are the ethical standards that developmental researchers must follow?

Ethical principles that guide psychological research include protection from harm, informed consent, confidentiality, knowledge of results, and protection from deception.

## KEY TERMS

behavior genetics (p. 5)
behaviorism (p. 3)
case studies (p. 22)
classical conditioning (p. 15)
cognitive-developmental theories (p. 13)
cohort (p. 10)
control group (p. 23)
correlation (p. 22)
critical period (p. 5)
cross-cultural research (p. 24)
cross-sectional design (p. 20)
dependent variable (p. 23)

developmental science (p. 2)
developmental theories (p. 11)
eclecticism (p. 19)
ego (p. 12)
experiment (p. 23)
experimental group (p. 23)
hypothesis (p. 20)
id (p. 12)
independent variable (p. 23)
information-processing theories (p. 14)
internal models of experience (p. 6)

learning theories (p. 15)
libido (p. 11)
longitudinal design (p. 20)
maturation (p. 4)
naturalistic observation (p. 22)
negative reinforcement (p. 16)
nonnormative changes (individual differences) (p. 10)
normative age-graded changes (p. 10)
normative history-graded changes (p. 10)
norms (p. 3)

operant conditioning (p. 15)
positive reinforcement (p. 15)
psychoanalytic theories (p. 11)
psychosexual stages (p. 12)
psychosocial stages (p. 12)
punishment (p. 16)
scaffolding (p. 13)
sensitive period (p. 5)
sequential design (p. 20)
superego (p. 12)
zone of proximal development (p. 13)

# Prenatal Development

Before the advent of modern medical technology, cultures devised spiritual practices that were intended to ensure a healthy pregnancy with a happy outcome. For instance, *godh bharan* is a centuries-old Hindu ceremony that honors a woman's first pregnancy. In the seventh month of her pregnancy, the mother-to-be dresses in formal garments that are given to her by her mother. A relative ties a yellow thread around the pregnant woman's wrist as ceremony attendees pronounce blessings on the unborn child. The purpose of the thread is to provide mother and baby with the spiritual protection required for a complication-free birth.

**zygote** The single cell formed from separate sperm and egg cells at conception.

**ovum** The cell released monthly from a woman's ovaries, which, if fertilized, forms the basis for the developing organism.

**fallopian tube** The tube between the ovary and the uterus down which the ovum travels to the uterus and in which conception usually occurs.

**uterus** The female organ in which the embryo/fetus develops (popularly referred to as the *womb*).

**sperm** The cells produced in a man's testes that may fertilize an ovum following intercourse.

**chromosomes** The structures, arrayed in 23 pairs, within each cell in the body that contain genetic information. Each chromosome is made up of many segments, called genes.

**gametes** Sperm and ova. These cells, unlike all other cells of the body, contain only 23 chromosomes rather than 23 pairs.

**deoxyribonucleic acid (DNA)** The chemical of which chromosomes are composed.

**Learning Objective 2.1** - - - - - - - - - →
What are the characteristics of the Zygote?

◉―|Watch the **Video** *Period of the Zygote* at **MyDevelopmentLab**

As rates of adverse pregnancy outcomes declined in the twentieth century, the *godh bharan* has become more celebratory than protective in nature. Likewise, a uniquely American prenatal institution, the baby shower, has also grown in popularity as pregnancy and childbirth have become safer. And as U.S.-based entertainment media have spread across the world, *godh bharan* ceremonies and others like it have increasingly come to resemble American baby showers.

The growing popularity and homogenization of prenatal celebrations suggest that the technological advances that have reduced maternal and fetal mortality rates have transformed the subjective and social experience of pregnancy from one of fear and dread to one of joy and anticipation. These advances have also been accompanied by innovations that have allowed researchers and parents-to-be to gain insight into prenatal developmental processes that were shrouded in mystery just a few decades ago. As you explore this chapter, you will become acquainted with some of these insights and, we hope, gain a greater appreciation for the amazing process of prenatal development.

## Conception and Genetics

The first step in the development of a human being is that moment of *conception*, when two single cells—one from a male and the other from a female—join together to form a new cell called a **zygote**. This event sets in motion powerful genetic forces that will influence the individual over the entire lifespan. ◉―|Watch at **MyDevelopmentLab**

## The Process of Conception

Ordinarily, a woman produces one **ovum** (egg cell) per month from one of her two ovaries. The ovum is released from an ovary roughly midway between two menstrual periods. If it is not fertilized, the ovum travels from the ovary down the **fallopian tube** toward the **uterus**, where it gradually disintegrates and is expelled as part of the next menstrual flow. If a couple has intercourse during the crucial few days when the ovum is in the fallopian tube, one of the millions of **sperm** ejaculated as part of each male orgasm may travel the full distance through the woman's vagina, cervix, and uterus into the fallopian tube and penetrate the ovum. A child is conceived. The zygote then continues on its journey down the fallopian tube and eventually implants itself in the wall of the uterus. (See *Thinking about Research*.)

**THE BASIC GENETICS OF CONCEPTION** Except in individuals with particular types of genetic abnormality, the nucleus of each cell in the human body contains a set of 46 **chromosomes**, arranged in 23 pairs. These chromosomes include all the genetic information for that individual, governing not only individual characteristics like hair color, height, body shape, temperament, and aspects of intelligence, but also all those characteristics shared by all members of our species, such as patterns of physical development and inborn biases of various kinds.

The only cells that do not contain 46 chromosomes are the sperm and the ovum, collectively called **gametes**, or *germ cells*. In the early stages of development, gametes divide as all other cells do (a process called *mitosis*), with each set of 23 chromosome pairs duplicating itself. In the final step of gamete division, however, called *meiosis*, each new cell receives only one chromosome from each original pair. Thus, each gamete has only 23 chromosomes instead of 23 pairs. When a child is conceived, the 23 chromosomes in the ovum and the 23 in the sperm combine to form the 23 pairs that will be part of each cell in the newly developing body.

The chromosomes are composed of long strings of molecules of a chemical called **deoxyribonucleic acid (DNA)**. In an insight for which they won the Nobel Prize in 1953, James Watson and Francis Crick deduced that DNA is in the shape of a double helix, somewhat

## Assisted Reproductive Technology

Physicians define *infertility* as the failure to conceive after 12 consecutive months of unprotected intercourse (Mitchell, 2002). To help them conceive and deliver healthy babies, many infertile couples turn to *assisted reproductive techniques (ART)*. One such technique is *in vitro fertilization*. The first step in IVF involves using hormones to stimulate the woman's ovaries to produce multiple eggs. The eggs are then extracted from the ovaries and combined with sperm in a laboratory dish. If conception takes place, one or more embryos—ideally at the six-to-eight-cell stage of development—are transferred to the woman's uterus in the hope that a normal pregnancy will develop. The eggs used in IVF can come from the woman who will carry the child or from a donor. Likewise, the sperm can be from the woman's partner or a donor.

However, IVF is not a highly successful procedure. Less than one-third of such procedures result in a live birth (CDC,

*An eight-celled embryo is ideal for an IVF transfer. Pictured here is an embryo on the day of transfer into a woman's uterus.*

2009). The older a woman is, the lower the probability that she will be able to have a successful IVF pregnancy. Roughly 40% of 20- to 29-year-old IVF patients achieve a live birth, but only 17% or so of IVF procedures involving women over age 40 are successful (CDC, 2009). Moreover, IVF is expensive and is typically not covered by health insurance (Jain, Harlow, & Hornstein, 2002). As of this writing, surveys show that just 15 states in the United States require that health insurance providers cover IVF treatment (Kaiser Family Foundation, 2010).

Successful IVF carries a different set of risks. The overall rate of birth defects is 30 to 40% higher among IVF newborns than naturally conceived infants (Hansen, Bower, Milne, de Klerk, & Kurincauk, 2005). One key factor influencing this difference is that multiple births are far more frequent among IVF patients, primarily because doctors typically transfer several zygotes at once in order to increase the likelihood of at least one live birth (CDC, 2009). Consequently, 29% of IVF patients deliver twins, and another 2% give birth to triplets (CDC, 2009). Multiple births are associated with premature birth, low birth weight, and birth defects. Thus, specialists in reproductive medicine aim to reduce the frequency of multiple births (Jain, Missmer, & Hornstein 2004).

Despite the risks associated with IVF, most women who achieve successful pregnancies as a result of this technique

**Learning Objective 2.1a**
What risks are associated with assisted reproductive technology?

deliver babies who are healthy and normal. Further, studies have shown that children conceived through IVF who are of normal birth weight and who do not have any birth defects develop identically to peers who were conceived naturally (Levy-Shiff et al., 1998; van Balen, 1998). Such findings should give encouragement and hope to those couples who must turn to assisted reproductive technology to fulfill their desire to have children.

### CRITICAL ANALYSIS

1. Look back at the discussion of research ethics in Chapter 1. Would it be ethical to use assisted reproductive technology to experimentally manipulate variables associated with conception, such as the timing of conception in relation to the seasons of the year, in order to determine the effects of such variables on development during infancy and childhood? Why or why not?

2. The use of assisted reproductive technology to help postmenopausal women get pregnant is controversial. What are the arguments for and against this practice?

---

like a twisted ladder. The remarkable feature of this ladder is that the rungs are constructed so that the entire helix can "unzip"; then each half can guide the duplication of the missing part, thus allowing multiplication of cells so that each new cell contains the full set of genetic information.

The string of DNA that makes up each chromosome can be subdivided further into segments called **genes**, each of which controls or influences a particular feature of an organism or a portion of some developmental pattern. A gene controlling or influencing a specific characteristic always appears in the same place (the *locus*; plural is *loci*) on the same chromosome in every individual of the same species. For example, the locus of the gene that determines whether you have type A, B, or O blood is on chromosome 9, and similar genes for blood type are found on chromosome 9 in every other human being. In February, 2001, scientists working on a remarkable group of studies known as the *Human Genome Project (HGP)* announced that they had identified the locus of every human gene (U.S. Department of Energy, 2001) (see Figure 2.1 on page 32). ◉ Watch at MyDevelopmentLab

There are actually two types of chromosomes. In 22 of the chromosome pairs, called *autosomes*, the members of the pair look alike and contain exactly matching genetic loci. The 23rd pair, however, operates differently. The chromosomes of this pair, which determine the child's sex and are therefore called the *sex chromosomes*, come in two varieties, referred to as the X and the Y chromosomes.

◉ Watch the **Video** *Junk DNA* at **MyDevelopmentLab**

*This photo shows the moment of conception, when a single sperm has pierced the coating around the ovum.*

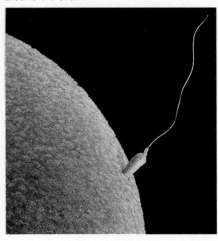

**FIGURE 2.1** Human Chromosome #20
This figure represents the genetic "map" of human chromosome #20; the map was produced by scientists associated with the Human Genome Project. Researchers have produced equally specific maps for all 23 human chromosomes. These maps include genes for normal traits (e.g., eye color) as well as for genetic disorders.

Creutzfeldt-Jakob disease
Gerstmann-Straussler disease
Insomnia, fatal familial
Hallervorden-Spatz syndrome
Alagille syndrome
Corneal dystrophy
Inhibitor of DNA binding, dominant negative
Facial anomalies syndrome
Gigantism
Retinoblastoma
Rous sarcoma
Colon cancer
Galactosialidosis
Severe combined immunodeficiency
Hemolytic anemia
Obesity/hyperinsulinism
Pseudohypoparathyroidism, type 1a
McCune-Albright polyostotic fibrous dysplasia
Somatotrophinoma
Pituitary ACTH secreting adenoma
Shah-Waardenburg syndrome

Diabetes insipidus, neurohypophyseal
SRY (sex-determining region Y)
McKusick-Kaufman syndrome
Cerebral amyloid angiopathy
Thrombophilia
Myocardial infarction, susceptibility to
Huntington-like neurodegenerative disorder
Anemia, congenital dyserythropoietic
Acromesomelic dysplasia, Hunter-Thompson type
Brachydactyly, type C
Chondrodysplasia, Grebe type
Myeloid tumor suppressor
Breast cancer
Maturity onset diabetes of the young, type 1
Diabetes mellitus, noninsulin-dependent
Graves disease, susceptibility to
Epilepsy, nocturnal frontal lobe and benign neonatal, type 1
Epiphyseal dysplasia, multiple
Electro-encephalographic variant pattern
Pseudohypoparathyroidism, type 1b

*Explore the Concept Dominant and Recessive Traits at MyDevelopmentLab*

**gene** A uniquely coded segment of DNA in a chromosome that affects one or more specific body processes or developments.

**homozygous** Term describing the genetic pattern when the two genes in the pair at any given genetic locus both carry the same instructions.

A normal human female has two X chromosomes in this 23rd pair (an XX pattern), while a normal human male has one X and one Y chromosome (an XY pattern). The X chromosome is considerably larger than the Y chromosome and contains many genetic loci not found on the Y.

Note that the sex of the child is determined by the sex chromosome it receives from the sperm. Because a woman has only X chromosomes, every ovum carries an X. But because a man has both X and Y chromosomes, when the father's gametes divide, half the sperm will carry an X, and half a Y. If the sperm that fertilizes the ovum carries an X, then the child inherits an XX pattern and is a girl. If the fertilizing sperm carries a Y, then the combination is XY, and the child is a boy.

Geneticists have pushed this understanding a step further, discovering that only one very small section of the Y chromosome actually determines maleness—a segment referred to as *SRY* (*sex-determining region of the Y chromosome*). Sometime between 4 and 8 weeks after conception, SRY genetic codes signal the male embryo's body to begin secreting hormones called *androgens*. These hormones cause male genitalia to develop. If androgens are not present, female genitalia develop, no matter what the embryo's chromosomal status is.

**Learning Objective 2.2**
In what ways do genes influence development?

**heterozygous** Term describing the genetic pattern when the two genes in the pair at any given genetic locus carry different instructions, such as a gene for blue eyes from one parent and a gene for brown eyes from the other parent.

**genotype** The pattern of characteristics and developmental sequences mapped in the genes of any specific individual, which will be modified by individual experience into the phenotype.

**phenotype** The expression of a particular set of genetic information in a specific environment; the observable result of the joint operation of genetic and environmental influences.

## Genotypes, Phenotypes, and Patterns of Genetic Inheritance

When the 23 chromosomes from the father and the 23 from the mother come together at conception, they provide a mix of "instructions." When the two sets of instructions are the same at any given locus (such as genes for type A blood from both parents), geneticists say that the genetic pattern is **homozygous**. When the two sets of instructions differ, the genetic pattern is said to be **heterozygous**, such as a gene pair that includes a gene for type A blood from one parent and a gene for type O blood from the other. How are these differences resolved? Geneticists are still a long way from having a complete answer to this question, but some patterns are very clear. Table 2.1 gives a few examples of physical characteristics that follow the rules you'll be reading about in this section. *Explore at MyDevelopmentLab*

**GENOTYPES AND PHENOTYPES** First, it's important to know that geneticists (and psychologists) make an important distinction between the **genotype**, which is the specific set of "instructions" contained in a given individual's genes, and the **phenotype**, which is the set of actual observed characteristics of the individual. The phenotype is a product of three things: the genotype, environmental influences from the time of conception onward, and the interaction between the two. A child might have a genotype associated with high IQ, but if his mother drinks too much alcohol during the pregnancy, there may be damage to his nervous

| Table 2.1 | NORMAL TRAITS | |
| --- | --- | --- |
| **Dominant** | **Recessive** | **Polygenic** |
| Freckles | Flat feet | Height |
| Coarse hair | Thin lips | Body type |
| Dimples | Rh negative blood | Eye color |
| Curly hair | Fine hair | Skin color |
| Nearsightedness | Red hair | Personality |
| Broad lips | Blond hair | |
| Rh positive blood | Type O blood | |
| Types A and B blood | | |
| Dark hair | | |

*Source:* Tortora and Grabowski, 1993. *Principles of anatomy and physiology.* New York: HarperCollins.

system, resulting in mild retardation. Another child might have a genotype including the mix of genes that contribute to a "difficult" temperament, but if his parents are particularly sensitive and thoughtful, he may learn other ways to handle himself.

**DOMINANT AND RECESSIVE GENES** Whenever a given trait is governed by a single gene, as is true of some 1,000 individual physical characteristics, inheritance patterns follow well-understood rules. Figure 2.2 offers a schematic look at how the **dominant/recessive pattern of inheritance** works, using the genes for curly and straight hair as an example. Because straight hair is controlled by a recessive gene, an individual must inherit the straight-hair gene from both parents in order for her phenotype to include straight hair. A child who

**dominant/recessive pattern of inheritance** The pattern of genetic transmission in which a single dominant gene influences a person's phenotype, but an individual must have two recessive genes to express a recessive trait.

**FIGURE 2.2** The Genetics of Hair Type Examples of how the genes for curly and straight hair pass from parents to children.

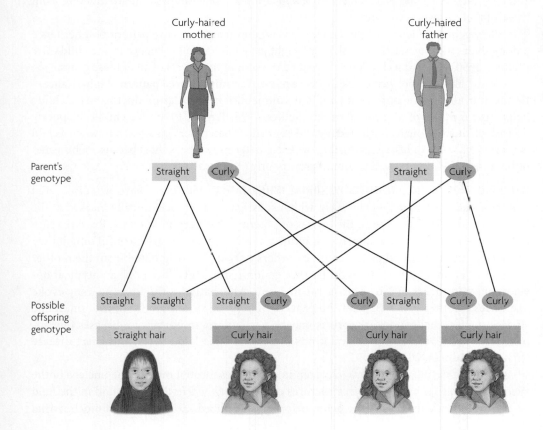

polygenic pattern of inheritance
Any pattern of genetic transmission in which multiple genes contribute to the outcome, such as is presumed to occur for complex traits such as intelligence or temperament.

multifactorial pattern of inheritance
The pattern of genetic transmission in which both genes and environment influence the phenotype.

receives only one gene for straight hair will have curly hair, but she may pass the straight-hair gene on to her offspring.

Since curly hair is controlled by a dominant gene, a child who inherits a gene for curly hair from either parent will actually have curly hair. However, her hair may not be as curly as that of the parent from whom she received the gene. Genes vary in *expressivity*, a term that simply means that the same gene may be expressed differently in two individuals who have it.

The dominant/recessive pattern doesn't always work in such a straightforward way. For example, humans carry genes for three kinds of blood type: A (dominant), B (dominant), and O (recessive). Each individual has only two of these genes. If one gene is A and the other is O, then the individual's blood type is A. As you know, an individual must inherit two recessive O genes to have type O blood. But what happens if an individual receives an A and a B gene? Since both are dominant, the individual has type AB blood, and the genes are said to be *co-dominant*.

**POLYGENIC AND MULTIFACTORIAL INHERITANCE**   In the **polygenic pattern of inheritance**, many genes influence the phenotype. There are many polygenic traits in which the dominant/recessive pattern is also at work. For example, children get several genes for skin color from each parent (Barsh, 2003). Dark skin is dominant over light skin, but blended skin colors are possible. Thus, when one parent has dark skin and the other has fair skin, their children most likely will have skin that is somewhere between the two. The dark-skinned parent's dominant genes will insure that the children are darker than the fair parent, but the fair-skinned parent's genes will prevent the children from having skin as dark as that of the dark-skinned parent.

Eye color is another polygenic trait with a dominant/recessive pattern (Liu, 2010). Scientists don't know for sure how many genes influence eye color. They do know, however, that the genes don't cause specific colors. Instead, they cause the colored part of the eye to be dark or light. Dark colors (black, brown, hazel, and green) are dominant over light colors (blue and gray). However, blended colors are also possible. People whose chromosomes carry a combination of genes for green, blue, and gray eyes can have phenotypes that include blue-gray, blue-green, or gray-green eye color. Likewise, genes that cause different shades of brown can combine their effects to produce variations in children's phenotypes that are different from those of their brown-eyed parents.

Many genes influence height, and there is no dominant/recessive pattern of inheritance among them. Most geneticists think each height gene has a small influence over a child's size (Tanner, 1990) and that a child's height will be the sum of the effects of all of these genes.

Height, like most polygenic traits, is also a result of a **multifactorial pattern of inheritance**— that is, it is affected by both genes and environment. For this reason, doctors use a child's height as a measure of his general health (Sulkes, 1998; Tanner, 1990). If a child is ill, poorly nourished, or emotionally neglected, he will be smaller than others his age. Thus, when a child is shorter than 97% of his agemates, doctors try to determine if he is short because of his genes or because something is causing him to grow poorly (Tanner, 1990).

**GENOMIC IMPRINTING AND MITOCHONDRIAL INHERITANCE**   Scientists have also discovered a process called *genomic imprinting* in which some genes are biochemically marked at the time ova and sperm develop in the bodies of potential mothers and fathers. Research into the significance of genomic imprinting indicates that some genes are harmful only if they come from the father and others cause disorders only if they originated from the mother (Jirtle & Weidman, 2007). It could be that genomic imprints "turn on" an atypical developmental process or "turn off" a normal one. Alternatively, the imprints may evoke responses in other genes that set the process of atypical development in motion. Some studies suggest that genomic imprints may be particularly important in diseases that appear later in life, including several kinds of cancer, Type II diabetes, and heart disease (Jirtle & Weidman, 2007).

In *mitochondrial inheritance*, children inherit genes located outside the nucleus of the zygote. These genes are carried in structures called *mitochondria* that are found in the fluid that surrounds the nucleus of the ovum before it is fertilized. Consequently, mitochondrial genes are passed only from mother to child. Geneticists have learned that several serious disorders, including some types of blindness, are transmitted in this way. In most such cases, the mother herself is unaffected by the harmful genes (Chinnery, 2006).

**TWINS AND SIBLINGS**    In most cases, babies are conceived and born one at a time. However, 3 out of every 100 births in the United States today are multiple births (Martin et al., 2010). This number has risen dramatically in recent decades, in large part because widely prescribed new medications given to infertile women frequently stimulate multiple ovulation. The great majority of multiple births in the United States are twins; triplets or higher multiples occur only about once in every 1,000 births (Martin et al., 2010).

Roughly two-thirds of twins are **fraternal twins**. Fraternal twins develop when two ova have been produced and both have been fertilized, each by a separate sperm. Such twins, also called **dizygotic twins**, are no more alike genetically than any other pair of siblings and may not even be of the same sex. The remaining one-third of twins are **identical twins** (also called **monozygotic twins**). In such cases, a single fertilized ovum apparently initially divides in the normal way, but then for unknown reasons separates into two parts, with each part developing into a separate individual. Because identical twins develop from precisely the same original fertilized ovum, they have identical genetic heritages. You'll remember from Chapter 1 that comparison of the degree of similarity of these two types of twins is a major research strategy in the important field of behavior genetics.

**fraternal (dizygotic) twins**    Children carried in the same pregnancy but who develop from two separately fertilized ova. They are no more alike genetically than other pairs of siblings.

**identical (monozygotic) twins**    Children carried in the same pregnancy who develop from the same fertilized ovum. They are genetic clones of each other.

**germinal stage**    The first stage of prenatal development, beginning at conception and ending at implantation of the zygote in the uterus (approximately the first 2 weeks).

**blastocyst**    Name for the mass of cells from roughly 4 to 10 days after fertilization.

**embryo**    The name given to the developing organism during the period of prenatal development between about 2 weeks and 8 weeks after conception, beginning with implantation of the blastocyst in the uterine wall.

## Development from Conception to Birth

Little was known about prenatal development until fairly recently. Consequently, there was a lot of confusion about the connection between the experiences of the pregnant woman and the intrauterine development and experiences of the child. For example, pregnancy has traditionally been divided into three *trimesters* of equal length, so doctors as well as expectant couples tended to think of prenatal development as consisting of three analogous stages. Of course, technology has changed all this. Scientists have learned that there are indeed three stages of prenatal development, but the developing child has already reached the *third* stage before the mother ends her first trimester.

## The Stages of Prenatal Development

The period of gestation of the human infant is 38 weeks (about 265 days). These 38 weeks are divided into three stages of unequal length, identified by specific changes within the developing organism (see Table 2.2 on page 36).

**THE GERMINAL STAGE**    The **germinal stage** begins at conception and ends when the zygote is implanted in the wall of the uterus. After conception, the zygote spends roughly a week floating down the fallopian tube to the uterus. Cell division begins 24 to 36 hours after conception; within 2 to 3 days, there are several dozen cells and the whole mass is about the size of the head of a pin. Approximately 4 days after conception, the mass of cells, now called a **blastocyst**, begins to subdivide, forming a sphere with two layers of cells around a hollow center. The outermost layer will form the various structures that will support the developing organism, while the inner layer will form the **embryo** itself. When it touches the wall of the uterus, the outer cell layer of the blastocyst breaks down at the point of contact. Small tendrils develop and attach the cell mass to the uterine wall, a process called *implantation*. When implantation is complete (normally 10 days to 2 weeks after conception), the blastocyst has perhaps 150 cells (Tanner, 1990). The sequence is illustrated schematically in Figure 2.3.

◄------------Learning Objective 2.3
What happens in each of the stages of prenatal development?

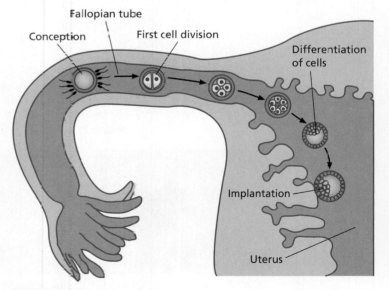

**FIGURE 2.3** Migration of the Zygote
This schematic shows the normal progression of development for the first 10 days of gestation, from conception to implantation.

Table
2.2

# MILESTONES IN PRENATAL DEVELOPMENT

| Stage/Time Frame | | Milestones |
|---|---|---|
| GERMINAL | Day 1: Conception | Sperm and ovum unite, forming a zygote containing genetic instructions for the development of a new and unique human being. |
| | Days 10 to 14: Implantation | The zygote burrows into the lining of the uterus. Specialized cells that will become the placenta, umbilical cord, and embryo are already formed. |
| EMBRYONIC | Weeks 3 to 8: Organogenesis | All of the embryo's organ systems form during the 6-week period following implantation. |
| | Weeks 9 to 38: Growth and Organ Refinement | The fetus grows from 1 inch long and 1/4 ounce to a length of about 20 inches and a weight of 7–9 pounds. By week 12, most fetuses can be identified as male or female. Changes in the brain and lungs make viability possible by week 24; optimum development requires an additional 14 to 16 weeks in the womb. Most neurons form by week 28, and connections among them begin to develop shortly thereafter. In the last 8 weeks, the fetus can hear and smell, is sensitive to touch, and responds to light. Learning is also possible. |
| FETAL | | |

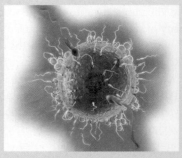

Sperm and egg

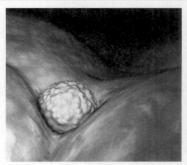

Zygote

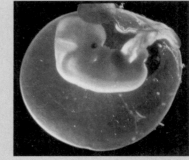

6-week fetus

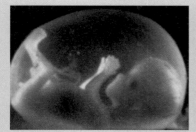

12-week fetus

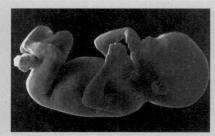

14-week fetus

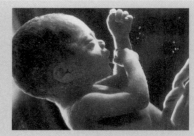

Well-developed fetus (age not given)

*Sources*: Kliegman, 1998; Tortora & Grabowski, 1993.

**THE EMBRYONIC STAGE** The **embryonic stage** begins when implantation is complete. The blastocyst's outer layer of cells specializes into two membranes, each of which forms critical support structures. The inner membrane becomes a sac or bag called the **amnion**, filled with liquid (amniotic fluid) in which the embryo floats. The outer membrane, called the **chorion**, develops into two organs, the **placenta** and the **umbilical cord**. The placenta, which is fully developed by about 4 weeks of gestation, is a platelike mass of cells that lies against the wall of the uterus. It serves as the liver and kidneys for the embryo until the embryo's own organs begin to function. It also provides the embryo with oxygen and removes carbon dioxide from its blood.

Connected to the embryo's circulatory system via the umbilical cord, the placenta also serves as a critical filter between the mother's circulatory system and the embryo's. Nutrients such as oxygen, proteins, sugars, and vitamins from the maternal blood can pass through to the embryo or fetus; digestive wastes and carbon dioxide from the infant's blood pass back through to the mother, whose own body can eliminate them. At the same time, many (but not all) harmful substances, such as viruses or the mother's hormones, are filtered out because they are too large to pass through the various membranes in the placenta. Most drugs and anesthetics, however, do pass through the placenta, as do some disease organisms.

While the support structures are developing, the mass of cells that will form the embryo itself is differentiating further into several types of cells that form the rudiments of skin, sense receptors, nerve cells, muscles, circulatory system, and internal organs—a process called *organogenesis*.

A heartbeat can be detected roughly 4 weeks after conception; the beginnings of lungs and limbs are also apparent at this time. By the end of the embryonic period, rudimentary fingers and toes, eyes, eyelids, nose, mouth, and external ears are all present, as are the basic parts of the nervous system; these and other developmental milestones are summarized in Table 2.2. The embryonic stage ends when organogenesis is complete and bone cells begin to form, typically about 8 weeks after conception.

**THE FETAL STAGE** Once organogenesis is complete, the developing organism is known as a **fetus** and the final phase of prenatal development, the **fetal stage**, begins (lasting from approximately 8 weeks until birth). From a weight of about 1/4 ounce and a length of 1 inch, the fetus grows to a baby weighing about 7 pounds and having a length of about 20 inches, who is ready to be born. In addition, this stage involves refinements of the organ systems that are essential to life outside the womb (see Table 2.3).

**embryonic stage** The second stage of prenatal development, from week 2 through week 8, when the embryo's organs form.

**amnion** The sac, or bag, filled with liquid in which the embryo/fetus floats during prenatal life.

**chorion** The outer layer of cells of the blastocyst during prenatal development, from which both the placenta and the umbilical cord are formed.

**placenta** An organ that develops between the fetus and the wall of the uterus during gestation.

**umbilical cord** The cord connecting the embryo/fetus to the placenta, containing two arteries and one vein.

**fetus** The name given to the developing organism from about 8 weeks after conception until birth.

**fetal stage** The third stage of prenatal development, from week 8 to birth, when growth and organ refinement take place.

| Table 2.3 | MILESTONES OF THE FETAL STAGE | |
|-----------|---|---|
| **Period** | **What Develops** | |
| Weeks 9–12 | Fingerprints; grasping reflex; facial expressions; swallowing and rhythmic "breathing" of amniotic fluid; urination; genitalia appear; alternating periods of physical activity and rest | |
| Weeks 13–16 | Hair follicles; responses to mother's voice and loud noises; 8–10 inches long; weighs 6 ounces | |
| Weeks 17–20 | Fetal movements felt by mother; heartbeat detectable with stethoscope; lanugo (hair) covers body; eyes respond to light introduced into the womb; eyebrows; fingernails; 12 inches long | |
| Weeks 21–24 | Vernix (oily substance) protects skin; lungs produce surfactant (vital to respiratory function); viability becomes possible, although most born now do not survive | |
| Weeks 25–28 | Recognition of mother's voice; regular periods of rest and activity; 14–15 inches long; weighs 2 pounds; good chance of survival if born now | |
| Weeks 29–32 | Very rapid growth; antibodies acquired from mother; fat deposited under skin; 16–17 inches long; weighs 4 pounds; excellent chance of survival if delivered now | |
| Weeks 33–36 | Movement to head-down position for birth; lungs mature; 18 inches long; weighs 5–6 pounds; virtually 100% chance of survival if delivered | |
| Weeks 37+ | Full-term status; 19–21 inches long; weighs 6–9 pounds | |

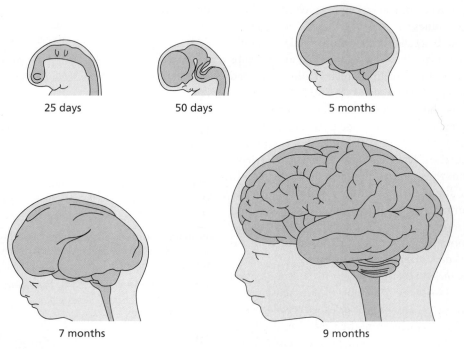

25 days    50 days    5 months

7 months    9 months

**FIGURE 2.4** The Prenatal Brain
Stages in the prenatal development of the brain, beginning with the neural tube in the embryonic period.

(*Source:* From drawings by Tom Prentiss in "The Development of the Brain" by W. Maxwell Cowan in *Scientific American*, September 1979, pp. 112–114+. Adapted by permission of Nelson H. Prentiss.)

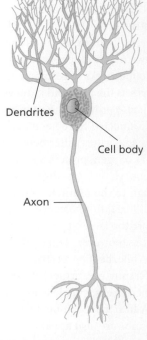

Dendrites

Cell body

Axon

**FIGURE 2.5** Structure of the Neuron
The structure of a single developed neuron. The cell bodies are the first to be developed, primarily between 10 and 20 weeks of gestation. Axons and dendrites begin to develop in the last 2 months of gestation and continue to increase in size and complexity for several years after birth.

**viability** The fetus's capacity for survival outside the womb.

**neurons** The cells in the nervous system that are responsible for transmission and reception of nerve impulses.

**neuronal proliferation** The rapid development of neurons between the 10th and 18th week of gestation.

**neuronal migration** The movement of neurons to specialized regions of the brain.

**cell body** The part of the cell that contains the nucleus and in which all the cell's vital functions are carried out.

**synapses** Tiny spaces across which neural impulses flow from one neuron to the next.

**axons** Tail-like extensions of neurons.

**dendrites** Branchlike protrusions from the cell bodies of neurons.

By the end of week 23, a small number of babies have attained **viability**, the ability to live outside the womb (Moore & Persaud, 1993). However, most babies born this early die, and those who do survive struggle for many months. Remaining in the womb just 1 week longer, until the end of week 24, greatly increases a baby's chances of survival. The extra week probably allows time for lung function to become more efficient. In addition, most brain structures are completely developed by the end of the 24th week. For these reasons, most experts accept 24 weeks as the average age of viability.

**THE FETAL BRAIN** As you learned earlier, the foundational structures of all of the body's organ systems are formed during the embryonic stage. Yet most of the formation and fine-tuning of the brain take place during the fetal stage (see Figure 2.4). **Neurons**, the specialized cells of the nervous system, actually begin developing during the embryonic stage, in week 3. But the pace of neural formation picks up dramatically between the 10th and 18th weeks, a process known as **neuronal proliferation**.

Between the 13th and 21st weeks, **neuronal migration** takes place, a process in which newly formed neurons migrate to the specialized regions of the brain where they will reside for the rest of the individual's life (Johnson, M. 2011). While migrating, neurons consist only of **cell bodies**, the part of the cell that contains the nucleus and in which all the cell's vital functions are carried out (see Figure 2.5). Once they have reached their final destinations in the fetal brain, the neurons begin to develop connections. These connections, called **synapses**, are tiny spaces between neurons across which neural impulses travel from one neuron to the next. Several changes in fetal behavior signal that the process of synapse formation is under way. For instance, the fetus exhibits alternating periods of activity and rest and begins to yawn (Walusinski, Kurjak, Andonotopo, & Azumendi, 2005; see Figure 2.6). When observed, these changes tell physicians that fetal brain development is proceeding normally.

Synapse formation requires the growth of two neuronal structures. **Axons** are tail-like extensions that can grow to be several feet in length. **Dendrites** are tentaclelike branches that

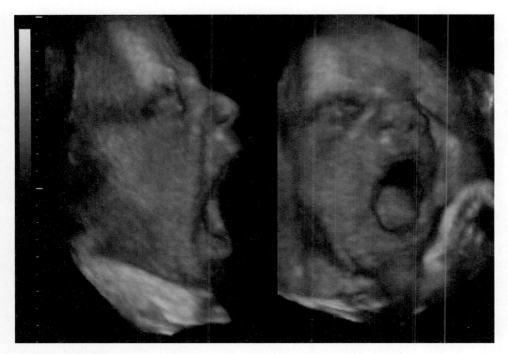

**FIGURE 2.6** Fetal Yawning

Fetal yawning appears between the 10th and 15th week. Its presence signals the beginning of sleep stages in the fetal brain.

(*Source:* O. Walusinski et al., "Fetal yawning: A behavior's birth with 4D US revealed," *The Ultrasound Review of Obstetrics & Gynecology,* 5 (2005), 210–217. Reprinted with permission.)

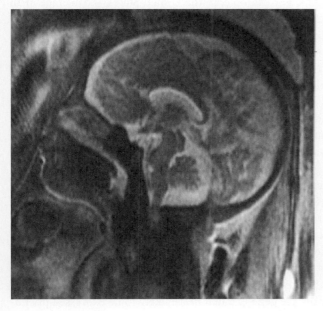

**FIGURE 2.7** A Normal Third-Trimester Fetal Brain

Glial cells that develop during the last few months of prenatal development hold neurons together and give form and structure to the fetal brain.

(*Source:* S. Brown, J. Estroff, and C. Barnewolf, "Fetal MRI," *Applied Radiology,* 33 (2004): 9–25. Copyright © 2004 by Applied Radiology/Anderson Publishing. Reprinted with permission.)

extend out from the cell body (see Figure 2.5). Dendrite development is thought to be highly sensitive to adverse environmental influences such as maternal malnutrition and defects in placental functioning (Dieni & Rees, 2003). ✳Explore at MyDevelopmentLab

Simultaneously with neuronal migration, **glial cells** begin to develop. These cells are the "glue" that hold the neurons together to give shape to the brain's major structures. As glial cells develop, the brain begins to assume a more mature appearance, one that can be observed using magnetic resonance imaging (MRI) and other modern technologies that you will read more about later in the chapter (see Figure 2.7).

✳Explore the **Concept** *Dendritic Spreading: Forming Interconnections in the Brain* at MyDevelopmentLab

**glial cells** The "glue" that holds neurons together to give form to the structures of the nervous system.

# Sex Differences in Prenatal Development

Because nearly all prenatal development is controlled by maturational sequences that are the same for all members of our species—male and female alike—there aren't very many sex differences in prenatal development. Still, there are a few, and they set the stage for some of the physical differences that are evident at later ages.

Sometime between 4 and 8 weeks after conception, the male embryo begins to secrete androgens, including the male hormone testosterone from the rudimentary testes. If this hormone is not secreted or is secreted in inadequate amounts, the embryo will be "demasculinized," even to the extent of developing female genitalia. Female embryos do not appear to secrete any equivalent hormone prenatally. However, the accidental presence of male hormone at the critical time (such as from some drug the mother may take, or from a genetic disorder called *congenital adrenal hyperplasia*) acts to "defeminize," or to masculinize, the female fetus, sometimes resulting in malelike genitalia and frequently resulting in masculinization of later behavior, such as more rough-and-tumble play (Cohen-Bendahan, van de Beek, & Berenbaum, 2005). Several hormones that affect the prenatal development of genitalia (particularly testosterone in males) also appear to affect the pattern of brain development, resulting in subtle brain differences between males and females and affecting patterns of growth-hormone secretions in adolescence, levels of physical aggression, and the relative dominance of the right and left hemispheres of the brain (Ruble & Martin, 1998; Todd et al., 1995). Although early research has raised some very intriguing questions, the evidence in this area is still fairly sketchy; it is clear that whatever role such prenatal hormones play in brain architecture and functioning is highly complex (Baron-Cohen, Lutchmaya, & Knickmeyer, 2006).

Girls progress a bit faster in some aspects of prenatal development, particularly skeletal development. They are 4 to 6 weeks ahead in bone development at birth (Tanner, 1990). Despite the more rapid development of girls, boys are slightly heavier and longer at birth, with more muscle tissue and fewer fat cells. For example, in the United States, the average birth length and weight for boys is 20 inches and 7 pounds 11 ounces, compared with slightly more than 19 inches and 7 pounds 3 ounces for girls (Levine, 2011).

Boys are considerably more vulnerable to all kinds of prenatal problems. Many more boys than girls are conceived—on the order of about 120 to 150 male embryos for every 100 female ones—but more of the males are spontaneously aborted. At birth, there are about 105 boys for every 100 girls. Boys are also more likely to experience injuries at birth (perhaps because they are larger), and they have more congenital malformations (Zaslow & Hayes, 1986). Male fetuses also appear to be more sensitive to variables such as cocaine which may negatively affect prenatal development (Levine et al., 2008). The striking sex difference in vulnerability to certain problems seems to persist throughout the lifespan. Males have shorter life expectancy, higher rates of behavior problems, more learning disabilities, and usually more negative responses to stressors such as maternal insensitivity (Warren & Simmens, 2005). One possible explanation for at least some of this sex difference may lie in the basic genetic difference. Because many genes for problems or disorders are recessive and are carried on the X chromosome, the XX combination affords a girl more protection against "bad" recessive genes that may be carried on one X chromosome; the dominant gene on the corresponding X chromosome would be expressed instead. Because boys have only one X chromosome, such a recessive gene is much more likely to be expressed phenotypically in a boy.

Early studies suggest that male fetuses, on average, are more physically active than females (DiPietro, Hodgson, Costigan, Hilton, & Johnson, 1996; DiPietro, Hodgson, Costigan, & Johnson, 1996). However, other studies have shown that a sex difference in wakefulness is responsible for these findings (de Medina, Visser, Huizink, Buitelaar, & Mulder, 2003). That is, male fetuses are awake more often than female fetuses are and, as a result, appear to be more active. When activity levels are measured within periods of wakefulness, male and female fetuses are equally active. By contrast, research showing that female fetuses are more responsive to external stimuli does seem to indicate that there is a real sex difference in responsiveness (Groome et al., 1999).

# Prenatal Behavior

◄------------Learning Objective 2.5
What behaviors have scientists observed in fetuses?

In recent years, techniques such as ultrasound imaging have provided researchers with a great deal of information about fetal behavior. Some researchers suggest that establishing norms for fetal behavior would help health-care providers better assess fetal health and predict postnatal problems (DiPietro et al., 2010; Nijhuis, 2003). Thus, in recent years, the number of research studies examining fetal behavior has increased significantly. These studies have produced rather remarkable findings, some of which are shown in Figure 2.8.

For one thing, researchers have learned that the fetus responds to sounds with heart rate changes, head turns, and body movements as early as the 25th week of gestation (Joseph, 2000). Researchers have also shown that it is possible to observe fetal brain activity by scanning the mother's abdomen with the same kinds of techniques used to examine brain function postnatally—techniques such as magnetic resonance imaging (MRI). Studies using these techniques have found that late-term fetuses exhibit neurological as well as behavioral responses to sounds (Moore et al., 2001).

Research also suggests that the fetus can distinguish between familiar and novel stimuli by the 32nd or 33rd week (Sandman, Wadhwa, Hetrick, Porto, & Peeke, 1997). In one classic study, pregnant women recited a short children's rhyme out loud each day between weeks 33 and 37. In week 38, researchers played a recording of either the same rhyme the mother had been reciting or another rhyme and measured the fetal heart rate. Fetal heart rates dropped during the playing of the familiar rhyme, but not during the unfamiliar rhyme, suggesting that the fetuses had learned the sound patterns of the rhyme (DeCasper, Lecaneut, Busnel, Granier-DeFerre, & Maugeais, 1994). The ability to learn in this way seems to emerge between 24 and 38 weeks (Krueger, Holditch-Davis, Quint, & DeCasper, 2004; Pressman, DiPietro, Costigan, Shupe, & Johnson, 1998).

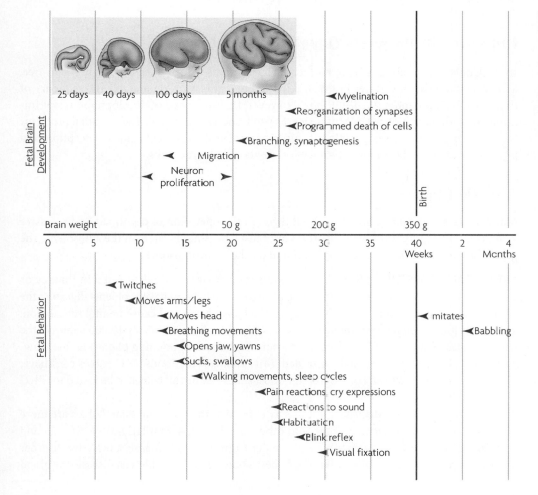

**FIGURE 2.8** Correlations between Fetal Behavior and Brain Development
Researchers have discovered numerous correlations between fetal brain development and behavior.

(*Source:* O. Walusinski et al., "Fetal yawning: A behavior's birth with 4D US revealed," *The Ultrasound Review of Obstetrics & Gynecology, 5* (2005), 210–217. Reprinted with permission.)

**teratogens** Substances such as viruses and drugs or events that can cause birth defects.

Evidence for fetal learning also comes from studies in which newborns appear to remember stimuli to which they were exposed prenatally: their mother's heartbeats, the odor of the amniotic fluid, and stories or pieces of music they heard in the womb (Righetti, 1996; Schaal, Marlier, & Soussignan, 1998). In another classic study of prenatal learning, pregnant women read a children's story such as Dr. Seuss's *The Cat in the Hat* out loud each day for the final 6 weeks of their pregnancies. After the infants were born, they were allowed to suck on special pacifiers that turned a variety of sounds off and on. Each kind of sound required a special type of sucking. Researchers found that the babies quickly adapted their sucking patterns in order to listen to the familiar story, but did not change their sucking in order to listen to an unfamiliar story (DeCasper & Spence, 1986). In other words, babies preferred the sound of the story they had heard in utero.

Developmentalists are trying to find out if prenatal learning affects later development, and if so, how (Bornstein et al., 2002). In one study, pregnant women wore waistbands equipped with speakers through which they exposed their fetuses to an average of 70 hours of classical music per week between 28 weeks of gestation and birth (Lafuente et al., 1997). By age 6 months, the babies who had heard the music were more advanced than control infants in many motor and cognitive skills. Of course, the exact meaning of this result is difficult to assess, but it does suggest that the prenatal sensory environment may be important in later development.

Researchers have also been able to identify individual differences in fetal behavior. You have already read about the sex difference in wakefulness. As is true of most sex differences, however, the range of individual differences within each gender is far greater than the difference in *average* activity levels between male and female fetuses. Some studies have shown that very active fetuses, both males and females, tend to become infants who are very active (DiPetro, Ghera, & Costigan, 2008). Moreover, these children are more likely to be labeled "hyperactive" by parents and teachers. In contrast, fetuses who are less active than average are more likely to have mental retardation (Accardo et al., 1997).

## Problems in Prenatal Development

In the United States, about 97% of mothers deliver infants who are healthy and problem-free, a phenomenon that illustrates just how remarkably regular and predictable the sequence of prenatal development is (CDC, 2011a). However, this sequence of development is not immune to modification or outside influence, as you'll soon see in detail. The potential problems fall into two general classes: genetic and chromosomal problems that begin at conception, and problems caused by damaging substances or events called **teratogens**.

**Learning Objective 2.6** ------------→
What are the effects of the major dominant, recessive, and sex-linked diseases?

## Genetic Disorders

Many disorders appear to be transmitted through the operation of dominant and recessive genes (see Table 2.4). *Autosomal* disorders are caused by genes located on the autosomes. The genes that cause *sex-linked* disorders are found on the X chromosome.

**AUTOSOMAL DISORDERS**  Most recessive autosomal disorders are diagnosed in infancy or early childhood. For example, one recessive gene causes a baby to have problems digesting the amino acid phenylalanine. Toxins build up in the baby's brain and cause mental retardation. This condition, called *phenylketonuria (PKU)*, is found in about 1 in every 10,000 babies in the United States (Seashore, 2011). If a baby consumes no foods containing phenylalanine, however, she will not become mentally retarded. Milk is one of the foods PKU babies can't have, so early diagnosis is critical. For this reason, most states require all babies to be tested for PKU soon after birth.

Like many recessive disorders, PKU is associated with race. Caucasian babies are more likely to have the disorder than infants in other racial groups. Similarly, West African and African American infants are more likely to suffer from *sickle-cell disease*, a recessive disorder that causes red blood cell deformities (Raj & Bertolone, 2010). In sickle-cell disease, the blood

| Table 2.4 | GENETIC DISORDERS | |
| --- | --- | --- |
| **Autosomal Dominant** | **Autosomal Recessive** | **Sex-Linked Recessive** |
| Huntington's disease | Phenylketonuria | Hemophilia |
| High blood pressure | Sickle-cell disease | Fragile-X syndrome |
| Extra fingers | Cystic fibrosis | Red-green color blindness |
| Migraine headaches | Tay-Sachs disease | Missing front teeth |
| Schizophrenia | Kidney cysts in infants | Night blindness |
| | Albinism | Some types of muscular dystrophy |
| | | Some types of diabetes |

*Sources:* Amato, 1993; Tortora and Grabowski, 1993.

can't carry enough oxygen to keep the body's tissues healthy. However, with early diagnosis and antibiotic treatment, more than 80% of children diagnosed with the disease survive to adulthood (Raj & Bertolone, 2010).

Almost one-half of West Africans have either sickle-cell disease or sickle-cell trait (Amato, 1998). Persons with *sickle-cell trait* carry a single recessive gene for sickle-cell disease, which causes a few of their red blood cells to be abnormal. Doctors can identify carriers of the sickle-cell gene by testing their blood for sickle-cell trait. Once potential parents know that they carry the gene, they can make informed decisions about future childbearing. In the United States, about 1 in 500 African Americans has sickle-cell disease, and 1 in 12 African Americans has sickle-cell trait (Raj & Bertolone, 2010). Sickle-cell disease and sickle-cell trait also occur more frequently in people of Mediterranean, Caribbean, Indian, Arab, and Latin American ancestry than in those of European ancestry (Raj & Bertolone, 2010).

About 1 in every 3,000 babies born to Jewish couples of Eastern European ancestry suffers from another recessive disorder, *Tay-Sachs disease*. By the time he is 1 to 2 years old, a Tay-Sachs baby is likely to have severe mental retardation and blindness. Very few survive past the age of 3 (Kaelbling, 2009).

Disorders caused by dominant genes, such as *Huntington's disease*, are usually not diagnosed until adulthood (Amato, 1998). This disorder causes the brain to deteriorate and affects both psychological and motor functions. Until recently, children of people with Huntington's disease had to wait until they became ill themselves to know for sure that they carried the gene. Now, doctors can use a blood test to identify the Huntington's gene. Thus, people who have a parent with this disease can make better decisions about their own childbearing and can prepare for living with a serious disorder when they get older. ⊙ Watch at **MyDevelopmentLab**

**SEX-LINKED DISORDERS**   Most sex-linked disorders are caused by recessive genes (see Figure 2.9). One fairly common sex-linked recessive disorder is *red-green color blindness*. People with this disorder have difficulty distinguishing between the colors red and green when they are next to each other. The prevalence of red-green color blindness is 8% in men and 0.5% (1/2 percent) in women (U.S. National Library of Medicine Genetics Home Reference, 2008). Most people learn ways of compensating for the disorder and thus live perfectly normal lives.

A more serious sex-linked recessive disorder is *hemophilia*. The blood of people with hemophilia lacks the chemical components that

⊙ Watch the **Video** *Genetic Counseling* at **MyDevelopmentLab**

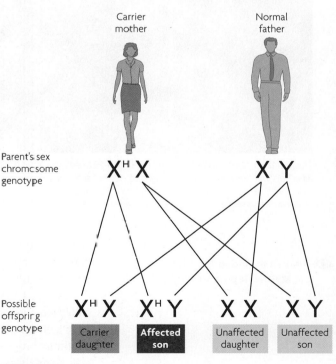

**FIGURE 2.9** Sex-Linked Inheritance
Compare this pattern of sex-linked transmission of a recessive disease (hemophilia) with the pattern shown in Figure 2.2.

## Fetal Assessment and Treatment

Shilpa and Rudy Patel are preparing for the birth of their first child. Like many other couples, they are hoping that their child will be healthy. In their case, however, there is real cause for concern because a genetic disorder known as *fragile-X syndrome* runs in Shilpa's family. **Watch** at **MyDevelopmentLab**

One procedure that can be used to test Shilpa's fetus is known as *chorionic villus sampling (CVS)*. CVS and another procedure, *amniocentesis*, can be used to identify chromosomal errors and many genetic disorders prior to birth (Curry, 2002). In CVS, cells are extracted from the placenta and subjected to a variety of laboratory tests during the early weeks of prenatal development. In amniocentesis, a needle is used to extract amniotic fluid containing fetal cells between weeks 14 and 16 of gestation. Fetal cells filtered out of the fluid are then tested in a variety of ways to diagnose chromosomal and genetic disorders. In addition, *ultrasonography* has become a routine part of prenatal care in the United States because of its usefulness in monitoring fetal growth in high-risk pregnancies. When an ultrasound test suggests that there may be some kind of brain or spinal cord abnormality, follow-up tests using magnetic resonance imaging are sometimes employed (Levine, 2002). These images are more detailed than those that are produced by ultrasonography.

Many laboratory tests that use maternal blood, urine, and/or samples of amniotic fluid also help health-care providers monitor fetal development. For example, the presence of a substance called *alpha-fetoprotein* in a mother's blood is associated with a number of prenatal defects, including abnormalities in the brain and spinal cord. Doctors can also use a laboratory test to assess the maturity of fetal lungs (Springer, 2010). This test is critical when doctors have to deliver a baby early because of a pregnant woman's health.

*Fetoscopy* involves insertion of a tiny camera into the womb to directly observe fetal development. Fetoscopy makes it possible for doctors to surgically correct some kinds of defects (Springer, 2010) and has made techniques such as fetal blood transfusions and bone marrow transplants possible. Specialists also use fetoscopy to take samples of blood from the umbilical cord. Fetal blood tests can help doctors identify a bacterial infection that is causing a fetus to grow too slowly (Springer, 2010). Once diagnosed, the infection can be treated by injecting antibiotics into the amniotic fluid to be swallowed by the fetus or by injecting drugs into the umbilical cord (Springer, 2010).

### Learning Objective 2.6a
What techniques are used to assess and treat problems in prenatal development?

### REFLECTION

1. How do you think you would respond to the news that a child you were expecting was carrying some kind of genetic defect?
2. Suppose Shilpa and Rudy learn that their baby is a girl. Will this news make them more or less concerned about the effect that carrying the fragile-X defect may have on their child's development? Why?

*This amazing photo shows the tiny hand of a 21 week old fetus grasping the finger of the surgeon who had just completed an operation to correct a serious malformation of the fetus's spine.*

**Watch** the **Video** *Prenatal Ultrasound* at **MyDevelopmentLab**

cause blood to clot. Thus, when a person with hemophilia bleeds, the bleeding doesn't stop naturally. Approximately 1 in 5,000 baby boys is born with this disorder, which is almost unknown in girls (Agaliotis, Zaiden, & Ozturk, 2009).

About 1 in every 4,000 males and 1 in every 8,000 females has a sex-linked disorder called *fragile-X syndrome* (Jewell, 2009). A person with this disorder has an X chromosome with a "fragile," or damaged, spot. Fragile-X syndrome can cause mental retardation that becomes progressively worse as children get older (Jewell, 2009). Fragile-X syndrome is also strongly associated with autism, a disorder that interferes with children's capacity to form emotional bonds with others (Cohen et al., 2005). Fortunately, fragile-X syndrome is one of several disorders that can be diagnosed before birth (see *Developmental Science in the Real World*).

# Chromosomal Errors

←----------- **Learning Objective 2.7**

How do trisomies and other disorders of the autosomes and sex chromosomes affect development?

Over 50 different chromosomal anomalies have been identified, and most result in miscarriage. When babies do survive, the effects of chromosomal errors tend to be dramatic.

**TRISOMIES** A *trisomy* is a condition in which an individual has three copies of a particular autosome. The most common is **Down syndrome** (also called **trisomy 21**), in which the child has three copies of chromosome 21. Roughly 1 in every 800-1,000 infants is born with this abnormality (Chen, 2010). These children have distinctive facial features, most notably a flattened face and somewhat slanted eyes with an epicanthic fold on the upper eyelid (an extension of the normal eyelid fold), reduced total brain size, and often other physical abnormalities such as heart defects. Typically, they have mental retardation. ◉─|**Watch** at **MyDevelopmentLab**

The risk of bearing a child with trisomy 21 varies with the age of the mother. Among women over 35, the chances of conceiving a child with the disorder are 1 in 385 (Chen, 2010). At 40, the risk rises to 1 in 106, and at 45, the chances are 1 in 30. Paternal age is a factor as well (Fisch et al., 2003). Interestingly, with mothers younger than 35, the father's age has no effect on trisomy 21 risk. However, a man over 40 who conceives a child with a woman over 35 is twice as likely to father a child with Down syndrome as a younger father is.

Scientists have identified children with trisomies of the 13th and 18th pairs of chromosomes as well (Best & Greg, 2009; Chen, 2009). These disorders have more severe effects than trisomy 21. Few children with trisomy 13 or trisomy 18 live past the age of 1 year. As with trisomy 21, the chances of having a child with one of these disorders increase with a woman's age.

**SEX-CHROMOSOME ANOMALIES** A second class of anomalies, associated with an incomplete or incorrect division of either sex chromosome, occurs in roughly 1 out of every 400 births (Berch & Bender, 1987). The most common is an XXY pattern, called Klinefelter's syndrome, which occurs in approximately 1 out of every 1,000 males. Affected boys most often look quite normal, although they have characteristically long arms and legs and underdeveloped testes. Most do not have mental retardation, but language and learning disabilities are common. Somewhat rarer is an XYY pattern. These children also develop as boys; typically they are unusually tall, with mild retardation.

A single-X pattern (XO), called Turner's syndrome, and a triple-X pattern (XXX) may also occur, and in both cases the child develops as a girl. Girls with Turner's syndrome—perhaps 1 in every 3,000 live female births (Tanner, 1990)—show stunted growth and are usually sterile. Without hormone therapy, they do not menstruate or develop breasts at puberty. Neuroimaging studies show that Turner syndrome is associated with abnormal development in both the cerebellum and the cerebrum (Brown et al., 2002). These girls also show an interesting imbalance in their cognitive skills: They often perform particularly poorly on tests that measure spatial ability but usually perform at or above normal levels on tests of verbal skill (Golombok & Fivush, 1994). Girls with an XXX pattern are of normal size but are slow in physical development. In contrast to girls with Turner's syndrome, they have markedly poor verbal abilities and overall low IQ, and they do particularly poorly in school compared with other children with sex-chromosome anomalies (Bender et al., 1995; Rovet & Netley, 1983).

*Note the distinctive facial characteristics of this child with Down Syndrome*

◉─|**Watch** the **Video** *Down Syndrome* at **MyDevelopmentLab**

# Teratogens: Maternal Diseases

←----------- **Learning Objective 2.8**

How do maternal diseases and environmental hazards affect prenatal development?

Deviant prenatal development can also result from variations in the environment in which the embryo and fetus is nurtured. A particular teratogen, such as a drug or a disease in the mother, will result in a defect in the embryo or fetus only if it occurs during a particular period of days or weeks of prenatal life. The general rule is that each organ system is most vulnerable to disruption at the time when it is developing most rapidly (Moore & Persaud, 1993). Figure 2.10 on page 46 shows times when different parts of the body are most vulnerable to teratogens. As you can see, the first 8 weeks are the period of greatest vulnerability for all the organ systems. ◉─|**Simulate** at **MyDevelopmentLab**

**RUBELLA** The first few weeks of gestation comprise a critical period for a negative effect from rubella (also called German measles). Most infants exposed to rubella in the first trimester show some degree of hearing impairment, visual impairment, and/or heart deformity

◉─|**Simulate** the **Experiment** *Teratogens and Their Effects* at **MyDevelopmentLab**

**Down syndrome (trisomy 21)** A genetic anomaly in which every cell contains three copies of chromosome 21 rather than two. Children born with this genetic pattern have characteristic physical features and usually have mental retardation.

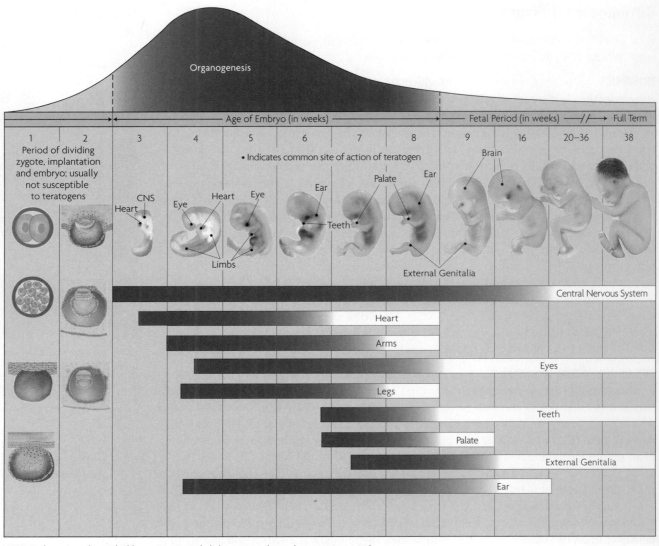

NOTE: Dark portions denote highly sensitive periods; light portions denote less sensitive periods.

**FIGURE 2.10** The Timing of Teratogen Exposure
The timing of teratogen exposure is crucial. Notice that teratogens have the most impact during the embryonic stage, except on certain body parts such as the brain and ears, which continue to be at risk for teratogenic effects because they continue to grow and develop during the fetal period.

(*Source:* From C. Moore, J. Barresi, and C. Thompson, "The cognitive basis of future-oriented prosocial behavior," *Social Development,* 7 (1998): 198–218. Copyright © 1998 by Blackwell Publishers, Inc. Reprinted with permission.)

(Ezike & Ang, 2009) Fortunately, rubella is preventable. A vaccine is available, and it should be given to all children as part of a regular immunization program (American College of Obstetrics and Gynecology [ACOG], 2002). Adult women who were not vaccinated as children can be vaccinated later, but the vaccination must be done at least 3 months before a pregnancy to provide complete immunity. Moreover, the vaccine itself can be teratogenic, another good reason to wait several weeks before attempting to conceive.

**HIV/AIDS**    In the United States, over 6,000 babies are born to women with HIV/AIDS each year (CDC, 2011b). These grim numbers are counterbalanced by some good news, though. First, only about a quarter of infants born to mothers with HIV actually become infected (Springer, 2010). Even more encouraging is the finding that infected women who are treated with *antiretroviral drugs* during their pregnancies have a markedly lower risk of transmitting the disease to their children—as low as 2% (CDC, 2007a). Because most women with HIV are asymptomatic and are unaware they are infected, the Centers for Disease Control recommends routine HIV counseling and voluntary testing for all pregnant women early in their pregnancies so that they can begin taking antiretroviral drugs, should that be necessary.

**HIV/AIDS AND PREGNANCY ACROSS CULTURES**   As you probably know, HIV/AIDS is far more prevalent in some African nations than in any other part of the world. For instance, in South Africa, about 30% of pregnant women are HIV-positive (Johnson, L. 2011). Thanks to international efforts to make antiretroviral drugs available to pregnant women in Africa, the rate of mother-to-fetus transmission of the virus has dropped dramatically in Africa, just as it has in the United States. However, ignorance and fear continue to hamper prevention efforts. For example, one study involving 79 pregnant women with HIV aged 18 to 38, in Burkina Faso, West Africa, found that most participants did not intend to inform their partners about their HIV status because they feared being stigmatized (Issiaka et al., 2001). Moreover, none were aware of community organizations from which individuals with HIV could obtain information and support. Such findings suggest that the need for basic HIV education in the developing world is critical.

**CYTOMEGALOVIRUS AND OTHER SEXUALLY TRANSMITTED DISEASES**   A much less well known but remarkably widespread and potentially serious sexually transmitted disease (STD) is *cytomegalovirus (CMV)*, a virus in the herpes group. It is now thought to be the single most prevalent infectious cause of both congenital mental retardation and deafness. CMV typically has few, if any, symptoms in an adult. In most cases, an affected person doesn't even know she carries this virus, although in an active phase it sometimes creates symptoms that suggest mononucleosis, including swollen glands and low fever. In infants who are infected prenatally or during birth, however, the virus can sometimes produce crippling disabilities.

Roughly half of all women of childbearing age have antibodies to CMV (CDC, 2006a), indicating that they have been infected at some time. Perhaps 2% of babies whose mothers have CMV antibodies become infected prenatally or as a result of breastfeeding (Schleiss, 2010).

Like CMV, the herpes virus can be transmitted to the fetus during delivery if the mother's disease is in the active phase at that time. Not only will the child then periodically experience the genital sores characteristic of the disease, but he or she may suffer other complications, most notably meningoencephalitis, a potentially serious inflammation of the brain and spinal cord. Because of this increased risk, many physicians now recommend surgical delivery (cesarean section) of infants of mothers with herpes, although vaginal delivery is possible if the disease is inactive.

Two additional STDs, *syphilis* and *gonorrhea*, also cause birth defects (Di Mario, Say, & Lincetto, 2007). Unlike most teratogens, a syphilis infection is most harmful during the last 26 weeks of prenatal development and causes eye, ear, and brain defects. Gonorrhea, which can cause the infant to be blind, is also usually transmitted during birth. For this reason, doctors usually treat the eyes of newborns with a special ointment that prevents damage from gonorrhea.

**CHRONIC ILLNESSES**   Conditions such as heart disease, diabetes, and lupus, can also negatively affect prenatal development (Ross & Mansano, 2010). And recent research indicates that prenatal exposure to some maternal health conditions, such as the fluctuations in metabolism rate characteristic of diabetes, may predispose infants to developmental delays (Levy-Shiff, Lerman, Har-Even, & Hod, 2002). One of the most important goals of the new specialty of *fetal-maternal medicine* is to manage the pregnancies of women who have such conditions so that the health of both mother and fetus will be supported. For example, pregnancy often affects a diabetic woman's blood sugar levels so drastically that it becomes impossible for her to keep them under control. In turn, erratic blood sugar levels may damage the fetus's nervous system or cause it to grow too rapidly (Allen & Kisilevsky, 1999; Kliegman, 1998). To prevent such complications, a fetal-maternal specialist must find a diet, a medication, or a combination of the two that will stabilize the mother's blood sugar but will not harm the fetus. With the advent of sophisticated communication technologies, specialists are also capable of monitoring fetal development 24 hours a day while the mother goes about her normal activities (See *Technology and the Developing Child* on page 48.).

**ENVIRONMENTAL HAZARDS**   There are a number of substances found in the environment that may have detrimental effects on prenatal development. For example, women who work with mercury (e.g., dentists, dental technicians, semiconductor manufacturing workers) are advised to limit their exposure to this potentially teratogenic substance (March of Dimes, 2011). Consuming large amounts of fish may also expose pregnant women to high levels of mercury (because of industrial pollution of the oceans and waterways). Fish may also contain elevated levels of another problematic industrial pollutant known as polychlorinated biphenyls, or PCBs. For these reasons, researchers recommend that pregnant women limit their consumption of fish, especially fresh tuna, shark, swordfish, and mackerel (March of Dimes, 2011).

There are several other environmental hazards that pregnant women are advised to avoid (March of Dimes, 2011):

- *Lead*, found in painted surfaces in older homes, pipes carrying drinking water, lead crystal glassware, and some ceramic dishes
- *Arsenic*, found in dust from pressure-treated lumber
- *Cadmium*, found in semiconductor manufacturing facilities
- *Anesthetic gases*, found in dental offices, outpatient surgical facilities, and hospital operating rooms
- *Solvents*, such as alcohol and paint thinners
- *Parasite-bearing substances*, such as animal feces and undercooked meat, poultry, or eggs

**Learning Objective 2.9**
What are the potential adverse effects of tobacco, alcohol, and other drugs on prenatal development?

## Teratogens: Drugs

There is now a huge literature on the effects of prenatal drugs, especially controlled substances such as heroin and marijuana (Barth, 2001). Sorting out the effects of drugs has proved to be an immensely challenging task because many women use multiple substances: Women who drink alcohol are also more likely than nondrinkers to smoke; those who use cocaine are also likely to take other illegal drugs or to smoke or drink to excess, and so on. In addition, many women who use drugs have other problems, such as depression, that may be responsible for the apparent effects of the drugs they use (Pajulo, Savonlahti, Sourander, Helenius, & Piha, 2001). Furthermore, the effects of drugs may be subtle, visible only many years after birth in the form of minor learning disabilities or increased risk of behavior problems.

**SMOKING**   Research suggests that smoking during pregnancy may cause genetic damage in the developing fetus (de la Chica, Ribas, Giraldo, Egozcue, & Fuster, 2005). In addition, the link between smoking and low birth weight is well established. Infants of mothers who smoke are on average about half a pound lighter at birth than infants of nonsmoking mothers (Mohsin, Wong, Baumann, & Bai, 2003) and are nearly twice as likely to be born with a weight below 2,500 grams (5 pounds 8 ounces), the common definition of low birth weight. The primary problem-causing agent in cigarettes is nicotine, which constricts the blood vessels, reducing blood flow and nutrition to the placenta.

The effects of smoking on both height and weight are still evident when the children of smoking and nonsmoking mothers reach school age (Cornelius, Goldschmidt, Day, & Larkby, 2002). Medical researchers have also found that prenatal smoking increases children's risk of a number of health problems (DiFranza, Aligne, & Weitzman, 2004). These problems include susceptibility to respiratory infections, asthma, and ear infections.

Prenatal exposure to tobacco also appears to have long-term effects on children's cognitive and social development. Some studies suggest that there are higher rates of learning problems and antisocial behavior among children whose mothers smoked during pregnancy (DiFranza, Aligne, & Weitzman, 2004). Moreover, children of women who smoked during pregnancy are more likely than their schoolmates to be diagnosed with attention-deficit hyperactivity disorder (Lindblad & Hjern, 2010). ◉ Watch at **MyDevelopmentLab**

**DRINKING** The effects of alcohol on the developing fetus range from mild to severe. At the extreme end of the continuum are children who exhibit a syndrome called **fetal alcohol syndrome (FAS)**, which affects 1 to 2 of every 1,000 infants in the United States (Vaux & Rosenkrantz, 2010). Projecting these figures to all children born in the United States means that up to 12,000 children with FAS are born every year. These children, whose mothers were usually heavy drinkers or alcoholics, are generally smaller than normal, with smaller brains and often with distinct physical anomalies or deformities. They frequently have heart defects, and their faces have certain distinctive features (visible in the two photos below), including a somewhat flattened nose and nose bridge and often an unusually long space between nose and mouth. However, the disorder is often difficult to diagnose. Experts recommend that physicians who suspect that a child may have FAS carry out a multidisciplinary assessment, one that includes a comprehensive medical and behavioral history of both the mother and the child as well as neuropsychological testing (Vaux & Rosenkrantz, 2010).

The best single study of the consequences of prenatal alcohol exposure has been done by Ann Streissguth and her colleagues (Baer, Sampson, Barr, Connor, & Streissguth, 2003), who followed a group of over 500 women who drank moderate to heavy amounts of alcohol while pregnant and their children. Streissguth tested the children repeatedly, beginning immediately after birth, again later in infancy, at age 4, at school age, and again at ages 11, 14, and 21. She found that the mother's alcohol consumption in pregnancy was associated with sluggishness and weaker sucking in infancy; lower scores on measures of intelligence at 8 months, 4 years,

**fetal alcohol syndrome (FAS)** A pattern of abnormalities, including mental retardation and minor physical anomalies, often found in children born to alcoholic mothers.

◉ Watch the **Video** *Effects of Prenatal Smoking on Children's Development* at **MyDevelopmentLab**

*These two children, from different countries and different racial backgrounds, have both been diagnosed as having fetal alcohol syndrome (FAS). Both are mentally retarded and have relatively small heads. Note also the short nose and low nasal bridge typical of FAS children.*

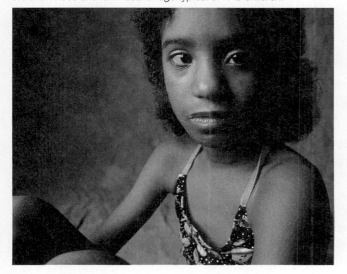

and 7 years; and problems with attention and vigilance at 4, 7, 11, and 14. Teachers also rated the 11-year-olds on overall school performance and on various behavior problems, and on both of these measures, children whose mothers had consumed the most alcohol during pregnancy were rated significantly worse. Streissguth also asked mothers about their diet, their education, and their life habits. She found that the links between a mother's alcohol consumption and poor outcomes for the child held up even when all these other variables were controlled statistically. Investigators have also found that these children's deficiencies in information-processing skills persist into adulthood (Connor, Sampson, Bookstein, Barr, & Streissguth, 2001). Moreover, they are more likely than peers who were not prenatally exposed to alcohol to have alcohol abuse problems themselves (Baer et al., 2003). 👁️ Watch at **MyDevelopmentLab**

👁️ Watch the **Video** *Fetal Alcohol Damage* at **MyDevelopmentLab**

**COCAINE** Significant numbers of pregnant women in the United States (and presumably elsewhere in the world) also take various illegal drugs, most notably cocaine. Early studies found a number of associations between prenatal cocaine exposure and developmental problems such as low birth weight and brain damage (Ornoy, 2002). However, most such studies ignored the fact that most cocaine-using pregnant women are poor and abuse multiple substances, making it difficult to separate the effects of cocaine from those of poverty and other drugs. Studies that separate the effects of all such factors suggest that cocaine alone has no long-term effects on cognitive or social development (Dharan & Parviainen, 2009). However, cocaine can lead to pregnancy complications, such as disruption of placental function and premature labor, that may adversely affect the developing fetus.

**MARIJUANA AND HEROIN** Prenatal exposure to marijuana appears to interfere with a child's growth (Marrou, 2009). Even at age 6, children whose mothers used the drug during pregnancy are smaller on average than their non-drug-exposed peers (Cornelius et al., 2002). Researchers also have evidence suggesting that prenatal exposure to marijuana adversely affects the developing brain (Wang et al., 2004). These findings may help explain why a number of studies have shown that the behavior of infants and children who were prenatally exposed to the drug differs from that of their agemates. For example, some studies suggest that learning disabilities and attention problems are more common among children whose mothers used marijuana during pregnancy (Fried & Smith, 2001).

Both heroin and methadone, a drug often used in treating heroin addiction, can cause miscarriage, premature labor, and early death (Brockington, 1996; Dharan, Parviainen, Newcomb, & Poleshuck, 2006). Further, 60–80% of babies born to heroin- or methadone-addicted women are addicted to these drugs as well. Addicted babies have high-pitched cries and suffer from withdrawal symptoms, including irritability, uncontrollable tremors, vomiting, convulsions, and sleep problems. These symptoms may last as long as 4 months.

The degree to which heroin and methadone affect development depends on the quality of the environment in which babies are raised. Babies who are cared for by mothers who continue to be addicted themselves usually don't do as well as those whose mothers stop using drugs or who are raised by relatives or foster families (Brockington, 1996). By age 2, most heroin- or methadone-addicted babies in good homes are developing normally.

**Learning Objective 2.10** ----------→
What are the risks associated with legal drugs, maternal diet, age, emotional distress, and poverty?

# Other Teratogens and Maternal Factors

A variety of additional factors, from vitamins to environmental pollutants to maternal emotions, can affect prenatal development. A few are listed in Table 2.5, and others are discussed in more detail in this section.

**PRESCRIPTION AND OVER-THE-COUNTER DRUGS** In general, doctors advise against taking any unnecessary medicines during pregnancy. But some pregnant women must take drugs in order to treat health conditions that may be threatening to their own and their unborn child's life. For instance, pregnant women with epilepsy must take antiseizure medication because the seizures themselves are potentially harmful to the unborn child. Other drugs that pregnant women may have to risk taking, even though they can be harmful, include medications that treat heart conditions and diabetes, those that control asthma symptoms, and some kinds of psychiatric drugs. In all such cases, physicians weigh the benefits of medication against

Table
2.5

## SOME IMPORTANT TERATOGENS

| Teratogen | Possible Effects on Fetus |
| --- | --- |
| **Maternal Diseases** | |
| Cancer | Fetal or placental tumor |
| Toxoplasmosis | Brain swelling, spinal abnormalities |
| Chicken pox | Scars, eye damage |
| Parvovirus | Anemia |
| Hepatitis B | Hepatitis |
| Chlamydia | Conjunctivitis, pneumonia |
| Tuberculosis | Pneumonia or tuberculosis |
| **Drugs** | |
| Inhalents | FAS-like syndrome, premature labor |
| Accutane/vitamin A | Facial, ear, heart deformities |
| Streptomycin | Deafness |
| Penicillin | Skin disorders |
| Tetracycline | Tooth deformities |
| Diet pills | Low birth weight |

*Sources:* Amato, 1998; Kliegman, 1998.

potential teratogenic effects and look for a combination of drug and dosage that will effectively treat the mother's health condition while placing her unborn child at minimal risk.

In contrast to prescription drugs, most people, pregnant or otherwise, take over-the-counter medicines on a casual, as-needed basis without consulting a doctor. Many of these drugs, such as acetaminophen, are safe for pregnant women unless taken to excess (Organization of Teratology Information Specialists, 2005). However, experts advise pregnant women to discuss the medicines they usually take with physicians at the outset of their pregnancies. These discussions should deal with both drugs and any vitamins or supplements that the pregnant woman usually takes. Their doctors will advise them as to which of the substances are safe and which are risky. Often, too, physicians can suggest safer alternatives; typically most look to older drugs that have been thoroughly tested (Vogin, 2005).

**DIET**   Both the general adequacy of a pregnant woman's diet, measured in terms of calories, and the presence of certain key nutrients are critical to prenatal development (Christian & Stewart, 2010). Dieticians recommend that expectant mothers take in about 300 calories more per day than before they were pregnant (March of Dimes, 2011). When a woman experiences severe malnutrition during pregnancy, particularly during the final 3 months, she faces a greatly increased risk of stillbirth, low infant birth weight, or infant death during the first year of life (Di Mario, Say, & Lincetto, 2007). Autopsies show that infants born to malnourished mothers have smaller brains, with fewer and smaller brain cells than normal (Georgieff, 1994).

A vital specific nutrient whose importance during pregnancy has become clear is folic acid, a B vitamin found primarily in liver, beans, leafy green vegetables, broccoli, orange juice, fortified breakfast cereals, and grain products, especially wheat germ. Inadequate amounts of this nutrient have been clearly linked to the risk of neural tube defects such as *spina bifida*, a deformity in which the lower part of the spine does not close (Ellenbogen, 2009). Many (but not all) such children are retarded; most have some lower-body paralysis. Because the neural tube develops primarily during the very earliest weeks of pregnancy, before a woman may even know she is pregnant, it is important for women who plan a pregnancy to ingest at least the minimum level of folic acid: 400 micrograms daily. To help raise the normal intake above the desired level, new regulations by the Food and Drug Administration in the United States now require that 140 micrograms of folic acid be added to each 100 grams of enriched flour, thus greatly increasing the likelihood that the majority of women will receive sufficient quantities of folic acid. Since the mandate was instituted, the number of infants born with spina bifida in the United States has been reduced by about one-third (Ellenbogen, 2009).

There are also risks associated with gaining too much weight during pregnancy. In particular, women who gain too much weight are more likely to have a cesarean section delivery (Takimoto, 2006); they are also prone to postpartum obesity, which carries a whole set of health risks, including heart disease and diabetes (Amorim et al., 2007). Gains within the recommended ranges appear optimal, although there is wide variability from one woman to the next.

Finally, women who are obese before they become pregnant have some additional risks, regardless of the amount of weight they gain. Such women are about twice as likely to have infants with neural tube defects, regardless of their intake of folic acid (Scialli, 2007). Research shows that, for obese women, weight-loss diets that include all of the nutrients needed for prenatal development are safe (Kiel et al., 2007).

**THE MOTHER'S AGE** Have you heard sensationalized media reports about women giving birth in their 50s and even into their 60s? Such late-in-life births are very rare, but it is the case that the average age at which women give birth for the first time has increased over the past few decades. In 1970, the average age at which a woman in the United States delivered her first child was 21.4 years. By contrast, in 2008, the average age was 25 years (Martin et al., 2010). The shift is largely due to the increasing prevalence of first births among women in their late thirties and early forties.

In most cases, older mothers have uncomplicated pregnancies and deliver healthy babies, but the risks associated with pregnancy do increase somewhat as women get older (Martin et al., 2010). Their babies are also at greater risk of weighing less than 5.5 pounds at birth, a finding that is partly explained by the greater incidence of multiple births among older mothers. Still, infants born to women over the age of 35, whether single or multiple births, are at higher risk of having problems such as heart malformations and chromosomal disorders.

At the other end of the age continuum, when comparing the rates of problems seen in teenage mothers with those seen in mothers in their 20s, almost all researchers find higher rates of problems among the teens. However, teenage mothers are also more likely to be poor, less likely to receive adequate prenatal care, less likely to be married, and more poorly educated about pregnancy and birth than older mothers are (Martin et al., 2005). Thus, it is very hard to sort out the causal factors.

**STRESS AND EMOTIONAL STATE** The idea that emotional or physical stresses are linked to poor pregnancy outcomes is firmly established in folklore (DiPietro, 2004). Results from studies in animals suggest that these beliefs are justified: Exposure of the pregnant female to stressors such as heat, light, noise, shock, or crowding significantly increases the risk of low-birth-weight offspring as well as later problems in the offspring (Schneider, 1992). Likewise, studies in humans show that stressful life events, emotional distress, and physical stress are all linked to slight increases in problems of pregnancy, such as low birth weight (DiPietro, 2004). Moreover, studies involving experimentally induced stressors (e.g., requiring a pregnant woman to take some kind of cognitive test) show that they seem to cause short-term changes in fetal activity, heart rate, and other responses (DiPietro, Costigan, & Gurewitsch, 2003). Whether such changes are sufficient to affect development in any meaningful way is as yet unknown.

Similarly, maternal emotions are associated with measures of fetal response such as activity level. Researcher Janet DiPietro and her colleagues have found that the fetuses of women who have positive emotions toward their condition are less active than those of mothers who feel more negatively about their pregnancies (DiPietro, Hilton, Hawkins, Costigan, & Pressman, 2002). The long-term effects of this association, if there are any, have been difficult to identify. Some developmental scientists argue that the real connection is a matter of maternal genes and/or parenting style; emotionally negative and depressed mothers may use ineffective parenting strategies or simply be more likely, for genetic reasons, to have children who are less emotionally positive than their peers (Lau, Riisdijk, Gregory, McGuffin, & Elev, 2007).

One fairly consistent finding, however, is that the fetuses of mothers who have been diagnosed with depression tend to grow more slowly than others (Yonkers et al., 2009). Developmentalists hypothesize that this effect may result directly from emotion-related hormones or it may be an indirect effect of the mother's emotional state. A mother with depression may eat less, or her weakened immune system may limit her ability to fight off viruses and bacteria, either of which may retard fetal growth. Consequently, many psychologists suggest that providing stressed and/or depressed pregnant women with social support and counseling may lead to improvements in both maternal and fetal health (Wilen & Mounts, 2006).

**POVERTY**  The basic sequence of fetal development is clearly no different for children born to poor mothers than for children born to middle-class mothers, but many of the problems that can negatively affect prenatal development are more common among the poor. For example, in the United States, mothers who have not graduated from high school are about twice as likely as mothers with a college education to have a low-birth-weight infant or a stillborn infant. Poor women are also likely to have their first pregnancy earlier and to have more pregnancies overall, and they are less likely to be immunized against such diseases as rubella. They are also less likely to seek prenatal care, and if they do, they seek it much later in their pregnancies. A significant portion of this difference could be overcome in the United States: Devoting the resources needed to provide good, universal prenatal care could significantly reduce not only the rate of infant death but also the rate of physical abnormalities and perhaps even mental retardation. Equal access to care is not the only answer. In Canada, for example, in which such care is universally available, social class differences in low-birth-weight deliveries and in infant mortality rates remain (Spencer, 2003).

## THINK CRITICALLY

- In your view, what are the advantages and disadvantages of genetic counseling for couples who want to have a child but who are concerned about a genetic or chromosomal disorder that runs in one or both of their families?
- With the advent of antiretroviral drugs, the rate of mother-to-fetus transmission of HIV has been greatly reduced. Do you think that these findings justify mandatory testing and treatment of pregnant women who are at high risk of having HIV/AIDS? Why or why not?

## CONDUCT YOUR OWN RESEARCH

In every culture, there are traditional beliefs about pregnancy, many of which are myths. For example, you may have heard that labor is more likely to begin during a full moon or that boys "carry high" but girls "carry low." Other once-popular ideas include the notion that eating spicy foods or having sex will bring on premature labor. Survey your classmates, friends, and relatives to find out what kinds of things they have heard about pregnancy. If you have access to people from different cultures, analyze the similarities and differences in these beliefs across groups.

## Conception and Genetics

**2.1** What are the characteristics of the zygote?

At conception, 23 chromosomes from the sperm join with 23 from the ovum to make up the set of 46 that will be reproduced in each cell of the new baby's body. Each chromosome consists of a long string of deoxyribonucleic acid (DNA) made up of segments called genes. The baby's sex is determined by the 23rd pair of chromosomes, a pattern of XX for a girl and XY for a boy.

**2.1a** What risks are associated with assisted reproductive technology?

Assisted reproductive technology fails to result in a live birth in about two-thirds of cases. In addition, it is more likely to lead to multiple birth than natural conception. As a result, infants conceived through ART techniques have higher rates of premature birth and other problems.

**2.2** In what ways do genes influence development?

Geneticists distinguish between the genotype, which is the pattern of inherited characteristics, and the phenotype, which is the result of the interaction of genotype and environment. Genes are transmitted from parent to child according to complex patterns of inheritance that include dominant/recessive, polygenic, multifactorial, and sex-linked. What are the characteristics of the zygote?

## Development from Conception to Birth

**2.3** What happens in each of the stages of prenatal development?

During the first days after conception, called the germinal stage of development, the zygote (the initial cell formed by egg and sperm) divides, travels down the fallopian tube, and is implanted in the wall of the uterus. The second stage, the period of the embryo, which lasts until 8 weeks after fertilization, includes the development of the various structures that support fetal development, such as the placenta, as well as primitive forms of all organ systems. The final 30 weeks of gestation, called the fetal period, are devoted primarily to enlargement and refinements in all the organ systems.

**2.4** How do male and female fetuses differ?

During the embryonic period, the XY embryo secretes the hormone testosterone, which stimulates the growth of male genitalia and shifts the brain into a "male" pattern. Boys are more active, have more slowly developing skeletons, are bigger at birth, and are more vulnerable to most forms of prenatal stress.

**2.5** What behaviors have scientists observed in fetuses?

The fetus is responsive to stimuli and appears to learn in the womb. Temperamental differences in the womb (such as activity level) persist into infancy and childhood, and some aspects of the prenatal sensory environment may be important to future development.

## Problems in Prenatal Development

**2.6** What are the effects of the major dominant, recessive, and sex-linked diseases?

Dominant disorders are not usually manifested until adulthood. Huntington's disease, a fatal affliction of the nervous system, is one such disorder. Recessive disorders affect individuals earlier in life, often leading to mental retardation and/or early death. These disorders include phenylketonuria, sickle-cell disease, and Tay-Sachs disease. A fairly common sex-linked disorder is red-green color blindness. Hemophilia and fragile-X syndrome are more serious sex-linked disorders that affect males far more often than females.

**2.6a** What techniques are used to assess and treat problems in prenatal development?

Techniques such as fetoscopy, ultrasonography, chorionic villus sampling, and amniocentesis are used to diagnose chromosomal and genetic disorders, and along with laboratory tests identify problems in fetal development. A few such problems can be treated prior to birth with surgery and/or medication.

**2.7** How do trisomies and other disorders of the autosomes and sex chromosomes affect development?

Abnormal numbers of chromosomes or chromosomal damage cause a number of serious disorders, including Down syndrome.

**2.8** How do maternal diseases and environmental hazards affect prenatal development?

Some diseases contracted by the mother, including rubella, AIDS, sexually transmitted diseases like genital herpes and CMV, and chronic illnesses, may cause abnormalities or disease in the child. Environmental hazards include pollutants such as mercury and lead as well as parasite-bearing substances such as animal feces. Their effect on the fetus varies with the timing of the exposure.

**2.8a** How has technology changed the way that health professionals manage high-risk pregnancies?

Health professionals can closely monitor the conditions of both expectant mothers and fetuses with small devices that women can use or wear as they go about their normal activities.

**2.9** What are the potential adverse effects of tobacco, alcohol, and other drugs on prenatal development?

Drugs such as alcohol and nicotine appear to have harmful effects on the developing fetus; drug effects depend on the timing of exposure and the dosage.

**2.10** What are the risks associated with legal drugs, maternal diet, age, emotional distress, and poverty?

Some prescription and over-the-counter drugs have teratogenic effects. Physicians need to know what drugs pregnant women take regularly so that they can provide guidance as to the appropriate use of such drugs during pregnancy. If a mother suffers from poor nutrition, she faces an increased risk of stillbirth, low birth weight, and infant death during the first year of life. Older mothers and very young mothers also run increased risks, as do their infants. Long-term, severe depression or chronic physical illness in the mother may increase the risk of complications during pregnancy or difficulties in the infant. A number of prenatal risk factors are associated with poverty, including earlier age at first pregnancy and lack of access to prenatal care.

## KEY TERMS

amnion (p. 37)
axons (p. 38)
blastocyst (p. 35)
cell body (p. 38)
chorion (p. 37)
chromosomes (p. 30)
dendrites (p. 38)
deoxyribonucleic acid (DNA) (p. 30)
dominant/recessive pattern of inheritance (p. 33)

Down syndrome (trisomy 21) (p. 45)
embryo (p. 35)
embryonic stage (p. 37)
fallopian tube (p. 30)
fetal alcohol syndrome (FAS) (p. 49)
fetal stage (p. 37)
fetus (p. 37)
fraternal (dizygotic) twins (p. 35)
gametes (p. 30)
genes (p. 32)

genotype (p 32)
germinal stage (p. 35)
glial cells (p 39)
heterozygous (p. 32)
homozygous (p. 32)
identical (monozygotic) twins (p. 35)
multifactorial pattern of inheritance (p. 34)
neuronal migration (p. 38)
neuronal proliferation (p. 38)
neurons (p. 38)

ovum (p. 30)
phenotype (p. 32)
placenta (p. 37)
polygenic pattern of inheritance (p. 34)
sperm (p. 30)
synapses (p. 38)
teratogens (p. 42)
umbilical cord (p. 37)
uterus (p. 30)
viability (p. 38)
zygote (p. 30)

# Birth and Early Infancy

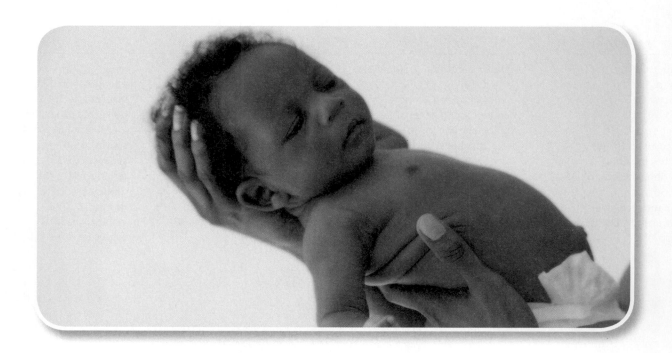

## LEARNING OBJECTIVES

### Birth

**3.1** What decisions must parents make about the birth process in industrialized societies?

**3.2** What are the events and risks associated with each stage of the birth process?

**3.3** What are some of the possible consequences of low birth weight?

### Behavior in Early Infancy

**3.4** What reflexes and behavioral states are exhibited by infants?

**3.4a** In what ways are the acoustic qualities of infants' cries and developmental outcomes related?

**3.5** What kinds of motor, sensory, and perceptual abilities do newborns have?

**3.6** What types of learning do infants exhibit?

**3.6a** How do music therapists use operant conditioning to improve preterm infants' sucking abilities?

**3.7** How do newborns differ in temperament, and what skills do they bring to social interactions?

### Health and Wellness in Early Infancy

**3.8** What are the infant's nutritional, health care, and immunization needs?

**3.8a** What is the evidence concerning breast- and bottle-feeding?

**3.9** What kinds of illnesses typically occur in infancy?

**3.10** What factors contribute to infant mortality?

When Mahajabeen Shaikh gave birth to twins, the larger of the two, Hiba, weighed a robust 20 ounces, small but sufficient for her gestational age of 26 weeks. But the other twin, Rumaisa, weighed just 8.6 ounces, a birth weight that gave her the distinction of being the smallest surviving infant ever born. Remarkably, experts in neonatal medicine at Chicago's Loyola University told Mahajabeen and her husband, Mohammed Rahman, that the odds favored a normal infancy and childhood for both girls (Associated Press, 2005).

Encouraged by the doctors' prognosis, Mahajabeen and Mohammed watched hopefully as their twins grew stronger each day. By the time the girls reached 5 months of age, both were out of the hospital and developing normally. When the family returned to Loyola on the twins' first birthday, both girls eagerly dug into the cake the hospital provided to celebrate the occasion. Rumaisa was still much smaller than Hiba, but, like her sister, she was healthy and thriving. However, their case is remarkable. There are only 58 documented cases of surviving newborns who weighed 13 ounces or less (Muraskas & Hasson, 2004). Further, most of those who do survive have lifelong health or neurological problems. ◉ Watch at **MyDevelopmentLab**

◉ **Watch** the **Video** *Medical Miracle: Partial Liquid Ventilation* at **MyDevelopmentLab**

Fortunately, most infants are born on time and do not require intensive care. In most cases, too, expectant mothers do not deliver under emergency circumstances and can choose the setting in which their babies will be born. We begin our discussion of birth and early infancy with an overview of the array of birth choices available today.

## Birth

For parents, birth is an experience that combines great physical stress with a wide variety of emotions: the joy of seeing the baby for the first time, curiosity about what kind of individual she will be, worry about possible physical problems, anxiety about the ability to parent effectively, and so on. For the child, of course, birth marks her entrance into the family and community.

## Birth Choices

◀----------**Learning Objective 3.1**

In the industrialized world, parents must make a number of choices in advance of the delivery. Parents may worry about whether they are making the best choices both for themselves and for the baby.

What decisions must parents make about the birth process in industrialized societies?

**DRUGS DURING LABOR AND DELIVERY** One key decision about the birth process concerns the use of pain-relieving drugs. Four types of pain relief are used (American College of Obstetricians and Gynecologists [ACOG], 2004). *Systemic analgesics* are usually given as injections. They relieve pain without causing loss of consciousness, much as an acetaminophen tablet (Tylenol) relieves a headache. *Local anesthetics* are also injected and cause numbness in a very small area, somewhat like the shot of novacaine that a dentist gives prior to filling a tooth. Local anesthetics are often given when a procedure called an *episiotomy* is necessary (a small incision that increases the size of the vagina). *Regional analgesics*, usually called *epidural blocks*, are the most commonly used form of pain relief. Just over 60% of women in the United States receive this form of pain relief during labor (Osterman & Martin, 2011).

*Rumaisa Rahman is shown here at a few weeks old. The smallest surviving infant, she weighed just 8.6 ounces at birth.*

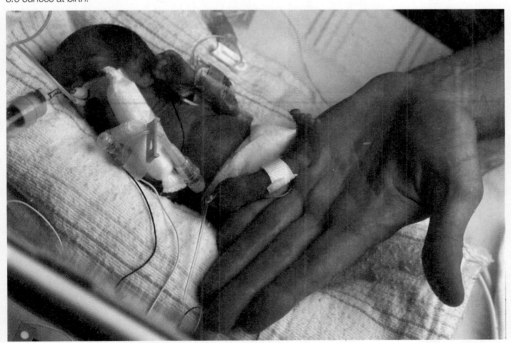

These couples, like so many today, are taking a child-birth class together. Having the father present at the delivery as coach seems to reduce the mother's pain and even shorten the length of labor.

Epidural blocks cause a complete loss of sensation below the point in the spine where the pain-relieving drug is injected. *General anesthesia* both relieves pain and induces unconsciousness. Because general anesthesia is the fastest acting form of pain relief, it is most commonly used in emergency situations.

Nearly all drugs given during labor pass through the placenta and enter the fetal bloodstream. Because the newborn lacks the enzymes necessary to break down such drugs quickly, the effect of any drug lasts longer in the baby than it does in the mother. Not surprisingly, then, drugged infants may show signs of being under the influence of such drugs (Gowen, 2011). For example, they may have slower or faster than normal heartbeats, depending on which drugs their mothers were given. In rare cases, infants of anesthetized mothers experience seizures.

Because of these risks, many women choose to avoid drugs altogether. The general term *prepared childbirth* is commonly used to refer to this particular choice.

Prepared childbirth involves several components. First, a woman selects someone to serve as a labor coach. *Prepared childbirth classes* psychologically prepare the woman and her labor coach for the experience of labor and delivery. For example, they learn to use the term *contraction* instead of *pain*. Further, believing that her baby will benefit from prepared childbirth provides the woman with the motivation she needs to endure labor without the aid of pain-relieving medication. Finally, relaxation and breathing techniques provide her with behavioral responses that replace the negative emotions that typically result from the physical discomfort of contractions. Aided by her coach, the woman focuses attention on her breathing rather than on the pain.

**THE LOCATION OF BIRTH** Another choice parents must make is where the baby is to be born. At the turn of the century, only about 5% of babies in the United States were born in hospitals; today, the figure is 99% (Martin et al., 2010). The remaining 1% are born at home or in free-standing birth centers. Limited research in Canada and the United States (e.g., Janssen, Holt, & Myers, 1994; Johnson & Davis, 2005) indicates that such nonhospital deliveries, if planned and attended by a midwife or equivalent professional, are no riskier than deliveries in hospitals.

The father's presence during labor and delivery has become the norm in the United States, so much so, in fact, that it has become difficult to study this variable. Decades ago, when hospital policies varied greatly with regard to the presence of fathers in the delivery room, it was possible to compare father-present to father-absent deliveries. Such studies found that when fathers were present, laboring women experienced less pain, requested less medication, delivered sooner, and experienced fewer complications than when fathers were absent (Henneborn & Cogan, 1975).

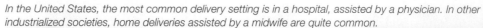

In the United States, the most common delivery setting is in a hospital, assisted by a physician. In other industrialized societies, home deliveries assisted by a midwife are quite common.

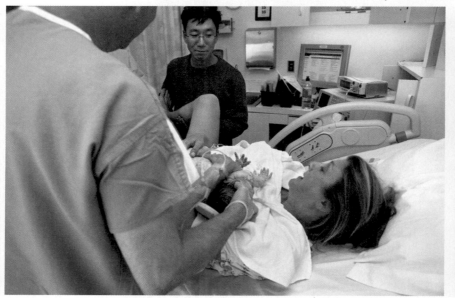

# The Process of Birth

◄----------Learning Objective 3.2
What are the events and risks associated with each stage of the birth process?

Labor typically progresses through three stages. Occasionally, complications occur. Once the child is born, his health is assessed, and the family begins getting to know its newest member.

**THE STAGES OF LABOR**   Stage 1 covers the period during which two important processes occur: **dilation** and **effacement**. The cervix (the opening at the bottom of the uterus) must open up like the lens of a camera (dilation) and flatten out (effacement). At the time of actual delivery of the infant, the cervix must normally be dilated to about 10 centimeters (about 4 inches). This part of labor has been likened to what happens when you put on a sweater with a neck that is too tight. You have to pull and stretch the neck of the sweater with your head in order to get it on. Eventually, you stretch the neck wide enough so that the widest part of your head can pass through. A good deal of the effacement may actually occur in the last weeks of the pregnancy, as may some dilation. It is not uncommon for women to be 80% effaced and 1 to 3 centimeters dilated when they begin labor. The contractions of the first stage of labor, which are at first widely spaced and later more frequent and rhythmical, serve to complete both processes. ◉⎤Watch at MyDevelopmentLab

Customarily, stage 1 is itself divided into phases. In the early (or *latent*) phase, contractions are relatively far apart and are typically not very uncomfortable. In the *active* phase, which begins when the cervix is 3 to 4 centimeters dilated and continues until dilation has reached 8 centimeters, contractions are closer together and more intense. The last 2 centimeters of dilation are achieved during a period usually called the *transition* phase. It is this period, when contractions are closely spaced and strong, that women typically find the most painful.

Fortunately, transition is relatively brief, especially in second or later pregnancies. Figure 3.1 shows the duration of the several subphases, although neither the figure nor the average numbers convey the wide individual variability that exists. Among women delivering a first child, stage 1 labor may last as little as 3 hours or as long as 20 (Biswas & Craigo, 1994; Kilpatrick & Laros, 1989). The average is about 8 hours for first births and 6 for subsequent deliveries (Albers, 1999). The times are generally longer for women receiving anesthesia than for those delivering by prepared childbirth.

At the end of the transition phase, the mother will normally have the urge to help the infant come out by "pushing." When the birth attendant (physician or midwife) is sure the cervix is fully dilated, she or he will encourage this pushing, and the second stage of labor—the actual delivery—begins. The baby's head moves past the stretched cervix, into the birth canal, and finally out of the mother's body. Most women find this part of labor markedly less distressing than the transition phase. The average length of stage 2 is about 50 minutes for first infants and 20 minutes for later deliveries (Moore & Persaud, 1993). It rarely takes longer than 2 hours.

Most infants are delivered head first, facing down toward the mother's spine. Three to four percent, however, are oriented differently, either feet first or bottom first (called *breech* presentations) (ACOG, 2007). Several decades ago, most breech deliveries were accomplished with the aid of medical instruments such as forceps; today, nearly four-fifths of breech presentations are delivered by cesarean section (ACOG, 2007)—a procedure discussed more fully in the next section. Stage 3, typically quite brief, is the delivery of the placenta (also called the *afterbirth*) and other material from the uterus. You can see all these steps presented in Figure 3.2 on page 60.

**COMPLICATIONS**   Birth complications that interfere with a child's vital functions can lead to brain damage and, as a result, cause a variety of later developmental problems. One such complication is an insufficiency of oxygen for the infant, a state called **anoxia**. During the period immediately surrounding birth, anoxia may occur because the umbilical circulation system fails to continue supplying blood oxygen until the baby breathes or because the umbilical cord has been squeezed in some way during labor or delivery. Long-term effects of anoxia have been hard to pin down. Prolonged anoxia is often (but not invariably) associated with such major consequences as cerebral palsy or mental retardation (Venerosi, Valanzano, Cirulli, Alleva, & Calamandrei, 2004).

◉⎤**Watch** the **Video** *Labor* at **MyDevelopmentLab**

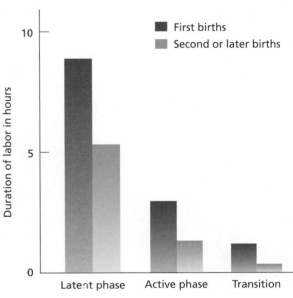

**FIGURE 3.1** Phases of Labor
Typical pattern of timing of the phases of stage 1 of labor for first births and for subsequent births. The relatively long latent phase shown here counts from 0 centimeters dilated, which increases the total hours somewhat. The average length of stage 1 is about 8 hours for a first birth and 6 hours for later births.

(*Source:* The course and conduct of normal labor and delivery. In A. H. DeCherney & M. L. Pernoll (Eds.), *Current obstetric and gynecologic diagnosis & treatment* (pp. 202–227). Norwalk, CT: Appleton & Lange.)

**dilation**   A key process in the first stage of childbirth, during which the cervix widens sufficiently to allow the infant's head to pass into the birth canal. Full dilation is 10 centimeters.

**effacement**   The flattening of the cervix, which, along with dilation, is a key process of the first stage of childbirth.

**anoxia**   A shortage of oxygen. This is one of the potential risks at birth, and it can result in brain damage if it is prolonged.

**FIGURE 3.2** Phases of Delivery
The sequence of steps during delivery is shown clearly in these drawings.

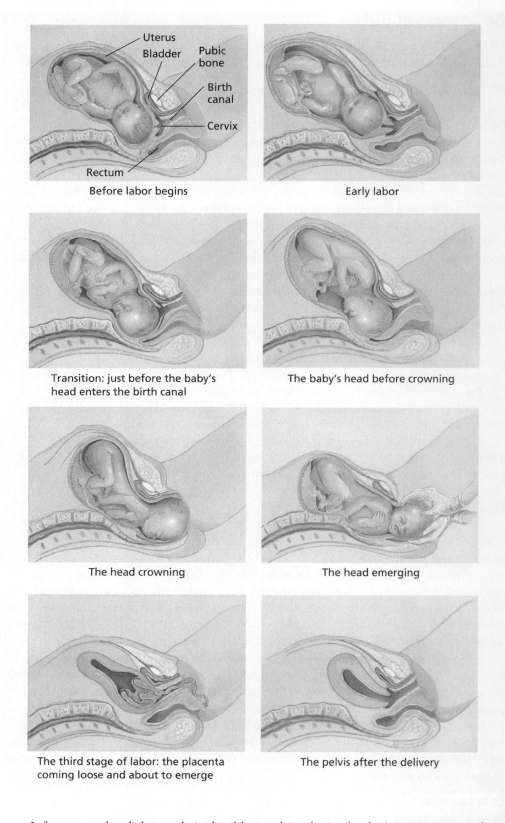

Uterus
Bladder Pubic bone
Birth canal
Cervix
Rectum

Before labor begins

Early labor

Transition: just before the baby's head enters the birth canal

The baby's head before crowning

The head crowning

The head emerging

The third stage of labor: the placenta coming loose and about to emerge

The pelvis after the delivery

Infants may also dislocate their shoulders or hips during birth. Some experience fractures, and in others, nerves that control facial muscles are compressed, causing temporary paralysis on one side of the face. Such complications are usually not serious and resolve themselves with little or no treatment.

**cesarean section (C-section)** Delivery of the child through an incision in the mother's abdomen.

**CESAREAN DELIVERIES** Sometimes it is necessary to deliver a baby surgically through incisions made in the abdominal and uterine walls. There are several situations that justify the use of this operation, called a **cesarean section** (or **C-section**). Factors that call for the procedure include fetal distress during labor, labor that fails to progress in a reasonable amount of time, a fetus that is too large to be delivered vaginally, and maternal health conditions that may be aggravated by vaginal delivery (e.g., cardiovascular disease, spinal injury) or may be dangerous to a vaginally delivered fetus (e.g., herpes) (ACOG, 2008a). Thus, in many situations, cesarean sections prevent maternal and fetal complications and, no doubt, save lives. Predictably, surveys show that 99% of childbirth-related maternal deaths occur in the developing nations of the world in which lack of access to high-quality medical care restricts cesarean rates to 2% to 5% of all births (World Health Organization, 2010). Despite the benefits of cesarean delivery, many observers claim that the current rate of cesarean deliveries in the United States is too high when compared to rates in similar countries. In the Netherlands, for example, only 14% of births are by C-section, while in the United States about one-third of all deliveries involve the procedure (EURO-PERISTAT Project, 2008; Martin et al., 2010). Critics of the frequency with which C-sections occur in the United States say that many of these operations are unnecessary. Are their claims justified?

One factor behind current C-section statistics is that, as you learned earlier, more older women are having babies (Martin et al., 2010). These women are more likely to conceive twins and other multiples. In such cases, surgical delivery almost always increases the odds in favor of the babies' postnatal health. Thus, the benefits of cesarean delivery outweigh its risks.

By contrast, surveys suggest that about 3% of C-sections performed in the United States are entirely elective (ACOG, 2007). In these cases, women who have no medical problems, and who are carrying healthy fetuses, request a surgical delivery, and their physicians comply. The ethics committee of the American College of Obstetrics and Gynecology (2008b) has ruled that elective surgical deliveries are ethical as long as the practitioner is certain that, for the patients who request them, vaginal deliveries carry equal risk.

**ASSESSING THE NEWBORN**    Most physicians evaluate an infant's status immediately after birth and then again 5 minutes later, to detect any problems that may require special care. The most frequently used assessment system is the *Apgar score*, developed by a physician, Virginia Apgar (1953). The newborn is given a score of 0, 1, or 2 on each of the five criteria listed in Table 3.1 A maximum score of 10 is fairly unusual immediately after birth, because most infants are still somewhat blue in the fingers and toes at that stage. At the 5-minute assessment, however, 85–90% of infants are scored as 9 or 10, meaning that they are getting off to a good start. Any score of 7 or better indicates that the baby is in no danger. A score of 4, 5, or 6 usually means that the baby needs help establishing normal breathing patterns; a score of 3 or below indicates a baby in critical condition, requiring active intervention, although babies with such low Apgar scores can and often do survive (Casey, McIntire, & Leveno, 2001).

**Table 3.1 — EVALUATION METHOD FOR APGAR SCORE**

| Aspect of Infant Observed | Score Assigned | | |
| --- | --- | --- | --- |
| | 0 | 1 | 2 |
| Heart rate | Absent | <100/min. | >100/min. |
| Respiratory rate | No breathing | Weak cry and shallow breathing | Good strong cry and regular breathing |
| Muscle tone | Flaccid | Some flexion of extremities | Well flexed |
| Response to stimulation of feet | None | Some motion | Cry |
| Color | Blue; pale | Body pink, extremities blue | Completely pink |

*Source:* Francis, P. L., Self, P. A., & Horowitz, F. D. (1987). The behavioral assessment of the neonate: An overview. In J. D. Osofsky (Ed.), *Handbook of infant development* (2nd ed., pp. 723–779). New York: Wiley-Interscience.

**low birth weight (LBW)** Term for any baby born with a weight below 2,500 grams (5.5 pounds), including both those born too early (preterm) and those who are small for date.

**very low birth weight (VLBW)** Term for any baby born with a weight below 1,500 grams (3.3 pounds).

**extremely low birth weight (ELBW)** Term for any baby born with a weight below 1,000 grams (2.2 pounds).

**preterm infant** An infant born before 38 weeks gestational age.

**small-for-date infant** An infant who weighs less than is normal for the number of weeks of gestation completed.

Another test used to assess newborns, widely used by researchers, is the Brazelton Neonatal Behavioral Assessment Scale (Brazelton, 1984). In this test, a skilled examiner checks the neonate's responses to a variety of stimuli; his reflexes, muscle tone, alertness, and cuddliness; and his ability to quiet or soothe himself after being upset. Scores on this test can be helpful in identifying children who may have significant neurological problems. More interestingly, several investigators (e.g., Francis, Self, & Horowitz, 1987) have found that teaching parents how to administer this test to their own infants turns out to have beneficial effects on the parent-infant interaction, apparently because it heightens the parent's awareness of all the subtle cues the baby provides.

**THE FIRST GREETING** Many parents experience intense joy as they greet the infant for the first time, accompanied often by laughter, exclamations of delight at the baby's features, and first tentative and tender touching. Here are one mother's reactions to seeing her new daughter:

> She's big, isn't she? What do you reckon? (Doctor makes a comment.) Oh look, she's got hair. It's a girl—you're supposed to be all little. Gosh. Oh, she's lovely. Oh, she's opened her eyes (laughs). Oh, lovely (kisses baby). (MacFarlane, 1977, pp. 64–65)

Most parents are intensely interested in having the baby look at them right away. They are delighted if the baby opens her eyes and will try to stimulate her to do so if she doesn't. The parents' initial tentative touches also seem to follow a pattern: The parent first touches the infant rather gingerly with the tip of a finger and then proceeds gradually to stroking with the full hand (MacFarlane, 1977). The tenderness seen in most of these early encounters is striking.

**Learning Objective 3.3**
What are some of the possible consequences of low birth weight?

## Low Birth Weight

The optimal weight range for infants—the weight that is associated with the lowest risk of later death or disability—is between about 3,000 and 5,000 grams (6.6 to 11 pounds) (Rees, Lederman, & Kiely, 1996). Several different labels are used to describe infants whose weight falls below this optimal range. All babies below 2,500 grams (5.5 pounds) are described with the most general term of **low birth weight (LBW)**. Those below 1,500 grams (3.3 pounds) are usually called **very low birth weight (VLBW)**, and those below 1,000 grams (2.2 pounds) are called **extremely low birth weight (ELBW)**. The incidence of low birth weight has declined in the United States in the past decade but is still high: About 8% of all newborns weigh below 2,500 grams (Martin et al., 2010). About 12% of those small babies weighed less than 1,500 grams. Babies who weigh more than 1,500 grams and who receive good neonatal care have close to a 100% chance of survival. However, in the VLBW and ELBW groups, the more the infant weighs, the greater his chances of survival.

**CAUSES OF LOW BIRTH WEIGHT** Low birth weight occurs for a variety of reasons, of which the most obvious and common is that the infant is born before the full 38 weeks of gestation. Any baby born before 38 weeks of gestation is labeled a **preterm infant**. Multiple births are especially likely to end in preterm delivery. In addition, mothers who suffer from chronic illnesses and those who develop a serious medical condition during pregnancy are more likely to deliver preterm infants (Sola, Rogido, & Partridge, 2002). In most cases of preterm delivery, labor begins spontaneously. However, because of a condition in the fetus or in the mother, physicians sometimes elect to deliver babies prior to 38 weeks of gestation via C-section.

It is also possible for an infant to have completed the full 38-week gestational period but still weigh less than 2,500 grams or to weigh less than would be expected for the number of weeks of gestation completed, however long that may have been. Such an infant is called a **small-for-date infant**. Infants in this group appear to have suffered from prenatal malnutrition, such as might occur with constriction of blood flow caused by the mother's smoking, or from other significant problems prenatally. Such infants generally have poorer prognoses than do equivalent-weight infants who weigh an appropriate amount for their gestational age, especially if the small-for-date infant is also preterm (Sola, Rogido, & Partridge, 2002).

**HEALTH STATUS OF LOW-BIRTH-WEIGHT INFANTS** All low-birth-weight infants share some characteristics, including markedly lower levels of responsiveness at birth and in the early months of life. Those born more than 6 weeks before term also often suffer from **respiratory distress syndrome**. Their poorly developed lungs lack an important chemical, called a *surfactant*, that enables the air sacs to remain inflated; some of the sacs collapse, resulting in serious breathing difficulties (Sola, Rogido, & Partridge, 2002). Beginning in 1990, neonatologists began treating this problem by administering a synthetic or animal-derived version of surfactant, a therapy that has reduced the rate of death among very low-birth-weight infants by about 30% (Hamvas et al., 1996; Schwartz, Anastasia, Scanlon, & Kellogg, 1994).

### LONG-TERM CONSEQUENCES OF LOW BIRTH WEIGHT

Thankfully, two-thirds to three-fourths of premature infants are indistinguishable from peers by the time they reach school age (Bowen, Gibson, & Hand, 2002; Foulder-Hughes & Cooke, 2003a). But the remainder experience difficulties in school. The two critical predictive factors for such children seem to be birth weight and gestational age (Foulder-Hughes & Cooke, 2003b; McGrath & Sullivan, 2002). The lower a child's birth weight and the earlier the gestational age at which he was born, the greater the risk that he will exhibit school problems. Researchers have found that children who were born prior to the 27th week and who weighed less than 2.2 pounds are far more likely to suffer from problems in elementary school than LBW children who were born later and/or weighed more than 2.2 pounds (Shum, Neulinger, O'Callaghan, & Mohay, 2008). Moreover, this difference persists through fourth grade in many cases. However, research also shows that these children do show progress over time, indicating that their difficulties do not necessarily suggest the presence of a permanent disability (Fussell & Burns, 2007).

*Low-birth-weight infants like this one are not only small; they are also more wrinkled and skinny, because the layer of fat under the skin has not fully developed. They are also more likely to have significant breathing difficulties, because their lungs lack surfactant.*

However, it is also important for parents to know that the type of care a premature infant receives contributes to how rapidly she develops (White-Traut et al., 2002). For example, a relatively recent innovation in the care of preterm newborns is an intervention called "kangaroo care" in which parents are shown how to increase the amount of skin-to-skin contact infants engage in with them. An important part of the intervention involves allowing parents to hold these tiny newborns for very long periods of time. Researchers have found that babies who receive kangaroo care grow and develop more rapidly than preterm infants given conventional neonatal care (Feldman & Eidelman, 2003; Tessier et al., 2003). An added bonus is that kangaroo care improves premature infants' ability to tolerate the discomforts associated with medical procedures such as drawing blood (Cong, Ludington-Hoe, McCain, & Fu, 2009).

Advocates of massage therapy for preterm infants also cite the necessity for skin-to-skin contact. Their research shows that preterm newborns gain weight faster and are more responsive to their environment after a few sessions of massage therapy (Field, Diego, & Hernandez-Reif, 2010). Surveys show that about 40% of newborn nurseries in the United States provide premature infants with some kind of massage intervention (Field, Hernandez-Reif, Feijo, & Freedman, 2006). Similarly, researchers have found that the physical contact that results from "double-bedding" of preterm twins increases such infants' chances for positive developmental outcomes (Diamond & Amso, 2008).

As preterm infants get older, Susan Landry and her colleagues have found, those whose mothers are good at identifying and shaping their attention behaviors develop more rapidly than those whose mothers are less so (Dieterich, Hebert, Landry, Swank, & Smith, 2004). Of course, responsive parenting is important for full-term babies' development as well. But Landry has found that consistent parental responsiveness over the first several years of life is more critical to preterm than to full-term infants' development (Landry, Smith, & Swank, 2006).

**respiratory distress syndrome** A problem frequently found in infants born more than 6 weeks before term, in which the infant's lungs lack a chemical (surfactant) needed to keep air sacs inflated.

# Behavior in Early Infancy

👁Watch the Videos *Reflexes: Babinski* and *Reflexes: Moro* at **MyDevelopmentLab**

Who is this small stranger who brings both joy and strain? What qualities and skills does the newborn bring to the interaction process? He cries, breathes, looks around a bit. But what else can he do in the early hours and days? On what skills does the infant build?

**Learning Objective 3.4** ------------➔
What reflexes and behavioral states are exhibited by infants?

## Reflexes and Behavioral States

One important part of the infant's repertoire of behaviors is a large collection of **reflexes**, which are physical responses triggered involuntarily by specific stimuli. In addition, newborns typically display a behavioral cycle that includes periods of alertness, sleepiness, and hunger.

**REFLEXES**  Some reflexes persist into adulthood, such as your automatic eyeblink when a puff of air hits your eye or the involuntary narrowing of the pupil of your eye when you're in a bright light. Others, sometimes referred to as **adaptive reflexes**, are essential to the infant's survival but gradually disappear in the first year of life. Sucking and swallowing reflexes are prominent in this category, as is the **rooting reflex**—the automatic turn of the head toward any touch on the cheek, a reflex that helps the baby get the nipple into his mouth during nursing. These reflexes are no longer present in older infants or adults but are clearly highly adaptive for the newborn.

*The Moro reflex*

Newborns also have a large collection of **primitive reflexes**, controlled by the medulla and the midbrain, both of which are close to being fully developed at birth. For example, if you make a loud noise or startle a baby in some other way, you'll see her throw her arms outward and arch her back, a pattern that is part of the **Moro reflex** (also called the *startle reflex*). Stroke the bottom of her foot, and she will splay out her toes; this reaction is called the **Babinski reflex**.  👁Watch at **MyDevelopmentLab**

Primitive reflexes disappear over the first year of life (see Table 3.2), apparently superseded by the action of the cortex, which by this age is much more fully developed. Yet, even though these reflexes represent neurologically primitive patterns, they are nonetheless linked to important

*The Babinski reflex*

**reflexes**  Automatic body reactions to specific stimulation, such as the knee jerk or the Moro reflex. Adults have many reflexes, but the newborn also has some primitive reflexes that disappear as the cortex develops.

**adaptive reflexes**  Reflexes that are essential to the infant's survival but that disappear in the first year of life.

**rooting reflex**  The reflex that causes an infant to automatically turn toward a touch on the cheek, open the mouth, and make sucking movements.

**primitive reflexes**  Collection of reflexes seen in young infants that gradually disappear during the first year of life, including the Moro and Babinski reflexes.

| | Table 3.2 | EXAMPLES OF PRIMITIVE AND ADAPTIVE REFLEXES | |
|---|---|---|---|
| **Reflex** | **Stimulation** | **Response** | **Developmental Pattern** |
| Tonic neck | While baby is on his back and awake, turn his head to one side. | Baby assumes a "fencing" posture, with arm extended on the side toward which the head is turned. | Fades by 4 months |
| Grasping | Stroke the baby's palm with your finger. | Baby will make a strong fist around your finger. | Fades by 3 to 4 months |
| Moro | Make a loud sound near the baby, or let the baby "drop" slightly and suddenly. | Baby extends legs, arms, and fingers, arches his back, and draws back his head. | Fades by about 6 months |
| Walking | Hold baby under arms with feet just touching a floor or other flat surface. | Baby will make step-like motions, alternating feet as in walking. | Fades by about 8 weeks in most infants |
| Babinski | Stroke sole of the baby's foot from toes toward heel. | Baby will fan out his toes. | Fades between 8 and 12 months |
| Rooting | Stroke baby's cheek with finger or nipple. | Baby turns head toward the touch, opens mouth, and makes sucking movements. | After 3 weeks, transforms into a voluntary head-turning response |

later behavior patterns. The tonic neck reflex (described in Table 3.2), for example, forms the foundation for the baby's later ability to reach for objects, because it focuses the baby's attention on the hand; the grasp reflex, too, is linked to the later ability to hold onto objects.

In a similar way, the walking reflex may be linked to later voluntary walking. In an early study, Zelazo and his colleagues (1972) stimulated the walking reflex repeatedly in some babies every day from the 2nd to the 8th week after birth. By 8 weeks, these stimulated babies took many more steps per minute when they were held in the walking position than did nonstimulated babies. And at the end of the first year, the stimulated babies learned to walk alone about a month sooner than did comparison babies who had not had their walking reflex stimulated.

The late Esther Thelen (1941–2004) cited Zelazo's findings regarding the walking reflex as an example of her **dynamic systems theory**, the notion that several factors interact to influence development (Thelen & Smith, 1996). Thelen noted that infants gain a proportionately substantial amount of weight at about the same time that they no longer show the walking reflex. Consequently, Thelen claimed that infants no longer exhibit the walking reflex because their muscles are not yet strong enough to handle the increased weight of their legs. True walking, according to Thelen, emerges both as a result of a genetic plan for motor skill development and because of a change in the ratio of muscle strength to weight in infants' bodies. This latter change is strongly influenced by environmental variables, especially nutrition and opportunities to freely move about. Thus, the streams of influence that are incorporated into dynamic systems theory include inborn genetic factors and environmental variables such as the availability of adequate nutrition and opportunities to practice motor skills.

Opportunities to practice motor skills seem to be particularly important for young children who have disorders, such as cerebral palsy, that impair motor functioning (Kerr, McDowell, & McDonough, 2007). Consequently, developmentalists are fairly certain that severely restricting a baby's movement slows down acquisition of motor skills, and many are beginning to accept the idea that a baby's movement experiences in normal environments may also influence motor skill development.

Thus, primitive reflexes are not just curiosities. They can be informative, as when a baby fails to show a reflex that ought to be there or displays a reflex past the point at which it normally disappears. For example, infants exposed to narcotics or those suffering from anoxia at birth may show only very weak reflexes; infants with Down syndrome have only very weak Moro reflexes and sometimes have poor sucking reflexes. When a primitive reflex persists past the normal point, it may suggest some neurological damage or dysfunction (Scerif et al., 2005; Schott & Rossor, 2003). Reflexes are also the starting point for many important physical skills, including reaching, grasping, and walking. ◉─Watch at **MyDevelopmentLab**

**BEHAVIORAL STATES** Researchers have described five different states of sleep and wakefulness in neonates, referred to as **states of consciousness**, summarized in Table 3.3. Most

**Moro reflex** The reflex that causes infants to extend their legs, arms, and fingers, arch the back, and draw back the head when startled (for example, by a loud sound or a sensation of being dropped).

**Babinski reflex** A reflex found in very young infants that causes them to splay out their toes in response to a stroke on the bottom of the foot.

**dynamic systems theory** The view that several factors interact to influence development.

**states of consciousness** The periodic shifts in alertness, sleepiness, crankiness, and so on that characterize an infant's behavior.

◉─Watch the **Video** Reflexes: Palmar Grasp at **MyDevelopmentLab**

| Table 3.3 | THE BASIC STATES OF INFANT SLEEP AND WAKEFULNESS |
|---|---|
| **State** | **Characteristics** |
| Deep sleep | Eyes closed, regular breathing, no movement except occasional startles |
| Active sleep | Eyes closed, irregular breathing, small twitches, no gross body movement |
| Quiet awake | Eyes open, no major body movement, regular breathing |
| Active awake | Eyes open, with movements of the head, limbs, and trunk; irregular breathing |
| Crying and fussing | Eyes may be partly or entirely closed; vigorous diffuse movement with crying or fussing sounds |

*Sources:* Based on the work of Hutt, Lenard, and Prechtl, 1969; Parmelee, Wenner, and Schulz, 1964; Prechtl and Beintema, 1964.

**colic** A pattern of persistent and often inconsolable crying, totaling more than 3 hours a day, found in some infants in the first 3 to 4 months of life.

infants move through these states in the same sequence: from deep sleep to lighter sleep to fussing and hunger and then to alert wakefulness. After they are fed, they become drowsy and drop back into deep sleep. The cycle repeats itself about every 2 hours.

Neonates sleep as much as two-thirds of the time—as much in the daytime as at night (Gahagan, 2011). By 6 or 8 weeks of age, most infants somewhat decrease their total amount of sleep per day and show signs of day/night sleep rhythms (called *circadian rhythms*). Babies this age begin to string two or three 2-hour cycles together without coming to full wakefulness; at which point, we say that the baby can "sleep through the night." By 6 months, babies are still sleeping a bit over 14 hours per day, but the regularity and predictability of the sleep are even more noticeable (Iglowstein, Jenni, Molinari, & Largo, 2003). Most 6-month-olds have clear nighttime sleep patterns and nap during the day at more predictable times. Of course, babies vary a lot around these averages (see Figure 3.3).

Crying is yet another normal part of an infant's cycle of behavioral states (see *Thinking about Research* on page 68). One researcher studying normal newborns found that they cried from 2% to 11% of the time (Korner, Hutchinson, Koperski, Kraemer, & Schneider, 1981). The percentage frequently increases over the first few weeks, peaking at 2–3 hours of crying a day at 6 weeks and then dropping off to less than 1 hour a day by 3 months (Needlman, 1996). Such a peak in crying at 6 weeks has been observed in infants from a number of different cultures, including cultures in which mothers have almost constant body contact with the infant (St. James-Roberts, Bowyer, Varghese, & Sawdon, 1994), which suggests that this crying pattern is not unique to the United States or to other Western cultures. Initially, infants cry most in the evening; later, their most intense crying occurs just before feedings.

Moreover, parents across a variety of cultures use very similar techniques to soothe crying infants. Most babies stop crying when they are picked up, held, and talked or sung to. Encouraging them to suck on a pacifier also usually helps. Parents sometimes worry that picking up a crying baby will lead to even more crying. But research suggests that prompt attention to a crying baby in the first 3 months actually leads to less crying later in infancy (Cecchini, Lai, & Langher, 2008). It is important for health-care professionals to make new parents aware of these findings, because studies suggest that parents of newborns who learn to effectively manage bouts of crying have more confidence in their new roles (Meijer & Wittenboer, 2007).

The basic function of a baby's cry, obviously, is to signal need. Because babies can't move to someone, they have to bring someone to them, and crying is the main way they have to attract attention. In fact, infants have a whole repertoire of cry sounds, with different cries for pain, anger, or hunger. The anger cry, for example, is typically louder and more intense, and the pain cry normally has a very abrupt onset—unlike the more basic kinds of hunger or distress cries, which usually begin with whimpering or moaning.

For the 15–20% of infants who develop **colic**, a pattern involving intense bouts of crying totaling 3 or more hours a day, nothing seems to help (Deshpande, 2009). Typically, colic appears at about 2 weeks of age and then disappears spontaneously at 3 or 4 months of age. The crying is generally worst in late afternoon or early evening. Neither psychologists nor physicians know why colic begins, or why it stops without any intervention. It is a difficult pattern to live with, but the good news is that it does go away.

Finally, the infant behavioral state most enjoyed by many caregivers is the one in which babies are awake and alert. However, newborns are in this state only 2 to 3 hours each day, on average, and the total amount of waking time is unevenly distributed over a 24-hour period. In other words, 15 minutes of waking time may happen at 6:00 a.m., then 30 minutes at 1:00 p.m., another 20 minutes at 4:00 p.m., and so on. Over the first 6 months, advances in neurological development enable infants to remain awake and alert for longer periods of time as their patterns of sleeping, crying, and eating become more regular.

**CROSS-CULTURAL DIFFERENCES IN RESPONSES TO INFANT SLEEP PATTERNS** Cultural beliefs play an important role in parents' responses to infants' sleep patterns. For example, parents in the United States typically see a newborn's erratic sleep cycle as a behavior problem that requires "fixing" through parental intervention (Harkness, 1998). Put differently, parents in the United States live by the clock themselves and are thus motivated to train their infants to adapt to the cultural context into which they have been born (Cole & Packer, 2011).

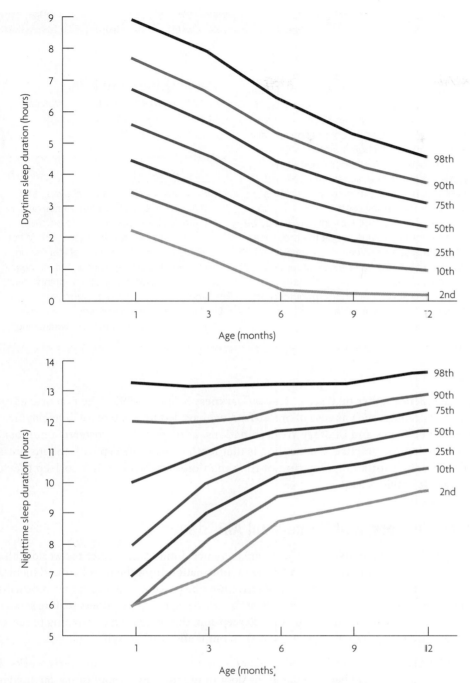

**FIGURE 3.3** Daytime and Nighttime Sleep across the First Year
This figure shows the percentile ranks among infants for various amounts of sleep (e.g., the 98th percentile means that 98% of babies sleep less; the 2nd percentile means that 2% of babies sleep less). As you can see, daytime napping declines as the duration of nighttime sleep increases over the first year of life.

(*Source:* From Ivo Iglowstein, Oskar G. Jenni, Luciano Molinari, and Remo H. Largo, Sleep Duration from Infancy to Adolescence: Reference Values and Generational Trends, *Pediatrics,* Feb. 2003; *111,* 302–307. Copyright © 2003 by the American Academy of Pediatrics. Adapted with permission.)

As a result, American parents focus a great deal of attention on trying to force babies to sleep through the night.

By contrast, in the majority of cultures in the world (and in Western cultures until perhaps 200 years ago), babies sleep in the same bed with their parents, typically until they are weaned, a pattern often called *cosleeping.* Such an arrangement is established for any of a number of reasons, including lack of alternative sleeping space for the infant. More often, cosleeping seems to reflect a basic collectivist value, one that emphasizes contact and

## Variations in Infants' Cries

Many babies with known medical abnormalities have different-sounding cries, including those with Down syndrome, encephalitis, meningitis, and many types of brain damage (Soltis, 2004). This observation has been extended to babies who appear physically normal but who are at risk for later problems because of some perinatal problem, such as preterm or small-for-date babies. Such babies typically make crying sounds that are acoustically distinguishable from those of a normal, low-risk baby. In particular, the cry of such higher-risk babies has a more grating, piercing quality.

On the assumption that the baby's cry may reflect some basic aspect of neurological integrity, Lester (1987) wondered whether one could use the quality of the cry as a diagnostic test. In a classic research study, he found that among preterm babies, those with higher-pitched cries in the first days of life had lower scores on an IQ test at age 5 years. The same kind of connection has also been found among both normal babies and those exposed to methadone prenatally. In all these groups, the higher the pitch and more grating the cry, the lower the child's later IQ or motor development (Huntington, Hans, & Zeskind, 1990). Eventually, it may be possible for physicians to use the presence of such a grating or piercing cry as a signal that the infant may have some underlying physical problem or as a way of making better guesses about the long-term outcomes for babies at high risk for later problems (Soltis, 2004).

### Learning Objective 3.4a
In what ways are the acoustic qualities of infants' cries and developmental outcomes related?

#### CRITICAL ANALYSIS

1. Suppose you did a study showing that the more irritable the infant's cries are, the more likely parents are to develop hostile attitudes toward their infant. What would be the implications of this finding for neurological explanations of the correlation between the quality of infants' cries and later developmental problems?
2. What kind of research would be necessary to establish norms for infant crying?

---

interdependence rather than separateness (Harkness & Super, 1995). The practical advantages of cosleeping, such as ease of breast-feeding, have led to an increase in its popularity in the United States and in other Western nations, a trend that has fostered a number of new studies on the practice. One finding is that mothers who cosleep with infants breast-feed their babies for a longer period of time than mothers who do not cosleep (Taylor, Donovan, & Leavitt, 2008).

## Motor, Sensory, and Perceptual Abilities

**Learning Objective 3.5**
What kinds of motor, sensory, and perceptual abilities do newborns have?

Although the motor abilities of newborns are extremely limited, they enter the world with all of the equipment they need to begin taking in information from the world around them. As you learned in Chapter 2, some aspects of **sensation**, the process of taking in raw information through the senses, are well established prior to birth (e.g., hearing). Others require some refinement over the early months and years. **Perception**, the attribution of meaning to sensory information, develops rapidly during the early months and years as well.

**MOTOR SKILLS**  The infant's motor skills emerge only gradually in the early weeks. By 1 month, a baby can hold her chin up off the floor or mattress. By 2 months, she can hold her head steady while she's being held and is beginning to reach for objects near her. These improving motor skills follow two broad patterns originally identified by Gesell: Development proceeds from the head downward, in a pattern called **cephalocaudal**, and from the trunk outward, in another pattern called **proximodistal** (Gesell, 1952). Thus, the baby can hold up her head before she can sit or roll over and can sit before she can crawl.

Another interesting feature of young babies' motor skills is how repetitively they perform their limited range of movements (Adolph & Berger, 2005). They kick, rock, wave, bounce, bang, rub, scratch, or sway repeatedly and rhythmically. These repeated patterns become particularly prominent at about 6 or 7 months of age, although you can see instances of such behavior even in the first weeks, particularly in finger movements and leg kicking. These movements do not seem to be totally voluntary or coordinated, but they also do not appear to be random. For instance, Thelen (1995) has observed that kicking movements peak just before the baby begins to crawl, as if the rhythmic kicking were a part of the preparation for crawling. Thelen's work has revealed certain patterns and order in the seemingly random movements of

**sensation**   The process of taking in raw information through the senses.

**perception**   The attribution of meaning to sensory information.

**cephalocaudal**   One of two basic patterns of physical development in infancy (the other is proximodistal), in which development proceeds from the head downward.

**proximodistal**   One of two basic patterns of physical development in infancy (the other is cephalocaudal), in which development proceeds from the center outward—that is, from the trunk to the limbs.

the young infant, but even this understanding does not alter the fact that, by contrast with perceptual abilities, the baby's initial motor abilities are quite limited.

**CULTURAL PRACTICES AND MOTOR DEVELOPMENT**    When we discuss phenomena as fundamental as motor development, it is tempting to conclude that they arise exclusively from genetic origins. However, there are important differences in these developmental phenomena. For example, more than 50 years ago, developmental scientists discovered that African infants, especially those born in rural areas, reach some motor milestones earlier than babies in other parts of the world, a phenomenon that was called *African infant precocity* (e.g., Geber & Dean, 1957). Subsequent studies found that a pattern of traditional cultural practices that both intentionally and coincidentally promote motor development was the most likely explanation for these findings (Berry, Poortinga, Segall, & Dasen, 2002). For instance, African mothers in traditional settings engage in activities that specifically target muscular and motor development. These activities include vigorous massage of babies' muscles and manipulation of their extremities in ways that mimic motor actions such as walking. African mothers also encourage infants to practice motor skills such as sitting up (Super, 1976). Coincidentally, mothers carry infants on their backs, a practice that promotes development of the head and trunk muscles. However, African infant precocity does not persist into early childhood probably because parental practices that encourage motor development in young children differ less across cultures than they do for infants (Lynn, 1998).

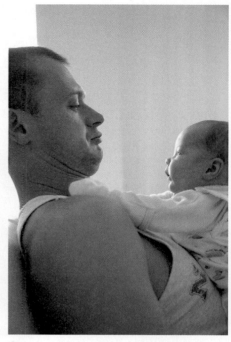

Observe adults interacting with young infants and you will see that, like this father, many adults seem to know just where to position a baby so that her eyes are the optimal distance from the adult's eyes to facilitate sustained eye contact (8 to 10 inches).

**SENSORY AND PERCEPTUAL ABILITIES**    Babies come equipped with a surprisingly mature set of perceptual skills. The newborn can do several things:

- Focus both eyes on the same spot, with 8–10 inches being the best focal distance; discriminate his mother's face from other faces almost immediately; and, within a few weeks, follow a moving object with his eyes—although not very efficiently.
- Easily hear sounds within the pitch and loudness range of the human voice; roughly locate objects by their sounds; discriminate some individual voices, particularly his mother's voice.
- Taste the four basic tastes (sweet, sour, bitter, and salty) plus a fifth taste called umami, which is elicited by an amino acid found in meat, fish, and legumes.
- Identify familiar body odors, including discriminating his mother's smell from the smell of a strange woman.

In contrast to the baby's motor skills, his perceptual skills are extraordinarily well developed for the interactions he will have with the people in his world. He hears best in the range of the human voice, and he can discriminate his mother (or other regular caregiver) from others on the basis of smell, sight, or sound almost immediately. The distance at which he can focus his eyes best, about 8–10 inches, is approximately the distance between his eyes and his mother's face during nursing.

## Learning

Infants use their motor, sensory, and perceptual skills to act on the people and objects in their environment. Such actions enable them to establish a foundational understanding of the world upon which to construct their future cognitive and social development. Thus, all three types of skills facilitate early **learning**, or change due to experience.

**CLASSICAL CONDITIONING**    The bulk of the research on learning in newborns suggests that they can be classically conditioned, although it is difficult (Herbert, Eckerman, Goldstein, & Stanton, 2004). Conditioning that relates to feeding in some way is most likely to be successful, perhaps because this activity is so critical for the infant's survival. As one example, Elliott Blass and his colleagues (1984) gave 1- and 2-day-old infants sugar water in a bottle (the unconditional stimulus), which prompted sucking (the unconditioned response). Then, just before they were given the sugar water, the babies' foreheads were stroked (the conditional stimulus). After several such repetitions, the experimenters stroked the infants' foreheads

◄ ----------- **Learning Objective 3.6**
What types of learning do infants exhibit?

**learning**    Change due to experience.

## Helping Preterm Infants Learn to Suck

Most preterm infants are born with poorly developed sucking abilities and must be tube fed in order to sustain growth. Florida State University professor of music Jayne Standley demonstrated that operant conditioning techniques can improve preterm newborns' sucking ability. Standley developed a special pacifier called a *PAL* (pacifier activated lullaby) with an embedded remote control device that activates a CD player whenever a baby sucks on it (Standley, 2003). In several pioneering studies, Standley found that the sucking rates of newborns who used PALs to activate recordings of lullabies sung by young women with high voices increased. As a result,

their sucking abilities strengthened so rapidly that they were able to transition from tube to nipple feeding far more quickly than control group infants who did not use PALs.

Subsequent studies have replicated Standley's original findings (e.g., Standley et al., 2010). As a result, the Food and Drug Administration has approved the routine use of PALs in neonatal intensive care units, and the devices are now common in NICUs across the United States.

### FIND OUT MORE

*Use your Internet search skills to answer these questions.*

**Learning Objective 3.6a**
How do music therapists use operant conditioning to improve preterm infants' sucking abilities?

1. What does research say about the use of music as a reinforcer for other types of infant behavior?
2. How does gestational age influence the response of a preterm infant to PAL therapy?

without giving the sugar water to see if the infants would begin sucking—which they did, thus showing classical conditioning.

By the time infants are 3 or 4 weeks old, classical conditioning is no longer difficult to establish; it occurs easily with many different responses. In particular, this means that the conditioned emotional responses you read about in Chapter 1 may begin to develop as early as the first week of life. Thus, the mere presence of Mom or Dad or another favored person may trigger the sense of "feeling good," a response that may contribute to the child's later attachment to the parent.

**OPERANT CONDITIONING**   Newborns also clearly learn by operant conditioning; see *Technology and the Developing Child*. The fact that conditioning of this kind can take place means that the neurological basis for learning to occur is present at birth. Results like this also tell us something about the sorts of reinforcements that are effective with very young children. It is surely highly significant for the whole process of mother-infant interaction that the mother's voice is an effective reinforcer for virtually all babies.

**SCHEMATIC LEARNING**   The fact that babies can recognize voices and heartbeats in the first days of life is also important, because it suggests that another kind of learning is going on as well. This third type of learning, sometimes referred to as **schematic learning**, draws both its name and many of its conceptual roots from Piaget's theory. The basic idea is that from the beginning the baby organizes her experiences into expectancies, or known combinations. These expectancies, often called *schemas*, are built up over many exposures to particular experiences but thereafter help the baby to distinguish between the familiar and the unfamiliar. Carolyn Rovee-Collier (1986) has suggested that we might think of classical conditioning in infants as being a variety of schematic learning. When a baby begins to move her head as if to search for the nipple as soon as she hears her mother's footsteps coming into the room, this is not just some kind of automatic classical conditioning, but the beginning of the development of expectancies. From the earliest weeks, the baby seems to make connections between events in her world, such as between the sound of her mother's footsteps and the feeling of being picked up or between the touch of the breast and the feeling of a full stomach. Thus, early classical conditioning may be the beginnings of the process of cognitive development.

**HABITUATION**   A concept related to schematic learning is habituation. **Habituation** is the automatic reduction in the strength or vigor of a response to a repeated stimulus. For example, suppose you live on a fairly noisy street, where the sound of cars going by is repeated over and over during each day. After a while, you not only don't react to the sound, you quite literally

**schematic learning**   The development of expectancies concerning what actions lead to what results or what events tend to go together.

**habituation**   An automatic decrease in the intensity of a response to a repeated stimulus, enabling a child or adult to ignore the familiar and focus attention on the novel.

do not perceive it as being loud. The ability to do this—to dampen down the intensity of a physical response to some repeated stimulus—is obviously vital in our everyday lives. If we reacted constantly to every sight and sound and smell that came along, we'd spend all our time responding to these repeated events, and we wouldn't have energy or attention left over for things that are new and deserve attention. The ability to dishabituate is equally important. When a habituated stimulus changes in some way, such as a sudden extra-loud screech of tires on the busy street by your house, you again respond fully. The reemergence of the original response strength is a sign that the perceiver—infant, child, or adult—has noticed some significant change. ◉ Watch at MyDevelopmentLab

A rudimentary capacity to habituate and to dishabituate is built in at birth in human babies, just as it is in other species. In 10-week-old babies, this ability is well developed. An infant will stop looking at something you keep putting in front of her face; she will stop showing a startle reaction (Moro reflex) to loud sounds after the first few presentations but will again startle if the sound is changed; she will stop turning her head toward a repeating sound (Swain, Zelazo, & Clifton, 1993). Such habituation itself is not a voluntary process; it is entirely automatic. Yet in order for it to work, the newborn must be equipped with the capacity to recognize familiar experiences. That is, she must have, or must develop, schemas of some kind.

The existence of these processes in the newborn has an added benefit for researchers: It has enabled them to figure out what an infant responds to as "the same" or "different." If a baby is habituated to some stimulus, such as a sound or a specific picture, the experimenter can then present slight variations on the original stimulus to see the point at which dishabituation occurs. In this way, researchers have begun to get an idea of how the newborn baby or young infant experiences the world around him—a point you'll read more about in Chapter 5.

## Temperament and Social Skills

Clearly, many aspects of early development are universal, such as reflexes and the capacity to respond to conditioning. However, there are also important individual differences among infants.

**TEMPERAMENT** Babies vary in the way they react to new things, in their typical moods, in their rate of activity, in their preference for social interactions or solitude, in the regularity of their daily rhythms, and in many other ways. Developmentalists collectively call these differences **temperament**. You'll be reading a great deal more about temperament in Chapter 9, but because the concept will come up often as we go along, it is important at this early stage to introduce some of the basic terms and ideas.

In classic research, developmentalists Alexander Thomas and Stella Chess (1977) described three categories of infant temperament, the **easy child**, the **difficult child**, and the **slow-to-warm-up child**. Easy children, who comprised approximately 40% of Thomas and Chess's original study group, approach new events positively. They try new foods without much fuss, for example. They also exhibit predictable sleeping and eating cycles, are usually happy, and adjust easily to change. ◉ Watch at MyDevelopmentLab

By contrast, the difficult child is less predictable with regard to sleep and hunger cycles and is slow to develop regular cycles. These children react vigorously and negatively to new things, are more irritable, and cry more. Thomas and Chess point out, however, that once the difficult baby has adapted to something new, he is often quite happy about it, even though the adaptation process itself is trying. In Thomas and Chess's original sample, about 10% of children were clearly classifiable in this group.

Children in the slow-to-warm-up group are not as negative in responding to new things or new people as are the difficult children. They show instead a kind of passive resistance. Instead of spitting out new food violently and crying, the slow-to-warm-up child may let the food drool out and may resist mildly any attempt to feed her more of the same. These infants

**temperament**   Inborn predispositions that form the foundations of personality.

**easy child**   An infant who adapts easily to change and who exhibits regular patterns of eating, sleeping, and alertness.

**difficult child**   An infant who is irritable and irregular in behavior.

**slow-to-warm-up child**   An infant who may seem unresponsive but who simply takes more time to respond than other infants do.

◉ Watch the **Video** *Habituation* at **MyDevelopmentLab**

← - - - - - - - - - -Learning Objective 3.7
How do newborns differ in temperament, and what skills do they bring to social interactions?

*Of course, you can't evaluate a baby's temperament on the basis of one picture, but you might guess that young Benjamin, smiling delightedly, has an easier temperament than Eleanor, who seems to be quite displeased with the food that is being offered to her.*

◉ Watch the **Video** *Temperament: Difficult* at **MyDevelopmentLab**

show few intense reactions, either positive or negative, although once they have adapted to something new, their reaction is usually fairly positive. Approximately 15% of Thomas and Chess's sample followed this pattern.

While these differences in style or pattern of response tend to persist through infancy into later childhood, no psychologist studying temperament suggests that such individual differences are absolutely fixed at birth. Inborn temperamental differences are shaped, strengthened, bent, or counteracted by the child's relationships and experiences. Infants enter the world with somewhat different repertoires or patterns of behavior, and those differences not only affect the experiences an infant may choose, but also help to shape the emerging pattern of interaction that develops between infant and parents. For example, toddlers and preschoolers with difficult temperaments are more often criticized or physically punished by their parents than are easy children, presumably because their behavior is more troublesome (Vitaro, Barker, Boivin, Brendgen, & Tremblay, 2006). Yet once it is established, such a pattern of criticism and punishment itself is likely to have additional consequences for a child. Nonetheless, not all parents of difficult children respond in this way. A skilled parent, especially one who correctly perceives that the child's "difficultness" is a temperamental quality and not a result of the child's willfulness or the parent's ineptness, can avoid some of the pitfalls and can handle the difficult child more adeptly.

**THE EMERGENCE OF EMOTIONAL EXPRESSION**    There is really no way to know just what emotion a baby actually feels. The best we can do is to try to judge what emotion a baby appears to express through his body and face. Researchers have done this by confronting babies with various kinds of events likely to prompt emotions, photographing or videotaping those encounters, and then asking adult judges to say which emotion the baby's face expresses (Izard, 2007).

Table 3.4 summarizes the current thinking about the ages at which various important emotional expressions first appear. As you can see, some rudimentary emotional expressions are visible at birth, including a sort of half-smile that delights parents even though they cannot figure out how to elicit it consistently. Within a few weeks, though, babies begin to show a full social smile. Happily, one of the earliest triggers for this wonderful baby smile is the kind of high-pitched voice that all adults seem to use naturally with infants. So adults seem to be preprogrammed to behave in just the ways that babies will respond to positively. Within a few weeks, babies will also smile in response to a smiling face, especially a familiar face.

Within a few months, babies' emotional expressions differentiate even further, so that they express sadness, anger, and surprise. Four-month-olds also begin to laugh—and there are few things in life more delightful than the sound of a giggling or laughing baby! Fear appears as a discrete emotional expression at about 7 months.

Interactions between infants and caregivers follow rhythmic patterns that are very much like conversations in which speakers take turns. First the father smiles, then the baby smiles. Next, the father tickles the baby's stomach, then the baby giggles and waves his arms. In response, the father makes a silly face, and so on.

**TAKING TURNS**    Yet another social skill the baby brings to interactions is the ability to take turns. As adults, we take turns all the time, most clearly in conversations and eye contacts. In fact, it's very difficult to have any kind of social encounter with someone who does not take turns. Kenneth Kaye (1982) argues that the beginnings of this turn-taking can be seen in very young infants in their eating patterns. As early as the first days of life, a baby sucks in a "burst-pause" pattern. He sucks for a while, pauses, sucks for a while, pauses, and so on. Mothers enter into this process, such as by jiggling the baby during the pauses, thus creating an alternating pattern: suck, pause, jiggle, pause, suck, pause, jiggle, pause. The rhythm of the interaction is really very much like a conversation. It is not clear whether this conversational quality of very early interaction occurs because the adult figures out the baby's natural rhythm and adapts her own responses to the baby's timing or whether some mutual adaptation is going on. Nonetheless, it is extremely intriguing that this apparent turn-taking is seen in infants only days old.

## Table 3.4 THE EMERGENCE OF EMOTIONAL EXPRESSIONS IN INFANCY AND TODDLERHOOD

| Age | Emotion Expressed | Examples of Stimuli That Trigger That Expression |
|---|---|---|
| At birth | Interest | Novelty or movement |
| | Distress | Pain |
| | Disgust | Offensive substances |
| | Neonatal smile (a "half smile") | Appears spontaneously for no known reason |
| 3 to 6 weeks | Pleasure/social smile (precursor to joy) | High-pitched human voice; clapping the baby's hands together; a familiar voice; a nodding face |
| 2 to 3 months | Sadness | Painful medical procedure |
| 7 months | Wariness (precursor to fear) | A stranger's face |
| | Frustration (precursor to anger) | Being restrained; being prevented from performing some established action |
| | Surprise | Jack-in-the-box |
| | Fear | Extreme novelty; heights (such as in the visual cliff experiment) |
| | Anger | Failure or interruption of some attempted action, such as reaching for a ball that has rolled under a couch |
| | Joy | Immediate delighted response to an experience with positive meaning, such as the caregiver's arrival or a game of peekaboo |

*Sources:* Izard and Malateste, 1987; Mascolo and Fischer, 1995; Sroufe, 1996.

## Health and Wellness in Early Infancy

You may have heard references to the increasing life expectancy in the United States. At the beginning of the 20th century, Americans' average life expectancy was only about 49 years, but by the first decade of the twenty-first century, it was 78 years (U. S. Census Bureau, 2011). One of the most significant factors behind this statistic is the reduction in infant mortality that occurred in industrialized societies during the 20th century. Improved medical technology and better understanding of newborns' nutritional and health-care needs are responsible for this trend. Sadly, though, many infants die in the first year of life. In fact, infancy continues to be associated with a higher death rate than any other period of life except old age (Kochanek et al., 2011). Many such deaths are due to genetic disorders, but others result from causes that are more easily preventable.

## Nutrition, Health Care, and Immunizations

◄------------ Learning Objective 3.8

What are the infant's nutritional, health-care, and immunization needs?

Newborns, of course, are completely physically dependent on their caretakers. To develop normally, they need adequate nutrition, regular medical care, and protection against diseases.

## Breast or Bottle?

Expectant mother Suzanne found it easy to decide where she wanted to give birth and whom she wanted to serve as her labor coach, but worried a great deal about how she would feed her baby. She had heard that breast-feeding was best, but she expected to return to work within a few weeks after the birth. Consequently, she was leaning toward bottle-feeding but was seeking information that would reassure her that her baby would develop properly on formula.

Several decades of extensive research in many countries comparing large groups of breast- and bottle-fed infants make it clear that breast-feeding is nutritionally superior to bottle-feeding (Krebs & Primak, 2011). On average, breast-fed infants are less likely to suffer from such problems as diarrhea, gastroenteritis, bronchitis, ear infections, and colic, and they are less likely to die in infancy (AAP, 2005). Breast milk also appears to promote the growth of nerves and the intestinal tract, to contribute to more rapid weight and size gain, and to stimulate better immune system function. Research also suggests that breast-feeding may protect infants from becoming overweight in later years. For these reasons, physicians strongly recommend breast-feeding if it is at all possible, even if the mother can nurse for only a few weeks after birth or if her breast milk must be supplemented with formula feedings (Krebs & Primak, 2011).

For mothers who cannot breast-feed at all, nutrition experts point out that infants who are fed high-quality, properly sterilized formula typically thrive on it (AAP, 2005). It is also reassuring to know that the social interactions between mother and child seem to be unaffected by the type of feeding. Bottle-fed babies are held and cuddled in the same ways as breast-fed babies, and their mothers appear to be just as sensitive and responsive to their babies and just as bonded to them as are mothers of breast-fed infants (Field, 1977). 👁 Watch at MyDevelopmentLab

### Learning Objective 3.8a
What is the evidence concerning breast- and bottle-feeding?

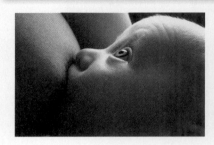

#### REFLECTION
1. If Suzanne were your friend and asked you for advice regarding this important decision, what would you tell her?
2. The research linking breast-feeding to obesity protection was correlational. What other variables might explain this relationship?

👁 Watch the Video *Breast-feeding* at MyDevelopmentLab

**NUTRITION** Eating is not among the states listed in Table 3.3 on page 65, but it is certainly something that newborn babies do frequently! Given that a newborn's natural cycle seems to be about 2 hours long, she may eat as many as ten times a day. Gradually, the baby takes more and more milk at each feeding and doesn't have to eat so often. By 2 months, the average number is down to five or six feedings each day, dropping to about three feedings by age 8 to 12 months (Overby, 2002). Breast-fed and bottle-fed babies eat with the same frequency, but these two forms of feeding do differ in other important ways (see *Developmental Science in the Real World*).

Up until 6 months, babies need only breast milk or formula accompanied by appropriate supplements (Krebs & Primak, 2011). For example, pediatricians usually recommend vitamin $B_{12}$ supplements for infants whose nursing mothers are vegetarians (Moilanen, 2004). Doctors may recommend supplemental formula feeding for infants who are growing poorly, but breast milk meets the nutritional needs of most infants.

There is no evidence to support the belief that solid foods encourage babies to sleep through the night. In fact, early introduction of solid food can actually interfere with nutrition. Pediatricians usually recommend withholding solid foods until 4 to 6 months of age (Krebs & Primak, 2011 Krebs). The first solids should be single-grain cereals, such as rice, with added iron. Parents should introduce their baby to no more than one new food each week. If parents follow a systematic plan, food allergies can be easily identified (Krebs & Primak, 2011).

**HEALTH CARE AND IMMUNIZATIONS** Infants need frequent medical check-ups. While much of *well-baby care* may seem routine, it is extremely important to babies' development. For example, babies' motor skills are usually assessed during routine visits to a doctor's office or a health clinic. An infant whose motor development is less advanced than expected for his age may require additional screening for developmental problems such as mental retardation (Levine, 2011).

One of the most important elements of well-baby care is vaccination of the infant against a variety of diseases (see Table 3.5 on page 75). Although immunizations later in childhood provide good protection against these diseases, the evidence suggests that

## Table 3.5

### RECOMMENDED IMMUNIZATION SCHEDULE FOR CHILDREN FROM BIRTH TO 6 YEARS

| Vaccine | Recommended Age |
|---|---|
| Hepatitis B | Birth–18 months |
| Rotavirus | 2–6 months |
| Diphtheria, Tetanus, Pertussis | Four doses: 2 months, 4 months, 6 months, 16–18 months |
| Haemophilus Influenzae Type b (Hib) | Four doses: 2 months, 4 months, 6 months, 12–15 months |
| Pneumococcal | Four doses: 2 months, 4 months, 6 months, 12–15 months |
| Polio | Three doses: 2 months, 4 months, 6–18 months |
| Influenza | 6 months to 6 years |
| Measles, Mumps, Rubella | 12–15 months |
| Varicella | 12–15 months |
| Hepatitis A | Two doses: 12 months–2 years |
| Meningococcal | 2–6 years |

*Source:* AAP, 2008.

immunization is most effective when it begins in the first month of life and continues across childhood and adolescence (Levine, 2011). Even adults need occasional "booster" shots to maintain immunity.

## Illnesses

←------------Learning Objective 3.9

What kinds of illnesses typically occur in infancy?

Virtually all babies get sick, most of them repeatedly. Among infants around the world, three types of illnesses are most common: diarrhea, upper respiratory infections, and ear infections.

**DIARRHEA**   Worldwide, one of the most common and deadly illnesses of infancy and early childhood is diarrhea, accounting for the deaths of an estimated 3.5 million infants and children each year. In developing countries, 1 out of 4 deaths of children under age 5 is due to diarrhea; in some countries, the rate is even higher (Cheng, McDonald, & Thielman, 2005). In the United States, diarrhea rarely leads to death in infants, but virtually every infant or young child has at least one episode of diarrhea each year; about 1 in 10 cases is severe enough for the child to be taken to a doctor (Kilgore, Holman, Clarke, & Glass, 1995). In most cases, the cause of the illness is a viral or bacterial infection, the most common of which is *rotavirus*, a microorganism that is spread by physical contact with others who are infected with the disease (Bishop, 2011).

Virtually all deaths from diarrhea could be prevented by giving fluids to rehydrate the child (Laney, 2002). In serious cases, this rehydration should involve a special solution of salts (*oral rehydration salts*, or *ORS*). The World Health Organization has for some years been involved in a program of training health professionals around the world in the use of ORS, with some success (Muhuri, Anker, & Bryce, 1996). Still, diarrhea remains a very serious illness for infants and children in many parts of the world.

**UPPER RESPIRATORY INFECTIONS**   A second common illness during infancy is some kind of upper respiratory infection. In the United States, the average baby has seven colds in the first

**otitis media (OM)** An inflammation of the middle ear that is caused by a bacterial infection.

**sudden infant death syndrome (SIDS)** The unexpected death of an infant who otherwise appears healthy; also called crib death. The cause of SIDS is unknown.

year of life (Smith, 2011). (That's a lot of nose-wipes!) Interestingly, research in a number of countries shows that babies in child-care centers have about twice as many such infections as do those reared entirely at home, presumably because babies in group-care settings are exposed to a wider range of germs and viruses (e.g., Lau, Uba, & Lehman, 2002). In general, the more different people a baby is exposed to, the more colds she is likely to get. This is not as bad as it may seem at first. The heightened risk of infection among infants in child care drops after the first few months, while those reared entirely at home have very high rates of illness when they first attend preschool or kindergarten. Attendance at child care thus simply means that the baby is exposed earlier to the various microorganisms typically carried by children.

**EAR INFECTIONS** Otitis media (OM), an inflammation of the middle ear that is caused by a bacterial infection, is the leading cause of children's visits to physicians' offices in the United States (Waseem, 2007). More than 90% of children have had at least one episode of OM in the first year of life, and about one-third have 6 or more bouts before age 7. Thanks to antibiotic drugs, most cases of OM clear up quickly. However, physicians have become concerned in recent years about the increasing resistance of the bacteria that cause otitis media to antibiotics. As a result, many physicians now recommend a "wait-and-see" response to cases of OM (AAP, 2004). If the child develops a high fever or the infection continues for 3 to 4 days, then antibiotics are prescribed. Placebo-controlled studies suggest that 75% of cases of OM clear up on their own within 7 days of initial diagnosis (AAP, 2004).

In a few children, OM becomes chronic, defined as an episode of otitis media that remains uncured after 6 months of antibiotic treatment (Waseem, 2007). In such cases, some physicians recommend that children undergo surgery to insert tubes in the ears. The tubes allow fluid to escape from the middle ear through the ear drum. Such drainage is needed because chronic fluid in the ears not only increases the frequency of infections but also interferes with hearing. Researchers have found that even mild hearing losses cause children to have difficulties with speech perception and can slow down the pace of language development. As a result, children in whom chronic fluid in the ears goes untreated are more likely to fail in school than are those with normal hearing (Tharpe, 2006).

**Learning Objective 3.10**----------➤
What factors contribute to infant mortality?

# Infant Mortality

A small minority of babies face not just a few sniffles but the possibility of death. In the United States, about 7 babies out of every 1,000 die before age 1 (Mathews & MacDorman, 2010). The rate has been declining steadily for the past few decades (down from 20 per 1,000 in 1970), but the United States continues to have a higher infant mortality rate than other industrialized nations. Almost two-thirds of these infant deaths occur in the first month of life and are directly linked to either congenital anomalies or low birth weight (Mathews & MacDorman, 2010). Fewer than 3 deaths per 1,000 births occur in the remainder of the first year.

**SUDDEN INFANT DEATH SYNDROME** A sizeable fraction of deaths in the first year are attributable to **sudden infant death syndrome (SIDS)**, in which an apparently healthy infant dies suddenly and unexpectedly. In the United States, SIDS is the leading cause of death in infants more than 1 month of age (CDC, 2011). SIDS occurs worldwide; for unexplained reasons, however, the rate varies quite a lot from country to country. For example, rates are particularly high in the United Kingdom and Argentina and particularly low in Japan and the Netherlands (Hauck & Tanabe, 2010).

Physicians have not yet uncovered the basic cause of SIDS, although they have learned a fair amount about the groups that are at higher risk: babies with low birth weight, male babies, African American babies, and babies with young mothers. SIDS is also more common in the winter and among babies who sleep on their stomachs (Task Force on Sudden Infant Death Syndrome, 2005), especially on a soft or fluffy mattress, pillow, or comforter. The growing evidence on the role of sleeping position persuaded pediatricians in many countries to change their standard advice to hospitals and families about the best sleeping position for babies. The American Academy of Pediatrics, for example, has been recommending since 1992 that healthy infants should be positioned on their sides or backs when they are put down to sleep

**What does a safe sleep environment look like?**

Lower the risk of sudden infant death syndrome (SIDS).

Don't forget Tummy Time when the baby is awake and is being watched.

Use a firm mattress in a safety-approved crib covered by a fitted sheet.

Make sure nothing covers the baby's head.

Place your baby on his or her back to sleep for naps and at night.

Do not use pillows, blankets, sheepskins, or pillow-like bumpers in your baby's sleep area.

Use sleep clothing, such as a one-piece sleeper, instead of a blanket.

Do not let anyone smoke near your baby.

Keep soft objects, stuffed toys, and loose bedding out of your baby's sleep area.

**FIGURE 3.4** The Back to Sleep Campaign Since the *Back to Sleep Campaign* began in 1994 as a joint project of the American Association of Pediatrics, the National Institute for Child Health and Human Development, and several government agencies, the SIDS death rate has declined by 50%. The campaign features brochures and other educational materials with illustrations such as this one. *Source:* Adapted from www.nichd.hih.gov/SIDS

(see Figure 3.4). Physicians in many other countries have made similar recommendations, a change in advice that has been followed by a significant drop in SIDS cases in every country involved (Fein, Durbin, & Selbst, 2002; Willinger, Hoffman, & Hartford, 1994). In the United States, for example, the number of SIDS cases has dropped by 50% since 1992 (NICHD, 2010). Still, sleeping position cannot be the full explanation, because, of course, most babies who sleep on their stomachs do not die of SIDS.

Smoking by the mother during pregnancy or by anyone in the home after the child's birth is another important contributor to SIDS. Babies exposed to such smoke are about four times as likely as are babies with no smoking exposure to die of SIDS (CDC, 2006d). Thus, in addition to advising pregnant women not to smoke, health-care professionals warn parents against allowing smoking in the home after the baby is born.

Imaging studies of the brains of infants at high risk for SIDS, such as those who display apnea in the early days of life, suggest that neuronal development progresses at a slower rate in these children than in others who do not exhibit such risk factors (Morgan et al., 2002). Babies' patterns of sleep reflect these neurological differences and also predict SIDS risk. Infants who show increasingly lengthy sleep periods during the early months are at lower risk of dying from SIDS than babies whose sleep periods do not get much longer as they get older (Cornwell & Feigenbaum, 2006). Likewise, autopsies of SIDS babies have revealed that their brains often show signs of delayed myelination and deficiencies in the neurotransmitter serotonin (Duncan et al., 2010).

FIGURE 3.5 Infant Mortality across
Ethnic Groups
As you can see, infant mortality rates vary
widely across U.S. racial and ethnic groups.

(*Sources:* Mathews & MacDorman, 2010;
MacDorman & Atkinson, 1999.)

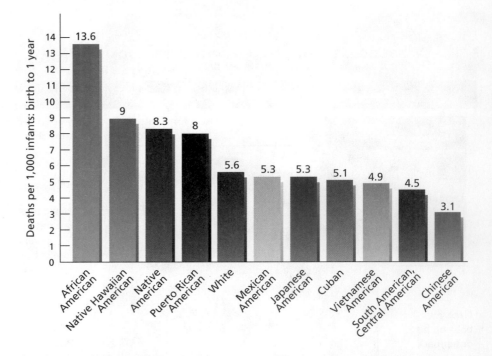

**FIGURE 3.6** Early Prenatal Care and
Ethnicity
Wide disparities exist across ethnic groups with
regard to access to prenatal care, although this
factor cannot fully explain group differences in
infant mortality. Note, for instance, that African
Americans and Mexican Americans have similar
rates of early prenatal care but vary widely in
infant mortality.

(*Source:* National Center for Health Statistics
(NCHS). (2006, 2010))

**ETHNIC DIFFERENCES IN INFANT MORTALITY** Large variations in infant mortality rates exist across ethnic groups in the United States, as shown in Figure 3.5 (Mathews & MacDorman, 2010). Rates are lowest among Asian American infants; about 5 of every 1,000 die each year. Among White American babies, the rate is approximately 6 deaths per 1,000. The three groups with the highest rates of infant death are Native Americans (8.3 deaths per 1,000), Native Hawaiians (9 deaths per 1,000), and African Americans (13.6 deaths per 1,000). One reason for these differences is that Native American and African American infants are two to three times more likely to suffer from congenital abnormalities and low birth weight—the two leading causes of infant death—than babies in other groups. Furthermore, SIDS is two to three times as common among them.

Because babies born into poor families, regardless of ethnicity, are more likely to die than those whose families are better off economically, some observers have suggested that poverty explains the higher rates of infant death among Native Americans and African Americans, the two groups with the highest rates of poverty. However, infant mortality rates among Hispanic American groups suggest that the link between poverty and infant mortality is not so

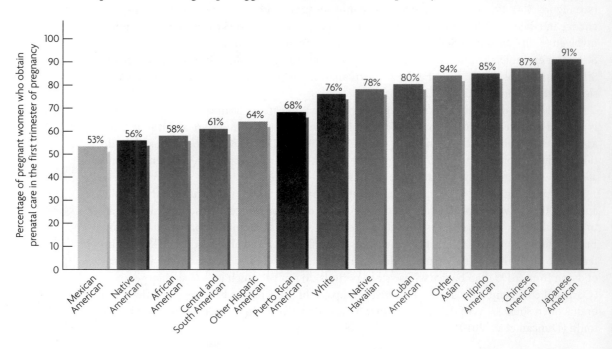

straightforward. The infant mortality rate among Mexican American babies is 5.3 per 1,000, and the mortality rate for infants of Cuban, South, and Central American ancestry is just under 5 per 1,000 (Mathews & MacDorman, 2010). These groups are almost as likely to be poor as African Americans and Native Americans. In contrast, Puerto Rican families are not likely to be poorer than other Hispanic American families, but the mortality rate is 8 per 1,000 among their infants. Similarly, rates of early prenatal care—defined as consulting a doctor or midwife during the first trimester of pregnancy—are nearly identical for African American women and Hispanic American women (National Center for Health Statistics [NCHS], 2010). Consequently, access to prenatal care cannot explain differences in infant mortality across these groups (see Figure 3.6 on page 78).

Interestingly, mortality rates among the babies of immigrants of all racial and ethnic groups are lower than those among babies of U.S.-born mothers. This finding also challenges the poverty explanation for racial and ethnic group differences in infant mortality, because immigrant women are more likely to be poor and less likely to receive prenatal care than women born in the United States (NCHS, 2010). Many researchers suggest that lower rates of tobacco and alcohol use among women born outside the United States may be an important factor.

## THINK CRITICALLY

- How would you go about raising public awareness of the advantages of breastfeeding, the importance of early immunizations, and the developmental risks associated with ear infections?
- Generate your own hypothesis to explain group differences in infant mortality. What kind of information would you need to test your hypothesis?

## CONDUCT YOUR OWN RESEARCH

You can find out more about women's childbearing-related worries by carrying out what researchers call a *free-response* study. Simply ask several women, both pregnant and nonpregnant if you can, to express their concerns in their own words. Write down what they say. When you have collected a number of responses, analyze them for common themes.

## SUMMARY  ✓•⌐Study and Review at MyDevelopmentLab

### Birth

**3.1  What decisions must parents make about the birth process in industrialized societies?**
Parents must decide whether to use pain-relieving drugs during delivery, whether their baby should be born in a hospital or other setting, and whether the father should be present for the delivery. Most drugs given to a woman during delivery pass through to the infant's bloodstream and have short-term effects on infant responsiveness. In uncomplicated, low-risk pregnancies, delivery at home or in a birth center may be as safe as hospital delivery. The presence of the father during delivery has a variety of positive consequences, including reducing the mother's experience of pain, but being present for the birth does not appear to affect the father's attachment to the infant.

**3.2  What are the events and risks associated with each stage of the birth process?**
The normal birth process has three stages: dilation and effacement, delivery, and placental delivery. Several types of

problems may occur at birth, including reduced oxygen supply to the infant (anoxia). Slightly more than one-quarter of all deliveries in the United States today are by cesarean section. Newborns are typically assessed using the Apgar score, which is a rating on five dimensions. Most parents show intense interest in the new baby's features, especially the eyes.

**3.3  What are some of the possible consequences of low birth weight?**
Infants born weighing less than 2,500 grams are designated as low birth weight (LBW); those below 1,500 grams are very low birth weight (VLBW); those below 1,000 grams are extremely low birth weight (ELBW). The lower the weight, the greater the risk of neonatal death or of significant lasting problems, such as low IQ score or learning disabilities.

### Behavior in Early Infancy

**3.4  What reflexes and behavioral states are exhibited by infants?**
Infants have a wide range of reflexes. Some, such as the sucking reflex, are essential for life. Other primitive reflexes

are present in the newborn but disappear in the first year. Cycles of sleeping, waking, and crying are present from the beginning.

**3.4a** In what ways are the acoustic qualities of infants' cries and developmental outcomes related?

Infants with developmental problems that are diagnosed at birth, such as Down syndrome, exhibit higher pitched cries than others. Those who appear normal at birth but develop later problems also have higher pitched cries. Because of these associations, some researchers believe that the pitch of a baby's cry can be used as an indicator of developmental risk.

**3.5** What kinds of motor, sensory, and perceptual abilities do newborns have?

Motor skills are only rudimentary at birth. Perceptual skills include the ability to focus both eyes; visually track slowly moving objects; discriminate the mother by sight, smell, and sound; and respond to smells, tastes, and touch.

**3.6** What types of learning do infants exhibit?

Within the first few weeks of life, babies are able to learn through association of stimuli (classical conditioning), from pleasant and unpleasant consequences (operant conditioning), from categorization of stimuli (schematic learning), and from repeated exposure to stimuli (habituation).

**3.6a** How do music therapists use operant conditioning to improve preterm infants' sucking abilities?

Research by music therapists has shown that preterm infants who are given special pacifiers called PALs that enable them to switch on a CD player practice their sucking behaviors more than control infants do. Thus, the music reinforces the sucking and, as a result, decreases the length of time that a preterm baby must be fed through a tube.

**3.7** How do newborns differ in temperament, and what skills do they bring to social interactions?

Babies differ from one another on several dimensions, including vigor of response, general activity rate, restlessness, irritability, and cuddliness. Thomas and Chess identified three temperamental categories: easy, difficult,

and slow-to-warm-up. Infants develop the ability to express a range of emotions, such as pleasure and distress, over the first year.

## Health and Wellness in Early Infancy

**3.8** What are the infant's nutritional, health-care, and immunization needs?

Breast milk or formula supplies all of an infant's nutritional needs until 6 months of age. Babies require periodic check-ups to track their growth and development. They also need to be immunized against a variety of diseases.

**3.8a** What is the evidence concerning breast- and bottle-feeding?

Pediatricians have concluded that breast-feeding is preferred because it is associated with lower levels of digestive problems, higher levels of immune system functioning, and is associated with positive growth patterns. However, bottle-fed babies can be equally healthy if they are fed high-quality, sterile formula in ways that foster social interactions with caregivers.

**3.9** What kinds of illnesses typically occur in infancy?

Common illnesses of childhood include diarrhea, upper respiratory infections, and ear infections. In the developing world, diarrhea is the leading cause of infant death. In the industrialized world, ear infections are the most serious of these illnesses, although they are rarely fatal. All forms of upper respiratory illness are more common among children in day care than among those reared at home.

**3.10** What factors contribute to infant mortality?

In the United States and other industrialized countries, most infant deaths in the first weeks are due to congenital anomalies or low birth weight; after the first weeks, sudden infant death syndrome (SIDS) is the most common cause of death in the first year. African American, Native Hawaiian, and Native American infants display higher rates of infant mortality than White Americans and other ethnic groups in the United States. Poverty may be a factor, but other groups with similar rates of poverty, such as Hispanic Americans, have lower infant mortality rates than African Americans, Native Hawaiians, and Native Americans.

## KEY TERMS

adaptive reflexes (p. 64)
anoxia (p. 59)
Babinski reflex (p. 65)
cephalocaudal (p. 68)
cesarean section (C-section) (p. 60)
colic (p. 66)
difficult child (p. 71)
dilation (p. 59)
dynamic systems theory (p. 65)

easy child (p. 71)
effacement (p. 59)
extremely low birth weight (ELBW) (p. 62)
habituation (p. 70)
learning (p. 69)
low birth weight (LBW) (p. 62)
Moro reflex (p. 65)
otitis media (OM) (p. 76)

perception (p. 68)
preterm infant (p. 62)
primitive reflexes (p. 64)
proximodistal (p. 68)
reflexes (p. 64)
respiratory distress syndrome (p. 63)
rooting reflex (p. 64)
schematic learning (p. 70)

sensation (p. 68)
slow-to-warm-up child (p. 71)
small-for-date infant (p. 62)
states of consciousness (p. 65)
sudden infant death syndrome (SIDS) (p. 76)
temperament (p. 71)
very low birth weight (VLBW) (p. 62)

# 4

# Physical Development

**midbrain** A section of the brain lying above the medulla and below the cortex that regulates attention, sleeping, waking, and other automatic functions; it is largely developed at birth.

**medulla** A portion of the brain that lies immediately above the spinal cord; it is largely developed at birth.

**cerebral cortex** The convoluted gray portion of the brain, which governs perception, body movement, thinking, and language.

*Most children who learn to water ski as toddlers are exposed to multiple experiential elements, such as infant swimming classes.*

Sometimes explaining an unusual outcome helps us better understand the factors that work together to produce more typical developmental events. For instance, have you ever tried to water-ski? If you spent more time treading water than you did gliding over the surface, you might feel somewhat embarrassed by the numerous YouTube home videos that depict water-skiing toddlers. You might be tempted to think that water-skiing toddlers have some special genetic endowment that enables them to master a skill that many adults find impossible. However, learning to water-ski in the early years of life isn't really all that remarkable when you think of it as the result of interactions between universal maturational variables and family-specific experiential factors.

On the maturational side, children possess the necessary neurological subsystem for water-skiing, the *vestibular sense*, at birth, but their nervous systems won't have developed the connections it needs to control the body until the end of the first year. Likewise, infants' skeletal and muscular systems must develop more fully before water-skiing is possible. In addition, as infants grow, their body proportions change such that they become less top-heavy, a basic requirement for maintaining an upright position on land or water.

On the experiential side, we must consider how families who are water-skiing enthusiasts might treat an infant differently than families with other interests. Infants in such families probably have opportunities to observe their parents and others having fun water-skiing. Frequent family boating outings may accustom them to the sound of the motor and the feeling of being in an unstable environment. Infant swimming classes probably help them learn how to maneuver in the water with a life jacket on.

All of the maturational and experiential elements come together between the first and second birthday when babies can walk and run proficiently, which also happens to be the time when most water-skiing parents introduce tots to the sport. The point that you should take away from our brief explanation of early water skiing is that the milestones of physical development that all children share—maturation of the brain, acquisition of motor skills, puberty, and the like—result from interactions between maturational and experiential factors that are similar to those that enable toddlers to ski. These common milestones are the subject of this chapter. As you read about them, you will gain a better understanding of the ways in which internal and external variables interact to produce them.

## The Brain and Nervous System

Figure 4.1 shows the main structures of the brain. At birth, the **midbrain** and the **medulla** are the most fully developed. These two parts, both in the lower part of the skull and connected to the spinal cord, regulate vital functions such as heartbeat and respiration as well as attention, sleeping, waking, elimination, and movement of the head and neck—all tasks a newborn can perform at least moderately well. The least developed part of the brain at birth is the **cerebral cortex**, the convoluted gray matter that wraps around the midbrain and is involved in perception, body movement, thinking, and language. Changes in the brain and nervous system continue throughout childhood and adolescence. There are several critical processes that contribute to these changes.

**Learning Objective 4.1** - - - - - - - - - - - - →
What are the major growth spurts in the brain?

## Growth Spurts

One of the most important principles of neurological development is that the brain grows in spurts rather than in a smooth, continuous fashion (Bergen & Woodin, 2011). Each of these spurts involves all of the major developmental processes you'll read about in the sections that follow, and each is followed by a period of stability. In infancy, the intervals of growth and stability are very short. There are short growth spurts at approximately 1-month intervals until the baby is about 5 months old. As the infant gets older, the periods of both growth and stability become longer, with spurts occurring at about 8, 12, and 20 months of age. Between ages 2 and 4, growth proceeds very slowly, and then there is another major spurt at age 4.

Interestingly, many growth spurts are *localized*; that is, they are restricted to one or a few parts of the brain rather than applying to the whole brain (Thompson et al., 2000). Neuropsychologists have correlated some of these localized brain growth spurts with milestones of cognitive development (Fischer & Rose, 1994). For example, the spurt at 20 months of age happens at the same time as most infants show evidence of goal-directed planning in their behavior. A toddler may move a chair from one location to another so that he can climb high enough to reach a forbidden object. Similarly, the spurt around age 4 is accompanied by attainment of an impressive level of fluency in both speaking and understanding language.

Two major growth spurts happen in the brain during middle childhood (Bauer, Lukowski, & Pathman, 2011). The first is linked to the striking improvements in fine motor skills and eye-hand coordination that usually emerge between 6 and 8 years of age (Gabbard, 2011). During the spurt experienced by 10- to 12-year-olds, the frontal lobes of the cerebral cortex (see Figure 4.1) become the focus of developmental processes (van der Molen & Molenaar, 1994). Predictably, logic and planning, two cognitive functions that improve dramatically during this period, are carried out primarily by the frontal lobes. In addition, this spurt is associated with improvements in memory function (Hepworth, Rovet, & Taylor, 2001).

There are also two major brain growth spurts in the teenage years. The first occurs between ages 13 and 15 (Spreen, Risser, & Edgell, 1995). For the most part, this growth spurt takes place in parts of the brain that control spatial perception as well as sensory, language, and motor functions (Bronk, 2011). Consequently, by the mid-teens, adolescents' abilities in these areas far exceed those of school-aged children.

Neuropsychologists Kurt Fischer and Samuel Rose believe that a qualitatively different neural network also emerges during this brain growth spurt, a network that enables teens to think abstractly and to reflect on their cognitive processes (Fischer & Rose, 1994). As evidence, they cite neurological and psychological research, from study after study, revealing that major changes in brain organization show up between ages 13 and 15 and qualitative shifts in cognitive functioning appear after age 15.

The brain growth spurt between 13 and 15 years of age is also associated with profound changes in the **prefrontal cortex (PFC)** (Gogtay et al., 2004; Kanemura, Aihara, Aoki, Araki, & Nakazawa, 2004). The PFC is the part of the frontal lobe that is just behind the forehead (see Figure 4.1). It is responsible for *executive processing*, a set of information processing skills that you will read more about in Chapter 6. These skills enable us to consciously control and organize our thought processes. Just prior to puberty, the neurons in the PFC rapidly form new synapses with those in other parts of the brain. Over the first few years of adolescence, the brain prunes away the least efficient of these synapses (Giedd, 2004; Giedd, Blumenthal, & Jeffries, 1999). As a result, by mid-adolescence, teenagers' executive processing skills far exceed those that they exhibited during middle childhood.

The second brain growth spurt begins around age 17 and continues into early adulthood (van der Molen & Molenaar, 1994). This time, the frontal lobes of the cerebral cortex are the focus of development (Davies & Rose, 1999).

**prefrontal cortex (PFC)** The part of the frontal lobe just behind the forehead that is responsible for executive processing.

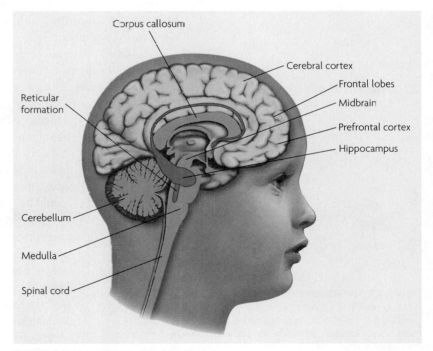

**FIGURE 4.1** Major Structures of the Brain
The medulla and the midbrain are largely developed at birth. In the first 2 years after birth, it is primarily the cortex that develops, although the dendrites continue to grow and synapses continue to form throughout the nervous system. The prefrontal cortex is the last part of the brain to mature.

You may recall that this area of the brain controls logic and planning. Thus, it is not surprising that older teens perform differently from younger teens when dealing with problems that require these cognitive functions.

Learning Objective 4.2 ------------→
What are synaptogenesis and pruning?

**synaptogenesis** The process of synapse formation.

**neurotransmitters** Chemicals that accomplish the transmission of signals from one neuron to another at synapses.

**pruning** The process of eliminating unused synapses.

**plasticity** The ability of the brain to change in response to experience.

◉ Simulate the **Experiments**
*Neurotransmitters* and *Action Potential*
at **MyDevelopmentLab**

◉ Watch the **Video** *Brain Building* at **MyDevelopmentLab**

◉ Watch the **Video** *Brain Development and Nutrition* at **MyDevelopmentLab**

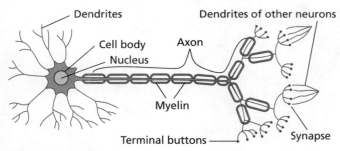

**FIGURE 4.2** The Neuron
A typical neuron has three major parts: (1) a cell body, which carries out the metabolic functions of the neuron; (2) branched fibers called dendrites, which are the primary receivers of impulses from other neurons; and (3) a slender, tail-like extension called an axon, the transmitting end of the neuron, which ends in many branches, each with an axon terminal. The axon is covered with myelin, a fatty substance that makes the transmission of neural impulses more efficient.

# Synaptic Development

**Synaptogenesis** is the process of creating connections (*synapses*) between neurons (Johnson, 2011). It involves the growth of both dendrites and axons (see Figure 4.2). Both play a role in neuronal communication, which is accomplished with chemicals called **neurotransmitters**, such as serotonin, dopamine, or endorphins. Neurotransmitters are stored in sacs at the ends of the terminal buttons and released when needed. They are picked up by *receptor sites* on the dendrites. So, as you can see, the synapses are where the action is, so to speak, in everything that goes on in the brain. ◉ Simulate at **MyDevelopmentLab**

Synaptogenesis occurs at a rapid rate in the cortex during the first 2 years after birth, resulting in a tripling of the overall weight of the brain during those years (Johnson, 2011). This burst in synaptogenesis, as well as other spurts that occur later in development, is followed by a period of **pruning**, when unnecessary connections are eliminated, making the whole system operate more efficiently. For example, early in development, each muscle cell seems to develop synaptic connections with several motor neurons in the spinal cord. But after the pruning process has occurred, each muscle fiber is connected to only one neuron. ◉ Watch at **MyDevelopmentLab**

Research on synaptogenesis and pruning supports the old dictum "Use it or lose it" (Nelson, de Haan, & Thompson, 2006). Supporting evidence comes from several kinds of research, including work with animals. For example, rats that are reared in highly stimulating environments have a denser network of neurons, dendrites, and synaptic connections as adults than rats that do not receive as much stimulation (Escorihuela, Tobena, & Fernández-Teruel, 1994). Animal studies also show that enriched environments help the young brain overcome damage caused by teratogens such as alcohol (Hannigan, O'Leary-Moore, & Berman, 2007). Also, in both nonhuman primates and humans, infants who experience significant sensory deprivation, such as from being blind in one eye, develop (or retain) less dense synaptic networks in the part of the brain linked to that particular function (Gordon, 1995). Thus, the early months appear to be a sensitive period for the retention of synapses

The brain possesses some degree of **plasticity**, the capacity to respond to experience, throughout the lifespan. However, plasticity is greatest during the first few years of life (Nelson, deHaan, & Thomas, 2006). Equally important is the point that the brain is also more vulnerable to deprivation in the early years than it is later in life. The brain of an adolescent who has a history of adequate nutrition is much better able to withstand the stress of a temporary period of malnutrition than the brain of an infant is. At the same time, though, if a teenager is malnourished so severely that his brain is damaged, he will probably be able to overcome the damage once adequate nutrition is restored, but he will do so at a slower pace than he would have under the same conditions earlier in life.

Finally, we must raise one additional point about plasticity. Nearly everything scientists know about the role of experience in brain development is derived from studies of children whose environments are deficient in some way (Nelson, de Haan, & Thomas, 2006). For instance, we know that inadequate nutrition can slow brain development and, consequently, interfere with both cognitive and social development (Liu, Raine, Venables, & Mednick, 2004). However, these findings do not imply that *supernutrition*, or a diet that provides nutrition beyond what is required for normal growth, accelerates brain growth and cognitive development. Indeed, this kind of fallacious conclusion, often inferred from studies emphasizing the importance of experience to brain development, leads to inappropriate beliefs. ◉ Watch at **MyDevelopmentLab**

# Myelination

◄----------- Learning Objective 4.3
How does the process of myelination influence brain function?

A second crucial process in neuronal development is the creation of sheaths, or coverings, around individual axons, which insulate them from one another electrically and improve the conductivity of the nerves. These sheaths are made of a substance called *myelin* (see Figure 4.2); the process of developing the sheaths is called **myelination**.

The sequence of myelination follows both cephalocaudal and proximodistal patterns. Thus, nerves serving muscle cells in the hands are myelinated earlier than those serving the feet. Myelination is most rapid during the first 2 years after birth, but it continues at a slower pace throughout childhood and adolescence. For example, the parts of the brain that are involved in vision reach maturity by the second birthday (Lippé, Perchet, & Lassonde, 2007). By contrast, the parts of the brain that govern motor movements are not fully myelinated until about age 6 (Todd, Swarzenski, Rossi, & Visconti, 1995).

Myelination leads to improvement in brain functions. For example, the **reticular formation** (see Figure 4.1 on page 83) is the part of the brain responsible for keeping your attention on what you're doing and for helping you sort out important and unimportant information. Myelination of the reticular formation begins in infancy but continues in spurts across childhood and adolescence. In fact, the process isn't complete until the mid-20s (Spreen et al., 1995). So, teenagers have longer attention spans than children, who, in turn, have longer attention spans than infants.

Also of importance is the myelination of the neurons that link the reticular formation to the frontal lobes. It is well documented that **selective attention**, the ability to focus cognitive activity on the important elements of a problem or situation, increases significantly during middle childhood (Wetzel, Widmann, Berti, & Schröger, 2006). It seems likely that myelination of linkages between the frontal lobes and the reticular formation work together to enable school-aged children to develop this important kind of concentration (Sowell et al., 2003).

To understand the importance of selective attention, imagine that your psychology instructor, who usually hands out tests printed on white paper, gives you a test printed on blue paper. You won't spend a lot of time thinking about why the test is blue instead of white; this is an irrelevant detail. Instead, your selective attention ability will prompt you to ignore the color of the paper and focus on the test questions. In contrast, some younger elementary school children might be so distracted by the unusual color of the paper that their test performance would be affected. As the nerves connecting the reticular formation and frontal lobes become more fully myelinated during the school years, children begin to function more like adults in the presence of such distractions.

The neurons of the **association areas**—parts of the brain where sensory, motor, and intellectual functions are linked—are myelinated to some degree by the time children enter school. However, from age 6 to age 12, the nerve cells in these areas become almost completely myelinated. Neuroscientists believe that this progression of the myelination process contributes to increases in information-processing speed. For example, suppose you were to ask a 6-year-old and a 12-year-old to identify pictures of common items—a bicycle, an apple, a desk, a dog—as rapidly as possible. Both would have equal knowledge of the items' names, but the 12-year-old would be able to produce the names of the items much more rapidly than the 6-year-old. Such increases in processing speed probably contribute to improvements in memory function you'll read about later in Chapter 6 (Johnson, 2011; Fletcher, 2011).

Neurons in other parts of the brain, such as the **hippocampus** (see Figure 4.1) are also myelinated in childhood (Tanner, 1990). The hippocampus is involved in the transfer of information to long-term memory. Maturation of this brain structure probably accounts for improvements in memory function, spatial cognition, and the ability to navigate (Nelson, de Haan, & Thomas, 2006). Moreover, maturation of the connections between the hippocampus and the cerebral cortex is probably responsible for the common finding that people's earliest memories involve events that happened when they were about 3 years old (Zola & Squire, 2003).

**myelination** The process by which an insulating layer of a substance called myelin is added to neurons.

**reticular formation** The part of the brain that regulates attention.

**selective attention** The ability to focus cognitive activity on the important elements of a problem or situation.

**association areas** Parts of the brain where sensory, motor, and intellectual functions are linked.

**hippocampus** A brain structure that is involved in the transfer of information to long-term memory.

# Lateralization

Equal in importance to synapse formation and myelination is the specialization in function that occurs in the two hemispheres of the brain. The **corpus callosum** (see Figure 4.1 on page 83), the brain structure through which the left and right sides of the cerebral cortex communicate, grows and matures more during the early childhood years than in any other period of life. The growth of this structure accompanies the functional specialization of the left and right hemispheres of the cerebral cortex. This process is called **lateralization**.
◉ Simulate at MyDevelopmentLab

**corpus callosum** The structure that connects the right and left hemispheres of the cerebral cortex.

**lateralization** The process through which brain functions are divided between the two hemispheres of the cerebral cortex.

**spatial perception** The ability to identify and act on relationships of objects in space; in most people, this skill is lateralized to the right cerebral hemisphere.

**relative right-left orientation** The ability to identify right and left from multiple perspectives.

◉ Simulate the Experiment *Split Brain* at **MyDevelopmentLab**

**LEFT- AND RIGHT-BRAIN DOMINANCE** Figure 4.3 illustrates how brain functions are lateralized in 95% of humans, a pattern known as *left-brain dominance*. In a small proportion of the remaining 5 percent, the functions are reversed, a pattern called *right-brain dominance*. However, most people who are not left-brain dominant have a pattern of *mixed dominance*, with some functions following the typical pattern and others reversed. (By the way, the terms *left-brain* and *right-brain* are sometimes used to describe personality or learning style. Such usage has nothing to do with the physical lateralization of functions in the two hemispheres of the brain.)

Neuroscientists suspect that our genes dictate which functions will be lateralized and which will not, because some degree of lateralization is already present in the human fetus (Gupta et al., 2005). For example, both fetuses and adults turn their heads in order to be able to listen to language with the right ear. Because sounds entering the right ear are routed to the left side of the brain for interpretation, such findings suggest that language begins to be lateralized in most fetuses. Full lateralization of language function, though, doesn't happen until near the end of the early childhood period (Spreen et al., 1995).

It appears that the experience of learning and using language, not simply genetically programmed maturation of the brain, is the impetus behind hemispheric specialization. Young children whose language skills are the most advanced also show the strongest degree of lateralization (Mills, Coffey-Corina, & Neville, 1994). Neuroscientists have not determined whether some children advance rapidly in language acquisition because their brains are lateralizing at a faster pace. It could also be that some children's brains are lateralizing language function more rapidly because they are learning it faster.

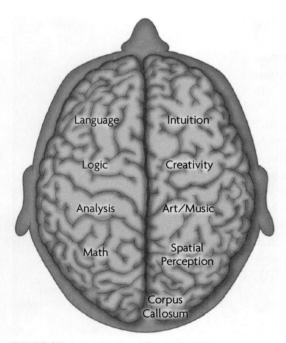

**FIGURE 4.3** Lateralization of Brain Functions
Brain functions are lateralized, as shown in the figure. Neurologists think that the basic outline of lateralization is genetically determined, whereas the specific timing of the lateralization of each function is determined by an interaction of genes and experiences.

**SPATIAL PERCEPTION** Lateralization is also linked to the development of **spatial perception**, the ability to identify and act on relationships of objects in space. For example, when you use a map to get from one place to another, you are using spatial perception to read the map and to relate it to the real world. Across early and middle childhood, spatial perception is lateralized to the right hemisphere of the brain in most people. Perception of objects such as faces lateralizes in the preschool years. However, complex spatial perception, such as map-reading, isn't strongly lateralized until after age 8 (Roberts & Bell, 2000). At the same time, the areas of the corpus callosum that are involved in interhemispheric communication related to spatial perceptual tasks grow rapidly (Thompson et al., 2000). As a result of both lateralization and corpus callosum growth, children beyond age 8 exhibit spatial perceptual skills that are superior to those of younger children.

A behavioral test of spatial perception lateralization that neuroscientists often use involves **relative right-left orientation**, the ability to identify right and left from multiple perspectives. Such tests usually show that most children younger than 8 know the difference between their own right and left. Typically, though, only those older than 8 understand the difference between statements like "it's on *your* right" and "it's on *my* right." Lateralization of spatial perception may also be related to the increased efficiency with which older children learn math concepts and problem-solving strategies. In addition, it is somewhat correlated to progress through Piaget's stages of cognitive development (van der Molen & Molenaar, 1994).

Differences in visual experiences have been postulated to explain sex differences in spatial perception and in a related function called **spatial cognition**, the ability to infer rules from and make predictions about the movement of objects in space. For example, when you are driving on a two-lane road and you make a judgment about whether you have enough room to pass the car ahead of you, you are using spatial cognition. From an early age, boys score much higher than girls, on average, when asked to perform spatial cognition tasks, perhaps because of boys' play preferences (Hyde, 2005). Some researchers argue that boys' greater interest in constructive activities such as building with blocks helps them develop more acute spatial perception. Research showing that the gender difference in spatial cognition is larger among children from middle- and high-income families than from low-income families seems to support this view, presumably because families with greater economic resources are better able to provide boys with the play materials that they specifically request (Bower, 2005).

**HANDEDNESS** **Handedness**, the tendency to rely primarily on the right or the left hand, is another important aspect of neurological lateralization (Tanner, 1990). Studies relating brain lateralization to handedness suggest that a common neurological process may be involved in both. About 95% of right-handers possess the typical pattern of language-on-the-left (Salpekar, Berl, & Kenealy, 2011). However, only 75% of left-handers are left-brain dominant. About 1% of left-handers have complete right-brain language specialization, and the rest have a mixed pattern of dominance (Pujol et al., 1999).

It used to be thought that right-handedness increased among humans as societies became more literate. The idea was that, when teaching children how to write, parents and teachers encouraged them to use their right hands. In this way, right-handedness became sort of a custom that was passed on from one generation to the next through instruction. By examining skeletons that predate the invention of writing, archaeologists have determined that the proportions of right- and left-handedness were about the same in illiterate ancient populations as they are among modern humans: 83% right-handed, 14% left-handed, and 3% ambidextrous (Steele & Mayes, 1995). These findings suggest that the prevalence of right-handedness is likely to be the result of genetic inheritance. Moreover, geneticists at the National Cancer Institute (NCI) have identified a dominant gene for right-handedness that they believe to be so common in the human population that most humans receive a copy of it from both parents (Klar, 2003). To further complicate the picture, an international team of researchers discovered another gene that predisposes children to be left-handed only when they receive the gene from their fathers (Francks et al., 2007).

Research comparing children's right-hand and left-hand performance on manual tasks, such as moving pegs from one place to another on a pegboard, also supports the genetic hypothesis. Most of these studies show that older children, teens, and adults are better at accomplishing fine-motor tasks with the nondominant hand than younger children are (Dellatolas et al., 2003; Roy, Bryden, & Cavill, 2003). Thus, experience in using the hands appears to moderate, rather than strengthen, the advantage of the dominant over the nondominant hand.

Of course, what developmentalists ultimately want to know is how being left- or right-handed affects a child's development. At one time left-handedness was regarded as a highly undesirable developmental outcome. This was due to superstitions about associations between left-handedness and the presence of evil spirits. As a result, parents and teachers encouraged left-handers to switch to right-handedness. Today, developmentalists and parents alike tend to believe that it is best to allow a child to follow her natural tendencies with regard to handedness.

Nevertheless, research does suggest that left-handedness is associated with poor developmental outcomes in both the cognitive and the socioemotional domain (Johnston, Nicholls, Shah, & Shields, 2008). But this association is probably the result of an underlying factor that influences both handedness and developmental outcomes. It's important to remember, too,

**spatial cognition** The ability to infer rules from and make predictions about the movement of objects in space.

**handedness** A strong preference for using primarily one hand or the other; it develops between 3 and 5 years of age.

**growth curve** The pattern and rate of growth exhibited by a child over time.

that only a small proportion of left-handed children ever display these deficits. Consequently, parents should avoid pushing a left-handed child to be right-handed in the interest of preventing developmental problems. Even if parents succeed in switching the child's hand preference, if there is a hidden risk factor present, the problem will still be there. Thus, research aimed at finding and moderating the effects of the underlying cause of the correlation between handedness and poor developmental outcomes is needed, rather than a campaign to change children's hand preferences.

## Size, Shape, and Skills

As you've seen, changes in children's nervous system have powerful influences on their development. But changes in other systems are influential as well.

Learning Objective 4.5 ----------→
What patterns of growth are evident in childhood and adolescence?

## Growth

By age 2, a toddler is about half as tall as he will be as an adult (hard to believe, isn't it?). You may also find it surprising that growth from birth to maturity is neither continuous nor smooth.

During the first phase, which lasts for about the first 2 years, the baby gains height very rapidly, adding 10 to 12 inches in length in the first year and tripling his body weight in the same span. At about age 2, the child settles down to a slower but steady addition of 2 to 3 inches and about 6 pounds a year until adolescence.

During the second phase, children's growth becomes more predictable from one point of measurement to the next. When health-care professionals measure children's height and weight, they use a statistic called a *percentile rank* to describe how the child compares to others of the same age. A percentile rank is the percentage of individuals whose measurements are equal to or less than those of the individual child who is being described. For example, if a child's weight is at the 25th percentile, 25% of children of his age weigh less than he does and 75% weigh more. In other words, a child who is at the 25th percentile is on the small side, compared to peers. One who is at the 50th percentile is about average, and another who is at the 75th percentile is larger than most children her age.

Individual children's height and weight percentile ranks can vary a great deal in the first 2 years of life. Thus, a child might accurately be described as "small for her age" at one check-up and "big for her age" at another check-up. But beginning around the age of 2 years, children's percentile ranks for height and weight begin to stabilize. When a child's percentile ranks for height and weight become stable, the child is said to have established his individual **growth curve**, or rate of growth. Figure 4.4, which is based on longitudinal data derived from several hundred children (Mei, Grummer-Strawn, Thompson, & Dietz, 2004), illustrates this pattern. As you can see, few children change ranks after 30 to 36 months of age. Thus, if a 3-year-old's growth curve is at the 25th percentile, his adult height will also be very near the 25th percentile.

The third phase is the dramatic adolescent "growth spurt," when the child may add 3 to 6 inches a year for several years, after which the rate of growth again slows until final adult size is reached. This growth spurt is, on average, larger for boys than for girls, but virtually all children show a period of more rapid growth sometime between the ages of about 9 and 15.

The shape and proportions of the child's body also change. In an adult, the head is about an eighth to a tenth of the total height. In a toddler, the head is proportionately far larger in order to accommodate the nearly adult-sized brain of the infant. And a child's hands and feet normally reach full adult size sometime in late elementary school or early adolescence, causing his appearance to be somewhat awkward. However, researchers have found no point in the adolescent growth process at which teenagers become consistently less coordinated or less skillful in physical tasks (Butterfield, Lehnhard, Lee, & Coladarci, 2004).

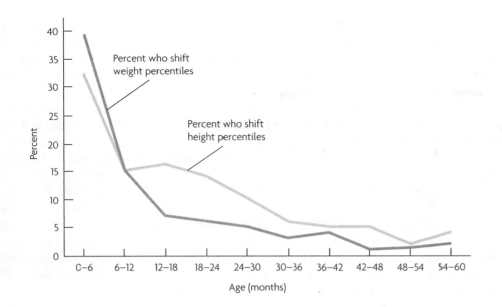

**FIGURE 4.4** Growth Curve Shifts from Birth to 5 Years
This figure shows the percentage of children in each age group who show changes in the percentile ranks for their height and weight from one check-up to the next.

(*Source:* Mei, Grummer-Strawn, Thompson, & Dietz, 2004.) Shifts in percentiles of growth during early childhood: Analysis of longitudinal data from California Child Health and Development Study. *Pediatrics, 113*, 617–627.

## Bones, Muscles, and Fat

The hand, wrist, ankle, and foot all have fewer bones at birth than they will have at full maturity. An adult has nine separate bones in his wrist, while a 1-year-old has only three; the remaining six bones develop over the period of childhood. Like many aspects of physical development, this process occurs earlier in girls than in boys. For example, the nine adult wrist bones are normally visible on x-rays, though not yet fully hardened or completely "articulated" (meaning they don't yet work as well together as they will in adulthood), by 51 months in girls but not until 66 months in boys (Needlman, 1996). Consequently, in the early years of school, girls display more advanced coordination in skills such as handwriting than boys do.

In one part of the body, though, the bones fuse rather than differentiate. The skull of a newborn is made up of several bones separated by spaces called **fontanels**. Fontanels allow the head to be compressed without injury during the birth process, and they give the brain room to grow. In most children, the fontanels are filled in by bone by 12 to 18 months, creating a single connected skull bone.

Bones also change in quality as well as in number over the course of development. An infant's bones are softer, with a higher water content, than an adult's bones. The process of bone hardening, called **ossification**, occurs steadily from birth through puberty, following such a regular and predictable pattern that physicians use **bone age** as the best single measure of a child's physical maturation; x-rays of the hand and wrist show the stage of development of wrist and finger bones. In infancy and toddlerhood, the sequence of development generally follows the cephalocaudal and proximodistal patterns. For example, bones of the hand and wrist harden before those in the ankles or feet.

Muscles—like bones—change in quality from infancy through adolescence, becoming longer and thicker and developing a higher ratio of muscle to water at a fairly steady rate throughout childhood. At adolescence, muscles go through a growth spurt, just as height does, so that adolescents become quite a lot stronger in just a few years. Both boys and girls show this increase in strength, but the increase is much greater in boys (Malina, 2007). For example, in a classic cross-sectional study in Canada involving 2,673 children and teenagers, Smoll and Schutz (1990) measured strength by having each child hang as long as possible from a bar, keeping his or her eyes level with the bar. As you can see in Figure 4.5, 9-year-old boys could maintain this flexed arm hang for about 40% longer than could girls of the same age; by age 17, boys could sustain it almost three times as long as girls. Similar results have been found for other measures of strength (Butterfield et al., 2004). This substantial difference in strength is

← - - - - - - - - - - - -**Learning Objective 4.6**
In what ways do bones, muscles, and fat change?

**fontanel** One of several "soft spots" in the skull that are present at birth but disappear when the bones of the skull grow together.

**ossification** The process of hardening by which soft tissue becomes bone.

**bone age** A measure of physical maturation based on x-ray examination of bones, typically the wrist and hand bones. Two children of the same chronological age may have different bone age because their rates of physical maturation differ.

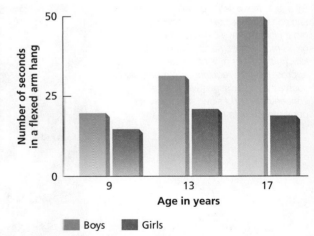

**FIGURE 4.5** Sex Differences in Strength
Both boys and girls get stronger between childhood and adolescence, but boys gain much more strength.

(*Source:* Smoll & Schutz, 1990, "Quantifying gender differences in physical performance: A developmental perspective." *Developmental Psychology, 26*, 360–369.)

**motor development** Growth and change in ability to perform both gross motor skills (such as walking or throwing) and fine motor skills (such as drawing or writing).

one reflection of the sex difference in muscle mass. In adult men, about 38% of total body mass is muscle, compared to only about 31% in adult women (Janssen, Heymsfield, Wang, & Ross, 2000). Such a sex difference in muscle mass (and accompanying strength) seems to be largely a result of hormone differences, although sex differences in exercise patterns or fitness may also play some role (Gabbard, 2011).

Another major component of the body is fat, most of which is stored immediately under the skin. This subcutaneous fat first develops beginning at about 34 weeks prenatally and has an early peak at about 9 months after birth (the so-called baby fat); the thickness of this layer of fat then declines until about age 6 or 7, after which it rises until adolescence. Once again, there is a sex difference in these patterns. From birth, girls have slightly more fat tissue than boys do, and this difference becomes gradually more marked during childhood. At adolescence, the difference grows still further. The size of the change is illustrated in results of the Canadian study cited earlier (Smoll & Schutz, 1990). Between ages 13 and 17, the percentage of body weight made up of fat rose from 21.8% to 24.0% among the girls in this study but dropped from 16.1% to 14.0% among the boys. So during and after puberty, proportions of fat rise among girls and decline among boys, while the proportion of weight that is muscle rises in boys and declines in girls.

**Learning Objective 4.7**
How does children's ability to use their bodies change?

# Using the Body

The ability to use the body to carry out physical activities involves interactions of several separate systems.

**STAMINA** *Stamina* is the capacity to sustain motor activity. For example, if you observe children on playgrounds, you will notice that preschoolers display short bursts of physical activity followed by periods of rest. School-aged children show a similar pattern, but their periods of activity are longer and their periods of rest are shorter than those of younger children because they possess more stamina (Gabbard, 2011).

Changes in stamina are linked to growth of the heart and lungs, which is especially evident during puberty. As the heart and lungs increase in size, the heart rate drops. Both of these changes are more marked for boys than for girls—another of the factors that increases boys' capacity for sustained effort relative to that of girls. Before puberty, boys and girls are fairly similar in physical strength, speed, and stamina, although even at these earlier ages, when a difference exists, it favors the boys. After puberty, boys have a clear advantage in all three areas (Smoll & Schutz, 1990).

◉ **Watch** the **Video** *Development of the Grasp Reflex* at **MyDevelopmentLab**

*By age 1, Nellie (left) not only can walk; she can navigate stairs. By age 5 or 6, most children have developed very good gross motor skills, needed to run and kick (middle). Yet a 5- or 6-year-old will approach a task requiring fine motor skills, such as using scissors, with tense concentration and slow, still imprecise body movements (right).*

## Table 4.1 — SEQUENCES OF DEVELOPMENT OF VARIOUS MOTOR SKILLS

| Age | Locomotor (Gross Motor) Skills | Manipulative (Fine Motor) Skills |
|---|---|---|
| 1–3 mos. | Stepping reflex; lifts head; sits with support | Holds object if placed in hand; begins to swipe at objects |
| 4–6 mos. | Rolls over; sits with self-support by 6 months; creeps | Reaches for and grasps objects, using one hand to grasp |
| 7–9 mos. | Sits without support | Transfers objects from one hand to the other; can grasp with thumb and finger ("pincer grasp") by 9 months |
| 10–12 mos. | Pulls self up to standing; walks grasping furniture, then walks without help; squats and stoops | Grasps a spoon across palm, but has poor aim of food at mouth |
| 13–18 mos. | Walks backward and sideways; runs (14–20 months) | Stacks two blocks; puts objects into small containers and dumps them out |
| 2–4 yrs. | Runs easily; walks up stairs using one foot per step; skips on both feet; pedals and steers a tricycle | Picks up small objects (e.g., Cheerios); holds crayon with fingers (age 2–3), then between thumb and first two fingers (age 3–4); cuts paper with scissors |
| 4–6 yrs. | Walks up and down stairs using one foot per step; walks on tiptoe; walks a thin line; jumps, throws, and catches fairly well | Threads beads but not needle (age 4–5); threads needle (age 5–6); grasps pencil maturely but writes or draws with stiffness and concentration |
| 6–9 yrs. | Kicks and hits stationary objects (e.g., ball) with force; intercepts moving objects on the run but must stop to hit, kick, or catch; running speed 4 to 5 yards per second | Uses mature grip when writing or drawing; uses downward motion to strike object with implement (e.g., hammer); bounces object with one hand with limited control |
| 9–12 yrs. | Kicks, hits, and catches moving objects on the run; substantial increase in vertical jump; running speed 5 to 6 yards per second | Uses downward or horizontal motion to strike object with implement as appropriate (e.g., hammer versus baseball bat); bounces object with one hand with good control |

*Sources*: Capute et al., 1984; Connolly and Dalgleish, 1989; Den Ouden, Rijken, Brand, Verloove-Vanhorick, and Ruys, 1991; Fagard and Jacquet, 1989, Gabbard, 2008; Gallahue and Ozmun, 1995; Hagerman, 1996; Needlman, 1996; Overby, 2002; Thomas, 1990.

**MOTOR DEVELOPMENT** Motor development includes both movement skills, often called *gross motor skills*, such as crawling, walking, running, and bike riding, and manipulative skills, often called *fine motor skills*, such as grasping or picking up objects, holding a crayon or a pencil, or threading a needle. Both gross motor and fine motor skills are present in some form at every age, as you can see in Table 4.1. As a general rule, however, gross motor skills develop earlier, with fine motor skills lagging behind. Thus, 6-year-olds can run, hop, skip, jump, and climb well; many can ride a two-wheeled bike. But children this age are not yet skilled at using a pencil or crayon or cutting accurately with scissors (see Figure 4.6). When they use such tools, their whole body gets involved—the tongue moving and the whole arm and back involved in the writing or cutting motion. In the elementary school years, fine motor skills improve rapidly, making it possible for most children not only to write more clearly and easily, but also to play a musical instrument, draw, and develop sports skills that require fine motor coordination. ◉ Watch at MyDevelopmentLab

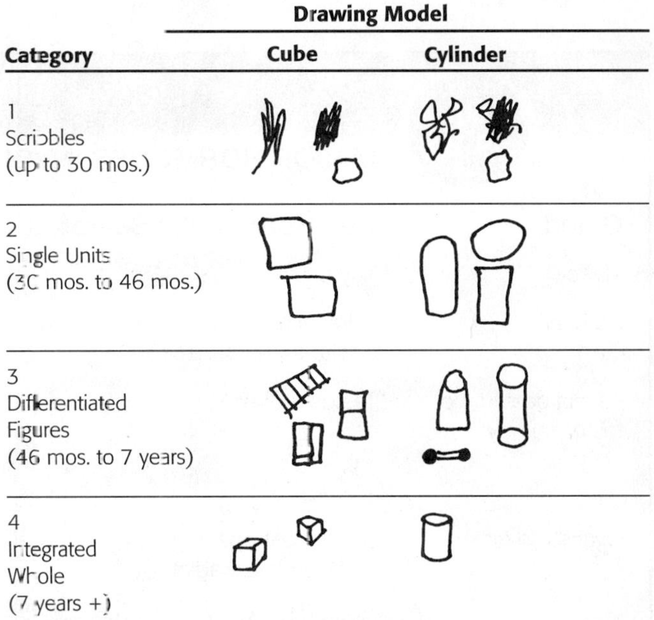

## The Endocrine and Reproductive Systems

One of the most obvious sets of physical changes involves the development of sexual maturity. The whole process is controlled by special chemical signals and is somewhat different in girls and boys.

| Category | Drawing Model | |
|---|---|---|
| | Cube | Cylinder |
| 1 Scribbles (up to 30 mos.) | | |
| 2 Single Units (30 mos. to 46 mos.) | | |
| 3 Differentiated Figures (46 mos. to 7 years) | | |
| 4 Integrated Whole (7 years +) | | |

**FIGURE 4.6** Stages in Children's Drawings
Examples of drawings in each category of two object forms.

(*Source*: Toomela, A. (1999). Drawing Development: Stages in the Representation of a Cube and a Cylinder. *Child Development, 70*, 1141–1150. Reprinted with permission from the Society for Research in Child Development.)

## Hormones

**Learning Objective 4.8** ------------➤
What are the contributions of the various hormones to physical development?

**endocrine glands** Glands (including the adrenals, the thyroid, the pituitary, the testes, and the ovaries) that secrete hormones governing overall physical growth and sexual maturing.

✳|Explore the **Concept** *The Endocrine System* at **MyDevelopmentLab**

**pituitary gland** Gland that provides the trigger for release of hormones from other glands.

**puberty** The series of hormonal and physical changes at adolescence that bring about sexual maturity.

**gonadotrophic hormones** Hormones secreted by the pituitary gland at the beginning of puberty that stimulate the development of glands in the testes and ovaries, which then begin to secrete testosterone or estrogen.

Hormones, which are secretions of the various **endocrine glands** in the body, govern pubertal growth and physical changes in several ways, which are summarized in Table 4.2. The **pituitary gland** provides the trigger for release of hormones from other glands; thus, it is sometimes called the *master gland*. For example, the thyroid gland secretes thyroxine only when it receives a signal from the pituitary in the form of a secretion of a specific thyroid-stimulating hormone. ✳|Explore at **MyDevelopmentLab**

The rate of growth of children is governed largely by thyroid hormone and pituitary growth hormone. Thyroid hormone is secreted in greater quantities for the first 2 years of life and then falls to a lower level and remains steady until adolescence (Tanner, 1990). Secretions from the testes and ovaries, as well as adrenal androgen, are also at very low levels in the early years of childhood. As Figure 4.7 shows, this changes at age 7 or 8, when adrenal androgen begins to be secreted in greater amounts—the first signal of the changes of puberty (Rosenthal & Gitelman, 2002).

Although **puberty** is often thought of as a single event, it is actually a series of milestones that culminate in the ability to reproduce. After the initial hormonal changes that happen around age 7 or 8, there is a complex sequence of additional hormonal changes. The pituitary gland begins secreting increased levels of **gonadotrophic hormones**. These in turn stimulate the development of glands in the testes and the ovaries that then secrete more of the so-called *sex hormones*—testosterone in boys and a form of estrogen called *estradiol* in girls.

Along with the gonadotrophic hormones, the pituitary gland secretes three other hormones that interact with the sex hormones and affect growth: *ACTH*, which signals the adrenal glands to secrete adrenal androgen; *thyroid-stimulating hormone*; and general *growth hormone*. Adrenal androgen, which is chemically very similar to testosterone, plays a particularly important role for girls, triggering the growth spurt and affecting pubic hair development. For boys, adrenal androgen is less significant, presumably because they already have so much male hormone in the form of testosterone in their bloodstreams. The increased levels of sex and growth hormones trigger two sets of body changes: development of the sex organs, and a much broader set of changes in the brain, bones, muscles, and other body organs.

| Table 4.2 | MAJOR HORMONES INVOLVED IN PHYSICAL GROWTH AND DEVELOPMENT | |
|---|---|---|
| **Gland** | **Key Hormone(s) Secreted** | **Aspects of Growth Influenced** |
| Thyroid | Thyroxine | Normal brain development and overall rate of growth |
| Adrenal | Adrenal androgen (chemically very similar to testosterone) | Some pubertal changes as well as the development of skeletal and muscular maturity |
| Leydig cells in the testes (in boys) | Testosterone | Crucial in the formation of male genitals prenatally; triggers the sequence of primary and secondary sex characteristic changes at puberty; stimulates increased output of growth hormone and affects bones and muscles |
| Ovaries (in girls) | Several estrogens, the most critical of which is estradiol | Development of the menstrual cycle, breasts, and pubic hair |
| Pituitary | Growth hormone (GH), thyroid-stimulating hormone (TSH), ACTH, and the gonadotrophic hormones | Growth hormone governs the rate of physical maturation; other pituitary hormones signal the respective sex glands to secrete; gonadotrophic hormones help control the menstrual cycle |

*Source:* Tanner, J. M. (1990). *Foetus into man* (revised and enlarged ed.). Cambridge, MA: Harvard University Press.

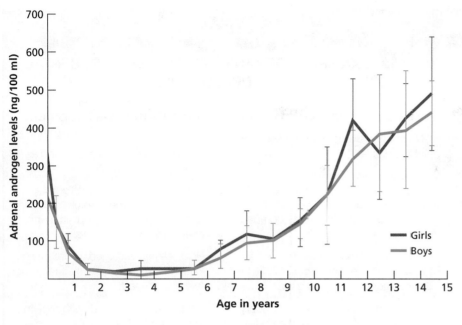

**FIGURE 4.7** Hormone Changes in Childhood and Adolescence
Changes in hormones prior to and at adolescence. The top graph shows changes in adrenal androgen, which are equivalent in boys and girls; the bottom graphs show increases in estradiol for girls in picograms per milliliter, and testosterone for boys in nanograms per milliliter.

(*Sources:* Androgen data from M. K. McClintock and G. Herdt, from "Rethinking Puberty: The Development of Sexual Attraction," *Current Directions in Psychological Science,* Vol. 5, No. 6 (December 1996), p. 181, Fig. 2. © 1996 American Psychological Association. By permission of Cambridge University Press. Estradiol and testosterone data from Elizabeth Susman, Fig. 2 from "Modeling Developmental Complexity in Adolescence: Hormones and Behavior in Context," p. 291, *Journal of Research on Adolescence,* 7, 1997. © 1997 by Lawrence Erlbaum Associates, Inc. By permission of the publisher and author.)

*Gains in coordination, strength, and stamina enable these adolescent girls to perform far better on the basketball court than was possible just a couple of years earlier.*

The most obvious changes of puberty are those associated with sexual maturity. Changes in *primary sex characteristics* include growth of the testes and penis in the male and of the ovaries, uterus, and vagina in the female. *Secondary sex characteristic* changes include breast development in girls, changing voice pitch and beard growth in boys, and the growth of body hair in both sexes. These physical developments occur in a defined sequence, customarily divided into five stages following a system originally suggested by J. M. Tanner (1990) (see Table 4.3 on page 94). Stage 1 describes the preadolescent stage, stage 2 the first signs of a pubertal change, stages 3 and 4 the intermediate steps, and stage 5 the final adult characteristic.

## Sequence of Changes in Girls and Boys

Studies of preteens and teens in both Europe and North America show that in girls, the various sequential changes are interlocked in a particular pattern, shown schematically in Figure 4.8 on page 94 (Malina, 1990). The first steps are the early changes in breasts and pubic hair, followed by the peak of the growth spurt and by the beginnings of stages 4 and 5, which involve further breast and pubic hair development. Usually, only after the growth spurt does first menstruation occur, an event called **menarche** (pronounced men-ARE-kee). Menarche typically occurs 2 years after the beginning of other visible changes and is succeeded only by the final stages of breast and pubic hair development. Among girls in industrialized countries today, menarche occurs, on average, between ages 12½ and 13½; 95% of all girls experience this event between the ages of 11 and 15 (Adelman & Ellen, 2002). ✳ Explore at MyDevelopmentLab

◄----------- **Learning Objective 4.9**
What are the sequences of pubertal changes in boys and girls?

**menarche** Onset of menstruation.

✳ Explore the **Concept** *Female Reproductive Organs* at **MyDevelopmentLab**

## Table 4.3 EXAMPLES OF TANNER'S STAGES OF PUBERTAL DEVELOPMENT

| Stage | Female Breast Development | Male Genital Development |
|---|---|---|
| 1 | No change except for some elevation of the nipple. | Testes, scrotum, and penis are all about the same size and shape as in early childhood. |
| 2 | Breast bud stage: elevation of breast and the nipple as a small mound. Areolar diameter increases compared to stage 1. | Scrotum and testes are slightly enlarged. Skin of the scrotum reddens and changes texture, but little or no enlargement of the penis. |
| 3 | Breast and areola both enlarged and elevated more than in stage 2, but no separation of their contours. | Penis slightly enlarged, at first mainly in length. Testes and scrotum are further enlarged. |
| 4 | Areola and nipple form a secondary mound projecting above the contour of the breast. | Penis further enlarged, with growth in breadth and development of glans. Testes and scrotum further enlarged, and scrotum skin still darker. |
| 5 | Mature stage. Only the nipple projects, with the areola recessed to the general contour of the breast. | Genitalia achieve adult size and shape. |

*Source:* Petersen, A. C., & Taylor, B. (1980). The biological approach to adolescence. In J. Adelson (Ed.), *Handbook of adolescent psychology* (pp. 117–158). New York: Wiley.

**secular trend** A pattern of change in some characteristic over several cohorts, such as systematic changes in the average timing of menarche or in average height or weight.

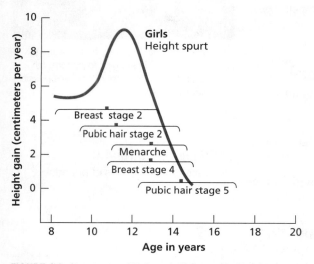

**FIGURE 4.8** Sequence of Pubertal Changes in Girls
The figure shows the normal sequence and timing of pubertal changes for girls. The red box on each black line represents the average age when the change occurs; the line indicates the range of normal times. Note the wide range of normality for all of these changes. Also note how relatively late in the sequence the growth spurt and menarche occur.

(*Sources:* Malina, 1990; Tanner, 1990.)

Interestingly, the timing of menarche changed rather dramatically from the mid-19th to the mid-20th century. In 1840, the average age of menarche in Western industrialized countries was roughly 17; the average dropped steadily from that time until the 1950s at a rate of about 4 months per decade among European populations, an example of what psychologists call a **secular trend** (Roche, 1979). The change was most likely caused by significant changes in lifestyle and diet, particularly increases in protein and fat intake along with reductions in physical exercise, that resulted in an increase in the proportion of body fat in females.

The stability of the average age of menarche at about 12.5 years over the past half century supports the notion that there is a genetic limit on the age range within which menarche may occur (Viner, 2002). However, increased consumption of fats and higher rates of obesity have led to higher proportions of body fat among today's girls, which, in turn, have triggered hormonal changes (Rosenfield, Lipton, & Drum, 2009). These changes have had little impact on the average age of menarche, but they have led to declines in the average ages at which girls show secondary sex characteristics (Rosenfield, Lipton, & Drum, 2009). On average, girls nowadays show these signs somewhat earlier than their mothers and grandmothers did, resulting in a lengthening of the average time between the appearance of secondary sex characteristics and menarche (Parent et al., 2003). Nevertheless, the appearance of breasts or pubic hair in girls younger than 8 years continues to be exceedingly rare, occurring in less than 1% of girls regardless of weight status. Thus, a girl younger than 8 who exhibits these signs may be diagnosed with *precocious puberty*, a diagnosis that requires follow-up to determine whether a tumor, hormonal disorder, or other condition or disease is responsible (Jospe, 2011).

For about 2 years after menarche, ovulation occurs in only 30% of girls' menstrual cycles (Adelman & Ellen, 2002). Over the next 2 years, that ovulation percentage rises to the adult rate of 80%. Such irregularity no doubt contributes to the widespread (but false) assumption among girls in their early teens that they cannot get pregnant because they are too young.

In boys, as in girls, the peak of the growth spurt typically comes fairly late in the sequence, as you can see in Figure 4.9. These data suggest that, on average, a boy completes stages 2 and 3 of genital development and stages 2 and 3 of pubic hair development before he reaches his growth peak. The development of a beard and the lowering of the voice occur near the end of the sequence. Precisely when in this sequence the boy begins to produce viable sperm is very difficult to determine. It appears that a boy can attain fertility as early as age 12 or as late as age 16 and still be within the normal range (Blake & Davis, 2011). Sequentially, fertility usually occurs just before a boy reaches his full adult height.

While the order of pubertal development seems to be highly consistent, there is quite a lot of individual variability. Figures 4.8 and 4.9 depict the normative, or average, pattern, but individual teenagers often deviate from the norm. For instance, a girl might move through several stages of pubic hair development before the first clear changes in the breasts become evident or might experience menarche much earlier in the sequence than normal. It is important to keep this variation in mind if you are trying to make a prediction about an individual teenager.

## The Timing of Puberty

In any random sample of 12- and 13-year-olds, you will find some who are already at stage 5, and others still at stage 1 in the steps of sexual maturation. In U.S. culture today, most young people seem to share the expectation that pubertal changes will happen sometime between ages 12 and 14. Coincidentally, most girls acquire a culturally undesirable *endomorphic*, or somewhat flabby, body type, as a result of puberty. Thus, early-developing girls should have more adjustment problems than average- or late-developing girls. Similarly, puberty provides most boys with a culturally admired *mesomorphic*, or lean and muscular, body type. Thus, early-developing boys should display better psychological and social adjustment than average- or late-developing boys.

Research in the United States indicates that girls who are early developers (who experience major body changes before age 10 or 11) show consistently more negative body images, such as thinking of themselves as too fat (Sweeting & West, 2002). Researchers have also consistently found that boys who are slightly ahead of their peers in pubertal development often occupy leadership roles and are more academically and economically successful in adulthood (Taga, Markey, & Friedman, 2006). On the negative side, substance use is associated with early puberty in both girls and boys, because, based on their appearance, early maturers are often invited to join groups of older teens among whom substance use is an important social activity (Costello, Sung, Worthman, & Angold, 2007).

The results of studies that examine the effects of pubertal timing have been somewhat clearer when researchers have instead asked teenagers about their internal models of earliness or lateness. The link between the internal model and the outcome is especially vivid in a classic study of ballet dancers by Jeanne Brooks-Gunn (Brooks-Gunn, 1987; Brooks-Gunn & Warren, 1985). She studied 14- to 18-year-old girls, some of whom were serious ballet dancers studying at a national ballet company school. A very lean, almost prepubescent body is highly desirable among such dancers. Brooks-Gunn therefore expected that dancers who were very late in pubertal development would actually have a better image of themselves than those who were on time. And that is exactly what she found (see Figure 4.10). Among the nondancers, menarche at the biologically average time was associated with a better body image than was late menarche, but exactly the reverse was true for the dancers. Thus, as predicted, it is the discrepancy between a teen girl's internal model of puberty and her experiential reality that predicts the effects of pubertal timing. Research has yet to examine the relationship between boys' internal models of puberty and their actual experiences.

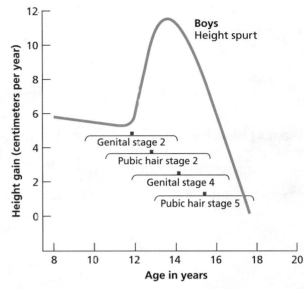

**FIGURE 4.9** Sequence of Pubertal Changes in Boys
The sequence of pubertal changes begins about 2 years later for boys than for girls, but as with girls, the height spurt occurs relatively late in the sequence.

(*Sources:* Malina, 1990; Tanner, 1990.)

### Learning Objective 4.10

How does the timing of puberty affect teens' development?

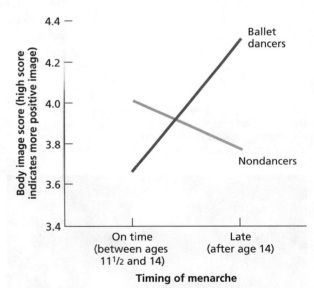

**FIGURE 4.10** Timing of Puberty and Body Image
Serious ballet dancers clearly prefer to have a very late puberty. In this study, dancers whose menarche was "on time" by ordinary standards actually had poorer body images than those who were objectively quite late, while the reverse was true for nondancers. Thus, it is perception of timing and not actual timing that is critical.

(*Source:* Brooks-Gunn & Warren, 1985, from Table 1, p. 291.)

# Sexual Behavior in Adolescence

◉⊸ Watch the Video *Adolescent Sexual Behavior* at MyDevelopmentLab

In the United States, most people become sexually active sometime before age 20, about half before they leave high school (see Figure 4.11). For some teens, being "sexually active" constitutes a single act of intercourse sometime during the high school years. However, many others have multiple partners and frequently engage in unprotected sex acts. ◉⊸ Watch at MyDevelopmentLab

Learning Objective 4.11 ---------➤
What are the ethnic, social, and academic factors that predict early sexual behavior?

## Prevalence and Predictors of Sexual Behavior

Figure 4.11 shows findings from a large-scale national survey of high school students in the United States (Eaton et al., 2010). As you can see from the figure, high school boys were found to be more sexually active than girls. Furthermore, the proportion of sexually experienced teens increased across grades 9 to 12. One statistic illustrated by the figure that is particularly worrisome to public health officials is the proportion of teens who have had multiple partners before leaving high school. Research has shown that the more partners a teenager (or an adult, for that matter) has, the more likely he or she is to contract a sexually transmitted disease. However, rates of sexual activity have declined substantially over the past three decades. In 1988, 60% of male and 51% of female 15- to 19-year-olds reported having had sex at least once in their lives. In 2008, the rates were 43% and 42%, respectively. (Abma, Martinez, & Cohen, 2010).

**ETHNIC AND AGE DIFFERENCES**  Sexual experience varies across ethnic groups in the United States (Abma, Martinez, & Cohen, 2010). Among female 15- to 19-year-olds, 39% of Whites, 43% of Hispanics, and 45% of African Americans are sexually experienced. Among males, 39% of Whites, 45% of Hispanics, and 61% of African Americans tell researchers that they have had sex at least once.

There are also age differences among students who are sexually active—defined as having had sex at least once within 3 months of responding to the survey. For example, roughly 15% of 15- to 17-year-olds and 38% of 18- to 19-year-old females reported sexual activity within the past four weeks, compared to 12% and 36% of males in the two ages groups, respectively (Abma, Martinez, & Cohen, 2010).

Among students who are sexually active, 63% say that they use condoms (CDC, 2006f). African Americans are more likely than students in other groups to report using condoms (69% versus 57% for Hispanic Americans and 63% for Whites). Birth control pills are used even less frequently. Only 21% of sexually active females report being on the pill. In addition, pill usage is far more common among White high school girls (27%) than among their African American and Hispanic American peers (9% and 11%, respectively).

*A number of factors determine the likelihood that teen couples like this one will become sexually active: the age at which they began dating, their moral and religious beliefs, their interest in school, and family variables such as socioeconomic status and parental supervision.*

**SOCIAL FACTORS**  Although sexual activity of boys is somewhat correlated with the amount of testosterone in their blood, social factors are much better predictors of teenagers' sexual activity than hormones (Halpern, Udry, Campbell, & Suchindran, 1993; Udry & Campbell, 1994). Those who begin sexual activity early are more likely to live in poor neighborhoods in which young people are not closely monitored by adults. They come from poorer families or from families in which sexual activity is condoned and dating rules are lax. They are more likely to use alcohol. Many were abused and/or neglected in early childhood (Herrenkohl, Herrenkohl, Egolf, & Russo, 1998).

Among girls, those who are sexually active are also more likely to have had early menarche, to have low interest in school, to have had their first date at a relatively early age, and to have a history of sexual abuse (Buzi, Roberts, Ross, Addy, & Markham, 2003; Ompad et al., 2006). In general, these same factors predict sexual activity among Whites, African Americans, and Hispanics. And in every group, the greater the number of these risk factors present for an individual teenager, the greater the likelihood that he or she will be sexually active.

Adolescents' moral beliefs and the activities in which they participate also predict to some extent whether they will become sexually active. For example, teens who believe premarital sex is morally wrong and who attend religious services frequently are less likely than their peers to become sexually active before reaching

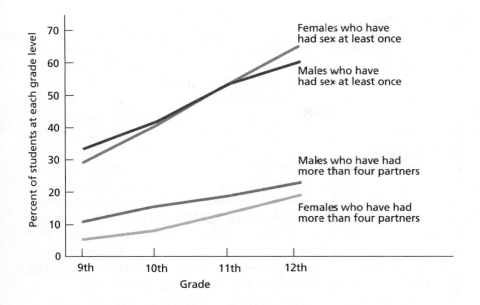

**FIGURE 4.11** Sexual Experience among High School Students in the United States
The graph illustrates the data from a representative sample of more than 15,000 high school students interviewed in 2009. As you can see, the number of students who have had sex at least once increases substantially from ninth to twelfth grade, and an alarming percentage of teens have had four or more partners by the end of the high school years.

(*Source* Eaton et al., 2010)

adulthood (Abma, Martinez, & Cohen, 2010). Rates of sexual activity are also lower among teens who are involved in sports or other after-school pursuits than among their peers who do not participate in such activities (Savage & Holcomb, 1999). Moreover, alcohol use is associated with 25–30% of adolescent sexual encounters; thus, teens who do not use alcohol are less likely to be sexually active than those who drink (Eaton et al., 2010). ◉ Watch at MyDevelopmentLab

◉ Watch the **Video** *Virginity Cool* at **MyDevelopmentLab**

**CULTURE, AGE AT MARRIAGE, AND TEEN SEXUAL ACTIVITY** Some observers claim that the trend towards later age at marriage is responsible for the widely held view in Western societies that sexual behavior in the teen years is a "problem." The problem, these observers say, is that the social demands of industrialized and technological cultures, such as the need for post-secondary education, conflict with the biological demands of the late adolescent and early adulthood years. They cite surveys such as the one shown in Figure 4.12 in support of the hypothesis that the cultural context in which sexual behavior occurs is of greater significance than the age at which it occurs.

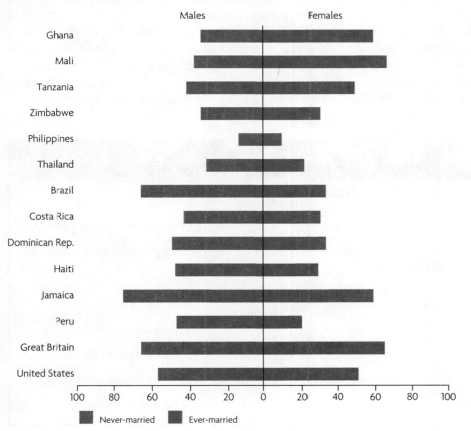

**FIGURE 4.12** Percentage of 15- to 19-Year-Olds Who Have Had Sexual Intercourse Across Cultures
In some traditional cultures, teens, especially females, begin having sex at early ages because they marry sooner than is typical among their peers in industrialized countries.

(*Source*: Singh, S., & Darroch, J. (2000). Adolescent pregnancy and childbearing: Levels and trends in industrialized countries. *Family Planning Perspectives, 32,* 14–23.

**Learning Objective 4.12** ----------➤

Which sexually transmitted diseases are common among sexually active teens?

**sexually transmitted diseases (STDs)** Category of disease spread by sexual contact, including chlamydia, genital warts, syphilis, gonorrhea, and HIV; also called venereal diseases.

👁─|Watch the **Video** *Intimate Danger* at **MyDevelopmentLab**

👁─|Watch the **Video** *Sexually Transmissible Infection: Ken, STI* at **MyDevelopmentLab**

👁─|Watch the **Video** *Cervical Cancer* at **MyDevelopmentLab**

👁─|Watch the **Video** *Aids in Black America* at **MyDevelopmentLab**

# Sexually Transmitted Diseases

Predictably, as rates of sexual behavior increase among teenagers, so do the rates of **sexually transmitted diseases (STDs)**, diseases spread by sexual contact. STD rates tend to be higher among younger sexually active individuals than among those who are older. In fact, more than half of all new STD cases each year in the United States occur in 15- to 24-year-olds. The rate of one STD, *chlamydia*, is higher among teenagers than in any other age group. About 3% of sexually active 15- to 19-year-old females in the United States have chlamydia (CDC, 2010). But chlamydia rates pale in comparison to those associated with the *human papilloma virus (HPV)*. About half of sexually active 15- to 19-year-old girls test positive for HPV (Quick Stats, 2007). If you read the entries in Table 4.4, you can readily see that the effects of STDs can be quite severe, especially "silent" infections such as chlamydia and HPV that often do not produce symptoms until they have caused a great deal of damage. 👁─|Watch at **MyDevelopmentLab**

Many teens are also woefully ignorant of sexually transmitted diseases and their potential consequences, although about 90% of high school students report having learned about sexually transmitted diseases (STDs) and other negative outcomes of risky sexual behavior in school (CDC, 2000; Abma, Martinez, & Cohen, 2010). Even when they are knowledgeable about STDs, many teens lack the assertiveness necessary to resist sexual pressure from a romantic partner or to discuss condom use. 👁─|Watch at **MyDevelopmentLab**

Two vaccines are available that protect young women against several types of HPV (CDC, 2011). The vaccines are recommended for all females between the ages of 9 and 26. However, researchers do not yet know how long the vaccines protective effects will last. Moreover, officials point out that there are other forms of HPV against which the vaccines offers no protection. For these reasons, public health officials state that girls and women who get the vaccines should continue to use condoms. 👁─|Watch at **MyDevelopmentLab**

Male teens who engage in same-sex intercourse are at higher risk of contracting HIV/AIDS than other groups. Among male teens who test positive for HIV, 60% acquired the virus in this way (CDC, 2007b). Moreover, about 60% of female adolescents who test positive for HIV became infected through sexual contact with a male who engaged in same-sex intercourse at some time in the past. Surveys showing that the disease is virtually nonexistent among homosexual male teens before age 15 but is present in about 10% of them by age 22 have prompted public health officials to heighten their efforts to educate young teens about HIV/AIDS (Valleroy et al., 2000). In addition, they have recommended universal screening for HIV for teens who engage in same-sex intercourse so that antiretroviral drugs can be prescribed as early in the course of the disease as possible. Education and screening programs are especially important among African American male teens, who account for 69% of all new cases of HIV/AIDS among 13- to 19-year-olds in the United States (CDC, 2007b). 👁─|Watch at **MyDevelopmentLab**

**Table 4.4**

## COMMON SEXUALLY TRANSMITTED DISEASES

| Disease | Symptoms | Treatment | Long-Term Consequences |
|---|---|---|---|
| Chlamydia | Painful urination; discharge; abdominal discomfort; one-third have no symptoms | Antibiotics | Pelvic inflammatory disease; sterility |
| Genital warts (HPV) | Painless growths on genitalia and/or anus | Removal of warts; no known cure | Increased risk of cervical cancer |
| Genital herpes | Painful blisters on genitalia | No known cure; can be controlled with various drugs | Risk of transmission to partners and to infants during birth |
| Gonorrhea | Discharge; painful urination | Antibiotics | Pelvic inflammatory disease |
| Syphilis | Sores on mouth, genitals | Antibiotics | Paralysis; brain damage; death |
| HIV/AIDS | Fatigue; fever; frequent infections | Antiretroviral drugs | Chronic infections; death |

To combat the spread of STDs among teens, many developmentalists and public health advocates say that more effective sex education programs are needed. Most suggest that programs that include social and decision-making skills training, along with information about STDs and pregnancy, are more likely to reduce the prevalence of sexual activity and increase the number of teens who protect themselves against disease and pregnancy when they do have sex than are information-only approaches. However, some studies show that even the most carefully designed sex education programs have little or no effect on teenagers' sexual behavior (Henderson et al., 2007). Information provided by peers and young adults who have had personal experiences with unplanned pregnancy and sexually transmitted diseases may influence teens' sexual decision-making to a greater degree than formal educational programs (Kidger, 2004). ◉—|Watch at **MyDevelopmentLab**

◉—|Watch the **Video** *Debate Over Abstinence-Only Education* at **MyDevelopmentLab**

## Teenage Pregnancy

◄----------**Learning Objective 4.13**
What are the factors associated with pregnancy in adolescence?

The rate of teenage pregnancy is higher in the United States than in any other Western industrialized country (Abma, Martinez, & Cohen, 2010). For example, the overall annual rate is about 40 pregnancies per 1,000 teens in the United States; it is only 27 pregnancies per 1,000 in the United Kingdom, 10 per 1,000 in Germany, and 4 per 1,000 in Japan (Abma, Martinez, & Cohen, 2010). Ethnic differences exist within the United States as well (Martin et al., 2010). Births to teenagers represent 17% of all births to African American women. Among Whites, only 8% of births involve teen mothers; among Hispanic women, about 14% of all births are to teenagers (Martin et al., 2010). ◉—|Watch at **MyDevelopmentLab**

◉—|Watch the **Video** *Teen Pregnancy* at **MyDevelopmentLab**

However, teen pregnancy statistics can be confusing, because they usually refer to all pregnancies among women under age 20. To clarify the extent of the teen pregnancy problem, it is useful to break down the statistics by adolescent subgroups. For example, in the United States, the annual pregnancy rate is 1 pregnancy per 1,000 for girls younger than 15; 22 per 1,000 among girls aged 15 to 17; and 70 per 1,000 among 18- to 19-year-olds (Martin et al., 2010). Looking at the numbers this way shows that teen pregnancy is far more frequent among older adolescents and, in fact, is most likely to happen after a girl leaves high school.

The age at which an adolescent becomes a parent is only one aspect of the teen pregnancy issue. Birth rates among teenagers have actually dropped in the entire U.S. population since the 1960s, including among 15- to 19-year-olds. What has increased is the rate of births to unmarried teens. In 1970, about three-quarters of teen mothers were married, whereas in 2003, more than 85% were unmarried (Martin et al., 2010).

Whether a girl becomes pregnant during her teenage years depends on many of the same factors that predict sexual activity in general (Miller, Benson, & Galbraith, 2001). The younger a girl is when she becomes sexually active, the more likely she is to become pregnant. Among teen girls from poor families, single-parent families, families with relatively uneducated parents, or whose mothers gave birth to them before age 20 pregnancy rates are higher (Martin et al., 2010).

In contrast, the likelihood of pregnancy is lower among teen girls who do well in school and have strong educational aspirations. Such girls are both less likely to be sexually active at an early age and more likely to use contraception if they are sexually active. Girls who have good communication about sex and contraception with their mothers are also less likely to get pregnant (Dogan-Até & Carrión-Basham, 2007).

When teen girls become pregnant, in most cases, they face the most momentous set of decisions they have encountered in their young lives. About one-third of teen pregnancies across all ethnic groups end in abortion, and about 14% result in miscarriages (Alan Guttmacher Institute, 2004). Among Whites, 7% of teens carry the baby to term and place it for adoption, while 1% of African American teens relinquish their babies to adoptive families.

The children of teen mothers are more likely than children born to older mothers to grow up in poverty, with all the accompanying negative consequences for the child's optimum development (Burgess, 2005). For instance, they tend to achieve developmental milestones more slowly than infants of older mothers (Pomerleau, Scuccimarri, & Malcuit, 2003). However, the children of teen mothers whose own parents help with child care, finances, and parenting skills are less likely to suffer such negative effects (Birch, 1998; Uno, Florsheim, & Uchino, 1998).

Moreover, social programs that provide teen mothers with child care and the support they need to remain in school positively affect both these mothers and their babies. Such programs also improve outcomes for teen fathers (Kost, 1997).

**Learning Objective 4.14**----------→
In what ways are gay, lesbian, bisexual, and transgendered teens different from and similar to their peers?

## Sexual Minority Youth

The emergence of a physical attraction to members of the opposite sex, or *heterosexuality*, is one of the defining features of adolescence for the great majority of teenagers. For some, though, adolescence is the time when they discover—or confirm a long-standing suspicion— that they are attracted to people of the same sex (*homosexuality*) or to both sexes (*bisexuality*). Still others become increasingly convinced that their psychological gender is inconsistent with their biological sex (*transgenderism*).

**GAY, LESBIAN, AND BISEXUAL ADOLESCENTS**    Surveys involving thousands of teens have found that about 92% identify themselves as exclusively heterosexual in *sexual orientation*, a person's preference for same- or opposite-sex partners (Austin et al., 2004; Remafedi, Resnick, Blum, & Harris, 1998). About 7% of teens report that they are still unsure of their sexual orientation, a status called *questioning* by researchers, and 1% classify themselves as exclusively gay, exclusively lesbian, or bisexual. By adulthood, 94% report being exclusively heterosexual, and just over 5% describe themselves as gay, lesbian, or bisexual, leaving only a very small proportion who are still questioning (Langer, Arnedt, & Sussman, 2004).

Several twin studies have suggested a genetic basis for homosexuality (Lippa, 2005). Most of these studies indicate that when one identical twin is homosexual, the probability that the other twin will also be homosexual is 50–60%, whereas the concordance rate is only about 20% for fraternal twins and only about 11% for pairs of biologically unrelated boys adopted into the same family (Dawood, Pillard, Horvath, Revelle, & Bailey, 2000; Kendler, Thornton, Gilman, & Kessler, 2000). Family studies also suggest that male homosexuality runs in families—that is, the families of most gay men have a higher proportion of homosexual males than do the families of heterosexual men (Kirk, Bailey, & Martin, 2000). Such findings strengthen the hypothesis that homosexuality has a biological basis (Dawood et al., 2000).

Additional studies suggest that prenatal hormone patterns may also be a causal factor in homosexuality (Lippa, 2005). For example, women whose mothers took the drug

*The process through which an individual comes to realize that he or she is homosexual appears to be a gradual one. Groups such as this one provide teens with the social support they need to cope with their own feelings and with the negative responses of some peers to their sexual orientation.*

diethyl-stilbestrol (DES, a synthetic estrogen) during pregnancy are more likely to be homosexual as adults than are women who were not exposed to DES in the womb (Meyer-Bahlburg et al., 1995). Moreover, there is evidence that many boys who demonstrate strong cross-sex play preferences in early childhood show homosexual preferences when they reach adolescence (Bailey & Zucker, 1995). Interestingly, too, studies show that the long bones in the legs and arms of school-aged children who grow up to be homosexual do not grow as rapidly as those of children who eventually become heterosexual (Martin & Nguyen, 2004). These findings indicate that maturational differences between homosexuals and heterosexuals are evident before puberty and involve body systems other than the sexual organs themselves. Taken together, prenatal hormone exposure studies, research examining early childhood activity preferences, and studies comparing the processes of physical maturation in heterosexuals and homosexuals are consistent with the hypothesis that homosexuality is programmed in at birth.

Such evidence does not mean that environment plays no role in homosexuality. For example, when one of a pair of identical twins is homosexual, the other twin does *not* share that sexual orientation 40–50% of the time. Something beyond biology must be at work, although developmentalists do not yet know what environmental factors may be involved.

Whatever the cause of variations in sexual orientation, the process through which an individual comes to realize that he or she is homosexual appears to be a gradual one (Diamond, 2007). Some researchers think that the process begins in middle childhood as a feeling of doubt about one's heterosexuality (Carver, Egan, & Perry, 2004; Wallien & Cohen-Kettenis, 2008). Retrospective studies have found that many gay men and lesbians recall having had homosexual fantasies during their teen years, but few fully accepted their homosexuality while still in adolescence (Wong & Tang, 2004). Instead, the final steps toward full self-awareness and acceptance of one's homosexuality appear to take place in early adulthood.

As homosexual teens grapple with questions about their sexual orientation, many report feeling isolated from and unaccepted by their peers (Galliher, Rostosky, & Hughes 2004; Martin & D'Augelli, 2003). Homosexual and questioning teens are also more likely to report being bullied by peers than heterosexual adolescents are (Berlan et al., 2010). Such findings help explain why rates of depression, attempted suicide, and substance abuse are higher among homosexual and questioning teens than heterosexual teens (Cato & Canetto, 2003; Corliss, 2010; Marshall, Friedman, Stall, & Thompson, 2009; Zhao, Montoro, Igartua, & Thombs, 2010). Many mental health professionals suggest that, to respond to these adolescents' needs, school officials provide emotional and social support for homosexual teens (Rostosky, Owens, Zimmerman, & Riggle, 2003; van Wormer & McKinney, 2003).

While homosexual adolescents clearly face unique challenges, they share many of the same concerns as their heterosexual peers. For example, both homosexual and heterosexual girls are more likely than boys to be dissatisfied with their physical appearance (Saewyc, Bearinger, Heinz, Blum, & Resnick, 1998). Consequently, dieting is more common among both homosexual and heterosexual girls than among boys of either sexual orientation. Like their heterosexual counterparts, homosexual male adolescents drink alcohol more often and engage in more risky behavior than do female teenagers.

**TRANSGENDERED TEENS** *Transgendered* teens and adults are those whose psychological gender is the opposite of their biological sex. Some studies suggest that transgendered individuals may have been exposed to atypical amounts of androgens in the womb (Lippa, 2005). However, most do not have such histories, so the cause of transgenderism remains a mystery. Nevertheless, transgendered adolescents usually report that, since early childhood, they have been more interested in activities that are associated with the opposite sex than in those that are typical for their own (Lippa, 2005). However, most children who are attracted to cross-gender activities, and even those who express a desire to be the opposite gender, do not exhibit transgenderism after puberty (Wallien & Cohen-Kettenis, 2008). Thus, such behaviors on the part of children are not considered to be predictive of the development of transgenderism in adolescence.

Because of their fear of being stigmatized, most teens who suspect that they are transgendered keep their feelings to themselves. The denial and anger that are often expressed

Watch the Video *Gender Identity Disorder: Denise* at **MyDevelopmentLab**

by family members when transgendered adolescents do venture to "come out" amplify these teens' distress (Zamboni, 2006). As a result, like gay, lesbian, and bisexual teens, transgendered teens are more likely to suffer from depression and are at higher risk of suicide than heterosexual adolescents are (Rosenberg, 2003). Watch at **MyDevelopmentLab**

## Health and Wellness

You read about infants' physical health in Chapter 3, and children have many of the same needs. However, their needs, and the focus of concerns about their health, change significantly after puberty, so it's important to separate our discussion of health issues and look first at childhood and then at adolescence.

**Learning Objective 4.15**
What are the health needs and concerns of children and adolescents?

## Health in Childhood

Typically, childhood is a fairly healthy period of life. However, children have many accidents, and the health habits formed during these years can persist for a lifetime, influencing individual health for good or for ill.

**HEALTH-CARE NEEDS**   Just as infants do, young children continue to require periodic medical check-ups and a variety of immunizations (Overby, 2002). At yearly check-ups, doctors monitor preschoolers' growth and motor development. Moreover, health-care professionals provide parents with strategies for dealing with everyday parenting issues. For example, parents frequently ask for advice regarding young children's sleeping habits (see *Developmental Science in the Real World*).

School-aged children benefit from regular medical care as well. For one thing, there are a few important immunizations that are usually administered during this period (Umetsu, 1998). In addition, many school-aged children have undiagnosed health problems. For example, 10–20% have difficulty sleeping (Owens, Spirito, McGuinn, & Nobile, 2000; Sadeh, Gruber, & Raviv, 2002). In most cases, parents of school children are unaware of such problems until a physician or nurse specifically asks a child about sleep patterns as part of a routine check-up. Sleep difficulties are associated with attention, concentration, and behavioral problems, so picking up on an undetected sleep problem, and correcting it, may improve a child's life considerably (Sadeh et al., 2002).

## DEVELOPMENTAL SCIENCE IN THE REAL WORLD

### A Good Night's Sleep for Kids (and Parents, Too!)

Every night Luis and Ramona go through the same ordeal when they put their 3-year-old son, Manny, to bed. The boy begs to sleep with them, but they always refuse. After four or five cycles of begging and sobbing, Manny finally becomes so exhausted that he can no longer stay awake. But the battle doesn't end at that point. Manny wakes up every night around 2:00 A.M. and slips into his parents' bed. Usually, Luis and Ramona are sleeping so soundly that Manny's late-night invasion goes unnoticed, and they awaken to find him in their bed the next morning.

Manny's nighttime behavior is all too familiar to many parents of preschoolers. Here are the bedtime strategies that most health-care professionals recommend:

- Provide the child with a structured, predictable daytime schedule, and stick to it as closely as possible every day.

- Set a regular bedtime that is 8 to 10 hours before the desired waking time.
- Discontinue daytime naps for a child who has difficulty getting to sleep or who awakens too early in the morning.
- Establish a routine set of "settling activities," such as a bath, story book, and goodnight kiss, and resist the child's efforts to prolong or modify the routine.
- Provide the child with a *transitional object* such as a doll or stuffed animal that is reserved especially for bedtime.

Making such adjustments can be challenging. However, research confirms that these kinds of changes can significantly reduce sleep-related conflicts (Borkowski, Hunter, & Johnson, 2001). Thus, a few days or even weeks of persistence on the parents' part may pay off in years of undisturbed sleep for parents and children alike.

**Learning Objective 4.15a**
What steps can parents take to minimize bedtime conflicts?

**REFLECTION**
1. If you were Manny's parent, what strategies would you use to try to prevent him from awakening at night and getting into your bed?
2. In your opinion, to what extent are parental concerns about where children sleep driven by cultural beliefs and standards of behavior?

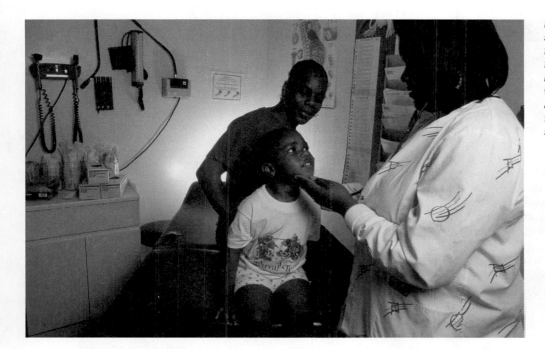

**GROWTH CURVES AND HEALTH**    Earlier in the chapter you learned that stabilization of a child's growth curve enables health-care professionals to predict her height at later ages. For this reason, the growth curve is critical to assessments of children's health (Overby, 2002). A downward deviation away from an established growth curve for height may be a sign that a child is suffering from an undiagnosed illness (Styne & Glaser, 2002). An upward deviation for weight may mean that the child is trending toward becoming overweight. The importance of growth curve assessment is one reason most health-care professionals assert that it is critical to young children's health that they be examined by the same physician, or at least in the same clinic, at each check-up (Children's Hospital of Philadelphia, 2008).

**ILLNESSES AND ACCIDENTS**    In the United States, the average preschooler has six to seven colds each year along with one or two episodes of gastrointestinal illness (Smith, 2011). Children who are experiencing high levels of stress or family upheaval are more likely to become ill (Guttman & Dick, 2004).

Another danger for children is accidents. In any given year, about a quarter of all children under 5 in the United States have at least one accident that requires some kind of medical attention, and accidents are the major cause of death in preschool and school-aged children (Borse & Sleet, 2009). At every age, accidents are more common among boys than among girls, presumably because of their more active and daring styles of play. The majority of accidents among children occur at home—falls, cuts, accidental poisonings, and the like. Drowning is the leading cause of accidental death in 1- to 4-year-olds; beyond age 5, motor vehicle accidents are the most frequent cause of death among children (Borse & Sleet, 2009). Moreover, as children become more active, more likely to participate in sports, and venture farther from home, their rates of various types of accidental injuries change. For instance, injuries due to falls are more common among 5- to 9-year-olds than they are among 10- to 14-year-olds. By contrast, 10- to 14-year-olds visit hospital emergency rooms seeking treatment for activity-related overexertion and for injuries resulting from bicycle accidents more frequently than those in the 5- to 9-year-old group do (Borse et al., 2008).

Bicycle-related mishaps become common in middle childhood (National Center for Injury Prevention and Control [NCIPC], 20-09). In fact, 80% of bicycle-related head injuries involve children. Research suggests that wearing a helmet while riding a bike reduces the chances of head injury by more than 85%. Consequently, many cities and states have enacted laws requiring both children and adult bicyclists to wear helmets. Finally, some "accidents" are actually the result of parental abuse (see *Thinking about Research*).

## Causes and Consequences of Child Abuse and Neglect

About 1 million cases of abuse and neglect in the United States each year come to the attention of law enforcement officials and/or health-care professionals (Fein, Durbin, & Selbst, 2002; Lamb & Lewis, 2011). Two-thirds involve *physical abuse*—the nonaccidental infliction of bodily injury on a child. Another quarter involve *sexual abuse*—physical contact between a child and adult that results in sexual gratification for the adult. About 5% are the result of *neglect*—failure to provide for a child's physical needs or to supervise him (Christian & Bloom, 2011). Sadly, about 1,700 infants and children die as a result of abuse or neglect each year, 80% of whom are under the age of 4 years (CDC, 2010).

Certain risk factors predispose parents to abuse and/or neglect their children. First, the risk of abuse is higher in any family experiencing significant stress, whether that stress arises from unemployment, poverty, neighborhood violence, a lack of social support, an especially difficult or demanding infant or one with physical disabilities (CDC, 2010). Second, some parents, particularly those who

were themselves abused, simply know no other way to deal with frustration and stress or with disobedience in their child, other than striking the child in some way. Other parents are depressed or unable to form the kind of emotional bond to the child that would help to prevent abuse (Christian & Bloom, 2010). Parental alcohol and drug dependence, too, play a significant role in a great many cases (Eiden, Foote & Schuetze, 2007).

Some children who are frequently or severely abused develop *post-traumatic stress disorder (PTSD)*. This disorder involves extreme levels of anxiety, flashback memories of episodes of abuse, nightmares, and other sleep disturbances. For some, these symptoms persist into adulthood (Koenen, Moffitt, Poulton, Martin, & Caspi, 2007). Abused children are also more likely than nonabused peers to exhibit delays in all domains of development (Cicchetti, Rogosch, Maughan, Toth, & Bruce, 2003). On the positive side, in studies involving abused and/or neglected children who were placed in foster care, differences between abused and nonabused

### Learning Objective 4.16
What are the consequences and suspected causes of child abuse and neglect?

children in physical, cognitive, and social development disappear within 1 year (Olivan, 2003). Thus, the critical factor in determining the short- and long-term effects of abuse is the quality of the post-abuse environment.

#### CRITICAL ANALYSIS

1. As a researcher, how might you set up a study to determine the qualities that distinguish abuse victims who experience long-term negative consequences from those who appear to experience no lasting effects?
2. What underlying factor or factors might explain the correlation between family stressors such as parental unemployment and child abuse?

**NUTRITION** Because children grow more slowly during the early childhood years than in infancy, they may seem to eat less than when they were babies. Moreover, food aversions often develop during the preschool years. For example, a child who loved carrots as an infant may refuse to eat them at age 2 or 3. Consequently, conflicts between young children and their parents often focus on the child's eating behavior (Overby, 2002).

During the school years, children become more open to new foods, but different kinds of nutritional problems arise. Many school-aged children make food choices without adult supervision for the first time in their lives. They use their allowances to purchase items from vending machines at school, or they stop at a corner store on the way to or from school. Not surprisingly, school-aged children's food choices in such circumstances are not always wise, and many consume a great deal of "junk" food—sodas, candy bars, and the like—of which their parents may not be aware.

⊙ **Watch** the **Video** *Kids and Food* at **MyDevelopmentLab**

### Learning Objective 4.16 ----------→
In what ways does excessive weight gain threaten the immediate and future health of children and adolescents?

## Excessive Weight Gain

**Excessive weight gain** is one of the most serious health issues of childhood and adolescence. It is a pattern in which children gain more weight in a year than is appropriate for their height, age, and sex. If a child gains excessive amounts of weight over a number of years, she is at risk of having weight problems and a number of serious health problems in adulthood. ⊙ **Watch** at **MyDevelopmentLab**

For adults, *obesity* has a fixed definition that is based on the **body mass index (BMI)**, a measure that estimates a person's proportion of body fat. Adults whose BMIs exceed 30 are classified as *obese* (CDC, 2007e). For children, standards for defining obesity must take into account the fact that some degree of increase in BMI occurs naturally in growing children as the ratio of fat to muscle in their bodies changes. Moreover, when prepubertal hormonal changes occur in the later years of middle childhood, girls' BMIs can become temporarily

**excessive weight gain** A pattern in which children gain more weight in a year than is appropriate for their age height, and sex.

**body mass index (BMI)** A measure that estimates a person's proportion of body fat.

distorted as the accompanying accumulation of fat tissue outpaces the growth of other kinds of tissue. Thus, it would be wrong to conclude that a 10- or 11-year-old girl was obese when what was really happening was that her body was in a transitional stage.

To determine whether an individual child's weight gain is appropriate, health-care professionals use a measure called **BMI-for-age**, a variation on the BMI that applies to adults (CDC, 2007e). A child's BMI-for-age is determined by calculating her BMI and comparing it to those of others her age. Different standards are used for boys and girls, because their BMIs do not increase at the same rate.

Children whose BMIs fall at the 95th percentile (the top 5%) are considered **obese**, and those whose BMIs exceed the 99th percentile are classified as **severely obese**. Children whose BMIs are between the 85th and 95th percentiles are classified as **overweight** (CDC, 2011). Because of growth spurts and the inherent instability of physical variables in childhood, multiple assessments are required before a child is actually classified as either, however. Surveys show that 15% of children aged 2 to 5 are overweight, and another 16% are at risk of becoming so by the time they reach school age (Pediatric Nutrition Surveillance, 2009). Rates increase dramatically in the middle childhood years. As you can see in Figure 4.13 on page 106, the prevalence of obesity and overweight among children and adolescents in the United States has grown at an alarming rate over the past five decades. Currently, almost 1 in 5 children between the ages of 6 and 11 is obese (Ogden & Carroll, 2010). Similar increases have been documented in every country in the world that tracks the prevalence of overweight among children and teenagers (Wang & Lobstein, 2006).

The older a child gets without stopping the pattern of excessive weight gain, the more likely the child is to be overweight into the adult years (Krebs & Primak, 2011). Research shows that a child who is still obese at the end of the middle childhood period is twice as likely to be obese in adulthood as a child who is obese at the beginning of this period (Krebs & Primak, 2011). In addition, more than half of children with obesity have one or more risk factors, such as elevated levels of cholesterol or high blood pressure, that predispose them to heart disease later in life (National Center for Chronic Disease Prevention and Health Promotion [NCCDPHP], 2000).

As you might suspect, overeating or eating too much of the wrong foods causes excessive weight gain in children just as it does in adults (NCCDPHP, 2000). However, both twin and adoption studies suggest that the tendency to gain excessive amounts of weight in childhood probably results from an interaction between a genetic predisposition for obesity and environmental factors that promote overeating or low levels of activity (Stunkard, Harris, Pedersen, & McClearn, 1990; Wardle, Carnell, Haworth, & Plomin, 2008). Whatever the genetic contribution might be, research suggests that a cultural pattern of decreases in physical activity and increases in the consumption of high-calorie convenience foods has led to the current epidemic of overweight children and adults (Taveras et al., 2010; See *Technology and the Developing Child*).  👁—⎤Watch at **MyDevelopmentLab**

It's important to keep in mind, though, that weight-loss diets for children can be fairly risky. Because they are still growing, the nutritional needs of overweight children differ from those of overweight adults (Krebs & Primak, 2011). Consequently, children require special diets developed and supervised by nutritional experts. Moreover, increasing the amount of exercise children get is just as important as changing their eating habits (Krebs & Primak, 2011). Experts on weight management in childhood recommend that parents of overweight and at-risk children take the following steps (CDC, 2007e):

- Provide plenty of vegetables, fruits, and whole-grain products.
- Include low-fat or non-fat milk or dairy products.
- Choose lean meats, poultry, fish, lentils, and beans for protein.
- Serve reasonably sized portions.
- Encourage everyone in the family to drink lots of water.
- Limit sugar-sweetened vegetables.
- Limit consumption of sugar and saturated fat.
- Limit children's TV, video game, and computer time.
- Involve the whole family in physical activities such as walking and bicycling.

*Like adults, children and adolescents who overeat and spend most of their time engaged in sedentary activities such as watching television are at risk for overweight and obesity.*

👁—⎤**Watch** the **Video** *Urban Sprawl and Obesity* at **MyDevelopmentLab**

**BMI-for-age**  Comparison of an individual child's BMI against established norms for his or her age group and sex.

**obese**  Describes a child whose BMI falls above the 95th percentile (the top 5%).

**severely obese**  Describes a child whose BMI-for-age is above the 99th percentile.

**overweight**  Describes a child whose BMI is at the 95th percentile.

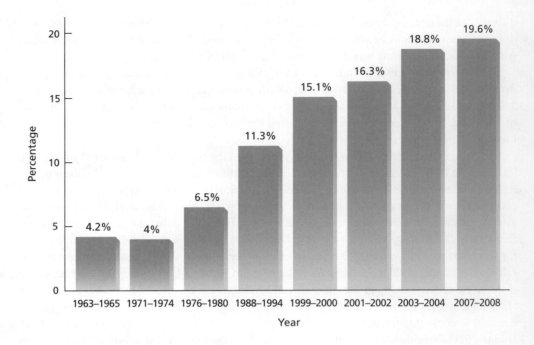

**FIGURE 4.13** Prevalence of Overweight among Children and Teens in the United States

The percentages of children and teens who are overweight have increased dramatically over the past five decades.

(*Source:* NCHS, 2007b; Ogden & Carroll, 2010)

The prevalence of overweight is somewhat less among adolescents than it is among school-aged children (NCHS, 2007b). One factor that may explain this age difference is that more teens than younger children actively try to lose weight, including those who do not have weight problems. Dieting in adolescence represents the culmination of a trend toward increasing awareness of the social desirability of thinness and knowledge of popular methods of weight loss that is evident among both boys and girls as early as age 7 (Kostanski, Fisher, & Gullone, 2004). Among teenagers, surveys suggest that 40% diet regularly, and 20% use extreme measures such as taking diet pills and fasting (CDC, 2006f; Neumark-Sztainer, Wall, Eisenberg, Story, & Hannan, 2006). As you will learn in Chapter 15, such extreme measures can be indicative of an *eating disorder*, a serious psychological disorder involving distortions of thinking and behavior that go far beyond habitual dieting. In most teens, however, habitual dieting is probably the result of an increased capacity for self-reflection (more on this in Chapter 6). ◉ Watch at **MyDevelopmentLab**

◉ Watch the **Video** *Body Image Part 1: Kianna, 12 Years Old* at **MyDevelopmentLab**

## TECHNOLOGY AND THE DEVELOPING CHILD

### Repetitive Strain Injury (RSI) of the Hand in Children and Teens

In many children's lives, digital play has replaced physical play (Krebs & Primak, 2011). As a result, health care providers are seeing increasing numbers of children and adolescents with *repetitive strain injuries* (RSI) involving the thumbs, fingers, hands, and wrists (Ferrie, 2007; Ince, Swearingen, & Yazici et al., 2009). The symptoms of RSI include pain, muscle spasms, weakness, tendonitis, and cysts on the wrists and finger joints. In some cases, these symptoms are so severe that children are unable to use their hands. Complete rest from the activity that caused RSI usually resolves the symptoms, but physical therapists who specialize in injuries of the hand point out

that RSI can be prevented (American Society of Hand Therapists, 2011). They recommend that parents limit the amount of time that children use video-game controllers, computer mice, cell phones, and other such devices. But other steps, such as monitoring the way that a child sits when she uses the computer or plays a video game, are equally important. Hand therapists have also devised a set of hand exercises that can be beneficial to adults and children alike who frequently use devices that are associated with RSI. You can read about these exercises and try them out yourself at http://www.asht.org/education/VideoGameInjury.cfm.

#### Learning Objective 4.16a
What is repetitive strain injury (RSI) of the hand, and how can it be prevented?

#### FIND OUT MORE
*Use your Internet search skills to answer these questions.*

1. What are the symptoms and potential long-term physical consequences of *video gamer's thumb*?
2. To what extent do devices such as computer keyboards and mice designed especially for young children prevent RSI?

# Poverty and Children's Health

◄----------- Learning Objective 4.17
How does poverty affect children's health?

As Table 4.5 suggests, children who live in poverty are at greater risk for a number of health problems than are their peers who are better off (Burgess, Propper, & Rigg, 2004; Case, Lubotsky, & Paxson, 2002; Currie, Shields, & Wheatley Price, 2004; Currie & Stable, 2003). Nevertheless, researchers typically do not study income in isolation from other variables. Instead, most examine the effects of **socioeconomic status (SES)**—a collective term that includes the economic, occupational, and educational factors that influence a family's relative position in society—on children's health. Such studies show that variables such as employment status, occupation, and parental educational levels predict children's health better than income alone does. Still, identifying risk factors tells us little about why those factors are important.

One possible explanation for this association is access to health care. Yet recent studies comparing poor families in the United States to those in Canada and the United Kingdom, where all citizens have access to free health care, have failed to fully support this hypothesis (Case, Lee, & Paxson, 2007). Children in poor families across all three nations have more health problems than those in more affluent households do. Thus, access to medical care is one piece of the SES-health relationship puzzle in the United States, but it isn't the whole story.

Looking beyond access to care, researchers have identified a number of other variables that may help to explain the association between poverty and children's health (Chen, 2004). For instance, tobacco use is more frequent among adults in low-income households (Gilman, Abrams, & Buka, 2003). As a result, children in lower SES homes are more likely to be exposed to nicotine prior to birth and to second-hand smoke in the early years. Table 4.6 lists several other such factors.

**socioeconomic status (SES)** A collective term that includes the economic, occupational, and educational factors that influence a family's relative position in society.

## Table 4.5 COMPARISON OF HEALTH PROBLEMS OF POOR AND NONPOOR CHILDREN

| Problem | Rate for Poor Children Compared to Nonpoor Children |
|---|---|
| Low birth weight | 1.5 to 2 times higher |
| Delayed immunization | 3 times higher |
| Asthma | Somewhat higher |
| Lead poisoning | 3 times higher |
| Neonatal mortality | 1.5 times higher |
| Deaths from accidents | 2 to 3 times higher |
| Deaths from disease | 3 to 4 times higher |
| Number reported to be in fair or poor health (rather than good health) | 2 times higher |
| Percentage with conditions limiting school activity | 2 to 3 times higher |
| Physical stunting (being in the 5th percentile or lower for height) | 2 times higher |
| Days sick in bed or lost school days | 40 percent higher |
| Severely impaired vision | 2 to 3 times higher |
| Severe iron-deficiency anemia | 2 times higher |

*Sources:* Brooks-Gunn, J., and Duncan, G. J., "The Effect of Poverty on Children," *The Future of Children*, 7(2), 1997, pp. 55–71; Starfield, B., "Childhood Morbidity: Comparisons, Clusters, and Trends," *Pediatrics, 88,* 1991, pp. 519–526.

**sensation-seeking** A strong desire to experience the emotional and physical arousal associated with risky behaviors such as fast driving and unprotected sex.

None of the factors in Table 4.6 alone, especially if it is experienced only temporarily, is sufficient to explain the relationship between poverty and children's health. But the presence of several of them in a child's life significantly increases the chances that the child will develop a health problem. However, there are a number of factors that help to protect children from the detrimental effects of the cumulative stressors associated with poverty. These factors include parental knowledge of child development and a strong social support network (Barrow, Armstrong, Varga, & Boothroyd, 2007; Seo, 2006). Thus, the ultimate effect that living in poverty has on the health of an individual child will depend on the combined effects of the risk and protective factors that are present in the child herself and in her environment. Poverty does not guarantee bad outcomes, but it stacks the deck against many children.

**Learning Objective 4.18**
How do psychologists explain risky behavior in adolescence?

**Watch** the **Video** *Teen Drinking* at **MyDevelopmentLab**

## Risky Behavior in Adolescence

For most individuals, adolescence is one of the healthiest periods of life. However, as adolescents gain independence, they encounter numerous health risks as a result of their own behavioral choices.　**Watch** at **MyDevelopmentLab**

**SENSATION-SEEKING**　Many teenagers appear to have what developmentalists describe as a heightened level of **sensation-seeking**, or a desire to experience high levels of arousal such as those that accompany high-speed driving or the highs that are associated with drugs. Sensation-seeking leads to recklessness (what most developmental researchers call "risky" or "high-risk" behavior), which, in turn, leads to markedly increased rates of accidents and injuries in this age range. For example, adolescents drive faster and use seat belts less

| Table 4.6 | CORRELATES OF POVERTY AND HEALTH |
|---|---|
| **Parent Characteristics** | **Environmental Characteristics** |
| Health status and history | Child-proofing of environment (e.g., safety latches on cabinets) |
| Depression | Cleanliness of home, neighborhood, child-care facilities |
| Parenting skills (e.g., consistent bedtime) | |
| Health habit instruction (e.g., teaching children how to brush their teeth) | Types of food available in the home |
| Smoking | Types of foods sold in neighborhood grocery stores |
| Substance abuse | Medicines available in neighborhood drug stores |
| Obesity | Seat belts, child safety seats in vehicles |
| Prenatal care compliance | Mold, pollution, and other respiratory irritants |
| Knowledge of child development | Access to health care |
| Enrollment in available health insurance, nutritional support programs | Safe, appropriate sites for motor play in neighborhood |
| Work schedule | Safe, appropriate toys in home |
| Unemployment | Access to high-quality child-care programs |
| Nonparental care arrangements | Level of violence in neighborhood |
| Education | |

*Source:* Ashiabi & O'Neal, 2007; Burgess, Propper, & Rigg, 2004; Dowd, 2007.

often than adults do (CDC, 2009). To reduce the number of accidents among teen drivers, many states in the United States have enacted laws that allow only "graduated" driver's licenses (Cobb, 2000). Sixteen-year-olds can drive in most such states, but they must remain accident- and ticket-free for a certain period of time before they can have privileges such as driving at night.

Risky behaviors may be more common in adolescence than in other periods because such behaviors help teenagers gain peer acceptance and establish autonomy from parents and from other authority figures (Jessor, 1992). However, neurological factors may be important as well. Developmental psychologist Laurence Steinberg suggests that sensation-seeking increases in adolescence because of changes in the brain that prompt teens to focus more on emotional gratification than they did in earlier years (Steinberg, 2008). Sensation-seeking declines, Steinberg says, as the prefrontal cortex matures and enables teens to gain better control of their impulses and to be better able to delay emotional gratification in favor of constructive goals such as academic achievement.

**ALCOHOL AND DRUG USE**    As you can see in Figure 4.14, illicit drug use is somewhat less common among recent cohorts than in past cohorts of teenagers (Johnston, O'Malley, Bachman, & Schulenberg, 2010). Researchers attribute this trend to declining approval of drug use among adolescents and to contemporary teens' better understanding of the negative consequences of taking drugs. Still, experts agree that drug use among teens continues to be a significant problem because of the risks to which teens expose themselves, such as drunk driving and the possibility of life-long addiction, when they use these substances.

Table 4.7 on page 110 lists the percentages of eighth-, tenth-, and twelfth-grade students who reported using each drug listed in the 12 months preceding the survey. Clearly, as was true in earlier cohorts, alcohol is the substance that teens use most often, but a surprising number of teenagers are using prescription drugs such as Ritalin, Adderall, OxyContin, and Vicodin. Similar percentages of teens use over-the-counter drugs such as cough medicines. (Note: The figures in the table for such drugs refer only to their use for purposes other than those for which they have been medically approved.) ◉—Watch at **MyDevelopmentLab**

◉—Watch the **Video** *Eliminating Meth* at **MyDevelopmentLab**

Teens who express the most interest in sensation-seeking are those who are most likely to use drugs and consume alcohol (Wu, Liu, & Fan, 2010). Furthermore, teens who are high sensation-seekers choose friends who are similar. Once such groups are formed, sensation-seeking becomes a central feature of their activities. So, for example, if one member tries marijuana or alcohol, others do so as well. However, teens who spend a lot of time alone may also be vulnerable to substance abuse. Researchers have found that shy adolescents, particularly those who are high in neuroticism, are more likely to use alcohol and drugs than are peers who are more outgoing (Kirkcaldy, Siefen, Surall, & Bischoff, 2004).

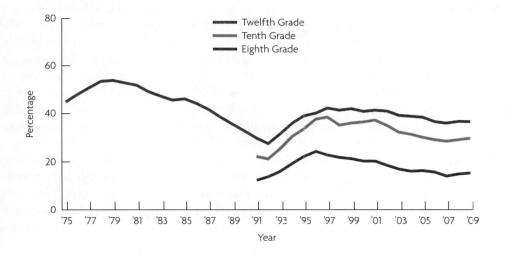

**FIGURE 4.14** Illicit Drug Use Trends among Teenagers
This figure shows the percentage of teens who admitted to using illicit drugs in the previous 12 months. As you can see, drug use rates have declined since the 1970s.

(*Source:* Johnston, L., O'Malley, P. M., Bachman, J., & Schulenberg, J. (2007). Monitoring the future: National results on adolescent drug use: Overview of key findings. NIH Publication No. 07-6202. June 22, 2007, from http://monitoringthefuture.org/).

## Table 4.7 — PERCENTAGES OF TEENS WHO HAVE USED ILLICIT DRUGS IN THE PAST 12 MONTHS

| Drug | 8th-graders | 10th-graders | 12th-graders |
|---|---|---|---|
| Alcohol | 34% | 56% | 67% |
| Marijuana | 12% | 25% | 32% |
| Vicodin* | 3% | 7% | 10% |
| Diet pills* | 5% | 8% | 8% |
| Tranquilizers* | 3% | 5% | 7% |
| Over-the-counter cold medicines* | 4% | 5% | 7% |
| Cocaine | 2% | 3% | 5% |
| OxyContin* | 3% | 4% | 4% |
| MDMA (Ecstasy) | 1% | 3% | 4% |
| Crack cocaine | 1% | 1% | 2% |
| Ritalin* | 3% | 4% | 4% |
| Methamphetamine | 2% | 2% | 3% |
| LSD | <1% | 2% | 2% |
| Heroin | 1% | 1% | 1% |

Source: Johnston et al., 2007.

*Recreational usage outside the scope of the purpose for which drug is medically approved.

The use of alcohol and other substances by teens leads to lowered inhibitions, just as it does in adults. However, the degree of disinhibition and the riskiness of the sensation-seeking activities that result from alcohol-induced disinhibition are greater in adolescents (Breyer & Winters, 2005). Furthermore, some studies suggest that the adolescent brain requires more alcohol, marijuana, and other drugs to experience a "high," thereby heightening the risk of immediate adverse responses and long-term dependence on these drugs. Once they become addicted to alcohol or drugs, the effects of these substances on the development of the prefrontal cortex may cause adolescents to lose the ability to judge the value of non-drug rewards, such as grades (Goldstein & Volkow, 2002). For this reason, alcohol and drugs represent enormous threats to a teenager's developmental pathway—yet another reason for parents to be vigilant in monitoring their adolescent children's activities and supporting their development in positive ways. ⊙ Watch at **MyDevelopmentLab**

⊙ **Watch** the **Video** *Teen Drinking Test* at **MyDevelopmentLab**

**SMOKING** Sensation-seeking seems to be less important in tobacco use. Surveys suggest that 11% of U.S. adolescents are regular smokers, and 44% have tried smoking (Johnston, O'Malley, Bachman, & Schulenberg, 2010). Smoking rates have dropped considerably since the mid-1970s, when about 30% of older teenagers were regular smokers. Researchers argue that, thanks to public education campaigns and the inclusion of antismoking information in school curricula, more teenagers are aware of the health consequences of smoking than in earlier cohorts. Moreover, many teens report that they oppose smoking because of its possible effect on their attractiveness to potential romantic partners. ⊙ Watch at **MyDevelopmentLab**

⊙ **Watch** the **Video** *Smoking* at **MyDevelopmentLab**

Peer influence plays an important role in teen smoking. When a nonsmoking teenager begins associating with a cohesive group of adolescents among whom smoking is a prominent behavior and a sign of group membership, he is likely to take up the habit too. In fact, some developmentalists advise parents that if their teen child's friends smoke, especially close friends and romantic partners with whom the child spends a lot of time, parents should probably assume that their child smokes as well (Holliday, Rothwell, & Moore, 2010).

Moreover, the period between ages 15 and 17 seems to be the time during which a teenager is most susceptible to peer influences with regard to smoking (West, Sweeting, & Ecob, 1999). Clearly, then, by monitoring the friends of their 15- to 17-year-olds and discouraging them from associating with smokers, parents may help prevent their teens from smoking (Mott, Crowe, Richardson, & Flay, 1999). ◉ Watch at **MyDevelopmentLab**

◉ **Watch** the **Video** Cognitive Dissonance: Need to Justify Our Actions at **MyDevelopmentLab**

Parental influence is important, too—a pattern that is especially clear for mothers and daughters (Kandel & Wu, 1995). When an adult stops smoking, the likelihood that her children will smoke decreases. Thus, another way to prevent teen smoking is to encourage parents to give up the habit. In addition, having a family rule against substance use—including drugs, alcohol, and tobacco—has a lot more influence on teenagers' decisions about using such substances than most parents think (Abdelrahman, Rodriguez, Ryan, French, & Weinbaum, 1998; Mott et al., 1999). Similarly, teens who view smoking as morally wrong are less likely to smoke than peers who do not think of smoking as a moral issue (Taylor et al., 1999). Thus, parents who think tobacco use is morally wrong should discuss their beliefs with their children.

## Mortality

◀----------- **Learning Objective 4.19**
What are the major causes of death among children and teenagers?

Those of us who live in countries with relatively low rates of infant and childhood mortality are accustomed to thinking of childhood as a basically healthy time. Yet worldwide, over 10% of children die before age 5; in many countries, the rate is higher than 20% (Public Health Policy Advisory Board, 2001). In less developed countries, the most common cause of death is diarrhea, confounded by malnutrition (Dillingham & Guerrant, 2004). In contrast, the leading cause of children's deaths in the United States is accidents, particularly motor vehicle accidents (Hoyert, Kung, & Smith, 2005).

Happily, the rate of childhood deaths in the United States has been declining for the past six decades (Kochanek et al., 2011), suggesting that, as a society, we have begun to control at least some of the causes of mortality, particularly through the use of car seats, seat belts, and bicycle helmets. However, the United States continues to have wide ethnic variation in mortality rates among children. African American children—especially African American boys—have the highest death rates, primarily because of much higher rates of accidents and homicides; Asian American children have the lowest rates, with White American children falling in between (Kochanek et al., 2011).

During the teen years, accidents continue to be the most frequent cause of death in most groups in the United States. However, among African Americans, homicide surpasses accidents as the leading cause of death after age 15 (Child Trends Data Bank, 2011). The ratio of African American to White teen girls who die as a result of homicide is almost as high, although homicide rates are a great deal lower among females than among males across all ethnic groups. Suicide and accident rates are lower among African American teens than in other ethnic groups (CDC, 2009). And deaths due to disease occur about as often among African Americans as among other teens. However, the very high incidence of homicide deaths raises the overall mortality rates for African American adolescents higher than that of teens in other groups.

## THINK CRITICALLY

- In this chapter you learned that boys develop fine motor skills at a slower pace than girls do. How do you think this sex difference affects boys' experiences in school?
- What would you say to the parent of an overweight child who said she believed that her son was just carrying some "baby fat" that he was sure to outgrow later in life?

## CONDUCT YOUR OWN RESEARCH

Studies of dieting behavior have shown that school-aged and teen girls are five or six times as likely as boys to have dieted at least ten times in the past year. Try asking about 20 male and 20 female students how many times they have deliberately tried to lose weight in the past year. Compare your findings to sex differences in dieting rates among children and teenagers. Develop a theory to explain any age differences that you find.

## The Brain and Nervous System

**4.1** **What are the major growth spurts in the brain?**
The brain develops in spurts. Several short spurts occur in the first years, followed by longer periods of growth at about ages 4, 6, 10, 13, and 17.

**4.2** **What are synaptogenesis and pruning?**
In most parts of the brain, synaptic development (synaptogenesis) reaches its first peak between 12 and 24 months, after which there is an eliminating (pruning) of unnecessary synapses. Periods of synaptic growth followed by pruning of redundant pathways continue to occur throughout childhood and adolescence.

**4.3** **How does the process of myelination influence brain function?**
Myelination of nerve fibers occurs rapidly in the early years but continues throughout childhood and adolescence. Myelination increases the efficiency of neural transmission. It is a gradual process; only the structures that are needed to support basic life functions are myelinated at birth. Brain structures that are critical to memory and other forms of complex information processing become myelinated later in childhood.

**4.4** **What are the milestones of the lateralization process?**
Significant changes in brain lateralization happen in early childhood. Some aspects of language function are lateralized. Others are not lateralized until the end of early childhood. Object perception is lateralized in early childhood, but complex spatial perception is not lateralized until age 8. Handedness is weakly related to brain lateralization, but the association between the two is poorly understood at the present time.

## Size, Shape, and Skills

**4.5** **What patterns of growth are evident in childhood and adolescence?**
Changes in height and weight are rapid during the first 2 years and then level off to a steady pace until adolescence, when a sharp growth spurt occurs.

**4.6** **In what ways do bones, muscles, and fat change?**
Bones increase in number in some joints (e.g., the wrist) but decrease in quantity in others (e.g., the skull). Bone hardening, or ossification, contributes to development of motor skills. Muscle tissue increases primarily in density and length of fibers, with a much larger increase at adolescence for boys than for girls. Fat cells are added in the early years and then again rapidly at adolescence, in this case more for girls than for boys.

**4.7** **How does children's ability to use their bodies change?**
Children of 6 or 7 have confident use of most gross motor skills, although there are refinements still to come; fine motor skills needed for many school tasks are not fully developed until sometime in the elementary school years.

**4.7a** **In what ways does the use of handheld electronic devices influence fine motor development?**
Some children who spend a lot of time using handheld electronic devices such as video games and cell phones develop painful repetitive strain injuries to their fingers, hands, and wrists. These injuries are painful and can interfere with fine motor development.

## The Endocrine and Reproductive Systems

**4.8** **What are the contributions of the various hormones to physical development?**
The physical changes of adolescence are triggered by a complex set of hormonal changes, beginning at about age 8. Very large increases in gonadotrophic hormones, which in turn trigger increased production of estrogen and testosterone, are central to the process.

**4.9** **What are the sequences of pubertal changes in boys and girls?**
In girls, sexual maturity is achieved in a set of changes beginning as early as age 8 or 9. Menarche occurs relatively late in the sequence. Boys achieve sexual maturity later, with the growth spurt occurring a year or more after the start of genital changes.

**4.10** **How does the timing of puberty affect teens' development?**
Variations in the rate of pubertal development have some psychological effects. In general, children whose physical development is markedly earlier or later than they expect or desire show more negative effects than do those whose development is "on time."

## Sexual Behavior in Adolescence

**4.11** What are the ethnic, social, and academic factors that predict early sexual behavior?

Sexual activity among teens has increased in recent decades in the United States. Compared to teens who delay sexual activity until leaving high school, teens who begin sexual activity earlier are less interested in school and more likely to come from poorer families or from families in which sexual activity is condoned, more likely to use alcohol, and more likely to have been abused.

**4.12** Which sexually transmitted diseases are common among sexually active teens?

Adolescents in the United States suffer from a variety of sexually transmitted diseases. The most common STDs among teens are chlamydia and the human papilloma virus (HPV). Most adults support sex education programs to combat the spread of STDs, but there is no consensus regarding the effectiveness of various approaches.

**4.13** What are the factors associated with pregnancy in adolescence?

The risk factors for teen pregnancy include early sexual activity, a low level of parental education, coming from a single-parent home, and being the daughter of a woman who gave birth in adolescence. Long-term consequences for girls who bear children during adolescence are negative on average, although a significant minority of such girls are able to overcome their early disadvantages.

**4.14** In what ways are gay, lesbian, bisexual, and transgendered teens different from and similar to their peers?

Research suggests that both heredity and environment contribute to the development of sexual orientation. Sexual attraction emerges in the early teens for both heterosexual and homosexual teens. Some gay and lesbian teens experiment with both same- and opposite-sex relationships before settling on a homosexual identity. Transgendered teens are those whose psychological gender does not match their biological sex. The cause of transgenderism is unknown, but prenatal hormones may be a factor.

## Health and Wellness

**4.15** What are the health needs and concerns of children and adolescents?

Like infants, older children benefit from regular medical check-ups. Many immunizations are required for initial and continued school enrollment. Acute illnesses are a normal part of children's early lives, and accidents are fairly common. Children of all ages need regular check-ups and immunizations.

**4.15a** What steps can parents take to minimize bedtime conflicts?

To minimize bedtime conflicts, parents should stick to daily routines, set a regular bedtime, discontinue naps, establish a bedtime routine, and provide the child with a transitional object such as a stuffed animal.

**4.15b** What are the causes and consequences of child abuse and neglect?

The risks of abuse and neglect increases when families are under stress and when parents are unfamiliar with non-physical ways of disciplining children. Parental depression, substance abuse, and lack of social support are additional contributing factors. Children who are abused may develop post-traumatic stress disorder. They may also exhibit developmental delays.

**4.16** In what ways does excessive weight gain threaten the immediate and future health of children and adolescents?

Excessive weight gain is a pattern in which children gain more weight in a year than is appropriate for their height, age, and sex. If a child gains excessive amounts of weight over a number of years, she is at risk of having weight problems and a number of serious health problems in adulthood.

**4.16a** What is repetitive strain injury (RSI) of the hand, and how can it be prevented?

RSI of the hand can develop as a result of using devices such as video-game controllers and computer mice for prolonged periods. It causes pain and other symptoms. Parents can reduce the chances that children will develop RSI by limiting the amount of time that they spend using electronic devices and following other preventive recommendations of hand therapists.

**4.17** How does poverty affect children's health?

Virtually all forms of physical disability, chronic illness, acute illness, and accidents are more frequent among children living in poverty. Explanations focus on limited access to health care and on more dangerous home and neighborhood situations among the poor, as well as on the effects of parental behaviors such as smoking and substance abuse on children's health.

**4.18** How do psychologists explain risky behavior in adolescence?

Increases in sensation-seeking in adolescence may be caused by changes in the brain. Peer influences and the desire to establish autonomy may also be contributing factors. Sensation-seeking behaviors (e.g., driving too fast) are a significant health risk for this age group. Tobacco, alcohol, and drug use are additional risks for some teens.

**4.19** What are the major causes of death among children and teenagers?

After early infancy, mortality rates are low among children, with most deaths being due to accidents. Among teens, homicide is a significant cause of death, especially for African American males.

# KEY TERMS

association areas (p. 85)
BMI-for-age (p. 105)
body mass index (BMI) (p. 104)
bone age (p. 89)
cerebral cortex (p. 82)
corpus callosum (p. 86)
endocrine glands (p. 92)
excessive weight gain (p. 104)
fontanel (p. 89)
gonadotrophic hormones (p. 92)
growth curve (p. 88)

handedness (p. 87)
hippocampus (p. 85)
lateralization (p. 86)
medulla (p. 82)
menarche (p. 93)
midbrain (p. 82)
motor development (p. 90)
myelination (p. 85)
neurotransmitters (p. 84)
obese (p. 105)
ossification (p. 89)

overweight (p. 105)
pituitary gland (p. 92)
plasticity (p. 84)
prefrontal cortex (PFC) (p. 83)
pruning (p. 84)
puberty (p. 92)
relative right-left orientation
    (p. 86)
reticular formation (p. 85)
secular trend (p. 94)
selective attention (p. 85)

sensation-seeking (p. 108)
sexually transmitted diseases
    (STDs) (p. 98)
severely obese (p. 105)
socioeconomic status (SES)
    (p. 107)
spatial cognition (p. 87)
spatial perception (p. 86)
synaptogenesis (p. 84)

# 5

# Perceptual Development

As Julio's school bus drove the familiar route from school to home, the kindergartner thought about how proud he was of himself for learning to recite the Pledge of Allegiance. His kindergarten class had worked on it for weeks, and he couldn't wait to get home and recite it for his mother. When the bus pulled to a stop in front of Julio's family's apartment building, he bounded out of the door and said to his waiting mother, 'Mama, I can say the whole pledge. Wanna hear it?"

**nativism** The view that perceptual abilities are inborn.

**empiricism** The view that perceptual abilities are learned.

Julio's mother answered, "Sure, but let's wait until we're inside."

Once inside the apartment, Julio put his backpack down on the sofa and squared his shoulders, clearing his throat as he straightened his shirt a bit. He beamed with pride as he began:

"I pledge allegiance to the flag of the newnited steaks of America and to the republic . . ."

When Julio finished, his mother applauded and praised him, but she felt compelled to correct his errors. "That's wonderful, son. I think it could still use a little more practice. For one thing, it's '*united*', not '*new*nited'," she said.

"What's 'united'?" Julio asked, looking puzzled.

"It means separate things are joined into one, like when you put a puzzle together and the pieces make one big picture," his mother replied.

"Oh, I get it . . . 'united,'" Julio said, trying out the new word.

Julio's mother carefully explained each word that he had misunderstood in the pledge and helped him practice reciting it until he could say it perfectly.

We have all heard children make errors like Julio's, and most of us find them to be endearing. You should recall from Chapter 3 that *sensation* is the process of taking in raw sensory information, and *perception* is the process of giving meaning to that information. To put it differently, sensory input comes into the brain from the outside, and we use information that is already stored in the brain to make sense of it. In Julio's case, he was unfamiliar with the word "united," so he connected the sensory information contained in the "ew" sound to a word that he did know, "new." Thus, for Julio, "united" became "newnited."

Julio's mother was able to explain the meanings of the words in the pledge so that he could properly perceive them. But how does the environment explain to babies what they need to know to give meaning to what they see, hear, smell, taste, and feel? As you will learn, some developmentalists argue that babies acquire such knowledge through observing and acting on the world. Others say that there are a few basic perceptual mechanisms that are present in the brain at birth. In this chapter, you will read about this debate, and you will learn what researchers on both sides have discovered about infants' and young children's ability to make sense of the world.

## Thinking about Perceptual Development

The study of perceptual development has been significant because it has been a key battleground in the dispute about nature versus nurture—though theorists who study perceptual development refer instead to the contrast between *nativism* and *empiricism*. **Nativism** is the view that most perceptual abilities are inborn. **Empiricism** argues that these skills are learned. This issue has been so central in studies of perception that researchers have focused almost all their attention on young infants; only by observing infants can they observe the organism when it is relatively uninfluenced by specific experience (Bornstein, Arterberry, & Mash, 2011).

**Learning Objective 5.1** - - - - - - - - - - - ➤
What are the three approaches to studying infants' perceptual skills?

## Ways of Studying Early Perceptual Skills

It took a while for psychologists to figure out how to study infants' perceptual skills. Babies can't talk and can't respond to ordinary questions, so how were researchers to decipher just what they could see, hear, or discriminate? Eventually, clever researchers figured out three basic methods for "asking" a baby about what he experiences. With the *preference technique*, devised by Robert Fantz (1956), the baby is simply shown two pictures or two objects, and the researcher keeps track of how long the baby looks at each one. If many infants shown the same pair of pictures consistently look longer at one picture than the other, this result not only indicates that babies see some difference between the two but also may reveal something about the kinds of objects or pictures that capture babies' attention. 👁 **Watch** at **MyDevelopmentLab**

Another strategy takes advantage of the processes of habituation and dishabituation you learned about in Chapter 3. Researchers first present a baby with a particular sight or sound over and over until he habituates—that is, until he stops looking at it or showing interest in it. Then experimenters present another sight or sound or object that is slightly different from the original one and watch to see if the baby shows renewed interest (dishabituation). If the baby does show renewed interest, they know he perceives the slightly changed sight or sound as "different" in some way from the original.

The third option is to use the principles of operant conditioning described in Chapter 1. For example, an infant might be trained to turn her head when she hears a particular sound, using the sight of an interesting moving toy as a reinforcement. After the learned response is well established, the experimenter can vary the sound in some systematic way to see whether the baby still turns her head.

*Success! The spoon is in the mouth! At 1 year, Genevieve isn't very skillful yet, but she is already able to coordinate the perceptual and motor skills involved in this complex task at least a bit.*

## Explanations of Perceptual Development

We noted earlier that the study of perception, more than any other topic in developmental psychology except perhaps intelligence, has been dominated by questions of nature versus nurture, or *nativism* versus *empiricism*. Certainly there are other theoretical issues worthy of study, but given the importance of the historical argument between the nativists and the empiricists, it's worthwhile to take a closer look at current understanding of this question about perceptual development.

**ARGUMENTS FOR NATIVISM**   It is not hard to find strong arguments for a nativist position on perceptual development. As researchers have become more and more clever in devising ways to test infants' perceptual skills, they have found more and more skills already present in newborns or very young infants: Newborns have good hearing, poor but adequate eyesight, and excellent touch and taste perception. They have at least some color vision and at least a rudimentary ability to locate the source of sounds around them. More impressive still, they are capable of making quite sophisticated discriminations from the earliest days of life, including being able to identify their mothers by sight, smell, or sound.

Newborn or very young babies also do not have to be taught what to look at. As you will learn later in the chapter, there are "rules" for looking, listening, and touching that can be detected at birth. Furthermore, studies on babies' object understanding point to the strong possibility that other "assumptions," or biases about the way the world is organized, may also be built-in.

The fact that the "rules" seem to change with age can also be explained in nativist terms, since the nervous system is undergoing rapid maturation during the early months of life. Furthermore, these rule changes seem to occur in bursts. One such set of changes seems to occur at about 2 to 3 months, when infants appear to shift away from focusing their eyes on contours or edges and toward more detailed visual analysis of objects or figures. At about the same age, a baby becomes able to track objects smoothly. Another shift seems to occur at about 4 months, when a whole host of discrimination skills, including depth perception and coordination of auditory and visual information, first become evident.

Finally, we can find support for a nativist position in comparisons of the perceptual development of babies born on time to those born post-term. In one classic study, Yonas (1981) compared the response of two groups of 6-week-old babies: a group of normal-term babies and a group of babies born 3 to 4 weeks late. Both sets of infants were tested for depth perception using the method of looming objects. Yonas found that the postterm infants showed more consistent reactions to the looming objects, even though both groups had had precisely

◄-----------**Learning Objective 5.2**
What are the arguments for the nativist and empiricist views of perceptual development?

👁 **Watch** the **Video** *Perception* at **MyDevelopmentLab**

the same number of weeks of experience with objects since birth. Thus, it looks as if it is maturational age, and not experience, that matters in this case, which strengthens a nativist, or biological, position.

**ARGUMENTS FOR EMPIRICISM**   On the other hand, however, we can find a great deal of evidence from research with other species that some minimum level of experience is necessary to support the development of the perceptual systems—the pattern of environmental effect Aslin calls *maintenance* (see Figure 1.1 on page 7). For example, animals deprived of light show deterioration of the whole visual system and a consequent decrease in perceptual abilities (Hubel & Weisel, 1963). Likewise, animals deprived of auditory stimuli display delayed or no development of auditory perceptual skills (Dammeijer, Schlundt, Chenault, Manni, & Anteunis, 2002).

It is also possible to find support for the negative version of Aslin's facilitation effect: Infants lacking sufficient perceptual stimulation may develop more slowly. Wayne Dennis's study of orphanage babies in Iran (1960) illustrates this possibility. The infants who didn't have a chance to look at things, to explore objects with hands and eyes and mouth, and who were deprived of the opportunity to move around freely were behind their peers in the development of both perceptual and motor skills.

Attunement may also occur. Evidence from studies of other species suggests that animals that are completely deprived of visual experiences in the early months of life never develop the same degree of depth perception as do those with full visual experience (Gottlieb, 1976b). The ability to integrate information from different senses also depends on early experience. For instance, you have a good idea about what a particular fabric feels like just by looking at it. That's because of experiences you have had in which you have used both vision and your sense of touch to take in information about fabrics. So, when you see different kinds of fabrics, your brain can make an educated guess about what they feel like without actually touching them. Studies with primates show that the capacity to create links among the various senses fails to develop unless information that requires multiple sensory modalities is present in the environment in the first few months after birth (Batterson, Rose, Yonas, Grant, & Sackett, 2008).

**INTEGRATING THE NATIVIST AND EMPIRICIST POSITIONS**   We can best understand the development of perceptual skills by thinking of it as the result of an interaction between inborn and experiential factors. The relationship between the built-in process and the role of the environment is a little like the difference between a computer's hardware and its software. The perceptual hardware (specific neural pathways, rules for examining the world, a bias toward searching for patterns, and the like) may be preprogrammed, while the software (the program that governs the child's response to a particular real environment) depends on specific experience. A child is able to make visual discriminations between people or among objects within the first few days or weeks of life. That's built into the hardware. The specific discriminations she learns and the number of separate objects she learns to recognize, however, will depend on her experience. She is initially able to discriminate all the sound contrasts that exist in any spoken language, but the specific sound contrasts she eventually focuses on and the actual language she learns depend on the language she hears. The basic system is thus adapted to the specific environment in which the child finds herself. A perfect example of this, of course, is the newborn's ability to discriminate her mother's face from a very similar woman's face. Such a discrimination must be the result of experience, yet the capacity to make the distinction must be built in. Thus, as is true of virtually all dichotomous theoretical disputes, both sides are correct. Both nature and nurture are involved.

## Sensory Skills

When developmentalists study sensory skills, they are asking just what information the sensory organs receive. Does the structure of the eye permit infants to see color? Are the structure of the ear and the cortex such that a very young infant can discriminate among different pitches? The common theme running through all of what you will read about sensory skills in this section is that newborns and young infants have far more sensory capacity than physicians or psychologists thought even as recently as a few decades ago. Perhaps because babies' motor skills are so obviously poor, we assumed that their sensory skills were equally poor. But we were wrong.

## Seeing

Several decades ago, most medical textbooks stated that newborn infants were blind. Now we know that the newborn has poorer visual skills than older children but is quite definitely not blind.

**VISUAL ACUITY**   In adults, the usual standard for **visual acuity**—how well one can see—is 20/20 vision. If you have 20/20 vision, you can see and identify something that is 20 feet away that the average person can also see at 20 feet. A person with 20/100 vision, in contrast, has to be as close as 20 feet to see something that the average person can see from 100 feet. In other words, the higher the second number, the poorer the person's visual acuity. At birth, an infant's visual acuity is in the range from 20/200 to 20/400, but it improves rapidly during the first year as a result of all the swift changes occurring in the brain described in Chapter 4, including myelination, dendritic development, and pruning. Most infants reach the level of 20/20 vision by about 6 months of age (Lewis, 2011).

**TRACKING OBJECTS IN THE VISUAL FIELD**   When an infant tries to get a spoon in her mouth, one of the things she needs to do is keep her eyes on her hand or the spoon as she moves it toward herself. This process of following a moving object with your eyes is called **tracking**. Because a newborn infant can't yet move independently, a lot of her experiences with objects are with things that move toward her or away from her. If she is to have any success in recognizing objects, she has to be able to keep her eyes on them as they move; she must be able to track.

Studies by Richard Aslin (1987) and others show that tracking is initially fairly inefficient but improves quite rapidly. Infants younger than 2 months show some tracking for brief periods if the target is moving very slowly, but a shift occurs somewhere around 6 to 10 weeks, and babies' tracking becomes skillful rather quickly. You can see the change graphically in Figure 5.1, taken from a study by Aslin.

**COLOR VISION**   Researchers have established that the types of cells in the eye necessary for perceiving red and green (the cones) are clearly present by 1 month, perhaps at birth; the cones required for perceiving blue are probably present by then as well (Bornstein, Arterberry, & Mash, 2011). Thus, infants can and do see and discriminate among various colors (Pereverzeva, Hui-Lin Chien, Palmer, & Teller, 2002).

Taken together, research findings on tracking and color vision certainly do not support the notion that an infant is blind at birth. While it is true that the infant's visual acuity is initially poor, it improves rapidly, and other visual capacities are remarkably well developed early on. There are also some interesting hints that some kind of "shifting of gears" may take place at approximately 2 months; a number of skills, including the scanning of objects and tracking, improve incrementally at about that age (Bronson, 1994). But we don't yet know whether such changes are the result of such neurological changes as the rapid proliferation of synapses and the growth of dendrites, of changes in the eye itself, or perhaps of the child's experience.

## Hearing and Other Senses

As you learned in Chapter 2, babies can hear long before they are born. However, like vision, hearing improves considerably in the early months of life. The other senses follow a similar course.

**visual acuity**   How well one can see.

**tracking**   Following a moving object with the eyes.

◄ - - - - - - - - - - - - **Learning Objective 5.3**
How do infants' visual skills change across the first months of life?

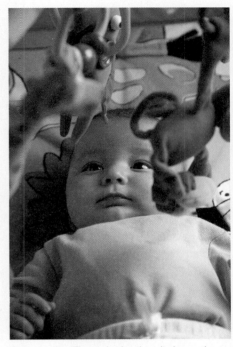

At 2 months, Eleanor's visual acuity is good enough that she can clearly see the colorful mobile hanging above her crib.

6-week-old          10-week-old

**FIGURE 5.1** Infants' Tracking Skills
The red line in each figure shows the trajectory of the moving line that babies tried to follow with their eyes in Aslin's experiment. The black line represents one baby's eye movements at 6 weeks and again at 10 weeks. At 6 weeks, the baby more or less followed the line, but not smoothly. By 10 weeks, the same baby's tracking skill was remarkably smooth and accurate.
(*Source:* Aslin, Richard N., "Motor Aspects of Visual Development in Infancy," *Handbook of Infant Perception: Vol. 1, From Sensation to Perception*, P. Salapatek and L. Cohen, eds. © 1987 by Academic Press. Adapted by permission.)

◄ - - - - - - - - - - - - **Learning Objective 5.4**
How do infants' senses of hearing, smell, taste, touch, and motion compare to those of older children and adults?

**AUDITORY ACUITY**    Although children's hearing improves up to adolescence, newborns' **auditory acuity**—how well they hear—is actually better than their visual acuity. Research evidence suggests that within the general range of pitch and loudness of the human voice, newborns hear nearly as well as adults do. Only with high-pitched sounds is their auditory acuity less than that of an adult; high-pitched sounds must be louder for a newborn to hear them than for older children or adults (Werner & Gillenwater, 1990).  👁—|**Watch** at **MyDevelopmentLab**

**DETECTING LOCATIONS**    Another basic auditory skill that exists at birth and improves with age is the ability to determine the location of a sound. Because your two ears are separated from one another, sounds arrive at one ear slightly before the other, which allows you to judge location. Only if a sound comes from a source equidistant from the two ears (along the midline) does this system fail. In this case, the sound arrives at the two ears at the same time and you know only that the sound is somewhere on your midline. Newborns can judge at least the general direction from which a sound has come because they turn their heads in roughly the right direction toward some sound. More specific location of sounds, however, is not well developed at birth. For example, Barbara Morrongiello has observed babies' reactions to sounds played at the midline and then sounds coming from varying degrees away from the midline. Among infants 2 months old, it takes a shift of about 27 degrees off midline before the baby shows a changed response; among 6-month-olds, only a 12-degree shift is needed, while by 18 months, discrimination of a 4-degree shift is possible—nearly the skill level seen in adults (Morrongiello, 1988; Morrongiello, Fenwick, & Chance, 1990).

**SMELLING AND TASTING**    Babies' senses of smell and taste have been studied much less than other senses. However, we do have some basic knowledge about them. As in adults, the two senses are intricately related—that is, if you cannot smell for some reason (for example, when you have a cold), your taste sensitivity is also significantly reduced. Smell is registered in the mucous membranes of the nose, which can discriminate nearly unlimited variations. The cells of these membranes are present very early on in prenatal development, even before the embryonic phase is complete (Kimura et al., 2009). Thus, babies come into the world with the equipment they need for smell and are apparently able to use the sense of smell to learn about the world even before they are born. Researchers have found that newborns recognize the odor of their own amniotic fluid and that babies as young as 1 week old can discriminate between their mother's and other women's odors (Bornstein, Arterberry, & Mash, 2011).

Taste is detected by the taste buds on the tongue, which register four basic tastes—sweet, sour, bitter, and salty—and a fifth taste called *umami*—the taste elicited by glutamate, an amino acid in meat, fish, and legumes. Newborns appear to respond differentially to the four basic tastes (Bornstein, Arterberry, & Mash, 2011). Some of the clearest demonstrations of this fact come from an elegantly simple set of early studies by Jacob Steiner (Ganchrow, Steiner, & Daher, 1983; Steiner, 1979). Newborn infants who had never been fed were photographed before and after flavored water was put into their mouths. By varying the flavor, Steiner could determine whether the babies reacted differently to different tastes. As you can see in Figure 5.2, babies responded quite differently to sweet, sour, and bitter flavors. Newborns can also taste umami. Generally, they express pleasure when researchers test them for sensitivity to this flavor (Nicklaus, Boggio, & Issanchou, 2005). Some researchers speculate that newborns' preferences for umami-flavored and sweet foods explain their attraction to breast milk, a substance that is naturally rich in sugars and glutamates.

**SENSES OF TOUCH AND MOTION**    The infant's senses of touch and motion may well be the best developed of all. The research you read about in Chapter 3 on the effects of massage on preterm infants illustrates that even the youngest infants are sensitive to touch (Dieter, Field, Hernandez-Reif, Emory, & Redzepi, 2003). Motion perception is clearly present even in the youngest infants, although a considerable degree of fine-tuning takes place over the first year of life (Bosworth & Birch, 2005).

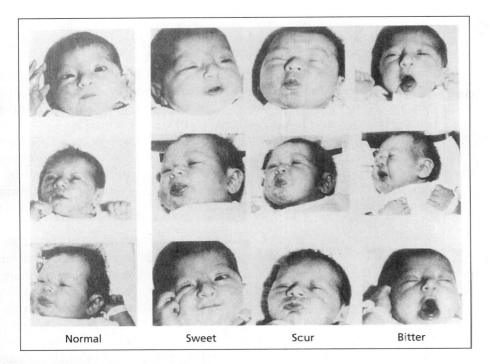

| Normal | Sweet | Sour | Bitter |

**FIGURE 5.2** Newborns' Responses to Tastes

These are three of the newborns Steiner observed in his experiments on taste response. The left-hand column shows each baby's normal expression; the remaining columns show the change in expression when they were given sweet, sour, and bitter tastes. What is striking is how similar the expressions are for each taste.

(*Source:* Steiner, J. E., "Human Facial Expressions in Response to Taste and Smell Stimulation," in *Advances in Child Development and Behavior*, Vol. 13, H. W. Reese and L. P. Lipsitt, eds. © 1979 by Academic Press. By permission.)

## Perceptual Skills

In studies of perceptual skills, developmentalists are asking what the individual does with the sensory information—how it is interpreted or combined. Researchers have found that very young infants are able to make remarkably fine discriminations among sounds, sights, and physical sensations, and they pay attention to and respond to patterns, not just to individual events.

### Looking

One important question to ask about visual perception is whether the infant perceives his environment in the same way as older children and adults. Can he judge how far away an object is by looking at it? Does he visually scan an object in an orderly way? Developmentalists believe that infants' patterns of looking at objects tell a great deal about what they are trying to gain from visual information.

**DEPTH PERCEPTION** One of the perceptual skills that has been most studied is depth perception. You need this ability any time you reach for something or decide whether you have room to make a left turn before an oncoming car gets to you. Similarly, an infant needs to be able to judge depth in order to perform all kinds of simple tasks, including judging how far away an object is so that he can reach for it, or how far it is to the floor if he has ideas about crawling off the edge of the couch, or how to aim a spoon toward a bowl of chocolate pudding.

It is possible to judge depth using any (or all) of three rather different kinds of information: First, *binocular cues* involve both eyes, each of which receives a slightly different visual image of an object; the closer the object is, the more different these two views are. In addition, information from the muscles of the eyes also tells you something about how far away

←----------- Learning Objective 5.5
How does visual perception change over the first months and years of life?

The experience of reaching for objects helps infants develop depth perception.

an object may be. Second, pictorial information, sometimes called *monocular cues*, requires input from only one eye. For example, when one object is partially in front of another one, you know that the partially hidden object is farther away—a cue called *interposition*. The relative size of two similar objects, such as telephone poles or two people you see in the distance, may also indicate that the smaller-appearing one is farther away. Linear perspective (the visual effect that makes railroad tracks seem to get closer together at a distance) is another monocular cue. Third, *kinetic cues* come from either your own motion or the motion of some object: If you move your head, objects near you seem to move more than objects farther away (a phenomenon called *motion parallax*). Similarly, if you see some object moving, such as a person walking across a street or a train moving along a track, the closer it is, the more distance it appears to cover in a given time.

How early can an infant judge depth, and which of these cues does he use? This is still an active area of research, so scientists do not have any final answers. The best conclusion at the moment seems to be that kinetic information is used first, perhaps by about 3 months of age; binocular cues are used beginning at about 4 months; and pictorial (monocular) cues are used last, perhaps at 5 to 7 months (Bornstein et al., 1992; Frichtel & Lécuyer, 2006).

In a remarkably clever early study, Eleanor Gibson and Richard Walk (1960) devised an apparatus called a visual cliff. You can see from the photo that it consists of a large glass table with a checkerboard pattern immediately below the glass; on the other side—the "cliff" side—the checkerboard is several feet below the glass. A baby placed on the apparatus could judge depth by several means, but it is primarily kinetic information that would be useful, since the baby in motion would see the nearer surface move more than the farther surface. If a baby has no depth perception, she should be equally willing to crawl on either side of the table, but if she can judge depth, she should be reluctant to crawl out on the "cliff" side.  ⊙ Watch at **MyDevelopmentLab**

⊙ **Watch** the **Video** *Eleanor Gibson, Richard Walk, and The Visual Cliff* at **MyDevelopmentLab**

⊙ **Simulate** the **Experiment** *The Visual Cliff* at **MyDevelopmentLab**

Since an infant had to be able to crawl in order to be tested in Gibson and Walk's procedure, the babies they studied were all 6 months old or older. Most of these infants did not crawl out on the cliff side but were quite willing to crawl out on the shallow side. In other words, 6-month-old babies have depth perception.  ⊙ Simulate at **MyDevelopmentLab**

However, the development of depth perception, or *stereopsis*, as the mature form of this visual perceptual skill is called, is far from complete at age 6 months. In order to exhibit adult levels of stereopsis, children's brains must be able to fully fuse the images they receive from the eyes into a single image. This process, called *binocular fusion*, develops over the first 10 years of life (Gabbard, 2011). The attainment of binocular fusion, and the improvements in stereopsis that accompany it, is the main reason that children's throwing and catching skills improve markedly in later childhood.

*In an experiment using a "visual cliff" apparatus, like the one used by Gibson and Walk, mom tries to entice her baby out onto the "cliff" side. But because the infant can perceive depth, he fears that he will fall if he comes toward her, so he stays put, looking concerned.*

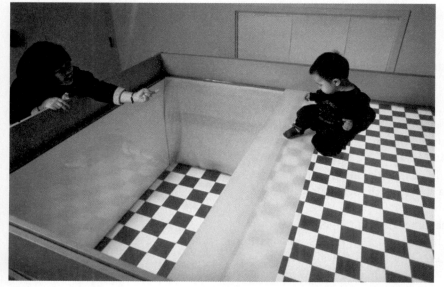

**WHAT BABIES LOOK AT**    In the first 2 months, a baby's visual attention is guided by a search for meaningful patterns (Bornstein, Arterberry, & Nash, 2011). Babies scan the world around them—not very smoothly or skillfully, to be sure, but nonetheless regularly, even in the dark. This general scanning continues until they come to a sharp light/dark contrast, which typically signals the edge of some object. Once she finds such an edge, a baby stops searching and moves her eyes back and forth across and around the edge. Thus, the initial rule seems to be: Scan till you find an edge and then examine the edge. Motion also captures a baby's attention at this age, so she will look at things that move as well as things with a noticeable light/dark contrast.

These rules seem to change between 2 and 3 months of age, perhaps because by then the cortex has developed more fully. At about this time, the baby's attention seems to shift from where an object is to what an object is. To put this another way, the baby seems to move from a strategy designed primarily for finding things to a strategy designed primarily for identifying things. Babies this age begin to scan rapidly across an entire figure rather than concentrating on edges. As a result, they spend more time looking at the internal features of some object or array of objects and are thus better able to identify the objects.

What is amazing about this shift at about 3 months is the degree of detail infants seem to be able to take in and respond to. They notice whether two pictures are placed horizontally or vertically, they can tell the difference between pictures with two things in them and pictures with three things in them, and they clearly notice patterns, even such apparently abstract patterns as "big thing over small thing."

One early study that illustrates this point particularly well was done by Albert and Rose Caron (1981), who used "training stimuli" in a habituation procedure. The babies were first shown a series of pictures that shared some particular relationship, such as "small over big." After the baby stopped being interested in the training stimuli (that is, after he habituated), the Carons showed him another figure (the "test stimulus") that either followed the same pattern or followed some other pattern, such as those in Figure 5.3. If the baby had really habituated to the pattern of the original pictures (small over big), he should show little interest in a picture like test stimulus A ("Ho hum, same old boring small over big thing"), but he should show renewed interest in test stimulus B ("Hey, here's something new!"). Caron and Caron found that 3- and 4-month-old children did precisely that. So even at this early age, babies find and pay attention to patterns, not just to specific stimuli.

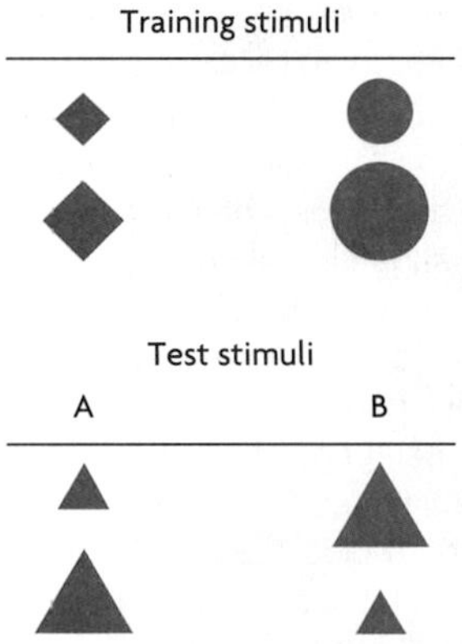

Researchers have also been interested in babies' perception of faces. Brain-imaging studies suggest that there is an area of the brain dedicated to face processing in both adults and infants as young as 3 months of age (Johnson, 2011). Moreover, among faces, babies clearly prefer some to others. They prefer attractive faces (an intriguing result discussed in *Thinking about Research* on page 124), and it now seems apparent that they prefer the mother's face from the earliest hours of life (Bushnell, 2001). Research indicates that recognition of the mother's voice directs the newborn's attention to her face (Sai, 2005). Recall from Chapter 3 that maternal voice recognition happens prenatally. After birth, once the association between the mother's voice and her face has happened, the newborn spends more time looking at her face than at other visual stimuli, setting the stage for the formation of a memory for the face.

Beyond the issue of preference, there is also the question of just what it is that babies are looking at when they scan a face. Before about 2 months of age, babies seem to look mostly at the edges of the faces (the hairline and the chin), a conclusion buttressed by the classic study by Pascalis and his colleagues (1995) that newborns could not discriminate mom's face from a stranger's if the hairline was covered. After 4 months, however, covering the hairline did not affect the baby's ability to recognize mom. In general, babies appear to begin to focus on the internal features of a face, particularly the eyes, at about 2 to 3 months.

**FIGURE 5.3** Pattern Recognition
In the Carons' study, the researchers first habituated each baby to a set of training stimuli (all "small over large" in this case). Then they showed each baby two test stimuli: one that had the same pattern as the training stimuli (A) and one that had a different pattern (B). Babies aged 3 and 4 months showed renewed interest in stimulus B but not stimulus A, indicating that they were paying attention to the pattern and not just specific stimuli.

(*Source: Pre-Term Birth and Psychological Development*, by S. Friedman and M. Sigman, "Processing of relational information as an index of infant risk," in A. J. Caron and R. F. Caron (Eds.), *Pre-Term Birth and Psychological Development*, pp. 227–228, © 1981 by Academic Press. Reprinted by permission.)

## Listening

◀-----------Learning Objective 5.6
How do infants perceive human speech and other auditory stimuli?

When we turn from looking to listening, we find similarly intriguing indications that very young infants not only make remarkably fine discriminations among individual sounds but also pay attention to patterns. Early studies established that babies as young as 1 month old can discriminate between speech sounds such as *pa* and *ba* (Trehub & Rabinovitch, 1972). Studies using conditioned head-turning responses have shown that by perhaps 6 months of age, babies can discriminate between two-syllable "words" such as *bada* and *baga* and can even respond to a syllable that is hidden inside a string of syllables, as in *tibati* or *kobako* (MacWhinney, 2011).

## Langlois's Studies of Babies' Preferences for Attractive Faces

Many studies on infant perception suggest that some perceptual rules are built-in. One such built-in rule appears to be a preference for attractive faces. In the first study in an classic series of experiments, Langlois and her colleagues (1987) tested 2- to 3-month-olds and 6- to 8-month-olds. Each baby was shown color slides of adult Caucasian women, half rated by adult judges as attractive, half rated as unattractive. On each trial, the baby saw two slides simultaneously, with each face approximately life-size, while the experimenter peeked through a hole in the screen to count the number of seconds the baby looked at each picture. Each baby saw some attractive/attractive pairs, some

unattractive/unattractive pairs, and some mixed pairs. With mixed pairs, even the 2- and 3-month-old babies consistently looked longer at the attractive faces. Several later studies, including some in which pictures of individuals of different races were used, produced similar findings (Langlois, Ritter, Roggman, Vaughn, 1991; Langlois, Roggman, Rieser-Danner, 1990).

It is hard to imagine what sort of learning experiences could account for such a preference in a 2-month-old. Instead, these findings raise the possibility that there is some inborn template for the "correct" or "most desired" shape and configuration for members of our species, and that we simply prefer those who match this template better.

### Learning Objective 5.5a
What were the findings of Langlois's classic study of infants' responses to faces that varied in attractiveness?

### CRITICAL ANALYSIS

1. If there is an inborn template that is used as a standard against which faces are compared, how might such a template affect our interactions with others?
2. How would researchers determine the degree to which attractiveness affects adults' perceptions of infants' faces? Why would such research be unable to tell us whether the concept of attractiveness is inborn?

---

Even more striking is the finding that babies are actually better at discriminating some kinds of speech sounds than adults are. Each language uses only a subset of all possible speech sounds. Japanese, for example, does not use the *l* sound that appears in English; Spanish makes a different distinction between *d* and *t* than occurs in English. It turns out that up to about 6 months of age, babies can accurately discriminate all sound contrasts that appear in any language, including sounds they do not hear in the language spoken to them. At about 6 months of age, they begin to lose the ability to distinguish pairs of vowels that do not occur in the language they are hearing; by age 1, the ability to discriminate nonheard consonant contrasts begins to fade, findings that provide powerful evidence for the influence of experience on speech perception (Dietrich, Swingley, & Werker, 2007; see *Technology and the Developing Child* on p. 125).

Some of the best evidence on this point comes from the work of Janet Werker and her colleagues (Werker, Maurer, & Yoshida, 2010). In their early studies, Werker's team tested 6- and 10-month-old infants on various consonant pairs, including one pair that is meaningful in English (*ba* versus *da*); a pair that occurs in a North American Indian language, Salish (*ki* versus *qi*); and one from Hindi, a language from the Indian subcontinent (*t.a* versus *ta*). Other infants were tested with both English and German vowel contrasts. Figure 5.4 shows the results on contrasts that do not occur in English for babies growing up in English-speaking families. You can see that at 6 months, these babies could still readily hear the differences between pairs of foreign consonants but were already losing the ability to discriminate foreign vowels. Infants aged 10 and 12 months could not readily hear either type of contrast. Similarly, Werker has found that 12-month-old Hindi infants can easily discriminate a Hindi contrast but not an English contrast. So each group of infants loses only the ability to distinguish pairs that do not appear in the language they are hearing.

Researchers have also found that babies are sensitive to the intonational and stress patterns of the speech they are listening to. For example, Anne Fernald (1993) has found that 5-month-olds will smile more when they hear

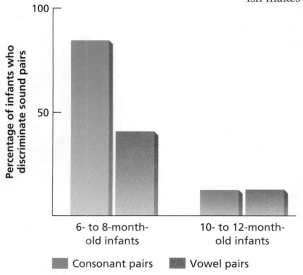

**FIGURE 5.4** Werker's Studies of Speech Perception
These data from Werker's studies are for babies growing up in English-speaking families, but she has similar results from infants in families that speak Hindi and families that speak Salish. In every case, 6-month-olds can still "hear" the distinctions between consonant pairs that do not occur in their family's language, but by 12 months that ability has largely disappeared. Discrimination of nonheard vowel pairs disappears even earlier.

(*Source:* "Listening to Speech in the First Year of Life: Experimental Influences on Phoneme Perception" by Werker and Desjardins, *Current Directions in Psychological Science*, Vol. 4, No. 3 (June 1995), p. 80, Fig. 2.)

# TECHNOLOGY AND THE DEVELOPING CHILD

## Cochlear Implants and Speech Development

A cochlear implant (CI) is a sound-receiving device that is surgically implanted behind the ear and transmits auditory information to electrodes implanted deep within the ear. Because speech production depends just as much on the brain's ability to interpret speech as it does on the ear's capacity for receiving speech sounds emitted by others, research shows that the earlier children get CIs, the more likely they are to develop normal speech (Flipsen, 2011; Flipsen & Colvard, 2006). In fact, the best results are achieved when children are implanted prior to age two (Nicholas & Geers, 2006, 2008). This is because speech perception develops in the early years of life, and in the absence of speech sounds, it doesn't develop at all. In fact, the speech of children who receive

CI treatment after the age of 7 may show no benefits whatever from the device.

The main drawback to early CI implantation is that the surgery destroys residual hearing. As a result, if CI implantation fails to bring about the desired results, the child will never be able to use conventional hearing aids. In addition, hearing impairments are difficult to diagnose in infancy. If there are doubts as to an individual child's hearing loss, surgery must wait until later in childhood when the diagnosis can be confirmed. Thus, the decision as to whether to allow a child to undergo CI surgery is never an easy one. Parents and physicians must weigh the benefits and risks associated with CIs, as well as a child's individual characteristics, to come to the best decision possible in each case.

**Learning Objective 5.6a**
How do cochlear implants affect the development of speech in children with hearing impairments?

### FIND OUT MORE

*Use your Internet search skills to answer these questions.*

1. What are the risks of CI surgery?
2. Some experts argue children with CIs should be taught sign language in addition to receiving speech therapy. What are the pros and cons of this "bilingual" approach?

---

tapes of adults saying something in a positive or approving tone than when they hear someone speaking in a negative tone, whether the words are in Italian, German, or English. By 8 months, babies demonstrate clear preferences for the language most often spoken by their mothers (MacWhinney, 2011). Even more impressive is a study showing that by 9 months of age, babies listening to English prefer to listen to words that use the typical English pattern of stress on the first syllable (such as *fal*ter, *com*et, or *gen*tle) rather than those that stress the second syllable (e.g., com*ply* or as*sign*) (Jusczyk & Hohne, 1997). Presumably, babies listening to another language would prefer listening to whatever stress pattern was typical of that language. All this research shows that very early on—from birth and perhaps even before birth—the baby is paying attention to crucial features of the language she hears, such as stress and intonation.

Pattern perception is also evident; research shows that, by 5 months of age, infants can recognize their own names (Newman, 2005). Studies that examine infants' responses to music show that babies have an uncanny ability to recognize patterns of sounds as well (Trehub, 2010 ). Infants respond to dissonant notes (i.e., tones that don't sound pleasant when played together) just as adults do (Trainor, Tsang, & Cheung, 2002). Likewise, they recognize familiar melodies, no matter what key they are played in. They also notice when a familiar melody is played on an instrument that differs from the one with which they were familiarized with the song (Trainor, Anonymous, & Tsang, 2004). Likewise, they can discriminate between songs that have different meters, such as waltzes and marches.

Interestingly, too, infants are able to recognize another universal in infant-directed singing—the distinction between play songs (e.g., "The Itsy-Bitsy Spider") and lullabies (e.g., "Rock-a-Bye Baby"). Babies respond to lullabies by turning their attention toward themselves and playing with their hands or sucking their thumbs (Rock, Trainor, & Addison, 1999). In contrast, they display externally directed responses to play songs and behave in ways that seem to encourage adults to continue singing (Rock et al., 1999). This ability to discriminate song type may arise out of the capacity to recognize the emotional characteristics of a piece of music, another aspect of musical perception that appears early in life (Adachi, Trehub, & Abe, 2004; Schmidt, Trainor, & Santesso, 2003).

**intermodal perception** Formation of a single perception of a stimulus that is based on information from two or more senses.

*At 3 weeks, this infant can already discriminate her mother's face from the face of another woman; she can also identify mom by voice and smell.*

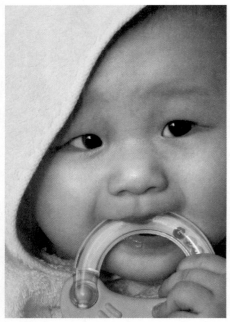

*Even though 4-month-old Leslie is not looking at this toy while she chews on it, she is nonetheless learning something about how it ought to look based on how it feels in her mouth and in her hands—an example of intermodal perception.*

# Combining Information from Several Senses

If you think about the way you receive and use perceptual information, you'll realize that you rarely have information from only one sense at a time. Ordinarily, you have both sound and sight, touch and sight, or still more complex combinations of smell, sight, touch, and sound. Psychologists have been interested in knowing how early an infant can combine such information. For example, how early can an infant integrate information from several senses, such as knowing which mouth movements go with which sounds? Even more complex, how early can a baby learn something via one sense and transfer that information to another sense (for example, at what age can a child recognize solely by feel a toy he has seen but never felt before)? This skill is usually called **intermodal perception**.

Piaget believed that intermodal perception was not present until quite late in the first year of life, after the infant had accumulated many experiences with specific objects and how they simultaneously looked, sounded, and felt. Other theorists, including the eminent perceptual psychologists James J. Gibson (1904–1979) and Eleanor J. Gibson (1910–2002), have argued that some intersensory integration or even transfer is built in at birth (Gibson, 2002). The baby then augments that inborn set of skills with specific experience with objects. Research favors the Gibsonian view: Empirical findings show that intermodal perception is possible as early as 1 month and is well developed by 6 months (Feigenson, 2011; Schweinle & Wilcox, 2004). Moreover, research comparing these skills in children born prematurely and those born at term suggests that basic maturational processes play an important role in their development (Espy et al., 2002).

Research also suggests that intermodal perception is important in infant learning. One group of researchers found that babies who habituated to a combined auditory-visual stimulus were better able to recognize a new stimulus than infants who habituated to either the auditory or the visual stimulus alone (Bahrick & Lickliter, 2000). For example, suppose you played a videotape of someone singing for one baby, played the videotape without the sound for another, and played an audio recording of the song for a third. Research suggests that the first baby would recognize a change in either the singer (visual stimulus) or the song (auditory stimulus) more quickly than either of the other two infants.

In older children, intermodal perception can be readily demonstrated. For instance, in several delightfully clever early experiments, Elizabeth Spelke showed that 4-month-old infants can connect sound rhythms with movement (1979). She showed babies two films simultaneously, one showing a toy kangaroo bouncing up and down, the other a donkey bouncing up and down, with one of the animals bouncing at a faster rate. Out of a loudspeaker located between the two films, the infant heard a tape recording of a rhythmic bouncing sound that matched the bounce pattern of one of the two animals. In this situation, babies showed a preference for looking at the film showing the bounce rate that matched the sound.

An even more striking illustration of the same basic process comes from the work of Jeffrey Pickens (1994). He showed 5-month-old babies two films side by side; each film showed a train moving along a track. Then out of a loudspeaker he played various sequences of engine sounds, such as getting gradually louder (thus appearing to come closer) or getting gradually fainter (thus appearing to be moving away). The babies in this experiment looked longer at the film of the train whose movement matched the pattern of engine sounds. That is, they appeared to have some understanding of the link between the pattern of sound and the pattern of movement—knowledge that demonstrates not only intermodal perception but also surprisingly sophisticated understanding of the accompaniments of motion.

# Ignoring Perceptual Information

Although babies are remarkably skillful at making perceptual discriminations of various kinds, they must acquire another, very different, kind of perceptual skill: the ability to ignore some kinds of perceptual data. Specifically, the child must acquire a set of rules called **perceptual constancies**.

When you see someone walking away from you, the image of the person on your retina actually becomes smaller. Yet you don't see the person getting smaller, but rather as the same size and moving farther away. When you do this, you are demonstrating **size constancy**; you are able to see the size as constant even though the retinal image has changed. Other constancies include the ability to recognize that shapes of objects are the same even though you are looking at them from different angles, called (logically enough) **shape constancy**, and the ability to recognize that colors are constant even though the amount of light or shadow on them changes, called **color constancy**.

Taken together, the several specific constancies add up to the larger concept of **object constancy**, which is the recognition that objects remain the same even when the sensory information you have about them has changed in some way. Babies begin to show signs of these constancies at 3 or 4 months of age and become more skilled over the first several years (Kav̆sek, 2002).

Shape constancy has perhaps the most obvious day-to-day relevance for a baby. She has to realize that her bottle is still her bottle even though it is turned slightly and thus presents a different shape to her eyes; she has to figure out that her toys are the same when they are in different positions. The beginnings of this understanding seem to be present by about 2 or 3 months of age. The classic study was done by Thomas Bower (1966), who first trained 2-month-old babies to turn their heads when they saw a particular rectangle. He then showed them tilted or slightly turned images of the same rectangle to see if the babies would respond to these as "the same," even though the retinal image cast by these tilted rectangles was actually a trapezoid and not a rectangle at all. Two-month-olds did indeed continue to turn their heads to these tilted and turned rectangles, showing that they had some shape constancy.

**perceptual constancies** A collection of mental rules that allow humans to perceive shape, size, and color as constant even when perceptual conditions (such as amount of light, angle of view, and the like) change.

**size constancy** The ability to see an object's size as remaining the same despite changes in size of the retinal image; a key element in size constancy is the ability to judge depth.

**shape constancy** The ability to see an object's shape as remaining the same despite changes in the shape of the retinal image; a basic perceptual constancy.

**color constancy** The ability to see the color of an object as remaining the same despite changes in illumination or shadow.

**object constancy** The general phrase describing the ability to see objects as remaining the same despite changes in sensory information about them.

**object permanence** The understanding that objects continue to exist even when they cannot be directly viewed.

## The Object Concept

Acquiring the various perceptual constancies is only part of a larger task facing the child; he must also figure out the nature of objects themselves. First of all, an infant must somehow learn to treat some combinations of stimuli as "objects" but not others, a process usually referred to as *object perception*. A still more sophisticated aspect of the infant's emerging concept of objects is the understanding that objects continue to exist even when they are out of view, an understanding usually referred to as **object permanence**.  ◉⊣Watch at **MyDevelopmentLab**

◉⊣Watch the **Video** *Hidden Elephant* at **MyDevelopmentLab**

## Object Perception

◀------------Learning Objective 5.9
What kinds of rules do infants appear to use in perceiving objects?

The most thorough and clever work on object perception in infants has been done by Elizabeth Spelke and her colleagues (Spelke & Kinzler, 2007). Spelke believes that babies are born with certain built-in assumptions about the nature of objects. One of these is the assumption that when two surfaces are connected to each other, they belong to the same object; Spelke calls this the *connected surface principle*. To study this (Spelke, 1982), she first habituated some 3-month-old babies to a series of displays of two objects other babies were habituated to the sight of one-object displays. Then the babies were shown two objects touching each other, such as two square blocks placed next to each other so that they created a rectangle. Under these conditions, the babies who had been habituated to two-object displays showed renewed interest, clearly indicating that they "saw" this as different, presumably as a single object. Babies who had seen the one-object displays during habituation showed no renewed interest. Spelke has also shown that babies as young as 2 and 3 months old are remarkably aware of the kinds of movements objects are capable of, even when the objects are out of sight. They expect an object to continue to move on its initial trajectory, and they show surprise if the object's movement violates this expectancy. They also seem to have some awareness that solid objects cannot pass through other solid objects.

In one experiment, Spelke (1991) used the procedure shown schematically in the upper part of Figure 5.5 on page 128. Two-month-old babies were repeatedly shown a series of

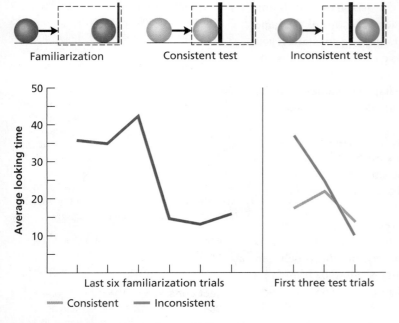

Familiarization      Consistent test      Inconsistent test

Last six familiarization trials      First three test trials

— Consistent    — Inconsistent

**FIGURE 5.5** Spelke's Classic Study of Object Perception

The top part of the figure shows a schematic version of the three conditions Spelke used. The graph below the conditions shows the actual results. You can see that the babies stopped looking at the ball and screen after a number of familiarization trials, but they showed renewed interest in the inconsistent version—a sign that the babies saw this as somehow different or surprising. The very fact that the babies found the inconsistent trial surprising is itself evidence that infants as young as 2 months have far more knowledge about objects and their behavior than most developmentalists had thought.

(*Source: Epigenesis of Mind: Essays on Biology and Cognition* by E. S. Spelke. Copyright 1991 by Taylor & Francis Group LLC-Books. Reproduced with permission of Taylor & Francis Group LLC-Books)

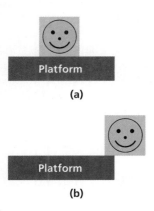

**(a)**

**(b)**

**FIGURE 5.6** Baillargeon's Study of Object Perception

Renée Baillargeon's research suggests that 2- and 3-month-old babies think that the smiling-face block will not fall under either of these conditions, but by 5 months, they realized that only the condition shown in (a) is stable. In condition (b), the block will fall.

(*Source:* "How Do Infants Learn About the Physical World?" by Baillargeon, R., *Current Directions in Psychological Science*, Vol. 3, No. 5 (October 1994), p. 134, Fig. 1.)

events like that in the "familiarization" section of the figure: A ball was rolled from the left-hand side to the right and disappeared behind a screen (the dashed line in Figure 5.5). The screen was then taken away and the baby could see that the ball was stopped against the wall on the right. After the baby got bored looking at this sequence (habituated), he or she was tested with two variations, one "consistent" and one "inconsistent." In the consistent variation, a second wall was placed behind the screen and the sequence was conducted as before, except now when the screen was removed, the ball could be seen resting up against the nearer wall. In the inconsistent variation, the ball was surreptitiously placed on the far side of the new wall. When the screen was removed, the ball was visible in this presumably impossible place. Babies in this experiment were quite uninterested in the consistent condition but showed sharply renewed interest in the inconsistent condition, as you can see in the lower part of Figure 5.5, which shows the actual results of the experiment.

Spelke is not suggesting that all of a child's knowledge of objects is built-in; she is suggesting that some rules are built-in and that others are learned through experience. Other researchers, such as Renée Baillargeon (1994, 2008), argue that basic knowledge is not built-in, but that strategies for learning are innate. According to this view, infants initially develop basic hypotheses about the way objects function—how they move, how they connect to one another. These early basic hypotheses are quite rapidly modified, based on the baby's experience with objects. For example, Baillargeon finds 2- to 3-month-old infants are already operating with a basic hypothesis that an object will fall if it isn't supported by something, but they have no notion of how much support is required. By about 5 months of age, this basic hypothesis has been refined, and they understand that the smiling-face block in the upper arrangement of Figure 5.6 (condition a) will stay supported, but the block in the bottom arrangement (condition b) will not (Baillargeon, 1994). However, developmental psychologist Leslie Cohen and his associates have conducted similar experiments with 8-month-olds, and they argue that infants respond to the stimuli used in such studies on the basis of novelty rather than because of an understanding of stable and unstable block arrangements (Cashon & Cohen, 2000). Such varying interpretations demonstrate just how difficult it is to make inferences about infants' thinking from their interactions with physical objects.

Studies have also examined the degree to which infants can make practical use of their understanding of objects and object movements. For example, 2-year-olds seem to experience difficulty when they are required to use this understanding to search for a hidden object (Kloos, Haddad, & Keen, 2006). In one study, 2-, 2.5-, and 3-year-olds were shown a display similar to that in the top portion of Figure 5.5 and responded in exactly the same way as younger infants to the consistent and inconsistent displays (Berthier, DeBlois, Poirier, Novak, & Clifton, 2000). Next, a board in which there were several doors took the place of the screen; however, the barrier protruded several inches above this board (see Figure 5.7). Across several trials, children were shown the ball rolling behind the board and were asked to open the door behind which they thought the ball would be found. Even though the children could clearly see behind which door the barrier was placed in every trial, none of the 2-year-olds and only a few of the 2.5-year-olds were able to succeed on this task, in contrast to the large majority of 3-year-olds. Developmentalists interpret such results to mean that infants gradually construct the object concept over the first 3 years of life (Mash, Novak, Berthier, & Keen, 2006).

# Object Permanence

◄------------Learning Objective 5.10
What is object permanence, and how
does it develop?

The study of object perception is a rather new area of research. In contrast, object permanence
has been extensively studied. This has happened in large part because this particular understanding was strongly emphasized in Piaget's theory of infant development (Piaget & Inhelder, 1969).

**STAGES IN THE DEVELOPMENT OF OBJECT PERMANENCE**    According
to Piaget's observations, replicated frequently by later researchers, the
first signs of object permanence appear at about 2 months of age. Suppose you show a toy to a child of this age and then put a screen in
front of the toy and remove the toy. When you then take away the
screen, the baby shows some indication of surprise, as if she knew
that something should still be there. The child thus seems to have a
rudimentary expectation about the permanence of an object. However, infants of this age show no signs of searching for a toy they may
have dropped over the edge of the crib or that has disappeared beneath a blanket or behind a screen. So, with young infants, there is
a fleeting concept of the permanence of objects, but it isn't yet well
developed enough to motivate them to search for a hidden object.

At about 6 or 8 months of age, this begins to change. Babies of
this age look over the edge of the crib for the dropped toy or over the
edge of the high chair for food that was spilled. (In fact, babies of this
age may drive their parents nuts playing "dropsy" in the high chair.)
Infants this age will also search for partially hidden objects. If you put
a favorite toy under a cloth but leave part of it sticking out, the infant
will reach for the toy, which suggests that in some sense the infant
recognizes that the whole object is there even though she can see only
part of it. Yet if you cover the toy completely with the cloth or put it
behind a screen, the infant will stop looking at it and will not reach
for it, even if she has seen you put the cloth over it.

This changes again somewhere between 8 and 12 months. At
this age, the "out of sight, out of mind" parental strategy no longer
works at all. Infants this age will reach for or search for a toy that has
been covered completely by a cloth or hidden by a screen. Thus, by
12 months, most infants appear to grasp the basic fact that objects
continue to exist even when they are no longer visible.

**OBJECT PERMANENCE AND CULTURAL PRACTICES**    It might seem that experiences manipulating objects contribute to the development of object permanence. However, Susan Goldberg's
classic longitudinal study of 38 Zambian infants (1972) indicated that this is not the case.
From shortly after birth, Zambian babies are carried about in slings on their mothers' backs.
They spend very little time on the floor or in any position in which they have much chance of
independent movement until they are able to sit up at about 6 months. At that point they are
usually placed on a mat in the yard of the house. From this vantage the baby can watch all the
activity around the house and in the neighborhood, but he has few objects to play with.

Yet despite this very limited experience manipulating objects, tests of object permanence
showed that, on average, the Zambian babies were ahead of U.S. babies on a measure of the
object concept at 6 months of age. At 9 and 12 months of age, the Zambian babies were slightly
behind U.S. babies, but Goldberg believes that this difference is due not to any cognitive failure but to the fact that at these ages the Zambian babies were quite unresponsive and passive
toward objects and thus were very difficult to test. She observed that Zambian adults actively
discourage older infants from touching and manipulating objects, and so, she hypothesized,
the infants may have interpreted the objects in the experiment to be things that they weren't
supposed to respond to. Nevertheless, Goldberg's research revealed a clear progression toward
object permanence across the first 18 months of life that was quite similar to that observed in
Western infants.

**FIGURE 5.7** Toddlers' Understanding of Object Movement
Researchers use devices such as this one to find out whether toddlers can
predict that a moving object will be stopped by the barrier that protrudes
above the wall of doors. Children younger than 3 typically fail to identify the
door behind which the object will be found.

*Infants who are carried in slings for several
hours each day have limited opportunities to
manipulate objects, yet researchers have found
that they better understand objects and their
movements at 6 months of age than babies
in other cultures do. However, in later infancy,
these babies develop object concepts more
slowly, because, according to researchers,
adults actively discourage them from touching
and manipulating objects.*

## Perception of Social Signals

The description of the infant's ability to discriminate faces presented earlier in this chapter treats faces as if they were purely physical objects, with fixed properties such as eye characteristics, hairlines, and so forth. But, of course, other people's faces also provide social signals in the form of varying emotional expressions. Variations in vocal intonations and body language similarly provide social cues. These are important bits of information for a baby to detect and decipher. Parents, teachers, and other adults convey a great deal of information through their emotional expression. In peer interactions, too, the ability to read another's emotion is essential for any kind of sustained cooperative play or for the subtle adaptations required for the formation of enduring friendships.

**Learning Objective 5.11** ----------→
How does infants' ability to perceive emotions change over the first year?

## Early Discrimination of Emotional Expressions

Research evidence suggests that infants begin to pay attention to social/emotional cues in faces at about 2 or 3 months of age. For example, at that age, infants begin to smile more to human faces than to a doll's face or another inanimate object, suggesting that at this early stage, the baby is already responding to the added social signals available in the human face (Nelson, de Haan, & Thomas, 2006). The orientation of the face seems to be one critical ingredient in this early preferential smiling. Albert Caron and his colleagues (1997) found that babies smile more only when the face is turned toward them; if the face is turned aside, the baby does not smile more.

Infants at this age are also beginning to notice and respond differently to variations in others' emotional expressions. Initially, they discriminate emotions best when they receive information on many channels simultaneously—such as when they see a particular facial expression and hear the corresponding emotion expressed in the adult's voice (Flom & Bahrick, 2007). For example, in one classic study Haviland and Lelwica (1987) found that when mothers expressed happiness with both face and voice, 10-week-old babies looked happy and interested and gazed at the mother; when the mothers expressed sadness, babies showed increased mouth movements or looked away; when the mothers expressed anger, some babies cried vigorously, while others showed a kind of still or "frozen" look.

By 5 to 7 months, babies can begin to "read" one channel at a time, responding to facial expression alone or vocal expression alone, even when the emotions are displayed by a stranger

---

## DEVELOPMENTAL SCIENCE IN THE REAL WORLD

### Infant Responses to Maternal Depression

Marsha, a new mother, had just been diagnosed with postpartum depression. Her doctor assured her that there was a good chance that the antidepressants she had begun taking, along with the psychotherapist he had recommended, would enable her to pull out of the depression in a few weeks. Still, Marsha told her psychotherapist that she worried about how her depression might affect her 1-month-old's development.

Marsha was right to be concerned about the effects of her depression on her baby's development. Developmentalists have found that babies who interact regularly with mothers who have depression express more negative and fewer positive emotions. They smile less, show more sad and angry facial expressions, and are more disorganized and distressed (Field,) 2010). Some studies suggest that such

effects may be the result of prenatal exposure to depression-related hormones. Further, studies have shown that these hormones are passed from mother to infant prenatally or via breast-feeding (Field, 2011).

At the same time, it seems clear that maternal behaviors influence how an infant whose mother has depression develops. When mothers with depression exhibit sensitive parenting behaviors, their infants are less likely to display negative effects (Candelaria, Teti, & Black, 2011). Thus, parent training may provide an avenue through which the potential negative effects of maternal depression can be moderated. Indeed, several studies have shown that training can increase the frequency of sensitive behaviors in mothers with depression (Doesum, Hosman, & Riksen-Walraven, 2005).

**Learning Objective 5.11a**
How does the emotional behavior of infants of mothers with depression differ from that of infants of mothers without depression?

#### REFLECTION

1. How might researchers study whether genetics plays a role in the correlation between maternal and infant depression?
2. Based on this discussion, what items might be included in a brief observational checklist that health-care professionals could use to identify problem behaviors in depressed mothers?

rather than mom or dad (Flom & Bahrick, 2007). Specifically, they can tell the difference between happy and sad voices and between happy, surprised, and fearful faces. They also seem to have some preliminary understanding that vocal and facial emotional expressions typically go together. 👁️ Watch at **MyDevelopmentLab**

Late in the first year of life, infants take another important step and link the information about a person's emotional expression with the environmental context. For example, a 12-month-old, faced with some new and potentially fearful event such as a new toy or a strange adult, may first look at mom's or dad's face to check for the adult's emotional expression. If mom looks pleased or happy, the baby is likely to explore the new toy with more ease or to accept the stranger with less fuss. If mom looks concerned or frightened, the baby responds to those cues and reacts to the novel situation with equivalent concern or fear. Researchers have described this as a process of **social referencing** (Thompson, Winer, & Goodvin, 2011; Walker-Andrews, 1997). Not only do babies use the emotions of others to guide their own responses, but recent research suggests that, by 12 months of age, they can use nonverbal cues to identify the cause of another person's emotional response (Moses, Baldwin, Rosicky, & Tidball, 2001). Moreover, 1-year-olds can calm themselves when their caregivers behave in expected ways (Cole, Martin, & Dennis, 2004). For example, a baby who is frustrated by hunger will calm down when she sees her caregiver preparing to nurse her or to provide her with some other kind of nourishment. However, infants' basic ability to perceive emotions carries potential risks for those whose mothers have depression (see *Developmental Science in the Real World*).

**social referencing** Using another person's emotional reaction to some situation as a basis for deciding one's own reaction. A baby does this when she checks her parent's facial expression or body language before responding positively or negatively to something new.

👁️ **Watch** the **Video** *Social Referencing* at **MyDevelopmentLab**

## Cross-Cultural Commonalities and Variations

It is reasonable to ask whether children in every culture learn about emotions in this same way. The Utka, an Inuit band in northern Canada, have two words for fear, distinguishing between fear of physical disaster and fear of being treated badly. Some African languages have no separate words for fear and sorrow. Samoans use the same word for love, sympathy, and liking, and Tahitians have no word at all that conveys the notion of guilt. These examples, drawn by James Russell (1989) from the anthropological literature, remind us that we need to be very careful when we talk about the "normal" process of a child learning about emotional expression and emotional meaning. From an English-speaking, Western perspective, emotions such as fear and anger seem like "basic" emotions that all infants understand early and easily. But what would be the developmental sequence for a child growing up in a culture in which fear and sorrow are not distinguishedv? 👁️ **Simulate** at **MyDevelopmentLab**

The work of Paul Ekman (1972, 1973, 1989, 2007) has provided evidence of a strong cross-cultural similarity in people's facial expressions when conveying certain of these same "basic" emotions, such as fear, happiness, sadness, anger, and disgust. (Figure 5.8 shows two such common expressions.) In all cultures studied so far, adults understand these facial expressions as having the same core meaning. Cultural variations are laid on top of these basic expressive patterns, and cultures have different rules about which emotions may be expressed and which must be masked. One could hypothesize that infants and toddlers are quite good at discriminating and understanding the core, shared patterns; even 2-year-olds can recognize and categorize happy and sad expressions. Beyond that basic understanding, the child must then slowly learn all the cultural overlays—the links between emotion and situation that hold for each culture, the specific meanings of emotional language, and the scripts that govern the appropriate expression of emotion in a given culture. This is no small task.

◄----------- Learning Objective 5.12
What cross-cultural differences in emotional perception have been noted?

👁️ **Simulate** the **Experiment** *Emotion and Motivation* at **MyDevelopmentLab**

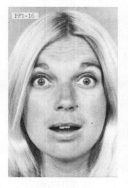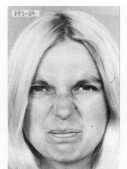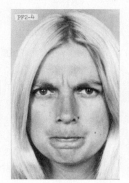

**FIGURE 5.8** Basic Emotions
What emotion is being expressed in each of these photos? If you said happiness, sadness, fear, surprise, disgust, and anger, you agree with virtually all observers, in many countries, who have looked at these pictures.

(Copyright Paul Ekman, PH.D./ Paul Ekman Group, LLC.)

◉ Watch the Video *Robot Facial Expressions* at MyDevelopmentLab What is remarkable is just how much of this information the preschooler already comprehends and reflects in his own behavior. ◉ Watch at MyDevelopmentLab

## THINK CRITICALLY

- How would nativists and empiricists explain infants' responses to music?
- Research shows that infants lack object permanence prior to about 8 months of age. How might this feature of infant perception be useful to caregivers?

## CONDUCT YOUR OWN RESEARCH

If you have access to a 3- to 6-month-old infant, you can replicate the research findings showing that infants respond differently to play songs and lullabies. Ask the baby's mother or father to sing the two types of songs and note whether the infant displays the kinds of behavior described in the text. Recall that researchers have found that lullabies elicit inwardly directed behaviors, such as thumb-sucking, and play songs elicit externally directed behaviors, such as babbling and smiling.

## SUMMARY  ✔•─ Study and Review at MyDevelopmentLab

### Thinking about Perceptual Development

**5.1  What are the three approaches to studying infants' perceptual skills?**
Studies of perceptual development have been greatly aided by methodological advances, such as Fantz's preference technique and the use of habituation or operant conditioning techniques with very young infants.

**5.2  What are the arguments for the nativist and empiricist views of perceptual development?**
A central issue in the study of perceptual development continues to be the nativism-empiricism debate. Many basic perceptual abilities, including strategies for examining objects, appear to be built into the system at birth or to develop as the brain develops over the early years. But specific experience is required both to maintain the underlying system and to learn fundamental discriminations and patterns.

### Sensory Skills

**5.3  How do infants' visual skills change across the first months of life?**
Color vision is present at birth, but visual acuity and tracking ability are relatively poor at birth. These skills develop rapidly during the first few months.

**5.4  How do infants' senses of hearing, smell, taste, touch, and motion compare to those of older children and adults?**
Basic auditory skills are more fully developed at birth; auditory acuity is good for the range of the human voice, and the newborn can locate at least the approximate direction of a sound. The sensory capacities for smelling and tasting and the senses of touch and motion are also well developed at birth.

### Perceptual Skills

**5.5  How does visual perception change over the first months and years of life?**
Depth perception is present in at least rudimentary form by 3 months of age. The baby initially uses kinetic cues, then binocular cues, and finally pictorial cues by about 5 to 7 months. Visual attention appears to follow definite rules, even in the first hours of life. Babies can discriminate the mother's face from other faces, and the mother's voice from other voices, almost immediately after birth.

**5.5a  What were the findings of Langlois's classic study of infants' responses to faces that varied in attractiveness?**
Langlois found that 2- and 3-month-old infants looked longer at faces that adults judged to be more attractive than at faces that adults judged to be less attractive. These findings suggest that templates for desirable configurations for human faces may be inborn.

**5.6  How do infants perceive human speech and other auditory stimuli?**
From the beginning, babies appear to attend to and discriminate among all possible speech sound contrasts; by the age of 1 year, the infant makes fine discriminations only among speech sounds that occur in the language she is actually hearing. Babies also attend to and discriminate among different patterns of sounds, such as melodies or speech inflections.

**5.6a  How do cochlear implants affect the development of speech perception?**
Many infants with inborn or acquired hearing losses can be helped with cochlear implants (CI). Speech perception develops most optimally when the device is implanted in the

first two years of life, but surgery may be delayed because of the difficulty in diagnosing hearing loss so early in life.

**5.7** What is intermodal perception, and when does it develop?

Intermodal perception, the ability to coordinate information from two or more senses, has been demonstrated in infants as young as 1 month old and is found reliably in 4-month-olds.

**5.8** What are perceptual constancies, and when are they important to perception?

Perceptual constancies are mental rules that enable humans to perceive the features of objects in the same way under varying conditions (e.g., viewing angle). Perceptual constancies such as size constancy, shape constancy, and color constancy are all present in at least rudimentary form by 4 months of age.

## The Object Concept

**5.9** What kinds of rules do infants appear to use in perceiving objects?

Young babies have quite complex understanding of objects, their properties, and their possible movements. They use the connected surface principle, the assumption that two connected surfaces belong to the same object, and also seem to know that objects fall when they are not supported. They also appear to discriminate between stable and unstable arrangements of objects such as block towers.

**5.10** What is object permanence, and how does it develop?

The understanding of object permanence (the realization that objects exist even when they are out of sight) begins

at 2 or 3 months of age and is quite well developed by 10 months.

## Perception of Social Signals

**5.11** How does infants' ability to perceive emotions change over the first year?

A baby's ability to discriminate among emotional expressions appears early in the first year. By 6 months of age, most infants can discriminate between emotional information contained in facial expressions and that represented by vocal tone. By 12 months, babies not only recognize nonverbal indicators of others' emotions but also change their own to match those of their caregivers (social referencing).

**5.11a** How does the emotional behavior of infants of mothers with depression differ from that of infants of mothers without depression?

Infants of mothers with depression express more negative and fewer positive emotions, smile less, show more sad and angry facial expressions, and are more disorganized and distressed. Prenatal exposure to stress- and depression-related hormones may explain these differences. Infants of mothers with depression whose mothers exhibit sensitive parenting behaviors are less likely to display long-term negative effects than those whose mothers do not show such behaviors.

**5.12** What cross-cultural differences in emotional perception have been noted?

Cross-cultural research has shown that facial expressions are given the same meaning in every culture studied so far. What varies across cultures to some degree is the situations associated with various emotions as well as social rules for expressing them.

## KEY TERMS

auditory acuity (p. 120)
color constancy (p. 127)
empiricism (p. 116)
intermodal perception (p. 126)

nativism (p. 116)
object constancy (p. 127)
object permanence (p. 127)
perceptual constancies (p. 127)

shape constancy (p. 127)
size constancy (p. 127)
social referencing (p. 131)

tracking (p. 119)
visual acuity (p. 119)

# 6

# Cognitive Development I: Structure and Process

When the last birthday party guest finally left, Sheilah busied herself with cleaning up the cake crumbs while the birthday boy, 7-year-old Rudy, looked through his gifts. One of them was an intriguing board game. "Mom," he said, "can you play this game with me now? Sheilah suggested that Rudy play the game with his 4-year-old sister, Marcella, instead. Rudy found Marcella in her room and began explaining the game to her. "You get one of these little guys and I get one. You put the guys on this square, and then you spin the spinner. Then you have to move your guy however many spaces it says on the spinner. If you land on one of these squares," he explained, pointing to a square with a star on it, "you get another turn. If you land on one with a stop sign, you have to skip a turn."

Marcella seemed to understand, so Rudy decided to let her go first. She flicked the spinner, and the arrow landed on four. "Okay," said Rudy, "you have to move your guy four spaces."

Marcella picked up her piece and began to count off the spaces, "1, 2, 3," when she suddenly stopped. "Four is a stop sign. I don't want to be on a stop sign. I'm gonna do the spinner again."

At this, Rudy became indignant. "You can't do it again; that's cheating," he yelled. "Mom," Rudy called loudly so that Sheilah could hear him in the other room, "I can't play with her 'cause she's a cheater."

Marcella began to sob as Rudy packed up the game and said, "Go play with your baby toys."

Scenes like this one are all too familiar to parents whose children are on either side of the transition from, in Piaget's terms, the *preoperational stage* to the *concrete operational stage*. Concrete operational 7-year-olds like Rudy have a strong preference for structured experiences with outcomes that depend on rules. They can imagine how much fun it would be to win a board game, but they know that to achieve a legitimate victory a player must abide by the rules. For preoperational 4-year-olds like Marcella, the world is more fluid. Like 7-year-olds, they can imagine winning a game, but they don't yet understand that the legitimacy of the outcome depends on the rules. That is, without rules, a game isn't a game at all. Thus, they prefer pretend play activities in which rules are easily changed and depend primarily on the whim of the player.

In this chapter, you will learn about Piaget's important discoveries, the theory he devised to explain them, and the ways in which other theorists have challenged both his

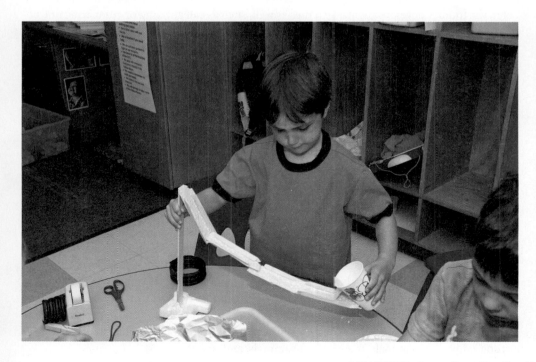

The metaphor of the child as a "little scientist," constructing his understanding of the world, comes directly from Piaget's theory.

findings and his theory. We will introduce you to developmentalists who accept Piaget's basic ideas but use principles from other theories to expand upon them. You will also read about Vygotsky's sociocultural approach to cognitive development. Finally, you will learn what research has revealed about the development of memory across the child and adolescent years.

## Piaget's Basic Ideas

Piaget set out to answer a fundamental question: How does a child's knowledge of the world change with age? In answering this question, Piaget's most central assumption was that the child is an active participant in the development of knowledge, constructing his own understanding. This idea, perhaps more than any other, has influenced the thinking of all developmentalists who have followed Piaget. In addition, after three decades of research devoted to challenging his assertion that cognitive functioning develops in stages, the whole concept of cognitive stages is enjoying a resurgence of interest among developmental psychologists (Feldman, 2004; Homer & Hayward, 2008; Kuhn, 2008; Shayer, 2008). Of course, the hundreds of studies that have been done since Piaget first proposed the stages have revealed a number of shortcomings in his original account of cognitive development (Birney & Sternberg, 2011). Still, the basic outline he first sketched more than 70 years ago of cognitive changes from infancy to adolescence appears to be fairly accurate.

**Learning Objective 6.1** - - - - - - - - - - - - →
What is the role of schemes in cognitive development?

## Schemes

A pivotal Piagetian concept—and one of the hardest to grasp—is that of a **scheme** (sometimes called a *schema*). This term is often used as a rough synonym for the word *concept* or the phrases *mental category* or *complex of ideas*, but Piaget used it even more broadly than that. He saw knowledge not as merely passive mental categories but as actions, either mental or physical; each of these actions is what he meant by a scheme. So a scheme is not really a category, but the *action* of categorizing in some particular fashion. Some purely physical or sensory actions are also schemes. If you pick up and look at a ball, you are using your "looking scheme," your "picking-up scheme," and your "holding scheme."

◉—|**Watch** the **Video** *Infant Perception* at **MyDevelopmentLab**

Piaget proposed that each baby begins life with a small repertoire of simple sensory or motor schemes, such as looking, tasting, touching, hearing, and grasping. For the baby, an object is a thing that tastes a certain way, feels a certain way when touched, or has a particular color. Later, the toddler develops mental schemes as well, such as categorizing or comparing one object to another. Over the course of development, the child gradually adds extremely complex mental schemes, such as deductive analysis or systematic reasoning. In fact, humans continue to add new schemes, both physical and mental, throughout the lifespan. So where, you might be wondering, do these new schemes come from? ◉—|Watch at **MyDevelopmentLab**

According to Piaget, as people act on their environments, an inborn mental process called **organization** causes them to derive generalizable schemes from specific experiences. For example, when an infant handles a spherical object, such as a ball, the scheme she constructs will be applied to all similar objects. So, when she observes a decorative glass ball, she will attempt to handle it in the same way she would a rubber ball. Schemes organize our thinking according to categories that help us determine what kinds of actions to take in response to variations in environmental characteristics.

**scheme** Piaget's word for the basic actions of knowing, including both physical actions (sensorimotor schemes, such as looking or reaching) and mental actions (such as classifying, comparing, and reversing). An experience is assimilated into a scheme, and the scheme is created or modified through accommodation.

**organization** The process of deriving generalizable schemes from specific experiences.

**figurative schemes** Mental representations of the basic properties of objects in the world.

**operative schemes** Mental representations of the logical connections among objects in the world.

According to Piaget, **figurative schemes** are mental representations of the basic properties of objects in the world. For instance, a child uses figurative schemes when she correctly labels dogs and cats, lists their characteristics (e.g., wet noses, fur, whiskers), and describes their typical behaviors (e.g., barking, wagging tails, mewing). Knowing that dogs and cats are different kinds of animals and that animals represent a category that is distinct from others (e.g., clothes, food, etc.) also involves figurative schemes. By contrast, **operative schemes** enable children to understand the logical connections among objects in the world and to reason about or operate on them. For example, operative schemes come into play when children understand that collies are dogs, dogs are mammals, mammals are animals, and so on.

# Adaptation

◄-----------Learning Objective 6.2
How do assimilation, accommodation, and equilibration change schemes?

Our schemes don't always work the way we expect them to. So, according to Piaget, the mental process he called **adaptation** complements organization by working to change schemes that don't quite fit the challenges offered by our environments. Three subprocesses are involved in adaptation.

**Assimilation** is the process of taking in, of absorbing some event or experience and making it part of a scheme. Piaget would say that when a baby handles a decorative glass ball in the same way she learned to manipulate a rubber ball, she has assimilated the ball to her ball-handling scheme. The key here is that assimilation is an active process. For one thing, we assimilate information selectively. That is, we pay attention only to those aspects of any experience for which we already have schemes. In other words, our minds function more like magnets, which attract only a limited range of metal objectives (those that contain iron), than a sponge, which absorbs any type of liquid with which it has contact. For example, when you listen to an instructor give a lecture, you may think that you are trying to write everything down in your notebook or store it in your brain, but in fact you are assimilating only the thoughts you can connect to some concept or model you already have.

The process complementary to assimilation is **accommodation**, which involves changing a scheme as a result of new information taken in by assimilation. The baby who grasps a glass ball for the first time will respond to the slipperiness of the surface, compared to what she expected based on her experience with rubber balls, and will accommodate her ball-handling scheme. In this way, she will develop a ball-handling scheme that can take into account different surface characteristics of different kinds of balls. Thus, in Piaget's theory, the process of accommodation is the key to developmental change. Through accommodation, we reorganize our thoughts, improve our skills, and change our strategies.

The third aspect of adaptation is **equilibration**, the process of bringing assimilation and accommodation into balance. This is not unlike what a scientist does when she develops a theory about some body of information. The scientist wants to have a theory that will make sense out of every observation—that is, one that has internal coherence. When new research findings come along, she assimilates them into her existing theory; if they don't fit perfectly, she makes modifications (accommodations) in the theory so that it will assimilate information that previously did not fit. However, if enough nonconfirming evidence accumulates, the scientist may have to throw out her theory altogether or change some basic theoretical assumptions; either response is a form of equilibration.

An analogy may be helpful. Suppose you have just transferred to a new college. Instead of consulting the campus map on the college's website, you try to find your way to your first class with only a hand-drawn map given to you by another student. As you make your way around the campus, you make corrections on your map—redrawing it and writing notes to yourself. The redrawn and revised map is certainly an improvement over the original version, but eventually you will find that it is both impossible to read and still seriously flawed. So you start over and draw a new map, based on all your information. You carry this around with you, revising it and writing on it until it, too, is so full of annotations that you need to start over. The corrections and annotations you make to your map are analogous to accommodations in Piaget's theory; the process of starting over and drawing a new map is analogous to equilibration. Each modification of an existing map or drawing of a new map allows you to more easily assimilate your driving or walking experiences. Put more simply, with each modification, your map works better than before. Moreover, the map you have constructed from your own experience will probably turn out to be more useful to you than the school's online map because it is linked to images and schemes, such as the appearance of a building's landscaping or the placement of bicycle racks and other objects, that serve as landmarks. This dynamic process of integrating schemes is another feature of equilibration.

Piaget thought that a child operated in a similar way, creating coherent, more or less internally consistent schemes. However, since the infant starts with a very limited repertoire of schemes (a very primitive initial map), the early structures the child creates are simply not going to be adequate. Such inadequacies, Piaget thought, force the child to make periodic major changes in the internal schemes.

Piaget saw three particularly significant reorganization, or equilibration, points in childhood, each ushering in a new stage of development. The first occurs at about 18–24 months,

**adaptation**   The processes through which schemes change.

**assimilation**   That part of the adaptation process proposed by Piaget that involves absorbing new experiences or information into existing schemes. Experience is not taken in "as is," however, but is modified (or interpreted) somewhat so as to fit the preexisting schemes.

**accommodation**   That part of the adaptation process proposed by Piaget by which a person modifies existing schemes as a result of new experiences or creates new schemes when old ones no longer handle the data.

**equilibration**   The third part of the adaptation process proposed by Piaget, involving a periodic restructuring of schemes to create a balance between assimilation and accommodation.

when the toddler shifts from the dominance of simple sensory and motor schemes to the use of the first symbols. The second equilibration point normally falls between ages 5 and 7, when the child adds a whole new set of powerful operative schemes Piaget calls **operations**. These are far more abstract and general mental actions, such as mental addition or subtraction. The third major equilibration point is in adolescence, when the child figures out how to "operate on" ideas as well as on events or objects.

The three major equilibration points yield four stages during which children use different ways of acting on the world around them. During the **sensorimotor stage**, from birth to 24 months, infants use their sensory and motor schemes to act on the world around them. In the **preoperational stage**, from 24 months to about 6 years, youngsters acquire symbolic schemes, such as language and fantasy, that they use in thinking and communicating. Next comes the **concrete operations stage**, during which 6- to 12-year-olds begin to think logically. The last phase is the **formal operations stage**, in which adolescents learn to think logically about abstract ideas and hypothetical situations.

# Causes of Cognitive Development

**Learning Objective 6.3** - - - - - - - - - - - - ➤
What are the four causes of cognitive development proposed by Piaget?

✳⊣**Explore** the **Concept** *Infants' Perceptual and Cognitive Milestones* at **MyDevelopmentLab**

**operation**    Term used by Piaget for a complex, internal, abstract scheme, first seen at about age 6.

**sensorimotor stage**    Piaget's term for the first major stage of cognitive development, from birth to about 24 months, when the child uses sensory and motor skills to act on the environment.

**preoperational stage**    Piaget's term for the second major stage of cognitive development, from about 24 months to about age 6, marked by the ability to use symbols.

**concrete operations stage**    Piaget's term for the stage of development between ages 6 and 12, during which children become able to think logically.

**formal operations stage**    Piaget's name for the fourth and final major stage of cognitive development, occurring during adolescence, when the child becomes able to manipulate and organize ideas or hypothetical situations as well as objects.

Since Piaget's stages represent a fixed sequence, you might think that they are controlled by an inborn genetic plan, much like the sequence of motor skill development you read about in Chapter 4. Piaget suggested that just such an inborn plan for cognitive development exists, but that it depends on environmental factors for its full expression. He proposed four main causes of cognitive development: two that are internal, and two that are found in a child's environment (Piaget & Inhelder, 1969). ✳⊣**Explore** at **MyDevelopmentLab**

As you learned in the preceding section, Piaget believed that equilibration was the chief process through which new stages of cognitive development are reached. He hypothesized that the process of equilibration is an inborn, automatic response to conflicts between a child's current schemes and the challenges of her environment. Likewise, he assumed that the basic pattern of brain maturation common to all human beings that you learned about in Chapter 4 contributed to cognitive development. So, he claimed, individual differences in the pace at which children proceed through the four stages of cognitive development may be partly explained by different rates of brain maturation, which may be the result of either inborn differences or environmental factors such as nutrition.

The two environmental factors Piaget posited to explain progression through the stages were social transmission and experience. *Social transmission* is simply information the child gets from other people. According to Piaget, parents, teachers, and others provide children with information, such as the names and characteristics of objects, as well as with models of more mature cognitive development. Say, for example, a preschooler believes that her dresser turns into a monster every night when the light is turned off. To reassure her, her parent turns the light on and off repeatedly to demonstrate that the dresser remains a piece of furniture whether the light is on or off. In so doing, the parent is demonstrating use of a logical scheme that has many applications to the physical world: "If this object was a dresser with the light on, it must still be a dresser when the light is off. Darkness cannot change the 'dresserness' of the dresser; it can't change one object into another." The parent's logical scheme conflicts with the magical scheme on which the child bases her belief that pieces of furniture can change into monsters in the dark. As a result, the experience stimulates the process of equilibration for the child. Piaget suggested that adults contribute a great deal to children's progression from one stage to the next through these kinds of informal demonstrations.

By *experience*, Piaget meant the child's own opportunities to act on the world and to observe the results of those actions. If you watch preschoolers playing on the beach or in a sandbox, you will notice that one of their favorite activities is to fill containers with sand, empty them out, and fill them up again. You might see a group of children making a "mountain" out of sand in this way. In so doing, they notice that the mountain doesn't hold together very well unless a little water is mixed with the sand, but then they see that too much water also prevents the mountain from holding together. Through this kind of experimentation and modification of actions, Piaget believed, children often stimulate their own cognitive development.

One place where children are exposed to many opportunities for both social transmission and experience is in school. In fact, studies all over the world have shown that children who attend school progress through Piaget's stages more rapidly than those who do not (Mishra, 2001). These studies lend weight to Piaget's claim that movement from one cognitive stage to another is not simply a matter of maturation but is the result of a complex interaction between internal and environmental variables. Each of these variables, Piaget suggested, is *necessary but not sufficient* to produce movement from one cognitive stage to the next. In other words, a certain degree of brain maturation is required for each stage, but brain development by itself cannot cause a child to progress to the next stage. All of the causal factors—equilibration, maturation, social transmission, and experience—must interact and support one another in order for cognitive development to proceed.

## Infancy

Piaget's theory assumes that the baby assimilates incoming information into the limited array of sensory and motor schemes she is born with—such as looking, listening, sucking, and grasping—and accommodates those schemes based on her experiences. This is the starting point for the entire process of cognitive development.

## Piaget's View of the Sensorimotor Period

◄------------Learning Objective 6.4
How did Piaget describe cognitive development in the first 2 years of life?

In the beginning, in Piaget's view, the baby is entirely tied to the immediate present, responding to whatever stimuli are available. She does not remember events or things from one encounter to the next and does not appear to plan or intend.

This pattern gradually changes during the first 24 months as the baby comes to understand that objects continue to exist even when they are out of sight (see Chapter 5) and as she becomes able to remember objects, actions, and individuals over periods of time. Yet Piaget insisted that in the sensorimotor period, the infant is not yet able to manipulate these early mental images or memories. Nor does she use symbols to stand for objects or events. It is the new ability to manipulate internal symbols, such as words or images, that marks the beginning of the next stage, the stage of preoperational thought, which emerges in most children sometime between 18 and 24 months.

The change from the limited repertoire of schemes available to the newborn to the ability to use symbols between 18 and 24 months is gradual, although Piaget identified six substages, summarized in Table 6.1 on page 140. Each substage represents some specific advance. Substage 2 is marked by the beginning of those important coordinations between looking and listening, reaching and looking, and reaching and sucking that are such central features of the 2-month-old's means of exploring the world. The term **primary circular reactions** refers to the many simple repetitive actions seen at substage 2, each organized around the infant's own body. The baby accidentally sucks his thumb one day, finds it pleasurable, and repeats the action. **Secondary circular reactions**, in substage 3, differ only in that the baby is now repeating some action in order to trigger a reaction outside his own body. The baby coos and mom smiles, so the baby coos again, apparently in order to get mom to smile again; the baby accidentally hits the mobile hanging above his crib, it moves, and he then repeats his arm wave, apparently with some intent to make the mobile move again. These initial connections between bodily actions and external consequences are fairly automatic, very like a kind of operant conditioning. During this substage, infants build the important schemes that underlie the *object concept*, a set of milestones discussed extensively in Chapter 5. Recall that **object permanence**, or the understanding that objects continue to exist even when they are out of sight, is one of the most important of these milestones.

Substage 4 brings with it the beginnings of a real understanding of causal connections. At this point, the infant moves into exploratory high gear. In substage 5, this exploratory behavior becomes even more marked with the emergence of what Piaget called **tertiary circular reactions**. In this substage, the baby is not content merely to repeat the original triggering action but tries out variations. He might try out many other sounds or facial

**primary circular reactions** Piaget's phrase to describe a baby's simple repetitive actions in substage 2 of the sensorimotor stage, organized around the baby's own body; the baby repeats some action in order to have some desired outcome occur again, such as putting his thumb in his mouth to repeat the good feeling of sucking.

**secondary circular reactions** Repetitive actions in substage 3 of the sensorimotor period, oriented around external objects; the infant repeats some action in order to have some outside event recur, such as hitting a mobile repeatedly so that it moves.

**object permanence** The understanding that objects continue to exist even when they cannot be directly perceived.

**tertiary circular reactions** The deliberate experimentation with variations of previous actions, characteristic of substage 5 of the sensorimotor period, according to Piaget.

## Table 6.1

## SUBSTAGES OF PIAGET'S SENSORIMOTOR STAGE

| Substage | Age | Piaget's Label | Characteristics |
|---|---|---|---|
| 1 | Birth–1 month | Reflexes | Use of built-in schemes or reflexes such as sucking or looking; no imitation; no ability to integrate information from several senses |
| 2 | 1–4 months | Primary circular reactions | Accommodation of basic schemes (grasping, looking, sucking), as baby practices them endlessly. Beginning coordination of schemes from different senses, such as looking toward a sound; baby does not yet link bodily actions to some result outside the body. |
| 3 | 4–8 months | Secondary circular reactions | Baby becomes much more aware of events outside his own body and makes them happen again, in a kind of trial-and-error learning. Imitation may occur, but only of schemes already in the baby's repertoire. Beginning understanding of the "object concept." |
| 4 | 8–12 months | Coordination of secondary schemes | Clear intentional means-ends behavior. The baby not only goes after what she wants, but may combine two schemes to do so, such as knocking a pillow away to reach a toy. Imitation of novel behaviors occurs, as does transfer of information from one sense to the other (cross-modal transfer). |
| 5 | 12–18 months | Tertiary circular reactions | "Experimentation" begins, in which the infant tries out new ways of playing with or manipulating objects. Very active, very purposeful trial-and-error exploration. |
| 6 | 18–24 months | Beginning of representational thought | Development of use of symbols to represent objects or events. Child understands that the symbol is separate from the object. Deferred imitation first occurs at this stage. |

Three-month-old Andrea may be showing a secondary circular reaction here, shaking her hand repeatedly to hear the sound of the rattle. A learning theorist would say that the pleasure she experiences from hearing the sound is reinforcing her hand-shaking behavior.

**Learning Objective 6.5**

What have researchers discovered about infants' ability to remember and to imitate others' actions?

expressions to see if they will trigger mom's smile or try moving his hand differently or in new directions in order to make the mobile move in new ways. At this stage, the baby's behavior has a purposeful, experimental quality. Nonetheless, Piaget thought that even in substage 5 the baby does not have internal symbols to stand for objects. The development of such symbols is the mark of substage 6 and a sign that the infant has become capable of learning from symbolic sources of information (see *Technology and the Developing Child* on page 141).

Piaget's descriptions of this sequence of development, largely based on remarkably detailed observations of his own three children, provoked a very rich array of research, some that confirms the general outlines of his proposals and some that does not. Research results described in Chapter 5, along with other research on infant memory and imitation, point to the conclusion that in a number of important respects, Piaget underestimated the ability of infants to store, remember, and organize sensory and motor information.

## Challenges to Piaget's View of Infancy

Although research has generally supported the sequence of cognitive development discovered by Piaget, there are many findings that challenge his view. As you learned in Chapter 5, research by Elizabeth Spelke and Renée Baillargeon, among others, has given us a more detailed account of infants' understanding of objects than Piaget's studies did. Their work suggests that infants have a much more sophisticated understanding of objects than Piaget concluded. Likewise, research examining infants' memory functioning and their capacity for imitation also suggests that Piaget may have underestimated their capabilities.

**MEMORY** One hint that infants are capable of greater feats of memory than Piaget proposed is research showing that habituation and dishabituation are already present at birth—research you read about in Chapter 3. A second source of evidence that quite young babies

# TECHNOLOGY AND THE DEVELOPING CHILD

## What Infants Learn from Television

Perhaps you are familiar with the ongoing controversy over the effects of the *Baby Einstein* video series and others like it on cognitive development. Researchers have found that watching such videos actually reduces infants' rate of vocabulary acquisition (Zimmerman, Christakis, & Meltzoff, 2007). Moreover, the more babies watch them, the less they interact with other people. (Fempek, Demers, Hanson, Kirkorian, & Anderson, 2011).

Developmentalists point out that researchers have long known infants in substages 1–5 of Piaget's sensori-motor stage are unlikely to learn anything of value from watching videos because they have not yet acquired the ability to process symbolic information (Troseth & DeLoache, 1998). In one study, researchers compared 6-, 12-, 18-, and 24-month old infants' patterns of looking at two kinds of videos: one of computer-generated geometric patterns (nonsymbolic stimulus) and another of a children's movie called *Follow That Bird* (symbolic stimulus). The two youngest groups showed no differences in their patterns of attention to the two videos, an indication

that they were unable to discern the meanings embedded in symbolic information. By contrast, 18- and 24-month-olds appeared to discriminate between the two videos, an indication that they were aware of the different types of information each presented (Richards & Cronise, 2000).

Given these findings, parents should probably keep in mind that for infants younger than 18 months or so, many so-called "educational" or "brain-stimulating" videos that target infant audiences may serve as more than reinforcement for the behavior of watching television. Recall from Chapter 1 that a reinforcer is any consequence that causes the behavior that it follows to increase. Most infant videos consist of rapidly changing arrays of the sorts of visual stimuli that infants are known to prefer–shapes, patterns, toys, faces, and so on–accompanied by music that is also attractive to them. Thus, when the infant looks at the television screen, she is rewarded with infant-friendly visual and auditory stimulation. In response, she increases the behavior of looking at the screen and learns to expect to be rewarded with attractive sensory stimuli whenever she does so. This makes her likely

to look at the screen whenever the television is on, regardless of what type of program that is on. Thus, the primary thing that infants learn from watching television is the behavior of watching television itself.

### Learning Objective 6.4a
What are infants in the various sensorimotor substages likely to learn from watching television?

### FIND OUT MORE

*Use your Internet search skills to answer these questions.*

1. You can search for the AAP's statement about television at www.aap.org. What rationale does the organization give for its recommendations?
2. How has the research of Jane Healy, PhD, raised awareness about the possible impact of media on early brain development?

---

can remember specific events over periods of time comes from a series of clever studies by Carolyn Rovee-Collier and her colleagues (Rovee-Collier & Cuevas, 2009). In her most widely used procedure, Rovee-Collier uses an ingenious variation of an operant conditioning strategy. She first hangs an attractive mobile over a baby's crib and watches to see how the baby responds. In particular, she is interested in how often the baby normally kicks her legs while looking at the mobile. After 3 minutes of this "baseline" observation, she attaches a string from the mobile to the baby's leg, as you can see in Figure 6.1, so that each time the baby kicks her leg, the mobile moves. Babies quickly learn to kick repeatedly in order to make this interesting new thing happen (what Piaget would call a secondary circular reaction). Within 3 to 6 minutes, 3-month-olds double or triple their kick rates, showing that learning has clearly occurred. Rovee-Collier then tests the baby's memory of this learning by coming back some days later and hanging the same mobile over the crib, but not attaching the string to the baby's foot. If the baby remembers the previous occasion, she should kick at a higher rate than she did when she first saw the mobile, which is precisely what 3-month-old babies do, even after a delay of as long as a week.

Such studies show that the young infant is cognitively a whole lot more sophisticated than developmentalists (and Piaget) had once supposed. At the same time, Rovee-Collier's work also offers some support for Piaget's views, since she observes systematic gains over the months of infancy in the baby's ability to remember. A 2-month-old can remember the kicking action for only 1 day; a 3-month-old can remember for over a week; and by 6 months, a baby can remember for more than 2 weeks. Rovee-Collier has also found that all these early infant memories are strongly tied to the specific context in which the original experience occurred. Even 6-month-olds do not recognize or remember the mobile if the investigator

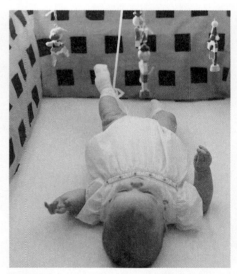

**FIGURE 6.1** Rovee-Collier's Studies of Infant Learning

This 3-month-old baby in one of Rovee-Collier's memory experiments will quickly learn to kick her foot in order to make the mobile move. And several days later, she will remember this connection between kicking and the mobile.

(*Source:* Rovee-Collier, 1993, p. 131. Rovee-Collier, C. (1993), "The capacity for long-term memory in infancy." *Current Directions in Psychological Science,* 2.)

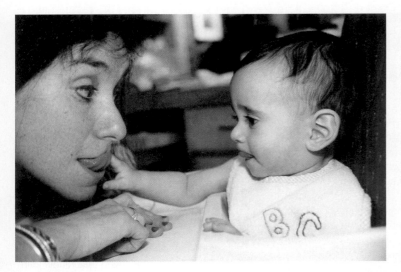

**FIGURE 6.2** Imitation
Although researchers still disagree on just how much young infants will imitate, everyone agrees that they will imitate the gesture of tongue protrusion.

makes even a very small change, such as hanging a different cloth around the crib in which the child was originally tested. Thus, babies do remember far more than Piaget believed—but their memories are highly specific. With age, their memories become less and less tied to specific cues or contexts (DeFrancisco & Rovee-Collier, 2008; Hsu & Rovee-Collier, 2006; Learmonth, Lamberth, & Rovee-Collier, 2004).

**IMITATION** Another active area of study has been the ability of the infant to imitate. If you look again at Table 6.1 on page 140, you'll see that Piaget thought that the ability to imitate emerged quite gradually over the early months. In broad terms, Piaget's proposed sequence has been supported. For example, imitation of someone else's hand movements or their actions with objects seems to improve steadily during the months of infancy, starting at 1 or 2 months of age; imitation of two-part actions develops only in toddlerhood, perhaps at 15 to 18 months (Poulson, Nunes, & Warren, 1989). In two areas, however, Piaget may have been wrong about infants' imitative abilities.

First, although Piaget thought babies could not imitate other people's facial gestures until about substage 4 (8–12 months), quite a lot of research now shows that newborns are able to imitate at least some facial gestures, particularly tongue protrusion (Nagy & Molnar, 2004), as shown in the photo in Figure 6.2. Nevertheless, newborns' capacity for imitation appears to be quite limited. Researchers have found that neonates imitate tongue-protrusion but not mouth-opening (Anisfeld et al., 2001). Taken together, studies of imitative behavior in newborns indicate that Piaget was probably wrong in his assertion that very young infants are incapable of imitation. However, it seems likely that he was accurate in his view that imitation is not a general strategy infants use for developing their understanding of the world until they are a bit older.

Piaget also argued that *deferred imitation*, in which a child sees some action and then imitates it at a later time when the model is no longer visible, became possible only in substage 6 (at about 18 months of age), since deferred imitation requires some kind of internal representation. Once again, more recent research points to earlier development of this ability (Jones & Herbert, 2009). Some studies show that babies as young as 6 months can defer their imitation for as long as 24 hours. By 14 months, toddlers can recall and later imitate someone's actions over a period of 2 days (Hanna & Meltzoff, 1993). This finding makes it clear that children of this age can and do learn specific behaviors through modeling, even when they have no chance to imitate the behavior immediately.

## The Preschool Years

Piaget's theory and research findings suggest that preschoolers' ability to use symbols such as words significantly enhances their ability to understand and act on the world around them. But their ability to reason about the world is still fairly poor.

**Learning Objective 6.6** ------------>
What are the characteristics of children's thinking during the preoperational stage?

## Piaget's View of the Preoperational Stage

Piaget saw evidence of symbol use in many aspects of the behavior of children aged 2 to 6. For example, children this age begin to pretend in their play. Such symbol use is also evident in the emergence of language and in the preschooler's primitive ability to understand scale models or simple maps (DeLoache, 1995). Thus, children's figurative schemes grow by leaps and bounds during this stage. By contrast, operative schemes develop slowly. As a result, the fragmentary, "in-progress" nature of preschoolers' operative schemes usually prevents them from generating valid conclusions to logical problems.

Other than symbol use, Piaget's description of the preoperational stage focused on all the other things the preschool-aged child still cannot do, giving an oddly negative tone to his description of this period. Piaget saw the preschooler's thinking as rigid, captured by appearances, insensitive to inconsistencies, and tied to her own perspective—a quality Piaget (1954) called **egocentrism**. The child is not being selfish; rather, she simply thinks (assumes) that everyone sees the world as she does.  ⊙ Watch at **MyDevelopmentLab**

Figure 6.3 illustrates a classic technique used to measure this egocentrism. The child is shown a three-dimensional scene with mountains of different sizes and colors. From a set of drawings, she picks out the one that shows the scene the way she sees it. Most preschoolers can do this without much difficulty. Then the examiner asks the child to pick out the drawing that shows how someone else sees the scene, such as a doll or the examiner. At this point, preschoolers have difficulty. Most often, they again pick the drawing that shows their own view of the mountains (Gzesh & Surber, 1985). In Piaget's view, for a child to be able to succeed at this task, she must shift from using herself as the only frame of reference to seeing things from another perspective. Piaget thought that preschool children could not yet do this.

The preschool child's focus on the appearance of objects is an equally important part of Piaget's description of this period, evident in some of the most famous of his studies, those on conservation (see Figure 6.4 on page 144). **Conservation** is the understanding that the quantity of a substance remains the same even when its appearance changes. Piaget's measurement technique involved first showing the child two equal objects or sets of objects, getting the child to agree that they were equal in some key respect, such as weight, quantity, length, or number, and then shifting, changing, or deforming one of the objects or sets and asking the child if they were still equal. Next, Piaget asked how the child knew the answer was correct. Children who were using preoperational schemes would give justifications, such as "the sausage has more clay because it is longer now." This kind of thinking reflects the child's tendency to think of the world in terms of one variable at a time, a type of thought Piaget called **centration**. By contrast, concrete operational thinkers are capable of **decentration**, a process in which multiple dimensions are considered. Thus, the older child says, "the sausage looks like more because its longer now, but you didn't add any clay or take any away so it must still be the same." Piaget insisted, based on his evaluations of both children's solutions and their reasoning, that children rarely exhibit a true understanding of conservation before age 5 or 6.  ⊙ Watch at **MyDevelopmentLab**

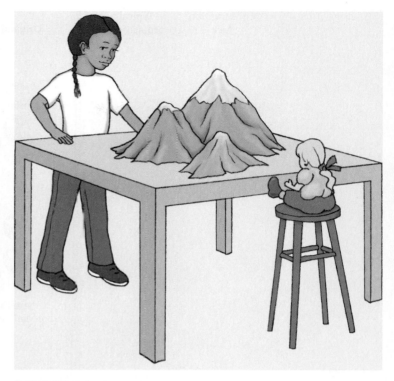

**FIGURE 6.3** Piaget's Three Mountains Task
The experimental situation shown here is similar to one Piaget used to study egocentrism in children. The child is asked to pick out a picture that shows how the mountains look to her, and then to pick out a picture that shows how the mountains look to the doll.

⊙ Watch the **Video** *The Preschool Years: Egocentrism* at **MyDevelopmentLab**

**egocentrism**  A cognitive state in which the individual (typically a child) sees the world only from his own perspective, without awareness that there are other perspectives.

⊙ Watch the **Video** *Concrete Operational Thinking* at **MyDevelopmentLab**

## Challenges to Piaget's View of Early Childhood

◄----------- **Learning Objective 6.7**
How has recent research challenged Piaget's view of this period?

Studies of conservation have generally confirmed Piaget's predictions (e.g., Desrochers, 2008). Although younger children can demonstrate some understanding of conservation if the task is made very simple, most children cannot consistently solve conservation problems until age 5 or 6 or later (e.g., Andreucci, 2003). Nevertheless, evidence suggests that preschoolers are somewhat more cognitively sophisticated than Piaget thought.

**EGOCENTRISM AND PERSPECTIVE TAKING**  Children as young as 2 and 3 appear to have at least some ability to understand that another person sees things or experiences things differently than they do. For example, children of this age will adapt their play or their speech to the demands of their companions. They play differently with older and younger playmates and talk differently to a younger child (Brownell, 1990; Guralnick & Paul-Brown, 1984).

However, such understanding is clearly not perfect at this young age. Developmental psychologist John Flavell has proposed two levels of perspective-taking ability. At level 1, the child knows that another person experiences something differently. At level 2, the child develops a whole series of complex rules for figuring out precisely what the other person sees or

**conservation**  The understanding that the quantity or amount of a substance remains the same even when there are external changes in its shape or arrangement.

**centration**  The young child's tendency to think of the world in terms of one variable at a time.

**decentration**  Thinking that takes multiple variables into account.

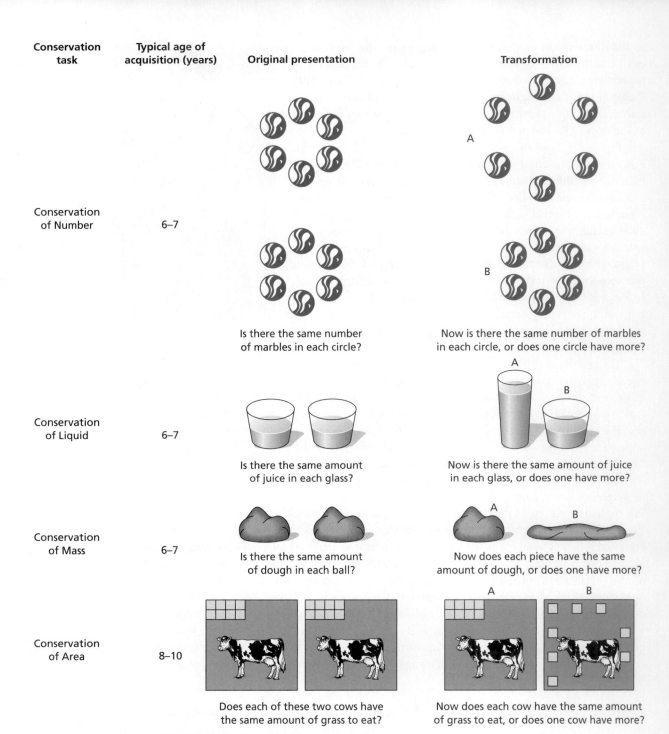

| Conservation task | Typical age of acquisition (years) | Original presentation | Transformation |
|---|---|---|---|
| Conservation of Number | 6–7 | Is there the same number of marbles in each circle? | Now is there the same number of marbles in each circle, or does one circle have more? |
| Conservation of Liquid | 6–7 | Is there the same amount of juice in each glass? | Now is there the same amount of juice in each glass, or does one have more? |
| Conservation of Mass | 6–7 | Is there the same amount of dough in each ball? | Now does each piece have the same amount of dough, or does one have more? |
| Conservation of Area | 8–10 | Does each of these two cows have the same amount of grass to eat? | Now does each cow have the same amount of grass to eat, or does one cow have more? |

**FIGURE 6.4** Piaget's Concrete Operational Tasks

Piaget's research involved several kinds of conservation tasks. He classified children's thinking as concrete operational with respect to a particular task if they could correctly solve the problem and provide a concrete operational reason for their answer. For example, if a child said, "The two circles of marbles are the same because you didn't add any or take any away when you moved them," the response was judged to be concrete operational. Conversely, if a child said, "The two circles are the same, but I don't know why," the response was not classified as concrete operational.

◉ Watch the **Video** *Conservation of Liquids* at **MyDevelopmentLab**

◉ Watch at **MyDevelopmentLab**

experiences (Flavell, Green, & Flavell, 1990). Two- and 3-year-olds have level 1 knowledge but not level 2 knowledge; the latter only begins to emerge in 4- and 5-year-olds. For example, a child of 4 or 5 understands that another person will feel sad if she fails or happy if she succeeds. The preschool child also begins to figure out that unpleasant emotions arise in situations in which the relationship between desire and reality is unequal. Sadness, for example, normally occurs when someone loses something or fails to acquire some desired object (Harris, 1989).

Some developmentalists have pointed out that the task of adopting another person's perspective can be challenging even for adults (Kesserling & Müller, 2010). For instance, a preschooler's egocentrism may impair his ability to communicate with a person who does not share his physical perspective. Similarly, the author of a cell phone user's manual may fail to provide users with clear instructions because of the difficulties that people who are know-ledgeable about a device have in adopting the cognitive perspective of those who are unfamiliar with it. Thus, egocentrism may be best thought of as a lifelong theme of cognitive development that is manifested differently in each of Piaget's stages.

**APPEARANCE AND REALITY**   The child's movement away from egocentrism seems to be part of a much broader change in her understanding of appearance and reality. Flavell has studied this understanding in a variety of ways (Flavell, 2004). In the most famous Flavell procedure, the experimenter shows the child a sponge that has been painted to look like a rock. Three-year-olds will say either that the object looks like a sponge and is a sponge or that it looks like a rock and is a rock. But 4- and 5-year-olds can distinguish the two; they realize that it looks like a rock but is really a sponge (Flavell, 1986). Thus, the older child understands that an object may not be what it seems.

Using similar materials, investigators have also asked whether a child can grasp the **false belief principle** (Lamb & Lewis, 2011). Individuals who understand the false belief principle can look at a problem or situation from another person's point of view in order to discern what kind of information can cause that person to believe something that isn't true. For example, after a child has felt the sponge/rock and has answered questions about what it looks like and what it "really" is, a researcher might ask something like this: "John [one of the child's playmates] hasn't touched this; he hasn't squeezed it. If John just sees it over here like this, what will he think it is? Will he think it's a rock or will he think that it's a sponge?" (Gopnik & Astington, 1988, p. 35). Most 3-year-olds think that the playmate will believe the object is a sponge because they themselves know that it *is* a sponge. By contrast, 4- and 5-year-olds realize that, because the playmate hasn't felt the sponge, he will have a false belief that it is a rock. Some studies show that 3-year-olds can perform more accurately if they are given a hint or clue. For example, if experimenters tell them that a "naughty" person is trying to fool their playmate, more of them will say that he will falsely think the sponge is rock (Bowler, Briskman, & Grice, 1999). But the child of 4 or 5 more consistently understands that someone else can believe something that isn't true and act on that belief.

## Theories of Mind

←-----------Learning Objective 6.8

Evidence like that just described has led researchers to examine children's understanding of others' thoughts and feelings in a new way. In the past 15 years, a number of developmentalists have examined a theoretical notion known as **theory of mind**, or a set of ideas that explain other people's ideas, beliefs, desires, and behavior (Flavell, 1999, 2000, 2004). As you might suspect, research indicates that adolescents and adults have a much more fully developed theory of mind than children do (Flavell & Green, 1999; Flavell, Green, & Flavell, 1998, 2000; Flavell, Green, Flavell, & Lin, 1999). However, research also suggests that the degree of sophistication in young children's theory of mind is probably greater than either Piaget or casual observers of children would expect.   ◉ Watch at **MyDevelopmentLab**

**UNDERSTANDING THOUGHTS, DESIRES, AND BELIEFS**   As early as 18 months, toddlers begin to have some understanding of the fact that people (but not inanimate objects) operate with goals and intentions (Meltzoff, 1995). By age 3, they understand some aspects of the links between people's thinking or feeling and their behavior. For example, they know that a person who wants something will try to get it. They also know that a person may still want something even if she can't have it (Lillard & Flavell, 1992). But 3-year-olds do not yet understand the basic principle that each person's actions are based on his or her own representation of reality and that a person's representation may differ from what is "really" there. For example, a person's *belief* about how popular she is has more influence on her behavior than her actual popularity. It is this new aspect of the theory of mind that clearly emerges at about age 4 or 5.

Furthermore, not until about age 6 do most children realize that knowledge can be derived through inference. For example, researchers in one study showed 4- and 6-year-olds

**false belief principle**   The understanding that another person might have a false belief and the ability to determine what information might cause the false belief. A child's understanding of the false belief principle is one key sign of the emergence of a representational theory of mind.

**theory of mind**   Ideas that collectively explain other people's ideas, beliefs, desires, and behavior.

What is a theory of mind, and how does it develop?

◉ **Watch** the **Videos** *False Belief Task* and *Theory of Mind* at **MyDevelopmentLab**

two toys of different colors (Pillow, 1999). Next, they placed the toys in opaque containers. They then opened one of the containers and showed the toy to a puppet. When asked whether the puppet now knew which color toy was in each container, only the 6-year-olds said yes.

Understanding of the reciprocal nature of thought seems to develop between age 5 and age 7 for most children. This is a particularly important development, because it is probably necessary for the creation of genuinely reciprocal friendships, which begin to become evident in the elementary school years (Sullivan, Zaitchik, & Tager-Flusberg, 1994). In fact, an individual preschooler's rate of development of theory of mind is a good predictor of her ability to judge others' trustworthiness (Maas, 2008).

**INFLUENCES ON THEORY OF MIND DEVELOPMENT**    Brain-imaging studies suggest that the development of a specific neural network in the cerebral cortex is strongly related to theory of mind development (Costa, Torriero, Oliveri, & Caltagirone, 2008). Moreover, developmentalists have found that a child's theory of mind is correlated with his performance on conservation tasks as well as egocentrism and understanding of appearance and reality (Melot & Houde, 1998; Yirmiya & Shulman, 1996). In addition, researchers have discovered links between working memory development and theory of mind (Benson & Sabbagh, 2010).

Recent findings suggest that interactions with siblings may be more important to theory of mind development than those with peers (Deneault et al., 2008; Hughes et al., 2005). In one study, researchers compared children with either older or younger siblings to those who had only co-twins or no siblings (Wright, Fineberg, Brown, & Perkins, 2005). They found that only children and twin-only children performed more poorly on theory of mind tasks than those who had either older or younger siblings. Various explanations have been proposed for what is called the *sibling advantage* in theory of mind development. To date, the best such theory focuses on the mentor-apprentice roles that often characterize siblings of different ages. You will learn more about these roles in Chapter 11.

Language skills, such as knowledge of words for feelings, desires, and thoughts—for example, *want*, *need*, *think*, and *remember*—are also related to theory of mind (Green, Pring, & Swettenham, 2004; Hughes et al., 2005). Furthermore, children whose parents discuss emotion-provoking past events with them develop a theory of mind more rapidly than their peers do (Ontai & Thompson, 2008). Indeed, some level of language facility may be a necessary condition for the development of theory of mind. Developmentalists have found that preschool children simply do not succeed at tests of false-belief skills until they have reached a certain threshold of general language skill (Milligan, Astington, & Dack, 2007).

Further support for this point comes from the finding that children with disabilities that affect language development, such as congenital deafness, mental retardation, or autism, develop a theory of mind more slowly than others (Rakhlin et al., 2011). Research has also demonstrated that, among such children, development of theory of mind is better predicted by language skills than by disability category (Porter, Coltheart, & Langdon, 2008).

*Research indicates that the sequence of development of theory of mind is highly similar across cultures.*

**Learning Objective 6.9**  - - - - - - - - - - - ➤
What does research indicate about the correlation between culture and theory of mind?

## False Belief and Theory of Mind Across Cultures

Research suggests that the false belief principle develops between ages 3 and 5 across a variety of cultures. For example, in one classic study Jeremy Avis and Paul Harris (1991) adapted the traditional false belief testing procedure for use with children in a pygmy tribe, the Baka, in Cameroon. The Baka are hunters and gatherers who live together in camps. Each child was tested in his or her own hut, using materials with which he or she was completely familiar. The child watched one adult named Mopfana (a member of the tribe) put some mango seeds into a bowl. Mopfana then left the hut, and a second adult (also a tribe member) told the child that they were going to play a game with Mopfana: They were going to hide the seeds in a cooking pot. Then the second adult asked the child what Mopfana was going to do when he came back. Would he look for the seeds in the bowl or in the pot? The second adult also asked the child whether Mopfana's heart would feel good or bad before he lifted the lid of the bowl. Younger children—2- and 3-year-olds and those who had recently turned 4—were much more likely to say that Mopfana would look for the seeds in the pot or to say that he would be sad before

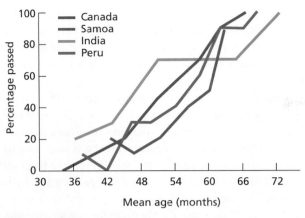
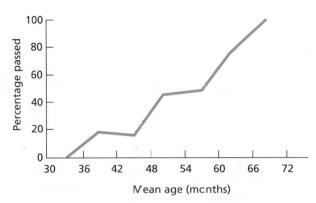

**FIGURE 6.5** False Belief Tasks across Cultures
Percentage of children passing the false-belief test as a function of age. In the left panel, data are plotted separately for Canada, Samoa, India, and Peru. In the right panel, results for these four cultures are combined. Data from 13 Samoan and all Thai children were excluded from this analysis because their birth dates were not available.

(*Source:* Callaghan et al. (2005). "Synchrony in the Onset of Mental State." *Psychological Science, 16*(5), 378–384, Fig. 1, p. 382, copyright © 2005 by Blackwell Publishers, Inc. Reprinted with permission.)

he looked in the bowl; older 4-year-olds and 5-year-olds were nearly always right on both questions.

In another classic study, when Flavell used his sponge/rock task with children in mainland China, he found that Chinese 3-year-olds are just as confused about this task as are American or British 3-year-olds, whereas 5-year-old Chinese children had no difficulty with it (Flavell, Zhang, Zou, Dong, & Qi, 1983). In these very different cultures, then, something similar seems to be occurring between ages 3 and 5. In these years, all children seem to understand something general about the difference between appearance and reality.

Research also suggests that certain aspects of theory of mind development may be universal. For example, similar sequences of such development have been found in the United States, China, Europe, and India (Cole & Packer, 2011; Liu, Wellman, Tardif, & Sabbagh, 2008). Figure 6.5 shows the results of one study comparing the performance of children from five cultures on a false-belief task (Callaghan et al., 2005). Moreover, participation in shared pretending has also been shown to be related to theory of mind development cross- culturally (Tan-Niam, Wood, & O'Malley, 1998).

## Alternative Theories of Early Childhood Thinking

◄ - - - - - - - - - - -**Learning Objective 6.10**
How do the theories of the neo-Piagetians and Vygotsky explain cognitive development?

In recent years, a number of interesting theoretical approaches have attempted to explain both Piaget's original results and more recent findings that appear to contradict them.

**NEO-PIAGETIAN THEORIES**   One set of alternative proposals is based on the information-processing model (explained in Chapter 1). These are called **neo-Piagetian theories** because they expand on, rather than contradict, Piaget's views (Morral, Gobbo, Marini, & Sheese, 2008). For example, the late neo-Piagetian Robbie Case explained age differences in cognitive development as a function of changes in children's use of their short-term memories (Case, 1985, 1992). Case used the term **short-term storage space (STSS)** to refer to working memory capacity. According to Case, there is a limit on how many schemes can be attended to in STSS. He referred to the maximum number of schemes that may be put into STSS at one time as **operational efficiency**. Improvements in operational efficiency occur through both practice (through tasks that require memory use, such as learning the alphabet) and brain maturation as the child gets older. Thus, a 7-year-old is better able to handle the processing demands of conservation tasks than a 4-year-old because of improvements in the operational efficiency of the STSS.

A good example of the function of STSS may be found by examining *matrix classification*, a task Piaget often used with both preschool and school-aged children (see Figure 6.6 on page 148).

**neo-Piagetian theory**   A theory of cognitive development that assumes that Piaget's basic ideas are correct but that uses concepts from information-processing theory to explain children's movement from one stage to the next.

**short-term storage space (STSS)**   A neo-Piagetian term for working memory capacity.

**operational efficiency**   A neo-Piagetian term for the number of schemes an individual can place into working memory at one time.

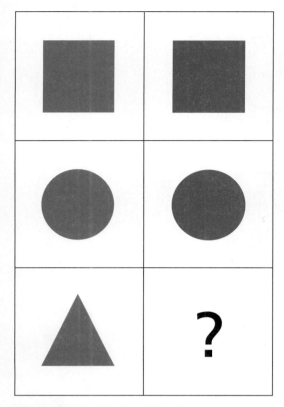

**FIGURE 6.6** Neo-Piagetian Matrix Task
Neo-Piagetians have used Piaget's matrix classification task in strategy training studies with young children. Before training, most preschoolers say that a green triangle or an orange circle belongs in the box with the question mark. After learning a two-step strategy in which they are taught to classify each object first by shape and then by color, children understand that an orange triangle is the figure that is needed to complete the matrix.

Matrix classification requires the child to place a given stimulus in two categories at the same time. Young children fail at such tasks because, according to neo-Piagetian theory, they begin by processing the stimulus according to one dimension (either shape or color) and then either fail to realize that it is necessary to reprocess the stimulus along the second dimension or forget to do so.

However, researchers have trained young children to perform correctly on such tasks by using a two-step strategy. They are taught to think of a red triangle, for example, in terms of shape first and color second. Typically, instruction involves a number of training tasks in which researchers remind children repeatedly that it is necessary to remember to reclassify stimuli with respect to the second variable. According to Case, both children's failure prior to instruction and the type of strategy training to which they respond illustrate the constraints imposed on problem-solving by the limited operational efficiency of the younger child's STSS. There is only room for one scheme at a time in the child's STSS, either shape or color. The training studies show that younger children can learn to perform correctly but do so in a way that is qualitatively different from the approach of older children. The older child's more efficient STSS allows her to think about shape and color at the same time and therefore to perform matrix classification successfully without any training.

However, it appears that children must be exposed to multiple training sessions that take place over a fairly extended period of time, as long as an entire year, in order to effect permanent changes in their matrix completion behaviors (Siegler & Svetina, 2002). Comparative research has shown that children who develop these skills on their own do so over an equivalent period of time and demonstrate transitional behaviors that are quite similar to those of children who are trained by experimenters. Thus, some developmentalists have suggested that there is no advantage to be gained by training children to exhibit skills that they are known to acquire in the natural course of cognitive development. Moreover, with regard to research methodology, when children must be trained over long periods of time, it becomes impossible to distinguish between the effects of training and those of the natural developmental processes that are occurring contemporaneously with such training.

**VYGOTSKY'S SOCIO-CULTURAL THEORY** In Chapter 1, you learned that psychologists' interest in Russian psychologist Lev Vygotsky's views on development has grown recently. Vygotsky's theory differs from both Piagetian and neo-Piagetian theory in its emphasis on the role of social factors in cognitive development. For example, two preschoolers working on a puzzle together discuss where the pieces belong. After a number of such dialogues, the participants internalize the discussion. It then becomes a model for an internal conversation the child uses to guide himself through the puzzle-solution process. In this way, Vygotsky suggested, solutions to problems are socially generated and learned. Vygotsky did not deny that individual learning takes place. Rather, he suggested that group learning processes are central to cognitive development. Consequently, from Vygotsky's perspective, social interaction is required for cognitive development (Thomas, 2005).

You'll recall that two important general principles of Vygotsky's theory are the *zone of proximal development* and *scaffolding*. Vygotsky also proposed specific stages of cognitive development from birth to age 7. Each stage represents a step toward the child's internalization of the ways of thinking used by adults in his society. ◉ Watch at **MyDevelopmentLab**

In the first period, called the *primitive stage*, the infant possesses mental processes that are similar to those of lower animals. He learns primarily through conditioning until language begins to develop in the second year. At that point, he enters the *naive psychology stage*, in which he learns to use language to communicate but still does not understand its symbolic character. For example, he doesn't realize that any collection of sounds could stand for the object "chair" as long as everyone agrees on the sounds; that is, if all English speakers agreed to substitute the word *blek* for *chair*, they could do so because they would all understand what *blek* meant.

Once the child begins to appreciate the symbolic function of language, near the end of the third year of life, he enters the *egocentric speech stage*. In this stage, he uses language as a

◉ Watch the Video *Scaffolding* at **MyDevelopmentLab**

guide to solving problems. In effect, he tells himself how to do things. For example, a 3-year-old walking down a flight of stairs might say to himself "Be careful." Such a statement would be the result of his internalization of statements made to him by more mature individuals in his environment.

Piaget also recognized the existence and importance of egocentric speech. However, he believed that egocentric speech disappeared as the child approached the end of the preoperational stage. In contrast, Vygotsky claimed that egocentric speech becomes completely internalized at age 6 or 7, when children enter the final period of cognitive development, the *ingrowth stage*. Thus, he suggested that the logical thinking Piaget ascribed to older children resulted from their internalization of speech routines they had acquired from older children and adults in the social world rather than from schemes they had constructed for themselves through interaction with the physical world.

At present, there is insufficient evidence to support or contradict most of Vygotsky's ideas (Miller, 2002). However, some of his ideas have been supported by research. For instance, researchers have found that private speech helps children solve problems (Villegas, Castellanos, & Gutiérrez, 2009). In addition, some intriguing research on children's construction of theory of mind ideas during social interactions lends weight to Vygotsky's major propositions. It seems that children in pairs and groups do produce more sophisticated theory of mind ideas than individual children who work on problems alone. For this reason, educators have used Vygotsky's theory as the basis for recommending that school children do assignments and work on projects in groups rather than individually (Norton & D'Ambrosio, 2008). However, the sophistication of a group's ideas appears to depend on the presence of at least one fairly advanced individual child in the group (Tan-Niam, Wood, & O'Malley, 1998). Thus, Vygotsky's theory may ignore the important contributions of individual thought to group interaction.

## The School-Aged Child

Like their younger counterparts, school-aged children develop figurative schemes at an impressive pace, especially when formal schooling introduces them to a breadth of ideas and basic facts about the world that take them beyond everyday experience. What is different about this stage, though, is that children's operative schemes begin to take shape and to provide them with a network of rules that provide logical frameworks for their figurative schemes. Consequently, the child develops a set of immensely powerful, abstract, general rules or strategies for examining and interacting with the world. Piaget called these new rules *concrete operations*.

## Piaget's View of Concrete Operations

◄----------- Learning Objective 6.11

What are concrete operations, and how do they represent an advance over earlier forms of thought?

Piaget defined concrete operations as a set of powerful, abstract schemes that are critical building blocks of logical thinking, providing internal rules about objects and their relationships.

**REVERSIBILITY**  Piaget thought that the most critical of all the concrete operations was **reversibility**—the understanding that both physical actions and mental operations can be reversed. The clay sausage in a conservation experiment can be made back into a ball; the water can be poured back into the shorter, fatter glass. This understanding of the basic reversibility of actions lies behind many of the gains made during this period.

For example, if you understand reversibility, then knowing that A is larger than B also tells you that B is smaller than A. The ability to understand hierarchies of classes, such as "Fido," "spaniel," "dog," and "animal," also rests on this ability to go backward as well as forward in thinking about relationships. Both Piaget's original observations and more recent research have demonstrated that at about age 7 or 8 the child first grasps the principle of **class inclusion**, the idea that subordinate classes are included in larger, superordinate classes. Bananas are included in the class "fruit," fruits are included in the class "food," and so forth. Preschool children understand that bananas are also fruit, but they do not yet fully understand the relationship between the classes—that the class "fruit" is superordinate, including all bananas as well as all other types of fruit, such as oranges and apples.

**reversibility**  One of the most critical of the operations Piaget identified as part of the concrete operations period: the understanding that actions and mental operations can be reversed.

**class inclusion**  The principle that subordinate classes of objects are included in superordinate classes.

*Inductive reasoning helps school-aged children figure out how to work devices such as smart phones.*

**inductive logic** Reasoning from the particular to the general, from experience to broad rules, characteristic of concrete operational thinking.

**deductive logic** Reasoning from the general to the particular, from a rule to an expected instance or from a theory to a hypothesis, characteristic of formal operational thinking.

**horizontal decalage** Piaget's term for school-aged children's inconsistent performance on concrete operations tasks.

Piaget also proposed that reversibility underlies the school-aged child's ability to use **inductive logic**: She can reason from her own experience to a general principle. For example, she can move from the observation that when you add another toy to a set and then count the set, it has one more toy than it did before, to a general principle that adding always makes more.

Elementary school children are pretty good observational scientists and enjoy cataloging, counting species of trees or birds, or figuring out the nesting habits of guinea pigs. What they are not yet good at is **deductive logic**, which requires starting with a general principle and then predicting some outcome or observation, like going from a theory to a hypothesis. For example, suppose someone asked you to think of all the ways human relationships and societies would be different if women were physically as strong as men. Answering this question requires deductive, not inductive, logic; the problem is hard because you must imagine things that you have not experienced. The concrete operational child is good at dealing with things he knows or can see and physically manipulate—that is, he is good with concrete, or actual things; he does not do well with mentally manipulating ideas or possibilities. Piaget thought that deductive reasoning did not develop until the stage of formal operations in adolescence.

**HORIZONTAL DECALAGE** Note that Piaget did *not* argue that all concrete operational skills popped out at the same moment, as if a light bulb had gone on in the child's head. He used the term **horizontal decalage** to refer to children's tendency to be able to solve some kinds of concrete operational problems earlier than others. The French word *decalage* means "shift." The shift into concrete operational thinking is "horizontal" because it involves applying the same kind of thinking—concrete operational logic—to new kinds of problems. A "vertical" decalage would be a shift from one kind of thinking to another, as happens when children move from the preoperational to the concrete operational stage.

An early longitudinal study of concrete operations tasks by Carol Tomlinson-Keasey and her colleagues (1979) demonstrated just how long the period of horizontal decalage may actually be. They followed a group of 38 children from kindergarten through third grade, testing them with five tasks each time: conservation of mass, weight, and volume; class inclusion; and hierarchical classification. You can see from Figure 6.7 that the children got better at all five tasks over the 3-year period, with a spurt between the end of kindergarten and the beginning

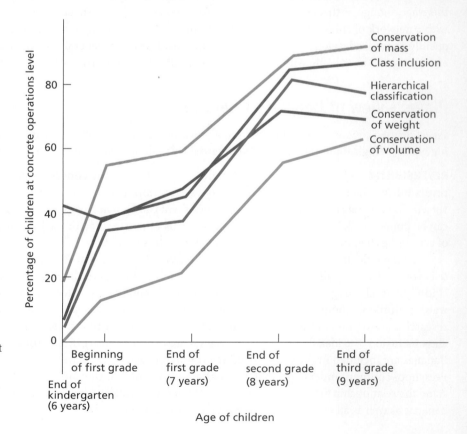

**FIGURE 6.7** Longitudinal Study of Concrete Operations
In this longitudinal study, children were tested with the same set of concrete operations tasks five different times, beginning in kindergarten and ending in the third grade.

(*Source:* Tomlinson-Keasey, C., Eisert, D. C., Kahle, L. R., Hardy-Brown, K.,& Keasey, B. (1979). "The structure of concrete operational thought." *Child Development, 50,* 1153–1163.)

of first grade (at about the age Piaget thought that concrete operations really developed) and another spurt during second grade. However, even at the end of third grade, not every child had mastered all of the concrete operations tasks.

Understanding the concept of horizontal decalage is especially important for teachers, parents, and others who interact with children every day. For example, a 9-year-old may grasp the logic of some mathematical relationships (e.g., If 6 + 2 = 8 and 4 + 4 = 8, then 6 + 2 = 4 + 4). Her understanding of such relationships demonstrates concrete operational thought. However, the same child, when asked by a parent to recall where she left her backpack, has difficulty applying concrete operational logic to the problem. As adults, we might use our concrete operations schemes to think of the problem this way: "If I had my backpack when I came in the door after school, and I didn't have it when I sat down in the living room, then it must be somewhere between the door and the living room." However, a 9-year-old who can grasp the concrete operational logic of mathematical relationships may demonstrate horizontal decalage by responding to the lost backpack problem with preoperational thinking: "I don't know where my backpack is; someone must have stolen it." In such situations, teachers or parents may think a child is being difficult or lazy; in reality, she simply may not yet be capable of using concrete operational thinking to solve everyday problems that seem simple to adults but are actually quite complex.

## Different Approaches to Concrete Operational Thought ◄----------- Learning Objective 6.12

What does Siegler's research suggest about concrete operational thinking?

Some psychologists have suggested that the problem of horizontal decalage calls into question Piaget's assertion that concrete operational thinking is a stage of cognitive development.

**SIEGLER'S WAVE THEORY**   The work of Robert Siegler (1996; Siegler & Chen, 2002) has shown that individual children may use a wide variety of types of rules—from very simple to quite sophisticated—on the same type of problem in different attempts on the same day (Siegler & Lin, 2010). For example, if you give first- or second-graders simple addition problems (3 + 6, 9 + 4, etc.), they may solve each problem in any of a variety of ways. If they have committed a particular sum to memory, they may retrieve the answer directly from memory without calculation—the strategy most adults use for simple addition problems. On other problems, children may simply count, starting at 1, until they reach the sum. So 6 + 3 becomes "One, two, three, four, five, six, . . . seven, eight, nine." Alternatively, they may use what some researchers call the *min strategy*, a somewhat more sophisticated rule in which the child starts with the larger number and then adds the smaller one by counting. In this method, the child arrives at the sum 3 + 6 by saying to herself, "Seven, eight, nine." The child mentally counts each number as it is added. So, when she begins at 6 and counts to 7, she knows that one number has been added. Similarly, she knows that two numbers have been added when she gets to 8, and three have been added when she arrives at 9. Finally, a child might use a still more sophisticated *decomposition strategy*, which involves dividing a problem into several simpler ones. For example, a child might add 9 + 4 by thinking, "10 + 4 = 14, 9 is one less than 10, 14 − 1 = 13, so 9 + 4 = 13" (Siegler, 1996, p. 94). (You may use this method for more complicated problems, such as multiplying 16 × 9. You might think, "9 × 10 = 90; 9 × 6 = 54; 54 + 90 = 144.")

With increasing age, elementary school children use counting less and less while increasing their use of retrieval, the min strategy, and decomposition—a finding that is entirely consistent with the notion of a gradual increase in use of more complex strategies. What Siegler has added to this information is the finding that the same child may use all these different strategies on different addition problems on the same day. So, it isn't that each child systematically shifts from one level of strategy to another, but rather that any given child may have a whole variety of strategies and may use some or all of them on different problems. Over time, the child's repertoire of likely strategies does indeed shift

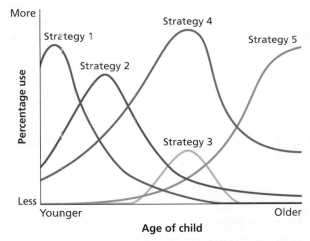

**FIGURE 6.8** Siegler's Wave Theory
Siegler's "overlapping wave" model of cognitive development is probably a better description of the way children move toward more complex forms of thinking than the steplike stage model Piaget originally proposed.

(*Source: Emerging Minds: The Process of Change in Children's Thinking* by Robert S. Siegler, © 1996 by Oxford University Press, Inc. Used by permission of Oxford University Press.)

**relational complexity** The number of elements in a problem and the complexity of the relationships among the elements.

**transitivity** The ability to make inferences about logical relationships in an ordered set of stimuli.

**seriation** The ability to use a rule to put an array of objects in order.

✳ Explore the Concept *Virtual Brain: Learning and Memory* at **MyDevelopmentLab**

toward more and more complex or sophisticated ones, just as Piaget and others have described. But the process is not steplike; instead, it is more like a series of waves, as shown in Figure 6.8 on page 151. When children add a new strategy, they do not immediately give up old ones; instead, they continue to use the old and the new for a while. Gradually, as the new strategies become more firmly established and better rehearsed, the less efficient or less effective strategies are dropped. ✳ Explore at **MyDevelopmentLab**

**RELATIONAL COMPLEXITY** Other theorists have explained children's success and failure on Piaget's concrete operational tasks as a result of variations in the **relational complexity** of the tasks themselves (Andrews & Halford, 2002). They argue that success on Piaget's tasks is determined by how many elements a problem has and how complicated the relationships among the elements are. Performance on Piaget's tasks improves across middle childhood, they claim, because improvements in the efficiency of the child's working memory enable him to cognitively manage more elements and more complex relationships among the elements of a problem.

One line of research on relational complexity deals with **transitivity**, the ability to make inferences about logical relationships in an ordered set of stimuli (Andrews & Halford, 1998). A simple example of a transitivity task is one in which a child is shown a stick *A* and asked to compare it to a slightly shorter stick *B*. Through questioning and discussion with the experimenter, the child concludes that *A* is longer than *B*. He is then asked to compare *B* to a slightly shorter stick *C*. Once he concludes that *B* is longer than *C*, he is asked whether *A* is longer or shorter than *C*. Children who infer that *A* must be longer than *C*, even though they did not directly compare *A* to *C*, exhibit transitivity. Researchers whose studies span 3 decades have found that few children younger than 6 can solve simple transitivity problems (Murray & Youniss, 1968; Andrews & Halford, 1998; Wright, Robertson, & Hadfield, 2011). When the complexity of transitivity problems is increased, as when sticks *B* and *C* are of equal length, even 8-year-olds have difficulty with transitivity (Andrews & Halford, 1998; Murray & Youniss, 1968). Thus, contrary to Piaget's view, there may not be a single transitivity scheme that is universally applicable to all such problems. Instead, a child's success on a transitivity problem may depend on how well the problem fits the capabilities of his information processing system at a particular point in development.

Relational complexity studies also focus on **seriation** tasks, problems that require children to use a rule to put an array of objects in order (Piaget & Inhelder, 1969). In Piaget's classic version of the seriation task, the researcher asks the child to arrange ten sticks of varying length from shortest to longest. Most children younger than 8 create ordered sets that include only three or four sticks rather than a single ordered array that includes all of them. In other words, they simplify the task by breaking it down into several less complex subtasks that they can accomplish (Halford, Bunch, & McCredden, 2007). In the process, however, they end up with an incorrect solution to the original problem.

## Adolescence

Piaget's research led him to conclude that a new level of thinking emerges fairly rapidly in early adolescence that enables teens to think logically about ideas that are not tied to concrete referents in the real world. Called *formal operations*, this stage is typically defined as the period during which adolescents learn to reason logically about abstract concepts.

**Learning Objective 6.13** ----------➤
What are the key elements of formal operational thinking?

## Piaget's View of Formal Operations

The formal operations stage has a number of key elements.

**SYSTEMATIC PROBLEM SOLVING** One important feature of formal operational thinking is the ability to search systematically and methodically for the answer to a problem. To study this ability, Piaget and his colleague Barbel Inhelder (Inhelder & Piaget, 1958) presented adolescents with complex tasks, mostly drawn from the physical sciences. In one of these tasks, participants were given various lengths of string and a set of objects of various weights that could be tied to one of the strings to make a swinging pendulum. They were shown how to start the pendulum by pushing the weight with differing amounts of force and by holding the weight at different heights. The participants' task was to figure out whether the length of the string, the weight of the object, the force of the push, or the height of the push (or a combination of these factors) determines the period of the pendulum, that is, the amount of time for one swing. (In case you've forgotten your high school physics, the answer is that only the length of the string affects the period of the pendulum.)

If you give this task to a concrete operational child, she will usually try out many different combinations of length, weight, force, and height in an inefficient way. She might try a heavy weight on a long string and then a light weight on a short string. Because she has changed both string length and weight in these two trials, however, there is no way she can draw a clear conclusion about either factor. In contrast, an adolescent using formal operational thinking is likely to be more organized, attempting to vary just one of the four factors at a time. She may try a heavy object with a short string, then with a medium string, then with a long one. After that, she might try a light object with the three lengths of string. Of course, not all adolescents (or all adults, for that matter) are quite this methodical in their approach. Still, there is a very dramatic difference between the overall strategy used by 10-year-olds and that used by 15-year-olds, which marks the shift from concrete to formal operations.

**LOGIC**  Another facet of the shift from concrete to formal operations is the appearance of what Piaget called hypothetico-deductive reasoning in the child's repertoire of skills. Piaget suggested that the concrete operational child can use inductive reasoning, which involves arriving at a conclusion or a rule based on a lot of individual experiences. **Hypothetico-deductive reasoning**, a more sophisticated kind of reasoning, involves using deductive logic, considering hypotheses or hypothetical premises, and then deriving logical outcomes. For example, the statement "If all people are equal, then you and I must be equal" involves logic of this type. Although children as young as 4 or 5 can understand some deductive relationships if the premises given are factually true, both cross-sectional and longitudinal studies support Piaget's assertion that only at adolescence are young people able to understand and use the basic principles of logic (Mueller, Overton, & Reene, 2001; Ward & Overton, 1990).

A great deal of the logic of science is hypothetico-deductive logic. Scientists begin with a theory and propose, "If this theory is correct, then we should observe such and such." In doing this, they are going well beyond their observations; they are conceiving of things they have never

**hypothetico-deductive reasoning**
Piaget's term for the form of reasoning that is part of formal operational thought and involves not just deductive logic but also the ability to consider hypotheses and hypothetical possibilities.

*Formal education, especially instruction in math and science, contributes to the development of formal operational thinking in early adolescence. Likewise, formal operational thinking enables teens to assimilate such instruction and use it to solve problems independently.*

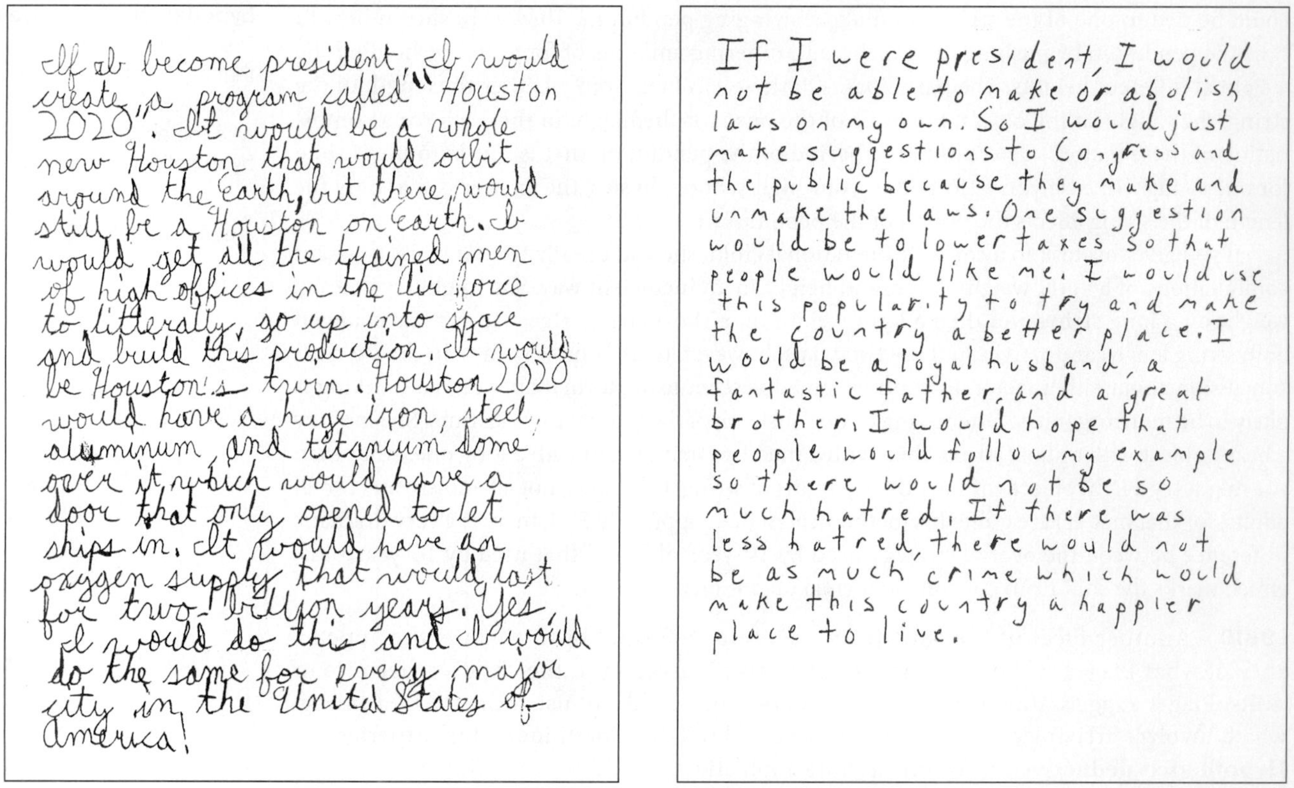
If I become president, I would create a program called "Houston 2020". It would be a whole new Houston that would orbit around the Earth, but there would still be a Houston on Earth. I would get all the trained men of high offices in the Air Force to litterally go up into space and build this production. It would be Houston's twin. Houston 2020 would have a huge iron, steel, aluminum and titanium dome over it which would have a door that only opened to let ships in. It would have an oxygen supply that would last for two billion years. Yes I would do this and I would do the same for every major city in the United States of America!

If I were president, I would not be able to make or abolish laws on my own. So I would just make suggestions to Congress and the public because they make and unmake the laws. One suggestion would be to lower taxes so that people would like me. I would use this popularity to try and make the country a better place. I would be a loyal husband, a fantastic father, and a great brother. I would hope that people would follow my example so there would not be so much hatred. If there was less hatred, there would not be as much crime which would make this country a happier place to live.

**FIGURE 6.9** Concrete versus Formal Operational Thinking
The same boy wrote both of these compositions. The one on the left was written when the boy was 10, and the other when he was 13. The compositions illustrate the difference between concrete operational and formal operational thinking in response to the hypothetical question "What would you do if you became president of the United States?"
(*Source:* Author.)

seen that ought to be true or observable. We can think of the change to this type of thinking at adolescence as part of a general decentering process that began much earlier. The preoperational child gradually moves away from his egocentrism and comes to be able to view things from the physical or emotional perspective of others. During the formal operations stage, the child takes another step by freeing himself even from his reliance on specific experiences. **Watch** at **MyDevelopmentLab**

**Watch** the **Video** *Egocentrism Task* at **MyDevelopmentLab**

Piaget also suggested that in many adolescents, hypothetico-deductive thinking leads to an outlook he called *naive idealism* (Piaget & Inhelder, 1969). Adolescents can use this powerful intellectual tool to think of an ideal world and to compare the real world to it. Not surprisingly, the real world often falls short of the ideal. As a result, some adolescents become so dissatisfied with the world that they resolve to change it. For many, the changes they propose are personal. For example, a teen whose parents have been divorced for years may suddenly decide she wants to live with the noncustodial parent because she expects that her life will be better. Another may express naive idealism by becoming involved in a political or religious organization.

The two compositions in Figure 6.9 illustrate how concrete operational and formal operational thinking lead to very different results when children are asked to reason deductively from an untrue premise. Both essays were written by the same boy, one at age 10 and the other at age 13, in response to the question "What would you do if you became president of the United States?" The 10-year-old boy's response is full of ideas about the president's ability to manipulate the concrete world. Significantly, it proposes building replicas of American cities in space, nicely illustrating the concrete operational thinker's tendency to replicate concrete reality when asked to think hypothetically. By contrast, the composition written at age 13 reflects both better deductive thinking and Piaget's notion of naive idealism. Moreover, it contains abstract ideas, such as the hypothesized relationship between hatred and crime, that are completely absent from the composition written at age 10. Thus, as Piaget's theory suggests, at 13, this boy not only knew more about the office of the president (e.g., that the president doesn't make laws singlehandedly), but he also thought quite differently about the world than he did at age 10. ⊙⎯Watch at MyDevelopmentLab

⊙⎯Watch the Video *Deductive Reasoning* at MyDevelopmentLab

## Post-Piagetian Work on Adolescent Thought

◄----------- Learning Objective 6.14
What does post-Piagetian research suggest about this stage?

A good deal of post-Piagetian research confirms Piaget's basic observations. Adolescents, much more than elementary school children, operate with possibilities in addition to reality, and they are more likely to use deductive logic. An 8-year-old thinks that "knowing" something is a simple matter of finding out the facts; a teenager is more likely to see knowledge as relative, as less certain (Bartsch, 1993). Deanna Kuhn and her colleagues (1995) have also found that teenagers and young adults, faced with disconfirming evidence, are more likely than younger children are to change their theories or their initial guesses; they are also more systematic in seeking out new information that will help hone their hypotheses—both hallmarks of formal operational reasoning.

A research illustration clearly illustrates the change in thinking. In an early cross-sectional study, Susan Martorano (1977) tested 20 girls at each of four grades (6th, 8th, 10th, and 12th) on 10 different tasks that required one or more of what Piaget called *formal operations skills*. Indeed, many of the tasks Martorano used were those Piaget himself had devised. Results from two of these tasks are shown in Figure 6.10. The pendulum problem is the same one described earlier; the balance problem requires a youngster to predict whether two different weights, hung at varying distances on either side of a scale, will balance. To solve this problem using formal operations, the teenager must consider both weight and distance simultaneously. You can see from the graph that a significant improvement in scores occurred between 8th and 10th grades (between ages 13 and 15).

**FORMAL OPERATIONS AND ADOLESCENT DECISION MAKING**    In a more practical vein, Catherine Lewis (1981) has shown that teenagers' new cognitive abilities alter the ways in which they go about making decisions. Older teenagers are more focused on the future, on possibilities, and on options when they consider decisions. Lewis asked 8th-, 10th-, and 12th-grade students to respond to a set of dilemmas, each of which involved a person facing a difficult decision, such as whether to have an operation to remove a facial disfigurement or how to decide which doctor to trust when different doctors give differing advice. Forty-two percent of the 12th graders, but only 11% of the 8th graders, mentioned future possibilities in their answers to these dilemmas.

Note, though, that even among the 12th graders in Lewis's study, nearly three-fifths did not show this type of future orientation. And take another look at Figure 6.10; only about 50–60% of 12th graders solved the two formal operations problems. In fact, only 2 of the 20 12th graders in Martorano's study used formal operational logic on all 10 problems. These findings reflect a common pattern in research on adolescent thinking: By no means do all teenagers (or adults) use these more abstract forms of logic and thought. Keating (1980) estimates that only about 50–60% of 18- to 20-year-olds in industrialized countries use formal operations at all, let alone consistently. In nonindustrialized countries, the rates are even lower (Keller, 2011). Moreover, rates of attainment of formal operations among secondary students in Europe have declined considerably over the past thirty years, leading developmentalists to speculate that changes in teaching strategies and the content of school curricula in recent decades may have had a negative effect on adolescents' cognitive development (Shayer & Ginsburg, 2009). Such findings suggest that social, cultural, and educational factors play a larger role in the development of formal operational thinking than Piaget assumed.

There are several possible explanations for such low levels of formal operational thought. One is that the parts of the brain needed to connect hypothetico-deductive thought to everyday problems may not be sufficiently developed to make these connections until the late teens. Neuroimaging studies comparing the brain activity of children, teens, and adults while they were engaged in a gambling task provide support for this hypothesis (Crone & van der Molen, 2004).

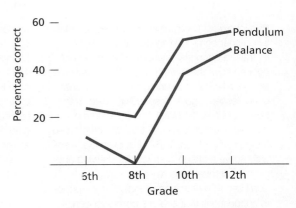

**FIGURE 6.10**  Performance on Two Formal Operations Tasks
These are the results from 2 of the 10 different formal operations tasks used in Martorano's cross-sectional study.

(*Source:* Martorano, 1977, p. 670. Copyright by the American Psychological Association Developmental analysis of performance on Piaget's formal operations tasks. *Developmental Psychology, 13,* 666–672.)

Expertise may also be a crucial factor. That is, most of us have some formal operational ability, but we can apply it only to topics or tasks with which we are highly familiar. Willis Overton and his colleagues (1987) have found considerable support for this possibility in their research. They have found that as many as 90% of adolescents can solve quite complex logic problems if the problems are stated using familiar content, while only half can solve identical logic problems when they are stated in abstract language.

Another possibility is that most everyday experiences and tasks do not require formal operations. Inductive reasoning or other simpler forms of logic are quite sufficient most of the time. We can elevate our thinking a notch under some circumstances, especially if someone reminds us that it would be useful to do so, but we simply don't rehearse formal operations very much.

Finally, psychologist David Elkind (1967) has proposed that, paradoxically, it is formal operational thinking itself that impairs adolescents' ability to make sound decisions about everyday matters. Elkind has proposed that the hypothetico-deductive capabilities associated with formal operational thought enable teenagers to construct unrealistic ideas about both the present and the future. In effect, these ideas lead teens to view their lives with either excessive optimism or excessive pessimism. Elkind's ideas have had a great deal of influence on the approaches taken by researchers to understanding teens' decisions with regard to risky behaviors such as drug use (see *Thinking about Research*).

**CULTURE AND FORMAL OPERATIONAL THINKING** The fact that formal operational thinking is found more often among young people or adults in Western or other industrialized cultures can be interpreted as being due to the fact that such cultures include high levels of technology and complex life-styles that demand more formal operational thought. By this argument, all nondevelopmentally disabled teenagers and adults are thought to have the capacity for formal logic, but only those of us whose lives demand its development will actually acquire it (Kuhn, 2008).

Notice that all these explanations undermine the very notion of a universal "stage" of thinking in adolescence. Yes, more abstract forms of thinking may develop in adolescence, but they are neither universal nor broadly used by individual teenagers or adults. Whether one develops or uses these forms of logic depends heavily on experience, expertise, and environmental demand.

⊙ **Watch** the **Video** *Imaginary Audience* at **MyDevelopmentLab**

---

**THINKING ABOUT RESEARCH**

## Elkind's Adolescent Egocentrism

Psychologist David Elkind hypothesized that another common manifestation of hypothetico-deductive reasoning is *adolescent egocentrism*, the belief that one's thoughts, beliefs, and feelings are unique. One component of adolescent egocentrism, Elkind said, is the *personal fable*, the belief that the events of one's life are controlled by a mentally constructed autobiography (Elkind, 1967). For example, a sexually active teenage girl might be drawing upon such a personal fable when she says "I just don't see myself getting pregnant" in response to suggestions that she use contraception. In contrast to this inappropriately rosy view of the future, a teen who is involved in a violent street gang may say "I'll probably get shot before I make 18" when advised to leave the gang and focus on graduating from high school.

Elkind also proposed that adolescent egocentrism drives teenagers to try out various attitudes, behaviors, and even clothing

choices in front of an *imaginary audience*, an internalized set of behavioral standards usually derived from a teenager's peer group. Think about the example of a teenaged girl who is habitually late for school because she changes clothes two or three times before leaving home. Each time the girl puts on a different outfit, she imagines how her peers at school will respond to it. If the imaginary audience criticizes the outfit, the girl feels she must change clothes in order to elicit a more favorable response

Many developmentalists have found Elkind's personal fable and imaginary audience to be helpful in explaining a variety of adolescents' risky behaviors. For example, both types of thinking come into play when teens decide to start smoking (Bright, McKillop, & Ryder, 2008). As Elkind suggests, then, the personal fable and imaginary audience may lead

adolescents to make poor decisions about risky behaviors.

### Learning Objective 6.13a
How does adolescent egocentrism affect teenagers' development?

#### CRITICAL ANALYSIS

1. In what ways might the personal fable and imaginary audience positively influence a teenager's decisions about risky behaviors such as drug use and unsafe sex? How might they negatively influence such decisions?
2. What are the roles of the imaginary audience and the personal fable in adults' perceptions of themselves?

⊙ **Watch** at **MyDevelopmentLab**

## Leading Questions and Children's Memory

Ari was alarmed when his 3-year-old son, Micah, told him about an incident involving a neighbor that Ari believed to be a possible case of sexual molestation, so he immediately called the police. Before the police arrived, Ari received a telephone call from a social worker, who advised Ari to write down everything that his son said spontaneously about the event but to avoid questioning him directly. Puzzled, Ari wondered, Who might be better than a parent to question a child about such a potentially traumatic event?

👁 Watch at **MyDevelopmentLab**

The social worker explained that pre-schoolers' memories are more suggestible than those of older children or adults (Ceci & Bruck, 1995; Hardy & Van Leeuwen, 2004). One common way that researchers study the suggestibility factor is to show the same film to children and adults. Then, while asking questions about what the participants saw, the investigators inject a question that assumes something that didn't really happen (e.g., "He was carrying a pipe wrench

when he came into the room, wasn't he?"). Young children are more affected than adults are by such misleading suggestions, because they have poor *source monitoring skills*, the ability to keep track of where a piece of information originated (Bright-Paul, Jarrold, & Wright, 2008). As a result, a young child who is being questioned has difficulty distinguishing between ideas that originated in his own memory and those that are contained in or implied by the interviewers' questions.

Studies of children's vulnerability to suggestive questions have led professionals who work with children who have been molested to advise parents to avoid directly questioning their children. Instead, say experts, parents should encourage children to speak spontaneously about what happened. When parents follow this advice, trained interviewers who know how to question preschoolers without unduly influencing them can have confidence in the information that they gain (Bruck, Ceci, & Hembrooke, 1998).

### Learning Objective 6.15a
How do children's source monitoring skills influence their responses to leading questions?

#### REFLECTION

1. Suppose when you pick your child up from child care, the teacher tells you that your child hit one of his classmates and asks you to talk to him about it. Based on the research regarding young children's memories, how should you proceed if you want to get the most accurate report possible about the incident from your child?

2. Think about possible conflicts between the rights of individuals who are accused of crimes and those of children who must be protected from people who would exploit them. How might research-based interviewing techniques help to protect both?

## Development of Information-Processing Skills

Human memory does not function as a mental tape recorder. Instead, memory is a constructive process, one that sometimes leads to errors and can even result in the invention of pseudomemories depicting events that never actually happened (Loftus, 1993). The constructive aspect of memory can begin quite early in life, as discussed in *Developmental Science in the Real World*. You may recall from Chapter 1 that the information-processing perspective is the view that has most often been used to study human memory. The information-processing model of memory postulates that information is processed, stored, and retrieved in different ways by the various components of the memory system, each of which has unique characteristics (see Figure 1.4 on page 21). Although information-processing theory is not truly a developmental theory, research derived from this perspective has shed considerable light on age-related changes in memory and other aspects of cognitive development (Lamb & Lewis, 2011). ✳ Explore at **MyDevelopmentLab**

👁 Watch the **Video** *Memory: Elizabeth Loftus* at **MyDevelopmentLab**

✳ Explore the **Concept** *Encoding, Storage, and Retrieval in Memory* at **MyDevelopmentLab**

## Changes in Processing Capacity and Efficiency ◄----------- Learning Objective 6.15

How do cognitive processing capacity and efficiency change with age?

One obvious place to look for an explanation of developmental changes in memory skills is in the "hardware" itself. With any computer, there are physical limits on the number of different operations that can be performed simultaneously or in a given space of time. In the human memory system, the limiting factor is the short-term memory, as you'll recall from Chapter 1. It seems likely that as the brain and nervous system develop in the early years of life, the capacity of short-term memory increases (Johnson, 2011).

This has turned out to be a very difficult hypothesis to test. The most commonly cited evidence in support of an increase in short-term memory capacity is the finding that over the years of childhood, children are able to remember longer and longer lists of numbers, letters, or words, a pattern clear in the data shown in Figure 6.11 on page 158. The difficulty with these results, however, is that they could also be simply another reflection of age

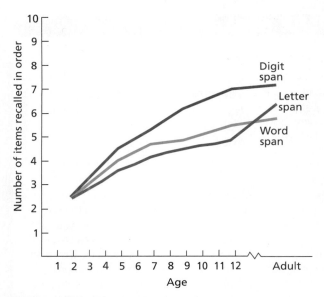

**FIGURE 6.11** Memory Span across Age
Psychologists have tried to measure basic memory capacity by asking research participants to listen to a list of numbers, letters, or words and then repeat the list items in order. This figure shows the number of such items that children of various ages are able to remember and recall accurately.

(*Source:* Dempster, 1981, from Figures 1–3, pp. 66–68. "Memory span: Sources of individual and developmental differences." *Psychological Bulletin, 89*, 63–100.)

⊙ **Watch** the **Video** *The Growing Child* at **MyDevelopmentLab**

differences in experience, because older children naturally have more experience with numbers, letters, and words. Thus, the memory-span data don't give a clear-cut answer to the question of whether basic processing capacity increases with age. Nevertheless, most developmental psychologists today agree that short-term memory capacity increases across childhood (Cowan, Nugent, Elliott, Ponomarev, & Saults, 1999).

Researchers have also produced persuasive evidence that processing efficiency increases steadily with age. The best evidence on this point is that cognitive processing gets steadily faster with age. Robert Kail (2007a) has found an exponential increase with age in processing speed on a wide variety of tasks, including such perceptual-motor tasks as tapping out a given rhythm or responding to a stimulus (for example, by pressing a button when you hear a buzzer) and cognitive tasks such as mental addition. He has found virtually identical patterns of speed increases in studies in Korea and the United States, adding a bit of cross-cultural validity to his results.

One plausible explanation for this common pattern is that over time, the brain and nervous system change physically in some fundamental way that allows increases in both response speed and mental processing. However, experience using the memory system also contributes to increases in processing efficiency. For example, playing video games seems to increase children's visual memory spans, at least temporarily (Loran-Royer, Munch, & Mesclé, 2010). However, one of the most important ways in which processing becomes more efficient is through the acquisition of **automaticity**, or the ability to recall information from long-term memory without using short-term memory capacity. For example, when children can respond to the question "How much is 7 times 7?" by saying "49" without thinking about it, they have achieved automaticity with respect to that particular piece of information. ⊙ **Watch** at **MyDevelopmentLab**

Automaticity is achieved primarily through practice (Meisinger & Bradley, 2008). It is critical to efficient information-processing because it frees up short-term memory space for more complex processing. Thus, the child or teenager who knows automatically what 7 x 7 is can use that fact in a complex multiplication or division problem without giving up any of the short-term memory space he is using to solve the problem. As a result, he is better able to concentrate on the "big picture" instead of expending effort trying to recall a simple multiplication fact. Not surprisingly, researchers have found that elementary school children who have automatized basic math facts in this way learn complex computational skills more rapidly (Ashkenazi, Rubinsten, & Henik, 2009). Similarly, kindergartners who display automaticity with regard to naming letters and objects are more likely to be fluent readers by the end of second grade than peers who require more time and effort to produce such names (Schatschneider, Fletcher, Francis, Carlson, & Foorman, 2004). Likewise, children who have practiced their handwriting skills to the point of automaticity can focus on the ideas they are writing about instead of the mechanical process of forming letters (Medwell & Wray, 2007). As a result, their compositions are longer, are better organized, and contain more elaboration.

**Learning Objective 6.16** ----------➤
What kinds of improvements in strategy use happen across childhood and adolescence?

## Memory Strategies

As we have noted, teenagers' and adults' working memories function more efficiently than those of children do. However, one of the most important principles in memory functioning is that the working memory, regardless of age or level of cognitive development, is limited in capacity. In order to deal with this limitation, the system creates **memory strategies**, ways of manipulating information that increase the chances that it will be remembered. Several common strategies are listed in Table 6.2. They emerge slowly over the entire course of childhood and adolescence, and even when children are familiar with a particular strategy, they often fail to use it.

**REHEARSAL STRATEGIES** Suppose you need to run the following errands: stop at the dry cleaner; buy some stamps; copy your IRS forms; and buy milk, bread, orange juice, carrots, lettuce, spaghetti, and spaghetti sauce at the grocery store. To remember such a list, you might

**automaticity** The ability to recall information from long-term memory without effort.

**memory strategies** Ways of manipulating information that increase the chances that it will be remembered.

## Table 6.2 — SOME COMMON STRATEGIES FOR REMEMBERING

| Strategy | Description |
|---|---|
| Rehearsal | Perhaps the most common strategy, which involves either mental or vocal repetition or repetition of movement (as in learning to dance). May be used by children as young as 2 years under some conditions. |
| Clustering | Grouping ideas, objects, or words into clusters to help in remembering them, such as "all animals," or "all the ingredients in the lasagna recipe," or "the chess pieces involved in the move called castling." This is one strategy that clearly benefits from experience with a particular subject or activity, since possible categories are learned or are discovered in the process of exploring or manipulating a set of materials. Primitive clustering is used by 2-year-olds. |
| Elaboration | Finding shared meaning or a common referent for two or more things to be remembered. The helpful mnemonic for recalling the names of the lines on the musical staff ("Every Good Boy Does Fine") is a form of elaboration, as is associating the name of a person you have just met with some object or other word. This form of memory aid is not used spontaneously by all individuals and is not used skillfully until fairly late in development, if then. |
| Systematic Searching | Scanning the memory for the whole domain in which something might be found. Children aged 3 and 4 can begin to do this to search for actual objects in the real world but are not good at doing this in memory. Search strategies may be first learned in the external world and then applied to inner searches. ⊙▶ Simulate at MyDevelopmentLab |

*Source:* Flavell, 1985. *Cognitive development* (2nd ed.). Englewood Cliffs, NJ: Prentice Hall.

use any one of several possible strategies, some of which are listed in Table 6.2. In this particular case, one option would be to rehearse the list over and over in your mind. Do children do this when they try to remember? One classic early study (Keeney, Cannizzo, & Flavell, 1967) indicated that school-aged children do but younger children do not. Keeney showed children a row of seven cards with pictures on them and told the children to try to remember all the pictures in the same order they were laid out. A helmet was then placed over the child's head to prevent the child from seeing the cards but allowed the experimenter to see if the child seemed to be rehearsing the list by muttering under his or her breath. Children under 5 almost never showed any rehearsal, but 8- to 10-year-old children usually did. Interestingly, when 5-year-olds were taught to rehearse, they were able to do so and their memory scores improved. Yet when these same 5-year-olds were given a new problem without being reminded to rehearse, they stopped rehearsing. That is, they could use the strategy if they were reminded to, but they did not produce it spontaneously—a pattern described as a **production deficiency**.

More recent work suggests that preschool-aged children show some kinds of strategies in their remembering if the task is quite simple, such as the game of hide-and-seek that Judy DeLoache (DeLoache, 1989; DeLoache, Simcock, & Marzolf, 2004) has used in her studies. In one of DeLoache's studies, the child watches the experimenter hide an attractive toy in some obvious place (e.g., behind a couch) and is then told that when a buzzer goes off she can go and find the toy. While playing with other toys during the 4-minute delay interval before the buzzer sounded, 2-year-olds often talked about, pointed to, or looked at the toy's hiding place—all of which seem clearly to be early forms of memory strategies.

These results and others like them indicate that there is no magic shift from nonstrategic to strategic behavior at age 5 or 6 or 7. Children as young as 2 use primitive strategies, but school-aged children seem to have larger repertoires of strategies and to use them more flexibly and efficiently, a quality of thinking that becomes increasingly evident in older schoolchildren (Tam, Jarrold, Baddeley, & Sabatos-DeVito, 2010). For example, when learning a list of words, 8-year-olds are likely to practice the words one at a time ("cat, cat, cat"), while older children practice them in groups ("desk, lawn, sky, shirt, cat"). The 8-year-olds, tested again a year later, show signs of a shift toward the more efficient strategy (Guttentag, Ornstein, & Siemens, 1987).

**CLUSTERING**  Another strategy that helps improve memory involves putting the items to be learned or remembered into some meaningful organization. For example, in trying to remember a list of items you need to buy at the grocery store, you could aid your memory by thinking of the items as ingredients in a recipe (e.g., "what I need to make spaghetti and meatballs").

⊙▶ Simulate the Experiment *Mnemonics* at **MyDevelopmentLab**

**production deficiency**  A pattern whereby an individual can use some mental strategy if reminded to do so but fails to use the strategy spontaneously.

**utilization deficiency** Using some specific mental strategy without deriving benefit from it.

Another common strategy is to mentally group the items into categories such as "fruits and vegetables" and "canned goods," a strategy called clustering, or chunking.

Studies of clustering often involve having children or adults learn lists of words that have potential categories built into them. For example, in a study of categorical clustering, a researcher would ask you to remember this list of words: *chair, spaghetti, lettuce, cat, desk, chocolate, duck, lion, table*. You would be given 2 minutes to try to memorize the list, using whatever method(s) you wished. Then the researcher would ask you to list the words you could recall. If you used some kind of clustering technique, you would be likely to list the same-category words together (*cat, duck, lion; chair, desk, table*; and *spaghetti, chocolate, lettuce*).

School-aged children show this kind of internal organization strategy when they recall things, while preschoolers generally do not. And among school-aged children, older children use this strategy more efficiently, using a few large categories rather than many smaller ones (Bjorklund & Muir, 1988; Schlagmüller & Schneider, 2002). Interestingly, research shows that children often spontaneously use such a strategy but derive no apparent memory benefit from it, a pattern called a **utilization deficiency** (Bjorklund, Miller, Coyle, & Slawinski, 1997; Schneider & Bjorklund, 1998)—in a sense the opposite pattern from a production deficiency, in which a child will use and benefit from a strategy if reminded to do so but will not use it spontaneously. Utilization deficiencies are intriguing to theorists because they suggest that the child assumes that using some kind of strategy is a good thing to do but does not fully understand how to go about it. This form of deficiency is more common in children younger than 6 or 7, but it occurs among older children and teenagers as well (Kron-Sperl, Schneider, & Hasselhorn, 2008).

**STRATEGY TRAINING** Training studies, in which children and adolescents are taught to use a particular memory strategy, suggest that teens benefit more from training than younger children do (Ghetti, Papini, & Angelini, 2006). For example, in one of the early strategy training studies, researchers taught elementary school and high school students a strategy for memorizing the manufacturing products associated with different cities, for example, "Detroit—automobiles" (Pressley & Dennis-Rounds, 1980). Once participants had learned the strategy and were convinced of its effectiveness, researchers presented them with a similar task: memorizing Latin words and their English translations. Experimenters found that only the high school students made an effort to use the strategy they had just learned to accomplish the new memory task. The elementary school children used the new strategy only when researchers told them to and demonstrated to them how it could be applied to the new task. The high school students' success seemed to be due to their superior ability to recognize the similarity between the two tasks—an aspect of metamemory, which will be discussed in the next section.

The differences between elementary school children's and adolescents' ability to learn strategies for processing meaningful text, such as newspaper articles or material in textbooks, are even more dramatic. In a classic study of text processing, experimenters asked 10-, 13-, 15-, and 18-year-olds to read and summarize a 500-word passage (about 1 page in a typical college textbook). The researchers (Brown & Day, 1983) hypothesized that participants would use four rules in writing summaries. First, they would delete trivial information. Second, their summaries would show categorical organization; that is, they would use terms such as *animals* rather than specific names of animals mentioned in the text. Researchers also speculated that participants would use topic sentences from the text in their summaries and would invent topic sentences for paragraphs that didn't have them.

The results of the research suggested that participants of all ages used the first rule, because all of their summaries included general rather than detailed or trivial information about the passage. However, the 10- and 13-year-olds used the other rules far less frequently than did the 15- and 18-year-olds. There were also interesting differences between the two older groups. Fifteen-year-olds used categories about as frequently as 18-year-olds did, but the oldest group used topic sentences far more effectively. This pattern of age differences in strategy use suggests that complex information-processing skills such as text summarizing improve gradually during the second half of adolescence.

Studies of text outlining reveal a similar pattern (Drum, 1985). Both elementary school and high school students know that an outline should include the main ideas of a passage along with supporting details. However, research suggests that 17-year-olds generate much more complete outlines than do 14-year-olds. Moreover, 11-year-olds' outlines usually include only a few of the main ideas of a passage and provide little or no supporting details for the main ideas they do include.

## Metamemory and Metacognition

◄------------Learning Objective 6.17

What are metamemory and metacognition, and what is their importance in cognitive development?

One way in which a child's information-processing "software" changes is in her increasing awareness of her own mental processes, or **metamemory** and **metacognition**—knowing about remembering and knowing about knowing. Such skills are a part of a larger category that information-processing theorists refer to as **executive processes**, cognitive skills that allow a person to devise and carry out alternative strategies for remembering and solving problems.

Research suggests that such skills emerge in early childhood (Schneider, 2010). For example, John Flavell's appearance/reality research has demonstrated that children between ages 3 and 5 know that in order to tell if a rock painted like a sponge is really a sponge or a rock, a person needs to touch or hold the object. Just looking at it doesn't give enough information (Flavell, 1993; O'Neill, Astington, & Flavell, 1992). In a similar vein, 4-year-olds (but not 3-year-olds) understand that to remember or forget something, one must have known it at a previous time (Lyon & Flavell, 1994). Flavell's research also suggests that by age 4, a child understands that there is a process called *thinking* that people do and that is distinct from knowing or talking (Flavell, Green, & Flavell, 1995). They also understand in some preliminary way that people can think about imaginary objects or events as well as real ones Despite these major advances, however, 4- and 5-year-olds do not yet understand that thinking occurs continuously (Wellman & Hickling, 1994). In particular, they don't realize that other people are thinking all the time, and when asked, they are bad at guessing what another person might be thinking about, even when the clues are quite clear—such as when the other person is reading or listening to something. All of these skills are much more highly developed in 7- and 8-year-olds, who seem to have figured out that their own and other people's thinking goes on constantly and follows certain rules.

These skills are of particular interest because performance on a whole range of everyday tasks is better if the child can monitor her own performance or can recognize when a particular strategy is called for and when it is not. Four- and 5-year-olds do show some such monitoring, but it is rarely seen earlier than that, and it clearly improves fairly rapidly across the elementary school years. For example, 10-year-olds are more likely than 8-year-olds to know that understanding a story requires that the reader or listener exert mental effort to prevent his or her mind from wandering (Parault & Schwanenflugel, 2000).

Among other things, some metacognitive ability is critical for learning to read skillfully. A child learning to read needs to recognize which words he knows and which he does not, or which sentences he understands and which he does not, and needs to have some idea of how to get the information he needs. He needs to be able to recognize the difference between easy sentences and hard ones so that he can concentrate more and put more effort into the harder ones. A variety of research reveals that younger and poorer readers are less adept at all these metacognitive tasks, while better or older readers can do them more readily and skillfully (Martini & Shore, 2008).

By age 14 or 15, the executive processing skills of an adolescent far exceed those of a younger child, and these skills continue to improve throughout adolescence and into the adult years (Schneider, 2010; van der Stel & Veenman, 2010). These gains result from improvements in working memory efficiency and increases in knowledge, which are largely attributable to the maturation of the prefrontal cortex (Giedd, 2004). As a result, teenagers outperform school-aged children on even simple memory tasks, such as remembering faces, and are far better than younger children at using complex strategies that aid memory (Gathercole, Pickering, Ambridge, & Wearing, 2004; Itier & Taylor, 2004). For example, one classic study of metamemory involved offering fifth-graders, eighth-graders, and college students the opportunity to earn money by remembering words (Cuvo, 1974). Researchers designated to-be-recalled words as being worth either 1 cent or 10 cents. Fifth-graders rehearsed 1-cent and 10-cent words equally. In contrast, eighth-graders and college students put more effort into rehearsing 10-cent words than 1-cent words. At the end of the rehearsal period, fifth-graders recalled equal

**metamemory** Knowledge about one's own memory processes.

**metacognition** General and rather loosely used term describing knowledge of one's own thinking processes: knowing what one knows, and how one learns.

**executive processes** Cognitive skills that allow a person to devise and carry out alternative strategies for remembering and solving problems.

**response inhibition** The ability to control responses to stimuli.

numbers of 1- and 10-cent words, while older participants remembered more 10-cent items. Further, college students outperformed eighth-graders in both rehearsal and recall. These findings suggest that the capacity to apply memory skills selectively based on the characteristics of a memory task appears early in the teen years and continues to improve throughout adolescence.

Another important skill that is facilitated by the development of executive processes is **response inhibition**, the ability to control responses to stimuli (Luna, Garver, Urban, Lazar, & Sweeney, 2004). Response inhibition is evident in situations that call for carefully considering the impact of your answer before responding to a question, such as in a job interview. Consequently, teens are less likely than school-aged children to immediately jump to a conclusion regarding the solution to a problem. Teens are likely to mentally work through the problem and be certain that they have taken into account all of the details involved in its solution before announcing that they have solved it.

**Learning Objective 6.18**
How does expertise influence memory function?

## Expertise

All of the apparent developmental changes that we have discussed may well turn out to be as much a function of expertise as they are of age. Piaget thought that children apply broad forms of logic to all their experiences in any given stage. If that's true, then the amount of specific experience a child has had with some set of materials shouldn't make a lot of difference. A child who understands hierarchical classification but who has never seen pictures of different types of dinosaurs still ought to be able to create classifications of dinosaurs about as well as a child who has played a lot with dinosaur models. A child who understands the principle of transitivity (if A is greater than B and B is greater than C, then A is greater than C) ought to be able to demonstrate this ability with sets of strange figures as well as she could with a set of toys familiar to her. But, in fact, that seems not to be the case.

Developmentalists now have a great deal of research showing that specific knowledge makes a huge difference (Kail, 2007b). Children and adults who know a lot about some subject or some set of objects (dinosaurs, baseball cards, mathematics, or whatever) not only categorize information in that topic area in more complex and hierarchical ways, but also are better at remembering new information on that topic and better at applying more advanced forms of logic to material in that area (Waters & Waters, 2010. Furthermore, such expertise seems to generalize very little to other tasks (Ericsson & Crutcher, 1990). A child who is a devout soccer fan will be better than a nonfan at recalling lists of soccer words or the content of a story about soccer, but the two children are likely to be equally good at remembering random lists of words (Schneider & Bjorklund, 1992; Schneider, Reimers, Roth, & Visé, 1995).

*These school-aged chess players, unless they are rank novices, would remember a series of chess moves or the arrangement of pieces on a chessboard far better than would nonplayers, regardless of their ages.*

Research on expertise also shows that even the typical age differences in strategy use or memory ability disappear when the younger group has more expertise than the older. For example, Michelene Chi, in her now-classic early study (1978), showed that expert chess players can remember the placement of chess pieces on a board much more quickly and accurately than can novice chess players, even when the expert chess players are children and the novices are adults—a finding since replicated several times (e.g., Schneider, Gruber, Gold, & Opwis, 1993). To paraphrase Flavell (1985), expertise makes any of us look very smart, very cognitively advanced; lack of expertise makes us look very dumb.

## THINK CRITICALLY

- Think of a common infant behavior such as a baby's repeatedly throwing a toy on the floor. How does the behavior seem to fit with Piaget's ideas about primary, secondary, and tertiary circular reactions?
- How does reversibility come into play when you watch a magician perform? Do you think an understanding of reversibility makes the performance more or less interesting for you than for a young child who has yet to develop reversibility?
- How would Piaget's theory be used to explain the finding that younger children do not benefit from memory strategy training as much as older children and teens do?

## CONDUCT YOUR OWN RESEARCH

You can use a deck of playing cards to examine memory improvement. Do your research with a 7-year-old and a 10-year-old, testing each child separately. For the first trial, select 12 cards, 3 from each suit, making sure that the cards are all of different values. Arrange the cards in front of the child randomly and allow 1 minute for the child to memorize the cards. When the minute has passed, take up the cards and ask the child to recall them. For the second trial, repeat the experiment with a different set of 12 cards, but tell the children that they may rearrange the cards if they think it will help their memory. The 7-year-old probably won't rearrange the cards by suit, but the 10-year-old will. This shows that the older child is attempting to use categories as a memory aid.

## SUMMARY ✓— Study and Review at MyDevelopmentLab

### Piaget's Basic Ideas

**6.1** **What is the role of schemes in cognitive development?**
Piaget assumed that the child was an active agent in his own development, constructing his own understandings and adapting to the environment through his actions on the world. Cognitive structures called schemes underlie the stages of cognitive development. Each stage involves a different type of scheme. The schemes are hierarchical in that each stage builds on the schemes that were constructed in earlier stages.

**6.2** **How do assimilation, accommodation, and equilibration change schemes?**
The complementary processes of assimilation (adding new information to an existing scheme) and accommodation (changing schemes to take in new information), as well as the process of equilibration by which they are balanced, are the means by which schemes adapt to the world.

Conflict between a child's existing schemes and his observations of the world leads to actions that eventually result in resolution of such conflicts, or equilibration, as Piaget called the process. Each stage of development represents a more adaptive equilibration.

**6.3** **What are the four causes of cognitive development proposed by Piaget?**
Equilibration interacts with maturation, social transmission, and experience to produce changes in children's thinking.

### Infancy

**6.4** **How did Piaget describe cognitive development in the first 2 years of life?**
Piaget's first stage is the sensorimotor period; the infant begins with a small repertoire of basic schemes, from which she moves toward symbolic representation in a series of six substages. In each stage, the infant uses sensory and motor

abilities to act on the world and to test hypotheses about the results of such actions. These tests involve repetitive behaviors, or circular reactions. The major milestones of this stage include object permanence, means-end behavior, and representational thought.

**6.4a** What are infants in the various substages of the sensorimotor stage likely to learn from watching television?

In substages 1 through 5, infants learn little from television because they do not understand the symbolic nature of media. The appealing sensory characteristics of video that has been designed to appeal to infants may reinforce the behavior of watching television. Such reinforcement may make infants likely to watch the television screen regardless of what type of program is playing.

**6.5** What have researchers discovered about infants' ability to remember and to imitate others' actions?

Post-Piagetian studies of infant cognition show infants' memory skills to be far more advanced than Piaget thought. Infants can imitate in the earliest weeks but do not show deferred imitation for several months.

## The Preschool Years

**6.6** What are the characteristics of children's thinking during the preoperational stage?

In Piaget's preoperational period, from 2 to 6 years, the child is able to use mental symbols to represent objects to himself internally. Despite this advance, the preschool-aged child still lacks many sophisticated cognitive characteristics. In Piaget's view, such children are still egocentric, rigid in their thinking, and generally captured by appearances.

**6.7** How has recent research challenged Piaget's view of this period?

Research on the cognitive functioning of preschoolers makes it clear that they are much less egocentric than Piaget thought. By age 4, children can distinguish between appearance and reality in a variety of tasks.

**6.8** What is a theory of mind, and how does it develop?

Preschoolers develop a surprisingly sophisticated theory of mind—that is, ideas of how other people's minds work. They understand that the actions of others are often based on thoughts and beliefs. The development of a theory of mind is influenced by general cognitive and language development. Engaging in pretend play with others seems to facilitate its development as well.

**6.9** What does research indicate about the correlation between culture and theory of mind?

Cross-cultural studies suggest that the development of the false belief principle and other features of theory of mind may be universal milestones of early childhood cognitive development.

**6.10** How do the theories of the neo-Piagetians and Vygotsky explain cognitive development?

Recent theorizing about the preschool period has been influenced by neo-Piagetian theories that explain Piaget's stages in information-processing terms. Vygotsky's sociocultural theory emphasizes the role of social interactions in children's cognitive development. Moreover, Vygotsky suggested that language provides the framework necessary to support many of the general concepts children acquire in the preschool years.

## The School-Aged Child

**6.11** What are concrete operations, and how do they represent an advance over earlier forms of thought?

In Piaget's third stage—concrete operations—occurring from age 6 to age 12, the child acquires powerful new mental tools called operations, such as reversibility.

**6.12** What does Siegler's research suggest about concrete operational thinking?

Recent research on this period confirms many of Piaget's descriptions of sequences of development but calls into question his basic concept of stages. Siegler's work shows that cognitive development is less steplike than Piaget proposed; children may use a variety of different strategies, varying in complexity, on the same kind of problem. Still, the repertoire of strategies does become more complex with age.

## Adolescence

**6.13** What are the key elements of formal operational thinking?

Piaget's fourth stage—formal operations—is said to develop from age 12 onward and is characterized by the ability to apply basic operations to ideas and possibilities as well as to actual objects and by the emergence of systematic problem solving and hypothetico-deductive logic.

**6.13a** How does adolescent egocentrism affect teenagers' development?

Psychologist David Elkind proposed that adolescent egocentrism leads teens to develop a personal fable that prevents them from realistically assessing risks. In addition, Elkind proposed that teens perform for an imaginary audience of peers. The imaginary audience leads them to think that others are constantly assessing their appearance and behavior. As a result, they become excessively focused on and critical of themselves.

**6.14** What does post-Piagetian research suggest about this stage?

Researchers have found clear evidence of such advanced forms of thinking in at least some adolescents.

## Development of Information-Processing Skills

**6.15** How do cognitive processing capacity and efficiency change with age?

Most theorists agree that there are age-related changes in the capacity of the mental "hardware" as well as improvements in speed and efficiency.

**6.15a** How do children's source monitoring skills influence their responses to leading questions?

Children are more susceptible to leading questions than adults are. The reason for this difference is that children are less likely to track information sources as they encode information in memory. Consequently, when they retrieve a piece of information from memory, they are unlikely to be able to determine if it came from their own memory of an event or from a leading question posed by an interviewer.

**6.16** What kinds of improvements in strategy use happen across childhood and adolescence?

Processing efficiency improves because of increasing use of various types of processing strategies with age, including strategies for remembering. Preschoolers use some strategies, but school-aged children use them more often and more flexibly. In adolescence, the number of strategies and the efficiency with which they are used improve substantially.

**6.17** What are metamemory and metacognition, and what is their importance in cognitive development?

Children's capacities to think about their own mental processes (metacognition) and to select appropriate memory strategies (metamemory) also contribute to improvements in memory functioning.

**6.18** How does expertise influence memory function?

Studies of expertise show that prior knowledge contributes to both individual and age-related differences in memory functioning and strategy use.

## KEY TERMS

accommodation (p. 137)
adaptation (p. 137)
assimilation (p. 137)
automaticity (p. 158)
centration (p. 143)
class inclusion (p. 149)
concrete operations stage (p. 138)
conservation (p. 143)
decentration (p. 143)
deductive logic (p. 150)
egocentrism (p. 143)
equilibration (p. 137)

executive processes (p. 161)
false belief principle (p. 145)
figurative schemes (p. 136)
formal operations stage (p. 138)
horizontal decalage (p. 150)
hypothetico-deductive
 reasoning (p. 153)
inductive logic (p. 150)
memory strategies (p. 158)
metacognition (p. 161)
metamemory (p. 161)
neo-Piagetian theory (p. 147)

object permanence (p. 139)
operation (p. 138)
operational efficiency (p. 147)
operative schemes (p. 136)
organization (p. 136)
preoperational stage (p. 138)
primary circular reactions
 (p. 139)
production deficiency (p. 159)
relational complexity (p. 152)
response inhibition (p. 162)
reversibility (p. 149)

scheme (p. 136)
secondary circular reactions
 (p. 139)
sensorimotor stage (p. 138)
seriation (p. 152)
short-term storage space
 (STSS) (p. 147)
tertiary circular reactions
 (p. 139)
theory of mind (p. 145)
transitivity (p. 152)
utilization deficiency (p. 160)

# 7

# Cognitive Development II: Individual Differences in Cognitive Abilities

If you go to youtube.com and search for clips of Jacob Barnett of Westfield, Indiana, you are likely to find one of several videos in which, at the age of 12, "Jake" explained his expansion of Einstein's theory of relativity. Astrophysics experts have confirmed that Jake's theory is original, insightful, perhaps even "brilliant," and addresses problems that researchers in the field have been unable to explain thus far. Consequently, just before Jake's thirteenth birthday, professors in the early college program at Indiana University-Purdue University Indianapolis (IUPUI) encouraged Jake to forego the college studies he had begun just a year earlier to join the university's staff of full-time researchers.

Despite these impressive accomplishments, there was a time in Jake's life when his parents feared that he might have some kind of intellectual disability. As a toddler, Jake did not speak and seemed to have difficulty relating to other children. Physicians and psychologists told his parents that he might have *autism*, a developmental disability that impairs a child's social and intellectual development. In response, Jake's parents began to use a variety of techniques to stimulate his development. By 3, Jake was not only speaking but was beginning to show signs that he was highly gifted.

By the end of his elementary school years, Jake's parents noticed that some of the autistic-type behaviors he had exhibited early in life were beginning to reemerge. A psychological evaluation suggested that Jake's behaviors indicated that he was simply bored with his school work. Indeed, tests showed that his intellectual development in mathematics and science was comparable to that of a college graduate. As a result, his parents withdrew him from school and enrolled him in an early college program at IUPUI. In other respects, however, Jake is a typical adolescent whose favorite activities include playing basketball and video games with his friends.

In this chapter, you will learn about gifted children like Jake as well as other children whose abilities fall far below those of typical children. We will also introduce you to the history of intelligence testing and the study of human intelligence. In addition, you will learn about some of the controversies surrounding group differences. ◉—Watch at **MyDevelopmentLab**

**intelligence** A set of abilities defined in various ways by different psychologists but generally agreed to include the ability to reason abstractly, the ability to profit from experience, and the ability to adapt to varying environmental contexts.

**Stanford-Binet** The best-known U.S. intelligence test. It was written by Lewis Terman and his associates at Stanford University and based on the first tests by Binet and Simon.

◉—Watch the **Video** *Are Intelligence Tests Valid?: Robert Guthrie* at **MyDevelopmentLab**

## Measuring Intellectual Power

At a conceptual level, most psychologists agree that **intelligence** includes the ability to reason abstractly, the ability to profit from experience, and the ability to adapt to varying environmental contexts. Consequently, most tests of intelligence include tasks that require examinees to use these abilities. Still, most of us have a greatly inflated notion of the permanence or importance of an IQ score. To acquire a more realistic view, it helps to know something about what such tests were designed to do and something about the beliefs and values of those who devised them.

## The First IQ Tests

◄- - - - - - - - - - Learning Objective 7.1

What were Binet's and Terman's approaches to measuring intelligence?

The first modern intelligence test was published in 1905 by two Frenchmen, Alfred Binet and Theodore Simon (1905). From the beginning, the test had a practical purpose—to identify children who might have difficulty in school. For this reason, the tasks that made up the test Binet and Simon devised were very much like some school tasks, including measures of vocabulary, comprehension of facts and relationships, and mathematical and verbal reasoning. For example, could a child describe the difference between wood and glass? Could a young child touch his nose, his ear, his head? Could he tell which of two weights was heavier?

Lewis Terman and his associates at Stanford University modified and extended many of Binet and Simon's original tasks when they translated and revised the test for use in the United States (Terman, 1916; Terman & Merrill, 1937). The several Terman revisions, called the **Stanford-Binet**, consist of six sets of tests, one set for children of each of six consecutive ages. A child taking the test begins with the set of tests for the age below his actual age,

**intelligence quotient (IQ)** Originally defined in terms of a child's mental age and chronological age, IQ is now computed by comparing a child's performance with that of other children of the same chronological age.

**mental age** Term used by Binet and Simon and Terman in the early calculation of IQ scores to refer to the age level of IQ test items a child could successfully answer. Used in combination with the child's chronological age to calculate an IQ score.

then takes the set for his age, then those for each successively older age until he has either completed all the tests for older ages or has reached a point where the remaining tests are too difficult for him.

Terman initially described a child's performance in terms of a score called an **intelligence quotient**, later shortened to **IQ**. This score was computed by comparing the child's chronological age (in years and months) with his **mental age**, defined as the level of questions he could answer correctly (Hegarty, 2007). For example, a child who could solve the problems for a 6-year-old but not those for a 7-year-old would have a mental age of 6. Terman devised a formula to calculate the IQ score:

$$\frac{\text{Mental Age}}{\text{Chronological Age}} \times 100$$

This formula results in an IQ score above 100 for children whose mental age is higher than their chronological age and an IQ score below 100 for children whose mental age is below their chronological age.

This old system for calculating IQ scores is not used any longer, even in the modern revisions of the Stanford-Binet. IQ score calculations are now based on a direct comparison of a child's performance with the average performance of a large group of other children of the same age, with a score of 100 still typically defined as average.

The majority of children achieve Stanford-Binet scores that are right around the average of 100, with a smaller number scoring very high or very low. Figure 7.1 shows the distribution of IQ scores that will result when the test is given to thousands of children. You can see that 67% (about two-thirds) of all children achieve scores between 85 and 115, while 96% achieve scores between 70 and 130. The groups that developmentalists refer to as "children who are gifted" or "children with mental retardation," both of which you'll read about in some detail in Chapter 15, clearly represent only very small fractions of the distribution.

One advantage of the modern method of calculating IQ scores is that it allows the test makers to restandardize the test periodically, so that the average remains at 100. Such readjustments are needed because IQ test scores have been rising steadily over the past 50 or 60 years. If the same standards were used today as were applied in 1932, when tests such as the Stanford-Binet were first devised, the average score would be 115 and not 100—an increase that has been found among children and adults all over the world (Dickens & Flynn, 2001; Flynn, 1994, 1999). That is, the average child today can solve problems that only an above-average child could solve 60 years ago. This historical shift upward in scores on cognitive ability tests is known as the *secular trend* in IQ scores. You may recall this term from Chapter 4, where you read about its use in relation to historical changes in the timing of menarche. The secular trend in IQ scores is also sometimes called the *Flynn effect*, because it was discovered by psychologist James Flynn (2007; Must et al., 2009) (see *Thinking about Research*).

**FIGURE 7.1** The Distribution of IQ Scores
The approximate distribution of scores on most modern IQ tests, along with the labels typically used for scores at various levels. The tests are designed and the scoring is standardized so that the average score is 100 and two-thirds of the scores fall between 85 and 115. Because of brain damage and genetic anomalies, there are slightly more children with low IQs than there are children with very high IQs.

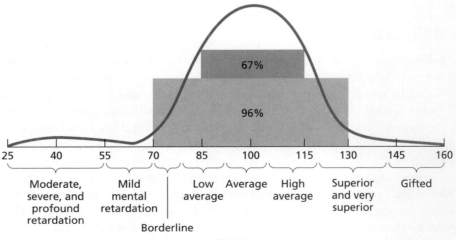

## The Flynn Effect

When thinking about the ways in which children's IQ scores have changed over the past 70 years, it's important to keep in mind that both maturational and experiential variables influence IQ scores. Most observers attribute gains in the maturational component of IQ scores to improvements in health and nutrition (Williams, 1998), most of which took place during the first half of the 20th century. Studies of test score changes in nations that have experienced significant improvements in the physical environment over the same period (e.g., Singapore, Estonia, and rural Kenya) lend weight to this hypothesis (Cocodia et al., 2003; Daley, Whaley, Sigman, Espinosa, & Neumann, 2003; Must, Must, & Raucik, 2003).

By contrast, scores on tests that reflect the experiential elements of the Flynn effect are continuing to increase in some industrial-

ized societies (Nettelbeck & Wilson, 2004). This increase is usually attributed to children's increased preschool attendance. In addition, test scores attained by today's children may reflect their tendency to be a bit more "testwise" than earlier cohorts simply because they take more tests and do more test-like activities in the early years of school (Cocodia et al., 2003).

Research also suggests that the experiential component of the Flynn effect can be reversed; that is, some types of experience can have negative effects on IQ scores (Shayer & Ginsburg, 2009; Teasdale & Owen, 2005). Studies in some European countries suggest that IQ scores may actually be falling, a finding that researchers attribute to declining enrollments in secondary schools in these countries (Teasdale & Owen, 2005, 2008). Thus, while questions about the secular trend in IQ scores are interesting in and of

themselves, the greatest value of research on the phenomenon may be the light it sheds on the contributions of schooling to intelligence test scores.

**Learning Objective 7.1a**
How has the Flynn effect influenced IQ scores?

### CRITICAL ANALYSIS

1. What are some possible alternative explanations for the finding that IQ scores may be falling in some European countries?
2. What are the advantages and disadvantages of intelligence tests that include both maturationally loaded and experientially based items?

## Modern IQ Tests

The three tests most frequently used by psychologists today are the Stanford-Binet V (the fifth revision of the original Stanford-Binet), the third edition of the Wechsler Preschool and Primary Scale of Intelligence (the **WPPSI-III**), and the fourth edition of the Wechsler Intelligence Scales for Children (the **WISC-IV**). The two Wechsler tests are derived from an intelligence test for children originally developed by psychologist David Wechsler (1974). The WPPSI-III is designed for children between the ages of 2½ and 7. Norms for the WISC-IV begin at age 6 and progress to age 16. (Several other well-known tests are listed in Table 7.1 on page 170.) All three tests feature both verbal and nonverbal problems ranging from very easy to very difficult. Children begin with the easiest problems of each type, continue with that type of item until they can go no further, and then go on to the next type of problem.

The WISC-IV is the test most often used in schools to diagnose children's learning problems. It consists of 15 different tests. Five of these tests, those that comprise the **verbal comprehension index**, rely strongly on verbal skills (for example, vocabulary, describing similarities between objects, general information). The remaining 10 tests demand nonverbal types of thinking, such as arranging pictures to tell a story and repeating digits back to the examiner. The nonverbal tests are divided among the **perceptual reasoning index**, **processing speed index**, and **working memory index**. Each of these groups of tests measures a different kind of nonverbal intelligence and generates its own IQ score. The WISC-IV also provides a comprehensive **full scale IQ** score that takes all four types of tests into account. Many psychologists find comparisons of the different kinds of IQ scores generated by the WISC-IV to be helpful in determining a child's intellectual strengths and weaknesses.

**INFANT TESTS**   Neither the Stanford-Binet nor either of the Wechsler tests can be used with children much younger than about 3. Infants and toddlers don't talk well, if at all, and most childhood tests rely heavily on language (see Table 7.1, on page 170). So how do developmentalists measure "intelligence" in an infant? This becomes an important question if they want

**Learning Objective 7.2**
What intelligence tests are used today, and how do they differ from earlier tests?

**WPPSI-III**   The third revision of the Wechsler Preschool and Primary Scale of Intelligence.

**WISC-IV**   The most recent revision of the Wechsler Intelligence Scales for Children, a well-known IQ test developed in the United States that includes both verbal and performance (nonverbal) subtests.

**verbal comprehension index**   Tests on the WISC-IV that tap verbal skills such as knowledge of vocabulary and general information.

**perceptual reasoning index**   Tests on the WISC-IV, such as block design and picture completion, that tap nonverbal visual-processing abilities.

**processing speed index**   Timed tests on the WISC-IV, such as symbol search, that measure how rapidly an examinee processes information.

**working memory index**   Tests on the WISC-IV, such as digit span, that measure working memory efficiency.

**full scale IQ**   The WISC-IV score that takes into account verbal and nonverbal scale scores.

Table
7.1

## INTELLIGENCE TESTS THAT MAY BE USED IN PLACE OF THE STANFORD-BINET AND THE WISC

| Test | Description |
|---|---|
| Peabody Picture Vocabulary Test (PPVT) | Not originally designed as an IQ test, but widely used as a quick measure of intelligence because the scores correlate so highly with Binet or Wechsler scores. Includes 150 pages, each page with four pictures, the pages arranged in order of increasing difficulty. The examiner says a word and asks the child to point to the appropriate picture, as in the example to the right. Widely used with preschool children. |
| Raven's Progressive Matrices | Each of the 36 items shows a pattern on a rectangular space, such as a set of dots covering the space. One section of the rectangle is blanked out, and the child must choose which of six alternative fill-in options will match the original matrix, as in the example to the right. Designed as a nonverbal measure of intelligence. |
| Kaufman Assessment Battery for Children (KABC) | Kaufman himself does not call this an intelligence test, although it is often used in this way. Suitable for children aged 2 1/2 to 12, it includes three tests of *sequential processing* (such as number recall) and seven tests of *simultaneous processing* (including face recognition), combined to provide an overall score based primarily on nonverbal measures. Six achievement subtests can also be given, including vocabulary, riddles, and reading. The test also allows flexible testing procedures, including the use of other languages, alternative wording, and gestures, all of which make the test one of the fairest for ethnic minorities and children from poverty-level families. |
| Cognitive Abilities Test (COGAT) | The COGAT is one of several intelligence tests that are administered to groups of children rather than in one-on-one testing sessions. These tests include items similar to those on individual tests, but they tend to be less reliable. Thus, they are typically used to screen children to determine who should be tested individually rather than to make decisions that require a great deal of precision, such as those associated with placing children in special education classes. |

PPVT item
(word is *emerge*)

Raven item

*Sources:* Portions adapted with the permission of The Free Press, a Division of Simon & Schuster, Inc., from *Bias in Mental Testing* by Arthur R. Jensen. Copyright © 1980 by Arthur R. Jensen.

to be able to identify, during infancy, those children who are not developing normally or to predict later intelligence or school performance.

Most "infant IQ tests," such as the widely used **Bayley Scales of Infant Development** (Bayley, 1969, 1993, 2005), have been constructed rather like IQ tests for older children in that they include sets of items of increasing difficulty. However, instead of testing school-like skills—skills an infant does not yet have—the items measure primarily sensory and motor skills, such as reaching for a dangling ring (an item for a typical baby at 3 months),

**Bayley Scales of Infant Development**
The best-known and most widely used test of infant "intelligence."

putting cubes in a cup on request (9 months), or building a tower of three cubes (17 months). Some more clearly cognitive items are also included, such as uncovering a toy hidden by a cloth, an item used with 8-month-old infants to measure an aspect of object permanence.

Bayley's test and others like it, such as the Denver Developmental Screening Test, have proved helpful in identifying infants and toddlers with serious developmental delays (Gardner et al., 2006). As a more general predictive tool to forecast later IQ scores or school performance, however, such tests have not been nearly as useful as many had hoped. On the whole, it looks as if what is being measured on typical infant tests is not the same as what is tapped by the commonly used intelligence tests for children and adults (Birney & Sternberg, 2011; Colombo, 1993).

**ACHIEVEMENT TESTS**   Another kind of test of intellectual skill with which you are probably familiar is the achievement test, which nearly all of you have taken in elementary and high school. **Achievement tests** are designed to test specific information learned in school, using items like those in Table 7.2. The child taking an achievement test doesn't end up with an IQ score, but his performance is compared to that of other children in the same grade across the country.

How is an achievement test different from an IQ test? An IQ test is intended to reveal something about how well a child can think and learn, while an achievement test tells something about what a child has already learned. Or to put it another way: Designers of IQ tests thought they were measuring a child's basic capacity (underlying **competence**), while an achievement test is intended to measure what the child has actually learned (**performance**). This is an important distinction. Each of us presumably has some upper limit of ability—what we could do under ideal conditions if we were maximally motivated, healthy, and rested.

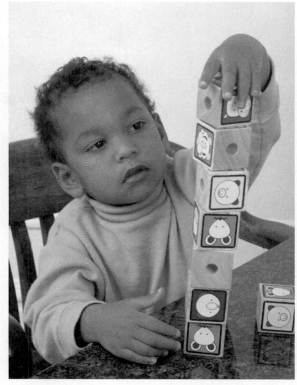

*At 22 months, James would clearly pass the 17-month item on the Bayley Scales of Infant Development that calls for the child to build a tower of three blocks.*

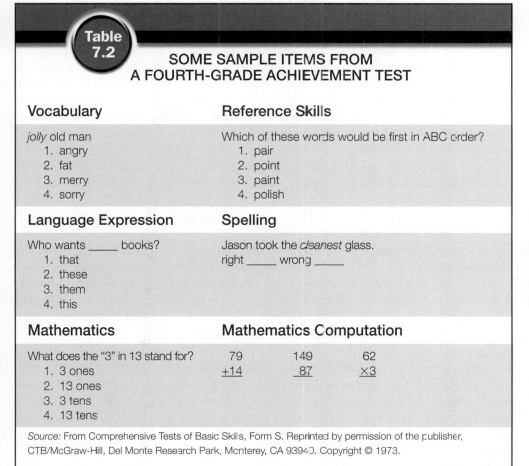

### Table 7.2

### SOME SAMPLE ITEMS FROM A FOURTH-GRADE ACHIEVEMENT TEST

**Vocabulary**

*jolly* old man
1. angry
2. fat
3. merry
4. sorry

**Reference Skills**

Which of these words would be first in ABC order?
1. pair
2. point
3. paint
4. polish

**Language Expression**

Who wants _____ books?
1. that
2. these
3. them
4. this

**Spelling**

Jason took the *cleanest* glass.
right _____ wrong _____

**Mathematics**

What does the "3" in 13 stand for?
1. 3 ones
2. 13 ones
3. 3 tens
4. 13 tens

**Mathematics Computation**

| 79 | 149 | 62 |
|----|-----|-----|
| +14 | 87 | ×3 |

*Source:* From Comprehensive Tests of Basic Skills, Form S. Reprinted by permission of the publisher, CTB/McGraw-Hill, Del Monte Research Park, Monterey, CA 93940. Copyright © 1973.

**achievement test**   Test designed to assess a child's learning of specific material taught in school, such as spelling or arithmetic computation; in the United States, achievement tests are typically given to all children in designated grades.

**competence**   A person's basic, underlying level of skill, displayed under ideal circumstances. It is not possible to measure competence directly.

**performance**   The behavior shown by a person under real-life rather than ideal circumstances. Even when researchers are interested in competence, all they can ever measure is performance.

Standardized tests are a common feature of the school experience. Some of these tests measure intelligence, while others focus on achievement of specific academic objectives.

Yet, since everyday conditions are rarely ideal, people typically perform below their hypothetical ability.

The creators of the widely used IQ tests believed that by standardizing the procedures for administering and scoring the tests, they could come close to measuring competence. But because scientists can never be sure that they are assessing any ability under the best of all possible circumstances, they have to settle for measuring performance at the time the test is taken. What this means in practical terms is that the distinction between IQ tests and achievement tests is one of degree rather than of kind. IQ tests include items that are designed to tap fairly fundamental intellectual processes such as comparison and analysis; achievement tests call for specific information the child has learned in school or elsewhere. Thus, the strong link between IQ and performance on achievement tests calls into question the notion that such tests are good measures of what has been taught and learned in a particular school. High scores in one school may simply mean that the students are brighter rather than indicating anything about the quality of the school's curriculum or the methods used by its teachers.

College entrance tests, such as the SAT, fall somewhere in between IQ and achievement tests. They are designed to measure basic "developed abilities," such as the ability to reason with words, rather than specific knowledge. But all three types of tests measure aspects of a child or young person's performance and not his or her competence.

## Stability of Test Scores

**Learning Objective 7.3**
How stable are IQ scores throughout childhood and adolescence?

One of the bits of folklore about IQ tests is that a particular IQ score is something you "have," like blue eyes or red hair—that a child who achieves a score of, say, 115 at age 3 will continue to score in about the same range at age 6 or 12 or 20. Psychologists use the term **reliability** to refer to the stability of a test score. By definition, a reliable test yields scores that are stable over time. That is, if a child takes a reliable test several times, her scores will be very similar at each testing. In this sense, IQ scores are, in fact, very stable, although there are also some exceptions to this general rule. One such exception is the weak link between scores on infant IQ tests such as the Bayley Scales and later IQ scores. The typical correlation between a Bayley score at 12 months and a Stanford-Binet IQ score at 4 years is only about .20 to .30 (Bee et al., 1982)—significant but not robust. Newer tests of infant intelligence, such as those based on habituation rates or other basic processes, may ultimately prove to be more helpful predictors of later IQ scores (Fagan, Holland, & Wheeler, 2007); currently, however, there is no widely used method that allows developmentalists to predict with any reliability which 1-year-olds will later have high or low IQ scores.

However, beginning at about age 3, consistency in performance on IQ tests such as the Stanford-Binet or the WISC-IV increases markedly (Birney & Sternberg, 2011). If such a test is taken twice, a few months or a few years apart, the scores are likely to be very similar. The correlations between adjacent-year IQ scores in middle childhood, for example, are typically in the range of .65 to .80 (Bartels, Rietveld, Van Baal, & Boomsma, 2002; Honzik, 1986). Moreover, correlations among IQ scores measured in late childhood, early adolescence, and adulthood are also quite high, typically ranging from .70 to .85, including adult IQs that are measured when people are in their 70s and 80s (Deary, Whiteman, Starr, Whalley, & Fox, 2004; Mortensen, Andresen, Kruuse, Sanders, & Reinisch, 2003). However, many children show quite wide fluctuations in their scores. When children are given IQ tests repeatedly over a period of years, the common finding is that about half show little or no significant fluctuation in their scores while the remaining half show at least small changes from one testing to another, with perhaps 15% showing rather substantial change (Sattler, 2008).

**reliability** The stability of a test score over multiple testing sessions.

One example comes from a classic New Zealand longitudinal study in which all 1,037 children born in the town of Dunedin over a 1-year period in the 1970s were followed through childhood and adolescence. Among many other measures the researchers measured the children's IQs with the WISC every 2 years starting at age 7. They found that over any 2-year period, 10% of the children's IQ scores changed as much as 15 points—a very large change (Caspi, Harkness, Moffitt, & Silva, 1996). Another 13% showed major changes over longer periods; 15 of the children showed cumulative shifts of more than 50 points over 6 years. In most cases, however, these large shifts represented "bounce" or "rebound" rather than permanent shifts upward or downward. That is, some children seemed to respond to specific life experiences—stresses or special advantages—with a decline or a rise in IQ score. A few years later, their IQ score returned to something closer to the original score.

Such fluctuations, while intriguing, occur against a background of increasing IQ test score stability with age. The general rule of thumb is that the older the child, the more stable the IQ score becomes. Older children may show some fluctuation in scores in response to major stresses such as parental divorce, a change in schools, or the birth of a sibling, but by age 10 or 12, IQ scores are normally quite stable.

Despite the evidence for stability, it is worth pointing out that IQ scores are not etched on a child's forehead at birth. Although these scores do become quite stable in late childhood, individual children can and do shift in response to especially rich or especially impoverished environments or to any stress in their lives (Sattler, 2008).

**validity** The degree to which a test measures what it is intended to measure.

## What IQ Scores Predict

◄------------Learning Objective 7.4
What do IQ scores predict?

The information on long-term stability of IQ test scores reveals something about the reliability of the tests. What about their validity? **Validity** has to do with whether a test is measuring what it is intended to measure. One way to assess a test's validity is to see whether scores on that test predict real behavior in a way that makes sense. In the case of IQ tests, the most central question is whether IQ scores predict school performance. That was what Binet originally intended his test to do; that is what all subsequent tests were designed to do. The research findings on this point are quite consistent: The correlation between a child's IQ test score and her grades in school or performance on other school tests typically falls between .45 and .60 (Brody, 1997; Peterson, Pihl, Higgins, Seguin, & Tremblay, 2003). A correlation in this range suggests a strong but by no means perfect relationship. It indicates that, on the whole, children with high IQ scores are more likely than their peers with average and low scores to be among the high achievers in school, and those who score low are likely to be among the low achievers. Still, some children with high IQ scores don't shine in school while some children with lower scores do.

IQ scores predict future grades as well as current grades. Preschool children with high IQ scores tend to do better when they enter school than those with lower scores; elementary school children with higher IQ scores do better later in high school. Further, IQ scores predict the total number of years of education a child is likely to complete. Higher-IQ elementary school children are more likely to complete high school and are more likely to decide to go on to college (Brody, 1997).

It is important to point out that these predictive relationships hold within each social class and ethnic group in the United States. Among the poor, among African Americans and Hispanic Americans, and among middle-class White Americans, children with higher IQs are most likely to get good grades, complete high school, and go on to college (Birney & Sternberg, 2011; Brody, 1992; Rushton & Jensen, 2005). Such findings have led a number of theorists to argue that intelligence adds to the child's *resilience*—a concept you learned

*IQ scores predict school achievement across all ethnic and socioeconomic groups. As a result, developmentalists argue that intelligence contributes to resilience regardless of the circumstances in which a child is growing up.*

about in Chapter 1. At the other end of the scale, low intelligence is associated with a number of negative long-term outcomes, including adult illiteracy, delinquency in adolescence, and criminal behavior in adulthood (Birney & Sternberg, 2011; Stattin & Klackenberg-Larsson, 1993).

Clearly, then, IQ tests can be said to be valid: They measure what they purport to measure, which is school performance. However, they do not measure everything. Most importantly, intelligence tests cannot tell you (or a teacher or anyone else) that a child has some specific, fixed, underlying intellectual capacity. IQ tests were originally designed to measure only the specific range of skills that are needed for success in school. They do this reasonably well, so, for this limited purpose, they are valid. But these tests do not predict how well a particular person may perform other cognitive tasks requiring skills such as creativity, insight, "street smarts," or ability to read social cues. ⊙—Watch at **MyDevelopmentLab**

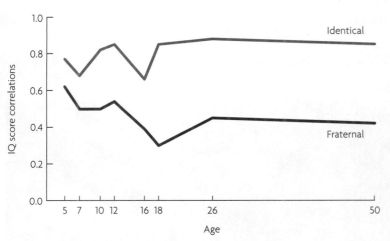

⊙—Watch the **Video** *SAT Alternatives: Robert Sternberg* at **MyDevelopmentLab**

## Explaining Individual Differences in IQ Scores

You will not be surprised to discover that the arguments about the origins of differences in IQ test scores nearly always boil down to a dispute about nature versus nurture. Both groups can muster research to support their views.

**Learning Objective 7.5** - - - - - - - - - ->
What do twin and adoption studies suggest about the effects of heredity and environment

## Twin and Adoption Studies

Both twin studies and studies of adopted children show strong hereditary influences on IQ scores. Identical twins are more like one another in IQ scores than are fraternal twins, and the IQs of adopted children are better predicted from the IQs of their natural parents than from those of their adoptive parents (Brody, 1992; Loehlin, Horn, & Willerman, 1994; Polderman et al., 2009; Rushton & Jensen, 2005; Scarr, Weinberg, & Waldman, 1993). This is precisely the pattern of correlations we would expect if there were a strong genetic element at work.

Further, as Figure 7.2 shows, correlations between the IQ scores of identical twins are stronger than those between the scores of fraternal twins throughout childhood, adolescence, and adulthood (Polderman et al., 2009; Posthuma, de Geus, & Boomsma, 2003). Neuroimaging studies suggest that these correlations arise from genes that affect the distribution of *gray matter* (nonmyelinated neurons) in the frontal lobes of the brain (Thompson et al., 2001).

⊙—Watch the **Video** *Mother-Child IQ Correlation* at **MyDevelopmentLab**

Remember, however, that if individual differences in IQ scores were fully attributable to heredity, the correlation between the scores of twins would be 1.0. Longitudinal studies suggest that heredity explains, at best, 80% of individual variation in IQ scores (Polderman et al., 2006). Thus, the take-away message from twin studies is that both heredity and environment contribute to IQ score differences. The importance of the environment is further highlighted by studies involving *virtual twins*, children of the same age who are adopted and raised as twins. As you can see in Figure 7.3, the IQ scores of virtual twins are more strongly correlated than those of biological siblings who are raised in separate homes (Segal, McGuire, Havelena, Gill, & Hershberger, 2007). ⊙—Watch at **MyDevelopmentLab**

Adoption studies provide support for an environmental influence on IQ scores, because the IQ scores of adopted children are clearly affected by the environment in which they have grown up (van IJzendoorn, Juffer, & Poelhuis, 2005). Early studies of adopted children involved mostly children born to poverty-level parents who were adopted into middle-class families. Such children typically have IQ scores 10 to 15 points higher than those of their birth mothers (Scarr et al., 1993), suggesting that the

**FIGURE 7.2** IQs of Fraternal and Identical Twins
This figure illustrates the combined findings of several longitudinal and cross-sectional studies of Dutch twins (Posthuma, de Geus, & Boomsma, 2003). You will notice that in childhood, when fraternal twins share the same environment, their IQ scores are more strongly correlated than in adulthood, when they presumably no longer live together. By contrast, the IQ scores of identical twins are even more strongly correlated in adulthood than during the childhood years. This pattern suggests conclusions about both heredity and environment. Specifically, at least with regard to IQ scores, the influence of heredity appears to increase with age, while that of the environment declines.

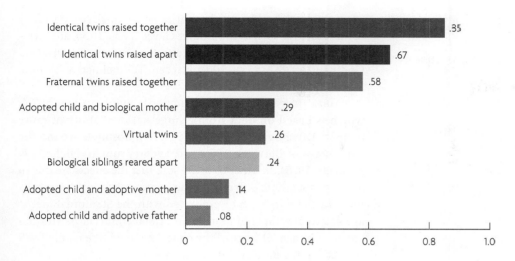

**FIGURE 7.3** IQ Correlations
Twin and adoption studies show that both heredity and environment influence IQ scores.

(*Sources:* Bouchard & McGue, 1981; Scarr, Weinberg, & Waldman, 1993; Segal et al., 2007.)
👁 Watch at **MyDevelopmentLab**

effect of being brought up by a middle-class adoptive family is to raise the child's IQ score. What this finding doesn't indicate is whether a less stimulating adoptive family would lower the test score of a child whose birth parents had average or above-average IQs. Information on that question comes from a French study by Christiane Capron and Michel Duyme (1989), who studied a group of 38 French children, all adopted in infancy. Approximately half of the children had been born to better-educated parents of higher social class, while the other half had been born to working-class or poverty-level parents. Some of the children in each group had then been adopted by higher-social-class parents, and the others by poorer families. Table 7.3 shows the children's IQ scores in adolescence. If you compare the two columns in the table, you can see the effect of rearing conditions: The children reared in upper-class homes had IQ scores that were about 11 points higher than those of children reared in lower-class families, regardless of the social class or education of the birth parents. At the same time, you can see a genetic effect if you compare the two rows in the table: The children born to upper-class parents had higher IQ scores than children from lower-class families, no matter what kind of environment they were reared in.

👁 Watch the **Video** *Twin Studies of Intelligence and Academic Achievement* at **MyDevelopmentLab**

## Family Characteristics and IQ Scores

◀------------ **Learning Objective 7.6**
How do shared and nonshared family characteristics affect IQ scores?

Adoption studies suggest that families make important contributions to children's intellectual development. Such factors are collectively known as the **shared environment**, because they affect all of the children in a household. Researchers have discovered a number of risk and protective factors in shared environments that are correlated with children's IQ scores.

**RISK FACTORS** Perhaps the most important risk factor in the shared environment is low socioeconomic status (SES). In Chapter 4 you learned that certain characteristics of low SES

**shared environment** Characteristics of a family that affect all children in the household.

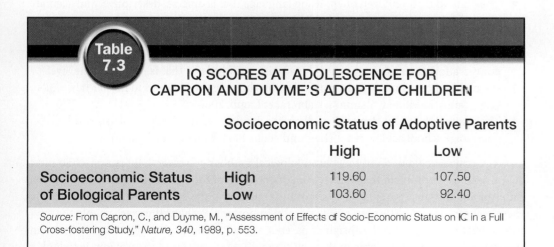

| Table 7.3 | | | |
|---|---|---|---|
| **IQ SCORES AT ADOLESCENCE FOR CAPRON AND DUYME'S ADOPTED CHILDREN** | | | |
| | | **Socioeconomic Status of Adoptive Parents** | |
| | | **High** | **Low** |
| **Socioeconomic Status of Biological Parents** | **High** | 119.60 | 107.50 |
| | **Low** | 103.60 | 92.40 |

*Source:* From Capron, C., and Duyme, M., "Assessment of Effects of Socio-Economic Status on IQ in a Full Cross-fostering Study," *Nature, 340,* 1989, p. 553.

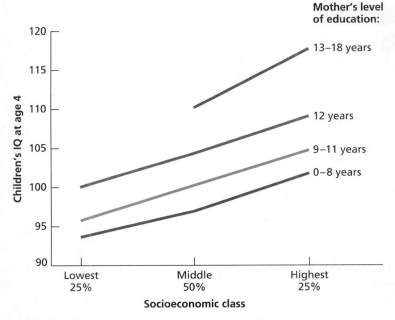

FIGURE 7.4 Socioeconomic Class, Maternal Education, and IQ
Each line represents the IQ scores of 4-year-old White children whose mothers had a particular level of education, and whose families fit in one of three broad socioeconomic class levels. Both elements are obviously related to the child's IQ.

(*Source:* Broman, S. H., Nichols, P. L., & Kennedy, W. A. (1975). *Preschool IQ: Prenatal and early developmental correlates.* Hillsdale, NJ: Erlbaum.)

**cumulative deficit** Any difference between groups in IQ or achievement test scores that becomes larger over time.

This kind of rich, complex, stimulating environment is consistently linked to higher IQ scores in children.

affect children's health (look back at Table 4.6, on page 108). Many of these factors, such as the mother's level of education, are correlated with children's scores on IQ tests as well (Gale, O'Callaghan, Godfrey, Law, & Martyn, 2004; Harden, Turkheimer, & Loehlin, 2007).

You can see this effect particularly vividly in Figure 7.4, which is based on data from a huge national study of more than 50,000 children born in 12 different hospitals around the United States between 1959 and 1966 (Broman, Nichols, & Kennedy, 1975). In order to make sure that the effects are due to SES and not ethnic differences, the figure shows only the results for White children who were tested with the Stanford-Binet at age 4, a total sample of more than 11,800 children. As you can see, the average IQ score of the children rises as the family's SES rises and as the mother's education rises.

Such differences are not found in the results of standardized tests of infant intelligence such as the Bayley Scales (Golden & Birns, 1983). Later in childhood, test score differences associated with SES appear in most studies (Cox, 1983; Misra, 1983), producing what is sometimes called a **cumulative deficit**. That is, the longer a child lives in poverty, the more negative the effect on IQ test scores and other measures of cognitive functioning (Turkheimer et al., 2003).

**PROTECTIVE FACTORS** When you read about correlations between poverty and IQ scores, it's easy to get the idea that children in low-income homes are doomed to have below-average intellectual abilities. However, there are several factors that help protect children against the risks associated with poverty. In fact, researchers have found that the quality of parent-child interactions may be a more important factor than income in determining a child's IQ (Robinson, Lanzi, Weinberg, Ramey, & Ramey, 2002). Research has shown that, no matter what the economic status of a child's family is, there are at least five dimensions of family interaction or stimulation that influence her IQ. Parents of children who have higher IQ scores or scores that increase with age tend to do several things:

- They provide an interesting and complex physical environment for their children, one that includes play materials that are appropriate for each child's age and developmental level (Englund, Luckner, Whaley, & Egeland, 2004; Luster, Lekskul & Oh, 2004).
- They are emotionally responsive to and involved with their children. They respond warmly and appropriately to a child's behavior, smiling when the child smiles, reacting when the child speaks, answering the child's questions, and responding to the child's cues in myriad other ways (La Paro, Justice, Skibbe, & Pianta, 2004).
- They talk to their children often, using language that is diverse, descriptive, and accurate (Fewell & Deutscher, 2003; Hart & Risley, 1995; Sigman et al., 1988).
- When they play with or interact with their children, they operate in what Vygotsky referred to as the *zone of proximal development* (described in Chapter 1), aiming their conversation, their questions, and their assistance at a level that is just above the level the children could manage on their own, thus helping the children to master new skills (e.g., Tamis-LeMonda, Shannon, Cabrera, & Lamb, 2004).
- They expect their children to do well and to develop rapidly. They emphasize and encourage school achievement (Englund et al., 2004; Murray et al., 2006).

You may have figured out the methodological problem in research on parent-child interactions: the same problem that surfaces in comparisons of the IQs of children in families that differ in SES. Because parents provide both the genes and the environment, it isn't clear that these environmental factors are really causally important. Perhaps these are simply the environmental features provided by brighter parents, and it is their genes and not the environment that cause the higher IQ scores in their children. The way around this problem is to look at the link between environmental factors and IQ in adopted children. In fact, the few studies of this type do point to the same critical environmental features. That is, adoptive parents who behave in the ways listed above have adopted children who score higher on IQ tests (Plomin, Leohlin, & DeFries, 1985; van IJzendoorn et al., 2005).

**DIFFERENCES WITHIN FAMILIES**  Within families, the experiences of individual children also differ in ways that affect IQ test scores. Taken together, such characteristics constitute the **nonshared environment**, factors that affect one child but not others in a family. Being the oldest of a large family, for example, is a very different experience from being the youngest or being in the middle. On average, first-born children have the highest IQ scores, with average scores declining steadily down the birth order (Abdel-Khalek & Lynn, 2008; Zajonc & Sulloway, 2007). One fairly typical set of data is illustrated in Figure 7.5, which is based on scores of nearly 800,000 students who took the National Merit Scholarship Examination in 1965, with the scores converted to the equivalent of IQ scores.

These differences are found consistently when IQ scores are averaged over many children or adults. However, when you look at individual families, the pattern is much weaker or not obvious at all. Another point is that the absolute differences in IQ scores are not huge, even in the aggregated data. Still, this pattern has been observed repeatedly in the United States and in several other nations, leaving developmentalists to wonder why such a pattern occurs. The late Robert Zajonc's (1923–2008) hypothesis was that, on average, the birth of each succeeding child "dilutes" the intellectual climate of the home (Zajonc & Sulloway, 2007). The oldest child initially interacts only with adults (parents) and thus has the most complex and enriching environment possible in that family at that time. Second or later children, in contrast, experience a lower average intellectual level simply because they interact with both other children and adults.

However, critics claim that Zajonc's theory, because it narrowly focuses on correlations between birth order and scores on conventional IQ tests, overlooks aspects of the environment that are unique to later-borns (Gillies & Lucey, 2006). These critics argue that later-borns must sometimes find ways to overcome the privileged position that first-borns occupy in the family system. For example, they may need to find a distinctive area of achievement to gain the same level of attention that parents give to first-borns. Moreover, in conflicts with first-borns, younger siblings must deal with older siblings' age-related advantages in physical and cognitive development. Thus, we might expect that later-borns would have opportunities to become skilled negotiators with (or manipulators of) near-age peers that first-borns do not have. In fact, this is exactly what the research shows (Gillies & Lucey, 2006). Thus, some aspects of the family environment may indeed be "diluted" by the time later-borns come along, but others are enhanced.

Some developmentalists have suggested that cultural beliefs about the significance of birth order may be just as important as any "dilution" that may occur as family size increases (Herrera, Zajonc, Wieczorkowska, & Cichomski, 2003). For example, among the Balinese, standard syllables signifying children's birth rank are added to their names. The rationale for this practice is that the higher a child's birth rank, the greater the status he or she must be afforded by members of the culture. As a result, every person a child meets instantly knows his or her status and the cultural prescriptions regarding how he or she is to be treated.

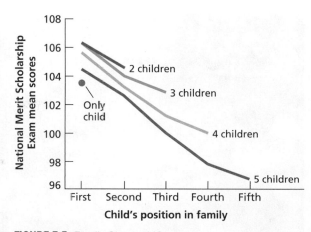

**FIGURE 7.5**  Family Size and IQ
These data from the 1965 National Merit Scholarship Examination show the commonly found relationship between test scores and family size and birth order. Within each family size, the average score is highest for the first-born and declines with each position in the birth-order sequence.

(*Sources:* Data from Breland, 1974, recalculated by Storter, 1990, Table 7, p. 32. Breland, H. M. (1974). "Birth order, family configuration and verbal achievement." *Child Development, 45,* 1011–1019.)

## Early Interventions and IQ Scores

Home environments and family interactions are not the only sources of environmental influence. Many young children also spend a very large amount of time in child care, special programs like Head Start, or preschool. How much effect do these environments have on a child's intellectual performance?

Attempts to answer this question have led to a messy body of research (Ripple & Zigler, 2010). Still, researchers agree generally on the effects. Children enrolled in Head

◄-----------Learning Objective 7.7
In what ways do early interventions affect IQ scores and school performance?

**nonshared environment**  Characteristics of a family that affect one child but not others in the household.

Children who have attended Head Start programs like this one are less likely to repeat a grade or to be assigned to special education classes.

Start or other enriched preschool programs outscore children who qualify for the program but do not enroll on tests of school readiness at age 5 (Zhai, Brooks-Gunn, & Waldfogel, 2011). They also show a gain of about 10 IQ points during the year of the Head Start experience compared to similar children without such experience. This IQ gain typically fades and then disappears within the first few years of elementary school (Barnett & Hustedt, 2005). However, research also suggests that the contributions made by Head Start teachers to children's beliefs about their ability to attain educational goals continue to be evident in adolescence (Slaughter-Defoe & Rubin, 2001).

On other measures, a clear residual effect can be seen as well. Children with Head Start or other quality preschool experience are less likely to be placed in special education classes, somewhat less likely to repeat a grade, and somewhat more likely to graduate from high school (Barnett & Hustedt, 2005). They also are healthier, have better immunization rates, and show better school adjustment than their peers (Ripple & Zigler, 2003; Zigler & Styfco, 1993). In addition, Head Start programs provide a useful context for identifying and helping children who exhibit behavior patterns, such as aggression, that put them at risk for adjustment difficulties in elementary school (Kamps, Tankersley, & Ellis, 2000).

Furthermore, one study that looked at adult outcomes of preschool attendance suggested lasting effects. Young adults who had attended a particularly good experimental preschool program, the Perry Preschool Project in Milwaukee, had higher rates of high school graduation, lower rates of criminal behavior, lower rates of unemployment, and a lower probability of being on welfare than did their peers who did not have the advantage of the preschool experience (Barnett, 1993). Thus, the potential effects of such early education programs may be broad—even though the programs appear to have no lasting effect on standardized IQ test scores (Ripple & Zigler, 2003).

More promising still—although far more expensive and complex—are enrichment programs that begin in infancy rather than at age 3 or 4 (Raikes, Chazan-Cohen, Love, & Brooks-Gunn, 2010). The best-designed and most meticulously reported of such infancy interventions has been carried out by Craig Ramey and his colleagues at the University of North Carolina (Ramey, Ramey, & Lanzi, 2007). Infants from poverty-level families whose mothers had low IQ scores were randomly assigned either to a special child-care program, 8 hours a day, 5 days a week, or to a control group that received nutritional supplements and medical care but no special enriched child care. The special child-care program, which began when the infants were 6 to 12 weeks of age and lasted until they began kindergarten, involved the kinds of optimal stimulation described earlier. When they reached kindergarten age, half the children in each group were enrolled in a special supplemental program that focused on family support and increasing educational activities at home. The remaining children had only the normal school experience.

The average IQ scores of the children at various ages are shown in Figure 7.6 on page 179. You can see that the IQ scores of the children who had been enrolled in the special child-care program were higher at every age, whether they were in the school-age supplementary program or not, although the scores for both groups declined in the elementary school years. What is not shown in the figure but is perhaps more practically significant is the fact that 44.0% of the control group children had IQ scores below 85, compared to only 12.8% of the children who had been in the special child-care program. In addition, the enriched infant-care group had significantly higher scores on both reading and mathematics achievement tests at age 12 and were only half as likely to have repeated a grade (Campbell & Ramey, 1994). And a follow-up study of the participants at age 21 revealed that the early advantage associated with participation in the program persisted into young adulthood (Pungello et al., 2010).

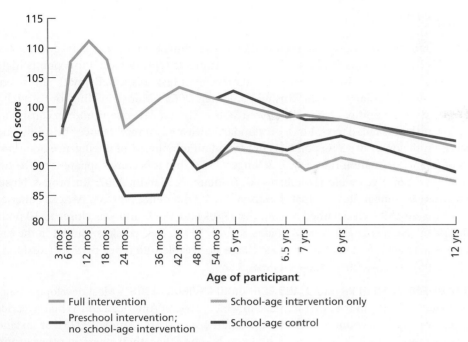

Full intervention          School-age intervention only

Preschool intervention;    School-age control
no school-age intervention

**FIGURE 7.6** Ramey's Studies of Early Intervention
In the Ramey study, children were randomly assigned in infancy to an experimental group with special child care (the "full intervention" group) or to a control group. From kindergarten through third grade, half of each group received supplementary family support, while the other half received none. Thus, the "preschool intervention" group had the intervention for 5 years, but nothing beyond that; the "school-age intervention" group had no intervention before school age but did have assistance in early elementary school. The difference in IQ between the intervention and control groups remained statistically significant even at age 12.

(*Source:* Campbell, F. A., and Ramey, C. T., "Effects of achievement: A follow-up study of children from low-income families," Fig. 1, p. 690, *Child Development*, 65 (1994), 684–698.)

## Interactions of Heredity and Environment

Putting together all the information about the influence of heredity and environment on IQ scores makes it clear that both factors are highly significant. Studies around the world and across several decades consistently yield estimates that at least half the variation in IQ scores within any population is due to heredity (Neisser et al., 1996; Plomin & Rende, 1991; Rogers, Rowe, & May, 1994; Rushton & Jensen, 2005; van Leeuwen, van den Berg, & Boomsma, 2008). The remaining half is clearly due to environment or to interactions between environment and heredity.

One useful way to think about this interaction is with the idea of a **reaction range**—a range within upper and lower boundaries of possible functioning established by one's genes. Where a child's IQ score falls within those boundaries is determined by environment. When a child's environment is improved, the child moves closer to the upper end of his reaction range. When the environment becomes worse, the child's effective intellectual performance falls toward the lower end of his reaction range. Thus, even though a reaction range of intelligence (as measured with an IQ test) is highly heritable, the IQ score within that range is determined by environment. Research showing that the IQ scores of identical twins are more weakly correlated in poor families than in those with more economic resources amply demonstrates this idea (Turkheimer, Haley, Waldron, D'Onofrio, & Gottesman, 2003).

## Explaining Group Differences in IQ or Achievement Test Scores

So far, we have sidestepped a difficult issue: group differences in IQ or achievement test scores. It's important to point out that individual variation in IQ and achievement is far greater than variation across groups. But you should be aware of what psychologists know, what they don't know, and how they explain these group differences.

Learning Objective 7.8

In what ways do heredity and environment interact to influence IQ scores?

**reaction range**   Term used by some psychologists for the range of possible outcomes (phenotypes) for some variable, given basic genetic patterning (the genotype). In the case of IQ scores, the reaction range is estimated at 20 to 25 points.

Learning Objective 7.9 ------------→
What ideas have theorists proposed
to explain ethnic group differences in
IQ scores?

# Ethnic Differences

Evidence points to several ethnic group differences in intellectual performance (Rushton & Jensen, 2005). First, Asian and Asian American students typically test 3 to 6 points higher on IQ tests and do consistently better on achievement tests (especially math and science tests) than do Caucasian children (Rushton & Jensen, 2005). More troubling for researchers and theorists is the finding that in the United States, African American children consistently score lower than Caucasian children on standard measures of intelligence. This difference, which is on the order of 12 IQ points, is not found on infant tests of intelligence or on measures of infant habituation rate (Fagan & Singer, 1983), but it becomes apparent by the time children are 2 or 3 years old (Dombrowski, Noonan, & Martin, 2007; Rushton & Jensen, 2005). There is some indication that the size of the IQ difference between African American and Caucasian children declined during the 1970s and 1980s and was closer to 10 points by the 1990s (Neisser et al., 1996; Williams & Ceci, 1997). Nevertheless, studies in the early years of the twenty-first century suggest that a noticeable difference persists (Rushton & Jensen, 2006). ◉─Watch at **MyDevelopmentLab**

◉─**Watch** the **Video** *Cultural Biases: Robert Guthrie* at **MyDevelopmentLab**

**GROUP DIFFERENCES IN PHYSICAL AND ECONOMIC ENVIRONMENTS** Most developmentalists argue that differences in the environments in which African American and White American children are reared account for the average difference in score (Brody, 1992). For instance, African American children are more likely to be poor than their peers in other groups. Aside from the effects of poverty on physical health that may affect test scores, some developmental scientists have argued that differences in the prevalence of computers, Internet access, and other types of information media in low-income families might explain ethnic group differences in cognitive test scores to some degree (see *Technology and the Developing Child*).

The greater prevalence of low birth weight among African American infants that you learned about in Chapter 4 may also contribute to cognitive test score differences according to at least one study (Dombrowski, Noonan, & Martin, 2007). Children who weighed less than

---

# TECHNOLOGY AND THE DEVELOPING CHILD
## The Digital Divide and Cognitive Test Scores

Less than a decade ago, developmentalists worried that the *digital divide*—differences in access to home computers and Internet service across low-, middle-, and high-income families—might widen the cognitive test score gap between disadvantaged children and their better-off peers (Kaiser Family Foundation, 2004). Few predicted that within a relatively short period of time, computers would become nearly as prevalent in low-income homes as they are among more advantaged families. Surveys suggest that about 90% of children in the United States have computers at home with only slight deviations from this percentage across income and ethnic groups, causing developmentalists to wonder whether widespread access to computers will shrink the group differences you have read about in this chapter (Rideout, Foehr, & Roberts, 2010).

Unfortunately, research in both Europe and the United States shows just the opposite. Studies suggest that low-income children's cognitive test scores actually decline as computers and broadband Internet services become more prevalent in their neighborhoods (Belo, Ferreira, & Telang, 2010; Malamud & Pop-Eleches, 2010; Vigdor & Ladd, 2010). Moreover, this effect has been found only among poor children. Home computers and Internet access seem to have no effect on the achievement of better-off children. In response to these findings, developmentalists' concerns have turned to questions as to why computers seem to have negative effects on poor children's academic development. To date, no consensus has emerged to explain these findings, but most proposed hypotheses focus on parental monitoring of children's computer activities (Vigdor & Ladd, 2010).

**Learning Objective 7.9a**
How are home computers and Internet access linked to achievement among poor children?

**FIND OUT MORE**

*Use your Internet search skills to answer these questions.*

1. Search for more information on this topic that will help you come up with your own hypothesis to explain why computer and Internet access lead to declines in achievement among poor children.

2. Look for information on the *Texas Technology Immersion Pilot*, a multi-year study of the effects of computers in school on children's achievement. How do the results of the TTIP compare to the findings described here?

---

## Stereotype Threat

Dr. Jones is a clinical psychologist who works at a large children's hospital. One of her duties is to administer individual intelligence tests to children who are patients in the hospital's neurology department. When she administers a test to a child, Dr. Jones doesn't refer to it as an "intelligence" test. Instead, she says, "I'm going to ask you some questions about words" or "I'm going to ask you to solve some problems." Dr. Jones uses this approach because her goal is to get the best performance possible out of each child she tests. She believes that if children are worried about the type of test they are taking or how their performance will be judged, they aren't likely to do their best. Dr. Jones is particularly concerned about how the performance of a child who is a member of a minority group might be affected by what she says about a test, because she is familiar with the research on *stereotype threat*.

Psychologists Claude Steele and Joshua Aronson (Steele & Aronson, 1995) define *stereotype threat* as a subtle sense of pressure members of a particular group feel when they are attempting to perform well in an area in which their group is characterized by a negative stereotype. According to Steele and Aronson, African American students experience stereotype threat whenever they are faced with an important cognitive test such as a college entrance exam or an IQ test, because of the general cultural stereotype that African Americans are less intellectually able than members of other groups. In order to avoid confirming the stereotype, says the theory, African Americans avoid putting forth their best effort, because to fail after having put forth one's best effort would mean that the stereotype was true.

Numerous studies have confirmed the existence of stereotype threat among both children and adults (Nussbaum & Steele, 2007; Rydell, Shiffrin, Boucher, Van Loo, & Rydell, 2010; Steele & Aronson, 2004; Suzuki & Aronson, 2005). However, stereotype threat appears to have a smaller effect on children's test performance than it does on that of adults. Nevertheless, Dr. Jones believes that it is best to err on the side of caution with respect to stereotype threat. Her conclusion is that refraining from using the term "intelligence test" does not harm children or threaten their performance, whereas using that term might cause them to be more anxious than they would be otherwise.

### Learning Objective 7.9b
How does stereotype threat theory explain ethnic group differences in cognitive test scores?

### REFLECTION

1. Do you agree with Dr. Jones's conclusion regarding erring on the side of caution?
2. How might parents and teachers moderate the effects of stereotype threat on children's test performance?

---

2,000 grams at birth averaged 86 at age 7, while those with normal birth weight averaged 94, a score that is within the average range of 90–110. Thus, studies that compare African American children's IQ test scores to those of children in other groups without taking into account the higher prevalence of low birth weight among African American children may overstate the size of group differences in average scores.

**CULTURAL DIFFERENCES ACROSS ETHNIC GROUPS**  Further evidence for the environmental hypothesis comes from studies of Asian American families, whose cultural beliefs tend to emphasize academic achievement more than either African American or White families. As teens, Asian Americans prioritize their time differently than do adolescents in other groups: Family and school take precedence over social activities with peers (Fuligni, Yip, & Tseng, 2002). Such differences have been cited in explanations of Asian American children's higher IQ scores.

Cultural differences also clearly contribute to observed differences between African American and Caucasian children's test scores, as African American psychologists have long pointed out (Fagan & Holland, 2007; Ogbu, 1994, 2004). One such cultural effect is discussed in *Developmental Science in the Real World*. We can see such differences at work in the way children from different subcultures respond to the testing situation itself. For example, in a classic study of adopted African American children, Moore (1986) found that those who had been reared in White families (and thus imbued with the values of the majority culture) not only had a higher average IQ score than those adopted into African American families (117 versus 103) but also approached the IQ-testing situation quite differently. They stayed more focused on the tasks and were more likely to try some task even if they didn't think they could do it. African American children adopted into middle-class African American families did not show this pattern of persistence and effort. They asked for help more often and gave up more easily when faced with a difficult task. When Moore then observed each adoptive mother teaching her child several tasks, he could see parallel differences. The White mothers were more encouraging and less likely to give the child the answer than were the African American mothers.

Findings like these suggest that the observed IQ differences among racial or ethnic groups are at least to some degree a reflection of cultural bias. Such bias arises from the fact that IQ tests and schools alike are designed by the majority culture to promote a particular form of intellectual activity, and many African American or other minority families rear their children in ways that do not promote or emphasize this particular set of skills (Guthrie, 2004). Consequently, some developmentalists have argued for banning intelligence testing altogether. However, most psychologists agree that there are still some good reasons for using IQ tests, as long as their limitations are understood. Likewise, studies examining a new approach to individualized assessment suggest that it may be possible for psychologists who are testing children from disadvantaged backgrounds to duplicate the test-familiarity advantage of middle-class children in the testing situation itself. In *dynamic assessment*, children are informed about the purpose of an intelligence test and are given a chance to practice with each kind of problem-solving task on the test prior to actually being tested. Studies show that dynamic assessment significantly increases the proportion of minority children who attain above-average scores (Lidz & Macrine, 2001). Further, whenever possible, intelligence testing of ethnic minority children should be carried out by testing professionals with ethnic backgrounds similar to those of the children being tested. Research has shown that children from minority groups get better scores under such conditions (Kim, Baydar, & Greek, 2003). Moreover, as we noted in Table 7.1, the Kaufman Assessment Battery for Children (KABC) (Kaufman & Kaufman, 2004) has been praised for its lack of bias. Minority group children tend to get higher scores on the KABC than they do on the Wechsler tests (Kaufman, Kaufman, Kaufman-Singer, & Kaufman, 2005). Thus, the KABC is used by many preschools, elementary schools, and clinicians to assess intelligence in minority group children.

**Learning Objective 7.10** - - - - - - - - - →
What factors contribute to cross-cultural differences in IQ and achievement test scores?

## Cross-Cultural Differences

The primary obstacle to cross-cultural studies of achievement is the lack of tests that are reliable and valid both within and across cultures (Oakland, 2009). For instance, researchers have had a very difficult time devising valid achievement tests for school systems in developing countries, especially those in the rural areas of such nations (Stemler et al., 2009). For example, researchers have found that conventional Western intelligence tests administered in the early childhood years predict school achievement for rural Zambian boys but not for girls (Serpell & Jere-Folotiya, 2008). It's unclear whether these results reflect a real gender difference or a problem with the validity of the intelligence and achievement measures themselves. Until such questions are resolved, studies comparing children's achievement in rural Zambia to that of children in the industrialized world—or even in urban areas of Zambia where Western notions of intelligence, achievement, and gender roles are more influential—are unlikely to yield meaningful results.

Because of these difficulties, comparisons of students in school systems that are very similar, at least with regard to educational objectives, predominate among international cross-cultural studies. For instance, comparisons of schoolchildren in North American, Europe, and Pacific Rim nations such as Japan are common. But because the surface characteristics of schools and the children themselves are quite similar across these nations, the reasons for achievement differences are often difficult to identify.

Nevertheless, studies that look for subtle variations beneath the surface have yielded important insights into the influence of educational practices on achievement. For example, studies have often found that children in the United States demonstrate substantially lower levels of performance in math and science than children in other industrialized nations (Provasnik & Gonzales, 2009). These comparisons have focused on Asian children because their scores have been found to be significantly higher than those of children in other nations. Harold Stevenson and others have argued that the differences between Asian and American children in performance on mathematics achievement tests result from differences in cultural emphasis on the importance of academic achievement, in the number of hours spent on homework, and in the quality of math instruction in the schools

(Chang & Murray, 1995; Geary, 1996; Schneider, Hieshima, Lee, & Plank, 1994; Stevenson & Lee, 1990; Stigler, Lee, & Stevenson, 1987). For example, Singaporean parents start teaching their children about numbers and mathematical reasoning long before the children begin school (Sharpe, 2002).

Moreover, teachers in Asian nations take a different approach to mathematics instruction than do teachers in the United States (Ni, Chiu, & Cheng, 2010). For example, in their pioneering studies comparing Asian and North American children, James Stigler and Harold Stevenson (1991) observed teaching practices in 120 classrooms in Japan, Taiwan, and the United States. Asian teachers typically devoted an entire class period to a single type of problem. In U.S. classrooms, in contrast, teachers rarely spent 30 or 60 minutes on a single coherent math or science lesson involving the whole class of children and a single topic. Instead, they shifted often from one topic to another during a single math or science lesson. They might do a brief bit on addition, then talk about measurement, then about telling

Asian and Asian American children tend to get higher scores on math and science tests than their peers in other groups do. What explanations can you think of for such a difference?

time, and then shift back to addition. Stigler and Stevenson also found striking differences in the amount of time teachers spent leading instruction for the whole class. In the U.S. classrooms they observed, group instruction occurred only 49% of the time; it occurred 74% of the time in Japan and 91% of the time in Taiwan. More recent studies have produced similar findings (NCES, 2003; Ni, Chiu, & Cheng, 2010).

Despite the fact that Stigler and Stevenson initiated their studies decades ago, their findings continue to inform developmentalists' understanding of cross-cultural differences in achievement due to the breadth and depth of the data they collected. More recent work has expanded researchers' knowledge about the factors that contribute to cross-cultural differences in achievement, particularly in math and science. For example, many studies have shown that Asian and American math instruction also differs with respect to emphasis on *computational fluency*, the degree to which an individual can automatically produce solutions to simple calculation problems (Geary et al., 1999). Research has demonstrated that computational fluency in the elementary school years is related to concurrent and future calculation skills; achievement in advanced math classes such as algebra; *number sense*, an intuitive grasp of mathematics; and to facility in solving word problems (Geary et al., 1999; Kail & Hall, 1999; Tolar, Lederberg, & Fletcher, 2009).

Asian and Western cultures differ with respect to beliefs about achievement as well. For example, developmentalists have found that North American parents and teachers emphasize innate ability, which they assume to be unchangeable, more than they emphasize effort. For Asians, the emphasis is just the opposite: They believe that people can become smarter by working harder (Hatano, 2004). Because of these differences in beliefs, some developmentalists claim, Asian parents and teachers have higher expectations for children and are better at finding ways to motivate them to do schoolwork. Moreover, Asian students see a more direct connection between their efforts and the educational outcomes they experience than either North American or European students do (McClure et al., 2011; Nóra, 2009).

## Sex Differences

◄------------Learning Objective 7.11

How do males and females differ with respect to IQ and achievement test performance?

Comparisons of overall IQ test scores for boys and girls do not reveal consistent differences (Camarata & Woodcock, 2006). It is only when researchers break down the overall score into several subscores that reflect separate skills that some patterns of sex differences emerge (Lippa, 2005). For example, more boys than girls test as gifted in mathematical reasoning (Halpern et al., 2007). This difference is evident as soon as children become developmentally capable of responding verbally to traditional ability tests, that is, around the age of 3 years

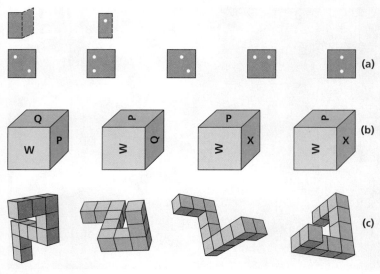

**FIGURE 7.7** Spatial Ability Tasks

Three examples of spatial ability tasks. (a) *Spatial visualization*. The figure at the top represents a square piece of paper being folded. A hole is punched through all the thicknesses of the folded paper. Which figure shows what the paper looks like when it is unfolded? (b) *Spatial orientation*. Compare the three cubes on the right with the one on the left. No letter appears on more than one face of a given cube. Which of the three cubes on the right could be a different view of the cube on the left? (c) *Mental rotation*. In each pair, can the three-dimensional objects be made congruent by rotation?

(*Source: Sex Differences in Cognitive Abilities,* by D. Halpern. Copyright 1986 by Taylor & Francis Group LLC-Books. Reproduced with permission of Taylor & Francis Group.)

◉⌐**Watch** the **Video** *Hands-On Learning in Elementary Math* at **MyDevelopmentLab**

◉⌐**Watch** the **Video** *Gender Differences: Robert Sternberg* at **MyDevelopmentLab**

(Locuniak & Jordan, 2008). Through the elementary school years, boys develop sophisticated mathematical strategies more rapidly than girls do (Carr & Alexeev, 2011). Moreover, these early sex differences predict differences in math achievement among boys and girls later in childhood (Jordan, 2010).

Some developmentalists attribute sex differences in mathematical reasoning to sex differences in spatial abilities. Such differences are evident in the early preschool years (Levine, Huttenlocher, Taylor, & Langrock, 1999). Boys have somewhat higher average scores on tests of spatial visualization, such as those illustrated in Figure 7.7. On measures of mental rotation, like that illustrated in part (c) of the figure, the sex difference is substantial and becomes larger with age (Hyde, 2005). Differences in such abilities are manifested in everyday tasks such as route learning. In learning to follow a new way to get from one place to another, both preschool and elementary school boys make fewer errors than girls (Beilstein & Wilson, 2000).

Where might such differences come from? The explanatory options should be familiar by now. Biological influences have been most often suggested as the cause of sex differences in spatial abilities (Hyde, 2005). Specifically, boys show greater coherence in brain function in areas of the brain devoted to spatial tasks, while girls display more organized functioning in parts of the brain where language and social information are processed (Hanlon, Thatcher, & Cline, 1999). Advocates of this position also point out that research with adults has demonstrated that hormonal differences between men and women, as well as hormonal variations among women, are linked to performance on spatial tasks (Halpern & Tan, 2001; Josephs, Newman, Brown, & Beer, 2003). As a result, some argue that hormonal differences between boys and girls or hormonal variations in the prenatal environment may affect spatial abilities.

However, longitudinal studies have also shown that parents' beliefs about their children's talents at age 6 predict those children's beliefs about their own abilities at age 17 (Fredricks & Eccles, 2002). For instance, parents are more likely to describe sons as competent in mathematics (Furnham 2000; Tiedemann, 2000). Parents are also more likely to characterize a daughter who performs well in math classes as a "hard worker," while a son who does well in mathematics is often described as "talented" (Räty, Vänskä, Kasanen, & Kärkkäinen, 2002). Not surprisingly, by the time children enter seventh grade, their mathematical self-concepts are well established and, typically, do not change across the high school years (Nagy et al., 2010). Thus, it isn't surprising that even the most mathematically talented girls are far less likely to aspire to careers in math and science than are boys (Ceci & Williams, 2010; Webb, Lubinski, & Benbow, 2002). ◉⌐Watch at **MyDevelopmentLab**

Environmental explanations notwithstanding, it is clear that males far outnumber females at the highest levels of mathematical giftedness, often quantified as scores in the top 1% on tests of quantitative reasoning, such as the math portion of the SAT (Lippa, 2005). Researchers have yet to find an adequate explanation for this sex difference. However, findings suggest that the disproportionate male to female ratio among the mathematically gifted may be but one manifestation of a larger phenomenon, that of greater variability among males than females. In other words, there are more males than females at the highest levels of mathematical ability, but the same is probably true of the lowest levels (Deary, Thorpe, Wilson, Starr, & Whalley, 2003). Such findings do not constitute an explanation for sex differences in mathematical giftedness. However, they do help us conceptualize these differences more dispassionately—that is, as "differences" rather than some form of "superiority" or "advantage" that has been unjustly conferred upon males. ◉⌐Watch at **MyDevelopmentLab**

# Alternative Views of Intelligence

Using IQ tests to define and explain individual and group differences in intelligence is called the *psychometric approach* (Birney & Sternberg, 2011; Shayer, 2008). Recently, developmentalists of diverse theoretical orientations have argued that this approach is too narrow. That is, many are beginning to believe that psychologists have placed too much emphasis on defining intelligence in terms of correlations between IQ tests and school achievement. Moreover, a number of developmentalists have suggested that we still do not really know what it is that intelligence tests measure. Thus, several alternative approaches to defining and measuring intelligence have been proposed in recent years.

## Information-Processing Theory

In Chapter 6, you read about developmental changes in information-processing strategies. Several developmentalists have argued that some of the same concepts can be used to explain what specific processes are measured on IQ tests.

←-----------Learning Objective 7.12
How do information-processing theorists explain individual differences in IQ scores?

**SPEED OF INFORMATION PROCESSING**    As you learned in Chapter 6, it is becoming increasingly clear that increases in speed or efficiency of processing underlie age-related changes in cognitive skills (Edmonds et al., 2008). Thus, it makes sense to hypothesize that differences in processing speed may also underlie individual differences in IQ scores (Thomas & Karmiloff-Smith, 2003). A number of investigators have found just such a link: Participants with faster reaction times or speed of performance on a variety of simple tasks also have higher average IQ scores on standard tests (McRorie & Cooper, 2004; Rinderman & Neubauer, 2004). A few studies have even linked speed of processing directly to central nervous system functioning and to IQ. For example, it is now possible to measure the speed of conduction of impulses along individual nerves, such as nerves in the arm. Philip Vernon (1993; Vernon & Mori, 1992; Shepher & Vernon, 2008) has found a correlation of about .45 between such a measure and IQ test score.

Most of this research has been done with adults, but a link between speed of reaction time and IQ scores has also been found in a few studies with children (Rindermann & Neubauer, 2004). Furthermore, there are some pretty clear indications that such speed-of-processing differences may be built in at birth. Indeed, the link between infant habituation (or recognition memory) and later IQ score seems to be primarily a result of basic variations in speed of processing (Rose & Feldman, 1997).

**OTHER LINKS BETWEEN IQ AND INFORMATION PROCESSING**    Other researchers have explored the connections between IQ and information processing by comparing the information-processing strategies used by typically developing children with those used by children with mental retardation. In one classic study, Judy DeLoache compared the searching strategies of groups of 2-year-olds who were either developing normally or showed delayed development (DeLoache & Brown, 1987). When the search task was very simple, such as looking for a toy hidden in an obvious location in a room, the two groups did not differ in search strategies or skill. But when the experimenter surreptitiously moved the toy before the child was allowed to search, typically developing children were able to search in alternative plausible places, such as in nearby locations; delayed children simply persisted in looking in the place where they had seen the toy hidden. They either could not change strategies once they had settled on a particular approach or did not have alternative, more complex strategies in their repertoires.

Other research underlines this difference in the flexibility of strategy use (Pretz & Sternberg, 2005). In several early studies, Joseph Campione and Ann Brown (1984; Campione, Brown, Ferrara, Jones, & Steinberg, 1985) found that both children with mental retardation and children with average and above- average IQs could learn to solve problems such as those in parts (a), (b), and (c) of Figure 7.8 on page 186, but the children with mental retardation could not transfer this learning to a more complex problem of the same general type, such as part (d), whereas children with average and above-average IQs could. Both sets of studies suggest that flexibility of use of any given strategy may be another key dimension of individual differences in intelligence.

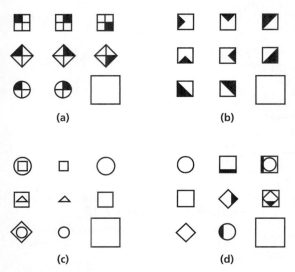

**FIGURE 7.8** Flexibility of Strategy Use

For parts (a) through (d), the child must figure out the "system" in each set and then describe what pattern should go in the empty box in the bottom right-hand corner. Part (a) shows rotation; part (b) shows addition of two elements; part (c) shows subtraction. The figure in part (d) is harder because the child must apply *two* principles at once, in this case both addition and rotation. Children with mental retardation and children with average and above-average IQs could do problems like those in parts (a), (b), and (c), but children with mental retardation did much more poorly on problems like the one in part (d).

(*Source:* Campione et al., 1985, Figure 1, p. 302, and Figure 4, p. 306. "Breakdowns in flexible use of information: Intelligence-related differences in transfer following equivalent learning performance." *Intelligence, 9*, 297–315. 1985, Figure 1, p. 302, and Figure 4, p. 306.)

**EVALUATING THE INFORMATION-PROCESSING APPROACH** The information-processing approach offers some important bridges between testing approaches to intelligence and cognitive-developmental theories such as those of Piaget and the neo-Piagetians (Anderson, 2005). It now looks as if children are born with some basic, inborn cognitive strategies (such as noting differences or similarities). It is also clear that these strategies or rules change during the early years of life, with more complex ones emerging and old ones being used more flexibly. Plain old experience is a key part of the process of change. The more a child plays with blocks, the better she will be at organizing and classifying blocks; the more a person plays chess, the better he will be at seeing and remembering relationships among pieces on the board. So some of the changes that Piaget thought of as changes in the underlying structure of intelligence are instead specific task learning. But there does seem to be some structural change as well, such as the emergence of new strategies, particularly metacognitive strategies.

Individual differences in what is normally thought of as intelligence can then be conceived of as resulting both from inborn differences in the speed or efficiency of the basic processes (differences in the hardware, perhaps) and from differences in expertise or experience. The child with a slower or less efficient processing system will move through all the various steps and stages more slowly; he will use the experience he has less efficiently or effectively and may never develop as complete a range of strategies as the child who is initially quicker. But when this less innately gifted child has sufficient expertise in some area, that specialized knowledge can compensate for the lower IQ.

This point is nicely illustrated in a study of expertise done in Germany (Schneider & Bjorklund, 1992). School-aged children who were experts (very knowledgeable) about soccer had better recall of soccer-related lists than did nonexperts. But high-IQ novices did as well as low-IQ experts on these same tasks. So rich knowledge in some area can compensate somewhat for lower IQ, but it does not result in equality. High-IQ experts will still be better than medium- or low-IQ experts in any given area.

The information-processing approach may also have some practical applications. Studies of recognition memory in infancy, for example, may give developmentalists a way to identify children with mental retardation very early in life or to sort out from among low-birth-weight infants those who seem at particular risk for later problems. Identifying the aspects of information processing that distinguish children with cognitive disabilities from typically developing peers may also allow developmentalists to identify specific kinds of training that would be useful for a child with mental retardation or for a child with a learning disability.

It is well to remember, though, that developmentalists do not yet have any tests of information-processing ability that could realistically replace the careful use of IQ tests in schools and clinics, although a few psychologists believe that a clinically useful biological measure of intelligence will be available within several decades (Tasbihsazan, Nettelbeck, & Kirby, 2003). Nor are the sequential theories of information-processing development yet able to explain all the observed differences among infants, preschoolers, and older children in performance on various Piagetian tasks. In short, information-processing theory is an important addition to psychologists' understanding of cognitive development, but it does not replace all the other approaches.

**Learning Objective 7.13**

What is the triarchic theory of intelligence?

## Sternberg's Triarchic Theory of Intelligence

Some developmentalists say that the problem with relying on IQ tests as the primary means of understanding and studying intelligence is that these tests fail to provide a complete picture of mental abilities. Psychologist Robert Sternberg, while conceding that conventional tests are good predictors of academic performance and other important outcomes (Sternberg 2011), argues that there are components of intellectual functioning that these tests measure poorly. He suggests that there are actually three aspects, or types, of intelligence (1985, 2003;

Sternberg & Wagner, 1993). Consequently, Sternberg's theory is known as the **triarchic theory of intelligence**. ✳―[Explore at MyDevelopmentLab

Sternberg has developed a test, the Sternberg Triarchic Abilities Test, to measure the three aspects of intelligence he hypothesizes (Sternberg, Castejon, Prieto, Hautamaeki, & Grigorenko, 2001). The first of the three, which Sternberg calls **analytical intelligence** (originally called *componential intelligence*), includes what is normally measured by IQ and achievement tests. Planning, organizing, and remembering facts and applying them to new situations are all part of analytical intelligence.

The second aspect Sternberg calls **creative intelligence** (originally labeled *experiential intelligence*). A person with well-developed creative intelligence can see new connections between things, is insightful about experiences, and questions what is sometimes called the "conventional wisdom" about various kinds of problems (Sternberg, 2001). A graduate student who comes up with good ideas for experiments, who can see how a theory could be applied to a totally different situation, who can synthesize many facts into a new organization, or who critically examines ideas that most professionals in the field accept as true is high in creative intelligence.

The third aspect Sternberg calls **practical intelligence** (originally labeled *contextual intelligence*), sometimes called "street smarts." People who have a high degree of practical intelligence are good at seeing how some bit of information may be applied to the real world or at finding some practical solution to a real-life problem—such as coming up with shortcuts for repetitive tasks or figuring out which of several different-sized boxes of cereal is the best buy. Practical intelligence may also involve being skilled at reading social cues or social situations, such as knowing how to persuade others to follow your suggestions, a key characteristic of leaders (Sternberg, 2008).

Sternberg's most basic point about these several types of intelligence is not just that standard IQ tests do not measure all three, but that in the world beyond the school walls, creative or practical intelligence may be required as much as or more than the type of skill measured on an IQ test (Sternberg & Grigorenko, 2006). These are important points to keep in mind when considering the origins of individual differences in IQ scores. What developmentalists know about "intelligence" is almost entirely restricted to information about analytical intelligence—the kind of intelligence most often demanded (and tested) in school. They know almost nothing about the origins or long-term consequences of variations in creative or practical intelligence.

**triarchic theory of intelligence** A theory advanced by Robert Sternberg, proposing the existence of three types of intelligence: analytical, creative, and practical.

**analytical intelligence** One of three types of intelligence in Sternberg's triarchic theory of intelligence; the type of intelligence typically measured on IQ tests, including the ability to plan, remember facts, and organize information.

**creative intelligence** One of three types of intelligence described by Sternberg in his triarchic theory of intelligence; includes insightfulness and the ability to see new relationships among events or experiences.

**practical intelligence** One of three types of intelligence in Sternberg's triarchic theory of intelligence; often called "street smarts," this type of intelligence includes skill in applying information to the real world or solving practical problems.

**multiple intelligences** Eight types of intelligence (linguistic, logical/mathematical, spatial, bodily kinesthetic, musical, interpersonal, intrapersonal, and naturalistic) proposed by Howard Gardner.

✳―[Explore the Concept *Sternberg's Triarchic Theory of Intelligence* at **MyDevelopmentLab**

## Gardner's Multiple Intelligences

◄-----------**Learning Objective 7.14**
What are the various types of intelligence proposed by Gardner?

Developmental psychologist Howard Gardner has also argued that a multidimensional view of intelligence provides both a better understanding of individual differences and, at least potentially, strategies for measuring these differences in more meaningful ways. Accordingly, he has proposed a theory of **multiple intelligences** (Gardner, 1983). This theory claims there are eight types of intelligence:

- Linguistic: People who are good writers or speakers, learn languages easily, or possess a lot of knowledge about language have greater than average linguistic intelligence.
- Logical/mathematical: Logical/mathematical intelligence enables individuals to learn math and to generate logical solutions to various kinds of problems.
- Spatial: Spatial intelligence is used in the production and appreciation of works of art such as paintings and sculpture.
- Bodily kinesthetic: Professional athletes possess high levels of this kind of intelligence.
- Musical: Musicians, singers, composers, and conductors possess musical intelligence.
- Interpersonal: Those in the "helping professions"—counselors, social workers, ministers, and the like—have high levels of interpersonal intelligence.
- Intrapersonal: People who are good at identifying their own strengths and choosing goals accordingly have high levels of intrapersonal intelligence.
- Naturalistic: Scientists are high in this type of intelligence, involving the ability to recognize patterns in nature.

**creativity**   The ability to produce original, appropriate, and valuable ideas and/or solutions to problems.

**divergent thinking**   The ability to produce multiple solutions to problems that have no clear answer.

👁—Watch the **Video** *Robert Sternberg on Giftedness* at **MyDevelopmentLab**

**Learning Objective 7.15** - - - - - - - - - →
How do theorists explain creativity?

Gardner's theory is based on observations of people with brain damage, mental retardation, and other conditions, such as savant syndrome. Gardner points out that brain damage usually causes disruption of functioning in very specific mental abilities rather than a general decline in intelligence. He also notes that many individuals with mental deficits have remarkable talents: some are gifted in music; others can perform complex mathematical computations in their heads. Gardner continues to refine his model. In recent years, he has proposed that a ninth type of intelligence, one that he calls *existential intelligence*, deals with the spiritual realm and enables us to contemplate the meaning of life (Halama & Strízenec, 2004). Critics claim that Gardner's view, while intuitively appealing, has little empirical support (White, 2006).

## Creativity

Finally, conventional intelligence tests do not measure **creativity**, the ability to produce original, appropriate, and valuable ideas and/or solutions to problems. While children's capacity for creativity appears to greatly depend on how much knowledge they have about a topic (Sak & Maker, 2006), researchers have found that creativity is only weakly related to IQ (Lubart, 2003).   👁—Watch at **MyDevelopmentLab**

Some developmentalists agree with the ideas proposed by psychologist J. P. Guilford (1897–1987) (Silvia et al., 2008). Guilford defined creativity as **divergent thinking** (Guilford, 1967). A child who uses divergent thinking can provide multiple solutions to problems that have no clear answer. In one creativity test, the Alternative Uses Test (Guilford, 1967), children are prompted to think of unusual uses of everyday objects such as bricks.

However, other theorists base their views on a model that was proposed by noted creativity researcher Paul Torrance (1915–2003). He argued that tests such as the Alternative Uses Test fail to capture all of the dimensions of creativity. To test his theory, Torrance devised the Torrance Tests of Creative Thinking (Torrance, 1998). The test examines how individuals respond to problems that involve interpretations of pictures, interpretations of verbal scenarios, and producing drawings in response to prompts (Torrance, 1998). Test-takers receive scores on four dimensions of creativity:

*Conventional intelligence tests do not measure creativity. Moreover, the creative skills that students learn when they work on school publications, as these teens are doing, are not measured by achievement tests.*

- Fluency:   The total number of ideas generated
- Flexibility:   Number of different categories represented in ideas
- Originality:   The degree to which ideas are unusual, statistically speaking
- Elaboration:   The amount of detail in ideas

Evidence for the validity of Torrance's test among adults was found in his own longitudinal study in which children who received high scores on the test in the 1950s were found to have a greater number of creative accomplishments in adulthood some 40 years later (Plucker, 1999). Moreover, the Torrance test proved to be more strongly correlated with life achievements of a creative nature than were research participants' childhood IQ scores.

## THINK CRITICALLY

- Given the variability in individual IQ scores, does it make sense to select children for special classes, such as those for the gifted, on the basis of a single test score? How else could you go about choosing students?
- A lot of effort has been expended trying to explain possible sex differences in mathematical ability. What are the practical implications of viewing such differences as genetic versus viewing them as caused by environmental factors?

## CONDUCT YOUR OWN RESEARCH

You can use Figure 7.8 on page 186 in a simple study that will help you learn more about stereotype threat. Randomly assign equal numbers of your male and female classmates or friends to "stereotype-threat" and "no-stereotype-threat" conditions. Tell those in the threat condition that the tasks in the figure measure sex differences in cognitive ability. Point out that men often outperform women on such tasks. Tell participants in the nonthreat condition that you have to collect data on the tasks for your psychology class. Score participants' responses to sets (a) through (d) as correct or incorrect according to the explanations provided in the figure caption. You should find that women in the threat condition make more errors than those in the nonthreat condition. Men should score about the same in both.

## SUMMARY ✓ Study and Review at MyDevelopmentLab

### Measuring Intellectual Power

**7.1 What were Binet's and Terman's approaches to measuring intelligence?**

Early tests of intelligence, such as that devised by Binet, were designed to identify children who might have difficulty in school. Scores were based on a child's mental age. Terman adapted Binet's test for use in the United States (the Stanford-Binet) and introduced the term *intelligence quotient (IQ)*. Modern intelligence tests compare a child's performance to that of others of the same age. Scores above 100 represent better than average performance; scores below 100 represent poorer than average performance.

**7.1a How has the Flynn effect influenced IQ scores?**

The Flynn effect is the tendency of IQ scores to rise over time. Flynn hypothesized that scores rise as general health, adequate nutrition, and educational opportunities increased across the twentieth century. Recent evidence showing both declines in school enrollment and IQ scores support the view that education is more likely to be responsible for the Flynn effect than are advances in the physical domain.

**7.2 What intelligence tests are used today, and how do they differ from earlier tests?**

The most commonly used individually administered tests for children are the current revisions of the Stanford-Binet and the Wechsler Intelligence Scales for Children (WISC). The WISC-IV provides separate IQ scores for verbal comprehension, perceptual reasoning, processing speed, and working memory. The Bayley Scales of Infant Development and other developmental screening instruments measure a variety of motor and cognitive milestones in the first 2 to 3 years. Standardized achievement tests are similar to intelligence tests but measure only information that is learned in school.

**7.3 How stable are IQ scores throughout childhood and adolescence?**

IQ scores are quite stable from one testing to the next, especially as a child gets older. But individual children's scores may still fluctuate or shift over the course of childhood.

**7.4 What do IQ scores predict?**

IQ test scores are quite good predictors of school performance and years of education, a correlation that gives one piece of evidence for the validity of the tests. An important limitation of IQ tests is that they do not measure many other facets of intellectual functioning that might be of interest.

### Explaining Individual Differences in IQ Scores

**7.5 What do twin and adoption studies suggest about the effects of heredity and environment on IQ scores?**

Studies of identical twins and of adopted children clearly show a substantial genetic influence on measured IQ scores. These studies also show that environment contributes to IQ scores.

**7.6 How do shared and nonshared family characteristics affect IQ scores?**

Poor children consistently score lower on IQ tests than do children from middle-class families; children whose families provide appropriate play materials and encourage intellectual development score higher on IQ tests. Children in large families may be subject to a dilution of family resources that produces successively lower IQ scores in each child.

**7.7 In what ways do early interventions affect IQ scores and school performance?**

Environmental influence is shown by increases in test performance or school success among children who have been in enriched preschool or infant-care programs. Children who participate in these programs are also less likely to require special education services and more likely to graduate from high school.

**7.8 In what ways do heredity and environment interact to influence IQ scores?**

One way to explain the interaction of heredity and environment is with the concept of reaction range: Heredity determines some range of potential; environment determines the level of performance within that range. In addition, parents' levels of intelligence shape the environments they create for children. The child is exposed to parental influence both genetically and environmentally.

## Explaining Group Differences in IQ or Achievement Test Scores

**7.9** What ideas have theorists proposed to explain ethnic group differences in IQ scores?

A consistent difference in IQ scores of about 10 to 12 points is found between African American and Caucasian children in the United States. It seems most likely that this difference is due to environmental and cultural differences between the two groups, such as differences in health and prenatal care and in the type of intellectual skills taught and emphasized at home.

**7.9a** In what ways are home computers and Internet access linked to achievement test scores among poor children?

Poor children's achievement test scores tend to decline as computer and Internet access increase in their neighborhoods. These effects have not been found among better-off children. Researchers do not yet have an explanation for these findings, but hypothesized causes focus on parental monitoring of children's computer activities.

**7.9b** How does stereotype threat theory explain ethnic group differences in cognitive test scores?

Stereotype threat theory proposes that minority test-takers are aware of cultural stereotypes regarding the performance of minorities on cognitive tests. As a result, when they take such tests, minority group members experience levels of performance anxiety that negatively impact their scores. Research supports stereotype threat theory, but it does not fully explain ethnic group differences in cognitive test scores.

**7.10** What factors contribute to cross-cultural differences in IQ and achievement test scores?

Some researchers have argued that the differences between Asian and American children in performance on mathematics achievement tests result not from genetic differences in capacity but from differences in cultural emphasis on the importance of academic achievement, the number of hours spent on homework, and the type (or approach) of math instruction in the schools.

**7.11** How do males and females differ with respect to IQ and achievement test performance?

Males and females do not differ on overall IQ test scores, but they do differ in some subskills. The largest differences are on measures of spatial reasoning, on which males are consistently better.

## Alternative Views of Intelligence

**7.12** How do information-processing theorists explain individual differences in IQ scores?

Information-processing theory provides developmentalists with an alternative approach to explaining individual differences in intelligence. Higher-IQ individuals, for example, appear to process information more quickly and to apply strategies or knowledge more broadly.

**7.13** What is the triarchic theory of intelligence?

Sternberg's triarchic theory of intelligence suggests that IQ tests measure only analytical intelligence, one of three aspects of intellectual ability. According to his theory, these tests measure neither creative nor practical intelligence.

**7.14** What are the various types of intelligence proposed by Gardner?

Gardner has proposed eight distinct types of intelligence: linguistic, logical/mathematical, spatial, bodily kinesthetic, musical, interpersonal, intrapersonal, and naturalistic.

**7.15** How do theorists explain creativity?

Guilford suggested that creativity involves divergent thinking. Torrance proposed four dimensions of creativity: fluency, flexibility, originality, and elaboration. Both devised tests to measure creativity that are still used by researchers.

## KEY TERMS

achievement test (p. 171)
analytical intelligence (p. 187)
Bayley Scales of Infant Development (p. 170)
competence (p. 171)
creative intelligence (p. 187)
creativity (p. 188)
cumulative deficit (p. 176)

divergent thinking (p. 188)
full scale IQ (p. 169)
intelligence (p. 167)
intelligence quotient (IQ) (p. 168)
mental age (p. 168)
multiple intelligences (p. 187)
nonshared environment (p. 177)

perceptual reasoning index (p. 169)
performance (p. 171)
practical intelligence (p. 187)
processing speed index (p. 169)
reaction range (p. 179)
reliability (p. 172)
shared environment (p. 175)
Stanford-Binet (p. 167)

triarchic theory of intelligence (p. 187)
validity (p. 173)
verbal comprehension index (p. 169)
WISC-IV (p. 169)
working memory index (p. 169)
WPPSI-III (p. 169)

# 8

# The Development of Language

## LEARNING OBJECTIVES

### Before the First Word: The Prelinguistic Phase

**8.1** What are the characteristics of cooing and babbling?

    **8.1a** How does gestural language develop among infants with hearing impairments?

**8.2** What have researchers learned about infants' receptive language skills?

### Learning Words and Word Meanings

**8.3** What are the trends in word learning over the first 2 years?

**8.4** How does word learning proceed in early and middle childhood?

**8.5** What are some proposed constraints on word learning?

### Learning the Rules: The Development of Grammar and Pragmatics

**8.6** How do children's first sentences differ from holophrases?

**8.7** What is the significance of the grammar explosion?

**8.8** What grammatical skills do children acquire in the preschool, elementary, and teen years?

**8.9** What are the milestones of pragmatics development?

### Explaining Language Development

**8.10** How do environmental theories explain language development?

**8.11** What kind of evidence supports the nativist theories?

**8.12** How do constructivist theories differ from other approaches?

### Individual and Group Differences in Language Development

**8.13** Are differences in the rate of language development related to later measures of proficiency?

**8.14** In what ways does language vary across cultural groups?

### Learning to Read and Write

**8.15** What is the role of phonological awareness in learning to read?

**8.16** What strategies do educators use to help children learn how to read?

    **8.16a** What does research say about the link between handwriting and brain development?

**8.17** What instructional strategies do educators use to help English-language learners?

    **8.17a** How does bilingualism influence language development?

Chimpanzees can fairly easily learn signs for individual objects or actions and can understand and follow quite complex instructions. Here Nim Chimpsky, one of the first chimps trained to use signs to communicate, signs "I see." But is it advisable to teach human infants to use sign language?

In recent years, countless programs geared toward teaching sign language to infants who can hear have been developed. The authors and publishers of these programs claim that acquiring sign language will speed up the language development process, enabling children to acquire larger vocabularies and more complex grammatical structures than others their age. Researcher Cyne Johnston and her colleagues at the Universities of Ottawa and Waterloo carried out an extensive review of sign-language training programs for hearing infants (Johnston, Durieux-Smith, & Bloom, 2005).

Johnston and her colleagues concluded that almost all of the studies had been carried out in ways that made it impossible to determine whether any of the training programs actually influenced language development. For the most part, the studies lacked experimental methods, such as random assignment, that would support claims of causality. Further, many failed to control variables, such as parental enthusiasm, that might account for program effects. Some involved very small numbers of participants and purely descriptive research methods such as naturalistic observation and case studies.

Based on their analysis, Johnston and her colleagues concluded that there is no evidence that teaching hearing babies to use sign language enhances their language development. The researchers did note, however, that teaching sign language to infants does not appear to be harmful to the process of spoken language development. Consequently, if parents find it useful or enjoyable to do so, there doesn't appear to be any reason why they shouldn't.

Do such conclusions mean that parents have no influence on infants' language development? Clearly not, because, at a minimum, a child must have linguistic input and be able to engage in linguistic interactions with other people in order to acquire language. Thus, as you'll see throughout this chapter, both maturation and experience are critical to language development.

**phonology**   The sound patterns of a particular language and the rules for combining them.

**semantics**   A particular language's system of meaning and the rules for conveying meaning.

**syntax**   The rules for forming sentences in a particular language.

**prelinguistic phase**   The period before a child speaks his or her first words.

**cooing**   Making repetitive vowel sounds, particularly the *uuu* sound; the behavior develops early in the prelinguistic period, when babies are between about 1 and 4 months of age.

👁—Watch the **Video** *Speech Development* at **MyDevelopmentLab**

**Learning Objective 8.1** ------------➤
What are the characteristics of cooing and babbling?

## Before the First Word: The Prelinguistic Phase

Language has several dimensions. The sound patterns that a particular language uses and the rules that govern those patterns are its **phonology**. **Semantics** refers to how language represents meaning. The rules a language uses for combining words into sentences is known as **syntax**. You will see each of these terms again as we trace the development of language from its early, preverbal beginnings to the emergence of true linguistic fluency many years later. The process of language development actually begins in the months before the baby speaks his first word, a period called the **prelinguistic phase**. 👁—Watch at **MyDevelopmentLab**

## Early Sounds and Gestures

A baby's early perceptual skill is not matched right away by much skill in producing sounds. From birth to about 1 month of age, the most common sound an infant makes is a cry, although infants also make other fussing, gurgling, and satisfied sounds. This sound repertoire expands at about 1 or 2 months with the addition of some laughing and **cooing**—making repetitive vowel sounds, like *uuuuuu*. Sounds like this are usually signals of pleasure in babies and may show quite a lot of variation, including increases and decreases in volume or pitch.

Consonant sounds appear only at about 6 or 7 months of age, when for the first time the baby has the muscle control needed to combine a consonant sound with a vowel sound. From 6 months on, there is a rapid increase in the amount of vowel-consonant combinations. This type of vocalization, called **babbling**, makes up about half of babies' noncrying sounds from about 6 to 12 months of age (Mitchell & Kent, 1990). ◉⊢Watch at MyDevelopmentLab

Much early babbling involves repetitive strings of the same syllables, such as *dadadada* or *nananana* or *yayayaya*. Adults find babbling delightful to listen to; Lois Bloom (1998), one of the foremost theorists and observers of children's language, points out that these new sound combinations are also much easier for adults to imitate than are the earlier baby sounds, because babbling has more of the rhythm and sound of adult speech. The imitative game that may then develop between parent and child is not only a pleasure for both but may help the baby to learn language.

Babbling is an important part of the preparation for spoken language in other ways as well. For one thing, developmentalists have observed that infants' babbling gradually acquires some of the intonational patterns of the language they are hearing—a process Elizabeth Bates refers to as "learning the tune before the words" (Bates, O'Connell, & Shore, 1987). At the very least, infants do seem to develop at least two such "tunes" in their babbling. Babbling with a rising intonation at the end of a string of sounds seems to signal a desire for a response; a falling intonation requires no response.

A second important thing about babbling is that when babies first start babbling, they typically babble all kinds of sounds, including some that are not part of the language they are hearing. Then, beginning at about 9 or 10 months of age, the sound repertoire of infants gradually begins to shift toward the set of sounds they are listening to, with the nonheard sounds dropping out—a pattern that clearly parallels the findings of Werker's research, illustrated in Figure 5.4 (page 124), and that reflects what psychologists know about early synaptic development and pruning (Werker & Tees, 2005). Findings like these do not prove that babbling is necessary for language development, but they certainly make it look as if babbling is part of a connected developmental process that begins at birth.

Another part of that connected developmental process appears to be a kind of gestural language that develops near the end of the first year (Goldin-Meadow, 2007a) (see *Thinking about Research* on page 194). These gestures are the first signs of **expressive language**—the sounds, signs, and symbols that communicate meaning (Savage-Rumbaugh et al., 1993). Pointing is the most common gesture infants use. However, it is not unusual to see a baby of this age ask for things by using a combination of gestures and sounds. A 10-month-old baby who apparently wants you to hand her a favorite toy may stretch and reach for it, opening and closing her hand, making whining sounds or other heartrending noises. At about the same age, babies enter into those gestural games much loved by parents, like "patty-cake," "soooo-big," or "wave bye-bye" (MacWhinney, 2011).

*Pointing is one of the earliest forms of gestural language. This preschooler probably began using such gestures several months before he spoke his first words.*

◉⊢Watch the **Video** *Baby Talk* at **MyDevelopmentLab**

◉⊢Watch the **Video** *Language Learning* at **MyDevelopmentLab**

## Receptive Language

◀------------Learning Objective 8.2

What have researchers learned about infants' receptive language skills?

Interestingly, the first signs that an infant understands the meaning of individual words spoken to her (which linguists call **receptive language**) also become evident at about 9 or 10 months (MacWhinney, 2011). Babies of this age are already actively learning the language they are listening to. Not only can they understand some simple instructions, but they can benefit from being exposed to a rich array of language. ◉⊢Watch at MyDevelopmentLab

These bits of information point to a whole series of changes that seem to come together at 9 or 10 months: the beginning of meaningful gestures, the drift of babbling toward the heard language sounds, the first participation in imitative gestural games, and the first comprehension of individual words. It is as if the child now understands something about the process of communication and is intending to communicate to the rest of the world.

**babbling** The repetitive vocalizing of consonant-vowel combinations by an infant, typically beginning at about 6 months of age.

**expressive language** Sounds, signs, or symbols used to communicate meaning.

**receptive language** Comprehension of spoken language.

## Sign Language and Gestures in Children Who Are Deaf

As you have learned, gestures play an important communicative role in the lives of babies who are approaching their first birthdays (Goldin-Meadow, 2007a). But consider the case of children who cannot hear and whose parents use sign language to communicate with them. You might think that children who acquire sign language would not also learn to use gestures, but that is not the case.

The milestones of both verbal and nonverbal language development in children who are deaf are highly similar to those of children who can hear. Children who are deaf show a kind of sign babbling that emerges between 5 and 7 months of age, much as children who can hear begin to babble sounds in these same months (Takei, 2001). Interestingly, children who are deaf also vocalize in ways that sound very much like the babbling of infants who can hear, an indication that babbling is more strongly influenced by maturation than by the environment. Then, a couple of months shy of their first birthdays, children who are deaf begin using simple gestures, such as pointing; this is just about the same time that we see such gestures in babies

who can hear (Goldin-Meadow, 2007b). At about 12 months of age, babies who are deaf display their first referential signs, which are analogous to the first spoken words of babies who can hear. Interestingly, though, these referential signs do not replace the gestures that appeared a few months earlier. Instead, like babies who can hear and who are just learning to speak, infants who are learning to sign use both referential signs and gestures to communicate.

Researcher Susan Goldin-Meadow (2007b) argues that, in both babies who can hear and babies who are deaf, gestural communication assumes a subordinate role to structured language once it begins to develop. Thus, at 1 year of age, infants who cannot hear use two forms of manual communication: the beginnings of structured sign language and gestures that amplify signed messages or communicate information that cannot be expressed in sign language. Similarly, infants who can hear are just beginning to develop structured spoken language, and they, too, use gestures as aids to communication. This marked similarity in the

### Learning Objective 8.1a
How does gestural language develop among infants with hearing impairments?

sequence and timing of the steps of early language in infants who are deaf and infants who can hear provides strong support for the argument that the human infant is somehow primed to learn language.

#### CRITICAL ANALYSIS

1. We noted that the emergence of vocalization in infants who are deaf at the same time that babbling appears in infants who can hear supports the idea that maturation strongly influences language development. Does the appearance of gestures in children who are deaf at about the same time as in children who can hear also support this hypothesis? Why?

2. In your view, what are the benefits and risks associated with being the hearing child of parents who are deaf?

## Learning Words and Word Meanings

Somewhere in the midst of all the babbling, the first words appear, typically at about 12 or 13 months (Fenson et al., 1994). Once she has learned the first few words, the infant begins the work of identifying specific links between words and the objects or actions for which they stand.

Learning Objective 8.3
What are the trends in word learning over the first 2 years?

## The First Words

For a child, a *word* can be any sound; it doesn't have to be a sound that matches words adults are using. Brenda, a little girl studied by Ronald Scollon (1976), used the sound *nene* as one of her first words. It seemed to mean primarily liquid food, since she used it for "milk," "juice," and "bottle," but she also used it to refer to "mother" and "sleep."

Typically, early word learning is very slow, requiring many repetitions for each word. In the first 6 months of word usage (roughly between 12 and 18 months of age), children may learn to say as few as 30 words. Most linguists (e.g., Nelson, 1985) have concluded that in this earliest word-use phase, the child learns each word as something connected to a set of specific contexts. The toddler has apparently not yet grasped that words are symbolic—that they refer to objects or events regardless of context.

Somewhere between 16 and 24 months, most children begin to add new words rapidly, as if they have figured out that things have names. According to Fenson's very large cross-sectional study, based on mothers' reports, the average 16-month-old has a speaking vocabulary of about 50 words; by 24 months of age, this speaking vocabulary has multiplied more than sixfold to about 320 words (Fenson et al., 1994). A parallel study in Italy by Elizabeth Bates and her colleagues (Caselli, Casadio, & Bates, 1997) showed that this rapid rate of vocabulary growth is not unique to children learning English. In this new phase, children seem to learn new words after very few repetitions and to generalize these new words to many more situations.

For the majority of children, this *naming explosion* is not a steady, gradual process; instead, a vocabulary spurt begins once the child has acquired about 50 words. You can see this pattern in Figure 8.1, which shows the vocabulary growth curves of six children studied longitudinally by Goldfield and Reznick (1990); the same pattern has been found by other researchers as well (e.g., Bloom, 1993; Ganger & Brent, 2001).

During this early period of rapid vocabulary growth, the majority of new words are names for things or people. Verblike words tend to develop later, perhaps because they label relationships between objects rather than just individual objects (Bates et al., 1994; Gleitman & Gleitman, 1992). For example, in Fenson's large cross-sectional study (1994), 63% of the words mothers said their children knew by age 2 were nouns, while only 8.5% were verbs. Studies of children learning other languages show very similar patterns, as you can see in Table 8.1.

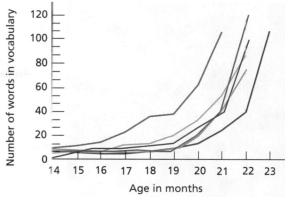

**FIGURE 8.1** Early Vocabulary Growth
Each line in this figure represents the vocabulary growth of one of the children followed by Goldfield and Reznick in their longitudinal study.

(*Source:* B. A. Goldfield and J. S. Reznick, Figure 3, p. 177, "Early lexical acquisition: Rate, content, and the vocabulary spurt," *Journal of Child Language, 17* (1990), 171–183. Reprinted with the permission of Cambridge University Press.)

## Table 8.1 — EARLY WORDS ACQUIRED BY CHILDREN IN FOUR CULTURES

| Words for people or things | German Boy | English Girl | Turkish Girl | Chinese Girl |
|---|---|---|---|---|
| | Mommy | Mommy | Mama | Momma |
| | Papa | Daddy | Daddy | Papa |
| | Gaga | babar | Aba | grandmother |
| | baby | baby | baby | horse |
| | dog | dog | food | chicken |
| | bird | dolly | apple | uncooked rice |
| | cat | kitty | banana | cooked rice |
| | milk | juice | bread | noodles |
| | ball | book | ball | flower |
| | nose | eye | pencil | wall clock |
| | moon | moon | towel | lamp |
| **Nonnaming words** | cry | run | cry | go |
| | come | all gone | come | come |
| | eat | more | put on | pick up |
| | sleep | bye-bye | went pooh | not want |
| | want | want | want | afraid |
| | no | no | hello | thank you |
| **Total percentage of naming words** | 67% | 69% | 57% | 59% |

*Source:* Gentner, Why nouns are learned before verbs: Linguistic relativity versus natural partitioning. In S. A. Kuczaj, II (Ed.), Language development: Vol. 2, Language, thought, and culture (pp. 301–334). Hillsdale, NJ: Erlbaum.

*Puppy, kitty, or . . . ? This toddler is likely to use the same animal name to refer to all types of creatures, an example of early language learners' tendency to employ words categorically in their everyday speech (overextension).*

Some studies suggest that noun learning may precede verb learning because infants lack the ability to consistently associate words with actions until about 18 months of age (Casasola & Cohen, 2000). However, studies in which researchers expose infants to languages that they have never heard before suggest that the fact that nouns occur more frequently than verbs in natural speech is an important factor. In such studies, infants demonstrate a remarkable ability to distinguish between object names and other types of words based on the frequency with which object names occur in a stream of speech (Hochmann, Endress, & Mehler, 2010). Thus, infants may learn nouns before verbs due to a built-in strategy that says something like "Learn the most frequent types of words first, then concentrate on the others." Research indicates that **underextension**—use of a word for only one specific object or in a single context—is most common at the earliest stages of vocabulary development, particularly before the naming explosion (MacWhinney, 2011), which suggests that most children initially think of words as belonging to only one thing, rather than as names for categories.

Once the naming explosion starts, however, the child appears to grasp the idea that words go with categories, and **overextension**—the use of a single word for an entire category of objects or in multiple contexts—becomes more common. At that stage, we're more likely to hear the word *kitty* applied to dogs or guinea pigs than we are to hear it used for just one animal or for a very small set of animals or objects (MacWhinney, 2011). As the child learns the separate labels that are applied to the different subtypes of furry four-legged creatures, overextension disappears.

Learning Objective 8.4 - - - - - - - - - - - - →
How does word learning proceed in early and middle childhood?

## Later Word Learning

During the preschool years, children continue to add words at remarkable speed. At age 2½, the average vocabulary is about 600 words, about a quarter of which are verbs (Bates et al., 1994); by age 5 or 6, total vocabulary has risen to perhaps 15,000 words—an astonishing increase of 10 words a day (Pinker, 1994). What accounts for this amazing rate of word learning? Researchers have found that a momentous shift in the way children approach new words happens around age 3. As a result of this shift, children begin to pay attention to words in whole groups, such as words that name objects in a single class (e.g., types of dinosaurs or kinds of fruit) or words with similar meanings.

Psychologists use the term **fast-mapping** to refer to this ability to categorically link new words to real-world referents (Carey & Bartlett, 1978). (*Referents* are the real objects and events to which words refer.) At the core of fast-mapping, say researchers, is a rapidly formed hypothesis about a new word's meaning (MacWhinney, 2011). The hypothesis is based on information derived from the child's prior knowledge of words and word categories and from the context in which the word is used. Once formed, the hypothesis is tested through use of the word in the child's own speech, often immediately after learning it. The feedback the child receives in response to use of the word helps him judge the accuracy of the hypothesis and the appropriateness of the category to which he has assumed that the word belongs. Perhaps this helps explain why preschoolers do so much talking and why they are so persistent at getting their listeners to actively respond to them.

Experimental studies have demonstrated that fast-mapping is evident as early as 18 months of age. In these studies, researchers teach toddlers new words that represent easily identifiable categories and then, after a period of time, measure their learning of related words. For example, fast-mapping should enable a child who has been taught the word *table* to acquire the word *chair* on her own more rapidly than a child who is unfamiliar with the word *table*. Such studies show that when children are tested a few weeks after receiving vocabulary instruction, they are more likely than children who were not instructed to understand and to use words that are related to, but are distinct from, those they were taught (e.g., Gershkoff-Stowe & Hahn, 2007).

In middle childhood, children continue to add vocabulary at the rate of 5,000 to 10,000 words a year. This figure comes from several careful studies by Jeremy Anglin (1993, 1995; Skwarchuk & Anglin, 2002), who estimates children's total vocabularies by

**underextension**   The use of words to apply only to specific objects, such as a child's use of the word *cup* to refer only to one particular cup.

**overextension**   The inappropriate use of a word to designate an entire category of objects, such as when a child uses the word *kitty* to refer to all animate objects.

**fast-mapping**   The ability to categorically link new words to real-world referents.

testing them on a sample of words drawn at random from a large dictionary. Figure 8.2 shows Anglin's estimates for first-, third-, and fifth-grade children. Anglin finds that the largest gain from third to fifth grade occurs in knowledge of the type of words he calls "derived words"—words such as *happily* or *unwanted*, which have a basic root to which some prefix or suffix is added. Anglin argues that at about age 8 or 9, the child shifts to a new level of understanding of the structure of language, figuring out relationships between whole categories of words, such as between adjectives and adverbs (*happy* and *happily*, *sad* and *sadly*) and between adjectives and nouns (*happy* and *happiness*). Once he understands such relationships, the child can understand and create whole sets of new words, and his vocabulary thereafter increases rapidly.

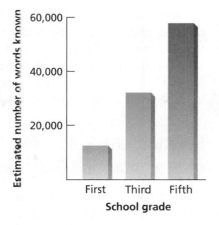

**FIGURE 8.2** Vocabulary Growth in Middle Childhood
Anglin's estimates of the total vocabulary of first- third-, and fifth-graders.

(*Source:* From "Word Learning and the Growth of Potentially Knowable Vocabulary" by Jeremy M. Anglin (1995), p. 7, Fig. 6. By permission of Jeremy M. Anglin.)

## Constraints on Word Learning

◄------------ Learning Objective 8.5

What are some proposed constraints on word learning?

A subject of hot debate among linguists is just how a child figures out which part of some scene a word may refer to. The classic example: A child sees a brown dog running across the grass with a bone in its mouth. An adult points and says "doggie." From such an experience, the toddler is somehow supposed to figure out that *doggie* refers to the animal and not to "running," "bone," "dog with bone," "brownness," "grass," or any other combination of elements in the whole scene.

Many linguists have proposed that a child could cope with this monumentally complex task only if he operated with some built-in biases, or **constraints** (e.g., Golinkoff, Mervis, & Hirsh-Pasek, 1994; Waxman & Kosowski, 1990; Woodward & Markman, 1998). For example, the child may have a built-in assumption that words refer to whole objects and not to their parts or attributes—this is referred to as the *whole object constraint* (Hollich, Golinkoff, & Hirsh-Pasek, 2007). The *mutual exclusivity constraint* leads children to assume that objects have only one name (Markman, Wasow, & Hansen, 2003).

Another built-in constraint is the **principle of contrast**, which is the assumption that every word has a different meaning. Thus, if a new word is used, it must refer to some different object or a different aspect of an object (Clark, 1990). For example, in a widely quoted early study, Carey and Bartlett (1978) interrupted a play session with 2- and 3-year-old children by pointing to two trays and saying, "Bring me the chromium tray, not the red one, the chromium one." These children already knew the word *red* but did not know the word *chromium*. Nonetheless, most of the children were able to follow the instruction by bringing the tray that was not red. Furthermore, a week later, about half of the children remembered that the word *chromium* referred to some color and that the color was "not red." Thus, they learned some meaning by contrast.

Early proponents of constraints argued that such biases are innate—built into the brain in some fashion. Another alternative is that the child learns the various constraints over time. For example, Carolyn Mervis and Jacquelyn Bertrand (1994) found that not all children between the ages of 16 and 20 months use the principle of contrast to learn the name of a new, unknown object. Children in their sample who did use this principle had larger vocabularies and were more likely to be good at sorting objects into categories. Results like these suggest that constraints may be a highly useful way for children to learn words quickly but that they may be a product of cognitive/linguistic development rather than the basis for it.

A more sweeping argument against the notion of built-in constraints comes from Katherine Nelson (1988), who points out that a child rarely

**constraint**   As used in discussions of language development, an assumption that is presumed to be built-in or learned early (a "default option") by which a child figures out what words refer to. Examples include the principle of contrast and the whole object constraint.

**principle of contrast**   The assumption that every word has a different meaning, which leads a child to assume that two or more different words refer to different objects.

*Suppose this little girl already knows the word flower. If her mother points to the flower and says "petal," is the girl likely to think that flower and petal mean the same thing? According to the principle of contrast, she will not be confused, because children approach word learning with the assumption that each word has a different meaning. Thus, she will assume that petal refers to some aspect of the flower whose name she doesn't yet know.*

encounters a situation in which an adult points vaguely and gives some word. Other theorists also emphasize that the situations in which children hear new words are rich with cues to help the children figure out what the words may refer to—including the parents' facial expressions, the emphasis in their words, and the entire context in which the new word is given (MacWhinney, 2011). To the extent that this is true, then, the child doesn't need a collection of constraints in order to figure out new words.

## Learning the Rules: The Development of Grammar and Pragmatics

After learning the first words, the next big step the child takes is to begin to string words into sentences. Children begin by combining single words, gestures, and vocal intonations. Next, they put two words together, then three, four, and more. The first two-word sentences are usually formed between the ages of 18 and 24 months.

### Holophrases and First Sentences

**Learning Objective 8.6**
How do children's first sentences differ from holophrases?

**holophrase**   A combination of a gesture and a single word that conveys more meaning than just the word alone; often seen and heard in children between 12 and 18 months old.

**telegraphic speech**   Term used by Roger Brown to describe the earliest sentences created by most children, which sound a bit like telegrams because they include key nouns and verbs but generally omit all other words and grammatical inflections.

Just as the first spoken words are preceded by apparently meaningful gestures, the first two-word sentences have gestural precursors as well. Toddlers often combine a single word with a gesture to create a "two-word meaning" before they actually use two words together in their speech. Bates suggests an example: A child may point to daddy's shoe and say "daddy," as if to convey "daddy's shoe." Or she may say "cookie!" while simultaneously reaching out her hand and opening and closing her fingers, as if to say "Give cookie!" (Bates et al., 1987). In both cases, the meaning conveyed by the use of a gesture and body language combined with a word is more than that of the word alone. Linguists call these word-and-gesture combinations **holophrases**; they are common between the ages of 12 and 18 months.

Once children actually begin speaking two-word sentences, they move rapidly through a series of steps or stages. The first sentences—which Roger Brown, a famous observer of child language, called *stage 1 grammar*—have several distinguishing features: They are short (generally two or three words), and they are simple. Nouns, verbs, and adjectives are usually included, but virtually all purely grammatical markers (which linguists call *inflections*) are missing. At the beginning, for example, children learning English do not normally add -*s* to the ends of nouns to make them plural, put the -*ed* ending on verbs to make the past tense, or use -'*s* for the possessive or auxiliary verbs such as *am* or *do*. For example, they might say "I tired" or "Me tired" rather than "I am tired," or "I not want it" rather than "I don't want it." Because only the really critical words are present in these early sentences, Brown (1973; Brown & Bellugi, 1964) described them as **telegraphic speech**. The child's language sounds rather like old-fashioned telegrams, in which people included all the essential words—usually nouns, verbs, and modifiers—but left out all the prepositions, auxiliary verbs, and the like because they had to pay for each word in a telegram.

Even at this earliest stage, children create sentences following rules—not adult rules, to be sure, but rules nonetheless. Children focus on certain types of words and put them together in particular orders. For example, young children frequently use a sentence made up of two nouns, such as "mommy sock" or "sweater chair" (Bloom, 1973). We might conclude from this that a two-noun form is a basic grammatical characteristic of early language, but such a conclusion misses the complexity. For instance, the child in Bloom's classic study who said "mommy sock" said it on two different occasions. The first time was when she picked up her mother's sock, and the second was when the mother put the child's own sock on the child's foot. In the

---

**Table 8.2**

**SOME MEANINGS CHILDREN EXPRESS IN THEIR EARLIEST SIMPLE SENTENCES**

| Meaning | Examples |
|---|---|
| Agent-action | Sarah eat; Daddy jump |
| Action-object | Eat cookie; read book |
| Possessor-possessed object | Mommy sock; Timmy lunch |
| Action-location | Come here; play outside |
| Object-location | Sweater chair; juice table |
| Attribute-object | Big book; red house |
| Nomination | That cookie; it dog |
| Recurrence | More juice; other book |

*Source:* Maratsos, 1983 Some current issues in the study of the acquisition of grammar. In J. H. Flavell & E. M. Markman (Eds.), *Handbook of child psychology* (pp. 707–786). New York: Wiley.

first case, "mommy sock" seemed to mean "mommy's sock," which is a possessive relationship. In the second instance, the child was conveying that "mommy is putting a sock on me," which is an agent-object relationship.

Table 8.2 lists some other meanings that children convey with their earliest sentences. Not all children express all these relationships or meanings in their early word combinations, and there does not seem to be a fixed order in which these meanings or constructions are acquired, but all children appear to express at least a few of these patterns in their earliest, simplest sentences (Maratsos, 1983).

## The Grammar Explosion

◄------------Learning Objective 8.7

What is the significance of the grammar explosion?

Just as a vocabulary explosion follows an early, slow beginning, so a *grammar explosion* follows several months of short, simple sentences. One sign of this change is that children's sentences get longer, as you can see in Figure 8.3, which shows the maximum sentence length reported by parents of toddlers of various ages, drawn from Fenson's study. Most 18- to 20-month-olds are still using one- and two-word sentences. By 24 months, children include four and five words in their longest sentences; by 30 months, their maximum sentence length has almost doubled again.

**VOCABULARY AND THE GRAMMAR EXPLOSION**   The grammar explosion is strongly linked to vocabulary development. That is, children whose grammar is more complex and advanced also have larger vocabularies. For example, Finnish researchers have found that the rate at which Finnish-speaking children acquire grammatical features of language such as verb inflections (e.g., in English adding –*ed* to signify the past tense) begins to increase rapidly when a child's speaking vocabulary reaches 50 words and levels off somewhat when they have vocabularies of about 250 words (Stolt, Haataja, Lapinleimu, H., & Lehtonen, 2009). Just what such a link may indicate about how children learn language is still a matter of debate. Is a large vocabulary necessary for grammar development? Alternatively, perhaps having begun to understand how to construct sentences, a child can also understand new words better and hence learn them more readily.

During the grammar explosion, children's speech ceases to be telegraphic, as they rather quickly add many of the inflections and function words. Within a few months, they use plurals, past tenses, auxiliary verbs such as *be* and *do*, prepositions, and the like. You can get a feeling for the sound of the change from Table 8.3 on page 200, which lists some of the findings of a classic case study of sentences spoken by a boy named Daniel, recorded by David Ingram (1981). The left-hand column lists some of Daniel's sentences at about 21 months of age, when he was still using the simplest forms; the right-hand column lists some of his sentences only 2½ months later (age 23 months), when he had shifted into a higher gear. As you can see, stage 2 grammar includes longer sentences and a few inflections, such as "doggies."

**ADDING INFLECTIONS**   Daniel obviously did not add all the inflections to his sentences at once. As you can see in Table 8.3, he uses only a few, such as -*s* for plural, although the beginning of a negative construction is apparent in "No book," and the beginning of a question form shows in "Where going?" even though he has not yet added the auxiliary verb to the question.

Within each language community, children seem to add inflections and more complex word orders in fairly predictable sequences. In a classic early study, Roger Brown (1973) found that the earliest inflection used by children learning English is most often -*ing* added onto a verb, as in "I playing" or "doggie running." Then come (in order) prepositions such as *on* and *in*; the plural -*s* on nouns; irregular past tenses such as *broke* or *ran*; possessives; articles (*a* and *the*); the -*s* on third-person verb forms, as in *he wants*; regular past tenses such as *played* and *wanted*; and the various forms of auxiliary verbs, as in *I am going*.

**QUESTIONS AND NEGATIVES**   There are also predictable sequences in the child's developing use of questions and negatives. In each case, the child seems to go through periods when he creates

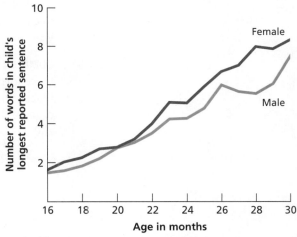

**FIGURE 8.3** Early Sentences
In their cross-sectional study, Fenson and his colleagues asked 1,130 parents of toddlers (aged 16 to 30 months) to describe the longest sentence used by their child.

(*Source:* From "Variability in Early Communicative Development" by Fenson, Dale, Reznick, Bates, Thal, and Pethick, *Monographs of the Society for Research in Child Development, 59*, No. 242 (1994), p. 82, Fig. 27.)

| Table 8.3 EXAMPLES OF DANIEL'S STAGE 1 AND STAGE 2 SENTENCES | |
| --- | --- |
| Stage 1 (Simple) Sentences, Age 21 Months | Stage 2 (More Complex) Sentences Age 23 Months |
| A bottle | A little boat |
| Here bottle | Doggies here |
| Hi Daddy | Give you the book |
| Horse doggie | It's a boy |
| Broke it | It's a robot |
| Kitty cat | Little box there |
| Poor Daddy | No book |
| That monkey | Oh cars |
| Want bottle | That flowers |
| | Where going? |

*Source:* Reprinted by permission of the publisher. D. Ingram, Early patterns of grammatical development, in R. E. Stark (Ed.), *Language behavior in infancy and early childhood,* tables 6 and 7, pp. 344–345. Copyright © 1981 by Elsevier Science Publishing Co., Inc.

types of sentences that he has not heard adults use but that are consistent with the particular set of rules he is using. For example, in the development of questions in English, there is a point at which the child puts a *wh* word (*who, what, when, where,* or *why*) at the beginning of a sentence but doesn't yet put the auxiliary verb in the right place, as in "Why it is resting now?" Similarly, in the development of negatives, there is a stage in which the child uses *not* or *-n't* or *no* but omits the auxiliary verb, as in "I not crying," "There no squirrels," or "This not fits" (Bloom, 1991). Then children rather quickly figure out the correct forms and stop making these mistakes.

**OVERREGULARIZATION**   Another intriguing phenomenon of this second phase of sentence construction is **overregularization**. What English-speaking 3- to 4-year-olds do is apply the basic rules to irregular words, thus making the language more regular than it really is (Maratsos, 2000). You can hear this phenomenon in children's creation of past tense forms such as "wented," "blowed," or "sitted," and plurals such as "teeths" or "blockses" (Fenson et al., 1994; Kuczaj, 1977, 1978). Stan Kuczaj has pointed out that young children initially learn a small number of irregular past tenses and use them correctly for a short time. Next, children rather suddenly seem to discover the rule of adding *-ed* and overgeneralize this rule to all verbs. Then, they relearn the exceptions one at a time. Even among preschoolers, this type of error is not hugely common, comprising only about 2–3% of all past tenses in English, according to one study (Marcus et al., 1992). These overregularizations nonetheless stand out because they are so distinctive and because they illustrate yet again that children create forms that they have not heard but that are logical within their current understanding of grammar.

**Learning Objective 8.8** -------------➤
What grammatical skills do children acquire in the preschool, elementary, and teen years?

# Later Grammar Learning

Even though most children are reasonably fluent in their first language (or languages) by age 3 or 4, there are still many refinements to be made. These refinements gradually appear in children's language over the course of the later preschool, elementary, and even early teen years.

**COMPLEX SENTENCES**   Soon after young children have figured out inflections and basic sentence forms such as negation and questions, they begin to create remarkably complex sentences, using conjunctions such as *and* and *but* to combine two ideas or using embedded clauses. Here are some examples, taken from the speech of 3- and 4-year-olds, from de Villiers and de Villiers (1992):

> I didn't catch it but Teddy did!
> I'm gonna sit on the one you're sitting on.
> Where did you say you put my doll?
> Those are punk rockers, aren't they?

Children add still more complex and difficult sentence forms to their repertoires throughout elementary school, and recurrent overregularization errors are eliminated (Bowerman, 1985). (However, children have trouble understanding and using passive forms, such as "The food is eaten by the cat" and do not use them much in spontaneous speech until they are 8 or 9.) But these are refinements. The really giant strides occur between ages 1 and about 4, as the child moves from single words to complex questions, negatives, and commands.

**FURTHER REFINEMENTS**   During middle childhood, children become skilled at managing the finer points of grammar (Prat-Sala, Shillcock, & Sorace, 2000; Ragnarsdottir, Simonsen,

**overregularization**   Young children's applications of basic rules to irregular words.

& Plunkett, 1999). For example, by the end of middle childhood, most children understand various ways of saying something about the past such as *I went, I was going, I have gone, I had gone, I had been going*, and so on. Moreover, they use such tenses correctly in their own speech. During the middle childhood years, children also learn how to maintain a topic of conversation, how to create unambiguous sentences, and how to speak politely or persuasively (Anglin, 1993).

**pragmatics** The rules for the use of language in communicative interaction, such as the rules for taking turns and the style of speech that is appropriate for different listeners.

## Pragmatics

◄------------Learning Objective 8.9
What are the milestones of pragmatics development?

Linguists are also interested in a third aspect of children's language—the way children learn to use speech, either to communicate with others (an aspect of language called **pragmatics**) or to regulate their own behavior. How early do children know what kind of language to use in specific situations? How early do they learn the "rules" of conversation—for example, that people conversing take turns?

Children seem to learn the pragmatics of language at a remarkably early age. For example, children as young as 18 months show adult patterns of gazing when they are talking with a parent: They look at the person who is talking, look away at the beginning of their own speaking turn, and then look at the listener again when they are signaling that they are about to stop talking (Rutter & Durkin, 1987).

Furthermore, a child as young as 2 years old adapts the form of his language to the situation he is in or the person he is talking to—a point made in Chapter 6 in the discussion of children's egocentrism. A child might say "Gimme" to another toddler as he grabs the other child's cup but say "More milk" to an adult. Likewise, whining is a special form of speech that toddlers use only when they are attempting to gain attention from an adult or persuade an adult to do something for them (Chan & Thompson, 2011).

Among older children, language is even more clearly adapted to the listener: 4-year-olds use simpler language when they talk to 2-year-olds than when they talk to adults (Tomasello & Mannle, 1985); first-graders explain things more fully to a stranger than to a friend (Sonnenschein, 1986) and are more polite to adults and strangers than to peers. Both of these trends are even clearer among fourth-graders. Thus, very early on—probably from the beginning—the child recognizes that language is meant to communicate, and he adapts the form of his language in order to achieve better communication.

Children also use language to help control or monitor their behavior. Such *private speech*, which may consist of fragmentary sentences, muttering, or instructions to the self, is detectable from the earliest use of words and sentences. For example, when 2- or 3-year-olds play by themselves, they give themselves instructions, stop themselves with words, or describe what they are doing: "No, not there," "I put that there," or "Put it" (Furrow, 1984).

Vygotsky hypothesized that the child uses private speech to communicate with herself for the explicit purpose of guiding her own behavior. He believed that such self-directing use of language is central to all cognitive development.

In young children, such self-directing speech is audible. In older children, it is audible only when the child is facing a challenging task; in other situations, it goes "underground." For example, you may recall from Chapter 6 that Flavell found that young elementary school children muttered to themselves while they were trying to remember lists; among 9- or 10-year-olds, this behavior is much less common (Bivens & Berk, 1990). Thinking of this set of findings in terms of the work on information processing described in Chapter 6 leads to the view that the child uses language audibly to remind himself of some new or complex processing strategy; as the child rehearses the strategy and learns it more flexibly, audible language is no longer needed. Such an interpretation is bolstered by the observation that even adults use audible language in problem solving when they are faced with especially difficult tasks.

*These children already know many of the social rules about how language is used, including rules about who is supposed to look at whom during a conversation.*

Even this brief foray into the research on children's use of language points out that a full understanding of language development requires knowledge of both cognitive development and children's social skills and understanding. From birth, the child is able to communicate feelings and thoughts through facial expressions, and somewhat later through gestures. But these are imperfect vehicles for communication; language is much more efficient. Such an argument reminds us once again that child development is not divided into tidy packages labeled "physical development," "social development," and "language development" but is instead a coherent, integrated process.

## Explaining Language Development

If merely describing language development is difficult, explaining it is still harder. Indeed, explaining how a child learns language has proved to be one of the most compelling challenges in developmental psychology.

**Learning Objective 8.10**- - - - - - - - - - ➤
How do environmental theories explain language development?

## Environmental Theories

The earliest theories of language were based either on learning theory or on the commonsense idea that children learn language by imitation. Imitation obviously has to play some part, because a child learns the language she hears. Still, imitation alone can't explain all language acquisition, because it cannot account for children's tendency to create words and expressions they have never heard, such as "footses" and "I goed."

*Behaviorist theories* such as Skinner's (1957) fare no better. Skinner argued that in addition to the role they play in imitation, parents shape language through systematic reinforcements, gradually rewarding better and better approximations of adult speech (the process of *shaping*). Yet when researchers have listened to parents talking to children, they find that parents don't seem to do anything like what Skinner proposed. Instead, parents are remarkably forgiving of all sorts of peculiar constructions and meaning (Brown & Hanlon, 1970; Hirsh-Pasek, Trieman, & Schneiderman, 1984); they reinforce children's sentences on the basis of whether the sentence is true rather than whether it is grammatically correct. Still, it seems obvious that what is said to a child has to play some role in the process of language formation.

**THE LINGUISTIC ENVIRONMENT**    Children who are exposed to less (and less varied) language in their earliest years don't seem to catch up later in vocabulary (MacWhinney, 2011). The data in Table 8.4 illustrate this point. These numbers come from the National Longitudinal Survey of Labor Market Experience of Youth (NLSY), a 12-year longitudinal study of a large sample of young women in the United States, begun when they were still teenagers. Table 8.4 shows one piece of information about the preschool-aged children of these young women: the percentage who had vocabulary scores below the 30th percentile on the most commonly used measure of vocabulary—the Peabody Picture Vocabulary Test (PPVT). Developmentalists know that the amount and quality of language a child hears varies with the family's income level: Poor mothers talk to their children less, use less complex sentences, and read to their children less. The data in Table 8.4 reveal that one consequence of poverty for children is a considerably higher risk of poor language skills.    ◉ Watch at **MyDevelopmentLab**

By age 30 months, the difference in vocabulary between poor and better-off children is already substantial, and the gap widens over the school years (Horton-Ikard & Ellis Weismer, 2007). Similarly, Catherine Snow (1997) has found that 4-year-old children reared in poverty use shorter and less complex sentences than do their better-off peers. Many factors no doubt contribute to these differences, but the richness and variety of the language a child hears are obviously highly significant (Pan, Rowe, Singer, & Snow, 2005). Researchers have found that attending a high-quality preschool program enhances low-income children's language development, perhaps because such programs expose children to richer and more varied language than they are receiving at home (Maier, Vitiello, & Greenfield, 2011). In addition, children

◉ **Watch** the **Video** *Stimulating Language Development* at **MyDevelopmentLab**

**Table 8.4**

| PERCENTAGE OF CHILDREN AGED 4 TO 7 WHO SCORE BELOW THE 30TH PERCENTILE ON THE PEABODY PICTURE VOCABULARY TEST, AS A FUNCTION OF POVERTY | | | |
|---|---|---|---|
| Type of Family | Number of Cases | Observed Percentage | Adjusted Percentage* |
| Recipients of Federal Aid to Families with Dependent Children, or AFDC ("welfare" families) | 196 | 60% | 52% |
| Poor but not receiving AFDC | 116 | 47% | 42% |
| Not poor | 659 | 27% | 30% |

*These percentages have been adjusted statistically to subtract out the effects of differences in parents' education, family structure, family size, and age, sex, and ethnicity of the child.

*Source:* From "The life circumstances and development of children in welfare families: A profile based on national survey data" by Zill, Moore, Smith, Stief, and Coiro, *Escape from poverty: What makes a difference for children,* P. L. Chase-Lansdale and J. Brooks-Gunn, eds., p. 45, Table 2.3. © 1995 by Cambridge University Press. By permission of Cambridge University Press.

who attend preschool are likely to be read to by teachers, another factor that fosters linguistic resilience among low-income children (Robb, Richert, & Wartella, 2009).

**INFANT-DIRECTED SPEECH (IDS)** Beyond the mere quantity of language directed at the child, the quality of the parents' language may also be important in helping the child learn language (Soderstrom, 2007). In particular, developmentalists know that adults talk to children in a special kind of very simple language, originally called *motherese* by many linguists and now more scientifically described as **infant-directed speech**. This simple language is spoken in a higher-pitched voice and at a slower pace than is speech to older children or other adults. The sentences are short and grammatically simple, with concrete vocabulary. When speaking to children, parents also repeat a lot, introducing minor variations ("Where is the ball? Can you see the ball? Where is the ball? There's the ball!"). They may also repeat the child's own sentences but in slightly longer, more grammatically correct forms—a pattern referred to as an *expansion* or a *recasting*. For example, if a child said "mommy sock," the mother might recast it as "Yes, this is mommy's sock," or if a child said "Doggie not eat," the parent might say "The doggie is not eating." ⊙⃟ **Watch** at **MyDevelopmentLab**

⊙⃟ **Watch** the **Video** *Child-Directed Speech* at **MyDevelopmentLab**

Developmentalists also know that babies as young as a few days old can discriminate between infant-directed speech and speech directed to other adults and that they prefer to listen to IDS, whether it is spoken by a female or a male voice (Cooper & Aslin, 1994; Pegg, Werker, & McLeod, 1992). This preference exists even when IDS is being spoken in a language other than the one normally spoken to the child. Janet Werker and her colleagues (1994), for example, have found that both English and Chinese infants prefer to listen to infant-directed speech, whether it is spoken in English or in Cantonese (one of the major languages of China). Moreover, other studies by Werker indicate that IDS helps infants identify sounds that are specific to the language that they are learning (e.g., the English *schwa*, the Spanish rolled *r*) by emphasizing those sounds more than others (Werker et al., 2007). Consequently, IDS may serve as an attention-getting device that helps infants acquire language.

The quality of infant-directed speech that seems to be critical to attracting infants' attention is its higher pitch. Once the child's attention is drawn by this special tone, the very simplicity and repetitiveness of the adult's speech may help the child to pick out repeating grammatical forms. Children's attention also seems to be drawn to recast sentences. For example, Farrar (1992) found that a 2-year-old was two or three times more likely to imitate a

**Infant-directed speech (IDS)** The simplified, higher-pitched speech that adults use with infants and young children.

correct grammatical form after he had heard his mother recast his own sentences than he was when the mother used that same correct grammatical form in her normal conversation. Experimental studies confirm this effect of recastings. Children who are deliberately exposed to higher rates of specific types of recast sentences seem to learn the modeled grammatical forms more quickly than do those who hear no recastings (Nelson, 1977).

Mothers' conversations with other adults also play a special role in language development. However, these conversations don't appear to interest an infant until she begins using language to communicate herself, usually between 18 and 24 months of age (Soderstrom & Morgan, 2007). Listening to them helps infants learn non-object words such as those that refer to colors and quantities (Tare, Shatz, & Gilbertson, 2007).

**Learning Objective 8.11**----------→
What kind of evidence supports the nativist theories?

👁—Watch the **Video** *Language Learning* at **MyDevelopmentLab**

## Nativist Theories

On the other side of the theoretical spectrum are the *nativist theories*, whose proponents argue that much of what the child needs for learning language is built into the organism (Matthews, 2006). Early nativist theorists such as Noam Chomsky (1965, 1975, 1986, 1988) were especially struck by two phenomena: the extreme complexity of the task the child must accomplish, and the apparent similarities in the steps and stages of children's early language development across languages and among all children. Newer cross-language comparisons make it clear that there is more variability than at first appeared, as will be described in the next section of this chapter. Nonetheless, nativist theories are alive and well and are becoming increasingly accepted. 👁—Watch at **MyDevelopmentLab**

One particularly influential nativist is Dan Slobin (1985a, 1985b), who assumes that every child is born with a basic language-making capacity, made up of a set of fundamental operating principles. Slobin argues that just as the newborn infant seems to come programmed with "rules to look by," infants and children are programmed with "rules to listen by." You've already encountered a good deal of evidence consistent with this proposal in earlier sections. Researchers have established that very young infants focus on individual sounds and syllables in the stream of sounds they hear, that they pay attention to sound rhythm, and that they prefer speech of a particular pattern (infant-directed speech). Slobin also proposes that babies are preprogrammed to pay attention to the beginnings and endings of strings of sounds and to stressed sounds—a hypothesis supported by research (e.g., Yu & Ballard, 2007). Together, these operating principles help to explain some of the features of children's early grammar. In English, for example, the stressed words in a sentence are normally the verb and the noun—precisely the words that English-speaking children use in their earliest sentences. In Turkish, on the other hand, prefixes and suffixes are stressed, and Turkish-speaking children learn both very early. Both of these patterns make sense if we assume that the preprogrammed rule is not "pay attention to verbness" or "nounness" or "prefixness" but "pay attention to stressed sounds."

**Learning Objective 8.12**----------→
How do constructivist theories differ from other approaches?

## Constructivist Theories

The fact that the nativist model is consistent with growing knowledge of apparently built-in perceptual skills and processing biases is certainly a strong argument in its favor. Even so, this is not the only compelling theoretical option. In particular, some theorists argue persuasively that what is important is not the built-in biases or operating principles but the child's construction of language as part of the broader process of cognitive development (Akhtar, 2004).

One prominent proponent of this view, Melissa Bowerman, puts the proposition this way: "When language starts to come in, it does not introduce new meanings to the child. Rather, it is used to express only those meanings the child has already formulated independently of language" (1985, p. 372). However, Bowerman (2007) also notes that as the child starts to use language to express the ideas he is beginning to grasp, the very act of creating linguistic frameworks for them helps him better understand them. Bowerman's perspective is supported by research showing that preschoolers use words that signify the present (e.g., now) at an earlier age than words that signify the past and future (e.g., yesterday, tomorrow) and that the

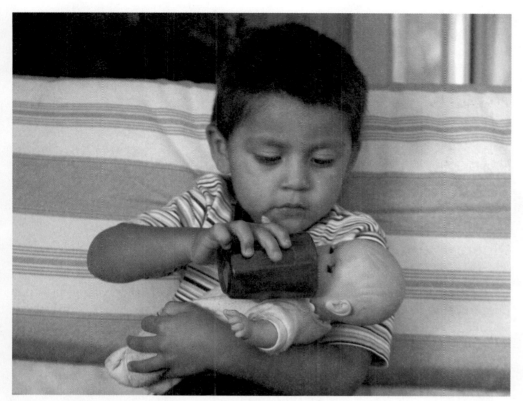

Constructivists point out that pretend play, a cognitive milestone, emerges at about the same time that two-word sentences show up in a child's speech, a phenomenon that supports their view that language development is a function of general cognitive development.

appearance of these words in their speech parallels changes in their understanding of time concepts (Grant & Suddendorf, 2011). Thus, from the constructivist perspective, cognitive and language development are interdependent processes, and research in the constructivist tradition looks for linkages between advances in the two domains. For example, symbolic play (such as pretending to drink from an empty cup) and imitation of sounds and gestures both appear at about the same time as the child's first words, suggesting some broad "symbolic understanding" that is reflected in a number of behaviors ⊙ Watch at MyDevelopmentLab

⊙ Watch the Video *Hand Gestures* at MyDevelopmentLab

We need not choose between Slobin's and Bowerman's approaches. Both may be true. The child may begin with built-in operating principles that aim her attention at crucial features of the language input. The child then processes that information according to her initial (perhaps built-in) strategies or schemes. Then she modifies those strategies or schemes as she receives new information, such as by arriving at some of the constraints about word meanings. The result is a series of rules for understanding and creating language. The strong similarities observed among children in their early language constructions come about both because all children share the same initial processing rules and because most children are exposed to very similar input from the people around them. But because the input is not identical, because languages differ, language development follows less and less similar pathways as the child progresses.

Finally, it seems clear that, as the nativists claim, some kind of capacity for processing linguistic information is "hard-wired" into the infant brain. However, many developmentalists have argued that this phenomenon is best understood when it is integrated into a constructivist view of language development. This integrated view proposes that the child begins with built-in operating principles that aim the child's attention at crucial features of the language input. The child then processes that information according to her initial (perhaps built-in) strategies or schemes. Then she modifies those strategies or rules as she receives new information—for example, arriving at some of the constraints on word meanings. The result is a series of rules for understanding and creating language. The strong similarities we see among children in their early language constructions come about both because all children share the same initial processing rules and because most children are exposed to very

**mean length of utterance (MLU)**   The average number of meaningful units in a sentence. Each basic word is one meaningful unit, as is each inflection.

similar input from the people around them. But because the input is not identical, because languages differ, language development follows less and less common pathways as the child progresses.

## Individual and Group Differences in Language Development

The description you've read of the sequence of language development is accurate on the average, but the speed with which children acquire language skill varies widely. There also seem to be important style differences.

**Learning Objective 8.13**
Are differences in the rate of language development related to later measures of proficiency?

## Differences in Rate

There is a great deal of individual variation in language development. Some children begin to use words at 8 months, while others do not do so until 18 months. Similarly, the normal range of variation in vocabulary size among 2-year-olds is from a low of 10 words to a high of several hundred (MacWhinney, 2011).

You can see the range of normal variation in sentence construction very clearly in Figure 8.4, which shows the average number of meaningful units per sentence [referred to by linguists as the **mean length of utterance (MLU)**] of 10 children, from longitudinal studies by Roger Brown (1973), Ira Blake (1994), and Lois Bloom (1991). The figure includes a line at the MLU level that normally accompanies a switch from simple, uninflected two-word sentences to more complex forms.

You can see that Eve was the earliest to make this transition, at about 20 months, while Adam and Sarah passed over this point nearly a year later. These variations are confirmed in Fenson's much larger cross-sectional study of more than 1,000 toddlers whose language was described by their parents. In this group, the earliest age at which parents reported more complex sentences than simple sentences was about 22 months, with an average of about 27 months. However, as many as a quarter of children had not reached this point by 30 months (Fenson et al., 1994).

**FIGURE 8.4** Classic Studies of Mean Length of Utterance
The 10 children whose language is charted here, studied by three different linguists, moved at markedly different times from simple one- and two-word sentences to more complex sentences.

(*Sources*: Reprinted and adapted by permission of the publisher from (1) *A First Language: The Early Stages*, by Roger Brown, p. 55, Cambridge, Mass.: Harvard University Press, Copyright © 1973 by the President and Fellows of Harvard College; (2) Lois Bloom, *Language Development from Two to Three*, Cambridge University Press, 1991, p. 92, Table 3.1; (3) I. K. Blake, "Language Development and Socialization in Young African-American Children," in Greenfield and Cocking (eds.), *Cross-Cultural Roots of Minority Children*, Lawrence Erlbaum Associates, 1994, p. 169, Table 9.1 and p. 171, Fig. 9.1.)

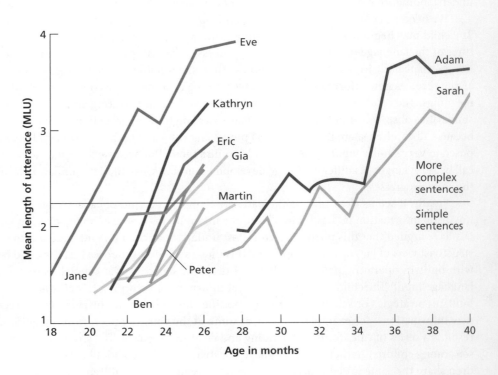

At present, MLU is frequently used by physicians, teachers, and others to identify children who need additional screening to determine whether they have some kind of language disability (Hewitt, Hammer, Yount, & Tomblin, 2005). The majority of children who are behind schedule during the early months of language development eventually catch up to their agemates without any special interventions. One study found that 97% of late-talking infants' language development was within the average range by age 6 (Ellis & Thal, 2008). *Speech-language therapy (SLT)* can help many of those who don't catch up on their own, especially when SLT is targeted to the specific elements (e.g., verb tenses) that are lacking in these children's expressive language (e.g., Leonard, Camarata, Pawtowska, Brown, & Camarata, 2008). The subset who do not catch up is primarily made up of children who also have poor receptive language (Ellis & Thal, 2008). Research suggests that some kind of problem with the fast-mapping process may be responsible for the leveling off in vocabulary growth that many of these children exhibit around the age of 3 (Alt, Plante, & Creusere, 2004). Such children appear to remain behind in language development and perhaps in cognitive development more generally. In practical terms, this means that parents of a child who is significantly delayed in understanding as well as speaking language should seek professional help to try to diagnose the problem and begin appropriate intervention.

How can these variations in speed of early language development be explained? The alternative possibilities should be familiar by now. One possibility is that the rate of language development may be something one inherits—in the same way that intelligence or the rate of physical development may be affected by heredity. Twin studies designed to test this possibility show that vocabulary size (but not grammatical complexity) is more similar in identical twins than in fraternal twins (Haworth et al., 2009; Mather & Black, 1984). However, adoption studies show that 2-year-olds' language skill can be predicted about equally well from the IQ scores or the language skills of either their biological or their adoptive parents (Plomin & DeFries, 1985). So it seems that parents who talk more, who read to their children more and elicit more language from them, and who respond appropriately to their children's language may have children who develop language more rapidly, regardless of genetic inheritance. Overall, as with IQ, it seems obvious that both the particular genes the child inherits and the environment in which the child grows up contribute to her rate of language development.

## Cross-Cultural Universals and Differences in Language Development

◄------------ Learning Objective 8.14
In what ways does language vary across cultural groups?

In the early years of research on children's language development, linguists and psychologists were strongly impressed by the apparent similarities across languages in children's early language. You've already seen some evidence that supports this impression in Table 8.1 on page 195, which illustrated large similarities in early vocabularies. Studies in a wide variety of language communities, including Turkish, Serbo-Croatian, Hungarian, Hebrew, Japanese, a New Guinean language called Kaluli, German, and Italian, have revealed important similarities in young children's language (Maitel, Dromi, Sagi, & Bornstein, 2000). For example, the prelinguistic phase seems to be identical in all language communities. All babies coo, then babble; all babies understand language before they can speak it; babies in all cultures begin to use their first words at about 12 months.

Moreover, a one-word phase seems always to precede a two-word phase in every language, with the latter appearing at about 18 months. Likewise, across all languages studied so far, prepositions describing locations are added in essentially the same order. Words for "in," "on," "under," and "beside" are learned first; then the child learns the words for "front" and "back" (Slobin, 1985b). Finally, children everywhere seem to pay more attention to the ends of words than to the beginnings, so they learn suffixes before they learn prefixes.

Interestingly, the universal tendency of children to attend to the ends of statements produces cross-cultural differences in language learning. Such differences happen because different languages use different kinds of words at the ends of sentences. In English, the last word in a statement is most likely to be a noun. However, in Mandarin (spoken in China) and Korean, the last word is often a verb. Consequently, while children who are learning English tend to use more nouns than verbs in their first attempts at speaking, children learning Mandarin and Korean produce just as many verbs as nouns (MacWhinney, 2011). Further, this linguistic difference is associated with cross-cultural variations in the way mothers speak to their babies. Those who speak languages that often use verbs at the ends of statements talk about verbs more to their babies. By contrast, mothers who speak English and other noun-focused languages more often explain nouns to infants.

Another interesting cross-linguistic difference is that the specific word order a child uses in early sentences is not the same for all children in all languages. In some languages, a noun/verb sequence is fairly common; in others, a verb/noun sequence may be heard. In addition, particular inflections are learned in highly varying orders from one language to another. Japanese children, for example, begin very early to use a special kind of marker, called a *pragmatic marker*, which tells something about the feeling or the context of what is being said. For instance, the word *yo* is used at the end of a sentence when the speaker is experiencing some resistance from the listener; the word *ne* is used when the speaker expects approval or agreement. Japanese children begin to use these markers very early, much earlier than children whose languages contain inflections.

Most strikingly, children learning certain languages do not appear to go through a stage of using simple two-word sentences with no inflections. Children learning Turkish, for example, use essentially the full set of noun and verb inflections by age 2 and never go through a stage of using uninflected words. Their language is simple, but it is rarely ungrammatical from the adult's point of view (Aksu-Koc & Slobin, 1985; Maratsos, 1998).

Finally, cross-cultural studies of language development provide us with several good examples of how such research informs our understanding of universals in human development. For example, researchers at one time thought that individual differences in the types of words babies use might be universal (e.g., Shore, 1995). This difference was termed a *style* of language acquisition. Early studies suggested that some toddlers exhibited a *referential* style that focused on labeling objects, while others showed an *expressive* style that concentrated more on social and emotional words. Further research, however, demonstrated that these differences, while somewhat useful for describing the development of English- and Spanish-speaking children, were not manifested in the development of children who were learning other languages (Camaioni & Longobardi, 1995; Galián, Carranza, Escudero, Ato, & Ato, 2006). As a result, researchers took a closer look at English-speaking toddlers, and they found that the apparent style difference disappears with age and has no impact on later language development (Hoff, 2009).

*Toddlers learning English use more nouns than verbs, while those learning Korean use about equal number of nouns and verbs.*

## Learning to Read and Write

Finally, throughout the industrialized world, and increasingly in developing nations, using language to read and write is just as critical to a child's development as using spoken language. Certainly, spoken language forms the foundation on which children build literacy skills. However, learning to read and write taps into children's cognitive and motor skills as well. ◉—Watch at **MyDevelopmentLab**

◉—Watch the **Video** *Literacy* at **MyDevelopmentLab**

## The Early Foundation: Phonological Awareness

◀----------- Learning Objective 8.15
What is the role of phonological awareness in learning to read?

One specific component of early childhood language development—*phonological awareness*—seems to be especially important to learning to read (Lundberg, 2009). **Phonological awareness** is a child's awareness of the rules governing sound patterns that are specific to his or her own language. It also includes the child's knowledge of that particular language's system for representing sounds with letters. Researchers measure English-speaking children's phonological awareness with questions like these: "What would *bat* be if you took away the [b]? What would *bat* be if you took away the [b] and put [r] there instead?"

Developmentalists now have abundant evidence that children who are more phonologically aware at age 3, 4, or 5 later learn to read much more easily and score higher on tests of reading comprehension in later childhood than children who are less phonologically aware (Kim, Petscher, Schatschneider, & Foorman, 2010). Furthermore, if you train preschoolers or kindergartners in phonological awareness, their reading skills in first grade improve—a result that has been found in studies in Scandinavia and Germany as well as the United States (Al Otaiba et al., 2008).

Of course, a child doesn't have to acquire phonological awareness in early childhood. Phonological skills can be learned in elementary school through formal instruction (Petrill et al., 2010). Electronic games that focus on letter-sound connections seem to be especially useful for helping school-aged children who lack phonological awareness catch up with their peers (Saine, Lerkanen, Ahonen, Tolvanen, & Lyytinen, 2010). ◉—Watch at **MyDevelopmentLab**

However, numerous studies have shown that the greater a child's phonological awareness *before* he enters school, the faster he learns to read (Christensen, 1997; Gilbertson & Bramlett, 1998; Schatschneider, Francis, Foorman, Fletcher, & Mehta, 1999; Wood & Terrell, 1998). In addition, phonological awareness in the early childhood years is related to rate of literacy learning for languages as varied as Korean, English, Punjabi, and Chinese (Cheung et al., 2010; Chiappe, Glaeser, & Ferko, 2007; McBride-Chang & Ho, 2000). Large gains in phonological awareness appear to take place between children's fourth and fifth birthdays, just before most children enter kindergarten (Justice et al., 2005).

Researchers have also found that many of the everyday activities preschoolers engage in foster the development of phonological awareness. For example, among English-speaking children, learning and reciting nursery rhymes contributes to phonological awareness (Bryant, MacLean, & Bradley, 1990; Bryant, MacLean, Bradley, & Crossland, 1990; Layton, Deeny, Tall, & Upton, 1996; MacLean, Bryant, & Bradley, 1987; Morris & Leavey, 2006). For Japanese children, a traditional game called *shiritori*, in which one person says a word and another comes up with a word that begins with its ending sound, helps children develop these skills (Kobayashi, Haynes, Macaruso, Hook, & Kato, 2005). Educators have also found that using such games to teach phonological awareness skills to preschoolers is just as effective as using more formal tools such as flash cards and worksheets (Brennan & Ireson, 1997).

Young children with good phonological awareness skills often use a strategy called **invented spelling** when they attempt to write (see Figure 8.5 on page 210). In spite of the

*Young children can learn phonological awareness skills either through formal means, as these preschoolers are doing, or informally through word games and rhymes.*

◉—Watch the **Video** *Chi Hae: Raising an Eleven Month Old, Parts 1 and 2* at **MyDevelopmentLab**

**phonological awareness** Understanding of the rules governing the sounds of a language as well as knowledge of the connection between sounds and the way they are represented in written language.

**invented spelling** A strategy young children with good phonological awareness skills use when they write.

**FIGURE 8.5** Invented Spelling
Translation: *A snake came to visit our class.* A 5-year-old used a strategy called "invented spelling" to write this sentence about a snake's visit (hopefully accompanied by an animal handler!) to her kindergarten class. Invented spelling requires a high level of phonological awareness. Research suggests that children who have well-developed phonological awareness skills by the time they reach kindergarten learn to read more quickly.

(*Source:* Author.)

ASNAK KAME tovisit AWReCLAS

many errors they make, children who use invented spelling before receiving formal instruction in reading and writing are more likely to become good spellers and readers later in childhood (Dixon & Kaminska, 2007). Thus, the evidence suggests that one of the best ways parents and preschool teachers can help young children prepare for formal instruction in reading is to engage them in activities that encourage word play and invented spelling.

**Learning Objective 8.16**
What strategies do educators use to help children learn how to read?

◉ Watch the Video *Dyslexia Detector* at **MyDevelopmentLab**

## Becoming Literate in School

Children who are learning to read a language that is based on the *alphabetic principle*, the principle that letters stand for sounds, benefit from specific instruction in sound-letter correspondences, a type of instruction called **systematic and explicit phonics** (Armbruster, Lehr, & Osborn, 2003). *Systematic* means that instruction must follow a plan, beginning with simple, one-letter/one-sound correspondences (e.g., the letter *b* for the sound /b/) and moving to those that involve two or more letters. The plan must be carefully developed so that instruction corresponds in meaningful ways to the spelling system of the language that is being learned. *Explicit* means that letter-sound correspondences are taught intentionally. ◉ Watch at **MyDevelopmentLab**

Effective phonics curricula also provide beginning readers with ample opportunities for daily practice in using their knowledge of sound-symbol correspondences so that they can develop automaticity. Phonics researchers argue that children cannot comprehend written language easily until they can decode it automatically and fluently (Rego, 2006). Their view is based on the finding that working memory is limited in capacity. Therefore, when decoding words is automatic, working memory capacity is freed up for the task of comprehending what has been read.

Advocates for the **whole language approach**, an approach to reading instruction that places more emphasis on the meaning of written language than on its structure, say that most children are capable of inferring letter-sound correspondences on their own as long as they have enough exposure to print (Strauss & Altwerger, 2007). The key, say these educators, is to motivate children to interact with written language in meaningful and enjoyable ways. Thus, they argue that reading curricula should include high-quality children's literature rather than phonics workbooks. Moreover, they recommend that teachers directly instruct children in phonics skills only when children ask questions about letters and sounds.

Research suggests that thinking that reading instruction must follow *either* the phonics *or* the whole language approach is a mistake. Instead, advocates of the **balanced approach** argue for comprehensive reading instruction that includes systematic and explicit phonics along with other instructional strategies derived from the whole language approach (Iaquinta, 2006). They argue that exposing children to good literature and helping them acquire a love of reading are important elements in any reading curriculum.

Once children have learned the basic reading process, learning about meaningful word parts, such as prefixes and suffixes, helps them become more efficient readers and to better understand what they read (Adams & Henry, 1997; Berninger, Abbott, Nagy, & Carlisle, 2010). Instruction in comprehension strategies, such as identifying the purpose of a particular text, also helps improve reading skill and understanding (Johnston, Barnes, & Desrochers, 2008). Of course, all along the way, children need to be exposed to good literature, both by reading on their own and by having teachers and parents read to them.

Some of the strategies used to teach reading also help children learn writing—the other component of literacy. For example, instruction in sound-symbol connections helps children learn to spell as well as to read (Rego, 2006). Of course, good writing is far more than just spelling; it requires instruction and practice, just as reading does. Specifically, children need explicit instruction in language mechanics—such as how to construct simple, compound, and complex sentences—to become good writers (Saddler, 2007). They also need to learn to

**systematic and explicit phonics** Planned, specific instruction in sound-letter correspondences.

**whole language approach** An approach to reading instruction that places more emphasis on the meaning of written language than on its structure.

**balanced approach** Reading instruction that combines explicit phonics instruction with other strategies for helping children acquire literacy.

organize writing tasks into phases such as planning, drafting, editing, and revising (Graham & Harris, 2007). Interestingly, too, handwriting skills help children not only become better writers but also contribute to the development of reading skills (see *Technology and the Developing Child*). 👁—Watch at **MyDevelopmentLab**

Despite educators' best efforts, many children fall behind their classmates in literacy during the early school years. In general, reading researchers have found that poor readers have problems with sound-letter combinations (Gersten et al., 2008). Thus, many children who have reading difficulties benefit from highly specific phonics approaches that provide a great deal of practice in translating letters into sounds and vice versa (Koppenhaver, Hendrix, & Williams, 2007; Ryder, Tunmer, & Greaney, 2008).

However, curriculum flexibility is also important in programs for poor readers. Some do not improve when phonics approaches are used. In fact, programs that combine sound-letter practice and comprehension training, have proven to be highly successful in helping poor readers catch up, especially when the programs are implemented in the early elementary years (Gersten et al., 2008). Consequently, teachers need to be able to assess the effectiveness of whatever approach they are using and change it to fit the needs of individual students.

## Learning a Second Language

Worldwide patterns of population growth and movement have led to tremendous increases in the number of children attending school in the United States, Canada, Great Britain, and Australia whose first language is not English. About two-thirds of these children speak English well enough to function in school, but the rest essentially do not speak English. Educators in English-speaking countries use the term **English-language learners (ELLs)** to refer to non–English-speaking children—either immigrant children or native-born children.

◀ - - - - - - - - - -Learning Objective 8.17
**English-language learners (ELLs)**
School children who do not speak English well enough to function in English-only classes.

👁—Watch the **Video** *Linda: Child Struggling with Reading, Part 1* at **MyDevelopmentLab**

**Learning Objective 8.17**
What instructional strategies do educators use to help English-language learners

---

# TECHNOLOGY AND THE DEVELOPING CHILD
## Handwriting and Brain Development

You might be surprised to learn that, in the age of keyboarding and thumb typing, handwriting instruction is still included in the literacy curriculum. While it is true that children as young as 8 or 9 years of age can learn to use a keyboard, research has shown that handwriting instruction activates the language learning areas of the brain in ways that keyboarding does not. In one study, researchers measured the impact of letter-learning lessons with and without handwriting instruction on brain activity in young children (James, 2010). The brains of children who were taught how to write the letters showed more adult-like patterns of activation when they were subsequently tested over the lessons. The researchers concluded that the physical involvement of the hands in letter instruction facilitates learning the letters.

Of course, keyboarding is a physical activity as well. So, why doesn't keyboarding enhance letter learning in the same way? Researchers hypothesize that writing by hand links a specific pattern of motor actions to

each letter that is stored in the brain as part of a network that includes other information about the letter (James & Gauthier, 2009). The act of writing the letter then activates this network and strengthens it. With keyboarding, the pattern of motor actions is nearly the same regardless of which letter is typed. As a result, learning to key in letters does not become part of the networks of meaning associated with them. Research showing strong correlations among handwriting, letter knowledge, and composition skills also supports the network hypothesis (Berninger et al., 1997; Graham, Weintraub, & Berninger, 2001).

Recent technological innovations have added a new dimension to handwriting practice. Software for touch-sensitive devices such as the iPad enables children to use these devices for handwriting practice. Moreover, touch pads have become important input devices in their own right. Some users find handwriting apps to be a quicker and more efficient way to input information into such devices than on-screen or peripheral keyboards. So, an

**Learning Objective 8.16a**
What does research say about the link between handwriting and literacy development?

"old-fashioned" skill like handwriting may turn out to be important to mastering the "new-fangled" technology of the touch pad.

### FIND OUT MORE
*Use your Internet search skills to answer these questions.*

1. Search for information on research by Dr. Steven Graham of Vanderbilt University and Dr. Virginia Berninger of the University of Washington on teaching composition skills to children.
2. Some innovative approaches to helping older adults with dementia and other types of brain dysfunction involve teaching them to write Chinese and Japanese characters. What is the rationale for these approaches?

**bilingual education** As practiced in the United States, a school program for students who are not proficient in English in which instruction in basic subject matter is given in the children's native language during the first 2 or 3 years of schooling, with a gradual transition to full English instruction over several years.

**structured immersion** An alternative to traditional bilingual education used in classrooms in which all children speak the same non-English native language. All basic instruction is in English, paced so that the children can comprehend, with the teacher translating only when absolutely necessary.

**English-as-a-second-language (ESL)** An alternative to bilingual education; children who are not proficient in English attend academic classes taught entirely in English but then spend several hours in a separate class to receive English-language instruction.

👁 Watch the **Video** *Bilingual Family* at **MyDevelopmentLab**

About 21% of school-aged children in the United States speak a language other than English at home; about 5% of school children speak no English whatsoever (National Center for Education Statistics [NCES], 2011). However, as you probably realize, these children are not equally distributed across the country. Some cities have relatively few, while others, as Table 8.5 shows, enroll a large number of such pupils. Furthermore, in many urban areas in North America, ELL children come from widely varying linguistic backgrounds. In Toronto, for example, school children speak more than 80 different languages (Toronto District School Board, 2001). In the U.S. cities of Los Angeles, New York, Chicago, and Washington, DC, more than 100 languages are spoken in the homes of children (NCES, 2008). Because the issues involved in educating ELL children are so diverse across nations and even across regions within nations, there is no one-size-fits-all instructional strategy for helping these children learn to speak, read, and write English.

In the United States, some ELL children, mostly those whose first language is Spanish, participate in a bilingual education program (Osorio-O'Dea, 2001). In **bilingual education**, instruction is presented in the children's native language during the first 2 or 3 years of schooling, and teachers make a gradual transition to instructing totally in English over the next few years. Such programs have been developed for Spanish-speaking children because they constitute by far the largest group of ELL students in U.S. schools (Planty et al., 2008). In other English-speaking countries, bilingual education is available to children from large non–English-speaking groups as well. For example, schools in Canada have provided both English- and French-speaking students in Quebec, a primarily French-speaking province, with bilingual education for decades. (See *Developmental Science in the Real World*.) 👁 Watch at **MyDevelopmentLab**

An alternative to bilingual education is **structured immersion**, used in classrooms in which all the children speak the same non-English native language and the teacher speaks both English and the children's native language. In such classrooms, the basic instruction is in English, paced so that the children can comprehend, with the teacher translating only when absolutely necessary. French language programs of this kind for English-speaking children have been very successful in Quebec (Allen, 2004; Holobow, Genesee, & Lambert, 1991). In these programs, students are taught exclusively in French for 2 years of elementary school. During the remaining elementary years, they receive bilingual instruction. Research shows that, in the early grades, these pupils are somewhat behind monolingual English-speakers in literacy skills. However, when these children reach high school age, they get higher scores on reading achievement tests than their monolingual peers.

However, it is often logistically impossible to provide bilingual education or structured immersion for most ELL children. For one thing, if a school system has only a handful of students who speak a particular language, it is not financially feasible to establish a separate curriculum for them. In addition, it may be impossible to find bilingual teachers for children whose language is spoken by very few people outside their country of origin. For these reasons, most ELL school children in the United States are enrolled in **English-as-a-second-language (ESL)** programs (NCES, 2011). In ESL programs, children attend academic classes that are conducted entirely in English and spend part of each day in English-language classes.

Research has shown that no particular approach to second-language learning is more successful than any other (Mohanty & Perregaux, 1997). There is some indication that programs that include a home-based component, such as those that encourage parents to learn the new language along with their children, may be

| Table 8.5 PERCENTAGE OF ELL SCHOOL-AGED CHILDREN IN THE FIFTEEN LARGEST CITIES IN THE UNITED STATES | |
|---|---|
| New York City, NY | 46% |
| Los Angeles, CA | 66% |
| Chicago, IL | 37% |
| Houston, TX | 50% |
| Philadelphia, PA | 21% |
| Phoenix, AZ | 45% |
| San Antonio, TX | 35% |
| San Diego, CA | 42% |
| Dallas. TX | 54% |
| San Jose, CA | 51% |
| Jacksonville, FL | 9% |
| Indianapolis, IN | 14% |
| San Francisco, CA | 49% |
| Austin, TX | 37% |
| Columbus, OH | 16% |

*Source:* Kids Count Data Center, 2010.

## One Language or Two?

Chan, a Chinese American, and Luisa, a Mexican American, are the proud parents of a 3-month-old girl. Chan is fluent in Mandarin and English, and Luisa is a Spanish-English bilingual. Their own experiences have convinced them that being bilingual is a great asset. They hope to provide their daughter with an even greater asset—that of being fluent in three languages. However, they are somewhat worried about the advisability of raising a child with more than one language in the home.

Knowing two or more languages clearly provides social and economic benefits to an adult (Bialystok, 2007). However, research suggests that there are cognitive advantages *and* disadvantages to growing up bilingual. On the positive side, children who are bilingual have a clear advantage in *metalinguistic ability*, the capacity to think about language (Bialystok, Shenfield, & Codd, 2000). In addition, most bilingual children display more advanced executive processing skills on language tasks than do monolingual children (Carlson & Meltzoff, 2008). These two advan-

tages enable bilingual children to more easily grasp the connection between sounds and symbols in the beginning stages of learning to read (van der Leij, Bekebrede, & Kotterink, 2010).

On the negative side, infants in bilingual homes reach some milestones later than those learning a single language. For example, bilingual infants' receptive and expressive vocabularies are as large as those of monolingual infants, but the words they know are divided between two languages (Patterson, 1998). In addition, children growing up in bilingual homes in which the two languages vary greatly in how they are written (e.g., English and Chinese) may acquire reading skills in both languages more slowly than peers in monolingual homes (Bialystok, Majumder, & Martin, 2003; Guglielmi, 2008).

However, research indicates that bilingual children who are equally fluent in both languages encounter few, if any, learning problems in school (Vuorenkoski, Kuure, Moilanen, & Peninkilampi, 2000). When the language in which they are less fluent is the language

in which their schooling is conducted, they are at risk for learning problems (Anderson, 1998; Thorn & Gathercole, 1999). Therefore, parents who choose bilingualism should probably take into account their ability to fully support children's acquisition of fluency in both languages.

### Learning Objective 8.17a
How does bilingualism influence language development?

### REFLECTION

1. What kind of linguistic environment would you provide for your child if you were in the same position as Chan and Luisa?
2. In your opinion, how likely is it that the little girl will achieve her parents' goal of fluency in three languages? What factors will influence her eventual level of fluency in each of the three languages?

---

especially effective (Koskinen et al., 2000). But it seems that any structured program, whether bilingual education or ESL, fosters higher achievement among non–English-speaking children than simply integrating them into English-only classes, an approach called **submersion**. Although most children in submersion programs eventually catch up to their English-speaking peers, many educators believe that instruction that supports children's home language and culture as well as their English-language skills enhances their overall development (Cushner, McClelland, & Safford, 2012).

With respect to overall achievement, ELL students' performance in school is very similar to that of English-speaking children (NCES, 2008). In fact, in U.S. schools, native-born English-speaking children are more likely to fail one or more grades than children whose home language is either Asian or European. Native-born Spanish-speaking children fail at about the same rate as English speakers. In fact, studies suggest that, with the help of special programs designed to ease their transition into a new language, ELL children can outperform their monolingual peers on standardized tests of reading achievement as early as second grade, even if they enter school with no knowledge whatever of English (Lesaux & Siegel, 2003). Thus, there is no evidence that a child who enters school with limited English skills has any greater risk of failure than a child whose first language is English.

One cautionary note is important, however: An ELL student does not have an increased risk of failure as long as the school provides some kind of transition to English-only instruction *and* school officials take care to administer all standardized tests in the language with which the child is most familiar (Cushner et al., 2012). The first is necessary to optimize the ELL

**submersion** An approach to education of non–English-speaking students in which they are assigned to a classroom where instruction is given in English and are given no supplemental language assistance; also known as the "sink or swim" approach.

*In many North American cities, a substantial proportion of school children come from homes in which a language other than English is spoken. With support, these children can become fluent in English and can excel in school.*

child's potential for achievement. The second ensures that non–English-speaking children are not misclassified as having mental retardation or learning disablities because of their limited English skills.

## THINK CRITICALLY

- Much of the research that you read about in this chapter was based on a very small number of case studies. Why do you think the researchers chose to use the case study method? What are the advantages and disadvantages of the case study method with regard to the study of language development?
- In what way are studies of animal communication useful in the study of human language development?

## CONDUCT YOUR OWN RESEARCH

As noted in this chapter, Vygotsky and Piaget differed about the function of private speech. You can observe children using private speech in a preschool, kindergarten, or first-grade classroom. (Remember to get permission from school officials and from the children's parents.) Focus on one child at a time, keeping a record of the child's self-directed statements. Determine the proportion of such statements that appear to be for the purpose of guiding behavior, as Vygotsky suggested. An example of such a statement might be a preschooler's utterance of "this goes here" while putting a puzzle together. After you have collected data on several children, decide whether you agree with Vygotsky.

## SUMMARY ✓●─Study and Review at MyDevelopmentLab

### Before the First Word: The Prelinguistic Phase

**8.1** What are the characteristics of cooing and babbling?
Cooing is the first type of communicative sound that a baby produces. It is made up of repetitive vowel sounds. Vocalizations that include strings of consonant and vowel sounds appear around 6 months of age and are called babbling. Babbling gradually changes until it reflects only those sounds that are included in the language that the baby is learning to speak.

**8.1a** How does gestural language develop in children who are deaf?
Infants who are deaf develop nonverbal language similarly to hearing infants. As they acquire sign language, they display a sort of sign babbling that is similar to the vocal babbling of hearing children. They also vocalize. Referential signs appear in their nonverbal communication about the same time that the hearing infants speak their first words. Research shows that nonverbal gestures clearly differ from symbolic signs in young children who are deaf and develop similarly to those of hearing children.

**8.2** What have researchers learned about infants' receptive language skills?
By 10 months of age, infants understand 30 or more words, though their speaking vocabulary is still extremely limited. By 13 months, an infant's receptive vocabulary increases to 100 words. Babies as young as 9 to 12 months understand simple instructions.

### Learning Words and Word Meanings

**8.3** What are the trends in word learning over the first 2 years?
The earliest words appear at about 1 year of age. The first words are simple and are typically used only for specific objects or situations. Vocabulary grows slowly at first and then usually spurts in a naming explosion. By 16 months of age, most children have a vocabulary of about 50 words. The earliest words are typically highly specific and context-bound in meaning; later, children typically overextend word usage.

**8.4** How does word learning proceed in early and middle childhood?
Children continue to learn new words throughout the preschool years and add approximately 10 words a day by the time they are ready to begin elementary school. Fast-mapping, the use of categories to learn new words, enables them to acquire new words rapidly.

**8.5** What are some proposed constraints on word learning?
Many (but not all) linguists have concluded that in determining word meanings, a child has built-in constraints or biases, such as the assumption that words refer to objects or actions but not both and the principle of contrast. Others linguists believe that such constraints exist but are acquired rather than built-in.

## Learning the Rules: The Development of Grammar and Pragmatics

**8.6** How do children's first sentences differ from holophrases?
Linguists use the term *holophrase* to refer to infants' use of single words, or single words combined with gestures, as sentences. As holophrases become less frequent around age 18 months, two-word sentences begin to appear in the child's speech. The young child can use these simple sentences to convey many different meanings, including location, possession, and agent-object relationships.

**8.7** What is the significance of the grammar explosion?
During the grammar explosion, the child quickly adds many grammatical inflections and learns to create questions and negative sentences.

**8.8** What grammatical skills do children acquire in the preschool, elementary, and teen years?
By age 3 or 4, most children can construct remarkably complex sentences. Later skills are primarily refinements of established skills, such as learning to understand and use passive sentences.

**8.9** What are the milestones of pragmatics development?
As early as age 2, children adapt their language to the needs of the listener and begin to follow culturally specific customs of language usage. Children also use language to regulate their own behavior.

## Explaining Language Development

**8.10** How do environmental theories explain language development?
Several theories have been offered to explain language development. Two early environmental explanations, one based on imitation and one on reinforcement, have been largely set aside. More recently, emphasis has been placed both on the helpful quality of the simpler form of adult-to-child language called *infant-directed speech*, and on the role of expansions and recastings of children's sentences.

**8.11** What kind of evidence supports the nativist theories?
Nativist theories assume that the child is born with a set of operating principles that focus him on relevant aspects of language input. Children's production of words that suggest the use of rules (e.g., "feets" rather than "feet"; "breaked" rather than "broke") rather than imitation of mature speech supports the nativist view.

**8.12** How do constructivist theories differ from other approaches?
Constructivist approaches differ from the learning and nativist perspectives in that they argue that language development is guided by the same processes that shape general cognitive development. Constructivist theorists hold that a child constructs language at the same time and in the same way as he constructs all cognitive understandings.

## Individual and Group Differences in Language Development

**8.13** Are differences in the rate of language development related to later measures of proficiency?
Children show differences in the rate of development of both vocabulary and grammar, differences explained by both heredity and environmental influences. Despite these variations in rate of early development, however, most children eventually learn to speak skillfully.

**8.14** In what ways does language vary across cultural groups?
The sequence of language development is remarkably consistent across all languages. There are a few exceptions, however. For example, children learning Turkish produce sentences during the two-word stage that differ with regard to the use of inflections from those of children learning other languages.

## Learning to Read and Write

**8.15** What is the role of phonological awareness in learning to read?
Development of an awareness of the sound patterns of a particular language during early childhood is important in learning to read and write. Children seem to acquire this skill through word play. Phonological awareness helps children establish connections between spoken and written language.

**8.16** What strategies do educators use to help children learn how to read?
In school, children need specific instruction in sound-letter correspondences, word parts, and comprehension strategies to become good readers. They also need to be exposed to good literature and to have lots of appropriate practice in using literacy skills.

**8.16a** What does research say about the link between handwriting and brain development?
Brain-imaging studies suggest that children who learn to write letters at the same time they are acquiring other information about them develop more adult-like patterns of brain activation than children who do not receive handwriting instruction. Researchers believe that the unique motor actions associated with writing each letter are stored along with meaningful information about the letter. Writing practice may activate the networks of meaning associated with letters and strengthens them. Touch pads may make handwriting instruction as important to computer use as keyboarding instruction is.

**8.17** What instructional strategies do educators use to help English-language learners?

Children with limited English perform as well as English-speaking peers when they receive specific kinds of support in school. In bilingual education classes, academic instruction takes place in children's first language and English is taught as a separate subject. In ESL programs, children receive academic instruction in English along with specific instruction in English. In structured immersion programs, a bilingual teacher provides most instruction in English and translates only when absolutely necessary. Research has not produced a clear answer as to which approach is most effective.

**8.17a** How does bilingualism influence language development?

Children who learn two or more languages in early childhood develop better metalinguistic skills than children who are monolingual. They also show better executive processing skills for language tasks. However, bilingual children may reach language development milestones later than monolingual children do. In some cases, reading skills develop more slowly in bilingual children.

## KEY TERMS

babbling (p. 193)
balanced approach (p. 210)
bilingual education (p. 212)
constraint (p. 197)
cooing (p. 192)
English-as-a-second-language (ESL) (p. 212)
English-language learners (ELLs) (p. 211)

expressive language (p. 193)
fast-mapping (p. 196)
holophrase (p. 198)
infant-directed speech (p. 203)
invented spelling (p. 209)
mean length of utterance (MLU) (p. 206)
overextension (p. 196)

overregularization (p. 200)
phonological awareness (p. 209)
phonology (p. 192)
pragmatics (p. 201)
prelinguistic phase (p. 192)
principle of contrast (p. 197)
receptive language (p. 193)
semantics (p. 192)
structured immersion (p. 212)

submersion (p. 213)
syntax (p. 192)
systematic and explicit phonics (p. 210)
telegraphic speech (p. 198)
underextension (p. 196)
whole language approach (p. 210)

# Personality Development: Alternative Views

Brady is a healthy 9-month-old whose parents delight in introducing him to all kinds of new experiences. Recently they brought home an electronic version of one of Brady's favorite television characters, *Sesame Street's* "Elmo," that sings and dances when he is switched on. When Brady's parents showed him the Elmo doll for the first time, the little boy laughed and began excitedly waving his arms and kicking his legs. After a few minutes, though,

Brady began to cry. His parents concluded that he had had enough of Elmo for a while and put the toy away.

What do you think Brady's behavior suggested, if anything, about his future personality? His motor responses to an electronic Elmo doll might lead you to believe that he would probably grow up to be an outgoing, adventurous child. So, you might be surprised to learn that research suggests just the opposite. As you'll soon learn, infants who react strongly to environmental stimuli tend to develop into shy preschoolers. By contrast, those who react to stimuli such as the Elmo doll with emotionally calm displays of intense interest are more likely to be outgoing. Such findings show that, at least to some degree, the patterns of behavior we display in our earliest months stay with us throughout our lives (Rothbart, 2011).

Thinking about the differences in how infants react to stimuli and how those differences are manifested later in life captures the essence of what psychologists mean when they use the term *personality*. Formally, this term is defined as the individual's enduring patterns of responses to and interactions with others and the environment. Practically, it pervades all of children's relationships, thereby exerting just as powerful an influence on developmental outcomes as their cognitive abilities. What causes such differences? When we look for answers to this question, we inevitably encounter the debate that pervades every discussion of human development: the nature-nurture controversy.

There is little doubt that heredity is an important factor. However, learning influences personality as well. Thus, parenting that relies solely on either the notion that personality is inborn or the idea that it is learned is likely to be ineffective. Instead, parents need to have a better idea of how and when inborn traits and learning, as well as a number of other factors, come into play. In this chapter, we will review how various theorists have approached the explanation of personality development. When you finish reading this chapter, you will have a better appreciation for the complexities of human personality. You will see that, like most developmental variables, it isn't simply a matter of *either* inborn traits *or* environmental influences.

## Defining Personality

Most developmentalists define **personality** as the individual's enduring patterns of responses to and interactions with others and the environment. Over the years, researchers and theorists have disagreed vehemently about how many *dimensions*, or clusters of characteristics, are needed to explain personality and how they should be measured. However, over the past two decades, a consensus has emerged on certain principles. The first is that infant temperament makes a sizeable contribution to later personality. The second principle is that five basic dimensions emerge as the core of an individual's personality during early and middle childhood and the ways in which these dimensions are manifested in an individual's life are fairly stable across adolescence and adulthood. ◉ Watch at **MyDevelopmentLab**

## Temperament

You read about temperament in Chapters 1 and 3, so the concept is not completely new. Most developmentalists who study temperament conceive of these qualities as the emotional substrate of personality, the set of core qualities or response patterns that are visible in infancy (see *Developmental Science in the Real World* on page 219). ◉ Watch at **MyDevelopmentLab**

**THREE VIEWS OF TEMPERAMENT** One of the most influential temperament category systems was proposed by Stella Chess (1914–2007) and Alexander Thomas (1913–2003). Chess and Thomas (1984) proposed three temperament types—*difficult*, *easy*, and *slow-to-warm-up*—that reflected profiles on nine different dimensions—a system described in Chapter 3. In contrast, Arnold Buss and Robert Plomin originally proposed only three key dimensions: activity level, emotionality (primarily negative emotionality), and sociability (Buss, 1989; Buss & Plomin, 1984, 1986).

◉ Watch the **Video** *Social and Personality Development* at **MyDevelopmentLab**

**Learning Objective 9.1**
What are the dimensions of temperament that most psychologists agree on?

◉ Watch the **Video** *Positive Psychology* at **MyDevelopmentLab**

**personality** The collection of relatively enduring patterns of reacting to and interacting with others and the environment that distinguishes each child or adult.

## Temperamental Surgency in the Toddler Classroom

Benita works in a child-care center and is assigned to the toddler room. She has noticed that one of the tykes, an 18-month-old boy named Thomas, seems to dominate the others. The little boy is bright, cheerful, and physically active, and he makes friends easily. However, when Benita plays naming games with the toddlers, Thomas blurts out an answer whenever Benita asks "What's this?" before his peers have a chance to answer. Benita wonders whether she should make a special effort to reduce Thomas's domineering behavior.

Developmental scientists often employ Chess and Thomas's (1984) goodness-of-fit model—the notion that the appropriateness of the environment for a given child's temperament is more important than the temperament itself—to explain interactions between infants' temperaments and their capacity to adjust to different settings. For instance, some temperamental profiles predispose infants to adjust easily to the structure of a child-care center, whereas others increase the chances that they will develop behavior problems (De Schipper et al.,

2004). In general, infants who are classified as easy according to Chess and Thomas's system more readily adjust to child-care centers than do infants in the difficult category. Such research suggests that what Benita may be seeing in Thomas's behavior is a conflict between his temperament and the demands of the environment in which he is being cared for.

Thomas possesses an above-average level of a dimension of temperament that researchers call *surgency*—a cluster of traits that includes sociability, high activity level, generally positive emotional states, and impulsiveness (Rothbart & Putnam, 2002). Some studies suggest that surgency is observable in infants as young as 3 months of age. Moreover, surgency is a highly stable facet of temperament that persists throughout childhood and into adulthood (Degnan et al., 2011). Surgent children's impulsiveness predisposes them to develop behavior problems in structured settings such as child-care centers. Despite their generally positive emotional state, surgent children can become frustrated when they are prevented from behaving

impulsively. In some cases, this frustration leads them to behave aggressively toward their peers. Thus, Benita's challenge is to find a way to encourage Thomas to allow the other children to respond to her questions without causing him to become so frustrated that he expresses his impulsiveness in less positive ways.

### REFLECTION

1. How might Benita use the principles of operant conditioning that you learned about in Chapter 1 to reduce Thomas's behavior of blurting out answers?
2. If you were Thomas's parent, how would you respond if Benita expressed her concerns about his impulsive behavior to you?

> **Learning Objective 9.1a**
> How is temperamental surgency manifested in the preschool classroom?

The questionnaire they devised to measure these three qualities has been widely used by researchers studying infants, children, and adults. Yet another key figure has been Jerome Kagan, who has focused on only a single dimension, which he calls *behavioral inhibition*—an aspect of what most people mean by "shyness" (Kagan, Reznick, & Snidman, 1990; Kagan, Snidman, & Arcus, 1993). None of these conceptualizations has been universally accepted.

**AN EMERGING CONSENSUS**  In recent years, researchers have come to favor the dimension approach proposed by Buss, Plomin, and Kagan rather than Chess and Thomas's categorical approach (Walters, 2011) Nevertheless, temperament researchers are still struggling to determine just what the key dimensions of temperament are (Thompson, Winer, & Goodvin, 2011). However, over the past two decades, a consensus has emerged, one that is reflected in the writings of the leading researchers in the field (Caspi & Shiner, 2006; Kagan & Herschkowitz, 2005; Rothbart, 2007). Many theorists are now emphasizing the following five key dimensions of temperament:

- *Activity level.*  A tendency to move often and vigorously, rather than to remain passive or immobile.
- *Approach/positive emotionality.*  A tendency to move toward rather than away from new people, situations, or objects, usually accompanied by positive emotion. This dimension is similar to what Buss and Plomin call *sociability*.
- *Inhibition and anxiety.*  The flip side of approach is a tendency to respond with fear or to withdraw from new people, situations, or objects.
- *Negative emotionality/irritability/anger.*  A tendency to respond with anger, fussiness, loudness, or irritability; a low threshold of frustration. This dimension appears to be what Thomas and Chess are tapping with their concept of the "difficult" child and what Buss and Plomin call *emotionality*.
- *Effortful control/task persistence.*  An ability to stay focused, to manage attention and effort.

*Kagan's research suggests that Chinese infants are less irritable in temperament than infants in Western cultures.*

**TEMPERAMENT ACROSS CULTURES** Despite knowing something about temperament, researchers are still left with several huge questions to answer. One such question concerns the universality of these dimensions of temperament. Early research by Daniel Freedman (1979) suggested that Chinese and Native American infants were less active than Caucasian American or Japanese babies. Kagan and his colleagues (1994) replicated part of these results in their comparison of Chinese, Irish, and Caucasian American 4-month-olds. They found that the Chinese infants were significantly less active, less irritable, and less vocal than were babies in the other two groups. The Caucasian American infants showed the strongest reactions to new sights, sounds, or smells. Similarly, Chisholm (1989) has replicated Freedman's research on Native American babies, finding them to be significantly less irritable, less excitable, and more able to quiet themselves than Caucasian American babies.

Since such differences are evident in newborns, they cannot be the result of systematic shaping by the parents. But the parents bring their temperaments as well as their cultural training to interactions with their newborns, which may tend to strengthen or perpetuate the babies' temperamental differences. For instance, Freedman and other researchers have observed that both Japanese and Chinese mothers talk to their infants much less than Caucasian mothers do. These differences in mothers' behavior were present from the mothers' first encounters with their infants after delivery, so the pattern is not a response to the babies' quieter behavior. Nonetheless, a correspondence between a mother's culturally defined behaviors and a baby's temperamental pattern is likely to strengthen the pattern in the child, which would tend to make the cultural differences larger over time (Chen, Wang, & De Souza, 2006). In addition, cultural values that emphasize some temperamental characteristics may shape parents' responses to infants, thereby increasing cross-cultural differences in temperament over time (Gartstein, Slobodskaya, Putna, & Knisht, 2009).

The distinction between temperament and personality is a little like the difference between a genotype and a phenotype. The genotype sets the basic pattern, but the eventual outcome depends on the way the basic pattern is affected by specific experience, one component of which is the cultural contexts in which children grow up. What is measured as personality later in childhood or adulthood reflects how the basic pattern has been affected by myriad life experiences (Karreman et al., 2010). If this interactive model is correct, then variations in temperament ought to bear some (perhaps even considerable) resemblance to personality in adulthood, although the matchup will probably not be perfect.

**Big Five** The five primary dimensions of adult personality identified by researchers: extraversion, agreeableness, conscientiousness, neuroticism, and openness/intellect.

**extraversion** One of the Big Five personality traits; a person who scores high on this trait is characterized by assertiveness, energy, enthusiasm, and outgoingness.

**agreeableness** One of the Big Five personality traits; a person who scores high on this trait is characterized by trust, generosity, kindness, and sympathy.

**openness/intellect** One of the Big Five personality traits; a person who scores high on this trait is characterized by curiosity, imagination, insight, originality, and wide interests.

**conscientiousness** One of the Big Five personality traits; a person who scores high on this trait is characterized by efficiency, organization, planfulness, and reliability.

**Learning Objective 9.2** ------------>
How do advocates for the Big Five approach define personality?

**neuroticism** One of the Big Five personality traits; a person who scores high on this trait is characterized by anxiety, self-pity, tenseness, and emotional instability.

## The Big Five

Researchers now agree that personality in childhood and later in life can be adequately described as a set of variations across five dimensions—the so-called **Big Five** personality traits (see Table 9.1). If you compare these five traits to the dimensions of infant temperament that you read about earlier, you will notice similarities. **Extraversion**, along with its opposite *introversion*, for instance, is quite similar to the temperamental dimensions of approach/positive emotionality and inhibition. **Agreeableness** and **openness/intellect** also draw on approach/positive emotionality as well as effortful control. **Conscientiousness** has much in common with effortful control, and **neuroticism** resembles negative emotionality.

## Table 9.1

## THE BIG FIVE PERSONALITY TRAITS

| Trait | Basic Feature(s) | Qualities of Individuals High in the Trait |
|---|---|---|
| Extraversion | The extent to which a person actively engages the world versus avoiding social experiences | Active, assertive, enthusiastic, outgoing, talkative |
| Agreeableness | The extent to which a person's interpersonal interactions are characterized by warmth and compassion versus antagonism | Affectionate, forgiving, generous, kind, sympathetic, trusting |
| Openness/Intellect | Reflects the depth, complexity, and quality of a person's mental and experiential life | Artistic, curious, imaginative, insightful, original, having wide interests |
| Conscientiousness | The extent and strength of a person's impulse control | Efficient, organized, planful, reliable, responsive, thorough, able to delay gratification in the service of more distant goals |
| Neuroticism; also called emotional (in)stability | The extent to which a person experiences the world as distressing or threatening | Anxious, self-pitying, tense, touchy, unstable, worrying |

Sources: Caspi, 1998, p. 316; John et al., 1994, Table 1, p. 161; McCrae and Costa, 1994.

The usefulness of the Big Five for describing personality has been demonstrated in studies of adults in a variety of countries, including some non-Western cultures, which lends some cross-cultural validity to this list. At the very least, researchers know that this set of dimensions is not unique to American adults (Lucas & Donnellan, 2011; Lüdtke, Trautwein, & Köller, 2004; McCrae & Terracciano, 2005).

There is also good evidence that the Big Five are stable traits: Among adults, personality test scores on these five dimensions have been shown to be stable over periods as long as a decade or more (Costa & McCrae, 2009). In addition, the usefulness of the Big Five as a description of personality has been validated by a variety of studies linking scores on these dimensions to behavior in a wide variety of real-life situations (Caspi et al., 2005; Furnham, Petrides, Tsaousis, Pappas, & Garrod, 2005). For example, the Big Five predict what

The temperamental characteristic of effortful control, which these preschoolers seem to have, is linked to the Big Five trait of conscientiousness.

kinds of information both teens and adults reveal about themselves on social networking sites (Golbeck, Robles, & Turner, 2011; see *Technology and the Developing Child*). These traits predict variations in emotion as well. For instance, workers who get high scores on measures of extraversion tend to have higher levels of job satisfaction and feel subjectively happier while at work when they are employed in positions that involve a great deal of interaction with others such as sales (Saksvik & Hetland, 2011). Thus, the Big Five appear to be useful descriptions of personality.

A growing body of research suggests that the Big Five provide a useful description of personality structure in late childhood and adolescence as well as adulthood (e.g., Deal, Halverson, Martin, Victor, & Baker, 2007; Soto, John, Gosling, & Potter, 2011). For example, Cornelis van Lieshout and Gerbert Haselager (1994), in a large early study of children and adolescents in the Netherlands, found that the five clearest dimensions on which they could characterize their young participants matched the Big Five very well, and this was true for both boys and girls and for preschoolers as well as adolescents. In this sample, agreeableness and emotional (in)stability (the equivalent of the neuroticism dimension) were the most evident dimensions of personality, followed by conscientiousness, extraversion, and openness.

Similar results have come from longitudinal studies in the United States, in which researchers have found that measures of the Big Five in childhood predict academic achievement and a variety of social and mental health variables in adolescence (Hendriks et al., 2011; Vrshek-Schallhorn et al., 2011; Witt, Massman, & Jackson, 2011). In one particularly influential and now-classic study, Oliver John and his colleagues (1994) studied a random sample of nearly 500 boys initially selected from among all fourth-graders in the Pittsburgh public school system and followed until age 13. Like the Dutch researchers, John found strong evidence that the five-factor model captured the personality variations among these preteen boys.

John's study was also helpful as a test of the validity of the five-factor model because he gathered information on other aspects of the boys' behavior. For example, Figure 9.1 contrasts the personality profiles of boys who reported delinquent activity versus boys who reported none. As John predicted, delinquent boys were markedly lower than nondelinquent boys in

---

# TECHNOLOGY AND THE DEVELOPING CHILD

## Facebook and the Big Five

A majority of teens these days spend an hour a day or more on social networking sites such as Facebook (Rideout, Foehr, & Roberts, 2010). To find out what Facebook users' pages reveal about their personalities, researchers set up a Facebook application that allowed them to administer a Big Five personality test while gathering information from respondents' own Facebook pages at the same time (Golbeck, Robles, & Turner, 2011). The researchers then correlated the personality test results with features of respondents' pages. They found that teens and adults who were high in extraversion had more friends than those who were lower in this trait, but their friends tended not to know each other. By contrast, respondents who were more introverted had fewer friends, but their friend networks had many associations. In addition, respondents who scored higher on conscientiousness used fewer swear words than those

who scored lower. Likewise, respondents with high scores on the neuroticism dimension tended to use more emotionally negative words, while those who scored high in agreeableness tended to use more emotionally positive words. Finally, respondents who scored high in openness posted longer comments on books and other reading materials than those who scored lower.

These findings suggest that employers who scan job applicants' Facebook pages to assess their personalities and determine how well they will fit in with the organization's standards of employee behavior may be on the right track (Niller, 2011). Similarly, 82% of college admissions offices screen applicants' Facebook pages and compare potential students' online self-presentations to those that are implied in their applications (Kaplan Test Prep Survey, 2011). Thus, teens who are looking for their first job or applying to selective

### Learning Objective 9.2a
What do teens' Facebook pages reveal about their personalities?

colleges should probably think carefully about what they reveal about themselves online.

### FIND OUT MORE

*Use your Internet search skills to answer these questions.*

1. Based on the correlations described here, what does your own Facebook page suggest about your personality? What about your friends' pages?
2. How might you use the research discussed here as a guide to what to post (and what not to post) on your Facebook page when you are looking for your first post-college-graduation job?

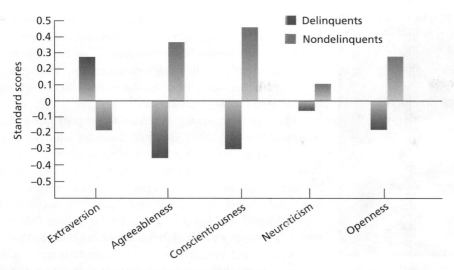

**FIGURE 9.1** John's Study of the Big Five and Delinquency
Twelve-year-olds who report more delinquent acts have personality profiles quite different from those of nondelinquent 12-year-olds—a set of results that helps to validate the usefulness of the Big Five personality traits as a description of children's personality.

(*Source:* O. P. John et al., from "The 'little five': Exploring the nomological network of the five factor model of personality in adolescent boys," *Child Development*, 65, 160–178.)

both agreeableness and conscientiousness. John also found that boys higher in conscientiousness did slightly better in school, just as would be expected. Subsequent studies supported John's findings. However, some of these studies also found a positive correlation between neuroticism and delinquency (e.g., Retz et al., 2004). Likewise, research examining relationships among the Big Five and delinquency in adolescent girls shows that neuroticism predicts criminal behavior among them as well (ter Laak et al., 2003). In addition, the link between a low level of conscientiousness and delinquency holds for girls.

These results are impressive and point to the usefulness of the five-factor model, but it is still too soon to tell whether the Big Five will turn out to be the optimal way of describing children's personality. In particular, researchers may need more than five dimensions to describe children. For example, both John and his colleagues in their U.S. study and van Lieshout and Haselager in their Dutch study found two additional dimensions that describe children's personality: irritability and activity level. With regard to activity level, longitudinal studies have provided support for the hypothesis that this particular dimension of temperament persists through childhood and gradually becomes subsumed by the extraversion dimension of the Big Five during the adolescent years (Eaton, 1994; Soto et al., 2008). Such studies point to the need for long-term studies in which links between early temperament and later personality can be more clearly identified.

## Genetic and Biological Explanations of Personality

Many researchers maintain that the evidence that heredity plays a strong role in the determination of personality is powerful and must be taken into account in any theoretical explanation of individual differences (Plomin, 2001, 2004). The genetic approach includes a number of persuasive propositions. However, there are many critics of this perspective. ⊙ Watch at **MyDevelopmentLab**

⊙ Watch the **Video** *Twins Separated at Birth: Reunited* at **MyDevelopmentLab**

### The Biological Argument

◄-----------**Learning Objective 9.3**
What is the focus of the biological approach to personality?

Broadly expressed, the argument that the origins of personality are biological is based on four major propositions.

*Proposition 1: Each individual is born with genetically determined characteristic patterns of responding to the environment and to other people.* Virtually every researcher who studies

This 1-year-old may just be having a bad day. But if this is typical behavior, one sign of a "difficult" temperament, she will be at higher risk for a variety of problems at later ages.

👁 Watch the Video *Happy Brains* at **MyDevelopmentLab**

👁 Watch the Video *How to Be Happy* at **MyDevelopmentLab**

temperament shares the assumption that temperamental qualities are inborn, carried in the genes. This idea is not so very different from the notion of "inborn biases," or "constraints," you have read about in earlier chapters, except that in this case the focus is on individual rather than shared behavioral dispositions. 👁 Watch at **MyDevelopmentLab**

There is clear, strong evidence to support this assertion (Gagne & Saudino, 2010; Ganiban, Saudino, Ulbricht, Neiderhiser, & Reiss, 2008), both in studies of adult personality and in studies of childhood temperament. Studies of twins in many countries show that identical twins are much more alike in their temperament or personality than are fraternal twins (Rose, 1995). Hill Goldsmith and his colleagues (1997) combined the results from many studies in which twins have been rated by their parents on Buss and Plomin's three temperament categories. Their research shows that the correlations on each dimension are a great deal higher for pairs of identical twins than for pairs of fraternal twins, indicating a strong genetic effect. Further support for the genetic hypothesis comes from researchers who have found that non-twin siblings are far more similar in personality than many parents believe them to be. Developmentalist Kimberly Saudino (Saudino, Wertz, Gagne, & Chawla, 2004) compared parents' ratings of siblings' activity levels to computerized assessments of videotapes of the children's behavior. She found that the parental ratings differed significantly across siblings but the computerized assessments did not. She found a similar pattern when she compared parents' ratings of siblings' shyness to those of objective observers. Such findings mean that parents tend to exaggerate temperamental differences among their children. Thus, studies that rely on parental ratings may fail to capture similarities across siblings that may have a genetic basis. 👁 Watch at **MyDevelopmentLab**

*Proposition 2: Genetic differences operate via variations in fundamental physiological processes.* Many (but not all) temperament theorists take Proposition 1 a step further and trace the basic differences in behavior to variations in underlying physiological patterns, particularly to variations in the reactivity of underlying neural systems (Gunnar et al., 2003; Plomin, 2004).

As an example, Kagan has suggested that differences in behavioral inhibition are based on differing thresholds for arousal in those parts of the brain—the amygdala and the hypothalamus—that control responses to uncertainty (Schwartz, Wright, Shin, Kagan, & Rauch, 2003). Arousal of these parts of the brain leads to increases in muscle tension and heart rate. Shy or inhibited children are thought to have a low threshold for such a reaction. That is, they more readily become tense and alert in the presence of uncertainty, perhaps even interpreting a wider range of situations as uncertain. What we inherit, according to this view, is not "shyness" or some equivalent behavioral pattern but a tendency for the brain to react in particular ways.

In support of this argument, Kagan reports correlations in the range of .60 between a measure of behavioral inhibition in children aged 2 to 5 and a series of physiological measures, such as muscle tension, heart rate, dilation of the pupil of the eye, and chemical composition of both urine and saliva, which strongly suggest that temperament is based on physiological responses and is not simply a set of learned habits (1994; Kagan et al., 1990). Moreover, Kagan and his associates have found that behavioral measures of inhibition taken in infancy are correlated with measures of brain reactivity to stimuli at ages 10 to 12; the correlation held for adults as well (Schwartz et al., 2003; Woodward et al., 2001). Other researchers have demonstrated that temperamental differences are associated with different levels of activity in the left and right hemispheres of the brain (Fox, Henderson, Rubin, Calkins, & Schmidt, 2001; McManis, Kagan, Snidman, & Woodward, 2002).

Remarkably, too, differences in infant temperament at four months of age seem to predict differences in brain structure in early adulthood. The cerebral cortices of young adults who showed early signs of shyness as infants are thicker on the right than on the left side of the brain while the opposite pattern has been found among adults who displayed early signs of outgoingness as infants (Schwartz et al., 2010). The implications of these results for adult behavior are not clear, but they suggest that the neurological foundations of infant temperament may be part of an underlying pattern of lifespan development.

*Proposition 3: Temperamental dispositions persist through childhood and into adulthood.* No theorist in the biological camp proposes that initial temperamental dispositions remain unchanged by experience. Still, if temperamental patterns create a bias toward particular behaviors, temperament ought to exhibit at least some stability over time. Such stability ought to show itself in the form of at least modest correlations between measures of a given temperamental dimension at different ages.

Although the research evidence is somewhat mixed, there is growing evidence of consistency in temperamental ratings over rather long periods of infancy and childhood (Degnan et al., 2011; Kagan & Fox, 2006; Rothbart, Ahadi, Hersey & Fisher, 2001). In one study, researchers found that temperamental ratings in the first few months of life were strongly related to ratings at age 5 (Degnan et al., 2011). In another study involving 450 Australian children, researchers found that mothers' reports of children's irritability, cooperation/manageability, inflexibility, rhythmicity, persistency, and tendency to approach (rather than to avoid) contact were all quite consistent from infancy through age 8 (Pedlow, Sanson, Prior, & Oberklaid, 1993). Similarly, in a longitudinal study of American children from age 1 to age 12, Diana Guerin and Allen Gottfried (1994a, 1994b) found strong consistency in parents' reports of their children's overall "difficultness" as well as approach versus withdrawal, positive versus negative mood, and activity level. In fact, research suggests that temperament differences are stable from the preschool years into adulthood (Caspi, 1998, 2000; Caspi & Shiner, 2006; Rothbart, 2011).

Kagan has also found considerable consistency over the childhood years in his measure of inhibition, which is based on direct observation of the child's behavior rather than on the mother's or father's ratings of the child's temperament. He reports that half of the babies in his longitudinal study who had shown high levels of crying and motor activity in response to a novel situation when they were 4 months old were still classified as highly inhibited at age 8, while three-fourths of those rated as uninhibited at 4 months remained in that category 8 years later (Kagan et al., 1993). Furthermore, the inhibited toddlers in Kagan's sample were less likely than their more uninhibited peers to be rated as highly aggressive or delinquent at age 11 (Schwartz, Snidman, & Kagan, 1996).

Thus, babies who readily and positively approach the world around them continue to be more positive as young teenagers; cranky, temperamentally difficult babies continue to show many of the same temperamental qualities 10 years later; and strongly behaviorally inhibited babies are quite likely to continue to show such "shyness" at later ages. Such consistency is probably stronger among children whose temperamental patterns are initially fairly extreme, such as highly inhibited youngsters or those with particularly clear patterns of negative emotionality (e.g., Rubin, Hastings, Stewart, Henderson, & Chen, 1997), but even among children with less extreme patterns, researchers find some degree of consistency.

*Proposition 4: Temperamental characteristics interact with the child's environment in ways that may either strengthen or modify the basic temperamental pattern.* Despite all the clear evidence for genetic/biological influences on temperament, genetics is clearly not destiny; there is still a good deal of room for environmental influences. For example, the extent to which parents direct the behavior of their children and express warmth toward them seems to be a significant factor in shaping the children's tendency toward positive affect and approach rather than withdrawal (Degnan, Henderson, Fox, & Rubin, 2008; Rubin & Coplan, 2004). In most cases, the resultant personality develops through some interaction between the child's temperamental tendencies and the environment the child encounters or creates. One factor that tends to strengthen a child's built-in qualities is the fact that we all—including young children—choose our experiences (Ganiban et al., 2011). Highly sociable children seek out contact with others; children low on the activity dimension are more likely to choose sedentary activities like working puzzles or playing board games rather than baseball. Similarly, temperament may affect the way a child interprets a given experience—a factor that helps to account for the fact that two children in the same family may experience the family pattern of interaction quite differently.

This child, clinging to her mom's leg, might be rated as relatively high in "behavioral inhibition." Her mother also may be reinforcing her by expressing approval of the clinging or shy behavior.

Imagine, for example, a family that moves often, such as a military family. If one child in this family has a strong built-in pattern of behavioral inhibition, the myriad changes and new experiences will likely trigger repeated fear responses. This child comes to anticipate each new move with dread and is likely to interpret his family life as highly stressful. A second child in the same family, with a more strongly approach-oriented temperament, finds the many moves stimulating and energizing and is likely to think of his childhood in a much more positive light.

A third environmental factor that often reinforces built-in temperamental patterns is the tendency of parents (and others in the child's world) to respond differently to children with different temperaments. The sociable child, who may smile often, is likely to elicit more smiles and more positive interactions with adults, simply because she has reinforced their behavior by her positive temperament. Buss and Plomin (1984) have proposed the general argument that children in the middle range on temperament dimensions typically adapt to their environment, while those whose temperament is extreme—for example, extremely difficult children—force their environment to adapt to them. Parents of difficult children, for example, adapt to the children's negativity by punishing them more, although often less consistently, than do parents of more adaptable children (Coplan, Reichel, & Rowan, 2009; Lengua & Kovacs, 2005). This pattern may well contribute to the higher rates of significant emotional problems in such children.

Buss and Plomin's proposal, while it may be accurate, doesn't convey the additional complexities of the process. First, sensitive and responsive parents can moderate the more extreme forms of infant or child temperament; a particularly nice example comes from the work of Megan Gunnar (1994) and her colleagues, who studied a group of highly inhibited toddlers who differed in the security of their attachment to their mothers. As you will learn in Chapter 11, *securely attached* infants use their caregivers as a "safe base" for exploring the world and are easily consoled after a separation from them. *Insecurely attached* infants do not consistently use the caregivers as a safe base and may even avoid them after a period of separation. In a classic series of studies, Gunnar found that insecurely attached inhibited toddlers showed the usual physiological responses to challenging or novel situations. Securely attached temperamentally inhibited toddlers, on the other hand, showed no such indications of physiological arousal in the face of novelty or challenge. Thus, secure attachment appears to have modified a basic physiological/temperamental response. Another example, also involving inhibited/fearful children, comes from the work of Kenneth Rubin and his colleagues (1997), who found that highly inhibited children with oversolicitous mothers showed more persistent inhibition across situations than did those whose mothers were more relaxed and less intrusive or intense. ⊙▸ Simulate at MyDevelopmentLab

Thus, while many forces within the environment tend to reinforce a child's basic temperament and thus create stability and consistency of temperament/personality over time, environmental forces can also push a child toward new patterns or aid a child in controlling extreme forms of basic physiological reactions.

⊙▸ Simulate the Experiment *Attachment Classifications in the Strange Situation* at **MyDevelopmentLab**

**Learning Objective 9.4** - - - - - - - - - - - ➤
What are some important criticisms of the biological approach?

## Critique of Biological Theories

The biological approach to the origins of personality has two great strengths. First, it is strongly supported by a large body of empirical research. There is simply no refuting the fact that built-in genetic and physiological patterns underlie what we think of as temperament or personality. This approach thus provides a powerful counterweight to the longtime dominance of psychoanalytic and learning theories of personality development, both of which strongly emphasized environmental influences.

Paradoxically, the second strength of this approach is that it is not purely biological; it is an interactionist approach, very much in keeping with much of the current theorizing about development. The child is born with certain behavioral tendencies, but his eventual personality depends on the transactions between his initial characteristics and the responses of his environment.

On the other side of the ledger, though, there appear to be a number of problems, not the least of which is the continuing lack of agreement on the basic dimensions of temperament. Researchers have used such varying definitions and measures that it is often difficult to compare the results of different investigations.

A second problem has been that many biologically oriented temperament theories have not been fundamentally developmental theories. They allow for change through the mechanism of interaction with the environment, but they do not address the question of whether there are systematic age differences in children's responses to new situations or to people; they do not focus on whether the child's emerging cognitive skills have anything to do with changes in the child's temperamental patterns. They do not, in a word, address how the shared developmental patterns may interact with inborn individual differences.

## Learning Explanations of Personality

Instead of focusing on what the child brings to the equation, learning theorists have looked at the reinforcement patterns in the environment as the primary cause of differences in children's personality patterns. Of course, theorists in this tradition do not reject biology. Albert Bandura, arguably the most influential theorist in this group, agrees that biological factors (such as hormones) or inherited propensities (such as temperament, presumably) also affect behavior. But he and others of this persuasion look to the environment as the major source of influence.

## The Learning Argument

◄ - - - - - - - - - - - Learning Objective 9.5
What are the basic propositions of learning explanations of personality?

The learning camp includes several distinct schools of thought. Some investigators, often called *radical behaviorists*, argue that only the basic principles of classical and operant conditioning are needed to account for variations in behavior, including personality. Others, among them Bandura, emphasize not only observational learning but also important cognitive elements. However, like the biological explanations, all of the learning approaches are organized around a set of basic propositions. Both groups of learning theorists agree with the first two propositions listed below; the remaining propositions emerge primarily from Bandura's work.

*Proposition 1: Behavior is strengthened by reinforcement.* If this rule applies to all behavior, then it should apply to attachment patterns, shyness, sharing behavior, and competitiveness. Children who are reinforced for clinging to their parents, for example, should show more clinging than children who are not reinforced for it. Similarly, a nursery school teacher who pays attention to children only when they get rowdy or aggressive should find that the children in her care get steadily more rowdy and aggressive over time.

*Proposition 2: Behavior that is reinforced on a partial schedule should be even stronger and more resistant to extinction than behavior that is consistently reinforced.* You read about partial reinforcement in Chapter 1, so you have some idea of what is involved. Most parents are inconsistent in their reinforcement of their children, so most children are on partial schedules of some kind, whether the parents intend that or not. That is, they are sometimes reinforced for a particular behavior, but not every time. Because behavior that is rewarded in this way is highly persistent—highly resistant to extinction, in the language of learning theory—partial reinforcement is a major factor in the establishment of those distinctive and stable patterns of behavior defined as personality. ✳ Explore at MyDevelopmentLab

✳ Explore the Concept *Process of Extinction and Spontaneous Recovery* at MyDevelopmentLab

An immense collection of studies supports these first two propositions. For example, in several studies, experimenters systematically rewarded some children for hitting an inflated rubber clown on the nose. When the researchers later watched the children in free play with peers, they found that the children who had been rewarded showed more hitting, scratching, and kicking than did children who hadn't been rewarded for punching the clown (Walters & Brown, 1963). Partial reinforcement in the form of inconsistent behavior from parents also

By observing and working next to his dad, this 3-year-old is not only learning how to cut fire wood; he is also learning his father's attitude about work and perhaps the beginnings of self-efficacy.

has the expected effect. For example, one study (Sears, Maccoby, & Levin, 1977) found that parents who permit fairly high levels of aggression in their children, but who occasionally react by punishing them quite severely, have children who are more aggressive than do parents who neither permit nor punish aggression.

*Proposition 3: Children learn new behaviors largely through modeling.* Bandura has argued that the full range of social behaviors, from competitiveness to nurturance, is learned not just by direct reinforcement but also by watching others behave in those ways. Thus, the child who sees her parents taking a casserole next door to the woman who has just been widowed will learn generosity and thoughtful behavior. The child who sees her parents hitting each other when they are angry will most likely learn violent ways of solving problems.

Children learn from television, too, and from their peers, their teachers, and their brothers and sisters. A boy growing up in an environment where he observes playmates and older boys hanging around street corners, shoplifting, or selling drugs is going to learn those behaviors. His continuous exposure to such antisocial models makes it that much harder for his parents to reinforce more constructive behavior. These many effects of observational learning have been demonstrated experimentally in literally hundreds of studies (Bandura, 1973, 1977, 2008).

However, learning from modeling is not an entirely automatic process. Bandura points out that what a child (or adult) learns from watching someone else will depend on four things: what she pays attention to and what she is able to remember (both cognitive processes), what she is physically able to copy, and what she is motivated to imitate. Because attentional abilities, memory, and other cognitive processes change with age through infancy and childhood, what a baby or child can or will learn from any given modeled event also changes through development (Grusec, 1992).

*Proposition 4: From reinforcement and modeling, children learn not only overt behavior but also ideas, expectations, internal standards, and self-concepts.* The child learns standards for his own behavior and expectancies about what he can and cannot do—which Bandura (1997) calls **self-efficacy**—from specific reinforcements and from modeling. In this way, the child internalizes what he has learned. Once those standards and those expectancies or beliefs are established, they affect the child's behavior in consistent and enduring ways and form the core of what can be called personality (Bandura, Caprara, Barbaranelli, Gerbino, & Pastorelli, 2003).

Learning Objective 9.6 - - - - - - - - - - - - →
What are some criticisms of the learning perspective?

## Critique of Learning Models

Several implications of the learning approach to personality are worth emphasizing. First of all, learning theories can explain either consistency or inconsistency in children's behavior. The behavior of a child who is friendly and smiling both at home and at school, for example, could be explained by saying that the child is being reinforced for that behavior in both settings rather than by assuming that the child has strong "approach tendencies" or a "gregarious temperament." Similarly, if the child is helpful at school but defiant at home, learning theorists invoke the principle that different reinforcement contingencies are at work in the two settings. To be sure, because individuals tend to choose settings that support or reward their accustomed behavior and because a person's behavior tends to elicit similar responses (reinforcements) from others in many settings, there is a bias toward consistency. But learning theorists have less trouble accounting for normal "situational variability" in behavior than do other theorists.

A related implication is that learning theorists are supremely optimistic about the possibility of change. Children's behavior can change if the reinforcement system (or their beliefs about themselves) changes, so problem behavior can be modified. In contrast, biologically oriented temperament theorists, while agreeing that environmental variations can alter or

**self-efficacy** Bandura's term for an individual's belief in his or her ability to accomplish tasks.

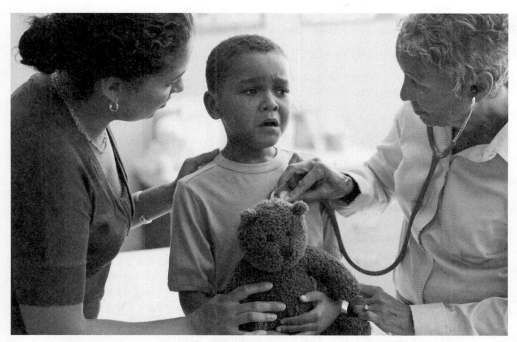

Bandura's principle of reciprocal determinism suggests that the effects of anxiety-provoking experiences on a child's personality, such as being examined by a doctor, are influenced by the environment's responses to his behavior as well as his own temperament and level of cognitive development.

shift the child's built-in temperamental tendencies, are more pessimistic about the likelihood of change, particularly for children whose temperamental pattern is extreme. Extremely inhibited children, for example, tend to remain that way even in supportive environments; extremely irritable, angry, inattentive children ("difficult" children in Chess and Thomas's conceptualization) are highly likely to become aggressive, difficult schoolchildren with a higher-than-normal likelihood of developing antisocial or delinquent patterns later, unless they learn extremely good strategies for self-control (e.g., Eisenberg et al., 2005; Moffitt & Harrington, 1996).

The great strength of the learning view of personality and social behavior is that it gives an accurate picture of the way in which many specific behaviors are learned. It is perfectly clear that children *do* learn through modeling; it is equally clear that children (and adults) will continue to perform behaviors that "pay off" for them.

The cognitive elements in Bandura's theory add further strength, offering a beginning integration of learning models and cognitive-developmental approaches (Mischel, 2007). Bandura's concept of **reciprocal determinism**, shown in Figure 9.2, attempts to explain how the different sets of factors emphasized in these theories interact to influence personality. Each of the three components of Bandura's model influences—and is influenced by—the other two. Moreover, the personal factors include cognitive elements, such as the child's stage of cognitive development, that earlier learning theories ignored (see *Thinking about Research* on page 230).

If we were to apply Piaget's language to Bandura's theory, we might define self-efficacy as a "self-scheme"—a concept of one's own capacities, qualities, standards, and experiences. New experiences are then assimilated to that scheme. You will recall from Chapter 6 that one of the characteristics of the process of assimilation as Piaget proposed it is that new information or experiences are modified as they are taken in. Similarly, Bandura is saying that once the child's self-concept is established, it affects what behaviors he chooses to perform, how he reacts to new experiences, whether he persists or gives up on some new task, and the like. If a child believes he is unpopular, for example, then he will not be surprised if others do not choose to sit by him in the lunchroom; if someone does sit next to him, he's likely to explain it in such a way that he retains his central belief, such as by saying to himself, "There must have been no place else to sit." In this way, the underlying scheme isn't modified (accommodated) very much.

**reciprocal determinism** Bandura's model in which personal, behavioral, and environmental factors interact to influence personality development.

**FIGURE 9.2** Bandura's Reciprocal Determinism
Bandura suggests that three components—the external environment, individual behaviors, and cognitive factors such as beliefs, expectancies, and personal dispositions (i.e., personality traits)—are all influenced by each other and play reciprocal roles in shaping personality.

## Locus of Control and Adolescent Health

You may have noticed that the same outcome can have quite different effects on two individual children. For instance, one child responds to getting a bad grade in school by studying harder, while another concludes that studying is of no use because school is just too hard. In Bandura's model of reciprocal determinism, an outcome produces different expectations in individuals because it is interpreted differently by them. Varying interpretations result from many factors. A trait called *locus of control,* a set of beliefs about the causes of events, is one of the most influential of these factors (Rotter, 1990).

Locus of control develops across the middle childhood and early teen years and is well established by mid-adolescence. An individual with an *external locus of control* attributes the causes of experiences (for example, school failure) to factors outside herself. A high school student with an external locus of control might claim that she failed a class because it was too difficult, an explanation that implies that she believes she has no control over what happens to her. A person with an *internal locus of control* views variables inside a person as responsible for outcomes. A high school student with an internal locus of control would say that he failed a class because he didn't study enough, a judgment that suggests that he believes he has control over academic outcomes.

An external locus of control predisposes a teenager to procrastinate, to avoid confronting problems, and to develop a self-defeating form of perfectionism (i.e., unwillingness to pursue a goal unless success is guaranteed) (Janssen & Carton, 1999; Periasamy & Ashby, 2002). Not surprisingly, research shows that adolescents with an external locus of control are less successful in school than their peers with an internal locus of control (Pennington, 2000). Perhaps more striking, though, are the associations that have been found between locus of control and health outcomes such as interest in quitting among teens who smoke cigarettes (Radtke, Scholz, Keller, Knauper, & Hornung, 2011). Another such finding is that teens with an external locus of control are less likely than those with an internal locus to follow medical advice regarding the prevention of sexually transmitted diseases (Gwandure & Mayekiso, 2010).

### Learning Objective 9.6a
What is locus of control, and how does it affect teens' development?

These findings suggest that having an external locus of control increases teenagers' vulnerability to a variety of health threats. Moreover, researchers have found that an external locus of control is quite resistant to change. Thus, they are searching for more effective strategies for identifying and intervening with teens who exhibit an external locus of control (Young & Bradley, 1998).

#### CRITICAL ANALYSIS

1. What kind of research would be required to test the effectiveness of an intervention program aimed at changing teenagers' locus of control?
2. How would a social cognitive theorist, such as Bandura, explain the process through which individuals develop locus of control beliefs?

---

Just as biological temperament theorists argue that inborn temperament serves as a central mediating force, shaping the child's choices and behavior, so in social learning theory self-efficacy (or self-scheme) acts as a central mediator, leading to stable differences in behavior of the kind we typically call personality. Self-efficacy can be modified (accommodated) if the child accumulates enough experience or evidence that doesn't fit with the existing scheme (that is, in learning theory language, if the reinforcement contingencies change in some dramatic way). If an "unpopular" child noticed that classmates regularly chose to sit next to him at lunch even when there were other seats available, he might eventually change his self-scheme, coming to think of himself as "somewhat popular." However, since the child (like an adult) will choose activities or situations that fit his sense of self-efficacy, such as sitting in the corner where no one is likely to see him, he will be partially protected from such nonconfirming experiences.

The learning theories, particularly the more radical versions, also have significant weaknesses. First, from the perspective of many psychologists, these theories still place too much emphasis on what happens to the child and not enough on what the child is doing with the information she has (Thomas, 2000). Bandura's theory is much less vulnerable to this charge, but most learning theories of personality are highly mechanistic and focused on external events. Second, like biological temperament theories, learning theories are not really developmental. They can say how a child might acquire a particular behavior pattern or belief, but they do not take into account the underlying developmental changes that are occurring. Do 3-year-olds and 10-year-olds develop a sense of self-efficacy in the same way? Do they learn the same amount or in the same way from modeling? Given Bandura's emphasis on the cognitive aspects of the modeling process, a genuinely developmental social learning theory could emerge in the coming years. Still, despite these limitations, all the theories in this group offer useful descriptions of one source of influence on the child's developing pattern of behavior.

# Psychoanalytic Explanations of Personality

Like many temperament theorists and those social learning theorists like Bandura, psycho-analytic theorists believe that the interaction between the child's inborn characteristics and the environment plays a central role in shaping differences in personality. However, unlike most temperament or learning approaches, psychoanalytic theories are clearly developmental as well, describing systematic changes in children's sense of self, in their needs or drives, and in their relationships with others.

## The Psychoanalytic Argument

◄ - - - - - - - - - - - -Learning Objective 9.7
What are the major points of the psychoanalytic approach to personality?

You read about psychoanalytic theories in Chapter 1, so the major propositions of this approach should be familiar.

*Proposition 1: Behavior is governed by unconscious as well as conscious motives and processes.* Freud emphasized three sets of instinctual drives: the sexual drive (libido); life-preserving drives, including avoidance of hunger and pain; and aggressive drives. Erikson emphasizes a more cognitive process, the drive for identity.

*Proposition 2: Personality structure develops over time, as a result of the interaction between the child's inborn drives and needs and the responses of the key people in the child's world.* Because the child is often prevented from achieving instant gratification of his various drives, he is forced to develop new skills—planning, talking, delaying, and other cognitive techniques that allow gratification of the basic needs in more indirect ways. Thus, the ego is created, and it remains the planning, organizing, thinking part of the personality. The superego, in turn, develops because parents and other adults try to restrain certain kinds of gratification; the child eventually incorporates these adult standards into his own personality.

*Proposition 3: Development of personality is fundamentally stagelike, with each stage centered on a particular task or a particular basic need.* You'll read about both Freud's and Erikson's stages in some detail below. The key point is simply that there are stages in these theories.

*Proposition 4: The specific personality a child develops depends on the degree of success the child has in moving through the various stages.* In each stage, the child requires a particular kind of supportive environment in order to successfully resolve that particular dilemma or meet that need. A child lacking the needed environment will have a very different personality from one whose environment is partially or wholly adequate. However, while each stage is important, all the psychoanalytic theorists strongly emphasize the crucial significance of the very earliest stages and focus especially on the adequacy of the relationship between the baby and the central caregiver, usually the mother. This is not quite like saying that infancy is a sensitive period for personality development; rather, Freud and later psychoanalytic theorists argue that the earliest relationship establishes a pattern and sets the child on a particular pathway through the remainder of the stages.

All four of these general propositions are contained in both Freud's and Erikson's theories, but both the details and the emphases differ in important respects. In Freud's theory, for example, cognitive skills develop only because the child needs them to obtain gratification; they have no independent life. In Erikson's theory (and in many other variations of psycho-analytic theory), cognitive skills are part of a set of ego functions that are presumed to develop independently, rather than arising entirely in the service of basic gratification.

Basic physical maturation is also more central to Freud's theory than to Erikson's. In Freud's theory, the stages shift from one to the next in part because of maturation of the nervous system. In each stage, the child is attempting to gratify basic physical ("sexual") needs through stimulation of a particular part of the body—that part of the body that is most sensitive at that time. As neurological development proceeds, maximum body sensitivity shifts from the mouth to the anus to the genitals, and this maturational change is part of what drives the stage changes. Erikson acknowledges such physical changes but places greater emphasis on shifts in the demands of the social environment. For Erikson, each stage centers on a specific social conflict, resulting in a psychosocial crisis. For example, stage 4 ("industry versus inferiority") begins at about age 6, because that is when the child goes off to school;

in a culture in which schooling is delayed, the timing of the developmental task might be delayed as well.

Because of such theoretical differences, Erikson and Freud have described the stages of development differently. Because both sets of stages have become part of the vocabulary of developmental psychology, you need to be conversant with both.

## Freud's Psychosexual Stages

Learning Objective 9.8 How does Freud's theory explain personality development?

Freud proposed five **psychosexual stages**, which are summarized in Table 9.2.

**THE ORAL STAGE: BIRTH TO 1 YEAR** The mouth, lips, and tongue are the first centers of pleasure for the baby, and his earliest attachment is to the one who provides pleasure in the mouth, usually his mother. For normal development, the infant requires some optimal amount of oral stimulation—not too much and not too little. If the optimal amount of stimulation is unavailable, then some libidinal energy may remain attached to ("fixated on," in Freud's terms) the oral mode of gratification. Such an individual, Freud thought, will continue to have a strong preference for oral pleasures in later life, as you can see in the right-hand column in Table 9.2.

**THE ANAL STAGE: 1 TO 3 YEARS** As the body matures, the baby becomes more and more sensitive in the anal region. And as she matures physically, her parents begin to place great emphasis on toilet training and express approval when she manages to perform in the right place at the right time. These two forces together help to shift the major center of physical and sexual sensitivity from the oral to the anal region.

The key to the child's successful completion of this stage (according to Freud) is how parents manage toilet training. If toilet training becomes a major battleground, then some fixation of energy at this stage may occur—with the possible adult consequences of excessive orderliness and stinginess or the opposite of these.

**psychosexual stages** The stages of personality development suggested by Freud, consisting of the oral, anal, phallic, latency, and genital stages.

**Oedipus conflict** The pattern of events that Freud believed occur between ages 3 and 5, when the child experiences a sexual desire for the parent of the opposite sex; the resulting fear of possible reprisal from the parent of the same sex is resolved when the child identifies with that parent.

**THE PHALLIC STAGE: 3 TO 5 YEARS** At about 3 or 4 years of age, the genitals become increasingly sensitive, ushering in a new stage. One sign of this new sensitivity is that children of both sexes normally begin to masturbate at about this age. In Freud's view, the most important event that occurs during the phallic stage is the so-called **Oedipus conflict**. He described the sequence of events more fully (and slightly more believably!) for boys.

According to Freud, during the phallic stage, the boy, having discovered his penis, rather naively wishes to use this newfound source of pleasure to please his oldest source of

| Table 9.2 | | FREUD'S STAGES OF PSYCHOSEXUAL DEVELOPMENT | | |
|---|---|---|---|---|
| **Stage** | **Age (years)** | **Sensitive Zones** | **Major Developmental Task (potential source of conflict)** | **Personality Traits of Adults "Fixated" at This Stage** |
| Oral | 0–1 | Mouth, lips, tongue | Weaning | Oral behavior, such as smoking and overeating; passivity and gullibility |
| Anal | 1–3 | Anus | Toilet training | Orderliness, stinginess, obstinacy, or the opposites |
| Phallic | 3–5 | Genitals | Oedipus conflict; identification with same-sex parent | Vanity, recklessness, or the opposites |
| Latency | 5–12 | No specific area; sexual energy is latent | Development of ego defense mechanisms | None; fixation does not normally occur |
| Genital | 12–18 and adulthood | Genitals | Mature sexual intimacy | None; adults who have successfully integrated earlier stages should emerge with a sincere interest in others and mature sexuality. |

pleasure, his mother. He becomes envious of his father, who has access to the mother's body in a way that the boy does not. The boy also sees his father as a powerful and threatening figure who has ultimate power—the power to castrate. The boy is caught between desire for his mother and fear of his father's power.

Most of these feelings and the resultant conflict are unconscious. The boy does not have overt sexual feelings or behave sexually toward his mother. But unconscious or not, the result of this conflict is anxiety. How can the little boy handle this anxiety? In Freud's view, the boy responds with a defensive process called *identification*: The boy "incorporates" his image of his father and attempts to match his own behavior to that image. By trying to make himself as much like his father as possible, the boy not only reduces the chance of an attack from the father; he takes on some of the father's power as well. Furthermore, it is the "inner father," with his values and moral judgments, that serves as the core of the child's superego.

In elementary school, boys play with boys, girls play with girls. How would Freud explain this?

According to Freud, a parallel process occurs in girls. The girl sees her mother as a rival for her father's sexual attentions and has some fear of her mother (though less than the boy has of his father, since the girl may assume she has already been castrated). In this case, too, identification with the mother is thought to be the "solution" to the girl's anxiety.

**THE LATENCY STAGE: 5 TO 12 YEARS** Freud thought that after the phallic stage came a sort of resting period before the next major change in the child's sexual development. The child has presumably arrived at some preliminary resolution of the Oedipus conflict and now experiences a kind of calm after the storm. One of the obvious characteristics of this stage is that the identification with the same-sex parent that defined the end of the phallic stage is now extended to others of the same sex. So it is during these years that children's peer interactions are almost exclusively with members of the same sex and that children often have "crushes" on same-sex teachers or other adults.

**THE GENITAL STAGE: 12 TO 18 AND OLDER** The further changes in hormones and the genital organs that take place during puberty reawaken the sexual energy of the child. During this period, a more mature form of sexual attachment occurs. From the beginning of this period, the child's sexual objects are people of the opposite sex. Freud placed some emphasis on the fact that not everyone works through this period to a point of mature heterosexual love. Some people have not had a satisfactory oral period and thus do not have a foundation of basic love relationships. Some have not resolved the Oedipus conflict and arrived at a complete or satisfactory identification with the same-sex parent, a failure that may affect their ability to cope with rearoused sexual energies in adolescence.

Optimal development at each stage, according to Freud, requires an environment that satisfies the unique needs of each period. The baby needs sufficient oral and anal stimulation; the 4-year-old boy needs a father present with whom to identify and a mother who is not too seductive. An inadequate early environment will leave a residue of unresolved problems and unmet needs, which are then carried forward to subsequent stages. This emphasis on the formative role of early experience, particularly early family experience, is a hallmark of psychoanalytic theories. In this view, the first 5 or 6 years of life are critical for the development of the individual personality.

## Erikson's Psychosocial Stages

◄-----------Learning Objective 9.9
How does Erikson's theory explain personality development?

Erikson shared most of Freud's basic assumptions, but there are some crucial differences between the two theories. First, Erikson placed less emphasis on the centrality of sexual drive and instead focused on a stepwise emergence of a sense of identity. Second, although he agreed with Freud that the early years are highly important, Erikson argued that identity is not fully formed at the end of adolescence but continues to move through further developmental

Simulate the Experiment Development at MyDevelopmentLab

stages in adult life. You can see in Table 9.3 the eight **psychosocial stages** that Erikson proposed, three of which are reached only in adulthood. ▶ Simulate at **MyDevelopmentLab**

In Erikson's view, maturation plays a relatively small role in the sequence of stages. Far more important are common cultural demands on children of a particular age, such as the demand that the child become toilet trained at about age 2, that the child learn school skills at age 6 or 7, or that the young adult form an intimate partnership. Each stage, then, centers on a particular *dilemma*, or social task. Thus, Erikson called his stages psychosocial stages rather than psychosexual stages.

**BASIC TRUST VERSUS BASIC MISTRUST: BIRTH TO 1 YEAR** The first task (or dilemma) occurs during the first year of life, when the child must develop a sense of basic trust in the predictability of the world and in his ability to affect the events around him. Erikson believed that the behavior of the major caregiver (usually the mother) is critical to the child's successful or unsuccessful resolution of this task. Children who reach the end of the first year with a firm sense of trust are those whose parents are loving and respond predictably and reliably to the child. A child who has developed a sense of trust will go on to other relationships, carrying this sense with him. Those infants whose early care has been erratic or harsh may develop mistrust, and they too carry this sense with them into later relationships.

Erikson never said, by the way, that the ideal or "correct" resolution to any of the dilemmas was to arrive at the ego quality at one end of the continuum. In the first stage, for example, there is some risk in being too trusting. The child also needs to develop some healthy mistrust, such as learning to discriminate between dangerous and safe situations.

**AUTONOMY VERSUS SHAME AND DOUBT: 2 TO 3 YEARS** Erikson saw the child's greater mobility during the toddler years as forming the basis for the sense of independence or autonomy. But if the child's efforts at independence are not carefully guided by the parents and she experiences repeated failures or ridicule, then the results of all the new opportunities for exploration may be shame and doubt instead of a basic sense of self-control and self-worth. Once again, the ideal is not for the child to have *no* shame or doubt; some doubt is

**psychosocial stages** The stages of personality development suggested by Erikson, involving tasks centered on trust, autonomy, initiative, industry, identity, intimacy, generativity, and ego integrity.

### Table 9.3 ERIKSON'S EIGHT PSYCHOSOCIAL STAGES OF DEVELOPMENT

| Approximate Age (years) | Ego Quality to Be Developed | Some Tasks and Activities of the Stage |
|---|---|---|
| 0–1 | Basic trust versus basic mistrust | Develop trust in mother or central caregiver and in one's own ability to make things happen, a key element in an early secure attachment |
| 2–3 | Autonomy versus shame, doubt | Develop walking, grasping, and other physical skills that lead to free choice; complete toilet training; child learns control but may develop shame if not handled properly |
| 4–5 | Initiative versus guilt | Learn to organize activities around some goal; become more assertive and aggressive |
| 6–12 | Industry versus inferiority | Absorb all the basic cultural skills and norms; including school skills and tool use |
| 13–18 | Identity versus role confusion | Adapt sense of self to physical changes of puberty, make occupational choice, achieve adult-like sexual identity, and search for new values |
| 19–25 | Intimacy versus isolation | Form one or more intimate relationships that go beyond adolescent love; marry and form family groups |
| 26–40 | Generativity versus stagnation | Bear and rear children, focus on occupational achievement or creativity, and train the next generation |
| 41+ | Ego integrity versus despair | Integrate earlier stages and come to terms with basic identity; accept self |

needed for the child to understand which behaviors are acceptable and which are not, which are safe and which are dangerous. But the ideal does lie toward the autonomy end of the continuum.

**INITIATIVE VERSUS GUILT: 4 TO 5 YEARS**   This phase, roughly equivalent to Freud's phallic stage, is also ushered in by new skills or abilities in the child. The 4-year-old is able to plan a bit, to take the initiative in reaching particular goals. The child tries out these new cognitive skills and attempts to conquer the world around him. He may try to go out into the street on his own; he may take a toy apart, and then find he can't put it back together and throw the parts at his mother. It is a time of vigorous action and of behaviors that parents may see as aggressive. The risk is that the child may go too far in his forcefulness or that the parents may restrict and punish too much—either of which can produce guilt. Some guilt is needed, since without it the child would develop no conscience and no self-control. The ideal interaction between parent and child is certainly not total indulgence, but too much guilt can inhibit the child's creativity and interactions with others.

**INDUSTRY (COMPETENCE) VERSUS INFERIORITY: 6 TO 12 YEARS**   The beginning of schooling is a major force in ushering in this stage. The child is now faced with the need to win approval by developing specific competences—learning to read, to do math, and to succeed at other school skills. The task of this period is thus simply to develop the repertoire of abilities society demands of the child. If the child is unable to develop the expected skills, she will develop instead a basic sense of inferiority. Yet some failure is necessary so that the child can develop some humility; as always, balance is an issue. Ideally, the child must have sufficient success to encourage a sense of competence but should not place so much emphasis on competence that failure is unacceptable or that she becomes a "workaholic."

**IDENTITY VERSUS ROLE CONFUSION: 13 TO 18 YEARS**   The task that faces the child during puberty is a major one in which the adolescent reexamines his identity and the roles he must occupy. Erikson suggested that two "identities" are involved—a sexual identity and an occupational identity. What should emerge for the adolescent from this period is a reintegrated sense of self, of what one wants to do and be, and of one's appropriate sexual role. The risk is that the child may suffer confusion, arising from the profusion of roles opening up at this age.

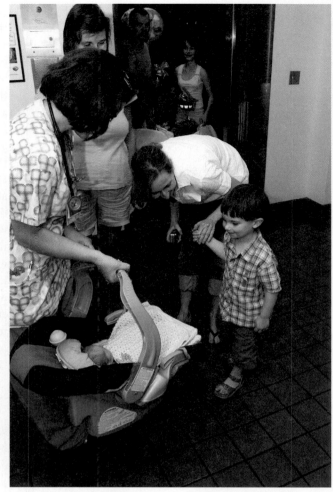

This preschooler, who is in the stage Erikson calls initiative versus guilt, may develop resentful or aggressive thoughts about his new baby brother. If so, the guilt he feels may help him inhibit any actions that may arise from these feelings.

## Evidence and Applications

◀------------Learning Objective 9.10
What evidence is there to support the psychoanalytic perspective on personality?

Empirical explorations of Freud's or Erikson's theories are relatively rare, largely because both theories are so general that specific tests are very difficult to perform. For example, to test Freud's notion of fixation, researchers would need much more information about how to determine whether a given child is fixated at some stage. What is a sign that a child is fixated at the oral or the anal stage? Is there some automatic connection between how early a child is weaned and such ostensibly oral adult behavior as smoking or overeating? When researchers have searched for such direct linkages, they have not found them.

Despite these difficulties, researchers have managed to observe instances of some of Freud's psychosexual stages. For instance, one 4-year-old boy, after his mother told him that she loved him, said, "And I love you too, and that's why I can't ever marry someone else" (Watson & Getz, 1990a, p. 29). In their studies of Oedipal behavior, Malcolm Watson and Kenneth Getz (1990a, 1990b) have indeed found that children of about 4 or 5 are likely to make comments like this. More generally, they have found that 4-year-olds, more than any other age group, show more affectionate behavior toward the opposite-sex parent and more aggressive or antagonistic behavior toward the same-sex parent. You can see the results of a study of aggressive and antagonistic behavior in Figure 9.3, on page 236. Whether Freud's

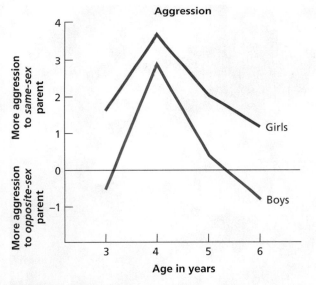

**FIGURE 9.3** Age and Parent-Directed Aggression
This figure graphs data from the detailed reports of parents on their children's affectionate and aggressive behavior toward them. Scores above 0 mean that the child was more aggressive toward the same-sex parent than toward the opposite-sex parent; scores below 0 mean the reverse.

(*Source:* Watson & Getz, 1990b, from Table 3, p. 499. "The relationship between Oedipal behaviors and children's family role concepts." *Merrill-Palmer Quarterly, 36*, 487–506.)

**Learning Objective 9.11** - - - - - - - - - ->
What are some criticisms of psychoanalytic theories?

explanation of this phenomenon is the correct one remains to be seen, but these observations are certainly consistent with his theory.

A second research area that has its roots in psychoanalytic theory is the current work on the security or insecurity of children's early attachments. Both Erikson and Freud argued that the quality of the child's first relationship with the central caregiver will shape her relationships with other children and other adults at later ages. You'll be reading a great deal more about early attachments in Chapter 11, but here it is sufficient to note that research in this area provides a good deal of support for the basic psychoanalytic hypothesis that the quality of the child's earliest relationship affects the whole course of her later development. Dozens of longitudinal studies have assessed children's attachment security at age 1 or 2 and then followed them over a period of years—in some cases throughout childhood and adolescence. The consistent finding is that children who had a more secure attachment in infancy have more positive relationships with others and are more socially skillful later on (Thompson, Winer, & Goodvin, 2011). Thus, the relationship formed during the earliest stage of psychosocial development seems to create a prototype for later relationships, as Erikson proposed. Recall, too, the result from the study by Gunnar (1994) described earlier: Temperamentally inhibited toddlers who have formed a secure attachment to their mothers show little or no physiological sign of fearfulness in a novel setting. Thus, the quality of the child's early attachment can at least partially override basic temperamental tendencies as the personality is formed.

## Critique of Psychoanalytic Theories

Freud's and Erikson's psychoanalytic theories are attractive for several reasons. Perhaps their greatest strength is that they provide us with a better account of the complexities of personality development than other perspectives, especially the learning theories (Seligman, 2005). In psychoanalytic theory, a particular characteristic of the environment, such as inconsistent parenting, is not hypothesized to have a specific effect on development. Instead, psychoanalysts predict that the effects of such factors depend on how individual children perceive them, the stage of development in which children experience them, and, in Erikson's case, the cultural context in which they occur.

Moreover, psychoanalytic theories focus on the importance of the emotional quality of the child's relationship with caregivers. These theories suggest that the child's needs or tasks change with age, so that the parents must constantly adapt to the changing child. One of the implications of this observation is that "good parenting" should not be thought of as if it were a global quality. Some parents may be very good at meeting the needs of an infant but terrible at dealing with a teenager's identity struggles; others may have the opposite pattern. The child's eventual personality and her overall emotional health thus depend on the interaction, or *transaction*, that develops in a particular family. This is an attractive element of psychoanalytic theories, because research within developmental psychology is increasingly supporting a transactional conception of the process of development (Blatt, 2008).

Psychoanalytic theory has also given psychologists a number of helpful concepts, such as defense mechanisms and identification, that have been so widely adopted that they have become a part of everyday language as well as theory. These strengths have led to a resurgence of influence of both Erikson's theory and several related psychoanalytic approaches.

The great weakness of all the psychoanalytic approaches is the fuzziness of many of the concepts. Identification may be an intriguing theoretical notion, but how can it be measured? How do researchers detect the presence of specific defense mechanisms? Without more precise operational definitions, it is impossible to test the theories. The general concepts of psychoanalytic theories have furthered an understanding of development only when other theorists or researchers have offered more precise definitions or clearer methods for measuring some psychoanalytic construct, such as the concept of security of attachment that you will read about in Chapter 11. Psychoanalytic theory may thus sometimes offer a provocative way of thinking about personality, but it is not a precise theory of development.

# A Possible Synthesis

◄------------Learning Objective 9.12

How can elements of the biological, learning, and psychoanalytic approaches be combined into a comprehensive explanation of personality?

You have read about three different views of the origins of those unique, individual patterns of behavior we call personality. Each view can be at least partially supported with research evidence; each has clear strengths. Do developmentalists need to choose just one of them, or can the views be combined in a way that makes sense? Some argue that theories as different as these cannot ever be combined, because they make such different assumptions about the child's role in the process of personality development (Lerner, Theokas, & Bobek, 2005; Overton & Reese, 1973). Nonetheless, combinations of these varying perspectives, like the one shown in Figure 9.4, may still be fruitful. This model suggests that the child's inborn temperament is a beginning point—an initial, highly significant bias in the system. Arrow 1 suggests a direct relationship between that inborn temperament and the eventual personality seen in the child and later in the adult.

Arrow 2 suggests a second direct effect, between the pattern of the child's environment and his eventual personality and social behavior. Whether the parents respond reliably and appropriately to the infant will affect his trust, or the security of his attachment, which will show up in a range of behaviors later; whether the parents reinforce aggressive or friendly behavior will influence the child's future as well.

These direct effects are straightforward, even obvious, but most of what happens is much more complicated than that. The way the child is treated is influenced by her temperament (arrow 3), and both that basic temperament and the family environment affect the child's self-scheme, or self-concept—her expectations for others and herself, her beliefs about her own abilities (arrows 4 and 5). This self-scheme (including the child's sense of self-efficacy), in turn, helps to shape the child's overt behavior, which reflects her "personality" (arrow 6).

This system does not exist in a vacuum. In keeping with the ecological approach of Bronfenbrenner and others, arrow 7 suggests that the parents' ability to maintain a loving and supportive relationship with their child is influenced by the parents' own outside experiences, such as whether they like their jobs or whether they have enough emotional support to help them weather their own crises.

For example, Mavis Hetherington (1989) reports that children with difficult temperaments show more problem behavior in response to their parents' divorce than do children with easier temperaments, but this difference exists only if the mother is also depressed and has inadequate social support. In this study, those difficult children whose divorcing mothers were not depressed did not show heightened levels of problems. Thus, the child's temperament clearly seems to have an impact, but the effect of temperament can be and is modified by the parents' pattern of response.

Another illustration of the intricacy of the system comes from the work of Susan Crockenberg (e.g., Crockenberg & Leerkes, 2004). In one early study (1981), Crockenberg studied a group of 48 mothers and infants over the first year of life. She measured each child's irritability (an aspect of temperament) when the baby was 5 to 10 days old and assessed the security of the child's at-

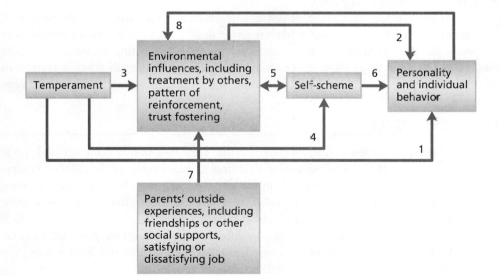

**FIGURE 9.4** An Interactive Model of Personality

Here is one version of a complex interactive model describing the formation of individual personality. The effects of inborn temperament and environmental influences are not merely additive. That is, the whole is greater than the sum of its parts. Each affects the other, helping to create the child's unique self-scheme, which in turn affects the child's experiences. All this occurs within the context of the family, which is itself influenced by the parents' own life experiences. What developmentalists think of as personality is a complex product of all these forces.

## Table 9.4 — INFLUENCE OF CHILD'S TEMPERAMENT AND MOTHER'S SOCIAL SUPPORT ON THE CHILD'S SECURE OR INSECURE ATTACHMENT

| Child Irritability | Mother's Social Support | Securely Attached Children | Insecurely Attached Children |
|---|---|---|---|
| High | Low | 2 | 9 |
| High | High | 12 | 1 |
| Low | Low | 7 | 2 |
| Low | High | 13 | 2 |

*Source:* From S. B. Crockenberg, Table 5, 862, "Infant Irritability, Mother Responsiveness, and Social Support Influences on the Security of Infant-Mother Attachment," *Child Development, 52*, 1981, p. 857–865.

tachment to the mother when the child was 12 months old. We might expect that irritable babies would be more likely to be insecurely attached, merely because they are more difficult to care for. In fact, Crockenberg found a small effect of this kind (see Table 9.4). But Crockenberg didn't stop there. She also measured the level of the mother's social support—the degree of help she received from family and friends in dealing with the strains of having a new child or other life changes she might be experiencing. The results of the study show that insecure attachment in the child was most likely when the mother had an irritable infant and low levels of support. If the baby was irritable, but the mother had good support, the child nearly always developed secure attachment. Only when two difficult conditions occurred together did a poor outcome result for the child.

In a later study, Crockenberg (1987) found that a higher level of anger and noncompliant behavior (perhaps reflections of what is called *neuroticism* in the Big Five) was common in toddlers who had been irritable as infants and whose mothers were angry and punitive toward them. Furthermore, such angry and punitive behavior by the mother was more likely if the mother had experienced rejection in her own childhood and if she experienced little support from her partner. Clearly, Crockenberg's work reveals a system of effects.

Returning to Figure 9.4, you'll see that arrow 8 emphasizes the transactional elements of the system. Once the child's unique pattern of behaviors and attitudes (personality) is formed, this pattern affects the environment she will encounter, the experiences she will choose, and the responses of the people around her, which in turn affect her behavior (Feinberg, Reiss, Niederhiser, & Hetherington, 2005).

No doubt even this fairly complex system underestimates the intricacy of the process of personality development in the child. Most research does not yet encompass all the pieces of the puzzle. But the very fact that developmental psychologists are turning toward such complex models is a very good thing. Development *is* complex, and developmentalists will not be able to describe it or explain it until they begin to examine and try to measure all these separate forces.

## THINK CRITICALLY

- Suppose that parents received an "owners' manual" for their children at birth, and that one of the features of the owners manual was a complete description of the child's temperament. In what way would having such information so early in a child's life affect parents' responses to children? How might parental access to such information facilitate or impede the development of children's personalities?
- As you learned in the chapter, children with difficult temperaments are punished more often than those who are more easy-going. How would you explain this finding using the interactive model in Figure 9.4 on page 237.

## CONDUCT YOUR OWN RESEARCH

As Freud's description of the latency stage would predict, researchers have found that the tendency for school-aged children to segregate themselves by gender is universal. There also appear to be universal rules defining socially acceptable contact between preadolescent boys and girls (Sroufe, Bennett, England, Urban, & Schulman, 1993). Some examples of acceptable girl-boy interactions are (1) accidental contact; (2) contact compelled by an adult, as when a teacher forces a boy to work with a girl in class; (3) and contact accompanied by verbal taunts, insults, or mild physical aggression such as pushing. You can observe both gender-segregated play and rule-governed cross-gender contact on any school playground. As you watch children at play, note the following: (1) the number of contacts between boys and girls; (2) the type of contact (accidental, compelled, or aggressive); (3) children's comments to or about a boy or girl who violates gender segregation rules; and (4) the kinds of activities exhibited by boys' groups and girls' groups. Use your data to hypothesize some additional rules governing children's relations with peers of the same sex and of the opposite sex.

## SUMMARY ✓•[Study and Review at MyDevelopmentLab

### Defining Personality

**9.1 What are the dimensions of temperament that most psychologists agree on?**
Researchers studying infants and young children have studied temperament rather than personality. Temperament is now widely seen as a set of built-in, behavior tendencies that form the emotional substrate of personality. There are sizeable differences among temperament theorists regarding how best to characterize the basic dimensions of temperament, but there is general agreement on five key dimensions: activity level, approach/positive emotionality, inhibition and anxiety, negative emotionality/irritability/anger, and effortful control/task persistence.

**9.1a How is temperamental surgency manifested in the preschool classroom?**
Temperamental surgency is a cluster of traits that includes sociability, high activity level, generally positive emotional states, and impulsiveness. Preschoolers with these traits may experience a conflict between their temperaments and the demands of the preschool classroom. Their impulsiveness may cause them to be labeled as "problem children" by teachers. Teachers' efforts to control their impulsiveness may cause these children to become frustrated and aggressive.

**9.2 How do advocates for the Big Five approach define personality?**
Researchers studying adult personality have agreed on a set of five dimensions (the Big Five) that capture most of the variation among individuals: extraversion, agreeableness, conscientiousness, neuroticism, and openness/intellect. Recent research suggests that the same five dimensions may give an accurate picture of variations in children's and adolescents' personalities as well.

**9.2b What do teens' Facebook pages reveal about their personalities?**
Teens and adults who are high in extraversion tend to have more Facebook friends, but their friends typically do not know each other. Introverts show the opposite pattern—fewer friends with more connections between them. Those who are low in conscientiousness post messages that contain swear words. Messages with negative emotion words are associated with neuroticism, while those with positive emotion words are associated with agreeableness.

### Genetic and Biological Explanations of Personality

**9.3 What is the focus of the biological approach to personality?**
Biological explanations of temperament and personality, focusing on genetic differences in patterns or styles of reacting to people and the environment, are well supported by research. Evidence is also accumulating that specific differences in neurological and chemical responses underlie many observed variations in behavior. However, temperament is clearly not totally determined by heredity or ongoing physiological processes, although the child's built-in temperament does shape her interactions with the world and affect others' responses to her.

**9.4 What are some important criticisms of the biological approach?**
Critics point out that theorists do not agree on the basic dimensions of temperament. In addition, biological theories ignore important factors such as children's cognitive interpretations of events.

### Learning Explanations of Personality

**9.5 What are the basic propositions of learning explanations of personality?**
Traditional learning theorists emphasize the role of basic learning processes, such as reinforcement, in shaping

individual behaviors, including patterns of interaction with others. Social/cognitive learning theorists such as Bandura also emphasize the role of observational learning as well as the role of the child's learned expectancies, standards, and self-efficacy beliefs in creating more enduring patterns of response.

**9.6**  **What are some criticisms of the learning perspective?**
Critics argue that learning theories place too much importance on what is happening to the child and pay too little attention to how the child acts on his environment. They also suggest that learning theories explain only how children acquire specific behaviors, not the underlying processes that drive personality development.

**9.6a**  **What is locus of control, and how does it affect teens' development?**
Locus of control is a personality trait that represents how an individual explains the causes of events. People with an internal locus of control view their own behavior and traits as causes of the outcomes they experience in life. People with an external locus of control view uncontrollable forces such as luck as more important. Teens with an external locus of control are less successful in school and are less likely to follow medical advice and to practice safe sex than those with an internal locus of control.

## Psychoanalytic Explanations of Personality

**9.7**  **What are the major points of the psychoanalytic approach to personality?**
Psychoanalytic theorists emphasize the importance of unconscious motives and processes as well as the stagelike emergence of personality. This approach views the relationship of the child with significant adults, particularly in early infancy, as critical. While Freud's and Erikson's theories share a common set of assumptions, they differ with respect to the importance of the libido. In addition, Freud proposed that personality development was completed in childhood, while Erikson claimed that change continued throughout the lifespan.

**9.8**  **How does Freud's theory explain personality development?**
Freud emphasized the unconscious emotional struggles that arise as a child adapts to the demands of the family environment. In addition, his psychosexual stages are strongly affected by maturation. Particularly significant is the phallic stage, beginning at about age 3 or 4, when the Oedipus conflict arises and is resolved through the process of identification.

**9.9**  **How does Erikson's theory explain personality development?**
Erikson agreed with Freud that the struggle that takes place between the child's desires and needs and the demands of the environment shapes personality. However, he placed more emphasis on the culture at large than did Freud, who emphasized primarily the child's immediate family. Erikson's psychosocial stages are influenced both by social demands and by the child's physical and intellectual skills. Each of the major stages has a central task, or dilemma, relating to some aspect of the development of identity.

**9.10**  **What evidence is there to support the psychoanalytic perspective on personality?**
Psychoanalytic theories have been broadly confirmed in some aspects, such as the impact of early attachment on later functioning.

**9.11**  **What are some criticisms of psychoanalytic theories?**
Critics point out that psychoanalytic theories are difficult to test because of their imprecision.

## A Possible Synthesis

**9.12**  **How can elements of the biological, learning, and psychoanalytic approaches be combined into a comprehensive explanation of personality?**
Elements of all three views can be combined into a transactional, or interactionist, view of personality development. Temperament may serve as the base from which personality grows, both by affecting behavior directly and by affecting the way others respond to the child. Both the child's temperament and the specific pattern of response from the people in the child's environment affect the child's self-concept, or self-scheme, which then helps to create stability in the child's unique pattern of behavior.

## KEY TERMS

| | | | |
|---|---|---|---|
| agreeableness (p. 220) | extraversion (p. 220) | openness/intellect (p. 220) | psychosocial stages (p. 234) |
| Big Five (p. 220) | neuroticism (p. 220) | personality (p. 218) | reciprocal determinism (p. 229) |
| conscientiousness (p. 220) | Oedipus conflict (p. 232) | psychosexual stages (p. 232) | self-efficacy (p. 228) |

# Concepts of Self, Gender, and Sex Roles

Consider the case of identical twins who were born in the mid-1960s. When an accident during a routine circumcision left one twin with a severely damaged penis, doctors recommended that his parents allow him to undergo sex reassignment surgery and that they raise him as a girl. Their thinking was that the child would be better able to develop a healthy sense of self with surgically sculpted female genitalia than with mutilated male genitalia. The parents agreed, and "John" became "Joan."

Joan's parents exposed her to all the typical female experiences and never hinted that she might have ever been anything other than a girl. Still, by the time she reached adolescence, Joan was convinced that she was different

Watch the Video *Intersexuals* at **MyDevelopmentLab**

from others in some fundamental way. When her parents revealed the truth, Joan became John once again. She, now he, underwent sex reassignment surgery and eventually married. Though John and his wife adopted children and, to outsiders, appeared to be a normal couple, he was never really happy. Unfortunately, in May 2004, John committed suicide. Watch at **MyDevelopmentLab**

The John/Joan case provides compelling evidence for the view that the development of *gender*, the psychological component of maleness and femaleness, is strongly influenced by the physiological aspects of *biological sex*, the physical component of maleness and femaleness (Bostwick & Martin, 2007; Reiner & Gearhart, 2004). However, some individuals develop a sense of gender that is the opposite of their biological sex, despite being physically normal in every way. Thus, developmentalists have concluded that factors beyond the physical domain also make significant contributions to gender development. Watch at **MyDevelopmentLab**

Watch the Video *Gender Versus Sex: Florence Denmark* at **MyDevelopmentLab**

How children develop a coherent sense of self is the topic of this chapter. First, we will explore how children come to understand "self" as a concept. Next, we will turn to the topic of self-esteem. Finally, we will return to the critical issue of how individuals integrate biological sex and psychological gender and incorporate them into a sense of self.

## The Concept of Self

Developmentalists' thinking about the child's emerging sense of self has been strongly influenced by both Freud and Piaget. Freud emphasized what he called the symbiotic relationship between the mother and young infant, while Piaget's theory has provided the basis for explanations of the sense of self that emphasize the child's knowledge of and thinking about himself. Even more influential than either Freud or Piaget, however, has been the thinking of the early American psychologist William James (1890, 1892), who compartmentalized the global **self-concept** into one component he called the "I" and another he termed the "me." The "I" self is often called the **subjective self**; it is that inner sense that "I am," "I exist." The "me" aspect is sometimes called the **objective self**; it is the individual's set of properties or qualities that are objectively known or knowable, including physical characteristics, temperament, and social skills. Simulate at **MyDevelopmentLab**

Simulate the Experiment *Multiple Selves* at **MyDevelopmentLab**

**Learning Objective 10.1**
What is the subjective self?

## The Subjective Self

Most developmentalists argue that the baby has some primitive sense of a subjective self from the beginning (Harter, 2006b). In the early months, the baby's task is to begin to coordinate the various sources of information he has about his own actions and their impact. In particular, over the first year, the infant develops a sense of himself as an agent in the world—as able to make things happen. The delight the baby shows when he is able to make a mobile move or create a noise by squeezing a squeaky toy is evidence of the baby's emerging sense of himself as an agent—the first step in the formation of a self-concept. Albert Bandura argues that the roots of the sense of self-efficacy are found during this first year, when the infant realizes he can control certain events in the world.

This sense of efficacy or control occurs not just with inanimate objects but perhaps even more centrally in interactions with adults, who respond appropriately to the child's behavior—smiling back when the baby smiles, making funny faces when the baby does particular things, playing repetitive games like peek-a-boo while changing diapers or feeding the baby. Of course the baby is not "causing" these things to happen in most cases; it is the parents who are initiating the games or patterns. But within these games and patterns are myriad repetitions of sequences in which the baby does something and the parent responds with some predictable behavior. From the baby's perspective, he has "made it happen," and his sense of self, of efficacy or agency, is established.

**self-concept** One's knowledge of and thoughts about the set of qualities attributed to the self.

**subjective self** The component of the self-concept that involves awareness of the "I," the self that is separate from others.

**objective self** The component of the self-concept that involves awareness of the self as an object with properties.

Piaget also argued that a critical element in the development of the subjective self is the understanding of object permanence that develops at about 9 to 12 months. Just as the infant is figuring out that mom and dad continue to exist when they are out of sight, he is figuring out—at least in some preliminary way—that he exists separately and has some permanence.

## The Objective Self

◄ - - - - - - - - - - - **Learning Objective 10.2**

What does acquisition of an objective self add to the infant's self-concept?

The second major step in the development of a self-concept is for the toddler to come to understand that she is also an object in the world. Just as a ball has properties—roundness, the ability to roll, a certain feel in the hand—so the self also has properties, such as gender, size, a name, and qualities like shyness or boldness, coordination or clumsiness. It is this self-awareness that is the hallmark of the "me" self.

**STUDYING SELF-AWARENESS**   The most common procedure psychologists use to measure self-awareness involves a mirror. First the baby is placed in front of a mirror, just to see how she behaves. Most infants of about 9 to 12 months will look at their own images, make faces, or try to interact with the baby in the mirror in some way. After allowing this free exploration for a time, the experimenter, while pretending to wipe the baby's face with a cloth, puts a spot of rouge on the baby's nose and then again lets the baby look in the mirror. The crucial test of self-recognition, and thus of awareness of the self, is whether the baby reaches for the spot of rouge on her own nose rather than for the spot on the nose in the mirror. 👁 **Watch** at **MyDevelopmentLab**

👁 **Watch** the **Video** *Self-Awareness* at **MyDevelopmentLab**

The results from one of Michael Lewis's studies using this procedure are shown in Figure 10.1 on page 244. As you can see, very few of the 9- to 12-month-old children in this study touched their noses, but by 21 months, three-quarters of the children showed that level of self-recognition. The figure also shows the rate at which children refer to themselves by name when they are shown a picture of themselves, which is another commonly used measure of self-awareness. You can see that this development occurs at almost exactly the same time as self-recognition in a mirror. Both are present by about the middle of the second year of life (Lewis & Ramsay, 2004). Neuroimaging studies suggest that brain maturation underlies the appearance of this milestone (Lewis & Carmody, 2008).

Once the toddler achieves such self-awareness, his behavior is affected in a wide range of ways. Self-aware toddlers begin to insist on doing things for themselves and show a newly proprietary attitude toward toys or other treasured objects ("Mine!"). Looked at this way, much of the legendary behavior in the "terrible twos" can be understood as an outgrowth of self-awareness. In a quite literal sense, toddlers are self-willed for the first time.

Another behavioral change ushered in by the toddler's newly emerging self-awareness is the expression of such self-conscious emotions as embarrassment, pride, or shame. These emotions are not normally expressed until late in the second year of life, presumably because they all involve some aspect of self-evaluation, not present until the toddler has achieved at least minimal self-awareness (Lewis, Allesandri, & Sullivan, 1992; Lewis, Sullivan, Stanger, & Weiss, 1989; Thompson, Winer, & Goodvin, 2011). According to Lewis, emotions such as shame or pride require the child to be aware of some standards of conduct and to compare himself to those standards— a development that also occurs late in the second year of life. It is only at this age, for example, that children begin to use words like *dirty* to describe themselves or an object, suggesting that they are judging themselves or others against some standard. The child then expresses shame when he feels he has

At 4 months, Lucy's pleasure at looking at herself in a mirror comes from the fact that this is an interesting moving object to inspect—not from any understanding that this is herself in the mirror.

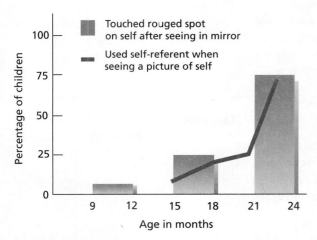

**FIGURE 10.1** Self-Recognition in Infancy
Mirror recognition and self-naming develop at almost exactly the same time.

(*Source:* Lewis & Brooks, 1978, pp. 214–215. Self-knowledge and emotional development. In M. Lewis & L. A. Rosenblum (Eds.), The development of affect (pp. 205–226). New York: Plenum Press.)

not met the standard, or pride when he is able to meet the standard—to build the block tower as high as the teacher wants, say, or to wash his hands so that they are clean, or the like. One aspect of this phase of development is that after age 2, children become increasingly eager for adult approval, using the adult's response to gauge whether they have met some standard or lived up to some expectation. By school age, children are beginning to internalize those standards and expectations and thus become more autonomous in their self-judgments (Combrinck-Graham & Fox, 2007). Likewise, they internalize their parents' rules and regulations, thereby becoming better able to regulate their emotional expression and behavior.

**EARLY SELF-DEFINITIONS**   Having achieved an initial self-awareness, the preschool child begins to define "who I am" by learning about her own qualities and her social roles. The 2-year-old not only knows her own name; she can probably also tell you if she is a girl or a boy and whether she is big or little. By about age 5 to 7, a child can give you quite a full description of herself on a whole range of dimensions. For example, Susan Harter (2006b) has found that children of this age have clear notions of their own competence on a variety of specific tasks, such as solving puzzles, counting, knowing a lot in school, climbing or skipping or jumping rope, or being able to make friends.

Beginning in the second year, children also seem to become aware of themselves as players in the social game. By age 2, the toddler has already learned a variety of social "scripts"—routines of play or interaction with others. Case (1991) points out that the toddler next begins to develop an implicit understanding of her own roles in these scripts. So she begins to think of herself as a "helper" in some situations or as "the boss" when she is telling another child what to do. You can see this clearly in sociodramatic play among preschoolers, who begin to take explicit roles: "I'll be the daddy and you be the mommy" or "I'm the teacher." As part of the same process, the preschool child also gradually understands her place in the network of family roles—she knows that she has sisters, brothers, father, mother, and so on.

These are major advances in the child's understanding. Yet the self-definition is still tied to concrete characteristics. For one thing, each facet of a preschool child's self-concept seems to be quite separate, rather like a list: "I'm good at running"; "I don't like to play with dolls"; "I live in a big house"; "I have blue eyes" (Harter, 2006b). These separate aspects of the self-scheme, or internal working model of the self, have not yet coalesced into a global sense of self-worth (Harter, 2006a). Children this age do not say "I am a terrible person" or "I really like myself." Their perceptions of themselves are more tied to specific settings and specific tasks. Moreover, a preschooler's self-concept tends to focus on his own visible characteristics—whether he's a boy or girl, what he looks like, what or who he plays with, where he lives, what he is good or bad at doing—rather than on more enduring, inner qualities.

**CULTURE AND SELF-DESCRIPTIONS**   Interestingly, too, the cultural context in which a child is growing up may influence preschool-age children's self-descriptions. For example, researchers have found that young children's inclusion of role terms (e.g., "daughter," "grandchild") in their self-descriptions varies across cultural groups. Preschoolers in Asian American families are more likely to include such descriptors than their European American counterparts are (Wang, 2006a). These differences may emerge from differences in the ways that parents from these two groups guide the formation of children's self-understanding through discussions of important events in their lives (Wang, 2006b). In Asian cultures, where family associations tend to be more highly valued than other types of social relationships, parents may encourage children to think of themselves in terms of family roles to a greater degree than parents in more individualistic and peer-oriented cultures.

**Learning Objective 10.3** - - - - - - - - - - ▶
In what way is the ability to regulate emotions related to social functioning?

# The Emotional Self

Another facet of self that emerges during the early years is the child's ability to understand and regulate her own expressions of emotion (Eisenberg, Spinrad, & Eggum, 2010). Part of this process is the development of *impulse control*, sometimes called *inhibitory control*—the growing ability to inhibit a response, for example, to wait rather than to weep, to yell rather than to hit, to go slowly rather than to run (Kochanska & Aksan, 2006). When an infant is upset, it is the parents who help to regulate that emotion by cuddling, soothing, or removing the child from the upsetting situation. Over the preschool years, this regulation process is gradually taken over more and more by the child as the various prohibitions and instructions are internalized. A 2-year-old is only minimally able to modulate feelings or behavior in this way; by age 5 or 6, however, most children have made great strides in controlling the intensity of their expressions of strong feelings, so they don't automatically hit someone or something when they are angry, cry inconsolably when they are frustrated, or sulk when they are denied (Sroufe, 1996).

A second aspect of the child's regulation of emotion is the need to learn the social rules of specific emotional expressions. For example, as early as age 3, children begin to learn that there are times when they ought to smile—even when they do not feel completely happy (Liew, Eisenberg, & Reiser, 2004). Thus, they begin to use the "social smile," a facial expression that is quite distinct from the natural, delighted smile. Similarly, children gradually learn to use abbreviated or constricted forms of other emotions, such as anger or disgust (Thompson & Goodvin, 2011), and they learn to conceal their feelings in a variety of situations. Equally, the preschool child learns to use her own emotional expressions to get things she wants, crying or smiling as needed. This control of emotions, in turn, rests at least partially on her grasp of the links between her behavior and others' perception of her behavior, an understanding that develops rapidly between ages 3 and 4 as a consequence of the child's growing theory of mind (see Chapter 6).

Expressive interactions with others help infants learn to regulate emotions in social settings. For instance, it is in the context of human interactions that the spontaneous social smile of the 2-month-old that he shows only to those closest to him develops into the intentional social smile of the 3-year-old that is exhibited to loved ones and strangers alike.

The ability to regulate emotions during the preschool years is strongly predictive of a wide variety of social skills later in life (Eisenberg, Hofer, & Vaughan, 2007; Rubin, Burgess, Dwyer, & Hastings, 2003). For instance, self-control in early childhood is related to children's ability to obey moral rules and to think about right and wrong during the school years (Kochanska & Aksan, 2006). Further, young children who are skilled in controlling negative emotions, such as anger, are less likely to display behavior problems during the school years (Eisenberg et al., 1999; Eisenberg et al., 2005). Research also suggests that children who poorly control their negative emotions are less popular with peers (Thompson & Goodvin, 2011).

The process of acquiring emotional control is one in which control shifts slowly from the parents to the child and interacts with the child's characteristics (Houck & Lecuyer-Marcus, 2004). For example, preschoolers who have consistently exhibited "difficult" behavior since infancy are more likely to have self-control problems in early childhood (Schmitz et al., 1999). Similarly, preschoolers who were born prematurely or who were delayed in language development in the second year of life experience more difficulties with self-control during early childhood (Carson, Klee, & Perry, 1998; Schothorst & van Engeland, 1996).

However, the way parents express emotions themselves is also related to their children's ability to regulate emotions. Generally, parents who are very expressive of their negative emotions tend to have children who poorly control their negative feelings (Eisenberg, Gershoff et al., 2001; Eisenberg, Liew, & Pidada, 2001). Interesting, too, is the finding that positive emotional expressivity in parents does not predict children's emotional self-regulation as consistently as negative emotional expressivity.

## Self-Concept at School Age

◄----------- **Learning Objective 10.4**

How do school-age children describe themselves?

Over the elementary school years, the child's concrete self-concept gradually shifts toward a more abstract, more comparative, more generalized self-definition. A 6-year-old might describe herself as "smart" or "dumb"; a 10-year-old is more likely to say he is "smarter than most other kids" (Harter, 2006b). The school-age child also begins to see her own (and other people's) characteristics as relatively stable and, for the first time, develops a global sense of her own self-worth.

A number of these themes are illustrated nicely in a classic study by Montemayor and Eisen (1977) of self-concepts in 9- to 18-year-olds. Using the question "Who am I?" these researchers found that the younger children they studied were still using mostly surface qualities to describe themselves, as in the description by this 9-year-old:

> My name is Bruce C. I have brown eyes. I have brown hair. I have brown eyebrows.
> I am nine years old. I LOVE! Sports. I have seven people in my family. I have great! eye
> site. I have lots! of friends. I live on 1923 Pinecrest Dr. I am going on 10 in September.
> I'm a boy. I have a uncle that is almost 7 feet tall. My school is Pinecrest. My teacher
> is Mrs. V. I play Hockey! I'm almost the smartest boy in the class. I LOVE! food. I love
> fresh air. I LOVE school. (pp. 317–318)

In contrast, look at the self-description of this 11-year-old girl in the sixth grade:

> My name is A. I'm a human being. I'm a girl. I'm a truthful person. I'm not very pretty.
> I do so-so in my studies. I'm a very good cellist. I'm a very good pianist. I'm a little bit
> tall for my age. I like several boys. I like several girls. I'm old-fashioned. I play tennis.
> I am a very good swimmer. I try to be helpful. I'm always ready to be friends with any-
> body. Mostly I'm good, but I lose my temper. I'm not well-liked by some girls and boys.
> I don't know if I'm liked by boys or not. (pp. 317–318)

This girl, like other youngsters of her age in Montemayor and Eisen's study, not only describes her external qualities but also emphasizes her beliefs, the quality of her relationships, and her general personality traits. Thus, as the child moves through the elementary school years (Piaget's concrete operations period), her self-definition becomes more complex, more comparative, less tied to external features, and more focused on feelings and ideas.

The increasingly comparative self-assessments seen in middle childhood are particularly visible in the school context. Kindergarten and first-grade children pay relatively little attention to how well others do at a particular task; in fact, the great majority will confidently tell you that they are the smartest kid in their class—an aspect of a general tendency at this age to identify self-qualities as positive (Harter, 2006b). By third grade, however, children begin to notice whether their classmates finish a test sooner than they do or whether someone else gets a better grade or more corrections on his spelling paper (Eccles & Roeser, 2011). Their self-judgments begin to include both positive and negative elements.

Teachers' behavior shows a related progression: In the first few grades, teachers emphasize effort and work habits. Gradually, they begin to use more comparative judgments. By junior high, teachers compare children not only to each other but to fixed standards, students at other schools, or national norms (Eccles & Roeser, 2011). These comparisons are sometimes subtle, but they can be powerful. Robert Rosenthal (1994), in a famous series of studies, has shown that a teacher's belief about a given student's ability and potential has a small but significant effect on his or her behavior toward that student and on the student's eventual achievement. This set of results has now been replicated many times. Rosenthal's standard procedure is to tell teachers at the beginning of a school year that some of the children in the class are underachievers and just ready to "bloom" intellectually, although in fact the children labeled in this way are chosen randomly. At the end of the year, those students labeled as having more potential have typically shown more academic gains than those who have not been labeled in this way.

Similarly, parents' judgments and expectations also play a role. For example, you may recall from Chapter 7 that parents in the United States are more likely to attribute a daughter's good performance in math to hard work but a son's good math grades to ability. Children absorb these explanations and adjust their behavior accordingly (Fredricks & Eccles, 2005).

The beliefs about their own abilities that students develop through this process of self-assessment are usually quite accurate. Students who consistently do well in comparison to others come to believe that they are academically competent. Further, and perhaps more important, they come to believe that they are in control of academic outcomes—in Bandura's terms, they have a strong sense of their own academic self-efficacy.

# Self-Concept and Identity in Adolescence

◀------------Learning Objective 10.5

How do Erikson's and Marcia's theories explain adolescent identity development?

The trend toward greater abstraction in self-definition continues during adolescence, and the self-concept blossoms into a mature sense of identity.

**SELF-DESCRIPTIONS**   Compare the answers of this 17-year-old to the "Who am I?" question with the ones you read earlier:

> I am a human being. I am a girl, I am an individual. I don't know who I am. I am a Pisces. I am a moody person. I am an indecisive person. I am an ambitious person. I am a very curious person. I am not an individual. I am a loner. I am an American (God help me). I am a Democrat. I am a liberal person. I am a radical. I am a conservative. I am a pseudoliberal. I am an atheist. I am not a classifiable person (i.e., I don't want to be). (Montemayor & Eisen, 1977, p. 318)

Obviously, this girl's self-concept is even less tied to her physical characteristics or even her abilities than is that of the 11-year-old. She is describing abstract traits or ideology. Figure 10.2 shows this shift from concrete to abstract self-definitions, based on the answers of all 262 participants in Montemayor and Eisen's study. Participants' answers to the "Who am I?" question were placed in one or more specific categories, such as references to physical properties ("I am tall," "I have blue eyes") or references to ideology ("I am a Democrat," "I believe in God"). Figure 10.2 makes it clear that physical appearance was still a highly significant dimension of self-concept in the preteen and early teen years but became less dominant in late adolescence.

The adolescent's self-concept also becomes more differentiated as the teen comes to see herself somewhat differently in each of several roles: as a student, with friends, with parents, and in romantic relationships (Harter, 2006b). Once these ideas are formed, they begin to influence adolescents' behavior. For example, teens who get high scores on measures of athletic self-concept are more likely to exercise than those who get lower scores (Anderson, Masse, Zhang, Coleman, & Chang, 2009). In addition, teens' academic self-concepts influence their decisions and feelings about behaviors such as completing homework (Bouchey & Harter, 2005; Goetz et al., 2011). As you can see, then, formation of a self-concept can lead to a pattern of behavior that produces evidence in support of the self-concept. That is, for example, teens who have confidence in their academic abilities take more difficult courses but they also tend to do their homework

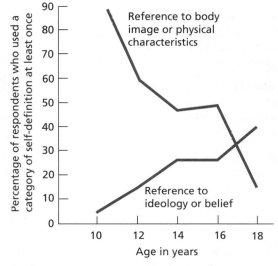

**FIGURE 10.2**  Age-Related Change in Self-Definitions As they get older, children and adolescents define themselves less by what they look like and more by what they believe or feel.

(*Source:* Montemayor & Eisen, 1977, from Table 1, p. 316. 'The development of self-conceptions from childhood to adolescence.' *Developmental Psychology, 13*, 314–319.)

*If you asked them to define themselves, these teenagers would surely give much more abstract and comparative answers than you would hear from a 6-year-old.*

**identity versus role confusion** As hypothesized by Erikson, the psychosocial stage in which a teen must develop a sense of personal identity or else enter adulthood with a sense of confusion about his or her place in the world.

**identity achievement** One of four identity statuses proposed by Marcia, involving the successful resolution of an identity "crisis" and resulting in a new commitment.

**moratorium** One of four identity statuses proposed by Marcia, involving an ongoing reexamination of identity but no new commitment.

**foreclosure** One of four identity statuses proposed by Marcia, involving an ideological or occupational commitment without a previous reevaluation.

**identity diffusion** One of four identity statuses proposed by Marcia, involving neither a current reevaluation of identity nor a firm personal commitment.

and study, behaviors that increases their chances of academic success. The outcomes they experience as a result of these behaviors further strengthen their academic self-concepts.

Adolescents' academic self-concepts seem to come both from internal comparisons of their performance to a self-generated ideal and from external comparisons to peer performance (Bouchey & Harter, 2005). It also appears that perceived competency in one domain affects how a teen feels about his ability in other areas. For example, if a high school student fails a math course, it is likely to affect his self-concept in other disciplines besides math. This suggests that teens' self-concepts are hierarchical in nature. Perceived competencies in various domains serve as building blocks for creating a global academic self-concept (Harter, 2006b).

**ERIKSON'S IDENTITY CRISIS** A somewhat different way to look at adolescent self-concept is through the lens of Erikson's theory. In this model, the central task (or dilemma) of adolescence is that of **identity versus role confusion**. During this stage, the adolescent's old identity will no longer suffice; a new identity must be forged, one that allows a place for the young person in each of the myriad roles of adult life—occupational roles, sexual roles, religious roles. Confusion about all these role choices is inevitable. The teen clique, or crowd, thus forms a base of security from which the young person can move toward a unique solution of the identity process. Ultimately, each teen must achieve an integrated view of himself, including his own pattern of beliefs, occupational goals, and relationships.

**MARCIA'S IDENTITY STATUSES** Nearly all the current work on the formation of adolescent identity has been based on James Marcia's descriptions of *identity statuses* (Marcia, 1966, 1980, 2010), which are rooted in but go beyond Erikson's general conception of the adolescent identity crisis. Following one of Erikson's ideas, Marcia argues that the formation of an adolescent identity has two key parts: a crisis and a commitment. By a "crisis," Marcia means a period of decision making when old values and old choices are reexamined. This may occur in a sort of upheaval (the classic notion of a crisis), or it may occur gradually. The outcome of the reevaluation is a commitment to some specific role, some particular ideology.

If you chart the two elements of crisis and commitment together, as in Figure 10.3, you can see that four different "identity statuses" are possible:

- **Identity achievement**: The young person has been through a crisis and has reached a commitment to ideological or occupational goals.
- **Moratorium**: A crisis is in progress, but no commitment has yet been made.
- **Foreclosure**: A commitment has been made without the person's having gone through a crisis. No reassessment of old positions has been made. Instead, the young person has simply accepted a parentally or culturally defined commitment.
- **Identity diffusion**: The young person is not in the midst of a crisis (although there may have been one in the past), and no commitment has been made. Diffusion may represent either an early stage in the process (before a crisis) or a failure to reach a commitment after a crisis.

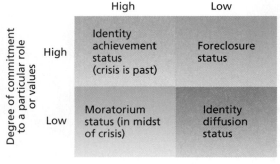

**FIGURE 10.3** Marcia's Identity Statuses
Marcia's four proposed identity statuses, based on Erikson's theory. To come to a fully achieved identity, according to this model, the young person must examine his or her values or goals and reach a firm commitment.

(*Source:* Marcia, 1980. Identity in adolescence. In J. Adelson (Ed.), Handbook of adolescent psychology (pp. 159–187). New York: Wiley.)

## Evidence for Erikson's and Marcia's Theories

Erikson's and Marcia's theories assume that some kind of identity crisis is both normal and healthy. These assumptions have not been entirely supported by the evidence. Researchers have found evidence for the beginnings of identity development in early adolescence, the so-called "tween" years (Meeus, 2011; See *Technology and the Developing Child* on page 249); however, the whole process of identity formation may occur later than Erikson thought (Kroger, 2007). In one combined analysis of eight separate cross-sectional studies, Alan Waterman (1985) found that most young people attained the identity achievement status in college, not during high school. Moreover, longitudinal research suggests that most adolescents experience a period of identity confusion before attaining any of the other statuses (Meeus, 2011). Thus, identity diffusion may be better thought of as the beginning of the identity development process than the outcome of a failed search for identity. In addition, identity statuses fluctuate during the teen years (Klimstra et al., 2010). That is, a teen who reaches Marcia's identity achieved status doesn't necessarily retain that status over time (Marcia, 2010; Meeus, 2011).

# TECHNOLOGY AND THE DEVELOPING CHILD

## Identity Play in Virtual Environments

In virtual environments such as Whyville.net, users choose from menus of physical characteristics, clothing, accessories, and the like to create avatars that represent themselves. These avatars are used to play games and chat with virtual friends, earn virtual money by working at virtual jobs, and purchase a wide variety of virtual products. Some developmentalists have wondered whether such environments might serve as *identity playgrounds* where "tweens," 8- to 12-year-olds on the brink of Erikson's identity crisis, try out different personas for the purpose of eliciting social feedback (Kafai, Fields, & Cook, 2007).

As both psychosocial and cognitive-developmental theory would predict, children's avatars change as they approach adolescence. Younger school-age children tend to create avatars that share their real-world characteristics (Subrahmanyam, 2008). By contrast, avatars created by "tweens" can vary widely from their real-world counterparts (Kafai, Fields, & Cook, 2010). When asked by researchers to explain the reasons behind the

characteristics and clothing that they choose for their avatars, tweens cite five main reasons:

- For aesthetic or artistic reasons
- To disguise their real identities
- To conform to or rebel against current trends
- To make the avatar look like their real selves
- To see how it feels to have a characteristic that they cannot have in real life (e.g., gender)

Some items in this list are consistent with the proposition that virtual environments serve as identity playgrounds for tweens. But is such behavior typical?

One factor to take into consideration is the degree to which participation in virtual environments is itself typical among tweens. Some researchers have found that only a minority of tweens use such websites to any great degree (Subrahmanyam & Greenfield, 2009). More often, tweens use the Internet to engage in chats, instant messaging, and e-mail with real-world peers. Of course, it's possible to take on false personae in these, but research suggests that online pretending of this kind is rare among

tweens (Gross, 2004). Moreover, online pretending is more often done to play pranks on others rather than as an exercise in identity exploration.

### Learning Objective 10.5a
To what extent do tweens use virtual environments to engage in identity play?

### FIND OUT MORE
*Use your Internet search skills to answer these questions.*

1. What are the similarities and differences across virtual environments that target younger children (e.g., Club Penguin, Webkinz) to those target tweens (e.g., Whyville)? To what extent, if any, are these differences suggestive of tweens' greater interest in identity development?

2. Search for studies on teen and adult self-representation in virtual environments (e.g., Second Life). How do the findings of these studies compare to the research on tweens cited here?

---

In addition, cognitive development may be more strongly related to identity formation than either Erikson or Marcia believed. Research suggests that teens who are most advanced in the development of logical thinking and other information-processing skills are also the most likely to have attained Marcia's identity achievement status (Peterson, Marcia, & Carpendale, 2004). This may help to explain why the process takes place at somewhat later ages than Erikson's and Marcia's theories predict. There is also evidence that the quest for personal identity continues throughout the lifespan, with alternating periods of instability and stability (Marcia, 2010). Consequently, adolescence may be only one such period among several.

For these reasons, both Marcia and Waterman agree that the various identity statuses do not form a clear developmental progression that all or most teens and young adults follow, even in Western cultures. Instead, the four identity statuses may more reasonably be thought of as different approaches young people may take to the task of identity formation, depending on culture as well as on the young person's individual situation (Marcia, 1993, 2010; Waterman, 1988). In this view, it is not correct to say that a young person who is in the foreclosure status has not achieved any identity. She has an identity, one she has adopted from parental or other societal rules without significant questioning.

**CULTURE AND THE IDENTITY CRISIS** The conception of an adolescent identity crisis is strongly influenced by cultural assumptions in industrialized Western societies, in which full adult status is postponed for almost a decade after puberty. In such cultures, young people do not normally or necessarily adopt the same roles or occupations as their parents. Indeed, they are encouraged to choose for themselves. In such a cultural system, adolescents are faced with what may be a bewildering array of options, a pattern that might well foster the sort of identity crisis Erikson described. As this hypothesis would predict, the proportion of study participants who fall within the identity diffusion category has increased substantially over the past 2 decades. Researchers interpret this trend as a natural consequence of contemporaneous increases in the amount of time that young people spend in college and other transitional settings, in the age at which they marry, in the age at which they have their first child, and so on (Born, 2007). Further, these studies suggest that, in the context of such dramatic historical and cultural shifts, it may be wrong to view identity diffusion as a negative developmental outcome.

**Learning Objective 10.6** - - - - - - - - - →
What is the process of ethnic identity development, according to Phinney?

# Ethnic Identity in Adolescence

Minority teens, especially those of color in a predominantly White culture, face another task in creating an identity in adolescence: They must also develop an ethnic identity, including self-identification as a member of some specific group, commitment to that group and its values and attitudes, and some evaluative attitudes (positive or negative) about the group to which they belong. Some of this self-identification occurs in middle childhood (Aboud & Doyle, 1995): 7- and 8-year-old minority children already understand the differences between themselves and majority children, and most often prefer their own subgroup.

Further steps in the ethnic identity process occur in adolescence as minority teens' general sense of identity grows (Meeus, 2011). Jean Phinney (1990, 2008; Phinney, Ferguson, & Tate, 1997; Phinney & Rosenthal, 1992) proposes that the development of a complete ethnic identity moves through three rough stages during adolescence. The first stage is an *unexamined ethnic identity*, equivalent to what Marcia calls a foreclosed status. For some subgroups in U.S. society, such as African Americans and Native Americans, this unexamined identity typically includes the negative images and stereotypes common in the wider culture. Indeed, it may be during adolescence, with the advent of the cognitive ability to reflect and interpret, that the young person becomes keenly aware of the way in which his own group is perceived by the majority.

The second stage in Phinney's model is the *ethnic identity search*, parallel to the crisis in Marcia's analysis of adolescent identity. This search is typically triggered by some experience that makes ethnicity relevant—perhaps an example of blatant prejudice or merely the wider realm of experience offered by high school. At this point, the minority teen begins to arrive at her own judgments.

This exploration stage is eventually followed by a *resolution of the conflicts and contradictions*—analogous to Marcia's status of identity achievement. This is often a difficult process, as teens become aware of what Prentice and Miller (2002) call *homegrown stereotypes*. These stereotypes involve instructions for how a group member is supposed to present herself to other members of the same group. They often include the notion that one's own beliefs are at variance with those of the group, but that certain behaviors are required when presenting oneself to the group in order to maintain their acceptance. For example, an African American teen might learn that she is supposed to behave in certain ways toward White peers in order to continue to be accepted by African American peers. Hispanic teens often report similar experiences. Some resolve this pressure by keeping their own ethnic group at arm's length. Some search for a middle ground, adopting aspects of both the majority and minority cultures, a pattern Phinney calls a "blended bicultural identity" (Phinney & Devich-Navarro, 1997). Others deal with it by creating essentially two identities (a pattern Phinney calls an "alternating bicultural identity"), as expressed by one young Hispanic teen interviewed by Phinney:

> *Being invited to someone's house, I have to change my ways of how I act at home, because of culture differences. I would have to follow what they do. . . . I am used to it now, switching off between the two. It is not difficult. (Phinney & Rosenthal, 1992, p. 160)*

*In addition to establishing a sense of personal identity, minority teens must also develop an ethnic identity. Some resolve this developmental task by creating a bicultural identity for themselves, one that allows them to interact comfortably with members of the majority group, individuals who belong to other minority groups, and members of their own group.*

*Cultures determine the kinds of behaviors that signify the transition from childhood to adulthood. For example, European American families might consider teens' quest for independence to be a sign of normal, healthy development. By contrast, to Asian American parents, increased willingness to fulfill family obligations, such as helping a younger sibling with homework, would be considered a more appropriate way for teens to express their growing understanding of the adult roles they will shortly assume.*

Still others resolve the dilemma by wholeheartedly choosing their own racial or ethnic group's patterns and values, even when that choice may limit their access to the larger culture.

In both cross-sectional and longitudinal studies, Phinney has found that African American teens and young adults do indeed move through these steps or stages toward a clear ethnic identity. Furthermore, there is evidence that African American, Asian American, and Mexican American teens and college students who have reached the second or third stage in this process—those who are searching for or who have reached a clear identity—have higher self-esteem and better psychological adjustment than do those who are still in the "unexamined" stage (Phinney, 1990). In contrast, among Caucasian American students, ethnic identity has essentially no relationship to self-esteem or adjustment.

Further, Phinney has found that ethnic identity seems to provide African American teens with an important protective factor. For one thing, those who possess a strong sense of ethnic identity get better grades than peers who do not (Oyserman, Harrison, & Bybee, 2001). The "bicultural" pattern of Phinney's last stage has been found to be a consistent characteristic of adolescents and adults who have high self-esteem and enjoy good relations with members of both the dominant culture and their own ethnic group (Berry & Sabatier, 2010; Phinney, 2008; Farver, Bhadha, & Narang, 2002; ). African American teens are also more likely than Asian American and Caucasian American youths to choose friends whose ethnic identity statuses are the same as their own (Hamm, 2000). As the discussion in *Developmental Science in the Real World* indicates, such research has led some developmentalists to propose programs aimed at helping African American teens acquire a strong sense of ethnic identity (Phinney, Kim-Jo, Osorio, & Vilhjalmsdottir, 2005).

## DEVELOPMENTAL SCIENCE IN THE REAL WORLD

### Adolescent Rites of Passage

An expression of intense concentration appeared on 13-year-old Aisha's face as she stood before a mirror, wrapping a brightly colored cloth around her head. She had learned the art of Gele head wrapping just a few hours earlier and wanted to demonstrate it for her mother and younger sister. Head wrapping is just one of many traditional African skills Aisha has learned in the rites of passage program she is attending at a local community college. The purpose of the program, one of hundreds across the United States, is to help Aisha and other African American teens develop a sense of ethnic identity.

Many developmentalists argue that the fuzziness of the adolescent-to-adult

transition in U.S. culture is more problematic for African American teens than for other American teens. They point out that other minority groups practice rites of passage that connect their young people with a centuries-long cultural heritage—such as the Jewish *bar mitzvah* and *bat mitzvah* and the *quinceañera* for young Hispanic girls. By contrast, the institution of slavery separated African Americans from the traditions of their ancestors.

Consequently, many African American churches and other institutions have devised formal initiation rites preceded by a period of instruction in traditional African cultural values and practices, typically called *rites of passage programs*. The goal of such programs is to enhance African American teens' sense of ethnic identity and self-esteem, thereby making them less vulnerable to institutional racism as well as drug abuse, pregnancy, and other risks associated with adolescence (Alford, 2007; Harvey & Rauch, 1997; Warfield-Coppock, 1997).

Research indicates that rites of passage programs can make a difference (Harvey & Hill, 2004). After participating in one such program, boys and girls in the fifth and sixth grades showed a number of positive effects (Cherry et al., 1998). They exhibited higher self-esteem, a stronger sense of racial identity, a lower incidence of school behavior

problems, and greater knowledge of African culture.

The experiences of many African American youth in rites of passage programs suggest that there may be some real advantage to providing teens with formal instruction and initiation into adult roles. What many see as a vestige of a bygone era may actually serve a very important function in adolescent identity development.

#### Learning Objective 10.6a
What role do rites of passage play in the development of ethnic identity?

#### REFLECTION

1. Rites of passage programs include three separate components that may explain their positive effects on teens: contact with adults, contact with peers, and information about ethnicity. Which factor do you think is most important and why?
2. When you were a teen, did you participate in any formal rites of passage, such as a confirmation, *bar mitzvah*, or *quinceañera*? If so, what effect did it have on you? If not, in what way do you think such a program might have been helpful to you?

**CULTURE AND ETHNIC IDENTITY DEVELOPMENT**   Of course, the search for identity is affected by cultural norms. It is likely that parent-teen conflict is common and even socially acceptable in North American and European families because these individualistic cultures associate separation from parents with psychological and social maturity. As a result, parents in North America and Europe expect to experience these conflicts and endorse adolescents' efforts to demonstrate independence. For example, many American parents think that part-time jobs help teens mature. Thus, if an American parent prohibits a teen from getting a job, but the adolescent presents a good argument as to why he should be allowed to work, the conflict is seen as a sign of maturity. In contrast, cultures that emphasize the community rather than the individual view teens' acceptance of family responsibilities as a sign of maturity. An issue such as whether a teen should get a job is decided in terms of family needs. If the family needs money, the adolescent might be encouraged to work. However, if the family needs the teen to care for younger siblings while the parents work, then a part-time job will be forbidden. If the teen argues about the parents' decision, the conflict is seen as representing immaturity rather than maturity.

Research involving Asian American teens helps to illustrate this point. Psychologists have found that first-generation Asian American teens often feel guilty about responding to the individualistic pressures of North American culture. Their feelings of guilt appear to be based on their parents' cultural norms, which suggest that the most mature adolescents are those who take a greater role in the family rather than try to separate from it (Chen, 1999). Thus, for many Asian American adolescents, achievement of personal and ethnic identity involves balancing the individualistic demands of North American culture against the familial obligations of their parents' cultures (Kiang, Harter, & Whitesell, 2007; Mio, 2010).

Phinney's stage model is a useful general description of the process of ethnic identity formation, but as research involving Asian American teens demonstrates, the details and content of ethnic identity differ markedly from one subgroup to another. Further, those groups that encounter more overt prejudice will have a different set of experiences and challenges than will those who may be more easily assimilated (Quintana, 2007); those whose own ethnic culture espouses values that are close to those of the dominant culture will have less difficulty resolving the contradictions than will those whose subculture is at greater variance with the majority. Whatever the specifics, young people of color and those from clearly defined ethnic groups have an important additional identity task in their adolescent years.

## Self-Esteem

Our discussion thus far has treated self-concept as if there were no values attached to the categories by which we define ourselves. Yet clearly one's self-concept contains an evaluative aspect, usually called *self-esteem*. Note, for example, the differences in tone in the answers to the "Who am I?" question quoted earlier in the chapter. The 9-year-old makes a lot of positive statements about himself, whereas the two older respondents offer more mixed evaluations.

**Learning Objective 10.7** - - - - - - - - - →
How does self-esteem develop?

## The Development of Self-Esteem

Over the years of elementary school and high school, children's evaluations of their own abilities become increasingly differentiated, with quite separate judgments about skills in academics or athletics, physical appearance, peer social acceptance, friendships, romantic appeal, and relationships with parents (Harter, 2006b). A consistent feature of self-competence judgments across domains is that they become less positive as children get older. The declines may be based on children's experiences. For example, social self-esteem, the assessment of one's own social skills, is higher in popular children than in those who are rejected by their peers (Jackson & Bracken, 1998).

Another striking feature of self-competence judgments is that they differ for boys and girls. Developmentalists believe that these differences are influenced both by cultural expectations and by children's own experiences. To fully understand this sex difference, it's important to understand that each component of self-esteem is valued differently by different children.

Initially, the standards and beliefs of the larger culture influence these values, so almost all young boys rate themselves as competent in sports, because they know that the culture values sports achievement in males. However, over time, children come to value domains in which they experience real achievements. So, as children get older, both boys and girls who view themselves as highly competent in sports, because of their own actual successes, also value sports achievement very highly (Jacobs et al., 2002). And lack of demonstrated skill in sports leads to a decline in the value placed on sports achievement among children of both genders.

As children develop domain-specific self-competence judgments, they also create for themselves a global self-evaluation that stands alongside these self-judgments. It is this global evaluation of one's own worth that is usually referred to as **self-esteem**. However, self-esteem is not merely the sum of all the separate assessments the child makes about his skills in different areas.

Instead, as Susan Harter's extremely interesting research on self-esteem reveals, each child's level of self-esteem is a product of two internal assessments (Harter, 1987, 1990, 1999). First, each child experiences some degree of discrepancy between what he would like to be and what he thinks he is—a gap between his ideal self and what he perceives to be his real self (Harter, 2006a). When that discrepancy is small, the child's self-esteem is generally high. When the discrepancy is large—when the child sees himself as failing to live up to his own goals or values—self-esteem is much lower. The standards are not the same for every child. Some value academic skills highly; others value sports skills or having good friends. The key to self-esteem, Harter proposes, is the amount of discrepancy between what the child desires and what the child thinks he has achieved. Thus, being good at something—singing, playing chess, or being able to talk to one's parents—won't raise a child's self-esteem unless the child values that particular skill.

Another major influence on a child's self-esteem, according to Harter, is the over-all sense of support the child feels from the important people around her, particularly parents, peers, and adult mentors (DuBois et al., 2002; Franco & Levitt, 1998; Ahrens, DuBois, Lozano, & Richardson, 2010). Both these factors are clear in the results of Harter's own research. She asked third-, fourth-, fifth-, and sixth-graders how important it was to them to do well in each of five domains and how well they thought they actually did in each. The total discrepancy between these sets of judgments made up the discrepancy score. (A high discrepancy score indicates that the child reported that she was not doing well in areas that mattered to her.) The social support score was based on children's replies to a set of questions about whether they

**self-esteem** A global evaluation of one's own worth; an aspect of self-concept.

*Playing ball with dad is a classic father-daughter activity in American culture. One of the side effects is likely to be that the daughter comes to believe that her father values skill in playing ball.*

thought others (parents and peers) liked them as they were, treated them as a person, or felt that they were important. The findings for the fifth- and sixth-graders were virtually identical, and both sets of results strongly supported Harter's hypothesis, as does other research, including studies of African American youth (DuBois, Felner, Brand, Phillips, & Lease, 1996; Luster & McAdoo, 1995): A low discrepancy score alone does not protect the child completely from low self-esteem if she lacks sufficient social support. And a loving and accepting family and peer group do not guarantee high self-esteem if the youngster does not feel she is living up to her own standards.

A particularly risky combination occurs when the child perceives that parental support is contingent on good performance in some area—getting good grades, making the first-string football team, being chosen to play the solo with the school orchestra, being popular with classmates. If the child does not measure up to the standard, he experiences both an increased discrepancy between ideal and achievement and a loss of support from the parents.

If we accept Harter's model and assume that self-esteem is a product of a person's comparison of her desired or valued qualities with her actual qualities, we still have to ask where each child's values and self-judgments come from. First, of course, a child's own direct experience with success or failure in various arenas plays an obvious role. Second, the value a child attaches to some skill or quality is obviously affected fairly directly by peers' and parents' attitudes and values. Peer standards (and general cultural standards) for appearance establish benchmarks for all children and teens. A child who is "too tall" or "too fat" or who deviates in some other way from the accepted norms is likely to feel a sense of inadequacy. Similarly, the degree of emphasis parents place on the child's performing well in some domain—whether schoolwork, athletics, or playing chess—is an important element in forming the child's aspirations in each area.

**Learning Objective 10.8**
How consistent is self-esteem across childhood and adolescence?

## Consistency of Self-Esteem over Time

A number of longitudinal studies of elementary school children and teens show that self-esteem is moderately stable in the short term but somewhat less so over periods of several years. The correlation between two self-esteem scores obtained a few months apart is generally about .60. Over several years, this correlation drops to something more like .40 (Alsaker & Olweus, 2002). So while it is true that a child with high self-esteem at age 8 or 9 is likely to have high self-esteem at age 10 or 11, it is also true that there is a good deal of variation around that stability.

Self-esteem seems to be particularly unstable in the years of early adolescence, especially at the time of the shift from elementary school to junior high school (Seidman & French, 2004). On average, self-esteem tends to rise in the later teen years (Harter, 2006a). However, both the decline in average self-esteem in the early teen years and the average increase that follows can obscure important individual differences (Harter & Whitesell, 2003). For example, adolescents with learning disabilities experience a great deal more instability in self-esteem than teens without learning disabilities do (Zhou & Liu, 2010).

Harter and others have found that a child who has low self-esteem is more likely than are her high self-esteem peers to have depression in both middle childhood and adolescence, especially when she also exhibits high levels of neuroticism (Harter, 1987; Renouf & Harter, 1990). Bear in mind, though, that this is correlational evidence. These findings don't prove that there is a causal connection between low self-esteem and depression. They only indicate that the two tend to go together.

## The Development of the Concepts of Gender and Sex Roles

As noted at the beginning of this chapter, biological sex and psychological gender are integral components of each individual's sense of self. Thus, in this final section, we turn our attention to the process through which sex and gender become woven into each child's self-concept. We begin by examining how children come to understand several important concepts that are associated with sex and gender.

# Developmental Patterns

←----------- **Learning Objective 10.9**
How do ideas about gender and sex roles change across childhood?

Those of us who want to understand ourselves—and developmentalists who may wish to advise parents about child-rearing—need to know more about the ways in which children learn about gender and sex roles.

**WHAT MUST BE LEARNED**   Acquiring an understanding of sex roles involves several related tasks. On the cognitive side, a child must learn the nature of the sex/gender category itself—that *boyness* or *girlness* is permanent, unchanged by such things as modifications in clothing or hair length. This understanding is usually called the **gender concept**. On the social side, the child has to learn what behaviors go with being a boy or a girl. That is, the child must learn the **sex role** (sometimes called the *gender role*) defined as appropriate for his or her gender in the particular culture.

All roles involve sets of expected behaviors, attitudes, rights, duties, and obligations. Teachers are supposed to behave in certain ways, as are employees, mothers, or baseball managers—all roles in our culture. Gender roles are somewhat broader than most other roles, but they are nonetheless roles—sets of expected behaviors, attitudes, rights, duties, and obligations involved in filling the role of "girl," "woman," "boy," or "man." Put another way, a gender role is a "job description" for being a male or a female in a given culture.

**Sex-typed behavior** is behavior exhibited by a child or an adult that matches culturally defined gender-role expectations for that person's gender (see *Thinking about Research* on page 256). A girl may know quite well that she is a girl and be able to describe the cultural sex roles for girls accurately but may still behave in a tomboyish way. Such a girl's sex-role behavior is less sex-typed than the behavior of a girl who adopts more traditional behavior patterns.

**THE GENDER CONCEPT**   Infants as young as 3 months of age distinguish between photos of male and female infants (Shirley & Campbell, 2000). As you'll read later, by as early as 18 months of age, children prefer playmates of the same sex. By 4, children can readily identify the gender of a speaker of their own age on the basis of vowel sounds in speech patterns (Perry, Ohde, & Ashmead, 2001).

Research suggests that the process of gender self-categorization is linked to cognitive development (Trautner, Gervai, & Nemeth, 2003). In other words, a child's understanding of gender progresses along with his or her general understanding of the world. Moreover, like general cognitive development, understanding of gender appears to involve a universal sequence of stages (Martin & Ruble, 2010).

The first stage is **gender identity**, which is simply a child's ability to label his own sex correctly and to identify other people as men or women, boys or girls. By 9 to 12 months, babies already treat male and female faces as if they were different categories, apparently using hair length as the primary differentiating clue (Ruble, Martin, & Berenbaum, 2006). Within the next year, they begin to learn the verbal labels that go with these different categories. By age 2, if you show children a set of pictures of a same-sex child and several opposite-sex children and ask "Which one is you?" most children can correctly pick out the same-sex picture (Thompson, 1975). Between ages 2 and 3, children learn to identify and label others correctly by sex, such as by pointing out "which one is a girl" or "which one is a boy" in a set of pictures (Ruble, Martin, & Berenbaum, 2006). Hair length and clothing seem to be especially important cues in these early discriminations. ◉▐Watch at **MyDevelopmentLab**

Next comes **gender stability**, the understanding that people stay the same gender throughout life. Researchers have measured this understanding by asking children such questions as "When you were a little baby, were you a little girl or a little boy?" or "When you grow up, will you be a mommy or a daddy?" Slaby and Frey, in their classic study (1975), found that most children understand this aspect of gender by about age 4, as Figure 10.4 on page 256 suggests.

*This mother is not only helping her daughter shop for clothes, she may also be transmitting information about sex roles and reinforcing traditional sex typing.*

◉▐**Watch** the **Video** *Understanding Self and Others* at **MyDevelopmentLab**

**gender concept**   The full understanding that gender is constant and permanent, unchanged by appearance.

**sex role**   The set of behaviors, attitudes, rights, duties, and obligations that are seen as appropriate for being male or female in any given culture.

**sex-typed behavior**   Behavior that matches a culturally defined sex role.

**gender identity**   The first stage in the development of gender concept, in which a child labels self and others correctly as male or female.

**gender stability**   The second stage in the development of gender concept, in which the child understands that a person's gender stays the same throughout life.

## Gender Differences in Temperament: Real or Imagined?

What kinds of temperamental differences come to mind when you think about boys and girls? You may think of boys as more irritable and girls as more fearful. But are these differences real, or are they simply stereotypes? In some studies, researchers have found that boys are more emotionally intense and less fearful than girls and that girls are generally more sociable (Calkins, Dedmon, Gill, Lomax, & Johnson, 2002; Gartstein & Rothbart, 2003). Nevertheless, temperamental differences between boys and girls are much smaller than the differences perceived by parents and other adults.

In one classic study, researchers found that adults viewing a videotape of an infant interpreted the baby's behavior differently depending on the gender label experimenters provided. Participants who were told the baby was a girl interpreted a particular behavior as expressing fear. Amazingly, participants who believed the infant was a boy labeled the same behavior anger (Condry & Condry, 1976).

Research on another dimension of temperament, emotionality, provides further examples of how perceived differences in temperament may affect parental responses to children's behavior. Most studies have

found that, even in infancy, girls are more responsive to others' facial expressions (McClure, 2000). This difference often leads to the perception that girls are more emotionally sensitive. However, studies of actual behavior reveal that boys are just as affectionate and empathetic as girls during infancy (Melson, Peet, & Sparks, 1991; Zahn-Waxler, Radke-Yarrow, Wagner, & Chapman, 1992).

Temperamental stereotyping may affect the quality of the parent-infant relationship. For example, parents of a calm, quiet girl may respond positively to her because they perceive her behavior to be consistent with their concept of "girlness." In contrast, parents of a physically active girl may develop a rejecting, disapproving attitude toward her because they view her behavior as excessively masculine. As a result of these judgments, parents may behave more affectionately toward a girl whom they perceive to be feminine than they do toward a daughter whom they view as masculine.

You should recognize these issues as yet another example of the nature-nurture debate. As you learned in Chapter 9, individual differences in temperament are inborn. Yet it is also clear that parents treat boys and

girls differently beginning very early in infancy. Thus, as children get older, gender differences in temperament are likely to be the result of both their inborn characteristics and the gender-based expectations and response patterns exhibited by their parents.

### Learning Objective 10.9a
What does research say about gender differences in temperament?

### CRITICAL ANALYSIS

1. In what ways might stereotypes influence the methods that researchers use to study gender differences in temperament?

2. How do differences between men and women, which have evolved over many years, contribute to expectations about how male and female infants differ in temperament? In other words, in your view, do adults engage in what might be called backward generalization from adults to infants with regard to their opinions about the existence of gender differences early in life?

---

**FIGURE 10.4** Early Sex-Role Stereotypes
In describing this self-portrait, the 5-year-old artist said, "This is how I will look when I get married to a boy. I am under a rainbow, so beautiful with a bride hat, a belt, and a purse." The girl knows she will always be female and associates gender with externals such as clothing (gender stability). She is also already quite knowledgeable about gender role expectations.
(*Source:* Author.)

The final stage in development of a gender concept, usually referred to as **gender constancy**, is the understanding that someone's biological sex stays the same even though he may appear to change by wearing different clothes or changing his hair length. For example, boys don't change into girls by wearing dresses. This is an appearance/reality problem very much like Flavell's sponge/rock test described in Chapter 6. The child must figure out that although a boy wearing a dress may look like a girl, he is really still a boy, just as the sponge painted to look like a rock may look like a rock but is really still a sponge. When children are asked the gender constancy question in this way, many 4-year-olds and most 5-year-olds can answer correctly, just as 4- and 5-year-olds understand other appearance/reality distinctions (Martin & Ruble, 2004). Sandra Bem has found that to reach this level of understanding, a child must have at least some grasp of the basic genital differences between boys and girls and some understanding that genital characteristics are what make a child "really" a boy or a girl. In her study, 4-year-olds who did not yet understand genital differences also did not show gender constancy (Bem, 1989). In sum, children as young as 2 or 3 know their own sex and that of people around them, but children do not have a fully developed concept of gender until they are 5 or 6. ◉ Watch at **MyDevelopmentLab**

◉ **Watch** the **Video** *Gender Constancy* at **MyDevelopmentLab**

**gender constancy** The final stage in development of gender concept, in which the child understands that gender doesn't change even though there may be external changes (in clothing or hair length, for example).

## Sex-Role Concepts and Stereotypes

◄ ‑ ‑ ‑ ‑ ‑ ‑ ‑ ‑ ‑ ‑ ‑ ‑ **Learning Objective 10.10**
What is the connection between gender stereotypes and sex-typed behavior?

Obviously, figuring out your gender and understanding that it stays constant is only part of the story. Learning what goes with, or ought to go with, being a boy or a girl is also a vital part of the child's task.

**SEX-ROLE STEREOTYPES**   Studies of children show that stereotyped ideas about sex roles develop early, even in families that espouse gender equality (Lippa, 2005). Even 2-year-olds already associate certain tasks and possessions with men and women, such as vacuum cleaners and food with women and cars and tools with men. By age 3 or 4, children can assign stereotypic occupations, toys, and activities to each gender (Ruble, Martin, & Berenbaum, 2006). By age 5, children begin to associate certain personality traits with males or females, and such knowledge is well developed by age 8 or 9 (Parmley & Cunningham, 2008).

Studies of children's ideas about how men and women (or boys and girls) ought to behave add an interesting further refinement to what developmentalists know about sex-role stereotypes, and an early study by William Damon (1977) illustrates this element particularly nicely. Damon told children aged 4 through 9 a story about a little boy named George who likes to play with dolls. George's parents tell him that only little girls play with dolls; little boys shouldn't. The children were then asked a batch of questions about the story, such as "Why do people tell George not to play with dolls?" or "Is there a rule that boys shouldn't play with dolls?" Four-year-olds in this study thought it was okay for George to play with dolls. There was no rule against it, and he should do it if he wanted to. Six-year-olds, in contrast, thought it was wrong for George to play with dolls. By about age 9, children had differentiated between what boys and girls usually do and what is "wrong." One boy said, for example, that breaking windows was wrong and bad, but that playing with dolls was not bad in the same way: "Breaking windows you're not supposed to do. And if you play with dolls, well you can, but boys usually don't."

Interestingly, more recent studies show that twenty-first century children express ideas about gender-typed behavior that are quite similar to those of their 1970s counterparts (Gee & Heyman, 2007; Gelman et al., 2004). These studies suggest that the 5- or 6-year-old, having figured out that she is permanently a girl or he is a boy, is searching for a rule about how boys and girls behave (Martin & Ruble, 2004). The child picks up information from watching adults, from watching television, from hearing evaluations of different activities (e.g., "Boys don't play with Barbies"). Initially they treat these as absolute, moral rules. Later they understand that these are social conventions, at which point sex-role concepts become more flexible (Martin & Ruble, 2004) (see Figure 10.5 on page 258).

In a similar way, many kinds of fixed, biased ideas about other people—such as biases against obese children, against those who speak another language, or against those of other races—are at their peak in the early school years and then decline throughout the remaining years of childhood and into adolescence (Martin & Ruble, 2010). Another way to put it is that children of 5 to 7 years of age have a strong sense of "us" versus "them," of in-group versus out-group. They classify other children as "like me" or "not like me" on some dimension, and they develop strong preferences for those who are like themselves and highly stereotyped (often negative) ideas about those who are not like themselves (Bennett & Sani, 2008a).

This entire stereotyping process seems to be totally normal, part of the child's attempt to create rules and order, to find patterns that can guide his understanding and his behavior. In fact, children's beliefs about the degree to which they "fit in" with peers of the same sex may be an important component of healthy psychological adjustment during the elementary school years (Egan & Perry, 2001). Thus, just as an English-speaking 2- or 3-year-old discovers the rule about adding -ed to a verb to make the past tense and then overgeneralizes that rule, so the 6- or 7-year-old discovers the "rules" about boys and girls, men

*Four-year-olds and 9-year-olds think it is okay for a boy to play with dolls, but many 6-year-olds think it is simply wrong for boys to do girl things or for girls to do boy things.*

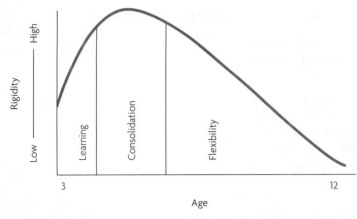

**FIGURE 10.5** Age-Related Change in Gender Stereotypes
As children learn about and consolidate their knowledge of gender-related phenomena, their stereotypes become more rigid. Once they have a better understanding of gender, their stereotypes become more flexible.

(*Source:* From Martin, C., Ruble, D. (2004), Children's search for gender cues: Cognitive perspectives on gender development, *Current Directions in Psychological Science,* 13, 67–70, fig. 1, p. 69.)

and women, "us" and "them," and overgeneralizes. In fact, most 6- and 7-year-olds believe that gender-role differences are built-in along with biological gender differences. By age 9, they understand that at least some differences in behavior between boys and girls are the result of training or experience (Taylor, 1996).

**SEX-ROLE STEREOTYPES ACROSS CULTURES** The content of sex-role stereotypes is remarkably similar in cultures around the world. John Williams and Deborah Best (1990), who have studied adults' gender stereotypes in 28 different countries and children's gender stereotypes in 24 countries, find that the most strongly stereotyped traits are weakness, gentleness, appreciativeness, and softheartedness for women and aggression, adventurousness, cruelty, and coarseness for men. There are a few differences, naturally. German children, for instance, choose "adventurous," "confident," and "steady" as female items, although these are more normally male items in other cultures. Pakistani children identify "emotional" with men; Japanese children associate independence and severity with neither sex. But these are variations on a common theme. Researchers have presented children with a story in which the sex of the main character was not explicitly stated. When asked to tell whether the character was better represented by a male or a female doll, in all 24 countries, 8-year-olds chose the male figure for stories about aggression, strength, cruelty, coarseness, and loudness, and they chose the female figure for stories about weakness. In 23 of 24 countries, 8-year-olds also chose the female character for gentleness, appreciativeness, and softheartedness. Thus, not only does every culture appear to have clear sex-role stereotypes, but the content of those stereotypes is remarkably similar across cultures.

Another of the interesting revelations of cross-cultural research is that the male stereotype and sex-role concept seem to develop a bit earlier and to be stronger than the female stereotype and sex-role concept—and this is true in virtually all countries studied. Whatever the reason for this phenomenon, it is clear that in Western societies, the qualities attributed to males are more highly valued than are female traits (Broverman, Broverman, Clarkson, Rosenkrantz, & Vogel, 1970; Lippa, 2005). Research has demonstrated that children assign higher status to a job with which they are unfamiliar when it is portrayed as being done by a man than when researchers tell them the job is usually performed by a woman (Liben, Bigler, & Krogh, 2001; Martin & Ruble, 2010).

It's also important to note that children's stereotypical beliefs about men and women are probably different from their beliefs about boys and girls (Bennett & Sani, 2008b). Consequently, children do not attribute higher status to boys in the same way as they do to men. For example, psychologist Gail Heyman showed second- and third-graders pictures of unfamiliar children and told them about behaviors the children had exhibited—behaviors that could be interpreted in several different ways (Heyman, 2001). Heyman found that both boys and girls were likely to classify the behavior as "bad" or "naughty" if the pictured child was a boy. Still, despite their beliefs about the gender-based status of adult occupations and apparent stereotypical negative bias toward boys, children as young as 4 years old recognize that excluding someone from an activity strictly on the basis of gender is morally wrong (Martin & Ruble, 2010).

**SEX-ROLE BEHAVIOR** The final element in the development of a sex-role concept is the actual behavior children show with those of their own sex and of the opposite sex. The unexpected finding here is that children's behavior is sex-typed earlier than are their ideas about sex roles or stereotypes. For example, by 18 to 24 months, children begin to show some preference for sex-stereotyped toys, such as dolls for girls or trucks or building blocks for boys, which is some months before they can normally identify their own gender (Miller, Trautner, & Ruble, 2006; Thommessen & Todd, 2010).

A similar pattern exists for playmate preference. Long before age 3, girls and boys begin to show a preference for same-sex playmates and are much more sociable with playmates of the same sex—at a time when they do not yet have a concept of gender stability (Lippa, 2005;

Maccoby, 1988, 1990; Maccoby & Jacklin, 1987). By school age, peer relationships are almost exclusively same-sex. You can see the early development of this preference in Figure 10.6, which shows the results of a seminal study of preschool play groups. The researchers counted how often children played with same-sex or opposite-sex playmates (La Freniere, Strayer, & Gauthier, 1984). You can see that by age 3, over 60% of play groups were same-sex groupings, and the rate rose for older children. Not only are preschoolers' friendships and peer interactions increasingly sex-segregated, it is also becoming clear that boy-boy interactions and girl-girl interactions differ in quality, even in these early years. One important part of same-sex interactions seems to involve instruction and modeling of sex-appropriate behavior. In other words, older boys teach younger boys how to be "masculine," and older girls teach younger girls how to be "feminine" (Danby & Baker, 1998).

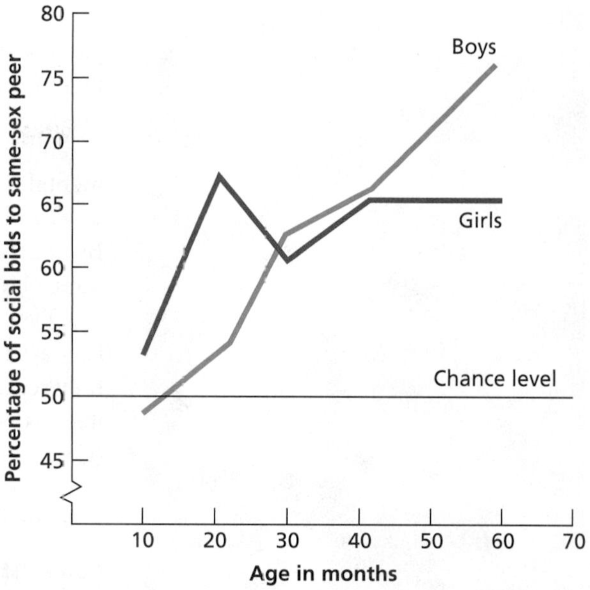

**SEX ROLES AND ADOLESCENT IDENTITY DEVELOPMENT** By the mid-teens, most adolescents have largely abandoned the automatic assumption that whatever their own gender does is better or preferable (Powlishta et al., 1994). However, increased flexibility may mean that teens experience more anxiety about how they should or should not behave, since cultural stereotypes are no longer seen as rigid dictates that must be followed. Because teens are actively searching for ways to incorporate gender into their own identities, parental attitudes as well as behavior become increasingly important in shaping teens' ideas about gender and sex roles (Castellino, Lerner, Lerner, & von Eye, 1998; Cunningham 2001; Ex & Janssens, 1998; Jackson & Tein, 1998; Raffaelli & Ontai, 2004).

**FIGURE 10.6** La Freniere's Classic Study of Playmate Preference
Same-sex playmate preference among preschoolers.

(*Source:* P. La Freniere, F. Strayer, and R. Gauthier, "The emergence of same-sex affiliative preference among pre-school peers: A developmental/ethological perspective," *Child Development*, 55. Society for Research in Child Development (1984): p. 1961, Fig. 1.)

# Explaining Sex-Role Development

‹- - - - - - - - - - - **Learning Objective 10.11**
How do social learning, cognitive-developmental, and gender schema theories explain sex-role development?

Theorists from most of the major traditions have tried their hand at explaining these patterns of sex-role development. Freud relied on the concept of identification to explain the child's adoption of appropriate sex-role behavior, but his theory founders on the fact that children begin to show clearly sex-typed behavior long before age 4 or 5, when Freud thought identification occurred.

**SOCIAL LEARNING THEORY** Social learning theorists, such as Albert Bandura (1977) and Walter Mischel (1966, 1970; Bandura & Bussey, 2004), have naturally emphasized the role of both direct reinforcement and modeling in shaping children's sex-role behavior and attitudes, as well as the availability of stereotypical sex-role models in the various media to which children are exposed. This approach has been far better supported by research than have Freud's ideas.

Social learning theorists point out that children are exposed to sex-role stereotypes in entertainment media. For example, gender stereotypes are particularly evident in young children's coloring books (Fitzpatrick & McPherson, 2010). Social learning theorists also point out that parents reinforce sex-typed activities in children as young as 18 months old, not only by buying different kinds of toys for boys and girls, but by responding more positively when their sons play with blocks or trucks or when their daughters play with dolls (Bussey & Bandura, 2004). Some evidence also suggests that toddlers whose parents are more consistent in rewarding sex-typed toy choice or play behavior, and whose mothers favor traditional family sex roles, learn accurate gender labels earlier than do toddlers whose parents are less focused on the gender-appropriateness of the child's play (Fagot & Leinbach, 1989; Fagot, Leinbach, & O'Boyle, 1992)—findings clearly consistent with the predictions of social learning theory.

Similarly, parents of school-age children are often guided by gender stereotypes when they select leisure-time activities for their children. For instance, parents more strongly encourage boys to participate in sports and in computer-based activities than they do girls (Fredricks & Eccles, 2005; Simpkins, Davis-Kean, & Eccles, 2005). They do so because of their beliefs about gender differences in various abilities. Research shows that, over time, children's own views about gender differences in athletic talent come into line with those of their parents and influence their activity preferences.

Social learning theorists argue that little boys prefer to play with trucks because parents buy them more trucks and reinforce them directly for such play.

**gender schema theory** A theory of the development of gender concept and sex-role behavior that proposes that, between about 18 months and age 2 or 3, a child creates a fundamental schema by which to categorize people, objects, activities, and qualities by gender.

Still, helpful as it is, a social learning explanation is probably not sufficient. In particular, parents differentially reinforce "boy" versus "girl" behavior less than you'd expect, and probably not enough to account for the very early and robust discrimination children seem to make on the basis of gender (Fagot, 1995; Gauvain, Fagot, Leve, & Kavanagh, 2002). Moreover, parents' reinforcement of gender-typed behavior is far from consistent (Power, 2000). Experimental studies have shown that parents neither encourage girls to engage in stereotypically female play behaviors nor discourage them from engaging in stereotypically male activities. By contrast, fathers, but not mothers, take more interest in the gender-appropriateness of boys' play behaviors. For the most part, though, parents treat boys and girls similarly.

Even children whose parents seem to treat their young sons and daughters in highly similar ways nonetheless learn gender labels and show same-sex playmate choices. Moreover, once they reach adulthood, the gender-related behavior of the large majority of girls who exhibited male-stereotypical behavior in childhood is indistinguishable from that of other women (Carr, 2007), despite the relative lack of discouragement girls experience when they exhibit tomboyish behavior. So, there seems to be something more to sex-role development than modeling and reinforcement.

**COGNITIVE-DEVELOPMENTAL THEORIES**   A second alternative, based strongly on Piagetian theory, is Lawrence Kohlberg's suggestion that the crucial aspect of the process of sex-role development is the child's understanding of the gender concept (1966; Kohlberg & Ullian, 1974). Once the child realizes that he is a boy or she is a girl forever, he or she becomes highly motivated to learn to behave in the way that is expected or appropriate for that gender. Specifically, Kohlberg predicted that systematic same-sex imitation should become evident only after the child has shown a full understanding of gender constancy. Most studies designed to test this hypothesis have supported Kohlberg: Children do seem to become much more sensitive to same-sex models after they understand gender constancy (Martin & Ruble, 2004). What Kohlberg's theory cannot easily explain, however, is the obvious fact that children show clearly differentiated sex-role behavior, such as toy preferences, long before they have achieved full understanding of the gender concept.

**GENDER SCHEMA THEORY**   The most fruitful current explanation of sex-role development is usually called **gender schema theory** (Bem, 1981; Martin, 1991; Martin & Halverson, 1981;

Social attitudes toward "tomboys," as these young female hockey players might be labeled, have changed a great deal in recent decades. As a result, girls are often encouraged to take up traditionally male activities. By contrast, boys who express interest in traditionally female activities, such as ballet, are still discouraged from participating in them.

Martin & Ruble, 2004), a model that has its roots in information-processing theories of cognitive development as well as in Kohlberg's theory. Just as the self-concept can be thought of as a "self-scheme" or "self-theory," so the child's understanding of gender can be seen in the same way. The gender schema begins to develop at about 18 months, once the child notices the differences between male and female, knows his own gender, and can label the two groups with some consistency; the gender schema is generally fully developed by age 2 or 3.

Why would children notice gender so early? Why is it such a significant characteristic? One possibility, suggested by Maccoby (1988), is that because gender is clearly an either/or category, children seem to understand very early that this is a key distinction. Thus, the category serves as a kind of magnet for new information. Another alternative is that young children pay a lot of attention to gender differences because their environment provides so many gender references. Adults and other children emphasize gender distinctions in innumerable small ways. The first question we ask about a new baby is "Is it a boy or a girl?" We buy blue baby clothes for boys and pink for girls; we ask toddlers whether their playmates are boys or girls. A preschool teacher emphasizes gender if she says "Good morning, boys and girls" or divides her charges into a boys' team and a girls' team (Bigler, 1995). In all these ways, adults signal to children that this is an important category and thus further the very early development of a gender scheme that matches cultural norms and beliefs. Whatever the origin of this early scheme, once it is established, a great many experiences are assimilated to it, and children may begin to show preferences for same-sex playmates or for gender-stereotyped activities (Martin, Ruble, & Berenbaum, 2006).

The key difference between gender-schema theory and Kohlberg's cognitive-developmental theory is that for the initial gender schema to be formed, children need not understand that gender is permanent. When they come to understand gender constancy at about 5 or 6, children develop a more elaborated rule, or schema, about "what people who are like me do" and they treat this "rule" the same way they treat other rules—as absolute. By early adolescence, teens understand that sex-role concepts are social conventions, and not rigid rules (Katz & Ksansnak, 1994). Indeed, a significant minority of teens and youths begin to define themselves as having both masculine and feminine traits—a point we'll return to in a moment.

Many of us, committed to the philosophical goal of equality for women, have taken the rigidity of children's early sex stereotypes ("Mommy, you can't be a psychology doctor, you have to be a psychology nurse") as evidence that there has been little progress toward gender equality. Gender schema theorists emphasize that such rule learning is absolutely normal, and so is the rigid stereotyping seen in children's ideas about sex roles between ages 5 and 8 or 9. Children are searching for order, for rules that help to make sense of their experiences. And a rule about "what men do" and "what women do" is a helpful schema for them.

**INDIVIDUAL GENDER SCHEMAS**    A different approach to the study of sex-role development can be found in research on individual gender schemas, or orientations. Researchers can ask, about any given child, adolescent, or adult, not only how closely the individual's behavior matches the sex-role stereotype, but also how the person thinks of herself or himself and gender-related qualities. In the early years of this research, the issue was usually phrased as masculinity versus femininity, and these were thought of as being on opposite ends of a single continuum. A person could be masculine or feminine but couldn't be both. Following the lead of Sandra Bem (1974) and Janet Spence and Robert Helmreich (1978), psychologists today most often conceive of masculinity and femininity as two separate dimensions, with masculinity centered around agentic/instrumental (assertive) qualities and femininity centered around expressive/communal (nurturing) qualities (Renk et al., 2006). A person can be high or low on either or both. Indeed, categorizing people as high or low on each of these two dimensions, based on each individual's self-description, yields four basic sex-role types, called masculine, feminine, androgynous, and undifferentiated—as you can see in Figure 10.7, on page 262. The masculine and feminine types are the traditional combinations in which a person sees himself or herself as high in one quality and low in the other. A **masculine** person, according to this conceptualization, is one who perceives himself or herself as having many traditional masculine qualities and few traditional feminine qualities. A **feminine** person shows the reverse pattern. In contrast, **androgynous** individuals see themselves as having both masculine and feminine traits; **undifferentiated** individuals describe themselves as lacking both kinds of traits—a group that sounds a lot like those with a "diffuse" identity in Marcia's system.

**masculine**    One of four sex-role types suggested by the work of Bem and others; a type characterized by high scores on masculinity measures and low scores on femininity measures.

**feminine**    One of four sex-role types suggested by the work of Bem and others; a type characterized by high scores on femininity measures and low scores on masculinity measures.

**androgynous**    One of four sex-role types suggested by the work of Bem and others; a type characterized by high levels of both masculine and feminine qualities.

**undifferentiated**    One of four sex-role types suggested by the work of Bem and others; a type characterized by low scores on both masculinity and femininity measures.

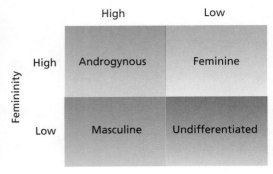

|  | High | Low |
|---|---|---|
| High | Androgynous | Feminine |
| Low | Masculine | Undifferentiated |

Femininity / Masculinity

**FIGURE 10.7** Sex-Role Orientation Categories
Thinking of masculinity and femininity as separate dimensions rather than as two ends of the same dimension leads to the creation of four sex-role types.

This categorization system says nothing about the accuracy of the child's or the adult's general sex-role schema. A teen girl, for example, could have a clear notion of the norms for male or female behavior and still perceive herself as having some stereotypically masculine qualities. In some sense, then, when developmentalists study masculinity, femininity, and androgyny, they are studying the intersection between the self-scheme and the gender scheme.

Either an androgynous or a masculine sex-role self-concept is associated with higher self-esteem among both boys and girls (Gurnáková & Kusá, 2004). This finding makes sense if we assume that there is a "masculine bias" in the United States and other Western societies, in that traditionally masculine qualities such as independence and competitiveness are more valued by both men and women than are many traditionally female qualities. If such a bias exists—and there is plenty of evidence that it does—then the teen boy's task is simpler than the teen girl's. He can achieve high self-esteem and success with his peers by adopting a traditional masculine sex role, whereas a girl who adopts a traditional feminine sex role is adopting a less valued role, with attendant risks of lower self-esteem and a reduced sense of competence (Massad, 1981; Rose & Montemayor, 1994).

Findings like these suggest the possibility that while the creation of rigid rules (or schemas) for sex roles is a normal and even essential process in young children, a blurring of those rules may be an important process in adolescence, particularly for girls, for whom a more masculine or androgynous self-concept is associated with more positive outcomes.

**Learning Objective 10.12** - - - - - - - - - ➔
In what ways might hormones influence gender-related behavior?

## Biological Approaches

The theories we have discussed so far flourished in an era when most developmentalists had turned away from the idea that hormonal differences between males and females contributed to sex-role development. Today, developmentalists are taking another look at decades-old experimental studies with animals showing that prenatal exposure to testosterone powerfully influences behavior after birth (Hines, 2010; Lippa, 2005; Zuloaga, Puts, Jordan, & Breedlove, 2008). Female animals exposed to testosterone behave more like male animals; for instance, they are more aggressive than females who do not experience prenatal exposure to testosterone. Similarly, when experimenters block the release of testosterone during prenatal development of male animal embryos, the animals exhibit behavior that is more typical of the females of their species.

Nature has provided some important evidence regarding the behavioral effects of prenatal exposure to testosterone in humans. Normally developing female embryos produce miniscule amounts of testosterone. Occasionally, however, genetic defects cause unusually large amounts of testosterone to be produced (Rosenthal & Gitelman, 2002). These defects can cause physical defects in the genitalia. In addition, girls with these conditions are more likely to exhibit stereotypically male behavior than are girls who do not have them (Lippa, 2005). Moreover, in adulthood, prenatal exposure to higher than normal levels of testosterone is associated with the likelihood that a woman will choose a typically masculine career (Sapienza, Zingales, & Maestripieri, 2009).

Hormonal influences have been proposed to explain the outcomes of cases involving sex reassignment of infants (like the one you read about at the beginning of the chapter) (Bostwick & Martin, 2007). Many sex reassignments arise from a genetic defect that causes male fetuses to develop deformed genitalia. This defect, however, interferes only with testosterone's effects on the sex organs (Rosenthal & Gitelman, 2002). The brains of these fetuses are exposed to normal amounts of testosterone throughout prenatal development. The hormonal hypothesis asserts that boys with this kind of genetic defect develop a masculine gender identity, despite being raised as girls, because their brains have been exposed prenatally to amounts of testosterone that are typical for male fetuses. As a result, like other boys, they come into the world with the tendency to look for "boy" things and to subtly incorporate such things into their developing self-concepts. According to this view, one could not reasonably expect to inculcate a sense of "femaleness" into these boys' self-concepts by raising them to believe they were girls. Moreover, research indicates that even when these individuals elect to retain the feminine identity with which they have been raised, they possess many attributes and exhibit a number of behaviors that are more typical of males than of females (Reiner & Gearhart, 2004).

Finally, note that our discussion of biological approaches has focused largely on research aimed at explaining the role played by biological factors in atypical development. It is always legitimate to question the degree to which findings based on such cases can be generalized to the more common course of development experienced by the majority of children. Although we must keep this caution in mind, research examining how variations in prenatal hormones caused by genetic defects influence behavior after birth suggests that hormones may be far more important in normal sex-role development than theorists once believed.

## THINK CRITICALLY

- The finding that children with difficult temperaments are punished more often than children with easy-going temperaments are could be interpreted several ways. What alternative explanations can you think of?
- If you were to create a mathematical model to explain gender-role development, how much weight (in percentages) would you give to each of these factors: hormones, imitation, reinforcement, models, peer influence, and cognitive development? Explain the reasons behind your weighting of the factors.

## CONDUCT YOUR OWN RESEARCH

You can replicate the classic study of Montemayor and Eisen simply by asking children and teens from 10 to 18 years of age to answer the question "Who am I?" (Remember to get parents' permission before involving children in any research project.) In each participant's response, count the number of references to physical characteristics and the number to beliefs or ideology. Plot your results on a graph like the one in Figure 10.2 on page 247. If your results differ from those of Montemayor and Eisen, try to determine what may have influenced your results. It may help to think about how the children you questioned might be different from those in the original study or how children's ideas about the self may have been influenced by historical and cultural changes in the three decades since Montemayor and Eisen's data were collected.

## SUMMARY ✓•─Study and Review at MyDevelopmentLab

### The Concept of Self

**10.1  What is the subjective self?**
The child's emerging self-concept has several elements, including the awareness of the self as separate from others and the understanding of self-permanence (which may collectively be called the subjective self). The subjective self develops in the first year of life.

**10.2  What does acquisition of an objective self add to the infant's self-concept?**
During the second year of life, the infant's self-concept expands beyond the subjective self to include an objective self, or a sense of self-awareness. As the objective self becomes better refined in early childhood, the child begins to classify herself according to easily identifiable categories such as gender ("boy" or "girl") and age ("little kids" and "big kids").

**10.3  In what way is the ability to regulate emotions related to social functioning?**
Children gain an understanding of their emotions during early childhood. The ability to regulate emotion during early childhood predicts how well children function in social settings during the school years.

**10.4  How do school-age children describe themselves?**
The self-concept becomes steadily more abstract in the elementary and high school years, coming to include not only actions but also likes and dislikes, beliefs, and more general personality characteristics.

**10.5  How do Erikson's and Marcia's theories explain adolescent identity development?**
During adolescence, there may be a reevaluation of the self, a process Erikson called the identity crisis. In theory, adolescents move from a diffuse sense of future occupational or ideological identity, through a period of reevaluation, to a commitment to a new self-definition. Marcia's theory proposes four identity statuses that may be exhibited as a result of the identity formation process: identity achievement, moratorium, foreclosure, and identity diffusion. Research findings raise doubts about whether the identity-formation process has such a clear developmental aspect.

**10.5a  To what extent do tweens use virtual environments to engage in identity play?**
In virtual environments, children and teens create avatars that represent themselves. Children tend to create avatars

that share their real-world characteristics. Some avatars created by "tweens" (9- to 12-year-olds) vary widely from their real-world counterparts. However, online identity play seems to be confined to a minority of teens rather than a typical feature of information-age identity development.

**10.6   What is the process of ethnic identity development, according to Phinney?**

Minority-group adolescents construct an ethnic identity. For many, a sense of belonging to two cultures, the dominant society as well as their own ethnic group, appears to be the most adaptive resolution of this process.

**10.6a   What role do rites of passage play in the development of ethnic identity?**

Rites of passage provide teens with public recognition of their maturational status with regard to adults. Some African American communities have devised rites of passage programs that teach teens about African history and culture. The programs usually end with a ceremony of some kind that initiates participants into adult culture.

## Self-Esteem

**10.7   How does self-esteem develop?**

Beginning at about age 7 or 8, the child develops a global evaluation of his or her self-worth (self-esteem). Self-esteem is shaped both by the degree of discrepancy between a child's goals and his accomplishments and by the degree of emotional support the child perceives from parents and peers. Self-esteem develops out of a child's experiences with success and failure, the value he ascribes to the activities at which he succeeds or fails, and the feedback he gets from peers and parents about his performance.

**10.8   How consistent is self-esteem across childhood and adolescence?**

Self-esteem is fairly stable across childhood but somewhat less so in early adolescence. Children with high self-esteem and greater feelings of self-efficacy show lower levels of depression.

## The Development of the Concepts of Gender and Sex Roles

**10.9   How do ideas about gender and sex roles change across childhood?**

Children generally acquire gender identity (the ability to correctly identify their own gender and that of others) by about age 2 or 3. They develop gender stability (knowing that people stay the same gender throughout life) by about 4, and they understand gender constancy (that people don't change gender by changing appearance) by about 5 or 6.

**10.9a   What does research say about gender differences in temperament?**

Studies show that gender stereotypes influence adults' interpretations of and generalization about infants' behavior. Some gender differences do exist such as boys' greater emotional intensity, girls' greater sensitivity to facial expressions, and girls' greater sociability. However, the differences are much smaller than most people believe.

**10.10   What is the connection between gender stereotypes and sex-typed behavior?**

In early elementary school, children create quite rigid rules about what boys and girls ought to do or are allowed to do. Older children are aware that such rules are social conventions and do not treat them as incontrovertible. Sex-typed behavior is evident from about 18 months of age.

**10.11   How do social learning, cognitive-developmental, and gender schema theories explain sex-role development?**

Theorists of several different traditions have attempted to explain observed patterns in sex-role development. Learning theories emphasize modeling and parental expectations. Cognitive-developmental theories propose that gender development occurs in stages. The most widely accepted theory is gender schema theory, which proposes that children begin to acquire a rule about what boys do and what girls do as soon as they figure out the difference between boys and girls, and that this schema forms the basis of both stereotyping and sex-typed behavior. Young people also differ in the extent to which they see themselves as having feminine or masculine qualities or traits. Those who describe themselves with qualities from both sets are said to be androgynous. Both girls and boys who describe themselves as androgynous or masculine have somewhat higher self-esteem, at least in U.S. culture.

**10.12   In what ways might hormones influence gender-related behavior?**

Animal studies show that prenatal exposure to testosterone leads to masculine behavior in females, while lack of exposure to this hormone causes male animals to behave in ways that are more typical of females. Research involving children with genetic defects suggests that testosterone may also influence sex-typed behavior in humans.

## KEY TERMS

androgynous (p.261)
feminine (p. 261)
foreclosure (p. 248)
gender concept (p. 255)
gender constancy (p. 256)
gender identity (p. 255)

gender schema theory (p. 260)
gender stability (p. 255)
identity achievement (p. 248)
identity diffusion (p. 248)
identity versus role confusion
    (p. 248)

masculine (p. 261)
moratorium (p. 248)
objective self (p. 242)
self-concept (p. 242)
self-esteem (p. 253)

sex role (p. 255)
sex-typed behavior (p. 255)
subjective self (p. 242)
undifferentiated (p. 261)

# 11

# The Development of Social Relationships

## LEARNING OBJECTIVES

### Relationships with Parents

**11.1** How did Bowlby and Ainsworth characterize affectional bonds, attachments, and internal working models?

**11.2** What factors influence the parent's bond to the child?

**11.3** How does the child's attachment to the parent change across infancy, early childhood, and middle childhood?

**11.4** What are the characteristics of parent-child relationships in adolescence?

### Variations in the Quality of Attachments

**11.5** How does the behavior of securely and insecurely attached infants differ?

**11.6** How does infant temperament influence the attachment process?

**11.7** To what degree are attachment classifications stable, and what are their long-term consequences?

### Relationships with Peers

**11.8** What are the characteristics of infants' and preschoolers' peer interactions?

**11.9** How do peer relationships change during the school years?

**11.10** What are the characteristics and consequences of variations in social status?

**11.11** What is the significance of peer groups and romantic relationships in adolescence?

**11.12** What are the characteristics of sibling relationships?

**11.12a** How does the resource dilution hypothesis explain differences between only children and those who have siblings?

### Behavior with Peers

**11.13** What is prosocial behavior, and when does it appear?

**11.13a** How can parents increase the chances that their children will demonstrate altruistic and helpful behavior?

**11.14** In what ways do boys and girls of different ages differ in the exhibition of aggression?

**11.15** What is trait aggression, and how does it differ from typical age-related forms of aggression?

**11.15a** What are the similarities and differences between cyberbullying and bullying in other social contexts?

In 2011, the nation of South Sudan finally attained the independence its residents had been seeking for decades. Among those who cheered the event were the survivors of a tragic saga that began to unfold during the late 1980s, when government-backed forces drove millions of Christian and animist families in southern Sudan from their homes (Omer, 2011). These desperate families headed for the Kenyan and Ethiopian borders in hopes of finding refuge. Sadly, tens of thousands of the refugees died, and their deaths left many children without parents. These children, some as young as 4 years of age, knew that they faced certain death if they returned home. Lacking adults to support them, the children banded together, the older children protecting the younger ones, and kept on the move. Little did they know that they would spend years walking in the hostile East African desert, a deadly hot and dry land more than twice the size of Texas.

Miraculously, thousands of these children, referred to as "Lost Boys" despite the fact that many were girls, made it to refugee camps in Kenya and Ethiopia. Ultimately, international relief agencies helped many of the children resettle in the United States. Many of them were successful in school, graduated from college, and went on to establish careers and families of their own, showing few hints of the degree of hardship and deprivation that they suffered earlier in their lives (Geltman et al., 2005).

Developmental scientists attribute the resilience of the Lost Boys to the intense bonds that they developed with one another during their ordeal (Geltman et al., 2005). These bonds helped the children compensate emotionally for the loss of their parents. Thus, the Lost Boys' story serves as a reminder that socioemotional connections can be just as important to development as physical care.

In this chapter, you will be introduced to the important ideas and discoveries of John Bowlby, Mary Ainsworth, and other developmental scientists regarding emotional bonds between infants and caregivers. We will next discuss the impact of these early relationships on those that come along later in life. A look at peer relationships, along with positive and negative patterns of peer interaction, rounds out our discussion of social relationships.

## Relationships with Parents

The parent-child relationship has been at the center of much theorizing and research in developmental psychology. To understand the major research findings, you need a basic knowledge of the theoretical foundation on which most research studies have been based.

**Learning Objective 11.1** ----------→
How did Bowlby and Ainsworth characterize affectional bonds, attachments, and internal working models?

## Attachment Theory

The strongest theoretical influence in studies of infant-parent relationships is attachment theory, particularly the work of John Bowlby and Mary Ainsworth (Ainsworth & Bowlby, 1991). Bowlby's thinking had roots in psychoanalytic thought, particularly in the emphasis on the significance of the earliest relationship between mother and child. To this theoretical base, he added important evolutionary and ethological concepts. In his view, an attachment relationship has survival value because it ensures that the infant will receive nurturance. The relationship is built and maintained by an interlocking repertoire of inborn behavior patterns that create and sustain proximity between parent and child. For example, infants cry, smile, and make eye contact, all behaviors that elicit caregiving from others. Similarly, there are universal ways in which parents, particularly mothers, respond to these behaviors—for example, picking the infants up when they cry or speaking to them in a high-pitched voice.

**AFFECTIONAL BONDS AND ATTACHMENTS** In Bowlby's and Ainsworth's writings, this mutual pattern of responding is key to the development of affectional bonds and attachments. Ainsworth defines an **affectional bond** as an enduring tie to a partner viewed as unique (1989).

An **attachment** is a type of affectional bond in which a person's sense of security is bound up in the relationship. When you are attached, you feel (or hope to feel) a special sense of security and comfort in the presence of the other, and you can use the other as a safe base from which to explore the rest of the world.

In these terms, the child's relationship with the parent is an attachment, but the parent's relationship with the child is an affectional bond rather than a true attachment, since the parent does not use the infant as a safe base. A relationship with one's adult partner or with a very close friend, however, is an attachment in the sense Ainsworth and Bowlby meant the term. There is a certain kind of security that an adult draws from being in such a relationship; knowing that one can rely on the acceptance and support of a romantic partner or a close friend no matter what happens in many ways parallels the safe base function attachment relationships serve for children.

Because attachments are internal states, developmentalists cannot observe them directly. Instead, they deduce their existence by observing **attachment behaviors**, which are all those behaviors that allow a child or an adult to achieve and retain physical proximity to someone else to whom he is attached. These could include smiling, making eye contact, calling out to the other person across a room, touching, clinging, or crying. Attachment behaviors are elicited primarily when the individual has need of care or support or comfort.

*In this relationship, the son is attached to his dad, but (in Ainsworth's terms) the father's relationship to his son is an affectional bond rather than an attachment.*

**INTERNAL WORKING MODELS**   According to Bowlby, once an attachment to another person has been established, the child begins to construct a mental representation of the relationship that becomes a set of expectations that the child has for future interactions with the same person. Bowlby coined the term **internal working model** to describe this mental representation and suggested that it includes such elements as the child's confidence (or lack of it) that the attachment figure will be available or reliable, the child's expectation of rebuff or affection, and the child's sense of assurance that the attachment figure is really a safe base for exploration. The internal model begins to be formed late in the child's first year of life and becomes increasingly elaborated and better established over the first 4 or 5 years (Schermerhorn, Cummings, & Davies, 2008). More importantly, the model affects the child's behavior: The child tends to re-create, in each new relationship, the pattern with which he is familiar.

**attachment**   A type of affectional bond in which the presence of the partner adds a special sense of security, a "safe base," for the individual.

## The Parent's Bond to the Child

◄----------- **Learning Objective 11.2**
What factors influence the parent's bond to the child?

If you read any popular magazines, you have probably come across articles proclaiming that mothers (or fathers) must have immediate contact with their newborn infant if they are to become properly bonded with the baby. As you'll see, the formation of an attachment relationship to a child is far too complex to be completely dependent on a single, early experience.

**THE DEVELOPMENT OF INTERACTIVE SKILL**   What is essential in the formation of an early bond is the opportunity for the parent and infant to develop a mutual, interlocking pattern of attachment behaviors, a smooth "dance" of interaction. The baby signals her needs by crying or smiling; she looks at her parents when they look at her. The parents, in their turn, enter into this interactive dance with their own repertoire of caregiving behaviors. They pick the baby up when she cries, wait for and respond to her signals of hunger or some other need, and so on. Some researchers and theorists have described this as the development of *synchrony* (Feldman, 2007; Isabella, Belsky, & von Eye, 1989).

Even though most adults show these behaviors with many infants, they do not form an attachment relationship with every baby they coo at in a restaurant or a grocery store. For an adult, the critical ingredient for the formation of a bond seems to be the opportunity to develop real synchrony—to practice the dance until the partners follow one another's lead smoothly and pleasurably. This takes time and many rehearsals. In general, the smoother and more

**attachment behaviors**   The collection of (probably) instinctive behaviors of one person toward another that bring about or maintain proximity and caregiving, such as the smile of the young infant; behaviors that reflect an attachment.

**internal working model**   As applied to social relationships, a cognitive construction of the workings of relationships, such as expectations of support or affection, trustworthiness, and so on. The earliest relationships may form the template for such a cognitive construction.

Ryan's dad, like many fathers, is far more likely to play with him by tossing him around than is his mom.

predictable the process becomes, the more satisfying it seems to be to the parents and the stronger their attachment to the infant becomes.

**FATHER-CHILD BONDS**   Most of the research you have read about so far has involved studies of mothers. Still, many of the same principles seem to hold for fathers as well (Lewis & Lamb, 2003). In particular, fathers seem to direct the same repertoire of attachment behaviors toward their infants as do mothers in the early weeks of a baby's life (Figueiredo, Costa, Pacheco, & Pais, 2007; George, Cummings, & Davies, 2010).

After the earliest weeks of life, however, signs of some specialization of parental behaviors with infants become evident (Brown, McBride, Shin, & Bost, 2007). Studies in the United States show that fathers spend more time playing with a baby, using more physical roughhousing (Lamb & Lewis, 2011). Mothers spend more time in routine caregiving, and they talk to and smile at the baby more (Brown, McBride, Shin, & Bost, 2007). This does not mean that fathers have a weaker affectional bond with the infant; it does mean that the behaviors they show toward the infant are typically somewhat different from those mothers show. Nevertheless, by 6 months of age, infants are just as likely to show signs of attachment to their fathers as to their mothers (Feldman, 2003). These signs include laughing and wriggling with delight in short, intense bursts while interacting with their fathers. By contrast, the signs of attachment to mothers are more likely to include slow, gradual smiles. Babies demonstrate through these signs that the specific features of synchronous interaction are different for mothers and fathers.

**SEX DIFFERENCES IN PARENTING ACROSS CULTURES**   Developmentalists caution against leaping to the conclusion that sex differences in parenting are somehow built-in; instead, they appear to rest on cultural patterns. Researchers in England and in India have found higher levels of physical play by fathers than by mothers, but other researchers in Sweden, Israel, Italy, China, and Malaysia have not (Parke & Buriel, 1998).

The few studies of paternal behavior that have been done in non-Western cultural settings indicate that father involvement is beneficial to infants' development regardless of cultural context. However, the elements of father involvement that benefit infants are not the same in every culture. For example, in cultures that value gender equality, *paternal control*, a pattern in which fathers interrupt and redirect infants' behavior in line with cultural expectations for the child's age and gender, hinders infants' social development (e.g., Feldman & Nasalha, 2010). By contrast, in cultures with strong patriarchal traditions and distinctive role prescriptions for mothers and fathers, such as some Middle Eastern societies, paternal control positively influences infants' social development (e.g., Feldman & Nasalha, 2010). Thus, it appears that judgments about and interpretations of paternal behavior must consider the cultural context in which the behavior occurs.

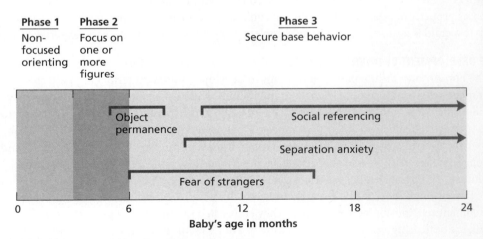

**FIGURE 11.1** Attachment in Developmental Context
This schematic shows how the various threads of development of attachment are woven together.

# The Child's Attachment to the Parent

◄------------Learning Objective 11.3

How does the child's attachment to the parent change across infancy, early childhood, and middle childhood?

Like the parent's bond to the baby, the baby's attachment emerges gradually. Bowlby (1969) suggested three phases in the development of the infant's attachment. These are presented schematically in Figure 11.1.

**PHASE 1: NONFOCUSED ORIENTING AND SIGNALING**   Bowlby believed that a baby begins life with a set of innate behavior patterns that orient him toward others and signal his needs. Mary Ainsworth described these as *proximity-promoting* behaviors: They bring people closer. In the newborn's repertoire, these behaviors include crying, making eye contact, clinging, cuddling, and responding to caregiving efforts by being soothed.

At this stage, there is little evidence that the baby is attached to the parents. Nonetheless, the roots of attachment are established. The baby is building up expectancies and schemas about interaction patterns with the parents, as well as developing the ability to discriminate mom and dad from others in many contexts.

**PHASE 2: FOCUS ON ONE OR MORE FIGURES**   By 3 months of age, the baby begins to aim her attachment behaviors somewhat more narrowly. She may smile more at the people who regularly take care of her and may not smile readily at a stranger. The infant does not yet have a complete attachment, though. The child still favors a number of people with her proximity-promoting behaviors, and no one person has yet become the "safe base." Children in this phase show no special anxiety at being separated from their parents and no fear of strangers.

**PHASE 3: SECURE BASE BEHAVIOR**   Only at about 6 months of age, according to Bowlby, does the baby form a genuine attachment—about the same time that he develops some preliminary understanding that objects and people continue to exist when they are out of sight (object permanence). For the first time, the infant uses the "most important" person as a safe base from which to explore the world around him—one of the key signs that an attachment exists. Because the 6- to 7-month-old begins to be able to move about the world more freely by creeping and crawling, he can move toward the caregiver as well as entice the caregiver to come to him. Attachment behaviors therefore shift from mostly "come here" (proximity-promoting) signals to what Ainsworth calls *proximity-seeking* behaviors, which might be thought of as "go there" behaviors. Once the child has developed a clear attachment, several related behaviors also appear. One of these is *social referencing*, which you read about in Chapter 5. The 10-month-old uses his ability to discriminate among various facial expressions to guide his safe-base behavior. He begins to check out mom's or dad's facial expression before deciding whether to venture forth into some novel situation.

**FEAR OF STRANGERS AND SEPARATION ANXIETY**   Fear of strangers and separation anxiety are two forms of distress that are rare before 5 or 6 months; they appear sometime between 6 and 9 months, rise in frequency until about 12 to 16 months, and then decline after about 24 months. The research findings are not altogether consistent, but it looks as though fear of strangers normally appears first, at about the same time as babies show fearful reactions in other situations. Anxiety at separation starts a bit later but continues to be visible for a longer period, a pattern diagrammed in Figure 11.1. 👁—Watch at **MyDevelopmentLab**

Such increases in stranger fear and separation anxiety have been observed in children from a number of different cultures and in both home-reared and child-care-reared children in the United States, which suggests that some basic age-related developmental timetables underlie this pattern (Kagan & Herschkowitz, 2005; Kagan, Kearsley, & Zelazo, 1978). Virtually all children show at least mild forms of these two types of distress, although the intensity of the reaction varies widely. Some babies protest briefly; others are virtually inconsolable. Some of this variation undoubtedly reflects basic temperamental differences in behavioral inhibition (Kagan et al., 1994). Heightened fearfulness may also be a response to some upheaval or stress in the child's life, such as a recent move or a change in the daily schedule. Whatever the origin of such variations in fearfulness, the pattern does eventually diminish in most toddlers, typically by the middle of the second year.

*A few months ago, this baby probably would have let himself be held by just about anyone without a fuss; now all of a sudden he's afraid of strangers. Parents are often puzzled by this behavior, but it is absolutely normal.*

👁—Watch the **Video** *Separation Anxiety* at **MyDevelopmentLab**

**ADOPTION AND ATTACHMENT**   Infants who are adopted before the age of 6 months are generally indistinguishable from non-adopted children in the development of attachments to caregivers (Rutter et al., 2010). However, studies of adopted infants reveal that the emotional quality of an infant's environment has an impact on the attachment process even during the earliest months of life. That is, adopted infants younger than 6 months of age who have histories of abuse or institutionalization are somewhat less likely than other infants to develop attachments despite the early age at which they joined their adoptive families (Rutter et al., 2010).

Infants who are adopted after the age of 6 months tend to have far more difficulty forming attachments than those who are adopted earlier. This is especially true if such infants have histories of abuse and/or neglect or have lived in institutions for long periods of time (Merz & McCall, 2010; Tottenham et al., 2010). One study found that 91% of children who had been adopted after being abused, neglected, or institutionalized suffered from emotional problems even after having been in their adoptive families for an average of 9 years (Smith, Howard, & Monroe, 1998). One key factor seems to be support from mental health professionals who are trained specifically to work with adoptive families. When families receive such support, their infants are less likely to encounter problems in the process of developing attachments (Juffer, van IJzendoorn, & Bakermans-Kranenburg, 2008).

In the Efe culture, infants are cared for by several women. Nevertheless, Efe infants prefer their biological mothers over other women.

**ATTACHMENTS TO MOTHERS AND FATHERS**   From the age of 7 or 8 months, when strong attachments are first seen, infants prefer either the father or the mother to a stranger. And when both the father and the mother are available, an infant will smile at or approach either or both, except when she is frightened or under stress. When that happens, especially between the ages of 8 and 24 months, the child typically turns to the mother rather than the father (Lamb, Bornstein, & Teti, 2002).

As you might expect, the strength of the child's attachment to the father at this early age seems to be related to the amount of time dad has spent with the child (Caldera, 2004; Ross, Kagan, Zelazo, & Kotelchuk, 1975). But greatly increased time with the father does not seem to be the only element, since Michael Lamb and his Swedish colleagues (1983) found that infants whose fathers were their major caregivers for at least a month in the first year of the child's life were nonetheless more strongly attached to their mothers than to their fathers. For the father to be consistently preferred over the mother would probably require essentially full-time paternal care. As this option becomes more common, it will be possible to study such father-child pairs to see whether babies develop a preference for the father.

**CULTURES WITH SHARED INFANT CARETAKING**   You may be wondering whether attachment patterns vary when an infant has more than one primary caretaker (Tronick, 2007). In one classic study, Edward Tronick and his colleagues (1992) studied a pygmy group called the Efe, who forage in the forests of Zaire. They live in small groups of perhaps twenty individuals in camps, each consisting of several extended families. Infants in these communities are cared for communally in the early months and years of life. They are carried and held by all the adult women, and they interact regularly with many different adults. They may even be nursed by women other than their mothers, although they normally sleep with their mothers.

Tronick and his colleagues report two things of particular interest about early attachment in this group. First, Efe infants seem to use virtually any adult or older child in their world as a safe base, which suggests that they may have no single central attachment. Second, beginning at about 6 months of age, the Efe infant nonetheless seems to insist on being with his mother more and to prefer her over other women, although other women continue to help care for the child. Thus, even in an extremely communal rearing arrangement, some sign of a central attachment is evident, although it may be less dominant.

**ATTACHMENTS IN EARLY CHILDHOOD**   By age 2 or 3, although the child's attachment to the mother and father remains powerful, most attachment behaviors have become less continuously visible. Children of this age can even use a photograph of their mother as a "safe base" for exploration in a strange situation (Passman & Longeway, 1982), which reflects another cognitive advance. By age 3 or 4, a child can also use shared plans offered by parents ("I'll be home after your nap time") to lessen her potential anxiety at separation (Crittenden, 1992).

Bowlby referred to this new form of attachment as a **goal-corrected partnership** (Bowlby, 1969). The infant's goal, to put it most simply, is always to have the attachment figure within sight or touch. The preschooler's goal is also to be "in contact" with the parent, but "contact" no longer requires constant physical presence. The preschooler not only understands that his mother will continue to exist when she isn't there; he now also understands that the relationship continues to exist even when the partners are apart. This enables the toddler or preschooler to modify ("correct") her goal of contact with her attachment figure by engaging in collaborative planning: agreeing on when and how the two will be together, for example, or what the child will do if she gets scared or anxious, or who the replacement security person will be.

*Although teens have more conflicts with parents than do younger children, they continue to maintain strong attachments to them.*

**ATTACHMENTS IN MIDDLE CHILDHOOD**   In elementary school, overt attachment behaviors such as clinging and crying are even less visible, so it is easy to lose sight of the fact that children this age are still strongly attached to their parents (Bokhorst, Sumter, & Westenberg, 2010). The elementary school child may take primary responsibility for maintaining contact with the parent (Kerns, 1996), but she wants to know that mom and dad are there when she needs them. Such a need is most likely to arise when the child faces some stressful situation, perhaps the first day of school, an illness or upheaval in the family, or the death of a pet. Because fewer experiences are new and potentially stressful to the 7- or 8-year-old than to the preschooler, there is much less obvious safe-base behavior and less open affection expressed by the child to the parent (Maccoby, 1984). These changes do not, however, signify that the child's attachment to the parent has weakened. In fact, extended separations from parents can be extremely stressful for school-aged children (Smith, Lalonde, & Johnson, 2004). Moreover, school-aged children who have close, warm relationships with their parents tend to be socially competent with peers (Michiels, Grietens, Onghena, Kuppens, 2010).

## Parent-Child Relationships in Adolescence

◄------------Learning Objective 11.4
What are the characteristics of parent-child relationships in adolescence?

In adolescence, the form of attachment behaviors shifts somewhat, because teenagers seek both to establish autonomy from the parents and to maintain their sense of relatedness (attachment) with them. The push for autonomy shows itself in increasing conflict between parent and adolescent; the maintenance of connection is seen in the continued strong attachment of child to parent.

**INCREASES IN CONFLICT**   The rise in conflict with parents as children enter adolescence has been repeatedly documented (e.g., Steinberg & Silk, 2002). In the great majority of families, there is an increase in mild bickering or conflicts over everyday issues such as chores or personal rights—whether the adolescent should be allowed to wear a bizarre hair style or certain clothing or the age at which privileges such as dating should be granted (Cunningham, Swanson, Spencer, & Dupree, 2003).

This increase in discord is widely found, but it is important not to assume that it signifies a major disruption of the quality of the parent-child relationship. Laurence Steinberg, one of the key researchers in this area, estimates that relatively few families in the United States experience a substantial or pervasive deterioration in the quality of parent-child relationships in the years of early adolescence (Steinberg & Silk, 2002). Those families at highest risk for

**goal-corrected partnership**   Term used by Bowlby to describe the form of the child-parent attachment in the preschool years, in which the two partners, through improved communication, negotiate the form and frequency of contact between them.

**individuation** The process of psychological, social, and physical separation from parents that begins in adolescence.

persistently heightened conflict are those in which the parents have a history of low levels of warmth and supportiveness toward their child in earlier years and continue this pattern during adolescence (Rueter & Conger, 1995; Silverberg & Gondoli, 1996). When parents express warmth and supportiveness and are open to hearing the teenager's opinions and disagreements, the period of heightened conflict seems to be relatively brief.

If the rise in conflict doesn't signal that the relationship is falling apart, what does it mean? A variety of theorists have suggested that the temporary discord, far from being a negative event, may instead be a developmentally healthy and necessary part of the adolescent's identity formation. In order to become his own person, the teenager needs to push away from the parents, disagree with them, try out his own limits—a process of **individuation** not unlike that seen in the toddler who begins to say "no" to parents during that famous period called the terrible twos (Grotevant & Cooper, 1985).

The pattern of causes for parent-teen conflict is obviously complex. Hormonal changes may be causally linked to increases in assertiveness, perhaps especially among boys. Parents' reactions to pubertal changes may also be highly important parts of the mix. Visible pubertal changes, including menarche, alter parents' expectations of the teenager and increase their concern about guiding and controlling the adolescent to help her avoid the pitfalls of too great a level of independence.

**ATTACHMENT TO PARENTS** Paradoxically, in the midst of this distancing and temporarily heightened family conflict, teenagers' underlying emotional attachment to their parents remains strong. Results from a classic study by Mary Levitt and her colleagues (1993) illustrate the point. Levitt interviewed African American, Hispanic American, and Caucasian American children aged 7, 10, and 14. All the children were shown a drawing with a set of three concentric circles. They were asked to place in the innermost circle the names of those "people who are the most close and important to you—people you love the most and who love you the most." In the next circle outward, children were asked to place the names of "people who are not quite as close but who are still important—people you really love or like, but not quite as much as the people in the first circle." The last circle contained names of somewhat more distant members of this personal "convoy." For each person listed, the interviewer then asked about the kind of support that person provided.

Levitt found that for all three racial or ethnic groups, at all three ages, parents and other close family were by far the most likely to be placed in the inner circle. Even 14-year-olds rarely placed friends in this position. So the parents remain central. At the same time, it is clear from Levitt's results that peers become increasingly important sources of support, as you can see in Figure 11.2. This figure shows the total amount of support the children and adolescents described from each source. Friends clearly provided more support for the 14-year-olds than they did for the younger children, a pattern that is clear for all three groups.

In general, a teenager's sense of well-being or happiness is more strongly correlated with the quality of his attachment to his parents than to the quality of his attachments to his peers (Nichikawa, Hägglöf, & Sundbom, 2010; van Brakel, Muris, Bögels, & Thomassen, 2006). In fact, good relationships with parents and peers seem to go hand in hand during the teen years (Allen, Porter, McFarland, Marsh, & McElhaney, 2005; Turnage, 2004; Weimer, Kerns, & Oldenburg, 2004; Zimmermann, 2004). Furthermore, the stronger the sense of connectedness (attachment) a teenager has with his parents, the less likely he is to engage in any of the risky or delinquent behaviors you learned about in Chapter 4 (Brook, Whiteman, Finch, & Cohen, 2000; Resnick et al., 1997). Thus, even while the teenager is becoming more autonomous, the parents continue to provide a highly important psychological safe base.

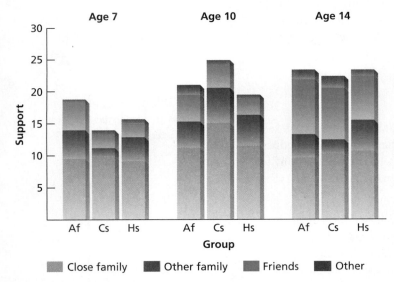

**FIGURE 11.2** The Social Convoy
African American (Af), Caucasian American (Cs), and Hispanic American (Hs) children and teens were asked about the amount and type of support they received from various members of their "social convoy." Note that for teens, friends become more significant sources of support, but parents do not become substantially *less* important.

(*Source:* M. Levitt, N. Guacci-Franco, and J. Levitt. "Convoys of social support in childhood and early adolescence: Structure and function," *Developmental Psychology, 29* (1993): p. 815.)

# Variations in the Quality of Attachments

Go to a child-care center and watch the way the babies or toddlers greet their parents at the end of the day. Some are calmly pleased to see mom or dad; others may run to the parent, crying and clinging; still others may show little interest. These children may all have formed an attachment to their parents, but the quality of those attachments differs markedly.

## Secure and Insecure Attachments

All attachment theorists share the assumption that the first attachment relationship is the most influential ingredient in the creation of the child's working model. Variations in this first attachment relationship are almost universally described using Mary Ainsworth's category system (Ainsworth et al., 1978). She distinguished between *secure attachment* and two types of *insecure attachment*, which she assessed using a procedure called the Strange Situation. ◉ Watch at MyDevelopmentLab

The **Strange Situation** consists of a series of episodes in a laboratory setting, typically used when the child is between 12 and 18 months of age. The child first spends time with the mother and then with the mother and a stranger; then the child is left alone with the stranger, then completely alone for a few minutes, then reunited with the mother, then left alone again, and finally reunited first with the stranger and then with the mother. Ainsworth suggested that children's reactions to these situations indicated one of three types of attachment: **secure attachment**, shown by a child who uses the parent as a safe base and is readily consoled after separation, and two types of **insecure attachment**, shown by a child who either shows little preference for mother over a stranger (the *insecure/detached* or *insecure/avoidant* child) or is wary of strangers and upset at separation but is not reassured by the mother's return (the *insecure/resistant* or *insecure/ambivalent* child). Mary Main has suggested a fourth type of attachment, which she calls *insecure/disorganized/disoriented* (Main & Solomon, 1990).

Some of the characteristics of the different types of attachment are listed in Table 11.1 below. As you read the descriptions, note that whether the child cries when he is separated from his mother is not a helpful indicator of the security of his attachment. It is the entire pattern of the child's responses to the Strange Situation that is critical, not any one response.

◄----------- Learning Objective 11.5
How does the behavior of securely and insecurely attached infants differ?

◉ Watch the **Video** *Attachment* at **MyDevelopmentLab**

**strange situation** A series of episodes used by Mary Ainsworth and others in studies of attachment. The child is observed with the mother, with a stranger, alone, when reunited with the stranger, and when reunited with the mother.

**secure attachment** An internal working model of relationships in which the child uses the parent as a safe base and is readily consoled after separation, when fearful, or when otherwise stressed.

**insecure attachment** An internal working model of relationships in which the child does not as readily use the parent as a safe base and is not readily consoled by the parent if upset. Includes three subtypes of attachment: avoidant, ambivalent, and disorganized/ disoriented.

| Table 11.1 | CATEGORIES OF SECURE AND INSECURE ATTACHMENT IN AINSWORTH'S STRANGE SITUATION |
|---|---|
| **Category** | **Behavior** |
| Secure attachment | Child readily separates from mother and easily becomes absorbed in exploration; when threatened or frightened, child actively seeks contact and is readily consoled; child does not avoid or resist contact if mother initiates it. When reunited with mother after absence, child greets her positively or is easily soothed if upset. Clearly prefers mother to stranger. |
| Insecure attachment (detached/avoidant) | Child avoids contact with mother, especially at reunion after an absence. Does not resist mother's efforts to make contact, but does not seek much contact. Shows no preference for mother over stranger. |
| Insecure attachment (resistant/ambivalent) | Child shows little exploration and is wary of stranger. Greatly upset when separated from mother, but not reassured by mother's return or her efforts at comforting. Child both seeks and avoids contact at different times. May show anger toward mother at reunion, and resists both comfort from and contact with stranger. |
| Insecure attachment (disorganized/disoriented) | Dazed behavior, confusion, or apprehension. Child may show contradictory behavior patterns simultaneously, such as moving toward mother while keeping gaze averted. |

*Sources*: Ainsworth et al., 1978; Carlson and Sroufe, 1995; Main and Solomon, 1990.

Watch the **Video** Attachment in Infants at **MyDevelopmentLab**

**ORIGINS OF SECURE AND INSECURE ATTACHMENTS** Studies of parent-child interactions suggest that one crucial ingredient for a secure attachment is *emotional availability* on the part of the caregiver (Biringen, 2000). An emotionally available caregiver is one who is able and willing to form an emotional attachment to the infant. For example, economically or emotionally distressed parents may be so distracted by their own problems that they can't invest emotion in the parent-infant relationship. Such parents may meet the baby's physical needs—feeding, changing diapers, and so on—but be unable to respond emotionally. **Watch** at **MyDevelopmentLab**

A number of studies (including some cross-cultural research) further suggest that both acceptance of the infant by the parents and some aspect of sensitivity to the child—a quality that has been measured and given various labels, including *synchrony, mutuality,* and *contingent responsiveness*—are also necessary for the formation of an attachment relationship (Posada et al., 2002). This key quality is more than merely love and affection. To be rated as sensitive, or high in contingent responsiveness, the parents must be attuned to the child's signals and cues and respond appropriately. They smile when the baby smiles, talk to the baby when he vocalizes, pick him up when he cries, and so on (Ainsworth & Marvin, 1995; Sroufe, 1996). Developmentalists' certainty that this type of responsiveness is a key ingredient in the formation of secure attachment has been strengthened by experimental studies showing that training mothers who demonstrate insensitivity to become more sensitive is highly effective. Such studies show long-term effects on both mothers' behavior and infants' attachment security (van Doesum, Riksen-Walraven, Hosman, & Hoefnagels, 2008).

Each of the several subvarieties of insecure attachment also has additional distinct antecedents. For example, a disorganized/disoriented pattern of attachment seems especially likely when the child has been abused or has parents who had some trauma in their own childhoods, such as either abuse or the early death of a parent (Cassidy & Berlin, 1994; Main & Hesse, 1990). An insecure pattern is more common when the mother is inconsistently or unreliably available to the child. Mothers may show such unavailability or periodic neglect for a variety of reasons, but a common one is depression (van Doesum et al., 2008). When the mother rejects the infant or regularly (rather than intermittently) withdraws from contact with the infant, the infant is more likely to show an avoidant pattern of attachment.

**ATTACHMENT QUALITY ACROSS CULTURES** Studies in a variety of countries have pointed to the possibility that secure attachments may be influenced by culture as well (Carlson & Harwood, 2003; van IJzendoorn & Sagi-Schwartz, 2008). The most thorough analyses have come from a Dutch psychologist, Marinus van IJzendoorn, who has examined the results of 32 separate studies in 8 different countries. Table 11.2 shows the percentage of babies classi-fied in each category for each country. We need to be cautious about overgeneralizing the information in this table, because in most cases there are only one or two studies from a given country, normally with quite small samples. The single study from China, for example, included only 36 babies. Still, the findings are thought-provoking.

The most striking thing about the data in Table 11.2 is their consistency. In each of the eight countries, a secure attachment is the most common pattern, found in more than half of all babies studied; in five of the eight countries, an avoidant pattern is the more common of the two forms of insecure attachment. Only in Israel and Japan is this pattern significantly reversed. How can such differences be explained?

One possibility is that the Strange Situation is simply not an appropriate measure of attachment security in all cultures. For example, because Japanese babies are rarely separated from their mothers in the first year of life, being left totally alone in the midst of the Strange Situation may be far more stressful for them, which might result in more intense,

*Japanese babies spend more time with their mothers than do infants in Western cultures. As a result, they may exhibit more distress during the Strange Situation and be inappropriately classified as ambivalently attached.*

Table 11.2

## SECURE AND INSECURE ATTACHMENTS IN DIFFERENT CULTURES

| Country | Number of Studies | Percentage of Children Showing Each Type of Attachment | | |
|---|---|---|---|---|
| | | Secure | Avoidant | Ambivalent |
| West Germany | 3 | 56.6 | 35.3 | 8.1 |
| Great Britain | 1 | 75.0 | 22.2 | 2.3 |
| Netherlands | 4 | 67.3 | 26.3 | 6.4 |
| Sweden | 1 | 74.5 | 21.6 | 3.9 |
| Israel | 2 | 64.4 | 6.8 | 28.8 |
| Japan | 2 | 67.7 | 5.2 | 25.0 |
| China | 1 | 50.0 | 25.0 | 25.0 |
| United States | 18 | 64.8 | 21.1 | 14.1 |
| Overall average | | 65% | 21% | 14% |

*Source:* van IJzendoorn, M. H., & Kroonenberg, P. M. (1988). "Cross cultural patterns of attachment: A meta-analysis of the Strange Situation." *Child Development, 59*, 150–151. Table 1.

inconsolable crying and hence a classification of ambivalent attachment. The counter-argument is that comparisons of toddlers' reactions in the Strange Situation suggest few cultural differences in such behaviors as proximity-seeking or avoidance of the mother, all of which lead to more confidence that the Strange Situation is tapping similar processes among children in many cultures (Sagi, van IJzendoorn, & Koren-Karie, 1991; van IJzendoorn & Sagi-Schwartz, 2008).

It is also possible that the meaning of a "secure" or "avoidant" pattern is different in different cultures, even if the percentages of each category are similar. German researchers, for example, have suggested that, in their culture, an insecure-avoidant classification may reflect not indifference by the mother but rather explicit training toward greater independence in the baby (Grossmann, Grossmann, Spangler, Seuss, & Unzner, 1985).

On the other hand, research in Israel (Sagi, 1990) shows that the attachment classification derived from the Strange Situation predicts the baby's later social skills in much the same way as it does for samples in the United States, which suggests that the classification system is valid in both cultures. The most plausible hypothesis is that the same factors in mother-infant interaction contribute to secure and insecure attachments in all cultures and that these patterns reflect similar internal models. But it will take more research like the Israeli work, in which the long-term outcomes of the various categories are studied, before developmentalists can be sure if this is correct.

## Temperament and Attachment

← - - - - - - - - - - -**Learning Objective 11.6**

How does infant temperament influence the attachment process?

The general timing of the development of attachment behaviors is the same in virtually all children. However, the emotional intensity of the relationship varies considerably from child to child. For example, infants differ widely in how much fear they show toward strangers or toward novel situations. Some of this difference may reflect basic temperamental variations (Kagan, 1994). Heightened fearfulness may also be a response to some upheaval or stress in the child's life, such as a recent move or a parent's job change.

goodness-of-fit   The degree to which
an infant's environment and his or her
temperament work together.

Individual differences in infant temperament may also be related to security of attachment (Zeanah & Fox, 2004). Generally speaking, easy infants, as defined by the Thomas and Chess system (which you read about in Chapter 9), are more likely to be securely attached than babies in the other two categories (Goldsmith & Alansky, 1987; Seifer, Schiller, Sameroff, Resnick, & Riordan, 1996; Vaughn et al., 1992). The relationship makes sense if you think about the traits of infants in the difficult and slow-to-warm-up groups. Difficult infants actively resist comfort; consequently, a parent may be discouraged from establishing a nurturing relationship with a difficult infant. Likewise, slow-to-warm-up babies are less responsive to parental behaviors directed toward them, and the parents of these infants may reduce the frequency of behaviors directed to their unresponsive babies. The result is that the kind of give-and-take relationships most easy infants experience with their parents may never develop for babies who are difficult or slow-to-warm-up (Laible, Panfile, & Makariev, 2008).

It's important to remember, however, that a correlation is just a correlation and certainly does not suggest that all easy infants develop secure attachment or that all babies of the other two temperamental types are insecurely attached. In fact, the majority of infants in all three temperament categories are securely attached (van IJzendoorn et al., 1992). In addition, if infant temperament dictated attachment quality, it would be highly unlikely to see infants who are securely attached to one parent but insecurely attached to the other. In reality, this is a very common research finding (e.g., Goossens & van IJzendoorn, 1990).

For these reasons, developmentalists propose that it is not temperament, per se, that influences attachment. Rather, attachment is influenced by the **goodness-of-fit** between the infant's temperament and his or her environment (Thomas & Chess, 1977). For example, if the parents of an irritable baby boy are good at tolerating his irritability and persist in establishing a synchronous relationship with him, then his irritability doesn't lead to the development of an insecure attachment.

**Learning Objective 11.7** ----------→

To what degree are attachment classifications stable, and what are their long-term consequences?

*This elementary school child appears to be securely attached to her parent. Research on the stability of attachment classifications suggests that the secure quality of the relationship was established when the girl was an infant.*

## Stability and Long-Term Consequences of Attachment Quality

Do variations in the quality of a child's early attachment persist over time? This question is a particularly important one for those researchers and therapists who are concerned that the effects of early abuse or neglect or other sources of insecure attachment might be permanent.

**STABILITY OF ATTACHMENT CLASSIFICATION**   Both consistency and inconsistency are evident in attachment relationships over time (Ranson & Urichuk, 2008). According to a review of the relevant research carried out by Judith Crowell and Stuart Hauser (2008), one important finding that has surfaced in many longitudinal studies is that secure attachments seem to be more stable than insecure attachments. In addition, the stability of an attachment classification appears to depend on an individual's life circumstances. When the child's family environment or life circumstances are reasonably consistent, the security or insecurity of attachment usually remains constant as well, even over many years (Weinfield & Egeland, 2004).

The very fact that a child's security can change from one time to another does not refute the notion of attachment as an internal working model. Bowlby suggested that for the first 2 or 3 years of life, the particular pattern of attachment shown by a child is in some sense a property of each specific relationship. For example, studies of toddlers' attachments to mothers and fathers show that some infants are securely attached to one parent and insecurely attached to the other (Minzi, 2010). It is the quality of the particular relationship that determines the child's security with that specific adult. If that relationship changes markedly, the security of the baby's attachment to that individual may change, too. However, Bowlby argued that by age 4 or 5, the internal working model becomes more general, more a property of the child, more generalized across relationships, and thus more resistant to change. At that point, the child tends to impose her working model on new relationships, including relationships with teachers and peers. Thus, a child may "recover" from an initially insecure attachment or lose a secure one. Consistency over time is more typical, however, both because children's relationships tend to be reasonably stable for the first few years and because once the internal model is clearly formed, it tends to perpetuate itself.

**LONG-TERM CONSEQUENCES OF SECURE AND INSECURE ATTACHMENT**    Ainsworth's classification system has proved to be extremely helpful in predicting a remarkably wide range of other behaviors in children, both toddlers and older children. Dozens of studies (e.g., Brumariu & Kerns, 2010; Carlson, Sampson, & Sroufe, 2003; Diener, Isabella, Behunin, & Wong, 2008) show that, compared to children rated as insecurely attached, children rated as securely attached to their mothers in infancy are later more sociable, more positive in their behavior toward friends and siblings, less clinging and dependent on teachers, less aggressive and disruptive, more empathetic, and more emotionally mature in their approach to school and other settings outside the home.

At adolescence, those who were rated as securely attached in infancy or who are classed as secure on the basis of recent interviews are more socially skilled, have more intimate friendships, are more likely to be rated as leaders and to have higher self-esteem and better grades (Bauminger, Finzi-Dottan, Chason, & Har-Even, 2008; Kobak, Zajac, & Smith, 2009; Woodhouse, Ramos-Marcuse, Ehrlich, Warner, & Cassidy, 2010). Those with insecure attachments—particularly those with avoidant attachments—not only have less positive and supportive friendships in adolescence but are also more likely to become sexually active early and to practice riskier sex (Carlson, Sroufe, & Egeland, 2004;).

One particularly clear demonstration of some of these links comes from a longitudinal study by Alan Sroufe and his colleagues (Sroufe, Egeland, Carlson, & Collins, 2005). These researchers assessed the security of attachment of a group of several hundred infants and then followed the children through childhood and adolescence, testing and observing them at regular intervals. Some of their observations were of participants who had been invited to attend a specially designed summer camp during early adolescence. The counselors rated each child on a range of characteristics, and observers noted how often children spent time together or with the counselors. Naturally, neither the counselors nor the observers knew what the children's initial attachment classification had been. Those children with histories of secure attachment in infancy were rated as higher in self-confidence and social competence. They complied more readily with requests from counselors, expressed more positive emotions, and had a greater sense of their ability to accomplish things. Secure children created more friendships, especially with other securely attached youngsters, and engaged in more complex activities when playing in groups. In contrast, the majority of the children with histories of insecure attachment showed some kind of deviant behavior pattern, such as isolation from peers, bizarre behavior, passivity, hyperactivity, or aggressiveness. Only a few of the originally securely attached children showed any of these patterns.

**QUALITY OF ATTACHMENT IN ADULTHOOD**    Longitudinal studies show that the effects of attachment status persist into adulthood (Jones, 2008; Tideman, Nilsson, Smith, & Stjernqvist, 2002). Some studies show that men and women who were securely attached to their parents are more sensitive to their intimate partners' needs (Mikulincer & Shaver, 2005).

Adults' internal models of attachment affect the way they behave with their own children as well. To assess the degree to which they do so, psychologist Mary Main and her colleagues developed a standardized attachment status interview for use with adults (Main, Hesse, & Goldwyn, 2008; Main, Kaplan, & Cassidy, 1985). They found that an adult's internal working model of attachment can be classified as one of three types:

- *Secure/autonomous/balanced.*    These individuals value attachment relations and see their early experiences as influential, but they are objective in describing both good and bad qualities. They speak coherently about their early experiences and have thoughts about what motivated their parents' behavior.
- *Dismissing or detached.*    These adults minimize the importance or the effects of 0early family experience. They may idealize their parents, perhaps even denying the existence of any negative childhood experiences. They emphasize their own personal strengths.
- *Preoccupied or enmeshed.*    These adults often talk about inconsistent or role-reversed parenting. They are still engrossed with their relationship with their parents, still actively struggling to please them or very angry at them. They are confused and ambivalent, but still engaged.

**parallel play** Form of play seen in toddlers, in which children play next to, but not with, one another.

When adults' models of attachment are related to the security of attachment displayed by their children, the expected pattern emerges strongly: Adults with secure models of attachment to their own parents are much more likely to have infants or toddlers with secure attachments. Those adults with dismissing models are more likely to have infants with avoidant attachments; those with preoccupied attachments are more likely to have infants with ambivalent attachments. Across 20 studies, the typical finding is that three-quarters of the mother-infant pairs share the same attachment category (van IJzendoorn, 1995, 1997). Diane Benoit has even found marked consistency across three generations: grandmothers, young mothers, and infants (Benoit & Parker, 1994).

The cross-generational similarity appears to be a result of each mother's own behavior toward her child, which varies as a function of her own internal working model of attachment (Steele, Hodges, Kaniuk, Hillman, & Henderson, 2003). Mothers who are themselves securely attached are more responsive and sensitive in their behavior toward their infants or young children. By contrast, mothers with dismissing or preoccupied attachments display behaviors that may interfere with the development of secure attachment in their children. When Emma Adam and her colleagues observed interactions between mothers and their 2-year-old children in a variety of settings (Adam, Gunnar, & Tanaka, 2004), they found that preoccupied mothers tended to display more anger, intrusiveness (actions that interfered with a child's goals), and negative emotions in interactions with their children than did mothers in the secure category. Moreover, dismissing mothers were less likely than secure mothers to exhibit positive emotions when interacting with their toddlers.

## Relationships with Peers

Children's relationships with parents and peers are interactive (Chen, He, Chang, & Liu, 2005). That is, good parenting is most effective when children associate with peers who exhibit social competence. Conversely, antisocial peers can undermine the potentially positive effects of good parenting. Thus, developmentalists no longer think of parental and peer relationships as independent sets of influences. In this section, we'll discuss how peer relationships change over the years of childhood and adolescence.

**Learning Objective 11.8**
What are the characteristics of infants' and preschoolers' peer interactions?

👁 **Watch** the **Video** *Play in Early Childhood* at **MyDevelopmentLab**

*By age 3, most children actually play together with one another in coordinated ways, rather than merely playing side by side.*

## Peer Relationships in Infancy and the Preschool Years

Children first begin to show some positive interest in other infants as early as 6 months of age. If you place two babies of that age on the floor facing each other, they will touch each other, pull each other's hair, and reach for each other's clothing. In 10-month-olds, these behaviors are even more evident. By 14 to 18 months of age, two or more children can play together with toys— occasionally cooperating, but more often simply playing side by side with different toys, a pattern Mildred Parten (1932) first described as **parallel play**. Toddlers of this age express interest in one another, gazing at or making noises at each other. Only at around 18 months of age, however, do toddlers show evidence of coordinated play, such as when one toddler chases another or imitates the other's action with some toy. By 3 or 4, children appear to prefer to play with peers rather than alone, and their play with one another is much more cooperative and coordinated, including various forms of group pretend play. 👁 **Watch** at **MyDevelopmentLab**

The first signs of playmate preferences or friendships also emerge in the toddler and preschool years (Hay, Payne, & Chadwick, 2004). By age 3 or 4, more than half of children have at least one mutual friendship, and many have already developed an enduring "best friend" relationship (Sebanc, Kearns, Hernandez, & Galvin, 2007).

To be sure, these early "friendships" are not nearly as deep or intimate as those between pairs of older children or adolescents. Toddler friends ignore each other's bids for interaction as often as not. Still, these pairs show unmistakable signs that their relationship is more than merely a passing fancy. They display more mutual liking, more reciprocity, more extended interactions, more positive and less negative behavior, more forgiveness, and more supportiveness in a novel situation than is true of nonfriend pairs at this same age (Dunn, 1993; Hartup, Laursen, Stewart, & Eastenson, 1988; Newcomb & Bagwell, 1995).

There is every reason to believe that early play with such a friend is a highly important arena for children to practice a host of social skills (Sebanc, 2003). Often, they must subdue their own desires in the interests of joint play, which requires some awareness of the other's feelings and wishes as well as an ability to modulate one's own emotions. Research on friendships reveals that play with peers, especially play with friends, may be a crucial ingredient in the development of these skills (Rubin et al., 2011).

## Peer Relationships at School Age

← - - - - - - - - - - - -**Learning Objective 11.9**
How do peer relationships change during the school years?

Over the past few decades, peer relationships have become increasingly important among school-aged children. Gradually, the amount of time that they spend interacting in school, in after-school care settings, and via electronic communication has come to exceed the amount of time that they spend in other activities (Neufeld & Maté, 2005; Rideout, Foehr, & Roberts, 2010). As a result, controversies have emerged regarding the degree to which this shift toward increased time with peers and decreased time with parents is beneficial or harmful to children. For instance, clinical psychologist Gordon Neufeld (Neufeld & Maté, 2005) has argued that spending more time with parents than with peers is essential for children's mental health. By contrast, researcher Judith Rich Harris has suggested precisely the opposite (2009).

**FRIENDSHIPS**    Compared to preschoolers, school-aged children develop a larger collection of **reciprocal friendships**—pairs in which each child names the other as a friend or as a "best friend." Thomas Berndt, in several studies (Berndt & Hoyle, 1985; Berndt, 2002), has found that most first-graders have only one such reciprocal friendship. This number gradually rises through elementary school, so that by eighth grade, the average child has two or three reciprocal friendships. Cross-cultural studies show that best-friend relationships and the belief that having a best friend is important are universal features of school-aged children's social development (Schraf & Hertz-Lazarowitz, 2003). ◉┤**Watch** at **MyDevelopmentLab**

◉─┤**Watch** the **Video** *Friends* at **MyDevelopmentLab**

Children in this age range also behave differently with friends than they do with strangers, just as preschoolers do. They are more open and more supportive with chums, smiling and looking at each other, laughing and touching each other more than non-friends; they talk more with friends and cooperate with and help each other more. Pairs of friends are also more successful than are non-friend pairs at solving problems or performing some task together (Newcomb & Bagwell, 1995). Yet school-aged children are also more critical of friends and have more conflicts with them than they do with strangers (Hartup, 1996). At the same time, when such conflicts with friends occur, children are more concerned about resolving them than they are disagreements with non-friends. Thus, friendships constitute an arena in which children can learn how to manage conflicts (Newcomb & Bagwell, 1995).

**SEX DIFFERENCES IN FRIENDSHIP QUALITY**    As you learned in Chapter 10, children's preference for same-sex playmates emerges early in life. Over the elementary school years, this preference increases. By third grade or so, almost all of children's relationships involve others of the same sex (Maccoby, 2002; Martin & Ruble, 2010). Gender differences in interaction patterns both contribute to and are reinforced by the phenomenon of gender segregation in middle childhood.

In their classic study, Waldrop and Halverson (1975) refer to boys' relationships as *extensive* and to girls' relationships as *intensive*. Boys' friendship groups are larger and more accepting of newcomers than are girls'. Boy friends play more outdoors and roam over a larger area in their play. Girl friends are more likely to play in pairs or in smaller groups, and they spend more playtime indoors or near home or school (Benenson, 1994; Gottman, 1986).

Interestingly, the ability to regulate emotion is associated with sex differences in friendship patterns (Dunsmore, Noguchi, Garner, Casey, & Bhullar, 2008). Among girls, those who are best able to manage their emotions have the greatest number of friends. For boys, the association is the opposite: skilled emotional management is linked to having fewer friends. These findings help to explain sex differences in social interactions among school-aged

**social status** A term used by psychologists to refer to how well an individual child is liked by his or her peers.

**popular children** Children who are described as well-liked by a majority of peers.

**neglected children** Children who are seldom described by peers as either liked or disliked.

**rejected children** Unpopular children who are explicitly avoided and not chosen as playmates or friends.

**Learning Objective 11.10** ---------➔

What are the characteristics and consequences of variations in social status?

👁─Watch the **Video** *The In Crowd* at **MyDevelopmentLab**

👁─Watch the **Video** *Peer-Neglected Child* at **MyDevelopmentLab**

*Some children prefer solitary activities and are not distressed about their lack of inclusion in peer groups.*

children. Compared to those of girls, boys' groups and boys' friendships appear to be focused more on competition and dominance, patterns in which open displays of emotions are often advantageous (Maccoby, 1995). By contrast, the ability to restrain emotions is critical to interactions among girls, which typically emphasize agreement, compliance, and self-disclosure.

None of these observed differences should obscure the fact that the interactions of male and female friends have a great many characteristics in common. For example, collaborative and cooperative exchanges are the most common forms of communication in both boys' and girls' friendships in these years. Nor should we necessarily conclude that boys' friendships are less important to them than are girls'. Nevertheless, it seems clear that there are differences in form and style that may well have enduring implications for the patterns of friendship over the life span.

## Social Status

One important aspect of individual differences in peer relationships is the degree to which peers like an individual child. Typically, this variable is called **social status**. Psychologists know a great deal about children in the three traditional status categories—popular, neglected, and rejected. **Popular children** are those who are most often described as well-liked and who are selected as playmates by peers. **Neglected children** are seldom described by peers as either liked or disliked, and **rejected children** are those who are actively disliked and avoided by their peers. 👁─Watch at **MyDevelopmentLab**

**POPULAR AND NEGLECTED CHILDREN** Some of the characteristics that differentiate popular children from others are things outside a child's control. In particular, extraverted, physically attractive, and physically larger children are more likely to be popular (Rubin, Coplan, Chen, Bowker, & McDonald, 2011). However, being very different from one's peers may also cause a child to be neglected or rejected. For example, shy children usually have few friends (Fordham & Stevenson-Hinde, 1999). Similarly, highly creative children are often rejected, as are those who have difficulty controlling their emotions (Aranha, 1997; Maszk, Eisenberg, & Guthrie, 1999).

Most studies show that popular children behave in positive, supporting, nonpunitive, and nonaggressive ways toward most other children. They explain things, take their playmates' wishes into consideration, take turns in conversation, and are able to regulate the expression of their strong emotions. In addition, popular children are usually good at accurately assessing others' feelings (Sallquist et al., 2009). Most are also good at looking at situations from others' perspectives (Fitzgerald & White, 2003).

Neglected children share many characteristics of peers who are popular. They often do quite well in school, but they are more prone to depression and loneliness than are popular children (Rubin et al., 2011). This is especially true for girls, who seem to value popularity more than boys do (Oldenburg & Kerns, 1997). Peer neglect may be associated with depression because brain-imaging studies show that peer neglect stimulates the same areas of the brain as physical pain (Eisenberger, 2003). In addition, some neglected children have unrealistic expectations about adults' ability to "fix" their situation (Galanaki, 2004). They may think, "Why doesn't the teacher *make* them be my friends?" Such thoughts may lead to feelings of hopelessness. 👁─Watch at **MyDevelopmentLab**

Nevertheless, many neglected children and teens aren't the least bit concerned about their lack of popularity (McElhaney, Antonishak, & Allen, 2008). Many such children are shy and prefer solitary activities; thus, their neglected status may simply be a function of their own personalities. However, a child's neglected status can change, suggesting that it is a function of both the social context and an individual child's personality. In fact, neglected children often move to the popular category when they become part of a new peer group.

**REJECTED CHILDREN**   There are two types of rejected children. *Withdrawn/rejected* children realize that they are disliked by peers (Rubin et al., 2011). After repeated attempts to gain peer acceptance, these children eventually give up and become socially withdrawn. As a result, they often experience feelings of loneliness.

*Aggressive/rejected* children are often disruptive and uncooperative but usually believe that their peers like them (Rubin et al., 2011). Many appear to be unable to control the expression of strong feelings (Eisenberg, Fabes, et al., 1995; Pettit, Clawson, Dodge, & Bates, 1996). They interrupt their play partners more often and fail to take turns in a systematic way.

**CAUSES AND CONSEQUENCES OF PEER REJECTION**   A growing body of research shows that rejection by one's peers in elementary school—especially when the rejection is because of excessive aggressiveness—is one of the very few aspects of childhood functioning that consistently predicts behavior problems or emotional disturbances later in childhood, in adolescence, and in adulthood (e.g., Ladd & Troop-Gordon, 2003). The link between early unpopularity and later behavior problems might be explained in any of several ways. Early problems with peers might be merely the most visible reflection of a general maladjustment that later manifests itself as delinquency or emotional disturbance. Alternatively, developmentalists might hypothesize that a failure to develop friendships itself causes problems that later become more general. Or, the basic difficulty could lie in a seriously warped internal working model of relationships that leads to peer rejection in elementary school and to delinquency. Or, all of the above might be true. Happily, however, not all rejected children remain rejected, and when a rejected child's status changes, the negative outcomes associated with rejection diminish (Ladd, Herald-Brown, & Reiser, 2008).

**CULTURE, PERSONALITY, AND SOCIAL STATUS**   Earlier we told you that extraverted children are more likely to be popular than shy children are. Researchers usually find just the opposite when they examine peer acceptance beyond the borders of Europe and North America. Particularly in Asian societies, children who are quiet and reserved are more likely to be popular than their more boisterous peers (Rubin et al., 2011). Thus, some developmentalists argue that peer acceptance among children may function as an important source of reinforcement for children who possess the personality traits that are most valued by adults in their cultures. Moreover, the criteria that children use to judge others may be an indication of the degree to which, by school age, they have picked up on the subtleties of the cultures in which they are growing up.

*A pattern of persistent aggression, and the peer rejection that so often accompanies it, is linked to a variety of long-term problems for children.*

## Peer Relationships in Adolescence

Many of the friendship patterns just discussed change at adolescence. For example, the sheer number of peer interactions increases rather dramatically across the teen years, a trend that is common across historical eras but has been accentuated by the advent of personal electronic communications devices. Recent surveys show that 69% of 11- to 14-year-olds and 85% of 15- to 18-year-olds have their own cell phones (Rideout, Foehr, & Roberts, 2010). Teens in both groups spend an average of two hours each day talking with and texting their friends. Many teenagers have one group of friends with whom they communicate by phone, another with whom they exchange online instant messages and e-mail, and yet another with which they associate through social networking (Foehr, 2006). As a result, teenagers have a wider range of acquaintances than their parents did in adolescence. However, they do not necessarily have more close friends.

Personality traits become more important in friend selection during adolescence (Tani, Rossi, & Smorti, 2005). Cross-sectional studies also suggest children's belief in the importance of popularity and peer acceptance strengthens slowly over the elementary school years and peaks during early adolescence (LaFontana & Cillessen, 2010). During these years, by age 12 to 15 or so, teens place more emphasis on popularity and peer acceptance than they do on any other dimension of peer relations. As adolescents get older, the quality of peer relationships becomes more important to them than popularity. Consequently, as adolescents approach adulthood, their friendships become increasingly intimate, in the sense that the friends share more of their inner feelings and secrets and are more knowledgeable about each

**Learning Objective 11.11**

What is the significance of peer groups and romantic relationships in adolescence?

other's feelings. Loyalty and faithfulness become centrally valued characteristics of friendship. These adolescent friendships are also more likely to endure for a year or longer (Bowker, 2004). Mixed-sex groups begin to appear, conformity to peer group values and behaviors increases, and parents' influence on the child wanes, even though the child's attachment to the parents remains strong.

**FUNCTIONS OF ADOLESCENT PEER GROUPS**   Just as individual relationships change, the function of the peer group changes in adolescence. In elementary school, peer groups primarily serve as a setting for mutual play (and for all the learning about relationships and the natural world that is part of such play). For teenagers, the peer group is the vehicle for the transition to adulthood, bringing with it the potential for both positive and negative influences on development (Eccles & Roeser, 2011).

One sign of this shift is that teenagers begin to confide primarily in their peers, rather than in their parents. You've seen one illustration of this change in Figure 11.2 (see page 272). An equally striking set of findings comes from classic research by Duane Buhrmester (1996). Figure 11.3 shows the combined findings from several studies in which children, teenagers, or adults were asked to rate the level of intimate disclosure they experienced with parents, friends, and a romantic partner. You can see three clear stages. Before adolescence, children report higher levels of self-disclosure with their parents. At adolescence, this changes in a major way: Self-disclosure with parents declines dramatically, while self-disclosure with friends becomes dominant. Then in adulthood, a second shift occurs as a romantic partner takes the role of primary confidant.

Another aspect of this change in the centrality of peer relationships is a strong clannishness and intense conformity to the group. Such conformity, which Erikson saw as an entirely normal aspect of adolescence, seems to peak at about age 13 or 14 (at about the same time that developmentalists observe a drop in self-esteem); conformity then wanes as the teenager begins to arrive at a sense of identity that is more independent of the peer group.   ◉ Watch at **MyDevelopmentLab**

◉─Watch the **Video** *Peer Pressure* at **MyDevelopmentLab**

It is also very clear that peers do indeed put pressure on each other to conform to peer group behavior standards. However, it is also true that peer group pressures are less potent and less negative than popular cultural stereotypes might suggest (Teitelman, Ratcliffe, & Cederbaum, 2008). Adolescents, like adults, choose their friends, and they are likely to choose to associate with a group that shares their values, attitudes, and behaviors. If the discrepancy between their own ideas and those of their friends becomes too great, teens are more likely to move toward a more compatible group of friends than to be persuaded to shift toward the first group's values or behaviors. Furthermore, teenagers report that explicit peer pressure is most likely to be pressure toward positive activities, such as school involvement, and away from misconduct.

One important exception to this rather rosy view of the impact of peer pressure occurs among teens who spend time with peers who lean toward aggressive, delinquent, or disruptive behavior (Véronneau, Vitaro, Pedersen, & Tremblay, 2008). Such peer subgroups often do provide explicit pressure toward misconduct or lawbreaking, to which some teens are susceptible. Whether an adolescent will be drawn to such a group in the first place, and whether he will be pushed toward more deviant behavior once he begins to "hang out" with such a group, appears to depend a good deal on his individual qualities—such as whether he has good social skills or has already shown some disruptive behavior before adolescence.

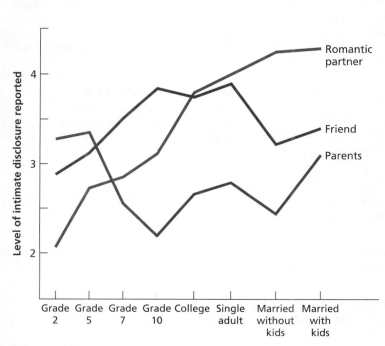

**FIGURE 11.3** Time Spent with Parents and Peers
Before adolescence, parents are most often a child's closest confidants; in adolescence, it is peers in whom the young person confides.

(*Source:* From "Need fulfillment, interpersonal competence, and the developmental context of early adolescent friendship" by D. Buhrmester, *The Company They Keep: Friendship in Childhood and Adolescence*, W. M. Bukowski, A. F. Newcomb, and W. W. Hartup (eds.), p. 168, Fig. 8.2.)

**CHANGES IN PEER GROUP STRUCTURE IN ADOLESCENCE**   The structure of the peer group also changes over the years of adolescence. The classic, widely quoted early study is Dexter Dunphy's observation of the formation, dissolution, and interaction of teenage groups in a high school in Sydney, Australia, between 1958 and 1960 (Dunphy, 1963). Dunphy identified two important subvarieties of groups. The first type, which he called a **clique**, is made up of four to six young people who appear to be strongly attached to one another. Cliques have strong cohesiveness and high levels of intimate sharing. However, most cliques also feature a considerable amount of within-group aggression aimed at maintaining the groups' status hierarchies (Closson, 2009). Typically, aggressive acts within cliques are perpetrated by dominant members against lower-status members (Closson, 2009). Furthermore, research suggests that cliques that are perceived as highly popular by non-members tolerate higher levels of within-group aggression than less popular cliques do. Thus, even though teens may enhance their popularity by associating with popular cliques, being accepted by these groups may require adolescents to endure being targeted by the groups' high-status members. ◉—|Watch at **MyDevelopmentLab**

In the early years of adolescence, cliques are almost entirely same-sex groups—a residual of the preadolescent pattern. Gradually, however, cliques combine into larger sets Dunphy called **crowds**, which include both males and females. Finally, the crowd breaks down again into heterosexual cliques and then into loose associations of couples. In Dunphy's study, children associated with their peers in crowds between approximately ages 13 and 15—the very years when researchers have observed the greatest conformity to peer pressure.

Bradford Brown and other researchers have changed Dunphy's labels somewhat (Brown, 1990; Brown, Bakken, Ameringer, & Mahon, 2008). Brown uses the word *crowd* to refer to the "reputation-based" group with which a young person is identified, either by choice or by peer designation. In most U.S. schools, there are any number of crowds—"jocks," "brains," "nerds," "dweebs," "punks," "druggies," "toughs," "normals," "populars," "preppies," or "loners." Studies in junior and senior high schools in the United States make it clear that teenagers can readily identify each of the major crowds in their school, and they offer quite stereotypic—even caricatured—descriptions of them (e.g., "The partiers goof off a lot more than the jocks do, but they don't come to school stoned like the burnouts do"). Each of these descriptions serves as what Brown calls an "identity prototype" (Brown, Mory, & Kinney, 1994, p. 133): Labeling others and labeling oneself as belonging to one or more of these groups help to create or reinforce the adolescent's own identity. Such labeling also helps the adolescent identify potential friends or foes. Thus, being identified as a member of one crowd or another channels each adolescent toward particular activities and particular relationships. Furthermore, within any given school, the various crowds are organized into a fairly clear, widely understood pecking order—that is, more status is attributed to some groups than to others. In U.S. schools, the groups labeled "jocks," "populars," or "normals" (or the equivalent) are typically at the top, with "brains" somewhere in the middle, and "druggies," "loners," and "nerds" at the bottom (Brown et al., 1994).

In one study of sixth-graders, researchers found that individual differences in achievement and overall academic motivation were predictable from crowd membership at the beginning of the year (Kindermann, 2007). Cross-group variations in school engagement—as measured by participation in extracurricular activities, interest in school subjects, and so on—appeared to explain this relationship. That is, students who were members of highly engaged crowds tended to be higher achievers and to be more strongly motivated to achieve than those who belonged to crowds that were less engaged.

In a study of peer group effects at the high school level, researchers found that teens who belong to a "brains" crowd are more likely to graduate from college, and those who belong to a "criminals" group are more likely to engage in antisocial behavior after leaving high school (Barber, Eccles, & Stone, 2001). Thus, the high school crowd with which a given individual adolescent chooses to associate may be indicative of the sense of personal identity he or she will build on in adulthood.

Within (and sometimes across) these crowds, adolescents create smaller friendship groups Brown calls *cliques* (with a definition that is very similar to Dunphy's meaning for the same term). Brown, like Dunphy, notes that in early adolescence, cliques are almost entirely same-sex; by late adolescence, they have become mixed in gender, often composed of groups of dating couples.

**clique**  A group of four to six friends with strong affectional bonds and high levels of group solidarity and loyalty; the term is used by researchers to describe a self-chosen group of friends.

**crowd**  A larger and looser group of friends than a clique, normally made up of several cliques that have joined together; a reputation-based group, common in adolescent subculture, with widely agreed-upon characteristics.

◉—|Watch the **Video** *Adolescent Cliques* at **MyDevelopmentLab**

*At a certain age, children move from one kind of clique to another.*

Whatever specific clique or crowd a teenager may identify with, theorists agree that the peer group performs the highly important function of helping the teenager shift from friendships to "partner" social relationships. The 13- or 14-year-old can begin to try out her new relationship skills in the wider group of the clique or crowd. Only after the adolescent develops some confidence do the beginnings of dating and of more committed pair relationships become evident.

**HETEROSEXUAL RELATIONSHIPS**   Of all the changes in social relationships in adolescence, perhaps the most profound for most teens is the shift from the total dominance of same-sex friendships to heterosexual relationships (Richards, Crowe, Larson, & Swarr, 1998). At the beginning of adolescence, teens are still fairly rigid about their preferences for same-sex friends (Bukowski, Sippola, & Hoza, 1999). Over the next year or two, they become more open to opposite-sex friendships (Harton & Latane, 1997; Kuttler, LaGreca, & Prinstein, 1999). The skills they gain in relating to opposite-sex peers in such friendships and in mixed-gender groups, as well as interactions with opposite-sex parents, prepare them for romantic relationships, which begin to become common among teens at around age 15 or so (Bucx, & Seiffge-Krenke, 2010; Feiring, 1999; Seiffge-Krenke & Connolly, 2010). Thus, while post-pubertal sexual desires are often assumed to be the basis of emergent romantic relationships, it appears that social factors are just as important.

Besides their social importance, these new relationships are clearly part of the preparation for assuming a full adult sexual identity. Physical sexuality is part of that role, but so are the skills of personal intimacy with the opposite sex, including flirting, communicating, and reading the form of social cues used by the other gender. In Western societies, adolescents learn these skills first in larger crowds or cliques and then in dating pairs (Zani, 1993). In fact, some studies suggest that engaging in such behaviors in group settings contributes more to the development of competence in romantic relationships than dating does (Laursen & Mooney, 2007).

By age 12 or 13, most adolescents have a prototypical understanding of what it means to be "in love." Interestingly, even though the actual progression toward romantic relationships happens faster for girls, boys report having had the experience of falling in love for the first time at an earlier age. Moreover, by the end of adolescence, the average boy believes he has been in love several more times than the average girl (Montgomery & Sorell, 1998).

The sense of being in love is an important factor in adolescent dating patterns (Montgomery & Sorell, 1998). In other words, teenagers prefer to date those with whom they believe they are in love, and they view falling out of love as a reason for ending a dating relationship. In addition, for girls but not for boys, romantic relationships are seen as a context in which self-disclosure can take place. Put another way, girls seem to want more psychological intimacy from these early relationships than their partners do (Feiring, 1999).

**HETEROSEXUAL RELATIONSHIPS ACROSS CULTURES**   Interpretations of research on couple formation must take into account the general finding that the development of romantic relationships in adolescence varies across cultures (Seiffge-Krenke & Connolly, 2010). In one study that compared Chinese and Canadian 16- and 17-year-olds, researchers found that far fewer Chinese than Canadian teens were involved in or desired to be involved in romantic relationships (Li et al., 2010). Analyses of these findings suggested that the underlying variable was cross-cultural variation in the centrality of peer and parental relationships. Chinese teens, on average, felt emotionally closest to their parents, while their Canadian counterparts reported greater emotional closeness to friends. However, among Chinese teens who reported being emotionally closer to friends than to parents, romantic relationships were more frequent than among peers who felt closer to their parents. Thus, these findings suggest that, across cultures, peer associations in early adolescence are foundational to the development of romantic relationships later in the teen years.

**HOMOSEXUAL TEENS** Romantic relationships emerge somewhat differently in the lives of homosexual teens. Like their heterosexual peers, homosexual teenagers become aware of same-sex attraction at around age 11 or 12 (Rosario, Scrimshaw, & Hunter, 2004). In contrast to the case among heterosexual teens, boys notice and act on same-sex attraction at somewhat earlier ages than girls do (Grov, Bimbi, Nanin, & Parsons, 2006).

There are many boys and girls, however, who experience some degree of attraction to both sexes prior to self-identifying as gay or lesbian. Thus, many homosexual teens go through a period of sexual discovery that begins with experimentation with heterosexual relationships. Shortly thereafter, these teenagers begin to experiment with same-sex relationships. By age 15 or so, most have classified themselves as primarily heterosexual or committed to a gay, lesbian, or bisexual orientation (Rosario, Scrimshaw, & Hunter, 2004). Many of those who are gay, lesbian, or bisexual participate in clubs and extracurricular activities that are designed to help sexual minority youth form social connections. In the company of these like-minded peers, gay, lesbian, and bisexual teens meet potential romantic partners and find important sources of social support (Rosario, Scrimshaw, & Hunter, 2004).

Researchers have found that homosexual teenagers today are more comfortable than those in past cohorts about revealing their sexual orientation to their parents and to their peers (Riley, 2010). Nevertheless, a comprehensive review of research on the coming-out process found that it varies across ethnic groups (Heatherington & Lavner, 2008). White teens appear to be most comfortable with and most likely to reveal their sexual orientations to parents and peers, while Asians Americans are least comfortable and least likely to disclose. Hispanic and African American adolescents fall between these two groups. Fear of disclosure is associated with concerns about parents' and peers' negative responses and, especially among Asian teens, a desire to respect traditional cultural values.

## Sibling Relationships

Playmates and friends play a highly significant role in children's development, but so, too, can brothers and sisters. This causes some observers to wonder whether children without siblings are not being deprived of important developmental experiences (see *Thinking about Research* on page 286). The Biblical story of Cain and Abel might lead us to believe that rivalry or jealousy is the key ingredient of sibling relationships. Yet rivalry is not the only quality of early sibling relationships; observations of preschoolers interacting with their siblings point toward other ingredients as well. Toddlers and preschoolers help their brothers and sisters, imitate them, and share their toys. Judy Dunn, in a detailed longitudinal study of a group of 40 families in England, observed that the older child often imitated a baby brother or sister; by the time the younger child was a year old, however, he or she began imitating the older sibling, and from then on most of the imitation consisted of the younger child copying the older one (Dunn & Kendrick, 1982). ◉⊣Watch at **MyDevelopmentLab**

Young brothers and sisters also hit each other, snatch toys, and threaten and insult each other. The older child in a pair of preschoolers is likely to be the leader and is therefore likely to show more of both aggressive and helpful behaviors (Abramovitch, Pepler, & Corter, 1982). For both members of the pair, however, the dominant feature seems to be ambivalence. Both supportive and negative behaviors are evident in about equal proportions. In Abramovitch's research, such ambivalence occurred whether the pair were close in age or further apart and whether the older child was a boy or a girl. Naturally there are variations on this theme; some pairs show mostly antagonistic or rivalrous behaviors, and some show mostly helpful and supportive behaviors. Most sibling pairs show both types of behaviors.

How do those themes play out in middle childhood? As a general rule, sibling relationships seem to be less central in the lives of school-aged children than are relationships with either friends or parents (Buhrmester, 1992). Children of elementary school age are less likely to turn to a sibling for affection than to parents, and they are less likely to turn to a brother or sister for companionship or intimacy than they are to a friend. Nevertheless, research indicates that sibling interactions—especially those that involve resolution of conflicts—strongly

◀------------Learning Objective 11.12
What are the characteristics of sibling relationships?

◉⊣Watch the **Video** *Sibling Rivalry* at **MyDevelopmentLab**

## The Resource Dilution Hypothesis

People often speculate that only children, those without siblings, are deprived of an important developmental experience and may be "spoiled" by their parents. However, some studies suggest that only children may actually have an advantage over those who have siblings and that this advantage may be due to birth order rather than the absence of siblints (Holmgren, Molander, & Nilsson, 2006; Kristensen & Bjerkedal, 2007). The *resource dilution hypothesis* explains these findings as the result of the progressive "watering down" of the parents' material and psychological resources with each additional birth (Downey, 2001). Thus, from this perspective, parents have the greatest influence on the oldest child, an advantage that is shared by only children and the oldest child in a multi-child family.

Critics of the resource dilution hypothesis point out that it ignores the relationship-building opportunities that these children contribute to their older siblings' development

(Gillies & Lucey, 2006). In support of their argument, critics cite research that suggests that later-borns have an advantage over their older siblings with regard to a variety of social skills, including the ability to negotiate solutions to interpersonal conflicts (Ross, Ross, Stein, & Trabasso, 2006). Likewise, firstborns who have siblings outperform only children on measures of social negotiation. Firstborns with younger siblings also appear to gain self-reliance skills from serving as surrogate parents for younger siblings and report that they feel closer to their siblings than they do to their friends (Brody, Kim, Murray, & Brown, 2003; Pollett & Nettle, 2009). Regardless of birth order, too, affectionate sibling relationships moderate the effects of stressful life events such as parental divorce, and they enable children to advance more rapidly than only children do with regard to understanding others' mental states and behaviors (Rubin et al., 2011). Thus, only and firstborn children may get more of the kind of

### Learning Objective 11.12a
How does the resource dilution hypothesis explain differences between only children and those who have siblings?

attention from parents that is critical to cognitive development, but sibling relationships appear to make positive contributions to children's social and emotional development.

### CRITICAL ANALYSIS

1. What kinds of sibling relationships would harm rather than help a child's social and emotional development?
2. In what kinds of situations might you expect only children to show social skills that are superior to those of children who have siblings?

influence children's understanding of social relationships and equip them with skills that are important in adult relationships (Bettner, 2007; Thompson & Halberstadt, 2008).

Sibling relationships also vary enormously. On the basis of direct studies of young children as well as retrospective reports by young adults about their sibling relationships when they were of school age, researchers have identified several patterns or styles of sibling relationships: (1) a *caregiver relationship*, in which one sibling serves as a kind of quasi-parent for the other, a pattern that seems to be more common between an older sister and younger brother than for any other combination of siblings; (2) a *buddy relationship*, in which both members of the pair try to be like one another and take pleasure in being together; (3) a *critical* or *conflictual relationship*, which includes attempts by one sibling to dominate the other, teasing, and quarreling; (4) a *rival relationship*, which contains many of the same elements as a critical relationship but is also low in any form of friendliness or support; and (5) a *casual* or *uninvolved relationship*, in which the siblings have relatively little to do with one another (Murphy, 1993; Stewart, Beilfuss, & Verbrugge, 1995). Rivalrous or critical relationships seem to be more common between siblings who are close together in age (4 or fewer years apart) and in families in which the parents are less satisfied with their marriage (Buhrmester & Furman, 1990; McGuire, McHale, & Updegraff, 1996). Buddy relationships appear to be somewhat more common in pairs of sisters (Buhrmester & Furman, 1990), while rivalry seems to be highest in boy-boy pairs (Stewart et al., 1995).

## Behavior with Peers

The broad sketch of peer relationships from toddlerhood through adolescence that you have just read makes clear the various roles that peers play in children's development over these years. It also points out how central such relationships are. What it does not convey are all the changes in the actual content and quality of children's peer interactions. To fill in some of the gaps, we will consider two specific categories of behavior representing two ends of a continuum: prosocial behavior and aggression.

# Prosocial Behavior

◄------------Learning Objective 11.13

What is prosocial behavior, and when does it appear?

**Prosocial behavior** is defined by psychologists as voluntary behavior intended to benefit another with no obvious self-gain. In everyday language, prosocial behavior is essentially what we mean by *altruism*, and it changes with age, just as other aspects of peer behavior change.

Prosocial behaviors first become evident in children of about 2 or 3—at about the same time they begin to show real interest in play with other children. They will offer to help another child who is hurt, offer a toy, or try to comfort another person (Tomasello, 2009). As pointed out in Chapter 6, children this young are only beginning to understand that others feel differently than they do, but they obviously understand enough about the emotions of others to respond in supportive and sympathetic ways when they see other children or adults hurt or sad.

**prosocial behavior** Voluntary behavior intended to benefit another, such as giving away or sharing possessions, money, or time, with no obvious self-gain; altruism.

## DEVELOPMENTAL SCIENCE IN THE REAL WORLD

### Rearing Helpful and Altruistic Children

Eight-year-old Marisol, perched on a kitchen stool that allowed her to reach the counter, slowly poured cake mix from the box into a large mixing bowl, taking care not to spill any. Her father, Rick, stood by her side ready to assist if his daughter needed help. "Good job," he said as the last of the mix fell into the bowl. "Now we add the eggs." With that, Rick painstakingly showed Marisol how to break an egg. Rick thought to himself that the cake would be finished a lot sooner if he did it himself, without Marisol. But Rick was committed to helping his daughter learn the skills needed to be a contributing member of the Ruiz household.

Teaching children to be helpful can be time-consuming. Helping them learn to be altruistic—that is, to want to help others even when there is no reward involved—can be even more difficult. However, research on the development of prosocial behavior can provide insights into the process (Eisenberg & Fabes, 1998):

- **Capitalize on the child's capacity for empathy.** If your child injures someone, point out the consequences of that injury for the other person: "When you hit Susan, it hurts her."
- **Create a loving and warm family climate.** When parents express affection and warmth regularly toward their

**Learning Objective 11.13a**
How can parents increase the chances that their children will demonstrate altruistic and helpful behavior?

children, the children are more likely to be generous and altruistic.
- **Provide rules or guidelines about helpful behavior.** Direct instructions foster prosocial behavior: "I'd like you to help Keisha with her puzzle" or "Please share your candy with John."
- **Provide prosocial attributions.** Attribute your child's helpful or altruistic action to the child's own internal character: "You're such a helpful child!"
- **Have children do helpful things.** Assign them regular household tasks such as helping to cook or clean, taking care of pets, or watching younger siblings.
- **Model thoughtful and generous behavior.** Stating the rules will do little good if parents' own behavior does not match what they say! Children (and adults) are simply much more likely to do generous or thoughtful things if they see other people—especially other people in authority, such as parents—being generous and thoughtful.

*Having children do helpful things, as these third-graders are doing by sorting recyclable material, is one way to increase altruistic behavior in kids.*

#### REFLECTION

1. How might teachers and parents model generosity?
2. Why do you think that a loving and warm family climate promotes altruistic behavior?

**aggression** Behavior that is aimed at harming or injuring another person or object.

**instrumental aggression** Aggressive behavior intended to achieve a goal, such as obtaining a toy from another child.

**hostile aggression** Aggressive verbal behavior intended to hurt another's feelings.

**Learning Objective 11.14** - - - - - - - - - ➤
In what ways do boys and girls of different ages differ in the exhibition of aggression?

👁—⎤Watch the **Video** *Reactive Aggression* at
**MyDevelopmentLab**

After these early years, researchers have noted a number of trends. One such trend is the appearance of prosocial reciprocity in the later preschool years. For example, a 4- or 5-year-old child is more likely to offer to share a toy with a child who has previously offered a toy to her (Fujisawa, Kutsukake, & Hasegawa, 2008). Older children and adolescents are more likely than preschoolers to provide physical and verbal assistance to someone in need (Eisenberg, 1992). However, not all prosocial behaviors show this pattern of increase with age. Comforting another child, for example, appears to be more common among children in preschool and early elementary grades than among older children (Eisenberg, 1988, 1990).

Developmentalists also know that children vary a lot in the amount of altruistic behavior they show, and that young children who show relatively more empathy and altruism are also those who regulate their own emotions well. They show positive emotions readily and negative emotions less often (Eisenberg et al., 1996). They are also more popular with peers (Mayeux & Cillissen, 2003). These variations in children's levels of empathy or altruism seem to be related to specific kinds of child rearing (see *Developmental Science in the Real World* on page 287).

# Aggression

If you have watched children in pairs or groups, then you know that, while children do support and share with their friends, they also tease, fight, yell, criticize, and argue over objects and territory. Researchers who have studied this more negative side of children's interactions have looked mostly at **aggression**, which can be defined as behavior apparently intended to injure some other person or object. 👁—⎤Watch at **MyDevelopmentLab**

**INSTRUMENTAL AND HOSTILE AGGRESSION**  Every child shows at least some aggression, but the form and frequency of aggression change over the years of childhood. When 2- or 3-year-old children are upset or frustrated, they are more likely to throw things or to hit each other. Typically, children of this age behave aggressively in order to achieve a goal, such as getting a toy from another child. This kind of aggression is known as **instrumental aggression**. Once the goal is achieved, the aggression stops.

As their verbal skills improve, children shift away from overt physical aggression toward greater use of verbal aggression, such as taunting or name-calling. The purpose of aggression changes as well. Among older preschoolers, **hostile aggression**, the goal of which is to hurt another's feelings rather than to do physical harm, becomes more common. In the elementary school and adolescent years, physical aggression becomes still less common, and children learn the cultural rules about when it is acceptable to display anger or aggression and how much one can acceptably display. In most cultures, this means that anger is increasingly disguised and aggression is increasingly controlled with increasing age (Underwood, Coie, & Herbsman, 1992).

**SEX DIFFERENCES IN AGGRESSION**  One interesting exception to the general pattern of declining physical aggression with age is that in all-boy pairs or groups, at least in the United States, physical aggression seems to remain both relatively high and constant over the years of childhood. Indeed, at every age, boys show more physical aggression and more assertiveness than do girls, both within friendship pairs and in general (Coie & Dodge, 1998).

The social consequences of aggressive behavior vary with gender. For girls, aggression seems to lead consistently to peer rejection. Among boys, however, aggression may result in either popularity or rejection (Rodkin, Farmer, Pearl, & Van Acker, 2000; Xie, Cairns, & Cairns, 1999). In fact, aggressiveness seems to be a fairly common characteristic of popular African American boys. In addition, irrespective of their general popularity, the close friends of aggressive boys tend to be aggressive as well. Furthermore, aggressiveness seems to precede these relationships. In other words, boys who are aggressive seek out other boys like themselves as friends (Hanish, Martin, Fabes, & Barcelo, 2008). Yet being friends doesn't seem to make either member of an aggressive friendship pair more aggressive (Poulin & Boivin, 2000). Research also suggests that children have more positive attitudes toward aggressive peers whose aggressive acts are seen as mostly retaliatory in nature and toward those who engage in prosocial as well as aggressive behaviors (Coie & Cillessen, 1993; Newcomb,

Bukowski, & Pattee, 1993; Poulin & Boivin, 1999). Social approval may not increase boys' aggressiveness, but it does seem to help maintain it, because interventions to reduce aggressive behavior typically have little effect on aggressive boys who are popular (Phillips, Schwean, & Saklofske, 1997).

**RELATIONAL AGGRESSION**  The findings of studies examining sex differences in aggression have been so clear and so consistent that most psychologists have concluded that boys are simply "more aggressive" in every possible way. But that conclusion may turn out to be wrong, or at least misleading. Instead, it appears that girls express aggressiveness in a different way, using what has been labeled relational aggression instead of either physical aggression or nasty words (Putallaz et al., 2007). Physical aggression hurts others through physical damage or threat of such damage; **relational aggression** is aimed at damaging another person's self-esteem or peer relationships, such as by cruel gossiping, by making facial expressions of disdain, or by ostracizing or threatening to ostracize the other ("I won't invite you to my birthday party if you do that"). Another important difference between hostile and relational aggression is that acts of hostile aggression are more likely to draw adult attention, especially when they involve hitting or other actions that can cause physical harm. Consequently, they may occur less frequently than acts of relational aggression. By contrast, children can engage in relational aggression in ways that escape the notice of adults—such as passing notes containing derogatory statements about peers or subtly moving away from a child who is the target of aggression during recess. As a result, some children may become habitual victims of relational aggression.

Girls are much more likely to use relational aggression than are boys, especially toward other girls, a difference that begins as early as the preschool years and becomes very marked by the fourth or fifth grade. For example, in one early study of nearly 500 children in the third through sixth grades, Nicki Crick found that 17.4% of the girls but only 2% of the boys were high in relational aggression—almost precisely the reverse of the rates of physical aggression (Crick & Grotpeter, 1995).

What might be the origins of such sex differences in the form of aggression used? One obvious possibility is that hormone differences play a part. For one thing, higher rates of physical aggression in males have been observed in every human society and in all species of primates. Thus, differing rates of physical aggression appear to have at least some biological basis. However, peer reinforcement may also play a role. Researchers have found that children as young as 3 years of age believe that girls are more likely to display relational aggression and boys are more likely to show physical aggression (Giles & Heyman, 2005). Thus, just as children encourage their peers to engage in other types of stereotypical behavior, they may provide rewards for boys and girls who display gender-appropriate aggressive behaviors. Likewise, they may actively sanction peers of both sexes for engaging in gender- inappropriate forms of aggression.

## Trait Aggression

◄------------Learning Objective 11.15
What is trait aggression, and how does it differ from typical age-related forms of aggression?

There are a few children, most of them boys, for whom a high level of aggressive behavior in early childhood is predictive of a lifelong pattern of antisocial behavior, a finding that has been supported by cross-cultural research (Derzon, 2001; Kosterman, Graham, Hawkins, Catalano, & Herrenkohl, 2001; Moffitt, 2007). Researchers have searched for causes of this kind of aggression, which psychologists often refer to as *trait aggression*, to distinguish it from developmentally normal forms of aggression.

Some psychologists have looked for a genetic basis for trait aggression and have produced some supportive data (Brendgen et al., 2008; Rhee & Waldman, 2011; Yaman et al., 2010). Others suggest that trait aggression is associated with being raised in an aggressive environment, such as an abusive family (Dodge, 1993). Family factors other than abuse, such as lack of affection and the use of coercive discipline techniques, also appear to be related to trait aggression, especially in boys (Chang, Schwartz, Dodge, & McBride-Chang, 2003; Campbell et al., 2010).

Still other developmentalists have discovered evidence that aggressive children may shape their environments in order to gain continuing reinforcement for their behavior. For example, as early as 4 years of age, aggressive boys tend to prefer other aggressive boys as playmates and

**relational aggression**  Aggression aimed at damaging another person's self-esteem or peer relationships, such as by using ostracism or threats of ostracism, cruel gossiping, or facial expressions of disdain.

to form stable peer groups with them. These groups develop their own patterns of interaction and reward each other with social approval for aggressive acts (Hanish et al., 2008). This pattern of association among aggressive boys continues through middle childhood and adolescence.

Finally, a large body of research suggests that highly aggressive children lag behind their peers in understanding others' intentions (Meece & Mize, 2010). Research demonstrating that teaching aggressive children how to think about others' intentions reduces aggressive behavior also supports this conclusion (Crick & Dodge, 1996; Webster-Stratton & Reid, 2003). Specifically, this research suggests that aggressive school-aged children seem to reason more like 2- to 3-year-olds about intentions. For example, they are likely to perceive a playground incident (such as one child accidentally tripping another during a soccer game) as an intentional act that requires retaliation. Training helps aggressive school-aged children acquire an understanding of others' intentions that most children learn between the ages of 3 and 5. Thus, trait aggression may originate in some kind of deviation from the typical developmental path during the early childhood period.

**BULLIES AND VICTIMS** As children get older, they tend to take on consistent roles across aggressive interactions—perpetrator, victim, assistant to the perpetrator, reinforcing onlooker, nonparticipant onlooker, defender of the victim, and so on (Andreou & Metallidou, 2004; Veenstra, Lindenberg, Munniksma, & Dijkstra, 2010). Habitual perpetrators are commonly referred to as *bullies*. Male bullies are more likely to be physically and verbally aggressive toward their victims, while female bullies are more likely to exhibit relational aggression (Von Marées & Petermann, 2010). Apart from these gender differences, developmentalists have learned a great deal about the characteristics that distinguish bullies from non-bullies. 👁️⎯**Watch** at **MyDevelopmentLab**

Children's personality and physical traits to some degree determine the non-bully roles they assume. For example, shy children usually occupy the nonparticipant onlooker role, while children who are emotionally unstable are more likely to serve as assistants to the perpetrator or as reinforcing onlookers (Tani, Greenman, Schneider, & Fregoso, 2003). Likewise, studies show that certain characteristics are found among habitual victims across a wide variety of cultural settings (Eslea et al., 2004). Among boys, victims are often physically smaller or weaker than their peers. Whether boys or girls, victims seldom assert themselves

👁️⎯**Watch** the **Video** *Peer Acceptance* at **MyDevelopmentLab**

---

# TECHNOLOGY AND THE DEVELOPING CHILD
## Cyberbullying

As you have learned, children and teens who are aggressive typically lack empathy and are especially vulnerable to situational factors that contribute to poor moral decision making. These factors are prominent in research that has examined why some adolescents engage in *cyberbullying*, a form of aggression in which electronic communications are used to intentionally inflict harm on others (Ang & Goh, 2010). In fact, two-thirds of cyberbullies exhibit aggressive behavior in other contexts as well (Twyman, Saylor, Taylor, & Comeaux, 2010).

Because they lack empathy, cyberbullies typically have little sensitivity to the speed with which electronic communications of an aggressive nature, such as digitally altered or embarrassing photos, can spread throughout

a peer context such as a school or neighborhood (Smith & Slonje, 2010). They may even regard the spreading of such information as a measure of cyberbullying success and display little concern about how such experiences affect their victims. In addition, acting aggressively with anonymity and in a way that distances the perpetrator from the immediate responses of the victim can contribute to cyberbullying. The anonymity factor may help explain why one-third of cyberbullies do not exhibit bullying behavior in other social contexts (Twyman et al., 2010).

### FIND OUT MORE

*Use your Internet search skills to answer these questions.*

### Learning Objective 11.15a
What are the similarities and differences between cyberbullying and bullying in other social contexts?

1. What are some strategies that adults can use to explain the rules of "netiquette" to children? In your opinion, to what extent might knowing these rules deter children from becoming cyberbullies?

2. How does cyberbullying among school-aged children and adolescents differ? Visit http://www.stopcyberbullying.org to start searching for answers to this question.

with their peers, making neither suggestions for play activities nor prosocial actions. Instead, they submit to whatever suggestions others make. Other children do not like this behavior and thus do not like the victims (Crick & Grotpeter, 1996; Schwartz, Dodge, & Coie, 1993). The consequences of such victimization can include loneliness, school avoidance, low self-esteem, and significant depression at later ages (Kochenderfer & Ladd, 1996; Olweus, 1995).

Bullies are distinctive because they are more aggressive toward adults than non-bullies, cannot empathize with their victims' pain or unhappiness, feel little or no guilt or shame about their actions, and are often impulsive (Menesini et al., 2003). However, bullying is a complex phenomenon that must be understood as resulting from characteristics of bullies themselves, the family environments in which they are being raised, and the social settings in which bullying incidents occur (Curtner-Smith, Smith, & Porter, 2010; Rubin et al., 2011; see *Technology and the Developing Child* on page 290). Studies suggest that four factors lie behind the development of bullying behavior (Olweus, 1995):

- Indifference toward the child and lack of warmth from the parents in the early years
- Failure by parents to set clear and adequate limits on aggressive behavior
- The parents' use of physical punishment
- A difficult, impulsive temperament in the child

## THINK CRITICALLY

- Compare and contrast the interaction patterns of adolescents in high schools to those of adults on campus or in workplaces. To what degree do crowds and cliques develop in such settings, and what roles do they play in academic and workplace functioning?
- In what ways do adults exhibit relational aggression? Do gender differences in types of aggression appear to persist into the adult years?

## CONDUCT YOUR OWN RESEARCH

A playground where toddlers and preschoolers play while their parents watch would be an ideal place to carry out a naturalistic observation of safe base behavior. Before you observe any children and parents, be sure to introduce yourself to the parents and explain that you are doing an assignment for your child development class. For a set period of time—say, 15 minutes—observe an individual child and note how many times he or she looks at, speaks to, or moves toward the parent. Repeat the procedure for several other children. Categorize the children as younger or older and compare the number of safe base behaviors for each age group. You should find that the younger the children are, the more frequently they make contact with their parent (their safe base).

## SUMMARY ✓•—Study and Review at MyDevelopmentLab

### Relationships with Parents

**11.1** How did Bowlby and Ainsworth characterize affectional bonds, attachments, and internal working models?
Bowlby and Ainsworth distinguished between an affectional bond (an enduring tie to a partner viewed as unique) and an attachment, which involves feelings of security and having a safe base. An attachment is deduced from the existence of attachment behaviors. Once established, an attachment relationship becomes the basis of an internal working model that the child applies to future interactions with the attachment figure and with others.

**11.2** What factors influence the parent's bond to the child?
For parents to form a strong bond to their infant, what is most crucial is not immediate contact at birth but the development and repetition of mutually reinforcing and interlocking attachment behaviors.

**11.3** How does the child's attachment to the parent change across infancy, early childhood, and middle childhood?
Bowlby proposed that the child's attachment to the caregiver develops through a series of steps, from rather indiscriminate aiming of attachment behaviors toward anyone within reach, through a focus on one or more figures, to

secure base behavior, beginning at about 6 months of age, which signals the presence of a clear attachment. Attachment behaviors become less visible during the preschool years, except when the child is stressed. School-aged children exhibit less safe base behavior than infants and preschoolers do, but extended separations can still be stressful.

**11.4** What are the characteristics of parent-child relationships in adolescence?

The child's basic attachment to the parents remains strong in adolescence, despite an increase in parent-child conflict, the greater independence of the teenager, and the increased role of the peer group.

**11.5** How does the behavior of securely and insecurely attached infants differ?

Children differ in the security of their first attachments. The secure infant uses the parent as a safe base for exploration and can be readily consoled by the parent. Insecurely attached infants display a variety of patterns, including ambivalence toward and avoidance of parents. Some insecurely attached infants exhibit a disorganized pattern in which they sometimes move toward and sometimes move away from parents. Differences in attachment classification are correlated with patterns of parental responsiveness.

**11.6** How does infant temperament influence the attachment process?

An infant's temperament may affect attachment. Behaviorally inhibited infants exhibit more stranger and separation anxiety than other infants. Infants with difficult temperaments often actively resist the kinds of comfort that foster the development of secure attachments. As a result, they are more likely than other infants to develop insecure attachments.

**11.7** To what degree are attachment classifications stable, and what are their long-term consequences?

The security of an initial attachment is reasonably stable and is fostered by sensitivity and contingent responsiveness by the parent. Securely attached children appear to be more socially skillful, more curious and persistent in approaching new tasks, and more mature. An adult's internal working model of attachment, based on the security of his or her own attachment to parents in childhood, influences parenting behavior.

## Relationships with Peers

**11.8** What are the characteristics of infants' and preschoolers' peer interactions?

Cooperative play emerges around 18 months, although infants still typically play by themselves. By 3 or 4, children would rather play with peers than alone.

**11.9** How do peer relationships change during the school years?

By the time they reach school age, most children have formed individual friendships and show preferential positive behavior toward their friends. Friendships become more common and more stable in the elementary school years, and more intimate in adolescence. In elementary school, peer interactions are focused mostly on common activities; in adolescence, peer groups also become a vehicle for the transition from dependence to independence.

**11.10** What are the characteristics and consequences of variations in social status?

Popularity among peers, in elementary school or later, is most consistently based on the amount of positive and supportive social behavior shown by a child toward peers. Socially rejected children are often characterized by high levels of aggression or bullying and low levels of agreement and helpfulness. Aggressive/rejected children are likely to show behavior problems in adolescence and a variety of disturbances in adulthood.

**11.11** What is the significance of peer groups and romantic relationships in adolescence?

Reputation-based groups, or crowds, are an important part of adolescent social relationships, particularly in the early high school years. Smaller groups of friends, or cliques, are also significant and gradually shift from being same-sex groups to mixed-sex groups to dating pairs. On average in Western cultures, dating begins at about age 15, but there is wide variability.

**11.12** What are the characteristics of sibling relationships?

Sibling relationships are often thought of as rivalrous, but there are many variations. Siblings in caregiver relationships act as surrogate parents for brothers and sisters. Those in buddy relationships try to act alike and enjoy being together. Rival relationships are characterized by conflict, and siblings in uninvolved relationships have little to do with one another.

**11.12a** How does the resource dilution hypothesis explain differences between only children and those who have siblings?

The resource dilution hypothesis assumes that the advantages that only children display over those who have siblings are due to birth order. This hypothesis argues that parental resources become "watered down" with each additional child. Critics say that the hypothesis ignores the social-developmental advantages of sibling relationships, such as superior conflict management skills.

## Behavior with Peers

**11.13** What is prosocial behavior, and when does it appear?
Prosocial behavior, such as helpfulness or generosity, is apparent as early as age 2 or 3 and generally increases throughout childhood.

**11.13a** How can parents increase the chances that their children will demonstrate altruistic and helpful behavior?
Developmentalists advise parents to look for opportunities to help children development empathy. They should also create a loving and warm family climate, provide children with guidelines for helpful behavior, praise them for prosocial behavior, and model thoughtful and generous behavior.

**11.14** In what ways do boys and girls of different ages differ in the exhibition of aggression?
Physical aggression decreases as children's language skills improve. Thus, older preschoolers and school-aged children are more likely than toddlers to use verbal aggression rather than physical aggression. At all ages, boys exhibit more physical aggression than girls do; girls show more relational aggression.

**11.15** What is trait aggression, and how does it differ from typical age-related forms of aggression?
Some children develop a pattern of aggressive behavior, known as trait aggression, that continues to cause problems for them throughout childhood and adolescence. Unlike more typical forms of aggression, trait aggression changes little with age.

**11.15a** What are the similarities and differences between cyberbullying and bullying in other social contexts?
Two-thirds of cyberbullies display bullying behavior in other contexts. They have the same characteristics as bullies (e.g., lack of empathy). However, one-third of cyberbullies do not appear to be bullies outside the digital environment. The anonymity offered by cyberbullying may encourage them to behave in such ways.

## KEY TERMS

affectional bond (p. 266)
aggression (p. 288)
attachment (p. 267)
attachment behaviors (p. 267)
clique (p. 283)
crowd (p. 283)

goal-corrected partnership (p. 271)
goodness-of-fit (p. 276)
hostile aggression (p. 288)
individuation (p. 272)
insecure attachment (p. 273)
instrumental aggression (p. 288)

internal working model (p. 267)
neglected children (p. 280)
parallel play (p. 278)
popular children (p. 280)
prosocial behavior (p. 287)
reciprocal friendship (p. 279)

rejected children (p. 280)
relational aggression (p. 289)
secure attachment (p. 273)
social status (p. 280)
strange situation (p. 273)

# 12

# Thinking about Relationships: Social-Cognitive and Moral Development

For more than 20 years, developmental psychologist Thomas Lickona of the State University of New York at Cortland has been helping parents and teachers apply the findings of developmental research to the nurturance of children's and adolescents' moral development, a process often called *character education*. Most recently, Lickona has advocated an approach called the *Smart and Good Schools Model* (Davidson, Khmelkov, & Lickona, 2010). Lickona's model defines *character* as having two components: *performance character* (the "smart" component) and *moral character* (the "good"

294

component). The first of these involves the tendency to work hard and do one's best regardless of personal interest in or potential material gain from specific tasks such as school work. The second involves actions that can be judged to be right or wrong according to the culture in which a person lives. Thus, the *Smart and Good Schools Model* includes curricula that are geared to fostering development in both the performance and moral domains of character. 👁—Watch at **MyDevelopmentLab**

Interestingly, these two components of character are evident in teachers' characterizations of "good" students and students' explanations of the distinguishing characteristics of "caring" teachers. What asked to list the hallmarks of a good student, teachers cite elements of performance character such as diligence and perseverance as well as elements of moral character such as honesty (Lickona & Davidson, 2005). Similarly, school-age children define caring teachers as those who are both good at teaching (performance character) and fair in grading (moral character) (Wentzel, 1997). Moreover, the *Smart and Good Schools Model* argues that most teachers and most teaching situations contribute to character development because of the many intentional messages that teachers convey to students in both domains:

*"Late work is unacceptable." (performance character)*
*"You should not interrupt others." (moral character)*

As a developmental scientist, Lickona argues that character education, like any other kind of instruction, must be based on a sound understanding of child development. A developmentally appropriate approach to character education begins with an understanding that how individuals think about relationships, a process called *social cognition*, is at the heart of character. Thus, we begin this chapter with a discussion of how thinking about social relationships changes over the years of childhood and adolescence and end with an examination of moral development, the process of learning to distinguish between right and wrong in accordance with cultural values.

**social cognition** Thinking about and understanding the emotions of and interactions and relationships among people.

👁—Watch the **Videos** *Signature Strengths as Character Education* and *Schools Teaching Respect* at **MyDevelopmentLab**

## The Development of Social Cognition

The topic of **social cognition** should not be entirely new to you. You have read about many facets of social cognition in previous chapters. The infant's emerging ability to recognize individuals and to use facial expressions and other body language for social referencing is one kind of social cognition, as is the growing understanding of others' emotions and the development of a theory of mind in the preschool years. However, there are several other important components of social cognition. 👁—Watch at **MyDevelopmentLab**

👁—Watch the **Video** *Social Cognition* at **MyDevelopmentLab**

## Some General Principles and Issues

◄-----------**Learning Objective 12.1**
What are the general principles of social-cognitive development?

One way to think about social cognition is simply to conceive of it as the application of general cognitive processes or skills to a different topic—in this case, people or relationships. In this view, the child's understanding of self, others, and social relationships is based on her overall level of cognitive development, such as her level of perspective-taking skills (Rubin, Coplan, Chen, Baskirk, & Wojslawowica, 2005; Selman, 1980). Indeed, many of the same principles that seem to apply to general cognitive development hold for social cognitive development as well; that is, children's social cognition develops in certain directions:

- *From outer to inner characteristics.* Younger children pay attention to the surface of things, to what things look like; older children look for principles, for causes.
- *From observation to inference.* Young children initially base their conclusions only on what they can see or feel; as they grow, they make inferences about what ought to be or what might be.

Watch the **Video** *Development of Social Cognition* at **MyDevelopmentLab**

- *From definite to qualified.* Young children's "rules" are very definite and fixed (such as sex-role rules); by adolescence, rules begin to be qualified.
- *From observer's view to general view.* Children become less egocentric with time—less tied to their own individual views, more able to construct a model of some experience or some process that is true for everyone.

All of these dimensions of change describe children's emerging social cognition, just as they describe the development of thinking about objects. But thinking about people or relationships also has some special features that makes it different from thinking about physical objects (Quinn et al., 2011). Watch at **MyDevelopmentLab**

One obvious difference is that people, unlike rocks or glasses of water, behave intentionally. In particular, people often attempt to conceal information about themselves; thus, the ability to "read" other people's cues is a key social-cognitive skill. Further, unlike relationships with objects, relationships with people are mutual and reciprocal. Dolls, sets of blocks, or bicycles don't talk back, get angry, or respond in unexpected ways, but people do all these things. In learning about relationships, children must learn enough about other people's motives and feelings to predict such responses.

Children also have to learn special rules about particular forms of social interactions—such as rules about politeness, about when you can and cannot speak, and about power or dominance hierarchies—all of which are forms of *social scripts* (Schank & Abelson, 1977). The existence of such scripts allows children to develop strong expectations about how people will behave, in what order, in which settings. Furthermore, these scripts change with age.

These illustrations make it clear that the development of sophisticated social cognition is more than a simple process of applying basic cognitive processes and strategies to the arena of social interaction. The child must also come to understand the ways in which social relationships are different from interactions with the physical world, and she must learn special rules and strategies. Let's begin with the child's growing ability to describe other people.

**Learning Objective 12.2**

In what ways do children's descriptions of other people change across childhood and adolescence?

Watch the **Video** *Black Doll White Doll* at **MyDevelopmentLab**

## Describing Other People

Research suggests that there is a shift from observation (what children see) to inference (how they interpret what they see) in children's descriptions of others, as well as a clear change in focus from outer to internal characteristics. There seem to be at least three steps. Up to perhaps ages 6 to 8, children's descriptions of others are focused almost exclusively on external features. Children in this age range describe others' hair color, their relative size, their gender, where they live, and what they like to do. Race is another characteristic that frequently crops up in such descriptions (see *Developmental Science in the Real World* on page 297). This description by a 7-year-old boy, taken from a classic study in England by Livesley and Bromley, is typical: Watch at **MyDevelopmentLab**

> *He is very tall. He has dark brown hair, he goes to our school. I don't think he has any brothers or sisters. He is in our class. Today he has a dark orange [sweater] and gray trousers and brown shoes. (1973, p. 213)*

When young children do use internal or evaluative terms to describe people, they are likely to use quite global terms, such as *nice* or *mean* and *good* or *bad*. Further, young children do not seem to see these qualities as lasting or general traits of the individual, applicable in all situations or over time (Heyman, 2009). In other words, the young child has not yet developed a concept that might be thought of as "conservation of personality."

Then, beginning at about age 7 or 8, at just about the time children seem to develop a global sense of self-esteem, a rather dramatic shift occurs in their descriptions of others. They begin to focus more on the inner traits or qualities of another person and to assume that those traits will be apparent in many situations (Gnepp & Chilamkurti, 1988). Children this age still describe others' physical features, but such descriptions seem to be intended more as examples or elaborations of more general points about internal qualities. You can see the change when you compare the 7-year-old's description above with this (widely quoted) description by a child who is nearly 10:

## Learning and Unlearning Prejudice

Mara was excited about her new job teaching first grade in a public school that had a multi-ethnic student population. She became concerned on her first day, however, when she overheard many of the 6-year-olds in her class making remarks about one another's ethnicity. Even more alarming to her was her young pupils' tendency to sort themselves according to ethnicity and to express dismay when a child of a different ethnicity sat by them or tried to join their games. Mara wanted to know how she could help her students learn to be more tolerant.

Research suggests that ethnic group schemas are well established by age 5 (Pezdek, Blandon-Gitlin, & Moore, 2003). Once these schemas are formed, children use them to make judgments about others (Macrae & Quadflieg, 2010). These early judgments probably reflect young children's egocentric thinking. Essentially, children view those like themselves as desirable companions and those who are unlike them—in gender, ethnicity, and other categorical variables—as undesirable (Doyle & Aboud, 1995). There is some evidence that these judgments increase in strength as children move through the elementary school years (Nesdale, Durkin, Maass, & Griffiths, 2005). These findings suggest

that the characteristics of Piaget's concrete operational stage, the goal of which is to construct a mental model of the outside world, may contribute to school-aged children's tendency to attribute an inappropriate amount of importance to external traits such as ethnicity.

Of course, cognitive development doesn't happen in a social vacuum, and by age 5, most White children in English-speaking countries have acquired an understanding of their culture's ethnic stereotypes and prejudices (Bigler & Liben, 1993). Likewise, African American, Hispanic American, and Native American children become sensitive very early in life to the fact that people in their own groups are viewed negatively by many Whites. Some studies suggest that this early awareness of stereotypes negatively influences minority children's self-esteem (Jambunathan & Burts, 2003).

Psychologists speculate that the combination of immature cognitive development, acquisition of cultural stereotypes, and teachers' lack of awareness may foster prejudicial attitudes. The key to preventing the development of prejudice, they say, is for preschool teachers to discuss ethnicity openly and to make conscious efforts to help children acquire

**Learning Objective 12.2a**

What can parents and teachers do to prevent children from developing racial prejudice?

nonprejudiced attitudes (Cushner, McClelland, & Safford, 1992). For example, they can assign children of different ethnic groups to do projects together.

Ideally, all children should learn to evaluate their own and others' behavior according to individual criteria rather than group membership, and minority children need to be especially encouraged to view their ethnicity positively. Preschool teachers are in a position to provide young children with a significant push toward these important goals.

### REFLECTION

1. How might Mara implement some of the strategies suggested here for reducing prejudice in her classroom?
2. In your view, what is the role of entertainment media in the development of ethnic prejudice?

---

*He smells very much and is very nasty. He has no sense of humour and is very dull. He is always fighting and he is cruel. He does silly things and is very stupid. He has brown hair and cruel eyes. He is sulky and 11 years old and has lots of sisters. I think he is the most horrible boy in the class. He has a croaky voice and always chews his pencil and picks his teeth and I think he is disgusting. (Livesley & Bromley, 1973, p. 217)*

This description still includes many external, physical features, but it goes beyond such concrete surface qualities to the level of personality traits, such as a lack of humor or cruelty.

In adolescence, young people's descriptions begin to include more comparisons of one trait with another or one person with another, more recognition of inconsistencies and exceptions, more shadings of gray (Shantz, 1983), as in this description by a 15-year-old:

*Andy is very modest. He is even shyer than I am when near strangers and yet is very talkative with people he knows and likes. He always seems good tempered and I have never seen him in a bad temper. He tends to degrade other people's achievements, and yet never praises his own. He does not seem to voice his opinions to anyone. He easily gets nervous. (Livesley & Bromley, 1973, p. 221)*

Some findings from two early studies by Carl Barenboim illustrate these changes (1977, 1981). He asked children ranging in age from 6 to 16 to describe three people. Any descriptions that involved comparing a child's behaviors or physical features with another child, or with a norm, he called *behavioral comparisons* (such as "Billy runs a lot faster than Jason" or "She draws the best in our whole class"). Statements that involved some internal personality construct he called *psychological constructs* (such as "Sarah is so kind" or "He's a real stubborn idiot!"); any that included qualifiers, explanations, exceptions, or mentions

A preschool child would no doubt label this boy's emotion as "sad." A teenager would understand that the emotion might be much more complicated, such as sadness mixed with anger at himself or some other form of ambivalence.

FIGURE 12.1 Children's Descriptions of Others

Barenboim's two studies of children's descriptions of others show clear shifts toward greater emphasis on psychological constructs. Study 1 involved children aged 10 to 16; study 2 involved children 6 to 11.

(*Source:* From C. Barenboim, "The development of person perception in childhood and adolescence: From behavioral comparisons to psychological constructs to psychological comparisons," *Child Development*, 52, Society for Research in Child Development (1981): p. 134, Fig. 1.)

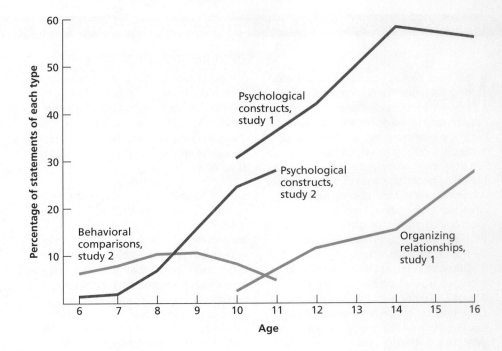

of changes in character he called *organizing relationships* (e.g., "He's only shy around people he doesn't know" or "Usually she's nice to me, but sometimes she can be quite mean"). Figure 12.1 shows the combined findings from the two studies. You can see that behavioral comparisons were most common at around age 8 or 9, psychological constructs increased with age, and organizing relationships did not appear at all until age 10 and were still increasing at age 16.

## Reading Others' Feelings

Learning Objective 12.3
How do children vary individually and across age with regard to understanding others' emotions?

Both cognitive skill and social information are obviously involved in understanding others' emotions. You need to be able to identify various body signals, including facial expressions; you need to understand various kinds of emotions and know that it is possible for people to feel several emotions at the same time; you need to understand the social context; and you need to have a theory of mind that helps you link the context with the other person's likely feelings. For example, you need the basic understanding that another person will be happy or sad depending on how well he does at something important to him.

Research on children's understanding of others' emotions suggests that they acquire these various forms of knowledge gradually over the years from about age 1 to adolescence (Pons, Harris, & de Rosnay, 2004; Thompson, Winer & Goodvin, 2011). You already know from Chapter 5 that by 10 to 12 months of age, babies can tell the difference between positive and negative facial and vocal expressions—at that age, they already show social referencing behavior. By age 3 or 4, the child's emotion-recognition repertoire has expanded considerably, and she has some preliminary understanding of the links between other people's emotions and their situations, such as that someone would be sad if she failed. And by age 10, the child understands and can read some emotional blends, even expressions of ambivalence. Despite these general age trends, developmentalists point out that the developmental pathway from recognizing emotions to understanding them well enough to make predictions about others' and their own emotional behavior is probably distinct for each emotion (Izard et al., 2011). That is, the development of children's understanding of anger probably differs somewhat from the development of their understanding of sadness.

**INDIVIDUAL DIFFERENCES IN EMOTION KNOWLEDGE** Not all children (or all adults) are equally skilled in their ability to read other people's emotions, a point emphasized in a growing body of research examining the construct of *emotional intelligence* (Goleman, 1995; Lopes et al., 2011; Salovey & Mayer, 1990). These individual differences turn out to be quite significant for a child's overall social development and social competence. For example, preschoolers who know and use more emotion-related words (*angry*, *sad*, and so on) are more popular with peers (Fabes, Eisenberg, Hanish, & Spinrad, 2001).

Carroll Izard and his colleagues (1997) have shown such a linkage longitudinally. In a group of economically disadvantaged children, Izard found that those who had better and more accurate emotion knowledge in preschool later showed greater social competence and fewer behavior problems in first grade. Such a linkage suggests the possibility that an intervention program designed to improve children's basic emotional competence—their ability both to read others and to control their own emotional expressions—might have wide-ranging benefits. One such intervention, the PATHS program, is described in *Thinking about Research*.

**THE DEVELOPMENT OF EMPATHY**   To explore the development of children's ability to read the emotions and cues of others, psychologists have also studied the development of empathy. **Empathy** involves two aspects: apprehending another person's emotional state or condition and then matching that emotional state oneself. An empathizing person experiences the same feeling he imagines the other person to feel, or a highly similar feeling. Empathy is the basis for *sympathy*, a general feeling of sorrow or concern for the other person (Sallquist, 2009). Generally speaking, empathy seems to be the earlier response developmentally; among older children and adults, sympathy often seems to grow out of an initial empathetic response (Eisenberg et al., 2007).

The most thorough analysis of the development of empathy and sympathy has been offered by Martin Hoffman (2007), who describes four broad steps, summarized in Table 12.1, on page 300. The first stage, *global empathy*, which seems to be a kind of automatic empathetic distress response, is visible in quite young infants. Hoffman describes one example:

*An 11-month-old girl, on seeing a child fall and cry, looked as if she was about to cry herself, and then put her thumb in her mouth and buried her head in her mother's lap, which is what she would do if she herself were hurt. (1988, pp. 509–510)*

**empathy**   As defined by Hoffman, "a vicarious affective response that does not necessarily match another's affective state but is more appropriate to the other's situation than to one's own" (1982, p. 285).

---

## THINKING ABOUT RESEARCH

### Preventing Violence by Increasing Children's Emotional Competence

Research reveals that most violent youths have poor social-reasoning skills and a poor understanding of others' emotions (Gleason, Jensen-Campbell, & Richardson, 2004). Although programs aimed at improving these skills in teenagers have met with limited success (Armstrong, 2003), research indicates that addressing such deficits in younger children may help to prevent violence in the teen years (DeRosier & Marcus, 2005). One violence prevention initiative geared toward younger children uses the PATHS (Promoting Alternative Thinking Strategies) program, a set of 60 lessons designed to teach elementary school children about emotions and how to read them (Kusché & Greenberg, 1994; Pinderhughes et al., 2010).

Researchers used the PATHS curriculum with a group of 900 excessively aggressive early elementary school children in 395 different classrooms in four U.S. cities in a project known as the Fast Track Project (Conduct Problems Prevention Research Group, 2007).

The children were divided into experimental and control groups. In special class sessions, children in the experimental group learned how to recognize others' emotions. They also learned strategies for controlling their own feelings, managing aggressive impulses, and resolving conflicts with peers.

After several years of implementation, the program produced the following effects among children in the experimental group:

- Better recognition of emotions
- More competence in social relationships
- Lower ratings of aggressiveness by peers
- Lowered risk of being placed in special education classes
- Less use of physical punishment by parents

This project provides support for the linkage between emotion knowledge and social competence. It also gives psychologists, teachers, parents, and law enforcement officials some degree of optimism

### Learning Objective 12.3a
How does increasing children's social competence influence violent behavior?

about the prospects for changing the developmental trajectories of aggressive children (Foster, Jones, & Conduct Problems Prevention Research Group, 2007; Pinderhughes et al., 2010).

#### CRITICAL ANALYSIS

1. Was the Fast Track Project a true experiment? Why or why not?
2. Suppose you were a researcher who wanted to replicate the results of the Fast Track Project. Which of its several components would you choose to manipulate if you had only enough resources to study one of the independent variables? Explain why.

| Table 12.1 | STAGES IN THE DEVELOPMENT OF EMPATHY PROPOSED BY HOFFMAN | |
|---|---|---|
| **Stage** | **Description** | |
| Stage 1: Global empathy | Observed during the first year. If the infant is around someone expressing a strong emotion, he may match that emotion—for example, by beginning to cry when he hears another infant crying. | |
| Stage 2: Egocentric empathy | Beginning at about 12 to 18 months of age, when children have developed a fairly clear sense of their separate selves, they respond to another's distress with some distress of their own, but they may attempt to "cure" the other person's problem by offering what they themselves would find most comforting. They may, for example, show sadness when they see another child hurt, and go get their own mother to help. | |
| Stage 3: Empathy for another's feelings | Beginning as young as age 2 or 3 and continuing through elementary school, children note others' feelings, partially match those feelings, and respond to the other's distress in nonegocentric ways. Over these years, children become able to distinguish a wider (and more subtle) range of emotions. | |
| Stage 4: Empathy for another's life condition | In late childhood or adolescence, some children develop a more generalized notion of others' feelings and respond not just to the immediate situation but to the other individual's general situation or plight. Thus, a young person at this level may become more distressed by another person's sadness, if she knows that the sadness is chronic or that the person's general situation is particularly tragic, than if she sees it as a more momentary problem. | |

*Sources*: Hoffman, 1982, 1988, 2000.

This initial response changes as early as 12 or 18 months, as soon as the child has a clear understanding of the difference between self and others. The toddler still shows a matching emotion but understands that the distress is the other person's and not her own. Nonetheless, her solution to the other's distress is still likely to be egocentric, such as offering the distressed person a teddy bear (Eisenberg & Fabes, 1998).

Children's empathetic and sympathetic responses become more and more subtle over the preschool and elementary school years, as they become better readers of others' emotions. By middle childhood, many children can even empathize with several different emotions at once, as when they see another child make a mistake and fall down during a game. The observing child may see and empathize with both the hurt and the sense of shame or embarrassment, and she may be aware that the child may prefer not to be helped. In adolescence, a still more abstract level emerges, when the child moves beyond the immediate situation and empathizes (or sympathizes) with another person's general plight (See *Technology and the Developing Child* on page 301).

Children as young as 2 or 3 show this kind of empathetic response to other people's distress or delight.

Notice that both developmental progressions—reading others' emotions and empathizing with them—reflect several of the general principles listed earlier in this chapter and parallel the changes Piaget described. In particular, there is a shift from observation to inference: With increasing age, the child's empathetic response is guided less by just the immediate, observed emotions seen in others, such as facial expressions or body language, and more by the child's inferences or deductions about the other person's feelings. This is not a swift change. For example, research in England by Paul Harris and his associates (1981) showed that not until adolescence do young people become fully aware that other people may hide their emotions or act differently from the way they feel "inside."

As you might expect, not all children show equal amounts of such empathetic responses. Some biological disposition toward empathy appears to be part of the story, as evidenced by the greater similarity in levels of empathy among identical twins than among fraternal twins (Volbrecht, Lemery-Chalfant, Aksan, Zahn-Waxler, & Goldsmith, 2007). On the environmental side, many of the same factors that contribute to

# TECHNOLOGY AND THE DEVELOPING CHILD

## Cinema Therapy for Children

*Cinema therapy*, a process in which a therapist "prescribes" watching and discussing a video in which the central character is dealing with issues that are similar to those of the client, has become an accepted therapeutic intervention for many mental health issues (Mann, 2004). Cinema therapy can be helpful for adults, but what about children? Can a grieving child, for example, be helped by watching and discussing a film such as *Bambi* or *The Lion King*? Research examining how children respond to such stories in print suggests that children younger than 8, whose capacity for empathy is limited, are unable to connect a fictional character's difficulties to their own life struggles (Boyd & Naus, 2003). However, children can be repeatedly exposed to video representations of such stories far more easily than is possible with print media. Research shows that with repeated viewing

children are more likely to identify with a struggling character and, as a result, may come to view their own challenges differently (Byrd, Forisha, & Ramsdell, 2006).

Thanks to the widespread availability of video cameras and editing software, some therapists have added a new wrinkle to cinema therapy for children. In the latest iteration of this therapeutic approach, children and teens make movies about characters who are facing issues that are similar to those in their own lives (Flanders & Halla-Poe, 2010). Proponents of this approach argue that watching and discussing commercial videos with children can help therapists understand their young clients' perspectives. Creating videos, by contrast, helps children act out behavioral changes that they may use as models for changes in their own lives. Thus, video creation may turn out to be the most effective form of cinema therapy.

### Learning Objective 12.3b
What are the recommendations of developmentalists for the use of cinema therapy with children?

**FIND OUT MORE**

*Use your Internet search skills to answer these questions.*

1. Visit http://www.taproot.com to view a video about the therapeutic use of video-making. What is your response to the recommendations of the website's authors?
2. Search the Internet to find out what psychologists recommend with regard to the use of video to help children build character strengths such as empathy.

---

greater altruistic behavior also appear to contribute to more empathetic responses in young children. For example, greater maternal response to distress is linked to increased empathy among toddlers (e.g., Davidov & Grusec, 2006). Like altruistic or kind behavior, empathy is also fostered by parental explanations about the consequences of the child's actions for others and by parental discussions of emotions (e.g., Miller, Eisenberg, Fabes, Shell, & Gular, 1989). Finally, developmentalists have some preliminary evidence that children who are high in *effortful control*, the temperamental capacity to regulate emotion in order to accomplish goals, are also high in empathy (Valiente et al., 2004). Whatever its source, empathy appears to be critical to controlling aggressive impulses, as children who are high in empathy tend to be low in aggressiveness (Strayer & Roberts, 2004).

## Describing Friendships

Preschool children seem to understand friendships mostly in terms of common activities. If you ask a young child how people make friends, the answer is usually that they "play together" or spend time physically near each other (Hartup, 2006). Children this age think of friendship as something that involves sharing toys or giving things to one another.

Gradually, this view of friendship begins to shift away from an emphasis on activities (Dunn, Cutting, & Fisher, 2002). Extensive studies by Thomas Berndt (1983, 1986, 2004) show that the key ingredient of friendships for elementary school children seems to be reciprocal trust: Friends are seen as special people with desired qualities other than mere proximity, as people who are generous with one another, who help and trust one another. Children this age also understand that friendship has a temporal dimension: Friends are people with whom one has a history of connection and interaction, rather than people one has just met or played with once, as Figure 12.2, on page 302 suggests. Likewise, over the elementary school years, children develop an understanding of gradations in

------------Learning Objective 12.4
How does children's understanding of friendship change as they get older?

*During the preschool years, friendships are based on shared activities. As children get older, reciprocal trust becomes more important than activities.*

---

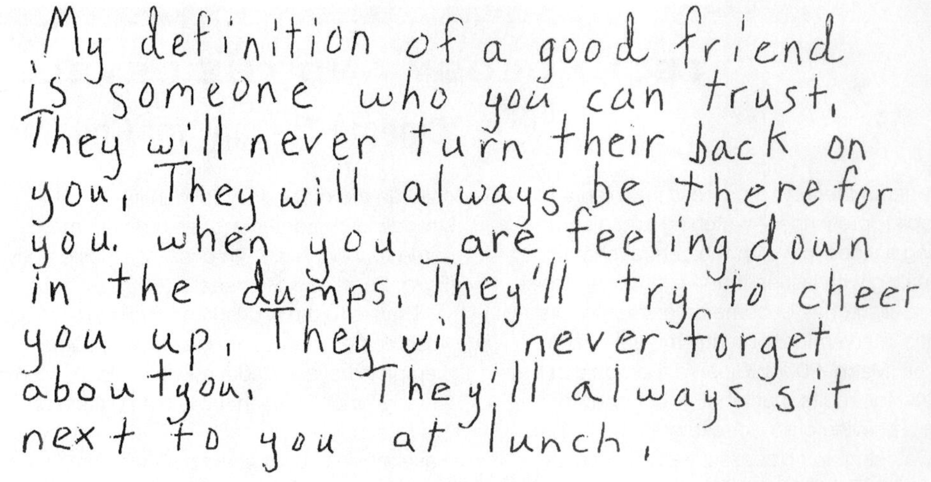

*My definition of a good friend is someone who you can trust. They will never turn their back on you. They will always be there for you. when you are feeling down in the dumps. They'll try to cheer you up, They will never forget about you.    They'll always sit next to you at lunch,*

**FIGURE 12.2** A 10-Year-Old's Explanation of Friendship
This essay on friendship written by a 10-year-old illustrates the way older school-aged children think about friends.
(*Source:* Author.)

friendships. That is, they understand the difference between "best friends" and other kinds of friends (Schraf & Hertz-Lazarowitz, 2003). Important, too, is the finding that improvements in children's understanding of peer relationships are linked to the quantity and quality of children's friendships (Rose & Asher, 2004).

By about age 11 or 12, children begin to talk about intimacy as an important ingredient in friendship; by middle adolescence, they expect a friend to be a confidant and to be supportive and trustworthy (Hartup, 2006). Understanding of friendship also becomes more qualified, more shaded. Research suggests that in late adolescence, young people understand that even very close friendships cannot fill every need and that friendships are not static: They change, grow, or dissolve as each member of the pair changes (Damon, 1977). A really good friendship, then, is one that adapts to these changes. ◉ Watch at MyDevelopmentLab

Some research findings from an early cross-sectional study by Brian Bigelow and John La Gaipa (1975) illustrate this pattern of change. These researchers asked several hundred children in Canada to write an essay about how their expectations of friends differed from their expectations of other acquaintances. The answers were scored along many dimensions, three of which are shown in Figure 12.3. You can see that references to demographic similarity (e.g., "We live in the same neighborhood") were highest among fourth-graders, whereas comments about loyalty and commitment were highest among seventh-graders. References to intimacy potential (e.g., "I can tell her things about myself I can't tell anyone else") did not appear at all until seventh grade but then increased in eighth grade.

◉ Watch the **Video** *Friendship During Middle Childhood* at **MyDevelopmentLab**

**FIGURE 12.3** Changes in Children's Ideas about Friendship
Some of the changes in children's ideas about friendship are clear from these findings from Bigelow and La Gaipa's study.

(*Source:* Table 1, p. 858. Bigelow, B. J., & La Gaipa, J. J. (1975). Children's written descriptions of friendships: A multidimensional analysis. *Developmental Psychology, 11,* 857–858.)

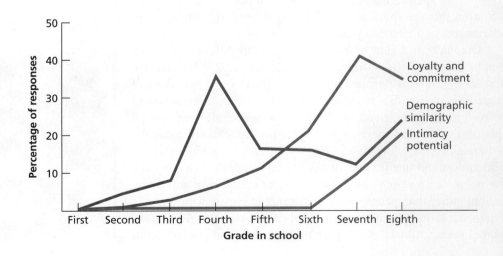

# Understanding Rules and Intentions

◄----------- Learning Objective 12.5

A somewhat different facet of the child's emerging social cognition is her understanding of different categories for social rules. Beginning in the elementary school years, children understand the important distinction between what Elliot Turiel (1983) calls *conventional rules* and *moral rules*. **Conventional rules** are arbitrary, created by a particular group or culture. School rules about wearing uniforms, not running in the hall, and asking permission before you leave the room are all conventional rules, as are cultural rules about appropriate dress for boys and girls. By age 7 or 8, children begin to grasp the fact that such rules are arbitrary and may vary from one group to another or from one situation to another. Children know that they should follow such rules when in the specified group or situation but need not follow them at other times. **Moral rules**, in contrast, are seen as universal and obligatory, reflecting basic principles that guarantee the rights of others. Not running in the hall is a conventional rule; not hitting other people is a moral rule. Children judge the breaking of moral rules as far more serious than the breaking of conventional rules (Smetana, 2006). Breaking conventional rules is seen as impolite or disruptive but is not typically condemned. Children's judgments of moral transgressions, however, are harsher.

Of course, as adults, we distinguish between intentional and unintentional rule violations, but do children make this same distinction? Working from his assumptions about young children's egocentrism, Piaget suggested that young children are incapable of such discriminations. However, research has demonstrated that young children do understand intentions to some degree (Zhang & Yu, 2002). For one thing, it's quite common for preschoolers to say "It was an accident ... I didn't mean to do it" when they are punished. Such protests suggest that children understand that intentional wrongdoing is punished more severely than unintentional transgressions of the rules. Likewise, researchers have pointed out that children must understand intentions in order to determine whether a promise has been fulfilled. Studies show that children as young as 4 years can make such judgments (Maas, 2008).

Several studies suggest that children can make judgments about actors' intentions both when presented with abstract problems and when motivated by a personal desire to avoid punishment (Thompson, 2009). In one classic study, 3-year-olds listened to stories about children playing ball (Nelson, 1980). Pictures were used to convey information about intentions (see Figure 12.4). The children were more likely to label a child who intended to harm a playmate as "bad" or "naughty" than to judge negatively a child who accidentally hit another child in the head with the ball. However, children's judgments were also influenced by outcomes. In other words, they were more likely to say a child who wanted to hurt his playmate was "good" if he failed to hit the child with the ball. These results suggest that children know more about intentions than Piaget thought, but they are still limited in their ability to base judgments entirely on intentions.

**conventional rules** As defined by Turiel, arbitrary, socially defined rules specific to a particular culture, subculture, group, or setting, such as "Don't run in the halls" or "Smoking allowed only in designated areas."

**moral rules** As defined by Turiel, universal and obligatory rules reflecting basic principles that guarantee the rights of others.

**FIGURE 12.4** A Test of Children's Understanding of Intentionality
Pictures like these have been used to assess young children's understanding of an actor's intentions.

## Moral Development

One of parents' and teachers' greatest concerns is helping children learn to be good people, to do the "right" thing according to the standards and values of their culture. **Moral development** has been explained in terms of psychoanalytic, learning, and cognitive-developmental theories. The cognitive-developmental theories, especially that of Lawrence Kohlberg, have been the most influential for the past several decades.

**Learning Objective 12.6** ----------➤
How do psychoanalytic, learning, and cognitive-developmental theories differ in their explanations of moral development?

## Dimensions of Moral Development

The psychoanalytic, learning, and cognitive-developmental theories each focus on a different aspect of moral development.

**MORAL EMOTIONS** Psychoanalytic theory emphasizes emotions in explaining moral development. According to Freud, the child learns moral rules by identifying with the same-sex parent during the phallic stage. The rules a child learns from her same-sex parent form her *superego*, or her internal moral judge. The superego has two parts: a conscience and an ego ideal. The **conscience** is a list of things that "good boys" and "good girls" don't do, such as telling lies. The **ego ideal** is a list of things that "good boys" and "good girls" do, such as obeying parents. When a child disobeys her conscience, she feels guilt. When she fails to live up to the standards set by the ego ideal, she feels shame. Freud believed children learn to obey the rules of their consciences and ego ideals to avoid these uncomfortable feelings.

To better understand Freud's idea about how the superego works, think about a hungry 7-year-old at the grocery store. He can figure out how to take a candy bar without anyone noticing. However, his superego classifies this behavior as stealing, and thinking about stealing a candy bar makes him feel guilty. This creates a conflict for him. If he steals the candy, he'll feel guilty. If he doesn't, he'll be hungry. If he has a healthy personality, Freud believed, he will obey his superego even though doing so will mean remaining hungry.

Erikson's views on moral development were similar to Freud's. However, Erikson believed that children learn moral rules from both parents. Erikson's theory also claimed that pride is just as important for moral development as guilt and shame. For example, if the boy decides not to take the candy, he will not only avoid feeling guilty but also feel pride in his ability to resist temptation.

Recently, there has been a resurgence of interest in moral emotions among developmentalists (Eisenberg, Eggum, & Edwards, 2010; Nunner-Winkler, 2007; Thompson & Newton, 2010). Research has shown, as Freud and Erikson predicted, that feelings of guilt, shame, and pride develop before age 6 (Kochanska & Aksan, 2006). Moreover, as both theorists predicted, the quality of parent-child relationships contributes to the development of moral emotions. For instance, children who have been abused display less understanding than do nonabused children of situations that produce guilt and pride in most people (Koenig, Cicchetti, & Rogosch, 2004).

Researchers infer that young children are experiencing shame when they try to hide an act they know to be wrong. However, it is not until the later school years, at age 10 or so, that children connect shame exclusively to moral wrongs (Olthof, Ferguson, Bloemers, & Deij, 2004). Adolescents' understanding of shame, predictably, is more complex. They tell researchers that people experience shame when they fail to live up to their own standards of behavior as well as when their wrongdoing is exposed to others.

Some research suggests that connections between moral emotions and moral behavior are weaker than Freud believed, because they depend on cognitive development (Hoffman, 2007). Younger children seem to think they should feel guilty or ashamed only if a parent or teacher sees them commit a violation of a moral rule. Thus, a 7-year-old candy thief is unlikely to feel guilty unless he gets caught in the act. Later, after age 9 or 10, when children are more likely to make behavioral choices based on how guilty, ashamed, or proud they think they will feel. For example, when the boy who wants the candy is older, he will be more likely to choose not to take the candy because he knows resisting temptation will make him feel proud of himself.

**moral development** The process of learning to distinguish between right and wrong in accordance with cultural values.

**conscience** The list of "don'ts" in the superego; violation of any of these leads to feelings of guilt.

**ego ideal** The list of "dos" in the superego; violation of any of these leads to feelings of shame.

**MORAL BEHAVIOR**    Another way of looking at moral development is through the lens of learning theorist B. F. Skinner's operant conditioning model, which proposes that consequences teach children to obey moral rules. According to Skinner, adults reward children for morally acceptable behavior with praise. At the same time, they punish children for morally unacceptable behavior. As a result, acceptable behavior increases and unacceptable behavior decreases as children get older.

Consequences certainly do influence children's behavior. However, punishment may actually interfere with moral development. For example, if a child's parent spanks him in the grocery store parking lot for having a stolen a candy bar, the parent hopes that the spanking will teach him that stealing is wrong. But the child may learn only that he can't steal when he's with the parent. Similarly, when punishment is severe or embarrassing, children may be distracted from making the connection between their behavior and the punishment. A child who has stolen candy may be so angry at his parent for embarrassing him with a public spanking that he concentrates all his attention on his anger. As a result, he fails to realize that his choice to steal caused the spanking (Hoffman, 1988).

An approach that combines punishment with reasoned explanations may be more effective. On discovering that a 7-year-old had stolen a candy bar, a parent using this approach would respond by telling the child privately that it is wrong to take things that don't belong to you even if you are very hungry. Next, the parent would require the child to right the wrong by admitting his crime, apologizing to the cashier or manager, and paying for the candy. Finally, the 7-year-old would probably have to repay his parents in some way if they gave him the money to pay for the stolen candy. Such a process allows the child to learn both that it is wrong to steal and that, when he breaks a moral rule, he must do something to set things right (Zahn-Waxler, Radke-Yarrow, & King, 1979).

As you may recall from Chapter 1, social-learning theorist Albert Bandura claims that children learn more from observing others than from either rewards or punishments. His theory states that, when a child sees someone rewarded for a behavior, he believes that he will also be rewarded if he behaves in the same way. Similarly, when he sees a model punished, he assumes that he will also experience punishment if he imitates the model's behavior (Bandura, 1977, 1989). For example, a story about a child who was praised by a parent for resisting the temptation to steal may teach the child who hears or reads it that resisting temptation is praiseworthy. Conversely, when a child is exposed to a story about a boy or girl who steals and doesn't get caught, he may learn that it's possible to steal without getting caught.

As Bandura's theory predicts, children learn a lot about moral behavior, both acceptable and unacceptable, from models' behavior. Models can even influence children to change their moral behavior. For example, if a 7-year-old sees another child steal candy after he decides not to, he may change his mind.

**MORAL REASONING**    *Moral reasoning* is the process of making judgments about the rightness or wrongness of specific acts. Piaget studied moral development by observing children playing games. As he watched them play, Piaget noticed that younger children seemed to have less understanding of the games' rules. Following up on these observations, Piaget questioned children of different ages about rules. Their answers led him to propose a two-stage theory of moral development (Piaget, 1932).

Children in Piaget's **moral realism stage**, which he found to be typical of children younger than 8, believe that the rules of games can't be changed because they come from authorities, such as parents, government officials, or religious figures. For example, one 6-year-old told Piaget that the game of marbles was invented on Noah's ark. He went on to explain that the rules can't be changed because the "big ones," meaning adults and older children, wouldn't like it (Piaget, 1965, p. 60).

Moral realists also believe that all rule violations result in punishment. For example, Piaget told children a story about a child who fell into a stream when he tried to use a rotten piece of wood as a bridge. Children younger than 8 told him that the child was being punished for something "naughty" he had done in the past.

After age 8, Piaget proposed, children move into the **moral relativism stage**, in which they learn that people can agree to change rules if they want to. They realize that the important

**moral realism stage**    The first of Piaget's stages of moral development, in which children believe that rules are inflexible.

**moral relativism stage**    The second of Piaget's stages of moral development, in which children understand that many rules can be changed through social agreement.

**preconventional morality** The first
level of moral development proposed by
Kohlberg, in which moral judgments are
dominated by consideration cf what will be
punished and what feels good.

thing about a game is that all the players follow the same rules, regardless of what those are. For example, 8- to 12-year-olds know that a group of children playing baseball can decide to give each batter four strikes rather than three. They understand that their agreement doesn't change the game of baseball and that it doesn't apply to other people who play the game. Children in this stage also get better at following the rules of games.

Eight- to twelve-year-olds also know that rule violations don't result in punishment unless you get caught. As a result, they view events like falling into a stream because of using a rotten piece of wood as a bridge as accidents. They understand that accidents are not caused by "naughty" behavior. Children older than 8 also understand the relationship between punishment and intentions. For example, looking back at the situation of a 7-year-old taking a candy bar from a store, Piaget's research suggests that children over 8 would distinguish between a child who unintentionally left without paying for the candy and another who deliberately took it. Older children would likely say that both children should return or pay for the candy, but only the one who intentionally stole it should be punished.

Research supports Piaget's claim that children over 8 give more weight to intentions than to consequences when making moral judgments (Zelazo, Helwig, & Lau, 1996). Although their thinking is more mature than that of preschoolers, school-aged children's moral reasoning is still highly egocentric. For example, every parent has heard the exclamation "It's not fair!" when a child fails to receive the same treat or privilege as a sibling. However, it is rare, if not completely unknown, for a child to protest the fairness of his receiving something that was not also given to a sibling. Thus, school-aged children still have a long way to go before they are capable of mature moral reasoning. To understand this developmental process, we must turn to the work of Lawrence Kohlberg (1927–1987).

**Learning Objective 12.7** ----------▶
What kinds of moral reasoning do people use at Kohlberg's preconventional, conventional, and postconventional levels?

## Kohlberg's Levels and Stages of Moral Development

Piaget (1932) was the first to offer a description of the development of moral reasoning, but Kohlberg's work has had the most powerful impact on developmentalists' thinking (Colby, Kohlberg, Gibbs, & Lieberman, 1983; Dawson, 2002; Kohlberg, 1964, 1976, 1980, 1981). Building on and revising Piaget's ideas, Kohlberg pioneered the practice of assessing moral reasoning by presenting children with a series of hypothetical dilemmas in story form, each of which highlighted a specific moral issue, such as the value of human life. One of the most famous is the dilemma of Heinz:

> In Europe, a woman was near death from a special kind of cancer. There was one drug that the doctors thought might save her. It was a form of radium that a druggist in the same town had recently discovered. The drug was expensive to make, but the druggist was charging ten times what the drug cost him to make. He paid $200 for the radium and charged $2000 for a small dose of the drug. The sick woman's husband, Heinz, went to everyone he knew to borrow the money, but he could only get together about $1000, which is half of what it cost. He told the druggist that his wife was dying, and asked him to sell it cheaper or let him pay later. But the druggist said, "No, I discovered the drug and I'm going to make money from it." So Heinz got desperate and broke into the man's store to steal the drug for his wife. (Kohlberg & Elfenbein, 1975, p. 621) ◉–Watch at **MyDevelopmentLab**

◉–Watch the **Video** *Kohlberg and the Heinz Dilemma* at **MyDevelopmentLab**

After hearing this story, the child or young person is asked a series of questions, such as whether Heinz should have stolen the drug. What if Heinz didn't love his wife? Would that change anything? What if the person dying was a stranger? Should Heinz steal the drug anyway? On the basis of answers to dilemmas like this one, Kohlberg concluded that there were three main levels of moral reasoning, each with two stages, as summarized briefly in Table 12.2. ✳–Explore at **MyDevelopmentLab**

✳–Explore the **Concept** *Ages and Stages of Cognitive and Moral Development* at **MyDevelopmentLab**

**LEVELS AND STAGES** At Level I, **preconventional morality**, the child's judgments of right and wrong are based on sources of authority who are close by and physically superior to her—usually the parents. Just as the elementary school child's descriptions of others are largely external, her standards for judging rightness or wrongness are also external rather than internal. In particular, it is the outcome or consequences of actions that determine the rightness or wrongness of those actions.

## Table 12.2 — KOHLBERG'S STAGES OF MORAL DEVELOPMENT

| Stage | Description |
|---|---|
| **LEVEL I: Preconventional Morality** | |
| Stage 1: Punishment and obedience orientation | The child decides what is wrong on the basis of what is punished. Obedience is valued for its own sake, but the child obeys because adults are physically more powerful. |
| Stage 2: Individualism, instrumental purpose, and exchange | The child follows rules when it is in her immediate interest. What is good is what brings pleasant results. |
| **LEVEL II: Conventional Morality** | |
| Stage 3: Mutual interpersonal expectations, relationships, and interpersonal conformity | Moral actions are those that live up to the expectations of the family or other significant group. "Being good" becomes important for its own sake. |
| Stage 4: Social system and conscience | Moral actions are those so defined by larger social groups or the society as a whole. One should fulfill duties one has agreed to and uphold laws, except in extreme cases. |
| **LEVEL III: Principled or Postconventional Morality** | |
| Stage 5: Social contract orientation (or utility and individual rights) | Acting so as to achieve the "greatest good for the greatest number." The teenager or adult is aware that most values are relative and laws are changeable, although rules should be upheld in order to preserve the social order. Still, there are some basic nonrelative values, such as the importance of each person's life and liberty. |
| Stage 6: Universal ethical principles | The adult develops and follows self-chosen ethical principles in determining what is right These ethical principles are part of an articulated, integrated, carefully thought-out, and consistently followed system of values and principles. |

*Sources*: Kohlberg, 1976; Lickona, 1978.

In stage 1 of this level—*the punishment and obedience orientation*—the child relies on the physical consequences of some action to decide whether it is right or wrong. If she is punished, the behavior was wrong; if she is not punished, it was right. She is obedient to adults because they are bigger and stronger.

In stage 2—*individualism, instrumental purpose, and exchange*—the child begins to do things that are rewarded and to avoid things that are punished. (For this reason, the stage is sometimes referred to as *naive hedonism*.) If something feels good or brings pleasant results, it is good. Some beginning of concern for other people is apparent during this stage, but only if that concern can be expressed as something that benefits the child herself as well. So she can enter into agreements such as "If you help me, I'll help you." The following responses to variations of the Heinz dilemma, drawn from studies of children and teenagers in a number of different cultures, illustrate stage 2:

*The majority of teenagers use stage 3 moral reasoning: What is good is what family or peers define as good and right. Do you think that the level of moral reasoning a teenager shows has any connection to his or her conformity to peers?*

conventional morality  The second level of moral development proposed by Kohlberg, in which a person's judgments are dominated by considerations of group values and laws.

principled (postconventional) morality  The third level of moral development proposed by Kohlberg, in which considerations of justice, individual rights, and social contracts dominate moral judgment.

*He should steal the drug for his wife because if she dies he'll have to pay for the funeral, and that costs a lot. (Taiwan)*

*He should steal the drug because "he should protect the life of his wife so he doesn't have to stay alone in life." (Puerto Rico)*

**Researcher:** *Suppose it wasn't his wife who was starving but his best friend. Should he steal the food for his friend?*

**Child:** *Yes, because one day when he is hungry his friend would help. (Turkey)* (Snarey, 1985, p. 221)

At Level II, **conventional morality**, the young person shifts from judgments based on external consequences and personal gain to judgments based on rules or norms of a group to which he or she belongs, whether that group is the family, the peer group, a church, or the nation. What the chosen reference group defines as right or good is right or good in the child's view, and the child internalizes these norms to a considerable extent.

Stage 3 (the first stage of Level II) is the stage of *mutual interpersonal expectations, relationships, and interpersonal conformity* (sometimes also called the *good boy/nice girl stage*). Children at this stage believe that good behavior is what pleases other people. They value trust, loyalty, respect, gratitude, and maintenance of mutual relationships. Andy, a boy Kohlberg interviewed who was at stage 3, said:

*I try to do things for my parents, they've always done things for you. I try to do everything my mother says, I try to please her. Like she wants me to be a doctor and I want to, too, and she's helping me get up there. (Kohlberg, 1964, p. 401)*

Another mark of stage 3 is that the child begins to make judgments based on intentions as well as on outward behavior. If someone "means well" or "didn't mean to do it," the wrongdoing is seen as less serious than if the person did it "on purpose."

In stage 4, the second stage of conventional morality, the child turns to larger social groups for her norms. Kohlberg labeled this the stage of *social system and conscience*. Children reasoning at this stage focus on doing their duty, respecting authority, following rules and laws. The emphasis is less on what is pleasing to particular people (as in stage 3) and more on adhering to a complex set of regulations. The regulations themselves are not questioned.

The transition to Level III, **principled morality** (also called **postconventional morality**), is marked by several changes, the most important of which is a shift in the source of authority. At Level I, children see authority as totally outside themselves; at Level II, the judgments or rules of external authority are internalized, but they are not questioned or analyzed; at Level III, a new kind of personal authority emerges and allows a person to make individual judgments and choices based on self-chosen principles.

In stage 5 at this level—called the *social contract orientation* by Kohlberg—people show evidence of the beginning of such self-chosen principles. Rules, laws, and regulations are still seen as important because they ensure fairness, and they are seen as logically necessary for society to function. However, people operating at this level also recognize that rules, laws, and regulations sometimes need to be ignored or changed. The system of government in the United States is based on moral reasoning of this kind, since it provides means for changing laws and for allowing personal protests against a given law, such as the civil rights protests of the 1960s and the Vietnam War protests of the 1960s and 1970s.

Stage 6, the second stage in Level III, is simply a further extension of this same pattern, with the individual searching for the highest level of moral principles possible and then trying to live in a way that is consistent with them. Kohlberg referred to this stage as the *universal ethical principles orientation*. People who reason in this way assume personal responsibility for their own actions on the basis of fundamental and universal principles, such as justice and basic respect for persons (Kohlberg, 1978; Kohlberg, Boyd, & Levine, 1990). In their case studies of modern adults who reason and act at this level, Ann Colby and William Damon (1992) note that another quality such people share is "open receptivity"—a willingness to examine their ideas and convictions, even while they act firmly and generously in support of their ideals. Such people are not common. Two famous examples are Mahatma Gandhi and Mother Teresa, both of whom devoted their lives to humanitarian causes.

It is very important to understand that what defines the stage or level of a person's moral development is not the specific moral choices the person makes but the form of reasoning used to justify the choices. For example, either choice—that Heinz should steal the drug or that he should not—can be justified with logic at any given stage. You have already read some examples of stage 2 justifications for Heinz's stealing the drug; the following is a stage 5 justification of the same choice, drawn from a study in India:

> *What if Heinz was stealing to save the life of his pet animal instead of his wife? If Heinz saves an animal's life his action will be commendable. The right use of the drug is to administer it to the needy. There is some difference, of course—human life is more evolved and hence of greater importance in the scheme of nature—but an animal's life is not altogether bereft of importance. . . . (Snarey, 1985, p. 223, drawn originally from Vasudev, 1983, p. 7)*

If you compare this answer to those presented earlier, you can clearly see the difference in the form of reasoning used, even though the action being justified is precisely the same.

Kohlberg argued that this sequence of moral development is both universal and hierarchically organized, just as Piaget thought his proposed stages of cognitive development were universal and hierarchical. That is, each stage follows and grows from the preceding one and has some internal consistency. Individuals should not move backward, or "down" the sequence, but only upward through the stages, if they move at all. Kohlberg did not suggest that all individuals eventually progress through all six stages or even that the stages are always associated with specific ages, but he insisted that their order is invariant and universal.

Kohlberg thought that there were at least a few people, such as Mother Teresa, whose moral reasoning was based on universal ethical principles.

**AGE AND MORAL REASONING**  Kohlberg's own findings, confirmed by many other researchers (e.g., Walker, de Vries, & Trevethan, 1987), show that preconventional moral reasoning (stages 1 and 2) is dominant in elementary school, with stage 2 reasoning still evident among many early adolescents. Conventional reasoning (stages 3 and 4) emerges in middle adolescence and remains the most common form of moral reasoning in adulthood. Postconventional reasoning (stages 5 and 6) is relatively rare, even in adults. For example, in one study of men in their forties and fifties, only 13% were rated as using stage 5 moral reasoning (Gibson, 1990).

Two research examples illustrate these overall age trends. The first, illustrated in Figure 12.5, comes from Kohlberg's own longitudinal study of 58 boys, first interviewed when they were 10, and followed for more than 20 years (Colby et al., 1983). Table 12.3 on page 310 shows cross-sectional data from a study by Lawrence Walker and his colleagues (1987). They studied 10 boys and 10 girls at each of four ages, interviewing the parents of each child as well. Note that Walker scored each response on a 9-point scale rather than using just the five main stages. This system, which has become quite common, allows for the fact that many people's reasoning falls between two specific stages.

The results of these two studies, although not identical, point to remarkably similar conclusions about the order of emergence of the various stages and about the approximate ages at which they predominate. In both studies, stage 2 reasoning dominates at ages 9 to 10, and stage 3 reasoning is most common at about ages 15 to 16.

**SEQUENCE OF STAGES**  The evidence also seems fairly strong that Kohlberg's stages occur in the sequence he proposed. For example, in three long-term longitudinal studies of teenagers and young adults, one in the United States (Colby et al., 1983), one in Israel (Snarey, Reimer, & Kohlberg, 1985), and one in Turkey (Nisan & Kohlberg, 1982), the changes in participants' reasoning nearly always occurred in the hypothesized order. Participants did not skip stages, and only about 5–7% of them showed any indication of regression (movement down the sequence of stages rather than up). Similarly, when Walker (1989) retested the participants in his study 2 years later, he found that only 6% had moved down (most only half a stage), while 22% had moved up, and none had skipped a stage. Such a rate of regression is about what researchers would expect to find, given the fact that the measurements of stage reasoning

**FIGURE 12.5** Responses to Kohlberg's Moral Dilemmas across Age
These findings are from Colby and Kohlberg's long-term longitudinal study of a group of boys who were asked about Kohlberg's moral dilemmas every few years from age 10 through early adulthood. Note that postconventional, or principled, reasoning was quite uncommon, even in adulthood.

(*Source:* From Colby et al., "A longitudinal study of moral judgment," *Monographs of the Society for Research in Child Development,* 48 (1–2, Serial No. 200), Society for Research in Child Development (1983): p. 46, Fig. 1.)

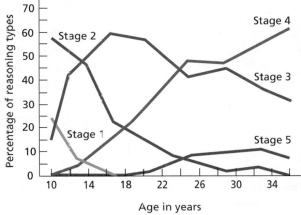

## Table 12.3

### PERCENTAGES OF CHILDREN AND PARENTS WHO SHOW MORAL REASONING AT EACH OF KOHLBERG'S STAGES

| Age | Stage | | | | | | | | |
|---|---|---|---|---|---|---|---|---|---|
| | 1 | 1–2 | 2 | 2–3 | 3 | 3–4 | 4 | 4–5 | 5 |
| 6 (grade 1) | 10% | 70% | 15% | 5% | – | – | – | – | – |
| 9 (grade 4) | – | 25% | 40% | 35% | – | – | – | – | – |
| 12 (grade 7) | – | – | 15% | 60% | 25% | – | – | – | – |
| 15 (grade 10) | – | – | – | 40% | 55% | 5% | – | – | – |
| Parents | – | – | – | 1% | 15% | 70% | 11% | 3% | – |

*Source:* From Walker et al., "Moral stages and moral orientations in real-life and hypothetical dilemmas," *Child Development, 60* (1987): p. 849, Table 1.

are not perfect. On the whole, the available evidence suggests that moral judgment changes over time in the sequence Kohlberg described (Rest, 1983).

**MORAL REASONING STAGES ACROSS CULTURES**    Variations of Kohlberg's dilemmas have been presented to children or adults in numerous countries and subcultures, both Western and non-Western, industrialized and nonindustrialized (Boom, Wouters, & Keller, 2007; Gibbs, Basinger, Grime, & Snarey, 2007; Monga, 2007). John Snarey, who has reviewed and analyzed these many studies, notes several things in support of Kohlberg's claim that the stages are universal: (1) Studies of children consistently find an increase in stage of reasoning with age; (2) the few longitudinal studies report "strikingly similar findings" (1985, p. 215), with participants progressing through the stage sequence with few reversals; and (3) cultures differ in the highest level of reasoning observed. In urban societies (both Western and non-Western), stage 5 is typically the highest stage observed, while in those cultures Snarey calls "folk societies," stage 4 is typically the highest. Collectively, this evidence provides quite strong support for the universality of Kohlberg's stage sequence.

Learning Objective 12.8 ----------→

## Causes and Consequences of Moral Development

What are the causes and consequences of age-related changes in moral reasoning?

The most obvious reason for the correlations between Kohlberg's stages and chronological age and for a consistent sequence of stages is that moral reasoning is strongly tied to cognitive development. Further, although the stages have often been criticized for failing to predict moral behavior, research does suggest that there is a link between moral reasoning and moral behavior.

**MORAL REASONING AND COGNITIVE DEVELOPMENT**    It appears that children must have a firm grasp of concrete operational thinking before they can develop or use conventional moral reasoning. Likewise, formal operational thinking appears to be necessary for advancement to the postconventional level. To be more specific, Kohlberg and many other theorists suggest that the decline of egocentrism that occurs as an individual moves through Piaget's concrete and formal operations stages is the cognitive-developmental variable that matters most in the development of moral reasoning. The idea is that the greater a child's or adolescent's ability to look at a situation from another person's perspective, the more advanced she is likely to be in moral reasoning. Psychologists use the term **role-taking** to refer to this ability (Selman, 1980). Research has provided strong support for the hypothesized links between role-taking and moral development (Kuhn, Kohlberg, Languer, & Haan, 1977; Walker, 1980).

**role-taking**    The ability to look at a situation from another person's perspective.

Nevertheless, cognitive development isn't enough. Kohlberg thought that the development of moral reasoning also required support from the social environment. Specifically, he claimed, to foster mature moral reasoning, a child's or teenager's social environment must provide him with opportunities for meaningful, reciprocal dialogue about moral issues. Research shows that media portrayals of morally deviant behavior, especially violent behavior, negatively influences children's moral reasoning suggesting that environmental factors may also interfere with moral development (Krcmar & Vieira, 2005). Thus, Kohlberg agreed with advocates of character education, as described at the beginning of the chapter, that moral development must be deliberately and systematically encouraged by parents and teachers.

Longitudinal research relating parenting styles and family climate to levels of moral reasoning suggests that Kohlberg was right (Pratt, Arnold, & Pratt, 1999; Volling, Mahoney, & Rauer, 2009). Parents' ability to identify, understand, and respond to children's and adolescents' less mature forms of moral reasoning seems to be particularly important to the development of moral reasoning. It is important because individuals of all ages have difficulty understanding and remembering moral arguments that are more advanced than their own level (Narvaez, 1998). Thus, a parent who can express her own moral views in terms of a child's level of understanding is more likely to be able to influence that child's moral development.

**MORAL REASONING AND MORAL BEHAVIOR**   Level of moral reasoning appears to be positively correlated with prosocial behavior and negatively related to antisocial behavior (Schonert-Reichl, 1999). In other words, higher levels of prosocial behavior are found among children and teens who are at higher levels of moral reasoning (compared to their peers). Alternatively, the highest levels of antisocial behavior are found among adolescents at the lowest levels of moral reasoning. Moreover, attitudes toward the acceptability of violence also vary with levels of moral reasoning. Individuals at lower levels have more tolerant attitudes toward violence (Sotelo & Sangrador, 1997).

Another connection between moral reasoning and behavior proposed by Kohlberg is that the higher the level of moral reasoning a young person shows, the stronger the link to behavior. For example, Kohlberg and others simply asked participants whether there is a link between one's stage of moral reasoning and the probability of making some moral choice, such as not cheating. In one early study, Kohlberg (1975) found that only 15% of college students reasoning at stage 5 of the principled level cheated when they were given an opportunity, while 55% of those at the conventional level and 70% of those at the preconventional level cheated.

A similar result comes from studies in which the moral reasoning of highly aggressive or delinquent youngsters is compared to that of nondelinquent peers. The repeated finding is that delinquents (male or female) have lower levels of moral reasoning than do nondelinquents, even when the two groups are carefully matched for levels of education, social class, and IQ (Chudzik, 2007; Ma, 2003; Smetana, 1990). In one study of this type, Virginia Gregg and her colleagues (1994) found that only 20% of a group of incarcerated male and female delinquents were reasoning at stage 3 or higher, while 59% of a carefully matched comparison group of nondelinquents were reasoning at this level. Like younger children who act out more in school, delinquents are most likely to use highly self-oriented reasoning, at Kohlberg's stage 2 (Richards, Bear, Stewart, & Norman, 1992).

Delinquents appear to be behind their peers in moral reasoning because of deficits in role-taking skills. For example, researchers have found that teenagers who can look at actions they are contemplating from their parents' perspective are less likely to engage in delinquent behavior than adolescents who cannot do so (Wyatt & Carlo, 2002). Most delinquent teens also seem to be unable to look at their crimes from their victims' perspectives or to assess hypothetical crimes from the victims' perspectives. Thus, programs aimed at helping delinquents develop more mature levels of moral reasoning usually focus on heightening their awareness of the victim's point of view. However, few such programs have been successful (Armstrong, 2003; Moody, 1997; Putnins, 1997).

Finally, despite the abundance of evidence for a link between moral reasoning and behavior, no one has found the correspondence to be perfect. After all, in Kohlberg's studies, 15% of the stage 5 moral reasoners did cheat, and a quarter of stage 4 and stage 5 reasoners who thought it morally right to participate in a sit-in did not do so. As Kohlberg says, "One can reason in terms of principles and not live up to those principles" (1975, p. 672).

**Learning Objective 12.9** ·········➤
How do Eisenberg's and Gilligan's approaches to moral development differ from Kohlberg's?

# Alternative Views

Most of the moral dilemmas Kohlberg posed for participants in his studies deal with wrong-doing—with stealing, for example, or disobeying laws. Few of the dilemmas reveal anything about the kind of reasoning children use in justifying prosocial behavior. You learned in Chapter 11 that altruistic behavior is evident in children as young as 2 and 3, but how do children explain and justify such behavior?

**EISENBERG'S MODEL OF PROSOCIAL REASONING**    Nancy Eisenberg and her colleagues evaluated children's empathy and prosocial behavior by gaining their responses to dilemmas involving self-interest (1989). One story for younger children, for example, involves a child walking to a friend's birthday party. On the way, he comes upon another child who has fallen and hurt himself. If the party-bound child stops to help, he will probably miss the cake and ice cream. What should he do? In response to dilemmas like this, preschool children most often use what Eisenberg calls **hedonistic reasoning**, in which the child is concerned with self-oriented consequences rather than moral considerations. Preschoolers asked about what they would do if they came upon an injured child on their way to a birthday party say things like "I'd help because he'd help me the next time" or "I wouldn't help because I'd miss the party." This approach gradually shifts to one Eisenberg calls **needs-oriented reasoning**, in which the child expresses concern rather directly for the other person's need, even if the other's need conflicts with the child's own wishes or desires. Children operating on this basis say things like "He'd feel better if I helped." These children do not express their choices in terms of general principles or indicate any reflectiveness about generalized values; they simply respond to the other's needs.

Still later, typically in adolescence, children say they will do good things because it is expected of them, a pattern highly similar to Kohlberg's stage 3. Finally, in late adolescence, some young people give evidence that they have developed clear, internalized values that guide their prosocial behavior: "I'd feel a responsibility to help because of my values" or "If everyone helped, society would be a lot better."

Some sample data from Eisenberg's longitudinal study of a small group of U.S. children illustrate the shift from hedonistic to needs-oriented reasoning; see Figure 12.6 on page 313. By early adolescence, hedonistic reasoning has virtually disappeared and needs-oriented reasoning has become the dominant form. However, when Eisenberg and her colleagues conducted follow-up studies of participants in early adulthood, they found that age-related changes in pro-social reasoning reflected individual differences in personality as well as a universal developmental process (Eisenberg et al., 2007).

Culture also contributes to the development of prosocial reasoning. In one study, Eisenberg and her team of researchers (Eisenberg, Hertz-Lazarowitz, & Fuchs, 1990; Boehnke, Silbereisen, Eisenberg, & Reykowski, 1989) found a pattern of prosocial reasoning development among German, Polish, Italian, and city-dwelling Israeli children resembling the one shown in Figure 12.6. However, kibbutz-reared Israeli elementary school children showed little needs-oriented reasoning (Eisenberg, 1986). Instead, this particular group of Israeli children was more likely to reason on the basis of internalized values and norms and the humanness of recipients, a pattern consistent with the strong emphasis on egalitarianism and communal values in the kibbutzim. These findings suggest that culture may perhaps play a larger role in children's moral reasoning than in their reasoning about justice, although that is still a highly tentative conclusion.

There are obviously strong parallels between the sequences of changes in the prosocial reasoning Eisenberg has described and Kohlberg's levels and the stages of moral reasoning. Children seem to move from a self-centered orientation ("What feels good to me is right")

**hedonistic reasoning**    A form of prosocial moral reasoning described by Eisenberg in which the child is concerned with consequences to self rather than moral considerations, roughly equivalent to Kohlberg's stage 2.

**needs-oriented reasoning**    A form of prosocial moral reasoning proposed by Eisenberg in which the child expresses concern directly for the other person's need, even if the other's need conflicts with the child's own wishes or desires.

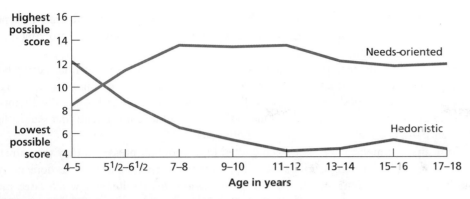

FIGURE 12.6 Eisenberg's Longitudinal Study of Prosocial Reasoning

Every 2 years Eisenberg asked the same group of children what a person should do when confronted with each of a series of dilemmas about doing good, such as helping someone who is hurt. She then analyzed their form of reasoning, using a measure for which the minimum score was 4 and the maximum was 16.

(*Source:* Eisenberg et al., "Pro-social development in late adolescence," *Child Development, 66*, 1995, pp. 1179–1197.)

to a stance in which social approval guides reasoning about both justice and moral behavior ("What is right is what other people define as right; I should do good things because others will approve of me if I do"). Much later, some young people seem to develop internalized, individualized norms to guide both kinds of reasoning. Despite these obvious parallels, though, researchers have typically found only moderate correlations between children's reasoning about prosocial dilemmas such as Eisenberg's and their reasoning about Kohlberg's justice or fairness dilemmas. The sequences of steps may be similar, but as was true of so much of the cognitive development you read about in Chapter 6, children's reasoning in one area doesn't necessarily generalize to a related area.

Eisenberg's research, as well as the work of others in the same field, helps to broaden Kohlberg's original conception, without changing the fundamental arguments. In contrast, Carol Gilligan has questioned some of the basic tenets of Kohlberg's model.

**GILLIGAN'S ETHIC OF CARING**   Carol Gilligan (1982; Gilligan & Wiggins, 1987) is fundamentally dissatisfied with Kohlberg's focus on justice and fairness as the defining elements of moral reasoning. Gilligan argues that there are at least two distinct "moral orientations": justice and caring. Each has its own central injunction: not to treat others unfairly (justice), and not to turn away from someone in need (caring). Boys and girls learn both of these injunctions, but Gilligan has hypothesized that girls are more likely to operate from an orientation of caring or connection, while boys are more likely to operate from an orientation of justice or fairness. Because of these differences, she argues, they tend to perceive moral dilemmas quite differently.

Given the emerging evidence on sex differences in styles of interaction and in friendship patterns, which you read about in Chapter 11, Gilligan's hypothesis makes some sense. Perhaps girls, focusing more on intimacy in their relationships, judge moral dilemmas by different criteria. In fact, however, research on moral dilemmas has not shown that boys are more likely to use justice as the basis for their moral reasoning or that girls more often use caring. Several studies of adults have shown such a pattern (e.g., Lambert et al., 2009; Lyons, 1983; Mitchell, 2002), but studies of children, adolescents, and college students generally have not (Jadack, Hyde, Moore, & Keller, 1995; Pratt, Skoe, & Arnold, 2004). What matters far more than gender in determining whether a given child or adult will use a caring or a justice orientation in addressing a moral dilemma is the nature of the dilemma itself. Dilemmas relating to interpersonal relationships, for example, are more likely to be addressed using a caring orientation, whereas dilemmas explicitly involving issues of fairness are more likely to be addressed with a justice orientation.

*Gilligan argues that females are much more likely to use an "ethic of caring" than an "ethic of justice" as a basis for their moral judgments, while the reverse is true among males. Such a difference may exist among adults, but research on children and adolescents shows no such pattern.*

It may be that adult women are more likely than men to interpret moral dilemmas as personal, but both men and women use both caring and justice arguments in resolving moral dilemmas (Turiel, 1998).

For example, Lawrence Walker scored children's answers to moral dilemmas using both Kohlberg's fairness scheme and Gilligan's criteria for a caring orientation. He found no sex difference either for hypothetical dilemmas like the Heinz dilemma or for real-life dilemmas suggested by the children themselves (Walker et al., 1987). Only among adults did Walker find a difference in the direction that Gilligan hypothesized.

Gilligan's arguments have often been quoted in the popular press as if they were already proven, when in fact the empirical base is really quite weak. Gilligan herself has done no systematic studies of children's (or adults') caring orientation. Yet despite these weaknesses, most developmentalists are not ready to discard all of her underlying points (Sherblom, 2008). Most agree to credit Gilligan's model with helping to broaden the study of moral development beyond the cognitively oriented perspective offered by Kohlberg.

## THINK CRITICALLY

- How might an understanding of social-cognitive development affect parental responses to children's misbehavior?
- Suppose that Gilligan's view of moral development is correct, and adult women focus on an ethic of caring when thinking about moral issues while men focus on an ethic of justice. What do you think the implications of such a difference would be for male-female relationships, for men and women as political leaders, or for other social phenomena?

## CONDUCT YOUR OWN RESEARCH

You can replicate Carl Barenboim's classic research by asking children of different ages to describe three specific people. You might begin by asking children to name the three peers they like best. Next, ask them to describe these children. Try to interview children across the same age range as those who participated in Barenboim's studies (6–16 years). Using the examples on page 297–298 in the text as a guide, count the number of physical/behavioral, psychological, and organizing relationship remarks made by the children you interview. Sum the remarks across the ages of the children you interview, and use the sums to create a graph like the one in Figure 12.1 on page 298.

## SUMMARY  ✓• Study and Review at MyDevelopmentLab

### The Development of Social Cognition

**12.1**  What are the general principles of social-cognitive development?
Many of the general principles that describe overall cognitive development also describe developmental changes in social cognition, including a shift in focus from outer to inner characteristics, from observation to inference, from definite to qualified judgment, and from a particular to a general view. Social and moral reasoning differ from other aspects of cognition, however, in that a child must learn that unlike objects, people behave with intention, mask feelings, and operate by special socially defined scripts or rules.

**12.2**  In what ways do children's descriptions of other people change across childhood and adolescence?
Children's descriptions of other people shift from a focus on external features to a focus on personality traits and to more qualified, comparative descriptions during

adolescence; this progression parallels the shifts in children's self-descriptions.

**12.2a**  What can preschool teachers do to prevent children from developing racial prejudice?
Research shows that young children use racial categories to make judgments about others. They are also aware of social attitudes toward people of different races at an early age. Psychologists recommend that preschool teachers discuss ethnicity openly and make conscious efforts to ensure that children of different ethnicities interact in constructive ways.

**12.3**  How do children vary individually and across age with regard to understanding others' emotions?
Children learn to interpret many basic emotional expressions fairly early, but they can correctly read more complex emotions and emotional blends only later. The ability to read others' emotions and intentions is an important element in a child's general social competence; those who are

less skilled, who have less "emotion knowledge," are more likely to be rejected by their peers. Empathy—the ability to match or approximate the emotion of another—is seen in young infants, but it becomes less egocentric and more subtle through the preschool and elementary school years.

**12.3a What are the recommendations of developmentalists for the use of cinema therapy with children?**
Cinema therapy is the use of films to help individuals with mental health issues. Unless young children watch videos repeatedly, they are unlikely to identify with the characters and understand how the characters' problems relate to their own. Thus, for children, making films about their own mental health issues may be a more effective form of cinema therapy than watching movies that were made for commercial purposes.

**12.3b How does increasing children's social competence influence violent behavior?**
The PATHS program increases the social competence of aggressive children by helping them become more aware of others' feelings. PATHS lessons also teach aggressive children to recognize and control their own emotions. Experimental research suggests that the PATHS program is an effective tool for reducing school violence.

**12.4 How does children's understanding of friendship change as they get older?**
Children's thinking about their relationships, especially friendships, also changes developmentally, moving from definitions of friends as people who share physical space or activities, to definitions emphasizing trust, and finally, during adolescence, to definitions emphasizing intimacy.

**12.5 What changes in children's understanding of rules and intentions emerge during the elementary school years?**
In elementary school, children begin to understand the distinction between conventional rules and moral rules. They also distinguish between intentional and unintentional acts.

## Moral Development

**12.6 How do psychoanalytic, learning, and cognitive-developmental theories differ in their explanations of moral development?**
Psychoanalytic theories of moral development emphasize emotions, whereas learning theories focus on reinforcement and modeling. Cognitive-developmental theorists study moral reasoning and assert that moral development is strongly related to general cognitive development.

**12.7 What kinds of moral reasoning do people use at Kohlberg's preconventional, conventional, and postconventional levels?**
Kohlberg described six distinct stages in children's (and adults') reasoning about moral issues. These six stages are divided into three levels. The child moves from preconventional morality (dominated by punishment and "what feels good"), to conventional morality (dominated by group norms or laws), to postconventional or principled morality (dominated by social contracts and basic ethical principles).

**12.8 What are the causes and consequences of age-related changes in moral reasoning?**
Both cognitive-developmental and environmental variables, such as the opportunity to discuss moral issues, contribute to advancement through Kohlberg's stages. A child's or adult's stage predicts prosocial and antisocial behavior and attitudes to some degree.

**12.9 How do Eisenberg's and Gilligan's approaches to moral development differ from Kohlberg's?**
Alternative models of moral reasoning include Eisenberg's stages of prosocial reasoning (reasoning about why to do something good) and Gilligan's proposed caring orientation. Gilligan's hypothesis that girls are more likely than boys to use caring, rather than justice, as a basis for moral judgments has not been supported by research with children, adolescents, and college students.

## KEY TERMS

conscience (p. 304)
conventional morality (p. 308)
conventional rules (p. 303)
ego ideal (p. 304)

empathy (p. 299)
hedonistic reasoning (p. 312)
moral development (p. 304)
moral realism stage (p. 305)

moral relativism stage (p. 305)
moral rules (p. 303)
needs-oriented reasoning (p. 312)
preconventional morality (p. 306)

principled (postconventional) morality (p. 308)
role-taking (p. 310)
social cognition (p. 295)

# The Ecology of Development: The Child within the Family System

## LEARNING OBJECTIVES

### Understanding the Family System

**13.1** How does family systems theory explain family interactions?

**13.2** How do the various systems in Bronfenbrenner's model interact to influence children's development?

  **13.2a** How do video calling applications expand the microsystems of children in immigrant families?

### Dimensions of Family Interaction

**13.3** What are the individual characteristics of children and parents that contribute to family interactions?

**13.4** How do emotional warmth and parental responsiveness influence parent-child relationships?

**13.5** How do parents' methods of control and communication affect development?

  **13.5a** What does research say about the effects of spanking?

### Parenting Styles

**13.6** What are the four parenting styles proposed by Maccoby and Martin?

**13.7** What did Steinberg and Dornbusch's study reveal about parenting styles?

**13.8** How do parenting styles differ across ethnic and socioeconomic groups?

### Family Structure, Divorce, and Parental Employment

**13.9** How is family structure related to development?

**13.10** How does divorce affect children's behavior?

  **13.10a** What steps can parents take to minimize the effects of divorce on children's development?

**13.11** How do parents' employment patterns affect children?

**13.12** What is the importance of social support to the family system?

---

If you have read William Golding's novel *The Lord of the Flies* or have seen one of the film versions, you know that the former teacher put forward a rather pessimistic view of human nature. In the story, a group of boys ranging in age from 6 or so to early adolescence are stranded on an island with no adult supervision. The hero, Ralph, attempts to establish a civilized community for the boys, based on the rules of the English society from which they have come. Exploiting the tendency of the younger boys toward fearfulness and superstition, his nemesis, Jack, sets up a "culture" in which he enjoys absolute power.

Although there have been many interpretations of Golding's work, one message seems clear: Children need adults to become civilized, or, to put it differently, to channel their natural impulses into behaviors that will enhance both their own development and the collective good of humankind. While most developmentalists would probably find Golding's characterization of unsupervised children and adolescents a bit too pessimistic, they would probably, nonetheless, agree with the basic premise that children require relationships with adults in order to develop optimally. But will just any adult do, or is there a need for a special adult-child relationship to serve as a context in which culture is transmitted from one generation to the next? In other words, do children really need families?

Questions like these are the subject of this chapter. We will begin with an examination of the complex theories that have been proposed to explain interactions among family members and the larger social contexts within which families exist. Afterward, we will turn our attention to the characteristics of family relationships and the contributions of individuals to them. Finally, you will read about changes in family structure and other aspects of family life that influence children's development.

**family systems theory** The view that the family is an integrated network of factors that work together to influence a child's development.

## Understanding the Family System

Family influences on children's development are often studied within the broader context of a *systems perspective*. The primary idea behind the systems approach is that multiple factors work together holistically. That is, the combined interactive effects of all the variables included in the catch-all term *family influences* are greater than the sum of any of the individual factors. For example, a parent's approach to discipline influences a child's development. At the same time, the child's own temperament influences her development. But when the two factors are combined, a different, or *interactive*, effect is produced that is more important than either factor alone. So, a particular approach to discipline may have one effect on a child with an easygoing temperament and a completely different effect on a child with a difficult temperament. Before we discuss Bronfenbrenner's *bioecological theory*, which is arguably the most important developmental systems theory that has been proposed, we will consider a few of the basic principles of the systems perspective as it has been applied to the study of families.

## Family Systems Theory

← - - - - - - - - - - - -**Learning Objective 13.1**
How does family systems theory explain family interactions?

In search of a comprehensive explanation of the family and how it shapes individuals, developmental scientists have turned to *systems theory* (Lamb & Lewis, 2011). Systems theorists emphasize that any system—biological, economic, or psychological—has two key properties. First and foremost, a system has "wholeness and order," which is another way of saying that the whole is greater than the sum of its parts. The whole consists of the parts and their relationship to one another. Often an analogy is made between a system and a melody. A melody is far more than a set of individual notes; it is the relationship of notes to one another that creates the melody. Thus, **family systems theory** is the view that the family is an integrated network of factors that work together to influence a child's development. The influence of the system as a whole on development is greater than the sum of the individual factors that make up the family.

A second feature of any system is that it is adaptive; that is, when any part of a system changes or some new element is added, the system "assimilates" if it can, but "accommodates" if it must. So systems resist change as much as they can by absorbing new data or new parts into the existing structure; if that doesn't work—as it often doesn't—only then will the system change. For example, when a family's second child is born, the parents may try to keep to their old routines as much as possible; the presence of this new individual in the family system will, however, inevitably force accommodations. This will be particularly true if the new baby is temperamentally very different from the first child.

FIGURE 13.1 Belsky's Model of Family
Interaction

Developmentalist Jay Belsky proposed this
model of family interaction to illustrate the
system of mutual influences that work
together to affect children's development.

(*Source:* From fig. 1, p. 6, Belsky, J. (1981).
Early human experience: A family perspective.
*Developmental Psychology, 17,* 3–23. Reprinted
with permission.)

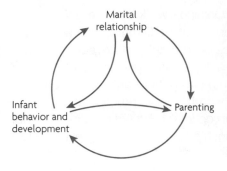

You can see that these two features of systems—
wholeness and adaptability—cause change in any
one part of a system to affect every other part. This
was suggested in a systems model of family functioning proposed by developmental psychologist
Jay Belsky (1981). As Figure 13.1 illustrates, systems
such as the one proposed by Belsky have feedback
loops. For example, a husband who is suffering from
depression is likely to be more negative toward his
wife than he used to be, and this negativity will put
a strain on their relationship. The worsening of the
relationship, coupled with the man's depression, will cause these parents to treat their children
differently—they will be less attentive in general, and more critical and strict when they do
pay attention. The children will react with changes of their own, perhaps becoming defiant,
and in response the parents will then become more strict and demanding. In this way, a cycle
is set in motion.

How do the various systems in
Bronfenbrenner's model interact to
influence children's development?

*The late Urie Bronfenbrenner changed the way
developmentalists think about the complexity
of the contexts in which children grow up.
His bioecological model was influenced by his
life history. At the age of 6, Bronfenbrenner
came to the United States from Russia with his
parents. With his wife, Liese, he raised six children. He was one of the founders of the Head
Start program in the 1960s. At the time of his
death, he had thirteen grandchildren and one
great-grandchild.*

# Bronfenbrenner's Bioecological Approach

Of all the various systems theories, none has been more influential than that of the late developmental psychologist Urie Bronfenbrenner (1917–2005) (1979, 1989, 2001). For Bronfenbrenner,
the family is the filter through which the larger society influences child development. As such,
the family can help the larger culture achieve the goal of socializing new members, but it can also
serve as a buffer against harmful elements in the culture-at-large. Thus, according to Bronfenbrenner, although other institutions can substitute for it to some degree, the family is "the most
efficient means of making human beings human" (Bronfenbrenner, quoted in EBC, 1991).

Of course there are many developmental theories, such as Freud's psychoanalytic theory,
that emphasize the importance of the child's family. What distinguishes Bronfenbrenner's bioecological approach from other developmental theories is his attempt to explain how all of the
various environmental influences on children's development are related to one another. Moreover, Bronfenbrenner also provides an explanation for how all of these interrelated influences
mesh with the child's own biological make-up. For this reason, his theory is now known as the
*bioecological approach.*

Just how does Bronfenbrenner achieve such a comprehensive account of the role played
by environmental factors in individual development? The fundamental premise of his theory
is that the bioecological system in which the child develops can be thought of as a series of
layers, or concentric circles. The innermost circle, made up of elements Bronfenbrenner calls
*microsystems,* includes all those settings in which the child has direct personal experience,
such as the family, a child-care center or a school, a job setting (for a teenager), and, thanks to
technological innovations, extended family members that may live near or far from the child's
own immediate family (see *Technology and the Developing Child*).

The next layer, which Bronfenbrenner calls *exosystems,* includes a whole range of system
elements that the child does not experience directly but that influence the child because they
affect one of the microsystems, particularly the family. The parents' work and workplace is one
such element, as is the parents' network of friends.

Finally, Bronfenbrenner describes a *macrosystem* that includes the larger cultural or
subcultural setting in which both the microsystems and the exosystems are embedded. The
poverty or wealth of the family, the neighborhood in which the family lives, the ethnic identity of the family, and the larger culture in which the entire system exists are all parts of this
macrosystem.

Figure 13.2 presents these three layers schematically for two hypothetical 4-year-old
American children—one from the majority White culture living in an intact middle-class
family with two employed parents, the other a Hispanic American child living with both
parents and a grandmother in a working-class, largely Spanish-speaking neighborhood,
whose mother stays at home full-time. If you try to imagine yourself living within each
of these systems, you can get a feeling for the many complex ways in which they differ

# TECHNOLOGY AND THE DEVELOPING CHILD

## Expanding the Microsystem with Digital Communications

When information technology product marketer Dennis Shiao was a child, he and his sister delighted in making audiotapes of themselves speaking Chinese that they then mailed to their grandparents back in China (Shiao, 2011). As you can imagine, back in the 1960s when Shiao was a child, it took quite a long time for the audiotapes to travel by mail from the United States to China (Note: That's why we call it "snail mail."). Nevertheless, recording them and knowing they would eventually reach their grandparents helped the Shiao children maintain connections with their family's cultural heritage.

Nowadays, many immigrant families are using Skype, FaceTime, and other video-calling applications for precisely the same purpose (Bittle et al., 2009). These tools enable families to not only communicate frequently with family members but also to feel included in important family events such as marriages, births, deaths, and so on. Thus, digital communications technologies help immigrant families deal with *acculturative stress*, the stress that occurs when people move to a new culture where the language and customs are unfamiliar to them (Bacigalupe & Lambe, 2011). Moreover, the availability of these tools helps families maintain children's skills in their first language and a sense of connectedness to their cultural heritage just as the tapes that Dennis Shiao and his sister made did for them.

### FIND OUT MORE

*Use your Internet search skills to answer these questions.*

### Learning Objective 13.2a

How do video calling applications expand the microsystems of children in immigrant families?

1. What do surveys reveal about the percentage of transnational Skype calls that are made by U.S. immigrants to their home countries?
2. For what purposes other than keeping in touch with extended family and friends do immigrants use video conferencing applications and other forms of Internet-based communication?

---

and how all their pieces interact with one another. Bronfenbrenner's point is that until developmentalists really understand the ways in which all the elements in such complex systems interact to affect the child, they will not understand development (Lerner, Lewin-Bizan, & Warren, 2011).

It is probably obvious that trying to understand child development in this way is immensely difficult. Nonetheless, let's plunge in, using Bronfrenbrenner's model as a general framework. In this chapter, we will focus on the most important element of the microsystem: the family itself. In Chapter 14, we will move beyond the family to consider other dimensions of the microsystem such as nonparental care settings and schools. We will also examine some of the factors in the exosystem, such as parental employment, and in the larger cultural context, or the macrosystem.

**FIGURE 13.2** Bronfenbrenner's Bioecological Model

Two hypothetical children, growing up in widely different ecological settings, illustrate the layers in Bronfenbrenner's model. To understand how the environment affects a child, developmentalists would need to study every aspect of this complex system simultaneously—a tall order.

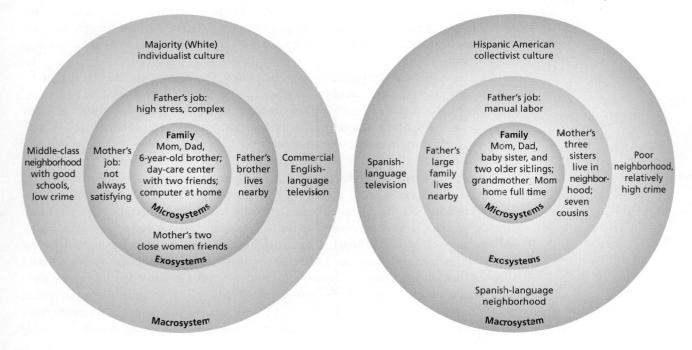

# Dimensions of Family Interaction

Researchers who have focused most directly on patterns of parent-child interaction have identified several major dimensions on which families differ and which seem to be significant for the child. These include the individual characteristics of children and parents, the emotional tone and responsiveness of parents, the manner in which parents exercise control of children's behavior, and the quality and amount of communication. Remember that, while it is useful for instructional purposes to focus exclusively on the family system for a bit, keep in mind that we are only temporarily ignoring the larger contexts within which the family exists in order to better understand its unique characteristics.

**Learning Objective 13.3**
What are the individual characteristics of children and parents that contribute to family interactions?

*It is probably obvious that loving a child is a critical ingredient in the child's optimum development—but sometimes it doesn't hurt to restate the obvious.*

# Individuals in the Family System

Each individual in the family system carries within himself or herself a variety of factors that are relevant to how he or she interacts with others in the system.

**CHILDREN'S CHARACTERISTICS** Children's temperaments contribute to the general tenor of the family system (Burt, McGue, Krueger, & Iacono, 2005). For example, in a family in which one child has a very difficult temperament, a great deal of time and energy may be devoted to keeping the child happy (Turecki, 2000). As a result, parents may be too frazzled to meet the needs of other children, and the difficult child's siblings may become resentful of her.

Children's relationships with their parents and siblings may also be affected by their place in the family sequence (referred to as **birth order**, or ordinal position). Parents generally have higher expectations for maturity in their first-born child and may well be more responsive to or more child-centered with that child. Perhaps responding to the higher expectations, oldest children (firstborns or only children) have higher average IQ scores and are somewhat more achievement-oriented, as you learned in Chapter 11 (Zajonc & Sulloway, 2007).

Differential treatment of siblings goes beyond parental expectations based on birth order, a point you may remember from the discussion of the *nonshared environment* in Chapter 7. Several studies by Judy Dunn (2007) in both the United States and England have shown that parents may express warmth and pride toward one child and scorn toward another. Similarly, parents may be very strict with one child and very lenient with her siblings. Children recognize and respond to these differences quite early in life. Responses may include resentment and increased hostility toward siblings from children who are treated more harshly than are their brothers and sisters. However, the causes and effects of differential treatment of siblings are difficult to study, because they are confounded with children's ages, their gender, and their temperaments.

Children's ages are an especially important influence on parent-child relationships, as we noted in Chapter 11's discussion of *goal-corrected partnerships*, a pattern in which parents expect older preschoolers to accept more responsibility for themselves than they did when they were infants and toddlers. Similarly, parents' expectations rise when children enter school, and the goal of parenting often becomes training the child to regulate his or her own behavior (Lamb & Lewis, 2011).

Researchers have learned that there are several parenting variables that contribute to the development of this kind of self-regulation. For example, the degree of self-regulation a parent expects influences the child's self-regulatory behavior. Higher expectations, together with parental monitoring to make certain that expectations are met, are associated with greater self-regulatory competence (Rodrigo, Janssens, & Ceballos, 1999). However, research has revealed that children's responses to the elements of parenting that contribute to self-regulatory behavior, such as expectations and monitoring, interact with a group of plasticity genes, or, to put it in more practical terms, "capacity for responding to parenting" genes (Belsky & Beaver, 2011). The impact of individual differences in these genes is that some children's are more negatively influenced by poor parenting and more positively influenced by good parenting than their peers. Furthermore, the effects of these genes are greater among boys than among girls. These findings provide us with yet another example of the need to think of nature and nurture as interactive processes.

Plasticity genes may also affect the ways in which children respond to other types of parenting factors (Belsky & Beaver, 2011). For example, it is clear that parents treat boys and girls differently, beginning in infancy, as we noted in Chapter 10. One such early-appearing difference is that parents sing more expressively to same-sex than to opposite-sex infants (Trehub, Hill, & Kamenetsky, 1997). Such differences may contribute in some way to the formation of same-sex alliances between parents and children that may be important later in childhood.

Other kinds of variations in parents' interactions with boys and girls are demonstrated by both mothers and fathers. For example, in one classic study, researchers found that adults viewing a videotape of an infant interpreted the baby's behavior differently depending on the gender label provided by the researchers. Participants who were told that the baby was a girl interpreted a particular behavior as expressing "fear." Amazingly, those who believed the infant to be male labeled the same behavior "anger" (Condry & Condry, 1976). More recent research employing this technique suggests that the current cohort of adults is somewhat less likely to stereotype infant behavior in this way, although, like their counterparts in the 1970s, they attend to and comment on motor activity more when they believe a target infant is a boy (Pomerleau, Malcuit, Turgeon, & Cossette, 1997). Thus, temperamental stereotyping may affect the quality of the parent-child relationship.

Some studies also suggest that there are sex differences in parents' expectations with respect to school-aged children's self-regulatory behavior. For example, mothers make different kinds of demands on boys and girls. They appear to provide both with the same types of guidance, but they are more likely to give boys more autonomy over their own behavior than they give girls. Nevertheless, they are also more likely to hold girls to a higher standard of accountability for failure (Moorman & Pomeranz, 2010). Developmentalists speculate that this difference may lead to stronger standards of behavior for girls later in development.

However, the opposite may be true with regard to children who have behavioral difficulties, such as those associated with attention deficit hyperactivity disorder (ADHD). Parents are more likely to attribute such problems to causes outside the child's control when the child is a girl (Maniadaki, Sonuga-Barke, & Kakouros, 2005). By contrast, parents of boys with ADHD are likely to view their sons' behavior as intentional. As a result, the strictness of rules and the harshness of disciplinary techniques is more likely to be increased in response to a son's ADHD symptoms than to a daughter's. Researchers speculate that this pattern, rather than producing higher behavioral standards among boys than among girls, may set up a pattern of hostile and manipulative interactions between parents and sons. Thus, again, we see that parent-child relationships are bidirectional in nature. That is, the effects of any pattern of parent behavior depend to some degree on the characteristics of children. Likewise, children's characteristics influence how parents respond to them.

**THE PARENTS' CHARACTERISTICS**   The parents bring their own life histories, their own personalities, and their relationship with each other into the family dynamics as well (Bornstein, Hahn, & Haynes, 2011). Not surprisingly, for example, parents who are high in the trait of neuroticism tend to view their children's behavior more negatively than parents who are more optimistic (Kurdek, 2003). Similarly, significant depression in either parent has a profound effect on the entire family system. You already know from Chapter 11 that an insecure attachment is more likely when the mother is diagnosed with depression. Parents with depression also perceive their children as more difficult and problematic and are more critical of them, even when objective observers cannot identify any difference in the behavior of such children and the children of mothers who do not have depression (Richters & Pellegrini, 1989; Webster-Stratton & Hammond, 1988). Thus, a parent's depression changes not only her behavior but her perception of the child's behavior, both of which alter the family system.

**warmth versus hostility** The key dimension of emotional tone used to describe family interactions.

**responsiveness** An aspect of parent-child interaction; a responsive parent is sensitive to the child's cues and reacts appropriately, following the child's lead.

**Learning Objective 13.4** ----------→

How do emotional warmth and parental responsiveness influence parent-child relationships?

Perhaps most broadly, the quality of the parents' own relationship with each other spills over into their relationship with their children (Cowan, Cowan, & Barry, 2011). Couples with satisfying marital relationships are more warm and supportive toward their children; those whose marriage is full of discord also have more negative relationships with their children (Erel & Burman, 1995; Parke & Buriel, 1998). Their children show heightened risks of anxiety, depression, and delinquent behavior (Harold & Conger, 1997). In general, fathers' relationships with their children seem to be more strongly affected by the quality of their marital relationship than do mothers' relationships, but the spillover occurs for both parents.

## Warmth and Responsiveness

One key family dimension that has an effect on the child is the relative **warmth versus hostility** of the home. "Warmth" has been difficult to define and measure, but it seems intuitively obvious that it is highly important for the child, and research has supported this intuition. A warm parent cares about the child, expresses affection, frequently or regularly puts the child's needs first, shows enthusiasm for the child's activities, and responds sensitively and empathetically to the child's feelings (Maccoby, 1980). On the other end of this continuum are parents who overtly reject their children—saying in words or by their behavior that they do not love or want them.

Such differences have profound effects. Psychologists have found that children in warm and loving families are more securely attached in the first 2 years of life; have higher self-esteem; are more empathetic, more altruistic, and more responsive to others' hurts or distress; and have higher IQ scores in preschool and elementary school and do better in school (Domitrovich & Bierman, 2001; Maccoby, 1980; Pettit, Bates, & Dodge, 1997; Simons, Robertson, & Downs, 1989). They are also less likely to show high levels of aggression or delinquent behavior in later childhood or in adolescence (Goldstein, Davis-Kean, & Eccles, 2005; Hipwell et al., 2008). In addition, teens who were reared in low-warmth families are more likely to have suicidal thoughts and other mental health problems (Lai & McBride-Chang, 2001; Xia & Qian, 2001).

As Bronfenbrenner's model would predict, high levels of affection can even buffer a child against the negative effects of otherwise disadvantageous environments (Stansfield, Head, Bartley & Fonagy, 2008). Several studies of children and teens growing up in poor, dangerous neighborhoods show that the single ingredient that most clearly distinguishes the lives of those who do not become delinquent from those who do is a high level of maternal love (Glueck & Glueck, 1972; McCord, 1982). Similarly, in a longitudinal study, Gregory Pettit and his colleagues (Pettit, Bates, & Dodge, 1997) found that children who were growing up in poverty but whose parents provided more "supportive parenting" (including warmth) were less likely to develop aggressive or delinquent behavior than equally poor children in less emotionally supportive families. At the other end of the continuum from parental warmth, parental hostility is linked to declining school performance and higher risk of delinquency (Melby & Conger, 1996). When such hostility is expressed as physical abuse or neglect, the consequences for the child may be even more severe, as we discussed in Chapter 4.

Fostering a secure attachment of the child to the parent appears to be one of the key consequences of emotional warmth (Stansfield et al., 2008). You already know from Chapter 11 that securely attached children are more skillful with their peers, more exploratory, more sure of themselves. Warmth also makes children generally more responsive to guidance, so the parents' affection and warmth increase the potency of the things they say to their children as well as the efficiency of their discipline (MacDonald, 1992).

A second key element of family interaction patterns is **responsiveness** by the parent to the child, a concept you've encountered in earlier chapters. Responsive parents are those who pick up on the child's signals appropriately and then react in sensitive ways to the child's needs (Ainsworth & Marvin, 1995; Sroufe, 1996). Children of parents who do more of this learn language somewhat more rapidly, show higher IQ scores and more rapid cognitive development, and are more likely to be securely attached, more compliant with adult requests, and more socially competent (e.g., Bornstein, 1989; Kochanska, 1997; van den Boom, 1994). Further evidence for the importance of responsiveness comes from research showing that training new parents to be more responsive reduces the odds that an infant will develop an insecure or disorganized attachment (Juffer, Bakermans-Kranenburg, & van IJzendoorn, 2005).

Neuroimaging studies have shed new light on the importance of parental warmth and responsiveness. These studies suggest that the cerebral cortex contains networks of **mirror neurons**, specialized cells that allow the brain to mentally simulate behaviors and emotions that primates observe in others (Sinigaglia & Rizzolatti, 2011). *Simulation theory* proposes that these mental models shape children's understanding of others' emotions and behavior (Gallese, 2005). Thus, according to this perspective, a child whose parents exhibit warmth develops a neurological model for parental warmth that may carry over to his other social relationships and to his own parenting behavior in adulthood.

**mirror neurons** Specialized cells in the cerebral cortex that simulate the behavior and emotions of others.

## Methods of Control and Communication Patterns

←------------Learning Objective 13.5
How do parents' methods of control and communication affect development?

It is the nature of children to do things their parents do not want them to do, ask for things they cannot have, or refuse to obey their parents' requests or demands. Parents are inevitably faced with the task of controlling the child's behavior and training the child to follow basic rules, a process popularly known as *discipline*. Parental control of children's behavior, a third aspect of family interaction, relies on several elements.

One element of control is the consistency of rules—making it clear to the child what the rules are, what the consequences are of disobeying (or obeying) them, and then enforcing them consistently. Some parents are very clear and consistent; others waver or are fuzzy about what they expect or will tolerate. Studies of families show that parents who are clear and consistent have children who are much less likely to be defiant or noncompliant, more competent and sure of themselves, and less likely to become delinquent or show significant behavior problems than are children from families with less consistent rules.

One piece of research that illustrates this pattern nicely is Lawrence Kurdek and Mark Fine's classic study of 850 junior high school students (Kurdek & Fine, 1994). They measured the level of control in the family by asking the young adolescents to rate the accuracy of each of the following three statements:

Someone in my family makes sure that my homework is done.
Generally, someone in my family knows where I am and what I'm doing.
Someone in my family keeps a close eye on me.

Kurdek and Fine also had information about each child's self-esteem and sense of self-efficacy, which they combined into a measure of "psychosocial competence." You can see the relationship between these two pieces of information in Figure 13.3, on page 324. Greater family control was clearly associated with greater psychosocial competence.

Such a link between good parental control and positive outcomes for the child has been found among African American as well as White and Hispanic American youth (Mogro-Wilson, 2008). For example, Craig Mason and his colleagues (1996; Walker-Barnes & Mason, 2004) have found that among working-class Black families, those in which the parents maintained the most consistent monitoring and control over their adolescents had teenagers who were least likely to show problem behavior. Interestingly and importantly, the link between parental control and lower rates of problem behavior in Mason's study was especially clear in cases in which the child had many peers who were engaging in problem behavior. Thus, the parents, by applying consistent rules and monitoring the child's activities, could at least partially counteract the negative effects of their children's "hanging out" with misbehaving peers (Darling, Cumsille, & Martínez, 2008).

To understand the process of control, you must understand the role of punishment, the technique that most parents use to enforce their rules. Punishment is most often aimed at getting a child to stop doing something prohibited, such as writing on the wall, hitting his brother, or staying out

*This dad seems to be willing to listen carefully to his son, even though the boy is angry and may be accusatory.*

## To Spank or Not to Spank?

In keeping with Bronfenbrenner's model, parents' beliefs regarding the best way to discipline children are influenced by the larger culture (Giles-Sims & Lockhart, 2005). In the United States, many parents believe that spanking is the most effective form of punishment.

In the short term, spanking a child usually does get the child to stop a behavior, and it seems to temporarily reduce the chance that the child will repeat the behavior (Gershoff, 2002). But, even in the short term there are some negative side effects. The child may stop misbehaving, but after a spanking he is likely to be crying, which may be almost as distressing as the original misbehavior. Another short-term side effect is that the parent is being negatively reinforced for spanking whenever the child stops misbehaving. Thus, the parent is being "trained" to use spanking the next time, and a cycle is being built up.

In the longer term, the effects of spanking are clearly negative (Gershoff, 2002). The child observes the parent using physical force as a method of solving problems or getting people to do what she wants. By repeatedly pairing her presence with the unpleasant or painful event of spanking, the parent is undermining her own positive value for the child. Spanking also frequently carries a strong underlying emotional message—anger, rejection, irritation, dislike of the child. Even very young children read such emotional messages quite clearly (Rohner, Kean, & Cournoyer, 1991). Spanking thus helps to create a family climate of rejection instead of warmth, with all the attendant negative consequences.

Finally, research evidence suggests that children who are spanked—like children who are abused—at later ages are less popular with their peers and show higher levels of aggression, lower self-esteem, more emotional instability, higher rates of depression and distress, and higher levels of delinquency and later criminality (Christie-Mizell, Pryor, & Grossman, 2008; Fine, Trentacosta, Izard, Mostow, & Campbell, 2004). As adults, children who have been spanked regularly are more likely to be depressed than are those who were never or rarely spanked (Straus, 1995), and they also have higher risks of various other types of adult problems, including unemployment, divorce or violence within a relationship, and criminality (Maughan, Pickles, & Quinton, 1995). All these negative effects are especially clear if the physical punishment is harsh and erratic, but the risks for these poor outcomes are increased even with fairly mild levels of physical punishment.

Developmentalists who oppose spanking do not mean to suggest that parents should never punish a child. They are saying that physical punishment, such as spanking, is not a good way to go about it. Yelling at the child is also not a good alternative strategy. Strong verbal aggression by a parent toward a child is also linked to many poor outcomes in the child, including increased risk of delinquency and adult violence (Straus, 1991b).

### Learning Objective 13.5a
What does research say about the effects of spanking?

### CRITICAL ANALYSIS

1. Why would it be unethical to use the experimental method to study the effects of spanking?
2. What kinds of variables (e.g., parents' personality traits) might explain the correlation between spanking and poor developmental outcomes?

---

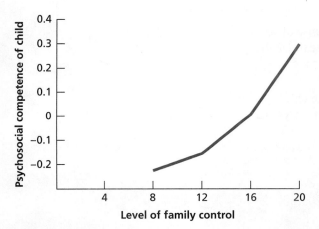

**FIGURE 13.3** Parental Control and Self-Esteem
Junior high school students who report higher levels of parental control and supervision also describe themselves as having higher self-esteem and self-efficacy.

(*Source:* From Kurdek, L., and Fine, M., fig. 1, p. 1143. "Family acceptance and family control as predictors of adjustments in young adolescents," *Child Development*, 65 (1994), 1137–1146. By permission of the Society for Research in Child Development.)

past a curfew, but it may also be used to try to push a child to do something that he is resisting, such as cleaning his room. Punishments almost invariably involve some aversive consequence for the child, ranging from withholding privileges or treats, assigning extra chores, sending a child to his room, or "grounding" the child to more severe forms of verbal scolding and even spanking. The most controversial of these is spanking. Because of the importance of the question, the pros and cons of physical punishment are explored in *Thinking about Research*, but there are two points about punishment strategies in general that you should understand.

First, as developmentalist Gerald Patterson says, "Punishment 'works.' If you use it properly it will produce rapid changes in the behavior of other people" (1975, p. 19). The operative word here, though, is *properly*. The most effective punishments—those that produce long-term changes in a child's behavior without unwanted or negative side effects—are those used early in some sequence of misbehavior, with the lowest level of emotion possible and the mildest level of punishment possible. Taking a desired toy away when the child first hits a sibling with it or consistently removing small privileges when a child misbehaves will produce the desired results, especially if the parent is also warm, clear about the rules, and consistent. It is far less effective to wait until the sibling's screams have reached a piercing level or until the fourth time a teenager has gone off without telling you where she's going and then weigh in with yelling, critical comments, and strong punishment.

Second, to a considerable degree, parents "get back what they put in" with respect to punishment. As you learned in Chapter 9, children learn by observation as well as by doing; therefore so they learn the adults' ways of coping with stress and their forms of punishment.

Yelling at children to get them to stop doing something, for example, may bring a brief change in their behavior (which reinforces the parent for yelling, by the way), but it also increases the chances that the children will yell back on other occasions.

Yet another dimension of the family system is the quality of the communication between parent and child. Developmentalists have conducted much less research on the quality of communication within families than on some of the other dimensions, so they are a long way from understanding all the ramifications of communication style. However, in general, children from families with open communication are seen as more emotionally or socially mature (Baumrind, 1971; Bell & Bell, 1982). Some studies also show that children in such families attain higher levels of academic achievement (Scott, 2004). Moreover, individuals who grow up in families characterized by open communication have good social skills in adulthood (Koesten, 2004).

## Parenting Styles

Each of the dimensions of family interaction discussed in the previous section has a demonstrable effect on the child, but if psychologists want to use a systems theory approach, it is not enough to look at each dimension independently. They also have to think about how the dimensions interact to create styles or patterns of child rearing.

## Types of Parenting Styles

The most influential proposal about styles of child rearing has come from Diana Baumrind (1973), who has looked at combinations of the various dimensions of parenting: (1) warmth, or nurturance; (2) level of expectations, which she calls "maturity demands"; (3) the clarity and consistency of rules, referred to as control; and (4) communication between parent and child. Baumrind saw three specific combinations of these characteristics: ✱ Explore at MyDevelopmentLab

- The **permissive style** is high in nurturance but low in maturity demands, control, and communication.
- The **authoritarian style** is high in control and maturity demands but low in nurturance and communication.
- The **authoritative style** is high in all four.

Eleanor Maccoby and John Martin (1983) extended Baumrind's category system, proposing a model that has been widely influential. They emphasized two dimensions, as you can see in Figure 13.4: the degree of control or demand and the level of acceptance/responsiveness. The intersection of these two dimensions creates four parenting types, three of which correspond fairly closely to Baumrind's authoritarian, authoritative, and permissive types. Maccoby and Martin's fourth type, the uninvolved **neglecting style**, was not identified by Baumrind in her early work, although their research shows clearly that this is a parenting style that deserves more study.

**THE AUTHORITARIAN TYPE**   Authoritarian parents are highly demanding of their children but at the same time quite unresponsive. Children growing up in such families do less well in school, are typically less skilled with peers, and have lower self-esteem than children from other types of families (Baumrind, 1991; Maccoby & Martin, 1983). Some of these children appear subdued; others may show high levels of aggressiveness or other indications of being out of control (Caputo, 2004).

**THE PERMISSIVE TYPE**   Children growing up with indulgent or permissive parents, who are tolerant and warm but exercise little authority, also show some negative outcomes. They do slightly less well in school in adolescence, and they are likely to be aggressive—particularly if the parents are specifically permissive toward aggressiveness—and to be somewhat immature in their behavior with peers and in school. They are less likely to take responsibility and are less independent (Maccoby & Martin, 1983).

←----------- Learning Objective 13.6
What are the four parenting styles proposed by Maccoby and Martin?

✱ Explore the Concept *Baumrind's Parenting Styles* at **MyDevelopmentLab**

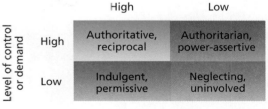

FIGURE 13.4 Maccoby and Martin's Parenting Styles Maccoby and Martin expanded on Baumrind's categories of parenting style in this two-dimensional typology.

(*Source:* Adapted from E. E. Maccoby and J. A. Martin. "Socialization in the context of the family: Parent-child interaction." In E. M. Hetherington (Ed.), *Handbook of Child Psychology*. Wiley, 1983, p. 39, Fig. 2. © 1983 by Wiley. By permission.)

**THE AUTHORITATIVE TYPE**   The most consistently positive outcomes have been associated with the authoritative parenting pattern, in which the parents are high in both control and warmth, setting clear limits, expecting and reinforcing socially mature behavior, and at the same time responding to the child's individual needs. Note that parents who use this style of parenting do not let the child rule the roost. Authoritative parents are quite willing to discipline the child appropriately if the child misbehaves. They are less likely to use physical punishment than are authoritarian parents, preferring instead to use time out or other mild punishments, but it is important to understand that such parents are not wishy-washy. Children reared in such families typically show higher self-esteem and are less likely to use alcohol or drugs in adolescence (Luyckx, Tildesley, Soenens, & Andrews, 2011). They are more independent but at the same time are more likely to comply with parental requests, and they may show more altruistic behavior as well. They are self-confident and achievement-oriented in school and get better grades in elementary school, high school, and college (e.g., Crockenberg & Litman, 1990; Dornbusch, Ritter, Liederman, Roberts, & Fraleigh, 1987; Jackson, Pratt, Hunsberger, & Pancer, 2005; Steinberg, Elmen, & Mounts, 1989; Weiss & Schwarz, 1996).

**THE NEGLECTING TYPE**   The most consistently negative outcomes are associated with the fourth parenting pattern, the neglecting or uninvolved type. You may remember from the discussion of secure and insecure attachments in Chapter 11 that one of the characteristics often found in the families of children rated as insecurely attached is the "psychological unavailability" of the mother. The mother may be depressed or may be overwhelmed by problems in her life, or she simply may not have made any deep emotional connection with the child. Whatever the reason, such children continue to show disturbances in their relationships with peers and with adults for many years. At adolescence, for example, youngsters from neglecting families are more impulsive and antisocial and much less achievement-oriented in school (Block, 1971; Caputo, 2004; Lamborn, Mounts, Steinberg, & Dornbusch, 1991; Pulkkinen, 1982). Lack of parental monitoring appears to be critical: Children and teens whose neglecting parents show poor monitoring are far more likely to become delinquent and to engage in sexual activity in early adolescence (Patterson, Reid, & Dishion, 1992; Pittman & Chase-Lansdale, 2001; Walker-Barnes & Mason, 2004).

**Learning Objective 13.7** - - - - - - - - - →
What did Steinberg and Dornbusch's study reveal about parenting styles?

# Parenting Styles and Development

The best single piece of research demonstrating the effects of the several parenting styles is a study of nearly 11,000 high school students in California and Wisconsin that was conducted by Laurence Steinberg and Sanford Dornbusch and their colleagues. Of this sample, 6,902 were followed over a 2-year period, providing valuable longitudinal information (Steinberg, Lamborn, Darling, Mounts, & Dornbusch, 1994). The researchers measured parenting styles by asking the teenagers to respond to questions about their relationship with their parents and their family life, including questions about both parental acceptance/responsiveness and parental control or demand—the dimensions that define Maccoby and Martin's category system. For example, the teenagers were asked to indicate the extent to which each of the following statements was true for them:

> I can count on my parents to help me out if I have some kind of problem.
> When [my father] wants me to do something, he explains why.
> My parents know exactly where I am most afternoons after school.

On the basis of participants' answers to such questions, Steinberg and Dornbusch were able to classify most of their families in the Maccoby and Martin category system and could then look at the relationship between these family styles and a variety of behaviors in the teenagers. They found that teenagers from authoritative families showed the most optimal pattern on every measure they used. These teenagers had higher self-reliance, higher social competence, better grades, fewer indications of psychological distress, and lower levels of school misconduct, drug use, and delinquency. Teenagers from authoritarian families had the lowest scores on the several measures of social competence and self-reliance; those from neglecting

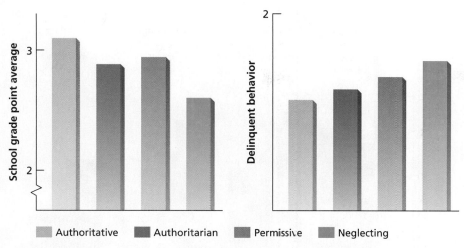

**FIGURE 13.5** Steinberg and Dornbusch's Study of Parenting Style and Delinquency
School grades and delinquency both varied as a function of parental style in Steinberg and Dornbusch's large sample of teenagers. Delinquent behavior in this case reflected the adolescent's own report of the frequency with which he or she carried a weapon, stole, or got into trouble with the police.
(*Source:* Steinberg et al., 1994, from Table 5, p. 762.)

families had the least optimal scores on measures of problem behaviors and school achievement (Steinberg et al., 1994). Figure 13.5 above illustrates two of these results: variations in grade point average and self-reported delinquent acts (including carrying a weapon, stealing, and getting into trouble with the police).

In an analysis of the data for the nearly 7,000 students on whom they had 2 years of information, Steinberg and Dornbusch found that students who described their parents as most authoritative at the beginning of the study showed more improvement in academic competence and self-reliance and the smallest increases in psychological symptoms and delinquent behavior over the 2 years, suggesting that the family style has a causal and continuing effect. These results have been replicated by many other researchers across a variety of cultures (e.g., Álvarez, Martín, Vergeles, & Martín, 2003).

These results are impressive, and they have been replicated in more recent cohorts of adolescents (Steinberg, Blatt-Eisengart, & Cauffman, 2006). However, the family system is, in fact, more complex than the simple comparison of the four parenting types may make it sound. For example, authoritative parents not only create a good family climate and thereby support and motivate their child optimally, but they also behave differently toward the child's school. They are much more likely to be involved with the school, attending school functions or talking to teachers, and this involvement seems to play a crucial role. When an otherwise authoritative parent is not also involved with the school, the outcomes for the student are not so clearly positive. Similarly, a teenager whose parent is highly involved with the school, but is not authoritative, shows less optimal outcomes. It is the combination of authoritativeness and school involvement that is associated with the best results (Steinberg, Lamborn, et al., 1992).

## Culture, Ethnicity, Socioeconomic Status and Parenting Styles

◄------------Learning Objective 13.8
How do parenting styles differ across ethnic and socioeconomic groups?

An additional complexity appears in analyses of relationships between parenting styles and developmental outcomes within each of several ethnic groups. Steinberg and Dornbusch's sample was large enough to allow them to do this for subgroups of African American, Hispanic American, and Asian American youth and their families, as well as for Whites (Steinberg et al., 1991). The results suggest both common processes and unique cultural variations.

Figure 13.6 on page 328 shows the percentage of families from each of the four ethnic groups involved in this study that could be classed as authoritative, broken down further by social class and by the intactness of the family. The authoritative pattern was most common

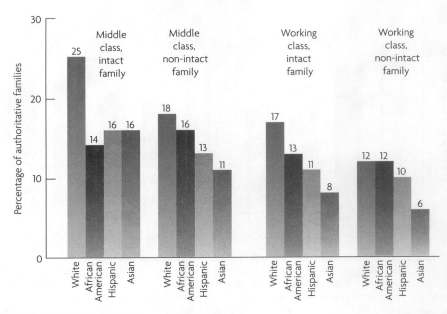

**FIGURE 13.6** Social Class, Ethnicity, and Parenting Style

As this figure suggests, authoritative parenting is more common among middle-class parents as well as in intact families (in which the child lives with both natural parents) of all ethnicities.

(*Source:* Steinberg et al., 1991.)

among Whites and least common among Asian Americans, but in each group, authoritative parenting was more common among the middle class and (with one exception) more common among intact families than in single-parent or stepparent families.

The more important question is whether the same predictive relationships between family style and child outcomes apply to all the groups. For some outcomes, the answer is "yes." In all four groups, for example, teenagers from authoritative families showed more self-reliance and less delinquency than did those from nonauthoritative families (Steinberg et al., 1991).

On the other hand, school performance was not linked to authoritative parenting in the same ways in all four groups. In this study, good grades were linked to such a parenting style for Whites and for Hispanic Americans, but only very weakly for Asian Americans—a group

*Asian parents very often score high on measures of authoritarian parental style. But their high level of strictness and control is embedded in a particular set of cultural values, and it thus has a different meaning for the child and a different effect on the child's behavior than such a style might have in a non-Asian family. This is yet another illustration of the fact that psychologists must be careful in generalizing theories and results across cultures.*

of students who do extremely well in school even though their parents are among the least authoritative. However, other researchers have found that the pattern of outcomes associated with authoritative and authoritarian parenting among other groups does hold true for Asian families (Chen, Dong, & Zhou, 1997). Among African American families, research results have been inconsistent with regard to linkages between parenting styles and academic achievement (Lamborn, Dornbusch, & Steinberg, 1996; Norwood, 1997).

How can developmentalists explain these differences? Taking a cue from Bronfenbrenner's model, Steinberg and Dornbusch hypothesized that ethnic differences in beliefs about the importance of education (part of the macrosystem) play a part in producing variations in educational outcomes across groups (Steinberg, Dornbusch, & Brown, 1992). They found that an additional key element is the belief students and parents hold about the importance of education for later success in life. All four ethnic groups studied share a belief that doing well in school will lead to better chances later, but the groups disagree on the consequences of doing poorly in school. Asian American students, more than any other group, believe that a good job is unlikely to follow a bad education, whereas

Hispanic Americans and African Americans are more optimistic about the risks associated with poor school performance. Perhaps as a result of their greater fear of academic failure, Asian American students spend much more time on homework than do other groups.

Another possibility is that the four styles suggested by Maccoby and Martin are themselves ethnocentric and simply do not (perhaps cannot) capture the elements that make individual cultural patterns unique (Parke & Buriel, 1998). For example, Ruth Chao (Chao & Tseng, 2002) notes that Chinese American parents, who require obedience, usually score high on traditional measures of authoritarian parenting. But in Asian cultures, strictness and a demand for obedience are perceived as aspects of concern and caring, not as reflections of lack of warmth. For the Chinese, says Chao, the key concept in parenting is training, which means teaching or educating, and training carries with it not only the element of control but also high involvement and closeness to the child. Chinese parents control their children not in order to dominate them—a motivation implicit in the authoritarian style as Baumrind described it—but rather to ensure that harmonious relations within the family and the culture will be maintained. According to Chao, the traditional measures of the authoritarian style simply fail to capture these values and thus badly misrepresent the quality of parent-child interactions within Chinese families.

Similarly, authoritative parenting may be less common in African American families because such families are more likely to be poor than those in other groups. One-third of African American and Hispanic American children live in poverty, compared to 17% of Whites, and 14% of Asian Americans (Child Trends Data Bank, 2011). As Figure 13.6 shows, authoritative parenting is less common among poor parents than among middle-class parents in all four major U.S. ethnic groups. Moreover, in Chapter 4 you learned that poverty is associated with a number of risk factors that threaten children's physical and psychological well-being (see Table 4.5 on page 107). Thus, it seems possible that African American parents believe that authoritarian parenting, rather than authoritative parenting, is an optimal adaptation to the circumstances in which they are bringing up their children (Pezzella, 2006).

## Family Structure, Divorce, and Parental Employment

So far, we haven't considered how the structure of a child's family influences interaction patterns and individual development. To fully understand how families influence development, we need to consider whether **family structure** (the configuration of individuals in a particular child's household) matters and how changes in family structure, such as divorce, contribute. ◉ Watch at **MyDevelopmentLab**

### Family Structure

Most of you probably know that the proportion of two-parent families in the United States has declined over the past 30 years. In 1970, almost 95% of children lived in such families, in 2007, only about 70% of children were living in two-parent homes, one of the lowest rates of two-parent households across the nations represented in Figure 13.7 on page 330 (Organization for Economic Cooperation and Development, 2010; U.S. Census Bureau, 2010). Most of the remaining 30% of children live in single-parent homes that are headed by women. Some children are being raised by same-sex couples.

**FAMILIES HEADED BY TWO BIOLOGICAL PARENTS** The broadest statement psychologists can make about the effects of family structure is that the optimal situation for children, at least in the United States, appears to include two biological parents who are married (Lamb & Lewis, 2010). Among Whites, children of married biological parents fare somewhat better than those of cohabiting biological parents (Manning & Brower, 2006). However, African American and Hispanic American children seem to be just as likely to thrive in homes headed by long-term cohabiting biological parents as in households headed by married biological parents.

As you probably know, though, many two-parent homes are far from happy and harmonious. Researchers have found that, among other variables, hostility in the parents' relationship is associated with a higher incidence of behavior problems in children (Katz & Woodin, 2002). Conversely, the greater the parents' satisfaction with their relationship, the better able

**family structure** The configuration of individuals in a child's household.

◉ Watch the **Video** *Divorce and Coparenting* at **MyDevelopmentLab**

◀----------- Learning Objective 13.9
How is family structure related to development?

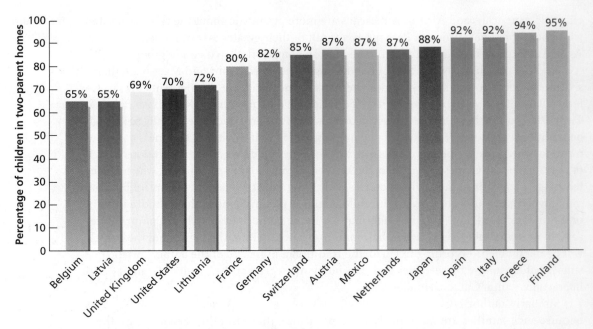

**FIGURE 13.7 Two-Parent Families around the World**
Children in the United States are less likely to live in two-parent families than children in many other industrialized nations.

(*Source:* Organization for Economic Cooperation & Development, 2010)

**blended family** A family that is established when a single parent marries a nonparent or parent.

their children are to regulate feelings of sibling rivalry (Volling, McElwain, & Miller, 2002). Such findings underscore the concept of the family as a system in which each relationship affects all others in some way.

**BLENDED FAMILIES** **Blended families** are established when a divorced or never-married single parent marries a parent or nonparent. Because children in such families are likely to have experienced periods during which they were living in single-parent homes, it's impossible to say whether any associated developmental outcomes are the result of the family structure itself or of the number of changes in living arrangements that the children have had to deal with over the years. Nevertheless, it's important to note that children living in such families have higher rates of delinquency and lower school grades than do those who live with two natural parents who are married (Lee, Burkham, Zimiles, & Ladewski, 1994) (see Figure 13.8). As a general rule, among preschoolers and school-aged children these negative effects are more pronounced for boys than for girls. ◉━Watch at **MyDevelopmentLab**

◉━Watch the **Video** *Blended Families* at **MyDevelopmentLab**

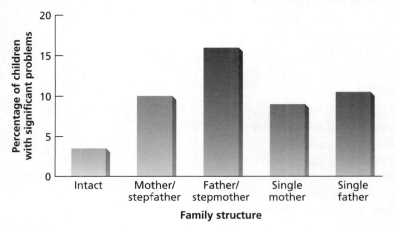

**FIGURE 13.8 Family Structure and Behavior Problems**
Children living with a stepparent, especially those living with their father and a stepmother, are more likely than those in intact families to show behavior problems of one type or another.

(*Source:* Lee, Burkham, Zimilies, & Ladewski, 1994, from Table 1, p. 417.)

In adolescence, the pattern of gender differences shifts. Associations between blended family status and poor developmental outcomes are stronger for teenaged girls than for teenaged boys (Brown & Amatea, 2000). The structure that has been studied most involves a divorced or never-married mother who marries after a period of singlehood. In such families, girls seem to have a great deal more difficulty getting along with a new stepfather than their brothers do. Many are critical of the new stepfather and treat him as an intruder. Others sulk and try to avoid contact with him. Girls in this situation are more likely to become depressed. They are also more likely than boys to become involved with drugs.

The reasons for this pattern are unknown. Some developmentalists speculate that the daughter may feel displaced from a special or more responsible position in the family system that she held when her mother was single (Brown & Amatea, 2000). In contrast, the teenaged boy may have more to gain by the addition of the stepfather because he acquired a male role model.

Whatever the explanation, findings like these remind us once again that family systems are astonishingly complex.

**SINGLE-PARENT FAMILIES** Single-parent households are quite diverse. As you can see in Figure 13.9 below, female-headed households are far more common than those headed by males. Consequently, most research on single-parent families focuses on female-headed households.

In contrast to stereotypes, some single mothers are very financially secure. In fact, about 8% in the United States have incomes in excess of $100,000 per year (U.S. Census, 2010). However, on average, female-headed families are far more likely to be poor than are two-parent households. Approximately one-quarter of female-headed families live in poverty, compared to just 4% of two-parent households (U.S. Census Bureau, 2010). Thus, the developmental outcomes that are found among the children of single mothers may be due to poverty, to family structure, or to an interaction between the two. ◉ Watch at **MyDevelopmentLab**

Children of single mothers are about twice as likely as other children to drop out of high school, twice as likely to have a child before age 20, and less likely to have a steady job in their late teens or early 20s (McLanahan & Sandefur, 1994). Children of adolescent mothers are particularly at risk. Differences between children of teenagers and those whose mothers are older are evident in early childhood. Some studies suggest that preschoolers whose mothers are single teenagers display less advanced cognitive and social development than their peers (Furstenberg, Brooks-Gunn, & Chase-Lansdale, 1989). Other research indicates that, when the children of teen mothers become teens themselves, they are more likely to exhibit behaviors such as truancy, fighting with peers, and early sexual activity than peers whose mothers are older (Levine, Pollack, & Comfort, 2001). ◉ Watch at **MyDevelopmentLab**

As gloomy as these findings may seem, keep in mind that many single mothers (and fathers, too) maintain strong links with an **extended family**, a family structure that includes parents, grandparents, aunts, uncles, cousins, and so on. Extended families seem to serve a protective function for children who are growing up in single-parent homes.
◉ Watch at **MyDevelopmentLab**

(Wilson, 1995). Grandmothers, for example, appear to be important sources of emotional warmth for the children of teenaged mothers (Coley & Chase-Lansdale, 1998). Moreover, extended family members often help single and divorced mothers with financial and emotional support as well as with child care. In the United States, such

*In the United States, many two-parent homes are formed when a single parent marries another single parent or a non-parent.*

◉ Watch the **Video** *Single Mothers* at **MyDevelopmentLab**

◉ Watch the **Video** *Sexuality in Adolescence: The Pregnant Teen* at **MyDevelopmentLab**

◉ Watch the **Video** *Becoming a Grandparent* at **MyDevelopmentLab**

**extended family** A family structure that includes parents, grandparents, aunts, uncles, cousins, and so on.

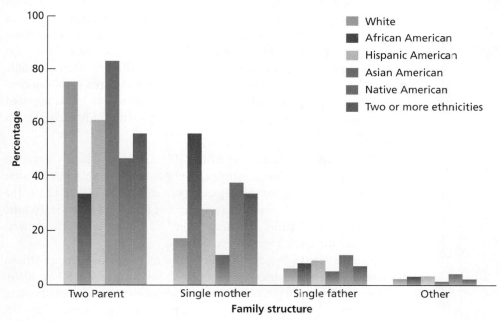

**FIGURE 13.9** Family Structure and Ethnicity
Household types for U.S. children under 18 years of age.

(*Source:* Aud & Fox, 2010)

Many single parents manage to overcome substantial obstacles and give their children the support and supervision they need. Support from extended family members, especially grandparents, is one of the key factors that enables single parents to do so.

👁—Watch the **Video** *A Family with Two Fathers* at **MyDevelopmentLab**

*The same factors that influence interactions in families headed by a man and a woman contribute to the well-being of children who are being raised by same-sex couples.*

networks are more common among minorities than among Whites (Harrison, Wilson, Pine, Chan, & Buriel, 1990).

**GAY AND LESBIAN FAMILIES**   Questions about children's sex-role identity and sexual orientation have dominated research on gay and lesbian parenting (Bailey, Brobow, Wolfe, & Mikach, 1995). Studies have generally shown that children raised by gay and lesbian parents develop sex-role identities in the same way as children of heterosexual parents. They are also just as likely to be heterosexual, although they may be more likely to question their sexual orientation than children of heterosexual parents are (Bos & Sandfort, 2010; Golombok & Tasker, 1996).

To help answer general questions about cognitive and social development among the children of gay and lesbian parents, researchers have conducted comprehensive reviews of the small number of studies that have been done. Such reviews have typically found that the majority of studies suggest that children raised by gay and lesbian parents do not differ from those raised by heterosexuals (Fitzgerald, 1999; Lambert, 2005; Patterson, 1997). However, most such studies have involved a very small number of families and children (Schumm, 2004). Moreover, in almost all cases, the children involved have been conceived and reared in heterosexual relationships prior to being parented by a same-sex couple. Thus, the findings of these studies can't be attributed conclusively to the effects of being raised by a gay or lesbian parent. 👁—Watch at **MyDevelopmentLab**

One study, though, involved 80 school-aged children who had been conceived by artificial insemination (Chan, Raboy, & Patterson, 1998). Researchers compared these children across four types of family structures: lesbian couples, single lesbian mothers, heterosexual couples, and single heterosexual mothers. The study found no differences in either cognitive or social development among the children. However, it did find that the same variables—parenting stress, parental conflict, parental affection—predicted developmental outcomes in all four groups. These findings, much like those contrasting two-parent and single-parent families, suggest that children's development depends more on how parents interact with them than on family configuration. Longitudinal research that shows that children of lesbian couples conceived through artificial insemination are as well or better adjusted than their peers in other types of families is supportive of this conclusion (Bos & Gartrell, 2010).

**FAMILY STRUCTURE, CULTURE, AND ETHNICITY**   Looking at family structure across ethnic groups further illustrates family diversity in the United States. You can get some feeling for the degree of variation from Figure 13.10. The figure graphs estimates of the percentages of five family types among White, African American, Hispanic American, Asian American, and Native American children in the United States.

You can see that single-parent families are far more common among African Americans and Native Americans than among other groups (Aud & Fox, 2010). A difference in the proportion of births to unmarried women is one contributing factor. As Figure 13.10 on page 333 shows, births to single women have increased rather dramatically across all ethnic groups in the United States in the past few decades (National Center for Health Statistics, 2010). However, the rates

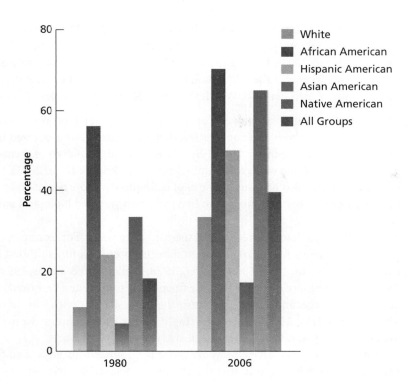

**FIGURE 13.10** Births to Unmarried Women
Percentage of births to unmarried women
across ethnic groups in the United States.
The rate of births to unmarried women has
increased across all groups in the United
States over recent decades. These statistics
are one reason for the growing number of
school-aged and teenaged children who
live in single-parent homes.

(*Source:* National Center for Health Statistics,
2010.)

of such births are much higher among African American and Native American women than
in other groups. (By the way, in all groups, more than three-quarters of single women giving birth
are over the age of 20. Thus, teenage pregnancy contributes very little to the statistics on single
motherhood.)

A second factor is that, although many African American and Native American single
mothers eventually marry, adults in these groups—whether parents or not—are less likely
to marry (Goodwin & Mosher, 2010). Among 40- to 44-year-olds in the United States, just
12% of Asian American, 14% of White American, and 16% of Hispanic American adults
have never married, compared to 30% of African Americans and 27% of Native Americans
(Goodwin & Mosher, 2010; U.S. Census Bureau, 2008). As a result, African American and
Native American children are far more likely than children in other groups to spend all of
their childhood years living in poverty. In both groups, as well as among Hispanic Americans, nearly half of all female-headed households live in poverty (U.S. Census Bureau, 2003).

Of course, statistics can't explain why African American and Native American families are more likely than those of other groups to be headed by single parents. Sociologists
speculate that, in the case of African Americans, lack of economic opportunities for men
renders them less able to take on family responsibilities (Cherlin, 1992). Others add that
grandparents and other relatives in both groups traditionally help support single mothers. For instance, among Native Americans, a traditional cultural value sociologists call *kin
orientation* views parenting as the responsibility of a child's entire family, including grandparents and aunts and uncles. As a result, Native American single parents, especially those
who live in predominantly Native American communities, receive more material and emotional support than do single parents in other groups and may feel less pressure to marry
(Ambert, 2001).

## Divorce

◄------------Learning Objective 13.10
How does divorce affect children's
behavior?

There can be little doubt that divorce is traumatic for children. However, this statement must
be followed by a note of caution. Some of the negative effects of divorce are due to factors that
were present *before* the divorce, such as difficult temperament in the child or excessive marital
conflict between the parents (Cherlin, Chase-Lansdale, & McRae, 1998). It's also important to

Many single parents manage to overcome substantial obstacles and give their children the support and supervision they need.

👁—Watch the Video *Being a Single Parent* at **MyDevelopmentLab**

👁—Watch the Video *Divorce and Adolescence* at **MyDevelopmentLab**

keep in mind that divorce is not a unitary variable; children are probably affected by a multitude of divorce-related factors: parental conflict, poverty, disruptions of daily routine, and so on (Bailey & Zvonkovic, 2003). For this reason, children whose parents separate or stay in conflict-ridden marriages, even if they do not actually divorce, may experience many of the same effects (Ingoldsby, Shaw, Owens, & Winslow 1999). 👁—Watch at **MyDevelopmentLab**

**CHILDREN AND DIVORCE**   In the first few years after a divorce, children typically show declines in school performance and show more aggressive, defiant, negative, or depressed behavior (Bonde, Obel, Nedergard, & Thomsen, 2004). By adolescence, the children of divorced parents are more likely than peers to engage in criminal behavior (Price & Kunz, 2003). Children living in stepparent families also have higher rates of delinquency, more behavioral problems in school, and lower grades than do those who live with their married biological parents do (Jeynes, 2007).

The negative effects of divorce seem to persist for many years. For example, children whose parents divorce have a higher risk of mental health problems in adulthood (Chase-Lansdale, Cherlin, & Kiernan, 1995; Cherlin et al., 1998; Wallerstein & Lewis, 1998). Many young adults whose parents are divorced lack the financial resources and emotional support needed to succeed in college, and a majority report that they struggle with fears of intimacy in relationships (Cartwright, 2006). Not surprisingly, adults whose parents were divorced are themselves more likely to divorce. 👁—Watch at **MyDevelopmentLab**

As a general rule, these negative effects are more pronounced for boys than for girls. However, some researchers have found that the effects are delayed in girls, making it more difficult to associate the effects with the divorce. Consequently, longitudinal studies often find that girls show equal or even greater negative effects (Amato, 1993; Hetherington, 1991a, 1991b). Age differences in the severity of the reaction have been found in some studies but not others. For example, one longitudinal study found that the effects of parental divorce were most severe in a group of 12-year-olds who experienced the divorce in early childhood rather than during the school years (Pagani, Boulerice, Tremblay, & Vitaro, 1997).

Ethnicity, incidentally, does not appear to be a causal factor. Yes, a larger percentage of African American children grow up in single-parent families. But the same negative outcomes occur in Caucasian American single-parent families, and the same positive outcomes are found in two-parent minority families. For example, the school dropout rate for Caucasian American children from single-parent families is higher than that for Hispanic American or African American children reared in two-parent families (McLanahan & Sandefur, 1994).

**UNDERSTANDING THE EFFECTS OF DIVORCE**   How are developmentalists to understand all these various findings? First, divorce reduces the financial and emotional resources available to support the child. With only one parent, the household typically has only one income and only one adult to respond to the child's emotional needs. Data from the United States indicate that a woman's income drops an average of 40–50% after a divorce (Bradbury & Katz, 2002).

Second and perhaps most importantly, single parenthood, divorce, and stepparent-hood all increase the likelihood that the family climate or style will shift away from authoritative parenting (Barber & Demo, 2006). This is evident in the first few years after a divorce, when the custodial parent (usually the mother) is distracted or has symptoms of depression and less able to manage warm control; it is evident in families with a stepparent as well, where rates of authoritative parenting are lower than in families that are headed by children's married biological parents (look back at Figure 13.6 on page 328).

Remember, an authoritarian or neglecting parenting style is linked to poor outcomes whether the parenting style is triggered by a divorce, a stressful remarriage, the father's loss of a job, or any other stress (Goldberg, 1990). Ultimately, it is this process within the family, rather than any particular type of disruption, that is significant for the child (see *Developmental Science in the Real World*). Predictably, studies show that children whose parents maintain high levels of warmth and responsiveness during and shortly after a divorce are far less likely to show negative effects (Sandler, Miles, Cookston, & Braver, 2008).

## When Divorce is Unavoidable

Adriana and Martin have decided to end their marriage, but they are concerned about how their divorce might affect their two children. Like most parents, they know that divorce can be traumatic for children, and they want to do their best to minimize such effects. They have gone to a family therapist to find out how best to achieve this goal. After determining that the couple was sure that their differences could not be reconciled and that there was no alternative to divorce, the therapist advised them that they would not be able to eliminate all of the short-term disruptive effects of such an event on their children. However, the therapist did suggest some specific things that Adriana and Martin could do to soften or reduce the effects:

- *Try to keep the number of separate changes the child has to cope with to a minimum.* If at all possible, keep the children in the same school or child-care setting and the same house or apartment (Austin, 2008).
- *If the children are teenagers, consider having each child live with the parent of the same gender.* The data are not totally consistent, but it looks as if this may be a less stressful arrangement (Lee et al., 1994).

- *The custodial parent should help the children stay in touch with the noncustodial parent.* Likewise, the noncustodial parent should maintain as much contact as possible with the children, calling and seeing them regularly, attending school functions, and so on (Cashmore, Parkinson, & Taylor, 2008).
- *Keep the conflict to a minimum.* Most of all, try not to fight in front of the children. Open conflict has negative effects on children whether the parents are divorced or not (Sandler, Miles, Cookston & Braver, 2008). Thus, divorce is not the sole culprit—divorce combined with open conflict between the adults has worse effects.
- *Parents should not use the children as go-betweens or talk disparagingly about their ex-spouses to them.* Children who feel caught in the middle between the two parents are more likely to show various kinds of negative symptoms, such as depression or behavior problems (Buchanan, Maccoby, & Dornbusch, 1991).
- Older children should be included in the *decision-making process.* When children participate in deciding where and with

whom they will live, how often they will see the noncustodial parent, and so on, families experience less postdivorce conflict and agreements tend to be more stable than when children's input is not sought (Cashmore & Parkinson, 2008; McIntosh, Wells, Smyth, & Long, 2008).

In the midst of the emotional upheaval that accompanies divorce, these are not easy prescriptions to follow. However, if divorcing parents are able to do so, their children will probably suffer less.

### REFLECTION

1. What specific strategies can Adriana and Martin employ to achieve the goal of reducing conflict?
2. If you were in this situation, where would you turn for emotional and moral support? Why?

### Learning Objective 13.10a
What steps can parents take to minimize the impact of divorce on their children's development?

## Parental Employment

**Learning Objective 13.11**
How do parents' employment patterns affect children?

Most of the work on the impact of fathers' employment on children's development focuses on fathers who have lost their jobs. Early research suggested that both parents become less consistent in their behavior toward their children, less affectionate, and less effective at monitoring them when the father is unemployed (Conger, Patterson, & Ge, 1995). However, as dual-career families have become more common, research has begun to reveal a different pattern. It seems that, when either parent loses his or her job, it is the responses of the still-employed parent that matter most when it comes to predicting the effects of parental unemployment on children's development. Specifically, when the still-employed parent, whether mother or father, displays higher levels of warmth and supportiveness following the other's job loss, children appear to be protected from the potentially negative effects of parental unemployment (Bacikova-Sleskova, Geckova, van Dijk, Groothoff, & Reijneveld, 2011).

Similarly, nearly all the research on mothers' employment compares mothers who work with those who do not. Predictably, most studies show that children benefit from maternal employment in single-parent families, presumably because of the economic benefits of the mother's job (Chase-Landale et al., 2011; Mahatmya & Lohman, 2011). By contrast, there is no clear pattern in the research on maternal employment in two-parent families. Some studies show that children are unaffected (e.g., Lucas-Thompston, Goldberg, & Prause, 2010). Others have found associations between maternal employment and negative outcomes such as depression in the child (Chambliss et al., 2010).

*In the United States today, nearly two-thirds of women with children under age 6 and three-quarters of women with school-aged or adolescent children work at least part-time (NICHD Early Child Care Research Network, 2003). In general, the effects seem to be neutral or beneficial for the children.*

Recent studies have revealed a pattern of associations between maternal employment and child obesity (Morissey, Dunifon, & Kalil, 2011). It appears that the more hours a mother works, the more likely her child is to be overweight (Cawley & Liu, 2007). Closer analyses suggest that there are several factors underlying this correlation. First, and predictably, the more hours a mother works, the less time she spends cooking, and the more likely she is to purchase prepared foods. Second, and again predictably, the more hours a mother works, the less time she spends in active, physical play with children. The link between maternal employment and obesity is weaker in two-parent families where fathers help with meal preparation and engage children in physical activities. However, fathers' contributions do not entirely offset the effects of maternal employment on children's obesity risk. What appears to help is a family pattern in which both parents, regardless of work hours, partner with children to do physically demanding chores such as yard work and home repair projects (Benson, 2011).

Learning Objective 13.12 ---------→
What is the importance of social support to the family system?

## Social Support for Parents

A second aspect of parents' lives that affects the family system is the quality of their network of relationships and their satisfaction with the social support they receive from that network. The general point is fairly self-evident: Parents who have access to adequate emotional and physical support—from each other or from friends and family—are able to respond to their children more warmly, more consistently, and with better control (Crowley & Curenton, 2011; Herwig, Wirtz, & Bengel, 2004). Children whose parents have access to more assistance from friends complete more years of school than do children whose parents have less support of this type (Hofferth, Boisjoly, & Duncan, 1995). The effect of social support on parents is particularly evident when they are experiencing stress of some kind, such as job loss, chronic poverty, teenage childbirth, a temperamentally difficult child or an infant with a handicap, divorce, or even just fatigue.

You may recall that Chapter 9 mentioned a study by Susan Crockenberg (1981) that illustrates the point nicely. She found that temperamentally irritable infants had an increased likelihood of ending up with an insecure attachment to their mothers only when the mother lacked adequate social support. When the mother felt that she had enough support, similarly irritable children were later securely attached. There are many other examples of this "buffering effect" of social support:

- New mothers who lack social and emotional support are more likely to suffer from postpartum depression than are those with adequate support (Cutrona & Troutman, 1986). Divorced parents who have help and emotional support from friends or family members are much more able to maintain a stable and affectionate environment for their children than are those who grapple with divorce in isolation (Hetherington, 1989).

- Mothers with depression benefit from programs aimed at increasing social support networks (Herwig, Wirtz, & Bengel, 2004).
- Among African American single mothers, those who have enough aid and emotional support from kin show a more authoritative style of parenting than do single mothers lacking such aid (Taylor et al., 1993).
- Professional women who have chosen to become full-time parents receive affirmation and practical advice on transitioning their families from two- to one-income status from organizations for stay-at-home parents (Crowley & Curenton, 2011).

As a general rule, social support seems to allow parents to mobilize the best parenting skills they have in their repertoire. The key is not the objective amount of contact or advice received, but rather the parent's satisfaction with the level and quality of the support he or she is experiencing. The moral seems to be that at times of greatest difficulty or stress, you need the emotional and physical support of others the most. Yet if you wait until that difficult moment to look around and see who is there to help, you may not find what you need. Social networks must be developed and nurtured over time. But they certainly seem to pay dividends for parents, and thus for children.

## THINK CRITICALLY

- What other variables might account for the relationships among parenting style, ethnicity, socioeconomic status, and developmental outcomes?
- Given what you have learned in this chapter, how would you answer someone who asked you whether it is worse for an unhappy couple to get divorced or to stay together even though they fight all the time?

## CONDUCT YOUR OWN RESEARCH

It is likely that a significant proportion of your friends and classmates have experienced a parental divorce. Recruit a few of them to participate in a study of young adults' memories regarding parental divorce. Ask volunteers to tell you how old they were when their parents divorced. Then ask them each to write a brief summary of how the divorce affected them immediately and in the long term. Categorize the summaries by age to determine whether volunteers' experiences vary according to the age at which they confronted parental divorce.

*Parents' working conditions represent one of the most important ways in which institutions outside the home influence families and, as a result, influence the development of individual children. Therefore, when workers succeed in improving the conditions under which they work, their efforts may produce long-term benefits for the entire society as well as immediate benefits for themselves and their families.*

## SUMMARY ✓•⎯ Study and Review at MyDevelopmentLab

### Understanding the Family System

**13.1  How does family systems theory explain family interactions?**
Family systems theory proposes that the family is an integrated network of factors that work together to influence a child's development. Changing one aspect of family life changes all the others. The influence of the system as a whole on development is greater than the sum of the individual factors that make up the family.

**13.2  How do the various systems in Bronfenbrenner's model interact to influence children's development?**
Bronfenbrenner conceived of the child's bioecological system as composed of three layers: microsystems, such as the family or the school, in which the child is directly involved; exosystems, such as the parent's jobs, which affect the child indirectly by influencing some aspect of a microsystem; and the macrosystem, including the ethnic subculture and the broader society or culture within which the family exists.

**13.2a  How do video calling applications such as Skype expand the developmental microsystems of children in immigrant families?**
Video calling applications help immigrant families and their children deal with acculturative stress, the stress that occurs when people move to a new culture where the language and customs are unfamiliar to them, by enabling them to easily keep in touch with extended family members in their home countries. These tools also help give children direct contact with extended family members that would be impossible without them. As a result, immigrants can maintain language skills that link them to their cultural heritage.

### Dimensions of Family Interaction

**13.3  What are the individual characteristics of children and parents that contribute to family interactions?**
The family system is affected by a child's temperament, birth order, age, and gender. Parental characteristics that

affect the family system include a parent's depression, the parent's working model of attachment, and the quality of the parents' relationship.

**13.4 How do emotional warmth and parental responsiveness influence parent-child relationships?**

Children in families that provide high levels of warmth and affection have more secure attachments and better peer relationships than children in families that are more cold or rejecting. Parents who are responsive to children's needs also positively affect children's development.

**13.5 How do parents' methods of control and communication affect development?**

Parents who have clear rules and standards and enforce those rules and expectations consistently have children with the greatest self-esteem and the greatest competence across a broad range of situations. Open communication in the family system is associated with social maturity in children.

**13.5a What does research say about the effects of spanking?**

Spanking reduces unacceptable behavior in the short-run. Long-term effects include the child's observation of his/her parent behaving in a physically aggressive and emotionally rejecting way.

## Parenting Styles

**13.6 What are the four parenting styles proposed by Maccoby and Martin?**

Four styles of parenting suggested by several theorists are authoritarian, authoritative, permissive, and neglecting. The authoritative style appears to be the most generally effective for producing confident, competent, independent, and affectionate children. The most negative outcomes are found with the neglecting style.

**13.7 What did Steinberg and Dornbusch's study reveal about parenting styles?**

Research by Steinberg and Dornbusch suggests that parenting styles are related to a variety of developmental outcomes, including academic achievement, social functioning, mental health, and delinquency.

**13.8 How do parenting styles differ across ethnic and socioeconomic groups?**

Research has revealed ethnic differences in the ways in which parenting style affects children. In particular, Asian American children generally do very well in school despite low rates of authoritative parenting, which may indicate that the categorization of family styles is culture-specific.

## Family Structure, Divorce, and Parental Employment

**13.9 How is family structure related to development?**

The structure of the family has an impact on family functioning, which in turn affects children's behavior. Children reared in single-parent families are at higher risk for a variety of negative outcomes, including dropping out of school, teen parenthood, and delinquency. Having a stepparent is also associated with heightened risks of poorer outcomes for children. Family interaction variables that predict developmental outcomes function in the same ways in gay and lesbian families as in other types of families.

**13.10 How does divorce affect children's behavior?**

For most children, divorce results in a decline in standard of living and a decrease in authoritative parenting. Some of the negative effects of divorce may be attributable to family conflict that occurred prior to the divorce itself.

**13.10a What steps can parents take to minimize the impact of divorce on children's development?**

Family therapists recommend that divorcing parents minimize changes, help children stay in touch with noncustodial parents, keep conflict to a minimum, avoid using the children as go-betweens, and, if children are teens, consider allowing them to live with the parent of the same gender.

**13.11 How do parents' employment patterns affect children?**

Parents' employment status may affect children directly by increasing or decreasing the family's economic resources, but it may also affect them indirectly through its influence on the parents themselves. For example, employment changes the mother's self-image, increasing her economic power and altering the distribution of labor. Loss of job by a father disrupts the family system, increasing authoritarian parenting and reducing marital satisfaction.

**13.12 What is the importance of social support to the family system?**

Having adequate physical and emotional support from a network of friends and/or relatives enables parents to employ effective parenting strategies. Such support is especially critical for families exposed to stressors such as job loss, chronic poverty, teenage parenthood, children with difficult temperaments or disabilities, and divorce.

## KEY TERMS

| | | | |
|---|---|---|---|
| authoritarian style ( (p. 325) | blended family (p. 330) | family systems theory (p. 317) | permissive style (p. 325) |
| authoritative style (p. 325) | extended family (p. 331) | mirror neurons (p. 323) | responsiveness (p. 322) |
| birth order (p. 320) | family structure (p. 329) | neglecting style (p. 325) | warmth versus hostility (p. 322) |

# Beyond the Family:
# The Impact of the Broader Culture

D o you know what momentous event happened on November 10, 1969? Here's a hint. It seemed relatively insignificant at the time, but it influenced the lives of millions of children and continues to do so today. In fact, there's a good chance that it influenced your own daily routine when you were a preschooler.

November 10, 1969, was the date on which *Sesame Street* made its debut (Palmer, 2003). When the program hit the airwaves, it was an instant success. Incredibly, by the end of its first year, fully half of the 12 million children in the United States were watching *Sesame Street* every day. Still, critics pointed out that the popularity of the show gave no indication as to whether it was achieving its educational goals. In response, psychologists began to study the program's effects on its young viewers. To date, many such studies have been done, and there is little doubt that *Sesame Street* has a positive impact on children's development in both the cognitive and the social-emotional domains (e.g., Wright et al., 2001). Moreover, the creators of *Sesame Street* demonstrated that psychological research can serve as a solid foundation on which to build entertainment media for children that are both effective and commercially successful.

Given these positive findings, you might be surprised to learn that *Sesame Street* has been criticized by some developmentalists, including the late Urie Bronfenbrenner, whose bioecological model of development you learned about in Chapter 13. Although they recognized the value of the program for children's cognitive development, Bronfenbrenner and others criticized the disconnect between the urban setting in which the live characters and muppets interact on the show and the characteristics—poverty, crime, lack of educational and job opportunities—of real-world urban neighborhoods (Morrow, 2005). However, the larger, more general criticism that Bronfenbrenner (1967) expressed about television was its capacity for diminishing the importance of the family. Simply put, more time with television means less time with mother, father, siblings, grandparents, and so on. For Bronfenbrenner, the threat or promise of any factor outside the child's immediate environment depends on how it affects the family system. Thus, as you read about the effects of nonparental care, schooling, socioeconomic status, and culture, keep in mind that these factors affect children both directly and indirectly through their impact on the family system itself.

## Nonparental Care

In 1970, only 18% of married women with children under age 6 were in the U.S. labor force; today, 64% of mothers in this group are employed (Bureau of Labor Statistics, 2010). More than half of women with children under age 1—including more than half of women living with a husband—now work outside the home at least part-time (Han, Ruhm, Waldfogel, & Washbrook, 2008). It is now typical for infants as well as school-aged children to spend a significant amount of time being cared for by someone other than a parent (FIFCFS, 2010).

**Learning Objective 14.1**
Why is it difficult to study the effects of nonparental care?

## Difficulties in Studying Nonparental Care

It might seem that the effect on development of nonparental care could easily be determined by comparing children who receive nonparental care to those who are cared for entirely by their parents. However, both "nonparental care" and "parental care" are among those variables that are actually complex interactions among numerous variables rather than single factors whose effects can be studied independently. Thus, interpretation of research on nonparental care has to take into account a variety of issues.

First, an enormous variety of different care arrangements are all lumped together in the general category of "nonparental care" (see Figure 14.1). Children who are cared for by grandparents in their own homes as well as those who are enrolled in child care centers both receive nonparental care. In addition, these care arrangements begin at different ages for different children and last for varying lengths of time. Some children have the same nonparental caregiver over many years; others shift often from one care setting to another. Moreover, nonparental care varies widely in quality (Corapci, 2010).

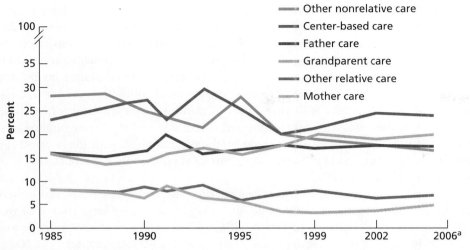

**FIGURE 14.1** Nonparental Care Arrangements for Children under Age 4 in the United States
For children under 4 whose mothers are employed, multiple nonparental care arrangements have been the norm for the past two decades. Many children are cared for in more than one type of setting.
(*Source:* FIFCFS, 2010.)

Not only are there a wide variety of child care arrangements across families, but it is common for children to experience more than one type of arrangement (FIFCS, 2010). For example, a child may attend a center-based program two days a week and be cared for by a relative on the other days. Child care arrangements also vary by ethnicity (U.S. Census Bureau, 2011). Hispanic American children are far less likely to be enrolled in child care centers than African American and Caucasian American children. Among children who are not enrolled in center care, African American and Hispanic American youngsters are more likely to be cared for by relatives than by nonrelatives; the opposite is true of Caucasian American children. In addition, mothers also differ in their attitudes toward the care arrangements they have made (Rose & Elicker, 2010). Some mothers with children in nonparental care would rather be at home taking care of their children; others are happy to be working. The reverse is also true: Some mothers who are at home full time would rather be working, and some are delighted to be at home. Thus, families who place their children in nonparental care are also different in a whole host of ways from those who care for their children primarily at home. Researchers have no way of knowing whether effects attributed to nonparental care are actually the result of these or other family differences.

Most of the research developmentalists have to draw on does not take these complexities into account. Researchers have frequently compared children "in child care" with those "reared at home" and assumed that any differences between the two groups were attributable to the child care experience. Recent studies are often better, but developmentalists are still a long way from having clear or good answers to even the most basic questions about the impact of child care on children's development. However, because the issue is so critical, you need to be aware of what is and is not yet known.

The number of infants in the United States who experience center based care is increasing.

## Effects of Early Nonparental Care on Development ← - - - - - - - - Learning Objective 14.2

Despite the difficulties involved in studying nonparental care, researchers have provided developmentalists and parents alike with at least some information about how nonparental care affects children's development. Studies have looked at a number of important outcomes. Attachment, for example, has been the focus of numerous studies. Developmental scientists have also examined the effects of nonparental care on children's cognitive and social functioning.

How does early nonparental care affect infants' and young children's development?

**ATTACHMENT**    One vital question is whether an infant or toddler can develop a secure attachment to her mother and father if she is repeatedly separated from them (Bowlby, 2007). Researchers know that the majority of infants develop secure attachments to parents who go to work every day, so it is clear that regular separations do not preclude secure attachment. Still, the early research created enough concern that psychologist Jay Belsky, in a series of papers and in testimony before a congressional committee, sounded an alarm (Belsky, 1985, 1992; Belsky & Rovine, 1988). Combining data from several studies, he concluded that there was a slightly heightened risk of insecure attachment among infants who entered child care before their first birthday, compared with those cared for at home throughout the first year. Subsequent analyses supported Belsky's conclusion (Lamb, Sternberg, & Prodromidis, 1992).

To search for answers to the questions raised by Belsky's research, 25 researchers at 14 universities got together in 1991 to design and carry out a very large study that would address all these questions (NICHD Early Child Care Research Network, 2006). They enrolled over 1,300 infants and their families in the study, including African American and Hispanic American families, mothers with little education as well as those with college or graduate degrees, and both single mothers and two-parent families.

The results of the study are surprisingly clear: Child care, in itself, is unrelated to the security of the child's attachment. Only among infants whose mothers are relatively insensitive to their needs at home does child care or nonparental care potentially have some negative effects. For these children, low-quality care is linked to less secure attachment. Only the infants who experience the combination of two poor conditions—an insensitive mother and poor care—have a higher risk of being insecurely attached. Infants with insensitive mothers whose nonparental care is of good quality are just as likely as any other child to be securely attached.

**COGNITIVE DEVELOPMENT**    Surveys show that school readiness is the primary goal of parents who choose center-based care for toddlers and preschoolers (Gamble, Ewing, & Wilhelm, 2009) There is some evidence that high-quality care has positive effects on children's overall cognitive and language skills (Vandell et al., 2010). Other research suggests that this positive effect is even larger among infants and children from poor families, who show significant and lasting gains in IQ scores and later school performance after attending highly enriched child care throughout infancy and early childhood—research you'll recall from Chapter 7 (Loeb, Fuller, Kagan, & Carrol, 2004; Pungello et al., 2010).

However, the picture is not entirely rosy. Several studies in the United States point to possible negative effects of day-care experience on cognitive development. For instance, one study found that children who were first enrolled in nonparental care in the year before they entered school obtained lower scores on reading and math achievement tests at the end of kindergarten than peers who were cared for at home (Herbst & Tekin, 2008).

**PERSONALITY**    When researchers look at the impact of nonparental child care on children's personality, they find yet another somewhat confusing story. A number of investigators have found that children in child care are more sociable and more popular and have better peer-play skills than do those reared primarily at home (Scarr & Eisenberg, 1993). However, this is by no means the universal finding. Many other researchers find nonparental care linked to heightened aggression with peers and lower compliance with teachers and parents, both during the preschool years and at later ages (NICHD Early Child Care Research Network, 2004; Nomaguchi, 2006).

What is it about nonparental care that appears to predispose infants to become aggressive, disobedient kindergartners? Perhaps an examination of what Bronfenbrenner would call the *biological context* can provide an answer. Researchers have found that levels of the stress hormone *cortisol* increase from morning to afternoon in infants who are enrolled in center-based care (Gunnar, Kryzer, Van Ryzin, & Phillips, 2010; Sumner, Bernard, & Dozier, 2010). By contrast, cortisol levels decrease over the course of the day in home-reared infants. Interestingly, cortisol levels of home-reared and center-care infants are identical on weekends and holidays. Thus, some developmentalists argue that the higher levels of cortisol experienced

## Choosing a Child Care Center

Rey is a single father who needs to find someone to care for his 14-month-old son while he is at work. Up until now, Rey's mother has been caring for the boy, but she has decided to return to work herself. Rey has heard about studies showing that high-quality care can enhance children's development, but he isn't exactly sure what is meant by the term "high-quality." Here are a few pointers Rey could use to find a high-quality child care center (NICHD Early Child Care Research Network, 2006).

- *A low teacher/child ratio.* For children younger than 2, the ratio should be no higher than 1:4; for 2- to 3-year-olds, ratios between 1:4 and 1:10 appear to be acceptable.
- *A small group size.* The smaller the number of children cared for together—whether in one room in a child care center or in a

home—the better for the child. For infants, a maximum of 6 to 8 per group appears best; for 1- to 2-year-olds, between 6 and 12 per group; for older children, groups as large as 15 or 20 appear to be acceptable.

- *A clean, colorful space, adapted to child play.* It is not essential to have lots of expensive toys, but the center must offer a variety of activities that children find engaging, organized in a way that encourages play.
- *A daily plan.* The daily curriculum should include some structure, some specific teaching, and some supervised activities. However, too much regimentation is not ideal.
- *Sensitive caregivers.* The adults in the child care setting should be positive, involved, and responsive to the children, not merely custodial.

**Learning Objective 14.2a**
What is a "high quality" child care center?

- *Knowledgeable caregivers.* Training in child development and infant curriculum development helps caregivers provide a child care setting that meets criteria for good quality.

### REFLECTION

1. What do you think Rey should do to ease his son's transition from his mother's care to a child care center?
2. One of the criteria is "sensitive caregivers." What kinds of caregiver behaviors might be indicative of this criterion?

by center-care infants affect their rapidly developing brains in ways that lead to problem behaviors. However, there is no direct evidence yet to support this hypothesis.

Some developmentalists argue that nonparental care arrangements probably vary in the degree to which they induce stress in infants and young children. In other words, they say, quality of care may be just as important as quantity of care (Vandell et al., 2010). For example, some researchers have found that, when infants are cared for in high-quality centers, the amount of time they spend in such care is unrelated to social behavior (Love et al., 2003). Thus, developmentalists urge parents, especially those who must leave their infants in center-based care for extended periods of time, to make every effort to ensure that the arrangement they choose has the characteristics discussed in *Developmental Science in the Real World.*

Another point to keep in mind is that individual differences have been found to interact with nonparental care. For example, infants who are behaviorally inhibited, in Jerome Kagan's terms, may be more sensitive to the stresses associated with center-based care (Bohlin & Hagekull, 2009). For this reason, more research that takes temperament into account is needed before we can say for certain that nonparental care has uniformly negative effects on children's social and personality development (Pluess & Belsky, 2009).

**A FINAL WORD**   Finally, it is important to understand that, on average, the differences between children in nonparental care and their home-reared peers, both positive and negative, are very small (NCIHD Early Child Care Research Network, 2003). Moreover, studies that have attempted to examine all of the complex variables associated with parental and non-parental care, such as parents' level of education, have shown that family variables are more important than the type of child care arrangements a family chooses (Anme et al., 2010; Belsky et al., 2007). Developmental psychologist Sandra Scarr, a leading child care researcher, has suggested that the kind of child care parents choose is an extension of their own characteristics and parenting styles (Scarr, 1997). For example, poorly educated parents may choose child care arrangements that do not emphasize infant learning. Similarly, parents whose focus is on intellectual development may not place a high priority on the emotional aspects of a particular child care arrangement. Thus, Scarr claims, child care effects are likely to be parenting effects in disguise.

How does self-care affect school-aged
children's development?

# Before- and After-School Care

Once children reach school age, the issues surrounding nonparental care change to some degree, for both parents and researchers. Many families require care arrangements only for brief periods of time before and after school. Parents of most younger school children provide such arrangements, but as children get older, many families allow children to supervise themselves. In the United States, more than 1.1 million children are at home by themselves after school for an hour or more each weekday (Afterschool Alliance, 2010). They are often referred to as *self-care children*. Self-care arrangements differ so much from child to child that it is impossible to say whether, as a group, self-care children differ from others. For example, some self-care children are home alone but are closely monitored by neighbors or relatives, while others are completely without supervision of any kind (Brandon, 1999). Consequently, the global category "self-care children" isn't very useful in research. To compare self-care children to others and to make predictions, investigators have to focus on variables that may affect self-care—such as the crime rate of the neighborhood in which self-care occurs. Thus, developmentalists have learned that the effects of self-care on a child's development depend on behavioral history, age, gender (with girls less negatively affected), the kind of neighborhood the child lives in, and how well parents monitor the child during self-care periods (Casper & Smith, 2002; NICHD Early Child Care Research Network, 2004; Posner & Vandell, 1994; Steinberg, 1986).

Research consistently demonstrates that self-care children are more poorly adjusted in terms of both peer relationships and school performance. They tend to be less socially skilled and to have a greater number of behavior problems. However, some of these differences between self-care children and others arise from the effect of self-care on children who already have social and behavioral difficulties before self-care begins. Investigators have found that children who have such problems in the preschool years, before they experience any self-care, are the most negatively affected by the self-care experience (Pettit, Laird, Bates, & Dodge, 1997).

With respect to age, most developmentalists agree that children under the age of 9 or 10 should not care for themselves. In fact, most cities and/or states have laws specifying the age at which a child may be legally left at home alone for long periods of time. In some areas, this age is in the mid-teens. Thus, parents considering self-care should check with local child protective services to find out the specific regulations in their area.

From a developmental perspective, children younger than 9 do not have the cognitive abilities necessary to evaluate risks and deal with emergencies. Children who start self-care in the early elementary years are vulnerable to older self-care children in their neighborhoods who may hurt or even sexually abuse them and are more likely to have adjustment difficulties in school (Pettit et al., 1997). High-quality after-school programs can help these younger children attain a higher level of achievement (Peterson, Ewigman, & Kivlahan, 1993; Zigler & Finn-Stevenson, 1993).

Children older than 12 may be cognitively able to manage self-care, but they, too, benefit from participation in well-supervised after-school programs. Even part-time participation in supervised activities after school seems to make a difference in the adjustment of self-care children (Pettit et al., 1997). Good programs provide children with opportunities to play, do homework, and get help from adults (Clark, Harris, White-Smith, Allen, & Ray, 2010; Posner & Vandell, 1994; Shernoff & Vandell, 2007).

Self-care has the most negative effects for children in low-income neighborhoods with high crime rates (Marshall et al., 1997). Self-care children in such areas may use after-school time to "hang out" with socially deviant peers who are involved in criminal activity or who have negative attitudes about school. Predictably, then, the positive effects of organized after-school programs on academic achievement are greater for children in low-income neighborhoods (Mason & Chuang, 2001; Posner & Vandell, 1994).

When everything is taken into consideration, the most important factor in self-care seems to be parental monitoring. Many parents, particularly single mothers, enlist the help of neighbors and relatives to keep an eye on their self-care children (Brandon & Hofferth, 2003). Most require children to call them at work when they get home from school to talk about their school day and get instructions about homework and chores. For example, a working mother might tell a fifth-grader, "By the time I get home at 5:00, you should be finished with your math and spelling. Don't work on your history project until I get home and can help you with it. As soon as you finish your math and spelling, start the dishwasher." Research suggests that children whose periods of self-care are monitored in this way are less likely to experience the potential negative effects of self-care (Galambos & Maggs, 1991).

## The Impact of Schools

School is another vitally important microsystem experienced by virtually all children in the great majority of cultures. School normally begins between ages 5 and 7, and in industrialized countries, it typically continues through age 16 or older. During these 10 or more years, the child learns an enormous number of facts and develops new and much more complex forms of thinking. What role does the schooling itself play in this set of cognitive changes and in other changes in the social domain? ◉ Watch at **MyDevelopmentLab**

## Early Childhood Education

The term **early childhood education** applies to programs that provide instruction to children between birth and age 8. There are many theoretical models in the field of early childhood education. In general, such models fall into two broad categories: *developmental approaches* and *academic approaches*.

**DEVELOPMENTAL APPROACHES**   The goal of **developmental approaches** is to support children through the natural course of physical, cognitive, and socioemotional development. Examples of developmental approaches with which you may be familiar are the *Waldorf* approach, the *Reggio Emilia* model, and the *Montessori* method. All of these approaches place more emphasis on the natural course of child development than they do on teaching children specific skills such as letter identification. As a result, children who attend preschools that take these approaches spend a great deal of time exploring and experimenting with educational materials.

Although there are thousands of "Montessori" schools in the United States, including some that are operated by public school systems, a true Montessori school is one that is staffed by teachers who have been specifically trained in the methods and materials that are unique to the Montessori approach. The goal of the Montessori method, founded by Italian physician Maria Montessori in the early years of the 20th century, is to enable each child to achieve his or her full developmental potential. The main idea behind the Montessori classroom is that the child is allowed to freely choose his activities, but the range of activities available is limited to those which support the child's development. In other words, Montessori educators control the environment in ways that support the child's natural development rather than trying to control the child herself. For example, Montessori classrooms provide young children with materials that strengthen the small muscles in their hands and fingers, thereby supporting the development of fine motor skills.

Because Montessori materials look like toys to children, teachers never have to say, "Susie, you need to work on your fine motor skills today." Instead, teachers monitor children's progress toward developmental goals and encourage children to choose activities that support the goals. For example, they might give children a few spring-type clothespins and something to clip them on, such as a piece of cardboard or a paper plate. In addition, Montessori teachers help children learn to cooperate and take turns using learning materials.

**ACADEMIC APPROACHES**   **Academic approaches** to early childhood education focus on teaching young children the skills they need to succeed in elementary school. Academically-oriented preschool programs employ curricula that are based on learning goals. Instruction tends to be teacher-directed, and the activities in which children engage are highly similar to those that are found in elementary schools. For this reason, computers play a more prominent role in the academic preschool approach than in other models of early childhood education (see *Technology and the Developing Child* on page 346.)

**early childhood education**   Educational programs for children between birth and 8 years.

**developmental approach**   An approach to early childhood education that supports children's development of naturally occurring milestones.

**academic approach**   An approach to early childhood education that provides children with instruction in skills needed for success in school.

◉─⎡Watch the **Video** *Kindergarten: Ready for Success* at **MyDevelopmentLab**

◄------------**Learning Objective 14.4**
How do the various approaches to early childhood education differ, and how does preschool affect children's development?

# TECHNOLOGY AND THE DEVELOPING CHILD
## Computers in the Preschool Classroom

Most educators today regard computers as a necessity in the preschool classroom. However, as we pointed out in the *Technology and The Developing Child* feature in Chapter 7, neither educators nor parents should assume that computers are a certain pathway to academic achievement or any other culturally-valued developmental outcome. Research has revealed both advantages and disadvantages to the use of computers in the early childhood classroom.

Young children can indeed learn academic skills by using computers. Computer programs have been used to teach prereading and mathematics skills to preschoolers from a variety of backgrounds (Boone, Higgins, Notari, & Stump, 1996; Elliot & Hall, 1997). Playing computer games also appears to improve children's fine motor skills and reaction times (Yuji, 1996). However, developmentalists have also found an inverse relationship between computer time and social development in young children: The more time a child spends on the computer, the lower he scores on measures of social development (Seo, Chun, Jwa, & Choi, 2011). Thus, there is good reason to limit young childrens' computer time in the classroom setting so as not to interfere with the social benefits of attending preschool. One way of promoting both computer use and social interaction is to require preschoolers to work on computers in pairs (NETC, 2005).

Most early childhood educators view the computer as a means of providing a child with additional learning opportunities rather than as a replacement for traditional activities (Ihmeideh, 2010; Lynch & Warner, 2004). Still, computers probably cannot provide the kinds of benefits preschoolers receive from physical interactions with three-dimensional objects such as blocks and media such as sand and fingerpaints. In addition, an interactive computer storybook may be both fun and educational for a child, but it can't replace the human interaction that takes place when a parent or teacher reads a story to a child.

### Learning Objective 14.4a
What are the advantages and disadvantages of computers in the preschool classroom?

### FIND OUT MORE
*Use your Internet search skills to answer these questions.*
1. How much emphasis do parents place on computers in the classroom when they choose a preschool for their children?
2. What concerns do Montessori early educators express about computers in the preschool classroom?

---

One common goal in academic prekindergarten programs is that children will learn to associate letters with the sounds they represent. Children are instructed in letter-sound relationships by teachers in a variety of ways. On one day, a teacher might conduct a whole-class session in which she holds up flash cards with letters and demonstrates the sounds they represent. The children imitate her a few times, and then she asks them to provide the sound for each letter as she holds up the card. On another day, a teacher might work with children in groups of three or four and ask them to look through a story book and find all the letters that represent the /m/ sound.

It is important to point out that the developmental and academic approaches are not mutually exclusive. A preschool program can include elements of both. In fact, as you might guess because of the developmental characteristics of young children, it would be practically impossible to design a preschool program in which every minute of the day was taken up with academic activities. For example, recall from Chapter 4 that the reticular formation, the brain structure that controls attention, is far from mature during these years. As a result, young children simply cannot be expected to sit still, receive instruction, and complete academic tasks such as filling in blanks on worksheets for several hours each day.

**DEVELOPMENTALLY APPROPRIATE PRACTICES** The National Association for the Education of Young Children (NAEYC) is an organization that evaluates early childhood programs and accredits those that meet its standards. The NAEYC standards do not endorse any particular approach to early childhood education. Instead, they focus on **developmentally appropriate practices**, an approach to curriculum development that takes into account the universal features of child development, individual differences across children, and the social and cultural contexts in which development occurs (NAEYC, 2009). According to these broad criteria, any kind of preschool program, regardless of its purpose or theoretical foundation, can be judged as either developmentally appropriate or developmentally inappropriate.

For example, the fact noted earlier—that the reticular formation in the brains of young children is still immature—is a universal that, according to the NAEYC standards, must be considered when early childhood educators design preschool programs. Thus, such programs

**developmentally appropriate practices** Early childhood education practices based on an understanding of developmental universals, individual differences, and contextual variables.

should not depend on children's ability to pay attention to external stimuli, such as a teacher's lecture, for long periods of time. In addition, teachers should expect young children to be easily distracted and should be tolerant of their need for a great deal of repetition. Moreover, children differ in the rate at which their reticular formations mature. So, the standard of developmental appropriateness also requires that teachers be tolerant of such individual differences. Even among children of similar ages, one child may require an instruction to be repeated twice, for instance, while another may require it to be repeated seven times. The social and cultural contexts in which children are developing affect their capacity to pay attention, too, and developmentally appropriate practices require that this factor be considered in the design of the curriculum. For example, parents who are high school graduates are more likely than parents who did not complete high school to provide their children with the kinds of activities that encourage them to develop the attention skills required in preschool (Suizzo & Stapleton, 2007). Thus, when early childhood educators design programs for children whose parents are likely to be poorly educated, they should assume that such children will require a bit more time to develop needed attention skills than would be required in a program in which most children's parents were high school graduates.

**THE EFFECTS OF EARLY CHILDHOOD EDUCATION**    In Chapter 7, you learned that early childhood programs have positive effects on the cognitive development of economically disadvantaged children. Similarly, early interventions are critical to the development of children with disabilities that affect cognitive functioning, and they help prepare young English-language learners for the task of acquiring academic skills in a new language (Fuller, 2007). Such programs are also instrumental in helping children who were born prematurely catch up with their peers (Blair, 2002).

Despite these positive findings, sociologist Bruce Fuller (2007), who conducted an extensive review of preschool programs across the United States, argues that research does not support the assumption that research on early education programs for children with disadvantages applies to nondisadvantaged children. Fuller points to studies showing that, while typically developing children from middle- and upper-income homes tend to display cognitive gains as a result of attending preschool, the magnitude of these gains is quite small and the gains have not always been found to persist over the elementary years. In addition, universal preschool programs that were implemented in the early 1990s in Oklahoma and Georgia and that have been attended by tens of thousands of children from homes across the socioeconomic spectrum have failed to improve academic performance at the elementary school level in those states. Fuller warns that the studies you read about earlier, showing that time spent in child care is linked to aggressive behavior, also apply to academically-oriented preschools. Thus, he and others ask whether the cognitive benefits of preschool outweigh its social risks for nondisadvantaged children.

One approach to the benefits/risk question is to determine whether there is an optimal amount of time for preschool attendance—that is, a number of hours that ensures cognitive gains without enhancing social risks. Fuller cites research showing that 15 hours a week is about the right amount of time to achieve the goal of balancing cognitive gains and social risks for 2- to 4-year-olds.

**EXPLAINING THE EFFECTS OF PRESCHOOL**    What explains this pattern of findings? It may be that the nature of the young brain's executive functioning and self-regulatory abilities gives preschoolers less ability than older children to benefit from formal educational experiences (Blair, 2002). This assertion does not mean that early education is pointless, but what it does imply is that expectations for the effects of early education must take into account the developmental characteristics of young children.

Research also suggests that a neurological transition occurs between the fifth and sixth birthdays, precisely when most children in the United States are enrolled in kindergarten, that enables children to benefit much more from formal education than they did at earlier ages (Tsujimoto, Yamamoto, Kawaguchi, Koizumi, & Sawaguchi, 2004). Even so, there may be limits on the effectiveness of time spent in kindergarten as well. One team of researchers tracked reading and math achievement in a nationally representative sample of more than 14,000 full-day and part-day kindergarten students across the elementary school years (Votruba-Drzal,

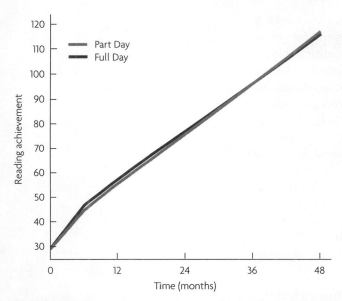

**FIGURE 14.2** Reading Achievement and Kindergarten Program Researchers found that children who attended part-day and full-day kindergarten did not differ in reading achievement across kindergarten, first, second, and third grade.

(*Source:* Votruba-Drzal, E., Li-Grining, C., & Maldonado-Carreño, C. (2008). A developmental perspective on full- versus part-day kindergarten and children's academic trajectories through fifth grade. *Child Development, 79,* 957–978, Fig. 1, p. 967. Copyright © 2008 by Blackwell Publishers, Ltd. Reproduced with permission Blackwell Publishers, Ltd.)

Li-Grining, & Maldonado-Carreño, 2008). As you can see in Figure 14.2, they found that children who attended full-day kindergarten displayed no long-term advantages over those who attended part-day programs. Moreover, by fifth grade, the researchers found that children who had attended part-day kindergartens displayed slightly higher levels of achievement than those who had been enrolled in full-day programs. However, as the researchers noted, disadvantaged children were more likely to attend full-day kindergartens than nondisadvantaged children were. As a result, instead of calling into question the effectiveness of full-day kindergarten, these findings may be yet another indicator that intensive educational interventions are vital to minimizing the achievement gap between disadvantaged youngsters and their nondisadvantaged peers.

Taken together, the research on the effects of preschool suggests that parents of typically developing children who have adequate economic resources should probably not assume that formal preschool is essential for their children's academic success (Fuller, 2007). Nor does full-day kindergarten appear to be critical for such children (Votruba-Drzal, Li-Grining, & Maldonado-Carreño, 2008). Furthermore, learning experiences in the home and in nonparental care settings that are less structured than preschool and kindergarten classrooms may contribute as much—or more—to children's intellectual development as formal educational experiences do (Morrison, Bachman, & Connor, 2005). From a policy perspective, Fuller argues that public resources are likely to yield the greatest dividends when they are focused on high-quality preschool programs for disadvantaged children and on effective elementary school programs for all children.

**Learning Objective 14.5** - - - - - - - - - - →

What factors contribute to effective schooling at the elementary level, and how does elementary school influence children's development?

# Elementary School

As noted earlier, for children all over the world, formal education is well under way by the time they reach the age of 6 or 7. Many people identify kindergarten with school entrance. However, in terms of school organization in the United States, kindergarten is the last year of preschool, and attendance is optional in all but 9 states (National Center for Education Statistics, 2011). By contrast, every state requires children to enroll in first grade, the first year of *elementary school*. The elementary school curriculum is more academic in nature than is that of kindergarten or the earlier years of preschool. Literacy (reading), numeracy (math), and the acquisition of skills and knowledge needed for more advanced studies are the primary focus of elementary schools.

In general, studies show that teachers who display a teaching style similar to the approach that authoritative parents take to raising children—an approach that combines clear goals, good control, good communication, and high nurturance—are the most effective (MacIver, Reuman, & Main, 1995). In addition, at least in the United States, there is evidence that elementary schools with smaller classes, fewer than 20 pupils or so, are more effective than those with larger classes (Ecalle, Magnan, & Gibert, 2007). Quality considerations aside, there are a number of factors, such as parental involvement, that help smooth children's transition to elementary school and enhance their chances for academic success. Moreover, because of its academic focus and the amount of time that children spend in school, formal education is one of the most important influences on the cognitive development of 6- to 12-year-olds.

**FITTING IN AND ADAPTING TO ELEMENTARY SCHOOL**   When parents come to parent-teacher conferences, attend school events, and get involved in supervising homework, children are more strongly motivated, feel more competent, and adapt better to school (Center for Public Education, 2011). They learn to read more readily, get better grades through elementary school, and stay in school for more years (Brody, Stoneman, & Flor, 1995; Grolnick & Slowiaczek, 1994; Reynolds & Bezruczko, 1993). This effect of parent involvement has been found among groups of poor children as well as among the middle class (e.g., Luster & McAdoo, 1996; Reynolds & Bezruczko, 1993), which confirms that the effect is not just a social class difference in disguise. That is, among poverty-level children, those whose parents are most involved with their school and schooling have a better chance of doing well in school than do equally poor children whose parents have little or no connection to the school.

Parental involvement is important not just for the child, but for the parent and for the school. Schools that invite and encourage parents to participate help to create a stronger sense of community, linking parents with one another and with the teachers. Stronger communities, in turn—whether they are in poverty-stricken inner cities or middle-class suburbs—provide better supervision and monitoring of the children in their midst, which benefits the children. Parents who get involved with their children's school also learn ways to help their children; they may even be motivated to continue their own education (Haynes et al., 1996).

A child's early success in school is also affected by whether his own personality or temperament matches the qualities valued and rewarded within the school setting. For example, Karl Alexander and his colleagues (1993) found that children who are enthusiastic, interested in new things, cheerful, and easygoing do better in the early years of school than those who are more withdrawn, moody, or high-strung.

Research also indicates that how a child starts out in the first few years of school has a highly significant effect on the rest of her school experience and success. Children who come to school with good skills quickly acquire new academic skills and knowledge and thereby adapt to later school demands more easily. Children who enter school with poor skills, or with less optimal temperamental qualities, learn less in the early years and are likely to move along a slower achievement trajectory throughout their school years. Such a slow trajectory is not set in stone. Parental involvement can improve the chances of a less advantaged child, as can a particularly skillful kindergarten or first-grade teacher (Pianta, Steinberg, & Rollins, 1995). The key point is that the child does not enter school as a blank slate; she brings her history and her personal qualities with her.

**EFFECTS ON COGNITIVE DEVELOPMENT**   In contrast to the inconsistent findings regarding the effects of early childhood education, there is no doubt that elementary schooling has profound effects on children's cognitive development (Kagan & Herschkowitz, 2005). For example, the data in Figure 14.3 on page 350 are taken from a classic study comparing working memory function in school-aged children in Boston, all of whom attended school, to that

*A range of research reveals that children's school performance improves when their parents participate in school activities such as parent-teacher conferences.*

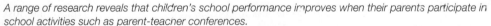

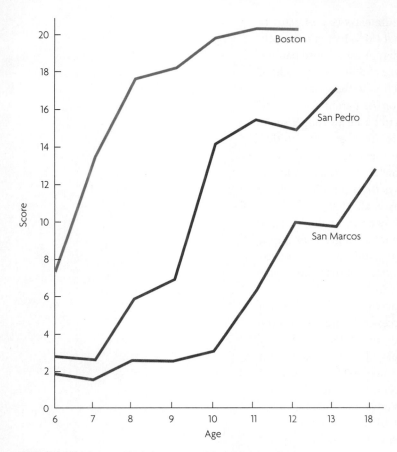

**FIGURE 14.3** Memory Performance and School Attendance

Kagan and his colleagues compared the memory performance of children who attended school regularly (Boston) and children who attended school irregularly (San Pedro, Guatemala) to that of children who did not attend school at all (San Marcos, Guatemala). School attendance was strongly correlated with memory performance.

(*Source:* From Kagan, J., Klein, R., Finley, G., Rogoff, B., Nolan, E., & Greenbaum, C. (1979). A cross-cultural study of cognitive development. *Monographs of the Society for Research in Child Development, 44,* pp. 1–77, fig. 7, p. 41. Copyright © 1979 by Blackwell Publishers, Ltd. Reproduced with permission of Blackwell Publishers, Ltd.)

of children in two Guatemalan communities (Kagan et al., 1979). Children in San Pedro attended school, while those in San Marcos did not. However, San Pedro children did not necessarily attend school consistently, and most did not enroll until after age 7. The scores in the figure were derived from tasks that required children to remember lists and arrangements of everyday objects and pictures of such objects. As you can see, schooling was associated with a substantial difference in memory function across groups.

Other cross-cultural studies—in Hong Kong and in Mexico, Peru, Colombia, Liberia, Zambia, Nigeria, Uganda, and many other countries—support the conclusion that school experiences are indeed causally linked to the emergence of some advanced cognitive skills. The links are both indirect and direct. One example of an indirect effect is that mothers in non-Western cultures who have attended Western-style schools engage in more teacher-like behavior with their children than their peers who have little or no formal education (Chavajay & Rogoff, 2002). Such a shift in a mother's role and behavior is likely to affect a child's cognitive development. A direct effect of schooling is that children who attend school acquire complex concepts and information-processing strategies that their nonschooled peers do not develop (Kagan & Herschkowitz, 2005). Schooled children are also better at generalizing a concept or principle they have learned to some new setting than those who do not attend school.

Schooling also affects the rate at which children move through Piaget's concrete operations stage (Mishra, 2001). You might think that rate of cognitive development doesn't matter, so long as everyone ends up in the same place. However, longitudinal studies show that the rate of progression through concrete operations predicts how well children will reason in adolescence and adulthood (Bradmetz, 1999). Thus, the cognitive-developmental advantage a child gains by attending school is one that probably lasts a lifetime.

A different way to measure the impact of schooling on cognitive development is to compare children whose birthdays fall just before the arbitrary school district cutoff date for entrance into kindergarten or first grade to those whose birthdays fall after the cutoff date. If a particular school district sets September 15 as the cutoff, for example, then a child born on September 10 is eligible for first grade five days after he turned 6, whereas a child born on September 20 is not eligible for another year, even though he is only 10 days younger. A year later, these two children are still essentially the same age, but one has had a year of school and the other has not, so investigators can look at the effect of schooling with age held constant (e.g., Morrison, Smith, & Dow-Ehrensberger, 1995; Stelzl, Merz, Ehlers, & Remer, 1995).

Studies comparing early versus late school starters in the United States show that schooling itself, rather than merely age, has a direct effect on some kinds of cognitive skills, such as the ability to use good memory strategies. In one such study, Fred Morrison and his colleagues (1995) found that a big improvement in the use of memory strategies occurred in first grade; children of the same age who spent the year in kindergarten because they just missed the cutoff did not show the same gain in memory skill—although these children would, of course, acquire such skill in the following year, when they were in first grade.

**Learning Objective 14.6** - - - - - - - - - →

How do children's achievement goals change during the transition to secondary school?

## The Transition to Secondary School

There are many places in the world, including some in North America, where children attend a lower school for 8 years before moving on to a high school. Such an arrangement is known as an 8-4 system. Because students typically show achievement declines after entering high school, educators have developed two models that include a transitional school—a junior high, middle school, or intermediate school— between elementary and high school. The junior high model typically includes 6 years of elementary school followed by 3 years of junior high and 3 years of high school. The middle school model comprises 5 elementary grades, 3 middle school grades, and 4 years of high school.

However, neither the junior high nor the middle school model seems to have solved the transition problem. Students show losses in both achievement and self-esteem across both transition points in the 6-3-3 and 5-3-4 systems. Further, students in both systems show greater losses during the transition to high school than those in 8-4 systems (Alspaugh, 1998; Anderman, 1998; Linnenbrink, 2010). Consequently, educators and developmentalists are searching for explanations and practical remedies.

One potential explanation for transition-related achievement declines is that students' academic goals change once they enter middle school. Researchers classify such goals into two very broad categories: task goals and ability goals. **Task goals** are based on personal standards and a desire to become more competent at something. For example, a runner who wants to improve her time in the 100-meter dash has a task goal. An **ability goal** is one that defines success in competitive terms. A person pursuing an ability goal wants to be better than another person at something. For example, a runner who wants to be the fastest person on his team has an ability goal. Longitudinal research shows that most fifth-graders have task goals, but by the time children have been in sixth grade a few months, most have shifted to ability goals (Anderman & Anderman, 1999; Anderman & Midgley, 1997).

A student's goal approach influences her behavior in important ways. Task goals are associated with a greater sense of personal control and positive attitudes about school (Anderman, 1999; Guttman, 2006). A student who takes a task-goal approach to her schoolwork tends to set increasingly higher standards for her performance and attributes success and failure to her own efforts. For example, a task-goal–oriented student is likely to say she received an A in a class because she worked hard or because she wanted to improve her performance.

In contrast, students with ability goals adopt relative standards—that is, they view performance on a given academic task as good so long as it is better than someone else's. Consequently, such students are more strongly influenced by the group with which they identify than by internal standards that define good and bad academic performance. Ability-goal– oriented students are also more likely than others to attribute success and failure to forces outside themselves. For example, such a student might say he got an A in a class because it was easy or because the teacher liked him. Moreover, such students are likely to have a negative view of school (Anderman, 1999).

Because middle schools emphasize ability grouping more than elementary schools, it is likely that many middle-school students change their beliefs about their own abilities during these years (Anderman, Maehr, & Midgley, 1999; Roeser & Eccles, 1998). Thus, high-achieving elementary students who maintain their levels of achievement across the sixth-grade transition gain confidence in their abilities (Pajares & Graham, 1999). In contrast, high achievers, average achievers, and low achievers who fail to meet expectations in middle school undergo a change in self-concept that likely leads to a decline in self-esteem. Once an ability-goal–oriented student adopts the belief that his academic ability is less than adequate, he is likely to stop putting effort into his schoolwork. In addition, such students are likely to use ineffective cognitive strategies when attempting to learn academic material (Young, 1997). Consequently, achievement suffers along with self-esteem. Fortunately, however, teachers and administrators can increase the chances that middle-school students will adopt task goals by making it clear to students that learning is more important than outperforming peers on standardized tests or report-card grades (Anderman & Anderman, 2009).

Educators have devised a number of strategies to address this shift in goal structure. One such approach is based on research demonstrating that the availability of supportive adults outside a child's family makes the transition easier (Galassi, Gulledge, & Cox, 1997; Wenz-Gross, Siperstein, Untch, & Widaman, 1997). For example, some schools pair students with an adult mentor, either a teacher or a volunteer from the community, either for a transitional period or throughout the middle-school years. In one such program, a homeroom teacher monitors

**task goal** A goal orientation associated with a desire for self-improvement.

**ability goal** A goal orientation associated with a desire to be superior to others.

This high school girl has quite firmly developed beliefs about her abilities and potentials, based on her past school successes and failures. These beliefs contribute significantly to her level of engagement in schooling and will affect important life choices, such as whether to go to college or whether to drop out of school altogether.

several students' daily assignment sheets, homework, grades, and even school supplies. The homeroom teacher also maintains communication with each child's parents regarding these issues. So, if a student in this program isn't doing his math homework or doesn't have any pencils, it is the homeroom teacher's responsibility to tell his parents about the problem. The parents are then responsible for follow-up.

Research suggests that programs of this level of intensity are highly successful in improving middle-schoolers' grades (Hanlon et al., 2009; Rosenblatt & Ellis, 2008). Their success probably lies in the fact that the homeroom teacher functions very much like an elementary school teacher—and despite cultural expectations to the contrary, a sixth-grader is developmentally a child, whether he is in elementary school or middle school. It isn't surprising that a strategy that makes a middle school more like an elementary school—a school designed for children, not adolescents—is successful. In fact, some observers think that middle schools have failed to meet their goal of easing the transition to secondary schooling because they have simply duplicated high school organization and imposed it on students who are not developmentally ready for it, rather than providing them with a real transition (Alspaugh, 1998).

One approach aimed at making middle schools truly transitional involves organizing students and teachers into teams. For example, in some schools, sixth, seventh, and eighth grades are physically located in different wings of the school building. In such schools, each grade is like a school-within-a-school. Teachers in each grade-level team work together to balance the demands of different subject-area classes, assess problems of individual students, and devise parent involvement strategies. Preliminary research suggests that the team approach helps to minimize the negative effects of the middle-school transition. As a result, it has become the recommended approach of the National Middle School Association in the United States (NMSA, 2004).

Regardless of the type of school they attended prior to high school—middle school, junior high, or grade school—for many teens, a general pattern of success or failure that continues into the adult years is set early in high school. For example, a teen who fails one or more courses in the first year of high school is far less likely than his or her peers to graduate (Neild, 2009). It appears that minority students have a particularly difficult time recovering from early failure.

However, some psychologists emphasize the positive aspects of transition to high school, claiming that participation in activities that are usually offered only in high school allows students opportunities to develop psychological attributes that can't be acquired elsewhere. To demonstrate the point, researchers asked high school students to use pagers to signal them whenever they were experiencing high levels of intrinsic motivation along with intense mental effort (Larson, 2000). The results showed that students experienced both states in elective classes and during extracurricular activities far more often than in required academic classes (Larson & Brown, 2007). In other words, a student engaged in an art project or sports practice is more likely to experience this particular combination of states than one who is in a history class. Consequently, educators may be able to ease the transition to high school for many students by offering a wide variety of elective and extracurricular activities and encouraging students to participate.

**Learning Objective 14.7** ---------→
What have researchers learned about disengaged and engaged students?

## Engagement in and Disengagement from Secondary School

Some secondary school students benefit little from extracurricular and elective activities because they choose not to be involved in them. For some, the demands of part-time jobs limit the time they have to participate, causing some developmentalists to question the value of these work experiences (see *Thinking about Research* on page 353). Such concerns arise out of research showing that secondary school students fall into two distinct groups. Some students are highly "engaged" in the schooling process, to use Laurence Steinberg's term. They not only enjoy school but are involved in all aspects of it, participating in extracurricular and elective activities, doing their homework, and so on. Others are "disengaged" from schooling,

## The Effects of Teenaged Employment

In the United States, surveys of teenagers suggest that deciding on a career is one of the central themes of adolescent identity development (Mortimer, Zimmer-Gembeck, Holmes, & Shanahan, 2002). Moreover, many teens believe that engaging in part-time work during high school will help them with this aspect of identity achievement. Parents, too, often encourage their adolescent children to obtain part-time employment on the grounds that it "builds character" and teaches young people about "real life." As a result, American adolescents spend more time in paid work than their counterparts in other countries do (e.g., Österbacka & Zick, 2009).

Are American teens and parents right about such beneficial effects of work? Longitudinal research involving individuals who graduated from high school in the late 1980s revealed that the more hours participants worked during high school, the more likely they were to use drugs (alcohol, cigarettes, marijuana, cocaine), to display aggression toward peers, to argue with parents, to get inadequate sleep, and to be dissatisfied with life (Bachman & Schulenberg, 1993). More recent studies have shown a similar pattern among teenagers who were in high school during the late 1990s (Bachman, Safron, Sy, & Schulenberg, 2003). Moreover, as adults, individuals who worked while in high school are less likely than peers who did not work to go to college. Thus, working may actually decrease teens' chances for successful careers during adulthood, precisely the opposite of what many adolescents and parents believe.

A quite different answer to the question of the impact of teenaged employment comes from research that takes into consideration the kind of work teenagers do, as well as how many hours they spend on the job (Mortimer & Harley, 2002). These findings indicate that unskilled work that affords little opportunity for independence and little chance to learn long-term job skills is much more likely to be associated with poor outcomes than is complex, skilled work. They also suggest that adolescents who have skill-based work experiences develop increased feelings of competence. In addition, those students who see themselves as gaining useful skills through their work also seem to develop confidence in their ability to achieve economic success in adulthood (Grabowski, Call, & Mortimer, 2001).

It is not clear how we should add up the results of these several studies. At the very least, this mixture of results should make parents think twice before encouraging teenagers to work. However, parents need to consider the quality of work a teen will do before assuming that a job will negatively affect his or her development.

### CRITICAL ANALYSIS

1. Teenaged employment may be correlated with developmental outcomes because teens who work differ from those who do not in ways that are also related to such outcomes. What variables do you think might distinguish teens who choose to work from their peers who don't?

2. Are there developmental outcomes not addressed by the research described in this discussion that you think might be positively affected by teenaged employment?

particularly from the academic part of the process. Steinberg argues that a child's level of engagement or disengagement is critical for the child and her future.

**DISENGAGED STUDENTS**　Educational researchers report that dropping out is the end result of a pattern of disengagement from school (Yazzie-Mintz, 2010). A classic, large-scale survey of high school students by Steinberg (1996) paints quite a gloomy picture of the typical level of engagement of U.S. high school students, based on interviews with and observations of over 20,000 teenagers and their families. A high proportion don't take school or their studies seriously; outside of class, they don't often participate in activities that reinforce what they are learning in school (such as doing their homework); the peer culture denigrates academic success and scorns those students who try to do well in school. Some of the specifics that support these conclusions are summarized in Table 14.1 on page 354.

Furthermore, a great many U.S. parents are just as disengaged from their children's schooling as their teenagers are. In Steinberg's study, more than half the high school students said they could bring home grades of C or worse without their parents getting upset; a third said their parents didn't know what they were studying at school; only about a fifth of the parents in this study consistently attended school programs. To use the terminology presented in Chapter 13, parents of disengaged students are most likely to be classed as permissive or authoritarian; parents of engaged students are most likely to be rated as authoritative (Steinberg, 1996).

Table
14.1

## STEINBERG'S EVIDENCE FOR WIDESPREAD DISENGAGEMENT
## FROM SCHOOLING AMONG U.S. TEENAGERS

- Over one-third of students said they get through the school day mostly by "goofing off with their friends."

- Two-thirds of students said they had cheated on a school test in the past year; nine out of ten said they had copied homework from someone else.

- The average U.S. high school student spends only about 4 hours a week on homework, compared with students in other industrialized countries, who spend 4 hours a *day*.

- Half the students said they did not do the homework they were assigned.

- Two-thirds of U.S. high school students hold paying jobs; half work 15 or more hours a week.

- Only about 20% of students said their friends think it is important to get good grades in school.

- Nearly 20% of students said they do not try as hard as they can in school because they are afraid of what their friends might think.

*Source:* L. Steinberg, *Beyond the Classroom* (New York: Simon & Schuster, 1996).

**THOSE WHO DROP OUT**    At the extreme end of the continuum of uninvolvement are teenagers who drop out before completing high school. The good news is that the dropout rate has declined significantly over the past several decades. Nevertheless, surveys show that about 8% of 16- to 24-year-olds in the United States left school prior to graduating (National Center for Education Statistics [NCES], 2011).

Hispanic Americans have the highest drop-out rate at 18%, compared with 9% for African Americans and 5% for Whites (NCES, 2011). Just under 4% of Asian Americans leave high school, and about 15% of Native American students do so (Freeman & Fox, 2005). Across all ethnic groups, kids growing up in poor families—especially poor families with a single parent—are considerably more likely to drop out of high school than are those from more economically advantaged or intact families (NCES, 2011).

Longitudinal studies have found three strong predictors of dropping out: a history of academic failure, a pattern of aggressive behavior, and a tendency to engage in risky behaviors

*Based on the U.S. average, about a tenth of these ninth-graders will drop out before finishing high school.*

*While engaged students like these are likely to have the advantage of higher IQ, they are also interested in school and expend effort to do well.*

(Farmer et al., 2003). With respect to risky behaviors, decisions about sexual intercourse seem to be especially critical. For girls, giving birth and getting married are strongly linked to dropping out.

In addition, many students report leaving school because they find it to be boring or irrelevant (Bridgeland, DiIulio, & Morison, 2006; Yazzie-Mintz, 2010). Many see themselves as falling behind and unable to catch up. Others report having felt a strong desire to follow the example of older peers who had dropped out. Moreover, parents of dropouts have a history of neither monitoring their children's behavior outside of school nor their progress in school (Bridgeland, DiIulio, & Morison, 2006). Thus, parental indifference, or perceived parental indifference, may play a key role in a teen's decision to leave school.

**ENGAGED STUDENTS: THOSE WHO ACHIEVE**    The other side of the coin are those engaged students who do well in school. Engaged students spend more time on homework, cut class less often, and pay more attention in class (Yazzie-Mintz, 2010). They also tend to spend their time with other students who are engaged or who at least do not ridicule them for making some effort in school. They are likely to have authoritative parents who expect them to get good grades and who are involved with them and with the school (Furlong & Christenson, 2008).

## Homeschooling

◀------------Learning Objective 14.8
Why do some parents choose to homeschool their children?

A growing number of parents in the United States are educating their children at home. In 1965, there were only about 2,500 homeschooled children in the United States; by the end of the first decade of the twenty-first century, 1.5 million, or about 3%, of school-aged children in the United States were homeschooled (NCES, 2011). In recent years, homeschooling has grown at a particularly rapid pace among minority families, especially African Americans (Jonsson, 2003). In 1997, there were only about 20,000 homeschooled African American children in the United States. In 2002, the number had grown to approximately 120,000. Homeschooling movements in other nations have experienced similar growth rates. In New Zealand, for example, the number of families involved in homeschooling more than doubled between 1993 and 2003 (New Zealand Ministry of Education, 2003).

Why would parents want to take on the daunting task of teaching their children at home? As you can see in Figure 14.4 on page 356, the most frequent reason for homeschooling is parents' desire to include religious training in their children's education (NCES, 2009). Special circumstances contribute to the decision to homeschool as well. For instance, some parents who must travel frequently for business reasons choose homeschooling because it allows their families to travel with them. Others want to include activities such as gardening

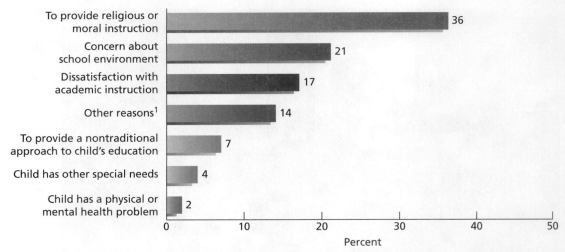

To provide religious or moral instruction — 36
Concern about school environment — 21
Dissatisfaction with academic instruction — 17
Other reasons[1] — 14
To provide a nontraditional approach to child's education — 7
Child has other special needs — 4
Child has a physical or mental health problem — 2

Percent

[1]"Other reasons" parents gave for homeschooling include family time, finances, travel, and distance.

**FIGURE 14.4** Reasons for Homeschooling
Homeschool parents cite several reasons for choosing to educate their children at home.
(*Source:* National Center for Education Statistics, 2009)

in their children's formal education, and homeschooling allows them the time to do so. Homeschooling also works well for children who are involved in time-consuming pursuits such as elite-level athletic training.

Many homeschool parents have children with disabilities and prefer teaching them at home to having them receive special-education services from local schools (NCES, 2009). The one-on-one teaching these children get at home often helps them achieve more than their peers with disabilities in public schools are able to (Duvall, Delquadri, & Ward, 2004; Ensign, 1998). In addition, children with disabilities who are homeschooled don't have to deal with teasing from peers.

Research on homeschooling is sparse. Advocates point to studies showing that homeschooled children are socially competent, and emotionally well adjusted, and score above average on standardized achievement tests (Ray, 2010). College entrance exam scores of homeschooled students are particularly impressive, ranging from an average score at the 59th percentile for students who were educated at home for one year to an average at the 92nd percentile for those who spent all of their school years in home education (Ray, 1999). However, opponents of homeschooling, a group that includes most professional educators, claim that comparisons of homeschooling and public education are misleading (Jonsson, 2003). They point out that researchers have studied only homeschooled children whose families volunteered to participate in research studies. In contrast, most public school achievement test data are based on representative samples or on populations of entire schools.

When comparing homeschooled children to those who attend school, it is also important to know that parents who choose homeschooling differ in significant ways from other families (Ray, 2010). For example, nearly 90% of homeschooling families are headed by a married couple, compared to about 70% of all families with children in the United States (NCES, 2009; U.S. Census Bureau, 2011). In addition, homeschooling parents tend to have more education than is typical across households in the United States; about half of homeschooling parents possess college degrees, compared to only a third of public school parents (Basham, 2001; NCES, 2009). As a result, homeschooling households tend to have somewhat higher incomes than those of children who attend public school, even though parents' higher education levels are offset to some degree by the fact that most homeschooling families are one- rather than two-income households (NCES, 2009). Thus, most homeschooling families in the United States have annual incomes between $25,000 and $75,000.

Professional educators argue that homeschooled children miss out on the kinds of socialization opportunities that school attendance provides (Jonsson, 2003). However, advocates of homeschooling counter that homeschooled children have the opportunity to become closer to their parents than children who attend conventional schools. Moreover, homeschoolers typically band together to create music, art, athletic, and social programs for their children (Ray,

2009). Consequently, most homeschooled children have as many opportunities for socializing with peers as children who attend school (Jonsson, 2003).

## The Impact of Entertainment Media

Entertainment media—television, movies, MP3 players, video games, computers, and the like—are a pervasive part of most children's environments. Of all of these, children and teens devote the most time to television (Rideout, Foehr, & Roberts, 2010)). In Chapter 4, you learned that the sedentary nature of these activities contributes to the development of obesity in many children. In this section, we will more closely examine the effects of these forms of entertainment on cognitive and social development. ●—Watch at **MyDevelopmentLab**

●—Watch the **Video** *Baby TV* at **MyDevelopmentLab**

## Television and Video Games

◄-----------**Learning Objective 14.9**
What are the effects of television and video games on children's development

"But the kids on TV look so happy when they eat it! Don't you want me to be happy?" the 7-year-old son of one of the authors sobbed when his request for a sugary cereal was denied. The effect of advertising on children's food preferences is well documented (Chapman, Nicholas, & Supramaniam, 2006; Livingstone & Helsper, 2006). However, it is just one of many effects that television has on children's lives. Video games carry risks as well.

**TELEVISION AND DEVELOPMENT**    Albert Bandura demonstrated the effects of televised violence on children's behavior in his classic "Bobo doll" studies (Bandura, Ross, & Ross, 1961). In these experiments, children were found to imitate adults' violent treatment of an inflatable clown that was depicted on film. Recent research suggests that such effects persist into the adult years. Psychologist L. Rowell Huesmann and his colleagues (2003) found that individuals who had watched the greatest number of violent television programs in childhood were the most likely to engage in actual acts of violence as young adults. Brain-imaging studies suggest that these long-term effects may be the result of patterns of neural activation that underlie emotionally laden behavioral scripts that children learn while watching violent programming (Murray et al., 2006). These patterns of neural activation may also explain the finding that repeated viewing of TV violence leads to emotional desensitization regarding violence and to the belief that aggression is a good way to solve problems (Funk, Bechtoldt-Baldacci, Pasold, & Baumgardner, 2004; Van Mierlo & Van den Bulck, 2004).

Of course, television isn't all bad. Researchers have found that science-oriented programs such as *Cyberchase* and *Fetch!* are effective teaching tools (Calvert & Kotler, 2003).

*In the United States, most children of this age watch television every day.*

Likewise, programs designed to teach racial tolerance to school-aged children have consistently shown positive effects on children's attitudes and behavior (Persson & Musher-Eizenman, 2003; Shochat, 2003). However, such programs are far less popular among boys than they are among girls (Calvert & Kotler, 2003). Moreover, even among girls, their popularity declines as children progress through middle childhood years. Perhaps these findings are best summed up by adapting an old cliché: "You can lead a child to quality TV programming, but you can't make him watch it." Thus, parental regulation of television viewing is the key to ensuring that exposure to TV will have more positive than negative effects on a child's development.

**TELEVISION AND RISKY BEHAVIOR**   The messages conveyed in the popular media about sex, violence, and drug and alcohol use may influence teens' risky behavior. In the United States, 11- to 14-year-olds spend 8 to 9 hours a day watching television, listening to music, and playing video games—more time than they spend in school (Rideout, Foehr, & Roberts, 2010). Surprisingly, most teenagers report that their parents have few, if any, rules regarding media use (Rideout, Foehr, & Roberts, 2010). However, research indicates that media messages interact with individual differences in sensation-seeking (Greene, Krcmar, Rubin, Walters, & Hale, 2002). Thus, teens who are highest in sensation-seeking are those who are most strongly influenced by media portrayals of risky behavior.   ◉ Watch at **MyDevelopmentLab**

◉ Watch the **Video** *Peer Pressure Part 1: Tim, 18 Years Old* at **MyDevelopmentLab**

Prime-time television programs contain about five sexual incidents per hour, and only 4% of these impart information about the potential consequences of sex (Kaiser Family Foundation, 2005). Sexual incidents are more frequent in movies than they are on television, but also rarely if ever include information about the health consequences of unprotected sex and other risky behaviors. One survey found that 75% of 200 movies surveyed portrayed characters using alcohol, tobacco, and/or engaging in unsafe sex practices (Gunasekera, Chapman, & Campbell, 2005). Nearly 70% included portrayals of tobacco use and 32% included alcohol-related intoxication. None of the films included references to the health consequences of unsafe sex, smoking, or alcohol use.

**VIDEO GAMES**   Surveys indicate that 8- to 14-year-olds spend between 1 and 2 hours each day playing video games (Rideout, Foehr, & Roberts, 2010) Developmentalists have looked at how these games affect children's cognitive and social/emotional development. Some studies suggest that video game playing enhances children's spatial-cognitive skills and may even eliminate the well-documented gender difference in this domain (Feng, Spence, & Pratt, 2007; Ferguson, 2010). Similarly, children who perform poorly in school may gain a sense of competence from mastering video games, especially those that are complex and require sophisticated strategies, that helps to offset the deterioration of self-esteem that may be brought on by school failure (Przbyiski, Rigby, & Ryan, 2010).   ◉ Watch at **MyDevelopmentLab**

◉ Watch the **Video** *Addicted to Video Games* at **MyDevelopmentLab**

Nevertheless, research suggests even short-term exposure to violent video games in laboratory settings increases research participants' general level of emotional hostility (Anderson & Dill, 2000; Bushman & Huesmann, 2006). Apparently, increases in emotional hostility and decreases in the capacity to empathize with others, which are engendered by violent video games, are the motivating forces behind the increases in aggressive behavior that often result from playing such games for extended periods of time (Funk, Buchman, Jenks, & Bechtoldt, 2003; Gentile, Lynch, Linder, & Walsh, 2004).

Critics of video-game research argue that many such studies are methodologically flawed and, as a result, exaggerate the potential negative effects of violent games (Ferguson & Kilburn, 2010). These researchers point out that the effect of a particular game often depends on who is playing it. For example, violent video games appear to be part of an overall pattern linking preferences for violent stimuli to aggressive behavior. The more violent television programs children watch, the more violent video games they prefer, and the more aggressively they behave toward peers (Mediascope, 1999b). This finding holds for both boys and girls. Most girls aren't interested in violent games and respond negatively to the hyper-sexualized female characters that most such games include (Behm-Morowitz & Mastro, 2009). However, like boys, the minority of girls who enjoy playing violent video games tend to be more physically aggressive than average. Consequently, parents who notice that aggressive and violent themes characterize most of their children's leisure-time interests as well as their interactions with peers should worry about their children playing video games (Funk, Buchman, Myers, & Jenks, 2000).

## Computers and Electronic Multitasking

◄------------Learning Objective 14.10

What are the roles of computers and electronic multitasking in children's development?

Surveys show that more than 90% of school-aged children and adolescents in the United States use computers on a regular basis. About 60% regularly use the Internet (Rideout, Foehr, & Robers, 2010). Remarkably, adolescents spend an average of 6 hours each day using multiple electronic devices (Foehr, 2006).

**COMPUTERS** Computer and Internet use rates are nearly identical for boys and girls. By contrast, a "digital divide" exists across socioeconomic groups with parent education being the key variable. Over 90% of families with children that are headed by college graduates have Internet access, as do 74% of homes headed by high school graudates. However, the proportions of children who use computers and the Internet at home have increased dramatically among all income groups over the past decade, and there is good evidence that the digital divide is disappearing at a rapid rate (Rideout, Foehr, & Roberts, 2010). Most children and teens use computers for school work, to play games, and social networking.

Apart from teacher-directed activities such as homework, children use computers in much the same ways as they use other environments (Rideout, Foehr, & Roberts, 2010). For the most part, children younger than 10 years of age play when they are on a computer. Consequently, educators and parents need to keep an eye on children who are supposed to be doing school work on their computers and to be aware of the tendency of children to test digital boundaries, such as age limits for social networking sites, just as they do physical boundaries. And, as we pointed out in the *Technology and the Developing Child* feature in Chapter 7, computer access can actually lead to declines in achievement if parents and teachers do not monitor how children actually use them (Belo, Ferreira, & Telang, 2010; Malamud & Pop-Eleches, 2010; Vigdor & Ladd, 2010).

Like television, however, the Internet is a mixed blessing. One issue is that advertising occurs in far more subtle forms online than it does on television. If a child working on a school report enters the term "nutrition" in a search engine, for example, many of the links that show up will appear to be informational but, on closer inspection, will be found to have been designed to sell some kind of food product (Moore & Rideout, 2007). Others will lead children to online games that are nothing more than ploys to introduce children to new products. Similarly, a child who is searching for information on a health topic may stumble onto sexually explicit materials. Once again, adult monitoring is essential when children are using computers.

*Some studies suggest that children in the United States now spend more time playing video games than they do watching television.*

**ELECTRONIC MULTITASKING**   Computers are an important element in the *electronic multitasking environment* in which many adolescents immerse themselves these days (Foehr, 2006). In one observational study of school computer labs, researchers found that many students worked on papers and other assignments in a split-screen format, with one part of the screen devoted to their work and another to a game (Jones, 2003). And many of these students were listening to music on their MP3 players at the same time. Some may also have been instant-messaging friends on the computers they were using. Interestingly, neuroscientists have located a network of neurons in the prefrontal cortex of the adult brain that allows humans to rapidly shift their focus from one task to another while keeping multiple goals in mind—the essence of multitasking (Koechlin, Basso, Pietrini, Panzer, & Grafman, 1999). As you learned in Chapter 4, the prefrontal cortex is an important site of brain development in the teen years. Thus, multitasking may emerge in adolescence along with the other newly developed forms of cognitive functioning that teens delight in exercising (e.g., Piaget's *naive idealism*). Still, research shows that, although multitasking may be a good temporary strategy for managing information overload, it is an inefficient approach for processing information in meaningful ways (Law, Logie, & Pearson, 2006). Something, and often something quite important, inevitably gets lost in the mix.

Moreover, developmentalists caution that habitual multitasking may increase levels of sensation-seeking, thereby increasing teens' chances of engaging in risky behavior (Foehr, 2006). In fact, multitasking itself can be quite a risky behavior when it takes the form of text-messaging while driving. Multitasking is also linked to increased anxiety levels (Bailey & Konstan, 2006). For these reasons, mental health professionals such as psychiatrist Edward Hallowell have developed therapeutic interventions to help teens and adults break the multitasking habit (Hallowell, 2007).

## Macrosystem Effects: The Impact of the Larger Culture

Finally, we consider explicitly the question of contexts and cultures. Each family, and thus each child, is embedded in a series of overlapping contexts, each of which affects the way the family itself interacts as well as all other parts of the system.

**Learning Objective 14.11** - - - - - - - - →
What are the effects of poverty on children and families?

## Socioeconomic Status and Development

In Chapter 4, you learned about the effects of *socioeconomic status (SES)*—a collective term that includes the economic, occupational, and educational factors that influence a family's relative position in society—on children's health. We discussed the impact of socioeconomic status on children's cognitive development in Chapter 7, and the association between poverty and single-parenthood in Chapter 13. In this chapter, we deal with SES as a factor that operates at both the microsystem and the exosystem levels of Bronfenbrenner's model. For instance, when poverty prevents a child from getting enough to eat, it operates as part of the microsystem. When the stores in the neighborhood in which the child lives do not offer a variety of healthy foods because of the low incomes of the residents, poverty functions at the exosystem level. Likewise, when parents' lack of transportation prevents them from obtaining employment, poverty not only functions as an exosystem factor but also becomes part of a self-perpetuating developmental context in which a child's development is hindered by a lack of material resources.

**CHARACTERISTICS OF CHILD POVERTY**   In the United States, *poverty* is defined as a yearly income of less than $22,491 for a family of four (U.S. Census Bureau, 2011 ). As you can see in Figure 14.5 on page 361, the child poverty rate in the United States declined from 22% in 1993 to 19% in 2008 (U.S. Census Bureau, 2010). However, you will notice that children are more likely than those in other age groups to live in poor households. In addition, another 39% of children in the United States live in *low-income* households, those in which the total family income is between 100% and 200% of the official federal poverty level (Douglas-Hall & Chau, 2007). Thus, more than half of all children in the United States live in families that have either insufficient funds or just enough to get by.

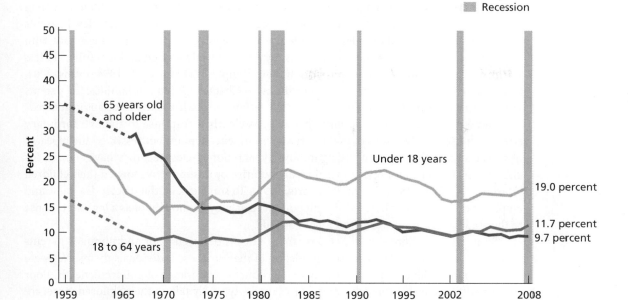

Note: The data points are placed at the midpoints of the respective years.
Data for people aged 18 to 64 and 65 and older are not available from 1960 to 1965.

**FIGURE 14.5** Poverty and Age
The graph shows the percentage of people in the United States living in poverty from 1959 to 2008, including children under 18.

(*Source:* U.S. Census Bureau, 2010.)

Child poverty rates vary across ethnic groups, as you can see in Figure 14.6 below (Douglas-Hall & Chau, 2007). Children reared by single mothers are far more likely than other children to be living in poverty. About 26% of single parents have incomes below the poverty line, compared to just 4% of two-parent families (U.S. Census Bureau, 2008b). Research shows that children in low-income and poor households are at greater risk of a number of health problems than are their peers who are better off financially. This association exists in other countries as well (Bradshaw & Richardson, 2009).

For most children, the deleterious effects of low income are transient, because most families do not remain in poverty throughout their children's early years. Long-term studies suggest that about 8% of families with children in the United States experience chronic low-income status (U.S. Department of the Treasury, 2008). Similar results have been obtained in longitudinal studies in the United Kingdom (Burgess, Propper, & Rigg, 2004).

**THE EFFECTS OF POVERTY ON FAMILIES**  Among many other things, poverty reduces options for parents. They may not be able to afford prenatal care, so their children are more likely to be born with some sort of disability. When the mother works, she is likely to have fewer choices of affordable child care. Poor children spend more time in poor-quality child care and shift more from one care arrangement to another. Poor families also live in smaller and less adequate housing, often in decaying neighborhoods with high rates of violence, and many of them move frequently, so their children change schools often. The parents are less likely to feel they have adequate social support, and the children often lack a stable group of playmates (Dodge, Pettit, & Bates, 1994). Overall, poor environments are more chaotic, and people living in poverty are more highly stressed with fewer psychological and social resources (Brooks-Gunn, 1995; McLoyd & Wilson, 1991).

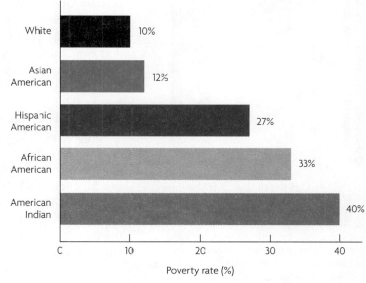

**FIGURE 14.6** Child Poverty Rates across Ethnic Groups in the United States, 2006
Although overall poverty rates have declined considerably in the United States over the past three decades, the rate among some ethnic groups continues to be alarmingly high.

(*Source:* From A. Douglas-Hall and M. Chau, 2007. *Basic Facts about Low-Income Children, Birth to Age 18.* Reprinted by permission of NCCP (National Center for Children in Poverty).)

Mothers and fathers living in poverty also interact with their children differently than parents in working-class or middle-class families in the United States. Poverty-level parents talk and read to their children less, provide fewer age-appropriate toys, spend less time with them in intellectually stimulating activities, explain things less often and less fully, are less warm, and are stricter and more physical in their discipline (Dodge et al., 1994; Evans, 2004; Sampson & Laub, 1994). In the terms introduced in Chapter 13, in poor families, the parents are more likely to be either neglecting or authoritarian and are less likely to be authoritative.

Some of this pattern of parental behavior is clearly a response to the extraordinary stresses and special demands of the poverty environment—a point buttressed by the repeated observation that those parents living in poverty who nonetheless feel they have enough social support are much less likely to be harshly punitive or unsupportive toward their children (Hashima & Amato, 1994; Taylor & Roberts, 1995). To some extent, the stricter discipline and emphasis on obedience observed among poor parents may be thought of as a logical response to the realities of life in a very poor neighborhood.

Some of the differences in child-rearing patterns between poor and nonpoor parents may also result from straightforward modeling of the way these individuals themselves were reared; some inadequate practices may be a product of ignorance of children's needs. Poor parents with relatively more education, for example, typically talk to their children more, are more responsive, and provide more intellectual stimulation than do equally poor parents with lower levels of education (Kelley, Sanchez-Hucles, & Walker, 1993). Whatever the cause, children reared in poverty experience both different physical conditions and quite different interactions with their parents.

**THE EFFECTS OF POVERTY ON CHILDREN** Not surprisingly, children raised in poverty turn out differently (Huston & Bentley, 2010). Children from poverty environments have higher rates of illness and disabilities, as you saw in Chapter 4. And, as you learned in Chapter 7, they also typically have lower IQ scores and move through the sequences of cognitive development more slowly—effects that have been found in studies in which researchers controlled for many possible confounding factors, such as the mother's IQ and the family structure (McLoyd, 1998). Children living in poverty are half as likely as their more well-off peers to know the alphabet and to be able to count before they enter school (U.S. Census Bureau, 2001). They are twice as likely as nonpoor children to repeat a grade and are less likely to go on to college (Brooks-Gunn, 1995; Huston, 1994; Zill, Moore, Smith, Steif, & Coiro, 1995). Children from low-income homes also exhibit more behavior problems than their better-off peers (Qi & Kaiser, 2003). As adults, children from low-income families are more likely to be poor, thus continuing the cycle through another generation. All these effects are greater for those children who live in poverty in infancy and early childhood and for those who have lived in poverty continuously than for children who have experienced some mixture of poverty and greater affluence (Bolger, 1997; Duncan et al., 1994; Shanahan, Sayer, Davey, & Brooks, 1997; Smith, Brooks-Gunn, & Klebanov, 1997).

Figure 14.7 shows one of these effects, drawn from research by Greg Duncan and his colleagues (1994). Duncan collected information on family income for a large sample of families over the years from the child's birth to age 5. He looked at the child's IQ score at age 5 as a function of whether the family had been poor in every one of those 5 years or in only some years. The figure compares the IQ scores of each of these groups to the benchmark IQ of children who never lived in poverty. It's clear that constant poverty has a greater negative effect than occasional poverty, and both are worse than not being poor. In this analysis, Duncan controlled for the mother's education and the structure of the household (single mother versus two parents, for example), so the differences observed seem to be real effects of poverty.

The effects of poverty are more severe for children who are also exposed to street gangs and street violence, to drug pushers, to overcrowded homes, and to higher risks of abuse (Brooks-Gunn, Duncan, & Aber, 1997). Surveys in a number of large cities indicate that nearly half of inner-city elementary and high school students have witnessed at least one violent crime in the past year (Osofsky, 1995); nearly all have heard gunfire, seen someone being beaten up, or observed a drug deal (White, Bruce, Farrell, & Kliewer, 1997); as many as

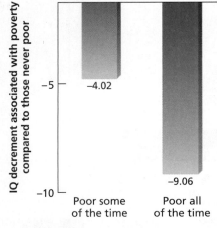

**FIGURE 14.7** Duration of Poverty and IQ Scores

In this analysis, the zero line represents the average IQ score of a group of 5-year-old children in Duncan's study who had never lived in poverty. Average IQ scores of children who had lived in poverty some of the time or all of the time are compared to that benchmark. You can see that children who spent all of their first 5 years living in poverty had considerably lower average IQs than those who lived in poverty only part of the time, and both groups were significantly lower than the benchmark group.

(*Source:* Duncan et al., 1994, from Table 3, p. 306.)

*It's not hard to see why some refer to scenes of urban poverty like this as "war zones."*

30% have seen a homicide by the time they are 15 (Garbarino & Kostelny, 1997). Predictably, children who are victimized or who witness violent crimes are more likely to suffer from emotional problems than are peers who are spared these experiences (Puruggganan, Stein, Johnson Silver, & Benenson, 2003).

A growing body of evidence shows that the effect of living in a concentrated pocket of poverty is to intensify all of the ill effects of family poverty. For example, many children living in such neighborhoods show all the symptoms of posttraumatic stress disorder (Garbarino, 2002), including sleep disturbances, irritability, inability to concentrate, angry outbursts, and hypervigilance. Many experience flashbacks or intrusive memories of traumatic events. And because they are likely to have missed out on many of the forms of intellectual stimulation and consistent family support that would allow them to succeed in school, they have high rates of behavior problems and academic failure. Fewer than half of urban poor children graduate from high school (NCES, 2011). The reasons for such school failure are complex, but there is little doubt that the chronic stress experienced by these children is one highly significant component.

**THE ROLES OF STRESS AND PROTECTIVE FACTORS** Studies of resilient and vulnerable children suggest that certain characteristics or circumstances may help protect some children from the detrimental effects of the cumulative stressors associated with poverty. Among the key protective factors are the following:

- High IQ of the child (Koenon et al., 2007)
- Competent adult parenting, such as an authoritative style (good supervision or monitoring of the child seems especially important) (Eamon & Mulder, 2005)
- Parental knowledge about child development (Seo, 2006)
- Availability of intellectually stimulating toys and activities in the home (Huston & Bentley, 2010)
- An optimistic outlook (in the child) (Lam et al., 2004)
- Effective schools (Woolley & Grogan-Kaylor, 2006)
- A secure initial attachment of the child to the parent (Li-Grining, 2007)
- A strong community helping network, including friends, family, or neighbors (Barrow et al., 2007)
- Stable parental employment (Terrisse, 2000)
- Strong sense of ethnic identity (Thomas, Townsend, & Belgrave, 2003)
- Participation in early childhood programs (Smokowski et al., 2004)

Thus, the effects of poverty depend on the combined effects of the number of stressors the child must cope with and the range of competencies or advantages the child brings to the situation. Poverty does not guarantee bad outcomes, but it stacks the deck against many children.

Learning Objective 14.12 - - - - - - - - ->
How do the values of African Americans, Hispanic Americans, and Asian Americans differ?

## Race and Ethnicity

In the United States, because poverty is so much more common among some ethnic groups than others, socioeconomic status and ethnic group membership are strongly linked. Because of this overlap, it is sometimes tempting to focus attention solely on socioeconomic status as the most powerful factor, ignoring the additional impact of ethnicity. For example, what difference does it make to a child to grow up in a family whose cultural roots emphasize collectivism rather than individualism? You have learned something about these questions throughout the book, but here we will take one final look at what is known about ethnic effects, using the several major groups in the United States as illustration.

These Irish Americans marching in a St. Patrick's Day parade fit the definition of an ethnic group, but they are not a race.

We should begin with a definition of **ethnicity**. According to Parke and Buriel, "Ethnicity refers to an individual's membership in a group sharing a common ancestral heritage based on nationality, language, and culture" (1998, p. 496); the group is an **ethnic group**. Ethnicity may include a biological or racial component, but that is not an essential part of the definition. Thus, race and ethnicity are not the same. Ethnicity refers primarily to social and cultural characteristics, whereas race normally designates a group with specific physical characteristics. Thus, African Americans and Asian Americans may be viewed as both ethnic and racial categories, whereas Hispanic Americans, Polish Americans, or Italian Americans would be regarded only as ethnic groups.

**AFRICAN AMERICANS**    African Americans, who make up about 13% of the total population (U.S. Census Bureau, 2011), have a culture that has been shaped by their African heritage, their experience of slavery, and a continuing experience of discrimination and segregation. The central values of this culture include the following (Hill, Soriano, Chen, & LaFromboise, 1994):

- Collectivism or communalism, as opposed to individualism; identity is collective as well as personal.
- Person-centered rather than object-centered values; relationships with people are more important than material possessions.
- Mutuality and reciprocity; a belief that "what goes around, comes around," that each person's actions will eventually have repercussions for that individual.
- A strong religious or spiritual orientation, involving acknowledgment of a higher power.
- An emphasis on the importance of children for family continuity.
- Harmony and a sense of connection with nature, including a belief in the "oneness of being" of all humanity.
- Role flexibility.

These values, especially the emphasis on collectivism or communalism and the importance of children, have contributed to a pattern of family structure that is quite different from that of the majority Caucasian American culture. Caucasian Americans think of "the family" as a father, a mother, and several children. Within the African American culture, "family" has a much broader definition, including many variations of extended family structures—a pattern that likely has its roots in West African culture (Stewart, 2007; Sudarkasa, 1993). Martin and Martin, in their book *The Black Extended Family*, defined the African American family as a multigenerational, interdependent kinship system that is welded together by a sense of obligation to relatives; is organized around a dominant figure; extends across geographic boundaries to connect family units to an extended family network; and has a built-in mutual aid system for the welfare of its members and the maintenance of the family as a whole (1978, p. 1). Thus, the key is not just that three or

**ethnicity**    An individual's membership in an ethnic group.

**ethnic group**    "A subgroup whose members are perceived by themselves and others to have a common origin and culture, and shared activities in which the common origin or culture is an essential ingredient" (Porter & Washington, 1993, p. 140).

more generations often live in the same household but that contact with nonresident kin is frequent and integral to the functioning of the family unit. When asked, African Americans overwhelmingly report a strong sense of family solidarity (Hatchett & Jackson, 1993; Wilson, 1986, 1989).

Within this subculture, marriage does not play the dominant role in family formation that it does among Caucasian Americans: Fewer African American adults marry, and divorce is more common (U.S. Census Bureau, 2008b). One result is that a much larger percentage of African American children are born to or reared by unmarried mothers (Martin et al., 2007). However, because of the cultural emphasis on the importance of children and on communalism, these single mothers occupy a different niche within the African American culture than do single mothers in the majority culture. The latter group are more likely to receive financial help from their parents but to live independently; an African American single mother is more likely to live in an extended family with her own mother or grandmother (DeLeire & Kalil, 2002).

Some African Americans teach their children about African culture by celebrating Kwanzaa. The Kwanzaa candles represent unity, self-determination, collective work and responsibility, cooperative economics, purpose, creativity, and faith.

These extended family structures allow individuals to pool their economic resources; they also provide important social and emotional support to the members of the household. The presence of the children's grandmother seems to provide especially helpful support for the young single mother; African American children from such three-generation families do better in school and show fewer behavior problems than do African American children reared by single mothers in households without a grandmother (DeLeire & Kalil, 2002). There is also some evidence that the presence of the grandmother increases the chance that an infant will develop a secure rather than an insecure attachment (Egeland & Sroufe, 1981). Thus, the extended family not only has a cultural history but also seems to be a successful adaptive strategy for many African American families.

Religion also appears to play a special, positive role within the African American culture. The church is a place for participation and belonging, an institution in which those who take on specific roles achieve prestige and status, as well as an institution that can provide help in times of physical or emotional need (Dupree, Watson, & Schneider, 2005). For African American children, participation in church activities seems to be a plus as well; a few studies suggest that those who are more active in a church are more likely to be successful in other arenas, such as in school or on the job (Lee, 1985).

The culture of African American families is also profoundly shaped by the persistence of prejudice. African American adolescents who are most aware of such prejudice are most likely to see school achievement as irrelevant (Taylor, Casten, Flickinger, Roberts, & Fulmore, 1994). Even the process of grieving for lost loved ones appears to be complicated by this consciousness of historical racial prejudice. Researchers have found that African Americans' memories of relatives who have passed away are often framed in terms of how racial prejudice interfered with the individual's pursuit of life goals (Rosenblatt & Wallace, 2005). When these memories are shared with children, it is likely that they increase children's awareness of the notion that African Americans often encounter obstacles in life that members of other groups do not. On a positive note, though, these stories may also enhance children's feelings of pride in their family histories and sense of ethnic identity.

This Hispanic American family has obviously assimilated some of the larger American culture: They are celebrating Thanksgiving. At the same time, they have doubtless retained many features of their own culture, including the centrality of family loyalty.

**HISPANIC AMERICANS**   Some of the statements made above about African Americans are also true of Hispanic Americans, for whom poverty is also endemic. The term *Hispanic* was chosen by the Department of Commerce to denote any person with family roots in Spanish-speaking countries or from Central or South America. The term *Latino*, which many people prefer, is the Spanish word for the same group. Hispanic people represent the fastest-growing minority group in the United States. In 1980, only 6% of the population was Hispanic. By 2010, the proportion had grown to 16% (U.S. Census Bureau, 2011).

A number of subgroups, differing somewhat in values and cultural traditions, comprise the Hispanic population in the United States. Just over 60% are Mexican, 9% are Puerto Rican, and 3.5% are Cuban in origin (U.S. Census Bureau, 2011). The rest are from other Central and South American

countries. Within this diverse group, Puerto Ricans have the highest poverty rates; their divorce rates are comparable to those among African Americans. Both Mexican Americans and Cuban Americans have divorce rates closer to the rate among White Americans.

These subgroups, however, share a number of cultural values, all of which are aspects of a basic collectivist world view (Hill et al., 1994; Parke & Buriel, 1998; Giese & Snyder, 2009):

- Preference for group participation or group work rather than individual effort (*allocentrism*).
- Strong commitment to and adherence to family; placing the family before the individual; self-identity is embedded in the family (*familia*).
- Avoidance of personal conflict; keeping the peace at all costs (*simpatía*).
- Respect for and deference to authority, such as parents, elders, teachers, or government officials (*respeto*).
- High value placed on personal relationships, which are seen as more important than reputation or material gain; feelings and needs of others are paramount; competition is discouraged (*personalismo*).

In addition, of course, there is also the common thread of the Spanish language. The great majority of Hispanic Americans today either speak only Spanish or are bilingual. Because of recent rapid immigration, more than half of Hispanic American school-aged children have only limited English proficiency; a shift toward English as the dominant language generally occurs among second- or third-generation Hispanic Americans, but many if not most continue to speak Spanish in the home (Hakimzadeh & Cohn, 2007). Many Hispanic American communities also have Spanish-language newspapers and radio and TV stations; in many neighborhoods, Spanish is the dominant tongue.

The significance of family life within Hispanic American culture is hard to exaggerate. The nuclear family is the core of this kin system, although contact with extended family members and with "fictive kin" is frequent (Howes, Guerra, & Zucker, 2007). *Fictive kin*, also common in extended African American family systems, might include a child's godparents or other friends who develop a long-term connection with the family and with each child (Keefe & Padilla, 1987).

This pattern seems to be stronger in first-generation immigrants, who rely almost exclusively on family members for emotional support and problem solving. The children of immigrants seem to have more extensive non-kin networks, and many shift somewhat toward an individualist set of values—with accompanying increases in intrafamily stress (Delgado-Gaitan, 1994; Parke & Buriel, 1998). In both newly immigrated and second-generation families, however, the extended family clearly plays a more central role in the daily life of Hispanic Americans than it does in the majority culture.

This emphasis on the central role of the family is reflected in the values taught to children so that they will become *bien educado*. Literally translated, *bien educado* means "well educated"; the phrase does not primarily connote formal education, however, but rather the ability to function well in any social setting without disrespect or rudeness. Thus, *bien educado* includes politeness, respect, loyalty, and attachment to the extended family and cooperation with others. Hispanic American mothers emphasize the importance of a child's showing proper demeanor in public; a Caucasian American mother, in contrast, is likely to be pleased or even proud when her child behaves in some independent and even slightly naughty way (Harwood, 1992).

These values are taught in the home through all the mechanisms you have read about throughout this book: modeling, direct reinforcement, and style of family interaction. A number of studies suggest that the more fully Hispanic American parents identify with their ethnic heritage, the more likely it is that the child will show these valued qualities, such as concern for others (Knight, Cota, & Bernal, 1993). Moreover, when children of Hispanic immigrants achieve a bicultural identity that includes a strong identification with their parents' culture, along with a sense of belonging in the dominant culture of the United States, they attain higher levels of both social adjustment and academic achievement (Coatsworth, Maldonado-Molina, Pantin, & Szapocznik, 2005).

**ASIAN AMERICANS**  About 5% of residents in the United States describe themselves as "Asian." Like Hispanic culture, Asian American culture places great emphasis on family loyalty, respect for elders, and family honor. Asian American families also resemble Hispanic American families in other respects: They often include three generations in the same household (U. S. Census Bureau, 2011); they are generally hierarchically organized, with the father as the obvious head; and there is a strong emphasis on the interdependence of family members. Despite these surface similarities to other ethnic groups, the mixture of values in Asian American families includes several that are distinct (American Psychological Association, 1993; Park, 2005; Parke & Buriel, 1998):

- Pacifism, self-discipline, and self-control—all values linked to Confucianism, and thus common among Asian groups with a strong Confucian heritage (Chinese, Korean, and Vietnamese particularly, with lesser influence among Japanese).
- An emphasis on hierarchy and respect in social systems and personal relationships (parents are superior to children, men to women), also based on Confucianism.
- Strong family links; young people are expected to obey elders; family solidarity and harmonious relationships are highly valued; family needs come before individual needs.
- A strong belief that each person controls his or her own destiny.
- A powerful work ethic and belief in the importance of achievement.

The Asian American family model includes a striking combination of indulgence, physical contact, comfort, and care on the one hand and high expectations for both obedience and achievement on the other. Children are taught that empathy for others is highly important and yet respecting the privacy of others is also critical (Barry, Bernard, & Beitel, 2008). Overall, children are highly valued, although the family's collective needs normally take precedence over the child's individual needs (Paiva, 2008).

Asian Americans also believe in individual effort as one of the primary roads to success (Harrison et al., 1990; Stevenson, 1988). In Caucasian American culture, ability rather than hard work is seen as the key to success. This difference is not trivial. If you believe in ability as the key ingredient, then there is not much point in pressing for greater effort, and you will accept mediocre performance from your child. An Asian American parent, in contrast, believing in the centrality of effort, takes a very different attitude toward both success and failure by a child. The parent takes success more or less for granted but responds to failure by insisting on more effort. Because of these different belief systems, Asian American parents spend more time tutoring their children and have higher standards for their children's achievement. They are also less likely to be satisfied with their children's schools, believing that schools, too, can always do better. Yet despite what (to Caucasian American eyes) seems like strong pressure to achieve, Asian and Asian American students do not report high feelings of stress or anxiety, whereas high-achieving Caucasian American adolescents do report frequent feelings of stress (Crystal et al., 1994).

Given all these differences, it isn't surprising that Asian American children as a group achieve at higher levels in schools than any other U.S. ethnic group, just as Asian children from Japan, China, Taiwan, and Korea regularly outperform U.S. children and teenagers on standardized tests of math and science, as you learned in Chapter 7. Similarly, you should recall from the discussion of schooling earlier in the chapter that a greater proportion of Asian Americans than any other group in the United States complete high school and college.

Asian cultures emphasize respect for elders.

**ETHNICITY IN PERSPECTIVE** What conclusions can be drawn about the role of ethnicity (or, more broadly, culture) in children's development from these three brief (and necessarily simplistic) sketches? Sadly, not many. First and foremost, of course, you have been reading almost entirely about subgroups within U.S. culture, which tells little about other cultural systems. And even within these limits, most research involves comparisons of each ethnic group with children or families in the majority culture. Until recently, most of this research assumed that the dominant culture was right or "normal" and that all other variations were inferior or "deviations" from the standard. That assumption has faded, but developmentalists have very little concurrent information about these groups and even less data about whether the same processes operate in each subgroup. What they are left with is a kind of snapshot of each group, with no way to tell which characteristics are the most crucial, which attitudes or values the most significant.

For example, if developmentalists look for reasons for good or poor school performance in different subcultures, what conclusions can they draw? Bilingualism cannot be the sole factor, because both Asian Americans and Hispanic Americans are typically bilingual; child-rearing style cannot be the sole factor, because Asian American parents are likely to be authoritarian (by current research definitions), yet their children do well in school. Doubtless it is the pattern of values and parental behavior that is crucial, and not any single variable (Knafo, Daniel, & Khoury-Kassabri, 2008). Cultures and subcultures are incredibly complex systems; their effects come from the combinations of factors, not merely from the adding up of a set of separate variables. In addition, of course, it's essential to try to understand how each subculture, each set of values, combines or conflicts with the values of the majority culture. For a child growing up with one foot in one culture and one in another culture, these are highly important issues.

**Learning Objective 14.13** ----------➤
In what way does the culture as a whole affect children's development?

## The Culture as a Whole

A culture as a whole is also a system, made up of values, assumptions, and beliefs, a political and an economic system, patterns of personal relationships, and so forth. Each piece of that system affects all the other parts; changing one part changes the whole. The wide cultural consequences of the rapid increase in the number of women in the labor force in the United States and other industrialized countries is a very good example. It has led, among many other things, to a fast-growing demand for nonparental care (with consequent changes in children's lives), to changes in male-female relationships, to new political alignments, and to shifts in patterns of interactions within families, which in turn affect children in still other ways.

Throughout this text, you have learned about sequences of children's development that seem to occur regardless of cultural context. At the same time, examples of cultural differences are also evident. At the most visible and measurable level are cultural variations in children's specific beliefs, the social scripts they learn, and the pattern of family and kin relationships they experience.

An interesting example comes from the work of Giyoo Hatano and his colleagues (1993; Inagaki & Hatano, 2004), who compared beliefs about the nature of plants and animals among Japanese, Israeli, and American kindergarten, second-grade, and fourth-grade children. Piaget noted, and others have confirmed, that young children typically view the world through the lens of *animism*, which leads them to attribute not only life but also feelings and self-awareness to inanimate objects, to plants, and to animals. Later, they differentiate among these several facets of life and understand that plants are alive but have no self-awareness. Hatano's study confirms the broad features of this shift: Younger children in all three cultures had much stronger beliefs in animism. But Hatano also found differences in the developmental pattern, depending on the specific cultural beliefs about life.

Japanese culture includes the belief that plants are much like humans; in the Buddhist system, even a blade of grass is thought to have a mind. In contrast, in Israeli language and culture, plants are put into a quite different category from animals and humans. When children in Japan and Israel were asked whether a tree or a tulip was alive, 91% of the Japanese—but only 60% of the Israeli fourth-graders said that it was. One-fifth of Japanese fourth-graders attributed sensory properties to plants, saying that a tree or a tulip could feel chilly or could feel pain if it was hit with a stick. Overall, because of their stronger distinction between plants and animals, Israeli children were much slower than either Japanese or American children to come to the understanding that people, animals, and plants are all alive. This study thus illustrates both an underlying developmental pattern that seems to be shared across cultures and the cultural variations laid over that basic pattern.

It is not hard to generate similar examples. For instance, cultures may vary in the proportion of securely and insecurely attached children because of variations in their typical child-rearing styles or beliefs, even though the process by which a child becomes securely or insecurely attached is much the same from one culture to another. In a similar way, adolescents in all cultures need to change their identity to at least some extent in order to move into the adult world, but cultures that provide initiation rituals at puberty may make the process much simpler and less confusing.

Certainly, developmentalists need to know a great deal more about how cultural variations affect development. But as you learned in Chapter 1, they also have to ask a more subtle set of questions. In particular, they need to know whether the relationship between environmental events or a child's characteristics and some outcome for the child are the same in every culture. Is authoritative child-rearing optimal in all cultures, or is some other style better for preparing children for adult life in some settings? Are aggressive children unpopular in every culture, or are there some settings in which aggression is highly valued? Indeed, is unpopularity in childhood a major risk factor for adult dysfunction in every culture? As yet there are no answers, although researchers are beginning to ask the questions.

## THINK CRITICALLY

- What are some of the implications of Sandra Scarr's view that parents' choices regarding nonparental care are an extension of their values and parenting styles?
- Suppose a child's birthday is a few days after his local school district's cutoff date for enrolling in first grade. In light of the evidence about the effects of schooling that you read about in this chapter, what would be the pros and cons of sending the child to a private school for first grade so that he would be eligible for second grade in a public school the following year?

## CONDUCT YOUR OWN RESEARCH

In the section on nonparental care, you learned that many children are placed in multiple care settings. You can find out how frequently such arrangements occur in your own area by surveying parents at a local child care center. First, explain your project to the center director and get his or her permission to interview parents as they pick up their children each evening. Next, spend a few late afternoons at the center conducting your interviews. Ask parents how many days a week their children attend the center and whether they are also in other kinds of nonparental care. Also ask how many different kinds of care each child has experienced since birth. Keep records of both the number and the types of care arrangements each child is currently experiencing and has been exposed to in the past.

## SUMMARY  ✓⊸ Study and Review at MyDevelopmentLab

### Nonparental Care

**14.1  Why is it difficult to study the effects of nonparental care?**
Nonparental care is difficult to study because it involves so many variables. In addition, care arrangements interact with family variables such as income and parents' educational level. Often, it is impossible to separate the effects of nonparental care from the effects of these variables.

**14.2  How does early nonparental care affect infants' and young children's development?**
A major study showed that child care has no overall negative effect on the security of children's attachment to their parents. Child care often has positive effects on the cognitive development of less advantaged children, but it may have negative effects on advantaged children if there is a large discrepancy between the home environment and the level of stimulation in child care. How child care affects a child's personality depends on the quality of the care. An organized, structured situation is preferable. Infants' physiological responses to the stresses associated with nonparental care may underlie its association with developmental outcomes.

**14.2a  What is a "high-quality" child care center?**
Researchers have identified a number of factors that distinguish high-quality child care centers. These include low teacher/child ratio, small group size, spaces that are adapted to child play, daily lesson plans, and sensitive and knowledgeable caregivers.

**14.3 How does self-care affect school-aged children's development?**
Self-care is associated with several negative effects. Girls, children who live in safe neighborhoods, and children whose parents closely monitor their activities after school are the least likely to be negatively affected by self-care.

## The Impact of Schools

**14.4 How do the various approaches to early childhood education differ, and how does preschool affect children's development?**
Developmental approaches, such as the Montessori method, seek to support the attainment of naturally occurring developmental goals. Academic approaches instruct preschoolers in the skills necessary for success in elementary schools. Developmentally appropriate practices are based on an understanding of developmental universals, individual differences, and the social and cultural contexts of development. Preschool and full-day kindergarten programs may have limited benefits for children who do not have disabilities and who come from homes with adequate economic resources. Learning experiences in less formal settings may contribute as much to such children's development as structured educational programs do.

**14.4a What are the advantages and disadvantages of computers in the preschool classroom?**
Young children can learn prereading and math skills from educational software. Computer use may also improve fine motor skills. However, computer use may prevent preschoolers from engaging in social interaction with peers.

**14.5 What factors contribute to effective schooling at the elementary level, and how does elementary school influence children's development?**
Teaching style, class size, and parental involvement contribute to children's achievement in elementary school. A child's adaptation to school is affected by his readiness to learn to read as well as by his parents' involvement in the school and in his educational attainment. Experience with school appears to be causally linked to some aspects of cognitive development.

**14.6 How do children's achievement goals change during the transition to secondary school?**
Children demonstrate achievement losses at every school transition. Most children are motivated by task goals in elementary school, but ability goals become more common after the transition to middle school, where ability grouping is more evident than in earlier grades. When children fail to meet the demands of middle school, they lose confidence in their abilities and show lower levels of self-esteem. Likewise, students who perform poorly in the first year or two of high school are less likely to graduate, an outcome that affects their chances for academic and economic success in adulthood.

**14.7 What have researchers learned about disengaged and engaged students?**
By adolescence, children have a clearly developed idea of their comparative skills and abilities. These beliefs are a significant element in decisions about whether to finish high school or drop out. Disengaged students exhibit a pattern of behavior that includes academic failure, lack of participation in extracurricular activities, and increased rates of risky behavior. Engaged students are more interested in school and invest personal effort in school work and extracurricular activities.

**14.7a How does employment affect adolescents' development?**
Teen employment is associated with increased risk of drug use. Teens who work are also less likely to attend college. However, the effects of employment depend on the type of job that an adolescent performs. Skill-based jobs can enhance teens' chances for future occupational success.

**14.8 Why do some parents choose to homeschool their children?**
Some parents choose to homeschool their children for religious reasons. Others want to provide one-on-one instruction for a child with disabilities. Some parents choose homeschooling in order to protect their children from negative peer influences. Generally, homeschooled children exhibit few differences from their schooled peers, but research has been sparse and includes only those homeschooled children whose families have volunteered to participate.

## The Impact of Entertainment Media

**14.9 What are the effects of television and video games on children's development?**
Children who watch specifically educational TV programming can gain skills or positive attitudes. Experts agree that watching violence on television increases the level of aggression shown by a child. Video games may enhance children's spatial cognitive skills; however, those that are violent may also contribute to aggressive behavior.

**14.10 What are the roles of computers and electronic multitasking in children's development?**
Children use computers for school work and to play games. Computer and Internet use can raise children's grades and achievement test scores. Multitasking may interfere with learning, lead to increases in sensation-seeking, and increase anxiety.

## Macrosystem Effects: The Impact of the Larger Culture

**14.11 What are the effects of poverty on children and families?**
Children growing up in poverty, perhaps especially urban poverty, are markedly disadvantaged in many ways,

including having lower access to medical care and greater exposure to multiple stresses. They do more poorly in school and drop out of school at far higher rates. Some protective factors, including a secure attachment, higher IQ, authoritative parenting, and effective schools, can help to counterbalance poverty effects for some children.

**14.12** How do the values of African Americans, Hispanic Americans, and Asian Americans differ?

African American subculture includes a strong emphasis on extended family households and contact and on religion. Hispanic Americans, too, place great emphasis on family ties; their emphasis on family honor and solidarity is heightened by the use of a shared language. In their collectivist cultural system, kin contact is frequent and central to daily life. Asian Americans emphasize respect and loyalty to family as well, but they stress the central importance of effort (rather than inherent ability) as the path to achievement.

**14.13** In what way does the culture as a whole affect children's development?

Developmentalists have very little understanding of how cultural variations influence development. Some patterns of development and some basic developmental processes (such as moral development and attachment) appear to be independent of culture. Other processes and patterns are affected by cultural variation.

## KEY TERMS

ability goals (p. 351)
academic approaches (p. 345)
developmental approaches (p. 345)

developmentally appropriate practices (p. 346)

early childhood education (p. 345)
ethnic group (p. 364)

ethnicity (p. 364)
task goals (p. 351)

# 15

# Atypical Development

At the age of 3, Aletha was diagnosed with *autistic disorder*, a disorder that interferes with children's ability to communicate and form social relationships. Shortly after the diagnosis was made, Aletha's mother enrolled the girl in a program at the local elementary school for children with disabilities. The teachers helped Aletha and her mother learn how to use sign language to communicate. The little girl responded well to the program, and her mother was thankful to finally have a means of communicating with her daughter.

Everything seemed to be going well with Aletha until the day after her fourth birthday when Aletha's mother encouraged her to put two signs together to create a sentence. Aletha knew the signs for "car" and "go," so her mother demonstrated "car go" and attempted to get the girl to imitate her. Aletha suddenly bit herself on the forearm so hard that it began to bleed. From that day on, whenever Aletha's mother attempted to teach her a new sign, she was cooperative. However, when Aletha's mother tried to motivate Aletha to combine signs, the girl would start biting herself.

Desperate for a solution, Aletha's mother turned to the school's psychologist. He recommended that, whenever Aletha started biting herself, Aletha's mother stop the sign language lessons for a period of time instead of going back to working on individual signs. Eventually, the psychologist said, Aletha would learn that, if she wanted to keep doing what she enjoyed (learning individual signs) she would have to cooperate with her mother's attempts to challenge her to combine them. Aletha's mother protested that it didn't seem fair to punish a child with such a severe disability. The psychologist responded, "Part of Aletha is growing up in the same way as other children, and that part of her needs discipline and guidance. Like any parent, you try to get her to do something that you know is good for her, and like many children, disability or no, she resists. This 'normal' part of Aletha needs discipline and guidance so that it can help her overcome the limits of her disability as much as possible."

Aletha's mother's experience represents just one of several patterns in which nonnormative changes that threaten a child's well being, or *atypical developmental changes*, interact with factors that are characteristic of most or all children to produce a frustrating situation for parent and child alike. (Recall from Chapter 1 that nonnormative changes are those developmental changes which result from unique, unshared events.) Some nonnormative changes of this kind are evident from the earliest months of life. For example, Down syndrome, which you learned about in Chapter 2, is identified before birth. Others can be readily identified before a child's second birthday. Still others do not become known until a child enters school.

These nonnormative pathways are the topic of this chapter. Each such pathway presents parents with a unique set of challenges. The fact that many (even most) of them manage to adapt effectively to the presence of child who displays atypical development is testimony to the devotion and immense effort expended.

## Understanding Atypical Development

Perhaps the best starting point for our discussion is to develop a working definition of *atypical development*. There are many behaviors that might be called *atypical*, if we went by the literal definition of the term—that is, *not typical*. Most children do things that others would view as unusual, but in most cases these behaviors fall within the normal range of variation. By contrast, **atypical development** involves behaviors that are not only unusual, but also part of an enduring pattern that interferes with a child's development in significant ways.

## Types of Problems

As we have noted, at one time or another most children show some kind of behavior that their parents would describe as "unusual" or "abnormal" (Klass & Costello, 2003). For

**atypical development** An enduring pattern of behavior that is unusual, compared to the behavior of others of the child's age, and that interferes with the child's development in some significant way.

◄----------- Learning Objective 15.1
What kinds of problems fall within the domain of atypical development?

### Knowing When to Seek Professional Help

Lucinda is a 4-year-old girl who is currently engaged in an ongoing battle with her parents. The proper arrangement of spaghetti is the central dispute in this battle. Lucinda is convinced that spaghetti and spaghetti sauce should touch each other only in a person's mouth. Consequently, she insists on having her spaghetti served in two separate bowls, one for the pasta and another for the sauce. Furthermore, she requires a spoon for the sauce and a fork for the pasta. She becomes hysterical at even the slightest suggestion that she try having her spaghetti in its more conventional form. Her parents have begun to worry that she might have some kind of serious mental disorder and wonder whether they should consult a child psychologist.

Checklists developed by experts in developmental psychopathology can be helpful in distinguishing behavior that is difficult to manage from behavior that may indicate a disorder for which professional care is appropriate. One such checklist has been published by the National Mental Health Association (available at http://www.nmha.org).

Here are a few of the warning signs for children and teenagers:

- Changes in grades or behavior reports from teachers
- Changes in patterns of sleeping or eating
- Frequent stomachaches or other minor physical symptoms
- Obsessive concern with weight loss
- A sad facial expression that persists over a period of weeks
- Outbursts of rage that lead to destruction of property or aggression toward others
- Activity far in excess of that exhibited by children of the same age
- Frequent unyielding defiance of parental or teacher authority

Of course, every child or teenager who exhibits such behavior doesn't have a serious psychological disorder. Still, when a child's pattern of difficult behavior matches one or more of these signs, parents should probably adopt the "better safe than sorry" approach and consult a mental health professional.

**Learning Objective 15.1a**
What signs indicate that a child may need help from a mental health professional?

**REFLECTION**

1. According to the checklist, is Lucinda's spaghetti-eating behavior likely to be a sign of a psychological disorder? Why or why not?
2. What strategies might Lucinda's parents use to get her to try eating spaghetti the way most people do?

---

example, about 7% of school-aged children wet their pants frequently enough that their parents express concern about it to pediatricians (Gahagan, 2011). Such problems, although worthy of further investigation, almost always fall within the range of typical development and are not indicative of a deeper problem (see *Developmental Science in the Real World*). Usually, developmentalists label a child's development as atypical only if a problem persists for 6 months or longer or if the problem is at the extreme end of the continuum for that behavior.

Within the domain of atypical development, *psychological disorders* constitute one important category of problems. A **psychological disorder** is a pattern of behavior that is unusual in a child's culture and interferes with his or her psychological, social, and/or educational functioning. There are three main categories of psychological disorders in children and adolescents. The first two are **attention problems** (most particularly, attention deficit hyperactivity disorder), which impair the ability to concentrate, and **externalizing problems** (also described as *disruptive behavior disorders*), including both delinquency and excessive aggressiveness or defiance, in which the deviant behavior is directed outward. The third category, **internalizing problems** (also called *emotional disturbances*), includes such problems as depression, anxiety, or eating disorders, in which the deviant behavior is largely directed internally, against the individual herself. You will be reading more about each of these categories later in the chapter.

There are several other types of atypical development that fall outside these three basic categories. For example, individuals at both extremes of the IQ scale are atypical when compared to others of their age. Likewise, children who have average intelligence but who are several years behind their peers in school achievement are considered to be atypical. Children with severe social impairments constitute yet another group of children whose development is atypical. You will also learn about these groups of children.

**psychological disorder** A pattern of behavior that is unusual in a person's culture and interferes with his or her psychological, social, and/or educational functioning.

**attention problems** A category of psychopathologies that impair one's ability to concentrate, including attention deficit hyperactivity disorder, attention deficit disorder, and hyperkinetic disorder.

**externalizing problems** A category of psychopathologies that includes any deviant behavior primarily directed toward others, such as conduct disorders.

**internalizing problems** A category of psychopathologies that includes anxiety and depression and other conditions in which deviant behavior is directed inwardly, against the self.

# Theoretical Perspectives on Atypical Development

◄------------Learning Objective 15.2

How do the biological, psychodynamic, learning, and cognitive perspectives explain atypical development?

Many of the theoretical perspectives that you read about in earlier chapters have been invoked to explain atypical development (see Table 15.1). For instance, the *biological perspective* views atypical development as a symptom of an underlying physical cause, such as genetic inheritance, biochemical abnormalities or imbalances, structural abnormalities within the brain, and/or infection. Consequently, those taking the biological perspective generally favor biological treatments such as drugs.

Originally proposed by Freud, the *psychodynamic (psychoanalytic) perspective* maintains that atypical development stems from early childhood experiences and unresolved, unconscious emotional conflicts. The cause assumed by the psychodynamic approach also suggests the cure, psychoanalysis, which Freud developed to uncover and resolve such unconscious conflicts. More recent psychodynamic approaches do not adhere strictly to Freud's accounts of atypical development, but they do emphasize the role of psychological processes and the importance of psychotherapy in addressing behavioral problems that arise from atypical development.

In stark contrast to both the biological and the psychodynamic perspective, the *learning perspective* suggests that atypical behaviors do not result from any underlying cause. That is, the behaviors themselves are the problem, and such behaviors are thought to be learned and sustained in the same way as any other behavior. According to this view, children and adolescents who exhibit atypical development are victims of faulty learning. Behavior therapists use learning principles to eliminate distressing behavior and to establish new, more appropriate behavior in its place.

The *cognitive perspective* suggests that faulty thinking or distorted perceptions can contribute to some types of atypical development. For example, pessimistic thinking is involved in depression and anxiety. Treatment consistent with this perspective is aimed at changing thinking and perceptions (i.e., cognitive therapy), which presumably will lead to a change in behavior.

**Table 15.1**

## PERSPECTIVES ON ATYPICAL DEVELOPMENT

| Perspective | Causes of Psychological Disorders | Treatment |
|---|---|---|
| **Biological perspective** | Atypical development is a symptom of an underlying physical disorder caused by a structural or biochemical abnormality in the brain, by genetic inheritance, or by infection. | Diagnose and treat like any other physical disorder<br>Drugs or other physical treatment |
| **Psychodynamic perspective** | Atypical development stems from early childhood experiences and unresolved, unconscious sexual or aggressive conflicts. | Bring disturbing repressed material to consciousness and help patient work through unconscious conflicts<br>Psychotherapy |
| **Learning perspective** | Atypical behaviors are learned and sustained like any other behaviors, or there is a failure to learn adaptive behaviors. | Use classical and operant conditioning and modeling to extinguish atypical behavior and to increase adaptive behavior<br>Behavior therapy<br>Behavior modification |
| **Cognitive perspective** | Faulty thinking or distorted perceptions can cause atypical development. | Change faulty, irrational, and/or negative thinking<br>Cognitive therapy |

*Source:* Wood et al., WORLD OF PSYCHOLOGY, © 2008. Reproduced by permission of Pearson Education, Inc.

# Developmental Psychopathology

In recent years, psychologists have changed the way they think about atypical development. Instead of searching for a single grand theory that can explain everything, they focus on factors that seem to predispose children to problems as well as on variables that appear to protect them (Beauchaine & Hinshaw, 2008). Developmentalists' knowledge about the dynamics of atypical development in general, and psychopathology in particular, has been enormously enhanced by an approach called **developmental psychopathology** (Achenbach, 1974; Cicchetti, 2008). This approach has strongly influenced how both researchers and practitioners think about children's and teenagers' psychological problems (Munir & Beardslee, 2001). It emphasizes several key points.

Developmental psychopathology integrates perspectives from a variety of disciplines in order to better understand atypical development. Researchers who study cultural differences, such as anthropologists, have contributed much to developmental psychopathologists' understanding of atypical development (Achenbach, 2008). For example, as you learned in Chapter 13, authoritarian parenting may be a risk factor in one setting and a protective factor in another.

Similarly, the work of behavior geneticists and neuroscientists has become increasingly important in the study of atypical development, especially when their findings are combined with those of developmental psychologists. For example, behavior geneticists have known for some time that heredity contributes to atypical development, and developmental psychologists have been aware of the roles that abuse plays in poor developmental outcomes for some time as well (Phares & Compas, 1993). Neuroscience has enabled them to get a better idea of just how inherited risks interact with environmental risks. In one study, Dante Cicchetti and his colleagues found evidence that the genes that children inherit from parents who suffer from conditions such as depression produce patterns of neurotransmitter functioning that differ from those of children whose parents do not have such conditions (Cicchetti, Rogosch, & Sturge-Apple, 2007). These neurotransmitter differences produce variations in how children respond to abuse. Such findings suggest that inherited risks may produce atypical development only in the presence of high-risk environmental factors such as abuse. Similarly, factors such as abuse may produce atypical development only in children who have inherited vulnerabilities. At the same time, protective factors—such as loving relationships with caregivers—may moderate the interaction between inherited and environmental risk factors such that a child's development does not differ from that of other children (Charuvastra & Cloitre, 2008).

This kind of complex interplay between risk and protective factors is another hallmark of developmental psychopathology. Consider the risks associated with a difficult temperament, for example (Rothbart, 2007). These risks are magnified when they are combined with harsh parenting, an approach to child-rearing that parents have usually learned from their own parents. Yet parents who have higher levels of education than their own parents usually do not model the harsh child-rearing strategies of their own parents (Serbin & Karp, 2003). Thus, the developmental pathway that a child with the internal risk factor of difficult temperament follows is influenced by how his parents respond to him, a factor that can serve to either increase or decrease the chances of a poor developmental outcome. At the same time, the parents' own experiences as children and those that they have had since contribute to how they respond to the child. As this example illustrates, developmental psychopathology provides explanations of atypical development that are far more comprehensive than those derived from the classical theories.

Developmental psychopathologists also include normative age-graded changes, developmental milestones that all children experience, in their explanations of atypical development. For example, a child's stage of cognitive development influences how she interprets an event that can increase her risk of an atypical developmental outcome. A teenager and a preschooler, for example, may be affected quite differently by a risk factor such as abuse because of their cognitive-developmental differences (Abela & Hankin, 2008; Walker, 2002). Moreover, experiencing such a risk may lead to neurological changes that can affect the subsequent cognitive development of both the teenager and the preschooler (Gillespie & Nemeroff, 2007).

*Whether a child or teenager will show a behavior problem in response to stress such as moving to a new home will depend in part on whether he faces other stresses or life changes at the same time—such as perhaps his parents' divorce.*

**developmental psychopathology**
A relatively new approach to the study of deviance that emphasizes that normal and abnormal development have common roots and that pathology can arise from many different pathways.

Finally, the *lifespan perspective*, the view that change occurs throughout life, is fundamental to developmental psychopathology (Wicks-Nelson & Israel, 1997). A maladaptive change at one point in development may be moderated or even reversed later on. Likewise, an adaptive change at one point in life can be threatened by later events. For example, a child's need for physical and emotional support in infancy may lead her to develop the sense of trust that Erikson described in his account of psychosexual development. However, if someone violates her trust at a later point, she may become generally distrustful of others. This distrust may lead to changes in behavior that increase the risk of some kind of maladaptive outcome. For instance, she may isolate herself for fear of being disappointed again.

## Attention Problems and Externalizing Problems

You will recall that attention problems include disorders in which children's ability to concentrate seems to be impaired. Externalizing problems are disorders that involve outwardly directed inappropriate behaviors, such as aggression.

## Attention Deficit Hyperactivity Disorder

A glance at the diagnostic criteria for **attention deficit hyperactivity disorder (ADHD)**, listed in Table 15.2 on page 378, reveals that the hallmarks of this disorder are physical restlessness and problems with attention—precisely what the name implies. Russell Barkley (2005), one of the major researchers and theorists on ADHD, suggests that the underlying problem is a deficit in the child's ability to inhibit behavior—to keep himself from starting some prohibited or unhelpful behavior or from reacting to some compelling stimulus or to stop behaving in some fashion once he has started. In busy, complex environments with many stimuli (such as a classroom), children with ADHD are unable to inhibit their reactions to all the sounds and sights around them, so they appear restless and cannot focus sustained attention on a single activity.

**DEFINING THE PROBLEM** Whether this constellation of problems constitutes a single syndrome or several distinct subvarieties is still a matter of active debate. You'll note that the criteria in Table 15.2 on page 378 are divided into two sets, those dealing with attention problems and those dealing with hyperactivity, suggesting the existence of two subtypes of ADHD: (1) **ADHD/hyperactive/impulsive type**, in which a high activity level is the main problem, and (2) **ADHD/inattentive type**, in which an inability to sustain attention is the major difficulty (DSM-IV TR, 2000). In addition, some children are diagnosed with **ADHD/combined type**, signifying that they meet the criteria for both the hyperactive/impulsive and the inattentive type.

Diagnosing ADHD is made all the more difficult by the fact that a great many children are inattentive or overactive at least some of the time. Both teachers and parents can be tempted to label a boisterous or talkative child as having ADHD. There is no doubt that a good deal of mislabeling of this kind does occur. Further, experimental studies have shown that, on many attention tasks, children diagnosed with ADHD do not differ from nondiagnosed children at all (Lawrence et al., 2004). Where children with ADHD do seem to differ markedly from other children is in their capacity to sustain attention when engaged in boring, repetitive tasks (DSM-IV TR, 2000). They also seem to be less able than other children of the same age to control impulses.

**CULTURE, AGE, GENDER, AND ETHNICITY** ADHD is diagnosed more frequently in the United States than in other countries with similar cultures (Polanczyk, de Lima, Horta, Biederman, & Rohde, 2007). Between 8% and 10% of school-aged children in the United States are diagnosed with ADHD, compared to 3% to 5% of children in France, for example (Gahagan, 2011; Lecendreux, Konofal, & Faraone, 2011). Some developmentalists suggest that this cross-national difference is the result of overuse of the diagnosis in the United States, an assertion that has been refuted by research (Cuffe, Moore, & McKeown, 2005). Others suggest that educators and mental health professionals in other nations have failed to recognize the degree to which ADHD is prevalent in their children (Polanczyk et al., 2007). One very thorough review of cross-national differences in ADHD prevalence

**attention deficit hyperactivity disorder (ADHD)** A disorder in which a child shows both significant problems in focusing attention and physical hyperactivity.

**ADHD/hyperactive/impulsive type** ADHD in which hyperactivity is the main problem.

**ADHD/inattentive type** ADHD in which inattention is the main problem.

**ADHD/combined type** ADHD in which both hyperactivity and inattention are problems.

←------------Learning Objective 15.4
What diagnostic labels are given to children who have attention problems?

## Table 15.2 DIAGNOSTIC CRITERIA FOR ATTENTION DEFICIT HYPERACTIVITY DISORDER

- The child must show either significant *inattention* or significant *hyperactivity-impulsivity* (or both).

- Inattention is indicated by any six or more of the following:
  1. Often fails to give close attention to details or makes careless mistakes in schoolwork or other activities.
  2. Often has difficulty sustaining attention in tasks or play.
  3. Often does not seem to listen when spoken to directly.
  4. Often does not follow through on instructions and fails to finish chores, homework, or duties.
  5. Often has difficulty organizing tasks and activities.
  6. Often avoids, dislikes, or is reluctant to engage in tasks that require sustained mental effort.
  7. Often loses things necessary for tasks or activities (e.g., toys, pencils, books, tools).
  8. Is often easily distracted by extraneous stimuli.
  9. Is often forgetful in daily activities.

- Hyperactivity-impulsivity is indicated by the presence of six of the following, persisting over a period of at least six months:
  1. Often fidgets with hands or feet or squirms in seat.
  2. Often leaves seat in classroom or in other situations in which remaining seated is expected.
  3. Often runs about or climbs excessively or reports feeling of restlessness.
  4. Often has difficulty playing quietly.
  5. Is often "on the go" or often acts as if "driven by a motor."
  6. Often talks excessively.
  7. Often blurts out answers before questions are completed.
  8. Often has difficulty waiting for a turn.
  9. Often interrupts or intrudes on others.

- The onset of the problem must be before age 7.

- At least some of the symptoms must be present in two or more settings, such as home and school or school and play with peers.

- The behavior must interfere with developmentally appropriate social, academic, or occupational functioning.

*Source:* Reprinted with permission from the *Diagnostic and Statistical Manual of Mental Disorders*, 4th edition, Text Revision (Copyright © 2000). American Psychiatric Association.

suggested that underlying rates of ADHD-like behavior are highly similar around the world, but variations in the way the disorder is diagnosed lead to differences in ADHD rates across nations (Polanczyk et al., 2007).

Age is also related to ADHD prevalence. The data in Table 15.3 reveal that rates of ADHD diagnosis increase over the elementary school years (Visser & Lesesne, 2005). As school becomes more difficult, the characteristics of the disorder cause problems for more children. Many of those who are diagnosed in the later grades were able to succeed at the less challenging work in the early grades without additional help. Declines in diagnosis rates in adolescence may be attributable to maturational factors that help some children with ADHD compensate for attention difficulties.

The table also clearly shows the striking gender difference in ADHD diagnosis and treatment. Part of this difference is due to the finding that girls are more likely to exhibit symptoms of the inattentive and combined types of ADHD than the hyperactive type (Gahagan, 2011). Boys show the opposite pattern; that is, they are more likely to be hyperactive and disruptive. Thus, teachers and parents may be more likely to notice boys' problems and seek help for them. Girls' symptoms, by contrast, may be attributed to laziness, moodiness, or a lack of interest in school. However, the gender difference may also represent an overreaction to boys'

| Table 15.3 | AGE, GENDER, ETHNICITY, AND ADHD | | | |
| --- | --- | --- | --- | --- |
| | Percentage Diagnosed with ADHD | | Percentage Taking Medication for ADHD | |
| | Male | Female | Male | Female |
| **Age** | | | | |
| 4–8 | 6 | 2 | 4 | 2 |
| 9–12 | 14 | 10 | 9 | 4 |
| 13–17 | 14 | 10 | 7 | 2 |
| **Race** | | | | |
| White | 12 | 5 | 7 | 3 |
| Black | 12 | 4 | 6 | 2 |
| Multiracial | 14 | 6 | 7 | 3 |
| Other | 7 | 2 | 3 | 1 |
| **Ethnicity** | | | | |
| Hispanic | 5 | 3 | 2 | 1 |
| Non-Hispanic | 12 | 2 | 7 | 3 |
| **Primary Language in the Home** | | | | |
| English | 12 | 5 | 7 | 3 |
| Other | 2 | 1 | <1 | <1 |

*Source:* Visser & Lesene, 2005 From *Morbidity and Mortality Weekly Report*, a federal government publication.

greater general rowdiness. Thus, some speculate that gender differences in ADHD diagnosis result from "medicalization" of typical male behavior, a view that remains controversial (Timimi & Leo, 2009).

Table 15.3 also shows that ADHD diagnosis and medication rates in the United States are consistent across White, African American, and multiracial groups. However, rates are far lower among Hispanic American children (Visser & Lesesne, 2005). This difference could be due to a real difference in children's behavior across groups, overdiagnosis in non-Hispanic groups, or underdiagnosis in Hispanic Americans. With regard to the first of these possibilities, surveys of teachers suggest that the kinds of behavior problems that lead to a diagnosis of ADHD occur just as frequently among Hispanic American children as they do in others (Ham, 2004). As for the second possible explanation, extensive surveys of parents, teachers, and health-care professionals, together with the high degree of consistency in diagnosis rates across non-Hispanic subgroups, suggest that ADHD is not overdiagnosed among them (Cuffe, Moore, & McKeown, 2005). The data shown in the table regarding language and ADHD diagnosis support the third possibility: that ADHD is underdiagnosed among Hispanic American children. It is likely that language differences among parents, teachers, and health-care professionals prevent the establishment of the kind of communication among them that is needed to diagnose ADHD. In other words, Hispanic American children whose parents speak English are more likely to be diagnosed with ADHD, or, put differently, those whose families do not speak English are at increased risk of not being diagnosed and treated for this troubling condition. These findings highlight the need for multilingual professionals in schools and health-care settings.

Children with ADHD are more physically active than peers. Many, like this girl, are also exceptionally adventurous.

**ORIGINS OF THE PROBLEM** Where might ADHD come from? Because the behavioral pattern begins so early and has such a strong physical component, most clinicians have assumed that this problem has some kind of biological origin. Early research failed to confirm a biological hypothesis, but more recent evidence makes clear that ADHD is a neuropsychiatric disorder (Kagan & Herschkowitz, 2005). Three converging lines of evidence support that conclusion.

First, physicians and psychologists have known for some time that a biological treatment is very often effective in reducing or eliminating the deviant behavior. Many children with ADHD in the United States are treated with a stimulant medication called methylphenidate (the most commonly used brand-name drug is Ritalin). The drug works by stimulating the part of the brain that maintains attention. About 70–90% of children treated with this drug show improvement, including decreases in demanding, disruptive, and noncompliant behaviors; lessened aggressiveness and noncompliance; more attentiveness in the classroom; and improved performance on many academic tasks (Pelham et al., 2002; Ridderinkhof, Scheres, Oosterlaan, & Sergeant, 2005). This evidence is consistent with a biological explanation for ADHD. More specifically, it suggests that the problem may lie in one of the brain's neurotransmitters, because stimulant medications of the type used with children with ADHD act by altering the action of monoamine, one of the key neurotransmitters (Kado & Takagi, 1996).

Additional evidence for an underlying biological cause comes from research in behavior genetics, which suggests that a pattern of hyperactivity is inherited, at least in certain families (Gahagan, 2011). About one-quarter of the parents of hyperactive children themselves have a history of hyperactivity. Studies of twins also suggest there is a genetic contribution. Among identical twins, if one is diagnosed as hyperactive, the other is highly likely to have the same diagnosis; among fraternal twins, this concordance rate is much lower (Kado & Takagi, 1996). Evidence suggesting that inheritance may also indirectly influence the development of ADHD comes from research showing that temperament is related to ADHD. Children who are low in *effortful control* (look back at Chapter 9) are more likely to be diagnosed with the disorder than are their peers who get higher ratings on scales that measure this aspect of temperament (Chang & Burns, 2005). Likewise, longitudinal research has shown that infants who are very outgoing are more likely to be diagnosed with externalizing disorders, including ADHD, when they enter preschool than are infants who are less outgoing (Putnam & Stifter, 2005).

Finally, brain-imaging diagnostic methods have begun to reveal subtle differences in brain structure and brain function between individuals with and without ADHD (Kagan & Herschkowitz, 2005). For example, studies using magnetic resonance imaging (MRI) suggest that the brains of children with ADHD respond differently to emotion-provoking stimuli than those of other children (Schlochtermeier et al., 2011). In addition, electroencephalographic studies show different patterns of electrical activity in the brains of children with ADHD than in those of children without ADHD Barry et al., 2011).

**TREATING AND MANAGING ADHD** We noted earlier that 70–90% of children with ADHD respond to treatment with stimulant drugs (Pelham et al., 2002; Ridderinkhof, Scheres, Oosterlaan, & Sergeant, 2005). As Table 15.3 shows, about half of children with ADHD take these medications. Differences between diagnosis and medication rates are due partly to some parents' initial choices regarding treatment for the disorder. However, nonadherence to medical advice is probably a larger factor. Longitudinal studies show that one in five children who are prescribed medication for ADHD stops taking it within 4 to 6 months (Sanchez, Crismon, Barner, Bettinger, & Wilson, 2005). The primary reason for treatment termination is parents' view that their children should not be taking psychiatric medications.

Recently, too, researchers have warned against the routine prescribing of stimulant drugs for children who exhibit mild symptoms of ADHD. These researchers point to studies showing that methylphenidate increases the risk of cardiovascular disease and that newer medications (e.g., Adderall) are associated with changes in thinking that may increase a child's risk of developing a more serious psychological disorder (Gardner, 2007). As a result, physicians are prescribing drugs for mild cases of ADHD less often than in the past and are instead recommending that parents and teachers try behavioral approaches before resorting to medication (Gahagan, 2011). ◉─Watch at **MyDevelopmentLab**

◉─Watch the **Videos** *Attention Deficit Disorder, Medicating Kids with ADD,* and *Alternative Approaches to Treating ADHD* at **MyDevelopmentLab**

## Oppositional Defiant Disorder

◀────────Learning Objective 15.5
What behaviors are associated with oppositional defiant disorder?

Children with **oppositional defiant disorder (ODD)** display a pattern of negative, defiant, disobedient, and hostile behavior toward their parents and other authority figures, established prior to age 8 (DSM-IV TR, 2000). Many children who have ADHD are also diagnosed with ODD. Estimates of the prevalence of ODD among children with ADHD range from 21% to 60% (Austin, Reiss, & Burgdorf, 2007). Among children who are not diagnosed with ADHD, the prevalence of ODD has been estimated to fall between 2% and 16% (DSM-IV TR, 2000).

Children with ODD are difficult to manage, as you might guess. They tend to display defiant behaviors most often with the people they know best, such as their parents, siblings, teachers, and classmates. When interacting with people whom they do not know well, children with ODD often behave appropriately. For instance, many children with this disorder seem to be quite easy-going the first time they are interviewed by a psychologist or other mental health professional. Thus, diagnosing a child with ODD can be challenging. Diagnostic procedures must include assessments of the child's behavior across a variety of settings. Even so, it is not unusual for a child's parent and regular classroom teacher to report that his behavior fits the ODD profile, while others who interact less often with the child, such as a physical education or music teacher, report having no problems with the child.

The cause of ODD is unknown, but researchers have identified several important themes in its manifestation (Tynan, 2008). One is that, as is true of ADHD, males are diagnosed with ODD more often than females are. Temperament is a factor as well; most children with ODD displayed difficult temperaments in infancy. Some studies suggest that prenatal exposure to alcohol, nicotine, and other teratogens increases a child's chances of being diagnosed with ODD. Many parents of children with ODD suffer from emotional disturbances such as anxiety disorders and depression. A high degree of marital conflict is also often found among the parents of children with ODD.

If a child has both ADHD and ODD, medication may be prescribed for her ADHD symptoms, but the symptoms of ODD are treated with parent training (Tynan, 2008). Training is the treatment of choice because, by the time they consult with a mental health professional, parents of children with ODD have usually established a pattern for responding to their children's troublesome behavior that serves only to perpetuate it. Most such parents respond to their children's behavior by giving in to their demands in order to obtain brief reprieves from the perpetual hostility, argumentativeness, and disobedience. You should recognize this response pattern as negative reinforcement: The symptoms of ODD are an aversive stimulus that subsides temporarily when the parent gives the child whatever she wants. Thus, the behaviors of both the child and the parent are reinforced, and a maladaptive cycle is repeated each time the child misbehaves. In parent training sessions, therapists teach parents of children with ODD to break the cycle. They learn to set concrete limits for the child's behavior and to stick to promised consequences, no matter how difficult or outrageous the child's behavior becomes.

**oppositional defiant disorder (ODD)** A pattern of negative, defiant, disobedient, and hostile behavior toward parents and other authority figures, established prior to age 8.

**conduct disorder** Diagnostic term for a pattern of deviant behavior including high levels of aggressive, antisocial, or delinquent acts.

**childhood-onset conduct disorder** Conduct disorder beginning in childhood; the pattern is linked to rejection by peers and to conduct problems that persist into adolescence and adulthood.

## Conduct Disorder

◀────────Learning Objective 15.6
What are childhood-onset and adolescent-onset conduct disorders, and how do they differ from delinquency?

The broadest category of externalizing problems is what might be referred to in everyday speech as "antisocial behavior." The American Psychiatric Association's *Diagnostic and Statistical Manual of Mental Disorders* (or DSM) defines **conduct disorder** (CD) as a pattern of behavior that includes high levels of aggression, argumentativeness, bullying, disobedience, irritability, and threatening and loud behavior.

**CHILDHOOD-ONSET CONDUCT DISORDER** The features of oppositional defiant disorder are associated with **childhood-onset conduct disorder**, a pattern of behavior that includes high

**adolescent-onset conduct disorder**
A conduct disorder that begins only in adolescence; it is typically less severe and persistent than childhood-onset conduct disorder.

levels of aggression, argumentativeness, bullying, disobedience, irritability, and threatening and loud behavior and begins before a child is 10 years of age. Essentially, childhood-onset conduct disorder is diagnosed if a child has all the characteristics of ODD and also engages in threatening and/or aggressive behavior toward others and repetitively violates important social rules (e.g., stealing).

Very often, children who are diagnosed with childhood-onset conduct disorder begin life with a range of vulnerabilities, including difficult temperament, lower intelligence, or both (Bernstein & Pataki, 2011). In the preschool years, these children very often throw tantrums and defy parents. They are very difficult children to handle. If the parents are not up to the task of controlling the child, the child's behavior worsens and becomes overt aggression toward others, who then reject the child.

During the school years, these children are less likely than peers to be able to empathize with others' feelings, a social-cognitive deficit that leads to peer rejection (Bernstein & Pataki, 2011). Such peer rejection aggravates the problem, pushing the seriously aggressive child in the direction of other children with similar problems, who become the child's only supportive peer group. By adolescence, these youngsters are firmly established in delinquent or antisocial behavior, and their friends are drawn almost exclusively from among other delinquent teens. They are also highly likely to display a cluster of other problem behaviors, including drug and alcohol use, truancy or dropping out of school, and early and risky sexual behavior, including having multiple sexual partners.

There is also some indication that childhood-onset conduct disorder has a strong genetic component (Oosterlaan, Geurts, Knol, & Sergeant, 2005). Thus, the preschooler who already shows defiant and oppositional behavior as well as aggressiveness may have strong inborn propensities for such behavior. Moreover, brain imaging studies indicate that the brain structures that regulate emotion and planning in children with CD are less fully developed than those of children who do not have the disorder (Huebner et al., 2008). But whether that propensity develops into a full-fledged, persisting conduct disorder will depend on the interactions between the inborn tendency and other aspects of the child's life, including the parents' ability to handle the child's early defiance (Bernstein & Pataki, 2011).

**ADOLESCENT-ONSET CONDUCT DISORDER**    When a child exhibits the features of conduct disorder at age 11 or later, he is given the diagnosis of **adolescent-onset conduct disorder**. In contrast to those with childhood-onset conduct disorder, teens who are diagnosed with the adolescent-onset form of the disorder tend to manifest antisocial behaviors that are milder, more transitory, and more a function of hanging out with bad companions than a deeply ingrained behavior problem (DSM-IV TR, 2000). Moreover, the antisocial behavior patterns of those with adolescent-onset conduct disorder often change as their relationships change. Consequently, peer influence seems to be the most important factor in the development of adolescent-onset conduct disorder.

Parenting style and other relationship variables seem to be additional factors in this type of antisocial behavior. Several studies show that authoritarian parenting increases the risk of adolescent-onset conduct disorder (Smith & Farrington, 2004). Thus, it may be that parents who do not balance strict supervision with recognition of teenagers' need to understand the reasons behind parents' rules incite rebellion in some children. However, the cultural context in which parenting occurs matters as well. It seems that the combination of authoritarian parenting and a culture that endorses strict rules and strong enforcement of those rules does not increase the risk of conduct disorder in teens. For example, in most Middle Eastern societies, children whose parents display the authoritarian style are less likely to develop conduct disorder than peers whose families' approaches to discipline do not match the larger culture (Dwairy, 2008).

Permissive parenting is also associated with adolescent-onset conduct disorder. Most teens who develop the disorder have parents who do not monitor them sufficiently, often because there is only one parent in the home (Office of Juvenile Justice and Delinquency Prevention [OJJDP], 2006). Regardless of family structure, when parents provide good monitoring and emotional support, their adolescent children are unlikely to exhibit antisocial behavior even if they hang around with a tough crowd or have close friends who engage in such behavior (Mounts & Steinberg, 1995).  ◉⌐|Watch at **MyDevelopmentLab**

◉⌐|**Watch** the **Video** *Risk-Taking and Delinquency* at **MyDevelopmentLab**

**DELINQUENCY**  **Delinquency** is a narrower category of externalizing problems than conduct disorder; it refers only to intentional law breaking. Clearly, many children who break laws also show other forms of conduct disorder, so the two categories overlap a great deal. Still, the overlap is not total, so it is useful to look at delinquency separately.

Low IQ scores appear to be an important risk factor for delinquency, particularly for children with childhood-onset conduct disorder, for those who show more serious or violent forms of offenses, and for those who experience some school failure (Hämäläinen & Pulkkinen, 1996). The argument offered by Donald Lynam and others (1993) is that school failure reduces a young person's engagement with school and the values it represents. School failure also increases the child's or adolescent's frustration, which raises the likelihood of aggression of some kind. Thus, for many less intelligent young people, the social constraint on delinquent behavior offered by education is simply weaker.

In addition to IQ, variations in self-esteem are related to delinquent behavior. However, there is considerable debate as to whether low or high self-esteem predisposes an adolescent to engage in delinquent behavior. On one side, Brent Donnellan and his colleagues argue that children who develop low self-esteem in elementary school, perhaps brought on by school failure or peer rejection, are more prone to delinquency in later years (Donnellan, Trzesniewski, Robins, Moffitt, & Caspi, 2005). By contrast, Roy Baumeister and others have claimed that the development of an inappropriately high level of self-esteem during childhood, given an individual's real accomplishments, is associated with delinquency (Baumeister, Bushman, & Campbell, 2000; Baumeister, Campbell, Krueger, & Vohs, 2003; Baumeister, Smart, & Boden, 1996). Put differently, Baumeister hypothesizes that *narcissism*, the view that one is the center of the world, is more likely to be at the center of a delinquent teen's sense of self-worth than is low self-esteem. To date, both sides have produced evidence in support of their views (e.g., Witt , Donnellan, & Trzesniewski, 2011; Bushman, Baumeister, Thomaes, & Ryu, 2009) As a result, Donnellan has argued that a researcher should probably think of the kind of low self-esteem he measures as being qualitatively distinct from the narcissism that has been studied by Baumeister's group (Donnellan et al., 2005). He says that it is possible for a delinquent teen both to be narcissistic and to have low self-esteem when he judges himself against the criteria he knows to be part of a cultural definition of "good" people. What seems clear is that teens who display delinquent behavior have views of themselves that distinguish them from adolescents who do not engage in such behaviors.

It is important to emphasize, however, that unlike the broader category of conduct disorders, which are quite stable from childhood to adulthood, the milder forms of delinquency do not invariably or even commonly persist into adulthood. Many teens commit only occasional delinquent acts and show no further problem in adulthood. For them, mild delinquent behavior is merely a phase. It is those who show a syndrome of delinquent acts plus high-risk behavior and come from families with low warmth and ineffective control who are quite likely to engage in criminal acts as adults.

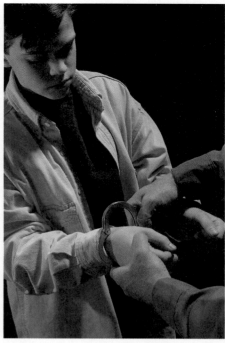

*Childhood-onset conduct disorder is typically more serious than adolescent-onset conduct disorder.*

## Internalizing Problems

As you learned earlier, internalizing problems are so named because they involve deviations from the typical developmental pathway that are directed internally, against the self. Such problems include disturbances of self-concept, as in eating disorders, and disturbances of emotions, as in depression.

## Eating Disorders

More than half of adolescent females and one-quarter of teen males in the United States report that they diet regularly; 5% use extreme measures such as taking diet pills (Eaton et al., 2010). However, dieting is quite different from an *eating disorder*, which is a category of psychiatric disorders in which eating behaviors go far beyond most people's everyday experiences with trying to lose weight. Most importantly, teens with eating disorders have distorted body images and may experience other types of distorted thinking. These disorders,

←------------**Learning Objective 15.7**
How do developmentalists define and explain eating disorders?

**delinquency**  A subcategory of conduct disorder involving explicit lawbreaking.

Watch the Video *Body Image and Eating Disorders* at **MyDevelopmentLab**

**bulimia** Eating disorder characterized by alternating periods of bingeing and purging.

**anorexia nervosa** Eating disorder characterized by self-starvation.

Watch the Videos *Anorexia Nervosa: Kim, Speaking Out: Natasha: Anorexia Nervosa,* and *Living with Anorexia Nervosa* at **MyDevelopmentLab**

*Girls who suffer from anorexia nervosa often have a distorted body image. They see themselves as too fat even when they are severely emaciated.*

which can be fatal, tend to make their first appearance in individuals' lives during the mid to late teens. They are more common among girls than boys, but gay, lesbian, and questioning youth are also at higher risk than their heterosexual peers of developing eating disorders (Austin et al., 2008). Watch at **MyDevelopmentLab**

**BULIMIA** Bulimia (sometimes called *bulimia nervosa*) involves three elements: (1) a preoccupation with eating and an irresistible craving for food, leading to episodes of binge eating; (2) an intense fear of fatness; and (3) some method of purging to counteract the effects of the binge eating so as to avoid weight gain. Typical purging methods are self-induced vomiting, excessive use of laxatives, or excessive exercise (Cushing & Waldrop, 2010). Alternating periods of normal eating and binge eating are common among individuals in all weight groups.

Only when binge eating occurs as often as twice a week and is combined with repeated episodes of some kind of purging is the syndrome properly called bulimia. People with bulimia are ordinarily not exceptionally thin, but they are obsessed with their weight, feel intense shame about their abnormal behavior, and often experience significant depression. The physical consequences of bulimia can include marked tooth decay (from repeated vomiting), stomach irritation, dehydration, lowered body temperature, disturbances of body chemistry, loss of hair, and, in extreme cases, cardiovascular problems (Osterhout, Scher, & Hilty, 2010).

It has been estimated that 5% of adolescent girls and young adult women in the United States show the full syndrome of bulimia (Blake & Davis, 2011). Adolescents most at risk for bulimia are those who live in cultures where slenderness is strongly emphasized, particularly those who wish to pursue a career that demands thinness, such as dance, gymnastics, modeling, or acting (Brownell & Fairburn, 1995). None of these behaviors is found in countries where food is scarce (Gordon, 2001).

**ANOREXIA NERVOSA** Anorexia nervosa is less common than bulimia but potentially more deadly. About 1.5% of teenaged girls in the United States are diagnosed with anorexia nervosa (Blake & Davis, 2011). Anorexia nervosa is characterized by extreme dieting, intense fear of gaining weight, and obsessive exercise. The weight loss eventually produces a variety of physical symptoms associated with starvation: sleep disturbance, cessation of menstruation, insensitivity to pain, loss of hair, low blood pressure, a variety of cardiovascular problems, and reduced body temperature. Researchers estimate that 4% to 8% of people with anorexia literally starve themselves to death; others die because of some type of cardiovascular dysfunction (Cushing & Waldrop, 2010). Watch at **MyDevelopmentLab**

**CAUSES OF EATING DISORDERS** Of the two eating disorders, bulimia is considerably easier to treat; people who have anorexia frequently have relapses or develop bulimia, even after extensive treatment (Blake & Davis, 2011). Explaining either disorder has proved to be exceptionally difficult. Both bulimia and anorexia typically begin with persistent dieting, reinforcing the idea that eating disorders represent the extreme end of a continuum that includes other forms of concern about weight (Cooper, 1995; Polivy & Herman, 1995). Such a link between dieting and eating disorders is further strengthened by evidence that in countries such as Taiwan, Singapore, and China, where dieting has become a recent fad, eating disorders, which were almost never seen in the past, are becoming more common (Lai, Tang, & Tse, 2005). Yet a great many young women (and some young men) diet regularly, even obsessively, but never develop an actual eating disorder. So, what moves a dieter from "normal" dieting into bulimia or anorexia?

Some theorists have proposed biological causes for eating disorders, such as some kind of brain dysfunction in the case of bulimia. Heredity may contribute to eating disorders, as well (Bernstein, 2010; Osterhout, Scher, & Hilty, 2010). Others argue for a psychoanalytic explanation, perhaps a fear of growing up. Childhood sexual abuse also appears to predispose girls to develop eating disorders (Perkins & Luster, 1997; Wonderlich et al., 2001). Family variables, such as the quality of a girl's parents' marriage, may also be important factors (Blake & Davis, 2011).

The most promising explanation of eating disorders, however, may lie in the discrepancy between the young person's internal image of a desirable body and her perception of her own body (McGee, Hewitt, Sherry, Parkin, & Flett, 2005). This explanation is supported by cross-cultural research demonstrating that adolescents in Western societies, who have the highest rates of eating disorders, are more likely to have negative body images than adolescents in non-Western societies (Makino, Tsuboi, & Dennerstein, 2004). Moreover, some developmentalists suggest that Western culture's emphasis on thinness as a requirement for attractiveness in a woman contributes to the prevalence of eating disorders.

Recent thinking, however, has placed more emphasis on the pre-existing psychological health of people who develop eating disorders than on cultural influences. Some researchers assert that the body images of individuals who suffer from eating disorders are the result of a general tendency toward distorted thinking (Dyl, Kittler, Phillips, & Hunt, 2006). In other words, these researchers say that people who have eating disorders tend to think in distorted ways about many things, not just their bodies. From this perspective, internalized images of the "perfect" body fuel the sales of diet products among psychologically healthy people, but they trigger a far more serious outcome, a true eating disorder, in individuals who have a tendency toward thought distortion. Thus, advertising may have a more powerful effect on an adolescent who has a general tendency toward distorted perceptions of herself and others than it does on teens who tend to view themselves and others more realistically. For instance, many young women who suffer from bulimia have also been diagnosed with *borderline personality disorder*, a psychiatric disorder in which individuals have irrational, unfounded fears that those they love will abandon them, as well as a host of other distorted perceptions (Halmi, 2003).

Longitudinal evidence seems to support this view. One study of young women who had been diagnosed with anorexia in adolescence, 94% of whom had recovered from their eating disorders, found that they were far more likely than the general population to suffer from a variety of mental disorders (Nilsson, Gillberg, Gillberg, & Rastam, 1999). Estimates of the proportion of young women who suffer from eating disorders and who also meet the criteria for some other type of psychiatric disorder range as high as 74% (Milos, Spindler, & Schnyder, 2004). An unusually high proportion of them, nearly 25%, have been diagnosed with *obsessive-compulsive disorder*, a disorder that involves an excessive need for control (American Psychiatric Association, 2000; Milos, Spindler, Ruggiero, Klaghofer, & Schnyder, 2002). These findings suggest that, for many teens, eating disorders may be a manifestation of some larger problem.

## Depression

You might be surprised to learn that, in some cases, emotional disorders in children are manifested as behaviors that are consistent with the criteria for attention deficit hyperactivity disorder and oppositional-defiant disorder (see *Thinking about Research* on page 386). Consequently, when children have behavior problems, mental health professionals often must rule out an emotional disorder as a possible cause before giving the child a diagnosis of ADHD, ODD, or childhood-onset conduct disorder. In addition, a child can be suffering from both a behavior disorder and **depression**, or feelings of sadness and despair that persist for more than 6 months (DSM-IV TR, 2000)

**DEFINING THE PROBLEM**  For many years, psychiatrists took the position that children or adolescents did not experience significant depression. This turned out to be quite wrong. Researchers have found abundant evidence that depression is actually quite common in adolescence and occurs at least occasionally among younger children. When a depressed mood lasts 6 months or longer and is accompanied by other symptoms, such as disturbances of sleeping and eating and difficulty concentrating, it is usually referred to as **clinical depression** or **major depressive disorder** (MDD). Although about 10% of children express feelings of deep sadness at some time or another, true clinical depression is very rare prior to adolescence. However, surveys and case studies suggest that, at any given time, 5% of adolescents in the United States are in the midst of an enduring depression (Benton, 2010). Some 11% of males and 22% of females report having experienced bouts of depression at some time during the teen years (Benton, 2010). The symptoms can include decreased or

**depression**  A combination of sad mood and difficulty carrying out daily functions.

**clinical depression (major depressive disorder)**  A combination of sad mood, sleeping and eating disturbances, and difficulty concentrating that lasts 6 months or longer.

◄ - - - - - - - - - - - **Learning Objective 15.8**
What factors predispose teens to major depressive disorder?

## Pediatric Bipolar Disorder

As you may know, 1% to 3% of adults suffer from a mood disorder called *bipolar disorder (BD)*. Adults who have BD alternate between periods of deep despair and *mania*. A person in a manic state has a great deal of energy, tends to be impulsive, has a reduced need for sleep, and exhibits high activity levels.

While it is generally agreed that BD is sometimes found in adolescents, the notion that school-aged children can be diagnosed with BD is controversial (Harris, 2005). The difficulty with applying the BD diagnosis to children is that mania has been found to exist only in individuals who have completed pubertal development (Harris, 2005). However, over the past two decades, a robust debate has arisen among mental health professionals about the claim that, in childhood, mania is manifested as episodes of explosive rage and a decreased need for sleep (Meyer, Fuhr, Hautzinger, & Schlarb, 2011; NIMH, 2001; Wozniak et al., 2005). Children who exhibit such episodes along with periods of depression are said to suffer from a form of BD called *pediatric bipolar disorder (PBD)*. However, there are many professionals who doubt the validity of the PBD diagnosis.

Developmentalists who are skeptical of the PBD diagnosis argue that most children who exhibit bouts of destructive rage are simply reeling from the effects of multiple risk factors rather than exhibiting a childhood form BD (Bossewitch, 2010). Specifically, say critics, children who are diagnosed with PBD are those who have difficult temperaments, suffer from extreme forms of developmental problems such as ADHD and/or ODD, and have been exposed to stress-inducing traumas such as family disruption (Harris, 2005). Moreover, they point out that, in adulthood, bipolar disorder is stable over the life-span, but longitudinal studies show that children who are diagnosed with PBD rarely grow into adults who fit the criteria for BD (Harris, 2005).

The strongest arguments against PBD are proposed by developmentalists who object to the use of powerful psychiatric drugs such as lithium to treat children who are diagnosed with the proposed disorder (Bossewitch, 2010; Harris, 2005; Olfman, 2006). These critics note that little is known about the effects of these drugs on the developing brain. Moreover, they point out that reliance on medications may cause parents not to receive other therapeutic interventions that might be

helpful in managing their children's difficult behavior. They strongly believe that a great deal more research is needed both on proposed diagnostic criteria and on the effects of psychiatric drugs on development before mental health professionals begin to routinely apply the PBD diagnosis.

### Learning Objective 15.8a

What are the arguments for and against diagnosing children with pediatric bipolar disorder?

### CRITICAL ANALYSIS

1. What is the significance of the finding that children with PBD rarely display BD in adulthood?
2. What kind of study would have to be done to determine how psychiatric drugs affect the developing brain? Look back at the discussion of research ethics in Chapter 1 and make a determination regarding the ethical requirements of such a study.

---

increased need for sleep, loss of interest in and enjoyment of usual activities, inappropriate feelings of guilt, loss of energy, problems with concentration, appetite change, and suicidal thoughts or actions (Scheffer, 2011).

As many as 50% of teens who suffer a major depressive episode experience a recurrence within 2 years (Scheffer, 2011). Further, depression has serious consequences. For one thing,

*Both depressed mood and significant clinical depressions rise in frequency in adolescence.*

depression can interfere with learning by slowing down the speed at which the brain processes information (Calhoun & Dickerson Mayes, 2005). Teens with depression are more likely than their nondepressed peers to use drugs (Rey, Sawyer, Raphael, Patton, & Lynskey, 2002). And a significant portion of teens with depression also say that they think about suicide (Fennig et al., 2005). **⊙▸⌐Simulate** at **MyDevelopmentLab**

**⊙▸⌐Simulate** the **Experiment**
*Experiment Ineffective Therapies* at
**MyDevelopmentLab**

Interestingly, during the preadolescent years, boys and girls are about equally likely to be unhappy or depressed; however, beginning somewhere between ages 13 and 15, girls are twice as likely to report high or chronic levels of depression (Scheffer, 2011). This sex difference persists throughout adulthood and has been found in a number of industrialized countries and among African Americans, Hispanic Americans, and Caucasian Americans (DSM-IV TR, 2000).

**CAUSES OF DEPRESSION**   Where does such depression come from, and why do girls experience more of it? The search for the developmental pathways leading to later depression begins with the clear finding that children growing up with parents with depression are much more likely than are those growing up with nondepressed parents to develop depression themselves (Eley et al., 2004). Of course, this finding could indicate a genetic factor, a possibility supported by at least a few studies of twins and adopted children (Petersen et al., 1993). Studies show that, in girls, the *hypothalamic-pituitary-adrenal (HPA) axis*, the network of structures that produces stress hormones, is more sensitive in girls than it is in boys (Oldenhinkel, & Bouma, 2011). Such research supports the argument that intra-familial correlations are biological in nature. Or, this link between parental and child depression could be explained in terms of the changes in the parent-child interaction that are caused by the parent's depression.

However, family and twin studies do not explain why the risk of depression increases in adolescence. Neuroimaging studies show that the sudden spike in depression rates in early adolescence may be related to some kind of dysfunction in the body's stress response system that is associated with the onset of puberty (Romeo, 2010). Pituitary dysfunction, in turn, may cause adolescents to be more sensitive to family stressors than younger children are. Any combination of stresses—such as the parents' divorce, the death of a parent or another loved person, the father's loss of job, a move, a change of schools, or lack of sleep—increases the likelihood of depression or other kinds of emotional distress to a greater degree among adolescents than among children (Compas, Ey, & Grant, 1993; Fredriksen, Rhodes, Reddy, & Way, 2004). **⊙▸⌐Watch** at **MyDevelopmentLab**

**⊙▸⌐Watch** the **Video** *Depression Among the Amish* at **MyDevelopmentLab**

## Adolescent Suicide

◄-----------Learning Objective 15.9
What risk factors are associated
with teen suicide?

In some teens, sadly, the suicidal thoughts that often accompany depression lead to action. Surveys suggest that 15% of high school students in the United States have thought seriously about taking their own lives, and 7% have actually attempted suicide (CDC, 2010). A very small proportion of teens, about 10 out of every 100,000, succeed in killing themselves (Xu, Kochanek, Murphy, & Tejada-Vera, 2010). However, public health experts point out that many teen deaths, such as those that result from single-car crashes, may be counted as accidental but are actually suicide (NCIPC, 2000).

Even though depression is more common among girls than boys, the likelihood of succeeding in committing suicide is almost five times as high among adolescent boys as among adolescent girls (Heron, 2007). In contrast, suicide *attempts* are estimated to be three times more common in girls than in boys (CDC, 2007). Girls, more often than boys, use less successful methods, such as self-poisoning.

The suicide rate is also nearly twice as high among Whites as among non-Whites, except for Native American youth, who attempt and commit suicide at higher rates than any other group (Heron, 2007). The rate among Native American teen males is about 25 per 100,000 per year, compared with about 12 per 100,000 among Caucasian American teen males, 9 per 100,000 among Asian American and Hispanic American adolescent males, and 7 per 100,000 among African American male youths. Similarly, Hispanic American teen males are more

# TECHNOLOGY AND THE DEVELOPING CHILD

## Suicide and Social Networking

A series of teen suicides in the Welsh town of Bridgend received a great deal of media attention (Salkeld & Koster, 2008). Several of the teens knew each other personally, but others were connected to the group only through online relationships. Many of them openly discussed the group's suicide plans on social networking sites, even going so far as to post messages about the dates on which they planned to kill themselves. None of the teachers or parents of these teens were aware that their children had been discussing suicide online, but many of their peers were.

Investigations of the Bridgend case and others like it have revealed that near-universal access to the Internet and teens' facility with the skills needed to create online videos and sophisticated websites have given those who desire to gain celebrity status through committing suicide in an attention-getting means

of doing so (Naito, 2007; Nicolis, 2007; Birbal et al., 2009). Furthermore, these tools enable teens to participate in suicide pact groups that, at least potentially, can span the globe. Digital messages about planned suicides like those that the Bridgend teens posted spread across the globe with lightning speed. Many contain embedded links that teens can follow to online memorials created by teen suicide victims prior to their deaths. Other embedded links point teens to online instructions for different ways of committing suicide (Scott & Temporini, 2010).

Research suggests that training parents and teachers to recognize signs of depression and substance abuse can help prevent suicide in individual teens (Galaif, Sussman, Newcomb, & Locke, 2007). However, group suicides that involve social media may be driven by a desire for fame as well as emotional difficulties such as depression.

**Learning Objective 15.9a**
What role does social networking play in adolescent group suicide?

Consequently, mental health professionals acknowledge that much more research needs to be done before they will be able to provide parents and teachers with advice on a way to prevent group suicides (Naito, 2007).

### FIND OUT MORE

*Use your Internet search skills to answer these questions.*

1. What types of suicide prevention resources are available on the Substance Abuse and Mental Health Services Administration (SAMHSA) website?
2. What role has the Internet played in cases of individual teen suicides?

---

likely to attempt suicide than Whites, although the rate of completed suicide among them is lower (NCIPC, 2011).

It is obviously very difficult to uncover the contributing factors in completed suicides, because the individuals are no longer available to be interviewed. Nonetheless, it does seem clear that some kind of significant psychopathology is virtually a universal ingredient, including but not restricted to depression. Behavior problems such as aggression are also common in the histories of completed suicides, as is a family history of psychiatric disorder or suicide, or a pattern of drug or alcohol abuse (Fennig et al., 2005; Garland & Zigler, 1993; Glowinski et al., 2001). In addition, psychologists suggest at least three other important elements (Shaffer, Garland, Gould, Fisher, & Trautman, 1988; Swedo et al., 1991):

- *Some triggering stressful event.* Studies of suicides suggest that the triggering event is often a disciplinary crisis with the parents or some rejection or humiliation, such as breaking up with a girlfriend or boyfriend or failure in a valued activity.
- *An altered mental state.* Such a state might be an attitude of hopelessness, reduced inhibitions from alcohol consumption, or rage.
- *An opportunity.* For example, a loaded gun available in the house or a bottle of sleeping pills in the parents' medicine cabinet creates an opportunity for a teen to carry out suicidal plans.

Suicide prevention efforts have focused on education, such as providing training to teachers or to teenagers on how to identify students who are at risk for suicide, in the hope that vulnerable individuals might be helped before they make an attempt (see *Technology and the Developing Child*). For example, self-mutilating behavior such as carving the skin with sharp objects is correlated with extreme feelings of loneliness and hopelessness, two emotions that often lead to suicide (Guertin, Lloyd-Richardson, Spirito, Donaldson, & Boergers, 2001). Thus, teachers who observe such behavior or its effects should refer students to school counselors.

Other professionals who work with teenagers should also take an active role in suicide prevention. For example, checklists have been developed to help physicians and nurses screen adolescents for potential suicide risk when they visit clinics for routine health care (Gould et al., 2005). Further, because teens who have been arrested attempt and complete suicide at higher rates than their peers, many experts on youth suicide recommend that adolescents be formally screened for suicide risk by a mental health professional within 24 hours of an arrest (Gallagher & Dobrin, 2005).

Special training in coping skills has also been offered to students, so that they might be able to find a nonlethal solution to their problems. Unfortunately, most such programs appear to be ineffective in changing student attitudes or knowledge (Shaffer, Garland, Vieland, Underwood, & Busner, 1991). These discouraging results are not likely to improve until psychologists know a great deal more about the developmental pathways that lead to this particular form of psychopathology.

Antidepressants are often prescribed for teens with depression who are considered to be at high risk for suicide (de Angelis, 2004). Most studies have shown that these medications can be just as effective in treating depression in adolescents as in adults (Findling, Feeny, Stansbrey, Delporto-Bedoya, & Demeter, 2004). However, in the United States, these drugs have yet to be approved by the Food and Drug Administration for treatment of depression in teenagers (de Angelis, 2004). Further, a large-scale British study found that antidepressants may actually increase the risk of suicide in some teens. These findings prompted the FDA to issue a warning against the routine use of these drugs with adolescents (U.S. Food and Drug Administration, 2004).

## Atypical Intellectual and Social Development

You may recall that, earlier in this chapter, we noted that some types of atypical development involve children's intellectual abilities. Some cause children to lag behind their peers. Others cause children to outpace them in cognitive functioning.

## Mental Retardation

**mental retardation** An intellectual disability defined most often as an IQ below 70 combined with poor adaptive behavior.

◄------------Learning Objective 15.10
What are the characteristics of children with mental retardation?

**Mental retardation,** or MR (also referred to by many educators today as *intellectual disability* or more generally as *developmental disability*), is normally diagnosed when a child has an IQ score below 70 and significant problems in adaptive behavior, such as an inability to dress or feed himself or a problem getting along with others or adjusting to the demands of a regular school classroom (Zeldin & Kao, 2010). Thus, a low IQ score is a necessary but not sufficient condition for a diagnosis of mental retardation. Low IQ scores are customarily divided into several ranges, and different labels are attached to children in each range, as you can see in Table 15.4 on page 390.

**COGNITIVE FUNCTIONING OF CHILDREN WITH MENTAL RETARDATION** Some researchers interested in information processing have tried to understand normal intellectual processing by looking at the ways in which the thinking of children with mental retardation differs from that of children with normal IQs (e.g., Calhoun & Dickerson Mayes, 2005). This research leads to several major conclusions about children with MR:

- They think and react more slowly than children with normal IQs.
- They think concretely and have difficulty with abstract reasoning.
- They require much more complete and repeated instruction in order to learn new information or a new strategy. (Children with normal IQs may discover a strategy for themselves or be able to proceed with only incomplete instruction.)
- They do not generalize or transfer something they have learned in one situation to a new problem or task. They thus appear to lack those "executive" functions that enable older children and adults with normal IQs to compare a new problem to familiar ones or to scan through a repertoire of strategies until they find one that will work.
- Intellectual deficits often interfere with the development of social skills, such as the ability to recognize and respond to facial expressions (Moore, 2001).

Table 15.4

## CATEGORIES OF MENTAL RETARDATION

| Classification | IQ Range | Percentage of Those with Mental Retardation | Characteristics of Persons at Each Level |
|---|---|---|---|
| Mild | 55–70 | 90% | Are able to grasp learning skills up to sixth-grade level. May become self-supporting and can be profitably employed in various vocational occupations. |
| Moderate | 40–55 | 6% | Probably are not able to grasp more than second-grade academic skills but can learn self-help skills and some social and academic skills. May work in sheltered workshops. |
| Severe | 25–40 | 3% | Can be trained in basic health habits; can learn to communicate verbally. Learn through repetitive habit training. |
| Profound | Below 25 | 1% | Have rudimentary motor development. May learn very limited self-help skills. |

Those with mental retardation (1–3%)

Moderate, severe, and profound (10%)

Mild (90%)

Total U.S. population

Total population of people with mental retardation

*Source:* Wood et al., WORLD OF PSYCHOLOGY, © 2008. Reproduced by permission of Pearson Education, Inc.

On simple, concrete tasks, children with mental retardation learn in ways and at rates similar to those of younger children with normal IQs. The more significant deficit is in higher-order processing. These children can learn, but they do so more slowly and require far more exhaustive and task-specific instruction.

It's important to note, too, that many of the things you have learned about child development apply to children with mental retardation. Children with intellectual disabilities go through the same Piagetian stages, although at a slower rate, and their motivational characteristics are very much like those of normal children (Blair, Greenberg, & Crnic, 2001). For example, on tasks that normal children are highly intrinsically motivated to learn, such as learning how to play a new video game, children with mental retardation are just as likely to display high levels of intrinsic motivation. And for tasks for which normal children often require extrinsic motivation, such as doing homework, children with intellectual disabilities are also likely to require parent- or teacher-provided incentives.

**CAUSES OF RETARDATION** Children with mental retardation can be divided into two distinct subgroups, depending on the cause of the retardation. The smaller subset, making up about 15–25% of the total, includes children whose retardation is caused by some evident physical damage. Included in this group are those with a genetic anomaly, such as Down syndrome, that probably causes parts of the brain associated with learning to function poorly (Pennington, Moon, Edgin, Stedron, & Nadel, 2003). Damage resulting in retardation can also be caused by a disease, a teratogen such as prenatal alcohol, or severe prenatal malnutrition; it can occur during the birth itself, such as from prolonged anoxia (Zeldin & Kao, 2010). A small subset of children acquire mental retardation as a result of an injury suffered after birth, often in an auto accident or a fall.

The majority of children with mental retardation show no obvious signs of brain damage or other physical disorder (Zeldin & Kao, 2010). In these cases, the cause of the retardation is some combination of genetic and environmental conditions. Typically, these children come from families in which the parents have low IQs or mental illness or the home life is highly disorganized or emotionally or cognitively deprived. To be sure, in these cases, too, the child's intellectual disability might have been exacerbated by the effects of teratogens or other hazards, such as prenatal alcohol or elevated levels of prenatal or postnatal lead, but it is not thought to be attributable solely to such physical causes.

Large-scale studies have shown quite conclusively that the several causes of retardation are not distributed evenly across the range of low IQ scores. The lower the IQ, the more likely it is that the cause is physical rather than environmental (Broman et al., 1987). One implication of this conclusion is that interventions such as the enriched child care and preschool Ramey devised (see Figure 7.7 on page 184) are more likely to be effective in countering the effects of family culture in causing milder retardation. This is not to say that educators should ignore environmental enrichment or specific early training for children whose retardation has a physical cause. Greater breadth of experience will enrich their lives and may help to bring their level of functioning closer to the top end of their "reaction range," allowing them to function much more independently (Baumeister, 2006).

## Learning Disabilities

◄------------Learning Objective 15.11

How do learning disabilities affect children's development?

Some children with normal IQs and essentially good adaptive functioning nonetheless have difficulty learning to read, write, or do arithmetic. The typical label for this problem is **learning disability (LD)**. Psychologists' definition of this problem includes the presumption that the difficulty arises from some kind of central nervous system dysfunction or damage, in much the same way that many definitions of ADHD assume some kind of biological underpinning. In fact, some children with attention deficit disorder are also diagnosed with learning disabilities so these two sets of problems overlap (Brook & Boaz, 2005). This overlap is far from complete, however, as most children diagnosed with learning disabilities do not suffer from ADHD.

**DIAGNOSING LEARNING DISABILITIES**  Diagnosing a learning disability is extremely tricky, and such a diagnosis is always a residual one—that is, a diagnosis arrived at only by eliminating other possible explanations of a problem. "Disability" is the label normally applied to the problem experienced by a child of average or above average intelligence, with normal vision and hearing, normal social-emotional development, but who has significant difficulty absorbing, processing, remembering, or expressing some type of information, such as written words or numbers. To avoid misdiagnosis, current policy in the United States is that children must show a lack of response to interventions designed to remediate such skill deficits before they can be classified as having a learning disability (Reynolds & Shaywitz, 2009). The specific form of a learning disability may vary widely, with some children displaying difficulties in reading only, some having trouble with reading and spelling (such as the boy whose writing sample is shown in Figure 15.1), and others having more difficulty with arithmetic.

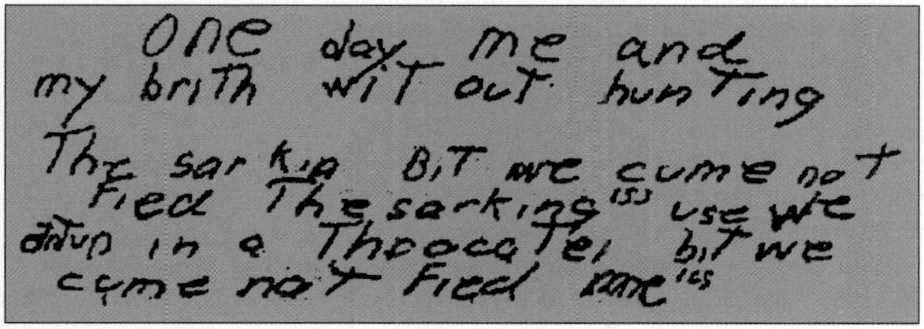

**FIGURE 15.1** Writing Sample by a Child with a Learning Disability
Shown is part of a story written by 13-year-old Luke, who has a significant and persistent learning disability. The little numbers next to some of the words are Luke's word counts. They demonstrate that despite his severe writing handicap, his counting abilities are intact.

(*Source:* From *Learning Disabilities: A Psychological Perspective* by Sylvia Farnham-Diggory, p. 61, Copyright © 1978 by Sylvia Farnham-Diggory. By permission of the author.)

**learning disability (LD)**  A term broadly used to describe an unexpected or unexplained problem in learning to read, spell, or calculate and more precisely used to refer to a neurological dysfunction that causes such effects.

*School can be a discouraging and frustrating place for a child with a learning disability.*

Because of such fuzziness in the definition, there is a good deal of dispute about just how many children really have a learning disability. Practically speaking, however, the learning disability label is used very broadly within school systems (at least in the United States) to describe children who have unexpected or otherwise unexplainable difficulty with schoolwork, particularly reading. About 5% of all children in the United States are currently labeled in this way (NCES, 2011).

**CAUSES OF LEARNING DISABILITIES**   Given such problems with the definition, it's not surprising that the search for causes of learning disabilities has been fraught with difficulties. The most central problem has been with the fundamental assumption that learning disabilities have a neurological basis. The difficulty is that children so labeled (like children with ADHD) rarely show signs of major brain damage on standard neurological tests—perhaps because many of the children are mislabeled or perhaps because the brain dysfunction is too subtle to detect with standard tests.

Happily, brain-imaging techniques now may make it possible to uncover subtle, but very real and significant, neurological differences between children with learning disabilities and those who are good readers. A frequently cited study by Sally Shaywitz and her colleagues (1998) used functional magnetic resonance imaging (fMRI) to identify the parts of the brain that become active when an individual is performing various reading-related tasks. When skillful adult readers in the study were working on these tasks, Shaywitz found that a series of brain regions were activated in turn, beginning with sections of the frontal lobe and then moving backward in the brain. Among the adults with learning disabilities who participated in this study, however, only the frontal lobe was fully activated, suggesting that their brains functioned quite differently on these tasks. This difference in brain activation patterns was especially vivid when the participants were working on tasks that required them to identify individual sounds, such as in a rhyming task—a finding that makes very good sense in light of all the research you read about in Chapter 8 that links good reading to phonological awareness.

In subsequent research, Shaywitz and her colleagues have found similar patterns of neurological activity in the brains of children with reading disabilities (Shaywitz, Mody, & Shaywitz, 2006). Such studies suggest that the brains of both children and adults with learning disabilities may not be "wired" in a way that allows them to efficiently analyze sounds into their phonological components. These findings may explain why interventions that provide explicit information about sound-symbol connections (which are typically not emphasized in conventional reading curricula), along with ample opportunities to practice newly acquired skills, have been found to be highly effective in helping people with learning disabilities become more fluent readers (Shaywitz, 2008).

**Learning Objective 15.12** ---------➤

What are the characteristics of gifted children?

# Giftedness

Some children lie at the other end of the intellectual continuum and are considered gifted. Finding good programs for such children is a continuing dilemma. But defining the term "gifted" precisely is difficult (Cramond, 2004). A number of authors (e.g., Gardner, 2002) have argued that people with exceptional specific talents, such as musical, artistic, mathematical, or spatial abilities, should be classed as gifted, along with those with very high IQ scores. This broadening of the definition of giftedness has been widely accepted among theorists, who agree that there are many kinds of exceptional ability, each of which may reflect unusual speed or efficiency with one or another type of cognitive function.

Within school systems, however, giftedness is still typically defined entirely by IQ test scores, such as all scores above 130 or 140. Some developmentalists suggest that it may be useful to divide the group of high-IQ children into two sets, the "garden-variety gifted," who have high IQ scores (perhaps 130 to 150) but no extraordinary ability in any one area, and the "highly gifted" with extremely high IQ scores and/or remarkable skill in one or more areas—a group Ellen Winner (von Károlyi & Winner, 2005) calls the profoundly gifted. These two groups may have quite different experiences at home and in school.

Gifted children show speedy and efficient processing on simple tasks and flexible use of strategies on more complex tasks. They learn quickly and transfer that learning broadly, and they have remarkably good problem-solving skills—they often leap directly to a solution that requires less gifted individuals many intermediate steps to figure out (von Károlyi & Winner, 2005). Further, they seem to have unusually good metacognitive skills: They know what they know and what they don't know, and they spend more time than average-IQ children in planning how to go about solving some problem (Shore & Dover, 2004).

One famous and remarkable early study of gifted children, by Lewis Terman, pointed to the latter conclusion. In the 1920s, Terman selected 1,500 children with high IQ scores from the California school system. These children—now adults in their 90s—have been followed regularly throughout their lives (e.g., Feldhusen, 2003; Holahan, 1988; Terman, 1925; Terman & Oden, 1959). Terman found that the gifted children he studied were better off than their less gifted classmates in many ways other than school performance. They were healthier, they had wider-ranging interests, and they were more successful in later life. Both the boys and the girls in this study went on to complete many more years of education than was typical in their era, and most had successful careers as adults.

Most research suggests that gifted children have about the same risk of social or emotional problems as normal-IQ children, which means that most are well adjusted and socially adept (Gottfried, Gottfried, Bathurst, & Guerin, 1994; Vida, 2005). Optimism about the social robustness of gifted children may have to be tempered somewhat, however, in the case of the profoundly gifted subgroup, such as those with IQs above 180. These children are so different from their peers that they are likely to be seen as strange or disturbing. They are often socially solitary and introverted as well as fiercely independent and nonconforming; they have difficulties finding peers who can play at their level and are often quite unpopular with classmates (Kennedy, 1995).

## Pervasive Developmental Disorders

◀------------Learning Objective 15.13

What behaviors are exhibited by children with pervasive developmental disorders?

Many of the atypical patterns of development we have discussed so far may indirectly cause difficulties in children's social relationships. By contrast, the defining feature of the group of disorders known as **pervasive developmental disorders (PDDs)**, or *autism spectrum disorders*, is the inability to form social relationships (Scheffer, 2011). In PDDs, the lack of social skills is itself the disorder rather than an indirect consequence of another atypical developmental pattern. The social difficulties of individuals with PDDs usually derive from their poor communication skills and inability to understand the reciprocal, or give-and-take, aspects of social relationships. Many of these children also exhibit odd, repetitive behaviors, such as hand-flapping. Some develop attachments to objects and become extremely anxious—or even enraged—when separated from them. Others engage in self-injurious behaviors such as head-banging. In the United States, just under 1% of all children have some kind of PDD (Kagan & Herschkowitz, 2005; NIMH, 2001b). The rates are similar in European countries (Lauritsen et al., 2004). The two most frequently diagnosed PDDs are *autistic disorder* and *Asperger's disorder*. ◉ Watch at MyDevelopmentLab

The distinguishing symptoms that are exhibited by children with **autistic disorder** include limited or nonexistent language skills, an inability to engage in reciprocal social relationships, and a severely limited range of interests (DSM-IV TR, 2000). Most are also mentally retarded, easily distracted, slow to respond to external stimuli, and highly impulsive (Scheffer, 2011). Some children are helped with symptoms of distractibility and impulsivity by the kinds of stimulant medications that are often prescribed for children with ADHD (Posey, Puntney, Sasher, Kem, & McDougle, 2004). ◉ Watch at MyDevelopmentLab

Many parents of children with autism report having noticed their children's peculiarities during the first few months of life. What strikes these parents is their infants' apparent lack of interest in people. However, in most cases, the disorder is not definitively diagnosed until children's failure to develop normal language skills makes it apparent that they are on an atypical developmental path. This usually occurs between the first and second birthday.

◉ Watch the **Video** *Against the Odds: Children with Autism* at **MyDevelopmentLab**

◉ Watch the **Video** *Autism: Dr. Kathy Pratt* at **MyDevelopmentLab**

**pervasive developmental disorders (PDDs)** A group of disorders in which children exhibit severe disturbances in social relationships.

**autistic disorder** A disorder in which children have much more limited language skills than others of the same age, an inability to engage in reciprocal social relationships, and a severely limited range of interests.

**Asperger's disorder** A disorder in which children possess the other characteristics of autistic disorder but have intact language and cognitive skills.

Children with autism who are capable of some degree of normal verbal communication and whose cognitive impairments are minimal are often called *high-functioning*. However, these children's communicative abilities are quite poor because of their limited ability to engage in social cognition. For example, most never fully develop a theory of mind (Peterson, Wellman, & Liu, 2005). As a result, they typically fail to understand how their statements are perceived by listeners and are incapable of engaging in normal conversations. In addition, the pitch and intonation of their speech is often abnormal. Some utter repetitive phrases, often in robot-like fashion, that are inappropriate for the situation in which they occur.

**Asperger's disorder** is often thought of as a mild form of autistic disorder. The diagnostic criteria for it are highly similar to those for autistic disorder (DSM-IV TR, 2000). However, children with Asperger's disorder have age-appropriate language and cognitive skills and often obtain high scores on IQ tests. Despite their normal language skills, children with Asperger's disorder are incapable of engaging in normal social relationships because, like children with autism who are high-functioning, they usually do not develop the capacity to understand others' thoughts, feelings, and motivations (a theory of mind). ◉—[Watch at **MyDevelopmentLab**

◉—[Watch the **Videos** *Speaking Out: David: Asperger's Syndrome* and *Living with Asperger's Syndrome* at **MyDevelopmentLab**

Because of their normal language and cognitive skills, most children with Asperger's disorder don't stand out from their peers until their second or third birthday, when other children begin to engage in cooperative play. However, normal children of this age vary widely, so children with Asperger's disorder are often assumed to be "late bloomers" or "going through a phase." Some are misdiagnosed with ADHD (Pozzi, 2003). Upon entering school, though, many begin to exhibit the odd behaviors that most people associate with pervasive developmental disorders. For example, they may become intensely focused on memorizing things that have little meaning to them, such as airline flight schedules. They may also engage in obsessive behaviors, such as counting and recounting the number of squares on a checkered tablecloth. By school age, their inability to form friendships like those of other children their age is usually quite apparent.

Pervasive developmental disorders were once thought to be the result of poor parenting. However, it is now well established that all of these disorders are of neurological origin (Kagan & Herschkowitz, 2005). However, there is no single brain anomaly or dysfunction that is associated with PDDs. Even for the individual disorders within this category, researchers have not found a single definitive neurological marker. In a few cases, specific genetic defects are known to lead to atypical neurological development and, in turn, cause children to develop pervasive developmental disorders. For instance, *fragile-X syndrome*, as you may recall from Chapter 2, can cause autistic disorder. For the most part, however, the cause of PDDs remains a mystery (Kagan & Herschkowitz, 2005).

*Sign language helps some non-verbal children with autism communicate with parents, teachers, and peers.*

Whatever the neurological mechanisms involved in PDDs, twin studies suggest that these disorders are hereditary. When one identical twin is diagnosed with a PDD, there is a 70% to 90% chance that the other twin will be diagnosed as well (Zoghbi, 2003). A wide variety of factors interact with genetic predispositions to trigger the appearance of these disorders (Rutter, 2005). When mothers are depressed, for example, infants have an increased risk of developing the symptoms of a PDD (Pozzi, 2003). However, media reports suggesting that immunizations may cause PDDs have proven to be unfounded (Rutter, 2005a).

You may have heard that vaccines containing a form of mercury called *thimerosal* are suspected of causing autism. However, researchers generally agree that the vaccine hypothesis is unfounded (Rutter, 2005a). In one important study, researchers tracked the development of more than half a million Danish children for several years in order to compare rates of autism among those who received vaccines with thimerosal and those who did not receive such immunizations (Madsen et al., 2002). Rates of autism were found to be nearly identical in the two groups. Furthermore, these researchers found that autism rates actually increased in Denmark after thimerosal was removed from all vaccines in the late 1990s (Madsen et al., 2003). Studies in the United States and Canada show a similar pattern. Although thimerosal has been removed from the vaccines that are routinely administered to infants and children, the prevalence of autism in both countries has continued to increase (Fombonne, Zakarian, Bennett, Meng, & McLean-Heywood, 2006; Schechter & Grether, 2008). Nevertheless, sensational media reports about the hypothesized link between immunizations and autism have contributed to the kinds of fears of vaccines that you read about earlier in the chapter.

Among some children with pervasive developmental disorders, symptoms actually get worse as the children get older (Sigman & McGovern, 2005). Sadly, the minimal language and social skills they appear to acquire through intensive educational programs in the early years of life sometimes deteriorate markedly before they reach adulthood. Many adults with these disorders live in sheltered environments and are employed in jobs that require minimal competencies.

The language skills of a child with a PDD are the best indicator of his or her prognosis in adulthood (DSM-IV TR, 2000). Consequently, children with Asperger's disorder have the best hope of attaining independence in adulthood. Thanks to their language and cognitive skills, many are capable of high levels of academic achievement. Indeed, expert reviews of the medical records of one of the most eminent German writers of the 20th century, Robert Walser, suggest that he probably suffered from Asperger's disorder (Fitzgerald, 2004). His social relationships, however, like those of almost all individuals with this disorder, continued to be impaired throughout his life.

**inclusive education** General term for education programs that assign children with physical, mental, or emotional disabilities to regular classrooms and that provide any special services required by the child in that classroom.

## Schooling for Atypical Children

← - - - - - - - - - - -**Learning Objective 15.14**
What have researchers learned about the effectiveness of inclusive education for children with disabilities?

Children who display atypical development require teachers and schools to make special adaptations. In 1975, largely as a result of pressure from parents of atypical or disabled children, Congress passed Public Law (PL) 94–142, called the Education for All Handicapped Children Act. It specifies that every child in the United States must be given access to an appropriate education in the least restrictive environment possible. PL 94–142 does not say that every child with a disability must be educated full-time in a regular classroom. The law allows schools to offer a continuum of services, including separate schools or special classrooms, although it also indicates that a child should be placed in a regular classroom as a first choice and removed from that setting only if her disability is such that she cannot be satisfactorily educated there. Table 15.5 on page 396 lists the categories of disabilities covered by the law as well as the percentage of school children with disabilities in each category.

PL 94–142 and the supplementary laws that followed it (including the Education of the Handicapped Act of 1986 and the Individuals with Disabilities Education Act of 1990, renewed in 2004) rest most centrally on the philosophical view that children with disabilities have a right to participate in normal school environments (e.g., Stainback & Stainback, 1985). Proponents have further argued that such **inclusive education** aids the child with a disability by integrating him into the nondisabled world, thus facilitating the development of important social skills as well as providing more appropriate academic challenges than are often found in separate classrooms or special programs for the disabled (Friend & Bursuck, 2006). Advocates of inclusion are convinced that children with mild mental retardation and those with learning disabilities will show greater academic achievement if they are in regular classrooms.

Schools and school districts differ widely in the specific model of inclusion they use, although virtually all models involve a team of educators, including the classroom teacher, one or more special education teachers, classroom aides, and sometimes volunteers. Some schools follow a plan called a *pull-out program*, in which the student with a disability is placed in a regular classroom only part of each day, with the remainder of the time spent working with a special education teacher in a special class or resource room. More common are full-inclusion systems in which the child spends the entire school day in a regular class but receives help from volunteers,

Lisa, the girl in the middle with Down syndrome, is in an inclusive elementary school classroom, participating as fully as possible in all activities and assignments.

Table 15.5

## DISABILITIES FOR WHICH CHILDREN IN THE UNITED STATES RECEIVED SPECIAL EDUCATION SERVICES

| Disability Category | Percentage of Special Education Students in the Category | Description of Disability |
|---|---|---|
| Learning Disability | 38 | Achievement 2 or more years behind expectations based on intelligence tests<br><br>Example: A fourth-grader with an average IQ who is reading at a first-grade level |
| Communication Disorder in Speech or Language | 22 | A disorder of speech or language that affects a child's education; can be a problem with speech or an impairment in the comprehension or use of any aspect of language<br><br>Example: A first-grader who makes errors in pronunciation like those of a 4-year-old and can't connect sounds and symbols |
| Mental Retardation | 7 | IQ below 70, together with impairments in adaptive functions<br><br>Example: A school-aged child with an IQ lower than 70 who is not fully toilet-trained and who needs special instruction in both academic and self-care skills |
| Other Health Impairments | 10 | A health problem that interferes with a child's education<br><br>Example: A child with severe asthma who misses several weeks of school each year |
| Serious Emotional Disturbance | 7 | An emotional or behavior disorder that interferes with a child's education<br><br>Example: A child whose severe temper tantrums cause him to be removed from the classroom every day |
| Autistic Spectrum Disorders | 5 | Behavior consistent with the criteria for any of the various autistic spectrum disorders in the DSM-IV TR (2000)<br><br>Example: A child with Asperger's syndrome who can manage the cognitive demands of regular classes but who needs help with communication and social skills |
| Multiple Disabilities | 2 | Need for special instruction and ongoing support in two or more areas to benefit from education<br><br>Example: A child with cerebral palsy who is also deaf, who thus requires both physical and instructional adaptations |
| Hearing Impairment | 1 | A hearing problem that interferes with a child's education<br><br>Example: A child who needs a sign-language interpreter in the classroom |
| Orthopedic Impairment | 1 | An orthopedic handicap that requires special adaptations<br><br>Example: A child in a wheelchair who needs a special physical education class |
| Visual Impairment | 0.4 | Impaired visual acuity or a limited field of vision that interferes with education<br><br>Example: A blind child who needs training in the use of Braille to read and write |
| Traumatic Brain Injury | .4 | An acquired injury to the brain caused by an external physical force, resulting in total or partial functional disability or psychosocial impairment, or both, that adversely affects a child's educational performance.<br><br>Example: A child with a history of traumatic brain injury who requires a learning environment with minimal distractions as well as extra time to complete assignments |

*Source:* National Center for Education Statistics, 2011.

aides, or special education teachers who come to the classroom to work with the child there. In some districts, a group of children with disabilities may be assigned to a single regular classroom; in others, no more than one such child is normally assigned to any one class (Friend & Bursuck, 2006).

There is little argument about the desirability of the overall goal: to provide every child with the best education possible, one that challenges the child and gives her the best possible chance to learn the basic intellectual and social skills needed to function in society. Thus, you may be surprised by the finding that teachers who have the most positive attitudes toward inclusion also have the highest burnout rates (Talmor, Reiter, & Feigin, 2005). Researchers speculate that teachers with idealistic views of inclusion probably work very hard to help students with disabilities succeed. When their efforts meet with limited success, they may suffer from feelings of failure and incompetence and may feel emotionally drained. In some schools, teachers are provided with co-teachers who carry some of the extra burdens involved in teaching a class that includes both typically developing children and children with disabilities. This practice appears to protect some teachers against burnout (Magiera & Zigmond, 2005). Moreover, students with disabilities receive much more direct instruction when both a regular teacher and a co-teacher are available

Clear answers to many of the questions about inclusion are still lacking. Still, educators and psychologists have struggled to summarize the information they do have, and most would agree with the following conclusions:

- Children with physical disabilities but no learning problem—such as blind children or some children with spina bifida—make the best academic progress when they are taught in the same way and in the same settings as children who do not have disabilities (Jenks, van Lieshout, & de Moor, 2008).
- For children with learning disabilities, however, full-inclusion programs may be less academically supportive than pull-out programs or resource rooms, because success for children with learning disabilities in a regular classroom depends heavily on the ability of the teacher to implement an individualized program. Co-teaching arrangements appear to be particularly helpful to children with learning disabilities (Magiera & Zigmond, 2005).
- Effective inclusion programs require that teachers be given additional training and substantial support from specialists, aides, or volunteers (Friend & Bursuck, 2006)—conditions that are sometimes not met because of budgetary or other reasons.

The above list of conclusions should convince you that there is no "magic bullet," no single solution for educators, for parents, or for children with disabilities. If you are planning to become a teacher, you will need to learn as much as possible about the needs of children with various kinds of disabilities as well as about successful strategies for teaching them; if you are a parent, you will need to inform yourself about all the educational alternatives so that you can become your child's consistent advocate within the school system.

## THINK CRITICALLY

- What implications for social and educational policy (if any) do you see in the fact that childhood-onset conduct disorders are likely to persist and ultimately to involve adult criminality and violence?
- Why do you think teenaged girls are more vulnerable to depression than teenaged boys are? What theory would you propose to explain the fact that girls attempt suicide more often than boys but are less likely to complete it?

## CONDUCT YOUR OWN RESEARCH

When a child is referred to a psychologist because her parents and teacher think she may have ADHD, the psychologist often compares the child's behavior to that of other children in the context in which it occurs. To get a feeling for how informative peer comparisons can be, ask an elementary school teacher to allow you to observe his or her class at a time when the children are supposed to be working independently. Observe a randomly selected sample of five children for a fixed period of time—say, 10 minutes each—and count the number of minutes each child spends working during the period. Be sure to watch only one child at a time. Convert your observations to percentages and average them. Next, follow the same procedure for every other child in the class. Prepare a chart showing how much each child's percentage of on-task behavior deviated from the average percentage of your randomly selected sample.

## SUMMARY ✓•─Study and Review at MyDevelopmentLab

### Understanding Atypical Development

**15.1**  **What kinds of problems fall within the domain of atypical development?**
Psychopathologies are most often divided into three broad groups: disorders of attention, including attention deficit hyperactivity disorder (ADHD); externalizing problems, including conduct disorders; and internalizing problems, including eating disorders and depression. Other types of atypical development affect children's intellectual and social functioning.

**15.1a**  **What signs indicate that a child may need help from a mental health professional?**
Parents should seek professional help for children who display some kind of sudden change in behavior, are obsessively concerned about their weight, exhibit a sad facial expression for an extended period of time, show outbursts of rage with destruction of property and/or aggression against others, are far more active than others, or defy authority without regard to the consequences of their behavior.

**15.2**  **How do the biological, psychodynamic, learning, and cognitive perspectives explain atypical development?**
Biological theories emphasize physical causes such as genetics, hormones, and neurological functioning. Psychodynamic theorists focus on unresolved emotional conflicts, while learning theorists propose that atypical behaviors are learned. Cognitive perspectives assert that atypical development is associated with faulty thinking.

**15.3**  **What is developmental psychopathology, and how has it changed the way psychologists approach questions about atypical development?**
Studies of psychopathology are more often being cast in a developmental framework, with emphasis on the complex pathways that lead to deviance or normality. Such an approach also emphasizes the importance of risk and protective factors, context, and a lifespan perspective.

### Attention Problems and Externalizing Problems

**15.4**  **What diagnostic labels are given to children who have attention problems?**
Attention deficit hyperactivity disorder (ADHD), the most common type of disorder of attention, includes both problems in focusing attention and excessive restlessness and activity. Long-term problems are greatest when ADHD is combined with a conduct disorder. ADHD appears to have an initial biological cause, but deviant behavioral patterns are aggravated or improved by subsequent experiences.

**15.5**  **What behaviors are associated with oppositional defiant disorder?**
Children with oppositional defiant disorder are disobedient and hostile toward authority figures. Many children with ODD also have ADHD. Parent training is important in the treatment of ODD.

**15.6**  **What are childhood-onset and adolescent-onset conduct disorders, and how do they differ from delinquency?**
Conduct disorders include patterns of both excessive aggressiveness and delinquency. Childhood-onset conduct disorders appear to have a genetic component and are exacerbated by poor family interactions and subsequent poor peer relations. Adolescent-onset conduct disorders are less serious and often result from peer influence. Delinquent acts (lawbreaking) increase in adolescence and are found not only among children with early-onset conduct disorders but also among some teens who show a brief period of delinquency but no long-term negative consequences.

### Internalizing Problems

**15.7**  **How do developmentalists define and explain eating disorders?**
Eating disorders, including bulimia and anorexia nervosa, probably result from a disordered body image. These disorders are most common in adolescent girls.

**15.8**  **What factors predispose teens to major depressive disorder?**
Depression is another type of internalizing problem, relatively uncommon in childhood but common in adolescence. Youngsters with depression are more likely to have a family history of parental depression, to have low self-esteem, or to have a history of being ignored by peers. Depression in adolescence is about twice as common among girls as among boys. No consensus has yet been reached on the explanation for this sex difference.

**15.8a What are the arguments for and against diagnosing children with pediatric bipolar disorder?**

Critics of the PBD diagnosis point to the fact that children and young teens rarely exhibit true mania. Advocates of the diagnosis argue that fits of rage are the childhood version of adult mania and recommend that children who display alternating periods of rage and sadness be treated in the same way as adults who have bipolar disorder. Critics express concern about the use of untested medications to treat children who have been diagnosed with this disorder and argue that psychotherapy should be tried before medications are prescribed. Advocates respond that children are not cognitively mature enough to benefit from psychotherapy and that trials of medications are justified when children need immediate help.

**15.9 What risk factors are associated with teen suicide?**

Depression sometimes leads to suicidal thoughts. Teenaged girls are more likely to attempt suicide, but teenaged boys are more likely to complete it. Risk factors for suicide include hopelessness, a triggering event, and an opportunity.

**15.9a What role does social networking play in adolescent group suicide?**

Teens who have entered into a suicide pact use social networking to post messages about their plans and invite others to join them. Some postings include embedded links to pro-suicide websites. Group suicides that involve social networking may be driven by a desire for fame and attention rather than by the factors that more typically contribute to suicide (e.g., depression).

## Atypical Intellectual and Social Development

**15.10 What are the characteristics of children with mental retardation?**

Children with mental retardation, normally defined as having an IQ below 70 combined with significant problems of adaptation, show slower development and more immature or less efficient information-processing strategies. Two types of children with mental retardation can be identified: those whose retardation has a clear physical cause, who are overrepresented among the severely retarded, and those without physical abnormalities, whose retardation is a result of genetic causes, such as low-IQ parents and/or deprived environments, and who are overrepresented among the mildly retarded.

**15.11 How do learning disabilities affect children's development?**

About 6.5% of school children in the United States are labeled as having a learning disability. There is still considerable dispute about how to identify a genuine learning disability, and many children may be misclassified. Recent research supports the hypothesis that learning disabilities have their roots in atypical brain function, although this conclusion remains tentative.

**15.12 What are the characteristics of gifted children?**

*Gifted* is a term applied to children with very high IQ or to those with unusual creativity or exceptional specific talents. Their information processing is unusually flexible and generalized. Gifted children appear to be socially well-adjusted, except for a small group who are unusually gifted and have a higher risk of psychopathology.

**15.13 What behaviors are exhibited by children with pervasive developmental disorders?**

Children with pervasive developmental disorders (PDDs), also known as autism spectrum disorders, have impaired social relationships. Those who have autistic disorder have limited language skills and are often mentally retarded. Asperger's disorder is a milder form of autistic disorder in which children have normal language and cognitive skills.

## Schooling for Atypical Children

**15.14 What have researchers learned about the effectiveness of inclusive education for children with disabilities?**

Inclusive education, in which children with disabilities are primarily educated in regular classrooms alongside non-disabled children, is consistent with special education law in the United States. Successful programs are those that focus on including children who most benefit from learning with nondisabled peers, provide co-teachers for children with learning disabilities, and provide regular teachers with training in inclusive teaching strategies.

## KEY TERMS

adolescent-onset conduct disorder (p. 382)
anorexia nervosa (p. 384)
Asperger's disorder (p. 394)
attention deficit hyperactivity disorder (ADHD) (p. 377)
ADHD/hyperactive/impulsive type (p. 377)
ADHD/inattentive type (p. 377)

ADHD/combined type (p. 377)
attention problems (p. 374)
atypical development (p. 373)
autistic disorder (p. 393)
bulimia (p. 384)
childhood-onset conduct disorder (p. 381)
clinical depression (major depressive disorder) (p. 385)

conduct disorder (p. 381)
delinquency (p. 383)
depression (p. 385)
developmental psychopathology (p. 376)
externalizing problems (p 374)
inclusive education (p. 395)
internalizing problems (p. 374)

learning disability (LD) (p. 391)
mental retardation (p. 389)
oppositional defiant disorder (p. 381)
pervasive developmental disorders (PDDs) (p. 393)
psychological disorder (p. 374)

# Putting It All Together: The Developing Child

At this point, it is likely that you know a good deal about the sequence of development of language and about sequential changes in cognitive functioning and in attachment, but you may not have a clear idea of how these different developmental sequences connect to one another. If your professor asked you to describe other developmental advances a child is making at the same time she is first using two-word sentences, you might have a difficult time answering. This epilogue will help to "put the child back together" by looking at how aspects of development fit together chronologically.

## Transitions, Consolidations, and Systems

The process of development can be thought of as being made up of a series of alternating periods of rapid growth (accompanied by disruption, or disequilibrium) and periods of comparative calm, or consolidation. Humans are continually changing, from conception to death, but the evidence suggests that there are particular times when the changes pile up or when one highly significant change occurs. The change might be a major physiological development such as puberty, a highly significant cognitive change such as the beginning of symbol usage at about 18 months, or some other major shift.

Such a significant change has two related effects. First, in systems-theory terms, any change inevitably affects the entire system. Thus, a rapid increase in skill in one area, such as language, demands adaptation in all parts of the developing system. Because a child learns to talk, her social interactions change, her thinking changes, and, no doubt, even her nervous system changes as new synapses are created and redundant or underused ones are pruned.

Similarly, a child's early attachment may affect her cognitive development by altering the way she approaches new situations, and the hormonal changes of puberty often affect parent-child relations.

Second, when the system changes in such a major way, the child sometimes seems to come "unglued" for a while. The old patterns of relationships, of thinking, of talking, don't work very well anymore, and it takes a while to work out new patterns. Erikson frequently used the word *dilemma* to refer to such a period of semi-upheaval. Klaus Riegel (1975) once suggested the term *developmental leaps*, which conveys nicely the sense of energy that often accompanies these pivotal periods. This epilogue will use the less vivid term *transition* to describe a time of change or upheaval and the term *consolidation* to describe an in-between time when change is more gradual. Together, these concepts may help you understand what is happening during each of the major age periods.

## From Birth to 24 Months

Figure E.1 shows the various changes during the first 24 months of life. The rows of the figure correspond roughly to the chapters of this book; you need to read up and down the columns, rather than just across the rows.

**FIGURE E.1** Milestones from Birth to 24 Months This summary chart shows some of the simultaneous developments during infancy. The several developmental changes that seem to be pivotal—transitional changes—are outlined in boxes.

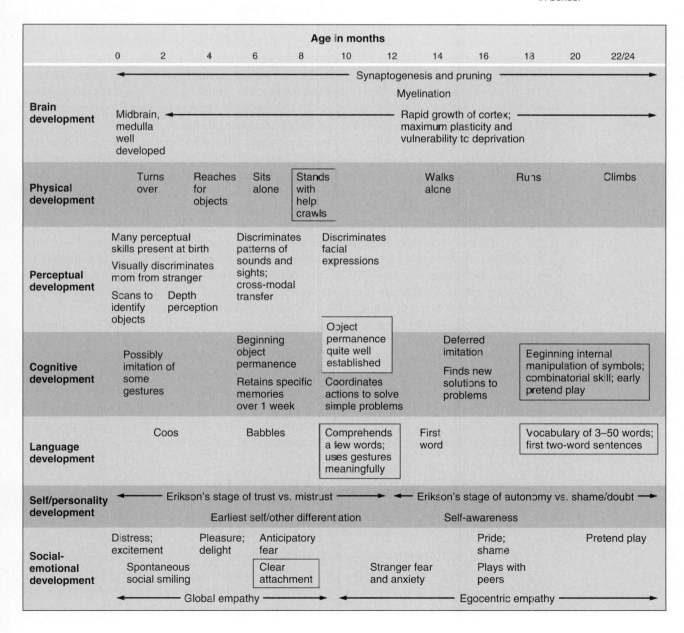

*Eight-month-old Laura has a whole set of new skills and understandings: She can crawl, she has a firm attachment to both parents, she can perhaps understand a few words, and she has a beginning understanding of object permanence. All these more or less simultaneous changes profoundly alter the system that is the child.*

The overriding impression one gets of the newborn infant—despite her remarkable skills and capacities—is that she is very much on "automatic pilot." There seem to be built-in rules, or schemes, that govern the way an infant looks, listens, explores the world, and relates to others.

One of the really remarkable things about these rules, as you learned in Chapters 3 and 5, is how well designed they are to lead both the child and the caregivers into the "dance" of interaction and attachment. Think of an infant being breast-fed. The baby has the needed rooting, sucking, and swallowing reflexes to take in the milk; when the baby is nursing, the mother's face is at the optimum distance from the baby's eyes for the infant to focus on it; the mother's facial features, particularly her eyes and mouth, are just the sort of visual stimuli that the baby is most likely to look at; the baby is particularly sensitive to the range of sounds produced by the human voice, especially the upper register, so the infant can easily hear the higher-pitched, lilting voice virtually all mothers use; and during breast-feeding the release of a hormone called cortisol in the mother has the effect of relaxing her and making her more alert to the baby's signals. Both the adult and the infant are thus "primed" to interact with one another.

Sometime around 6 to 8 weeks, there seems to be a change, when these automatic, reflexive responses give way to behavior that appears to be more intentional. The child now looks at objects differently, apparently trying to identify what an object is rather than merely where it is; at this age, she also begins to reliably discriminate one face from another, she smiles more, she sleeps through the night, and she generally becomes a more responsive creature.

Because of these changes in the baby (and also because most mothers by this time have recovered physically from childbirth and most mothers and fathers have begun to adjust to the immense change in their routines), big changes in mother-infant interaction patterns become evident at this time. The need for routine caretaking continues, of course, but as the child stays awake for longer periods, and smiles and makes eye contact more, exchanges between parent and child become smoother and more playful.

Once this transition has occurred, there seems to be a brief period of consolidation lasting perhaps 5 or 6 months. Of course, change continues during this consolidation period. Neurological change, in particular, is rapid, with the motor and perceptual areas of the cortex continuing to develop. The child's perceptual skills also show major changes in these months, with depth perception becoming stronger and clear cross-modal transfer and identification of patterns of sounds and sights emerging.

Despite all these changes, however, there is a kind of equilibrium in this period—an equilibrium that is altered by a series of changes that occur between about 7 and 9 months: (1) The infant forms a strong central attachment, followed a few months later by the development of separation anxiety and fear of strangers; (2) the infant begins to move around independently (albeit very slowly and haltingly at first); (3) communication between infant and parents changes substantially, as the baby begins to use meaningful gestures and to comprehend individual words; (4) the infant begins to understand object permanence, that objects and people can continue to exist even when they are out of sight. At the very least, these changes profoundly alter the parent-child interactive system, requiring the establishment of a new equilibrium (a new consolidation). The infant continues to build gradually on this set of new skills—learning a few spoken words, learning to walk, consolidating the basic attachment—until some time between 18 and 24 months of age, at which point the child's language and cognitive development appear to take another major leap forward.

## Central Processes

What causes all of these changes? Any short list of such causes will inevitably be a gross oversimplification, but four key processes seem to be at work.

**PHYSICAL MATURATION**   First, and most obviously, the biological clock is ticking very loudly indeed during the early months. Only at adolescence and again in old age is such an obvious maturational pattern at work. In infancy, the pre-patterned growth of neural dendrites and synapses appears to be the key. The shift in behavior at 2 months, for example, seems to be governed by just such built-in changes, as synapses in the cortex develop sufficiently to control behavior more fully.

Important as this built-in program is, it nonetheless depends on the presence of specific factors in the environment (Johnson, 2011). The brain may be "programmed" to create certain synapses, but the process has to be triggered by exposure to particular kinds of experience. Because virtually all infants encounter such a minimum environment, perceptual, motor, and cognitive developments are virtually identical from one baby to the next. But that does not mean that the environment is unimportant.

**THE CHILD'S EXPLORATIONS**   A second key process is the child's own exploration of the world around her. She is born ready to explore, to learn from her experience, but she still has to learn the specific connections between seeing and hearing, to tell the differences between mom's face and someone else's, to pay attention to the sounds emphasized in the language she is hearing, to discover that her actions have consequences, and so on.

Clearly, physiological maturation and the child's own explorations are intimately linked in a kind of perpetual feedback loop. The rapid changes in the nervous system, bones, and muscles permit more and more exploration, which in turn affects the child's perceptual and cognitive skills, and these in turn affect the architecture of the brain. For example, researchers have a good deal of evidence that the ability to crawl—a skill that rests on a host of maturationally-based physical changes—profoundly affects a baby's understanding of the world. Before the baby can move independently, he seems to locate objects only in relation to his own body; after he can crawl, he begins to locate objects with reference to fixed landmarks. This shift, in turn, probably contributes to the infant's growing understanding of himself as an object in space.

**ATTACHMENT**   A third key process is obviously the relationship between infant and caregiver. It seems likely that Bowlby was right about the built-in readiness of all infants to create an attachment, but the quality of the specific experience the child encounters seems to have a more formative effect on attachment formation than is true for other aspects of development. A wide range of environments are "good enough" to support physical, perceptual, and cognitive growth in these early months. For the establishment of a secure central attachment, however, the acceptable range seems to be narrower.

Still, attachment does not develop along an independent track. Its emergence is linked both to maturational change and to the child's own exploration. For example, the child's understanding of object permanence may be a necessary precondition for the development of a basic attachment.

This hypothesis might be turned on its head with the argument that the process of establishing a clear attachment may cause, or at least affect, the child's cognitive development. For example, a secure attachment seems to protect youngsters from the effects of maternal stress, in that infants of stressed mothers who are securely attached will progress through the sensorimotor stage more rapidly than infants of stressed mothers who are insecurely attached (Bergman, Sarkar, Glover, & O'Connor, 2010). Such a connection might exist because the securely attached child is simply more comfortable exploring the world around him from the safe base of his attachment figure, even when she is under stress. He thus has a richer and more varied set of experiences, which may stimulate more rapid cognitive (and neurological) development.

**INTERNAL WORKING MODELS**   Attachment might also be thought of as a subcategory of a broader process—the creation of internal working models. Seymour Epstein (2003) proposes that what the baby is doing is nothing less than beginning to create a *theory of reality*. In Epstein's view, such a theory includes at least four elements:

- A belief about the degree to which the world is a place of pleasure or pain
- A belief about the extent to which the world is predictable, controllable, and just versus chaotic, uncontrollable, and capricious
- A belief about whether people are desirable or threatening to relate to
- A belief about the worthiness or unworthiness of the self

The roots of this theory of reality, Epstein argues, lie in the experiences of infancy, particularly experiences with other people. Indeed, Epstein suggests that beliefs created in infancy are likely to be the most basic and therefore the most durable and resistant to change at later ages. Not all psychologists agree with Epstein about the broadness of the infant's theory of reality. However, virtually all agree that the baby begins to create at least two significant internal models, one of the self and one of relationships with others (attachment). Of the two, the attachment model seems to be the most fully developed at 18 or 24 months; the model of the self undergoes many elaborations in the years that follow. You'll recall from Chapter 10 that it is only at about age 6 or 7 that the child seems to have a sense of her global worth (Harter, 2006b).

## Influences on the Basic Processes

The process of creating these two internal models is universal. Nonetheless, infants can be deflected from the common trajectory by several kinds of influences.

**ORGANIC DAMAGE** The most obvious potential deflector of development is some kind of damage to the physical organism, from genetic anomalies, inherited disease, or teratogenic effects in utero. Yet even when damage does occur, nature and nurture interact: Recall from Chapter 2 that the long-term consequences of such damage may be more or less severe, depending on the richness and supportiveness of the environment the baby grows up in.

**FAMILY ENVIRONMENT** The specific family environment in which the child is reared also affects the developmental trajectory. On one end of the continuum are beneficial effects from an optimal environment that includes a variety of objects for the baby to explore, at least some opportunity to explore freely, and loving, responsive, and sensitive adults who talk to the infant often and respond to his cues (Allhusen et al., 2005). Among other things, such enriched environments may contribute to the development and retention of a more elaborate and complex network of neural connections. On the other end of the continuum are some environments that fall outside of the "good enough" range and thus fail to support the child's most basic development. A family that subjected an infant to severe neglect or abuse would fall into this category, as might one in which a parent suffered deep or lasting depression or one characterized by persisting upheaval or chronic poverty (Allhusen et al., 2005). In between these extremes are many variations in enrichment, in responsiveness, and in loving support, all of which seem to have at least some impact on the child's pattern of attachment, his motivation, the content of his self-concept, his willingness to explore, and his specific knowledge. The consequences of such differences become evident later in life, when the child faces the challenging tasks of school and the demands of relating to other children.

**INFLUENCES ON THE FAMILY** As you've already read many times before, the child is embedded in the family, and the family is part of a larger economic, social, and cultural system, all of which can have both direct and indirect effects on the child. The most obvious example is the impact of poverty or wealth: The parents' overall economic circumstances may have a very wide-ranging impact on a child's life experience. Poor families are less able to provide a safe and secure environment. Their infants are more likely to be exposed to environmental toxins such as lead; less likely to have regular health care, including immunizations; and more likely to have nutritionally inadequate diets. If they must place their infant in child care, poor parents may be unable to afford good quality care, and they are more likely to have to shift the baby from one care arrangement to another. Collectively, these are large differences. The effects do not become evident immediately; babies being reared in poverty-level families do not look much different from babies being reared in more affluent circumstances. By age 2, 3, or 4, though, the differences begin to be obvious.

## The Preschool Years

The main theme of the preschool period, as summarized in Figure E.2, is that the child is making a slow but immensely important shift from dependent baby to independent child. The toddler and then the preschooler can move around easily, can communicate more and more

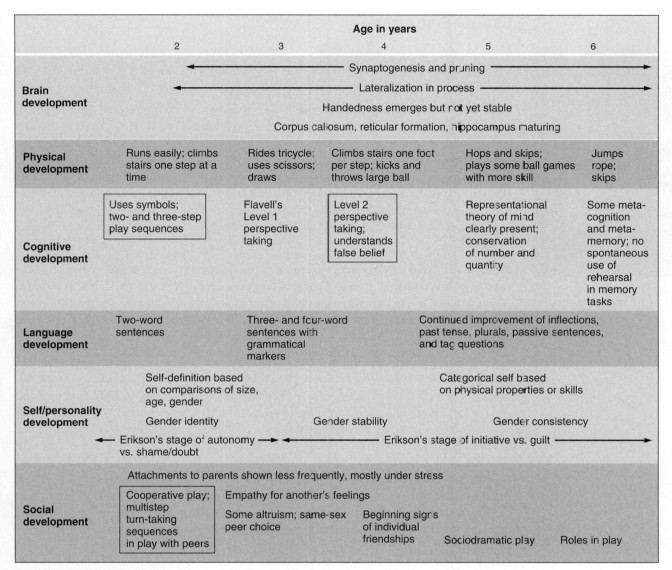

| | \multicolumn{5}{c|}{**Age in years**} |
| | 2 | 3 | 4 | 5 | 6 |
|---|---|---|---|---|---|
| **Brain development** | \multicolumn{5}{l|}{Synaptogenesis and pruning<br>Lateralization in process<br>Handedness emerges but not yet stable<br>Corpus callosum, reticular formation, hippocampus maturing} |
| **Physical development** | Runs easily; climbs stairs one step at a time | Rides tricycle; uses scissors; draws | Climbs stairs one foot per step; kicks and throws large ball | Hops and skips; plays some ball games with more skill | Jumps rope; skips |
| **Cognitive development** | Uses symbols; two- and three-step play sequences | Flavell's Level 1 perspective taking | Level 2 perspective taking; understands false belief | Representational theory of mind clearly present; conservation of number and quantity | Some meta-cognition and meta-memory; no spontaneous use of rehearsal in memory tasks |
| **Language development** | Two-word sentences | \multicolumn{2}{l|}{Three- and four-word sentences with grammatical markers} | \multicolumn{2}{l|}{Continued improvement of inflections, past tense, plurals, passive sentences, and tag questions} |
| **Self/personality development** | \multicolumn{2}{l|}{Self-definition based on comparisons of size, age, gender} | | \multicolumn{2}{l|}{Categorical self based on physical properties or skills} |
| | Gender identity | | Gender stability | | Gender consistency |
| | \multicolumn{2}{l|}{Erikson's stage of autonomy vs. shame/doubt} | \multicolumn{3}{l|}{Erikson's stage of initiative vs. guilt} |
| **Social development** | \multicolumn{5}{l|}{Attachments to parents shown less frequently, mostly under stress} |
| | Cooperative play; multistep turn-taking sequences in play with peers | \multicolumn{2}{l|}{Empathy for another's feelings<br><br>Some altruism; same-sex peer choice / Beginning signs of individual friendships} | Sociodramatic play | Roles in play |

**FIGURE E.2** Early Childhood Milestones
A brief summary of parallel developments during the preschool years.

clearly, has a growing sense of himself as a separate person with specific qualities, and has the beginning of cognitive and social skills that allow him to interact more fully and successfully with playmates. In these years, the child's thinking is decentering, to use Piaget's term: He shifts away from using himself as the only frame of reference and becomes less tied to physical appearances.

In the beginning, these newfound skills and this new independence are not accompanied by much impulse control. Two-year-olds are pretty good at doing; they are terrible at *not* doing. If frustrated, they hit things, and wail, scream, or shout (isn't language wonderful?). A large part of the conflict parents experience with children of this age arises because the parent must limit the child, not only for the child's own survival but also to help teach the child impulse control (Laible & Thompson, 2002).

The preschool years also stand out as the period in which the seeds of the child's (and perhaps the adult's) social skills and personality are sown. The attachment process that began in infancy continues to be formative, because it helps to shape the child's internal working model of social relationships. However, in the years from age 2 to 6, this early model is revised, consolidated, and established more firmly. The resultant interactive patterns tend to persist into elementary school and beyond. The 3-, 4-, or 5-year-old who develops the ability to share, to read others' cues well, to respond positively to others, and to control aggression and impulsiveness is likely to be a socially successful, popular 8-year-old. In contrast, the noncompliant, hostile preschooler is far more likely to become an unpopular, aggressive schoolchild (Caspi, 2000).

*The development of self-care skills is an important theme of the preschool years.*

## Central Processes

Many forces are at play in creating the changes of the preschool years, including two immense cognitive advances in this period: the toddler's new ability to use symbols, and the rapid development, between ages 3 and 5, of a more sophisticated theory of mind.

**PHYSICAL MATURATION** Synaptogenesis and pruning continue into early childhood, although at a slower pace than in infancy. Still, experience is crucial, as all the work on early interventions for disadvantaged children demonstrates (Ramey, Ramey, & Lanzi, 2007). In the midst of its growth spurts, the brain is organizing itself such that functions are beginning to show the pattern of lateralization that is found in adults. As a result, the brain becomes more efficient. The maturing of the reticular formation enhances the child's ability to pay attention, and that of the hippocampus leads to improved memory abilities. At the same time, advances in gross and fine motor skills enable the preschooler to function far more independently than in infancy.

**SYMBOL USE** The development of symbol use is reflected in many different aspects of the child's life. It is evident in the rapid surge of language development, in the child's approach to cognitive tasks, and in play, when the child pretends and has objects stand for something else. The ability to use language more skillfully, in turn, affects social behavior in highly significant ways. For example, the child increasingly uses verbal rather than physical aggression and negotiates with parents instead of having tantrums or using defiant behavior.

**THEORY OF MIND** The emergence of the child's more sophisticated theory of mind has equally broad effects, especially in the social arena, where her newfound abilities to read and understand others' behaviors form the foundation for new levels of interactions with peers and parents. It is probably not accidental that friendships between individual children are first visible at about the time that they also show the sharp drop in egocentrism that occurs with the emergence of the theory of mind.

The seminal role of cognitive changes is also evident in the growing importance of several basic schemes. Not only does the 2- or 3-year-old have an increasingly generalized internal model of attachment; she also develops a self-scheme and a gender scheme, each of which forms part of the foundation of both social behavior and personality.

**SOCIAL CONTACTS** Important as the physical and cognitive changes are, they are clearly not the only factors that contribute to developmental changes in the preschool years. Equally important are the child's contacts with adults and peers. When young children play together, they expand each other's experience with objects and suggest new ways of pretending to one another, thus fostering still further cognitive growth. When two children disagree about how to explain something or insist on their own different views, each child gains awareness that there are other ways of thinking or playing, thus creating opportunities to learn about others' mental processes. Just as Vygotsky suggested, social interactions are the arena in which much cognitive growth occurs. For example, in one study, Charles Lewis and others have found that children who have many siblings or who interact regularly with a variety of adult relatives show more rapid understanding of other people's thinking and acting than do children with fewer social partners (Carpendale & Lewis, 2006; McAlister & Peterson, 2007). Research also shows that children with secure attachments show a more rapid shift to understanding false belief and other aspects of a representational theory of mind than do children with insecure attachments (Carpendale & Lewis, 2006)—a result that points to the importance of the quality of social interactions as well as their quantity for the child's cognitive development Play with other children also forms the foundation of the child's emerging gender scheme. Noticing whether other people are boys or girls and what toys boys and girls play with is the first step in the long chain of sex-role learning.

Naturally enough, it is also social interactions, especially those with parents, that modify or reinforce the child's pattern of social behaviors. The parents' style of discipline becomes critical here. Gerald Patterson's work shows clearly that parents who lack the skills to control the toddler's impulsivity and demands for independence are likely to end up strengthening noncompliant and disruptive behavior (Granic & Patterson, 2006).

## Influences on the Basic Processes

The family's ability to support the child's development in the preschool years is affected not only by the skills and knowledge the parents bring to the process but also by the amount of stress they are experiencing from outside forces and the quality of support they have in their own lives. In particular, mothers who are experiencing high levels of stress are more likely to be punitive and negative toward their children, with resulting increases in the children's defiant and noncompliant behavior. Maternal negativity, in turn, is implicated in the persistence of noncompliant behavior into elementary school. This link is clear, for example, in Susan Campbell's (2006) longitudinal study of a group of noncompliant children. Campbell finds that among a group of 3-year-olds who were labeled "hard to manage," those who had improved by age 6 had mothers who had been less negative.

Stress is obviously not the only factor in the mother's level of negativity toward the child. Mothers with depression are also more likely to show negativity (Thompson, Winer, & Goodvin, 2011), as are mothers from working-class or poverty-level families, who may well have experienced negativity and harsh discipline in their own childhoods. Even so, stress and lack of personal social support are both part of the equation. Thus, preschoolers, like children of every age, are affected by broader social forces outside the family as well as by the family interaction itself.

## The Elementary School Years

Figure E.3 on page 408 summarizes the changes and continuities of middle childhood. There are obviously many gradual changes: increasing physical skill, less reliance on appearance, more attention to underlying qualities and attributes, and a greater role of peers. Major milestones in brain development include major growth spurts between ages 6 and 8 and again between ages 10 and 12, the gradual myelination of the association areas that occurs throughout this period, the full lateralization of spatial perception around age 8, improvements in reticular formation and hippocampus functioning, and the beginning of the final phase of prefrontal maturation at age 9 or so. Clearly, a great deal happens developmentally during the school years. But the momentous conjunction of neurological, physical, cognitive, and socioemotional development happening between ages 5 and 7, which enables the child to gain far more from educational experiences than she could in earlier years, merits special attention. This one interval during these years in which there seems to be a more rapid change is right at the beginning of middle childhood, at the point of transition from being a preschooler to being a schoolchild.

## The Transition between 5 and 7

Some kind of transition into middle childhood has been noted in a great many cultures. There seems to be widespread recognition that a 6-year-old is somehow qualitatively different from a 5-year-old: more responsible, more able to understand complex ideas. Among the Kipsigis of Kenya, for example, the age of 6 is said to be the first point at which the child has *ng'omnotet*, translated as "intelligence" (Harkness &; Super, 1985). The fact that schooling begins at this age seems to reflect an implicit or explicit recognition of this fundamental shift.

Psychologists who have studied development across this transition have pointed to a series of changes children undergo:

- Cognitively, there is a shift to what Piaget calls *concrete operational thinking*. The child now understands conservation problems, seriation, and class inclusion. More generally, the child seems to pay less attention to surface properties of objects and more to underlying continuities and patterns, to be captured less by appearance and to focus on the underlying reality. This can be seen not only in children's understanding of physical objects but also in their understanding of others, of relationships, and of themselves.
- Studies of information processing reveal a parallel rapid increase in the child's use of executive strategies.
- In terms of self-concept, a global judgment of self-worth first emerges at about age 7 or 8.
- In peer relationships, gender segregation becomes virtually complete by age 6 or 7, especially in individual friendships.

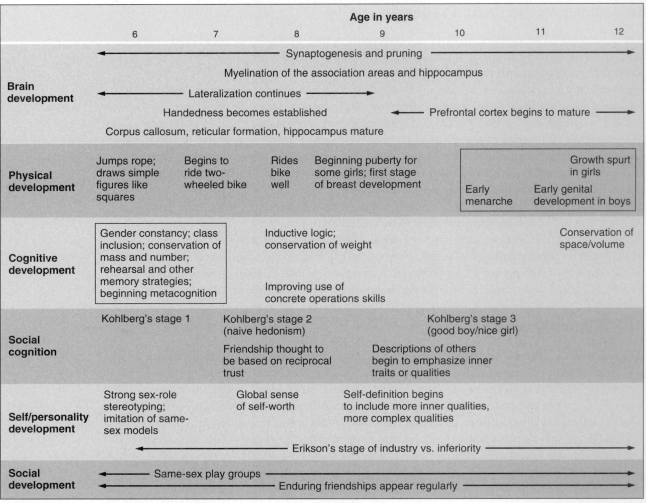

| | **Age in years** | | | | | | |
|---|---|---|---|---|---|---|---|
| | 6 | 7 | 8 | 9 | 10 | 11 | 12 |
| **Brain development** | Synaptogenesis and pruning — (6 to 12) | | | | | | |
| | Myelination of the association areas and hippocampus | | | | | | |
| | ← Lateralization continues → | | | | | | |
| | Handedness becomes established | | | ← Prefrontal cortex begins to mature → | | | |
| | Corpus callosum, reticular formation, hippocampus mature | | | | | | |
| **Physical development** | Jumps rope; draws simple figures like squares | Begins to ride two-wheeled bike | Rides bike well | Beginning puberty for some girls; first stage of breast development | | Early menarche | Growth spurt in girls / Early genital development in boys |
| **Cognitive development** | Gender constancy; class inclusion; conservation of mass and number; rehearsal and other memory strategies; beginning metacognition | | Inductive logic; conservation of weight / Improving use of concrete operations skills | | | | Conservation of space/volume |
| **Social cognition** | Kohlberg's stage 1 | Kohlberg's stage 2 (naive hedonism) / Friendship thought to be based on reciprocal trust | | Kohlberg's stage 3 (good boy/nice girl) / Descriptions of others begin to emphasize inner traits or qualities | | | |
| **Self/personality development** | Strong sex-role stereotyping; imitation of same-sex models | Global sense of self-worth | Self-definition begins to include more inner qualities, more complex qualities | | | | |
| | ← Erikson's stage of industry vs. inferiority → | | | | | | |
| **Social development** | ← Same-sex play groups → | | | | | | |
| | ← Enduring friendships appear regularly → | | | | | | |

**FIGURE E.3** Middle Childhood Milestones
A brief summary of parallel changes during the elementary school years.

*Going to school is a hugely formative experience for children.*

The confluence of these changes is impressive and seems to provide some support for the existence of the kind of stage Piaget hypothesized. There appears to be some kind of change in the basic structure of the child's thinking that is reflected in all aspects of the child's functioning. Still, impressive as these changes are, it is not so clear that what is occurring is a rapid, pervasive, structural change to a whole new way of thinking and relating. Children don't make this shift all at once in every area of their cognitive or social functioning. For example, while the shift from a concrete to a more abstract self-concept may become noticeable at age 6 or 7, it occurs quite gradually and is still going on at ages 11 and 12. Similarly, a child may grasp conservation of quantity at age 5 or 6 but typically does not understand conservation of weight until several years later.

Furthermore, expertise, or lack of it, strongly affects the pattern of a child's cognitive progress. Thus, while most psychologists agree that a set of important changes normally emerges together at about this age, most also agree that they do not represent a rapid or abrupt reorganization of the child's basic mode of operating.

## Central Processes

There seem to be three sets of developmental processes at work in the elementary school years: cognitive, social, and physical.

**COGNITIVE INFLUENCES** Of the developmental shifts seen during middle childhood, the cognitive changes seem to many psychologists the most central, comprising a necessary but not sufficient condition for the alterations in relationships and in the self-scheme that also occur during this period. A good illustration is the emergence of a global sense of self-worth, which seems to require not only a tendency to look beyond or behind surface characteristics but also the use of inductive logic. The child appears to arrive at a global sense of self-worth by some summative, inductive process.

Similarly, the quality of the child's relationships with peers and parents seems to rest, in part, on a basic cognitive understanding of reciprocity and perspective taking. The child now understands that others read him as much as he reads them. Children of 7 or 8 will say of their friends that they "trust each other," something you would be very unlikely to hear from a 5-year-old.

**PEER GROUP INFLUENCES**   A bias toward seeing cognitive changes as central has dominated theories and research on middle childhood for many decades, largely as a result of the powerful influence of Piaget's theory. This imbalance has begun to be redressed in recent years as the importance of the peer group and the child's social experience has become better understood. There are two reasons for this change in thinking. First, developmentalists have reawakened to the (perhaps obvious) fact that a great deal of the experience on which the child's cognitive progress is based occurs in social interactions. Second, they have realized that social relationships present the child with a unique set of demands, both cognitive and interactive, and have unique consequences for the child's social and emotional functioning. It is in the elementary school years, for example, that patterns of peer rejection or acceptance are consolidated, with reverberations through adolescence and into adult life.

**PHYSICAL INFLUENCES**   It is not completely clear just what role physical change plays in the various developmental changes of the elementary school years. Clearly, there are physical changes going on. Girls, in particular, begin the early steps toward puberty during elementary school. What developmentalists don't yet know is whether the rate of physical development in these years is connected in any way to the rate of the child's progress through the sequence of cognitive or social understandings. One thing is true: Bigger, more coordinated, early-developing children are likely to have slightly faster cognitive development and to be somewhat more popular with peers. Obviously, this is an area in which developmentalists need far more knowledge.

## Influences on the Basic Processes: The Role of Culture

Most of what you have read about middle childhood (and about other periods as well) is based on research on children growing up in Western cultures. Investigators must ask, therefore, whether the patterns they see are specific to particular cultures or whether they reflect underlying developmental processes common to all children everywhere.

With respect to middle childhood, there are some obvious differences in the experiences of children in Western cultures compared to those growing up in villages in Africa, in Polynesia, or in other parts of the world where families live by subsistence agriculture and schooling is not a dominant force in children's lives (Weisner, 1984). In many such cultures, children of 6 or 7 are thought of as "intelligent" and responsible and are expected to play almost adultlike roles. They are highly likely to be given the task of caring for younger siblings and to begin their apprenticeships in the skills they will need as adults, such as agricultural or animal husbandry skills, learning by working alongside the adults. In some West African and Polynesian cultures, it is also common for children of this age to be sent out to foster care with relatives or to apprentice with a skilled worker.

Such children obviously have a very different set of social tasks to learn in the middle childhood years than do children growing up in industrialized countries. They do not need to learn how to relate to or make friends with same-age strangers in a new environment (school). Instead, from an early age, they need to learn their place in an existing network of roles and relationships. For the Western child, the roles are less prescribed; the choices for adult life are far more varied.

Yet the differences in the lives of children in industrialized and nonindustrialized cultures should not obscure the very real similarities. In all cultures, middle childhood is the period in which children develop individual friendships, segregate their play groups by gender, develop the cognitive underpinnings of reciprocity, learn the beginnings of what Piaget called *concrete operations*, and acquire some of the basic skills that will be required for adult life. These are not trivial similarities. They speak to the power of the common process of development, even in the midst of obvious variations in experience.

## Adolescence

Figure E.4 summarizes the various threads of development during adolescence. A number of experts on this developmental period argue that it makes sense to divide the years between 12 and 20 into two subperiods, one beginning at 11 or 12 ("early adolescence"), the other perhaps at 16 or 17 ("late adolescence").

## Early and Late Adolescence

Early adolescence, almost by definition, is a time of transition, of significant change in virtually every aspect of the child's functioning. The 12- or 13-year-old is assimilating an enormous number of new physical, social, and intellectual experiences. While all this absorption is going on, but before the experiences have been digested, the young person is in a more or less continuous state of disequilibrium. Old patterns, old schemes no longer work very well,

**FIGURE E.4** Milestones of Adolescence
A brief summary of parallel developments during adolescence.

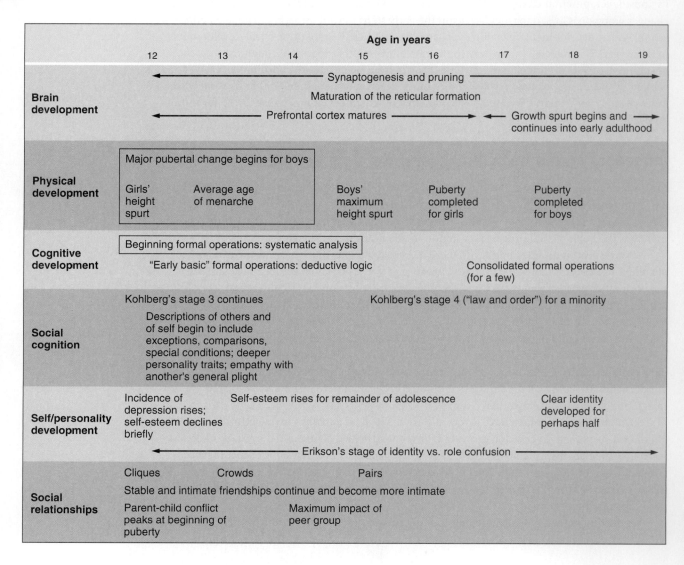

but new ones have not been established. It is during this early period that the peer group is so centrally important.

By contrast, late adolescence is more of a time of consolidation, when the young person establishes a cohesive new identity, with clearer goals and role commitments. Ultimately, the 16- or 17- or 18-year-old begins to make the needed accommodations, pulls the threads together, and establishes a new identity, new patterns of social relationships, new goals and roles.

**EARLY ADOLESCENCE**  In some ways, the early years of adolescence have a lot in common with the toddler years. Two-year-olds are famous for their negativism and for their constant push for more independence. At the same time, they are struggling to learn a vast array of new skills. Teenagers show many of these same qualities, albeit at much more abstract levels, thanks to the maturing of the prefrontal cortex. Many of them go through a period of negativism, particularly with parents, right at the beginning of the pubertal changes. And many of the conflicts with parents center on issues of independence—adolescents want to come and go when they please, listen to the music they prefer (at maximum volume), and wear the clothing and hair styles that are currently "in."

As is true of the negativism of 2-year-olds, it is easy to overstate the depth or breadth of the conflict between young teenagers and their parents. For the great majority of teenagers, there is no major turmoil—simply a temporary increase in the frequency of disagreements or disputes. The depiction of adolescence as full of storm and stress is as much an exaggeration as the stereotype of the "terrible twos." What is true is that both ages are characterized by a new push for independence, which is inevitably accompanied by more confrontations with parents over limits. While this push for independence is going on, young adolescents are also facing a new set of demands: new social skills, new and more complex school tasks, a need to form an adult identity. The sharp increase in the rate of depression (especially among girls) and the drop in self-esteem seen at the beginning of adolescence seem to be linked to this surplus of demands and changes. A number of investigators have found that those adolescents who must deal with the greatest number of simultaneous changes in the early adolescent years—changing to junior high school, moving to a new town or new house, perhaps a parental separation or divorce—also show the greatest declines in positive personality traits, such as effortful control (e.g., Laceulle, Nederhof, Karreman, Ormel, & van Aken, 2011). Young adolescents who can cope with these changes one at a time (for example, youngsters who are able to remain in the same school through eighth or ninth grade before shifting to high school) show fewer symptoms of stress.

Facing major stressful demands, the 2-year-old uses mom (or some other central attachment figure) as a safe base for exploring the world, returning for reassurance when she is fearful. Young adolescents seem to do the same with the family, using it as a safe base from which to explore the rest of the world, including the world of peer relationships. Parents of young adolescents must try to find a balance between providing the needed security, often in the form of clear rules and limits, and still allowing independence—just as parents of 2-year-olds must walk a fine line between allowing exploration and ensuring safety. Among teenagers, as among toddlers, the most confident and successful are those whose families manage this balancing act well.

Drawing a parallel between early adolescents and toddlers also makes sense in that both age groups face the task of establishing a separate identity. The toddler must separate herself from the symbiotic relationship with mom or another central caregiver. The child must figure out not only that she is separate but also that she has abilities and qualities. Physical maturation also allows her new levels of independent exploration. The young adolescent must separate himself from his family and from his identity as a child and begin to form a new identity as an adult.

**LATE ADOLESCENCE**  To carry the analogy we've been using further, late adolescence is more like the later preschool years. Major changes have been weathered, and a new balance has been achieved. The physical upheavals of puberty are mostly complete, the family system has changed to allow the teenager more independence and freedom, and the beginnings of a new identity have been created. This period is not without its strains, however. Most young people do not achieve a clear identity until college age, if then, so the identity process continues.

*Independence of a new and different kind.*

The task of forming emotionally intimate partnerships (whether sexual or not) is a key task of late adolescence, and it is accompanied by rising levels of self-esteem and declining levels of family confrontation or conflict.

## Central Processes and Their Connections

It seems clear that changes in one or another of the facets of development may be central to the constellation of transformations seen at a given age. In infancy, underlying physiological change and the creation of a first central attachment appear to have such key causal roles; in the preschool years, cognitive changes seem especially dominant; among school-aged children, both cognitive and social changes appear to be formative. In adolescence, every domain shows significant change. At this point, developmentalists simply do not have the research data to clarify the basic causal connections among the transformations in these various areas. Nevertheless, they have some information about linkages.

**THE ROLE OF PUBERTY**   One obvious factor to emphasize in discussions of adolescence is puberty itself. Puberty not only defines the beginning of early adolescence; it clearly affects all other facets of the young person's development, either directly or indirectly. There are several direct effects. Most clearly, the surges of pubertal hormones stimulate sexual interest while triggering body changes that make adult sexuality and fertility possible. These changes seem inescapably and causally linked to the gradual shift (for the great majority of teens) from same-sex peer groupings to mixed-sex crowds and finally to romantic relationships.

Hormone changes may also be directly implicated in the increases in confrontation or conflict between parents and children and in various kinds of aggressive or delinquent behavior. Lawrence Steinberg's (2005) research and that of other developmentalists suggests such a direct link. However, many studies find no such connections (e.g., Coe, Hayashi, Levine, 1988), so most theorists conclude that the links between pubertal hormones and changes in adolescent social behavior are considerably more complicated than they had first imagined.

One factor that complicates the analysis is that the physical changes of puberty have highly significant indirect effects as well as direct consequences. When a child's body grows and becomes more like that of an adult, the parents begin to treat the child differently, and the child begins to see himself as a soon-to-be-adult. Both of these changes may be linked to the brief rise in parent-adolescent confrontation and may help to trigger some of the searching self-examinations that are part of this period of life.

Physiological changes might conceivably also play some role in the shift to formal operations. There is some indication, for example, that synaptic and dendritic pruning continues through early adolescence, so a final reorganization of the brain may be occurring in these years. At the same time, any link between formal operational thinking and pubertal change cannot be inevitable, because all adolescents experience puberty, but not all make the transition to formal operations. The best guess at the moment is that neurological or hormonal changes at adolescence may be necessary for further cognitive gains, but they cannot be sufficient conditions for such developments.

**THE ROLE OF COGNITIVE CHANGES**   An equally attractive possibility to many theorists is the proposition that it is the cognitive changes that are pivotal in adolescent development. Of course, two important milestones in brain development make these changes possible: the maturation of the prefrontal cortex and the surge in development in the frontal lobes around age 17. So, the division between cognitive and physical changes is a somewhat artificial one. Nevertheless, it is clear that cognitive development facilitates many of the other changes seen in adolescence, including changes in self-concept, the process of identity formation, increases in level of moral reasoning, and changes in peer relationships.

There is ample evidence, for example, that the greater abstractness in the adolescent's self-concept and in her descriptions of others is intimately connected to the broader changes in cognitive functioning (Harter, 2006b). You will also remember from Chapter 12 that the shift in the child's thinking from concrete operations to at least beginning formal operations seems to be a necessary precondition for the emergence of more advanced forms of social cognition and moral judgment. Finally, some ability to use formal operations may also be necessary but not sufficient for the formation of a clear identity. One of the characteristics of formal operational thinking is the ability to imagine possibilities that you have never experienced and to manipulate ideas in your head. These new skills may help to foster the questioning of old values and old patterns that is a central part of identity formation. For example, several studies show that among high school and college students, those in Marcia's status of identity achievement or moratorium are much more likely also to be using formal operations reasoning than are those in the status of diffusion or foreclosure. In Rowe and Marcia's classic study (1980), the only individuals who showed full identity achievement were those who were also using full formal operations. But the converse was not true. That is, there were a number of participants in the study who used formal operations but had not yet established a clear identity. Thus, formal operational thinking may enable the young person to rethink many aspects of her life, but it does not guarantee that she will do so.

Overall, both the physical changes of puberty and the potential cognitive changes of formal operations appear to be central to the phenomena of adolescence, but the connections between them, and their impact on social behavior, remain unclear.

## Influences on the Basic Processes

There is not enough space in this epilogue (or perhaps in this entire text) to detail all the factors that influence the teenager's experience of adolescence. You have already read about many of these factors, including the timing of the child's pubertal development, the degree of personal or familial stress, and such cultural variations as the use of initiation rites. But one more general point is worth repeating: Adolescence, like every other developmental period, does not begin as a clean slate. The individual youngster's own temperamental qualities, behavioral habits, and internal models of interaction, established in earlier years of childhood, obviously have a profound effect on the experience of adolescence. Examples are easy to find:

- Teens who are high in neuroticism and introversion, who have low self-esteem, and who tend to blame external agents for their problems are at higher risk for mental health problems than are peers who have a more optimistic outlook on life (Martin et al., 2005).
- Alan Sroufe's classic longitudinal study (1989), described in Chapter 11, showed that those who had been rated as having a secure attachment in infancy were more self-confident and more socially competent with peers at the beginning of adolescence.
- Delinquency and heightened aggressiveness in adolescence are most often preceded by earlier behavior problems and by inadequate family control as early as the child's toddler years (Granic & Steinberg, 2006).
- Depression in the teenage years is more likely among those who enter adolescence with low self-esteem (Harter, 2006a).

## A Return to Some Basic Questions

With this brief overview in mind, let's now go back to some of the questions raised in Chapter 1 and see if the answers can be made any clearer.

## What Are the Major Influences on Development?

Throughout this text, you have read about the arguments for and against both nature and nurture, or nativism and empiricism, as basic explanations of developmental patterns. In every instance, you learned that the real answer lies in the interaction between the two. To make the point more clearly, we might go back to Aslin's five models of environmental and internal influences on development, illustrated in Figure 1.1. You'll recall that Aslin proposed one purely physical model (which he calls maturation), according to which some particular development occurs regardless of environmental input, and one purely environmental pattern (which he calls induction), according to which some development is entirely a function of experience. These two "pure"

*By late adolescence, the form of peer interaction has shifted from mixed-sex cliques to loose associations of pairs.*

alternatives make logical sense, but in actuality, probably neither occurs at all. All of development is a product of various forms of interaction between internal and external influences.

Even in the case of development that appears to be the most clearly biologically determined or influenced, such as physical development or early perceptual development, normal development can occur only if the child is growing in an environment that falls within an adequate or sufficient range. The fact that the vast majority of environments fall within that range in no way reduces the crucial importance of the environment. Similarly, even those aspects of development that seem most obviously to be products of the environment, such as the quality of the child's first attachment, rest on a physiological foundation and on instinctive patterns of attachment behaviors. The fact that all normal children possess that foundation and those instincts makes them no less essential for development.

**RUTTER'S FIVE PRINCIPLES OF THE INTERACTION OF NATURE AND NURTURE**   It is not enough merely to say that all development is a product of interaction between nature and nurture. Developmentalists want to be able to specify much more clearly just how that interaction operates. Michael Rutter and his colleagues (1997) have proposed a set of five general principles governing the interplay between nature and nurture; these go beyond Aslin's models and provide a helpful summary analysis:

- *"Individuals differ in their reactivity to the environment"* (p. 338). Some babies, children, and adults are highly reactive, highly sensitive to stress or strangeness; others react with much less volatility. Variations in such reactivity may rest on basic inborn temperamental differences, or they may be the product of cumulative experience.
- "There is a two-way interplay between individuals and their environments" (p. 338). It is important not to think of the influences of the environment as a one-way street. Influences go back and forth.
- *"The interplay between persons and their environments needs to be considered within an ecological framework"* (p. 339). Although research nearly always treats environmental events (for example, divorce) as if they were the same for everyone, they are not. The event itself will differ as a function of culture, poverty, family structure, and a whole host of other variables.
- *"People process their experiences rather than just serve as passive recipients of environmental forces"* (p. 339). It is the meaning each child attaches to an experience that governs the effect, not the experience itself. Thus, the "same" experience can have widely differing effects, depending on how the child (or adult) processes or interprets it.

- *"People act on their environment so as to shape and select their experiences"* (p. 339). Experiences are not distributed randomly and independently of how the child or adult behaves. We each choose behaviors and niches within the family or within other social groups.

**A CONTINUUM OF ENVIRONMENTAL INFLUENCES**   Another point, not included in Rutter's list, is that the form and extent of the interaction between nature and nurture may well vary as a function of the aspect of development in question. It may help to think of different facets of development along a continuum, with those most fully internally programmed on one end and those most externally influenced on the other.

Physical development defines one end of this continuum, since it is very strongly shaped by internal forces. Given the minimum necessary environment, physical maturational time-tables are extremely powerful and consistent, particularly during infancy and adolescence. Next along the continuum is probably language (although some experts might argue with this conclusion, given the possible dependence of language development on prior cognitive developments). Language seems to emerge with only minimal environmental support—though again, the environment must fall within some acceptable range. At the very least, the child must hear language spoken (or see it signed). Still, specific features of the environment seem to matter a bit more in the case of language development than is true for physical development. For example, parents who respond appropriately to their children's vocalizations seem to be able to speed up the process, an example of what Aslin calls *facilitation*.

Cognitive development falls somewhere in the middle of the continuum. Clearly, powerful internal forces are at work here. Developmentalists don't yet know whether the impressive regularity of the sequences of cognitive development arises from built-in processes such as assimilation and accommodation or from physiological changes such as synapse formation and pruning, or from some combination of causes. However, developmentalists do know that specific qualities of the environment affect both cognitive power and structure. Children with varied and age-appropriate toys, who receive encouragement for exploration and achievement, whose parents are responsive to their overtures—who experience, in Aslin's terms, not just facilitation but attunement—show faster cognitive development and higher IQ scores.

Social and emotional development lie at the other end of the continuum, where the impact of the environment seems to be the greatest, although even here genetic factors are obviously at work. Some aspects of temperament seem clearly to be built-in, or genetic, and attachment behaviors may be instinctive; both of these inborn factors certainly shape the child's earliest encounters with others. In this developmental area, however, the balance of nature and nurture seems to lean more toward nurture. In particular, the security of the child's attachment and the quality of the child's relationships with others outside of the family seem to be powerfully affected by the specific quality of the interactions within the family.

## Does Timing Matter?

It's also important to remember that the impact of any experience can vary depending on when it occurs during development. This issue has been explored in a variety of ways throughout the book.

**EARLY EXPERIENCE AS CRITICAL**   The most pervasive version of the timing question is whether the early years of life are a critical or sensitive period for the establishment of many of the trajectories of the child's later development. There are arguments on both sides. Some psychologists, such as Sandra Scarr, point to the fact that virtually all children successfully complete the sensorimotor period, and even children with mild and moderate retardation achieve some form of Piaget's concrete operations. The term that has been widely used to describe such developmental patterns is *canalization*, a notion borrowed from embryologist C. H. Waddington (1957). He suggested that development can be thought of metaphorically as a marble rolling down a gully on a hillside, as in Figure E.5 on page 416. When a gully is narrow and deep,

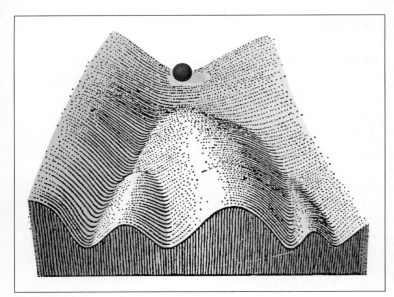

**FIGURE E.5** Canalization

Waddington's visual depiction of the concept of canalization. A narrow and deep gully depicts strong canalization. If infancy is highly canalized, it means that almost any environment will support or sustain that development.

(*Source:* From C. H. Waddington. "A catastrophic theory of evolution," *Annals of the New York Academy of Science*, 231 (1974): 32–42. By permission.)

development is said to be highly canalized. The marble will roll down that gully with little deviation. Other aspects of development, in contrast, might be better depicted with much flatter or wider gullies, with many side branches, where the marble will be more likely to deviate from a given path. Scarr and others argue that in the early years of life, development is highly canalized, with strong "self-righting" tendencies. Even if deflected, the baby's pattern of development rapidly returns to the bottom of the gully and proceeds along the normal track. Such self-righting is illustrated, for example, by the large percentage of low-birth-weight or other initially vulnerable babies who nonetheless catch up to their normal-birth peers in physical and cognitive development by age 2 or 3.

On the other side of the argument are a whole group of psychologists—much of whose thinking is rooted in psychoanalytic theory—who see infancy and early childhood as especially formative (e.g., Sroufe, 1983). They note that some prenatal influences are permanent; some effects of early cognitive impoverishment, malnutrition, or abuse may also be long-lasting. There is also a good deal of evidence that early psychological adaptations, such as the quality of the earliest attachment or the child's tendency toward aggressive behavior, tend to persist and shape the child's later experiences in a cumulative way.

It seems likely that both of these perspectives are valid: The early years of life are a sensitive period for some kinds of development and at the same time highly canalized. How can such an apparent paradox be resolved? There are at least two possible ways. First, canalization could be seen not just as a product of powerful built-in programming but as the result of such programming being expressed in a sufficiently supportive environment. It is only when a child's particular environment falls outside the range of sufficiently supportive environments that there is a so-called environmental effect. So, for a child reared in an extremely impoverished orphanage setting or a child who is regularly physically abused, environmental effects can be strongly negative and long-lasting. The earlier such a deviation from a sufficiently supportive environment occurs, the more pervasive the effects seem to be. In this way of looking at critical periods versus canalization,

*Nature and nurture interact in the parent-child relationship. Parents' patterns of nurturance are influenced both by their own traits and by their children's inborn temperaments.*

a normally supported infancy may be less pivotal in the pattern of the child's development than minor deviations during toddlerhood or the preschool years. But if the deviations in infancy are extreme enough to deflect the infant from the normal developmental path—as in the case of severe abuse or malnutrition—the effect is larger than for deviations at any other age.

Robert Cairns (Cairns, Elder, & Costello, 2001) offers a second resolution to the paradox when he points out that in any given period, some facets of development may be highly canalized and other facets may be strongly responsive to environmental variation. In infancy, for example, physical, perceptual, and perhaps linguistic development may be strongly canalized, but the development of internal working models of attachment is clearly affected by the child's specific family experiences. Indeed, all internal working models—whether of attachment, of gender identity and self- concept, or of peer relations—are likely to be more powerfully affected by early than by later experiences, simply because the model, once formed, affects and filters all later experience.

A particularly nice example of this kind of early effect comes from one of Alan Sroufe's classic studies of the long-term consequences of attachment security. Sroufe and his colleagues (Sroufe, Egeland, & Kreutzer, 1990) compared two groups of elementary school children. One group had formed secure attachments in infancy but for various reasons had not functioned well in the preschool years. The second group had shown poor adaptation at both ages. When these two groups of children were assessed at elementary school age, Sroufe found that those who had had a good early start "rebounded" better. They had better emotional health and social skills than did those who had had poor adaptation in infancy, even though both groups had functioned poorly as preschoolers. The infancy experience is not totally formative; the child's current circumstances also have a major impact. But, at least with respect to attachment security, early experience leaves a lingering trace.

**PSYCHOLOGICAL TASKS AT DIFFERENT AGES**   Another way to think about timing is to identify specific psychological tasks to be dealt with at different ages. Erikson's theory, for example, emphasizes a series of psychological dilemmas. Any experience that affects the way a child resolves a particular task will be formative at that time; at an earlier or later time, the same experience might have much less effect. Alan Sroufe and Michael Rutter (1984) have offered a broader list of age- related tasks, presented in Table E.1 on page 418. In this way of looking at things, the child is seen as focusing on different aspects of the environment at different times. Thus, during the period from age 1 to 21⁄2, when the child is focused on mastery of the world of objects, the quality and range of inanimate experiences to which the child has access may be of special importance.

Overall, most developmentalists today think that no specific age is "critical" for all aspects of development; most think, however, that for any aspect of development, some ages are more critical than others, and that patterns that affect later experience are set during those times. Moreover, on balance, it seems likely that developmental change is more qualitative than quantitative. Certainly, over the years of development, the child acquires more vocabulary words, more information-processing strategies. But these tools and skills are used in different ways by older children than they are by younger ones. Further, it seems clear that these qualitative changes occur in sequences. Such sequences are apparent in physical development, in cognitive development, and in social and moral development.

*If infancy is a critical period for some aspects of personality development, then these preschoolers' characters are already well formed. Whether or not this is true remains one of the most crucial theoretical and practical issues in developmental psychology.*

**STAGES**   Whether it is meaningful to speak of stages of development, however, is still an open question. Some hierarchically organized stages have certainly been identified, the most obvious example being Kohlberg's stages of moral reasoning. And researchers can certainly find examples of apparently stagelike changes across several developmental areas—for example, at about 18 to 24 months, the child seems to discover the ability to combine symbols, a change that is evident in two-word sentences, in thinking, and in multistep play with other children. There also appears to be a quite stagelike shift between ages 3 and 4, of which the theory of mind is the centerpiece. Nevertheless, each new skill or understanding seems to be acquired in a fairly narrow area first and is generalized more fully only later.

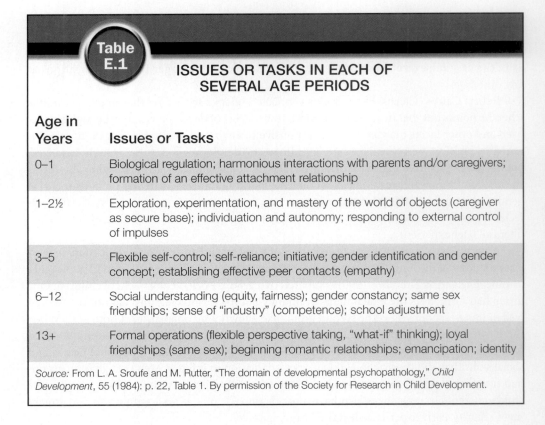

| Table E.1 | ISSUES OR TASKS IN EACH OF SEVERAL AGE PERIODS |
|---|---|

| Age in Years | Issues or Tasks |
|---|---|
| 0–1 | Biological regulation; harmonious interactions with parents and/or caregivers; formation of an effective attachment relationship |
| 1–2½ | Exploration, experimentation, and mastery of the world of objects (caregiver as secure base); individuation and autonomy; responding to external control of impulses |
| 3–5 | Flexible self-control; self-reliance; initiative; gender identification and gender concept; establishing effective peer contacts (empathy) |
| 6–12 | Social understanding (equity, fairness); gender constancy; same sex friendships; sense of "industry" (competence); school adjustment |
| 13+ | Formal operations (flexible perspective taking, "what-if" thinking); loyal friendships (same sex); beginning romantic relationships; emancipation; identity |

*Source:* From L. A. Sroufe and M. Rutter, "The domain of developmental psychopathology," *Child Development*, 55 (1984): p. 22, Table 1. By permission of the Society for Research in Child Development.

In fact, one of the things that differentiates the gifted or higher-IQ child from the child with a lower IQ or mental retardation is how quickly and broadly the child generalizes some new concept or strategy to new instances.

Despite this nonstagelike quality of most developmental change, it is nonetheless true that the patterns of relationships, of thinking, and of problem solving of two children of widely different ages (say, a 5-year-old and an 11-year-old) differ in almost every respect. So there is certainly orderliness in the sequences, and there are some links between them, but there probably are not major stages as Piaget proposed them.

**CONTINUITIES** In the midst of all this change, all these sequences, all the new ways of relating and thinking, there is also continuity. Each child carries forward some core of individuality. The notion of temperament certainly implies such a core, as does the concept of an internal working model. Thus, the specific behavior exhibited by a child may change—the clinging toddler may not become a clinging 9-year-old—but the underlying attachment model or the temperament that led to the clinging will still be at least partially present, manifesting itself in new ways. In particular, it has become increasingly clear that maladaptations often persist over time, as seen in the consistency of high levels of aggression or tantrum behavior and in the persistence of some of the maladaptive social interactions that flow from insecure attachments. The task of developmental psychologists is to understand both coherence (consistency) and the underlying patterns of transformation (development).

## What Is the Significance of Individual Differences?

The issue of individual continuities emphasizes the fact that development is individual as well as collective. By definition, and as the core of its basic approach, developmental psychology concerns itself with the typical rather than with deviations from what is expected. Still, you have read about individual differences in virtually every chapter, so you know that both inborn differences and emergent or environmentally produced variations are present for children in every aspect of development. It seems instructive to tie together many of the threads woven throughout this epilogue by returning to the dimension of individual difference you have read about several times—vulnerability versus resilience.

It may be useful to define these concepts somewhat differently than we did in earlier chapters, in terms of the range of environments that will be sufficiently supportive for optimal development. By this definition, a vulnerable infant is one with a narrow range of potentially supportive environments. For such a child, only the most stimulating, the most responsive, the most adaptive environment will do. When the child's environment falls outside that range, the probability of a poor outcome is greatly increased. A resilient child, in contrast, is one for whom any of a very wide range of environments will support optimal development. A resilient child may thus be more strongly canalized, and a vulnerable child less so.

Some kinds of vulnerabilities are inborn, caused by genetic abnormalities, prenatal trauma or stress, preterm birth, or malnutrition. Any child suffering from these problems will thrive only in a highly supportive environment. You've encountered this pattern again and again through the chapters of this book:

- Low-birth-weight infants typically have normal IQs if they are reared in middle-class homes, but they have a high risk of retardation if they are reared in nonstimulating poverty-level homes (Dombrowski et al., 2007).
- Infants with prenatal exposure to alcohol develop more normally if they are reared in a nurturing, stimulating home environment (Streissguth et al., 2005).
- Children born with cytomegalovirus are much more likely to have learning problems in school if they are reared in poverty-level environments than if they are reared in middle-class families (Hanshaw et al., 1976).

These examples are fairly straightforward. But "vulnerability" in this sense does not remain constant throughout life. A more general proposition, which you might think of as a working hypothesis, is that each time a given child's environment falls outside the range of acceptable supportiveness (that is, each time a mismatch occurs between the child's needs and what is available), the child becomes more vulnerable; on the other hand, every time the child's needs are met, the child becomes more resilient. For example, a temperamentally difficult child whose family environment is nonetheless sufficient to foster a secure attachment will become more resilient, more able to handle the next set of tasks; a temperamentally easy child who for some reason developed an insecure attachment would become more vulnerable to later stress or environmental insufficiency.

Furthermore, the qualities of the environment that are critical for a child's optimal development no doubt change as the child passes from one age to another. Responsive and warm interactions with parents seem particularly important in the period from perhaps 6 months to 18 months; richness of cognitive stimulation seems particularly critical between perhaps 1 year and 4 years; opportunity for practicing social skills with peers may be especially crucial at a later age. Thus, as the tasks change with age, the optimal environment changes also. Among other things, this means that the same family may be very good with a child of one age and not so good with a child of another age.

Most generally, the vulnerability/resilience model leads to the conclusion that even the most "vulnerable" child can show improvement if her environment improves markedly. Because some congenitally vulnerable children do not encounter sufficiently supportive environments, their vulnerability continues to increase. For this reason, early problems often persist. At the same time, improvement is possible, even likely. Most children manage to survive and thrive, despite stresses and vulnerabilities.

## A Final Point: The Joy of Development

To end both this epilogue and the text on an optimistic note, remember that in the midst of all the "crises" and "transitions" and "vulnerabilities," development has a special joyous quality. When a child masters a new skill, she is not just pleased—she is delighted and will repeat that new skill at length, quite obviously getting vast satisfaction from it. A 5-year-old who

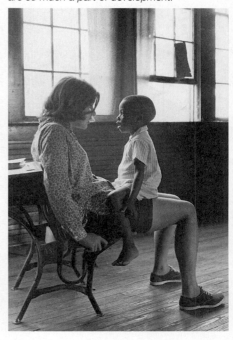

This photo has been used at the end of every edition of this text because it speaks so eloquently of the joy and discovery that are so much a part of development.

learns to draw stars may draw them on everything in sight, including paper, walls, clothes, and napkins, simply because it is so much fun to draw stars. A 10-year-old who learns to do cartwheels will delightedly display this new talent to anyone who will watch and will practice endlessly.

The same joyous quality can be part of the family's development as well. Confronting and moving successfully through any of the periodic and inevitable upheavals in family life can be immensely pleasing. Watching your child progress, liking your child, and enjoying being together are all deeply satisfying parts of rearing children. When parents cry at their son's or daughter's high school graduation or wedding, it is not merely sentiment. It is an expression of that sense of love, pride, and wonderment that they and their children have come so far.

## Chapter 1

1. What is the most accurate statement about the concept of internal models of experience?
   a. Babies are born with built-in biases in the way they experience the world.
   b. New experiences are filtered through a person's core ideas and assumptions.
   c. People fantasize a "model" of their spouses and children.
   d. The effect of an experience depends on the objective properties of the experience.
   e. By adulthood, men can comprehend model diagrams better than women.

2. An emphasis on individualism would most likely be found in which subculture?
   a. Asian American
   b. African American
   c. Native American
   d. Hispanic American
   e. European American

3. Freud's term for the unconscious, instinctual sexual drive is
   a. instinct.
   b. ego.
   c. erogenous zone.
   d. libido.
   e. superego.

4. Based on Spelke's research, we would expect that 2-month-old Timmy would
   a. pay special attention to objects that are stationary.
   b. understand that objects will move downward when not supported.
   c. believe that moving objects change direction randomly.
   d. have no preexisting conception about the behavior of objects.
   e. not be able to see a moving object.

5. Food, praise, or attention all serve as what type of reinforcer?
   a. negative
   b. classical
   c. intrinsic
   d. extrinsic
   e. positive

6. Bandura added all of the following concepts to traditional learning theory EXCEPT
   a. modeling.
   b. observational learning.
   c. classical conditioning.
   d. emphasis on cognitive elements.
   e. intrinsic reinforcements.

7. Seeing one's own behavior or beliefs in others whether they are actually present or not is the defense mechanism of
   a. denial.
   b. displacement.
   c. rationalization.
   d. repression.
   e. projection.

8. Dr. Meadows is a psychologist and conducts in-depth examinations of each of her patients. What research method is she using?
   a. naturalistic observation
   b. case study
   c. longitudinal study
   d. therapeutic intervention
   e. cross-sectional study

9. Which of Aslin's models describes a pattern with NO environmental effect?
   a. attunement
   b. facilitation
   c. induction
   d. maturation
   e. maintenance

10. In an experiment designed to study the effects of homework assignments on grades in school, the grades are the
    a. independent variable.
    b. control variable.
    c. dependent variable.
    d. cohort variable.
    e. concrete variable.

11. Of the following individuals, who advocated the empiricist side of the nature-nurture debate?
    a. Descartes
    b. Plato
    c. Locke
    d. Rousseau
    e. Hall

12. Studies of partial reinforcement show that
    a. it is the same thing as positive reinforcement.
    b. behaviors are learned faster using partial reinforcement.
    c. it works with children but not with adults.
    d. it makes behaviors more resistant to extinction.
    e. behaviors are weakened by partial reinforcement.

13. According to Bandura,
    a. direct reinforcement is not always necessary for learning to occur.
    b. observational learning occurs only if the observer is reinforced.
    c. reinforcement is important in observational learning but not in modeling.
    d. all learning can be explained using operant conditioning principles.
    e. intrinsic reinforcements are external reinforcements.

14. All of the following represent a similar point of view EXCEPT
    a. empiricists.
    b. Plato.
    c. Descartes.
    d. idealists.
    e. rationalists.

15. Piaget believed that cognitive development is
    a. characterized by great irregularities.
    b. shaped by the environment.
    c. an active process of exploration, manipulation, and examination.
    d. random and unpredictable.
    e. based on personality factors

16. When the large dog next door barked suddenly, 6-month-old Lara was startled. Now when she sees the dog, she cries. The dog's barking was a(n)
    a. conditioned stimulus.
    b. unconditional stimulus.
    c. conditioned response.
    d. unconditioned response.
    e. negative reinforcement.

17. Which of the following is an example of negative reinforcement?
    a. The audience applauds when Jim finishes his song.
    b. Maurice is spanked for talking back to his parents.
    c. Cathy stops telling lies when her parents spank her.
    d. Lucas throws a temper tantrum when he is told he can't have some candy.
    e. LaVera is no longer grounded, as her grades have improved.

18. Richard tries to make meaningful associations in order to remember information. He is trying to put the information in to which type of memory?
    a. sensory
    b. short-term
    c. working
    d. encoding
    e. long-term

19. Professor Robbs wants to eliminate cohort effects in his research. Which design should he avoid?
    a. correlational
    b. longitudinal
    c. sequential
    d. cross-sectional
    e. case study

20. One of a pair of identical twins was given extra practice in pre-walking movements, and the other twin was not given extra practice. The twin with extra practice walked several months earlier, but the other twin caught up within four months. This would illustrate which of Aslin's five types of environmental influence?
    a. facilitation
    b. maturation
    c. attunement
    d. induction
    e. maintenance

21. Dr. Messerman is researching cognitive development in children. During one of the research sessions, one child decides he does not want to participate anymore. Research ethics reqire that Dr. Messerman
    a. stop testing that child.
    b. wait a few days and test the child again.
    c. ask the parents to talk to the child.
    d. force the child to participate with the parents' consent.
    e. must terminate the research.

22. The concept of stages is not needed if development
    a. is strictly qualitative.
    b. involves reorganization.
    c. is made up of new strategies.
    d. involves attainment of new skills.
    e. consists only of additions.

23. A Freudian psychoanalyst would say that 1-year-old Zachary's personality is made up of
    a. only the ego.
    b. the id and the superego.
    c. the id and the ego.
    d. only the superego.
    e. only the id.

24. In order to determine the relationship between variables, a researcher should use a(n)
    a. average.
    b. correlation.
    c. deviation.
    d. range.
    e. median.

25. Freud proposed that the structure of personality has three parts, which he called
    a. assimilation, accommodation, and equilibration.
    b. physiological needs, love and belongingness needs, and self-actualization.
    c. id, ego, and superego.
    d. anal, oral, and phallic.
    e. libido, id, and instinct.

## Chapter 2

1. A well-known teratogen, toxoplasmosis, can cause
    a. behavior problems in adolescence.
    b. brain swelling and spinal abnormalities.
    c. serious malnutrition.
    d. lower IQ scores.
    e. facial deformities.

2. Bess has been told to eat plenty of beans, green leafy vegetables, and grain products during pregnancy. They will provide _____ that will help prevent neural tube defects.
    a. calcium
    b. folic acid
    c. vitamin A
    d. iron
    e. protein

3. Which of the following is an accurate statement concerning CMV?
    a. Symptoms are always severe in adults.
    b. It is not a serious disease.
    c. It is a virus in the herpes group.
    d. It cannot be transmitted prenatally.
    e. It causes syphilis.

4. Some studies suggest that age-related deterioration of a genomic imprint
    a. will always come from the mother's ovum.
    b. results in Prader-Willi syndrome if from the father.
    c. always leads to obesity and mental retardation.
    d. may be particularly important in diseases that appear later in life, such as heart disease.
    e. is an example of mitochondrial inheritance.

5. Quentin has type O blood, blond hair, freckles, dimples, and flat feet. Which of these traits is polygenic?
   a. type O blood
   b. blond hair
   c. freckles
   d. dimples
   e. flat feet

6. Which of the following is an accurate description of the placenta?
   a. It is a platelike mass of cells protecting the heart.
   b. It is fully developed by two weeks after conception.
   c. It serves as heart and lungs for the embryo.
   d. It is connected to the embryo's circulatory system through the umbilical cord.
   e. It develops during the germinal stage.

7. Effects of malnutrition during pregnancy are
   a. most damaging during the embryonic period, when organ systems differentiate.
   b. noticeable only under famine conditions.
   c. not noticeable, because the fetus is able to act as a parasite on the mother's body.
   d. most detrimental if malnutrition occurs during the last three months of pregnancy.
   e. damaging only when combined with maternal drug use.

8. It is difficult to identify the reason for higher rates of pregnancy problems among teens because, compared to older women, teens are
   a. less likely to get adequate prenatal care.
   b. more likely to be poor.
   c. less likely to be married.
   d. more poorly educated about pregnancy and birth .
   e. All of these.

9. Longitudinal studies have shown that very active fetuses are more likely to become school children who are labeled by teachers as
   a. hyperactive.
   b. mentally retarded.
   c. learning disabled.
   d. normal.
   e. gifted.

10. Duane and Jeanine are African American. A genetic counselor would most likely test them for
    a. sickle cell disease.
    b. PKU.
    c. cystic fibrosis.
    d. Tay Sachs.
    e. Huntington's disease.

11. Matt and Marcy are twins. From this statement you can be certain that they are _____ twins.
    a. identical
    b. monozygotic
    c. fraternal
    d. conjoined
    e. polygenic

12. Craig has a sex-linked disorder. Which of the following does he have?
    a. Huntington's
    b. Tay Sachs
    c. schizophrenia
    d. albinism
    e. hemophilia

13. Height is a trait that is all of the following EXCEPT
    a. polygenic.
    b. multifactorial.
    c. dominant.
    d. affected by environment.
    e. a measure of general health.

14. Infertility is defined as the failure to conceive after _____ consecutive months of unprotected intercourse.
    a. two
    b. four
    c. six
    d. 10
    e. 12

15. Adela has congenital adrenal hyperplasia. She is more likely than other women to have a daughter who
    a. is masculinized in both apperance and behavior.
    b. is extremely feminine in her behavior.
    c. is unaffected by this disorder.
    d. appears to be masculine as a child, but feminine as an adult.
    e. is shy and timid as a child.

16. Daniel's wife is pregnant. He has just read an article about the use of acetaminophen during pregnancy. He should tell his wife
    a. acetaminophen should not be used during the last three months of pregnancy.
    b. acetaminophen is off limits during pregnancy because it is always teratogenic to human fetuses.
    c. acetaminophen is safe during pregnancy, unless taken to excess.
    d. acetaminophen causes several chromosomal disorders.
    e. acetaminophen should be avoided completely because their newborn will be addicted to it.

17. The _____ exists in only rudimentary form at the end of embryonic period.
    a. amnion
    b. nervous system
    c. placenta
    d. circulatory system
    e. umbilical cord

18. Research on prenatal development suggests that the fetus can distinguish between familiar and novel stimuli by the
    a. end of the germinal period.
    b. end of the embryonic period.
    c. 20th week of prenatal development.
    d. 32nd or 33rd week prenatally.
    e. the first month after birth.

19. All of the following are dominant traits EXCEPT
    a. Type A blood.
    b. nearsightedness.
    c. flat feet.
    d. coarse hair.
    e. freckles.

20. Robert's wife is in the germinal stage of pregnancy, and he wants to know what is happening. You can tell him that the
    a. amnion and placenta are developing.
    b. "finishing" of organ systems is taking place.
    c. gametes are being formed through meiosis.
    d. the blastocyst is forming.
    e. the heart is formed and beating.

21. Which of these chromosomal disorders is associated with both mental retardation and autism?
    a. Down syndrome.
    b. Klinefelter's syndrome.
    c. Fragile-X syndrome.
    d. Turner's syndrome.
    e. Huntington's disease.

22. Research in fetal development has shown that
    a. fetuses are unresponsive to auditory stimuli.
    b. fetuses are unable to recognize patterns of sound.
    c. only embryonic chicks recognize different sounds.
    d. active fetuses become labeled as retarded after birth.
    e. the prenatal learning process parallels what happens postnatally.

23. Mrs. Robertson is having a prenatal test in which cells are extracted from the placenta. This test is
    a. amniocentesis.
    b. CVS.
    c. fetoscopy.
    d. ultrasound.
    e. sonography.

24. What type of cell division produces gametes?
    a. meiosis
    b. codominance
    c. mitosis
    d. splicing
    e. cloning

25. The pattern of characteristics and developmental sequences mapped in the genes of any specific individual is the
    a. gamete.
    b. genotype.
    c. phenotype.
    d. chromosome.
    e. zygote.

# Chapter 3

1. Mrs. Chevalier's infant son appears to be passive and shows few intense reactions. According to Thomas and Chess, this infant is
   a. active.
   b. difficult.
   c. easy.
   d. slow-to-warm-up.
   e. passive.

2. Which of the following would be considered an adaptive reflex?
   a. Babinski
   b. Moro
   c. sucking
   d. startle
   e. eyeblink

3. Margie is having her first baby and is about to go into the second stage of labor. You can tell her that for mothers giving birth for the first time, the second stage of labor typically lasts
   a. 10 minutes.
   b. 50 minutes.
   c. two to three hours.
   d. 12 hours.
   e. 16 hours.

4. Dr. Murphy specializes in treating children born below 1500 grams. Most of his patients
   a. seem to catch up to normal functioning children within five years of birth.
   b. usually die in the first three months of life.
   c. will develop either Klinefelter's or Turner's syndrome.
   d. will lag behind their peers for many years.
   e. will be mentally retarded.

5. What would be the Apgar score for a newborn with a heart rate of more than 100 beats per minute, a strong cry, some flexion, pink body and blue extremities, and no response to stimulation of feet?
   a. 4
   b. 6
   c. 7
   d. 8
   e. 10

6. Ray and Jane's baby weighs 2,300 grams. She is
   a. very low birth weight.
   b. preterm.
   c. low birth weight.
   d. small for date.
   e. extremely low birth weight.

7. Kelly was born before 38 weeks of gestation. She would, therefore, be labeled
   a. small for date.
   b. low birth weight.
   c. extremely low birth weight.
   d. preterm.
   e. pregestation.

8. Which of the following is the MOST accurate statement about colic?
   a. It involves intense bouts of crying for more than eight hours daily.
   b. It is worse in the early morning hours.
   c. It is caused by poor parenting practices.
   d. Neither psychologists nor physicians know why it begins.
   e. Improper diet causes colic.

9. Which of the following reflexes is controlled by the medulla and midbrain?
   a. swallowing
   b. sucking
   c. rooting
   d. eyeblink
   e. Moro

10. To test whether primitive reflexes are linked to important later behaviors, Zelazo and his colleagues stimulated the walking reflex of 2 to 8 week old babies. What did they find?
    a. The infant's leg muscles failed to develop properly.
    b. There was no difference in later motor skills.
    c. This was not a reflex, but actually precocious walking.
    d. Infants walked alone about a month earlier.
    e. Early walking motions impaired cognitive skills.

11. The Apgar scoring system is used to evaluate an infant's
    a. status immediately after birth and then again five minutes later.
    b. weight at birth and at one week after birth.
    c. social responses at one day and one week after birth.
    d. strength of crying, blood pressure, and birth weight immediately after birth.
    e. readiness to be taken home.

12. Roberta is in the first stage of labor and her contractions are closely spaced and very strong. She is most likely in which phase?
    a. active
    b. early
    c. latent
    d. transition
    e. middle

13. Billie suffered from anoxia during birth. This means that she
    a. was delivered through an abdominal incision.
    b. had low birth weight.
    c. was sluggish due to drugs administered during labor.
    d. had an insufficient supply of oxygen.
    e. will definitely have brain damage.

14. During the first stage of labor, the cervix flattens out in a process called
    a. dilation.
    b. effacement.
    c. flattening.
    d. gestation.
    e. compression.

15. Mike swings his arms out wide to catch a ball. In a few months, he will use his hands to catch the ball. This is an example of which type of development?
    a. cephalocaudal
    b. proximodistal
    c. primitive
    d. adaptive
    e. sensorimotor

16. Based on the research evidence, what would be the correct advice to give a friend if she asked you for information about alternative birthing locations (assuming there are no complications in the pregnancy)?
    a. Babies born at home or in birthing centers suffer no more complications than babies born in traditional hospital settings.
    b. Babies born at home or in birthing centers have a head start in their development and are better off in the long run.
    c. Birthing centers should be avoided because they have neither the advantages of home birth nor the safety features of hospitals.
    d. Home birth should be avoided because the risk of infection during birth is much higher than for traditional hospital births.
    e. The only safe place to give birth is in a hospital.

17. Katie is a new mother and wants to know the best way to deal with her crying infant. Her doctor will tell her that
    a. it is best to just ignore the crying.
    b. giving more attention will lead to more crying.
    c. crying is a sign of a spoiled child.
    d. she should always feed her infant when he cries.
    e. she should hold and talk to her infant.

18. Researchers have found that 2/3 to 3/4 of premature infants are no longer distinguishable from their peers of the same chronological age by
    a. three years of age.
    b. preschool age.
    c. the time they go to school.
    d. puberty.
    e. adolescence.

19. A newborn baby's perceptual skills include all of the following EXCEPT
    a. focusing both eyes on the same spot.
    b. hearing sounds within the pitch of the human voice.
    c. tasting sweet, sour, bitter, and salty.
    d. discriminating his mother's smell from another woman's.
    e. efficiently follow a moving object with his eyes.

20. The average number of feedings a day drops to three by what age?
    a. 1 month
    b. 2 months
    c. 6 to 8 months
    d. 8 to 12 months
    e. 20 to 24 months

21. On vacation, Anita ate Mexican food for the first time and easily adjusted to a new schedule and sleeping arrangements. Thomas and Chess would classify Anita's temperament as
    a. active.
    b. difficult.
    c. easy.
    d. slow-to-warm-up.
    e. passive.

22. Mrs. Winston's baby has had three colds in the first six months of his life. She is concerned that there is a problem. Her doctor tells her that in the United States, the average baby has _____ colds in the first year of life.
    a. one
    b. three

c. five

d. seven

e. nine

23. A baby's eyes are open, breathing is regular, and there is no major body movement. What state is this baby in?

a. active awake

b. crying and fussing

c. deep sleep

d. active sleep

e. quiet awake

24. Most infants are delivered

a. feet first, facing toward the mother's spine.

b. feet first, facing forward.

c. head first, facing toward the mother's spine.

d. head first, facing forward.

e. buttocks first, face forward.

25. Infants' motor skills are repetitive, and these repeated patterns become particularly prominent at what age?

a. 6 or 7 months

b. 12 months

c. 18 to 20 months

d. 24 months

e. 36 months.

# Chapter 4

1. Approximately what percent of children and adolescents are obese?

a. 3

b. 5

c. 10

d. 16

e. 20

2. Early developing girls are more likely to

a. show consistently more negative body images.

b. be regarded as leaders by their peers.

c. engage in delinquent behavior.

d. attain higher levels of economic success in adulthood.

e. delay becoming sexually active.

3. What part of the brain is involved in the transfer of information to long-term memory?

a. cerebellum

b. cortex

c. medulla

d. midbrain

e. hippocampus

4. Synaptogenesis in the first two years after birth results in the _____ of overall brain weight.

a. reduction by a quarter

b. reduction by a half

c. stabilization

d. doubling

e. tripling

5. During and after puberty, proportions of
   a. fat and muscle weight rise in both boys and girls.
   b. fat weight rises and muscle weight declines in girls.
   c. muscle weight increases and fat decreases in both boys and girls.
   d. fat and muscle weight increase in boys.
   e. fat and muscle weight do not change.

6. The _____ is the convoluted gray matter that is involved in perception, body movement, and language.
   a. medulla
   b. midbrain
   c. brainstem
   d. cortex
   e. hypothalamus

7. Anne Marie has been sexually active since she was 12 years old. Based on this, it would be most accurate to say that she probably
   a. experienced early menarche.
   b. was very involved in school.
   c. had her first date later than most girls.
   d. did not experience any abuse as a child.
   e. is a heavy drug user.

8. All of the following are secreted by the pituitary EXCEPT
   a. gonadotrophic hormones.
   b. GH.
   c. TSH.
   d. ACTH.
   e. MRI.

9. Because it provides the trigger for release of hormones from other glands, the _____ is sometimes called the _____ gland.
   a. thyroid; master
   b. adrenal; superior
   c. testes; superior
   d. ovaries; superior
   e. pituitary; master

10. Myelination is most rapid
    a. at birth.
    b. during the first two years after birth.
    c. during the preschool years.
    d. between three and five years.
    e. at puberty.

11. About half of sexually active 15- to 19-year-old girls test positive for
    a. chlamydia.
    b. gonorrhea.
    c. HPV.
    d. syphilis.
    e. herpes.

12. Longitudinal studies indicate that among recent cohorts of teens, when compared to earlier cohorts, illicit drug use
    a. has no lasting effects.
    b. has been increasing for the last 20 years.

    **c.** is likely associated with media influence.

    **d.** is more harmful to males than to females.

    **e.** is somewhat less common.

13. Lucy has added 12 inches to her length and tripled her body weight. How old is she?
    **a.** one year old
    **b.** two years old
    **c.** four years old
    **d.** six years old
    **e.** eleven years old

14. Which two glands are primarily responsible for the rate of growth?
    **a.** ovaries and testes
    **b.** adrenals and testes
    **c.** thyroid and pituitary
    **d.** pineal and ovaries
    **e.** leydig cells and testes

15. Research on pruning has shown all of the following to be true EXCEPT that
    **a.** pathways that are not used are pruned.
    **b.** pruning is a variation of what Aslin called attunement.
    **c.** it is important for adults to talk to babies.
    **d.** the pruning process is heavily dependent on experience.
    **e.** pruning begins at six years of age.

16. Socioeconomic status is determined by a combination of variables, including
    **a.** income, occupation, and ethnicity.
    **b.** age, ethnicity, and occupation.
    **c.** ethnicity, occupation, and neighborhood.
    **d.** age, education, and income.
    **e.** income, occupation, and education.

17. Jessica is going through puberty early and has developed adjustment problems because her body has become
    **a.** endomorphic.
    **b.** a culturally desirable body type.
    **c.** lean and muscular.
    **d.** ectomorphic.
    **e.** thin and wiry.

18. Girls have more fat tissue than boys in which age periods?
    **a.** at all ages from birth onward
    **b.** from birth to adolescence but not afterward
    **c.** from birth to age two and again in adolescence
    **d.** from puberty onward
    **e.** only in early infancy

19. LiAnn is guiding her friend toward a hidden prize. She tells her friend "it is on your right." LiAnn is at least
    **a.** one year old.
    **b.** three years old.
    **c.** five years old.
    **d.** six years old.
    **e.** eight years old.

20. The child's muscle fibers
    a. become longer, thicker, and less watery at a fairly steady rate during childhood.
    b. are greater in number than needed, and the excess will be pruned with exercise.
    c. do not develop according to a proximodistal/cephalocaudal sequence.
    d. are fully developed by six years of age.
    e. increase more rapidly in girls.

21. In industrialized countries, 95% of all girls experience menarche between the ages of
    a. 12 and 13.
    b. 12 and 14.
    c. 10 and 12.
    d. 11 and 15.
    e. 12 and 16.

22. What part of the brain becomes the focus of developmental processes during the 10- to 12-year-old neurological growth spurt?
    a. medulla
    b. midbrain
    c. frontal lobes
    d. parietal lobes
    e. brainstem

23. Research on sex education has shown that students prefer to get information about sex
    a. from their parents.
    b. from a teacher.
    c. in a church setting.
    d. from books they read.
    e. from friends.

24. Renaldo is four years old and is experiencing a neurological growth spurt. What skill will he be attaining?
    a. evidence of some goal-directed planning
    b. fluency in speaking and understanding language
    c. improvements in eye-hand coordination
    d. improvements in memory function
    e. motor coordination

25. Which of the following statements about neurological development is accurate?
    a. There is a major growth spurt at four years of age.
    b. Before five months of age, growth spurts occur every three months.
    c. As the infant grows older, periods of growth become shorter.
    d. Between ages two and four years of age, there are frequent growth spurts.
    e. The first major growth spurt occurs at four months.

## Chapter 5

1. A three-month-old infant is shown a series of drawings, each of which shows a small object above a larger object of the same shape. After a while, the baby looks for shorter periods of time at each new version of the small-above-large pattern. Then, a test figure is shown consisting of the opposite pattern and the baby shows renewed interest. These results indicate that the baby
    a. was able to notice the patterns among objects, not just the shapes of objects.
    b. cannot yet habituate to "old" patterns and dishabituate to "new" patterns.
    c. is very intelligent, as the skills for this task are not present until 18 months of age.
    d. habituated to the specific objects that were shown, but not to the arrangement.
    e. paid attention to specific stimuli rather than patterns.

2. Which of the following depth cues does an infant learn first?
   a. pictorial
   b. binocular
   c. kinetic
   d. monocular
   e. interposition

3. Interposition is an example of a
   a. kinetic cue.
   b. binocular cue.
   c. monocular cue.
   d. pictorial cue.
   e. motion cue.

4. Motion parallax is which type of depth cue?
   a. binocular
   b. kinetic
   c. monocular
   d. pictorial
   e. sensational

5. Greg is one month of age. He should be able to discriminate between speech sounds
   a. from female voices but not male voices.
   b. such as "pa" and "ba."
   c. that are actually two-syllable words.
   d. that are nouns but not verbs.
   e. hidden in longer sounds.

6. When researchers use reinforcement to study infant perception they are using the technique of
   a. selectivity.
   b. dishabituation.
   c. operant conditioning.
   d. preference.
   e. classical conditioning.

7. At about two to three months of age, a baby is more likely to look at his mother's
   a. chin.
   b. hairline.
   c. eyes.
   d. ears.
   e. nose.

8. Which of the following is the initial "rule to look by" used by a newborn?
   a. "Look at the inside of things to determine what they are."
   b. "Scan until you find a curved object, then examine the curve."
   c. "Scan until you find a face, then lock onto the face."
   d. "Scan until you find an edge, then examine that edge."
   e. "Look for a face, then examine the features."

9. Gabrielle can discriminate between two-syllable sounds. It is most likely that she acquired this ability at what age?
   a. one month
   b. three months
   c. four months
   d. six months
   e. twelve months

10. Research by Spelke, as well as that of Pickens, confirms that infants four months or older can
    a. recognize familiar faces.
    b. extend cross modal transfer to all senses.
    c. match sounds with appropriate movements.
    d. display excellent depth perception.
    e. integrate information from all senses.

11. The understanding that objects continue to exist even when they cannot be directly perceived is object
    a. continuance.
    b. transfer.
    c. modality.
    d. concept.
    e. permanence.

12. Maria's baby has just started to see colors. Her baby is how old?
    a. 12 months
    b. 9 months
    c. 6 months
    d. 3 months
    e. 1 month

13. Mr. Collins is anxious to know what perceptual skills his newborn son has. You can tell him his newborn will have all of the following EXCEPT
    a. good auditory acuity.
    b. adequate visual acuity.
    c. highly efficient depth perception.
    d. excellent tactual and taste perception.
    e. some color vision.

14. By two years of age, Tyler's visual attention is focused on the _____ of objects in his world.
    a. size
    b. meaningful patterns
    c. shape
    d. texture
    e. color

15. Jack can take something away from his baby and the baby loses interest. His baby is probably
    a. less than six months old.
    b. between six and ten months old.
    c. between eight and twelve months old.
    d. between ten and sixteen months old.
    e. over eight months old.

16. Spelke believes that infants are born with certain built-in assumptions about the nature of objects. One such assumption is what she calls the
    a. connected surface principle.
    b. A not B principle.
    c. intermodal transfer principle.
    d. interpersonal perception principle.
    e. intersensory integration principle.

17. Researchers interested in infant perception of faces have found that
    a. infants prefer to look at faces over other complex objects.
    b. faces are uniquely interesting to infants.
    c. when looking at faces, babies have no preference for type of face.
    d. babies prefer to look at male faces.
    e. babies prefer their mother's face.

18. Olivia wants her baby to be able to speak her native language as well as English. She should introduce her baby to her native language before six months because in the first six months, babies
    a. can learn at least three languages at one time.
    b. have not learned their native language.
    c. can accurately discriminate all sound contrasts found in any language.
    d. think all languages are part of a universal world language.
    e. are able to memorize words efficiently.

19. Because the nativism versus empiricism issue has been so central in studies of perception, the vast majority of the research on perceptual development has focused on
    a. young infants.
    b. laboratory rats.
    c. grade school children.
    d. primates.
    e. adults.

20. Dexter calls his newborn son by name, but as yet the baby does not respond to that name. At what age will his baby first recognize his own name?
    a. one month
    b. two months
    c. three months
    d. four months
    e. five months

21. When a baby understands that her bottle still exists even when she throws it down and it disappears under the sofa, she is demonstrating
    a. size constancy.
    b. shape constancy.
    c. object identity.
    d. object permanence.
    e. object constancy.

22. Monique is three months old. If she is developing normally, she has switched from a visual strategy designed to _____ things to a strategy designed to _____ things.
    a. identify; find
    b. judge; ignore
    c. find; identify
    d. ignore; judge
    e. judge; identify

23. Babies lose the ability to distinguish vowels that do not occur in the language they are hearing by _____ of age and the ability to discriminate nonheard consonant contrasts by _____ of age.
    a. three months; six months
    b. nine months; one year
    c. six months; nine months
    d. six months; one year
    e. one year; two years

24. At what age do babies begin to show signs of object constancies?
   a. at birth
   b. two or three weeks
   c. one month
   d. two or three months
   e. three or four months

25. No matter how her mother hands her bottle to her, Ginny still reaches for it, demonstrating that she has acquired
   a. size constancy.
   b. depth perception.
   c. shape constancy.
   d. object permanence.
   e. color constancy.

## Chapter 6

1. All of the following are part of Vygotsky's socio-cultural theory EXCEPT
   a. zone of proximal development.
   b. operational efficiency.
   c. scaffolding.
   d. naive psychology.
   e. the primitive stage.

2. Beyond the accomplishment of symbol use, Piaget's description of the preoperational stage
   a. focused mostly on all the things the preschool-age child cannot do.
   b. attributed too high a level of cognitive skill to preschool children.
   c. included his discovery that preschool children understand conservation.
   d. included psychoanalytic and behavioral concepts.
   e. focused primarily on solitary activities.

3. A three-year-old child's theory of mind would include the understanding that
   a. a person who wants something will try to get it.
   b. each person's actions are based on his own representation of reality.
   c. a person's representation of reality may not be accurate.
   d. people might act on an inaccurate representation of reality.
   e. thought is reciprocal.

4. When Joan adds two numbers by starting with the larger, and then adds the smaller by counting, she is using which strategy?
   a. decomposition
   b. vertical
   c. horizontal
   d. conservation
   e. min

5. Larry can solve some concrete operational problems presented to him, but not all of them. Piaget would refer to the tendency to solve some problems earlier than other similar problems as
   a. class inclusion.
   b. scaffolding.
   c. horizontal decalage.
   d. operational efficiency.
   e. formal operations.

6. According to Piaget, we derive generalizable schemes from specific experiences through an inborn mental process called
   a. adaptation.
   b. organization.
   c. equilibration.
   d. conservation.
   e. assimilation.

7. Research indicates that conservation
   a. involves understanding that all aspects of an object change when one aspect changes.
   b. is rarely exhibited before age five.
   c. does not occur until the end of concrete operations.
   d. means that a child is unable to take the perspective of other people.
   e. is the same as egocentrism.

8. Compared to 10-year-old Ed, 16-year-old Kevin will
   a. use less deductive logic.
   b. be more tied to empirical reality.
   c. know that knowledge is relative.
   d. rarely consider future possibilities.
   e. use more inductive logic.

9. Angelina has just started to use language and participate in "make believe." Which of Piaget's stages is she in?
   a. sensorimotor
   b. preoperational
   c. concrete operations
   d. formal operations
   e. postformal operations

10. Sixteen-year-old Marcy believes that her relationship with Nathan is deeper than anyone else has ever experienced, and, therefore, her parents could never understand what she feels. This type of thinking is
    a. concrete operational.
    b. post logical.
    c. preoperational.
    d. the result of the imaginary audience.
    e. the personal fable.

11. Which type of logic involves moving from the general to the particular?
    a. deductive
    b. inductive
    c. transductive
    d. conductive
    e. primitive

12. Research on the principle of false belief indicates that it
    a. develops between three and five years of age in a wide variety of cultures.
    b. is replaced by more sophisticated "true belief" types of thinking after the age of four or five.
    c. does not develop until adolescence in most cultures.
    d. is more likely to develop in children who have had insecure attachments.
    e. develops more rapidly in boys who are only children.

13. Piaget's most central assumption was that the child is
    a. a passive recipient of knowledge.
    b. an active participant in the development of knowledge.
    c. totally dependent on the environment.
    d. dependent on affordances from the environment.
    e. unable to construct an understanding of an event.

14. A set of ideas that explains other people's ideas, beliefs, desires, and behavior is a theory of
    a. mind.
    b. cognition.
    c. personality.
    d. mentality.
    e. beliefs.

15. Bruce understands that he is smaller than his older brother, but he does not consider his older brother to be larger than he is. Bruce lacks
    a. naive psychology.
    b. class inclusion.
    c. egocentrism.
    d. conservation.
    e. reversibility.

16. In Piaget's theory, the set of abstract, general rules for examining and interacting with the world are
    a. egocentric speech.
    b. formal operations.
    c. concrete operations.
    d. proximal rules.
    e. assimilation and accommodation.

17. Kurt does not want to go to school today because he believes that everybody will notice his new haircut, which he thinks is too short. This is an example of
    a. concrete operational thinking.
    b. preoperational thinking.
    c. the personal fable.
    d. the imaginary audience.
    e. post logical thinking.

18. Flavell has proposed that there are two levels of perspective-taking ability. At Level 2, the child
    a. develops a series of complex rules for figuring out what the other person sees or experiences.
    b. has formal operations in a rudimentary form.
    c. can think about what others are thinking about his thinking about them.
    d. is at least eight years old.
    e. is governed by both egocentrism and assimilation.

19. A child who uses inductive logic can
    a. start with a theory and then generate hypotheses from that theory.
    b. go from his or her own experience to a general principle.
    c. easily imagine possibilities that he has never experienced.
    d. generate specific hypotheses from a general theory.
    e. achieve formal operational thoughts.

20. According to Piaget, the infant in the sensorimotor stage
    a. is able to plan actions and display intentions.
    b. functions entirely in the immediate present.
    c. can use symbols to stand for objects.
    d. can remember events from one encounter to the next.
    e. can manipulate internal symbols.

21. Elkind hypothesized that adolescents often believe that the events of one's life are
    controlled by a mentally constructed autobiography called a(n)
    a. adolescent belief.
    b. imaginary audience.
    c. egocentric autobiography.
    d. personal fable.
    e. new look theory.

22. Derek has just shifted from relying on simple sensory and motor schemes to use of
    symbols. How old is Derek?
    a. 18 months
    b. 4 years
    c. 6 years
    d. 10 years
    e. 14 years

23. When a child understands that objects remain the same even when their appearance
    changes, the child has acquired
    a. centration.
    b. egocentrism.
    c. formal operations.
    d. conservation.
    e. habituation.

24. Mindy has learned to eat with a spoon. The first time she is given a fork she tries to eat
    her soup with it. Mindy has used the mental process called
    a. adaption.
    b. organization.
    c. equilibration.
    d. conservation.
    e. assimilation.

25. According to Piaget, a scheme (or schema) is a
    a. hypothesis that cannot be observed, tested, or disproved.
    b. strategy used by parents to distract their children.
    c. type of psychoanalytic defense mechanism.
    d. mental or physical action of categorizing.
    e. passive mental category.

## Chapter 7

1. Your child has been administered the Bayley Scales and has achieved a very high score. What
   can you predict about your child's adolescent IQ based on her score on the Bayley Scales?
   a. It will be well above average.
   b. It will be approximately one-half of the Bayley score.
   c. Little can be predicted from the Bayley score.
   d. Your child will be below average in intelligence.
   e. It will be double the Bayley score.

2. Research on the effect of social class on IQ has shown
   a. a cumulative deficit; social class differences widen with age.
   b. a social class effect on infant scales only.
   c. no difference in IQ based on social class.
   d. a decreasing effect of social class after the grade school years.
   e. no specific social class effects.

3. Who translated and revised Binet and Simon's test for use in the United States?
   a. Simon
   b. Terman
   c. Wechsler
   d. Piaget
   e. Sternberg

4. Research has shown that _____ is more important than family income in determining a child's IQ.
   a. sibling's IQ.
   b. good nutrition.
   c. limited television viewing.
   d. quality of parent-child interactions.
   e. activity level.

5. Planning, organizing, and remembering facts to apply to new situations is characteristic of which type of intelligence?
   a. analytical
   b. creative
   c. practical
   d. experiential
   e. componential

6. It is most realistic to say that IQ tests measure a child's _____ at the time the test is taken.
   a. performance
   b. basic capacity
   c. underlying competence
   d. metacognition
   e. consistency

7. Tests of mental rotation given to preschool children indicate that the sex difference
   a. is substantial and becomes larger with age.
   b. decreases with age.
   c. favors girls up until high school.
   d. favors boys until adolescence, when girls catch up.
   e. is very slight and decreases with age.

8. Which individual is most likely to experience stereotype threat?
   a. Dorothy, who is 14 and taking a history test
   b. Terrell, who is African American and playing football
   c. Roberto, who is 70 and taking a memory test
   d. Roger, who is 19 and taking a science course
   e. Margo, who is 17 and applying for college

9. Given the recent research in racial differences in math and science achievement test scores, we would expect which child to have the highest score?
   a. Keith, who is Caucasian
   b. Kim, who is Asian-American

    **c.** Consuela, who is Mexican American

    **d.** Takeesha, who is African-American

    **e.** Natasha, who is Eastern European

10. Artists and sculptors are high in which of Gardner's intelligences?

    **a.** intrapersonal

    **b.** bodily kinesthetic

    **c.** spatial

    **d.** logical mathematical

    **e.** naturalistic

11. Ninety-six percent of all children will achieve IQ scores between

    **a.** 10 and 100.

    **b.** 70 and 130.

    **c.** 85 and 115.

    **d.** 95 and 105.

    **e.** 100 and 115.

12. Research across ethnic and social class groups within the United States on intelligence indicates that

    **a.** IQ predicts performance only among middle-class children.

    **b.** intelligence adds to a child's resilience.

    **c.** there are genetically programmed differences in IQ.

    **d.** intelligence is a poor predictor of academic performance.

    **e.** social class and ethnicity determines intelligence.

13. According to Sternberg, intelligence that involves "street smarts" is

    **a.** creative.

    **b.** analytical.

    **c.** practical.

    **d.** experimental.

    **e.** componential.

14. The intelligence tests used most frequently by psychologists are the revised versions of the

    **a.** Denver Developmental Screening Test, the WPPSI-III, and the WISC IV.

    **b.** Terman Tests of Intellect, and the Bayley Scales of Infant Development.

    **c.** Stanford-Binet, the WPPSI-III, and the WISC IV.

    **d.** Denver Developmental Screening Test, the Terman Tests of Intellect, and the WPPSI-III.

    **e.** Bayley Scales of Infant Development, WPPSI-III, and Stanford-Binet.

15. Carrie's intelligence test score should correlate with her grades in school or performance on other school tests between

    **a.** .20 and .30.

    **b.** −.10 and −.30.

    **c.** −.45 and −.60.

    **d.** .45 and .60.

    **e.** .60 and .85.

16. An IQ score of 90 for a ten-year-old girl means that she

    **a.** scored 90 percent correct on the test.

    **b.** is better than 90 percent of all nine-year-olds taking the test.

    **c.** would be considered to be of average intelligence.

    **d.** has an IQ in the 90th percentile.

    **e.** is below average

17. In the industrialized world, tests of intelligence look very much like
    a. projective tests.
    b. unreliable tests.
    c. invalid tests.
    d. aptitude tests.
    e. achievement tests.

18. Research into racial differences in intellectual performance has shown consistently higher performance on achievement tests, particularly math and science, by children who are
    a. Puerto Rican and Cuban.
    b. Asian and Asian American.
    c. African American.
    d. of European heritage.
    e. Native American.

19. Research on speed of information processing has found that it is
    a. negatively related to IQ.
    b. linked to central nervous system functioning.
    c. related to higher IQs in children but not adults.
    d. a function of better athletic performance.
    e. not related to IQ.

20. Which of the following individuals developed a triarchic theory of intelligence?
    a. Binet
    b. Gardner
    c. Skinner
    d. Sternberg
    e. Piaget

21. Mariano has been shown a rectangle with a pattern covering all but a small part of it. He is asked to choose from six different patterned pieces the one that will fill in the rectangle. Mariano is taking which test?
    a. WISC-IV
    b. Stanford Binet
    c. Denver Developmental Screening Test
    d. Raven's Progressive Matrices
    e. Kaufman Assessment Battery for Children

22. Boys show greater coherence in brain functions in areas devoted to spatial tasks. This supports which explanation of sex differences in spatial abilities?
    a. biological
    b. cognitive
    c. learning
    d. cultural
    e. social

23. Although the IQs of African American children are somewhat lower than those of Caucasian children, the difference is within the reaction range of IQs. This indicates that the difference could be caused by all of the following EXCEPT
    a. low birth weight.
    b. inadequate nutrition.
    c. high blood levels of lead.
    d. parents who do not read to their children.
    e. genetic programming.

24. When compared to non-preschool peers, poor children with preschool experience
    a. function better in school.
    b. test dramatically higher.
    c. differ at least 20 points in IQ.
    d. exhibit more aggressive behaviors.
    e. have unrealistic expectations.

25. Dr. Madison is a counselor, and Ms. Rogers is a social worker. Both are likely to be high in which of Gardner's intelligences?
    a. interpersonal
    b. intrapersonal
    c. spatial
    d. logical
    e. naturalistic

# Chapter 8

1. The fact that parents are remarkably forgiving of all sorts of peculiar constructions and meaning in their children's speech is evidence AGAINST which theory of language development?
    a. imitation
    b. reinforcement
    c. innateness
    d. constructivist
    e. psychoanalytic

2. When Lisa sees a dog, she points and says "kitty." Lisa is demonstrating
    a. overextension.
    b. telegraphic speech.
    c. underextension.
    d. holophrasing.
    e. overregularization.

3. Which of the following babies is most likely to show a preference for the stress patterns of his or her native language?
    a. nine-month-old Eric
    b. seven-month-old Latisha
    c. five-month-old Sam
    d. three-month-old Bobbi
    e. one-month old Maria

4. Cross-cultural research indicates that children the world over do all of the following EXCEPT
    a. use one-word phrases before two-word phrases.
    b. add prepositions in the same order.
    c. pay more attention to the ends of words than the beginnings.
    d. use the same specific word order in early sentences.
    e. coo before they babble.

5. According to linguists, any sound or set of sounds that is used consistently to refer to some thing, action, or quality is considered to be
    a. babbling.
    b. a gesture.
    c. language.
    d. a word.
    e. an overextension.

6. All of the following changes occur at 9 or 10 months of age EXCEPT
   a. the beginning of meaningful gestures.
   b. telegraphic speech and holophrases.
   c. imitative gestural games.
   d. first comprehension of individual words.
   e. receptive language becomes evident.

7. Which of the following statements about babbling is CORRECT?
   a. In the development of babies' babbling, it can be said that they are "learning the words before the tune."
   b. When babies babble with a falling intonation at the end of a string of sounds, it seems to signal a desire for a response.
   c. When babies first start babbling, they typically babble all kinds of sounds, including some that are not part of the language they are hearing.
   d. At about 9 or 10 months of age, the sound repertoire in babbling gradually shifts to include the set of sounds they do not hear spoken.
   e. Babbling involves complex combinations of vowels that occur before cooing.

8. An infant first understands the meaning of individual words spoken to him at about
   a. 12 months.
   b. 9 or 10 months.
   c. 4 or 5 months.
   d. 24 months.
   e. 1 or 2 months.

9. When a child assumes that objects will have only one name, the child is influenced by
   a. the whole object constraint.
   b. the principle of contrast.
   c. the mutual exclusivity constraint.
   d. underextension.
   e. overextention.

10. Which of the following is an accurate statement about infant-directed speech?
    a. It is the behavior pattern shown by infants attached to their mothers.
    b. It is not effective in communicating with young children.
    c. It is sometimes called "motherese."
    d. It is spoken only by mothers and only to their own infants.
    e. It tends to slow down language acquisition.

11. From six months on, babies begin engaging in _____, which is a sound pattern consisting of consonants and vowels.
    a. cooing
    b. babbling
    c. gurgling
    d. fussing
    e. crying

12. Children's first use of questions and negatives
    a. is purely random.
    b. is an exact copy of the speech they hear.
    c. reveals a knowledge of rules.
    d. is characterized by overuse of auxiliary verbs.
    e. involves overextension.

13. Sounds, signs, or symbols that communicate meaning are called
    a. prelinguistic language.
    b. expressive language.

    c. prenatal language.

    d. cooing and babbling.

    e. phonology.

14. Which of the following is true of bilingual children?

    a. They have difficulty discriminating between the two languages.

    b. They have more difficulty with language tasks in school.

    c. They have an advantage in metalinguistic ability.

    d. They reach all language milestones earlier.

    e. They have difficulty focusing attention.

15. The fact that children say things such as "I wented," supports what conclusion about the role of imitation in language development?

    a. Imitation is the central process in language development.

    b. Imitation alone can't explain all language acquisition.

    c. Imitation in infancy improves language development in early childhood.

    d. Imitation is irrelevant in language development.

    e. Imitation slows language development.

16. The earliest theories of language reflected which of the following perspectives?

    a. psychoanalysis

    b. learning theory

    c. cognitive theory

    d. information processing

    e. humanistic theory

17. Skinner's theory of language states that children's language is shaped through systematic _____ of better and better approximations of adult speech.

    a. generation

    b. reinforcement

    c. imitation

    d. monitoring

    e. development

18. Research on the use of various meanings that children convey with earliest sentences (such as agent-action, action-location, and recurrence) has shown that

    a. all children express all the meanings in their earliest sentences.

    b. there is a fixed order in which the meanings are acquired.

    c. all children appear to express at least a few meanings in their earliest speech.

    d. most of the meanings are too difficult for children under five years of age.

    e. the meanings first appear in holophrastic speech.

19. A group of children are watching a guinea pig run around on the floor. Which one of the following comments from the children illustrates overextension?

    a. "See the guinea pig."

    b. "Look at the mouse."

    c. "Look at Tim."

    d. "That's not a rabbit."

    e. "That's my pet."

20. Carlos is bilingual, and his parents have asked a counselor what to expect when he goes to school. She should tell them that most bilingual children who are equally fluent in both languages

    a. have few, if any, learning problems in school.

    b. lose fluency in both languages.

    c. demonstrate few differences in verbal memory efficiency.

    d. have decreased metalinguistic ability.

    e. have difficulty focusing their attention.

21. The ability to categorically link new words to real-world referents is
    a. overextension.
    b. linguistic reference.
    c. expressive language.
    d. fast-mapping.
    e. underextension.

22. By one or two months of age, babies can
    a. tell the difference between individual letter sounds.
    b. understand that speech sounds are matched by the speaker's mouth movements.
    c. discriminate among syllables or words.
    d. show a preference for words in their native language.
    e. produce babbling sounds.

23. Japanese children learn at an early age to use a word at the end of the sentence that tells something about the feeling or context of what is being said. This is called a(n)
    a. extension.
    b. inflection.
    c. constraint.
    d. generalization.
    e. pragmatic marker.

24. Lawanda has not yet experienced the naming explosion. Therefore, her use of "car" is most likely to be for
    a. the family car only.
    b. all cars, including toys.
    c. all four-wheel vehicles.
    d. all methods of transportation.
    e. cars used only by people she knows.

25. All of the following contribute to phonological awareness EXCEPT
    a. learning and reciting nursery rhymes.
    b. shiritori.
    c. word play.
    d. reading to children.
    e. expressive jargon.

## Chapter 9

1. Leroy is full of original ideas and is very imaginative. He is high in which of the Big Five personality traits?
    a. agreeableness
    b. extraversion
    c. openness/intellect
    d. neuroticism
    e. conscientiousness

2. All of the following are strengths of the psychoanalytic theories EXCEPT
    a. They account for the complexities of personality development.
    b. They look at the child's perception of events.
    c. They consider the cultural context.
    d. They focus on the emotional quality of caregiver-child relationships.
    e. They stress the importance of reinforcement contingencies.

3. Both Piaget and Bandura would agree that the child's self-concept
    a. can be changed easily by peer interactions.
    b. can be modified by the parents but not the peers.

    **c.** affects schoolwork but not peer interactions.

    **d.** affects how the child performs and reacts to others.

    **e.** has little impact on basic attributes.

4. Murray is enthusiastic about whatever he does and talks to anyone he meets. He would score high on which dimension of personality?

    **a.** extraversion

    **b.** neuroticism

    **c.** openness/intellect

    **d.** conscientiousness

    **e.** agreeableness

5. Janice takes her toys apart and gets upset when they can't be fixed. Erikson would place her in the stage of

    **a.** trust versus mistrust.

    **b.** initiative versus guilt.

    **c.** industry versus inferiority.

    **d.** identity versus role confusion.

    **e.** autonomy versus shame and doubt.

6. The correct sequence of Freud's five psychosexual stages is

    **a.** anal, oral, phallic, latency, genital.

    **b.** oral, anal, phallic, latency, genital.

    **c.** latency, anal, oral, genital, phallic.

    **d.** anal, oral, genital, latency, phallic.

    **e.** phallic, anal, oral, latency, genital.

7. Although Piaget and Bandura agree on the impact that self-concept or self-scheme has once it develops, Piaget emphasizes _____, while Bandura emphasizes _____ as a causal factor.

    **a.** internal processes; reinforcement and modeling

    **b.** modeling; external processes

    **c.** reinforcement; modeling

    **d.** defenses; modeling

    **e.** internal processes; accommodation

8. The temperament dimensions of inhibition and anxiety

    **a.** are reflected in high scores on extraversion.

    **b.** are reflected in high scores on openness.

    **c.** contribute to low scores on neuroticism at later ages.

    **d.** reflect a tendency to respond with fear or withdraw from new people, situations, or objects.

    **e.** are the basis of emotionality.

9. Which of the following is an instinctual drive in Freud's theory?

    **a.** affiliation

    **b.** ambition

    **c.** accommodation

    **d.** aggression

    **e.** assimilation

10. All of the following are characteristic of the Big Five trait of agreeableness EXCEPT

    **a.** affectionate.

    **b.** forgiving.

    **c.** generous.

    **d.** enthusiastic.

    **e.** trusting.

11. Lillith is usually tense and she worries about every small event in her life. She is high in the Big Five trait of
    a. agreeableness.
    b. conscientiousness.
    c. openness/intellect.
    d. extraversion.
    e. neuroticism.

12. All of the following propositions are part of learning theory EXCEPT
    a. behavior is strengthened by reinforcement.
    b. genetic differences operate via variations in fundamental physiological processes.
    c. behavior that is reinforced on a partial schedule should be even stronger and more resistant to extinction than behavior that is consistently reinforced.
    d. children learn new behaviors largely through modeling.
    e. from reinforcement and modeling, children learn not only overt behavior but also ideas, expectations, internal standards, and self-concepts.

13. Which of the following is characteristic of someone high in extraversion?
    a. affectionate
    b. forgiving
    c. generous
    d. enthusiastic
    e. trusting

14. Until recently, Oliver's peer interactions were almost exclusively with other boys. Now he is more interested in girls. Oliver is in which stage of psychosexual development?
    a. oral
    b. anal
    c. phallic
    d. latency
    e. genital

15. Correlation between measures of behavioral inhibition in children and physiological measures, such as muscle tension, heart rate, dilation of the pupil of the eye, and the chemical composition of both urine and saliva indicate that
    a. temperament is a set of learned habits.
    b. behavioral inhibition is strongly related to the environment.
    c. parental influences cause behavioral inhibition in children.
    d. behavioral inhibition is predictive of greater adaptability in adulthood.
    e. temperament is based on physiological responses.

16. Which of the following traits is characteristic of fixation at the oral stage?
    a. vanity.
    b. orderliness.
    c. recklessness.
    d. stinginess.
    e. overeating.

17. There is an old adage: "Do what I say, not what I do." What do research results tell us about children's responses in a situation in which a parent says one thing but does another?
    a. Children will imitate what the parent does.
    b. Children will imitate what the parent says.
    c. Children will imitate behavior of the mother but not of the father.
    d. If the words and the behavior are not consistent, the child will not imitate at all.
    e. Learning from modeling is automatic.

18. Dr. O'Hara is a psychoanalytic theorist. When treating a client, he will place the most emphasis on the
    a. equal significance of all stages of development.
    b. genetic programming.
    c. crucial significance of the earliest stages of development.
    d. fallacy of emphasizing stages of development.
    e. social learning skills.

19. Biological temperament theorists argue that _____ serves as a central mediating process, whereas social learning theorists argue that _____ acts as a central mediator.
    a. self scheme; self-concept
    b. inborn temperament; self-concept
    c. ego; inborn temperament
    d. inborn personality; inborn temperament
    e. self scheme; ego

20. Rothbart and Bates define "temperament" as
    a. a measurement of one's level of attachment and familial responsiveness.
    b. a characteristic of individuals that is evident within the first month and lasts through the fifth year.
    c. a dimension of one's personality measuring introversion and extroversion.
    d. the way one interacts with others and relates to the world.
    e. individual differences in emotional, motor, reactivity and self-regulation.

21. Observational learning or modeling involves
    a. attaching a new response to an old stimulus.
    b. learning by watching someone else perform some action.
    c. an unconditioned and a conditioned stimulus.
    d. attaching an old response to a new stimulus.
    e. parents and children exclusively.

22. Which stage in Erikson's theory corresponds to Freud's phallic stage?
    a. identity vs. role confusion
    b. industry vs. inferiority
    c. autonomy vs shame and doubt
    d. initiative vs. guilt
    e. trust vs. mistrust

23. Anna trusts almost everyone and is generous and affectionate with her family and friends. Anna would score high in
    a. agreeableness.
    b. conscientiousness.
    c. neuroticism.
    d. openness/intellect.
    e. extraversion.

24. All of the following are propositions on which the biological explanation of personality is based EXCEPT
    a. each individual is born with genetically determined characteristic patterns of responding to the environment and to other people.
    b. children learn not only overt behavior but also ideas, expectations, internal standards, and self-concepts from reinforcement and modeling.
    c. genetic differences operate via variations in fundamental physiological processes.
    d. temperamental dispositions persist through childhood and into adulthood.
    e. temperamental characteristics interact with the child's environment in ways that may strengthen or modify basic temperamental patterns.

25. Crockenberg found that insecure attachment between a mother and infant is most likely to occur under which of the following conditions?
    a. an irritable infant and a low level of maternal social support
    b. an irritable infant and a high level of support for the family
    c. a passive infant and a low level of paternal social support
    d. a passive infant and a high level of support for the family
    e. a passive infant and an overindulging mother


## Chapter 10

1. Because children's self-judgments mature over the years, what are teachers able to do for the first time by junior high school?
    a. emphasize effort and attitude
    b. compare children to fixed standards and national norms
    c. emphasize work habits and organizational skills
    d. consider children as individuals
    e. give short-answer tests

2. Self-esteem is especially unstable
    a. in the preschool years.
    b. in minority group adolescents but not Caucasian adolescents.
    c. in African Americans and Hispanic Americans during childhood.
    d. in early adolescence.
    e. in eighth-grade girls but not boys.

3. Research in sex-role stereotypes has shown that
    a. more children agree on what men are than on what women are.
    b. male qualities are more highly valued in Western societies.
    c. the female role is more strongly stereotyped.
    d. children stereotype more strongly than do adults.
    e. the female sex-role concept develops earlier.

4. As an Asian American teen, Sue Lee may
    a. have an easier time achieving an independent identity than her Caucasian peers.
    b. be encouraged by her parents to be independent.
    c. assume a foreclosed identity before she fully achieves a sense of ethnic identity.
    d. experience conflict between the individualistic standards of Western society and the collectivist values of traditional Asian culture.
    e. separate from her parents at an early age.

5. The key difference between gender schema theory and Kohlberg's theory is that
    a. Kohlberg's theory is cognitive; gender schema is not.
    b. to form the initial gender schema, a child need not understand that gender is permanent.
    c. gender schema theory only applies to preschoolers; Kohlberg's theory applies to all ages.
    d. Kohlberg's theory is not research-based.
    e. gender schema theory is largely psychoanalytic.

6. At what age do we first see children choosing to play with sex-stereotyped toys?
    a. age 2
    b. age 3
    c. age 4
    d. age 5
    e. age 6

7. As teenagers progress through adolescence, their self-concept becomes more
   a. concrete.
   b. tied to their physical characteristics.
   c. specific.
   d. differentiated.
   e. negative.

8. Research by Michael Lewis indicates that by _____ months of age, three-quarters of children tested touch their noses in the spot-of-rouge mirror test.
   a. 9 to 12
   b. 12 to 14
   c. 16
   d. 21
   e. 24

9. Maggie describes herself as follows. "I'm a human being, a girl, and a truthful person. I try to be helpful." How old is she likely to be?
   a. three
   b. six
   c. nine
   d. twelve
   e. fifteen

10. What is the term for a global judgment of self worth?
    a. self-love
    b. social referencing
    c. self-concept
    d. self-esteem
    e. identity achievement

11. Which of the following children would be at the greatest risk for low self-esteem?
    a. Archie, who is intelligent but weak and uncoordinated, and loves to play chess
    b. Kelly, who doesn't succeed in many of the things she tries, but has a lot of social support
    c. Latisha, who is a talented musician and intends to pursue a career in music over her parents' objections
    d. Willie, who is not athletic and has parents who value sports participation highly
    e. Aisha, who is pleased with her sports performance

12. Which of the following sex-role types is similar to a diffuse identity in Marcia's terms?
    a. masculine
    b. feminine
    c. androgynous
    d. bisexual
    e. undifferentiated

13. All of the following influence a child's self-esteem EXCEPT
    a. the child's direct experience with success and failure.
    b. the standards of the peer group.
    c. parents' attitudes and values.
    d. emphasis placed on performance by parents.
    e. the age of the child.

14. The correlation between self esteem scores obtained a few months apart is about
    a. .85
    b. .70
    c. .60
    d. .40
    e. .35

15. Gender refers to the
    a. biological aspects of maleness and femaleness.
    b. physiological makeup of females and males.
    c. sex chromosomes.
    d. psychological aspects of femaleness and maleness.
    e. specific XX and XY chromosome patterns.

16. When Angie describes herself as coordinated but very shy, she is defining her
    a. fused self.
    b. subjective self.
    c. concrete self.
    d. objective self.
    e. ego self.

17. Jorge, the son of a physician, is a second-year medical student, a Catholic, and a moderate in politics, just like his father and his grandfather expected him to be. On the basis of this information, his identity status in Marcia's system would probably be
    a. identity achievement.
    b. moratorium.
    c. foreclosure.
    d. identity diffusion.
    e. role confusion.

18. DeShawn is African American. As he nears adolescence he is most likely to
    a. prefer his subgroup over the majority culture.
    b. reject his own ethnic group.
    c. develop an identity very early.
    d. commit to the values of the majority culture.
    e. develop identity diffusion.

19. Sex roles are
    a. behaviors appropriate for one's sex.
    b. not apparent in children until after puberty.
    c. only applicable to adults.
    d. strictly physical.
    e. the same as gender concepts.

20. According to Marcia's conception of identity status, a person with identity achievement
    a. is in a crisis, and has not made a commitment.
    b. has not experienced a crisis but has made a commitment.
    c. has not experienced a crisis and has not made a commitment.
    d. is in a crisis but has made a commitment.
    e. has experienced a crisis and made a commitment.

21. In the Erikson/Marcia framework, a person who is in the midst of reexamining his or her values and choices, but who has not yet decided on some specific role or some particular ideology, is in the status of
    a. achievement.
    b. moratorium.
    c. foreclosure.
    d. diffusion.
    e. confusion.

22. A person who sees himself or herself as having both masculine and feminine traits is
    a. undifferentiated.
    b. bisexual.
    c. gender-confused.

d. androgynous.

e. gender-neutral.

23. Olga regularly plays with dolls and rarely chooses to play with tools or trucks. She is exhibiting which type of behavior?

a. sex constant

b. sex-typed

c. gender constant

d. gender secure

e. role neutral

24. Phinney's second stage of ethnic identity search is parallel to Marcia's concept of

a. foreclosure.

b. commitment.

c. moratorium.

d. crisis.

e. diffusion.

25. Eduardo has recently learned a variety of social scripts. He is probably how old?

a. six months

b. one year

c. 18 months

d. two years

e. three years

# CHAPTER 11

1. According to Dunphy, a crowd is

a. smaller than a clique.

b. made up of four to six people.

c. made up of several cliques.

d. exclusively male or female.

e. highly cohesive.

2. After the first weeks of a baby's life, fathers in the United States, compared to mothers, spend

a. more time in routine caregiving.

b. the same amount of time smiling at the baby.

c. more time playing with the baby.

d. more time talking to the baby.

e. less time roughhousing with the baby.

3. Whenever Holly's mother returns after leaving her with a sitter for a period of time, Holly makes no effort to make contact with her mother. Ainsworth would say that Holly is exhibiting what type of attachment?

a. insecure/avoidant

b. insecure/ambivalent

c. securely attached

d. insecure/disorganized

e. insecure/disoriented

4. Latisha is in first grade. How many reciprocal friendships is she most likely to have?

a. 5

b. 4

c. 3

d. 2

e. 1

5. Researchers have found that neglected children
   a. do poorly in school.
   b. are more prone to aggression.
   c. may be shy and prefer solitary activities.
   d. are deeply troubled by their lack of popularity.
   e. cannot change their status.

6. Which of the following is an accurate finding of research on bullies and their victims?
   a. Victims vary greatly in characteristics.
   b. Bullies have high levels of anxiety.
   c. Bullies tend to be more aggressive to adults that do non-bullies.
   d. Parents of bullies tend to set excessive limits.
   e. Most elementary school children have been victimized by a bully.

7. Bonita is about to give birth, and she wants to know the best way to achieve bonding with her newborn. You can tell her that
   a. immediate contact is necessary for the formation of stable, long-term affectional bonding.
   b. she should develop a mutual interlocking pattern of attachment behaviors.
   c. she should avoid too much contact in the first few weeks so the baby is not overstimulated.
   d. she should ignore the baby's signals and develop a strict schedule for feeding and naps.
   e. she should provide contact with several adults on an ongoing basis.

8. As a preschooler, Patti's goal-corrected attachment to her parents involves
   a. having her parents within reach.
   b. having her parents within sight.
   c. collaborative planning for being together.
   d. physical proximity except at nap time.
   e. requiring her parents to be present at all times.

9. Which of the following is true of preschoolers' friendships?
   a. They are consistently aware of each other's needs.
   b. They end with their first quarrel.
   c. There is no benefit to these friendships.
   d. By age 4, most children have developed a "best friend" relationship.
   e. They are deep and longlasting.

10. Rivalrous or critical relationships seem to be more common when
    a. siblings are widely separated in age.
    b. parents are less satisfied with their marriage.
    c. the siblings are sisters.
    d. the siblings go to the same school.
    e. there is a single parent home.

11. Bowlby stated that early infant-parent relationships
    a. are mutually and reciprocally shaped by way of an extended series of reinforcements, punishments, and extinctions.
    b. have survival value and are built and maintained by an interlocking repertoire of instinctive behaviors that create and sustain proximity between parent and child.
    c. are rooted in the infant's id instincts, especially sexual drives, which become associated with various erogenous zones of the body.
    d. are reflexive, organized patterns of behavior, which gradually become modified through the process of assimilation/accommodation.
    e. are based on affectional bonds that build a permanent secure base for later development.

12. Compared to her brother, Greg, and his friends, when Samantha plays with her friends they are
    a. more likely to be in smaller groups.
    b. more accepting of newcomers.
    c. more likely to play outdoors.
    d. more likely to spend less time near home.
    e. more likely to roam over a larger area.

13. In a Strange Situation test, Jeannine does not become upset when her mother leaves the room, and when her mother returns, she runs to her and then quiets and returns to playing with toys. What type of attachment does this indicate?
    a. secure
    b. insecure/avoidant
    c. insecure/ambivalent
    d. insecure/disorganized
    e. secure/disoriented

14. Chris has been labeled as insecure (detached/avoidant). Which of the following would be an accurate description of his behavior?
    a. He rarely explores his surroundings.
    b. He is extremely wary of strangers.
    c. He seeks and avoids contact at the same time.
    d. He appears dazed and confused.
    e. He will not resist his mother's efforts to make contact.

15. Cross cultural research using the Strange Situation has indicated that
    a. all cultures define ambivalent behavior in the same way.
    b. child rearing practices and values are similar in most cultures.
    c. the same factors in mother-infant interactions contribute to secure attachment in most cultures.
    d. the Strange Situation is an unreliable measure in Israel but not in Germany or Sweden.
    e. attachment classification cannot predict an infant's later social skills.

16. Infants rated as _____ are likely to have mothers who are abusive or have had trauma in their own childhoods, such as abuse or the early death of a parent.
    a. avoidant
    b. ambivalent
    c. disorganized/disoriented
    d. secure
    e. detached

17. Which of the following is the most common pattern in a caregiver relationship among siblings?
    a. older and younger sisters
    b. older and younger brothers
    c. older brother and younger sister
    d. older sister and younger brother
    e. identical twin sisters

18. Bowlby argued that by age 4 or 5, the internal working model becomes more
    a. focused.
    b. ambivalent.
    c. general.
    d. likely to change.
    e. inaccurate.

19. Which of the following is an accurate statement about adolescent romantic relationships?
    a. The progression toward romantic relationships occurs earlier for boys.
    b. Girls report falling in love for the first time earlier than boys.
    c. Teens prefer to date those with whom they believe they are in love.
    d. Boys want more psychological intimacy than do girls.
    e. Self disclosure occurs at the same rate for both sexes.

20. Pedro and Ricardo are brothers, and Pedro attempts to dominate Ricardo by teasing him and quarreling with him. Their relationship is characterized as a _____ relationship.
    a. caregiver
    b. buddy
    c. critical or conflicting
    d. rival
    e. casual or uninvolved

21. Olivia is depressed and therefore unreliably available to her infant. Her infant is likely to be
    a. avoidant.
    b. ambivalent.
    c. disorganized/disoriented.
    d. secure.
    e. detached.

22. The most profound change in peer relationships in adolescence is the shift from
    a. several close friends to one best friend.
    b. proximity based friendships to interest based friendships.
    c. same-sex friendships to heterosexual relationships.
    d. one best friend to several close friends.
    e. cliques to authentic friendships.

23. Which type of aggression in early childhood is predictive of a lifelong pattern of antisocial behavior?
    a. hostile
    b. physical
    c. trait
    d. instrumental
    e. relational

24. All of the following are examples of relational aggression EXCEPT
    a. facial expressions of disdain.
    b. ostracism.
    c. cruel gossiping.
    d. physical harm.
    e. passing derogatory notes.

25. Attachment is mostly influenced by
    a. the temperament of the child.
    b. the goodness of fit between the infant's temperament and his environment.
    c. the goodness of fit between the parent's temperament and her environment.
    d. the temperament of the mother.
    e. the temperament of either parent.

# Chapter 12

1. Kohlberg's sixth stage of universal ethical principles orientation
    a. involves following specific religious doctrines.
    b. was his most important stage.
    c. involves the assumption of personal responsibility.

    **d.** remains the foundation for his entire theory.

    **e.** involves judicious application of rewards.

2. Gilligan describes two distinct moral orientations that she called
   a. obedience and reward.
   b. hedonistic and needs-oriented.
   c. personal and universal.
   d. justice and care.
   e. concrete and formal.

3. Research suggests that in late adolescence, young people understand that
   a. close friendships can fill all a person's needs.
   b. friendships are static.
   c. friendships involve doing everything together.
   d. friendships can dissolve as members change.
   e. a good friendship will last for life.

4. A concern for how others will judge one's actions is typical of which level of moral development?
   a. universal ethical principles
   b. conventional
   c. preconventional
   d. postconventional
   e. postoperational

5. When Freddie describes his friend Roger as being better at arithmetic than he is, Freddie is expressing what Barenboim calls
   a. a behavioral comparison.
   b. an organizing relationship.
   c. egocentric empathy.
   d. a psychological construct.
   e. a concrete operation.

6. Turiel describes conventional rules as
   a. universal.
   b. arbitrary.
   c. obligatory.
   d. moral.
   e. permanent.

7. Mel's decisions always seem to be based on rules and laws. Mel is in which of Kohlberg's stages of moral development?
   a. two
   b. three
   c. four
   d. five
   e. six

8. Maria has been carefully saving her allowance so that she can buy a car when she gets her license. But recently, her father has been out of work and has some bills he is not able to pay, so Maria gives him her savings. Eisenberg would say that Maria is using which type of reasoning?
   a. hedonistic
   b. needs-oriented
   c. egocentric
   d. postconventional
   e. conventional

9. People show evidence of the beginning of self-chosen principles in which of Kohlberg's stages?
   a. one
   b. two
   c. three
   d. four
   e. five

10. Children can first empathize with several different emotions at once by
    a. 5 years of age.
    b. middle childhood.
    c. early adolescence.
    d. middle adolescence.
    e. late adolescence.

11. Sam is 4 years old. He is most likely to say that Louis is his best friend because Louis
    a. is a generous person.
    b. is very smart.
    c. shares his toys.
    d. plays with lots of children.
    e. has a good personality.

12. A shift to judgments based on rules or norms of a group to which the individual belongs is characteristic of which level of moral development?
    a. preconventional
    b. conventional
    c. postconventional
    d. postformal
    e. postoperational

13. According to Kohlberg, the most important cognitive-developmental variable for the development of moral reasoning is
    a. sensorimotor thinking.
    b. stage three thinking
    c. hedonistic thinking.
    d. knowledge of intentions.
    e. decline of egocentrism.

14. Universal ethical principles orientation occurs in which of Kohlberg's stages?
    a. two
    b. three
    c. four
    d. five
    e. six

15. According to Kochanska's research, we would expect a child to demonstrate more signs of guilt if he is
    a. assertive.
    b. fearful.
    c. aggressive.
    d. calm.
    e. confident.

16. Studies of the relationship between level of moral reasoning and moral behavior have
    a. failed to support Kohlberg's prediction that reasoning and behavior should be positively correlated.
    b. shown that people at the principled level disobey more societal rules than people at the conventional level.

c. shown positive correlations between reasoning and behavior in children but not in adults.

d. supported Kohlberg's prediction that reasoning and behavior should be positively correlated.

e. shown a positive correlation between moral reasoning and antisocial behavior.

17. Faced with a choice of helping her sister finish a project or playing outside with her own friends, a child says, "I will help, but only if she promises to help me the next time." This child is reasoning at what level in Eisenberg's levels of prosocial reasoning?
   a. hedonistic orientation
   b. needs-oriented orientation
   c. approval-by-others orientation
   d. internalized orientation
   e. mutual interpersonal orientation

18. Who proposed a model of prosocial reasoning?
   a. Kohlberg
   b. Eisenberg
   c. Piaget
   d. Freud
   e. Skinner

19. In stage _____ of Kohlberg's theory of moral development, individuals focus less on what is pleasing to particular people and more on conforming to an unquestioned, complex set of regulations.
   a. two
   b. three
   c. four
   d. five
   e. six

20. What three emotions did Erikson believe were equally important in moral development?
   a. shame, guilt, embarrassment
   b. guilt, shame, pride
   c. guilt, humility, love
   d. shame, love, embarrassment
   e. anger, guilt, shame

21. In high school, students are not allowed to leave the premises for lunch. This is a(n)
   a. moral rule.
   b. universal rule.
   c. conventional rule.
   d. amoral rule.
   e. permanent rule.

22. Children's social cognition develops from
   a. inner to outer characteristics.
   b. qualified to definite rules.
   c. a general view to an observer's view.
   d. definite to fixed rules.
   e. observation to inference.

23. By about what age can children tell the difference between the positive and negative facial expressions of others?
   a. 6 to 8 months
   b. 10 to 12 months
   c. 18 months
   d. 2 years
   e. 3 years

24. Who proposed that consequences teach children to obey moral rules?
    a. Freud
    b. Erikson
    c. Piaget
    d. Skinner
    e. Kohlberg

25. Kohlberg's research, confirmed by others, indicates that preconventional reasoning is dominant in
    a. infancy.
    b. elementary school.
    c. adolescence.
    d. early adulthood.
    e. late adulthood.

## Chapter 13

1. Based on Steinberg and Dornbusch's research on high school students, what parental factors are most closely associated with children achieving the best grades?
    a. working-class status and white ethnic identity
    b. involvement with the school and permissive
    c. permissive style and middle-class status
    d. authoritative style and involvement with the school
    e. authoritative but with little time to attend school functions.

2. Mrs. Mastrovianni is a very nurturant mother and communicates well with her children. They know that she expects them to behave in a mature manner and obey her rules. Mrs. Mastrovianni would fit Baumrind's classification of
    a. authoritarian.
    b. authoritative.
    c. neglecting.
    d. permissive.
    e. social cognitive.

3. Cross-ethnic group research has shown that the relationship between authoritative parenting and self-reliance and less delinquency occurs in
    a. White families only.
    b. Hispanic American, Asian American, and White families only.
    c. all ethnic groups studied in the research.
    d. Asian American and White families only.
    e. African American families only.

4. A study of children conceived by artificial insemination and raised by lesbian parents and heterosexual parents has shown
    a. dramatically lower cognitive development in children raised by lesbian mothers.
    b. poorer social development in children raised by lesbian couples.
    c. no differences in cognitive or social development.
    d. the same variables predicted outcomes in all groups.
    e. that family configuration is extremely influential on development.

5. According to Steinberg and Dornbusch's research, teenagers who had the lowest scores on measures of problem behavior and school achievement had parents who were
    a. authoritative.
    b. authoritarian.
    c. inconsistent.

    **d.** permissive.

    **e.** neglecting.

6. What percentage of children in the United States were living in a two-parent family in 2007?

    **a.** 95%

    **b.** 50%

    **c.** 70%

    **d.** 30%

    **e.** 80%

7. Single-parent families are most common among

    **a.** Asian Americans and African Americans.

    **b.** African Americans and Native Americans.

    **c.** Hispanic Americans and Asian Americans.

    **d.** Caucasian-Americans and Hispanic Americans.

    **e.** Native-Americans and Caucasian Americans.

8. A "psychologically unavailable" mother is often found when children are rated

    **a.** mentally retarded.

    **b.** insecurely attached.

    **c.** learning disabled.

    **d.** overindulged.

    **e.** independent.

9. Among Native Americans, there is a traditional cultural value viewing parenting as the responsibility of the entire family that is called

    **a.** familial parenting.

    **b.** extended family.

    **c.** group parenting.

    **d.** communal parenting.

    **e.** kin orientation.

10. Steinberg and Dornbusch's research found that the authoritative parenting style was most common in parents who were

    **a.** Asian American.

    **b.** African American.

    **c.** Hispanic American.

    **d.** Native American.

    **e.** Caucasian American.

11. Jillian has high self-esteem, is altruistic and achievement oriented, and complies with most parental requests. Her parents are

    **a.** authoritarian.

    **b.** neglecting.

    **c.** permissive.

    **d.** rejecting.

    **e.** authoritative.

12. All of the following are sex differences in mothers' expectations with respect to school-aged children's self-regulatory behavior EXCEPT

    **a.** they hold boys to a higher standard of accountability.

    **b.** they make different demands on boys and girls.

    **c.** they give more autonomy to boys.

    **d.** they provide boys and girls with the same guidance.

    **e.** they expect boys to fail more often.

13. Baumrind proposed the following three styles of child rearing:
    a. secure, insecure, neglectful
    b. praising, punishing, diplomatic
    c. conventional, pre-conventional, post-conventional
    d. permissive, authoritarian, authoritative
    e. disorganized, permissive, authoritative

14. Approximately what percentage of Asian American children live in poverty?
    a. 33
    b. 17
    c. 14
    d. 5
    e. 1

15. Compared to later-born children, firstborn children are generally
    a. expected to grow up more slowly.
    b. punished more.
    c. less likely to go to college.
    d. more likely to rebel.
    e. less likely to achieve emminence.

16. Authoritative parents' approach to discipline is to
    a. use no punishment, only reinforcement.
    b. use more physical punishment with older children.
    c. use milder punishments such as time out.
    d. be inconsistent and severe.
    e. be unresponsive to communication.

17. All of the following are dimensions on which families differ that seem to be significant for the child EXCEPT
    a. emotional tone.
    b. responsiveness of parents.
    c. quality of communication.
    d. socioeconomic level.
    e. how control is exercised.

18. Research indicates that maternal employement is associated with
    a. obesity in children.
    b. relationship satisfaction among mothers.
    c. high achievement in children.
    d. relationship satisfaction in mothers' partners.
    e. lower rates of depression in children.

19. Mr. and Mrs. Miller tend to temperamentally stereotype their infants. This is likely to result in
    a. an expectation that their daughter will be more active.
    b. pushing their quiet son to be more active.
    c. a perception of their son as more emotionally sensitive.
    d. tolerating a higher activity level in their daughter.
    e. labeling their son as fearful more often than angry.

20. Tom is 23 years old. His parents divorced when he was young. He is likely to
    a. marry early and stay married.
    b. go on to college and succeed.
    c. be well adjusted as an adult.

    **d.** struggle with fears of intimacy.

    **e.** stay married for life.

21. Which of the variables below is a key determinant of the impact of parental unemployment on a child's development in a two-career family?

    **a.** the family's income

    **b.** the child's temperament

    **c.** increased levels of warmth and supportiveness in the still-employed parent

    **d.** the willingness of the still-employed parent to get a second job

    **e.** the quality of the child's attachment to the unemployed parent

22. By adolescence, children of divorce are more likely than peers to

    **a.** get a job.

    **b.** be sexually active earlier.

    **c.** avoid dating.

    **d.** become involved with sports.

    **e.** become more involved in school.

23. Among 45- to 49-year-olds in the United States, what percentage of White American women have never married?

    **a.** 9%

    **b.** 12%

    **c.** 14%

    **d.** 16%

    **e.** 30%

24. Carlotta has just been divorced. Her income will probably drop by how much?

    **a.** 10 percent

    **b.** 30 percent

    **c.** 45 percent

    **d.** 55 percent

    **e.** 60 percent

25. How do the demands of raising a difficult child affect the family system?

    **a.** Parents may be too frazzled to meet the needs of their other children.

    **b.** The quality of the parents' relationship may decline.

    **c.** Extended family members are less involved.

    **d.** none of the above.

    **e.** more achievement oriented.

## Chapter 14

1. Compared to poor parents with less education, poor parents with relatively more education typically

    **a.** provide about the same level of intellectual stimulation.

    **b.** are just about as responsive.

    **c.** are more authoritarian.

    **d.** talk more to their children.

    **e.** are less involved with their children.

2. Cheryl wants to win the school spelling bee. This is a(n)

    **a.** task goal.

    **b.** competence goal.

    **c.** ability goal.

    **d.** learning goal.

    **e.** cognitive goal.

3. Middle schools tend to emphasize
   a. ability grouping.
   b. internal control.
   c. cooperation over competition.
   d. mixed grouping.
   e. task grouping.

4. Research consistently demonstrates all of the following about self-care children EXCEPT
   a. they are less socially skilled.
   b. they have a greater number of behavioral problems.
   c. they are poorly adjusted in terms of peer relationships.
   d. they have poorer school performance.
   e. they are better able to control impulses.

5. Research on teen employment by Mortimer and colleagues has shown that
   a. unskilled work has no impact on school engagement.
   b. there is no difference in the effects of part-time or full-time work.
   c. school performance declines dramatically for all types of work.
   d. full-time work is better than part-time work.
   e. jobs that teach useful skills increase a teen's confidence in his or her ability.

6. In the United States, about what proportion of children under age 6 years in nonparental care are enrolled in center-based care?
   a. three-quarters
   b. two-thirds
   c. one-half
   d. one-third
   e. one-quarter

7. Which of the following best describes how most parents control their teens' TV watching?
   a. Most allow teens to watch television only after their homework is completed.
   b. Most use TV time as a reward for good grades.
   c. Most forbid teens to watch programs with sexual or violent content.
   d. Most have few, if any, rules for television.
   e. Most exhibit inconsistent enforcement of restrictions on television watching.

8. Research by Bachman & Schulenberg indicates that the more hours per week a teen spends in paid employment, the
   a. less engaged in school she will be.
   b. less drug usage and delinquent behavior he reports.
   c. less aggression she shows toward peers.
   d. fewer arguments he has with parents.
   e. more satisfied he is with his life.

9. Suppose that you are a parent with a one-year-old infant. You are looking for a good day care setting for your child, and you visit a series of day care centers in your town. Which of the following questions should you be sure to ask about the caregivers at each center?
   a. "What is the average age of your caregivers?"
   b. "Do your caregivers have PhDs?"
   c. "How much training have your caregivers had in child development?"
   d. "Did your caregivers experience day care themselves as children?"
   e. "Do your caregivers have children of their own?"

10. Several researchers have found that the most likely cause of the negative effects of nonparental care on a child's social competence is
    a. the length of time spent in child care.
    b. the age at which the child first enters child care.
    c. the socioeconomic level of the family.
    d. the ethnicity of the family.
    e. the relative quality of the care.

11. The results of the NICHD study led to which conclusion about the impact of day care on attachment?
    a. An insensitive mother is the only cause of an insecure attachment.
    b. No matter how sensitive the mother, day care is harmful.
    c. All mothers of day care children suffer from depresssion.
    d. The child's personality is the only factor.
    e. Day care itself was unrelated to the security of the child's attachment.

12. The largest body of research into the impact of television has focused on the potential impact of television on children's
    a. aggressiveness.
    b. school performance.
    c. physical development.
    d. assertiveness.
    e. social skills.

13. What was the response of the children after viewing adults acting violently towards a blow-up clown in Bandura's "Bobo doll" experiment?
    a. They showed no signs of inceased agression.
    b. Boys acted more aggressively but girls showed no increase in aggression.
    c. The children were found to imitate the aggressive acts of the adults.
    d. They showed complete disinterest in the bobo doll in the room.
    e. They engaged in more sociodramatic play.

14. Which of the following children is least likely to display aggressive behavior upon entering kindergarten?
    a. Marcus, is cared for by a neighbor two afternoons a week.
    b. Julius, who has never been in nonparental care.
    c. Joachim, who has been cared for by a nanny since age 2.
    d. Michael, who has been cared for by his grandmother since his fist birthday.
    e. Maria, who has been enrolled in center-based care since she was 3 weeks old.

15. Lucinda is on the middle school track team and competes in short-distance running events. Her goal is to improve her time in all of her events at every track meet she participates in. What type of goal does Lucinda have?
    a. competence
    b. ability
    c. athletic
    d. physical
    e. task

16. In a middle school, homeroom teachers monitor homework completion and grades. These teachers are performing the role of
    a. principals.
    b. counselors.
    c. coaches.
    d. mentors.
    e. advisors.

17. Which group of students has the highest dropout rate?
   a. Caucasian Americans
   b. African Americans
   c. Asian Americans
   d. Hispanic Americans
   e. Native Americans

18. What do people of the same ethnicity have in common?
   a. physical characteristic
   b. place of residence
   c. nationality, language, and culture
   d. political views
   e. None of these.

19. A characteristic of resilient children and adolescents is
   a. concrete operational thought.
   b. high self-esteem.
   c. gang membership.
   d. skepticism.
   e. dependence.

20. Steinberg's research of over 20,000 teenagers in high school and their families found that
   a. a high proportion don't take school seriously.
   b. the majority of students study every night.
   c. the peer culture encourages academic success.
   d. most after-school activities reinforce school work.
   e. most parents are engaged in their children's schooling.

21. Five-year-old Willie is in day care for about nine hours a day so his mother can work to support the family. When his mother picks him up, she is exhausted. According to Belsky, Willie is most at risk for
   a. early aggressive behavior.
   b. insecure attachment.
   c. poor cognitive development.
   d. more childhood illnesses.
   e. poor social skills.

22. One reason for the difficulties involved in studying the effects of nonparental care is that
   a. most children receive similar types of care.
   b. few children are cared for by non-relatives.
   c. children tend to be enrolled in more than one type of care at a time.
   d. family care is more popular than center-based care.
   e. only poor children are enrollened in center-based care in infancy.

23. Compared to other children, children raised in poverty
   a. have higher rates of illness and disabilities.
   b. have the same distribution of IQ scores.
   c. develop cognitively at the same rate.
   d. are less likely to repeat a grade.
   e. are less likely to be poor as adults.

24. Longitudinal research involving teenagers who were in high school in the late 1980's revealed that the more hours participants worked during high school, the more likely they were to
   a. avoid drug and alcohol use.
   b. get along with peers.
   c. get along with parents.
   d. be well rested.
   e. be dissatisfied with life.

25. Belsky found that infants who enter day care before their first birthdays are at a slightly heightened risk for
   a. mental retardation.
   b. poor motor skills.
   c. inadequate social skills.
   d. insecure attachment.
   e. lower cognitive skills.

# Chapter 15

1. Beginning at 13 to 15 years, girls are _____ as likely to report high or chronic levels of depression as boys.
   a. half
   b. equally
   c. twice
   d. three times
   e. four times

2. What do 4% to 8% of people with anorexia do?
   a. starve themselves to death
   b. fully recover from the disorder
   c. have symptoms of schizophrenia
   d. also show signs of bulimia
   e. none of the above

3. Wallie's ADHD would be categorized as which type of problem?
   a. internalizing
   b. mood
   c. externalizing
   d. anxiety based
   e. attention

4. Connie defies her parents and her teachers; Zeke has been labeled a delinquent. They both have which type of problem?
   a. attention
   b. externalizing
   c. internalizing
   d. psychosomatic
   e. neurotic

5. Autistic disorder and Asperger's disorder are the two most frequently diagnosed
   a. forms of mental retardation.
   b. attention problems.
   c. forms of depression.
   d. learning disabilities.
   e. pervasive developmental disorders.

6. Dorothea went to her doctor complaining of stomach irritation and hair loss. Her doctor also noted that she is dehydrated and has tooth decay and lowered body temperature. What is the most likely diagnosis?
   a. bulimia
   b. anorexia
   c. cancer
   d. severe infection
   e. conduct disorder

7. Neuroimaging studies of children with and without ADHD suggest that children with the disorder have
   a. the same brain structure as non-ADHD children.
   b. a lower level of neurotransmitters.
   c. a larger visual cortex than non-ADHD children.
   d. different responses to emotion-provoking stimuli.
   e. smaller frontal lobes.

8. Monica is preoccupied with eating. She eats huge amounts of food, then purges by using laxatives. Monica suffers from
   a. anorexia.
   b. depression.
   c. bulimia.
   d. anxiety.
   e. stress.

9. The profoundly gifted tend to
   a. be extroverted.
   b. be popular with classmates.
   c. have emotional problems.
   d. be viewed as normal by their peers.
   e. be overconforming.

10. Boris is a defiant and oppositional preschooler. Boris's risk of developing childhood-onset conduct disorder will be influenced by
   a. his temperament.
   b. exposure to anti-social peers.
   c. how his parents respond to his behavior.
   d. popularity with his peers.
   e. the type of preschool he attends.

11. All of the following present evidence that ADHD has a biological component EXCEPT
   a. The behavioral pattern begins very early and has a very strong physical component.
   b. Biological treatment, i.e., stimulant medication, is very often effective.
   c. If one identical twin is diagnosed as hyperactive, the other is likely to have the same diagnosis.
   d. Teachers often report that children first model the ADHD behaviors that they witness in other children prior to diagnosis.
   e. Brain imaging scans show subtle differences in the brains of individuals with ADHD and those without.

12. The developmental psychopathological approach emphasizes all of the following EXCEPT
   a. normal and abnormal development emerging from the same processes.
   b. normal and abnormal development being interrelated.
   c. the pathways to deviant and normal behavior.
   d. the same maladaptive behavior being reached by different pathways.
   e. maladaptive behavior is rarely being long-term.

13. A longitudinal study of youth growing up in a working-class neighborhood in the United States indicates that _____ of those who had had a serious depression by age 18 had also attempted suicide.
   a. one-half
   b. one-quarter
   c. one-third
   d. one-fifth
   e. two-thirds

14. Terrell has ADHD. He is most likely to be given which type of medication?
    a. stimulant
    b. depressant
    c. sedative
    d. antipsychotic
    e. antianxiety

15. Robinson suggests labeling children with high IQs (130 to 150), but without extraordinary ability in any one area as
    a. intelligent.
    b. gifted.
    c. garden-variety gifted.
    d. bright.
    e. superior.

16. In order to be diagnosed as bulimic, a person has to indulge in bingeing and purging at least
    a. every day.
    b. once a week.
    c. twice a week.
    d. once a month.
    e. twice a month.

17. Usually we label a child's development atypical or deviant only if a problem is at the extreme end of the continuum for that behavior, or if it persists for _____ or longer.
    a. two weeks
    b. one month
    c. three months
    d. six months
    e. one year

18. Kate has an eating disorder, and Jimmy suffers from anxiety. Both have
    a. externalizing problems.
    b. disturbances of conduct.
    c. internalizing problems.
    d. genetic disorders.
    e. attention problems.

19. What percent of children in the United States has some type of pervasive developmental disorder?
    a. 1
    b. 4
    c. 10
    d. 25
    e. 50

20. Developmental psychopathology integrates perspectives
    a. anthropology.
    a. sociology.
    b. geneology.
    c. neurology.
    d. all of the above.

21. Patrice had anorexia nervosa as a teen but is now recovered. She is most likely to have
    a. obsessive-compulsive disorder.
    b. antisocial personality disorder.
    c. schizophrenia.
    d. depression.
    e. a conduct disorder.

22. Besides high IQs, the gifted in Terman's study were
    a. healthier.
    b. taller.
    c. not interested in sports.
    d. not successful in later life.
    e. emotionally disabled.

23. Children with Asperger's differ from children with autism in that they
    a. have excellent social skills.
    b. good social relationships.
    c. age appropriate language skills.
    d. lower IQs.
    e. solid theories of mind.

24. A pattern of behavior that includes high levels of aggression, argumentativeness, bullying, disobedience, irritability, and threatening behavior is a(n)
    a. conduct disorder.
    b. ADHD.
    c. attention disorder.
    d. personality disorder.
    e. psychosomatic disorder.

25. Advocates of the developmental psychopathology approach do believe that
    a. change is possible only in early childhood.
    b. later change is unconstrained by earlier adaptations.
    c. maladaptive behavior is usually the result of a genetically controlled pathway.
    d. genes influence the development of psychopathology to some degree.
    e. history and roots of behavior are usually very similar among children with the same disorder.

# SELF-TESTS ANSWER KEY

## Chapter 1

| | | | |
|---|---|---|---|
| 1. b. | 8. b. | 14. a. | 20. a. |
| 2. e. | 9. d. | 15. c. | 21. a. |
| 3. d. | 10. c. | 16. b. | 22. e. |
| 4. b. | 11. c. | 17. e. | 23. e. |
| 5. e. | 12. d. | 18. e. | 24. b. |
| 6. c. | 13. a. | 19. d. | 25. c. |
| 7. e. | | | |

## Chapter 2

| | | | |
|---|---|---|---|
| 1. b. | 8. e. | 14. e. | 20. d. |
| 2. b. | 9. a. | 15. a. | 21. c. |
| 3. c. | 10. a. | 16. c. | 22. e. |
| 4. d. | 11. c. | 17. b. | 23. b. |
| 5. b. | 12. e. | 18. d. | 24. a. |
| 6. d. | 13. c. | 19. c. | 25. b. |
| 7. d. | | | |

## Chapter 3

| | | | |
|---|---|---|---|
| 1. d. | 8. d. | 14. b. | 20. d. |
| 2. c. | 9. e. | 15. b. | 21. c. |
| 3. b. | 10. d. | 16. a. | 22. d. |
| 4. d. | 11. a. | 17. e. | 23. e. |
| 5. b. | 12. d. | 18. c. | 24. c. |
| 6. c. | 13. d. | 19. e. | 25. a. |
| 7. d. | | | |

## Chapter 4

| | | | |
|---|---|---|---|
| 1. e. | 8. e. | 14. c. | 20. a. |
| 2. a. | 9. e. | 15. e. | 21. d. |
| 3. e. | 10. b. | 16. e. | 22. c. |
| 4. e. | 11. c. | 17. a. | 23. a. |
| 5. b. | 12. e. | 18. a. | 24. b. |
| 6. d. | 13. a. | 19. e. | 25. a. |
| 7. a. | | | |

## Chapter 5

| | | | |
|---|---|---|---|
| 1. a. | 8. d. | 14. b. | 20. e. |
| 2. c. | 9. d. | 15. a. | 21. d. |
| 3. c. | 10. c. | 16. a. | 22. c. |
| 4. b. | 11. e. | 17. e. | 23. d. |
| 5. b. | 12. e. | 18. c. | 24. e. |
| 6. c. | 13. c. | 19. a. | 25. c. |
| 7. c. | | | |

## Chapter 6

| | | | |
|---|---|---|---|
| 1. b. | 8. c. | 14. a. | 20. b. |
| 2. a. | 9. b. | 15. e. | 21. d. |
| 3. a. | 10. e. | 16. c. | 22. a. |
| 4. e. | 11. a. | 17. d. | 23. d. |
| 5. c. | 12. a. | 18. a. | 24. b. |
| 6. b. | 13. b. | 19. b. | 25. d. |
| 7. b. | | | |

## Chapter 7

| | | | |
|---|---|---|---|
| 1. c. | 8. c. | 14. c. | 20. d. |
| 2. a. | 9. b. | 15. d. | 21. d. |
| 3. b. | 10. c. | 16. c. | 22. a. |
| 4. d. | 11. b. | 17. e. | 23. e. |
| 5. a. | 12. b. | 18. b. | 24. a. |
| 6. a. | 13. c. | 19. b. | 25. a. |
| 7. a. | | | |

## Chapter 8

| | | | |
|---|---|---|---|
| 1. b. | 8. b. | 14. c. | 20. c. |
| 2. a. | 9. c. | 15. b. | 21. d. |
| 3. a. | 10. c. | 16. b. | 22. a. |
| 4. d. | 11. b. | 17. b. | 23. e. |
| 5. d. | 12. c. | 18. c. | 24. a. |
| 6. b. | 13. b. | 19. b. | 25. e. |
| 7. c. | | | |

## Chapter 9

| | | | |
|---|---|---|---|
| 1. c. | 8. d. | 14. e. | 20. e. |
| 2. e. | 9. d. | 15. e. | 21. b. |
| 3. d. | 10. d. | 16. e. | 22. d. |
| 4. a. | 11. e. | 17. a. | 23. a. |
| 5. b. | 12. b. | 18. c. | 24. b. |
| 6. b. | 13. d. | 19. b. | 25. a. |
| 7. a. | | | |

## Chapter 10

| | | | |
|---|---|---|---|
| 1. b. | 8. d. | 14. c. | 20. e. |
| 2. d. | 9. d. | 15. d. | 21. b. |
| 3. b. | 10. d. | 16. d. | 22. d. |
| 4. d. | 11. d. | 17. c. | 23. b. |
| 5. b. | 12. e. | 18. a. | 24. d. |
| 6. a. | 13. e. | 19. a. | 25. d. |
| 7. d. | | | |

## Chapter 11

| | | | |
|---|---|---|---|
| 1. c. | 8. c. | 14. e. | 20. c. |
| 2. c. | 9. d. | 15. c. | 21. a. |
| 3. a. | 10. b. | 16. c. | 22. c. |
| 4. e. | 11. b. | 17. d. | 23. c. |
| 5. c. | 12. a. | 18. c. | 24. d. |
| 6. c. | 13. a. | 19. c. | 25. b. |
| 7. b. | | | |

## Chapter 12

| | | | |
|---|---|---|---|
| 1. c. | 8. b. | 14. e. | 20. b. |
| 2. d. | 9. e. | 15. b. | 21. c. |
| 3. d. | 10. b. | 16. d. | 22. e. |
| 4. b. | 11. c. | 17. a. | 23. b. |
| 5. a. | 12. b. | 18. b. | 24. d. |
| 6. b. | 13. e. | 19. c. | 25. b. |
| 7. c. | | | |

# Chapter 13

| | | | |
|---|---|---|---|
| 1. d. | 8. b. | 14. e. | 20. d. |
| 2. b. | 9. e. | 15. b. | 21. c. |
| 3. c. | 10. e. | 16. c. | 22. b. |
| 4. c. | 11. e. | 17. d. | 23. a. |
| 5. e. | 12. a. | 18. a. | 24. c. |
| 6. c. | 13. d. | 19. b. | 25. a. |
| 7. b. | | | |

# Chapter 14

| | | | |
|---|---|---|---|
| 1. d. | 8. a. | 14. e. | 20. a. |
| 2. c. | 9. c. | 15. e. | 21. b. |
| 3. a. | 10. e. | 16. d. | 22. c. |
| 4. e. | 11. e. | 17. d. | 23. a. |
| 5. e. | 12. a. | 18. c. | 24. e. |
| 6. e. | 13. c. | 19. b. | 25. d. |
| 7. d. | | | |

# Chapter 15

| | | | |
|---|---|---|---|
| 1. c. | 8. c. | 14. a. | 20. e. |
| 2. a. | 9. c. | 15. c. | 21. a. |
| 3. e. | 10. c. | 16. c. | 22. a. |
| 4. b. | 11. d. | 17. d. | 23. c. |
| 5. e. | 12. e. | 18. c. | 24. a. |
| 6. a. | 13. d. | 19. a. | 25. d. |
| 7. d. | | | |

# GLOSSARY

**adaptive reflexes** Reflexes that are essential to the infant's survival but that disappear in the first year of life.

**ability goal** A goal orientation associated with a desire to be superior to others.

**academic approach** An approach to early childhood education that provides children with instruction in skills needed for success in school.

**accommodation** That part of the adaptation process proposed by Piaget by which a person modifies existing schemes as a result of new experiences or creates new schemes when old ones no longer handle the data.

**achievement test** Test designed to assess a child's learning of specific material taught in school, such as spelling or arithmetic computation; in the United States, achievement tests are typically given to all children in designated grades.

**adaptation** The processes through which schemes change.

**ADHD/combined type** ADHD in which both hyperactivity and inattention are problems.

**ADHD/hyperactive/impulsive type** ADHD in which hyperactivity is the main problem.

**ADHD/inattentive type** ADHD in which inattention is the main problem.

**adolescent-onset conduct disorder** A conduct disorder that begins only in adolescence; it is typically less severe and persistent than childhood-onset conduct disorder.

**affectional bond** An enduring tie to a partner, viewed as unique.

**aggression** Behavior that is aimed at harming or injuring another person or object.

**agreeableness** One of the Big Five personality traits; a person who scores high on this trait is characterized by trust, generosity, kindness, and sympathy—also shapes future experience.

**amnion** The sac, or bag, filled with liquid in which the embryo/fetus floats during prenatal life.

**analytical intelligence** One of three types of intelligence in Sternberg's triarchic theory of intelligence; the type of intelligence typically measured on IQ tests, including the ability to plan, remember facts, and organize information.

**androgynous** One of four sex-role types suggested by the work of Bem and others; a type characterized by high levels of both masculine and feminine qualities.

**anorexia nervosa** Eating disorder characterized by self-starvation.

**anoxia** A shortage of oxygen. This is one of the potential risks at birth, and it can result in brain damage if it is prolonged.

**Asperger's disorder** A disorder in which children possess the other characteristics of autistic disorder but have intact language and cognitive skills.

**assimilation** That part of the adaptation process proposed by Piaget that involves absorbing new experiences or information into existing schemes. Experience is not taken in 'as is,' however, but is modified (or interpreted) somewhat so as to fit the preexisting schemes.

**association areas** Parts of the brain where sensory, motor, and intellectual functions are linked.

**attachment** A type of affectional bond in which the presence of the partner adds a special sense of security, a 'safe base,' for the individual.

**attachment behaviors** The collection of (probably) instinctive behaviors of one person toward another that bring about or maintain proximity and caregiving, such as the smile of the young infant; behaviors that reflect an attachment.

**attention deficit hyperactivity disorder (ADHD)** A disorder in which a child shows both significant problems in focusing attention and physical hyperactivity.

**attention problems** A category of psychopathologies that impair one's ability to concentrate, including attention deficit hyperactivity disorder, attention deficit disorder, and hyperkinetic disorder.

**atypical development** An enduring pattern of behavior that is unusual, compared to the behavior of others of the child's age, and that interferes with the child's development in some significant way.

**auditory acuity** How well one can hear.

**authoritarian style** One of the three parental styles described by Baumrind, characterized by high levels of control and maturity demands and low levels of nurturance and communication.

**authoritative style** One of the three parental styles described by Baumrind, characterized by high levels of control, nurturance, maturity demands, and communication.

**autistic disorder** A disorder in which children have much more limited language skills than others of the same age, an inability to engage in reciprocal social relationships, and a severely limited range of interests.

**automaticity** The ability to recall information from long-term memory without effort.

**axons** Tail-like extensions of neurons.

**babbling** The repetitive vocalizing of consonant-vowel combinations by an infant, typically beginning at about 6 months of age.

**balanced approach** Reading instruction that combines explicit phonics instruction with other strategies for helping children acquire literacy.

**Bayley Scales of Infant Development** The best-known and most widely used test of infant 'intelligence.'

**behavior genetics** The study of the genetic contributions to behavior or traits such as intelligence or personality.

**behaviorism** The theoretical view that defines development in terms of behavior changes caused by environmental influences.

**Big Five** The five primary dimensions of adult personality identified by researchers: extraversion, agreeableness, conscientiousness, neuroticism, and openness/intellect.

**bilingual education** As practiced in the United States, a school program for students who are not proficient in English in which instruction in basic subject matter is given in the children's native language during the first 2 or 3 years of schooling, with a gradual transition to full English instruction over several years.

**birth order** A child's position in the sequence of children within a family, such as first-born, later-born, or only child.

**blastocyst** Name for the mass of cells from roughly 4 to 10 days after fertilization.

**blended family** A family that is established when a single parent marries a nonparent or parent.

**BMI-for-age** Comparison of an individual child's BMI against established norms for his or her age group and sex.

**body mass index (BMI)** A measure that estimates a person's proportion of body fat.

**bone age** A measure of physical maturation based on x-ray examination of bones, typically the wrist and hand bones. Two children of the same chronological age may have different bone age because their rates of physical maturation differ.

**bulimia** Eating disorder characterized by alternating periods of bingeing and purging.

**cell body** The part of the cell that contains the nucleus and in which all the cell's vital functions are carried out.

**centration** The young child's tendency to think of the world in terms of one variable at a time.

**cephalocaudal** One of two basic patterns of physical development in infancy (the other is proximodistal), in which development proceeds from the head downward.

**cerebral cortex** The convoluted gray portion of the brain, which governs perception, body movement, thinking, and language.

**cesarean section (C-section)** Delivery of the child through an incision in the mother's abdomen.

**childhood-onset conduct disorder** Conduct disorder beginning in childhood; the pattern is linked to rejection by peers and to conduct problems that persist into adolescence and adulthood.

**chorion** The outer layer of cells of the blastocyst during prenatal development, from which both the placenta and the umbilical cord are formed.

**chromosomes** The structures, arrayed in 23 pairs, within each cell in the body that contain genetic information. Each chromosome is made up of many segments, called genes.

**class inclusion** The principle that subordinate classes of objects are included in superordinate classes.

**classical conditioning** One of three major types of learning. An automatic, or unconditional response such as an emotion or a reflex comes to be triggered by a new cue, called the conditional stimulus, after having been paired several times with that stimulus.

**clinical depression (major depressive disorder)** A combination of sad mood, sleeping and eating disturbances, and difficulty concentrating that lasts six months or longer.

**clique** A group of four to six friends with strong affectional bonds and high levels of group solidarity and loyalty; the term is used by researchers to describe a self-chosen group of friends.

**cognitive-developmental theories** Developmental theories that emphasize children's actions on the environment and suggest that age-related changes in reasoning precede and explain changes in other domains.

**cohort** A group of individuals who share the same historical experiences at the same times in their lives.

**colic** A pattern of persistent and often inconsolable crying, totaling more than three hours a day, found in some infants in the first 3 to 4 months of life.

**color constancy** The ability to see the color of an object as remaining the same despite changes in illumination or shadow.

**competence** A person's basic, underlying level of skill, displayed under ideal circumstances. It is not possible to measure competence directly.

**concrete operations stage** Piaget's term for the stage of development between ages 6 and 12, during which children become able to think logically.

**conduct disorder** Diagnostic term for a pattern of deviant behavior including high levels of aggressive, antisocial, or delinquent acts.

**conscience** The list of 'don'ts' in the superego; violation of any of these leads to feelings of guilt.

**conscientiousness** One of the Big Five personality traits; a person who scores high on this trait is characterized by efficiency, organization, planfulness, and reliability.

**conservation** The understanding that the quantity or amount of a substance remains the same even when there are external changes in its shape or arrangement.

**constraint** As used in discussions of language development, an assumption that is presumed to be built-in or learned early (a 'default option') by which a child figures out what words refer to. Examples include the principle of contrast and the whole object constraint.

**control group** A group of participants in an experiment who receive either no special treatment or some neutral treatment.

**conventional morality** The second level of moral development proposed by Kohlberg, in which a person's judgments are dominated by considerations of group values and laws.

**conventional rules** As defined by Turiel, arbitrary, socially defined rules specific to a particular culture, subculture, group, or setting, such as 'Don't run in the halls' or 'Smoking allowed only in designated areas.'

**cooing** Making repetitive vowel sounds, particularly the uuu sound; the behavior develops early in the prelinguistic period, when babies are between about 1 and 4 months of age.

**corpus callosum** The structure that connects the right and left hemispheres of the cerebral cortex.

**correlation** A statistic used to describe the strength of a relationship between two variables. It can range from −1.00 to +1.00. The closer it is to +1.00 or −1.00, the stronger the relationship being described.

**creative intelligence** One of three types of intelligence described by Sternberg in his triarchic theory of intelligence; includes insightfulness and the ability to see new relationships among events or experiences.

**creativity** The ability to produce original, appropriate, and valuable ideas and/or solutions to problems.

**critical period** Any time period during development when an organism is especially responsive to and learns from a specific type of stimulation. The same stimulation at other points in development has little or no effect.

**cross-cultural research** Any study that involves comparisons of different cultures or contexts.

**cross-sectional design** A form of research study in which samples of participants from several different age groups are studied at the same time.

**crowd** A larger and looser group of friends than a clique, normally made up of several cliques that have joined together; a reputation-based group, common in adolescent subculture, with widely agreed-upon characteristics.

**cumulative deficit** Any difference between groups in IQ or achievement test scores that becomes larger over time.

**decentration** Thinking that takes multiple variables into account.

**deductive logic** Reasoning from the general to the particular, from a rule to an expected instance or from a theory to a hypothesis, characteristic of formal operational thinking.

**delinquency** A subcategory of conduct disorder involving explicit lawbreaking.

**dendrites** Branchlike protrusions from the cell bodies of neurons.

**deoxyribonucleic acid (DNA)** The chemical of which chromosomes are composed.

**dependent variable** The variable in an experiment that is expected to show the impact of manipulations of the independent variable; also called the outcome variable.

**depression** A combination of sad mood and difficulty carrying out daily functions.

**developmental approach** An approach to early childhood education that supports children's development of naturally occurring milestones.

**developmental psychopathology** A relatively new approach to the study of deviance that emphasizes that normal and abnormal development have common roots and that pathology can arise from many different pathways.

**developmental science** The study of age-related changes in behavior, thinking, emotions, and social relationships.

**developmental theories** Sets of statements that propose general principles of development.

**developmentally appropriate practices** Early childhood education practices based on an understanding of developmental universals, individual differences, and contextual variables.

**difficult child** An infant who is irritable and irregular in behavior.

**dilation** A key process in the first stage of childbirth, during which the cervix widens sufficiently to allow the infant's head to pass into the birth canal. Full dilation is 10 centimeters.

**divergent thinking** The ability to produce multiple solutions to problems that have no clear answer.

**dominant/recessive pattern of inheritance** The pattern of genetic transmission in which a single dominant gene influences a person's phenotype, but an individual must have two recessive genes to express a recessive trait.

**Down syndrome (trisomy 21)** A genetic anomaly in which every cell contains three copies of chromosome 21 rather than two. Children born with this genetic pattern have characteristic physical features and usually have mental retardation.

**dynamic systems theory** The view that several factors interact to influence development.

**early childhood education** Educational programs for children between birth and 8 years.

**easy child** An infant who adapts easily to change and who exhibits regular patterns of eating, sleeping, and alertness.

**eclecticism** The use of multiple theoretical perspectives to explain and study human development.

**effacement** The flattening of the cervix, which, along with dilation, is a key process of the first stage of childbirth.

**ego** In Freudian theory, the portion of the personality that organizes, plans, and keeps the person in touch with reality. Language and thought are both ego functions.

**ego ideal** The list of 'dos' in the superego; violation of any of these leads to feelings of shame.

**egocentrism** A cognitive state in which the individual (typically a child) sees the world only from his own perspective, without awareness that there are other perspectives.

**embryo** The name given to the developing organism during the period of prenatal development between about 2 weeks and 8 weeks after conception, beginning with implantation of the blastocyst in the uterine wall.

**embryonic stage** The second stage of prenatal development, from week 2 through week 8, when the embryo's organs form.

**empathy** As defined by Hoffman, 'a vicarious affective response that does not necessarily match another's affective state but is more appropriate to the other's situation than to one's own' (1982, p. 285).

**empiricism** The view that perceptual abilities are learned.

**endocrine glands** Glands (including the adrenals, the thyroid, the pituitary, the testes, and the ovaries) that secrete hormones governing overall physical growth and sexual maturing.

**English-as-a-second-language (ESL)** An alternative to bilingual education; children who are not proficient in English attend academic classes taught entirely in English but then spend several hours in a separate class to receive English-language instruction.

**English-language learners (ELLs)** School children who do not speak English well enough to function in English-only classes.

**equilibration** The third part of the adaptation process proposed by Piaget, involving a periodic restructuring of schemes to create a balance between assimilation and accommodation.

**ethnic group** A subgroup whose members are perceived by themselves and others to have a common origin and culture and shared activities in which the common origin or culture is an essential ingredient' (Porter & Washington, 1993, p. 140).

**ethnicity** An individual's membership in an ethnic group.

**excessive weight gain** A pattern in which children gain more weight in a year than is appropriate for their age height, and sex.

**executive processes** Cognitive skills that allow a person to devise and carry out alternative strategies for remembering and solving problems.

**experiment** A research method for testing a causal hypothesis, in which participants are assigned randomly to experimental and control groups and the experimental group is then provided with a particular experience that is expected to alter behavior in some fashion.

**experimental group** A group of participants in an experiment who receive a particular treatment intended to produce some specific effect.

**expressive language** Sounds, signs, or symbols used to communicate meaning.

**extended family** A family structure that includes parents, grandparents, aunts, uncles, cousins, and so on.

**externalizing problems** A category of psychopathologies that includes any deviant behavior primarily directed toward others, such as conduct disorders.

**extraversion** One of the Big Five personality traits; a person who scores high on this trait is characterized by assertiveness, energy, enthusiasm, and outgoingness.

**extremely low birth weight (ELBW)** Term for any baby born with a weight below 1,000 grams (2.2 pounds).

**fallopian tube** The tube between the ovary and the uterus down which the ovum travels to the uterus and in which conception usually occurs.

**false belief principle** The understanding that another person might have a false belief and the ability to determine what information might cause the false belief. A child's understanding of the false belief principle is one key sign of the emergence of a representational theory of mind.

**family structure** The configuration of individuals in a child's household.

**family systems theory** The view that the family is an integrated network of factors that work together to influence a child's development.

**fast-mapping** The ability to categorically link new words to real-world referents.

**feminine** One of four sex-role types suggested by the work of Bem and others; a type characterized by high scores on femininity measures and low scores on masculinity measures.

**fetal alcohol syndrome (FAS)** A pattern of abnormalities, including mental retardation and minor physical anomalies, often found in children born to alcoholic mothers.

**fetal stage** The third stage of prenatal development, from week 8 to birth, when growth and organ refinement take place.

**fetus** The name given to the developing organism from about 8 weeks after conception until birth.

**figurative schemes** Mental representations of the basic properties of objects in the world.

**fontanel** One of several 'soft spots' in the skull that are present at birth but disappear when the bones of the skull grow together.

**foreclosure** One of four identity statuses proposed by Marcia, involving an ideological or occupational commitment without a previous reevaluation.

**formal operations stage** Piaget's name for the fourth and final major stage of cognitive development, occurring during adolescence, when the child becomes able to manipulate and organize ideas or hypothetical situations as well as objects.

**fraternal (dizygotic) twins** Children carried in the same pregnancy but who develop from two separately fertilized ova. They are no more alike genetically than other pairs of siblings.

**full scale IQ** The WISC-IV score that takes into account verbal and nonverbal scale scores.

**gametes** Sperm and ova. These cells, unlike all other cells of the body, contain only 23 chromosomes rather than 23 pairs.

**gender concept** The full understanding that gender is constant and permanent, unchanged by appearance.

**gender constancy** The final stage in development of gender concept, in which the child understands that gender doesn't change even though there may be external changes (in clothing or hair length, for example).

**gender identity** The first stage in the development of gender concept, in which a child labels self and others correctly as male or female.

**gender schema theory** A theory of the development of gender concept and sex-role behavior that proposes that, between about 18 months and age 2 or 3, a child creates a fundamental schema by which to categorize people, objects, activities, and qualities by gender.

**gender stability** The second stage in the development of gender concept, in which the child understands that a person's gender stays the same throughout life.

**gene** A uniquely coded segment of DNA in a chromosome that affects one or more specific body processes or developments.

**genotype** The pattern of characteristics and developmental sequences mapped in the genes of any specific individual, which will be modified by individual experience into the phenotype.

**germinal stage** The first stage of prenatal development, beginning at conception and ending at implantation of the zygote in the uterus (approximately the first two weeks).

**glial cells** The 'glue' that holds neurons together to give form to the structures of the nervous system.

**goal-corrected partnership** Term used by Bowlby to describe the form of the child-parent attachment in the preschool years, in which the two partners, through improved communication, negotiate the form and frequency of contact between them.

**gonadotrophic hormones** Hormones secreted by the pituitary gland at the beginning of puberty that stimulate the development of glands in the testes and ovaries, which then begin to secrete testosterone or estrogen.

**goodness-of-fit** The degree to which an infant's environment and his or her temperament work together.

**growth curve** The pattern and rate of growth exhibited by a child over time.

**habituation** An automatic decrease in the intensity of a response to a repeated stimulus, enabling a child or adult to ignore the familiar and focus attention on the novel.

**handedness** A strong preference for using primarily one hand or the other; it develops between 3 and 5 years of age.

**hedonistic reasoning** A form of prosocial moral reasoning described by Eisenberg in which the child is concerned with consequences to self rather than moral considerations, roughly equivalent to Kohlberg's stage 2.

**heterozygous** Term describing the genetic pattern when the two genes in the pair at any given genetic locus carry different instructions, such as a gene for blue eyes from one parent and a gene for brown eyes from the other parent.

**hippocampus** A brain structure that is involved in the transfer of information to long-term memory.

**holophrase** A combination of a gesture and a single word that conveys more meaning than just the word alone; often seen and heard in children between 12 and 18 months old.

**homozygous** Term describing the genetic pattern when the two genes in the pair at any given genetic locus both carry the same instructions.

**horizontal decalage** Piaget's term for school-aged children's inconsistent performance on concrete operations tasks.

**hostile aggression** Aggressive verbal behavior intended to hurt another's feelings.

**hypothesis** A testable prediction based on a theory.

**hypothetico-deductive reasoning** Piaget's term for the form of reasoning that is part of formal operational thought and involves not just deductive logic but also the ability to consider hypotheses and hypothetical possibilities.

**id** In Freudian theory, the inborn, primitive portion of the personality, the storehouse of libido, the basic energy that continually pushes for immediate gratification.

**identical (monozygotic) twins** Children carried in the same pregnancy who develop from the same fertilized ovum. They are genetic clones of each other.

**identity achievement** One of four identity statuses proposed by Marcia, involving the successful resolution of an identity 'crisis' and resulting in a new commitment.

**identity diffusion** One of four identity statuses proposed by Marcia, involving neither a current reevaluation of identity nor a firm personal commitment.

**identity versus role confusion** As hypothesized by Erikson, the psychosocial stage in which a teen must develop a sense of personal identity or else enter adulthood with a sense of confusion about his or her place in the world.

**inclusive education** General term for education programs that assign children with physical, mental, or emotional disabilities to regular classrooms and that provide any special services required by the child in that classroom.

**individuation** The process of psychological, social, and physical separation from parents that begins in adolescence.

**inductive logic** Reasoning from the particular to the general, from experience to broad rules, characteristic of concrete operational thinking.

**infant directed speech (IDS)** The simplified, higher-pitched speech that adults use with infants and young children.

**insecure attachment** An internal working model of relationships in which the child does not as readily use the parent as a safe base and is not readily consoled by the parent if upset. Includes three subtypes of attachment: avoidant, ambivalent, and disorganized/disoriented.

**instrumental aggression** Aggressive behavior intended to achieve a goal, such as obtaining a toy from another child.

**intelligence** A set of abilities defined in various ways by different psychologists but generally agreed to include the ability to reason abstractly, the ability to profit from experience, and the ability to adapt to varying environmental contexts.

**intelligence quotient (IQ)** Originally defined in terms of a child's mental age and chronological age, IQ is now computed by comparing a child's performance with that of other children of the same chronological age.

**intermodal perception** Formation of a single perception of a stimulus that is based on information from two or more senses.

**internal models of experience** A theoretical concept emphasizing that each child creates a set of core ideas or assumptions about the world, the self, and relationships with others through which all subsequent experience is filtered.

**internal working model** As applied to social relationships, a cognitive construction of the workings of relationships, such as expectations of support or affection, trustworthiness, and so on. The earliest relationships may form the template for such a cognitive construction.

**internalizing problems** A category of psychopathologies that includes anxiety and depression and other conditions in which deviant behavior is directed inwardly, against the self.

**invented spelling** A strategy young children with good phonological awareness skills use when they write.

**lateralization** The process through which brain functions are divided between the two hemispheres of the cerebral cortex.

**learning** Change due to experience.

**learning disability (LD)** A term broadly used to describe an unexpected or unexplained problem in learning to read, spell, or calculate and more precisely used to refer to a neurological dysfunction that causes such effects.

**learning theories** Psychological theories that explain development in terms of accumulated learning experiences.

**libido** The term used by Freud to describe the basic, unconscious, instinctual sexual energy in each individual.

**longitudinal design** A form of research study in which the same participants are observed or assessed repeatedly over a period of months or years.

**low birth weight (LBW)** Term for any baby born with a weight below 2,500 grams (5.5 pounds), including both those born too early (preterm) and those who are small for date.

**masculine** One of four sex-role types suggested by the work of Bem and others; a type characterized by high scores on masculinity measures and low scores on femininity measures.

**maturation** Sequential patterns of change that are governed by instructions contained in the genetic code and shared by all members of a species.

**mean length of utterance (MLU)** The average number of meaningful units in a sentence. Each basic word is one meaningful unit, as is each inflection.

**medulla** A portion of the brain that lies immediately above the spinal cord; it is largely developed at birth.

**memory strategies** Ways of manipulating information that increase the chances that it will be remembered.

**menarche** Onset of menstruation.

**mental age** Term used by Binet and Simon and Terman in the early calculation of IQ scores to refer to the age level of IQ test items a child could successfully answer. Used in combination with the child's chronological age to calculate an IQ score.

**mental retardation** An intellectual disability defined most often as an IQ below 70 combined with poor adaptive behavior.

**metacognition** General and rather loosely used term describing knowledge of one's own thinking processes: knowing what one knows, and how one learns.

**metamemory** Knowledge about one's own memory processes.

**midbrain** A section of the brain lying above the medulla and below the cortex that regulates attention, sleeping, waking, and other automatic functions; it is largely developed at birth.

**mirror neurons** Specialized cells in the cerebral cortex that simulate the behavior and emotions of others.

**moral development** The process of learning to distinguish between right and wrong in accordance with cultural values.

**moral realism stage** The first of Piaget's stages of moral development, in which children believe that rules are inflexible.

**moral relativism stage** The second of Piaget's stages of moral development, in which children understand that many rules can be changed through social agreement.

**moral rules** As defined by Turiel, universal and obligatory rules reflecting basic principles that guarantee the rights of others.

**moratorium** One of four identity statuses proposed by Marcia, involving an ongoing reexamination of identity but no new commitment.

**Moro reflex** The reflex that causes infants to extend their legs, arms, and fingers, arch the back, and draw back the head when startled (for example, by a loud sound or a sensation of being dropped).

**motor development** Growth and change in ability to perform both gross motor skills (such as walking or throwing) and fine motor skills (such as drawing or writing).

**multifactorial pattern of inheritance** The pattern of genetic transmission in which both genes and environment influence the phenotype.

**multiple intelligences** Eight types of intelligence (linguistic, logical/mathematical, spatial, bodily kinesthetic, musical, interpersonal, intrapersonal, and naturalistic) proposed by Howard Gardner.

**myelination** The process by which an insulating layer of a substance called myelin is added to neurons.

**nativism** The view that perceptual abilities are inborn.

**naturalistic observation** A research method in which participants are observed in their normal environments.

**needs-oriented reasoning** A form of prosocial moral reasoning proposed by Eisenberg in which the child expresses concern directly for the other person's need, even if the other's need conflicts with the child's own wishes or desires.

**negative reinforcement** The process of strengthening a behavior by the removal or cessation of an unpleasant stimulus.

**neglected children** Children who are seldom described by peers as either liked or disliked.

**neglecting style** A fourth parenting style suggested by Maccoby and Martin, involving low levels of both acceptance and control.

**neo-Piagetian theory** A theory of cognitive development that assumes that Piaget's basic ideas are correct but that uses concepts from information-processing theory to explain children's movement from one stage to the next.

**neuronal migration** The movement of neurons to specialized regions of the brain.

**neuronal proliferation** The rapid development of neurons between the 10th and 18th week of gestation.

**neurons** The cells in the nervous system that are responsible for transmission and reception of nerve impulses.

**neuroticism** One of the Big Five personality traits; a person who scores high on this trait is characterized by anxiety, self-pity, tenseness, and emotional instability.

**neurotransmitters** Chemicals that accomplish the transmission of signals from one neuron to another at synapses.

**nonnormative changes (individual differences)** Changes that result from unique, unshared events.

**nonshared environment** Characteristics of a family that affect one child but not others in the household.

**normative age-graded changes** Changes that are common to every member of a species.

**normative history-graded changes** Changes that occur in most members of a cohort as a result of factors at work during a specific, well-defined historical period.

**norms** Average ages at which developmental events happen.

**obese** Describes a child whose BMI falls above the 95th percentile (the top 5%).

**object constancy** The general phrase describing the ability to see objects as remaining the same despite changes in sensory information about them.

**object permanence** The understanding that objects continue to exist even when they cannot be directly perceived.

**objective self** The component of the self-concept that involves awareness of the self as an object with properties.

**Oedipus conflict** The pattern of events that Freud believed occur between ages 3 and 5, when the child experiences a sexual desire for the parent of the opposite sex; the resulting fear of possible reprisal from the parent of the same sex is resolved when the child identifies with that parent.

**openness/intellect** One of the Big Five personality traits; a person who scores high on this trait is characterized by curiosity, imagination, insight, originality, and wide interests.

**operant conditioning** The type of learning in which the probability of a person's performing some behavior is increased or decreased because of the consequences it produces.

**operation** Term used by Piaget for a complex, internal, abstract scheme, first seen at about age 6.

**operational efficiency** A neo-Piagetian term for the number of schemes an individual can place into working memory at one time.

**operative schemes** Mental representations of the logical connections among objects in the world.

**oppositional defiant disorder (ODD)** A pattern of negative, defiant, disobedient, and hostile behavior toward parents and other authority figures, established prior to age 8.

**organization** The process of deriving generalizable schemes from specific experiences.

**ossification** The process of hardening by which soft tissue becomes bone.

**otitis media (OM)** An inflammation of the middle ear that is caused by a bacterial infection.

**overextension** The inappropriate use of a word to designate an entire category of objects, such as when a child uses the word kitty to refer to all animate objects.

**overregularization** Young children's applications of basic rules to irregular words.

**overweight** Describes a child whose BMI is at the 95th percentile.

**ovum** The cell released monthly from a woman's ovaries, which, if fertilized, forms the basis for the developing organism.

**parallel play** Form of play seen in toddlers, in which children play next to, but not with, one another.

**perception** The attribution of meaning to sensory information.

**perceptual constancies** A collection of mental rules that allow humans to perceive shape, size, and color as constant even when perceptual conditions (such as amount of light, angle of view, and the like) change.

**perceptual reasoning index** Tests on the WISC-IV, such as block design and picture completion, that tap nonverbal visual-processing abilities.

**performance** The behavior shown by a person under real-life rather than ideal circumstances. Even when researchers are interested in competence, all they can ever measure is performance.

**permissive style** One of the three parenting styles described by Baumrind, characterized by high levels of nurturance and low levels of control, maturity demands, and communication.

**personality** The collection of relatively enduring patterns of reacting to and interacting with others and the environment that distinguishes each child or adult.

**pervasive developmental disorders (PDDs)** A group of disorders in which children exhibit severe disturbances in social relationships.

**phenotype** The expression of a particular set of genetic information in a specific environment; the observable result of the joint operation of genetic and environmental influences.

**phonological awareness** Understanding of the rules governing the sounds of a language as well as knowledge of the connection between sounds and the way they are represented in written language.

**phonology** The sound patterns of a particular language and the rules for combining them.

**pituitary gland** Gland that provides the trigger for release of hormones from other glands.

**placenta** An organ that develops between the fetus and the wall of the uterus during gestation.

**plasticity** The ability of the brain to change in response to experience.

**polygenic pattern of inheritance** Any pattern of genetic transmission in which multiple genes contribute to the outcome, such as is presumed to occur for complex traits such as intelligence or temperament.

**popular children** Children who are described as well-liked by a majority of peers.

**positive reinforcement** The process of strengthening a behavior by the presentation of some pleasurable or positive stimulus.

**practical intelligence** One of three types of intelligence in Sternberg's triarchic theory of intelligence; often called 'street smarts,' this type of intelligence includes skill in applying information to the real world or solving practical problems.

**pragmatics** The rules for the use of language in communicative interaction, such as the rules for taking turns and the style of speech that is appropriate for different listeners.

**preconventional morality** The first level of moral development proposed by Kohlberg, in which moral judgments are dominated by consideration of what will be punished and what feels good.

**prefrontal cortex (PFC)** The part of the frontal lobe just behind the forehead that is responsible for executive processing.

**prelinguistic phase** The period before a child speaks his or her first words.

**preoperational stage** Piaget's term for the second major stage of cognitive development, from about 24 months to about age 6, marked by the ability to use symbols.

**preterm infant** An infant born before 38 weeks gestational age.

**primary circular reactions** Piaget's phrase to describe a baby's simple repetitive actions in substage 2 of the sensorimotor stage, organized around the baby's own body; the baby repeats some action in order to have some desired outcome occur again, such as putting his thumb in his mouth to repeat the good feeling of sucking.

**primitive reflexes** Collection of reflexes seen in young infants that gradually disappear during the first year of life, including the Moro and Babinski reflexes.

**principle of contrast** The assumption that every word has a different meaning, which leads a child to assume that two or more different words refer to different objects.

**principled (postconventional) morality** The third level of moral development proposed by Kohlberg, in which considerations of justice, individual rights, and social contracts dominate moral judgment.

**processing speed index** Timed tests on the WISC-IV, such as symbol search, that measure how rapidly an examinee processes information.

**production deficiency** A pattern whereby an individual can use some mental strategy if reminded to do so but fails to use the strategy spontaneously.

**prosocial behavior** Voluntary behavior intended to benefit another, such as giving away or sharing possessions, money, or time, with no obvious self-gain; altruism.

**proximodistal** One of two basic patterns of physical development in infancy (the other is cephalocaudal), in which development proceeds from the center outward'—that is, from the trunk to the limbs.

**pruning** The process of eliminating unused synapses.

**psychoanalytic theories** Developmental theories based on the assumption that age-related change results from maturationally determined conflicts between internal drives and society's demands.

**psychological disorder** A pattern of behavior that is unusual in a person's culture and interferes with his or her psychological, social, and/or educational functioning.

**psychosexual stages** The stages of personality development suggested by Freud: the oral, anal, phallic, latency, and genital stages.

**psychosocial stages** The stages of personality development suggested by Erikson, involving tasks centered on trust, autonomy, initiative, industry, identity, intimacy, generativity, and ego integrity.

**puberty** The series of hormonal and physical changes at adolescence that bring about sexual maturity.

**punishment** The removal of a desirable stimulus or the administration of an unpleasant consequence after some undesired behavior in order to stop the behavior.

**reaction range** Term used by some psychologists for the range of possible outcomes (phenotypes) for some variable, given basic genetic patterning (the genotype). In the case of IQ scores, the reaction range is estimated at 20 to 25 points.

**receptive language** Comprehension of spoken language.

**reciprocal determinism** Bandura's model in which personal, behavioral, and environmental factors interact to influence personality development.

**reciprocal friendship** A friendship in which each partner identifies the other as a friend; also, a quality of friendship in school-aged children, when friendship is for the first time perceived as being based on reciprocal trust.

**reflexes** Automatic body reactions to specific stimulation, such as the knee jerk or the Moro reflex. Adults have many reflexes, but the newborn also has some primitive reflexes that disappear as the cortex develops.

**rejected children** Unpopular children who are explicitly avoided and not chosen as playmates or friends.

**relational aggression** Aggression aimed at damaging another person's self-esteem or peer relationships, such as by using ostracism or threats of ostracism, cruel gossiping, or facial expressions of disdain.

**relational complexity** The number of elements in a problem and the complexity of the relationships among the elements.

**relative right-left orientation** The ability to identify right and left from multiple perspectives.

**reliability** The stability of a test score over multiple testing sessions.

**respiratory distress syndrome** A problem frequently found in infants born more than 6 weeks before term, in which the infant's lungs lack a chemical (surfactant) needed to keep air sacs inflated.

**response inhibition** The ability to control responses to stimuli.

**responsiveness** An aspect of parent-child interaction; a responsive parent is sensitive to the child's cues and reacts appropriately, following the child's lead.

**reticular formation** The part of the brain that regulates attention.

**reversibility** One of the most critical of the operations Piaget identified as part of the concrete operations period: the understanding that actions and mental operations can be reversed.

**role-taking** The ability to look at a situation from another person's perspective.

**rooting reflex** The reflex that causes an infant to automatically turn toward a touch on the cheek, open the mouth, and make sucking movements.

**scaffolding** The term used by Bruner to describe the process by which a teacher (or parent, older child, or other person in the role of teacher) structures a learning encounter with a child so as to lead the child from step to step—a process consistent with Vygotsky's theory of cognitive development.

**schematic learning** The development of expectancies concerning what actions lead to what results or what events tend to go together.

**scheme** Piaget's word for the basic actions of knowing, including both physical actions (sensorimotor schemes, such as looking or reaching) and mental actions (such as classifying, comparing, and reversing). An experience is assimilated into a scheme, and the scheme is created or modified through accommodation.

**secondary circular reactions** Repetitive actions in substage 3 of the sensorimotor period, oriented around external objects; the infant repeats some action in order to have some outside event recur, such as hitting a mobile repeatedly so that it moves.

**secular trend** A pattern of change in some characteristic over several cohorts, such as systematic changes in the average timing of menarche or in average height or weight.

**secure attachment** An internal working model of relationships in which the child uses the parent as a safe base and is readily consoled after separation, when fearful, or when otherwise stressed.

**selective attention** The ability to focus cognitive activity on the important elements of a problem or situation.

**self-concept** One's knowledge of and thoughts about the set of qualities attributed to the self.

**self-efficacy** Bandura's term for an individual's belief in his or her ability to accomplish tasks.

**self-esteem** A global evaluation of one's own worth; an aspect of self-concept.

**semantics** A particular language's system of meaning and the rules for conveying meaning.

**sensation** The process of taking in raw information through the senses.

**sensation-seeking** A strong desire to experience the emotional and physical arousal associated with risky behaviors such as fast driving and unprotected sex.

**sensitive period** A period during which particular experiences can best contribute to proper development. It is similar to a critical period, but the effects of deprivation during a sensitive period are not as severe as during a critical period.

**sensorimotor stage** Piaget's term for the first major stage of cognitive development, from birth to about 24 months, when the child uses sensory and motor skills to act on the environment.

**sequential design** A form of research study that combines cross-sectional and longitudinal designs in some way.

**seriation** The ability to use a rule to put an array of objects in order.

**severely obese** Describes a child whose BMI-for-age is above the 99th percentile.

**sex role** The set of behaviors, attitudes, rights, duties, and obligations that are seen as appropriate for being male or female in any given culture.

**sex-typed behavior** Behavior that matches a culturally defined sex role.

**sexually transmitted diseases (STDs)** Category of disease spread by sexual contact, including chlamydia, genital warts, syphilis, gonorrhea, and HIV; also called venereal diseases.

**shape constancy** The ability to see an object's shape as remaining the same despite changes in the shape of the retinal image; a basic perceptual constancy.

**shared environment** Characteristics of a family that affect all children in the household.

**short-term storage space (STSS)** A neo-Piagetian term for working memory capacity.

**size constancy** The ability to see an object's size as remaining the same despite changes in size of the retinal image; a key element in size constancy is the ability to judge depth.

**slow-to-warm-up child** An infant who may seem unresponsive but who simply takes more time to respond than other infants do.

**small-for-date infant** An infant who weighs less than is normal for the number of weeks of gestation completed.

**social cognition** Thinking about and understanding the emotions of and interactions and relationships among people.

**social referencing** Using another person's emotional reaction to some situation as a basis for deciding one's own reaction. A baby does this when she checks her parent's facial expression or body language before responding positively or negatively to something new.

**social status** A term used by psychologists to refer to how well an individual child is liked by his or her peers.

**socioeconomic status (SES)** A collective term that includes the economic, occupational, and educational factors that influence a family's relative position in society.

**spatial cognition** The ability to infer rules from and make predictions about the movement of objects in space.

**spatial perception** The ability to identify and act on relationships of objects in space; in most people, this skill is lateralized to the right cerebral hemisphere.

**sperm** The cells produced in a man's testes that may fertilize an ovum following intercourse.

**Stanford-Binet** The best-known U.S. intelligence test. It was written by Lewis Terman and his associates at Stanford University and based on the first tests by Binet and Simon.

**states of consciousness** The periodic shifts in alertness, sleepiness, crankiness, and so on that characterize an infant's behavior.

**Strange Situation** A series of episodes used by Mary Ainsworth and others in studies of attachment. The child is observed with the mother, with a stranger, alone, when reunited with the stranger, and when reunited with the mother.

**structured immersion** An alternative to traditional bilingual education used in classrooms in which all children speak the same non-English native language. All basic instruction is in English, paced so that the children can comprehend, with the teacher translating only when absolutely necessary.

**subjective self** The component of the self-concept that involves awareness of the 'I,' the self that is separate from others.

**submersion** An approach to education of non-English–speaking students in which they are assigned to a classroom where instruction is given in English and are given no supplemental language assistance; also known as the 'sink or swim' approach.

**sudden infant death syndrome (SIDS)** The unexpected death of an infant who otherwise appears healthy; also called crib death. The cause of SIDS is unknown.

**superego** In Freudian theory, the 'conscience' part of personality, which contains parental and societal values and attitudes incorporated during childhood.

**synapses** Tiny spaces across which neural impulses flow from one neuron to the next.

**synaptogenesis** The process of synapse formation.

**syntax** The rules for forming sentences in a particular language.

**systematic and explicit phonics** Planned, specific instruction in sound-letter correspondences.

**task goal** A goal orientation associated with a desire for self-improvement.

**telegraphic speech** Term used by Roger Brown to describe the earliest sentences created by most children, which sound a bit like telegrams because they include key nouns and verbs but generally omit all other words and grammatical inflections.

**temperament** Inborn predispositions that form the foundations of personality.

**teratogens** Substances such as viruses and drugs or events that can cause birth defects.

**tertiary circular reactions** The deliberate experimentation with variations of previous actions, characteristic of substage 5 of the sensorimotor period, according to Piaget.

**theory of mind** Ideas that collectively explain other people's ideas, beliefs, desires, and behavior.

**tracking** Following a moving object with the eyes.

**transitivity** The ability to make inferences about logical relationships in an ordered set of stimuli.

**triarchic theory of intelligence** A theory advanced by Robert Sternberg, proposing the existence of three types of intelligence: analytical, creative, and practical.

**umbilical cord** The cord connecting the embryo/fetus to the placenta, containing two arteries and one vein.

**underextension** The use of words to apply only to specific objects, such as a child's use of the word cup to refer only to one particular cup.

**undifferentiated** One of four sex-role types suggested by the work of Bem and others; a type characterized by low scores on both masculinity and femininity measures.

**uterus** The female organ in which the embryo/fetus develops (popularly referred to as the womb).

**utilization deficiency** Using some specific mental strategy without deriving benefit from it.

**validity** The degree to which a test measures what it is intended to measure.

**verbal comprehension index** Tests on the WISC-IV that tap verbal skills such as knowledge of vocabulary and general information.

**very low birth weight (VLBW)** Term for any baby born with a weight below 1,500 grams (3.3 pounds).

**viability** The fetus's capacity for survival outside the womb.

**visual acuity** How well one can see.

**warmth versus hostility** The key dimension of emotional tone used to describe family interactions.

**whole language approach** An approach to reading instruction that places more emphasis on the meaning of written language than on its structure.

**WISC-IV** The most recent revision of the Wechsler Intelligence Scales for Children, a well-known IQ test developed in the United States that includes both verbal and performance (nonverbal) subtests.

**working memory index** Tests on the WISC-IV, such as digit span, that measure working memory efficiency.

**WPPSI-III** The third revision of the Wechsler Preschool and Primary Scale of Intelligence.

**zone of proximal development** In Vygotsky's theory, the range of tasks that are slightly too difficult for a child to do alone but that can be accomplished successfully with guidance from an adult or more experienced child.

**zygote** The single cell formed from separate sperm and egg cells at conception.

# REFERENCES

Abdel-Khalek, A., & Lynn, R. (2008). Intelligence, family size and birth order: Some data from Kuwait. *Personality and Individual Differences, 44,* 1032–1038.

Abdelrahman, A., Rodriguez, G., Ryan, J., French, J., & Weinbaum, D. (1998). The epidemiology of substance use among middle school students: The impact of school, familial, community and individual risk factors. *Journal of Child & Adolescent Substance Abuse, 8,* 55–75.

Abela, J., & Hankin, B. (2008). Cognitive vulnerability to depression in children and adolescents: A developmental psychopathology perspective. In J. Abela & B. Hankin (Eds.), *Handbook of depression in children and adolescents* (pp. 35–78). New York: Guilford Press.

Abma, J., Martinez, G., & Cohen, C. (2010). Teenagers in the United States: Sexual activity, contraceptive use, and childbearing. *Vital Health Statistics, 23,* 1–86.

Aboud, F. E., & Doyle, A. B. (1995). The development of in-group pride in black Canadians. *Journal of Cross-Cultural Psychology, 26,* 243–254.

Abramovitch, R., Pepler, D., & Corter, C. (1982). Patterns of sibling interaction among preschool-age children. In M. E. Lamb & B. Sutton-Smith (Eds.), *Sibling relationships: Their nature and significance across the life-span* (pp. 61–86). Hillsdale, NJ: Erlbaum.

Accardo, P., Tomazic, T., Fete, T., Heaney, M., Lindsay, R., & William, B. (1997). Maternally reported fetal activity levels and developmental diagnoses. *Clinical Pediatrics, 36,* 279–283.

Achenbach, T. M. (1974). *Developmental psychopathology.* New York: The Ronald Press Company.

Achenbach, T. M. (1982). *Developmental psychopathology* (2nd ed.). New York: Wiley.

Achenbach, T. M. (1993). Taxonomy and comorbidity of conduct problems: Evidence from empirically based approaches. *Development and Psychopathology, 5,* 51–64.

Achenbach, T. M. (1995). Developmental issues in assessment, taxonomy, and diagnosis of child and adolescent psychopathology. In D. Cicchetti & D. J. Cohen (Eds.), *Developmental psychopathology: Vol. 1. Theory and methods* (pp. 57–80). New York: Wiley.

Achenbach, T. M. (2008). Multicultural perspectives on developmental psychopathology. In J. Hudziak (Ed.), *Developmental psychopathology and wellness: Genetic and environmental influences* (pp. 23–47). Arlington, VA: American Psychiatric Publishing.

Achenbach, T. M., & Edelbrock, C. S. (1981). Behavioral problems and competencies reported by parents of normal and disturbed children aged 4 through 16. *Monographs of the Society for Research in Child Development, 46*(1, Serial No. 188).

Adachi, M., Trehub, S., & Abe, J. (2004). Perceiving emotion in children's songs across age and culture. *Japanese Psychological Research, 46,* 322–336.

Adam, E., Gunnar, M., & Tanaka, A. (2004). Adult attachment, parent emotion, and observed parenting behavior: Mediator and moderator models. *Child Development, 75,* 110–122.

Adams, M., & Henry, M. (1997). Myths and realities about words and literacy. *School Psychology Review, 26,* 425–436.

Adams, M. J., Trieman, R., & Pressley, M. (1998). Reading, writing, and literacy. In W. Damon (Ed.), *Handbook of child psychology: Vol 4. Child psychology in practice* (5th ed., pp. 275–355). New York: Wiley.

Adelman, W., & Ellen, J. (2002). *Adolescence.* In A. Rudolph, R. Kamei, & K. Overby (Eds.), *Rudolph's fundamentals of pediatrics* (3rd ed., pp. 70–109). New York: McGraw-Hill.

Adolph, K., & Berger, S. (2005). Physical and motor development. In M. Bornstein & M. Lamb (Eds.), *Developmental science: An advanced textbook* (5th ed., pp. 223–283). Hillsdale, NJ: Erlbaum.

Afterschool Alliance. (2010). *America after 3 pm.* Retrieved August 13, 2010, from http://www.afterschoolalliance.org/documents/AA3PM_Key_Findings_2009.pdf

Agaliotis, D., Zaiden, R., & Ozturk, S. (2009). *Hemophilia, overview.* Retrieved June 27, 2010, from http://emedicine.medscape.com/article/210104-overview

Ahrens, K., DuBois, D., Lozano, P., & Richardson, L. (2010). Naturally acquired mentoring relationships and young adult outcomes among adolescents with learning disabilities. *Learning Disabilities Research & Practice, 25,* 207–216.

Ainsworth, M., & Bowlby, J. (1991). An ethological approach to personality development. *American Psychologist, 46,* 333–341.

Ainsworth, M. D. S. (1972). Attachment and dependency: A comparison. In J. L. Gewirtz (Ed.), *Attachment and dependency* (pp. 97–138). Washington, DC: Winston.

Ainsworth, M. D. S. (1982). Attachment: Retrospect and prospect. In C. M. Parkes & J. Stevenson-Hinde (Eds.), *The place of attachment in human behavior* (pp. 3–30). New York: Basic Books.

Ainsworth, M. D. S., Blehar, M., Waters, E., & Wall, S. (1978). *Patterns of attachment.* Hillsdale, NJ: Erlbaum.

Ainsworth, M. D. S., & Marvin, R. S. (1995). On the shaping of attachment theory and research: An interview with Mary D. S. Ainsworth (Fall 1994). *Monographs of the Society for Research in Child Development, 60* (244, Nos. 2–3), 3–21.

Akhtar, N. (2004). Nativist versus constructivist goals in studying child language. *Journal of Child Language, 31,* 459–462.

Aksan, N., & Kochanska, G. (2005). Conscience in childhood: Old questions, new answers. *Developmental Psychology, 41,* 506–516.

Aksu-Koc, A. A., & Slobin, D. I. (1985). The acquisition of Turkish. In D. I. Slobin (Ed.), *The crosslinguistic study of language acquisition: Vol. 1. The data* (pp. 839–878). Hillsdale, NJ: Erlbaum.

Al Otaiba, S., Connor, C., Lane, H., Kosanovich, M., Schatschneider, C., Dyrlund, A., Miller, M., & Wright, T. (2008). Reading first kindergarten classroom instruction and students' growth in phonological awareness and letter naming/decoding fluency. *Journal of School Psychology, 46,* 281–314.

Alan Guttmacher Institute. (2004). *U.S. teenage pregnancy statistics with comparative statistics for women aged 20–24.* Retrieved May 6, 2005, from http://www.guttmacher.org/pubs/teen_stats.html

Albers, L. (1999). The duration of labor in healthy women. *Journal of Perinatology, 19,* 114–119.

Alexander, K. L., Entwisle, D. R., & Dauber, S. L. (1993). First-grade classroom behavior: Its short- and long-term consequences for school performance. *Child Development, 64,* 801–814.

Alford, K. (2007). African-American males and the rites of passage experience. In S. Logan, R. Denby, & P. Gibson (Eds.), *Mental health care in the African-American community* (pp. 305–319). New York: Haworth Press.

Alho, O., Laära, E., & Oja, H. (1996). How should relative risk estimates for acute otitis media in children aged less than 2 years be perceived? *Journal of Clinical Epidemiology, 49*, 9–14.

Allen, C., & Kisilevsky, B. (1999). Fetal behavior in diabetic and non-diabetic pregnant women: An exploratory study. *Developmental Psychobiology, 35*, 69–80.

Allen, J., Porter, M., McFarland, F., Marsh, P., & McElhaney, K. (2005). The two faces of adolescents' success with peers: Adolescent popularity, social adaptation, and deviant behavior. *Child Development, 76*, 747–760.

Allen, K., & Rainie, L. (2002). *Parents online.* Retrieved March 16, 2004, from http://www.pewinternet.org

Allen, M. (2004). Minority language school systems: A profile of students, schools and communities. *Education Quarterly Review, 9*, 9–29.

Allhusen, V., Belsky, J., Booth-LaForce, C., Bradley, R., Brownell, C., Burchinal, M., et al. (2005). Duration and developmental timing of poverty and children's cognitive and social development from birth through third grade. *Child Development, 76*, 795–810.

Alsaker, F., & Olweus, D. (2002). Stability and change in global self-esteem and self-related affect. In T. Brinthaupt & R. Lipka (Eds.), *Understanding early adolescent self and identity: Applications and interventions* (pp. 193–223). Albany: State University of New York Press.

Alspaugh, J. (1998). Achievement loss associated with the transition to middle school and high school. *Journal of Educational Research, 92*, 20–25.

Alt, M., Plante, E., & Creusere, M. (2004). Semantic features in fast-mapping: Performance of preschoolers with specific language impairment versus preschoolers with normal language. *Journal of Speech, Language, & Hearing Research, 47*, 407–420.

Álvarez, J., Martín, A. F., Vergeles, M., & Martín, A. H. (2003). Substance use in adolescence: Importance of parental warmth and supervision. *Psicothema, 15*, 161–166.

Amato, P. R. (1993). Children's adjustment to divorce: Theories, hypotheses, and empirical support. *Journal of Marriage and the Family, 55*, 23–38.

Amato, S. (1998). Human genetics and dysmorphy. In R. Behrman & R. Kliegman (Eds.), *Nelson essentials of pediatrics* (3rd ed., pp. 129–146). Philadelphia: Saunders.

Ambert, A. (2001). *Families in the new millennium.* Boston, MA: Allyn & Bacon.

American Academy of Pediatrics (AAP). (2004). Clinical practice guideline: Diagnosis and management of acute otitis media. *Pediatrics, 113*, 1451–1465.

American Academy of Pediatrics (AAP). (2005). Breastfeeding and the use of human milk. *Pediatrics, 115*, 496–506.

American Academy of Pediatrics Committee on Infectious Diseases. (2000). Recommended childhood immunization schedule. *Pediatrics, 97*, 143–146.

American Academy of Pediatrics Committee on Psychosocial Aspects of Child and Family Health. (1998). Guidance for effective discipline. *Pediatrics, 101*, 723–728.

American College of Obstetricians and Gynecologists (ACOG). (2001, December 12). *ACOG addresses latest controversies in obstetrics.* Retrieved April 1, 2004, from http://www.acog.org

American College of Obstetricians and Gynecologists (ACOG). (2002, November 29). *Rubella vaccination recommendation changes for pregnant women.* Retrieved April 2, 2004, from http://www.acog.org

American College of Obstetricians and Gynecologists (ACOG). (2004a). *Ethics in obstetrics and gynecology.* Washington, DC: Author.

American College of Obstetricians and Gynecologists (ACOG). (2004b). *Pain relief during labor and delivery.* Retrieved August 6, 2008, from http://www.acog.org/publications/patient_education/bp086.cfm

American College of Obstetricians and Gynecologists (ACOG). (2007a). Cesarean delivery on maternal request: ACOG committee opinion no. 394. *Obstetrics & Gynecology, 110*, 1501.

American College of Obstetricians and Gynecologists (ACOG). (2007b). *If your baby is breech.* Retrieved August 6, 2008, from http://www.acog.org/publications/patient_education/bp079.cfm

American College of Obstetricians and Gynecologists (ACOG). (2008a). *Cesarean birth.* Retrieved August 6, 2008, from http:// www.acog.org/publications/patient_education/bp006.cfm

American College of Obstetricians and Gynecologists (ACOG). (2008b). *Surgery and patient choice.* Retrieved August 6, 2008, from http://www.acog.org/publications/patient_education/bp079.cfm

American Psychiatric Association. (2000). *Practice guidelines for eating disorders.* Retrieved June 9, 2005, from http://www.psych.org

American Psychological Association. (1993). *Violence and youth: Psychology's response: Vol. 1. Summary report of the American Psychological Association Commission on Violence and Youth.* Washington, DC: American Psychological Association.

American Society of Hand Therapists. (2011). *Portable electronics and video game injury prevention tips.* Retrieved June 10, 2011, from http://www.asht.org/education/VideoGameInjury.cfm

Amorim, A., Rössner, S., Neovius, M. Lourenço, P., & Linné, Y. (2007). Does excess pregnancy weight gain constitute a major risk for increasing long-term BMI? *Obesity, 15*, 1278–1286.

Anderman, E. (1998). The middle school experience: Effects on the math and science achievement of adolescents with LD. *Journal of Learning Disabilities, 31*, 128–138.

Anderman, E., Maehr, M., & Midgley, C. (1999). Declining motivation after the transition to middle school: Schools can make a difference. *Journal of Research & Development in Education, 32*, 131–147.

Anderman, E., & Midgley, C. (1997). Changes in achievement goal orientations, perceived academic competence, and grades across the transition to middle-level schools. *Contemporary Educational Psychology, 22*, 269–298.

Anderman, L. (1999). Classroom goal orientation, school belonging and social goals as predictors of students' positive and negative affect following the transition to middle school. *Journal of Research & Development in Education, 32*, 89–103.

Anderman, L., & Anderman, E. (1999). Social predictors of changes in students' achievement goal orientations. *Contemporary Educational Psychology, 24*, 21–37.

Anderman, L., & Anderman, E. (2009). Oriented towards mastery: Promoting positive motivational goals for students. In R. Gilman, E. Huebner, & M. Furlong (Eds.), *Handbook of positive psychology in schools* (pp. 161–173). New York: Routledge/Taylor & Francis Group.

Anderson, C., & Dill, K. (2000). Video games and aggressive thoughts, feelings, and behavior in the laboratory and in life. *Journal of Personality & Social Psychology, 78*, 772–790.

Anderson, C., Masse, L., Zhang, H., Coleman, K., & Chang, S. (2009). Contribution of athletic identity to child and adolescent physical activity. *American Journal of Preventive Medicine, 37*, 220–226.

Anderson, M. (2005). Marrying intelligence and cognition: A developmental view. In J. Pretz & R. Sternberg (Eds.), *Cognition and intelligence: Identifying the mechanisms of mind* (pp. 268–287). New York: Cambridge University Press.

Anderson, R. (1998). Examining language loss in bilingual children. *Multicultural Electronic Journal of Communication Disorders, 1.*

Andreou, E., & Metallidou, P. (2004). The relationship of academic and social cognition to behaviour in bullying situations among Greek primary school children. *Educational Psychology, 24*, 27–41.

Andreucci, C. (2003). Comment l'idée d'instabilité du volume vient aux enfants. *Enfance, 55*, 139–158.

Andrews, G., & Halford, G. (1998). Children's ability to make transitive inferences: The importance of premise integration and structural complexity. *Cognitive Development, 13*, 479–513.

Andrews, G., & Halford, G. (2002). A cognitive complexity metric applied to cognitive development. *Cognitive Psychology, 45*, 153–219.

Ang, R., & Goh, D. (2010). Cyberbullying among adolescents: The role of affective and cognitive empathy, and gender. *Child Psychiatry and Human Development, 41*, 387–397.

de Angelis, T. (2004). Should we be giving psychotropics to children? *APA Monitor on Psychology, 35*, 42.

Anglin, J. M. (1993). Vocabulary development: A morphological analysis. *Monographs of the Society for Research in Child Development, 58* (Serial No. 238).

Anglin, J. M. (1995, April). *Word learning and the growth of potentially knowable vocabulary.* Paper presented at the biennial meetings of the Society for Research in Child Development, Indianapolis.

Anisfeld, M., Turkewitz, G., Rose, S., Rosenberg, F., Sheiber, F., Couturier-Fagan, D., Ger, J., & Sommer, I. (2001). No compelling evidence that newborns imitate oral gestures. *Infancy, 2*, 111–122.

Anme, T., Tanaka, H., Shinohara, R., Sugisawa, Y., Tanaka, E., Tong, L., et al. (2010). Effectiveness of Japan's extended/night child care: A five-year follow up. *Procedia: Social and Behavioral Sciences, 2*, 5573–5580.

Apgar, V. A. (1953). A proposal for a new method of evaluation of the newborn infant. *Current Research in Anesthesia and Analgesia, 32*, 260–267.

Aranha, M. (1997). Creativity in students and its relation to intelligence and peer perception. *Revista Interamericana de Psicologia, 31*, 309–313.

Armbruster, B., Lehr, F., & Osborn, J. (2003). *Put reading first: The research building blocks of reading instruction.* Retrieved June 20, 2008, from http://www.nifl.gov/partnershipforreading/publications/PFRbooklet.pdf

Armstrong, T. (2003). Effect of moral reconation therapy on the recidivism of youthful offenders: A randomized experiment. *Criminal Justice & Behavior, 30*, 668–687.

Ashiabi, G., & O'Neal, K. (2007). Children's health status: Examining the associations among income poverty, material hardship, and parental factors. *PLoS ONE, 2*, e940.

Aslin, R. N. (1981). Experiential influences and sensitive periods in perceptual development: A unified model. In R. N. Aslin, J. R. Alberts, & M. R. Petersen (Eds.), *Development of perception. Psychobiological perspectives: Vol. 2. The visual system* (45–93). New York: Academic Press.

Aslin, R. N. (1987). Motor aspects of visual development in infancy. In P. Salapatek & L. Cohen (Eds.), *Handbook of infant perception: Vol. 1. From sensation to perception* (pp. 43–113). Orlando, FL: Academic Press.

Aslin, R. N. (2011). Perceptual constraints on implicit memory for visual features: Statistical learning in human infants. In L. Oakes, C. Cashon, M. Casasola, & D. Rakison (Eds.). *Infant perception and cognition: Recent advances, emerging theories, and future directions.* (pp. 111–124). New York: Oxford University Press.

Associated Press. (2005, February 8). "World's smallest baby goes home." Retrieved August 8, 2008, from http://www.cbsnews.com/stories/2005/02/08/health/main672488.shtml

Astington, J., & Jenkins, J. (1999). A longitudinal study of the relation between language and theory-of-mind development. *Developmental Psychology, 35*, 1311–1320.

Aud, S., & Fox, M. (2010). *Status and trends in the education of racial and ethnic groups.* Retrieved July 27, 2010, from http://nces.ed.gov/pubs2010/2010015.pdf

Austin, M., Reiss, N., & Burgdord, L. (2007). *ADHD comorbidity.* Retrieved October 24, 2008, from http://www.mhmrcv.org/poc/view_doc.php?type=doc&id=13851&cn=3

Austin, S., Ziyadeh, N., Farman, S., Prokop, L., Keliher, A., & Jacobs, D. (2008). Screening high school students for eating disorders: Results of a national initiative. *Prevention of Chronic Disease, 5*, 1–10.

Austin, S., Ziyadeh, N., Kahn, J., Camargo, C., Colditz, G., & Field, A. (2004). Sexual orientation, weight concerns, and eating-disordered behaviors in adolescent girls and boys. *Journal of the American Academy of Child & Adolescent Psychiatry, 43*, 1115–1123.

Austin, W. (2008). Relocation, research, and forensic evaluation, part I: Effects of residential mobility on children of divorce. *Family Court Review, 46*, 137–150.

Avis, J., & Harris, P. L. (1991). Belief-desire reasoning among Baka children: Evidence for a universal conception of mind. *Child Development, 62*, 460–467.

Bachman, J. G., Safron, D., Sy, S., & Schulenberg, J. (2003). Wishing to work: New perspectives on how adolescents' part-time work intensity is linked to educational disengagement, substance use, and other problem behaviours. *International Journal of Behavioral Development, 27*, 301–315.

Bachman, J. G., & Schulenberg, J. (1993). How part-time work intensity relates to drug use, problem behavior, time use, and satisfaction among high school seniors: Are these consequences or merely correlates? *Developmental Psychology, 29*, 220–235.

Bacigalupe, G., & Lambe, S. (2011). Virtualizing intimacy: Information communication technologies and transnational families in therapy. *Family Process, 50*, 12–26.

Bacikova-Sleskova, M., Geckova, A., van Dijk, J., Groothoff, J., & Reijneveld, S. (2011). Parental support and adolescents' health in the context of parental employment status. *Journal of Adolescence, 34*, 141–149.

Baer, J., Sampson, P., Barr, H., Connor, P., & Streissguth, A. (2003). A 21-year longitudinal analysis of the effects of prenatal alcohol exposure on young adult drinking. *Archives of General Psychiatry, 60*, 377–385.

Bahrick, L., & Lickliter, R. (2000). Intersensory redundancy guides attentional selectivity and perceptual learning in infancy. *Developmental Psychology, 36*, 190–201.

Bailey, B., & Konstan, J. (2006). On the need for attention-aware systems: Measuring effects of interruption on task performance, error rate, and affective state. *Computers in Human Behavior, 22*, 685–708.

Bailey, J., Brobow, D., Wolfe, M., & Mikach, S. (1995). Sexual orientation of adult sons of gay fathers. *Developmental Psychology, 31*, 124–129.

Bailey, J., Pillard, R., Dawood, K., Miller, M., Farrer, L., Trivedi, S., & Murphy, R. (1999). A family history study of male sexual orientation using three independent samples. *Behavior Genetics, 29*, 79–86.

Bailey, J., & Zucker, K. (1995). Childhood sex-typed behavior and sexual orientation: A conceptual analysis and quantitative review. *Developmental Psychology, 31*, 43–55.

Bailey, S., & Zvonkovic, A. (2003). Parenting after divorce: Nonresidential parents' perceptions of social and institutional support. *Journal of Divorce & Remarriage, 39*, 59–80.

Baillargeon, R. (1994). How do infants learn about the physical world? *Current Directions in Psychological Science, 3*, 133–140.

Baillargeon, R. (2008). Innate ideas revisited: For a principle of persistence in infants' physical reasoning. *Perspectives on Psychological Science, 3*, 2–13.

Baker-Ward, L. (1995, April). *Children's reports of a minor medical emergency procedure.* Paper presented at the biennial meetings of the Society for Research in Child Development, Indianapolis.

van Balen, F. (1998). Development of IVF children. *Developmental Review, 18*, 30–46.

Bandura, A. (1973). *Aggression: A social learning analysis.* Englewood Cliffs, NJ: Prentice Hall.

Bandura, A. (1977). *Social learning theory.* Englewood Cliffs, NJ: Prentice Hall.

Bandura, A. (1982). Self-efficacy mechanism in human agency. *American Psychologist, 37*, 122–147.

Bandura, A. (1986). *Social foundations of thought and action: A social cognitive theory.* Englewood Cliffs, NJ: Prentice Hall.

Bandura, A. (1989). Social cognitive theory. *Annals of Child Development, 6*, 1–60.

Bandura, A. (1997). *Self-efficacy. The exercise of control.* New York: Freeman.

Bandura, A. (2004). Swimming against the mainstream: The early years from chilly tributary to transformative mainstream. *Behaviour Research & Therapy, 42*, 613–630.

Bandura, A. (2008). Reconstrual of "free will" from the agentic perspective of social cognitive theory. In J. Baer, J. Kaufman, & R. Baumeister (Eds.), *Are we free? Psychology and free will* (pp. 86–127). New York: Oxford University Press.

Bandura, A., & Bussey, K. (2004). On broadening the cognitive, motivational, and sociostructural scope of theorizing about gender development and functioning: Comment on Martin, Ruble, and Szkrybalo (2002). *Psychological Bulletin, 130*, 691–701.

Bandura, A., Caprara, G., Barbaranelli, C., Gerbino, M., & Pastorelli, C. (2003). Role of affective self-regulatory efficacy in diverse spheres of psychosocial functioning. *Child Development, 74*, 769–782.

Bandura, A., Ross, D., & Ross, S. (1961). Transmission of aggression through imitation of aggressive models. *Journal of Abnormal & Social Psychology, 63*, 575–582.

Barber, B., & Demo, D. (2006). The kids are alright (at least, most of them): Links between divorce and dissolution and child well-being. In M. Fine & J. Harvey (Eds.), *Handbook of divorce and relationship dissolution* (pp. 289–312). Mahwah, NJ: Erlbaum.

Barber, B., Eccles, J., & Stone, M. (2001). Whatever happened to the jock, the brain, and the princess? Young adult pathways linked to adolescent activity involvement and social identity. *Journal of Adolescent Research, 16*, 429–455.

Barkley, R. (2005). *Attention-deficit hyperactivity disorder: A handbook for diagnosis and treatment* (3rd ed.). New York: Guilford Press.

Barenboim, C. (1977). Developmental changes in the interpersonal cognitive system from middle childhood to adolescence. *Child Development, 48*, 1467–1474.

Barenboim, C. (1981). The development of person perception in childhood and adolescence: From behavioral comparisons to psychological constructs to psychological comparisons. *Child Development, 52*, 129–144.

Barkley, R. A., Fischer, M., Edelbrock, C. S., & Smallish, L. (1990). The adolescent outcome of hyperactive children diagnosed by research criteria: I. An 8-year prospective follow-up study. *Journal of the American Academy of Child and Adolescent Psychiatry, 29*, 546–557.

Barnett, D., Manley, J., & Cicchetti, D. (1993). Defining child maltreatment: The interface between policy and research. In D. Cicchetti & S. Toth (Eds.), *Child abuse, child development, and social policy* (pp. 7–73). Norwood, NJ: Ablex.

Barnett, W. S. (1993). Benefit-cost analysis of preschool education: Findings from a 25-year follow-up. *American Journal of Orthopsychiatry, 63*, 500–508.

Barnett, W. S., & Hustedt, J. (2005). Head Start's lasting benefits. *Infants & Young Children, 18*, 16–24.

Baron-Cohen, S., Lutchmaya, S., & Knickmeyer, R. (2006). *Prenatal testosterone in mind.* Cambridge, MA: MIT Press.

del Barrio, V., Moreno-Rosset, C., Lopez-Martinez, R., & Olmedo, M. (1997). Anxiety, depression and personality structure. *Personality & Individual Differences, 23*, 327–335.

Barrow, F., Armstrong, M., Vargo, A., & Boothroyd, R. (2007). Understanding the findings of resilience-related research for fostering the development of African American adolescents. *Child and Adolescent Psychiatric Clinics of North America, 16*, 393–413.

Barry, D., Bernard, M., & Beitel, M. (2008, in press). East Asian child-rearing attitudes: An exploration of cultural, demographic and self-disclosure factors among U.S. immigrants. *International Journal of Psychology.*

Barry, R., Clarke, A., Hajos, M., Dupuy, F., McCarthy, R., & Seikowitz, M. (2011). EEG coherence and symptom profiles of children with attention-deficit/hyperactivity disorder. *Clinical Neurophysiology, 122*, 1327–1332.

Barsh, G. (2003). What controls variation in human skin color? *Public Library of Science: Biology, 1*, e27.

Bartels, M., Rietveld, M., Van Baal, G., & Boomsma, D. (2002). Genetic and environmental influences on the development of intelligence. *Behavior Genetics, 32*, 237–249.

Barth, R. (2001). Research outcomes of prenatal substance exposure and the need to review policies and procedures regarding child abuse reporting. *Child Welfare, 80*, 275–296.

Bartsch, K. (1993). Adolescents' theoretical thinking. In R. M. Lerner (Ed.), *Early adolescence: Perspectives on research, policy, and intervention* (pp. 143–157). Hillsdale, NJ: Erlbaum.

Basham, P. (2001). Home schooling: From the extreme to the mainstream. *Public Policy Sources/The Fraser Institute, 51.* Retrieved June 23, 2004, from http://www.fraserinstitute.ca/admin/books/files/homeschool.pdf

Bates, E., Marchman, V., Thal, D., Fenson, L., Dale, P., Reznick, J. S., Reilly, J., & Hartung, J. (1994). Developmental and stylistic variation in the composition of early vocabulary. *Journal of Child Language, 21*, 85–123.

Bates, E., O'Connell, B., & Shore, C. (1987). Language and communication in infancy. In J. D. Osofsky (Ed.), *Handbook of infant development* (2nd ed., pp. 149–203). New York: Wiley.

Bates, J. E. (1989). Applications of temperament concepts. In G. A. Kohnstamm, J. E. Bates, & M. K. Rothbart (Eds.), *Temperament in childhood* (pp. 321–356). Chichester, England: Wiley.

Batterson, V., Rose, S., Yonas, A., Grant, K., & Sackett, G. (2008). The effect of experience on the development of tactual-visual transfer in pigtailed macaque monkeys. *Developmental Psychobiology, 50*, 88–96.

Bauer, P., Lukowski, A., & Pathman, T. (2011). Neuropsychology of middle childhood development (6 to 11 years old). In A. Davis (Ed.), *Handbook of pediatric neuropsychology* (pp. 37–46). New York: Springer.

Baumeister, A. (2006). Mental retardation: Confusing sentiment with science. In H. Switzky & S. Greenspan (Eds.), *What is mental retardation?* (pp. 93–124). Washington, DC: American Association on Mental Retardation.

Baumeister, R., Bushman, B., & Campbell, W. (2000). Self-esteem, narcissism, and aggression: Does violence result from low self-esteem or from threatened egotism? *Current Directions in Psychological Science, 9*, 26–29.

Baumeister, R., Campbell, J., Krueger, J., & Vohs, K. (2003). Does high self-esteem cause better performance, interpersonal success, happiness, or healthier lifestyles? *Psychological Science in the Public Interest, 4*(1), 1–44.

Baumeister, R., Smart, L., & Boden, J. (1996). Relation of threatened egotism to violence and aggression: The dark side of high self-esteem. *Psychological Review, 103*, 5–33.

Bauminger, N., Finzi-Dottan, R., Chason, S., & Har-Even, D. (2008). Intimacy in adolescent friendship: The roles of attachment, coherence, and self-disclosure. *Journal of Social and Personal Relationships, 25*, 409–428.

Baumrind, D. (1971). Current patterns of parental authority. *Developmental Psychology Monograph, 4*(1, Part 2).

Baumrind, D. (1973). The development of instrumental competence through socialization. In A. D. Pick (Ed.), *Minnesota symposium on child psychology* (Vol. 7, pp. 3–46). Minneapolis: University of Minnesota Press.

Baumrind, D. (1991). The influence of parenting style on adolescent competence and substance use. *Journal of Early Adolescence, 11*, 56–95.

Bayley, N. (1969). *Bayley Scales of Infant Development.* New York: Psychological Corporation.

Bayley, N. (1993). *Bayley Scales of Infant Development: Birth to two years.* San Antonio, TX: Psychological Corporation.

Beauchaine, T., & Hinshaw, S. (2008). *Child and adolescent psychopathology.* New York: Wiley.

Bee, H. L., Barnard, K. E., Eyres, S. J., Gray, C. A., Hammond, M. A., Spietz, A. L., Snyder, C., & Clark, B. (1982). Prediction of IQ and language skill from perinatal status, child performance, family characteristics, and mother-infant interaction. *Child Development, 53*, 1135–1156.

Behm-Morawitz, E., & Mastro, D. (2009). The effects of the sexualization of female video game characters on gender stereotyping and female self-concept. *Sex Roles, 61*, 808–823.

Beilstein, C., & Wilson, J. (2000). Landmarks in route learning by girls and boys. *Perceptual & Motor Skills, 91*, 877–882.

Bell, L. G., & Bell, D. C. (1982). Family climate and the role of the female adolescent: Determinants of adolescent functioning. *Family Relations, 31*, 519–527.

Belo, R., Ferreira, P., & Telang, R. (2010). *The effects of broadband in schools: Evidence from Portugal.* Retrieved July 12, 2011, from http://cemapre.iseg.utl.pt/events/1e3/papers/Rodrigo%20Belo.pdf

Belsky, J. (1981). Early human experience: A family perspective. *Developmental Psychology, 17*, 3–23.

Belsky, J. (1985). Prepared statement on the effects of day care. In *Improving child care services: What can be done?* Select Committee on Children, Youth, and Families, House of Representatives, 98th Cong., 2d Sess. Washington, DC: U.S. Government Printing Office.

Belsky, J. (1992). Consequences of child care for children's development: A deconstructionist view. In A. Booth (Ed.), *Child care in the 1990s. Trends and consequences* (pp. 83–94). Hillsdale, NJ: Erlbaum.

Belsky, J. (2001). Developmental risks (still) associated with early child care. *Journal of Child Psychology & Psychiatry & Allied Disciplines, 42*, 845–859.

Belsky, J. (2002). Quantity counts: Amount of child care and children's socioemotional development. *Journal of Developmental and Behavioral Pediatrics, 23*, 167–170.

Belsky, J., & Beaver, K. (2011). Cumulative genetic plasticity, parenting and adolescent self-regulation. *Journal of Child Psychology and Psychiatry, 52*, 619–626.

Belsky, J., Lang, M. E., & Rovine, M. (1985). Stability and change in marriage across the transition to parenthood: A second study. *Journal of Marriage and the Family, 47*, 855–865.

Belsky, J., & Rovine, M. (1988). Nonmaternal care in the first year of life and the security of infant-parent attachment. *Child Development, 59*, 157–167.

Belsky, J., Vandell, D., Burchinal, M., Clarke-Stewart, A., McCartney, K., Owen, M., et al. (2007). Are there long-term effects of early child care? *Child Development, 78*, 681–701.

Bem, S. L. (1974). The measurement of psychological androgyny. *Journal of Consulting and Clinical Psychology, 42*, 155–162.

Bem, S. L. (1981). Gender schema theory: A cognitive account of sex-typing. *Psychological Review, 88*, 354–364.

Bem, S. L. (1989). Genital knowledge and gender constancy in preschool children. *Child Development, 60*, 649–662.

Benbow, C. P. (1988). Sex differences in mathematical reasoning ability in intellectually talented preadolescents: Their nature, effects, and possible causes. *Behavioral & Brain Sciences, 11*, 169–232.

Bender, S. L., Word, C. O., DiClemente, R. J., Crittenden, M. R., Persaud, N. A., & Ponton, L. E. (1995). The developmental implications of prenatal and/or postnatal crack cocaine exposure in preschool children: A preliminary report. *Journal of Developmental and Behavioral Pediatrics, 16*, 418–424.

Benenson, J. F. (1994). Ages four to six years: Changes in the structures of play networks of girls and boys. *Merrill-Palmer Quarterly, 40*, 478–487.

Bennett, M., & Sani, F. (2008a). Children's subjective identification with social groups: A self-stereotyping approach. *Developmental Science, 11*, 69–75.

Bennett, M., & Sani, F. (2008b). The effect of comparative context upon stereotype content: Children's judgments of ingroup behavior. *Scandinavian Journal of Psychology, 49*, 141–146.

Benoit, D., & Parker, K. C. H. (1994). Stability and transmission of attachment across three generations. *Child Development, 65*, 1444–1456.

Benson, J., & Sabbagh, M. (2010). Theory of mind and executive functioning: A developmental neuropsychological approach. In P. Zelazo, M. Chandler, & E. Crone (Eds.), *Developmental social cognitive neuroscience.* New York: Psychology Press.

Benson, L. (2011). The role of parental employment in childhood obesity. *Dissertation Abstracts Internation: Section B: The Sciences and Engineering, 42055.*

Benton, T. (2010). *Depression.* Retrieved August 16, 2010, from http://emedicine.medscape.com/article/914192-overview

Berch, D. B., & Bender, B. G. (1987, December). Margins of sexuality. *Psychology Today, 21*, 54–57.

Bergen, D., & Woodin, M. (2011). Neuropsychological development of newborns, infants, and toddlers (0 to 3 years old). In A. Davis (Ed.), *Handbook of pediatric neuropsychology* (pp. 15–30). New York: Springer.

Bergman, K., Sarkar, P., Glover, V., & O'Connor, T. (2010). Maternal prenatal cortisol and infant cognitive development: Moderation by infant-mother attachment. *Biological Psychiatry, 67*, 1026–1032.

Berndt, T. J. (1983). Social cognition, social behavior, and children's friendships. In E. T. Higgins, D. N. Ruble, & W. W. Hartup (Eds.), *Social cognition and social development: A sociocultural perspective* (pp. 158–192). Cambridge, England: Cambridge University Press.

Berndt, T. J. (1986). Children's comments about their friendships. In M. Perlmutter (Ed.), *Minnesota symposia on child psychology* (Vol. 18, pp. 189–212). Hillsdale, NJ: Erlbaum.

Berndt, T. J. (1992). Friendship and friends' influence in adolescence. *Current Directions in Psychological Science, 1,* 156–159.

Berndt, T. J. (2004). Children's friendships: Shifts over a half- century in perspectives on their development and their effects. *Merrill Palmer Quarterly Journal of Developmental Psychology, 50,* 206–223.

Berndt, T. J., & Hoyle, S. G. (1985). Stability and change in childhood and adolescent friendships. *Developmental Psychology, 21,* 1007–1015.

Berndt, T. J., & Murphy, L. M. (2002). Influences of friends and friendships: Myths, truths, and research recommendations. *Advances in Child Development and Behavior, 30,* 275–310.

Berninger, V., Abbott, R., Nagy, W., & Carlisle, J. (2010). Growth in phonological, orthographic, and morphological awareness in grades 1 to 6. *Journal of Psycholinguistic Research, 39,* 141–163.

Berninger, V., Abbott, R., Zook, D., Ogier, S., Lemos-Britton, Z., & Brooksher, R. (1999). Early intervention for reading disabilities: Teaching the alphabet principle in a connectionist framework. *Journal of Learning Disabilities, 32,* 491–503.

Berninger, V., Vaughan, K., Abbott, R., Abbott, S., Rogan, L., Brooks, A., et al. (1997). Treatment of handwriting problems in beginning writers: Transfer from handwriting to composition. *Journal of Educational Psychology, 89,* 652–666.

Bernstein, B. (2010). *Eating disorder, anorexia.* Retrieved August 16, 2010, from http://emedicine.medscape.com/article/805152-overview

Bernstein, B., & Pataki, C. (2011). *Conduct disorder.* Retrieved July 27, 2011, from http://emedicine.medscape.com/article/918213-overview#aw2aab6b5

Berry, J., Poortinga, Y., Poortinga, M., & Dasen, P. (2002). *Cross-cultural psychology: Research and applications.* Cambridge, UK: Cambridge University Press.

Berry, J., & Sabatier, C. (2010). Acculturation, discrimination, and adaptation among second generation immigrant youth in Montreal and Paris. *International Journal of Intercultural Relations, 34,* 191–207.

Berthier, N., DeBlois, S., Poirier, C., Novak, M., & Clifton, R. (2000). Where's the ball? Two- and three-year-olds reason about unseen events. *Developmental Psychology, 36,* 394–401.

Best, R., & Gregg, A. (2009). *Patau syndrome.* Retrieved June 27, 2010, from http://emedicine.medscape.com/article/947706-overview

Bettner, B. (2007). Recreating sibling relationships in marriage. *Journal of Individual Psychology, 63,* 339–344.

Bialystok, E., Majumder, S., & Martin, M. (2003). Developing phonological awareness: Is there a bilingual advantage? *Applied Linguistics, 24,* 27–44.

Bialystok, E., Shenfield, T., & Codd, J. (2000). Languages, scripts, and the environment: Factors in developing concepts of print. *Developmental Psychology, 36,* 66–76.

Bigelow, B. J., & La Gaipa, J. J. (1975). Children's written descriptions of friendships: A multidimensional analysis. *Developmental Psychology, 11,* 857–858.

Bigler, R. S. (1995). The role of classification skill in moderating environmental influences on children's gender stereotyping: A study of the functional use of gender in the classroom. *Child Development, 66,* 1072–1087.

Bigler, R. S., & Liben, S. (1993). The role of attitudes and interventions in gender-schematic processing. *Child Development, 61,* 1440–1452.

Billy, J. O. G., Brewster, K. L., & Grady, W. R. (1994). Contextual effects on the sexual behavior of adolescent women. *Journal of Marriage and the Family, 56,* 387–404.

Binet, A., & Simon, T. (1905). Méthodes nouvelles pour le diagnostic du niveau intellectual des anormaux [New methods for diagnosing intellectual level in the abnormal]. *Année Psychologie, 11,* 191–244.

Birbal, R., Maharaih, H., Birbal, R., Clapperton, M., Jarvis, J., Ragoonath, A., et al. (2009). Cybersuicide and the adolescent population: Challenges of the future. *International Journal of Adolescent Medicine and Health, 21,* 151–159.

Birch, D. (1998). The adolescent parent: A fifteen year longitudinal study of school-age mothers and their children. *International Journal of Adolescent Medicine & Health, 10,* 141–153.

Biringen, A. (2000). Emotional availability: Conceptualization and research findings. *American Journal of Orthopsychiatry, 70,* 104–114.

Birney, D., Citron-Pousty, J., Lutz, D., & Sternberg, R. (2005). The development of cognitive and intellectual abilities. In M. Bornstein & M. Lamb (Eds.), *Developmental science: An advanced textbook* (5th ed., pp. 327–358). Hillsdale, NJ: Erlbaum.

Birney, D., & Sternberg, R. (2011). The development of cognitive abilities. In M. Bornstein & M. Lamb (Eds.), *Developmental science: An advanced textbook* (6th ed., pp. 353–388). New York: Psychology Press.

Biswas, M. K., & Craigo, S. D. (1994). The course and conduct of normal labor and delivery. In A. H. DeCherney & M. L. Pernoll (Eds.), *Current obstetric and gynecologic diagnosis & treatment* (pp. 202–227). Norwalk, CT: Appleton & Lange.

Bittle, S., Rochkind, J., Ott, A., & Gasbarra, P. (2009). *A place to call home: What immigrants say now about life in America.* Retrieved July 24, 2011, from http://www.publicagenda.org/files/pdf/Immigration.pdf

Bivens, J. A., & Berk, L. E. (1990). A longitudinal study of the development of elementary school children's private speech. *Merrill-Palmer Quarterly, 36,* 443–463.

Bjorklund, D. F., Miller, P. H., Coyle, T. R., & Slawinski, J. L. (1997). Instructing children to use memory strategies: Evidence of utilization deficiencies in memory training studies. *Developmental Review, 17,* 411–441.

Bjorklund, D. F., & Muir, J. E. (1988). Remembering on their own: Children's development of free recall memory. In R. Vasta (Ed.), *Annals of child development* (Vol. 5, pp. 79–124). Greenwich, CT: JAI Press.

Blair, C. (2002). School readiness: Integrating cognition and emotion in a neurobiological conceptualization of children's functioning at school entry. *American Psychologist, 57,* 111–127.

Blair, C., Greenberg, M., & Crnic, K. (2001). Age-related increases in motivation among children with mental retardation and MA- and CA-matched controls. *American Journal on Mental Retardation, 106,* 511–524.

Blake, I. K. (1994). Language development and socialization in young African-American children. In P. M. Greenfield & R. R. Cocking (Eds.), *Cross-cultural roots of minority child development* (pp. 167–195). Hillsdale, NJ: Erlbaum.

Blake, K., & Davis, V. (2011). Adolescent medicine. In K. Marcdante, R. Kliegman, H. Jensen, & R. Behrman (Eds.), *Nelson's essentials of pediatrics* (6th ed., pp. 265–284). New York: Elsevier Health Publishers.

Blass, E. M., Ganchrow, J. R., & Steiner, J. E. (1984). Classical conditioning in newborn humans 2–48 hours of age. *Infant Behavior and Development, 7,* 223–235.

Blatt, S. (2008, in press). Polarities of experience: Relatedness and self-definition in personality development, psychopathology, and the therapeutic process. Washington, DC: American Psychological Association.

Block, J. (1971). *Lives through time.* Berkeley, CA: Bancroft.

Bloom, L. (1973). *One word at a time.* The Hague: Mouton.

Bloom, L. (1991). *Language development from two to three.* Cambridge, England: Cambridge University Press.

Bloom, L. (1993). *The transition from infancy to language: Acquiring the power of expression.* Cambridge, England: Cambridge University Press.

Bloom, L. (1997, April). *The child's action drives the interaction.* Paper presented at the biennial meetings of the Society for Research in Child Development, Washington, DC.

Bloom, L. (1998). Language acquisition in its developmental context. In W. Damon (Ed.), *Handbook of child psychology: Vol. 2. Cognition, perception, and language* (5th ed., pp. 309–370). New York: Wiley.

Blumberg, F., & Sokol, L. (2004). Boys' and girls' use of cognitive strategies when learning to play video games. *Journal of General Psychology, 131,* 151–158.

Boehnke, K., Silbereisen, R., Eisenberg, N., & Reykowski, J. (1989). Developmental pattern of prosocial motivation: A cross-national study. *Journal of Cross-Cultural Psychology, 20,* 219–243.

Bohlin, G., & Hagekull, B. (2009). Socio-emotional development: From infancy to young adulthood. *Scandinavian Journal of Psychology, 50,* 592–601.

Bokhorst, C., Sumter, S., & Westenberg, P. (2010). Social support from parents, friends, classmates, and teachers in children and adolescents aged 9 to 18 years: Who is perceived as most supportive? *Social Development, 19,* 417–426.

Bolger, K. (1997, April). *Children's adjustment as a function of timing of family economic hardship.* Paper presented at the biennial meetings of the Society for Research in Child Development, Washington, DC.

Bond, L., Braskamp, D., & Roeber, E. (1996). *The status report of the assessment programs in the United States.* Oakbrook, IL: North Central Regional Educational Laboratory. ERIC Document No. ED 401 333.

Bonde, E., Obel, C., Nedergard, N., & Thomsen, P. (2004). Social risk factors as predictors for parental report of deviant behaviour in 3-year-old children. *Nordic Journal of Psychiatry, 58,* 17–23.

Bong, M. (1998). Tests of the internal/external frames of reference model with subject-specific academic self-efficacy and frame-specific academic self-concepts. *Journal of Educational Psychology, 90,* 102–110.

van den Boom, D. C. (1994). The influence of temperament and mothering on attachment and exploration: An experimental manipulation of sensitive responsiveness among lower-class mothers with irritable infants. *Child Development, 65,* 1457–1477.

van den Boom, D. C. (1995). Do first-year intervention effects endure? Follow-up during toddlerhood of a sample of Dutch irritable infants. *Child Development, 66,* 1798–1816.

Boom, J., Wouters, H., & Keller, M. (2007). A cross-cultural validation of stage development: A Rasch re-analysis of longitudinal socio-moral reasoning data. *Cognitive Development, 22,* 213–229.

Boone, R., Higgins, K., Notari, A., & Stump, C. (1996). Hypermedia prereading lessons: Learner-centered software for kindergarten. *Journal of Computing in Childhood Education, 7,* 39–70.

Borkowski, M., Hunter, K., & Johnson, C. (2001). White noise and scheduled bedtime routines to reduce infant and childhood sleep disturbances. *Behavior Therapist, 24,* 29–37.

Born, A. (2007). Well-diffused? Identity diffusion and well-being in emerging adulthood. In M. Watzlawik & A. Born (Eds.), *Capturing identity: Quantitative and qualitative methods* (pp. 149–161). Lanham, MD: University Press of America.

Bornstein, M., Arterberry, M., & Mash, C. (2011). In M. Bornstein & M. Lamb (Eds.), *Developmental science: An advanced textbook* (6th ed., pp. 303–352). New York: Psychology Press.

Bornstein, M., DiPietro, J., Hahn, C., Painter, K., Haynes, O., & Costigan, K. (2002). Prenatal cardiac function and postnatal cognitive development: An exploratory study. *Infancy, 3,* 475–494.

Bornstei, M., Hahn, C., & Haynes, O. (2011). Maternal personality, parenting cognitions, and parenting practices. *Developmental Psychology, 47,* 658–675.

Bornstein, M. H. (Ed.). (1989). Maternal responsiveness: Characteristics and consequences. *New Directions for Child Development, 43.*

Bornstein, M. H. (1995). Parenting infants. In M. H. Bornstein (Ed.), *Handbook of parenting: Vol 1. Children and parenting* (pp. 3–39). Mahwah, NJ: Erlbaum.

Bornstein, M. H., Tamis-LeMonda, C. S., Tal, J., Ludemann, P., Toda, S., Rahn, C. W., Pecheux, M., Azuma, H., & Vardi, D. (1992). Maternal responsiveness to infants in three societies: The United States, France, and Japan. *Child Development, 63,* 808–821.

Borse, N., Gilchrist, J., Dellinger, A., Rudd, R., Ballesteros, M., & Sleet, D. (2008). *CDC childhood injury report: Patterns of unintentional injuries among 0-19 year olds in the United States, 2000-2006.* Retrieved August 6, 2010, from http://www.cdc.gov/safechild/images/CDC-ChildhoodInjury.pdf

Borse, N., & Sleet, D. (2009). CDC childhood injury report: Patterns of unintentional injuries among 0-19 year olds in the United States, 2000-2006. *Family & Community Health, 32,* 189.

Bos, H., & Gartrell, N. (2010). Adolescents of the USA National Lesbian Family Study: Can family characteristics counteract the negative effects of stigmatization? *Family Process, 49,* 559–572.

Bos, H., & Sandfort, T. (2010). Children's gender identify in lesbian and heterosexual two-parent families. *Sex Roles, 62,* 114–126.

Bossewitch, J. (2010). Pediatric bipolar and the media of madness. *Ethical Human Psychology and Psychiatry: An International Journal of Critical Inquiry, 12,* 254–268.

Bostwick, J., & Martin, K. (2007). A man's brain in an ambiguous body: A case of mistaken gender identity. *American Journal of Psychiatry, 164,* 1499–1505.

Bosworth, R., & Birch, E. (2005). Motion detection in normal infants and young patients with infantile esotropia. *Vision Research, 45,* 1557–1567.

Bouchard, T. J., Jr., & McGue, M. (1981). Familial studies of intelligence: A review. *Science, 212,* 1055–1059.

Bouchey, H., & Harter, S. (2005). Reflected appraisals, academic self-perceptions, and math/science performance during early adolescence. *Journal of Educational Psychology, 97,* 673–686.

Bowen, J., Gibson, F., & Hand, P. (2002). Educational outcome at 8 years for children who were born extremely prematurely: A controlled study. *Journal of Pediatrics & Child Health, 38,* 438–444.

Bower, B. (2005). Mental meeting of the sexes: Boys' spatial advantage fades in poor families. *Science News, 168,* 21.

Bower, T. G. R. (1966). The visual world of infants. *Scientific American, 215,* 80–92.

Bowerman, M. (1985). Beyond communicative adequacy: From piecemeal knowledge to an integrated system in the child's acquisition of language. In K. E. Nelson (Ed.), *Children's language* (Vol. 5, pp. 369–398). Hillsdale, NJ: Erlbaum.

Bowerman, M. (2007). Containment, support, and beyond: Constructing topological spatial categories in first language acquisition. In M. Aurnague, M. Hickmann, & L. Vieu (Eds.), *The categorization of spatial entities in language and cognition* (pp. 177–203). Amsterdam, Netherlands: John Benjamins Publishing Company.

Bowker, A. (2004). Predicting friendship stability during early adolescence. *Journal of Early Adolescence, 24*, 85–112.

Bowlby, J. (1969). *Attachment and loss: Vol. 1. Attachment.* New York: Basic Books.

Bowlby, R. (2007). Babies and toddlers in non-parental daycare can avoid stress and anxiety if they develop a lasting secondary attachment bond with one carer who is consistently accessible to them. *Attachment & Human Development, 9*, 307–319.

Bowler, D., Briskman, J., & Grice, S. (1999). Experimenter effects on children's understanding of false drawings and false beliefs. *Journal of Genetic Psychology, 160*, 443–460.

Boyd, D., & Naus, M. (2003). *Children's understanding of grief narratives: A preliminary study.* Paper presented at the annual meeting of the Society for Research in Child Development, Tampa, FL.

Bradbury, K., & Katz, J. (2002). Women's labor market involvement and family income mobility when marriages end. *New England Economic Review, Q4*, 41–74.

Bradley, R. H., Whiteside, L., Mundfrom, D. J., Casey, P. H., Kelleher, K. J., & Pope, S. K. (1994). Early indications of resilience and their relation to experiences in the home environments of low birth-weight, premature children living in poverty. *Child Development, 65*, 346–360.

Bradmetz, J. (1999). Precursors of formal thought: A longitudinal study. *British Journal of Developmental Psychology, 17*, 61–81.

Bradshaw, J., & Richardson, D. (2009). An index of child well-being in Europe. *Child Indicators Research, 2*, 319–351.

van Brakel, A., Muris, P., Bögels, S., & Thomassen, C. (2006). A multifactorial model for the etiology of anxiety in non-clinical adolescents: Main and interactive effects of behavioral inhibition, attachment, and parental rearing. *Journal of Child and Family Studies, 15*, 569–579.

Brandenburg, N. A., Friedman, R. M., & Silver, S. E. (1990). The epidemiology of childhood psychiatric disorders: Prevalence findings from recent studies. *Journal of the American Academy of Child and Adolescent Psychiatry, 29*, 76–83.

Brandon, P. (1999). Determinants of self-care arrangements among school-age children. *Children & Youth Services Review, 21*, 497–520.

Brandon, P., & Hofferth, S. (2003). Determinants of out-of-school child-care arrangements among children in single-mother and two-parent families. *Social Science Research, 32*, 129–147.

Brazelton, T. D. (1984). *Neonatal Behavioral Assessment Scale.* Philadelphia: Lippincott.

Breitmayer, B. J., & Ramey, C. T. (1986). Biological nonoptimality and quality of postnatal environment as codeterminants of intellectual development. *Child Development, 57*, 1151–1165.

Breland, H. M. (1974). Birth order, family configuration, and verbal achievement. *Child Development, 45*, 1011–1019.

Brendgen, M., Boivin, M., Vitaro, F., Bukowski, W., Dionne, G., Tremblay, R., & Pérusse, D. (2008). Linkages between children's and their friends' social and physical aggression: Evidence for a gene-environment interaction? *Child Development, 79*, 13–29.

Brennan, F., & Ireson, J. (1997). Training phonological awareness: A study to evaluate the effects of a program of metalinguistic games in kindergarten. *Reading & Writing, 9*, 241–263.

Breyer, J., & Winters, K. (2005). *Adolescent brain development: Implications for drug use prevention.* Retrieved April 15, 2008, from http://www.mentorfoundation.org/pdfs/prevention_perspectives/19.pdf

Bridgeland, J., DiIulio, J., & Morison, K. (2006). *The silent epidemic: Perspectives of high school dropouts.* Retrieved September 9, 2008, from http://www.gatesfoundation.org/nr/downloads/ed/thesilentepidemic3-06final.pdf

Bright, S., McKillop, D., & Ryder, D. (2008). Cigarette smoking among young adults: Integrating adolescent cognitive egocentrism with the Trans-Theoretical Model. *Australian Journal of Psychology, 60*, 18–25.

Bright-Paul, A., Jarrold, C., & Wright, D. (2008). Theory-of-mind development influences suggestibility and source monitoring. *Developmental Psychology, 44*, 1055–1068.

Briones, T., Klintsova, A., & Greenough, W. (2004). Stability of synaptic plasticity in the adult rat visual cortex induced by complex environment exposure. *Brain Research, 1018*, 130–135.

Brockington, I. (1996). *Motherhood and mental health.* Oxford, England: Oxford University Press.

Brody, G. H., Kim, S., Murry, V., & Brown, A. (2003). Longitudinal direct and indirect pathways linking older sibling competence to the development of younger sibling competence. *Developmental Psychology, 39*, 618–628.

Brody, G. H., Stoneman, Z., & Flor, D. (1995). Linking family processes and academic competence among rural African American youths. *Journal of Marriage and the Family, 47*, 567–579.

Brody, N. (1992). *Intelligence* (2nd ed.). San Diego, CA: Academic Press.

Brody, N. (1997). Intelligence, schooling, and society. *American Psychologist, 52*, 1046–1050.

Broman, C. L. (1993). Race differences in marital well-being. *Journal of Marriage and the Family, 55*, 724–732.

Broman, S. H., Nichols, P. L., & Kennedy, W. A. (1975). *Preschool IQ: Prenatal and early developmental correlates.* Hillsdale, NJ: Erlbaum.

Broman, S. H., Nichols, P. L., Shaughnessy, P., & Kennedy, W. (1987). *Retardation in young children.* Hillsdale, NJ: Erlbaum.

Bronfenbrenner, U. (1967, October 7). The split-level American family. *Saturday Review*, 60–66.

Bronfenbrenner, U. (1979). *The ecology of human development.* Cambridge, MA: Harvard University Press.

Bronfenbrenner, U. (1989). Ecological systems theory. *Annals of Child Development, 6*, 187–249.

Bronfenbrenner, U. (2001). The bioecological theory of human development. In N. Smelser & P. Baltes (Eds.), *International encyclopedia of the social and behavioral sciences* (pp. 6963–6970). New York: Elsevier.

Bronk, K. (2011). Neuropsychology of adolescent development. In A. Davis (Ed.), *Handbook of pediatric neuropsychology* (pp. 47–59). New York: Springer.

Bronson, G. W. (1994). Infants' transitions toward adult-like scanning. *Child Development, 65*, 1253–1261.

Bronson, P., & Merryman, A. (2009). *Nurture shock.* New York: Twelve, Hachette Book Group.

Brook, J., Whiteman, M., Finch, S., & Cohen, P. (2000). Longitudinally foretelling drug use in the late twenties: Adolescent personality and social-environmental antecedents. *Journal of Genetic Psychology, 161*, 37–51.

Brook, U., & Boaz, M. (2005). Attention deficit and hyperactivity disorder/learning disabilities (ADHD/LD): Parental characterization and perception. *Patient Education & Counseling, 57*, 96–100.

Brooks-Gunn, J. (1987). Pubertal processes and girls' psychological adaptation. In R. M. Lerner & T. T. Foch (Eds.), *Biological-psychosocial interactions in early adolescence* (pp. 123–154). Hillsdale, NJ: Erlbaum.

Brooks-Gunn, J. (1988). Commentary: Developmental issues in the transition to early adolescence. In M. R. Gunnar & W. A. Collins (Eds.), *Minnesota symposia on child psychology* (Vol. 21, pp. 189–208). Hillsdale, NJ: Erlbaum.

Brooks-Gunn, J. (1995). Children in families in communities: Risk and intervention in the Bronfenbrenner tradition. In P. Moen, G. H. Elder Jr., &

K. Lüscher (Eds.), *Examining lives in context: Perspectives on the ecology of human development* (pp. 467–519). Washington, DC: American Psychological Association.

Brooks-Gunn, J., & Duncan G. J. (1997). The effects of poverty on children. *The Future of Children, 7*(2), 55–71.

Brooks-Gunn, J., Duncan, G. J., & Aber, J. L. (Eds.). (1997). *Neighborhood poverty: Vol 1. Context and consequences for children.* New York: Russell Sage Foundation.

Brooks-Gunn, J., Guo, G., & Furstenberg, F. F., Jr. (1993). Who drops out of and who continues beyond high school? A 20-year follow-up of black urban youth. *Journal of Research on Adolescence, 3,* 271–294.

Brooks-Gunn, J., & Warren, M. P. (1985). The effects of delayed menarche in different contexts: Dance and nondance students. *Journal of Youth and Adolescence, 13,* 285–300.

Broverman, I. K., Broverman, D., Clarkson, F. E., Rosenkrantz, P. S., & Vogel, S. R. (1970). Sex-role stereotypes and clinical judgments of mental health. *Journal of Consulting and Clinical Psychology, 34,* 1–7.

Brown, A. (2000–2001). Prenatal infection and adult schizophrenia: A review and synthesis. *International Journal of Mental Health, 29,* 22–37.

Brown, A., & Day, J. (1983). Macrorules for summarizing text: The development of expertise. *Journal of Verbal Learning and Verbal Behavior, 22,* 1–14.

Brown, B. B. (1990). Peer groups and peer cultures. In S. S. Feldman & G. R. Elliott (Eds.), *At the threshold: The developing adolescent* (pp. 171–196). Cambridge, MA: Harvard University Press.

Brown, B. B., Bakken, J. P., Ameringer, S. W., & Mahon, S. D. (2008). A comprehensive conceptualization of the peer influence process in adolescence. In M. J. Prinstein & K. Dodge (Eds.), *Understanding peer influences in children and adolescents* (pp. 17–44). New York: Guilford Publications.

Brown, G., McBride, B., Shin, N., & Bost, K. (2007). Parenting predictors of father-child attachment security: Interactive effects of father involvement and fathering quality. *Fathering, 5,* 197–219.

Brown, L., Karrison, T., & Cibils, L. A. (1994). Mode of delivery and perinatal results in breech presentation. *American Journal of Obstetrics and Gynecology, 171,* 28–34.

Brown, N., & Amatea, E. (2000). *Love and intimate relationships.* New York: Psychology Press.

Brown, R. (1973). *A first language: The early stages.* Cambridge, MA: Harvard University Press.

Brown, R., & Bellugi, U. (1964). Three processes in the acquisition of syntax. *Harvard Educational Review, 334,* 133–151.

Brown, R., & Hanlon, C. (1970). Derivational complexity and order of acquisition. In J. R. Hayes (Ed.), *Cognition and the development of language* (pp. 155–207). New York: Wiley.

Brown, S., Estroff, J., & Barnewolf, C. (2004). Fetal MRI. *Applied Radiology, 33,* 9–25.

Brown, W., Kesler, S., Eliez, S., Warsofsky, I., Haberecht, M., Patwardhan, A., Ross, J., Neely, E., Zeng, S., Yankowitz, J., & Reiss, A. (2002). Brain development in Turner syndrome: A magnetic resonance imaging study. *Psychiatry Research: Neuroimaging, 116,* 187–196.

Brownell, C. A. (1990). Peer social skills in toddlers: Competencies and constraints illustrated by same-age and mixed-age interaction. *Child Development, 61,* 836–848.

Bruck, M., & Ceci, S. J. (1997). The suggestibility of young children. *Current Directions in Psychological Science, 6,* 75–79.

Bruck, M., Ceci, S. J., & Hembrooke, H. (1998). Reliability and credibility of young children's reports: From research to policy and practice. *American Psychologist, 53,* 136–151.

Brumariu, L., & Kerns, K. (2010). Parent-child attachment and internalizing symptoms in childhood and adolescence: A review of empirical findings and future directions. *Development and Psychopathology, 22,* 177–203.

Bryant, P. E., MacLean, M., & Bradley, L. (1990). Rhyme, language, and children's reading. *Applied Psycholinguistics, 11,* 237–252.

Bryant, P. E., MacLean, M., Bradley, L. L., & Crossland, J. (1990). Rhyme and alliteration, phoneme detection, and learning to read. *Developmental Psychology, 26,* 429–438.

Buchanan, C. M., Maccoby, E. E., & Dornbusch, S. M. (1991). Caught between parents: Adolescents' experience in divorced homes. *Child Development, 62,* 1008–1029.

Bucx, F., & Seiffge-Krenke, I. (2010). Romantic relationships in intra-ethnic and inter-ethnic adolescent couples in Germany: The role of attachment to parents, self-esteem, and conflict resolution skills. *International Journal of Behavioral Development, 34,* 128–135.

Buhrmester, D. (1992). The developmental courses of sibling and peer relationships. In F. Boer & J. Dunn (Eds.), *Children's sibling relationships: Developmental and clinical issues.* Hillsdale, NJ: Erlbaum.

Buhrmester, D. (1996). Need fulfillment, interpersonal competence, and the developmental contexts of early adolescent friendship. In W. M. Bukowski, A. F. Newcomb, & W. W. Hartup (Eds.), *The company they keep: Friendship in childhood and adolescence* (pp. 158–185). Cambridge, England: Cambridge University Press.

Buhrmester, D., & Furman, W. (1990). Perceptions of sibling relationships during middle childhood and adolescence. *Child Development, 61,* 1387–1398.

Bukowski, W., Sippola, L., & Hoza, B. (1999). Same and other: Interdependency between participation in same- and other-sex friendships. *Journal of Youth & Adolescence, 28,* 439–459.

Bureau of Labor Statistics. (2010). *Employment characteristics of families, 2009.* Retrieved July 17, 2010, from http://www.bls.gov/news.release/famee.nr0.htm

Burgess, S. (2005). The preschool home literacy environment provided by teenage mothers. *Early Child Development & Care, 175,* 249–258.

Burgess, S., Propper, C., & Rigg, J. (2004). *The impact of low income on child health: Evidence from a birth cohort study.* CASE Paper 85. Center for Analysis of Social Exclusion. Retrieved March 20, 2008, from http://sticerd.lse.ac.uk/dps/case/cp/CASEpaper85.pdf

Burt, S., McGue, M., Krueger, R., & Iacono, W. (2005). How are parent-child conflict and childhood externalizing symptoms related over time? Results from a genetically informative cross-lagged study. *Journal of Child Psychology and Psychiatry, 46,* 263–274.

Burton, L. (1992). Black grandparents rearing children of drug-addicted parents: Stressors, outcomes, and the social service needs. *Gerontologist, 31,* 744–751.

Bushman, B., Baumeister, R., Thomaes, S., & Ryu, E. (2009). Looking again, and harder, for a link between low self-esteem and aggression. *Journal of Personality, 77,* 427–446.

Bushman, B., & Huesmann, R. (2006). Short-term and long-term effects of violent media on aggression in children and adults. *Archives of Pediatric Adolescent Medicine, 160,* 348–352.

Bushnell, I. (2001). Mother's face recognition in newborn infants: Learning and memory. *Infant and Child Development, 10,* 67–74.

Buss, A. H. (1989). Temperaments as personality traits. In G. A. Kohnstamm, J. E. Bates, & M. K. Rothbart (Eds.), *Temperament in childhood* (pp. 39–58). Chichester, England: Wiley.

Buss, A. H., & Plomin, R. (1984). *Temperament: Early developing personality traits.* Hillsdale, NJ: Erlbaum.

Buss, A. H., & Plomin, R. (1986). The EAS approach to temperament. In R. Plomin & J. Dunn (Eds.), *The study of temperament: Changes, continuities and challenges* (pp. 67–80). Hillsdale, NJ: Erlbaum.

Bussey, K., & Bandura, A. (2004). Social cognitive theory of gender development and functioning. In E. Eagly, A. Beall, & R. Sternberg (Eds.), *The psychology of gender* (2nd ed., pp. 92–119). New York: Guilford.

Butterfield, S., Lehnhard, R., Lee, J., & Coladarci, T. (2004). Growth rates in running speed and vertical jumping by boys and girls ages 11–13. *Perceptual & Motor Skills, 99,* 225–234.

Buzi, R., Roberts, R., Ross, M., Addy, R., & Markham, C. (2003). The impact of a history of sexual abuse on high-risk sexual behaviors among females attending alternative school. *Adolescence, 38,* 595–605.

Byrd, M., Forisha, B., & Ramsdell, C. (2006, May 2). *Cinema therapy with children and their families.* Paper presented at the Minnesota Association of Children's Mental Health Child & Adolescent Mental Health Conference, Duluth, MA.

Cairns, R. B. (1991). Multiple metaphors for a singular idea. *Developmental Psychology, 27,* 23–26.

Cairns, R. B., & Cairns, B. D. (1994). *Lifelines and risks: Pathways of youth in our time.* Cambridge, England: Cambridge University Press.

Cairns, R., Elder, G., & Costello, E. (2001). *Developmental science.* Cambridge, UK: Cambridge University Press.

Caldera, Y. (2004). Paternal involvement and infant-father attachment: A Q-set study. *Fathering, 2,* 191–210.

Calkins, S., Dedmon, S., Gill, K., Lomax, L., & Johnson, L. (2002). Frustration in infancy: Implications for emotion regulation, physiological processes, and temperament. *Infancy, 3,* 175–197.

Callaghan, T., Rochat, P., Lillard, A., Claux, M., Odden, H., Itakura, S., Tapanya, S., & Singh, S. (2005). Synchrony in the onset of mental-state reasoning: Evidence from five cultures. *Psychological Science, 16,* 378–384.

Calvert, S., & Kotler, J. (2003). Lessons from children's television: The impact of the Children's Television Act on children's learning. *Applied Developmental Psychology, 24,* 275–335.

Camaioni, L., & Longobardi, E. (1995). Nature and stability of individual differences in early lexical development of Italian-speaking children. *First Language, 15,* 203–218.

Camarata, S., & Woodcock, R. (2006). Sex differences in processing speed: Developmental effects in males and females. *Intelligence, 34,* 231–252.

Campbell, F. A., & Ramey, C. T. (1994). Effects of early intervention on intellectual and academic achievement: A follow-up study of children from low-income families. *Child Development, 65,* 684–698.

Campbell, S. (2006). *Behavior problems in preschool.* New York: Guilford Press.

Campbell, S., Spieker, S., Vandergrift, N., Belsky, J., & Burchinal, M. (2010). Predictors and sequelae of trajectories of physical aggression in school-age boys and girls. *Development and Psychopathology, 22,* 133–150.

Campione, J. C., & Brown, A. L. (1984). Learning ability and transfer propensity as sources of individual differences in intelligence. In P. H. Brooks, C. McCauley, & R. Sperber (Eds.), *Learning and cognition in the mentally retarded.* Hillsdale, NJ: Erlbaum.

Campione, J. C., Brown, A. L., Ferrara, R. A., Jones, R. S., & Steinberg, E. (1985). Breakdowns in flexible use of information: Intelligence-related differences in transfer following equivalent learning performance. *Intelligence, 9,* 297–315.

Cantwell, D. P. (1990). Depression across the early life span. In M. Lewis & S. M. Miller (Eds.), *Handbook of developmental psychopathology* (pp. 293–310). New York: Plenum Press.

Capron, C., & Duyme, M. (1989). Assessment of effects of socio-economic status on IQ in a full cross-fostering study. *Nature, 340,* 552–554.

Capute, A. J., Palmer, F. B., Shapiro, B. K., Wachtel, R. C., Ross, A., & Accardo, P. J. (1984). Primitive reflex profile: A quantification of primitive reflexes in infancy. *Developmental Medicine and Child Neurology, 26,* 375–383.

Caputo, R. (2004). Parent religiosity, family processes, and adolescent outcomes. *Families in Society, 85,* 495–510.

Carey, S., & Bartlett, E. (1978). Acquiring a single new word. *Papers & Reports on Child Language Development, 15,* 17–29.

Carlson, E., Sampson, M., & Sroufe, A. (2003). Implications of attachment theory and research for developmental-behavioral pediatrics. *Journal of Developmental and Behavioral Pediatrics, 24,* 364–379.

Carlson, E., & Sroufe, A. (1995). Contribution of attachment theory to developmental psychopathology. In D. Cicchetti & D. J. Cohen (Eds.), *Developmental psychopathology: Vol. 1. Theory and methods* (pp. 581–617). New York: Wiley.

Carlson, E., Sroufe, A., & Egeland, B. (2004). The construction of experience: A longitudinal study of representation and behavior. *Child Development, 75,* 66–83.

Carlson, S., & Meltzoff, A. (2008). Bilingual experience and executive functioning in young children. *Developmental Science, 11,* 282–298.

Carlson, V., & Harwood, R. (2003). Alternative pathways to competence: Culture and early attachment relationships. In S. Johnson & V. Whiffen (Eds.), *Attachment processes in couple and family therapy* (pp. 85–99). New York: Guilford Press.

Caron, A. J., & Caron, R. F. (1981). Processing of relational information as an index of infant risks. In S. Friedman & M. Sigman (Eds.), *Preterm birth and psychological development* (pp. 219–240). New York: Academic Press.

Caron, A. J., Caron R. F., Roberts, J., & Brooks, R. (1997). Infant sensitivity to deviations in dynamic facial-vocal displays: The role of eye regard. *Developmental Psychology, 33,* 802–813.

Carpendale, J., & Lewis, C. (2006). *How children develop social understanding.* New York: Wiley-Blackwell.

Carr, C. (2007). Where have all the tomboys gone? Women's accounts of gender in adolescence. *Sex Roles, 56,* 439–448.

Carr, M., & Alexeev, N. (2011). Fluency, accuracy, and gender predict developmental trajectories of arithmetic strategies. *Journal of Educational Psychology, 103,* 617–631.

Carson, D., Klee, T., & Perry, C. (1998). Comparisons of children with delayed and normal language at 24 months of age on measures of behavioral difficulties, social and cognitive development. *Infant Mental Health, 19,* 59–75.

Carter, A., Garrity-Rokous, F., Chazan-Cohen, R., Little, C., & Briggs-Gowan, M. (2001). Maternal depression and comorbidity: Predicting early parenting, attachment security, and toddler social-emotional problems and competencies. *Journal of the American Academy of Child and Adolescent Psychiatry, 40,* 18–26.

Cartwright, C. (2006). You want to know how it affected me? Young adults' perceptions of the impact of parental divorce. *Journal of Divorce & Remarriage, 44,* 125–143.

Carver, P., Egan, S., & Perry, D. (2004). Children who question their heterosexuality. *Developmental Psychology, 40,* 43–53.

Casasola, M., & Cohen, L. (2000). Infants' association of linguistic labels with causal actions. *Developmental Psychology, 36,* 155–168.

Case, A., Lee, D., & Paxson, C. (2007). *The income gradient in children's health: A comment on Currie, Shields and Wheatley Price.* NBER Working Paper No. W13495. Retrieved March 19, 2008, from http://ssrn.com/abstract=1021973

Case, A., Lubotsky, D., & Paxson, C. (2002). Economic status and health in childhood: The origins of the gradient. *American Economic Review, 92,* 1308–1334.

Case, R. (1985). *Intellectual development: Birth to adulthood.* New York: Academic Press.

Case, R. (1991). Stages in the development of the young child's first sense of self. *Developmental Review, 11,* 210–230.

Case, R. (1992). *The mind's staircase: Exploring thought and knowledge.* Hillsdale, NJ: Erlbaum.

Caselli, C., Casadio, P., & Bates, E. (1997). *A cross-linguistic study of the transition from first words to grammar* (Technical Report No. CND-9701). Center for Research in Language, University of California, San Diego.

Casey, B., McIntire, D., & Leveno, K. (2001). The continuing value of the Apgar score for the assessment of newborn infants. *New England Journal of Medicine, 344,* 467–471.

Cashmore, J., & Parkinson, P. (2008). Children's and parents' perceptions on children's participation in decision making after parental separation and divorce. *Family Court Review, 46,* 91–104.

Cashmore, J., Parkinson, P., & Taylor, A. (2008). Overnight stays and children's relationships with resident and nonresident parents after divorce. *Journal of Family Issues, 29,* 707–733.

Cashon, C., & Cohen, L. (2000). Eight-month-old infants' perceptions of possible and impossible events. *Infancy, 1,* 429–446.

Caslyn, C., Gonzales, P., & Frase, M. (1999). *Highlights from the third international Mathematics and Science Study.* Washington, DC National Center for Educational Statistics.

Casper, L., & Smith, K. (2002). Dispelling the myths: Self-care, class, and race. *Journal of Family Issues, 23,* 716–727.

Caspi, A. (2000). The child is father of the man: Personality continuities from childhood to adulthood. *Journal of Personality & Social Psychology, 78,* 158–172.

Caspi, A., Harkness, A. R., Moffitt, T. E., & Silva, P. A. (1996). Intellectual performance: Continuity and change. In P. A. Silva & W. R. Stanton (Eds.), *From child to adult: The Dunedin Multidisciplinary Health and Development Study* (pp. 59–74). Aukland: Oxford University Press.

Caspi, A., & Moffitt, T. E. (1991). Individual differences are accentuated during periods of social change: The sample case of girls at puberty. *Journal of Personality and Social Psychology, 61,* 157–168.

Caspi, A., & Moffitt, T. E. (2006). Gene-environment interactions in psychiatry: Joining forces with neuroscience. *Nature Reviews: Neuroscience, 7,* 583–590.

Caspi, A., & Shiner, R. (2006). Personality development. In N. Eisenberg, W. Damon, & R. Lerner (Eds.), *Handbook of child psychology: Vol. 3, Social, emotional, and personality development* (6th ed., pp. 300–365). Hoboken, NJ: Wiley.

Cassidy, J., & Berlin, L. J. (1994). The insecure/ambivalent pattern of attachment: Theory and research. *Child Development, 65,* 971–991.

Castellino, D., Lerner, J., Lerner, R., & von Eye, A. (1998). Maternal employment and education: Predictors of young adolescent career trajectories. *Applied Developmental Science, 2,* 114–126.

Cato, J., & Canetto, S. (2003). Attitudes and beliefs about suicidal behavior when coming out is the precipitant of the suicidal behavior. *Sex Roles, 49,* 497–505.

Cawley, J., & Liu, F. (2007). *Maternal employment and childhood obesity: A search for mechanisms in time use data.* Retrieved July 24, 2011, from http://www.nber.org/papers/w13600.pdf

Cecchini, M., Lai, C., & Langher, V. (2007). Communication and crying in newborns. *Infant Behavior & Development, 30,* 655–665.

Ceci, S. J., & Bruck, M. (1995). *Jeopardy in the courtroom: A scientific analysis of children's testimony.* Washington, DC: American Psychological Association.

Ceci, S. J., & Williams, W. (2010). Sex differences in math-intensive fields. *Current Directions in Psychological Science, 19,* 275–279.

Centers for Disease Control (CDC). (1992). Pregnancy risks determined from birth certificate data—United States, 1989. *Morbidity & Mortality Weekly Report, 41*(30), 556–563.

Centers for Disease Control (CDC). (1995a). Chorionic villus sampling and amniocentesis: Recommendations for prenatal counseling. *Morbidity & Mortality Weekly Report, 44*(RR-9), 1–12.

Centers for Disease Control (CDC). (1995b). U.S. Public Health Service recommendations for human immunodeficiency virus counseling and voluntary testing for pregnant women. *Mortality & Morbidity Weekly Report, 44*(RR-7), 1–15.

Centers for Disease Control (CDC). (1996). Population-based prevalence of perinatal exposure to cocaine: Georgia, 1994. *Morbidity & Mortality Weekly Report, 45,* 887.

Centers for Disease Control (CDC). (2004a). Sexually transmitted disease surveillance 2001, supplement. chlamydia prevalence monitoring project. Retrieved May 4, 2005, from http://www.cdc.gov/std/Chlamydia2003/

Centers for Disease Control (CDC). (2004b). Surveillance summaries. *Morbidity & Mortality Weekly Report, 53,* 2–29.

Centers for Disease Control (CDC). (2006a). *Cytomegalovirus.* Retrieved August 4, 2008, from http://www.cdc.gov/cmv/facts.htm

Centers for Disease Control (CDC). (2006b). *HPV vaccine questions and answers.* Retrieved June 29, 2006, from http://www.cdc.gov/std/hpv/STDFact-HPV-vaccine.htm#vaccine

Centers for Disease Control (CDC). (2006c). *Sudden infant death syndrome (SIDS): Risk factors.* Retrieved June 8, 2007, from http://www.cdc.gov/SIDS/riskfactors.htm

Centers for Disease Control (CDC). (2007a). *HIV/AIDS: Pregnancy and childbirth.* Retrieved August 4, 2008, from http://www.cdc.gov/hiv/topics/perinatal/index.htm

Centers for Disease Control (CDC). (2007b). *HIV/AIDS surveillance in adolescents and young adults (through 2005).* Retrieved April 11, 2008, from http://www.cdc.gov/hiv/topics/surveillance/resources/slides/adolescents/index.htm

Centers for Disease Control (CDC). (2007c). *Suicide: Fact sheet.* Retrieved June 22, 2007, from http://www.cdc.gov/ncipc/factsheets/suifacts.htm

Centers for Disease Control (CDC). (2009a). *Teen driver facts.* Retrieved August 15, 2010, from http://www.cdc.gov/MotorVehicleSafety/Teen_Drivers/teendrivers_factsheet.html

Centers for Disease Control (CDC). (2009b). *Suicide.* Retrieved August 16, 2010, from http://www.cdc.gov/violenceprevention/pdf/Suicide-DataSheet-a.pdf

Centers for Disease Control (CDC). (2010). *STDs in adolescents and young adults.* Retrieved June 9, 2011, from http://www.cdc.gov/std/stats09/adol.htm

Centers for Disease Control (CDC). (2011a). *About BMI for children and teens.* Retrieved June 9, 2011, from http://www.cdc.gov/healthyweight/assessing/bmi/childrens_bmi/about_childrens_bmi.html

Centers for Disease Control (CDC). (2011b). *Birth defects: Data & Statistics.* Retrieved June 7, 2011, from http://www.cdc.gov/ncbddd/birthdefects/data.html.

Centers for Disease Control (CDC). (2011c). *HPV vaccine: Questions and answers.* Retrieved June 9, 2011, from http://www.cdc.gov/vaccines/vpd-vac/hpv/vac-faqs.htm

Centers for Disease Control (CDC). (2011d). *STDs and pregnancy: CDC fact sheet.* Retrieved June 21, 2011, from http://www.cdc.gov/std/pregnancy/STDfact-Pregnancy.htm.

Centers for Disease Control and Prevention. (2009). *Sexually transmitted disease surveillance, 2008.* Retrieved August 23, 2010, from http://www.cdc.gov/std/stats08/surv2008-Complete.pdf

Centers for Disease Control and Prevention. (2010). *Child maltreatment: Facts at a glance.* Retrieved August 29, 2011, from http://www.cdc .gov/ViolencePrevention/pdf/cm-datasheet-a.pdf

Centers for Disease Control and Prevention, American Society for Reproductive Medicine, Society for Assisted Reproductive Technology. (2009). *2007 assisted reproductive technology success rates: National summary and fertility clinic reports.* Retrieved August 22, 2010, from http://www.cdc.gov/art/ART2007/PDF/COMPLETE_2007_ART.pdf

Center for Public Education. (2011). *Back to school: How parent involvement affects student achievement (at a glance).* Retrieved September 10, 2011, from http://www.centerforpubliceducation.org/Main-Menu/ Public-education/Parent-Involvement

Chalfant, J. C. (1989). Learning disabilities: Policy issues and promising approaches. *American Psychologist, 44*, 392–398.

Chambliss, C., Termine, K., Norton, J., Barry, O., Bahm, J., Papas, A., et al. (2010). Relationship between a history of consistent maternal employment and depression in young adults. *Psychological Reports, 107*, 762–772.

Chan, R., Raboy, B., & Patterson, C. (1998). Psychosocial adjustment among children conceived via donor insemination by lesbian and heterosexual mothers. *Child Development, 69*, 443–457.

Chan, R., & Thompson, N. (2011). Whines, cries, and motherese: Their relative power to distract. *The Journal of Social, Evolutionary, and Cultural Psychology, 5*, 131–141.

Chang, F., & Burns, B. (2005). Attention in preschoolers: Associations with effortful control and motivation. *Child Development, 76*, 247–263.

Chang, L., & Murray, A. (1995, April). Math performance of 5- and 6-year-olds in Taiwan and the U.S.: Maternal beliefs, expectations, and tutorial assistance. Paper presented at the biennial meetings of the Society for Research in Child Development, Indianapolis.

Chang, L., Schwartz, D., Dodge, K., & McBride-Chang, C. (2003). Harsh parenting in relation to child emotion regulation and aggression. *Journal of Family Psychology, 17*, 598–606.

Chao, R., & Tseng, V. (2002). Parenting of Asians. In M. Bornstein (Ed.), *Handbook of parenting: Volume 4: Social conditions and applied parenting* (2nd ed., pp. 59–93). Mahwah, NJ: Erlbaum.

Chapa, J., & Valencia, R. R. (1993). Latino population growth, demographic characteristics, and educational stagnation: An examination of recent trends. *Hispanic Journal of Behavioral Sciences, 15*, 165–187.

Chapman, K., Nicholas, P., & Supramaniam, R. (2006). How much food advertising is there on Australian television? *Health Promotion International, 21*, 172–180.

Charuvastra, A., & Cloitre, M. (2008). Social bonds and post traumatic stress disorder. *Annual Review of Psychology, 59*, 301–328.

Chasel-Lansdale, P., Cherlin, A., Buttamannova, K., Fomby, P., Ribar, D., & Coley R. (2011). Long-term implications of welfare reform for the development of adolescents and young adults. *Children and Youth Services Review, 33*, 678–688.

Chase-Lansdale, P., Cherlin, A., & Kiernan, K. (1995). The long-term effects of parental divorce on the mental health of young adults: A developmental perspective. *Child Development, 66*, 1614–1634.

Chavajay, P., & Rogoff, B. (2002). Schooling and traditional collaborative social organization of problem solving by Mayan mothers and children. *Developmental Psychology, 38*, 55–66.

Chen, E. (2004). Why socioeconomic status affects the health of children: A psychosocial perspective. *Current Directions in Psychological Science, 13*, 112–115.

Chen, H. (2007). *Down syndrome.* Retrieved August 7, 2008, from http:// www.emedicine.com/ped/TOPIC615.HTM

Chen, H. (2009). *Trisomy 18.* Retrieved June 27, 2010, from http://emedi-cine.medscape.com/article/943463-overview

Chen, H. (2010). *Down syndrome.* Retrieved June 27, 2010, from http:// emedicine.medscape.com/article/943216-overview

Chen, X., He, Y., Chang, L., & Liu, H. (2005). The peer group as a context: Moderating effects on relations between maternal parenting and social and school adjustment in Chinese children. *Child Development, 76*, 417–434.

Chen, X., Wang, L., & DeSouza, A. (2006). Temperament, socioemotional functioning, and peer relationships in Chinese and North American children. In X. Chen, D. French, & B. Schneider (Eds.), *Peer relationships in cultural context* (pp. 123–147). New York: Cambridge University Press.

Chen, Z. (1999). Ethnic similarities and differences in the association of emotional autonomy and adolescent outcomes: Comparing Euro-American and Asian-American adolescents. *Psychological Reports, 84*, 501–516.

Chen, Z., Dong, Q., & Zhou, H. (1997). Authoritative and authoritarian parenting practices and social and school performance in Chinese children. *International Journal of Behavioral Development, 21*, 855–873.

Cheng, A., McDonald, J., & Thielman, N. (2005). Infectious diarrhea in developed and developing countries. *Journal of Clinical Gastroenterology, 39*, 757–773.

Cherlin, A. (1992). *Marriage, divorce, remarriage.* Cambridge, MA: Harvard University Press.

Cherlin, A., Chase-Lansdale, P., & McRae, C. (1998). Effects of parental divorce on mental health throughout the life course. *American Sociological Review, 63*, 239–249.

Cherry, V., Belgrave, F., Jones, W., Kennon, D., Gray, F., & Phillips, F. (1998). NTU: An Africentric approach to substance abuse prevention among African American youth. *Journal of Primary Prevention, 18*, 319–339.

Chess, S., & Thomas, A. (1984). *Origins and evolution of behavior disorders: Infancy to early adult life.* New York: Brunner/Mazel.

Cheung, H., Chung, K., Wong, S., McBride-Chang, C., Penney, T., & Ho, C. (2010). Speech perception, metalinguistic awareness, reading, and vocabulary in Chinese-English bilingual children. *Journal of Educational Psychology, 102*, 367–380.

Chi, M. T. (1978). Knowledge structure and memory development. In R. S. Siegler (Ed.), *Children's thinking: What develops?* (pp. 73–96). Hillsdale, NJ: Erlbaum.

Chiappe, P., Glaeser, B., & Ferko, D. (2007). Speech perception, vocabulary, and the development of reading skills in English among Korean- and English-speaking children. *Journal of Educational Psychology, 99*, 154–166.

de la Chica, R., Ribas, I., Giraldo, J., Egozcue, J., & Fuster, C. (2005). Chromosomal instability in amniocytes from fetuses of mothers who smoke. *JAMA: Journal of the American Medical Association, 293*, 1212–1222.

Children's Hospital of Philadelphia. (2008, March 3). *In early childhood, continuous care by one doctor best, study suggests.* Retrieved March 18, 2008, from http://www.sciencedaily.com/releases/ 2008/03/080303072646.htm

Child Trends Data Bank. (2011a). *Teen homicide, suicide, and firearms deaths.* Retrieved August 29, 2011, from http://www.childtrendsdata-bank.org/alphalist?q=node/124

Child Trends Data Bank. (2011b). *Children in poverty.* Retrieved September 10, 2011, from http://www.childtrendsdatabank.org/? q=node/221

Chinnery, P. (2006). Could it be mitochondrial? When and how to investigate. *Practical Neurology, 6*, 90–101.

Chisholm, J. S. (1989). Biology, culture, and the development of temperament: A Navaho example. In J. K. Nugent, B. M. Lester, & T. B. Brazelton (Eds.), *The cultural context of infancy: Vol. 1. Biology, culture, and infant development.* Norwood, NJ: Ablex.

Chomsky, N. (1965). *Aspects of a theory of syntax.* Cambridge, MA: MIT Press.

Chomsky, N. (1975). *Reflections on language.* New York: Pantheon Books.

Chomsky, N. (1986). *Knowledge of language: Its nature, origin, and use.* New York: Praeger.

Chomsky, N. (1988). *Language and problems of knowledge.* Cambridge, MA: MIT Press.

Chopak, J., Vicary, J., & Crockett, L. (1998). Predicting alcohol and tobacco use in a sample of rural adolescents. *American Journal of Health Behavior, 22,* 334–341.

Christensen, C. (1997). Onset, rhymes, and phonemes in learning to read. *Scientific Studies of Reading, 1,* 341–358.

Christian, C., & Bloom, N. (2011). Psychosocial issues. In K. Marcdante, R. Kliegman, H. Jensen, & R. Behrman (Eds.), *Nelson's essential of pediatrics* (pp. 81–103). New York: Elsevier Health Publishers.

Christian, P., & Stewart, C. (2010). Maternal micronutrient deficiency, fetal development, and risk of chronic disease. *The Journal of Nutrition, 140,* 437–445.

Christie-Mizell, C., Pryor, E., & Grossman, E. (2008). Child depressive symptoms, spanking, and emotional support: Differences between African American and European American youth. *Family Relations, 57,* 335–350.

Chudzik, L. (2007). Moral judgment and conduct disorder intensity in adolescents involved in delinquency: Matching controls by school grade. *Psychological Reports, 101,* 221–236.

Cicchetti, D. (2008). A multiple-levels-of-analysis perspective on research in development and psychopathology. In T. Beauchaine & S. Hinshaw (Eds.), *Child and adolescent psychopathology* (pp. 27–57). Hoboken, NJ: Wiley.

Cicchetti, D., Rogosch, F., Maughan, A., Toth, S., & Bruce, J. (2003). False belief understanding in maltreated children. *Development & Psychopathology, 15,* 1067–1091.

Cicchetti, D., Rogosch, F., & Sturge-Apple, M. (2007). Interactions of child maltreatment and 5-HTT and monoamine oxidase A polymorphisms: Depressive symptomatology among adolescents from low-socioeconomic status backgrounds. *Development and Psychopathology, 19,* 1161–1180.

Clark, E. V. (1990). On the pragmatics of contrast. *Journal of Child Language, 41,* 417–431.

Clark, R., Harris, A., White-Smith, K., Allen, W., & Ray, B. (2010). Promising practices: The positive effects of after-school programs for African American male development and educational progress. In W. Johnson (Ed.), *Social work with African American males: Health, mental health, and social policy* (pp. 117–146). New York: Oxford University Press.

Closson, L. (2009). Aggressive and prosocial behaviors within early adolescent friendship cliques: What's status got to do with it? *Merrill-Palmer Quarterly: Journal of Developmental Psychology, 55,* 406–435.

Coatsworth, J., Maldonado-Molina, M., Pantin, H., & Szapocznik, J. (2005). A person-centered and ecological investigation of acculturation strategies in Hispanic immigrant youth. *Journal of Community Psychology, 33,* 157–174.

Cobb, K. (2000, September 3). Breaking in drivers: Texas could join states restricting teens in effort to lower rate of fatal accidents. *Houston Chronicle,* A1, A20.

Cocodia, E., Kim, J., Shin, H., Kim, J., Ee, J., Wee, M., & Howard, R. (2003). Evidence that rising population intelligence is impacting formal education. *Personality & Individual Differences, 35,* 797–810.

Coe, C., Hayashi, K. T., & Levine, S. (1988). Hormones and behavior at puberty: Activation or concatenation? In M. R. Gunnar & W. A. Collins (Eds.), *Development during the transition to adolescence: Minnesota symposia on child psychology* (Vol. 21, pp. 17–42). Hillsdale, NJ: Erlbaum.

Cohen, D., Pichard, N., Tordjman, S., Baumann, C., Burglen, L., Excoffier, E., Lazar, G., Mazet, P., Pinquier, C., Verloes, A., & Heron, D. (2005). Specific genetic disorders and autism: Clinical contribution towards their identification. *Journal of Autism & Developmental Disorders, 35,* 103–116.

Cohen-Bendahan, C., van de Beek, C., & Berenbaum, S. (2005). Prenatal sex hormone effects on child and adult sex-typed behavior: Methods and findings. *Neuroscience and Biobehavioral Reviews, 29,* 353–384.

Coie, J. D. (1997a, April). *Initial outcome evaluation of the prevention trial.* Paper presented at the biennial meetings of the Society for Research in Child Development, Washington, DC.

Coie, J. D. (1997b, August). *Testing developmental theory of antisocial behavior with outcomes from the Fast Track Prevention Project.* Paper presented at the annual meeting of the American Psychological Association, Chicago.

Coie, J. D., & Cillessen, A. H. N. (1993). Peer rejection: Origins and effects on children's development. *Current Directions in Psychological Science, 2,* 89–92.

Coie, J. D., & Dodge, K. A. (1998). Aggression and antisocial behavior. In W. Damon (Ed.), *Handbook of child psychology: Vol. 3. Social, emotional, and personality development* (5th ed., pp. 779–862). New York: Wiley.

Coie, J. D., Terry, R., Lenox, K., Lochman, J., & Hyman, C. (1995). Childhood peer rejection and aggression as predictors of stable patterns of adolescent disorder. *Development and Psychopathology, 7,* 697–713.

Coiro, M. J. (1995, April). *Child behavior problems as a function of marital conflict and parenting.* Paper presented at the biennial meetings of the Society for Research in Child Development, Indianapolis.

Colby, A., & Damon, W. (1992). *Some do care: Contemporary lives of moral commitment.* New York: Free Press.

Colby, A., Kohlberg, L., Gibbs, J., & Lieberman, M. (1983). A longitudinal study of moral judgment. *Monographs of the Society for Research in Child Development, 48*(1–2, Serial No. 200).

Cole, M., & Packer, M. (2011). Culture in development. In M. Bornstein & M. Lamb (Eds.), *Developmental science: An advanced textbook* (6th ed., pp. 51–108). New York: Psychology Press.

Cole, P., Martin, S., & Dennis, T. (2004). Emotion regulation as a scientific construct: Methodological challenges and directions for child development research. *Child Development, 75,* 317–333.

Coley, R., & Chase-Lansdale, L. (1998). Adolescent pregnancy and parenthood: Recent evidence and future directions. *American Psychologist, 53,* 152–166.

Collet, J. P., Burtin, P., Gillet, J., Bossard, N., Ducruet, T., & Durr, F. (1994). Risk of infectious diseases in children attending different types of day-care setting. Epicreche Research Group. *Respiration, 61,* 16–19.

Colombo, J. (1993). *Infant cognition: Predicting later intellectual functioning.* Newbury Park, CA: Sage.

Combrinck-Graham, L., & Fox, G. (2007). Development of school-age children. In A. Martin, F. Volkmar, & M. Lewis (Eds.), *Lewis's child and adolescent psychiatry* (pp. 267–278). Philadelphia: Lippincott, Williams, & Wilkins.

Compas, B. E., Ey, S., & Grant, K. E. (1993). Taxonomy, assessment, and diagnosis of depression during adolescence. *Psychological Bulletin, 114*, 323–344.

Condry, J., & Condry, S. (1976). Sex differences: A study in the eye of the beholder. *Child Development, 47*, 812–819.

Conduct Problems Prevention Research Group. (2007). Fast Track randomized controlled trial to prevent externalizing psychiatric disorders: Findings from grades 3 to 9. *Journal of the American Academy of Child & Adolescent Psychiatry, 46*, 1250–1262.

Cong, X., Ludington-Hoe, S., McCain, G., & Fu, P. (2009). Kangaroo care modifies preterm infant heart rate variability in response to heel stick pain: Pilot study. *Early Human Development, 85*, 561–567.

Conger, R. D., Patterson, G. R., & Ge, X. (1995). It takes two to replicate: A mediational model for the impact of parents' stress on adolescent adjustment. *Child Development, 66*, 80–97.

Connolly, K., & Dalgleish, M. (1989). The emergence of a tool-using skill in infancy. *Developmental Psychology, 25*, 894–912.

Connor, P., Sampson, P., Bookstein, F., Barr, H., & Streissguth, A. (2001). Direct and indirect effects of prenatal alcohol damage on executive function. *Developmental Neuropsychology, 18*, 331–354.

Cooper, P. J. (1995). Eating disorders and their relationship to mood and anxiety disorders. In K. D. Brownell & C. G. Fairburn (Eds.), *Eating disorders and obesity: A comprehensive handbook* (pp. 159–164). New York: Guilford Press.

Cooper, R. P., & Aslin, R. N. (1994). Developmental differences in infant attention to the spectral properties of infant-directed speech. *Child Development, 65*, 1663–1677.

Coplan, R., Reichel, M., & Rowan, K. (2009). Exploring the associations between maternal personality, child temperament, and parenting: A focus on emotions. *Personality and Individual Differences, 46*, 241–246.

Corapci, F. (2010). Chaos and child development. In G. Evens & T. Wachs (Eds.), *Chaos and its influence on children's development: An ecological perspective* (pp. 67–82). Washington, DC: American Psychological Association.

Corliss, H., Rosario, M., Wypij, D., Wylie, S., Frazier, A., & Austin, S. (2010). Sexual orientation and drug use in a longitudinal study of U.S. adolescents. *Addictive Behaviors, 35*, 517–521.

Cornelius, M., Goldschmidt, L., Day, N., & Larkby, C. (2002). Alcohol, tobacco and marijuana use among pregnant teenagers: 6-year follow-up of offspring growth effects. *Neurotoxicology & Teratology, 24*, 703–710.

Cornwell, A., & Feigenbaum, P. (2006). Sleep biological rhythms in normal infants and those at high risk for SIDS. *Chronobiology International, 23*, 935–961.

Costa, A., Torriero, S., Oliveri, M., & Caltagirone, C. (2008). Prefrontal and temporo-parietal involvement in taking others' perspective: TMS evidence. *Behavioural Neurology, 19*, 71–74.

Costa, P. T., Jr., & McCrae, R. R. (1994). Set like plaster? Evidence for the stability of adult personality. In T. F. Hetherton & J. L. Weinberger (Eds.), *Can personality change?* (pp. 21–40). Washington, DC: American Psychological Association.

Costa, P. T., & McCrae, R. R. (2009). The five-factor model and the NEO Inventories. In J. Butcher (Ed.), *Oxford handbook of personality assessment (Oxford library of psychology)* (pp. 299–322). New York: Oxford University Press.

Costello, E., Sung, M., Worthman, C., & Angold, A. (2007). Pubertal maturation and the development of alcohol use and abuse. *Drug and Alcohol Dependence, 88*, S50–S59.

Cowan, C., Cowan, P., & Barry, J. (2011). Couples' groups for parents of preschoolers: Ten-year outcomes of a randomized trial. *Journal of Family Psychology, 25*, 240–250.

Cowan, N., Nugent, L. D., Elliott, E., Ponomarev, I., & Saults, J. (1999). The role of attention in the development of short-term memory: Age differences in the verbal span of apprehension. *Child Development, 70*, 1082–1097.

Cox, T. (1983). Cumulative deficit in culturally disadvantaged children. *British Journal of Educational Psychology, 53*, 317–326.

Cramer, P. (2000). Defense mechanisms in psychology today. *American Psychologist, 55*, 637–646.

Cramond, B. (2004). Can we, should we, need we agree on a definition of giftedness? *Roeper Review, 27*, 15–16.

Crawford, A., & Manassis, K. (2001). Familial predictors of treatment outcome in childhood anxiety disorders. *Journal of the American Academy of Child and Adolescent Psychiatry, 40*, 1182–1189.

Crick, N., & Dodge, K. (1996). Social information-processing mechanisms in reactive and proactive aggression. *Child Development, 67*, 993–1002.

Crick, N. R., & Grotpeter, J. K. (1996). Children's treatment by peers: Victims of relational and overt aggression. *Development and Psychopathology, 8*, 367–380.

Crittenden, P. M. (1992). Quality of attachment in the preschool years. *Development and Psychopathology, 4*, 209–241.

Crockenberg, S. B. (1981). Infant irritability, mother responsiveness, and social support influences on the security of infant-mother attachment. *Child Development, 52*, 857–865.

Crockenberg, S. B. (1987). Predictors and correlates of anger toward and punitive control of toddlers by adolescent mothers. *Child Development, 48*, 964–975.

Crockenberg, S. B., & Leerkes, E. (2004). Infant and maternal behaviors regulate infant reactivity to novelty at 6 months. *Developmental Psychology, 40*, 1123–1132.

Crockenberg, S. B., & Litman, C. (1990). Autonomy as competence in 2-year-olds: Maternal correlates of child defiance, compliance, and self-assertion. *Development Psychology, 26*, 961–971.

Crone, E., & van der Molen, M. (2004). Developmental changes in real life decision making: Performance on a gambling task previously shown to depend on the ventromedial prefrontal cortex. *Developmental Neuropsychology, 25*, 251–279.

Crowell, J. A., & Feldman, S. S. (1991). Mothers' working models of attachment relationships and mother and child behavior during separation and reunion. *Developmental Psychology, 27*, 597–605.

Crowell, J. A., & Hauser, S. (2008). AAIs in a high-risk sample: Stability and relation to functioning from adolescence to 39 years. In H. Steele & M. Steele (Eds.), *Clinical applications of the Adult Attachment Interview* (pp. 341–370). New York: Guilford Press.

Crowley, J., & Curenton, S. (2011). Organizational social support and parenting challenges among mothers of color: The case of Mocha Moms. *Family Relations, 60*, 1–14.

Crystal, D. S., Chen, C., Fuligni, A. J., Stevenson, H. W., Hsu, C., Ko, H., Kitamura, S., & Kimura, S. (1994). Psychological maladjustment and academic achievement: A cross-cultural study of Japanese, Chinese, and American high school students. *Child Development, 65*, 738–753.

Cuffe, S., Moore, C., & McKeown, R. (2005). Prevalence and correlates of ADHD symptoms in the National Health Interview Survey. *Journal of Attention Disorders, 9*, 392–401.

Cunningham, M. (2001). The influence of parental attitudes and behaviors on children's attitudes toward gender and household labor in early adulthood. *Journal of Marriage and the Family, 63*, 111–122.

Cunningham, M., Swanson, D., Spencer, M., & Dupree, D. (2003). The association of physical maturation with family hassles among African American adolescent males. *Cultural Diversity and Ethnic Minority Psychology, 9*, 276–288.

Currie, A., Shields, M., & Wheatley Price, S. (2004). Is the child health/family income gradient universal? Evidence from England. *Journal of Health Economics, 26*, 213–232.

Currie, J., & Stabile, M. (2003). Socioeconomic status and child health: Why is the relationship stronger for older children? *American Economic Review, 93*, 1813–1823.

Curry, C. (2002). An approach to clinical genetics. In A. Rudolph, R. Kamei, & K. Overby (Eds.), *Rudolph's fundamentals of pediatrics* (3rd ed., pp. 184–220). New York: McGraw-Hill.

Curtner-Smith, M., Smith, P., & Porter, M. (2010). Family-level perspective on bullies and victims. In E. Vernberg & B. Biggs (Eds.), *Preventing and treating bullying and victimization* (pp. 75–106). New York: Oxford University Press.

Cusher, K., McClelland, A., & Safford, P. (2012). *Human diversity in education: An integrative approach.* Boston, MA: McGraw-Hill

Cushner, K., McClelland, A., & Safford, P. (1992). *Human diversity in education.* New York: McGraw-Hill.

Cushing, T., & Waldrop, R. (2010). *Anorexia nervosa.* Retrieved August 16, 2010, from http://emedicine.medscape.com/article/912187-overview

Cutrona, C. E., & Troutman, B. R. (1986). Social support, infant temperament, and parenting self-efficacy: A mediational model of postpartum depression. *Child Development, 57*, 1507–1518.

Cuvo, A. (1974). Incentive level influence on overt rehearsal and free recall as a function of age. *Journal of Experimental Child Psychology, 13*, 167–181.

Daley, T., Whaley, S., Sigman, M., Espinosa, M., & Neumann, C. (2003). IQ on the rise: The Flynn effect in rural Kenyan children. *Psychological Science, 14*, 215–219.

Dammeijer, P., Schlundt, B., Chenault, M., Manni, J., & Anteunis. I. (2002). Effects of early auditory deprivation and stimulation on auditory brain-stem responses in the rat. *Acta Oto-Laryngologica, 122*, 703–708.

Damon, W. (1977). *The social world of the child.* San Francisco: Jossey-Bass.

Damon, W. (1983). The nature of social-cognitive change in the developing child. In W. F. Overton (Ed.), *The relationship between social and cognitive development* (pp. 103–142). Hillsdale, NJ: Erlbaum.

Danby, S., & Baker, C. (1998). How to be masculine in the block area. *Childhood: A Global Journal of Child Research, 5*, 151–175.

Dark, V. J., & Benbow, C. P. (1993). Cognitive differences among the gifted: A review and new data. In D. K. Detterman (Ed.), *Current topics in human intelligence: Vol. 3. Individual differences and cognition* (pp. 85–120). Norwood, NJ: Ablex.

Darling, N., Cumsille, P., & Martínez, L. (2008). Individual differences in adolescents' beliefs about the legitimacy of parental authority and their own obligation to obey: A longitudinal investigation. *Child Development, 79*, 1103–1118.

D'Asessandro, D., Kreiter, C., Kinzer, S., & Peterson, M. (2004). A randomized controlled trial of an information prescription for pediatric patient education on the Internet. *Archives of Pediatrics, 158*, 857–862.

Davidov, M., & Grusec, J. (2006). Untangling the links of parental responsiveness to distress and warmth to child outcomes. *Child Development, 77*, 44–58.

Davidson, M., Khmelkov, V., & Lickona, T. (2010). The power of character: Needed for, and developed from, teaching and learning. In T. Lovat, R. Toomey, & N. Clement (Eds.), *International research handbook on values education and student well-being* (pp. 427–454). New York: Spring Science + Business Media.

Davies, P., & Rose, J. (1999). Assessment of cognitive development in adolescents by means of neuropsychological tasks. *Developmental Neuropsychology, 15*, 227–248.

Dawood, K., Pillard, R., Horvath, C., Revelle, W., & Bailey, J. (2000). Familial aspects of male homosexuality. *Archives of Sexual Behavior, 29*, 155–163.

Dawson, T. (2002). New tools, new insights: Kohlberg's moral judgement stages revisited. *International Journal of Behavioral Development, 26*, 154–166.

De Schipper, J., Tavecchio, L., Van IJzendoorn, M., & Van Zeijl, J. (2004). Goodness-of-fit in center day care: Relations of temperament, stability, and quality of care with the child's adjustment. *Early Childhood Research Quarterly, 19*, 257–272.

Deal, J., Halverson, C., Martin, R., Victor, J., & Baker, S. (2007). The Inventory of Children's Individual Differences: Development and validation of a short version. *Journal of Personality Assessment, 89*, 162–166.

Deary, I., Thorpe, G., Wilson, V., Starr, J., & Whalley, L. (2003). Population sex differences in IQ at age 11: The Scottish mental survey 1932. *Intelligence, 31*, 533–542.

Deary, I., Whiteman, M., Starr, J., Whalley, L., & Fox, H. (2004). The impact of childhood intelligence on later life: Following up the Scottish mental surveys of 1932 and 1947. *Journal of Personality & Social Psychology, 86*, 139–147.

DeCasper, A. J., Lecaneut, J., Busnel, M., Granier-DeFerre, C., & Maugeais, R. (1994). Fetal reactions to recurrent maternal speech. *Infant Behavior and Development, 17*, 159–164.

DeCasper, A. J., & Spence, M. J. (1986). Prenatal maternal speech influences newborns' perception of speech sounds. *Infant Behavior and Development, 9*, 133–150.

DeFrancisco, B., & Rovee-Collier, C. (2008). The specificity of priming effects over the first year of life. *Developmental Psychobiology, 50*, 486–501.

Degnan, K., Hane, A., Henderson, H., Moas, O., Reeb-Sutherland, B., & Fox, N. (2011). Longitudinal stability of temperamental exuberance and social-emotional outcomes in early childhood. *Developmental Psychology, 47*, 765–780.

Degnan, K., Henderson, H., Fox, N., & Rubin, K. (2008). Predicting social wariness in middle childhood: The moderating roles of childcare history, maternal personality and maternal behavior. *Social Development, 17*, 471–487.

DeLeire, T., & Kalil, A. (2002). Good things come in threes: Single-parent multigenerational family structure and adolescent adjustment. *Demography, 39*, 393–413.

Delgado-Gaitan, C. (1994). Socializing young children in Mexican-American families: An intergenerational perspective. In P. M. Greenfield & R. R. Cocking (Eds.), *Crosscultural roots of minority child development* (pp. 55–86). Hillsdale, NJ: Erlbaum.

Dellatolas, G., de Agostini, M., Curt, F., Kremin, H., Letierce, A., Maccario, J., & Lellouch, J. (2003). Manual skill, hand skill asymmetry, and cognitive performance in young children. *Laterality: Asymmetries of Body, Brain, & Cognition, 8*, 317–338.

DeLoache, J. S. (1989a). The development of representation in young children. In H. W. Reese (Ed.), *Advances in child development and behavior* (Vol. 22, pp. 2–37). San Diego, CA: Academic Press.

DeLoache, J. S. (1989b). Young children's understanding of the correspondence between a scale model and a larger space. *Cognitive Development, 4*, 121–139.

DeLoache, J. S. (1995). Early understanding and use of symbols: The model model. *Current Directions in Psychological Science, 4*, 109–113.

DeLoache, J. S., Simcock, G., & Marzolf, D. (2004). Transfer by very young children in the symbolic retrieval task. *Child Development, 75*, 1708–1718.

Dempster, F. (1981). Memory span: Sources of individual and developmental differences. *Psychological Bulletin, 89*, 63–100.

Den Ouden, L., Rijken, M., Brand, R., Verloove-Vanhorick, S. P., & Ruys, J. H. (1991). Is it correct to correct? Developmental milestones in 555 "normal" preterm infants compared with term infants. *Journal of Pediatrics, 118*, 399–404.

Deneault, J., Ricard, M., Décarie, T., Morin, P., Quintal, G., Boilvin, M., Tremblay, R., & Pérusse, D. (2008). False belief and emotion understanding in monozygotic twins, dizygotic twins and non-twin children. *Cognition and Emotion, 22*, 697–708.

Dennis, W. (1960). Causes of retardation among institutional children: Iran. *Journal of Genetic Psychology, 96*, 47–59.

DeRosier, M. E., Kupersmidt, J. B., & Patterson, C. J. (1994). Children's academic and behavioral adjustment as a function of the chronicity and proximity of peer rejection. *Child Development, 65*, 1799–1831.

DeRosier, M. E., & Marcus, S. (2005). Building friendships and combating bullying: Effectiveness of S.S.GRIN at one-year follow-up. *Journal of Clinical Child & Adolescent Psychology, 34*, 140–150.

Derryberry, D., & Rothbart, M. K. (1998). Reactive and effortful processes in the organization of temperament. *Development and Psychopathology, 9*, 633–652.

Derzon, J. (2001). Antisocial behavior and the prediction of violence: A meta-analysis. *Psychology in the Schools, 38*, 93–106.

Desrochers, S. (2008). From Piaget to specific Genevan developmental models. *Child Development Perspectives, 2*, 7–12.

Deshpande, P. (2009). *Colic*. Retrieved July 7, 2010, from http://emedicine.medscape.com/article/927760-overview

DeWalt, D., & Hink, A. (2009). Health literacy and child health outcomes: A systematic review of the literature. *Pediatrics, 124*, S265-S274.

Dharan, V., & Parviainen, E. (2009). *Psychosocial and environmental pregnancy risks*. Retrieved June 27, 2010, from http://emedicine.medscape.com/article/259346-overview

Dharan, V., Parviainen, E., Newcomb, P., & Poleshuck, V. (2006). *Psychosocial and environmental pregnancy risks*. Retrieved August 4, 2008, from http://www.emedicine.com/med/TOPIC3237.HTM

Di Mario, S., Say, L., & Lincetto, O. (2007). Risk factors for stillbirth in developing countries: A systematic review of the literature. *Sexually Transmitted Diseases, 34*, S11–S21.

Diagnostic and statistical manual of mental disorders IV: Text revision (DSM-IV TR). (2000). Washington, DC: American Psychiatric Association.

Diamond, A., & Amso, D. (2008). Contributions of neuroscience to our understanding of cognitive development. *Current Directions in Psychological Science, 17*, 136–141.

Diamond, L. (2007). A dynamical systems approach to the development and expression of female same-sex sexuality. *Perspectives on Psychological Science, 2*, 142–161.

Dickens, W., & Flynn, J. (2001). Heritability estimates versus large environmental effects: The IQ paradox resolved. *Psychological Review, 108*, 346–369.

Diener, M., Isabella, R., Behunin, M., & Wong, M. (2008). Attachment to mothers and fathers during middle childhood: Associations with child gender, grade, and competence. *Social Development, 17*, 84–101.

Dieni, S., & Rees, S. (2003). Dendritic morphology is altered in hippocampal neurons following prenatal compromise. *Journal of Neurology, 55*, 41–52.

Dieter, J., Field, T., Hernandez-Reif, M., Emory, E., & Redzepi, M. (2003). Stable preterm infants gain more weight and sleep less after five days of massage therapy. *Journal of Pediatric Psychology, 28*, 403–411.

Dieterich, S., Hebert, H., Landry, S., Swank, P., & Smith, K. (2004). Maternal and child characteristics that influence the growth of daily living skills from infancy to school age in preterm and term children. *Early Education & Development, 15*, 283–303.

Dietrich, C., Swingley, D., & Werker, J. (2007). Native language governs interpretation of salient speech sound differences at 18 months. *Proceedings of the National Academy of Sciences, 104*, 16027–16031.

DiFranza, J., Aligne, C., & Weitzman, M. (2004). Prenatal and postnatal environmental tobacco smoke exposure and children's health. *Pediatrics, 113*, 1007–1015.

Digman, J. M. (1990). Personality structure: Emergence of the five-factor model. *Annual Review of Psychology, 41*, 417–440.

Dillingham, R., & Guerrant, R. (2004). Childhood stunting: Measuring and stemming the staggering costs of inadequate water and sanitation. *Lancet, 363*, 94–95.

DiPietro, J. (2004). The role of prenatal maternal stress in child development. *Current Directions in Psychological Science, 13*, 71–74.

DiPietro, J., Bornstein, M., Costigan, K., Pressman, E., Hahn, C., Painter, K., Smith, B., & Yi, L. (2002). What does fetal movement predict about behavior during the first two years of life? *Psychobiology, 40*, 358–371.

DiPietro, J., Costigan, K., & Gurewitsch, E. (2003). Fetal response to induced maternal stress. *Early Human Development, 74*, 125–138.

DiPietro, J., Ghera, M., & Costigan, K. (2008). Prenatal origins of temperamental reactivity in early infancy. *Early Human Development, 84*, 569–575.

DiPietro, J., Hilton, S., Hawkins, M., Costigan, K., & Pressman, E. (2002). Maternal stress and affect influence fetal neurobehavioral development. *Developmental Psychology, 38*, 659–668.

DiPietro, J., Hodgson, D., Costigan, K., Hilton, S., & Johnson, T. (1996). Fetal neurobehavioral development. *Child Development, 67*, 2553–2567.

DiPietro, J., Hodgson, D., Costigan, K., & Johnson, T. (1996). Fetal antecedents of infant temperament. *Child Development, 67*, 2568–2583.

DiPietro, J., Kivlighan, K., Costigan, K., Rubin, S., Shiffler, D., Henderson, J., & Pillion, J. (2010). Prenatal antecedents of newborn neurological maturation. *Child Development, 81*, 115–130.

Dishion, T. J. (1990). The family ecology of boys' peer relations in middle childhood. *Child Development, 61*, 874–892.

Dixon, M., & Kaminska, Z. (2007). Does exposure to orthography affect children's spelling accuracy? *Journal of Research in Reading, 30*, 184–197.

Dodge, K. A. (1990). Developmental psychopathology in children of depressed mothers. *Developmental Psychology, 26*, 3–6.

Dodge, K. A. (1993). Social-cognitive mechanisms in the development of conduct disorder and depression. *Annual Review of Psychology, 44*, 559–584.

Dodge, K. A. (1997, April). *Testing developmental theory through prevention trials*. Paper presented at the biennial meetings of the Society for Research in Child Development, Washington, DC.

Dodge, K. A., Pettit, G. S., & Bates, J. E. (1994). Socialization mediators of the relation between socioeconomic status and child conduct problems. *Child Development, 65*, 649–665.

Doesum, K., Hosman, C., & Riksen-Walraven, J. (2005). A model-based intervention for depressed mothers and their infants. *Infant Mental Health Journal, 26*, 157–176.

van Doesum, K., Riksen-Walraven, J., Hosman, C., & Hoefnagels, C. (2008). A randomized controlled trial of a home-visiting intervention aimed at preventing relationship problems in depressed mothers and their infants. *Child Development, 79*, 547–561.

Dogan-Até, A., & Carrión-Basham, C. (2007). Teenage pregnancy among Latinas. *Hispanic Journal of Behavioral Science, 29*, 554–579.

Domitrovich, C., & Bierman, K. (2001). Parenting practices and child social adjustment: Multiple pathways of influence. *Merrill-Palmer Quarterly, 47*, 235–263.

Donnellan, M., Trzesniewski, K., Robins, R., Moffitt, T., & Caspi, A. (2005). Low self-esteem is related to aggression, antisocial behavior, and delinquency. *Psychological Science, 16*, 328–335.

Dornbusch, S. M., Ritter, P. L., Liederman, P. H., Roberts, D. F., & Fraleigh, M. J. (1987). The relation of parenting style to adolescent school performance. *Child Development, 58*, 1244–1257.

Douglas-Hall, A., & Chau, M. (2007). *Basic facts abouty low-income children, birth to age 18*. New York: National Center for Children in Poverty, Mailman School of Public Health, Columbia University. Retrieved March 18, 2008, from http://nccp.org/publications/pub_762.html

Dowd, J. (2007). Early childhood origins of the income-health gradient: The role of maternal health behaviors. *Social Science and Medicine, 65*, 1202–1213.

Downey, D. (2001). Number of siblings and intellectual development: The resource dilution explanation. *American Psychologist, 56*, 497–504.

Drum, P. (1985). Retention of text information by grade, ability and study. *Discourse Processes, 8*, 21–52.

DuBois, D., Burk-Braxton, C., Swenson, L., Tevendale, H., Lockerd, E., & Moran, B. (2002). Getting by with a little help from self and others: Self-esteem and social support as resources during early adolescence. *Developmental Psychology, 38*, 822–839.

DuBois, D. L., Felner, R. D., Brand, S., Phillips, R. S. C., & Lease, A. M. (1996). Early adolescent self-esteem: A developmental-ecological framework and assessment strategy. *Journal of Research on Adolescence, 6*, 543–579.

Duncan, G. J. (1993, April). *Economic deprivation and childhood development.* Paper presented at the biennial meetings of the Society for Research in Child Development, New Orleans.

Duncan, G. J., Brooks-Gunn, J., & Klebanov, P. K. (1994). Economic deprivation and early childhood development. *Child Development, 65*, 296–318.

Duncan, J., Paterson, D., Hoffman, J., Mokler, D., Borenstein, N., Belliveau, R., et al. (2010). Brainstem serotonergic deficiency in sudden infant death syndrome. *Journal of the American Medical Association, 303*, 430–437.

Duncan, R. M. (1995). Piaget and Vygotsky revisited: Dialogue or assimilation? *Developmental Review, 15*, 458–472.

Dunn, J. (1992). Siblings and development. *Current Directions in Psychological Science, 1*, 6–9.

Dunn, J. (1993). *Young children's close relationships.* Newbury Park, CA: Sage.

Dunn, J. (2007). Siblings and socialization. In J. Grusec & P. Hastings (Eds.), *Handbook of socialization: Theory and research* (pp. 309–327). New York: Guilford Press.

Dunn, J., Cutting, A., & Fisher, N. (2002). Old friends, new friends: Predictors of children's perspective on their friends at school. *Child Development, 73*, 621–635.

Dunn, J., & Kendrick, C. (1982). Siblings and their mothers: Developing relationships within the family. In M. E. Lamb & B. Sutton-Smith (Eds.), *Sibling relationships: Their nature and significance across the lifespan* (pp. 39–60). Hillsdale, NJ: Erlbaum.

Dunn, J., & McGuire, S. (1994). Young children's nonshared experiences: A summary of studies in Cambridge and Colorado. In E. M. Hetherington, D. Reiss, & R. Plomin (Eds.), *Separate social worlds of siblings: The impact of nonshared environment on development* (pp. 111–128). Hillsdale, NJ: Erlbaum.

Dunphy, D. C. (1963). The social structure of urban adolescent peer groups. *Sociometry, 26*, 230–246.

Dunsmore, J., Noguchi, R., Garner, P., Casey, E., & Bhullar, N. (2008). Gender-specific linkages of affective social competence with peer relations in preschool children. *Early Education and Development, 19*, 211–237.

Dupree, L., Watson, M., & Schneider, M. (2005). Preferences for mental health care: A comparison of older African Americans and older Caucasians. *Journal of Applied Gerontology, 24*, 196–210.

Duvall, S., Delquadri, J., & Ward, D. (2004). A preliminary investigation of the effectiveness of homeschool instructional environments for students with attention-deficit/hyperactivity disorder. *School Psychology Review, 33*, 140–158.

Dwairy, M. (2008). Parental inconsistency versus parental authoritarianism: Associations with symptoms of psychological disorders. *Journal of Youth and Adolescence, 37*, 616–626.

Dyl, J., Kittler, J., Phillips, K., & Hunt, J. (2006). Body dysmorphic disorder and other clinically significant body image concerns in adolescent psychiatric inpatients: Prevalence and clinical characteristics. *Child Psychiatry and Human Development, 36*, 369–382.

Eamon, M., & Mulder, C. (2005). Predicting antisocial behavior among Latino young adolescents: An ecological systems analysis. *American Journal of Orthopsychiatry, 75*, 117–127.

Eaton, D., Kann, L., Kinchen, S., Shanklin, S., Ross, J., Hawkins, J., et al. (2010). Youth risk behavior surveillance-United States, 2009. *Morbidity and Mortality Weekly Report, 59*, 1–148.

Eaton, W. (1994). Temperament, development, and the five-factor model: Lessons from activity level. In C. Halverson & G. Kohnstamm (Eds.), *The developing structure of temperament and personality from infancy to adulthood* (pp. 173–187). Hillsdale, NJ: Erlbaum.

EBC (1991). *Childhood: In the land of giants.* [Television series]. New York: Public Broadcasting System.

Ecalle, J., Magnan, A., & Gibert, F. (2006). Class size effects on literacy skills and literacy interest in first grade: A large-scale investigation. *Journal of School Psychology, 44*, 191–209.

Eccles, J., & Roeser, R. (2011). School and community influences on human development. In M. Bornstein & M. Lamb (Eds.), *Developmental science: An advanced textbook* (6th ed., pp. 571–644). New York: Psychology Press.

Edmonds, C., Isaacs, E., Visscher, P., Rogers, M., Lanigan, J., Singhal, A., Lucas, A., Gringras, P., Denton, J., & Deary, I. (2008). Inspection time and cognitive abilities in twins aged 7 to 17 years: Age-related changes, heritability and genetic covariance. *Intelligence, 36*, 210–255.

Egan, S., & Perry, D. (2001). Gender identity: A multidimensional analysis with implications for psychosocial adjustment. *Developmental Psychology, 37*, 451–463.

Egeland, B., & Sroufe, L. A. (1981). Attachment and early maltreatment. *Child Development, 52*, 44–52.

Eiden, R., Foote, A., & Schuetze, P. (2007). Maternal cocaine use and caregiving status: Group differences in caregiver and infant risk variables. *Addictive Behaviors, 32*, 465–476.

Eisenberg, N. (1986). *Altruistic emotion, cognition, and behavior.* Hillsdale, NJ: Erlbaum.

Eisenberg, N. (1988). The development of prosocial and aggressive behavior. In M. H. Bornstein & M. E. Lamb (Eds.), *Developmental psychology: An advanced textbook* (2nd ed., pp. 461–496). Hillsdale, NJ: Erlbaum.

Eisenberg, N. (1990). Prosocial development in early and mid-adolescence. In R. Montemayor, G. R. Adams, & T. P. Gullotta (Eds.), *From childhood to adolescence: A transitional period?* (pp. 240–268). Newbury Park, CA: Sage.

Eisenberg, N. (1992). *The caring child*. Cambridge, MA: Harvard University Press.

Eisenberg, N. (2001). The core and correlates of affective social competence. *Social Development, 10*, 120–124.

Eisenberg, N., Eggum, N., & Edwards, A. (2010). Empathy-related responding and moral development. In W. Arsenio & E. Lemerise (Eds.), *Emotions, aggression, and morality in children: Bridging development and psychopathology* (pp. 115–135). Washington, DC: American Psychological Association.

Eisenberg, N., & Fabes, R. A. (1998). Prosocial behavior. In W. Damon (Ed.), *Handbook of child psychology: Vol 3. Social, emotional, and personality development* (5th ed., pp. 701–778). New York: Wiley.

Eisenberg, N., Fabes, R. A., Murphy, B., Karbon, M., Smith, M., & Maszk, P. (1996). The relations of children's dispositional empathy-related responding to their emotionality, regulation, and social functioning. *Developmental Psychology, 32*, 195–209.

Eisenberg, N., Fabes, R. A., Murphy, B., Maszk, P., Smith, M., & Karbon, M. (1995). The role of emotionality and regulation in children's social functioning: A longitudinal study. *Child Development, 66*, 1360–1384.

Eisenberg, N., Fabes, R. A., Murphy, B., Shepard, S., Guthrie, I., Mazsk, P., Paulin, R., & Jones, S. (1999). Prediction of elementary school children's socially appropriate and problem behavior from anger reactions at age 4–6 years. *Journal of Applied Developmental Psychology, 20*, 119–142.

Eisenberg, N., Guthrie, I., Cumberland, A., Murphy, B., Shepard, S., Zhou, Q., & Carlo, G. (2007). Prosocial development in early adulthood: A longitudinal study. *Journal of Personality and Social Psychology, 82*, 993–1006.

Eisenberg, N., Hertz-Lazarowitz, R., & Fuchs, I. (1990). Prosocial moral judgment in Israeli kibbutz and city children: A longitudinal study. *Merrill-Palmer Quarterly, 36*, 273–285.

Eisenberg, N., Hofer, C., & Vaugh, J. (2007). Effortful control and its socioemotional consequences. In J. Gross (Ed.), *Handbook of emotion regulation* (pp. 287–306). New York: Guilford Press.

Eisenberg, N., Liew, J., & Pidada, S. (2001). The relations of parental emotional expressivity with quality of Indonesian children's social functioning. *Emotion, 1*, 116–136.

Eisenberg, N., & Murphy, B. (1995). Parenting and children's moral development. In M. H. Bornstein (Ed.), *Handbook of parenting: Vol. 4. Applied and practical parenting* (pp. 227–257). Mahwah, NJ: Erlbaum.

Eisenberg, N., Sadovsky, A., Spinrad, T., Fabes, R., Losoya, S., Valiente, C., Reiser, M., Cumberland, A., & Shepard, S. (2005). The relations of problem behavior status to children's negative emotionality, effortful control, and impulsivity: Concurrent relations and prediction of change. *Developmental Psychology, 41*, 193–211.

Eisenberg, N., Spinrad, T., & Eggum, N. (2010). Emotion-related self-regulation and its relation to children's maladjustment. *Annual Review of Clinical Psychology, 6*, 495–525.

Eisenberger, N. (2003). Does rejection hurt? An fMRI study of social exclusion. *Science, 302*, 290–292.

Ekman, P. (1972). Universals and cultural differences in facial expressions of emotion. In J. Cole (Ed.), *Nebraska symposium on motivation, 1971* (pp. 207–282). Lincoln: University of Nebraska Press.

Ekman, P. (1973). Cross-cultural studies of facial expression. In P. Ekman (Ed.), *Darwin and facial expression* (pp. 169–222). New York: Academic Press.

Ekman, P. (1989). The argument and evidence about universals in facial expressions of emotion. In H. Wagner & A. Manstead (Eds.), *Handbook of social psychophysiology* (pp. 143–164). Chichester, England: Wiley.

Ekman, P. (2007). The directed facial action task: Emotional responses without appraisal. In J. Coan & J. Allen (Eds.), *Handbook of emotion elicitation and assessment* (pp. 47–53). New York: Oxford University Press.

Eley, T., Liang, H., Plomin, R., Sham, P., Sterne, A., Williamson, R., & Purcell, S. (2004). Parental familial vulnerability, family environment, and their interactions as predictors of depressive symptoms in adolescents. *Journal of the American Academy of Child Psychiatry, 43*, 298–306.

Elkind, D. (1967). Egocentrism in adolescence. *Child Development, 38*, 1025–1034.

Ellenbogen, R. (2009). *Neural tube defects in the neonatal period.* Retrieved June 27, 2010, from http://emedicine.medscape.com/article/963090-overview

Elliot, A., & Hall, N. (1997). The impact of self-regulatory teaching strategies on "at-risk" preschoolers' mathematical learning in a computer-mediated environment. *Journal of Computing in Childhood Education, 8*, 187–198.

Ellis, E., & Thal, D. (2008). Early language delay and risk for language impairment. *Perspectives on Language Learning and Education, 15*, 93–100.

Englund, M., Luckner, A., Whaley, G., & Egeland, B. (2004). Children's achievement in early elementary school: Longitudinal effects of parental involvement, expectations, and quality of assistance. *Journal of Educational Psychology, 96*, 723–730.

Ensign, J. (1998). *Defying the stereotypes of special education: Homeschool students.* Paper presented at the annual meeting of the American Education Research Association, San Diego, CA.

Epstein, S. (1991). Cognitive-experiential self theory: Implications for developmental psychology. In M. R. Gunnar & L. A. Sroufe (Eds.), *The Minnesota symposia on child development* (Vol. 23, pp. 79–123). Hillsdale, NJ: Erlbaum.

Epstein, S. (2003). Cognitive-experiential self-theory of personality. In T. Millon & M. Lerner (Eds.), *Comprehensive handbook of psychology, volume 5: Personality and social psychology* (pp. 159–184). Hoboken, NJ: Wiley & Sons.

Erel, O., & Burman, B. (1995). Interrelatedness of marital relations and parent-child relations: A meta-analytic review. *Psychological Bulletin, 118*, 108–312.

Ericsson, K. A., & Crutcher, R. J. (1990). The nature of exceptional performance. In P. B. Baltes, D. L. Featherman, & R. M. Lerner (Eds.), *Life-span development and behavior* (Vol. 10, pp. 188–218). Hillsdale, NJ: Erlbaum.

Escalona, K. S. (1981). The reciprocal role of social and emotional developmental advances and cognitive development during the second and third years of life. In E. K. Shapiro & E. Weber (Eds.), *Cognitive and affective growth: Developmental interaction* (pp. 87–108). Hillsdale, NJ: Erlbaum.

Escorihuela, R. M., Tobena, A., & Fernández-Teruel, A. (1994). Environmental enrichment reverses the detrimental action of early inconsistent stimulation and increases the beneficial effects of postnatal handling on shuttlebox learning in adult rats. *Behavioural Brain Research, 61*, 169–173.

Eslea, M., Menesini, E., Morita, Y., O'Moore, M., Mora-Merchan, J., Pereira, B., & Smith, P. (2004). Friendship and loneliness among bullies and victims: Data from seven countries. *Aggressive Behavior, 30*, 71–83.

Espy, K., Stalets, M., McDiarmid, M., Senn, T., Cwik, M., & Hamby, A. (2002). Executive functions in preschool children born preterm: Application of cognitive neuroscience paradigms. *Child Neuropsychology, 8*, 83–92.

EURO-PERISTAT Project. (2008). *European perinatal health report*. Retrieved July 4, 2010, from http://www.europeristat.com/bm.doc/european-perinatal-health-report.pdf

Evans, G. (2004). The environment of childhood poverty. *American Psychologist, 59*, 77–92.

Ex, C., & Janssens, J. (1998). Maternal influences on daughters' gender role attitudes. *Sex Roles, 38*, 171–186.

Ezike, E., & Ang, J. (2009). *Rubella*. Retrieved July 6, 2010, from http://emedicine.medscape.com/article/968523-overview.

Fabes, R., Eisenberg, N., Hanish, L., & Spinrad, T. (2001). Pre-schoolers' spontaneous emotion vocabulary: Relations to likability. *Early Education & Development, 12*, 11–27.

Fagan, J., & Holland, C. (2007). Racial equality in intelligence: Predictions from a theory of intelligence as processing. *Intelligence, 35*, 319–334.

Fagan, J. F., Holland, C., & Wheeler, K. (2007). The prediction, from infancy, of adult IQ and achievement. *Intelligence, 35*, 225–231.

Fagan, J. F., III, & Singer, L. T. (1983). Infant recognition memory as a measure of intelligence. In L. P. Lipsitt (Ed.), *Advances in infancy research* (Vol. 2, pp. 31–78). Norwood, NJ: Ablex.

Fagard, J., & Jacquet, A. (1989). Onset of bimanual coordination and symmetry versus asymmetry of movement. *Infant Behavior and Development, 12*, 229–235.

Fagot, B. I. (1995). Parenting boys and girls. In M. H. Bornstein (Ed.), *Handbook of parenting: Vol. 1. Children and parenting* (pp. 163–183). Mahwah, NJ: Erlbaum.

Fagot, B. I., & Hagan, R. (1991). Observations of parent reactions to sex-stereotyped behaviors: Age and sex effects. *Child Development, 62*, 617–628.

Fagot, B. I., & Leinbach, M. D. (1989). The young child's gender schema: Environmental input, internal organization. *Child Development, 60*, 663–672.

Fagot, B. I., Leinbach, M. D., & O'Boyle, C. (1992). Gender labeling, gender stereotyping, and parenting behaviors. *Developmental Psychology, 28*, 225–230.

Fantuzzo, J., Sekino, Y., & Cohen, H. (2004). An examination of the contributions of interactive peer play to salient classroom competencies for urban Head Start children. *Psychology in the Schools, 41*, 323–336.

Fantz, R. L. (1956). A method for studying early visual development. *Perceptual & Motor Skills, 6*, 13–15.

Farmer, T., Estell, D., Leung, M., Trott, H., Bishop, J., & Cairns, B. (2003). Individual characteristics, early adolescent peer affiliations, and school dropout: An examination of aggressive and popular group types. *Journal of School Psychology, 41*, 217–232.

Farnham-Diggory, S. (1978). On the logic and pitfalls of logograph research. *Journal of Experimental Child Psychology, 25*, 366–370.

Farrar, M. J. (1992). Negative evidence and grammatical morpheme acquisition. *Developmental Psychology, 28*, 90–98.

Farver, J. (1996). Aggressive behavior in preschoolers' social networks: Do birds of a feather flock together? *Early Childhood Research Quarterly, 11*, 333–350.

Farver, J., Bhadha, B., & Narang, S. (2002). Acculturation and psychological functioning in Asian Indian adolescents. *Social Development, 11*, 11–29.

Federal Interagency Forum on Child and Family Statistics (FIFCFS). (2010). *America's children in brief: Key national indictors of well-being, 2010*. Retrieved July 18, 2010, from http://www.childstats.gov/americaschildren/index.asp

Feigenson, L. (2011). Predicting sights from sounds: 6-month-olds' intermodal numerical abilities. *Journal of Experimental Child Psychology, 110*, 347–361.

Fein, J., Durbin, D., & Selbst, S. (2002). Injuries and emergencies. In A. Rudolph, R. Kamei, & K. Overby (Eds.), *Rudolph's fundamentals of pediatrics* (3rd ed., pp. 390–435). New York: McGraw-Hill.

Feinberg, M., Reiss, D., Neiderhiser, J., & Hetherington, E. (2005). Differential association of family subsystem negativity on siblings' maladjustment: Using behavior genetic methods to test process theory. *Journal of Family Psychology, 19*, 601–610.

Feiring, C. (1999). Other-sex friendship networks and the development of romantic relationships in adolescence. *Journal of Youth & Adolescence, 28*, 495–512.

Feldhusen, J. (2003). Lewis M. Terman: A pioneer in the development of ability tests. In B. Zimmerman & D. Schunk (Eds.), *Educational psychology: A century of contributions* (pp. 155–169). Mahwah, NJ: Erlbaum.

Feldman, D. (2004). Piaget's stages: The unfinished symphony of cognitive development. *New Ideas in Psychology, 22*, 175–131.

Feldman, R. (2003). Paternal socio-psychological factors and infant attachment: The mediating role of synchrony in father-infant interactions. *Infant Behavior and Development, 25*, 221–236.

Feldman, R. (2007). Parent-infant synchrony and the construction of shared timing: Physiological precursors, developmental outcomes, and risk conditions. *Journal of Child Psychology and Psychiatry, 48*, 329–354.

Feldman, R., & Eidelman, A. (2003). Skin-to-skin contact (Kangaroo Care) accelerates autonomic and neurobehavioural maturation in preterm infants. *Developmental Medicine & Child Neurology, 45*, 274–281.

Feldman, R., & Masalha, S. (2010). Parent-child and triadic antecedents of children's social competence: Cultural specificity, shared process. *Developmental Psychology, 46*, 455–467.

Feldman, S. S. (1987). Predicting strain in mothers and fathers of 6-month-old infants: A short-term longitudinal study. In P. W. Berman & F. A. Pedersen (Eds.), *Men's transitions to parenthood* (pp. 13–36). Hillsdale, NJ: Erlbaum.

Feng, J., Spence, I., & Pratt, J. (2007). Playing an action video game reduces gender differences in spatial cognition. *Psychological Science, 18*, 850–855.

Fennig, S., Geva, K., Zalzman, G., Weitzman, A., Fennig, S., & Apter, A. (2005). Effect of gender on suicide attempters versus nonattempters in an adolescent inpatient unit. *Comprehensive Psychiatry, 46*, 90–97.

Fenson, L., Dale, P. S., Reznick, J. S., Bates, E., Thal, D. J., & Pethick, S. J. (1994). Variability in early communicative development. *Monographs of the Society for Research in Child Development, 59*(5, Serial No. 242).

Ferguson, C. (2010). Blazing angels or resident evil? Can violent video games be a force for good? *Review of General Psychology, 14*, 68–81.

Ferguson, C., & Kilburn, J. (2010). Much ado about nothing: The misestimation and overinterpretation of violent video game effects in Eastern and Western nations: Comment on Anderson et al. (2010). *Psychological Bulletin, 136*, 174–178.

Fernald, A. (1993). Approval and disapproval: Infant responsiveness to vocal affect in familiar and unfamiliar languages. *Child Development, 64*, 657–674.

Fernald, A., Taeschner, T., Dunn, J., Papousek, M., Boysson-Bardies, B., & Fukui, I. (1989). A cross-language study of prosodic modifications in mothers' and fathers' speech to preverbal infants. *Journal of Child Language, 16*, 477–501.

Ferrie, B. (2007). *Video gamer's thumb*. Retrieved June 10, 2011, from http://occupational-therapy.advanceweb.com/Article/Video-Gamers-Thumb-2.aspx

Fewell, R., & Deutscher, B. (2003). Contributions of early language and maternal facilitation variables to later language and reading abilities. *Journal of Early Intervention, 26,* 132–145.

Field, T. (2010). Postpartum depression effects on early interactions, parenting, and safety practices: A review. *Infant Behavior & Development, 33,* 1–6.

Field, T. (2011). Prenatal depression effects on early development: A review. *Infant Behavior & Development, 33,* 409–418.

Field, T., Hernandez-Reif, M., Feijo, L., & Freedman, J. (2006). Prenatal, perinatal and neonatal stimulation: A survey of neonatal nurseries. *Infant Behavior & Development, 29,* 24–31.

Field, T. M. (1977). Effects of early separation, interactive deficits, and experimental manipulations on infant-mother face-to-face interaction. *Child Development, 48,* 763–771.

Field, T. M., Woodson, R., Greenberg, R., & Cohen, D. (1982). Discrimination and imitation of facial expressions by neonates. *Science, 218,* 179–181.

Figueiredo, B., Costa, R., Pacheco, A., & Pais, A. (2007). Mother-to-infant and father-to-infant initial emotional involvement. *Early Child Development and Care, 177,* 521–532.

Findling, R., Feeny, N., Stansbrey, R., Delporto-Bedoya, D., & Demeter, C. (2004). Special articles: Treatment of mood disorders in children and adolescents: Somatic treatment for depressive illnesses in children and adolescents. *Psychiatric Clinics of North America, 27,* 113–137.

Fine, L., Trentacosta, C., Izard, C., Mostow, A., & Campbell, J. (2004). Anger perception, caregivers' use of physical discipline, and aggression in children at risk. *Social Development, 13,* 213–228.

Fisch, H., Hyun, G., Goldern, R., Hensle, T., Olsson, C., & Liberson, G. (2003). The influence of paternal age on Down syndrome. *Journal of Urology, 169,* 2275–2278.

Fischer, K., & Rose, S. (1994). Dynamic development of coordination of components in brain and behavior: A framework for theory and research. In K. Fischer & G. Dawson (Eds.), *Human behavior and the developing brain* (pp. 3–66). New York: Guilford.

Fitzgerald, B. (1999). Children of lesbian and gay parents: A review of the literature. *Marriage & Family Review, 29,* 57–75.

Fitzgerald, D., & White, K. (2003). Linking children's social worlds: Perspective-taking in parent-child and peer contexts. *Social Behavior & Personality, 31,* 509–522.

Fitzgerald, M. (2004). The case of Robert Walser (1878–1956). *Irish Journal of Psychological Medicine, 21,* 138–142.

Fitzpatrick, M., & McPherson, B. (2010). Coloring within the lines: Gender stereotypes in contemporary coloring books. *Sex Roles, 62,* 127–137.

Flanders, L., & Halla-Poe, D. (2010). *Cinema therapy and the movie-making process.* Retrieved July 21, 2011, from http://ezinearticles.com/?Cinema-Therapy-and-The-MovieMaking-Process&id=5587558

Flannery, D. J., Montemayor, R., & Eberly, M. B. (1994). The influence of parent negative emotional expression on adolescents' perceptions of their relationships with their parents. *Personal Relationships, 1,* 259–274.

Flavell, J. H. (1985). *Cognitive development* (2nd ed.). Englewood Cliffs, NJ: Prentice Hall.

Flavell, J. H. (1986). The development of children's knowledge about the appearance-reality distinction. *American Psychologist, 41,* 418–425.

Flavell, J. H. (1993). Young children's understanding of thinking and consciousness. *Current Directions in Psychological Science, 2,* 40–43.

Flavell, J. H. (1999). Cognitive development: Children's knowledge about the mind. *Annual Review of Psychology, 50,* 21–45.

Flavell, J. H. (2000). Development of children's knowledge about the mental world. *International Journal of Behavioral Development, 24,* 14–23.

Flavell, J. H. (2004). Theory-of-mind development: Retrospect and prospect. *Merrill-Palmer Quarterly, 50,* 274–290.

Flavell, J. H., & Green, F. L. (1999). Development of intuitions about the controllability of different mental states. *Cognitive Development, 14,* 133–146.

Flavell, J. H., Green, F. L., & Flavell, E. R. (1989). Young children's ability to differentiate appearance-reality and level 2 perspectives in the tactile modality. *Child Development, 60,* 201–213.

Flavell, J. H., Green, F. L., & Flavell, E. R. (1990). Developmental changes in young children's knowledge about the mind. *Cognitive Development, 5,* 1–27.

Flavell, J. H., Green, F. L., & Flavell, E. R. (1995). Young children's knowledge about thinking. *Monographs of the Society for Research in Child Development, 60*(1, Serial No. 243).

Flavell, J. H., Green, F. L., & Flavell, E. R. (1998). The mind has a mind of its own: Developing knowledge about mental uncontrollability. *Cognitive Development, 13,* 127–138.

Flavell, J. H., Green, F. L., & Flavell, E. R. (2000). Development of children's awareness of their own thoughts. *Journal of Cognition and Development, 1,* 97–112.

Flavell, J. H., Green, F. L., Flavell, E. R., & Lin, N. (1999). Development of children's knowledge about unconsciousness. *Child Development, 70,* 396–412.

Flavell, J. H., Green, F. L., Wahl, K. E., & Flavell, E. R. (1987). The effects of question clarification and memory aids on young children's performance on appearance-reality tasks. *Cognitive Development, 2,* 127–144.

Flavell, J. H., Miller, P. H., & Miller, S. A. (1993). *Cognitive development* (3rd ed.). Englewood Cliffs, NJ: Prentice Hall.

Flavell, J. H., Zhang, X., Zou, H., Dong, Q., & Qi, S. (1983). A comparison of the appearance-reality distinction in the People's Republic of China and the United States. *Cognitive Psychology, 15,* 459–466.

Fletcher, K. (2011). Neuropscyhology of early childhood. In A. Davis (Ed.), *Handbook of pediatric neuropsychology* (pp. 31–36). New York: Springer.

Flipsen, P., Jr. (2011). Examining speech sound acquisition for children with cochlear implants using the GFTA-2. *The Volta Review, 111,* 25–37.

Flipsen, P., Jr., & Colvard, L. G. (2006). Intelligibility of conversational speech produced by children with cochlear implants. *Journal of Communication Disorders, 39,* 93–108.

Flom, R., & Bahrick, L. (2007). The development of infant discrimination of affect in multimodal and unimodal stimulation: The role of intersensory redundancy. *Developmental Psychology, 43,* 238–252.

Flynn, J. (1999). Searching for justice: The discovery of IQ gains over time. *American Psychologist, 54,* 5–20.

Flynn, J. (2007). *What is intelligence? Beyond the Flynn Effect.* New York: Cambridge University Press.

Foehn, U. G. (2006). Media multitasking among American youth: Prevalence, predictors and pairings—Key findings. Retrieved September 6, 2008, from http://www.kff.org/entmedia/7593.cfm

Foehr, U. (2006). *Media multitasking among American youth: Prevalence, predictors and pairings.* Retrieved September 8, 2011, from http://www.kff.org/entmedia/upload/7592.pdf

Fombonne, E., Zakarian, R., Bennett, A., Meng, L., & McLean-Heywood, D. (2006). Pervasive developmental disorders in Montreal, Quebec, Canada: Prevalence and links with immunizations. *Pediatrics, 118,* e139–e150.

Fordham, K., & Stevenson-Hinde, J. (1999). Shyness, friendship quality, and adjustment during middle childhood. *Journal of Child Psychology & Psychiatry & Allied Disciplines, 40*, 757–768.

Fossati, A., Borroni, S., Eisenberg, N., & Maffei, C. (2010). Relations of proactive and reactive dimensions of aggression to overt and covert narcissism in nonclinical adolescents. *Aggressive Behavior, 36*, 21–27.

Foster, E., Jones, D., & Conduct Problems Prevention Research Group. (2007). The economic analysis of prevention: An illustration involving the Fast Track Project. *Journal of Mental Health Policy and Economics, 10*, 165–175.

Foulder-Hughes, L., & Cooke, R. (2003a). Do mainstream schoolchildren who were born preterm have motor problems? *British Journal of Occupational Therapy, 66*, 9–16.

Foulder-Hughes, L., & Cooke, R. (2003b). Motor, cognitive, and behavioural disorders in children born very preterm. *Developmental Medicine & Child Neurology, 45*, 97–103.

Fox, N. A., Henderson, H., Rubin, K., Calkins, S., & Schmidt, L. (2001). Continuity and discontinuity of behavioral inhibition and exuberance: Psychophysiological and behavioral influences across the first four years of life. *Child Development, 72*, 1–21.

Fox, N. A., Kimmerly, N. L., & Schafer, W. D. (1991). Attachment to mother/attachment to father: A meta-analysis. *Child Development, 62*, 210–225.

Francis, P. L., Self, P. A., & Horowitz, F. D. (1987). The behavioral assessment of the neonate: An overview. In J. D. Osofsky (Ed.), *Handbook of infant development* (2nd ed., pp. 723–779). New York: Wiley-Interscience.

Francks, C., Maegawa, S., Lauren, J., Abrahams, B., Velayos-Baeza, A., Medland, S., et al. (2007). LRRTM1 on chromosome 2p12 is a maternally suppressed gene that is associated paternally with handedness and schizophrenia. *Molecular Psychiatry, 12*, 1129–1139.

Franco, N., & Levitt, M. (1998). The social ecology of middle childhood: Family support, friendship quality, and self-esteem. *Family Relations: Interdisciplinary Journal of Applied Family Studies, 47*, 315–321.

Fraser, A. M., Brockert, J. E., & Ward, R. H. (1995). Association of young maternal age with adverse reproductive outcomes. *New England Journal of Medicine, 332*, 1113–1117.

Fredricks, J., & Eccles, J. (2002). Children's competence and value beliefs from childhood through adolescence: Growth trajectories in two male sex-typed domains. *Developmental Psychology, 38*, 519–533.

Fredricks, J., & Eccles, J. (2005). Family socialization, gender, and sport motivation and involvement. *Journal of Sport & Exercise Psychology, 27*, 3–31.

Fredriksen, K., Rhodes, J., Reddy, R., & Way, N. (2004). Sleepless in Chicago: Tracking the effects of adolescent sleep loss during the middle school years. *Child Development, 75*, 84–95.

Freedman, D. G. (1979). Ethnic differences in babies. *Human Nature, 2*, 36–43.

Freeman, C., & Fox, M. (2005). *Status and trends in the education of American Indians and Alaska Natives.* Retrieved June 27, 2008, from http://nces.ed.gov/pubs2005/2005108.pdf

French, S., Seidman, E., Allen, L., & Aber, J. (2006). The development of ethnic identity during adolescence. *Developmental Psychology, 42*, 1–10.

Freud, S. (1905). *The basic writings of Sigmund Freud* (A. A. Brill, Trans.). New York: Random House.

Freud, S. (1920). *A general introduction to psychoanalysis* (J. Riviere, Trans.). New York: Washington Square Press.

Frey, K. S., & Ruble, D. N. (1992). Gender constancy and the "cost" of sex-typed behavior: A test of the conflict hypothesis. *Developmental Psychology, 28*, 714–721.

Frichtel, M., & Lécuyer, R. (2006). The use of perspective as a depth cue with a 2D display in 4- and 5-month-old infants. *Infant Behavior and Development, 30*, 409–421.

Fried, P., & Smith, A. (2001). A literature review of the consequences of prenatal marihuana exposure: An emerging theme of a deficiency in aspects of executive function. *Neurotoxicology & Teratology, 23*, 1–11.

Fujisawa, K., Kutsukake, N., & Hasegawa, T. (2008). Reciprocity of prosocial behavior in Japanese preschool children. *International Journal of Behavioral Development, 32*, 89–97.

Fuligni, A., Yip, T., & Tseng, V. (2002). The impact of family obligation on the daily activities and psychological well-being of Chinese American adolescents. *Child Development, 73*, 302–314.

Fuller, B. (2007). *Standardized childhood: The political and cultural struggle over early education.* Palo Alto, CA: Stanford University Press.

Funk, J., Bechtoldt-Baldacci, H., Pasold, T., & Baumgardner, J. (2004). Violence exposure in real-life, video games, television, movies, and the Internet: Is there desensitization? *Journal of Adolescence, 27*, 23–39.

Funk, J., Buchman, D., Jenks, J., & Bechtoldt, H. (2003). Playing violent video games, desensitization, and moral evaluation in children. *Journal of Applied Developmental Psychology, 24*, 413–436.

Funk, J., Buchman, D., Myers, B., & Jenks, J. (2000, August). *Asking the right questions in research on violent electronic games.* Paper presented at the annual meeting of the American Psychological Association, Washington, DC.

Furlong, M., & Christenson, S. (2008). Engaging students at school and with learning: A relevant construct for all students. *Psychology in the Schools, 45*, 365–368.

Furnham, A. (2000). Parents' estimates of their own and their children's multiple intelligences. *British Journal of Developmental Psychology, 18*, 583–594.

Furnham, A., Petrides, K., Tsaousis, I., Pappas, K., & Garrod, D. (2005). A cross-cultural investigation into the relationships between personality traits and work values. *Journal of Psychology: Interdisciplinary & Applied, 139*, 5–32.

Furrow, D. (1984). Social and private speech at two years. *Child Development, 55*, 355–362.

Furrow, D., & Nelson, K. (1984). Environmental correlates of individual differences in language acquisition. *Journal of Child Language, 11*, 523–534.

Furstenberg, F. F., Brooks-Gunn, J., & Chase-Lansdale, L. (1989). Teenaged pregnancy and childbearing. *American Psychologist, 44*, 313–320.

Fussell, J., & Burns, K. (2007). Attention deficit/hyperactivity disorder: A case study in differential diagnosis. *Clinical Pediatrics, 46*, 735–737.

Gabbard, C. (2008). *Lifelong motor development.* San Francisco: Benjamin Cummings.

Gabbard, C. (2011). *Lifelong motor development* (6th ed.). San Francisco, CA: Pearson Benjamin Cummings.

Gagne, J., & Saudino, K. (2010). Wait for it! A twin study of inhibitory control in early childhood. *Behavior Genetics, 40*, 327–337.

Gahagan, S. (2011). Behavioral disorders. In K. Marcdante, R. Kliegman, H. Jenson, & R. Behrman (Eds.), *Nelson essentials of pediatrics* (6th ed., pp. 45–62). New York: Elsevier Health Publishers.

Galaif, E., Sussman, S., Newcomb, M., & Locke, T. (2007). Suicidality, depression, and alcohol use among adolescents: A review of empirical findings. *International Journal of Adolescent Medicine and Health, 19*, 27–35.

Galambos, D. L., & Maggs, J. (1991). Out-of-school care of young adolescents and self-reported behavior. *Developmental Psychology, 27*, 644–655.

Galanaki, E. (2004). Teachers and loneliness: The children's perspective. *School Psychology International, 25*, 92–105.

Galassi, J., Gulledge, S., & Cox, N. (1997). Middle school advisories: Retrospect and prospect. *Review of Educational Research, 67*, 301–338.

Gale, C., O'Callaghan, F., Godfrey, K., Law, C., & Martyn, C. (2004). Critical periods of brain growth and cognitive function in children. *Brain, 127*, 321–329.

Galián, M., Carranza, J., Escudero, A., Ato, M., & Ato, E. (2006). Individual differences in the linguistic competence of referential and expressive subject. *Psicothema, 18*, 37–42.

Gallagher, C., & Dobrin, A. (2005). The association between suicide screening practices and attempts requiring emergency care in juvenile justice facilities. *Journal of the American Academy of Child and Adolescent Psychiatry, 44*, 485–493.

Gallahue, D. L., & Ozmun, J. C. (1995). *Understanding motor development* (3rd ed.). Madison, WI: Brown & Benchmark.

Gallese, V. (2005). Embodied simulation: From neurons to phenomenal experience. *Phenomenology and the Cognitive Sciences, 4*, 23–48.

Galliher, R., Rostosky, S., & Hughes, H. (2004). School belonging, self-esteem, and depressive symptoms in adolescents: An examination of sex, sexual attraction status, and urbanicity. *Journal of Youth & Adolescence, 33*, 235–245.

Gamble, W., Ewing, A., & Wilhelm, M. (2009). Parental perceptions of characteristics of non-parental child care: Belief dimensions, family and child correlates. *Journal of Child and Family Studies, 18*, 70–82.

Ganchrow, J. R., Steiner, J. E., & Daher, M. (1983). Neonatal facial expressions in response to different qualities and intensities of gustatory stimuli. *Infant Behavior and Development, 6*, 189–200.

Ganger, J., & Brent, M. (2001). Re-examining the vocabulary spurt and its implications: Is there really a sudden change in cognitive development? In A. Do, L. Domínguez, & A. Johansen (Eds.), *Proceedings of the 25th Annual Boston University Conference on Language Development* (pp. 296–306). Somerville, MA: Cascadilla Press.

Ganiban, J., Saudino, K., Ulbricht, J., Neiderhiser, J., & Reiss, D. (2008). Stability and change in temperament during adolescence. *Journal of Personality and Social Psychology, 95*, 222–236.

Ganiban, J., Ulbricht, J., Saudino, K., Reiss, D., & Neiderhiser, J. (2011). Understanding child-based effects on parenting: Temperament as a moderator of genetic and environmental contributions to parenting. *Developmental Psychology, 47*, 676–692.

Garbarino, J. (2002). Foreword: Pathways from childhood traumas to adolescent violence and delinquency. *Journal of Aggression, Maltreatment, & Trauma, 6*, xxv–xxxi.

Garbarino, J., & Kostelny, K. (1997). What children can tell us about living in a war zone. In J. D. Osofsky (Ed.), *Children in a violent society* (pp. 32–41). New York: Guilford Press.

Gardner, A. (2007). *Doctors' groups offer ADHD guide for parents.* Retrieved September 1, 2008, from http://health.usnews.com/usnews/health/healthday/071002/doctors-groups-offer-adhd-guide-for-parents.htm

Gardner, H. (1983). *Frames of mind: The theory of multiple intelligence.* New York: Basic Books.

Gardner, H. (2002). Learning from extraordinary minds. In M. Ferrari (Ed.), *The pursuit of excellence through education* (pp. 3–20). Mahwah, NJ: Erlbaum.

Gardner, J., Karmel, B., Freedland, R., Lennon, E., Flory, M., Miroschnichenko, I., Phan, H., Barone, A., & Harm, A. (2006). Arousal, attention, and neurobehavioral assessment in the neonatal period: Implications for intervention and policy. *Journal of Policy and Practice in Intellectual Disabilities, 3*, 22–32.

Garland, A. F., & Zigler, E. (1993). Adolescent suicide prevention: Current research and social policy implications. *American Psychologist, 48*, 169–182.

Garmezy, N. (1993). Vulnerability and resilience. In D. C. Funder, R. D. Parke, C. Tomlinson-Keasey, & K. Widaman (Eds.), *Studying lives through time: Personality and development* (pp. 377–398). Washington, DC: American Psychological Association.

Gartstein, M., & Rothbart, M. (2003). Studying infant temperament via the revised infant behavior questionnaire. *Infant Behavior & Development, 26*, 64–86.

Garstein, M., Slobodskaya, H., Putnam, S., & Knisht, I. (2009). A cross-cultural study of infant temperament: Predicting preschool effortful control in the United States of America and Russia. *European Journal of Developmental Psychology, 6*, 337–364.

Gathercole, S., Pickering, S., Ambridge, B., & Wearing, H. (2004). The structure of working memory from 4 to 15 years of age. *Developmental Psychology, 40*, 177–190.

Gaultney, J., & Gingras, J. (2005). Fetal rate of behavioral inhibition and preference for novelty during infancy. *Early Human Development, 81*, 379–386.

Gauvain, M., Fagot, B., Leve, C., & Kavanagh, K. (2002). Instruction by mothers and fathers during problem solving with their young children. *Journal of Family Psychology, 16*, 81–90.

Ge, X., & Conger, R. (1999). Adjustment problems and emerging personality characteristics from early to late adolescence. *American Journal of Community Psychology, 27*, 429–459.

Geary, D. C. (1996). International differences in mathematical achievement: Their nature, causes, and consequences. *Current Directions in Psychological Science, 5*, 133–137.

Geary, D. C., Bow-Thomas, C. C., Liu, F., & Siegler, R. S. (1996). Development of arithmetical competencies in Chinese and American children: Influences of age, language, and schooling. *Child Development, 65*, 2022–2044.

Geary, D. C., Lin, F., Chen, G., Saults, S. J., & Hoard, M. K. (1999). Contributions of computational fluency to cross-national differences in arithmetical reasoning abilities. *Journal of Educational Psychology, 91*, 716–719.

Geber, M., & Dean, R. (1957). Gesell tests on African children. *Pediatrics, 20*, 1055–1065.

Gee, C., & Heyman, G. (2007). Children's evaluation of other people's self-descriptions. *Social Development, 16*, 800–818.

Gee, C., & Rhodes, J. (2003). Adolescent mothers' relationship with their children's biological fathers: Social support, social strain and relationship continuity. *Journal of Family Psychology, 17*, 370–383.

Gelman, S., Taylor, M., Nguyen, S., Leaper, C., & Bigler, R. (2004). Mother-child conversations about gender: Understanding the acquisition of essentialist beliefs. *Monographs of the Society for Research in Child Development, 69*, 1–127.

Geltman, P., Grant-Knight, W., Mehta, S., Lloyd-Travaglini, C., Lustig, S., Landgraf, J., & Wise, P. (2005). The "Lost Boys of Sudan." *Archives of Pediatrics and Adolescent Medicine, 159*, 585–591.

Gentile, D., Lynch, P., Linder, J., & Walsh, D. (2004). The effects of violent video game habits on adolescent hostility, aggressive behaviors, and school performance. *Journal of Adolescence, 27*, 5–22.

Gentner, D. (1982). Why nouns are learned before verbs: Linguistic relativity versus natural partitioning. In S. A. Kuczaj, II (Ed.), *Language development: Vol. 2, Language, thought, and culture* (pp. 301–334). Hillsdale, NJ: Erlbaum.

George, M., Cummings, E., & Davies, P. (2010). Positive aspects of fathering and mothering, and children's attachment in kindergarten. *Early Child Development and Care, 180*, 107–119.

Georgieff, M. K. (1994). Nutritional deficiencies as developmental risk factors: Commentary on Pollitt and Gorman. In C. A. Nelson (Ed.), *The Minnesota symposia on child development* (Vol. 27, pp. 145–159). Hillsdale, NJ: Erlbaum.

Gershkoff-Stowe, L., & Hahn, E. (2007). Fast mapping skills in the developing lexicon. *Journal of Speech, Language, and Hearing Research, 50,* 682–696.

Gershoff, E. (2002). Corporal punishment by parents and associated child behaviors and experiences: A meta-analytic and theoretical review. *Psychological Bulletin, 128,* 539–579.

Gersten, R., Compton, D., Connor, C., Dimino, J., Santoro, L., Linan-Thompson, S., et al. (2008). *Assisting students struggling with reading: Response to intervention and multi-tier intervention for reading in the primary grades. A practice guide.* Retrieved August 10, 2010, from http://ies.ed.gov/ncee/wwc/pdf/practiceguides/rti_reading_pg_021809.pdf

Gesell, A. (1925). *The mental growth of the preschool child.* New York: Macmillan.

Gesell, A. (1952). *Infant development: The embryology of early behavior.* New York: Harper & Brothers.

Ghetti, S., Papini, S., & Angelini, L. (2006). The development of the memorability-based strategy: Insight from a training study. *Journal of Experimental Child Psychology, 94,* 206–228.

Gibbs, J., Basinger, K., Grime, R., & Snarey, J. (2007). Moral judgment development across cultures: Revisiting Kohlberg's universality claims. *Developmental Review, 27,* 443–500.

Gibson, D. R. (1990). Relation of socioeconomic status to logical and sociomoral judgment of middle-aged men. *Psychology and Aging, 5,* 510–513.

Gibson, E. (2002). *Perceiving the affordances: A portrait of two psychologists.* Hillsdale, NJ: Erlbaum.

Gibson, E. J., & Walk, R. D. (1960). The "visual cliff." *Scientific American, 202,* 80–92.

Giedd, J. (2004). Structural magnetic resonance imaging of the adolescent brain. *Annals of the New York Academy of Sciences, 1021,* 77–85.

Giedd, J., Blumenthal, J., & Jeffries, N. (1999). Brain development during childhood and adolescence: A longitudinal MRI study. *Nature Neuroscience, 2,* 861–863.

Giese, G., & Snyder, D. (2009). An outlook on the growing Hispanic market segment and the abilities of the U.S. banking industry to effectively penetrate the Hispanic market segment. *Journal of Business & Economics Research, 7,* 103–114.

Gilbertson, M., & Bramlett, R. (1998). Phonological awareness screening to identify at-risk readers: Implications for practitioners. *Language, Speech, & Hearing Services in Schools, 29,* 109–116.

Giles, J., & Heyman, G. (2005). Young children's beliefs about the relationship between gender and aggressive behavior. *Child Development, 76,* 207–121.

Giles-Sims, J., & Lockhart, C. (2005). Culturally shaped patterns of disciplining children. *Journal of Family Issues, 26,* 196–218.

Gillespie, C., & Nemeroff, C. (2007). Corticotropin-releasing factor and the psychobiology of early-life stress. *Current Directions in Psychological Science, 16,* 85–89.

Gillies, V., & Lucey, H. (2006). 'It's a connection you can't get away from': Brothers, sisters and social capital. *Journal of Youth Studies, 9,* 479–493.

Gilligan, C. (1982). *In a different voice: Psychological theory and women's development.* Cambridge, MA: Harvard University Press.

Gilligan, C., & Wiggins, G. (1987). The origins of morality in early childhood relationships. In J. Kagan & S. Lamb (Eds.), *The emergence of morality in young children* (pp. 277–307). Chicago: University of Chicago Press.

Gilman, S., Abrams, D., & Buka, S. (2003). Socioeconomic status over the life course and stages of cigarette use: Initiation, regular use, and cessation. *Journal of Epidemiology and Community Health, 57,* 802–808.

Gleason, K., Jensen-Campbell, L., & Richardson, D. (2004). Agreeableness as a predictor of aggression in adolescence. *Aggressive Behavior, 30,* 43–61.

Gleitman, L. R., & Gleitman, H. (1992). A picture is worth a thousand words, but that's the problem: The role of syntax in vocabulary acquisition. *Current Directions in Psychological Science, 1,* 31–35.

Glowinski, A., Bucholz, K., Nelson, E., Fu, Q., Madden, P., Reich, W., & Heath, A. (2001). Suicide attempts in an adolescent female twin sample. *Journal of the American Academy of Child and Adolescent Psychiatry, 40,* 1300–1307.

Glueck, S., & Glueck, E. (1972). *Identification of pre-delinquents: Validation studies and some suggested uses of Glueck table.* New York: Intercontinental Medical Book Corp.

Gnepp, J., & Chilamkurti, C. (1988). Children's use of personality attributions to predict other people's emotional and behavioral reactions. *Child Development, 50,* 743–754.

Goetz, T., Nett, U., Martiny, S., Hall, N., Pekrun, R., Dettmers, S., et al. (2011). Students' emotions during homework: Structures, self-concept antecedents, and achievement outcomes. *Learning and Individual Differences,* page numbers in press.

Gogtay, N., Giedd, J., Lusk, L., Hayashi, K., Greenstein, D., Vaituzis, A., Nugent, T., Herman, D., Clasen, L., Toga, A., Rapoport, J., & Thompson, P. (2004). Dynamic mapping of human cortical development during childhood through early adulthood. *Proceedings of the National Academy of Sciences, 17,* 17.

Golbeck, J., Robles, C., & Turner, K. (2011, May 7–12). *Predicting personality with social media.* Paper presented at the ACM CHI Conference on Human Factors in Computing Systems, Vancover, BC, Canada.

Goldberg, S. (1972). Infant care and growth in urban Zambia. *Human Development, 15,* 77–89.

Goldberg, W. A. (1990). Marital quality, parental personality, and spousal agreement about perceptions and expectations for children. *Merrill-Palmer Quarterly, 36,* 531–556.

Golden, M. & Birns, B. (1983). Social class and infant intelligence. In M. Lewis (Ed.), *Origins of intelligence: Infancy and early childhood* (2nd ed., pp. 347–398). New York: Plenum Press.

Goldfield, B. A. (1993). Noun bias in maternal speech to one-year-olds. *Journal of Child Language, 20,* 85–99.

Goldfield, B. A., & Reznick, J. S. (1990). Early lexical acquisition: Rate, content, and the vocabulary spurt. *Journal of Child Language, 17,* 171–183.

Goldin-Meadow, S. (2007a). The challenge: Some properties of language can be learned without linguistic input. *Linguistic Review, 24,* 417–421.

Goldin-Meadow, S. (2007b). Gesture with speech and without it. In S. Duncan, J. Cassell, & E. Levy (Eds.), *Gesture and the dynamic dimension of language: Essays in honor of David McNeill* (pp. 31–49). Amsterdam, Netherlands: John Benjamins Publishing Company.

Goldsmith, H. H., & Alansky, J. (1987). Maternal and infant temperamental predictors of attachment: A meta-analytic review. *Journal of Consulting and Clinical Psychology, 55,* 805–806.

Goldsmith, H. H., Buss, K. A., & Lemery, K. S. (1997). Toddler and childhood temperament: Expanded content, stronger genetic evidence, new evidence for the importance of environment. *Developmental Psychology, 33,* 891–905.

Goldstein, R., & Volkow, N. (2002). Drug addiction and its underlying neurobiological basis: Neuroimaging evidence for the involvement of the frontal cortex. *American Journal of Psychiatry, 159,* 1642–1652.

Goldstein, S., Davis-Kean, P., & Eccles, J. (2005). Parents, peers, and problem behavior: A longitudinal investigation of the impact of relationship perceptions and characteristics on the development of adolescent problem behavior. *Developmental Psychology, 41*, 401–413.

Goleman, D. (1995). *Emotional intelligence.* New York: Bantam Books.

Golinkoff, R. M., Mervis, C. B., & Hirsh-Pasek, K. (1994). Early object labels: The case for lexical principles. *Journal of Child Language, 21*, 125–155.

Golombok, S., & Fivush, R. (1994). *Gender development.* Cambridge, England: Cambridge University Press.

Golombok, S., & Tasker, F. (1996). Do parents influence the sexual orientation of their children? Findings from a longitudinal study of lesbian families. *Developmental Psychology, 32*, 3–11.

Goodwin, P., & Mosher, C. (2010). *Marriage and cohabitation in the United States: A statistical portrait based on cycle 6 (2002) of the National Survey of Family Growth.* Retrieved July 27, 2010, from http://www.cdc.gov/nchs/data/series/sr_23/sr23_028.pdf

Goossens, R., & van IJzendoorn, M. (1990). Quality of infants' attachments to professional caregivers: Relation to infant-parent attachment and day-care characteristics. *Child Development, 61*, 832–837.

Gopnik, A., & Astington, J. W. (1988). Children's understanding of representational change and its relation to the understanding of false belief and the appearance-reality distinction. *Child Development, 59*, 26–37.

Gordon, N. (1995). Apoptosis (programmed cell death) and other reasons for elimination of neurons and axons. *Brain & Development, 17*, 73–77.

Gordon, R. (2001). Eating disorders East and West: A culture-bound syndrome unbound. In M. Nasser, M. Katzman, & R. Bordon (Eds.), *Eating disorders and cultures in transition* (pp. 1–23). New York: Taylor & Francis.

Gottfried, A. W., Gottfried, A. E., Bathurst, K., & Guerin, D. W. (1994). *Gifted IQ: Early developmental aspects.* New York: Plenum Press.

Gottlieb, G. (1976a). Conceptions of prenatal development: Behavioral embryology. *Psychological Review, 83*, 215–234.

Gottlieb, G. (1976b). The roles of experience in the development of behavior and the nervous system. In G. Gottlieb (Ed.), *Neural and behavioral specificity.* New York: Academic Press.

Gottman, J. M. (1986). The world of coordinated play: Same- and cross-sex friendship in young children. In J. M. Gottman & J. G. Parker (Eds.), *Conversations of friends: Speculations on affective development* (pp. 139–191). Cambridge, England: Cambridge University Press.

Gould, M., Marrocco, F., Kleinman, M., Thomas, J., Mostkoff, K., Cote, J., & Davies, M. (2005). Evaluating iatrogenic risk of youth suicide screening programs: A randomized controlled trial. *Journal of the American Medical Association, 293*, 1635–1643.

Gowen, C. (2011). Fetal and neonatal medicine. In K. Marcdante, R. Kliegman, H. Jensen, & R. Behrman (Eds.), *Nelson's essential of pediatrics* (6th ed., pp. 213–264). New York: Elsevier Health Publishers.

Grabowski, L., Call, K., & Mortimer, J. (2001). Global and economic self-efficacy in the educational attainment process. *Social Psychology Quarterly, 64*, 164–197.

Graham, S., & Harris, K. (2007). Best practices in teaching planning. In S. Graham, C. Macarthur, & J. Fitzgerald (Eds.), *Best practices in writing instruction* (pp. 119–140). New York: Guilford Press.

Graham, S., Weintraub, N., & Berninger, V. (2001). Which manuscript letters do primary grade children write legibly? *Journal of Educational Psychology, 93*, 488–497.

Granic, I., & Patterson, G. (2006). Toward a comprehensive model of antisocial development: A systems dynamic systems approach. *Psychological Review, 113*, 101–131.

Grant, J., & Suddendorf, T. (2011). Production of temporal terms by 3-, 4-, and 5-year-old children. *Early Childhood Research Quarterly, 26*, 87–95.

Green, E., Deschamps, J., & Páez, D. (2005). Variation of individualism and collectivism within and between 20 countries: A typological analysis. *Journal of Cross-Cultural Psychology, 36*, 321–339.

Green, S., Pring, L., & Swettenham, J. (2004). An investigation of first-order false belief understanding of children with congenital profound visual impairment. *British Journal of Developmental Psychology, 22*, 1–17.

Greenberger, E., & Steinberg, L. (1986). *When teenagers work: The psychological and social costs of adolescent employment.* New York: Basic Books.

Greene, K., Krcmar, M., Rubin, D., Walters, L., & Hale, J. (2002). Elaboration in processing adolescent health messages: The impact of egocentrism and sensation seeking on message processing. *Journal of Communication, 52*, 812–831.

Greenfield, P. (1995). Profile: On teaching. Culture, ethnicity, race, and development: Implications for teaching theory and research. *SRCD Newsletter* (Winter), 3–4, 12.

Greenough, W. T. (1991). Experience as a component of normal development: Evolutionary considerations. *Developmental Psychology, 27*, 11–27.

Gregg, V., Gibbs, J. C., & Basinger, K. S. (1994). Patterns of developmental delay in moral judgment by male and female delinquents. *Merrill-Palmer Quarterly, 40*, 538–553.

Grenier, G. (1985). Shifts to English as usual language by Americans of Spanish mother tongue. In R. O. De La Garza, F. D. Bean, C. M. Bonjean, R. Romo, & R. Alvarez (Eds.), *The Mexican American experience: An interdisciplinary anthology* (pp. 347–358). Austin: University of Texas Press.

Grolnick, W. S., & Slowiaczek, M. L. (1994). Parents' involvement in children's schooling: A multidimensional conceptualization and motivational model. *Child Development, 65*, 237–252.

Groome, L., Mooney, D., Holland, S., Smith, L., Atterbury, J., & Dykman, R. (1999). Behavioral state affects heart rate response to low-intensity sound in human fetuses. *Early Human Development, 54*, 39–54.

Gross, E. (2004). Adolescent Internet use: What we expect, what teens report. *Journal of Applied Developmental Psychology, 24*, 713–738.

Grossmann, K., Grossmann, K. E., Spangler, G., Suess, G., & Unzner, L. (1985). Maternal sensitivity and newborns' orientation responses as related to quality of attachment in northern Germany. *Monographs of the Society of Research in Child Development, 50* (1–2, Serial No. 209), 233–256.

Grotevant, H. D., & Cooper, C. R. (1985). Patterns of interaction in family relationships and the development of identity exploration in adolescence. *Child Development, 56*, 415–428.

Grov, C., Bimbi, D., Nanin, J., & Parsons, J. (2006). Race, ethnicity, gender, and generational factors associated with the coming-out process among gay, lesbian, and bisexual individuals. *Journal of Sex Research, 43*, 115–121.

Grusec, J. E. (1992). Social learning theory and developmental psychology: The legacies of Robert Sears and Albert Bandura. *Developmental Psychology, 28*, 776–786.

Guerin, D. W., & Gottfried, A. W. (1994a). Developmental stability and change in parent reports of temperament: A ten-year longitudinal investigation from infancy through preadolescence. *Merrill-Palmer Quarterly, 40*, 334–355.

Guerin, D. W., & Gottfried, A. W. (1994b). Temperamental consequences of infant difficultness. *Infant Behavior and Development, 17,* 413–421.

Guertin, T., Lloyd-Richardson, E., Spirito, A., Donaldson, D., & Boergers, J. (2001). Self-mutilative behavior in adolescents who attempt suicide by overdose. *Journal of the American Academy of Child and Adolescent Psychiatry, 40,* 1062–1069.

Guglielmi, R. (2008). Native language proficiency, English literacy, academic achievement, and occupational attainment in limited-English-proficient students: A latent growth modeling perspective. *Journal of Educational Psychology, 100,* 322–342.

Guilford, J. (1967). *The nature of human intelligence.* New York: McGraw-Hill.

Gunasekera, H., Chapman, S., & Campbell, S. (2005). Sex and drugs in popular movies: An analysis of the top 200 films. *Journal of the Royal Society of Medicine, 98,* 464–470.

Gunnar, M. R. (1994). Psychoendocrine studies of temperament and stress in early childhood: Expanding current models. In J. E. Bates & T. D. Wachs (Eds.), *Temperament: Individual differences at the interface of biology and behavior* (pp. 175–198). Washington, DC: American Psychological Association.

Gunnar, M. R., Kryzer, E., Van Ryzin, M., & Phillips, D. (2010). The rise in cortisol in family day care: Association with aspects of care quality, child behavior, and child sex. *Child Development, 81,* 851–869.

Gunnar, M. R., Sebanc, A., Tout, K., Donzella, B., & Van Dulmen, M. (2003). Peer rejection, temperament, and cortisol activity in preschoolers. *Developmental Psychobiology, 43,* 346–358.

Gupta, R., Hasan, K., Trivedi, R., Pradhan, M., Das, V., Parikh, N., & Narayana, P. (2005). Diffusion tensor imaging of the developing human cerebrum. *Journal of Neuroscience Research, 81,* 172–178.

Guralnick, M. J., & Paul-Brown, D. (1984). Communicative adjustments during behavior-request episodes among children at different developmental levels. *Child Development, 55,* 911–919.

Gurnáková, J., & Kusá, D. (2004). Gender self-concept in personal theories of reality. *Studia Psychologica, 46,* 49–61.

Guthrie, R. (2004). *Even the rat was white.* Boston: Pearson Allyn & Bacon.

Guttentag, R. E., Ornstein, P. A., & Siemens, L. (1987). Children's spontaneous rehearsal: Transitions in strategy acquisition. *Cognitive Development, 2,* 307–326.

Guttman, A., & Dick, P. (2004). Infant hospitalization and maternal depression, poverty and single parenthood: A population-based study. *Child: Care, Health & Development, 30,* 67–75.

Guttman, L. (2006). How student and parent goal orientations and classroom goal structures influence African Americans during the high school transition. *Contemporary Educational Psychology, 31,* 44–63.

Gwandure, C., & Mayekiso, T. (2010). Predicting HIV risk using a locus of control-based model among university students. *Journal of Child and Adolescent Mental Health, 22,* 119–129.

Gzesh, S. M., & Surber, C. F. (1985). Visual perspective-taking skills in children. *Child Development, 56,* 1204–1213.

Haan, N. (1981). Adolescents and young adults as producers of their own development. In R. M. Lerner & N. A. Busch-Rossnagel (Eds.), *Individuals as producers of their own development* (pp. 155–182). New York: Academic Press.

Hack, M., Taylor, C. B. H., Klein, N., Eiben, R., Schatschneider, C., & Mercuri-Minich, N. (1994). School-age outcomes in children with birth weights under 750 g. *New England Journal of Medicine, 331,* 753–759.

Hagan, J. (1997). Defiance and despair: Subcultural and structural linkages between delinquency and despair in the life course. *Social Forces, 76,* 119–134.

Hagerman, R. J. (1996). Growth and development. In W. W. Hay, Jr., J. R. Groothuis, A. R. Hayward, & M. J. Levin (Eds.), *Current pediatric diagnosis and treatment* (12th ed., pp. 65–84). Norwalk, CT: Appleton & Lange.

Haith, M. M. (1980). *Rules that babies look by.* Hillsdale, NJ: Erlbaum.

Hakimzadeh, S., & Cohn, D. (2007). *English usage among Hispanics in the United States.* Retrieved September 9, 2008, from http://pewhispanic.org/reports/report.php?ReportID=82

Halama, P., & Strízenec, M. (2004). Spiritual, existential or both? Theoretical considerations on the nature of "higher" intelligences. *Studia Psychologica, 46,* 239–253.

Halford, G., Bunch, K., & McCredden, J. (2007). Problem decomposability as a factor in complexity of the dimensional change card sort task. *Cognitive Development, 22,* 384–391.

Hallowell, E. (2007). Crazy busy: Overstretched, overbooked, and about to snap! Strategies for handling your fast-paced life. New York: Ballantine Books.

Halmi, K. (2003). Classification, diagnosis and comorbidities of eating disorders. In M. Maj, K. Halmi, J. Lopez-Ibor, & N. Sartorius (Eds.), *Eating disorders* (pp. 1–33). New York: Wiley.

Halpern, C. T., Udry, J. R., Campbell, B., & Suchindran, C. (1993). Testosterone and pubertal development as predictors of sexual activity: A panel analysis of adolescent males. *Psychosomatic Medicine, 55,* 436–447.

Halpern, D., Benbow, C., Geary, D., Gur, R., Hyde, J., & Gernsbache, M. (2007). The science of sex differences in science and mathematics. *Psychological Science in the Public Interest, 8,* 1–51.

Halpern, D., & Tan, U. (2001). Stereotypes and steroids: Using a psychobiosocial model to understand cognitive sex differences. *Brain & Cognition, 45,* 392–414.

Ham, B. (2004, October 29). *Hispanic children less likely to get ADHD diagnosis.* Retrieved June 20, 2008, from http://www.cfah.org/hbns/news/ADHD10-29-04.cfm

Hämäläinen, M., & Pulkkinen, L. (1996). Problem behavior as a precursor of male criminality. *Development and Psychopathology, 8,* 443–455.

Hamm, J. (2000). Do birds of a feather flock together? The variable bases for African American, Asian American, and European American adolescents' selection of similar friends. *Developmental Psychology, 36,* 209–219.

Hamvas, A., Wise, P. H., Yang, R. K., Wampler, N. S., Noguchi, A., Maurer, M. M., Walentik, C. A., Schramm, W. F., & Cole, F. S. (1996). The influence of the wider use of surfactant therapy on neonatal mortality among blacks and whites. *New England Journal of Medicine, 334,* 1635–1640.

Han, W., Ruhm, C., Waldfogel, J., & Washbrook, E. (2008, June). The timing of mothers' employment after childbirth. *Monthly Labor Review,* 15–28.

Han, W., Waldfogel, J., & Brooks-Gunn, J. (2001). The effects of early maternal employment on later cognitive and behavioral outcomes. *Journal of Marriage and the Family, 63,* 336–354.

Hanish, L., Martin, C., Fabes, R., & Barcelo, H. (2008). The breadth of peer relationships among preschoolers: An application of the Q-connectivity method to externalizing behavior. *Child Development, 79,* 1119–1136.

Hanlon, H., Thatcher, R., & Cline, M. (1999). Gender differences in the development of EEG coherence in normal children. *Developmental Neuropsychology, 17,* 199–223.

Hanlon, T., Simon, B., O'Grady, K., Carswell, S., & Callaman, J. (2009). The effectiveness of an after-school program targeting urban African American youth. *Education and Urban Society, 42,* 96–118.

Hanna, E., & Meltzoff, A. N. (1993). Peer imitation by toddlers in laboratory, home, and day-care contexts: Implications for social learning and memory. *Developmental Psychology, 29*, 701–710.

Hannigan, J., O'Leary-Moore, S., & Berman, R. (2007). Postnatal environmental or experiential amelioration of neurobehavioral effects of perinatal alcohol exposure in rats. *Neuroscience & Biobehavioral Reviews, 31*, 202–211.

Hannon, E., & Trehub, S. (2005). Metrical categories in infancy and adulthood. *Psychological Science, 16*, 48–55.

Hansen, M., Bower, C., Milne, E., de Klerk, N., & Kurinczuk, J. (2005). Assisted reproductive technologies and the risk of birth defects: A systematic review. *Human Reproduction, 20*, 328–338.

Hanshaw, J. B., Scheiner, A. P., Moxley, A. W., Gaeav, L., Abel, V., & Scheiner, B. (1976). School failure and deafness after "silent" congenital cytomegalovirus infection. *New England Journal of Medicine, 295*, 468–470.

Harden, K., Turkheimer, E., & Loehlin, J. (2007). Genotype by environment interaction in adolescents' cognitive aptitude. *Behavior Genetics, 37*, 273–283.

Hardy, C., & Van Leeuwen, S. (2004). Interviewing young children: Effects of probe structures and focus of rapport-building talk on the qualities of young children's eyewitness statements. *Canadian Journal of Behavioral Science, 36*, 155–165.

Harkness, S. (1998). Time for families. *Anthropology Newsletter, 39*, 1, 4.

Harkness, S., & Super, C. M. (1985). The cultural context of gender segregation in children's peer groups. *Child Development, 56*, 219–224.

Harkness, S., & Super, C. M. (1995). Culture and parenting. In M. H. Bornstein (Ed.), *Handbook of parenting: Vol. 2. Biology and ecology of parenting* (pp. 211–234). Mahwah, NJ: Erlbaum.

Harold, G. T., & Conger, R. D. (1997). Marital conflict and adolescent distress: The role of adolescent awareness. *Child Development, 68*, 333–350.

Harrington, R., Rutter, M., & Fombonne, E. (1996). Developmental pathways in depression: Multiple meanings, antecedents, and endpoints. *Development and Psychopathology, 8*, 601–616.

Harris, J. (1998). *The nurture assumption: Why kids turn out the way they do: Parents matter less than you think and peers matter more.* New York: Free Press.

Harris, J. (2005). The increased diagnosis of "Juvenile Bipolar Disorder": What are we treating? *Psychiatric Services, 56*, 529–531.

Harris, J. (2009). *The nurture assumption: Why children turn out the way they do* (2nd ed.). New York: Free Press.

Harris, P. L. (1989). *Children and emotion: The development of psychological understanding.* Oxford: Basil Blackwell.

Harris, P. L., Olthof, T., & Terwogt, M. M. (1981). Children's knowledge of emotion. *Journal of Child Psychology and Psychiatry, 22*, 247–261.

Harrison, A. O., Wilson, M. N., Pine, C. J., Chan, S. Q., & Buriel, R. (1990). Family ecologies of ethnic minority children. *Child Development, 61*, 347–362.

Hart, B., & Risley, T. R. (1995). *Meaningful differences in the everyday experience of young American children.* Baltimore, MD: Brookes.

Harter, S. (1987). The determinants and mediational role of global self-worth in children. In N. Eisenberg (Ed.), *Contemporary topics in developmental psychology* (pp. 219–242). New York: Wiley-Interscience.

Harter, S. (1998). The development of self-representations. In W. Damon (Ed.), *Handbook of child psychology: Vol. 3. Social, emotional, and personality development* (5th ed., pp. 553–617). New York: Wiley.

Harter, S. (1999). *Developmental approaches to self processes.* New York: Guilford.

Harter, S. (2006a). The development of self-esteem. In M. Kernis (Ed.), *Self-esteem issues and answers: A sourcebook of current perspectives* (pp. 144–150). New York: Psychology Press.

Harter, S. (2006b). The self. In N. Eisenberg, W. Damon, & R. Lerner (Eds.), *Handbook of child psychology: Vol. 3, Social, emotional, and personality development* (6th ed., pp. 505–570). Hoboken, NJ: Wiley.

Harter, S., & Whitesell, N. R. (1996). Multiple pathways to self-reported depression and psychological adjustment among adolescents. *Development and Psychopathology, 8*, 761–777.

Harter, S., & Whitesell, N. R. (2003). Beyond the debate: Why some adolescents report stable self-worth over time and situation, whereas others report changes in self-worth. *Journal of Personality, 71*, 1027–1058.

Harton, H., & Latane, B. (1997). Social influence and adolescent lifestyle attitudes. *Journal of Research on Adolescence, 7*, 197–220.

Hartup, W. W. (1989). Social relationships and their developmental significance. *American Psychologist, 44*, 120–126.

Hartup, W. W. (1996). The company they keep: Friendships and their developmental significance. *Child Development, 67*, 1–13.

Hartup, W. W. (2006). Relationships in early and middle childhood. In A. Vangellisti & D. Perlman (Eds.), *The Cambridge handbook of personal relationships* (pp. 177–190). New York: Cambridge University Press.

Hartup, W. W., Laursen, B., Stewart, M. I., & Eastenson, A. (1988). Conflict and the friendship relations of young children. *Child Development, 59*, 1590–1600.

Harvey, A., & Hill, R. (2004). Afrocentric youth and family rites of passage program: Promoting resilience among at-risk African American youths. *Social Work, 49*, 65–74.

Harvey, A., & Rauch, J. (1997). A comprehensive Afrocentric rites of passage program for black male adolescents. *Health & Social Work, 22*, 30–37.

Harwood, R. L. (1992). The influence of culturally derived values on Anglo and Puerto Rican mothers' perceptions of attachment behavior. *Child Development, 63*, 822–839.

Hashima, P. Y., & Amato, P. R. (1994). Poverty, social support, and parental behavior. *Child Development, 65*, 394–403.

Haskins, R. (1989). Beyond metaphor: The efficacy of early childhood education. *American Psychologist, 44*, 274–282.

Hatano, G. (2004). The Japanese conception of and research on intelligence. In R. Sternberg (Ed.), *The international handbook of intelligence* (pp. 302–324). New York: Cambridge University Press.

Hatano, G., Siegler, R. S., Richards, D. D., Inagaki, K., Stavy, R., & Wax, N. (1993). The development of biological knowledge: A multi-national study. *Cognitive Development, 8*, 47–62.

Hatchett, S. J., & Jackson, J. S. (1993). African American extended kin systems: An assessment. In H. P. McAdoo (Ed.), *Family ethnicity: Strength in diversity* (pp. 90–108). Newbury Park, CA: Sage.

Hauck, F., & Tanabe, K. (2010). International trends in sudden infant death syndrome and other sudden unexpected deaths in infancy: Need for better diagnostic standardization. *Current Pediatric Reviews, 6*, 86–94.

Haviland, J. M., & Lelwica, M. (1987). The induced affect response: 10-week-old infants' responses to three emotional expressions. *Developmental Psychology, 23*, 97–104.

Haworth, C., Kovas, Y., Harlaar, N., Hayiou-Thomas, M., Petrill, S., Dale, P., et al. (2009). Generalist genes and learning disabilities: A multivariate genetic analysis of low performance in reading, mathematics, language and general cognitive ability in a sample of 8000 12-year-old twins. *Journal of Child Psychology and Psychiatry, 50*, 1318–1325.

Haynes, N. M., Ben-Avie, M., Squires, D. A., Howley, J. P., Negron, E. N., & Corbin, J. N. (1996). It takes a whole village: The SDP school. In J. P. Corner, N. M. Haynes, E. T. Joyner, & M. Ben-Avie (Eds.), *Rallying the whole village: The Comer process for reforming education* (pp. 42–71). New York: Teachers College Press.

Hedegaard, M., Henriksen, T. B., Secher, N. J., Hatch, M. C., & Sabroe, S. (1996). Do stressful life events affect duration of gestation and risk of preterm delivery? *Epidemiology, 7*, 339–345.

Heenan, J. (2005). *Character education transforms school.* Retrieved July 19, 2005, from http://www.cornerstonevalues.org/kew2.htm

Hegarty, P. (2007). From genius inverts to gendered intelligence: Lewis Terman and the power of the norm. *History of Psychology, 10*, 132–155.

Henderson, M., Wight, D., Raab, G., Abraham, C., Parkes, A., Scott, S., et al. (2007). Impact of a theoretically based sex education programme (SHARE) delivered by teachers on NHS registered conceptions and terminations: Final results of cluster randomised trial. *British Medical Journal, 334*(7585), 133–136.

Hendriks, A., Kuyper, H., Lubbers, M., & Van der Werf, M. (2011). Personality as a moderator of context effects on academic achievement. *Journal of School Psychology, 49*, 217–248.

Henneborn, W. J., & Cogan, R. (1975). The effect of husband participation on reported pain and the probability of medication during labour and birth. *Journal of Psychosomatic Research, 19*, 215–222.

Henry, B., Caspi, A., Moffitt, T., & Silva, P. (1996). Temperamental and familial predictors of violent and nonviolent criminal convictions: Age 3 to age 18. *Developmental Psychology, 32*, 614–623.

Hepworth, S., Rovet, J., & Taylor, M. (2001). Neurophysiological correlates of verbal and nonverbal short-term memory in children: Repetition of words and faces. *Psychophysiology, 38*, 594–600.

Herbert, J., Eckerman, C., Goldstein, R., & Stanton, M. (2004). Contrasts in infant classical eyeblink conditioning as a function of premature birth. *Infancy, 5*, 367–383.

Herbst, C., & Tekin, E. (2008). *Child care subsidies and child development.* Institute for the study of labor. Retrieved July 18, 2010, from http://papers.ssrn.com/sol3/papers.cfm?abstract_id=1305820

Heron, M. (2007). Deaths: Leading causes for 2004. *National Vital Statistics Reports, 56*, 1–96.

Herrenkohl, E., Herrenkohl, R., Egolf, B., & Russo, M. (1998). The relationship between early maltreatment and teenage parenthood. *Journal of Adolescence, 21*, 291–303.

Herrera, N., Zajonc, R., Wieczorkowska, G., & Cichomski, B. (2003). Beliefs about birth rank and their reflection in reality. *Journal of Personality & Social Psychology, 85*, 142–150.

Herwig, J., Wirtz, M., & Bengel, J. (2004). Depression, partnership, social support, and parenting: Interaction of maternal factors with behavioral problems of the child. *Journal of Affective Disorders, 80*, 199–208.

Hess, E. H. (1972). "Imprinting" in a natural laboratory. *Scientific American, 227*, 24–31.

Hetherington, E. (1989). Coping with family transitions: Winners, losers, and survivors. *Child Development, 60*, 1–14.

Hetherington, E. (1991a). Presidential address: Families, lies, and videotapes. *Journal of Research on Adolescence, 1*, 323–348.

Hetherington, E. (1991b). The role of individual differences and family relationships in children's coping with divorce and remarriage. In P. A. Cowen & M. Hetherington (Eds.), *Family transitions* (pp. 165–194). Hillsdale, NJ: Erlbaum.

Hetherington, E., Henderson, S., Reiss, D., Anderson, E., et al. (1999). Adolescent siblings in stepfamilies: Family functioning and adolescent adjustment. *Monographs of the Society for Research in Child Development, 64*, 222.

Heatherington, L., & Lavner, J. (2008). Coming to terms with coming out: Review and recommendations for family systems-focused research. *Family Psychology, 22*, 329–343.

Hewitt, L., Hammer, C., Yount, K., & Tomblin, B. (2005). Language sampling for kindergarten children with and without SLI: Mean length of utterance, IPSYN, and NDW. *Journal of Communication Disorders, 38*, 197–213.

Heyman, G., (2001). Children's interpretation of ambiguous behavior: Evidence for a "boys are bad" bias. *Social Development, 10*, 230–247.

Heyman, G. (2009). Children's reasoning about traits. In P. Bauer (Ed.), *Advances in child development*, (Vol. 37, pp. 105–144). San Diego, CA: Academic Press.

Hill, H. M., Soriano, F. I., Chen, S. A., & LaFromboise, T. D. (1994). Sociocultural factors in the etiology and prevention of violence among ethnic minority youth. In L. D. Eron, J. H. Gentry, & P. Schlegel (Eds.), *Reason to hope: A psychosocial perspective on violence and youth* (pp. 59–97). Washington, DC: American Psychological Association.

Hines, M. (2010). Sex-related variation in human behavior and the brain. *Trends in Cognitive Sciences, 14*, 448–456.

Hipwell, A., Keenan, K., Kasza, K., Loeber, R., Stouthamer-Loeber, M., & Bean, T. (2008). Reciprocal influences between girls' conduct problems and depression, and parental punishment and warmth. *Journal of Abnormal Child Psychology, 36*, 663–677.

Hirsh-Pasek, K., Trieman, R., & Schneiderman, M. (1984). Brown and Hanlon revisited: Mothers' sensitivity to ungrammatical forms. *Journal of Child Language, 11*, 81–88.

Hochmann, J., Endress, A., & Mehler, J. (2010). Word frequency as a cue for identifying function words in infancy. *Cognition, 115*, 444–457.

Hodge, K. P., & Tod, D. A. (1993). Ethics of childhood sport. *Sports Medicine, 15*, 291–298.

Hoff, E. (2009). *Language development* (4th ed.). Belmont, CA: Wadsworth Publishing.

Hofferth, S. L., Boisjoly, J., & Duncan, G. (1995, April). *Does children's school attainment benefit from parental access to social capital?* Paper presented at the biennial meetings of the Society for Research in Child Development, Indianapolis.

Hoffman, M. L. (1982). Development of prosocial motivation: Empathy and guilt. In N. Eisenberg (Ed.), *The development of prosocial behavior* (pp. 281–314). New York: Academic Press.

Hoffman, M. L. (1988). Moral development. In M. H. Bornstein & M. E. Lamb (Eds.), *Developmental psychology: An advanced textbook* (2nd ed., pp. 497–548). Hillsdale, NJ: Erlbaum.

Hoffman, M. L. (2000). *Empathy and moral development: Implications for caring and justice.* Cambridge, England: Cambridge University Press.

Hoffman, M. L. (2007). The origins of empathic morality in toddlerhood. In C. Brownell & C. Kopp (Eds.), *Socioemotional development in the toddler years: Transitions and transformations.* New York: Guilford Press.

Holahan, C. K. (1988). Relation of life goals at age 70 to activity participation and health and psychological well-being among Terman's gifted men and women. *Psychology and Aging, 3*, 286–291.

Hollich, G., Golinkoff, R., & Hirsh-Pasek, K. (2007). Young children associate novel words with complex objects rather than salient parts. *Developmental Psychology, 43*, 1051–1061.

Holliday, J., Rothwell, H., & Moore, L. (2010). The relative importance of different measures of peer smoking on adolescent smoking behavior: Cross-sectional and longitudinal analyses of a large British cohort. *Journal of Adolescent Health, 47*, 58–66.

Holmgren, S., Molander, B., & Nilsson, L. (2006). Intelligence and executive functioning in adult age: Effects of sibship size and birth order. *European Journal of Cognitive Psychology, 18,* 138–158.

Holobow, N., Genesee, F., & Lambert, W. (1991). The effectiveness of a foreign language immersion program for children from different ethnic and social class backgrounds: Report 2. *Applied Psycholinguistics, 12,* 179–198.

Homer, B., & Hayward, E. (2008). Cognitive and representational development in children. In K. Cartwright (Ed.), *Literacy processes: Cognitive flexibility in learning and teaching* (pp. 19–41). New York: Guilford Press.

Honzik, M. P. (1986). The role of the family in the development of mental abilities: A 50-year study. In N. Datan, A. L. Greene, & H. W. Reese (Eds.), *Life-span developmental psychology: Intergenerational relations* (pp. 185–210). Hillsdale, NJ: Erlbaum.

Horowitz, F. D. (1987). *Exploring developmental theories: Toward a structural/behavioral model of development.* Hillsdale, NJ: Erlbaum.

Horowitz, F. D. (1990). Developmental models of individual differences. In J. Colombo & J. Fagen (Eds.), *Individual differences in infancy: Reliability, stability, prediction* (pp. 3–18). Hillsdale, NJ: Erlbaum.

Horowitz, F. D. (2003). Child development and the PITS: Simple questions, complex answers, and developmental theory. In M. Hertzig & E. Farber (Eds.), *Annual progress in child psychiatry and child development: 2000–2001* (pp. 3–19). New York: Brunner-Routledge.

Horton-Ikard, R., & Ellis Weismer, S. (2007). A preliminary examination of vocabulary and word-learning in African-American toddlers from middle and low SES homes. *American Journal of Speech-Language Pathology, 16,* 381–392.

Houck, G., & Lecuyer-Marcus, E. (2004). Maternal limit setting during toddlerhood, delay of gratification, and behavior problems at age five. *Infant Mental Health Journal, 25,* 28–46.

Howard, K., Carothers, S., Smith, L., & Akai, C. (2007). Overcoming the odds: Protective factors in the lives of children. In J. Borkowski, J. Farris, T. Whitman, S. Carothers, K. Week, & D. Keogh (Eds.) *Risk and resilience: Adolescent mothers and their children grow up.* (pp. 205–232). Mahwah, NJ: Erlbaum.

Howes, C., Guerra, A., & Zucker, E. (2007). Cultural communities and parenting in Mexican-heritage families. *Parenting: Science and Practice, 7,* 235–270.

Hsu, V., & Rovee-Collier, C. (2006). Memory reactivation in the second year of life. *Infant Behavior and Human Development, 29,* 91–107.

Hubel, D. H., & Weisel, T. N. (1963). Receptive fields of cells in striate cortex of very young, visually inexperienced kittens. *Journal of Neurophysiology, 26,* 994–1002.

Huebner, T., Vioet, T., Marx, I., Konrad, K., Fink, G., Herpetz, S., & Herpetz-Dahlmann, B. (2008). Morphometric brain abnormalities in boys with conduct disorder. *Journal of the American Academy of Child & Adolescent Psychiatry, 47,* 540–547.

Huesmann, L. R., Lagerspetz, K., & Eron, L. D. (1984). Intervening variables in the television violence-aggression relation: Evidence from two countries. *Developmental Psychology, 20,* 746–775.

Huesmann, L. R., Moise-Titus, J., Podolski, C., & Eron, L. D. (2003). Longitudinal relations between children's exposure to TV violence and their aggressive and violent behavior in young adulthood: 1977–1992. *Developmental Psychology, 39,* 201–221.

Hughes, C., Jaffee, S., Happé, F., Taylor, A., Caspi, A., & Moffitt, T. (2005). Origins of individual differences in theory of mind: From nature to nurture? *Child Development, 76,* 356–370.

Huntington, L., Hans, S. L., & Zeskind, P. S. (1990). The relations among cry characteristics, demographic variables, and developmental test scores in infants prenatally exposed to methadone. *Infant Behavior and Development, 13,* 533–538.

Hurwitz, E., Gunn, W. J., Pinsky, P. F., & Schonberger, L. B. (1991). Risk of respiratory illness associated with day-care attendance: A nationwide study. *Pediatrics, 87,* 62–69.

Huston, A. C. (1994). Children in poverty: Designing research to affect policy. *Social Policy Report, Society for Research in Child Development, 8*(2), 1–12.

Huston, A. C., & Bentley, A. C. (2010). Development in societal context. *Annual Review of Psychology, 61,* 411–438.

Huston, A. C., & Rosenkrantz Aronson, S. (2005). Mothers' time with infant and time in employment as predictors of mother-child relationships and children's early development. *Child Development, 76,* 467–482.

Huston, A. C., & Wright, J. C. (1998). Mass media and children's development. In W. Damon (Ed.), *Handbook of child psychology: Vol. 4. Child psychology in practice* (5th ed., pp. 999–1058). New York: Wiley.

Hutt, S. J., Lenard, H. G., & Prechtl, H. E. R. (1969). Psychophysiological studies in newborn infants. In L. P. Lipsitt & H. W. Reese (Eds.), *Advances in child development and behavior* (Vol. 4, pp. 128–173). New York: Academic Press.

Huttenlocher, J. (1995, April). *Children's language in relation to input.* Paper presented at the biennial meetings of the Society for Research in Child Development, Indianapolis.

Hyde, J. (2005). The gender similarities hypothesis. *American Psychologist, 60,* 581–592.

Iaquinta, A. (2006). Guided reading: A research-based response to the challenges of early reading instruction. *Early Childhood Education Journal, 33,* 1573–1707.

Iglowstein, I., Jenni, O., Molinari, L., & Largo, R. (2003). Sleep duration from infancy to adolescence: Reference values and generational trends. *Pediatrics, 111,* 302–307.

Ihmeideh, F. (2010). The role of computer technology in teaching reading and writing: Preschool teachers' beliefs and practices. *Journal of Research in Childhood Education, 24,* 69–79.

van IJzendoorn, M. H. (1995). Adult attachment representations, parental responsiveness, and infant attachment: A meta-analysis on the predictive validity of the Adult Attachment Interview. *Psychological Bulletin, 117,* 387–403.

van IJzendoorn, M. H., Goldberg, S., Kroonenberg, P. M., & Frenkel, O. J. (1992). The relative effects of maternal and child problems on the quality of attachment: A meta-analysis of attachment in clinical samples. *Child Development, 63,* 840–858.

van IJzendoorn, M. H., Juffer, F., & Poelhuis, C. (2005). Adoption and cognitive development: A meta-analytic comparison of adopted and nonadopted children's IQ and school performance. *Psychological Bulletin, 131,* 301–316.

van IJzendoorn, M. H., & Kroonenberg, P. M. (1988). Cross-cultural patterns of attachment: A meta-analysis of the Strange Situation. *Child Development, 59,* 147–156.

van IJzendoorn, M., & Sagi-Schwarz, A. (2008). Cross-cultural patterns of attachment: Universal and contextual dimensions. In J. Cassidy & P. Shaver (Eds.), *Handbook of attachment: Theory, research, and clinical applications* (2nd ed., pp. 880–905). New York: Guilford Press.

Inagaki, K., & Hatano, G. (2004). Vitalistic causality in young children's naive biology. *Trends in Cognitive Sciences, 8,* 356–362.

Ince, D., Swearingen, C., & Yazici, Y. (2009). Wrist pain in 7 to 12 year olds playing with game consoles/handhelds: Younger children have more pain, independent from time spent playing. *Arthritis & Rheumatism, 60,* 1234–1234.

Ingoldsby, E., Shaw, D., Owens, E., & Winslow, E. (1999). A longitudinal study of interparental conflict, emotional and behavioral reactivity, and preschoolers' adjustment problems among low-income families. *Journal of Abnormal Child Psychology, 27,* 343–356.

Ingram, D. (1981). Early patterns of grammatical development. In R. E. Stark (Ed.), *Language behavior in infancy and early childhood* (pp. 327–358). New York: Elsevier/North-Holland.

Inhelder, B., & Piaget, J. (1958). *The growth of logical thinking from childhood to adolescence.* New York: Basic Books.

Interactive Digital Software Association. (1998). *Deep impact: How does the interactive entertainment industry affect the U.S. economy?* Retrieved from http://www.idsa.com

Isabella, R. A., Belsky, J., & von Eye, A. (1989). Origins of infant-mother attachment: An examination of interactional synchrony during the infant's first year. *Developmental Psychology, 25,* 12–21.

Issiaka, S., Cartoux, M., Zerbo, O., Tiendrebeogo, S., Meda, N., Dabis, F., & Van de Perre, P. (2001). Living with HIV: Women's experience in Burkina Faso, West Africa. *AIDS Care, 13,* 123–128.

Itier, R., & Taylor, M. (2004). Face inversion and contrast-reversal effects across development: In contrast to the expertise theory. *Developmental Science, 7,* 246–260.

Izard, C. E. (2007). Basic emotions, natural kinds, emotion schemas, and a new paradigm. *Perspectives on Psychological Science, 2,* 260–280.

Izard, C. E., & Abe, J. (2004). Developmental changes in facial expressions of emotions in the Strange Situation during the second year of life. *Emotion, 4,* 251–265.

Izard, C. E., Fantauzzo, C. A., Castle, J. M., Haynes, O. M., Rayias, M. F., & Putnam, P. H. (1995). The ontogeny and significance of infants' facial expressions in the first 9 months of life. *Developmental Psychology, 31,* 997–1013.

Izard, C. E., & Harris, P. (1995). Emotional development and developmental psychopathology. In D. Cicchetti & D. J. Cohen (Eds.), *Developmental psychopathology: Vol. 1. Theory and methods* (pp. 467–503). New York: Wiley.

Izard, C. E., Schultz, D., & Ackerman, B. P. (1997, April). *Emotion knowledge, social competence, and behavior problems in disadvantaged children.* Paper presented at the biennial meetings of the Society for Research in Child Development, Washington, DC.

Izard, C. E., Woodburn, E., Finlon, K., Krauthamer-Ewing, E., Grossman, S., & Seidenfeld, A. (2011). Emotion knowledge, emotional utilization, and emotion regulation. *Emotion Review, 3,* 44–52.

Jackson, D., & Tein, J. (1998). Adolescents' conceptualization of adult roles: Relationships with age, gender, work goal, and maternal employment. *Sex Roles, 38,* 987–1008.

Jackson, E., Campos, J. J., & Fischer, K. W. (1978). The question of decalage between object permanence and person permanence. *Developmental Psychology, 14,* 1–10.

Jackson, L., & Bracken, B. (1998). Relationship between students' social status and global and domain-specific self-concepts. *Journal of School Psychology, 36,* 233–246.

Jackson, L., Pratt, M., Hunsberger, B., & Pancer, S. (2005). Optimism as a mediator of the relation between perceived parental authoritativeness and adjustment among adolescents: Finding the sunny side of the street. *Social Development, 14,* 273–304.

Jacobs, J., Lanza, S., Osgood, D., Eccles, J., & Wigfield, A. (2002). Changes in children's self-competence and values: Gender and domain differences across grades one through twelve. *Child Development, 73,* 509–527.

Jadack, R. A., Hyde, J. S., Moore, C. F., & Keller, M. L. (1995). Moral reasoning about sexually transmitted diseases. *Child Development, 66,* 167–177.

Jahnke, H. C., & Blanchard-Fields, F. (1993). A test of two models of adolescent egocentrism. *Journal of Youth & Adolescence, 22,* 313–326.

Jain, T., Harlow, B., & Hornstein, M. (2002). Insurance coverage and outcomes of in vitro fertilization. *New England Journal of Medicine, 347,* 661–666.

Jain, T., Missmer, S., & Hornstein, M. (2004). Trends in embryo-transfer practice and in outcomes of the use of assisted reproductive technology in the United States. *New England Journal of Medicine, 350,* 1639–1645.

Jambunathan, S., & Burts, D. (2003). Comparison of perception of self-competence among five ethnic groups of preschoolers in the US. *Early Childhood Education, 173,* 651–660.

James, K. (2010). Sensori-motor experience leads to changes in visual processing in the developing brain. *Developmental Science, 13,* 279–288.

James, K., & Gauthier, I. (2009). When writing impairs reading: Letter perception's susceptibility to motor interference. *Journal of Experimental Psychology, 138,* 416–431.

James, W. (1890). *Principles of psychology.* Chicago: Encyclopaedia Britannica.

James, W. (1892). *Psychology: The briefer course.* New York: Holt.

Janssen, I., Heymsfield, S., Wang, Z., & Ross, R. (2000). Skeletal muscle mass and distribution in 468 men and women aged 18–88 yr. *Journal of Applied Physiology, 89,* 81–88.

Janssen, P. A., Holt, V. L., & Myers, S. J. (1994). Licensed midwife-attended, out-of-hospital births in Washington State: Are they safe? *Birth, 21,* 141–148.

Janssen, T., & Carton, J. (1999). The effects of locus of control and task difficulty on procrastination. *The Journal of Genetic Psychology, 160,* 436–442.

Jenkins, J. M., & Astington, J. W. (1996). Cognitive factors and family structure associated with theory of mind development in young children. *Developmental Psychology, 32,* 70–78.

Jenkins, J., Simpson, A., Dunn, J., Rasbash, J., & O'Connor, T. (2005). Mutual influence of marital conflict and children's behavior problems: Shared and nonshared family risks. *Child Development, 76,* 24–39.

Jenks, K., van Lieshout, E., & de Moor, J. (2008, in press). Arithmetic achievement in children with cerebral palsy or spina bifida meningomyelocele. *Remedial and Special Education.*

Jessor, R. (1992). Risk behavior in adolescence: A psychosocial framework for understanding and action. *Developmental Review, 12,* 374–390.

Jewell, J. (2009). *Fragile X syndrome.* Retrieved June 27, 2010, from http://emedicine.medscape.com/article/943776-overview

Jeynes, W. (2007). The impact of parental remarriage on children: A meta-analysis. *Marriage & Family Review, 40,* 75–102.

Jirtle, R., & Weidman, J. (2007). Imprinted and more equal. *American Scientist, 95,* 143–149.

John, O. P., Caspi, A., Robins, R. W., Moffitt, T. E., & Stouthamer-Loeber, M. (1994). The "little five": Exploring the nomological network of the five-factor model of personality in adolescent boys. *Child Development, 65,* 160–178.

Johnson, K., & Daviss, B. (2005). Outcomes of planned home births with certified professional midwives: Large prospective study in North America. *British Medical Journal, 330,* 1416.

Johnson, L. (2011). *HIV prevalence in pregnant women.* Retrieved June 21, 2011, from http://www.childrencount.ci.org.za/uploads/NSP-HIV-prevalence-in-pregnant-women.pdf.

Johnson, M. (2011). Developmental neuroscience, psychophysiology, and genetics. In M. Bornstein & M. Lamb (Eds.), *Developmental science: An advanced textbook* (6th ed., pp. 201–240). New York: Psychology Press.

Johnston, A., Barnes, M., & Desrochers, A. (2008). Reading comprehension: Developmental processes, individual differences, and interventions. *Canadian Psychology, 49,* 125–132.

Johnston, D., Nicholls, M., Shah, M., & Shields, M. (2008, in press). Nature's experiment? Handedness and early childhood development. *Demography.*

Johnston, J., Durieux-Smith, A., & Bloom, K. (2005). Teaching gestural signs to infants to advance child development: A review of the evidence. *First Language, 25,* 235–251.

Johnston, L. D., O'Malley, P. M., Bachman, J. G., & Schulenberg, J. E. (2010). *Monitoring the future national results on adolescent drug use: Overview of key findings, 2009* (NIH Publication No. 10-7583). Bethesda, MD: National Institute on Drug Abuse.

Jones, A. (2008). The AAI as clinical tool. In H. Steele & M. Steele (Eds.), *Clinical applications of the Adult Attachment Interview.* (pp. 175–194). New York: Guilford Press.

Jones, E., & Herbert, J. (2009). Imitation and the development of infant learning, memory, and categorization. *Revue de Primatologie, 1.* Retrieved September 3, 2011, from http://primatologie.revues.org/236

Jones, M. C. (1924). A laboratory study of fear: The case of Peter. *Pedagogical Seminary, 31,* 308–315.

Jones, S. (2003). *Let the games begin: Gaming technology and entertainment among college students.* Washington, DC: Pew Internet and American Life Project. Retrieved May 17, 2006, from http:// www .pewinternet.org/PPF/r/93/report_display.asp

Jonsson, P. (2003). The new face of homeschooling. *Christian Science Monitor Online.* Retrieved June 23, 2004, from http://www.csmonitor .com/2003/0429/p01s01-ussc.html

Jordan, N. (2010). Early predictors of mathematics achievement and mathematics learning difficulties. In R. Tremblay, R. Barr, R. Peters, & M. Boivin (Eds.), *Encyclopedia on early childhood development* [Online]. Retrieved August 11, 2010, from http://www.child-encyclopedia.com/documents/JordanANGxp.pdf

Jordan, N. C., Huttenlocher, J., & Levine, S. C. (1992). Differential calculation abilities in young children from middle- and low-income families. *Developmental Psychology, 28,* 644–653.

Joseph, R. (2000). Fetal brain behavior and cognitive development. *Developmental Review, 20,* 81–98.

Josephs, R., Newman, M., Brown, R., & Beer, J. (2003). Status, testosterone, and human intellectual performance. *Psychological Science, 14,* 158–163.

Jospe, N. (2011). Endocrinology. In K. Marcdante, R. Kliegman, H. Jensen, & R. Behrman (Eds.), *Nelson's essential of pediatrics* (6th ed., pp. 625–670). New York: Elsevier Health Publishers.

Juffer, F., van IJzendoorn, M., & Bakermans-Kranenburg, M. J. (2008). Supporting adoptive families with video-feedback intervention. In F. Juffer, M. Bakermans-Kranenburg, & M. van IJzendoorn (Eds.), *Promoting positive parenting: An attachment-based intervention* (pp. 139–153). New York: Taylor & Francis Group/Lawrence Erlbaum Associates.

Jusczyk, P., & Hohne, E. (1997). Infants' memory for spoken words. *Science, 277,* n.p.

Justice, L., Invernizzi, M., Geller, K., Sullivan, A., & Welsch, J. (2005). Descriptive-developmental performance of at-risk preschoolers on early literacy tasks. *Reading Psychology, 26,* 1–25.

Kado, S., & Takagi, R. (1996). Biological aspects. In S. Sandberg (Ed.), *Hyperactivity disorders of childhood* (pp. 246–279). Cambridge, England: Cambridge University Press.

Kaelbling, R. (2009). *GM2 Gangiosidoses.* Retrieved June 27, 2010, from http://emedicine.medscape.com/article/951943-overview

Kafai, Y., Fields, D., & Cook, M. (2010). Your second selves: Player designed avatars. *Games and Culture, 5,* 23–42.

Kagan, J. (1971). *Change and continuity in infancy.* New York: Wiley.

Kagan, J. (1989). *Unstable ideas: Temperament, cognition, and self.* Cambridge, MA: Harvard University Press.

Kagan, J. (2007). A trio of concerns. *Perspectives on Psychological Science, 2,* 361–376.

Kagan, J., Arcus, D., Snidman, N., Feng, W. Y., Hendler, J., & Greene, S. (1994). Reactivity in infants: A cross-national comparison. *Developmental Psychology, 30,* 342–345.

Kagan, J., & Fox, N. (2006). Biology, culture, and temperamental biases. In N. Eisenberg, W. Damon, & R. Lerner (Eds.), *Handbook of child psychology: Vol. 3, Social, emotional, and personality development* (6th ed., pp. 167–225). Hoboken, NJ: Wiley.

Kagan, J., & Herschkowitz, N. (2005). *A young mind in a growing brain.* Mahwah, NJ: Erlbaum.

Kagan, J., Kearsley, R., & Zelazo, P. (1978). *Infancy: Its place in human development.* Cambridge, MA: Harvard University Press.

Kagan, J., Klein, R., Finley, G., Rogoff, B., Nolan, E., & Greenbaum, C. (1979). A cross-cultural study of cognitive development. *Monographs of the Society for Research in Child Development, 44,* 1–77.

Kagan, J., Reznick, J. S., & Snidman, N. (1990). The temperamental qualities of inhibition and lack of inhibition. In M. Lewis & S. M. Miller (Eds.), *Handbook of developmental psychopathology* (pp. 219–226). New York: Plenum Press.

Kagan, J., Snidman, N., & Arcus, D. (1993). On the temperamental categories of inhibited and uninhibited children. In K. H. Rubin & J. B. Asendorpf (Eds.), *Social withdrawal, inhibition, and shyness in childhood* (pp. 19–28). Hillsdale, NJ: Erlbaum.

Kail, R. (1990). *The development of memory in children* (3rd ed.). New York: Freeman.

Kail, R. (1997). Processing time, imagery, and spatial memory. *Journal of Experimental Child Psychology, 64,* 67–78.

Kail, R. (2004). Cognitive development includes global and domain-specific processes. *Merrill-Palmer Quarterly, 50,* 445–455.

Kail, R. (2007a). Cognitive development includes global and domain-specific processes. In G. Ladd (Ed.), *Appraising the human developmental sciences: Essays in honor of Merrill-Palmer Quarterly* (pp. 56–66). Detroit: Wayne State University Press.

Kail, R. (2007b). Longitudinal evidence that increases in processing speed and working memory enhance children's reasoning. *Psychological Science, 18,* 312–313.

Kail, R., & Hall, L. (1999). Sources of developmental change in children's word-problem performance. *Journal of Educational Psychology, 91,* 660–668.

Kaiser Family Foundation. (2004). *Children, the digital divide, and federal policy.* Retrieved July 12, 2011, from http://www.kff.org/entmedia/loader.cfm?url=/commonspot/security/getfile.cfm&PageID=46360

Kaiser Family Foundation. (2005). *Sex on TV.* Retrieved June 21, 2007, from http://www.kff.org/entmedia/entmedia110905pkg

Kaiser Family Foundation. (2010). *Mandated coverage of infertility treatment.* Retrieved August 17, 2011, from http://www.statehealthfacts.org/comparetable.jsp?ind=686&cat=7

Kamps, D., Tankersley, M., & Ellis, C. (2000). Social skills interventions for young at-risk students: A 2-year follow-up study. *Behavioral Disorders, 25,* 310–324.

Kandel, D., & Wu, P. (1995). The contributions of mothers and fathers to the intergenerational transmission of cigarette smoking in adolescence. *Journal of Research on Adolescence, 5,* 225–252.

Kanemura, H., Aihara, M., Aoki, S., Araki, T., & Nakazawa, S. (2004). Development of the prefrontal lobe in infants and children: A three-dimensional magnetic resonance volumetric study. *Brain and Development, 25,* 195–199.

Kaplan Test Prep Survey. (2011). *School may be out for summer, but rising high school seniors plan to spend vacation months becoming stronger college applicants*. Retrieved July 13, 2011, from http://www.marketwatch.com/story/kaplan-test-prep-survey-school-may-be-out-for-summer-but-rising-high-school-seniors-plan-to-spend-vacation-months-becoming-stronger-college-applicants-2011-06-20

Kaplowitz, P. (2010). *Precocious puberty*. Retrieved August 13, 2010, from http://emedicine.medscape.com/article/924002-overview

von Károlyi, C., & Winner, E. (2005). Extreme giftedness. In R. Sternberg (Ed.), *Conceptions of giftedness* (2nd ed., pp. 377–394). New York: Cambridge University Press.

Karreman, A., de Haas, S., Van Tuijl, C., van Aken, M., & Dekovic, M. (2010). Relations among temperament, parenting, and problem behavior in young children. *Infant Behavior & Development, 33*, 39–49.

Kashima, Y., Kashima, E., Chiu, C., Farsides, T., Gelfand, M., Hong, Y., Kim, U., Strack, F., Werth, L., Yuki, M., & Yzerbyt, V. (2005). Culture, essentialism, and agency: Are individuals universally believed to be more real entities than groups? *European Journal of Social Psychology, 35*, 147–169.

Katz, L., & Woodin, E. (2002). Hostility, hostile detachment, and conflict engagement in marriages: Effects on child and family functioning. *Child Development, 73*, 636–652.

Katz, P. A., & Ksansnak, K. R. (1994). Developmental aspects of gender role flexibility and traditionality in middle childhood and adolescence. *Developmental Psychology, 30*, 272–282.

Kaufman, A., & Kaufman, N. (2004). *Kaufman Assessment Battery for Children (KABC) II*. Bloomington, MN: Pearson AGS.

Kaufman, J., Kaufman, A., Kaufman-Singer, J., & Kaufman, N. (2005). The Kaufman Assessment Battery for Children–Second Edition and the Kaufman Adolescent and Adult Intelligence Test. In D. Flanagan & P. Harrison (Eds.), *Contemporary intellectual assessment: Theories, tests, and issues* (pp. 344–370). New York: Guilford Press.

Kavsek, M. J. (2002). The perception of static subjective contours in infancy. *Child Development, 73*, 331–344.

Kaye, K. (1982). *The mental and social life of babies: How parents create persons*. Chicago: University of Chicago Press.

Keating, D. P. (1980). Thinking processes in adolescence. In J. Adelson (Ed.), *Handbook of adolescent psychology* (pp. 211–246). New York: Wiley.

Keefe, S. E., & Padilla, A. M. (1987). *Chicano ethnicity*. Albuquerque: University of New Mexico Press.

Keen, R. (2003). Representation of objects and events: Why do infants look so smart and toddlers look so dumb? *Current Directions in Psychological Science, 12*, 79–83.

Keeney, T. J., Cannizzo, S. R., & Flavell, J. H. (1967). Spontaneous and induced verbal rehearsal in a recall task. *Child Development, 38*, 935–966.

Keller, H. (2011). Culture and cognition: Developmental perspectives. *Journal of Cognitive Education and Psychology, 10*, 3–8.

Kelley, M. L., Sanchez-Hucles, J., & Walker, R. R. (1993). Correlates of disciplinary practices in working- to middle-class African-American mothers. *Merrill-Palmer Quarterly, 39*, 252–264.

Kendler, K., Thornton, L., Gilman, S., & Kessler, R. (2000). Sexual orientation in a U.S. national sample of twin and nontwin sibling pairs. *American Journal of Psychiatry, 157*, 1843–1846.

Kennedy, D. M. (1995). Glimpses of a highly gifted child in a heterogeneous classroom. *Roeper Review, 17*, 164–168.

Kerns, K. A. (1996). Individual differences in friendship quality: Links to child-mother attachment. In W. M. Bukowski, A. F. Newcomb, & W. W. Hartup (Eds.), *The company they keep: Friendship in childhood and adolescence* (pp. 137–157). Cambridge, England: Cambridge University Press.

Kerr, C., McDowell, B., & McDonough, S. (2007). The relationship between gross motor function and participation restriction in children with cerebral palsy: An exploratory analysis. *Child: Care, Health and Development, 33*, 22–27.

Kesselring, T., & Müller, U. (2010). The concept of egocentrism in the context of Piaget's theory. *New Ideas in Psychology, 28*, 327–345.

Kiang, L., Harter, S., & Whitesell, N. (2007). Relational expression of ethnic identity in Chinese Americans. *Journal of Social and Personal Relationships, 24*, 277–296.

Kidger, J. (2004). 'You realise it could happen to you': The benefits to pupils of young mothers delivering school sex education. *Sex Education, 4*, 185–197.

Kids Count Data Center. (2010). *Data across states*. Retrieved September 6, 2011, from http://datacenter.kidscount.org/data/acrossstates/Rankings.aspx?loct=3&by=a&order=a&ind=81&dtm=397&tf=38

Kiel, D., Dodson, E., Artal, R., Boehmer, T., & Leet, T. (2007). Gestational weight gain and pregnancy outcomes in obese women: How much is enough? *Obstetrics & Gynecology, 110*, 752–758.

Kilgore, P. E., Holman, R. C., Clarke, M. J., & Glass, R. I. (1995). Trends of diarrheal disease-associated mortality in US children, 1968 through 1991. *Journal of the American Medical Association, 274*, 1143–1148.

Kilpatrick, S. J., & Laros, R. K. (1989). Characteristics of normal labor. *Obstetrics and Gynecology, 74*, 85–87.

Kim, H., Baydar, N., & Greek, A. (2003). Testing conditions influence the race gap in cognition and achievement estimated by household survey data. *Journal of Applied Developmental Psychology, 23*, 567–582.

Kim, Y., Petscher, Y., Schatshneider, C., & Foorman, B. (2010). Does growth rate in oral reading fluency matter in predicting reading comprehension achievement? *Journal of Educational Psychology, 102*, 652–667.

Kimura, M., Umehara, T., Udagawa, J., Kawauchi, H., & Hiroki, O. (2009). Development of olfactory epithelium in the human fetus: Scanning electron microscopic observations. *Congenital Anomalies, 49*, 102–107.

Kindermann, T. (2007). Effects of naturally existing peer groups on changes in academic engagement in a cohort of sixth graders. *Child Development, 78*, 1186–1203.

Kirk, K., Bailey, J., & Martin, N. (2000). Etiology of male sexual orientation in an Australian twin sample. *Psychology, Evolution, & Gender, 2*, 301–311.

Kirk, S., Gallagher, J., & Anastasiow, N. (1993). *Educating exceptional children* (7th ed.). Boston: Houghton Mifflin.

Kirkcaldy, B., Siefen, G., Surall, D., & Bischoff, R. (2004). Predictors of drug and alcohol abuse among children and adolescents. *Personality & Individual Differences, 36*, 247–265.

Klaczynski, P., Fauth, J., & Swanger, A. (1998). Adolescent identity: Rational vs. experiential processing, formal operations, and critical thinking beliefs. *Journal of Youth & Adolescence, 27*, 185–207.

Klahr, D. (1992). Information-processing approaches to cognitive development. In M. H. Bernstein & M. E. Lamb (Eds.), *Developmental psychology: An advanced textbook* (3rd ed., pp. 273–335). Hillsdale, NJ: Erlbaum.

Klar, A. (2003). Human handedness and scalp hair-whorl direction develop from a common genetic mechanism. *Genetics, 165*, 269–276.

Klein, A., & Swartz, S. (1996). *Reading Recovery in California: Program overview*. San Francisco: San Francisco Unified School District.

Kliegman, R. (1998). Fetal and neonatal medicine. In R. Behrman & R. Kliegman (Eds.), *Nelson essentials of pediatrics* (3rd ed., pp. 167–225). Philadelphia: Saunders.

Klimstra, T., Luyckx, K., Hale, W., Frijns, T., van Lier, P., & Meeus, W. (2010). Short-term fluctuations in identity: Introducing a micro-level approach to identity formation. *Journal of Personality and Social Psychology, 99*, 191–202.

Kloos, H., Haddad, J., & Keen, R. (2006). Which cues are available to 24-month-olds? Evidence from point-of-gaze measures during search. *Infant Behavior and Development, 29*, 243–250.

Knafo, A., Daniel, D., & Khoury-Kassabri, M. (2008). Values as protective factors against violent behavior in Jewish and Arab high schools in Israel. *Child Development, 79*, 652–667.

Knight, G. P., Cota, M. K., & Bernal, M. E. (1993). The socialization of cooperative, competitive, and individualistic preferences among Mexican American children: The mediating role of ethnic identity. *Hispanic Journal of Behavioral Sciences, 15*, 291–309.

Kobak, R., Zajac, K., & Smith, C. (2009). Adolescent attachment and trajectories of hostile/impulsive behavior: Implications for the development of personality disorders. *Development and Psychopathology, 21*, 839–851.

Kobayashi, M., Haynes, C., Macaruso, P., Hook, P., & Kato, J. (2005). Effects of mora deletion, nonword repetition, rapid naming, and visual search performance on beginning reading in Japanese. *Annals of Dyslexia, 55*, 105–128.

Kochanek, K., Xu, J., Murphy, S., Minino, A., & Kung, H. (2011). Deaths: Preliminary data for 2009. *National Vital Statistics Reports, 59*, 1–69.

Kochanska, G. (1997). Mutually responsive orientation between mothers and their young children: Implications for early socialization. *Child Development, 68*, 94–112.

Kochanska, G., & Aksan, N. (2006). Children's conscience and self-regulation. *Journal of Personality, 74*, 1587–1617.

Koechlin, E., Basso, G., Pietrini, P., Panzer, S., & Grafman, J. (1999). Exploring the role of the anterior prefrontal cortex in human cognition. *Nature, 399*, 148–151.

Koenen, K. C., Moffitt, T. E., Poulton, R., Martin, J., & Caspi, A. (2007). Early childhood factors associated with the development of post-traumatic stress disorder: Results from a longitudinal birth cohort. *Psychological Medicine, 37*, 181–192.

Koenig, A., Cicchetti, D., & Rogosch, F. (2004). Moral development: The association between maltreatment and young children's prosocial behaviors and moral transgressions. *Social Development, 13*, 97–106.

Koeppe, R. (1996). Language differentiation in bilingual children: The development of grammatical and pragmatic competence. *Linguistics, 34*, 927–954.

Koesten, J. (2004). Family communication patterns, sex of subject, and communication competence. *Communication Monographs, 71*, 226–244.

Kohlberg, L. (1964). Development of moral character and moral ideology. In M. L. Hoffman & L. W. Hoffman (Eds.), *Review of child development research* (Vol. 1, pp. 283–332). New York: Russell Sage Foundation.

Kohlberg, L. (1966). A cognitive-developmental analysis of children's sex-role concept and attitudes. In E. E. Maccoby (Ed.), *The development of sex differences* (pp. 82–172). Stanford, CA: Stanford University Press.

Kohlberg, L. (1975). The cognitive-developmental approach to moral education. *Phi Delta Kappan*, 670–677.

Kohlberg, L. (1976). Moral stages and moralization: The cognitive-developmental approach. In T. Lickona (Ed.), *Moral development and behavior: Theory, research, and social issues* (pp. 31–53). New York: Holt.

Kohlberg, L. (1978). Revisions in the theory and practice of moral development. *New Directions for Child Development, 2*, 83–88.

Kohlberg, L. (1980). *The meaning and measurement of moral development.* Worcester, MA: Clark University Press.

Kohlberg, L. (1981). *Essays on moral development: Vol. 1. The philosophy of moral development.* New York: Harper & Row.

Kohlberg, L., Boyd, D. R., & Levine, C. (1990). The return of stage 6: Its principle and moral point of view. In T. E. Wren (Ed.), *The moral domain: Essays in the ongoing discussion between philosophy and the social sciences.* Cambridge: MIT Press.

Kohlberg, L., & Elfenbein, D. (1975). The development of moral judgments concerning capital punishment. *American Journal of Orthopsychiatry, 54*, 614–640.

Kohlberg, L., & Ullian, D. Z. (1974). Stages in the development of psychosexual concepts and attitudes. In R. C. Friedman, R. M. Richart, & R. L. Vande Wiele (Eds.), *Sex differences in behavior* (pp. 209–222). New York: Wiley.

Kopp, C. B., & Kaler, S. R. (1989). Risk in infancy: Origins and implications. *American Psychologist, 44*, 224–230.

Koppenhaver, D., Hendrix, M., & Williams, A. (2007). Toward evidence-based literacy interventions for children with severe and multiple disabilities. *Seminars in Speech & Language, 28*, 79–90.

Korner, A. F., Hutchinson, C. A., Koperski, J. A., Kraemer, H. C., & Schneider, P. A. (1981). Stability of individual differences of neonatal motor and crying patterns. *Child Development, 52*, 83–90.

Koskinen, P., Blum, I., Bisson, S., Phillips, S., Creamer, T. S., & Baker, T. K. (2000). Book access, shared reading, and audio models: The effects of supporting the literacy learning of linguistically diverse students in school and at home. *Journal of Educational Psychology, 92*, 23–36.

Kost, K. (1997). The effects of support on the economic well-being of young fathers. *Families in Society, 78*, 370–382.

Kostanski, M., Fisher, A., & Gullone, E. (2004). Current conceptualisation of body image dissatisfaction: Have we got it wrong? *Journal of Child Psychology and Psychiatry, 45*, 1317–1325.

Kosterman, R., Graham, J., Hawkins, J., Catalano, R., & Herrenkohl, T. (2001). Childhood risk factors for persistence of violence in the transition to adulthood: A social development perspective. *Violence & Victims, 16*, 355–369.

Krcmar, M., & Vieira, E. (2005). Imitating life, imitating television: The effects of family and television models on children's moral reasoning. *Communication Research, 32*, 267–294.

Krebs, N., Himes, J., Jacobson, D., Nicklas, T., & Styne, D. (2007). Assessment of child and adolescent overweight and obesity. *Pediatrics, 120*, S193–S228.

Krebs, N., & Primak, L. (2011). Pediatric nutrition and nutritional disorders. In K. Marcdante, R. Kliegman, H. Jensen, & R. Behrman (Eds.), *Nelson's essential of pediatrics* (pp. 103–122). New York: Elsevier Health Publishers.

Kristensen, P., & Bjerkedal, T. (2007). Explaining the relation between birth order and intelligence. *Science, 316*, 1717.

Kroger, J. (2007). Why is identity achievement so elusive? *Identity, 7*, 331–348.

Kron-Sperl, V., Schneider, W., & Hasselhorn, M. (2008). The development and effectiveness of memory strategies in kindergarten and elementary school: Findings from the Würzburg and Göttingen longitudinal memory studies. *Cognitive Development, 23*, 79–104.

Krueger, C., Holditch-Davis, D., Quint, S., & DeCasper, A. (2004). Recurring auditory experience in the 28- to 34-week-old fetus. *Infant Behavioral Development, 27*, 537–543.

Kuczaj, S. A., II. (1977). The acquisition of regular and irregular past tense forms. *Journal of Verbal Learning and Verbal Behavior, 49*, 319–326.

Kuczaj, S. A., II. (1978). Children's judgments of grammatical and ungrammatical irregular past tense verbs. *Child Development, 49,* 319–326.

Kuhn, D. (1992). Cognitive development. In M. H. Bornstein & M. E. Lamb (Eds.), *Developmental psychology: An advanced textbook* (3rd ed., pp. 211–272). Hillsdale, NJ: Erlbaum.

Kuhn, D. (2008). Formal operations from a twenty-first-century perspective. *Human Development, 51,* 48–55.

Kuhn, D., Garcia-Mila, M., Zohar, A., & Andersen, C. (1995). Strategies of knowledge acquisition. *Monographs of the Society for Research in Child Development, 60*(Serial No. 245).

Kuhn, D., Kohlberg, L., Languer, J., & Haan, N. (1977). The development of formal operations in logical and moral judgment. *Genetic Psychology Monographs, 95,* 97–188.

Kurdek, L. (2003). Correlates of parents' perceptions of behavioral problems in their young children. *Journal of Applied Developmental Psychology, 24,* 457–473.

Kurdek, L. A., & Fine, M. A. (1994). Family acceptance and family control as predictors of adjustment in young adolescents: Linear, curvilinear, or interactive effects? *Child Development, 65,* 1137–1146.

Kusché, C. A., & Greenberg, M. T. (1994). *The PATHS Curriculum.* Seattle: Developmental Research and Programs.

Kuttler, A., LaGreca, A., & Prinstein, M. (1999). Friendship qualities and social-emotional functioning of adolescents with close, cross-sex friendships. *Journal of Research on Adolescence, 9,* 339–366.

La Freniere, P., Strayer, F. F., & Gauthier, R. (1984). The emergence of same-sex affiliative preferences among preschool peers: A developmental/ethological perspective. *Child Development, 55,* 1958–1965.

La Paro, K., Justice, L., Skibbe, L., & Pianta, R. (2004). Relations among maternal, child, and demographic factors and the persistence of preschool language impairment. *American Journal of Speech-Language Pathology, 13,* 291–303.

Laceulle, O., Nederhof, E., Karreman, A., Ormel, M., & van Aken, M. (2011, in press). Stressful events and temperament change during early and middle adolescence: The TRAILS study. *European Journal of Personality.*

de Lacoste, M., Horvath, D., & Woodward, J. (1991). Possible sex differences in the developing human fetal brain. *Journal of Clinical and Experimental Neuropsychology, 13,* 831.

Ladd, G., Herald-Brown, S., & Reiser, M. (2008). Does chronic classroom peer rejection predict the development of children's classroom participation during the grade school years? *Child Development, 79,* 1001–1015.

Ladd, G., & Troop-Gordon, W. (2003). The role of chronic peer difficulties in the development of children's psychological adjustment problems. *Child Development, 74,* 1344–1367.

LaFontana, K., & Cillessen, A. (2010). Developmental changes in the priority of perceived status in childhood and adolescence. *Social Development, 19,* 130–147.

Lafuente, M., Grifol, R., Segarra, J., Soriano, J., Gorba, M., & Montesinos, A. (1997). Effects of the Firstart method of prenatal stimulation on psychomotor development: The first six months. *Pre- & Peri-Natal Psychology Journal, 11,* 151–162.

Lai, B., Tang, C., & Tse, W. (2005). Prevalence and psychosocial correlates of disordered eating among Chinese pregnant women in Hong Kong. *Eating Disorders: The Journal of Treatment & Prevention, 13,* 171–186.

Lai, K., & McBride-Chang, C. (2001). Suicidal ideation, parenting style, and family climate among Hong Kong adolescents. *International Journal of Psychology, 36,* 81–87.

Laible, D., Panfile, T., & Makariev, D. (2008). The quality and frequency of mother-toddler conflict: Links with attachment and temperament. *Child Development, 79,* 426–443.

Laible, D., & Thompson, R. (2002). Mother-child conflict in the toddler years: Lessons in emotion, morality, and relationships. *Child Development, 73,* 1187–1203.

Lam, C., Lam, M., Shek, D., & Tang, V. (2004). Coping with economic disadvantage. A qualitative study of Chinese adolescents from low-income families. *International Journal of Adolescent Medicine and Health, 16,* 343–357.

Lamb, M., Bornstein, M., & Teti, D. (2002). *Social development in infancy* (4th ed.). Mahwah, NJ: Erlbaum.

Lamb, M., & Lewis, C. (2011). The role of parent-child relationships in child development. In M. Bornstein & M. Lamb (Eds.), *Developmental science: An advanced textbook* (6th ed., pp. 469–518). New York: Psychology Press.

Lamb, M. E., Frodi, M., Hwang, C., & Frodi, A. M. (1983). Effects of paternal involvement on infant preferences for mothers and fathers. *Child Development, 54,* 450–458.

Lamb, M. E., Sternberg, K. J., & Prodromidis, M. (1992). Nonmaternal care and the security of infant-mother attachment: A reanalysis of the data. *Infant Behavior and Development, 15,* 71–83.

Lambert, E., Clarke, A., Tucker-Gail, K., & Hogan, N. (2009). Multivariate analysis of reasons for death penalty support between male and female college students: Empirical support for Gilligan's "ethic of care." *Criminal Justice Studies: A Critical Journal of Crime, Law, & Society, 22,* 239–260.

Lambert, S. (2005). Gay and lesbian families: What we know and where to go from here. *Family Journal: Counseling & Therapy, 13,* 43–51.

Lamborn, S. D., Dornbusch, S. M., & Steinberg, L. (1996). Ethnicity and community context as moderators of the relations between family decision making and adolescent adjustment. *Child Development, 67,* 283–301.

Lamborn, S. D., Mounts, N. S., Steinberg, L., & Dornbusch, S. M. (1991). Patterns of competence and adjustment among adolescents from authoritative, authoritarian, indulgent, and neglectful families. *Child Development, 62,* 1049–1065.

Lamke, L. K. (1982). Adjustment and sex-role orientation. *Journal of Youth & Adolescence, 11,* 247–259.

Landry, S., Smith, K., & Swank, P. (2006). Responsive parenting: Establishing early foundations for social, communication, and independent problem-solving skills. *Developmental Psychology, 42,* 627–642.

Laney, D. (2002). The gastrointestinal tract & liver. In A. Rudolph, R. Kamei, & K. Overby (Eds.), *Rudolph's fundamentals of pediatrics* (3rd ed., pp. 465–512).

Langer, G., Arndt, C., & Sussman, D. (2004). *Primetime Live poll: American sex survey analysis.* Retrieved June 22, 2007, from http://abcnews.go.com/Primetime/PollVault/story?id=156921&page=1

Langlois, J. H., Ritter, J. M., Roggman, L. A., & Vaughn, L. S. (1991). Facial diversity and infant preferences for attractive faces. *Developmental Psychology, 27,* 79–84.

Langlois, J. H., Roggman, L. A., Casey, R. J., Ritter, J. M., Rieser-Danner, L. A., & Jenkins, V. Y. (1987). Infant preferences for attractive faces: Rudiments of a stereotype? *Developmental Psychology, 23,* 363–369.

Langlois, J. H., Roggman, L. A., & Rieser-Danner, L. A. (1990). Infants' differential social responses to attractive and unattractive faces. *Developmental Psychology, 26,* 153–159.

Larson, R. (2000). Toward a psychology of positive youth development. *American Psychologist, 55,* 170–183.

Larson, R., & Brown, J. (2007). Emotional development in adolescence: What can be learned from a high school theater program? *Child Development, 78,* 1083–1099.

Lau, A., Uba, A., & Lehman, D. (2002). Infectious diseases. In A. Rudolph, R. Kamei, & K. Overby (Eds.), *Rudolph's fundamentals of pediatrics* (3rd ed., pp. 289–389).

Lau, J., Riisdijk, F., Gregory, A., McGuffin, P., & Elev, T. (2007). Pathways to childhood depressive symptoms: The role of social, cognitive, and genetic risk factors. *Developmental Psychology, 43,* 1402–1414.

Laub, J. H., & Sampson, R. J. (1995). The long-term effect of punitive discipline. In J. McCord (Ed.), *Coercion and punishment in long-term perspectives* (pp. 247–258). Cambridge, England: Cambridge University Press.

Lauritsen, M., Pedersen, C., & Mortensen, P. (2004). The incidence and prevalence of pervasive developmental disorders: A Danish population-based study. *Psychological Medicine, 34,* 1339–1346.

Laursen, B. (1995). Conflict and social interaction in adolescent relationships. *Journal of Research on Adolescence, 5,* 55–70.

Laursen, B., & Mooney, K. (2007). Individual differences in adolescent dating and adjustment. In R. Engels, M. Kerr, & H. Stattin (Eds.), *Friends, lovers and groups: Key relationships in adolescence* (pp. 81–91). New York: Wiley.

Law, A., Logie, R., & Pearson, D. (2006). The impact of secondary tasks on multitasking in a virtual environment. *Acta Psychologica, 122,* 27–44.

Lawrence, V., Houghton, S., Douglas, G., Durkin, K., Whiting, K., & Tannock, R. (2004). Children with ADHD: Neuropsychological testing and real-world activities. *Journal of Attention Disorders, 7,* 137–149.

Layton, L., Deeny, K., Tall, G., & Upton, G. (1996). Researching and promoting phonological awareness in the nursery class. *Journal of Research in Reading, 19,* 1–13.

Leaper, C., Breed, L., Hoffman, L., & Perlman, C. (2002). Variations in the gender-stereotyped content of children's television cartoons across genres. *Journal of Applied Social Psychology, 32,* 1653–1662.

Learmonth, A., Lamberth, R., & Rovee-Collier, C. (2004). Generalization of deferred imitation during the first year of life. *Journal of Experimental Child Psychology, 88,* 297–318.

Lebra, T. S. (1994). Mother and child in Japanese socialization: A Japan-U.S. comparison. In P. M. Greenfield & R. R. Cocking (Eds.), *Cross-cultural roots of minority child development* (pp. 259–274). Hillsdale, NJ: Erlbaum.

Lecendreux, M., Konofal, E., & Faraone, S. (2011). Attention deficit hyperactivity disorder and associated features among children in France. *Journal of Attention Disorders, 15,* 516–524.

Lee, C. C. (1985). Successful rural black adolescents: A psychological profile. *Adolescence, 20,* 129–142.

Lee, V. E., Burkham, D. T., Zimiles, H., & Ladewski, B. (1994). Family structure and its effect on behavioral and emotional problems in young adolescents. *Journal of Research on Adolescence, 4,* 405–437.

van Leeuwen, M., van den Berg, S., & Boomsma, D. (2008). A twin-family study of general IQ. *Learning and Individual Differences, 18,* 76–88.

Lengua, L., & Kovacs, E. (2005). Bidirectional associations between temperament and parenting and the prediction of adjustment problems in middle childhood. *Journal of Applied Developmental Psychology, 26,* 21–38.

Leonard, L., Camarata, S., Pawtowska, M., Brown, B., & Camarata, M. (2008). The acquisition of tense and agreement morphemes by children with specific language impairment during intervention: Phase 3. *Journal of Speech, Language, and Hearing Research, 51,* 120–125.

Lerner, R., Lewin-Bizan, S., & Warren, A. (2011). Concepts and theories of human development. In M. Bornstein & M. Lamb (Eds.), *Developmental science: An advanced textbook* (6th ed., pp. 3–50). New York: Psychology Press.

Lerner, R., Theokas, C., & Bobek, C. (2005). Concepts and theories of human development: Historical and contemporary dimensions. In M. Bornstein & M. Lamb (Eds.), *Developmental science: An advanced textbook* (5th ed., pp. 3–44). Hillsdale, NJ: Erlbaum.

Lesaux, N., & Siegel, L. (2003). The development of reading in children who speak English as a second language. *Developmental Psychology, 39,* 1005–1019.

Lester, R. (1987). A life-span perspective for early adolescence. In R. Lerner R & T. Foch T (Eds.), *Biological-psychosocial interactions in early adolescence* (pp. 9–34). Hillsdale, NJ: Erlbaum.

Leve, L. D., & Fagot, B. I. (1995, April). *The influence of attachment style and parenting behavior on children's prosocial behavior with peers.* Paper presented at the biennial meetings of the Society for Research in Child Development, Indianapolis.

Levine, D. (2002). MR imaging of fetal central nervous system abnormalities. *Brain & Cognition, 50,* 432–448.

Levine, D. (2011). Growth and development. In K. Marcdante & R. Kliegman (Eds.), *Nelson's essential of pediatrics* (pp. 13–44). New York: Elsevier Health Publishers.

Levine, D. (2011). Growth and development. In K. Marcdante, R. Kliegman, H. Jenson, & R. Behrman (Eds.). *Nelson essentials of pediatrics* (6th ed., pp. 13–44). Philadelphia, PA: Saunders.

Levine, J., Pollack, H., & Comfort, M. (2001). Academic and behavioral outcomes among the children of young mothers. *Journal of Marriage and the Family, 63,* 355–369.

Levine, S., Huttenlocher, J., Taylor A., & Langrock, A. (1999). Early sex differences in spatial skill. *Developmental Psychology, 35,* 940–949.

Levitt, M. J., Guacci-Franco, N., & Levitt, J. L. (1993). Convoys of social support in childhood and early adolescence: Structure and function. *Developmental Psychology, 29,* 811–818.

Levy, G. D., & Fivush, R. (1993). Scripts and gender: A new approach for examining gender-role development. *Developmental Review, 13,* 126–146.

Levy-Shiff, R., Lerman, M., Har-Even, D., & Hod, M. (2002). Maternal adjustment and infant outcome in medically defined high-risk pregnancy. *Developmental Psychology, 38,* 93–103.

Levy-Shiff, R., Vakil, E., Dimitrovsky, L., Abramovitz, M., Shahar, N., Har-Even, D., Gross, S., Lerman, M., Levy, L., Sirota, L., & Fish, B. (1998). Medical, cognitive, emotional, and behavioral outcomes in school-age children conceived by in-vitro fertilization. *Journal of Clinical Child Psychology, 27,* 320–329.

Lewis, C., & Lamb, M. E. (2003). Fathers' influences on children's development: The evidence from two-parent families. *European Journal of Psychology of Education, 18,* 211–228.

Lewis, D. (2011). Neurology. In K. Marcdante, R. Kliegman, H. Jenson, & R. Behrman (Eds.), *Nelson's essential of pediatrics* (pp. 671–712). New York: Elsevier Health Publishers.

Lewis, M. (1997). *Altering fate.* New York: Guilford Press.

Lewis, M., Allesandri, S. M., & Sullivan, M. W. (1992). Differences in shame and pride as a function of children's gender and task difficulty. *Child Development, 63,* 630–638.

Lewis, M., & Brooks, J. (1978). Self-knowledge and emotional development. In M. Lewis & L. A. Rosenblum (Eds.), *The development of affect* (pp. 205–226). New York: Plenum Press.

Lewis, M., & Carmody, D. (2008). Self-representation and brain development. *Developmental Psychology, 44,* 1329–1334.

Lewis, M., & Ramsay, D. (2004). Development of self-recognition, personal pronoun use, and pretend play during the 2nd year. *Child Development, 75,* 1821–1831.

Lewis, M., Sullivan, M. W., Stanger, C., & Weiss, M. (1989). Self development and self-conscious emotions. *Child Development, 60,* 146–156.

Li, Z., Connolly, J., Jiang, D., Pepler, D., & Craig, W. (2010). Adolescent romantic relationships in China and Canada: A cross-national comparison. *International Journal of Behavioral Development, 34,* 113–120.

Liben L., Bigler, R., & Krogh, H. (2001). Pink and blue collar jobs: Children's judgments of job status and job aspirations in relation to sex of worker. *Journal of Experimental Child Psychology, 79,* 346–363.

Lichter, D., & Eggebeen, D. (1994). The effect of parental employment on child poverty. *Journal of Marriage and the Family, 56,* 633–645.

Lickona, T. (1978). Moral development and moral education. In J. M. Gallagher & J. J. A. Easley (Eds.), *Knowledge and development* (Vol. 2, pp. 21–74). New York: Plenum.

Lickona, T., & Davidson, M. (2005). *Smart and good high schools: Integrating excellence and ethics for success in school, work, and beyond.* Cortland, NY: Center for the 4th and 5th Rs (Respect and Responsibility), Washington, DC: Character Education Partnership.

Lidz, C., & Macrine, S. (2001). An alternative approach to the identification of gifted culturally and linguistically diverse learners: The contribution of dynamic assessment. *School Psychology International, 22,* 74–96.

van Lieshout, C. F. M., & Haselager, G. J. T. (1994). The Big Five personality factors in Q-sort descriptions of children and adolescents. In C. F. Halverson, Jr., G. A. Kohnstamm, & R. P. Martin (Eds.), *The developing structure of temperament and personality from infancy to adulthood* (pp. 293–318). Hillsdale, NJ: Erlbaum.

Liew, J., Eisenberg, N., & Reiser, M. (2004). Preschoolers' effortful control and negative emotionality, immediate reactions to disappointment, and quality of social functioning. *Journal of Experimental Child Psychology, 89,* 298–313.

Li-Grining, C. (2007). Effortful control among low-income preschoolers in three cities: Stability, change, and individual differences. *Developmental Psychology, 43,* 208–221.

Lillard, A. S., & Flavell, J. H. (1992). Young children's understanding of different mental states. *Developmental Psychology, 28,* 626–634.

Lindahl, L., & Haimann, M. (1997). Social proximity in early mother-infant interactions: Implications for gender differences? *Early Development & Parenting, 6,* 83–88.

Lindblad, F., & Hjern, A. (2010). ADHD after fetal exposure to maternal smoking. *Nicotine & Tobacco Research, 12,* 408–415.

Linnenbrink, M. (2010). *Transition to the middle school building and academic achievement in Iowa.* Retrieved August 16, 2010, from http://intersect.iowa.gov/admin/ckfinder/userfiles/files/Intersect%20Middle%20Sch.pdf

Lippa, R. (2005). *Gender, nature, and nurture* (2nd ed.). Hillsdale, NJ: Erlbaum.

Lippé, R., Perchet, C., & Lassonde, M. (2007). Electrophysical markers of visuocortical development. *Cerebral Cortex, 17,* 100–107.

Liu, A., Wollstein, A., Hysi, P., Ankra-Badu, G., Spector, T., Park, D., et al. (2010). Digital quantification of human eye color highlights: Genetic association of three new loci. *Public Library of Science: Genetics, 6,* e1000934.

Liu, D., Wellman, H., Tardif, T., & Sabbagh, M. (2008). Theory of mind development in Chinese children: A meta-analysis of false-belief understanding across cultures and languages. *Developmental Psychology, 44,* 523–531.

Liu, J., Raine, A., Venables, P., & Mednick, S. (2004). Malnutrition at age 3 years and externalizing behavior problems at ages 8, 11, and 17 years. *American Journal of Psychiatry, 161,* 2005–2013.

Livesley, W. J., & Bromley, D. B. (1973). *Person perception in childhood and adolescence.* London: Wiley.

Livingstone, S., & Helsper, E. (2006). Does advertising literacy mediate the effects of advertising on children? A critical examination of two linked research literatures in relation to obesity and food choice. *Journal of Communication, 56,* 560–584.

Locuniak, M., & Jordan, N. (2008). Using kindergarten number sense to predict calculation fluency in second grade. *Journal of Learning Disabilities, 41,* 459.

Loeb, S., Fuller, B., Kagan, S., & Carrol, B. (2004). Child care in poor communities: Early learning effects of type, quality, and stability. *Child Development, 75,* 47–65.

Loehlin, J. C., Horn, J. M., & Willerman, L. (1994). Differential inheritance of mental abilities in the Texas Adoption Project. *Intelligence, 19,* 324–336.

Loftus, E. (1993). The reality of repressed memories. *American Psychologist, 48,* 518–537.

Lopes, P., Nezlek, J., Extremera, N., Hertel, J., Fernandez-Berrocal, P., Schütz, A., et al. (2011). Emotion regulation and the quality of social interaction: Does the ability to evaluate emotional situations and identify effective responses matter? *Journal of Personality, 79,* 429–467.

Loran-Royer, S., Munch, C., Mescle, H., & Lieury, A. (2010). Kawashima vs "Super Mario"? Should a game be serious in order to stimulate cognitive aptitudes? *European Review of Applied Psychology, 60,* 221–232.

Louhiala, P. J., Jaakkola, N., Ruotsalainen, R., & Jaakkola, J. J. K. (1995). Form of day care and respiratory infections among Finnish children. *American Journal of Public Health, 85,* 1109–1112.

Love, J., Harrison, L., Sagi-Schwartz, A., van IJzendoorn, M., Ross, C., Ungerer, J., Raikes, H., Brady-Smith, C., Boller, K., Brooks-Gunn, J., Constantine, J., Kisker, E., Paulsell, D., & Chazan-Cohen, R. (2003). Child care quality matters: How conclusions may vary with context. *Child Development, 74,* 1021–1033.

Lubart, T. (2003). In search of creative intelligence. In R. Sternberg & T. Lubart (Eds.), *Models of intelligence: International perspective* (pp. 279–292). Washington, DC: American Psychological Association.

Lucas, R., & Donnellan, B. (2011, in press). Personality development across the life span: Longitudinal analyses with a national sample from Germany. *Journal of Personality and Social Psychology.*

Lucas-Thompson, R., Goldberg, W., & Prause, J. (2010). Maternal work early in the lives of children and its distal associations with achievement and behavior problems: A meta-analysis. *Psychological Bulletin, 136,* 915–942.

Lüdtke, O., Trautwein, N., & Köller, O. (2004). A validation of the NEO-FFI in a sample of young adults: Effects of the response format, factorial validity, and relations with indicators of academic achievement. *Diagnostica, 50,* 134–144.

Luna, B., Garver, K., Urban, T., Lazar, N., & Sweeney, J. (2004). Maturation of cognitive processes from late childhood to adulthood. *Child Development, 75,* 1357–1372.

Lundberg, I. (2009). Early precursors and enabling skills of reading acquisition. *Scandinavian Journal of Psychology, 50,* 611–616.

Luster, T., Lekskul, K., & Oh, S. (2004). Predictors of academic motivation in first grade among children born to low-income adolescent mothers. *Early Childhood Research Quarterly, 19,* 337–353.

Luster, T., & McAdoo, H. P. (1995). Factors related to self-esteem among African American youths: A secondary analysis of the High/Scope Perry Preschool data. *Journal of Research on Adolescence, 5,* 451–467.

Luster, T., & McAdoo, H. P. (1996). Family and child influences on educational attainment: A secondary analysis of the High/Scope Perry Preschool data. *Developmental Psychology, 32,* 26–39.

Luyckx, K., Tildesley, E., Soenens, B., & Andrews, J. (2011). Parenting and trajectories of children's malaptive behaviors: A 12-year prospective community study. *Journal of Clinical Child and Adolescent Psychology, 40,* 468–478.

Lynch, S., & Warner, L. (2004). Computer use in preschools: Directors' reports of the state of the practice. *Early Childhood Research and Practice, 6*. Retrieved July 26, 2011, from http://ecrp.uiuc.edu/V6n2/lynch.html

Lynn, R. (1998). New data on black infant precocity. *Personality and Individual Differences, 25,* 801–804.

Lyon, T. D., & Flavell, J. H. (1994). Young children's understanding of "remember" and "forget." *Child Development, 65,* 1357–1371.

Lyons, N. P. (1983). Two perspectives: On self, relationships, and morality. *Harvard Educational Review, 53,* 125–145.

Lytton, H., & Romney, D. M. (1991). Parents' differential socialization of boys and girls: A meta-analysis. *Psychological Bulletin, 109,* 267–296.

Ma, H. (2003). The relation of moral orientation and moral judgment to prosocial and antisocial behaviour of Chinese adolescents. *International Journal of Psychology, 38,* 101–111.

Maas, F. (2008). Children's understanding of promising, lying, and false belief. *Journal of General Psychology, 135,* 301–321.

McAlister, A., & Peterson, C. (2007). A longitudinal study of child siblings and theory of mind development. *Cognitive Development, 22,* 258–270.

Maccoby, E. E. (1980). *Social development: Psychological growth and the parent-child relationship.* New York: Harcourt Brace Jovanovich.

Maccoby, E. E. (1984). Middle childhood in the context of the family. In W. A. Collins (Ed.), *Development during middle childhood: The years from six to twelve* (pp. 184–239). Washington, DC: National Academy Press.

Maccoby, E. E. (1988). Gender as a social category. *Developmental Psychology, 24,* 755–765.

Maccoby, E. E. (1990). Gender and relationships: A developmental account. *American Psychologist, 45,* 513–520.

Maccoby, E. E. (1995). The two sexes and their social systems. In P. Moen, G. H. Elder, Jr., & K. Luscher (Eds.), *Examining lives in context: Perspectives on the ecology of human development* (pp. 347–364). Washington, DC: American Psychological Association.

Maccoby, E. E. (2002). Gender and group process: A developmental perspective. *Current Directions in Psychological Science, 11,* 54–58.

Maccoby, E. E., & Jacklin, C. N. (1987). Gender segregation in childhood. In H. W. Reese (Ed.), *Advances in child development and behavior* (Vol. 20, pp. 239–288). Orlando, FL: Academic Press.

Maccoby, E. E., & Martin, J. A. (1983). Socialization in the context of the family: Parent-child interaction. In E. M. Hetherington (Ed.), *Handbook of child psychology: Socialization, personality, and social development* (Vol. 4, pp. 1–102). New York: Wiley.

MacDonald, K. (1992). Warmth as a developmental construct: An evolutionary analysis. *Child Development, 63,* 753–773.

MacFarlane, A. (1977). *The psychology of child birth.* Cambridge, MA: Harvard University Press.

MacIver, D., Reuman, D., & Main, S. (1995). Social structuring of the school: Studying what is, illuminating what could be. *Annual Review of Psychology, 46,* 375–400.

MacLean, M., Bryant, P., & Bradley, L. (1987). Rhymes, nursery rhymes, and reading in early childhood. *Merrill-Palmer Quarterly, 33,* 255–281.

Macrae, N., & Quadflieg, S. (2010). Perceiving people. In S. Fiske, D. Gilbert, & G. Lindzey (Eds.), *The handbook of social psychology* (5th ed., pp. 428–463). Hoboken, NJ: John Wiley & Sons.

MacWhinney, B. (2011). Language development. In M. Bornstein & M. Lamb (Eds.), *Developmental science: An advanced textbook* (page numbers in press). New York: Psychology Press.

Madsen, K., Hviid, A., Vestergaard, M., Schendel, D., Wohlfahrt, J., Thorsen, P., Olsen, J., & Melbye, M. (2002). A population-based study of measles, mumps, rubella vaccination and autism. *New England Journal of Medicine, 347,* 1477–1482.

Madsen, K., Lauritsen, M., Pederson, C., Thorsen, P., Plesner, A., Andersen, P., & Mortensen, P. (2003). Thimerosal and the occurrence of autism: Negative ecological evidence from Danish population-based data. *Pediatrics, 112,* 604–606.

Magiera, K., & Zigmond, N. (2005). Co-teaching in middle school classrooms under routine conditions: Does the instructional experience differ for students with disabilities in co-taught and solo-taught classes? *Learning Disabilities Research & Practice, 20,* 79–85.

Mahatmya, D., & Lohman, B. (2011). Predictors of late adolescent delinquency: The protective role of after-school activities in low-income families. *Children and Youth Services Review, 33,* no pagination specified.

Maier, M., Vitiello, V., & Greenfield, D. (2011). A multilevel model of child- and classroom-level psychosocial factors that support language and literacy resilience of children in Head Start. *Early Childhood Research Quarterly,* page numbers in press.

Main, M., & Hesse, E. (1990). Parents' unresolved traumatic experiences are related to infant disorganized attachment status: Is frightened and/or frightening parental behavior the linking mechanism? In M. T. Greenberg, D. Cicchetti, & E. M. Cummings (Eds.), *Attachment in the preschool years: Theory, research, and intervention* (pp. 151–182). Chicago: University of Chicago Press.

Main, M., Hesse, E., & Goldwyn, R. (2008). Studying differences in language usage in recounting attachment history: An introduction to the AAI. In H. Steele & M. Steele (Eds.), *Clinical applications of the Adult Attachment Interview* (pp. 31–68). New York: Guilford Press.

Main, M., Kaplan, N., & Cassidy, J. (1985). Security in infancy, childhood, and adulthood: A move to the level of representation. *Monographs of the Society for Research in Child Development, 50*(Serial No. 209), 66–104.

Main, M., & Solomon, J. (1990). Procedures for identifying infants as disorganized/disoriented during the Ainsworth Strange Situation. In M. T. Greenberg, D. Cicchetti, & E. M. Cummings (Eds.), *Attachment in the preschool years: Theory, research, and intervention* (pp. 121–160). Chicago: University of Chicago Press.

Maitel, S., Dromi, E., Sagi, A., & Bornstein, M. (2000). The Hebrew Communicative Development Inventory: Language-specific properties and cross-linguistic generalizations. *Journal of Child Language, 27,* 43–67.

Malamitsi-Puchner, A., Protonotariou, E., Boutsikou, T., Makrakis, E., Sarandakou, A., & Creatsas, G. (2005). The influence of the mode of delivery on circulating cytokine concentrations in the perinatal period. *Early Human Development, 81,* 387–392.

Malamud, O., & Pop-Eleches, C. (2010). *Home computer use and the development of human capital* (National Bureau of Economic Research Working Paper No. 15814).

Malina, R. M. (1990). Physical growth and performance during the transitional years (9–16). In R. Montemayor, G. R. Adams, & T. P. Gullotta (Eds.), *From childhood to adolescence: A transitional period?* (pp. 41–62). Newbury Park, CA: Sage.

Malina, R. M. (2007). Physical fitness of children and adolescents in the United States: Status and secular change. In G. Tomkinson & T. Olds (Eds.), *Pediatric fitness: Secular trends and geographic variability.* Basel, Switzerland: Karger.

Maniadaki, K., Sonuga-Barke, E., & Kakouros, E. (2005). Parents' causal attributions about attention deficit/hyperactivity disorder: The effect of child and parent sex. *Child: Care, Health & Development, 31,* 331–340.

Mann, D. (2004). *Movie therapy: Using movies for mental health.* Retrieved July 21, 2011, from http://www.cinematherapy.com/pressclippings/tullahomanews.pdf

Manning, W., & Brower, S. (2006). Children's economic well-being in married and cohabiting parent families. *Journal of Marriage and the Family, 68*, 345–362.

Maratsos, M. (1983). Some current issues in the study of the acquisition of grammar. In J. H. Flavell & E. M. Markman (Eds.), *Handbook of child psychology: Cognitive development* (pp. 707–786). New York: Wiley.

Maratsos, M. (1998). The acquisition of grammar. In W. Damon (Ed.), *Handbook of child psychology, Vol. 2: Cognition, perception, and language* (5th ed., pp. 421–466). New York: Wiley.

Maratsos, M. (2000). More overregularizations after all: New data and discussion on Marcus, Pinker, Ullman, Hollander, Rosen, & Xu. *Journal of Child Language, 27*, 183–212.

March of Dimes. (2004). *Environmental risks and pregnancy*. Retrieved September 21, 2004, from http://www.marchofdimes.com/professionals/681_9146.asp

March of Dimes. (2011). *Environmental risks and pregnancy*. Retrieved June 7, 2011, from http://www.marchofdimes.com/pregnancy/stayingsafe_indepth.html

Marcia, J. E. (1966). Development and validation of ego identity status. *Journal of Personality & Social Psychology, 3*, 551–558.

Marcia, J. E. (1980). Identity in adolescence. In J. Adelson (Ed.), *Handbook of adolescent psychology* (pp. 159–187). New York: Wiley.

Marcia, J. E. (2007). Theory and measure: The Identity Status Interview. In M. Watzlawik & A. Born (Eds.), *Capturing identity: Quantitative and qualitative methods* (pp. 1–14). Lanham, MD: University Press of America.

Marcia, J. E. (2010). Life transitions and stress in the context of psychosocial development. In T. Miller (Ed.), *Handbook of stressful transitions across the lifespan* (pp. 19–34). New York: Springer Science & Business Media.

Marcus, G. F., Pinker, S., Ullman, M., Hollander, M., Rosen, T. J. & Fei, X. (1992). Overregularization in language acquisition. *Monographs of the Society for Research in Child Development, 57*(4, Serial No. 228).

Markman, E., Wasow, J., & Hansen, C. (2003). Use of the mutual exclusivity assumption by young word learners. *Cognitive Psychology, 47*, 241–275.

Marrou, H., Tiemeier, H., Steegers, E., Jaddoe, V., Hofman, A., Verhulst, F., et al. (2009). Intrauterine cannabis exposure affects fetal growth trajectories: The Generation R study. *Journal of the American Academy of Child and Adolescent Psychiatry, 48*, 1173–1181.

Marschark, M. (1993). *Psychological development of deaf children*. New York: Oxford University Press.

Marshall, M., Friedman, M., Stall, R., & Thompson, A. (2009). Individual trajectories of substance use in lesbian, gay and bisexual youth and heterosexual youth. *Addiction, 104*, 974–981.

Marshall, N. L., Coll, C. G., Marx, F., McCartney, K., Keefe, N., & Ruh, J. (1997). After-school time and children's behavioral adjustment. *Merrill-Palmer Quarterly, 43*, 497–514.

Martin, C. L. (1991). The role of cognition in understanding gender effects. In H. W. Reese (Ed.), *Advances in child development and behavior* (Vol. 23, pp. 113–150). San Diego, CA: Academic Press.

Martin, C. L. (1993). New directions for investigating children's gender knowledge. *Developmental Review, 13*, 184–204.

Martin, C. L., & Halverson, C. F., Jr. (1981). A schematic processing model of sex typing and stereotyping in children. *Child Development, 52*, 1119–1134.

Martin, C. L., & Halverson, C. F., Jr. (1983). Gender constancy: A methodological and theoretical analysis. *Sex Roles, 9*, 775–790.

Martin, C. L., & Ruble, D. (2004). Children's search for gender cues: Cognitive perspectives on gender development. *Current Directions in Psychological Science, 13*, 67–70.

Martin, C. L., & Ruble, D. (2010). Patterns of gender development. *Annual Review of Psychology, 61*, 353–381.

Martin, E. P., & Martin, J. M. (1978). *The black extended family*. Chicago: University of Chicago Press.

Martin, E. W. (1995). Case studies on inclusion: Worst fears realized. *The Journal of Special Education, 29*, 192–199.

Martin, G., Richardson, A., Bergen, H., Roeger, L., & Allison, S. (2005). Perceived academic performance, self-esteem and locus of control as indicators of need for assessment of adolescent suicide risk: Implications for teachers. *Journal of Adolescence, 28*, 75–87.

Martin, J., & D'Augelli, A. (2003). How lonely are gay and lesbian youth? *Psychological Reports, 93*, 486.

Martin, J., Hamilton, B., Sutton, P., Ventura, S., Mathews, T., Kirmeyer, S., et al. (2010). Births: Final data for 2007. *National Vital Statistics Report, 58*, 1–125.

Martin, J., Hamilton, B., Sutton, P., Ventura, S., Menacker, F., & Kirmeyer, S. (2006). Births: Final data for 2004. *National Vital Statistics Reports, 55*, 1–102.

Martin, J., Hamilton, B., Sutton, P., Ventura, S., Menacker, F., Kirmeyer, S., et al. (2007). Births: Final data for 2005. *National Vital Statistics Reports, 56*, 1–104.

Martin, J., Hamilton, B., Sutton, P., Ventura, S., Menacker, F., & Munson, M. (2005). Births: Final data for 2003. *National Vital Statistics Reports, 54*, 1–116.

Martin, J., & Nguyen, D. (2004). Anthropometric analysis of homosexuals and heterosexuals: Implications for early hormone exposure. *Hormones & Behavior, 45*, 31–39.

Martini, R., & Shore, B. (2008). Pointing to parallels in ability-related differences in the use of metacognition in academic and psychomotor tasks. *Learning and Individual Differences, 18*, 237–247.

Martorano, S. C. (1977). A developmental analysis of performance on Piaget's formal operations tasks. *Developmental Psychology, 13*, 666–672.

Mascolo, M. F., & Fischer, K. W. (1995). Developmental transformations in appraisals for pride, shame, and guilt. In J. P. Tangney & K. W. Fischer (Eds.) *Self-conscious emotions: The psychology of shame, guilt, embarrassment, and pride* (pp. 64–113). New York: Guilford Press.

Mash, C., Novak, E., Berthier, N., & Keen, R. (2006). What do two-year-olds understand about hidden-object events? *Developmental Psychology, 42*, 263–271.

Mason, C. A., Cauce, A. M., Gonzales, N., & Hiraga, Y. (1996). Neither too sweet nor too sour: Problem peers, maternal control, and problem behavior in African American adolescents. *Child Development, 67*, 2115–2130.

Mason, M., & Chuang, S. (2001). Culturally-based after-school arts programming for low-income urban children: Adaptive and preventive effects. *Journal of Primary Prevention, 22*, 45–54.

Massad, C. M. (1981). Sex role identity and adjustment during adolescence. *Child Development, 52*, 1290–1298.

Maszk, P., Eisenberg, N., & Guthrie, I. (1999). Relations of children's social status to their emotionality and regulation: A short-term longitudinal study. *Merrill-Palmer Quarterly, 454*, 468–492.

Matarazzo, J. D. (1992). Biological and physiological correlates of intelligence. *Intelligence, 16*, 257–258.

Mather, P. L., & Black, K. N. (1984). Heredity and environmental influences on preschool twins' language skills. *Developmental Psychology, 20*, 303–308.

Mathews, T., & MacDorman, M. (2010). Infant mortality statistics from the 2006 period: Linked birth/infant death data set. *National Vital Statistics Reports, 58*, 1–32.

Matthews, R. (2006). The case for linguistic nativism. In R. Stainton (Ed.), *Contemporary debates in cognitive science* (pp. 81–96). Malden, MA: Blackwell Publishing.

Maughan, B., Pickles, A., & Quinton, D. (1995). Parental hostility, child-hood behavior, and adult social functioning. In J. McCord (Ed.), *Coercion and punishment in long-term perspectives* (pp. 34–58). Cambridge, England: Cambridge University Press.

Maye, J., Weiss, D., & Aslin, R. (2008). Statistical phonetic learning in infants: Facilitation and feature generalization. *Developmental Science, 11*, 122–134.

Mayeux, L., & Cillissen, A. (2003). Development of social problem solving in early childhood: Stability, change, and associations with social competence. *Journal of Genetic Psychology, 164*, 153–173.

McBride-Chang, C., & Ho, C. (2000). Developmental issues in Chinese children's character acquisition. *Journal of Educational Psychology, 92*, 50–55.

McClure, E. (2000). A meta-analytic review of sex differences in facial expression processing and their development in infants, children, and adolescents. *Psychological Bulletin, 126*, 242–453.

McClure, J., Meyer, L., Garisch, J., Fischer, R., Weir, K., & Walkey, F. (2011). Students' attributions for their best and worst marks: Do they relate to achievement? *Contemporary Educational Psychology, 36*, 71–81.

McCord, J. (1982). A longitudinal view of the relationship between parental absence and crime. In J. Gunn & D. P. Farrington (Eds.), *Abnormal offenders, delinquency, and the criminal justice system* (pp. 113–128). London: Wiley.

McCrae, R. R., & Costa, P. T., Jr. (1994). The stability of personality: Observations and evaluations. *Current Directions in Psychological Science, 3*, 173–175.

McCrae, R. R., & Terracciano, A. (2005). Universal features of personality traits from the observer's perspective: Data from 50 cultures. *Journal of Personality & Social Psychology, 88*, 547–561.

McElhaney, K., Antonishak, J., & Allen, J. (2008). "They like me, they like me not": Popularity and adolescents' perceptions of acceptance predicting social functioning over time. *Child Development, 79*, 720–731.

McGee, B., Hewitt, P., Sherry, S., Parkin, M., & Flett, G. (2005). Perfectionistic self-presentation, body image, and eating disorder symptoms. *Body Image, 2*, 29–40.

McGrath, M., & Sullivan, M. (2002). Birth weight, neonatal morbidities, and school age outcomes in full-term and preterm infants. *Issues in Comprehensive Pediatric Nursing, 25*, 231–254.

McGue, M. (1994). Why developmental psychology should find room for behavior genetics. In C. A. Nelson (Ed.), *The Minnesota symposia on child development* (Vol. 27, pp. 105–119). Hillsdale, NJ: Erlbaum.

McGuire, S., McHale, S. M., & Updegraff, K. (1996). Children's perceptions of the sibling relationship in middle childhood: Connections within and between family relationships. *Personal Relationships, 3*, 229–239.

McIntosh, J., Wells, Y., Smyth, B., & Long, C. (2008). Child-focused and child-inclusive divorce mediation: Comparative outcomes from a prospective study of post-separation adjustment. *Family Court Review, 46*, 105–124.

McLanahan, S. S., & Sandefur, G. (1994). *Growing up with a single parent: What hurts, what helps.* Cambridge, MA: Harvard University Press.

McLoyd, V. C. (1998). Socioeconomic disadvantage and child development. *American Psychologist, 53*, 185–204.

McLoyd, V. C., & Wilson, L. (1991). The strain of living poor: Parenting, social support, and child mental health. In A. C. Huston (Ed.), *Children in poverty: Child development and public policy* (pp. 105–135). Cambridge, England: Cambridge University Press.

McManis, M., Kagan, J., Snidman, N., & Woodward, S. (2002). EEG asymmetry, power, and temperament in children. *Developmental Psychobiology, 41*, 169–177.

McRorie, M., & Cooper, C. (2004). Psychomotor movement and IQ. *Personality & Individual Differences, 37*, 523–531.

de Medina, P., Visser, G., Huizink, A., Buitelaar, J., & Mulder, E. (2003). Fetal behavior does not differ between boys and girls. *Early Human Development, 73*, 17–26.

Medwell, J., & Wray, D. (2007). Handwriting: What do we know and what do we need to know? *Literacy, 41*, 10–15.

Meece, D., & Mize, J. (2010). Multiple aspects of preschool children's social cognition: Relations with peer acceptance and peer interaction style. *Early Child Development and Care, 180*, 585–604.

Mei, Z., Grummer-Strawn, L., Thompson, D., & Dietz, W. (2004). Shifts in percentiles of growth during early childhood: Analysis of longitudinal data from California Child Health and Development Study. *Pediatrics, 113*, 617–627.

Meijer, A., & Wittenboer, G. (2007). Contribution of infants' sleep and crying to marital relationship of first-time parent couples in the first year after childbirth. *Journal of Family Psychology, 21*, 49–57.

Meisinger, E., & Bradley, B. (2008). Classroom practices for supporting fluency development. In M. Kuhn & P. Schwanenflugel (Eds.), *Fluency in the classroom: Solving problems in the teaching of literacy* (pp. 36–54). New York: Guilford Press.

Melby, J. N., & Conger, R. D. (1996). Parental behaviors and adolescent academic performance: A longitudinal analysis. *Journal of Research on Adolescence, 6*, 113–137.

Melot, A., & Houde, O. (1998). Categorization and theories of mind: The case of the appearance/reality distinction. *Cahiers de Psychologie Cognitive/Current Psychology of Cognition, 17*, 71–93.

Melson, G., Peet, S., & Sparks, C. (1991). Children's attachments to their pets: Links to socioemotional development. *Children's Environmental Quarterly, 8*, 55–65.

Meltzoff, A. N. (1995). Understanding the intentions of others: Re-enactment of intended acts by 18-month-old children. *Developmental Psychology, 31*, 838–850.

Menesini, E., Sanchez, V., Fonzi, A., Ortega, R., Costabile, A., & Lo Feudo, G. (2003). Moral emotions and bullying: A cross-national comparison of differences between bullies, victims and outsiders. *Aggressive Behavior, 29*, 515–530.

Mervis, C. B., & Bertrand, J. (1994). Acquisition of the novel name-nameless category (N3C) principle. *Child Development, 65*, 1646–1662.

Merz, E., & McCall, R. (2010). Behavior problems in children adopted from psychosocially depriving institutions. *Journal of Abnormal Child Psychology, 38*, 459–470.

Meyer-Bahlburg, H. F. L., Ehrhardt, A. A., Rosen, L. R., Gruen, R. S., Veridiano, N. P., Vann, F. H., & Neuwalder, H. F. (1995). Prenatal estrogens and the development of homosexual orientation. *Developmental Psychology, 31*, 12–21.

Michiels, D., Grietens, H., Onghena, P., & Kuppens, S. (2010). Perceptions of maternal and paternal attachment security in middle childhood: Links with positive parental affection and psychosocial adjustment. In L. Newland, H. Freeman, & D. Coyl (Eds.), *Emerging topics on father attachment: Considerations in theory, context and development.* London: Routledge.

Mikulincer, M., & Shaver, P. (2005). Attachment security, compassion, and altruism. *Current Directions in Psychological Science, 14*, 34–38.

Miller, B., Benson, B., & Galbraith, K. (2001). Family relationships and adolescent pregnancy risk: A research synthesis. *Developmental Review, 21*, 1–38.

Miller, C., Trautner, H., & Ruble, D. (2006). The role of gender stereo-types in children's preferences and behavior. In L. Balter & C. Tamis-LeMonday (Eds.), *Child psychology: A handbook of contemporary issues* (2nd ed., pp. 293–323). New York: Psychology Press.

Miller, P. (2002). *Theories of development* (4th ed.). New York: Worth.

Milligan, K., Astington, J., & Dack, L. (2007). Language and theory of mind: Meta-analysis of the relation between language ability and false-belief understanding. *Child Development, 78*, 622–646.

Mills, D., Coffey-Corina, S., & Neville, H. (1994). Variability in cerebral organization during primary language acquisition. In G. Dawson & K. Fischer (Eds.), *Human behavior and the developing brain*. New York: Guilford.

Milos, G., Spindler, A., & Schnyder, U. (2004). Psychiatric comorbid-ity and Eating Disorder Inventory (EDI) profiles in eating disorder patients. *Canadian Journal of Psychiatry, 49*, 179–184.

Milos, G., Spindler, A., Ruggiero, G., Klaghofer, R., & Schnyder, U. (2002). Comorbidity of obsessive-compulsive disorders and duration of eating disorders. *International Journal of Eating Disorders, 31*, 284–289.

*Mini fetal monitor saves lives: High risk pregnancy specialists design fetal device to more closely monitor baby and mother*. (January 1, 2009). Retrieved June 7, 2011, from http://www.sciencedaily.com/videos/2009/0103-mini_fetal_monitor_saves_lives.htm

Minzi, M. (2010). Gender and cultural patterns of mothers' and fathers' attachment and links with children's self-competence, depression and loneliness in middle and late childhood. *Early Child Development and Care, 180*, 193–209.

Mio, J. (2010). On becoming an Asian American man: My journey through adulthood. In W. Liu, D. Iwamotor, & M. Chae (Eds.), *Culturally responsive counseling with Asian American men* (pp. 319–336). New York: Routledge/Taylor & Francis Group.

Mischel, W. (1966). A social learning view of sex differences in behavior. In E. E. Maccoby (Ed.), *The development of sex differences* (pp. 56–81). Stanford, CA: Stanford University Press.

Mischel, W. (1970). Sex typing and socialization. In P. H. Mussen (Ed.), *Carmichael's manual of child psychology* (Vol. 2, pp. 3–72). New York: Wiley.

Mischel, W. (2007). Toward a cognitive social learning reconceptualization of personality. In Y. Shoda, D. Cervone, & G. Downey (Eds.), *Persons in context: Building a science of the individual*. New York: Guilford Press.

Mishra, R. C. (2001). Cognition across cultures. In D. Matsumoto (Ed.), *Handbook of culture and psychology* (pp. 119–135). New York: Oxford University Press.

Misra, G. (1983). Deprivation and development: A review of Indian studies. *Indian Educational Review, 18*, 12–32.

Mitchell, A. (2002). Infertility treatment: More risks and challenges. *New England Journal of Medicine, 346*, 769–770.

Mitchell, K. (2002). Women's morality: A test of Carol Gilligan's theory. *Journal of Social Distress & the Homeless, 11*, 81–110.

Mitchell, P. R., & Kent, R. D. (1990). Phonetic variation in multisyllable babbling. *Journal of Child Language, 17*, 247–265.

Mittra, A., Choudhari, N., & Zadgaonkar, A. (2009). System simulation for a novel fetal monitoring methodology. *International Journal of Engineering Systems Modeling and Simulation, 1*, 92–100.

Moffitt, T. (2007). A review of research on the taxonomy of life-course persistent versus adolescence-limited antisocial behavior. In D. Flan-nery, A. Vazsonyi, & I. Waldman (Eds.), *The Cambridge handbook of violent behavior and aggression* (pp. 49–74). New York: Cambridge University Press.

Moffitt, T. E. (1990). Juvenile delinquency and attention deficit disorder: Boys' developmental trajectories from age 3 to age 15. *Child Development, 61*, 893–910.

Moffitt, T. E. (1993). Adolescence-limited and life-course-persistent anti-social behavior: A developmental taxonomy. *Psychology Review, 100*, 674–701.

Moffitt, T. E., & Harrington, H. L. (1996). Delinquency: The natural history of antisocial behavior. In P. A. Silva & W. R. Stanton (Eds.), *From child to adult: The Dunedin multidisciplinary health and development study* (pp. 163–185). Aukland: Oxford University Press.

Mogro-Wilson, C. (2008). The influence of parental warmth and control on Latino adolescent alcohol use. *Hispanic Journal of Behavioral Sciences, 30*, 89–105.

Mohanty, A., & Perregaux, C. (1997). Language acquisition and bilin-gualism. In J. Berry, P. Dasen, & T. Saraswathi (Eds.), *Handbook of cross-cultural psychology: Vol. 2. Basic processes and human development*. Boston: Allyn & Bacon.

Mohsin, M., Wong, F., Bauman, A., & Bai, J. (2003). Maternal and neonatal factors influencing premature birth and low birth weight in Australia. *Journal of Biosocial Science, 35*, 161–174.

Moilanen, B. (2004). Vegan diets in infants, children, and adolescents. *Pediatrics in Review, 25*, 174–176.

van der Molen, M., & Molenaar, P. (1994). Cognitive psychophysiol-ogy: A window to cognitive development and brain maturation. In G. Dawson & K. Fischer (Eds.), *Human behavior and the developing brain*. New York: Guilford.

Molfese, V. J., DiLalla, L. F., & Bunce, D. (1997). Prediction of the intel-ligence test scores of 3- to 8-year-old children by home environment, socioeconomic status, and biomedical risks. *Merrill-Palmer Quarterly, 43*, 219–234.

Monga, M. (2007). Managers' moral reasoning: Evidence from large Indian manufacturing organisations. *Journal of Business Ethics, 71*, 179–194.

Montemayor, R., & Eisen, M. (1977). The development of self-conceptions from childhood to adolescence. *Developmental Psychology, 13*, 314–319.

Montgomery, M., & Sorell, G. (1998). Love and dating experience in early and middle adolescence: Grade and gender comparisons. *Journal of Adolescence, 21*, 677–689.

Moody, E. (1997). Lessons from pair counseling with incarcerated juvenile delinquents. *Journal of Addictions & Offender Counseling, 18*, 10–25.

Moore, C., Barresi, J., & Thompson, C. (1998). The cognitive basis of future-oriented prosocial behavior. *Social Development, 7*, 198–218.

Moore, D. (2001). Reassessing emotion recognition performance in people with mental retardation: A review. *American Journal on Mental Retardation, 106*, 481–502.

Moore, E. G. J. (1986). Family socialization and the IQ test performance of traditionally and transracially adopted black children. *Developmental Psychology, 22*, 317–326.

Moore, E., & Rideout, V. (2007). The online marketing of food to children: Is it just fun and games? *Journal of Public Policy and Marketing, 26*, 202–220.

Moore, K. L., & Persaud, T. V. N. (1993). *The developing human: Clinically oriented embryology* (5th ed.). Philadelphia: Saunders.

Moore, R., Vadeyar, S., Fulford, J., Tyler, D., Gribben, C., Baker, P., James, D., & Gowland, P. (2001). Antenatal determination of fetal brain activity in response to an acoustic stimulus using functional magnetic resonance imaging. *Human Brain Mapping, 12*, 94–99.

Moorman, E., & Pomerantz, E. (2010). Ability mindsets influence the quality of mothers' involvement in children's learning: An experimental investigation. *Developmental Psychology, 46*, 1354–1362.

Morgan, C., Finan, A., Yarnold, R., Petersen, S., Horsfield, M., Rickett, A., & Wailoo, M. (2002). Assessment of infant physiology and neuronal development using magnetic resonance imaging. *Child: Care, Health, & Development, 28*, 7–10.

Morral, S., Gobbo, C., Marini, Z., & Sheese, R. (2008). *Cognitive development: Neo-Piagetian perspectives.* New York: Taylor & Francis Erlbaum.

Morris, T., & Leavey, G. (2006). Promoting phonological awareness in nursery-aged children through a Sure Start Early Listening programme. *International Journal of Early Years Education, 14,* 155–168.

Morrison, D. R., & Cherlin, A. J. (1995). The divorce process and young children's well-being: A prospective analysis. *Journal of Marriage and the Family, 57,* 800–812.

Morrison, F., Bachman, H., & Connor, C. (2005). *Improving literacy in America: Guidelines from research.* New Haven, CT: Yale University Press.

Morrison, F. J., Smith, L., & Dow-Ehrensberger, M. (1995). Education and cognitive development: A natural experiment. *Developmental Psychology, 31,* 789–799.

Morrissey, T., Dunifon, R., & Kalil, A. (2011). Maternal employment, work schedules, and children's body mass index. *Child Development, 82,* 66–81.

Morrongiello, B. A. (1988). Infants' localization of sounds along the horizontal axis: Estimates of minimum audible angle. *Developmental Psychology, 24,* 8–13.

Morrongiello, B. A., Fenwick, K. D., & Chance, G. (1990). Sound localization acuity in very young infants: An observer-based testing procedure. *Developmental Psychology, 26,* 75–84.

Morrow, R. (2005). *Sesame Street and the reform of children's television.* Baltimore: Johns Hopkins University Press.

Morse, P. A., & Cowan, N. (1982). Infant auditory and speech perception. In T. M. Field, A. Houston, H. C. Quay, L. Troll, & G. E. Finley (Eds.), *Review of human development* (pp. 32–61). New York: Wiley.

Mortensen, E., Andresen, J., Kruuse, E., Sanders, S., & Reinisch, J. (2003). IQ stability: The relation between child and young adult intelligence test scores in low-birthweight samples. *Scandinavian Journal of Psychology, 44,* 395–398.

Mortimer, J., & Harley, C. (2002). The quality of work and youth mental health. *Work & Occupations, 29,* 166–197.

Mortimer, J., Zimmer-Gembeck, M., Holmes, M., & Shanahan, M. (2002). The process of occupational decision making: Patterns during the transition to adulthood. *Journal of Vocational Behavior, 61,* 439–465.

Moseley, K., Freed, G., & Goold, S. (2011). Which sources of child health advice do parents follow? *Clinical Pediatrics, 50,* 50–56.

Moses, L., Baldwin, D., Rosicky, J., & Tidball, G. (2001). Evidence for referential understanding in the emotions domain at twelve and eighteen months. *Child Development, 72,* 718–735.

Moshman, D. (2005). *Rationality, morality, and identity.* Hillsdale, NJ: Erlbaum.

Mott, J., Crowe, P., Richardson, J., & Flay, B. (1999). After-school supervision and adolescent cigarette smoking: Contributions of the setting and intensity of after-school self-care. *Journal of Behavioral Medicine, 22,* 35–58.

Mounts, N., & Steinberg, L. (1995). An ecological analysis of peer influence on adolescent grade point average and drug use. *Developmental Psychology, 31,* 915–922.

Mueller, U., Overton, W., & Reene, K. (2001). Development of conditional reasoning: A longitudinal study. *Journal of Cognition & Development, 2,* 27–49.

Muhuri, P. K., Anker, M., & Bryce, J. (1996). Treatment patterns for childhood diarrhoea: Evidence from demographic and health surveys. *Bulletin of the World Health Organization, 74,* 135–146.

Munakata, Y. (2006). Information processing approaches to cognitive development. In W. Damon, R. Lerner, D. Kuhn, & R. Sieglers (Eds.). *Handbook of child psychology, Volume 2, Cognition, Perception, and Language* (6th ed.). (pp. 426–465). New York: John Wiley & Sons.

Munir, K., & Beardslee, W. (2001). A developmental and psychobiological framework for understanding the role of culture in child and adolescent psychiatry. *Child & Adolescent Psychiatric Clinics of North America, 10,* 667–677.

Muraskas, J., & Hasson, A. (2004). A girl with a birth weight of 280 g, now 14 years old. *New England Journal of Medicine, 324,* 1598–1599.

Murphy, S. O. (1993, April). *The family context and the transition to siblinghood: Strategies parents use to influence sibling-infant relationships.* Paper presented at the biennial meetings of the Society for Research in Child Development, New Orleans.

Murray, J., Liotti, M., Ingmundson, P., Mayberg, H., Pu, U., Zamarripa, F., Liu, Y., Woldorff, M., Gao, J., & Fox, P. (2006). Children's brain activations while viewing televised violence revealed by MRO. *Media Psychology, 8,* 25–37.

Murray, J., & Youniss, J. (1968). Achievement of inferential transitivity and its relation to serial ordering. *Child Development, 39,* 1259–1268.

Murray, L., Woolgar, M., Martins, C., Christaki, A., Hipwell, A., & Cooper, P. (2006). Conversations around homework: Links to parental mental health, family characteristics and child psychological functioning. *British Journal of Developmental Psychology, 24,* 125–149.

Must, O., Must, A., & Raudik, V. (2003). The secular rise in IQs: In Estonia, the Flynn effect is not a Jensen effect. *Intelligence, 31,* 461–471.

Must, O., te Njienhuis, J., Must, A., & van Vianen, A. (2009). Comparablity of IQ scores over time. *Intelligence, 37,* 25–33.

Nagy, E., & Molnar, P. (2004). Homo imitans or homo provocans? Human imprinting model of neonatal imitation. *Infant Behavior and Development, 27,* 54–63.

Nagy, G., Watt, H., Eccles, J., Trautwein, U., Ludtke, O., & Baumer, J. (2010). The development of students' mathematics self-concept in relation to gender: Different countries, different trajectories? *Journal of Research on Adolescence, 20,* 482–506.

Naito, A. (2007). Internet suicide in Japan: Implications for child and adolescent mental health. *Clinical Child Psychology and Psychiatry, 12,* 583–597.

Narvaez, D. (1998). The influence of moral schemas on the reconstruction of moral narratives in eighth graders and college students. *Journal of Educational Psychology, 47,* 218–228.

National Abortion and Reproductive Rights Action League (NARAL). (1997). *Limitations on the rights of pregnant women* [NARAL Factsheet]. Retrieved March 5, 2001, from http://www.naral.org/publications/facts

National Association for the Education of Young Children (NAEYC). (2009). *Developmentally appropriate practice in early childhood programs serving children from birth through age 8.* Retrieved September 10, 2011, from http://www.naeyc.org/files/naeyc/file/positions/position%20statement%20Web.pdf

National Center for Education Statistics (NCES). (2003). *Highlights from the TIMSS 1999 video study of eighth-grade mathematics teaching* (NCES Publication No. 2003011). Washington, DC: Author.

National Center for Education Statistics (NCES). (2008). *The condition of education 2008.* Retrieved June 27, 2008, from http:// nces.ed.gov/programs/coe/

National Center for Education Statistics (NCES). (2009). *Homeschooling.* Retrieved July 26, 2011, from http://nces.ed.gov/programs/coe/indicator_hsc.asp

National Center for Education Statistics (NCES). (2011a). *The condition of education.* Retrieved July 13, 2011, from http://nces.ed.gov/programs/coe/

National Center for Education Statistics (NCES). (2011b). *Digest of education statistics.* Retrieved July 26, 2011, from http://nces.ed.gov/programs/digest/d10/

National Center for Health Statistics (NCHS). (2007). *Prevalence of overweight among children and adolescents: United States 2003–2004*. Retrieved June 19, 2007, from http://www.cdc.gov/nchs/products/pubs/pubd/hestats/overweight/overwght_child_03.htm

National Center for Health Statistics (NCHS). (2010). *Health, United States, 2009*. Retrieved July 27, 2010, from http://www.cdc.gov/nchs/data/hus/hus09.pdf#009

National Center for Injury Prevention and Control (NCIPC). (2009). *Five leading causes of nonfatal unintentional injury, United States 2009*. Retrieved August 29, 2011, from http://webappa.cdc.gov/cgi-bin/broker.exe

National Center for Injury Prevention and Control (NCIPC). (2011). *Data & statistics (WISQARS)*. Retrieved September 10, 2011, from http://www.cdc.gov/injury/wisqars/index.html

National Institute for Child Health and Human Development (NICHD). (2010). *Back to sleep public education campaign*. Retrieved July 10, 2010, from http://www.nichd.nih.gov/sids/

National Institute of Mental Health (NIMH). (2001). NIMH research roundtable on prepubertal bipolar disorder. *Journal of the American Academy of Child & Adolescent Psychiatry, 40,* 871–878.

National Literacy Trust. (2003). *Mother tongues: What languages are spoken in the UK?* Retrieved July 9, 2005, from http://www.literacytrust.org.uk/Research/lostop3.html

National Middle School Association (NMSA). (2004). *Small schools and small learning communities*. Retrieved June 22, 2007, from http://www.nmsa.org/AboutNMSA/PositionStatements/SmallSchools/tabid/293/Default.aspx

Needlman, R. D. (1996). Growth and development. In R. E. Behrman, R. M. Kliegman, & A. M. Arvin (Eds.), *Nelson textbook of pediatrics* (15th ed., pp. 30–72). Philadelphia: Saunders.

Neisser, U., Boodoo, G., Bouchard, T. J., Jr., Boykin, A. W., Brody, N., Ceci, S. J., Halpern, D. F., Loehlin, J. C., Perloff, R., Sternberg, R. J., & Urbina, S. (1996). Intelligence: Knowns and unknowns. *American Psychologist, 51,* 77–101.

Nelson, C., de Haan, M., & Thomas, K. (2006). *Neuroscience of cognitive development: The role of experience and the developing brain.* New York: Wiley.

Nelson, K. (1977). Facilitating children's syntax acquisition. *Developmental Psychology, 13,* 101–107.

Nelson, K. (1985). *Making sense: The acquisition of shared meaning.* New York: Academic Press.

Nelson, K. (1988). Constraints on word learning. *Cognitive Development, 3,* 221–246.

Nelson, S. (1980). Factors influencing young children's use of motives and outcomes as moral criteria. *Child Development, 51,* 823–829.

Nesdale, D., Durkin, K., Maass, A., & Griffiths, J. (2005). Threat, group identification, and children's ethnic prejudice. *Social Development, 14,* 189–205.

Netherlands Twin Register. (2010). *More NTR information*. Retrieved July 3, 2010, from http://www.tweelingenregister.org/index_uk.html

Nettelbeck, T., & Wilson, C. (2004). The Flynn effect: Smarter not faster. *Intelligence, 32,* 85–93.

Neufeld, G., & Maté, G. (2005). *Hold on to your kids: Why parents need to matter more than peers.* New York: Ballantine Books.

Neumark-Sztainer, D., Wall, M., Eisenberg, M., Story, M., & Hannan, P. (2006). Overweight status and weight control behaviors in adolescents: Longitudinal and secular trends from 1999 to 2004. *Preventive Medicine, 43,* 52–59.

Newcomb, A. F., & Bagwell, C. L. (1995). Children's friendship relations: A meta-analytic review. *Psychological Bulletin, 117,* 306–347.

Newcomb, A. F., Bukowski, W. M., & Pattee, L. (1993). Children's peer relations: A meta-analytic review of popular, rejected, neglected, controversial, and average sociometric status. *Psychological Bulletin, 113,* 99–128.

New Zealand Ministry of Education. (2003). *Homeschooling in 2003.* Retrieved June 23, 2004, from http://www.minedu.govt.nz/index.cfm?layout=document&documentid=6893&indexid=6852&indexparentid=5611

Newman, R. (2005). The cocktail party effect in infants revisited: Listening to one's name in noise. *Developmental Psychology, 41,* 352–362.

Ni, Y., Chiu, M., & Cheng, Z. (2010). Chinese children learning mathematics: From home to school. In M. Bond (Ed.), *The Oxford handbook of psychology* (pp. 143–154). New York: Oxford University Press.

NICHD Early Child Care Research Network. (2003). Does amount of time spent in child care predict socioemotional adjustment during the transition to kindergarten? *Child Development, 74,* 976–1005.

NICHD Early Child Care Research Network. (2004). Are child developmental outcomes related to before- and after-school care arrangements? Results from the NICHD Study of Early Child Care. *Child Development, 75,* 280–295.

NICHD Early Child Care Research Network. (2006). *The NICHD study of early child care and youth development.* Retrieved September 6, 2008, from http://www.nichd.nih.gov/publications/pubs/upload/seccyd_051206.pdf

Nichikawa, S., Hägglöf, B., & Sundbom, E. (2010). Contributions of attachment and self-concept on internalizing and externalizing problems among Japanese adolescents. *Journal of Child and Family Studies, 19,* 334–342.

Nicholas, J., & Geers, A. (2006). When will they catch up? The role of age at cochlear implantation in the spoken language development of children with severe to profound hearing loss. *Journal of Speech, Language, and Hearing Research, 50,* 1048–1062.

Nicholas, J., & Geers, A. (2008). Expected test scores for preschoolers with a cochlear implant who use spoken language. *American Journal of Speech-Language Pathology, 17,* 121–138.

Nicholls, C. (2005). Death by a thousand cuts: Indigenous language bilingual education programmes in the northern territory of Australia, 1972–1998. *International Journal of Bilingual Education & Bilingualism, 8,* 160–177.

Nicklaus, S., Boggio, V., & Issanchou, S. (2005). Gustatory perceptions in children. *Archives of Pediatrics, 12,* 579–584.

Nicolis, H. (2007). Nonlinear dynamics and probabilistic behavior of adolescent suicidal outbreaks. *Nonlinear Dynamics, Psychology, and Life Sciences, 11,* 451–472.

Nijhuis, J. (2003). Fetal behavior. *Neurobiology of Aging, 24,* S41–S46.

Niller, E. (2011). *Facebook can serve as personality test*. Retrieved July 13, 2011, from http://abcnews.go.com/Technology/facebook-serve-personality-test/story?id=13592118

Nilsson, E., Gillberg, C., Gillberg, I., & Rastam, M. (1999). Ten-year follow-up of adolescent-onset anorexia nervosa: Personality disorders. *Journal of the American Academy of Child and Adolescent Psychiatry, 38,* 1389–1395.

Nisan, M., & Kohlberg, L. (1982). Universality and variation in moral judgment: A longitudinal and cross-sectional study in Turkey. *Child Development, 53,* 865–876.

Nolen-Hoeksema, S. (1994). An interactive model for the emergence of gender differences in depression in adolescence. *Journal of Research on Adolescence, 4,* 519–534.

Nomaguchi, K. (2006). Maternal employment, nonparental care, mother-child interactions, and child outcomes during preschool years. *Journal of Marriage and Family, 68,* 1341–1369.

Nóra, S. (2009). Attitude towards mathematics among Chinese and Hungarian secondary school students. *Magyar Pszichológiai Szemlei, 64,* 157–177.

Northwest Educational Technology Consortium (NETC). (2011). *Early connections: Technology in early childhood education.* Retrieved July 26, 2011, from http://www.netc.org/earlyconnections/techconnections.html

Norton, A., & D'Ambrosio, B. (2008). ZPC and ZPD: Zones of teaching and learning. *Journal for Research in Mathematics Education, 39,* 220–246.

Norwood, M. K. (1997, April). *Academic achievement in African-American adolescents as a function of family structure and child-rearing practices.* Paper presented at the biennial meetings of the Society for Research in Child Development, Washington, DC.

Nunner-Winkler, G. (2007). Development of moral motivation from childhood to early adulthood. *Journal of Moral Education, 36,* 399–414.

Nussbaum, A., & Steele, C. (2007). Situational disengagement and persistence in the face of adversity. *Journal of Experimental Social Psychology, 43,* 127–134.

Oates, J. (1998). Risk factors for infant attrition and low engagement in experiments and free play. *Infant Behavior and Development, 21,* 555–569.

Office of Juvenile Justice and Delinquency Prevention. (2006). *Juvenile offenders and victims: 2006 report.* Retrieved April 12, 2008, from http://ojjdp.ncjrs.gov/ojstatbb/nr2006/index.html

Ogbu, J. U. (1994). From cultural differences to differences in cultural frame of reference. In P. M. Greenfield & R. R. Cocking (Eds.), *Cross-cultural roots of minority child development* (pp. 365–391). Hillsdale, NJ: Erlbaum.

Ogbu, J. U. (2004). Collective identity and the burden of "acting white" in black history, community, and education. *Urban Review, 36,* 1–35.

Ogden, C., & Carroll, M. (2010). *Prevalence of obesity among children and adolescents: United States, trends 1963–1965 through 2007–2008.* Retrieved August 6, 2010, from http://www.cdc.gov/nchs/data/hestat/obesity_child_07_08/obesity_child_07_08.pdf

Oldehinkel, A., & Bouma, E. (2011). Sensitivity to the depressogeni effect of stress and HPA-axis reactivity in adolescence: A review of gender differences. *Neuroscience and Biobehavioral Reviews, 35,* 1757–1770.

Oldenburg, C., & Kerns, K. (1997). Associations between peer relationships and depressive symptoms: Testing moderator effects of gender and age. *Journal of Early Adolescence, 17,* 319–337.

O'Leary, S., Smith Slep, A., & Reid, M. (1999). A longitudinal study of mothers' overreactive discipline and toddlers' externalizing behavior. *Journal of Abnormal Child Psychology, 27,* 331–341.

Olfman, S. (2006). Introduction. In S. Olfman (Ed.), *No child left different* (pp. 1–14). Westport, CT: Greenwood Publishers.

Olivan, G. (2003). Catch-up growth assessment in long-term physically neglected and emotionally abused preschool age male children. *Child Abuse & Neglect, 27,* 103–108.

Olshan, A. F., Baird, P. A., & Teschke, K. (1989). Paternal occupational exposures and the risk of Down syndrome. *American Journal of Human Genetics, 44,* 646–651.

Olthof, T., Ferguson, T., Bloemers, E., & Deij, M. (2004). Morality- and identity-related antecedents of children's guilt and shame attributions in events involving physical illness. *Cognition & Emotion, 18,* 383–404.

Olweus, D. (1995). Bullying or peer abuse at school: Facts and intervention. *Current Directions in Psychological Science, 4,* 196–200.

Omer, S. (2011). *Birthday wish: 'Lost boys' pin hopes on independent South Sudan.* Retrieved July 21, 2011, from http://www.msnbc.msn.com/id/43657361/ns/world_news-africa/t/birthday-wish-lost-boys-pin-hopes-independent-south-sudan/

Ompad, D., Strathdee, S., Celentano, D., Latkin, C., Poduska, J., Kellam, S., & Ialongo, N. (2006). Predictors of early initiation of vaginal and oral sex among urban young adults in Baltimore, Maryland. *Archives of Sexual Behavior, 35,* 53–65.

O'Neill, D. K., Astington, J. W., & Flavell, J. H. (1992). Young children's understanding of the role that sensory experiences play in knowledge acquisition. *Child Development, 63,* 474–490.

Ontai, L., & Thompson, R. (2008). Attachment, parent-child discourse, and theory-of-mind development. *Social Development, 17,* 47–60.

Oosterlaan, J., Geurts, H., Knol, D., & Sergeant, J. (2005). Low basal salivary cortisol is associated with teacher-reported symptoms of conduct disorder. *Psychiatry Research, 134,* 1–10.

Organization for Economic Cooperation and Development. (2010). *Living arrangements of children.* Retrieved August 1, 2010, from http://www.oecd.org/dataoecd/63/5/41919559.pdf

Organization of Teratology Information Specialists. (2005). *Acetaminophen and pregnancy.* Retrieved June 7, 2007, from http://www.otispregnancy.org/pdf/acetaminophen.pdf

Ornoy, A. (2002). The effects of alcohol and illicit drugs on the human embryo and fetus. *Israel Journal of Psychiatry & Related Sciences, 39,* 120–132.

O'Shea, T. M., Klinepeter, K. L., Goldstein, D. J., Jackson, B. W., & Dillard, R. G. (1997). Survival and developmental disability in infants with birth weights of 501 to 800 grams, born between 1979 and 1994. *Pediatrics, 100,* 982–986.

Osofsky, J. D. (1995). The effects of exposure to violence on young children. *American Psychologist, 50,* 782–788.

Osorio-O'Dea, P. (2001). *CRS report for Congress: Bilingual education.* Retrieved June 23, 2008, from http://www.policyalmanac.org/education/archive/bilingual.pdf

Österbacka, E., & Zick, C. (2009). Transition to adulthood in Finland and the United States. *Social Indicators Research, 93,* 131–135.

Osterhout, C., Scher, L., & Hilty, D. (2010). *Bulimia nervosa.* Retrieved August 16, from http://emedicine.medscape.com/article/286485-overview

Osterman, M., & Martin, J. (2011). Epidural and spinal anesthesia use during labor: 27-state reporting area, 2008. *National Vital Statistics Reports, 59,* 1–14.

Overby, K. (2002). Pediatric health supervision. In A. Rudolph, R. Kamei, & K. Overby (Eds.), *Rudolph's fundamentals of pediatrics* (3rd ed., pp. 1–69). New York: McGraw-Hill.

Overton, W. F., & Reese, H. W. (1973). Models of development: Methodological implications. In J. R. Nesselroade & H. W. Reese (Eds.), *Life-span developmental psychology: Methodological issues* (pp. 65–86). New York: Academic Press.

Overton, W. F., Ward, S. L., Noveck, I. A., Black, J., & O'Brien, D. P. (1987). Form and content in the development of deductive reasoning. *Developmental Psychology, 23,* 22–30.

Owens, J., Spirito, A., McGuinn, M., & Nobile, C. (2000). Sleep habits and sleep disturbance in elementary school-aged children. *Journal of Developmental & Behavioral Pediatrics, 21,* 27–36.

Oyserman, D., Harrison, K., & Bybee, D. (2001). Can racial identity be promotive of academic efficacy? *International Journal of Behavioral Development, 25,* 379–385.

Pagani, L., Boulerice, B., Tremblay, R., & Vitaro, F. (1997). Behavioural development in children of divorce and remarriage. *Journal of Child Psychology & Psychiatry & Allied Disciplines, 38,* 769–781.

Paiva, N. (2008). South Asian parents' constructions of praising their children. *Clinical Child Psychology and Psychiatry, 13,* 191–207.

Pajares, F., & Graham, L. (1999). Self-efficacy, motivation constructs, and mathematics performance of entering middle school students. *Contemporary Educational Psychology, 24,* 124–139.

Pajulo, M., Savonlahti, E., Sourander, A., Helenius, H., & Piha, J. (2001). Antenatal depression, substance dependency and social support. *Journal of Affective Disorders, 65*, 9–17.

Palmer, A. (2003). The street that changed everything. *APA Monitor on Psychology, 34*, 90.

Pan, B., Rowe, M., Singer, J., & Snow, C. (2005). Maternal correlates of growth in toddler vocabulary production in low-income families. *Child Development, 76*, 763–782.

Papousek, H., & Papousek, M. (1991). Innate and cultural guidance of infants' integrative competencies: China, the United States, and Germany. In M. H. Bornstein (Ed.), *Cultural approaches to parenting* (pp. 23–44). Hillsdale, NJ: Erlbaum.

Parault, S., & Schwanenflugel, P. (2000). The development of conceptual categories of attention during the elementary school years. *Journal of Experimental Child Psychology, 75*, 245–262.

Parent, S., Tillman, G., Jule, A., Skakkebaek, N., Toppari, J., & Bourguignon, J. (2003). The timing of normal puberty and the age limits of sexual precocity: Variations around the world, secular trends, and changes after migration. *Endocrine Review, 24*, 668–693.

Park, N. (2005). Life satisfaction among Korean children and youth: A developmental perspective. *School Psychology International, 26*, 209–223.

Parke, R. D. (2004). The Society for Research in Child Development at 70: Progress and promise. *Child Development, 75*, 1–24.

Parke, R. D., & Buriel, R. (1998). Socialization in the family: Ethnic and ecological perspectives. In W. Damon (Ed.), *Handbook of child psychology: Vol 3. Social, emotional, and personality development* (5th ed., pp. 463–552). New York: Wiley.

Parmelee, A. H., Jr., Wenner, W. H., & Schulz, H. R. (1964). Infant sleep patterns from birth to 16 weeks of age. *Journal of Pediatrics, 65*, 576–582.

Parmley, M., & Cunningham, J. (2008). Children's gender-emotion stereotypes in the relationship of anger to sadness and fear. *Sex Roles, 58*, 358–370.

Parten, M. B. (1932). Social participation among preschool children. *Journal of Abnormal and Social Psychology, 27*, 243–269.

Pascalis, O., de Schonen, S., Morton, J., Derulle, C., & Fabre-Grenet, M. (1995). Mother's face recognition by neonates: A replication and extension. *Infant Behavior and Development, 18*, 79–85.

Passman, R. H., & Longeway, K. P. (1982). The role of vision in maternal attachment: Giving 2-year-olds a photograph of their mother during separation. *Developmental Psychology, 18*, 530–533.

Patterson, C. (1997). Children of lesbian and gay parents. *Advances in Clinical Child Psychology, 19*, 235–282.

Patterson, G. R. (1975). *Families: Applications of social learning to family life*. Champaign, IL: Research Press.

Patterson, G. R. (1996). Some characteristics of a developmental theory for early-onset delinquency. In M. F. Lenzenweger & J. J. Haugaard (Eds.), *Frontiers of developmental psychopathology* (pp. 81–124). New York: Oxford University Press.

Patterson, G. R., Reid, J. B., & Dishion, T. J. (1992). *Antisocial boys*. Eugene, OR: Castalia Press.

Patterson, J. (1998). Expressive vocabulary of bilingual toddlers: Preliminary findings. *Electronic Multicultural Journal of Communication Disorders, 1*. Retrieved April 11, 2001, from http://www.asha.ucf.edu/patterson.html

Pediatric Nutrition Surveillance. (2009). *Comparison of growth and anemia contributors*. Retrieved July 21, 2010, from http://www.cdc.gov/pednss/pednss_tables/tables_health_indicators.htm

Pedlow, R., Sanson, A., Prior, M., & Oberklaid, F. (1993). Stability of maternally reported temperament from infancy to 8 years. *Developmental Psychology, 29*, 998–1007.

Pegg, J. E., Werker, J. F., & McLeod, P. J. (1992). Preference for infant-directed over adult-directed speech: Evidence from 7-week-old infants. *Infant Behavior and Development, 15*, 325–345.

Peisner-Feinberg, E. S., & Burchinal, M. R. (1997). Relations between preschool children's child-care experiences and concurrent development: The Cost, Quality, and Outcomes Study. *Merrill-Palmer Quarterly, 43*, 451–477.

Pelham, W., Hoza, B., Pillow, D., Gnagy, E., Kipp, H., Greiner, A., Waschbusch, D., Trane, S., Greenhouse, J., Wolfson, L., & Fitzpatrick, E. (2002). Effects of methylphenidate and expectancy on children with ADHD: Behavior, academic performance, and attributions in a summer treatment program and regular classroom settings. *Journal of Consulting and Clinical Psychology, 70*, 320–335.

Pempek, T., Demers, L., Hanson, K., Kirkorian, H., & Anderson, D. (2011). The impact of infant-directed videos on parent-child interaction. *Journal of Applied Developmental Psychology, 32*, 10–19.

Pennington, B., Moon, J., Edgin, J., Stedron, J., & Nadel, L. (2003). The neuropsychology of Down syndrome: Evidence of hippocampal dysfunction. *Child Development, 74*, 75–93.

Pennington, D. (2000). *Social cognition*. Philadelphia: Taylor & Francis.

Pereverzeva, M., Hui-Lin Chien, S., Palmer, J., & Teller, D. (2002). Infant photometry: Are mean adult isoluminance values a sufficient approximation to individual infant values? *Vision Research, 42*, 1639–1649.

Periasamy, S., & Ashby, J. (2002). Multidimensional perfectionism and locus of control: Adaptive vs. maladaptive perfectionism. *Journal of College Student Psychotherapy, 17*, 75–86.

Perkins, D. F., & Luster, T. (1997, April). *The relationship between sexual abuse and a bulimic behavior: Findings from community-wide surveys of female adolescents*. Paper presented at the biennial meetings of the Society for Research in Child Development, Washington, DC.

Perlman, M., Claris, O., Hao, Y., Pandid, P., Whyte, H., Chipman, M., & Liu, P. (1995). Secular changes in the outcomes to eighteen to twenty-four months of age of extremely low birth weight infants, with adjustment for changes in risk factors and severity of illness. *Journal of Pediatrics, 126*, 75–87.

Perry, D., Kusel, S. K., & Perry, L. C. (1988). Victims of peer aggression. *Developmental Psychology, 24*, 807–814.

Perry, T., Ohde, R., & Ashmead, D. (2001). The acoustic bases for gender identification from children's voices. *Journal of the Acoustical Society of America, 109*, 2983–2998.

Persson, A., & Musher-Eizenman, D. (2003). The impact of a prejudice-prevention television program on young children's ideas about race. *Early Childhood Research Quarterly, 18*, 530–546.

Petersen, A. C. (1987). The nature of biological-psychosocial interactions: The sample case of early adolescence. In R. M. Lerner & T. T. Foch (Eds.), *Biological-psychosocial interactions in early adolescence* (pp. 35–62). Hillsdale, NJ: Erlbaum.

Petersen, A. C., Compas, B. E., Brooks-Gunn, J., Stemmler, M., Ey, S., & Grant, K. E. (1993). Depression in adolescence. *American Psychologist, 48*, 155–168.

Petersen, A. C., Sarigiani, P. A., & Kennedy, R. E. (1991). Adolescent depression: Why more girls? *Journal of Youth & Adolescence, 20*, 247–272.

Petersen, A. C., & Taylor, B. (1980). The biological approach to adolescence. In J. Adelson (Ed.), *Handbook of adolescent psychology* (pp. 117–158). New York: Wiley.

Peterson, C., & Bell, M. (1996). Children's memory for traumatic injury. *Child Development, 67*, 3045–3070.

Peterson, C. C., & Siegal, M. (1995). Deafness, conversation and theory of mind. *Journal of Child Psychology and Psychiatry, 36*, 459–474.

Peterson, C. C., & Siegal, M. (1999). Representing inner worlds: Theory of mind in autistic, deaf, and normal hearing children. *Psychological Science, 10*, 126–129.

Peterson, C. C., Wellman, H., & Liu, D. (2005). Steps in theory-of-mind development for children with deafness or autism. *Child Development, 76*, 502–517.

Peterson, D., Marcia, J., & Carpendale, J. (2004). Identity: Does thinking make it so? In C. Lightfoot, C. Lalonde, & M. Chandler (Eds.), *Changing conceptions of psychological life* (pp. 113–126). Mahwah, NJ: Erlbaum.

Peterson, J., Pihl, R., Higgins, D., Seguin, J., & Tremblay, R. (2003). Neuropsychological performance, IQ, personality, and grades in a longitudinal grade-school male sample. *Individual Differences Research, 1*, 159–172.

Peterson, L., Ewigman, B., & Kivlahan, C. (1993). Judgments regarding appropriate child supervision to prevent injury: The role of environmental risk and child age. *Child Development, 64*, 934–950.

Petrill, S., Hart, S., Harlaar, N., Logan, J., Justice, L., Schatschneider, C., et al. (2010). Genetic and environmental influences on the growth of early reading skills. *Journal of Child Psychology and Psychiatry, 51*, 660–667.

Pettit, G. S., Bates, J. E., & Dodge, K. A. (1997). Supportive parenting, ecological context, and children's adjustment: A seven-year longitudinal study. *Child Development, 68*, 908–923.

Pettit, G. S., Clawson, M. A., Dodge, K. A., & Bates, J. E. (1996). Stability and change in peer-rejected status: The role of child behavior, parenting, and family ecology. *Merrill-Palmer Quarterly, 42*, 295–318.

Pettit, G. S., Laird, R. D., Bates, J. E., & Dodge, K. A. (1997). Patterns of after-school care in middle childhood: Risk factors and developmental outcomes. *Merrill-Palmer Quarterly, 43*, 515–538.

Pezdek, K., Blandon-Gitlin, I., & Moore, C. (2003). Children's face recognition memory: More evidence for the cross-race effect. *Journal of Applied Psychology, 88*, 760–763.

Pezzella, F. (2006, November). *Authoritarian parenting: A race socializing protective factor that deters at risk African American males from delinquency and violence.* Paper presented at the annual meeting of the American Society of Criminology, Los Angeles.

Phares, V., & Compas, B. (1993). Fathers and developmental psychopathology. *Current Directions in Psychological Science, 2*, 162–165.

Phillips, D., Schwean, V., & Saklofske, D. (1997). Treatment effect of a school-based cognitive-behavioral program for aggressive children. *Canadian Journal of School Psychology, 13*, 60–67.

Phinney, J. S. (1990). Ethnic identity in adolescents and adults: Review of research. *Psychological Bulletin, 108*, 499–514.

Phinney, J. S. (2008). Ethnic identity exploration in emerging adulthood. In D. Browning (Ed.), *Adolescent identities: A collection of readings* (pp. 47–66). New York: The Analytic Press.

Phinney, J. S., & Devich-Navarro, M. (1997). Variations in bicultural identification among African American and Mexican American adolescents. *Journal of Research on Adolescence, 7*, 3–32.

Phinney, J. S., Ferguson, D. L., & Tate, J. D. (1997). Intergroup attitudes among ethnic minority adolescents: A causal model. *Child Development, 68*, 955–969.

Phinney, J. S., Horenczyk, G., Liebkind, K., & Vedder, P. (2001). Ethnic identity, immigration, and well-being: An interactional perspective. *Journal of Social Issues, 57*, 493–510.

Phinney, J. S., Kim-Jo, T., Osorio, S., & Vilhjalmsdottir, P. (2005). Autonomy and relatedness in adolescent-parent disagreements: Ethnic and developmental factors. *Journal of Adolescent Research, 20*, 8–39.

Phinney, J. S., & Rosenthal, D. A. (1992). Ethnic identity in adolescence: Process, context, and outcome. In G. R. Adams, T. P. Gullotta, & R. Montemayor (Eds.), *Adolescent identity formation* (pp. 145–172). Newbury Park, CA: Sage.

Piaget, J. (1952). *The origins of intelligence in children.* New York: International Universities Press.

Piaget, J. (1954). *The construction of reality in the child.* New York: Basic Books. (Originally published 1937)

Piaget, J. (1962). *Play, dreams, and imitation in childhood.* New York: W. W. Norton.

Piaget, J. (1965). *The moral judgment of the child.* New York: Free Press.

Piaget, J. (1970). Piaget's theory. In P. H. Mussen (Ed.), *Carmichael's manual of child psychology* (3rd ed., Vol. 1, pp. 703–732). New York: Wiley.

Piaget, J. (1977). *The development of thought: Equilibration of cognitive structures.* New York: Viking Press.

Piaget, J., & Inhelder, B. (1969). *The psychology of the child.* New York: Basic Books.

Pianta, R. C., & Egeland, B. (1994a). Predictors of instability in children's mental test performance at 24, 48, and 96 months. *Intelligence, 18*, 145–163.

Pianta, R. C., & Egeland, B. (1994b). Relation between depressive symptoms and stressful life events in a sample of disadvantaged mothers. *Journal of Consulting and Clinical Psychology, 62*, 1229–1234.

Pianta, R. C., Steinberg, M. S., & Rollins, K. B. (1995). Teacher-child relationships and deflections in children's classroom adjustment. *Development and Psychopathology, 7*, 295–312.

Pickens, J. (1994). Perception of auditory-visual distance relations by 5-month-old infants. *Developmental Psychology, 30*, 537–544.

Pietschnig, J., Voracek, M., & Formann, A. (2010). Mozart effect-schmozart effect: A meta-analysis. *Intelligence, 38*, 314.

Pillow, B. (1999). Children's understanding of inferential knowledge. *Journal of Genetic Psychology, 160*, 419–428.

Pinderhughes, E., Coie, J., Lochman, J., Bierman, K., Dodge, K., Greenberg, M., et al. (2010). The fast track project: Preventing severe conduct problems in school-age youth. In R. Murrihy, A. Kidman, & T. Ollendick (Eds.), *Clinical handbook of assessing and treating conduct problems in youth* (pp. 407–433). New York: Spring Science + Business Media.

Pinker, S. (1994). *The language instinct: How the mind creates language.* New York: Morrow.

Pittman, L., & Chase-Lansdale, P. (2001). African American adolescent girls in impoverished communities: Parenting style and adolescent outcomes. *Journal of Research on Adolescence, 11*, 199–224.

Planty, M., Hussar, W., Provasnik, S., Kena, G., Dinkes, R., Kewl-Ramani, A., Kemp, J., Kridl, B., & Livingston, A. (2008). *Condition of education 2007.* Retrieved August 17, 2008, from http://nces.ed.gov/pubsearch/pubsinfo.asp?pubid=2008031

Plomin, R. (1990). *Nature and nurture: An introduction to behavior genetics.* Pacific Grove, CA: Brooks/Cole.

Plomin, R. (1995). Genetics and children's experiences in the family. *Journal of Child Psychology and Psychiatry, 36*, 33–68.

Plomin, R. (2001). Genetics and behavior. *Psychologist, 14*, 134–139.

Plomin, R. (2004). Genetics and developmental psychology. *Merrill-Palmer Quarterly, 50*, 341–352.

Plomin, R., & DeFries, J. C. (1985). *Origins of individual differences in infancy: The Colorado Adoption Project.* Orlando, FL: Academic Press.

Plomin, R., Loehlin, J. C., & DeFries, J. C. (1985). Genetic and environmental components of "environmental" influences. *Developmental Psychology, 21*, 391–402.

Plomin, R., Reiss, D., Hetherington, E. M., & Howe, G. W. (1994). Nature and nurture: Genetic contributions to measures of the family environment. *Developmental Psychology, 30*, 32–43.

Plomin, R., & Rende, R. (1991). Human behavioral genetics. *Annual Review of Psychology, 42*, 161–190.

Plucker, J. (1999). Is the proof in the pudding? Reanalyses of Torrance's (1958 to present) longitudinal data. *Creativity Research Journal, 12*, 103–115.

Pluess, M., & Belsky, J. (2009). Differential susceptibility to rearing experience: The case of childcare. *Journal of Child Psychology and Psychiatry, 50*(4), 396–404.

Polanczyk, G., de Lima, M., Horta, B., Biederman, J., & Rohde, L. (2007). Worldwide prevalence of ADHD: A systematic review and metaregression analysis. *American Journal of Psychiatry, 164*, 942–948.

Polderman, T., de Geus, E., Hoekstra, R., Bartels, M., van Leeuwen, M., Verhulst, F., et al. (2009). Attention problems, inhibitory control, and intelligence index overlapping genetic factors: A study in 9-, 12-, and 18-year-old twins. *Neuropsychology, 23*, 381–391.

Polderman, T., Gosso, M., Posthuma, D., Van Beijsterveldt, T., Heutink, P., Verhulst, F., & Boomsma, D. (2006). A longitudinal twin study on IQ, executive functioning, and attention problems during childhood and early adolescence. *Acta Neurologica Belgica, 106*, 191–207.

Polivy, J., & Herman, C. P. (1995). Dieting and its relation to eating disorders. In K. D. Brownell & C. G. Fairburn (Eds.), *Eating disorders and obesity: A comprehensive handbook* (pp. 83–86). New York: Guilford Press.

Pollett, T., & Nettle, D. (2009). Birth order and adult family relationships: Firstborns have better sibling relationships than laterborns. *Journal of Social and Personal Relationships, 26*, 1029–1046.

Pomerleau, A., Malcuit, G., Turgeon, L., & Cossette, L. (1997). Effects of labelled gender on vocal communication of young women with 4-month-old infants. *International Journal of Psychology, 32*, 65–72.

Pomerleau, A., Scuccimarri, C., & Malcuit, G. (2003). Mother-infant behavioral interactions in teenage and adult mothers during the first six months postpartum: Relations with infant development. *Infant Mental Health Journal, 24*, 495–509.

Pons, F., Harris, P., & de Rosnay, M. (2004). Emotion comprehension between 3 and 11 years: Developmental periods and hierarchical organization. *Journal of Developmental Psychology, 1*, 127–152.

Porter, J., & Washington, R. (1993). Minority identity and self-esteem. *Annual Review of Sociology, 19*, 139–161.

Porter, M., Coltheart, M., & Langdon, R. (2008). Theory of mind in Williams syndrome assessed using a nonverbal task. *Journal of Autism and Developmental Disorders, 38*, 806–814.

Posada, G., Jacobs, A., Richmond, M., Carbonell, O., Alzate, G., Bustamante, M., & Quiceno, J. (2002). Maternal caregiving and infant security in two cultures. *Developmental Psychology, 38*, 67–78.

Posey, D., Puntney, J., Sasher, T., Kem, D., & McDougle, C. (2004). Guanfacine treatment of hyperactivity and inattention in pervasive developmental disorders: A retrospective analysis of 80 cases. *Journal of Child & Adolescent Psychopharmacology, 14*, 233–241.

Posner, J., & Vandell, D. (1994). Low-income children's after-school care: Are there beneficial effects of after-school programs? *Child Development, 65*, 440–456.

Posthuma, D., de Geus, E., & Boomsma, D. (2003). Genetic contributions to anatomical, behavioral, and neurophysiological indices of cognition. In R. Plomin, J. DeFries, I. Craig, & P. McGuffin (Eds.), *Behavioral genetics in the postgenomic era* (pp. 141–161). Washington, DC: American Psychological Association.

Poulin, F., & Boivin, M. (1999). Proactive and reactive aggression and boys' friendship quality in mainstream classrooms. *Journal of Emotional & Behavioral Disorders, 7*, 168–177.

Poulin, F., & Boivin, M. (2000). The role of proactive and reactive aggression in the formation and development of boys' friendships. *Developmental Psychology, 36*, 233–240.

Poulson, C. L., Nunes, L. R. D., & Warren, S. F. (1989). Imitation in infancy: A critical review. In H. W. Reese (Ed.), *Advances in child development and behavior* (Vol. 22, pp. 272–298). San Diego, CA: Academic Press.

Power, T. (2000). *Play and exploration in children and animals.* Hillsdale, NJ: Erlbaum.

Powlishta, K. K., Serbin, L. A., Doyle, A., & White, D. R. (1994). Gender, ethnic, and body type biases: The generality of prejudice in childhood. *Developmental Psychology, 30*, 526–536.

Pozzi, M. (2003). A three-year-old boy with ADHD and Asperger's syndrome treated with parent-child psychotherapy. *Journal of the British Association of Psychotherapists, 41*, 16–31.

Prat-Sala, M., Shillcock, R., & Sorace, A. (2000). Animacy effects on the production of object-dislocated description by Catalan-speaking children. *Journal of Child Language, 27*, 97–117.

Pratt, M., Arnold, M., & Pratt, A. (1999). Predicting adolescent moral reasoning from family climate: A longitudinal study. *Journal of Early Adolescence, 19*, 148–175.

Pratt, M., Skoe, E., & Arnold, M. (2004). Care reasoning development and family socialization patterns in later adolescence: A longitudinal analysis. *International Journal of Behavioral Development, 28*, 139–147.

Prechtl, H., & Beintema, D. (1964). *The neurological examination of the full-term newborn infant: Clinics in developmental medicine.* London: Heinemann.

Prentice, D., & Miller, D. (2002). The emergence of homegrown stereotypes. *American Psychologist, 57*, 352–359.

Pressley, M., & Dennis-Rounds, J. (1980). Transfer of a mnemonic keyword strategy at two age levels. *Journal of Educational Psychology, 72*, 575–582.

Pressman, E., DiPietro, J., Costigan, K., Shupe, A., & Johnson, T. (1998). Fetal neurobehavioral development: Associations with socioeconomic class and fetal sex. *Developmental Psychobiology, 33*, 79–91.

Pretz, J., & Sternberg, R. (2005). Unifying the field: Cognition and intelligence. In J. Pretz & R. Sternberg (Eds.), *Cognition and intelligence: Identifying the mechanisms of mind* (pp. 306–318). New York: Cambridge University Press.

Price, C., & Kunz, J. (2003). Rethinking the paradigm of juvenile delinquency as related to divorce. *Journal of Divorce & Remarriage, 39*, 109–133.

Provasnik, S., & Gonzales, P. (2009). *Condition of education, special analysis 2009.* Retrieved August 8, 2010, from http://nces.ed.gov/programs/coe/2009/analysis/

Przybylski, A., Rigby, C., & Ryan, R. (2010). A motivational model of video game engagement. *Review of General Psychology, 14*, 154–166.

Public Health Policy Advisory Board. (2001). *Health and the American child: A focus on mortality among children.* Washington, DC: Author.

Pujol, J., Deus, J., Losilla, J., & Capdevila, A. (1999). Cerebral lateralization of language in normal left-handed people studied by functional MRI. *Neurology, 52*, 1038–1043.

Pulkkinen L. (1982). Self-control and continuity from childhood to late adolescence. In P. Baltes & O. G. Brim, Jr. (Eds.), *Life span development and behavior* (Vol. 4, pp. 64–107). New York: Academic Press.

Pungello, E., Kainz, K., Burchinal, M., Wasik, B., Sparling, J., Ramey, C., et al. (2010). Early educational intervention, early cumulative risk, and the early home environment as predictors of young adult outcomes within a high-risk sample. *Child Development, 81*, 410–426.

Purugganan, O., Stein, R., Johnson Silver, E., & Benenson, B. (2003). Exposure to violence and psychosocial adjustment among urban school-aged children. *Journal of Developmental and Behavioral Pediatrics, 24*, 424–430.

Putallaz, M., Grimes, C., Foster, K., Kupersmidt, J., Coie, J., & Dearing, K. (2007). Overt and relational aggression and victimization: Multiple perspectives within the school setting. *Journal of School Psychology, 45,* 523–547.

Putnam, S., & Stifter, C. (2005). Behavioral approach-inhibition in toddlers: Prediction from infancy, positive and negative affective components, and relations with behavior problems. *Child Development, 76,* 212–226.

Putnins, A. (1997). Victim awareness programs for delinquent youths: Effects on moral reasoning maturity. *Adolescence, 32,* 709–714.

Qi, C., & Kaiser, A. (2003). Behavior problems of preschool children from low-income families: Review of the literature. *Early Childhood Special Education, 23,* 188–216.

Quick stats: Prevalence of HPV infection among sexually active females aged 14 to 59 years. (2007). *Morbidity and Mortality Weekly Report, 56,* 852.

Quinn, P., Anzures, G., Izard, C., Lee, K., Pascalis, O., Slater, A., et al. (2011). Looking across domains to understand infant representation of emotion. *Emotion Review, 3,* 197–206.

Quintana, S. (2007). Racial and ethnic identity: Developmental perspectives and research. *Journal of Counseling Psychology, 54,* 259–270.

Radtke, T., Scholz, U., Keller, R., Knauper, B., & Hurnung, R. (2011). Smoking-specific compensatory health beliefs and the readiness to stop smoking in adolescents. *British Journal of Health Psychology, 16,* 610–625.

Raffaelli, M., & Ontai, L. (2004). Gender socialization in Latino families: Results from two retrospective studies. *Sex Roles, 50,* 287–299.

Ragnarsdottir, H., Simonsen, H., & Plunkett, K. (1999). The acquisition of past tense morphology in Icelandic and Norwegian children: An experimental study. *Journal of Child Language, 26,* 577–618.

Raikes, H., Chazan, Cohen, R., Love, J., & Brooks-Gunn, J. (2010). In A. Reynolds, A. Rolnick, M. Englund, & J. Temple (Eds.), *Childhood programs and practices in the first decade of life: A human capital integration* (pp. 99–118). New York: Cambridge University Press.

Raj, A., & Bertolone, S. (2010). *Sickle cell anemia.* Retrieved June 27, 2010, from http://emedicine.medscape.com/article/958614-overview

Rakhlin, N., Kornilov, S., Reich, J., Babyonyshev, M., Koposov, R., & Grigorenko, E. (2011). The relationship between syntactic development and theory of mind: Evidence from a small-population study of a developmental language disorder. *Journal of Neurolinguistics, 24,* 476–496.

Ramey, C. T. (1993). A rejoinder to Spitz's critique of the Abecedarian experiment. *Intelligence, 17,* 25–30.

Ramey, C. T., & Campbell, F. A. (1987). The Carolina Abecedarian Project: An educational experiment concerning human malleability. In J. J. Gallagher & C. T. Ramey (Eds.), *The malleability of children* (pp. 127–140). Baltimore: Brookes.

Ramey, C. T., & Ramey, S. L. (2004). Early learning and school readiness: Can early intervention make a difference? *Merrill-Palmer Quarterly, 50,* 471–491.

Ramey, S. L., Ramey, C. T., & Lanzi, R. (2007). Early intervention: Background, research findings, and future directions. In J. Jacobson, J. Mulick, & J. Rojahn (Eds.), *Issues in clinical child psychology* (pp. 445–463). New York: Springer.

Ranson, K., & Urichuk, L. (2008). The effect of parent-child attachment relationships on child biopsychosocial outcomes: A review. *Early Child Development and Care, 178,* 129–152.

Rattaz, C., Goubet, N., & Bullinger, A. (2005). The calming effect of a familiar odor on full-term newborns. *Journal of Developmental and Behavioral Pediatrics, 26,* 86–92.

Räty, H., Vänskä, J., Kasanen, K., & Kärkkäinen, R. (2002). Parents' explanations of their child's performance in mathematics and reading: A replication and extension of Yee and Eccles. *Sex Roles, 46,* 121–128.

Rauscher, F., Shaw, G., & Ky, K. (1993). Music and spatial task performance. *Nature, 365,* 611.

Ray, B. (1999). *Home schooling on the threshold: A survey of research at the dawn of the new millennium.* Washington, DC: Home Education Research Institute.

Ray, B. (2009). *Home education reason and research: Common questions and research-based answers.* Salem, OR: National Home Education Research Institute.

Ray, B. (2010). Academic achievement and demographic traits of homeschool students: A nationwide study. *Academic Leadership: The Online Journal, 9.* Retrieved July 25, 2011, from http://www.academicleadership.org/article/Academic_Achievement_and_Demographic_Traits_of_Homeschool_Students_A_Nationwide_Study

Rees, J. M., Lederman, S. A., & Kiely, J. L. (1996). Birth weight associated with lowest neonatal mortality: Infants of adolescent and adult mothers. *Pediatrics, 98,* 1161–1166.

Rego, A. (2006). The alphabetic principle, phonics, and spelling: Teaching students the code. In J. Schumm (Ed.), *Reading assessment and instruction for all learners* (pp. 118–162). New York: Guilford Press.

Reiner, W., & Gearhardt, J. (2004). Discordant sexual identity in some genetic males with cloacal exstrophy assigned to female sex at birth. *New England Journal of Medicine, 350,* 333–341.

Reiss, D. (1998). Mechanisms linking genetic and social influences in adolescent development: Beginning a collaborative search. *Current Directions in Psychological Science, 6,* 100–105.

Remafedi, G., Resnick, M., Blum, R., & Harris, L. (1998). Demography of sexual orientation in adolescents. *Pediatrics, 89,* 714–721.

Renk, K., Donnelly, R., McKinney, C., & Agliata, A. (2006). In K. Yip (Ed.), *Psychology of gender identity: An international perspective* (pp. 49–68). Hauppauge, NY: Nova Science Publishers.

Renouf, A. G., & Harter, S. (1990). Low self-worth and anger as components of the depressive experience in young adolescents. *Development and Psychopathology, 2,* 293–310.

Resnick, M. D., Bearman, P. S., Blum, R. W., Bauman, K. E., Harris, K. M., Jones, J., Tabor, J., Beuhring, T., Sieving, R. E., Shew, M., Ireland, M., Bearinger, L. H., & Udry, J. R. (1997). Protecting adolescents from harm: Findings from the National Longitudinal Study on Adolescent Health. *Journal of the American Medical Association, 278,* 823–832.

Rest, J. R. (1983). Morality. In J. H. Flavell & E. M. Markman (Eds.), *Handbook of child psychology: Cognitive development* (Vol. 3, pp. 556–629). New York: Wiley.

Retz, W., Retz-Junginger, P., Hengesch, G., Schneider, M., Thome, J., Pajonk, F., Salahi-Disfan, A., Rees, O., Wender, P., & Rösler, M. (2004). Psychometric and psychopathological characterization of young male prison inmates with and without attention deficit/hyperactivity disorder. *European Archives of Psychiatry & Clinical Neuroscience, 254,* 201–208.

Rey, J., Sawyer, M., Raphael, B., Patton, G., & Lynskey, M. (2002). Mental health of teenagers who use cannabis: Results of an Australian survey. *British Journal of Psychiatry, 180,* 216–221.

Reynolds, A. J. (1994). Effects of a preschool plus follow-on intervention for children at risk. *Developmental Psychology, 30,* 787–804.

Reynolds, A. J., & Bezruczko, N. (1993). School adjustment of children at risk through fourth grade. *Merrill-Palmer Quarterly, 39,* 457–480.

Reynolds, C., & Shaywitz, S. (2009). Response to intervention: Ready or not? Or, from wait-to-fail to watch-them-fail. *School Psychology Quarterly, 24,* 130–145.

Rhee, S., & Waldman, I. (2011). Genetic and environmental influences on aggression. In P. Shaver & M. Mikulincer (Eds.), *Human aggression and violence: Causes, manifestations, and consequences.* Washington, DC: American Psychological Association.

Rholes, W. S., & Ruble, D. N. (1984). Children's understanding of dispositional characteristics of others. *Child Development, 55,* 550–560.

Ricci, C. M., Beal, C. R., & Dekle, D. J. (1995, April). *The effect of parent versus unfamiliar interviewers on young witnesses' memory and identification accuracy.* Paper presented at the biennial meetings of the Society for Research in Child Development, Indianapolis.

Rice, M. L., Huston, A. C., Truglio, R., & Wright, J. (1990). Words from "Sesame Street": Learning vocabulary while viewing. *Developmental Psychology, 26,* 421–428.

Richards, H. C., Bear, G. G., Stewart, A. L., & Norman, A. D. (1992). Moral reasoning and classroom conduct: Evidence of a curvilinear relationship. *Merrill-Palmer Quarterly, 38,* 176–190.

Richards, J., & Cronise, K. (2000). Extended visual fixation in the early preschool years: Look duration, heart rate changes, and attentional inertia. *Child Development, 71,* 602–620.

Richards, M., Hardy, R., Kuh, D., & Wadsworth, M. (2001). Birth weight and cognitive function in the British 1946 birth cohort: Longitudinal population-based study. *British Medical Journal, 322,* 199–203.

Richards, M. H., Crowe, P. A., Larson, R., & Swarr, A. (1998). Developmental patterns and gender differences in the experience of peer companionship during adolescence. *Child Development, 69,* 154–163.

Richters, J., & Pellegrini, D. (1989). Depressed mothers' judgments about their children: An examination of the depression-distortion hypothesis. *Child Development, 60,* 1068–1075.

Ridderinkhof, K., Scheres, A., Oosterlaan, J., & Sergeant, J. (2005). Delta plots in the study of individual differences: New tools reveal response inhibition deficits in AD/HD that are eliminated by methylphenidate treatment. *Journal of Abnormal Psychology, 114,* 197–215.

Rideout, V., Foehr, U., & Roberts, D. (2010). *Generation M2: Medial in the lives of 8- to 18-year-olds.* Retrieved August 12, 2010, from http://www.kff.org/entmedia/upload/8010.pdf

Riegel, K. F. (1975). Adult life crises: A dialectic interpretation of development. In N. Datan & L. H. Ginsberg (Eds.), *Lifespan developmental psychology: Normative life crises* (pp. 99–128). New York: Academic Press.

Riggs, L. L. (1997, April). Depressive affect and eating problems in adolescent females: An assessment of direction and influence using longitudinal data. Paper presented at the biennial meetings of the Society for Research in Child Development, Washington, D.C.

Righetti, P. (1996). The emotional experience of the fetus: A preliminary report. *Pre- & Peri-Natal Psychology Journal, 11,* 55–65.

Riley, B. (2010). GLB adolescent's "coming out." *Journal of Child and Adolescent Psychiatric Nursing, 23,* 3–10.

Rinderman, H., & Neubauer, A. (2004). Processing speed, intelligence, creativity, and school performance: Testing of causal hypotheses using structural equation models. *Intelligence, 32,* 573–589.

Ripple, C., & Zigler, E. (2003). Research, policy, and the federal role in prevention initiatives for children. *American Psychologist, 58,* 482–490.

Robb, M., Richert, R., & Wartella, E. (2009). Just a talking book? Word learning from watching baby videos. *British Journal of Developmental Psychology, 27*(1), 27–45.

Roberts, J., & Bell, M. (2000). Sex differences on a mental rotation task: Variations in electroencephalogram hemispheric activation between children and college students. *Developmental Neuropsychology, 17,* 199–223.

Robinson, H. B. (1981). The uncommonly bright child. In M. Lewis & L. A. Rosenblum (Eds.), *The uncommon child* (pp. 57–82). New York: Plenum Press.

Robinson, N. M., & Janos, P. M. (1986). Psychological adjustment in a college-level program of marked academic acceleration. *Journal of Youth & Adolescence, 15,* 51–60.

Robinson, N. M., Lanzi, R., Weinberg, R., Ramey, S., & Ramey, C. (2002). Family factors associated with high academic competence in former Head Start children at third grade. *Gifted Child Quarterly, 46,* 278–290.

Roche, A. F. (1979). Secular trends in human growth, maturation, and development. *Monographs of the Society for Research in Child Development, 44*(3–4, Serial No. 179).

Rock, A., Trainor, L., & Addison, T. (1999). Distinctive messages in infant-directed lullabies and play songs. *Developmental Psychology, 35,* 527–534.

Rodkin, P., Farmer, T., Pearl, R., & Van Acker, R. (2000). Heterogeneity of popular boys: Antisocial and prosocial configurations. *Developmental Psychology, 36,* 14–24.

Rodrigo, M., Janssens, J., & Ceballos, E. (1999). Do children's perceptions and attributions mediate the effects of mothers' child rearing actions? *Journal of Family Psychology, 13,* 508–522.

Roeser, R., & Eccles J. (1998). Adolescents' perceptions of middle school: Relation to longitudinal changes in academic and psychological adjustment. *Journal of Research on Adolescence, 8,* 123–158.

Rogers, J. (2007). The influences of age, culture, and beliefs on toilet training. *Continence, 1,* 84–86.

Rogers, J. L., Rowe, D. C., & May, K. (1994). DF analysis of NLSY IQ/achievement data: Non-shared environmental influences. *Intelligence, 19,* 157–177.

Rohner, R. P., Kean, K. J., & Cournoyer, D. E. (1991). Effects of corporal punishment, perceived caretaker warmth, and cultural beliefs on the psychological adjustment of children in St. Kitts, West Indies. *Journal of Marriage and the Family, 53,* 681–693.

Romeo, R. (2010). Adolescence: A central event in shaping stress reactivity. *Developmental Psychobiology, 52,* 244–253.

Rooks, J. P., Weatherby, N. L., Ernst, E. K. M., Stapleton, S., Rosen, D., & Rosenfield, A. (1989). Outcomes of care in birth centers: The National Birth Center Study. *New England Journal of Medicine, 321,* 1804–1811.

Rosario, M., Scrimshaw, E., & Hunter, J. (2004). Ethnic/racial differences in the coming-out process of lesbian, gay, and bisexual youths: A comparison of sexual identity development over time. *Cultural Diversity and Ethnic Minority Psychology, 10,* 215–228.

Rose, A. J., & Asher, S. (2004). Children's strategies and goals in response to help-giving and help-seeking tasks within a friendship. *Child Development, 75,* 749–763.

Rose, A. J., & Montemayor, R. (1994). The relationship between gender role orientation and perceived self-competence in male and female adolescents. *Sex Roles, 31,* 579–595.

Rose, K., & Elicker, J. (2010). Maternal child care preferences for infants, toddlers, and preschoolers: The disconnect between policy and preference in the USA. *Community, Work, & Family, 13,* 205–229.

Rose, R. J. (1995). Genes and human behavior. *Annual Review of Psychology, 56,* 625–654.

Rose, S. A., & Feldman, J. F. (1995). Prediction of IQ and specific cognitive abilities at 11 years from infancy measures. *Developmental Psychology, 31,* 685–696.

Rose, S. A., & Feldman, J. F. (1997). Memory and speed: Their role in the relation of infant information processing to later IQ. *Child Development, 68,* 630–641.

Rosenberg, M. (2003). Recognizing gay, lesbian, and transgender teens in a child and adolescent psychiatry practice. *Journal of the American Academy of Child & Adolescent Psychiatry, 42*, 1517–1521.

Rosenblatt, J., & Elias, M. (2008). Dosage effects of a preventive social-emotional learning intervention on achievement loss associated with middle school transition. *Journal of Primary Prevention, 29*(6), 535–555.

Rosenblatt, P., & Wallace, B. (2005). Narratives of grieving African Americans about racism in the lives of deceased family members. *Death Studies, 29*, 217–235.

Rosenfield, R., Lipton, R., & Drum, M. (2009). Thelarche, pubarche, and menarche attainment in children with normal and elevated body mass index. *Pediatrics, 123*, 84–88.

Rosenthal, R. (1994). Interpersonal expectancy effects: A 30-year perspective. *Current Directions in Psychological Science, 3*, 176–179.

Rosenthal, S., & Gitelman, S. (2002). Endocrinology. In A. Rudolph, R. Kamei, & K. Overby (Eds.), *Rudolph's fundamentals of pediatrics* (3rd ed., pp. 747–795). New York: McGraw-Hill.

Ross, G., Kagan, J., Zelazo, P., & Kotelchuk, M. (1975). Separation protest in infants in home and laboratory. *Developmental Psychology, 11*, 256–257.

Ross, H., Ross, M., Stein, N., & Trabasso, T. (2006). How siblings resolve their conflicts: The importance of first offers, planning, and limited opposition. *Child Development, 77*, 1730–1745.

Rostosky, S., Owens, G., Zimmerman, R., & Riggle, E. (2003). Associations among sexual attraction status, school belonging, and alcohol and marijuana use in rural high school students. *Journal of Adolescence, 26*, 741–751.

Rothbart, M. K. (2004). Temperament and the pursuit of an integrated developmental psychology. *Merrill-Palmer Quarterly, 50*, 492–505.

Rothbart, M. K. (2007). Temperament, development, and personality. *Current Directions in Psychological Science, 16*, 207–212.

Rothbart, M. K. (2011). *Becoming who we are: Temperament and personality in development*. New York: Guilford Press.

Rothbart, M. K., Ahadi, S., Hersey, K., & Fisher, P. (2001). Investigations of temperament at three to seven years: The Children's Behavior Questionnaire. *Child Development, 72*, 1394–1408.

Rothbart, M. K., & Putnam, S. (2002). Temperament and socialization. In L. Pulkkinen & A. Caspi (Eds.), *Paths to successful development: Personality in the life course* (pp. 19–45). New York: Cambridge University Press.

Rotter, J. (1990). Internal versus external control of reinforcement: A case history of a variable. *American Psychologist, 45*, 489–493.

Rovee-Collier, C. (1986). The rise and fall of infant classical conditioning research: Its promise for the study of early development. In L. P. Lipsitt & C. Rovee-Collier (Eds.), *Advances in infancy research* (Vol. 4, pp. 139–162). Norwood, NJ: Ablex.

Rovee-Collier, C. (1993). The capacity for long-term memory in infancy. *Current Directions in Psychological Science, 2*, 130–135.

Rovee-Collier, C., & Cuevas, K. (2009). The development of infant memory. In M. Courage & N. Cowan (Eds.), *The development of memory in infancy and childhood* (2nd ed., pp. 11–42). New York: Psychology Press.

Rovet, J., & Netley, C. (1983). The triple X chromosome syndrome in childhood: Recent empirical findings. *Child Development, 54*, 831–845.

Rowe, I., & Marcia, J. E. (1980). Ego identity status, formal operations, and moral development. *Journal of Youth & Adolescence, 9*, 87–99.

Roy, E., Bryden, P., & Cavill, S. (2003). Hand differences in pegboard performance through development. *Brain & Cognition, 53*, 315–317.

Rubin, K. H., Burgess, K., Dwyer, K., & Hastings, P. D. (2003). Predicting preschoolers' externalizing behaviors from toddler temperament, conflict, and maternal negativity. *Developmental Psychology, 39*, 164–176.

Rubin, K. H., Coplan, R., Chen, X., Baskirk, A., & Wojslawowica, J. (2005). Peer relationships in childhood. In M. Bornstein & M. Lamb (Eds.), *Developmental science: An advanced textbook* (5th ed., pp. 469–512). Hillsdale, NJ: Erlbaum.

Rubin, K. H., Coplan, R., Chen, X., Bowker, J., & McDonald, K. (2011). Peer relationships in childhood. In M. Bornstein & M. Lamb (Eds.), *Developmental science: An advanced textbook* (6th ed., pp. 519–570). New York: Psychology Press.

Rubin, K. H., Hastings, P. D., Stewart, S. L., Henderson, H. A., & Chen, X. (1997). The consistency and concomitants of inhibition: Some of the children, all of the time. *Child Development, 68*, 467–483.

Ruble, D. N. (1987). The acquisition of self-knowledge: A self-socialization perspective. In N. Eisenberg (Ed.), *Contemporary topics in developmental psychology* (pp. 243–270). New York: Wiley-Interscience.

Ruble, D. N., & Martin, C. L. (1998). Gender development. In W. Damon (Ed.), *Handbook of child psychology: Vol 3. Social, emotional, and personality development* (5th ed., pp. 933–1016). New York: Wiley.

Ruble, D. N., Martin, C. L., & Berenbaum, S. A. (2006). Gender development. In N. Eisenberg, W. Damon, & R. Lerner (Eds.), *Handbook of child psychology: Vol. 3. Social, emotional, and personality development* (6th ed., pp. 858–932). Hoboken, NJ: Wiley.

Rueter, M. A., & Conger, R. D. (1995). Antecedents of parent-adolescent disagreements. *Journal of Marriage and the Family, 57*, 435–448.

Runyan, D. K., Hunter, W. M., Socolar, R. R. S., Amaya-Jackson, L., English, D., Landsverk, J., Dubowitz, H., Browne, D. H., Bandiwala, S. I., & Mathew, R. M. (1998). Children who prosper in unfavorable environments: The relationship to social capital. *Pediatrics, 101*, 12–18.

Rushton, J., & Jensen, A. (2005). Thirty years of research on race differences in cognitive ability. *Psychology, Public Policy, & Law, 11*, 235–294.

Russell, J. A. (1989). Culture, scripts, and children's understanding of emotion. In C. Saarni & P. L. Harris (Eds.), *Children's understanding of emotion* (pp. 293–318). Cambridge, England: Cambridge University Press.

Rutter, D. R., & Durkin, K. (1987). Turn-taking in mother-infant interaction: An examination of vocalizations and gaze. *Developmental Psychology, 23*, 54–61.

Rutter, M. (1978). Early sources of security and competence. In J. S. Bruner & A. Garton (Eds.), *Human growth and development* (pp. 33–61). London: Oxford University Press.

Rutter, M. (1987). Continuities and discontinuities from infancy. In J. D. Osofsky (Ed.), *Handbook of infant development* (2nd ed., pp. 1256–1296). New York: Wiley-Interscience.

Rutter, M. (1989). Isle of Wight revisited: Twenty-five years of child psychiatric epidemiology. *Journal of the American Academy of Child and Adolescent Psychiatry, 28*, 633–653.

Rutter, M. (2002). Nature, nurture, and development: From evangelism through science toward policy and practice. *Child Development, 73*, 1–21.

Rutter, M. (2005a). Aetiology of autism: Findings and questions. *Journal of Intellectual Disability Research, 49*, 231–238.

Rutter, M. (2005b). Environmentally mediated risks for psychopathology: Research strategies and findings. *Journal of the American Academy of Child and Adolescent Psychiatry, 44*, 3–18.

Rutter, M., Dunn, J., Plomin, R., Simonoff, E., Pickles, A., Maughan, B., Ormel, J., Meyer, J., & Eaves, L. (1997). Integrating nature and nurture: Implications of person-environment correlations and interactions for developmental psychopathology. *Development and Psychopathology, 9*, 335–364.

Rutter, M., & Garmezy, N. (1983). Developmental psychopathology. In E. M. Hetherington (Ed.), *Handbook of child psychology: Vol 4. Socialization, personality, and social development* (pp. 775–912). New York: Wiley.

Rutter, M., Sonuga-Barke, E., Beckett, C., Castle, J., Kreppner, J., Kumsta, R., et al. (2010). Deprivation-specific psychological patterns: Effects of institutional deprivation. *Monographs of the Society for Research in Child Development, 75,* 1–231.

Rutter, M., & Sroufe, A. (2000). Developmental psychopathology: Concepts and challenges. *Development and Psychopathology, 12,* 265–296.

Rydell, R., Shiffrin, Boucher, K., Van Loo, K., & Rydell, M. (2010). Stereotype threat prevents perceptual learning. *Proceedings of the National Academy of the Sciences, 107,* 14042–14047.

Ryder, J., Tunmer, W., & Greaney, K. (2008). Explicit instruction in phonemic awareness and phonemically based decoding skills as an intervention strategy for struggling readers in whole language classrooms. *Reading and Writing, 21,* 349–369.

Saddler, B. (2007). Improving sentence construction skills. In S Graham, C. Macarthur, & J. Fitzgerald (Eds.), *Best practices in writing instruction* (pp. 163–178). New York: Guilford Press.

Sadeh, A., Gruber, R., & Raviv, A. (2002). Sleep, neurobehavioral functioning, and behavior problems in school-age children. *Child Development, 73,* 405–417.

Saewyc, E., Bearinger, L., Heinz, P., Blum, R., & Resnick, M. (1998). Gender differences in health and risk behaviors among bisexual and homosexual adolescents. *Journal of Adolescent Health, 23,* 131–188.

Safren, S., & Heimberg, R. (1999). Depression, hopelessness, suicidality, and related factors in sexual minority and heterosexual adolescents. *Journal of Consulting and Clinical Psychology, 67,* 859–866.

Sagi, A. (1990). Attachment theory and research from a cross-cultural perspective. *Human Development, 33,* 10–22.

Sagi, A., van IJzendoorn, M. H., & Koren-Karie, N. (1991). Primary appraisal of the Strange Situation: A cross-cultural analysis of preseparation episodes. *Developmental Psychology, 27,* 587–596.

Sai, F. (2005). The role of the mother's voice in developing mother's face preference: Evidence for intermodal perception at birth. *Infant & Child Development, 14,* 29–50.

Saigal, S., Szatmari, P., Rosenbaum, P., Campbell, D., & King, S. (1991). Cognitive abilities and school performance of extremely low birth weight children and matched term control children at age 8 years: A regional study. *Journal of Pediatrics, 118,* 751–760.

Saine, N., Lerkhanen, M., Ahonen, T., Tolvanen, A., & Lyytinen, H. (2010). Predicting word-level reading fluency outcomes in three contrastive groups: Remedial and computer-assisted remedial reading intervention, and mainstream instruction. *Learning and Individual Differences, 20,* 402–414.

Sak, U., & Maker, C. (2006). Developmental variation in children's creative mathematical thinking as a function of schooling, age, and knowledge. *Creativity Research, 18,* 279–291.

Saksvik, I., & Hetland, H. (2011). The role of personality in stress perception across different vocational types. *Journal of Employment Counseling, 48,* 3–16.

Salkeld, L., & Koster, O. (2008). *Coroner launches probe into 'Internet suicide cult' after seven youngsters in one town hang themselves.* Retrieved September 3, 2010, from http://www.dailymail.co.uk/news/article-509727/Coroner-launches-probe-internet-suicide-cult-SEVEN-youngsters-town-hang-themselves.html

Sallquist, J., Eisenberg, N., Spinrad, T., Reiser, M., Hofer, C., Zhou, Q., et al. (2009). Positive and negative emotionality: Trajectories across six years and relations with social competence. *Emotion, 9,* 15–28.

Salovey, P., & Mayer, J. (1990). Emotional intelligence. *Imagination, Cognition, and Personality, 9,* 185–211.

Salpekar, J., Berl, M., & Kenealy, L. (2011). Seizure disorders. In A. Davis (Ed.), *Handbook of pediatric neuropsychology* (pp. 931–942). New York: Springer.

Sampson, R. J., & Laub, J. H. (1994). Urban poverty and the family context of delinquency: A new look at structure and process in a classic study. *Child Development, 65,* 523–540.

Sanchez, R., Crismon, M., Barner, J., Bettinger, T., & Wilson, J. (2005). Assessment of adherence measures with different stimulants among children and adolescents. *Pharmacotherapy, 25,* 909–917.

Sandler, I., Miles, J., Cookston, J., & Braver, S. (2008). Effects of father and mother parenting on children's mental health in high- and low-conflict divorces. *Family Court Review, 46,* 282–296.

Sandman, C., Wadhwa, P., Hetrick, W., Porto, M., & Peeke, H. (1997). Human fetal heart rate dishabituation between thirty and thirty-two weeks. *Child Development, 68,* 1031–1040.

Sandven, K., & Resnick, M. (1990). Informal adoption among Black adolescent mothers *American Journal of Orthopsychiatry, 60,* 210–224.

Sapienza, P., Zingales, L., & Maestripieri, D. (2009). Gender differences in financial risk aversion and career choices are affected by testosterone. *PNAS Proceedings of the National Academy of Science of the United States of America, 106,* 15268–15273.

Sattler, J. (2008). *Assessment of children: Cognitive foundations* (5th ed.). San Diego, CA: Jerome M. Sattler, Publisher, Inc.

Saudino, K. J. (1998). Moving beyond the heritability question: New directions in behavioral genetic studies of personality. *Current Directions in Psychological Science, 6,* 86–90.

Saudino, K. J., & Plomin, R. (1997). Cognitive and temperamental mediators of genetic contributions to the home environment during infancy. *Merrill-Palmer Quarterly, 43,* 1–23.

Saudino, K. J., Wertz, A., Gagne, J., & Chawla, S. (2004). Night and day: Are siblings as different in temperament as parents say they are? *Journal of Personality & Social Psychology, 87,* 698–706.

Savage, M., & Holcomb, D. (1999). Adolescent female athletes' sexual risk-taking behaviors. *Journal of Youth & Adolescence, 28,* 583–594.

Savage-Rumbaugh, E. S., Murphy, J., Sevcik, R. A., Brakke, K. E., Williams, S. L., & Rumbaugh, D. M. (1993). Language comprehension in ape and child. *Monographs of the Society for Research in Child Development, 58*(3–4, Serial No. 223).

Scarr, S. (1997). Why child care has little impact on most children's development. *Current Directions in Psychological Science, 6,* 143–147.

Scarr, S., & Eisenberg, M. (1993). Child care research: Issues, perspectives, and results. *Annual Review of Psychology, 44,* 613–644.

Scarr, S., Weinberg, R. A., & Waldman, I. D. (1993). IQ correlations in transracial adoptive families. *Intelligence, 17,* 541–555.

Scerif, G., Karmiloff-Smith, A., Campos, R., Elsabbagh, M., Driver, J., & Cornish, K. (2005). To look or not to look? Typical and atypical development of oculomotor control. *Journal of Cognitive Neuroscience, 17,* 591–604.

Schaal, B., Marlier, L., & Soussignan, R. (1998). Olfactory function in the human fetus: Evidence from selective neonatal responsiveness to the odor of amniotic fluid. *Behavioral Neuroscience, 112,* 1438–1449.

Schank, R. C., & Abelson, R. (1977). *Scripts, plans, goals, and understanding.* Hillsdale, NJ: Erlbaum.

Schatschneider, C., Fletcher, J., Francis, D., Carlson, C., & Foorman, B. (2004). Kindergarten prediction of reading skills: A longitudinal comparative analysis. *Journal of Educational Psychology, 96,* 265–282.

Schatschneider, C., Francis, D., Foorman, B., Fletcher, J., & Mehta, P. (1999). The dimensionality of phonological awareness: An application of item response theory. *Journal of Educational Psychology, 91,* 439–449.

Schechter, R., & Grether, J. (2008). Continuing increases in autism reported to California's developmental services system: Mercury in retrograde. *Archives of General Psychiatry, 65,* 19.

Scheffer, R. (2011). Psychiatric disorders. In K. Marcdante, R. Kliegman, H. Jenson, & R. Behrman (Eds.). *Nelson Essentials of Pediatrics* (6th ed., pp. 63–80). Philadelphia: Saunders.

Schermerhorn, A., Cummings, M., & Davies, P. (2008). Children's representations of multiple family relationships: Organizational structure and development in early childhood. *Journal of Family Psychology, 22,* 89–101.

Schlagmüller, M., & Schneider, W. (2002). The development of organizational strategies in children: Evidence from a microgenetic longitudinal study. *Journal of Experimental Child Psychology, 81,* 298–319.

Schleiss, M. (2010). *Cytomegalovirus infection.* Retrieved June 27, 1010, from http://emedicine.medscape.com/article/963090-overview

Schlochtermeier, L., Stoy, M., Schlagenhauf, F., Wrase, J., Park, S., Friedel, E., et al. (2011). Childhood methylphenidate treatment of ADHD and response to affective stimuli. *European Neuropsychopharmacology, 21,* 646–654.

Schmidt, L., Trainor, L., & Santesso, D. (2003). Development of frontal electroencephalogram (EEG) and heart rate (ECG) responses to affective musical stimuli during the first 12 months of post-natal life. *Brain & Cognition, 52,* 27–32.

Schmitz, S., Fulker, D., Plomin, R., Zahn-Waxler, C., Emde, R., & DeFries, J. (1999). Temperament and problem behavior during early childhood. *International Journal of Behavioral Development, 23,* 333–355.

Schneider, B., Hieshima, J. A., Lee, S., & Plank, S. (1994). East-Asian academic success in the United States: Family, school, and community explanations. In P. M. Greenfield & R. R. Cocking (Eds.), *Crosscultural roots of minority child development* (pp. 323–350). Hillsdale, NJ: Erlbaum.

Schneider, M. L. (1992). The effect of mild stress during pregnancy on birthweight and neuromotor maturation in rhesus monkey infants *(Macaca mulatta). Infant Behavior and Development, 15,* 389–403.

Schneider, W. (2010). Metacognition and memory development in childhood and adolescence. In H. Waters & W. Schneider (Eds.), *Metacognition, strategy use, and instruction* (pp. 54–81). New York: Guilford Press.

Schneider, W., & Bjorklund, D. F. (1992). Expertise, aptitude, and strategic remembering. *Child Development, 63,* 461–473.

Schneider, W., & Bjorklund, D. F. (1998). Memory. In W. Damon (Ed.), *Handbook of child psychology: Vol. 2. Cognition, perception, and language* (5th ed., pp. 467–521). New York: Wiley.

Schneider, W., Gruber, H., Gold, A., & Opwis, K. (1993). Chess expertise and memory for chess positions in children and adults. *Journal of Experimental Child Psychology, 56,* 328–349.

Schneider, W., Reimers, P., Roth, E., & Visé, M. (1995, April). *Short- and long-term effects of training phonological awareness in kindergarten: Evidence from two German studies.* Paper presented at the biennial meetings of the Society for Research in Child Development, Indianapolis.

Schonert-Reichl, K. (1999). Relations of peer acceptance, friendship adjustment, and social behavior to moral reasoning during early adolescence. *Journal of Early Adolescence, 19,* 249–279.

Schothorst, P., & van Engeland, H. (1996). Long-term behavioral sequelae of prematurity. *Journal of the American Academy of Child and Adolescent Psychiatry, 35,* 175–183.

Schott, J., & Rossor, M. (2003). The grasp and other primitive reflexes. *Journal of Neurology, Neurosurgery & Psychiatry, 74,* 558–560.

Schraf, M., & Hertz-Lazarowitz, R. (2003). Social networks in the school context: Effects of culture and gender. *Journal of Social & Personal Relationships, 20,* 843–858.

Schumm, J. S., & Vaughn, S. (1995). Getting ready for inclusion: Is the stage set? *Learning Disabilities Research and Practice, 10,* 169–179.

Schumm, W. (2004). What was really learned from Tasker and Golombok's (1995) study of lesbian and single parent mothers? *Psychological Reports, 94,* 422–424.

Schwartz, C. E., Kunwar, P., Greve, D., Moran, L., Viner, J., Covino, J., et al. (2010). Structural differences in adult orbital and ventromedial prefrontal cortex predicted by infant temperament at 4 months of age. *Archives of General Psychiatry, 67,* 78–84.

Schwartz, C. E., Snidman, N., & Kagan, J. (1996). Early childhood temperament as a determinant of externalizing behavior in adolescence. *Development and Psychopathology, 8,* 527–537.

Schwartz, C. E., Wright, C., Shin, L., Kagan, J., & Rauch, S. (2003). Inhibited and uninhibited infants "grown up": Adult amygdalar response to novelty. *Science, 300,* 1952–1953.

Schwartz, D., Dodge, K. A., & Coie, J. D. (1993). The emergence of chronic peer victimization in boys' play groups. *Child Development, 64,* 1755–1772.

Schwartz, R. M., Anastasia, M. L., Scanlon, J. W., & Kellogg, R. J. (1994). Effect of surfactant on morbidity, mortality, and resource use in newborn infants weighing 500 to 1500 g. *New England Journal of Medicine, 330,* 1476–1480.

Schweinle, A., & Wilcox, T. (2004). Intermodal perception and physical reasoning in young infants. *Infant Behavior and Development, 27,* 246–265.

Scialli, A. (2007). Maternal obesity and pregnancy. *Birth Defects Research Part A: Clinical and Molecular Teratology, 76,* 73–77.

Scott, C., & Temporini, H. (2010). Forensic issues and the Internet. In E. Benedek, P. Ash, & C. Scott (Eds.), *Principles and practice of child and adolescent forensic mental health* (pp. 253–263). Arlington, VA: American Psychiatric Publishing.

Scott, J. (2004). Family, gender, and educational attainment in Britain: A longitudinal study. *Journal of Comparative Family Studies, 35,* 565–589.

Scullard, P., Peacock, C., & Davies, P. (2010). Googling children's health: Reliability of medical advice on the Internet. *Archives of Diseases of Childhood, 95,* 580.

Sears, R. R., Maccoby, E. E., & Levin, H. (1977). *Patterns of child rearing.* Stanford, CA: Stanford University Press. (Originally published 1957 by Row, Peterson)

Sebanc, A. (2003). The friendship features of preschool children: Links with prosocial behavior and aggression. *Social Development, 12,* 249–268.

Sebanc, A., Kearns, K., Hernandez, M., & Galvin, K. (2007). Predicting having a best friend in young children: Individual characteristics and friendship features. *Journal of Genetic Psychology, 168,* 81–95.

Segal, N., McGuire, S., Havelena, J., Gill, P., & Hershberger, S. (2007). Intellectual similarity of virtual twin pairs: Developmental trends. *Personality and Individual Differences, 42,* 1209–1219.

Seibt, B., & Förster, J. (2004). Stereotype threat and performance: How self-stereotypes influence processing by inducing regulatory foci. *Journal of Personality & Social Psychology, 87,* 38–56.

Seidman, E., Allen, L., Aber, J. L., Mitchell, C., & Feinman, J. (1994). The impact of school transitions in early adolescence on the self-system and perceived social context of poor urban youth. *Child Development, 65,* 507–522.

Seidman, E., & French, S. (2004). Developmental trajectories and ecological transitions: A two-step procedure to aid in the choice of prevention and promotion interventions. *Development and Psychopathology, 16*, 1141–1159.

Seifer, R., Schiller, M., Sameroff, A., Resnick, S., & Riordan, K. (1996). Attachment, maternal sensitivity, and infant temperament during the first year of life. *Developmental Psychology, 32*, 12–25.

Seiffge-Krenke, I., & Connolly, J. (2010). Adolescent romantic relationships across the globe: Involvement, conflict management, and linkages to parents and peer relationships. *International Journal of Behavioral Development, 34*, 97.

Seligman, S. (2005). Dynamic systems theories as a metaframework for psychoanalysis. *Psychoanalytic Dialogues, 15*, 285–319.

Selman, R. L. (1980). *The growth of interpersonal understanding.* New York: Academic Press.

Seo, H., Chun, H., Jwa, S., & Choi, M. (2011). *Early Child Development and Care, 181*, 245–265.

Seo, S. (2006). A study of infant developmental outcome with a sample of Korean working mothers of infants in poverty: Implications for early intervention programs. *Early Childhood Education Journal, 33*, 253–260.

Serbin, L., & Karp, J. (2003). Intergenerational studies of parenting and the transfer of risk from parent to child. *Current Directions in Psychological Science, 12*, 138–142.

Serbin, L. A., Powlishta, K. K., & Gulko, J. (1993). The development of sex typing in middle childhood. *Monographs of the Society for Research in Child Development, 58*(2, Serial No. 232).

Serpell, R., & Jere-Folotiya, J. (2008). Developmental assessment, cultural context, gender, and schooling in Zambia. *International Journal of Psychology, 43*, 88–96.

Shaffer, D., Garland, A., Gould, M., Fisher, P., & Trautman, P. (1988). Preventing teenage suicide: A critical review. *Journal of the American Academy of Child and Adolescent Psychiatry, 27*, 675–687.

Shaffer, D., Garland, A., Vieland, V., Underwood, M., & Busner, C. (1991). The impact of curriculum-based suicide prevention programs for teenagers. *Journal of the American Academy of Child and Adolescent Psychiatry, 30*, 588–596.

Shakib, S. (2003). Female basketball participation. *American Behavioral Scientist, 46*, 1405–1422.

Shanahan, M., Sayer, A., Davey, A., & Brooks, J. (1997, April). *Pathways of poverty and children's trajectories of psychosocial adjustment.* Paper presented at the biennial meetings of the Society for Research in Child Development, Washington, DC.

Shantz, C. U. (1983). Social cognition. In J. H. Flavell & E. M. Markman (Eds.), *Handbook of child psychology: Vol. 3. Cognitive development* (pp. 495–555). New York: Wiley.

Sharpe, P. (2002). Preparing for primary school in Singapore: Aspects of adjustment to the more formal demands of the primary one mathematics syllabus. *Early Child Development & Care, 172*, 329–335.

Shayer, M. (2008). Intelligence for education: As described by Piaget and measured by psychometrics. *British Journal of Educational Psychology, 78*, 1–29.

Shayer, M., & Ginsburg, D. (2009). Thirty years on—a large anti-Flynn effect? 13- and 14-year-olds, Piagetian test of formal operations norms 1976-2006/7. *British Journal of Educational Psychology, 79*, 409–418.

Shaywitz, S. (2008). Why some smart people can't read. In M. Immordino-Yang (Ed.), *The Jossey-Bass reader on the brain and learning* (pp. 242–250). San Francisco: Jossey-Bass.

Shaywitz, S. E., Mody, M., & Shaywitz, B. A. (2006). Neural mechanisms in dyslexia. *Current Directions in Psychological Science, 15*, 278–281.

Shaywitz, S. E., Shaywitz, B. A., Pugh, K. R., Fulbright, R. K., Constable, R. T., Mencl, W. E., Shankweiler, D. P., Liberman, A. M., Skudlarski, P., Fletcher, J. M., Katz, L., Marachione, K. E., Lacadie, C., Gatenby, C., & Gore, J. C. (1998). Functional disruption in the organization of the brain for reading in dyslexia. *Proceedings of the National Academy of Sciences, USA, 95*, 2636–2641.

Shepherd, L., & Vernon, P. (2008). Intelligence and speed of information-processing: A review of 50 years of research. *Personality and Individual Differences, 44*, 535–551.

Sherblom, S. (2008). The legacy of the "care challenge": Re-envisioning the outcome of the justice-care debate. *Journal of Moral Education, 37*, 81–98.

Shernoff, D., & Vandell, D. (2007). Engagement in after-school program activities: Quality of experience from the perspective of participants. *Journal of Youth and Adolescence, 36*, 891–903.

Shiao, D. (2011). *In this era of digital and social, the extended family is closer than ever.* Retrieved July 24, 2011, from http://allvirtual.wordpress.com/2011/07/16/in-this-era-of-digital-and-social-the-extended-family-is-closer-than-ever/

Shirley, L., & Campbell, A. (2000). Same-sex preference in infancy. *Psychology, Evolution & Gender, 2*, 3–18.

Shochat, L. (2003). *Our Neighborhood:* Using entertaining children's television to promote interethnic understanding in Macedonia. *Conflict Resolution Quarterly, 21*, 79–93.

Shore, B., & Dover, A. (2004). Metacognition, intelligence, and giftedness. In R. Sternberg (Ed.), *Definitions and conceptions of giftedness* (pp. 39–45). Thousand Oaks, CA: Corwin Press.

Shore, C. (1986). Combinatorial play, conceptual development, and early multiword speech. *Developmental Psychology, 22*, 184–190.

Shore, C. M. (1995). *Individual differences in language development.* Thousand Oaks, CA: Sage.

Shum, D., Neulinger, K., O'Callaghan, M., & Mohay, H. (2008). Attentional problems in children born very preterm or with extremely low birth weight at 7–9 years. *Archives of Clinical Neuropsychology, 23*, 103–112.

Siegel, B. (1996). Is the emperor wearing clothes? Social policy and the empirical support for full inclusion of children with disabilities in the preschool and early elementary grades. *Social Policy Report, Society for Research in Child Development, 10*(2–3), 2–17.

Siegler, R. (1996). *Emerging minds: The process of change in children's thinking.* New York: Oxford University Press.

Siegler, R., & Chen, Z. (2002). Development of rules and strategies: Balancing the old and the new. *Journal of Experimental Child Psychology, 81*, 446–457.

Siegler, R., & Svetina, M. (2002). A microgenetic/cross-sectional study of matrix completion: Comparing short-term and long-term change. *Child Development, 73*, 793–809.

Siegler, R. S., & Ellis, S (1996). Piaget on childhood. *Psychological Science, 7*, 211–215.

Siegler, R., & Lin, X. (2010). Self-explanations promote children's learning. In H. Waters & W. Schneider (Eds.), *Metacognition, strategy use, and instruction* (pp. 85–112). New York: Guilford Press.

Sigman, M., & McGovern, C. (2005). Improvement in cognitive and language skills from preschool to adolescence in autism. *Journal of Autism & Developmental Disorders, 35*, 15–23.

Sigman, M., Neumann, C., Carter, E., Cattle, D. J., D'Souza, S., & Bwibo, N. (1988). Home interactions and the development of Embu toddlers in Kenya. *Child Development, 59*, 1251–1261.

Silverberg, S. B., & Gondoli, D. M. (1996). Autonomy in adolescence: A contextualized perspective. In G. R. Adams, R. Montemayor, & T. P. Gullotta (Eds.), *Psychosocial development during adolescence: Progress in developmental contextualism* (pp. 12–61). Thousand Oaks, CA: Sage.

Silvia, P., Winterstein, B., Willse, J., Barona, C., Cram, J., Hess, K., Martinez, J., & Richard, C. (2008). Assessing creativity with divergent thinking tasks: Exploring the reliability and validity of new subjective scoring methods. *Psychology of Aesthetics, Creativity, and the Arts, 2,* 68–85.

Simonoff, E., Pickles, A., Meyer, J. M., Silberg, J. L., Maes, H. H., Loeber, R., Rutter, M., Hewitt, J. K., & Eaves, L. J. (1997). The Virginia twin study of adolescent behavioral development. *Archives of General Psychiatry, 54,* 801–808.

Simpkins, S., Davis-Kean, P., & Eccles, J. (2005). Parents' socializing behavior and children's participation in math, science, and computer out-of-school activities. *Applied Development Science, 9,* 14–30.

Singh, S., & Darroch, J. (2000). Adolescent pregnancy and childbearing: Levels and trends in industrialized countries. *Family Planning Perspectives, 32,* 14–23.

Singh, S., Wulf, D., Samara, R., & Cuca, Y. (2000). Gender differences in the timing of first intercourse: Data from 14 countries. *International Family Planning Perspectives, 26,* 21–28, 43.

Sinigaglia, C., & Rizzolatti, G. (2011). Through the looking glass: Self and others. *Consciousness and Cognition: An International Journal, 20,* 64–74.

Skinner, B. F. (1957). *Verbal behavior.* New York: Prentice Hall.

Skwarchuk, S., & Anglin, J. (2002). Children's acquisition of the English cardinal number words: A special case of vocabulary development. *Journal of Educational Psychology, 94,* 107–125.

Slaby, R. G., & Frey, K. S. (1975). Development of gender constancy and selective attention to same-sex models. *Child Development, 46,* 849–856.

Slaughter-Defoe, D., & Rubin, H. (2001). A longitudinal case study of Head Start eligible children: Implications for urban education. *Educational Psychologist, 36,* 31–44.

Slobin, D. I. (1985a). Crosslinguistic evidence for the language-making capacity. In D. I. Slobin (Ed.), *The crosslinguistic study of language acquisition, Vol. 2: Theoretical issues* (pp. 1157–1256). Hillsdale, NJ: Erlbaum.

Slobin, D. I. (1985b). Introduction: Why study acquisition crosslinguistically? In D. I. Slobin (Ed.), *The crosslinguistic study of language acquisition, Vol. 1: The data* (pp. 3–24). Hillsdale, NJ: Erlbaum.

Smetana, J. G. (1990). Morality and conduct disorders. In M. Lewis & S. M. Miller (Eds.), *Handbook of developmental psychopathology* (pp. 157–180). New York: Plenum Press.

Smetana, J. G., (2006). Social-cognitive domain theory: Consistencies and variations in children's moral and social judgments. In M. Killen & J. Smetana (Eds.), *Handbook of moral development* (pp. 119–153). Mahwah, NJ: Lawrence Erlbaum Associates.

Smith, A., Lalonde, R., & Johnson, S. (2004). Serial migration and its implications for the parent-child relationship: A retrospective analysis of the experiences of the children of Caribbean immigrants. *Cultural Diversity & Ethnic Minority Psychology, 10,* 107–122.

Smith, C., & Farrington, D. (2004). Continuities in antisocial behavior and parenting across three generations. *Journal of Child Psychology and Psychiatry, 45,* 230–247.

Smith, J. R., Brooks-Gunn, J., & Klebanov, P. K. (1997). Consequences of living in poverty for young children's cognitive and verbal ability and early school achievement. In G. J. Duncan & J. Brooks-Gunn (Eds.), *Consequences of growing up poor* (pp. 132–179). New York: Russell Sage Foundation.

Smith, P., & Slonje, R. (2010). Cyberbullying: The nature and extent of a new kind of bullying, in and out of school. In S. Jimerson, S. Swearer, & D. Espelage (Eds.), *Handbook of bullying in schools: An international perspective* (pp. 249–262). New York: Routledge/Taylor & Francis Group.

Smith, S. (2011). Infectious diseases. In K. Marcdante, R. Kliegman, H. Jensen, & R. Behrman (Eds.), *Nelson's essential of pediatrics* (pp. 355–462). New York: Elsevier Health Publishers.

Smith, S., Howard, J., & Monroe, A. (1998). An analysis of child behavior problems in adoptions in difficulty. *Journal of Social Service Research, 24,* 61–84.

Smokowski, P., Mann, E., Reynolds, A., & Fraser, M. (2004). Childhood risk and protective factors and late adolescent adjustment in inner city minority youth. *Children and Youth Services Review, 26,* 63–91.

Smoll, F. L., & Schutz, R. W. (1990). Quantifying gender differences in physical performance: A developmental perspective. *Developmental Psychology, 26,* 360–369.

Snarey, J. R. (1985). Cross-cultural universality of social-moral development: A critical review of Kohlbergian research. *Psychological Bulletin, 97,* 202–232.

Snarey, J. R., Reimer, J., & Kohlberg, L. (1985). Development of social-moral reasoning among kibbutz adolescents: A longitudinal cross-sectional study. *Developmental Psychology, 21,* 3–17.

Snow, C. E. (1997, April). Cross-domain connections and social class differences: Two challenges to nonenvironmentalist views of language development. Paper presented at the biennial meetings of the Society for Research in Child Development, Washington, DC.

Soderstrom, M. (2007). Beyond babytalk: Re-evaluating the nature and content of speech input to preverbal infants. *Developmental Review, 27,* 501–532.

Soderstrom, M., & Morgan, J. (2007). Twenty-two-month-olds discriminate fluent from disfluent adult-directed speech. *Developmental Science, 10,* 641–653.

Sola, A., Rogido, M., & Partridge, J. (2002). The perinatal period. In A. Rudolph, R. Kamei, & K. Overby (Eds.), *Rudolph's fundamentals of pediatrics* (3rd ed., pp. 125–183). New York: McGraw-Hill.

Soltis, J. (2004). The signal functions of early infant crying. *Brain and Behavior Sciences, 27,* 443–458.

Sonnenschein, S. (1986). Development of referential communication skills: How familiarity with a listener affects a speaker's production of redundant messages. *Developmental Psychology, 22,* 549–552.

Sotelo, M., & Sangrador, J. (1997). Psychological aspects of political tolerance among adolescents. *Psychological Reports, 81,* 1279–1288.

Soto, C., John, O., Gosling, S., & Potter, J. (2008). The developmental psychometrics of Big Five self-reports: Acquiescence, factor structure, coherence, and differentiation from ages 10 to 20. *Journal of Personality and Social Psychology, 94,* 718–737.

Soto, C., John, O., Gosling, S., & Potter, J. (2011). Age differences in personality traits from 10 to 65: Big five domains and facets in a large cross-sectional sample. *Journal of Personality and Social Psychology, 100,* 330–348.

Sowell, E., Peterson, B., Thompson, P., Welcome, S., Henkenius, A., & Toga, A. (2003). Mapping cortical change across the human life span. *Nature Neuroscience, 6,* 309–315.

Spelke, E., & Kinzler, K. (2007). Core knowledge. *Developmental Science, 10,* 89–96.

Spelke, E. S. (1979). Exploring audible and visible events in infancy. In A. D. Pick (Ed.), *Perception and its development: A tribute to Eleanor J. Gibson* (pp. 221–236). Hillsdale, NJ: Erlbaum.

Spelke, E. S. (1982). Perceptual knowledge of objects in infancy. In J. Mehler, E. C. T. Walker, & M. Garrett (Eds.), *Perspectives on mental representation* (pp. 409–430). Hillsdale, NJ: Erlbaum.

Spelke, E. S. (1985). Perception of unity, persistence, and identity: Thoughts on infants' conceptions of objects. In J. Mehler & R. Fox (Eds.), *Neonate cognition* (pp. 89–113). Hillsdale, NJ: Erlbaum.

Spelke, E. S. (1991). Physical knowledge in infancy: Reflections on Piaget's theory. In S. Carey & R. Gelman (Eds.), *The epigenesis of mind: Essays on biology and cognition* (pp. 133–169). Hillsdale, NJ: Erlbaum.

Spelke, E. S., von Hofsten, C., & Kestenbaum, R. (1989). Object perception in infancy: Interaction of spatial and kinetic information for object boundaries. *Developmental Psychology, 25,* 185–196.

Spence, J. T., & Helmreich, R. L. (1978). *Masculinity and femininity.* Austin: University of Texas Press.

Spencer, N. (2003). Social, economic, and political determinants of child health. *Pediatrics, 112,* 704–706.

Spiker, D. (1990). Early intervention from a developmental perspective. In D. Cicchetti & M. Beeghly (Eds.), *Children with Down syndrome: A developmental perspective* (pp. 424–448). Cambridge, England: Cambridge University Press.

Spreen, O., Risser, A., & Edgell, D. (1995). *Developmental neuropsychology.* New York: Oxford University Press.

Springer, S. (2010). *The fetus as a patient: Prenatal diagnosis and fetal therapy.* Retrieved June 27, 2010, from http://emedicine.medscape.com/article/947706-overview

Sroufe, A., Egeland, B., Carlson, E., & Collins, W. (2005). *The development of the person: The Minnesota study of risk and adaptation from birth to adulthood.* New York: Guilford Publications.

Sroufe, A., Egeland, B., & Kreutzer, T. (1990). The fate of early experience following developmental change: Longitudinal approaches to individual adaptation in childhood. *Child Development, 61,* 1363–1373.

Sroufe, L., Bennett, C., England, M., Urban, J., & Shulman, S. (1993). The significance of gender boundaries in preadolescence: Contemporary correlates and antecedants of boundary violations and maintenance. *Child Development, 64,* 455–466.

Sroufe, L. A. (1983). Infant-caregiver attachment and patterns of adaptation in preschool: The roots of maladaption and competence. In M. Perlmutter (Ed.), *The Minnesota symposia on child psychology* (Vol. 16, pp. 41–84). Hillsdale, NJ: Erlbaum.

Sroufe, L. A. (1988). The role of infant-caregiver attachment in development. In J. Belsky & T. Nezworski (Eds.), *Clinical implications of attachment* (pp. 18–40). Hillsdale, NJ: Erlbaum.

Sroufe, L. A. (1989). Pathways to adaptation and maladaptation: Psychopathology as developmental deviation. In D. Cicchetti (Ed.), *The emergence of a discipline: Rochester symposium on developmental psychopathology* (pp. 13–40). Hillsdale, NJ: Erlbaum.

Sroufe, L. A. (1990). A developmental perspective on day care. In N. Fox & G. G. Fein (Eds.), *Infant day care: The current debate* (pp. 51–60). Norwood, NJ: Ablex.

Sroufe, L. A. (1996). *Emotional development: The organization of emotional life in the early years.* Cambridge, England: Cambridge University Press.

Sroufe, L. A. (1997). Psychopathology as an outcome of development. *Development and Psychopathology, 9,* 251–268.

Sroufe, L. A., & Rutter, M. (1984). The domain of developmental psychopathology. *Child Development, 55,* 17–29.

Stainback, S., & Stainback, W. (1985). The merger of special and regular education: Can it be done? A response to Lieberman and Mesinger. *Exceptional Children, 51,* 517–521.

Standley, J. (2003). *Music therapy with premature infants: Research and developmental interventions.* Silver Spring, MD: American Music Therapy Association.

Standley, J., Cassidy, J., Grant, R., Cevasco, A., Szuch, C., Nguyen, J., et al. (2010). The effect of music reinforcement for non-nutritive sucking on nipple feeding of premature infants. *Pediatric Nursing, 36,* 138–145.

Stansfield, S., Head, J., Bartley, M., & Fonagy, P. (2008). Social position, early deprivation, and the development of attachment. *Social Psychiatry and Psychiatric Epidemiology, 43,* 516–526.

Starfield, B. (1991). Childhood morbidity: Comparisons, clusters, and trends. *Pediatrics, 88,* 519–526.

Stattin, H., & Klackenberg-Larsson, I. (1993). Early language and intelligence development and their relationship to future criminal behavior. *Journal of Abnormal Psychology, 102,* 369–378.

Steele, C., & Aronson, J. (1995). Stereotype threat and the intellectual test performance of African Americans. *Journal of Personality & Social Psychology, 69,* 797–811.

Steele, H., Holder, J., & Fonagy, P. (1995, April). *Quality of attachment to mother at one year predicts belief-desire reasoning at five years.* Paper presented at the biennial meetings of the Society for Research in Child Development, Indianapolis.

Steele, J., & Mayes, S. (1995). Handedness and directional asymmetry in the long bones of the human upper limb. *International Journal of Osteoarchaeology, 5,* 39–49.

Steele, M., Hodges, J., Kaniuk, J., Hillman, S., & Henderson, K. (2003). Attachment representations and adoption: Associations between maternal states of mind and emotion narratives in previously maltreated children. *Journal of Child Psychotherapy, 29,* 187–205.

Stein, K., Roeser, R., & Markus, H. (1998). Self-schemas and possible selves as predictors and outcomes of risky behaviors in adolescents. *Nursing Research, 47,* 96–106.

Steinberg, E., Tanofsky-Kraff, M., Cohen, M., Elberg, J., Freedman, R., Semega-Janneh, M., Yanovski, S., & Yanovski, J. (2004). Comparison of the child and parent forms of the Questionnaire on Eating and Weight Patterns in the assessment of children's eating-disordered behaviors. *International Journal of Eating Disorders, 36,* 183–194.

Steinberg, L. (1986). Latchkey children and susceptibility to peer pressure: An ecological analysis. *Developmental Psychology, 22,* 433–439.

Steinberg, L. (1996). *Beyond the classroom: Why school reform has failed and what parents need to do.* New York: Simon & Schuster.

Steinberg, L. (2005). Cognitive and affective development in adolescence. *Trends in Cognitive Sciences, 9,* 69–74.

Steinberg, L. (2008). A social neuroscience perspective on adolescent risk-taking. *Developmental Review, 28,* 78–106.

Steinberg, L., Blatt-Eisengart, I., & Cauffman, E. (2006). Patterns of competence and adjustment among adolescents from authoritative, authoritarian, indulgent, and neglectful homes: A replication in a sample of serious juvenile offenders. *Journal of Research on Adolescence, 16,* 47–58.

Steinberg, L., Darling, N. E., Fletcher, A. C., Brown, B. B., & Dornbusch, S. M. (1995). Authoritative parenting and adolescent adjustment: An ecological journey. In P. Moen, G. H. Elder, Jr., & K. Lüscher (Eds.), *Examining lives in context: Perspectives on the ecology of human development* (pp. 423–466). Washington, DC: American Psychological Association.

Steinberg, L., & Dornbusch, S. M. (1991). Negative correlates of part-time employment during adolescence: Replication and elaboration. *Developmental Psychology, 27,* 304–313.

Steinberg, L., Dornbusch, S. M., & Brown, B. B. (1992). Ethnic differences in adolescent achievement: An ecological perspective. *American Psychologist, 47,* 723–729.

Steinberg, L., Elmen, J. D., & Mounts, N. S. (1989). Authoritative parenting, psychosocial maturity, and academic success among adolescents. *Child Development, 60,* 1424–1436.

Steinberg, L., Lamborn, S. D., Darling, N., Mounts, N. S., & Dornbusch, S. M. (1994). Over-time changes in adjustment and competence among adolescents from authoritative, authoritarian, indulgent, and neglectful families. *Child Development, 65,* 754–770.

Steinberg, L., Lamborn, S. D., Dornbusch, S. M., & Darling, N. (1992). Impact of parenting practices on adolescent achievement: Authoritative parenting, school involvement, and encouragement to succeed. *Child Development, 63,* 1266–1281.

Steinberg, L., Mounts, N. S., Lamborn, S. D., & Dornbusch, S. D. (1991). Authoritative parenting and adolescent adjustment across varied ecological niches. *Journal of Research on Adolescence, 1*, 19–36.

Steinberg, L., & Silk, J. (2002). Parenting adolescents. In M. Bornstein, (Ed.), *Handbook of parenting: Volume 1: Children and parenting* (2nd ed.), (pp. 103–133). Mahwah, NJ: Erlbaum.

Steiner, J. E. (1979). Human facial expressions in response to taste and smell stimulation. In H. W. Reese & L. P. Lipsitt (Eds.), *Advances in child development and behavior* (Vol. 13, pp. 257–296). New York: Academic Press.

van der Stel, M., & Veenman, M. (2010). Development of metacognitive skillfulness: A longitudinal study. *Learning and Individual Differences, 20*, 220–224.

Stelzl, I., Merz, F., Ehlers, T., & Remer, H. (1995). The effect of schooling on the development of fluid and crystallized intelligence: A quasi-experimental study. *Intelligence, 21*, 279–296.

Stemler, S., Chamvu, F., Chart, H., Jarvin, L., Jere, J., Hart, L., et al. (2009). Assessing competencies in reading and mathematics in Zambian children. In E. Grigorenko (Ed.), *Multicultural psychoeducational assessment* (pp. 157–185). New York: Springer Publishing.

Sternberg, R. (2001). What is the common thread of creativity? Its dialectical relation to intelligence and wisdom. *American Psychologist, 56*, 360–362.

Sternberg, R. (2003). Construct validity of the theory of successful intelligence. In R. Sternberg, J. Lautrey, & T. Lubart (Eds.), *Models of intelligence: International perspectives* (pp. 55–80). Washington, DC: American Psychological Association.

Sternberg, R. (2008). The WICS approach to leadership: Stories of leadership and the structures and processes that support them. *The Leadership Quarterly, 19*, 360–371.

Sternberg, R. (2011). The theory of successful intelligence. In R. Sternberg & S. Kaufman (Eds.), *The Cambridge handbook of intelligence* (pp. 504–527). New York: Cambridge University Press.

Sternberg, R., Castejon, J., Prieto, M., Hautamaeki, J., & Grigorenko, E. (2001). Confirmatory factor analysis of the Sternberg Triarchic Abilities Test in three international samples: An empirical test of the triarchic theory of intelligence. *European Journal of Psychological Assessment, 17*, 1–16.

Sternberg, R., & Grigorenko, E. (2006). Cultural intelligence and successful intelligence. *Group & Organization Management, 31*, 37–39.

Sternberg, R. J. (1985). *Beyond IQ: A triarchic theory of human intelligence.* New York: Cambridge University Press.

Sternberg, R. J., & Davidson, J. E. (1985). Cognitive development in the gifted and talented. In F. D. Horowitz & M. O'Brien (Eds.), *The gifted and talented: Developmental perspectives* (pp. 37–74). Washington, DC: American Psychological Association.

Sternberg, R. J., & Wagner, R. K. (1993). The geocentric view of intelligence and job performance is wrong. *Current Directions in Psychological Science, 2*, 1–5.

Stevenson, H. W. (1988). Culture and schooling: Influences on cognitive development. In E. M. Hetherington, R. M. Lerner, & M. Perlmutter (Eds.), *Child development in life span perspective* (pp. 241–258). Hillsdale, NJ: Erlbaum.

Stevenson, H. W., & Lee, S. (1990). Contexts of achievement: A study of American, Chinese, and Japanese children. *Monographs of the Society for Research in Child Development, 55*(1–2, Serial No. 221).

Stevenson, H. W., Lee, S., Chen, C., Lummis, M., Stigler, J., Fan, L., & Ge, F. (1990). Mathematics achievement of children in China and the United States. *Child Development, 61*, 1053–1066.

Stewart, P. (2007). Who is kin? Family definition and African American families. *Journal of Human Behavior in the Social Environment, 15*, 163–181.

Stewart, R. B., Beilfuss, M. L., & Verbrugge, K. M. (1995, April). *That was then, this is now: An empirical typology of adult sibling relationships.* Paper presented at the biennial meetings of the Society for Research in Child Development, Indianapolis.

Stigler, J. W., Lee, S., & Stevenson, H. W. (1987). Mathematics classrooms in Japan, Taiwan, and the United States. *Child Development, 58*, 1272–1285.

Stigler, J. W., & Stevenson, H. W. (1991, Spring). How Asian teachers polish each lesson to perfection. *American Educator 12–20*, 43–47.

St. James-Roberts, I., Bowyer, J., Varghese, S., & Sawdon, J. (1994). Infant crying patterns in Manila and London. *Child: Care, Health and Development, 20*, 323–337.

Stolarova, M., Whitney, H., Webb, S., deRegnier, R., Georgieff, M., & Nelson, C. (2003). Electrophysiological brain responses of six-month-old low risk premature infants. *Infancy, 4*, 437–450.

Stolt, S., Haataja, L., Lapinleimu, H., & Lehtonen, L. (2009). Associations between lexicon and grammar at the end of the second year in Finnish children. *Journal of Child Language, 36*, 779–806.

Stoutjesdyk, D., & Jevne, R. (1993). Eating disorders among high performance athletes. *Journal of Youth & Adolescence, 22*, 271–282.

Straus, M. A. (1995). Corporal punishment of children and adult depression and suicidal ideation. In J. McCord (Ed.), *Coercion and punishment in long-term perspectives* (pp. 59–77). Cambridge, England: Cambridge University Press.

Strauss, S., & Altwerger, B. (2007). The logographic nature of English alphabetics and the fallacy of direct intensive phonics instruction. *Journal of Early Childhood Literacy, 7*, 299–319.

Strayer, J., & Roberts, W. (2004). Empathy and observed anger and aggression in five-year-olds. *Social Development, 13*, 1–13.

Streissguth, A., Bookstein, F., Barr, H., Sampson, P., O'Malley, K., & Young, J. (2005). Risk factors for adverse life outcomes in fetal alcohol syndrome and fetal alcohol effects. *Journal of Developmental & Behavioral Pediatrics, 25*, 228–238.

Streissguth, A. P., Barr, H. M., & Sampson, P. D. (1990). Moderate prenatal alcohol exposure: Effects on child IQ and learning problems at age 7½ years. *Alcoholism: Clinical and Experimental Research, 14*, 662–669.

Streissguth, A. P., Barr, H. M., Sampson, P. D., Darby, B. L., & Martin, D. C. (1989). IQ at age 4 in relation to maternal alcohol use and smoking during pregnancy. *Developmental Psychology, 25*, 3–11.

Streissguth, A. P., Bookstein, F. L., Barr, H. M., Sampson, P. D., O'Malley, K., & Young, J. (2004). Risk factors for adverse life outcomes in fetal alcohol syndrome and fetal alcohol effects. *Journal of Developmental and Behavioral Pediatrics, 25*, 228–238.

Streissguth, A. P., Bookstein, F. L., Sampson, P. D., & Barr, H. M. (1995). Attention: Prenatal alcohol and continuities of vigilance and attentional problems from 4 through 14 years. *Development and Psychopathology, 7*, 419–446.

Streissguth A. P., Landesman-Dwyer, S., Martin, J. C., & Smith, D. W. (1980). Teratogenic effects of alcohol in humans and laboratory animals. *Science, 209*, 353–361.

Streissguth, A. P., Martin, D. C., Barr, H. M., Sandman, B. M., Kirchner, G. L., & Darby, B. L. (1984). Intrauterine alcohol and nicotine exposure: Attention and reaction time in 4-year-old children. *Developmental Psychology, 20*, 533–541.

Streissguth, A. P., Martin, D. C., Martin, J. C., & Barr, H. M. (1981). The Seattle longitudinal prospective study on alcohol and pregnancy. *Neurobehavioral Toxicology and Teratology, 3*, 223–233.

Stunkard, A. J., Harris, J. R., Pedersen, N. L., & McClearn, G. E (1990). The body-mass index of twins who have been reared apart. *New England Journal of Medicine, 322,* 1483–1487.

Styne, D., & Glaser, N. (2002). Endocrinology. In R. Behrman & R. Klingman (Eds.), *Nelson essentials of pediatrics* (4th ed., pp. 711–766). Philadelphia: Saunders.

Subrahmanyam, K. (2009). Developmental implications of children's virtual worlds. *Washington & Lee Law Review, 66,* 1065–1083.

Subrahmanyam, K., & Greenfield, P. (2008). Media symbol systems and cognitive processes. In S. Calvert & B. Wilson (Eds.), *The handbook of children, media, and development* (pp. 166–187). New York: John Wiley & Sons.

Sudarkasa, N. (1993). Female-headed African American households: Some neglected dimensions. In H. P. McAdoo (Ed.), *Family ethnicity* (pp. 81–89). Newbury Park, CA: Sage.

Suizzo, M., & Stapleton, L. (2007). Home-based parental involvement in young children's education: Examining the effects of maternal education across U.S. ethnic groups. *Educational Psychology, 27,* 1–24.

Sulkes, S. (1998). Developmental and behavioral pediatrics. In R. Behrman & R. Kliegman (Eds.), *Nelson essentials of pediatrics* (3rd ed.). Philadelphia: Saunders.

Sullivan, K., Zaitchik, D., & Tager-Flusberg, H. (1994). Preschoolers can attribute second-order beliefs. *Developmental Psychology, 30,* 395–402.

Sumner, M., Bernard, K., & Dozier, M. (2010). Young children's full-day patterns of cortisol production. *Archives of Pediatrics & Adolescent Medicine, 164,* 567–571.

Super, C. (1976). Environmental effects on motor development. *Developmental Medicine & Child Neurology, 18,* 561–567.

Suzuki, L., & Aronson, J. (2005). The cultural malleability of intelligence and its impact on the racial/ethnic hierarchy. *Psychology, Public Policy, & Law, 11,* 320–327.

Swain, I. U., Zelazo, P. R., & Clifton, R. K. (1993). Newborn infants' memory for speech sounds retained over 24 hours. *Developmental Psychology, 29,* 312–323.

Swedo, S. E., Rettew, D. C., Kuppenheimer, M., Lum, D., Dolan, S., & Goldberger, E. (1991). Can adolescent suicide attempters be distinguished from at-risk adolescents? *Pediatrics, 88,* 620–629.

Sweeting, H., & West, P. (2002). Gender differences in weight related concerns in early to late adolescence. *Journal of Family Issues, 23,* 728–747.

Taga, K., Markey, C., & Friedman, H. (2006). A longitudinal investigation of associations between boys' pubertal timing and adult behavioral health and well-being. *Journal of Youth and Adolescence, 35,* 401–411.

Takei, W. (2001). How do deaf infants attain first signs? *Developmental Science, 4,* 71–78.

Takimoto, H. (2006). Malnutrition during pregnancy in Japan and proposals for improvement. *Acta Obstetrica et Gynaecologica Japonica, 58,* 1514–1518.

Talmor, R., Reiter, S., & Feigin, N. (2005). Factors relating to regular education teacher burnout in inclusive education. *European Journal of Special Needs Education, 20,* 215–229.

Tam, H., Jarrold, C., Baddeley, A., & Sabatos-De Vito, M. (2010). The development of memory maintenance: Children's use of phonological rehearsal and attentional refreshment in working memory tasks. *Journal of Experimental Child Psychology, 107,* 306–324.

Tamis-LeMonda, C., Shannon, J., Cabrera, N., & Lamb, M. (2004). Fathers and mothers at play with their 2- and 3-year-olds: Contributions to language and cognitive development. *Child Development, 76,* 1806–1820.

Tani, F., Greenman, P., Schneider, B., & Fregoso, M. (2003). Bullying and the Big Five: A study of childhood personality and participant roles in bullying incidents. *School Psychology International, 24,* 131–146.

Tani, F., Rossi, S., & Smorti, M. (2005). Friendship choice criteria in children and adolescents: A study on personality characteristics. *Eta Evolutiva, 81,* 33–43.

Tanner, J. M. (1990). *Foetus into man* (revised and enlarged ed.). Cambridge, MA: Harvard University Press.

Tan-Niam, C., Wood, D., & O'Malley, C. (1998). A cross-cultural perspective on children's theories of mind and social interaction. *Early Child Development & Care, 144,* 55–67.

Tare, M., Shatz, M., & Gilbertson, L. (2008). Maternal uses of non-object terms in child-directed speech: Color, number and time. *First Language, 28,* 87–100.

Tasbihsazan, R., Nettelbeck, T., & Kirby, N. (2003). Predictive validity of the Fagan Test of Infant Intelligence. *British Journal of Developmental Psychology, 21,* 585–597.

Taveras, E., Gillman, M., Kleinman, K., Rich-Edwards, J., & Rifas-Shiman, S. (2010). Racial/ethnic differences in early-life risk factors for childhood obesity. *Pediatrics, 125,* 686–695.

Taylor, M. G. (1996). The development of children's beliefs about social and biological aspects of gender differences. *Child Development, 67,* 1555–1571.

Taylor, R. D., Casten, R., Flickinger, S. M., Roberts, D., & Fulmore, C. D. (1994). Explaining the school performance of African-American adolescents. *Journal of Research on Adolescence, 4,* 21–44.

Taylor, R. D., & Roberts, D. (1995). Kinship support and maternal and adolescent well-being in economically disadvantaged African-American families. *Child Development, 66,* 1585–1597.

Taylor, W., Ayars, C., Gladney, A., Peters, R., Roy, J., Prokhorov, A., Chamberlain, R., & Gritz, E. (1999). Beliefs about smoking among adolescents: Gender and ethnic differences. *Journal of Child & Adolescent Substance Abuse, 8,* 37–54.

Teasdale, T., & Owen, D. (2005). A long-term rise and recent decline in intelligence test performance: The Flynn Effect in reverse. *Personality and Individual Differences, 39,* 837–843.

Teasdale, T., & Owen, D. (2008). Secular declines in cognitive test scores: A reversal of the Flynn Effect. *Intelligence, 36,* 121–126.

Teitelman, A., Ratcliffe, S., & Cederbaum, J. (2008). Parent-adolescent communication about sexual pressure, maternal norms about relationship power, and STI/HIV protective behaviors of minority urban girls. *Journal of the American Psychiatric Nurses Association, 14,* 50–60.

ter Laak, J., de Goede, M., Alevan, L., Brugman, G., van Leuven, M., & Hussmann, J. (2003). Incarcerated adolescent girls: Personality, social competence and delinquency. *Adolescence, 38,* 251–265.

Terman, L. (1916). *The measurement of intelligence.* Boston: Houghton Mifflin.

Terman, L. (1925). *Genetic studies of genius: Vol. 1. Mental and physical traits of a thousand gifted children.* Stanford: CA: Stanford University Press.

Terman, L., & Merrill, M. A. (1937). *Measuring intelligence: A guide to the administration of the new revised Stanford-Binet tests.* Boston: Houghton Mifflin.

Terman, L., & Oden, M. (1959). *Genetic studies of genius: Vol. 5. The gifted group at mid-life.* Stanford, CA: Stanford University Press.

Terrisse, B. (2000, April). *The resilient child: Theoretical perspectives and a review of the literature.* Paper presented to the Council of Ministers of Education, Ottawa, ON, Canada.

Tessier, R., Cristo, M., Velez, S., Giron, M., Line, N., Figueroa de Calume, Z., Ruiz-Palaez, J., & Charpak, N. (2003). Kangaroo Mother Care: A method for protecting high-risk low-birth-weight and premature infants against developmental delay. *Infant Behavior and Development, 26,* 384–397.

Tharenou, P. (1999). Is there a link between family structures and women's and men's managerial career advancement? *Journal of Organizational Behavior, 20,* 837–863.

Tharpe, A. (2006). *The impact of minimal and mild hearing loss on children.* Retrieved March 19, 2008, from http://www. medicalhomeinfo. org/screening/EHDI/June_26_2006_FINAL_MildHearingLoss.pdf

Thelen, E. (1983). Learning to walk is still an "old" problem: A reply to Zelazo. *Journal of Motor Behavior, 15,* 139–161.

Thelen, E. (1995). Motor development: A new synthesis. *American Psychologist, 50,* 79–95.

Thelen, E., & Adolph, K. E. (1992). Arnold L. Gesell: The paradox of nature and nurture. *Developmental Psychology, 28,* 368–380.

Thelen, E., & Smith, L. (1996). *A dynamic systems approach to the development of cognition and action.* Cambridge, MA: MIT Press.

Thomas, A., & Chess, S. (1977). *Temperament and development.* New York: Brunner/Mazel.

Thomas, D., Townsend, T., & Belgrave, F. (2003). The influence of cultural and racial identification on the psychosocial adjustment of inner-city African American children in school. *American Journal of Community Psychology, 32,* 217–228.

Thomas, M. (2000). *Comparing theories of child development* (5th ed.). Pacific Grove, CA: Brooks/Cole.

Thomas, M. (2005). Comparing theories of child development (6th ed.). Pacific Grove, CA: Wadsworth/Cengage.

Thomas, M., & Karmiloff-Smith, A. (2003). Connectionist models of development, developmental disorders, and individual differences. In R. Sternberg, J. Lautrey, & T. Lubart (Eds.), *Models of intelligence: International perspectives* (pp. 133–150). Washington, DC: American Psychological Association.

Thomas, R. (2005). *Comparing theories of child development* (6th ed.). Pacific Grove, CA: Brooks/Cole.

Thomas, R. M. (1990). Motor development. In R. M. Thomas (Ed.), *The encyclopedia of human development and education: Theory, research, and studies* (pp. 326–330). Oxford: Pergamon Press.

Thommessen, S., & Todd, B. (2010, April 2010). *Revisiting sex differences in play: Very early evidence of stereotypical preferences in infancy.* Paper presented at the annual meeting of the British Psychological Society, Stratford-upon-Avon, UK.

Thompson, J., & Halberstadt, A. (2008). Children's accounts of sibling jealousy and their implicit theories about relationships. *Social Development, 17,* 488–511.

Thompson, P., Cannon, T., Narr, K., van Erp, T., Poutanen, V., Huttunen, M., Lovist, J., Nordenstam, C., Kaprio, J., Khaledy, M., Dail, R., Zoumalan, C., & Toga, A. (2001). Genetic influences on brain structure. *Nature Neuroscience, 4,* 1253–1258.

Thompson, P., Giedd, J., Woods, R., MacDonald, D., Evans, A., & Toga, A. (2000). Growth patterns in the developing brain detected by using continuum mechanical tensor maps. *Nature, 404,* 190–193.

Thompson, R. (2009). Early foundations: Conscience and the development of moral character. In D. Narvaez & D. Lapsley (Eds.), *Personality, identity, and character: Explorations in moral psychology* (pp. 159–184). New York: Cambridge University Press.

Thompson, R., & Newton, E. (2010). Emotion in early conscience. In W. Arsenio & E. Lemerise (Eds.), *Emotions, aggression, and morality in children: Bridging development and psychopathology* (pp. 13–31). Washington, DC: American Psychological Association.

Thompson, R., Winer, A., & Goodvin, R. (2011). The individual child: Temperament, emotion, self, and personality. In M. Bornstein & M. Lamb (Eds.), *Developmental science: An advanced textbook* (6th ed., pp. 427–468). New York: Psychology Press.

Thompson, R. A. (1998). Early sociopersonality development. In W. Damon (Ed.), *Handbook of child psychology: Vol. 3. Social, emotional, and personality development* (5th ed., pp. 25–104). New York: Wiley.

Thompson, S. K. (1975). Gender labels and early sex role development. *Child Development, 46,* 339–347.

Thorn, A., & Gathercole, S. (1999). Language-specific knowledge and short-term memory in bilingual and non-bilingual children. *Quarterly Journal of Experimental Psychology: Human Experimental Psychology, 52A,* 303–324.

Tideman, E., Nilsson, A., Smith, G., & Stjernqvist, K. (2002). Longitudinal follow-up of children born preterm: The mother-child relationship in a 19-year perspective. *Journal of Reproductive & Infant Psychology, 20,* 43–56.

Tiedemann, J. (2000). Parents' gender stereotypes and teachers' beliefs as predictors of children's concept of their mathematical ability in elementary school. *Journal of Educational Psychology, 92,* 144–151.

Timimi, S., & Leo, J. (2009). *Rethinking ADHD.* London, UK: Palgrave Macmillan.

Todd, R. D., Swarzenski, B., Rossi, P. G., & Visconti, P. (1995). Structural and functional development of the human brain. In D. Cicchetti & D. J. Cohen (Eds.), *Developmental psychopathology: Vol. 1. Theory and methods* (pp. 161–194). New York: Wiley.

Tolar, T., Lederberg, A., & Fletcher, J. (2009). A structural model of algebra achievement: Computational fluency and spatial visualisation as mediators of the effect of working memory on algebra achievement. *Educational Psychology, 29,* 239–266.

Tomasello, M. (2009). *Why we cooperate.* Cambridge, MA: MIT Press.

Tomasello, M., & Mannle, S. (1985). Pragmatics of sibling speech to one-year-olds. *Child Development, 56,* 911–917.

Tomlinson-Keasey, C., Eisert, D. C., Kahle, L. R., Hardy-Brown, K., & Keasey, B. (1979). The structure of concrete operational thought. *Child Development, 50,* 1153–1163.

Toomela, A. (1999). Drawing development: Stages in the representation of a cube and a cylinder. *Child Development, 70,* 1141–1150.

Toronto District School Board (2001). *Facts and figures about the TDSB.* Retrieved October 6, 2001, from http://www.tdsb.on.ca/communications/TDSBFacts.html

Torrance, P. (1998). *Torrance Tests of Creative Thinking.* Bensenville, IL: Scholastic Testing Service.

Tortora, G., & Grabowski, S. (1993). *Principles of anatomy and physiology.* New York: Harper Collins.

Tottenham, N., Hare, T., Quinn, B., McCarry, T., Nurse, M., Gilhooly, T., et al. (2010). Prolonged institutional rearing is associated with atypically large amygdala volume and difficulties in emotion regulation. *Developmental Science, 13,* 46–61.

Townsend, G., & Belgrave, F. (2003). The influence of cultural and racial identification on the psychosocial adjustment of inner-city African American children in school. *American Journal of Community Psychology, 32,* 217–228.

Trainor, L., Anonymous, & Tsang, C. (2004). Long-term memory for music: Infants remember tempo and timbre. *Developmental Science, 7,* 289–296.

Trainor, L., Tsang, C., & Cheung, V. (2002). Preference for sensory consonance in 2- and 4-month-old infants. *Music Perception, 20,* 187–194.

Trautner, H., Gervai, J., & Nemeth, R. (2003). Appearance-reality distinction and development of gender constancy understanding in children. *International Journal of Behavioral Development, 27,* 275–283.

Trehub, S. (2010). In the beginning: A brief history of infant music perception [Special issue]. *Musicae Scientiae,* 71–87. Retrieved October 28,

2011, from http://www.utm.utoronto.ca/fileadmin/w3trehub/publications/TrehubMusicaeScientiaeProofs28Sept10.pdf

Trehub, S. E., Bull, D., & Thorpe, L. A. (1984). Infants' perception of melodies: The role of melodic contour. *Child Development, 55,* 821–830.

Trehub, S. E, Hill, D., & Kamenetsky, S. (1997). Parents' sung performances for infants. *Canadian Journal of Experimental Psychology, 51,* 385–396.

Trehub, S. E., & Rabinovitch, M. S. (1972). Auditory-linguistic sensitivity in early infancy. *Developmental Psychology, 6,* 74–77.

Trehub, S. E., Thorpe, L. A., & Morrongiello, B. A. (1985). Infants' perception of melodies: Changes in a single tone. *Infant Behavior and Development, 8,* 213–223.

Treiman, R. (2004). Spelling and dialect: Comparisons between speakers of African American vernacular English and White speakers. *Psychonomic Bulletin & Review, 11,* 338–342.

Tronick, E. Z. (2007). *The neurobehavioral and social-emotional development of infants and children.* New York: Norton & Co.

Tronick, E. Z., Morelli, G. A., & Ivey, P. K. (1992). The Efe forager infant and toddler's pattern of social relationships: Multiple and simultaneous. *Developmental Psychology, 28,* 568–577.

Troseth, G., & DeLoache, J. (1998). The medium can obscure the message: Young children's understanding of video. *Child Development, 69,* 950–965.

Tsujimoto, S., Yamamoto, T., Kawaguchi, H., Koizumi, H., & Sawaguchi, T. (2004). Children: An event-related optical topography study. *Cerebral Cortex, 14,* 703–712.

Tuna, J. M. (1989). Mental health services for children: The state of the art. *American Psychologist, 44,* 188–199.

Turecki, S. (2000). *The difficult child.* New York: Bantam Books.

Turiel, E. (1983). *The development of social knowledge: Morality and convention.* New York: Cambridge University Press.

Turiel, E. (1998). The development of morality. In W. Damon (Ed.), *Handbook of child psychology: Vol. 3. Social, emotional, and personality development* (5th ed., pp. 863–932). New York: Wiley.

Turkheimer, E., Haley, A., Waldron, M., D'Onofrio, B., & Gottesman, I. (2003). Socioeconomic status modifies heritability of IQ in young children. *Psychological Science, 14,* 623–628.

Turnage, B. (2004). African American mother-daughter relationships mediating daughter's self-esteem. *Child & Adolescent Social Work Journal, 21,* 155–173.

Twyman, K., Saylor, C., Taylor, L., & Comeaux, C. (2010). Comparing children and adolescents engaged in cyberbullying to matched peers. *Cyberpsychology, Behavior, and Social Networking, 13,* 195–199.

Tynan, D. (2008). *Oppositional defiant disorder.* Retrieved October 24, 2008, from http://www.emedicine.com/ped/TOPIC2791

Udry, J. R., & Campbell, B. C. (1994). Getting started on sexual behavior. In A. S. Rossi (Ed.), *Sexuality across the life course* (pp. 187–208). Chicago: University of Chicago Press.

Umberson, D., & Gove, W. R. (1989). Parenthood and psychological well-being. Theory, measurement, and stage in the family life course. *Journal of Family Issues, 10,* 440–462.

Umetsu, D. (1998). Immunology and allergy. In R. Behrman & E. Kliegman (Eds.), *Nelson essentials of pediatrics* (3rd ed.). Philadelphia: Saunders.

Underwood, M. K., Coie, J. D., & Herbsman, C. R. (1992). Display rules for anger and aggression in school-age children. *Child Development, 63,* 366–380.

Underwood, M. K., Kupersmidt, J. B., & Coie, J. D. (1996). Childhood peer sociometric status and aggression as predictors of adolescent childbearing. *Journal of Research on Adolescence, 6,* 201–224.

United States Census Bureau. (2011). *Statistical abstract of the United States.* Retrieved August 26, 2011, from http://www.census.gov/compendia/statab/

Uno, D., Florsheim, P., & Uchino, B. (1998). Psychosocial mechanisms underlying quality of parenting among Mexican-American and white adolescent mothers. *Journal of Youth & Adolescence, 27,* 585–605.

U.S. Census Bureau. (2001). *Statistical abstract of the United States: 2000.* Washington, DC: U.S. Government Printing Office.

U.S. Census Bureau. (2003). *2002, American Community Survey.* Retrieved June 18, 2004, from http://www.census.gov/acs/www/index.html

U.S. Census Bureau. (2008). *Statistical abstract of the United States.* Retrieved September 7, 2008, from http://www.census.gov/compendia/statab/index.html

U.S. Census Bureau. (2010a). *America's families and living arrangements, 2009.* Retrieved August 1, 2010, from http://www.census.gov/population/www/socdemo/hh-fam/cps2009.html

U. S. Census Bureau. (2010b). *Income, poverty, and health insurance in the United States: Tables and figures.* Retrieved August 12, 2010, from http://www.census.gov/hhes/www/poverty/data/incpovhlth/2008/tables.html

U. S. Census Bureau. (2011). *Statistical abstract of the United States.* Retrieved July 26, 2011, from http://www.census.gov/compendia/statab/

U.S. Department of Energy. (2001). *The Human Genome Program* [Online report]. Retrieved July 6, 2001, from http://www.ornl.gov/TechResources/Human_Genome/home.html

U.S. Department of the Treasury. (2008). *Income mobility in the U.S. from 1996 to 2005.* Retrieved March 13, 2008, from http://www.treas.gov/offices/tax-policy/library/incomemobilitystudy03-08revise.pdf

U.S. Food and Drug Administration. (2004, October 15). *Suicidality in children and adolescents being treated with antidepressant medication.* Retrieved May 12, 2005, from http://www.fda.gov/cder/drug/antidepressants/SSRIPHA200410.htm

U.S. National Library of Medicine Genetics Home Reference. (2008). *Color vision deficiency.* Retrieved August 14, 2008, from http://ghr.nlm.nih.gov/condition=colorvisiondeficiency

Valentine, J., DuBois, D., & Cooper, H. (2004). The relation between self-beliefs and academic achievement: A meta-analytic review. *Educational Psychologist, 39,* 111–133.

Valiente, C., Eisenberg, N., Fabes, R., Shepard, S., Cumberland, A., & Losoya, S. (2004). Prediction of children's empathy-related responding from their effortful control and parents' expressivity. *Developmental Psychology, 40,* 911–926.

Valleroy, L., MacKellar, D., Karon, J., Rosen, D., McFarland, W., Shehan, D., Stoyanoff, S., LaLota, M., Celentano, D., Koblin, B., Thieded, H., Katz, M., Torian, L., & Janssen, R. (2000). HIV prevalence and associated risks in young men who have sex with men. *Journal of the American Medical Association, 284,* 198–204.

Vandell, D., Belsky, J., Burchinal, M., Steinberg, L., & Vandergrift, N. (2010). Do the effects of early child care extend to age 15 years? Results from the NICHD study of early child care and youth development. *Child Development, 81,* 737–756.

Van Mierlo, J., & Van den Bulck, J. (2004). Benchmarking the cultivation approach to video game effects: A comparison of the correlates of TV viewing and game play. *Journal of Adolescence, 27,* 97–111.

Vartanian, L. (2001). Adolescents' reactions to hypothetical peer group conversations: Evidence for an imaginary audience? *Adolescence, 36,* 347–380.

Vaughn, B., Stevenson-Hinde, J., Waters, E., Kotsaftis, A., Lefever, G., Shouldice, A., Trudel, M., & Belsky, J. (1992). Attachment security and temperament in infancy and early childhood: Some conceptual clarification. *Developmental Psychology, 28,* 463–473.

Vaux, T., & Rosenkrantz, T. (2010). *Fetal alcohol syndrome*. Retrieved August 17, 2011, from http://emedicine.medscape.com/article/974016-overview

Veenstra, R., Lindenberg, S., Munniksma, A., & Dijkstra, J. (2010). The complex relationship between bullying, victimization, acceptance, and rejection: Giving special attention to status, affection, and sex differences. *Child Development, 81,* 480–486.

Venerosi, A., Valanzano, A., Cirulli, F., Alleva, E., & Calamandrei, G. (2004). Acute global anoxia during C-section birth affects dopamine-mediated behavioural responses and reactivity to stress. *Behavioural Brain Research, 154,* 155–164.

Vermeer, H., & van IJzendoorn, M. (2006). Children's elevated cortisol levels at daycare: A review and meta-analysis. *Early Childhood Research Quarterly, 21,* 390–401.

Vernon, P. A. (1993). Intelligence and neural efficiency. In D. K. Detterman (Ed.), *Current topics in human intelligence: Vol. 3. Individual differences and cognition* (pp. 171–187). Norwood, NJ: Ablex.

Vernon, P. A., & Mori, M. (1992). Intelligence, reaction times, and peripheral nerve conduction velocity. *Intelligence, 16,* 273–288.

Véronneau, M., Vitaro, F., Pedersen, S., & Tremblay, R. (2008). Do peers contribute to the likelihood of secondary school graduation among disadvantaged boys? *Journal of Educational Psychology, 100,* 429–442.

Victorian Infant Collaborative Study Group. (1991). Eight-year outcome in infants with birth weight of 500–999 grams: Continuing regional study of 1979 and 1980 births. *Journal of Pediatrics, 118,* 761–767.

Vida, J. (2005). Treating the "wise baby." *American Journal of Psychoanalysis, 65,* 3–12.

Vigdor, J., & Ladd, H. (2010). *Scaling the digital divide: Home computer technology and student achievement*. Retrieved July 12, 2011, from http://www.nber.org/papers/w16078

Villegas, J., Castellanos, E., & Gutiérrez, J. (2009). Representations in problem solving: A case study with optimization problems. *Electronic Journal of Research in Educational Psychology, 17,* 279–308.

de Villiers, P. A., & de Villiers, J. G. (1992). Language development. In M. H. Bornstein & M. E. Lamb (Eds.), *Developmental psychology: An advanced textbook* (3rd ed., pp. 337–418). Hillsdale, NJ: Erlbaum.

Viner, R. (2002). Is puberty getting earlier in girls? *Archives of Disease in Childhood, 86,* 8–10.

Visser, S., & Lesesne, C. (2005). Mental health in the United States: Prevalence of diagnosis and medication treatment for attention-deficit/hyperactivity disorder: United States, 2003. *Morbidity and Mortality Weekly Report, 54,* 842–847.

Vitaro, F., Barker, E., Boivin, M., Brendgen, M., & Tremblay, R. (2006). Do early difficult temperament and harsh parenting differentially predict reactive and proactive aggression? *Journal of Abnormal Child Psychology, 34,* 681–691.

Vitaro, F., Tremblay, R. E., Kerr, M., Pagani, L., & Bukowski, W. M. (1997). Disruptiveness, friends' characteristics, and delinquency in early adolescence: A test of two competing models of development. *Child Development, 68,* 676–689.

Vogin, J. (2005). *Taking medication while pregnant*. Retrieved June 7, 2007, from http://www.medicinenet.com/script/main/art.asp?articlekey=51639

Volbrecht, M., Lemery-Chalfant, K., Aksan, N., Zahn-Waxler, C., & Goldsmith, H. (2007). Examining the familial link between positive affect and empathy development in the second year. *Journal of Genetic Psychology, 168,* 105–129.

Volling, B., Mahoney, A., & Rauer, A. (2009). Sanctification of parenting, moral socialization, and young children's conscience development. *Psychology of Religion and Spirituality, 1,* 53–68.

Volling, B., McElwain, N., & Miller, A. (2002). Emotion regulation in context: The jealousy complex between young siblings and its relations with child and family characteristics. *Child Development, 73,* 581–600.

Von Marées, N., & Petermann, F. (2010). Bullying in German primary schools: Gender differences, age trends and influence of parents' migration and educational backgrounds. *School Psychology International, 31,* 178–198.

Votruba-Drzal, E., Li-Grining, C., & Maldonado-Carreño, C. (2008). A developmental perspective on full- versus part-day kindergarten and children's academic trajectories through fifth grade. *Child Development, 79,* 957–978.

Vrshek-Schallhorn, S., Czarlinski, J., Mineka, S., Zinbarg, R., & Craske, M. (2011). Prospective predictors of suicidal ideation during depressive episodes among older adolescents and young adults. *Personality and Individual Differences, 50,* 1202–1207.

Vuorenkoski, L., Kuure, O., Moilanen, I., & Peninkilampi, V. (2000). Bilingualism, school achievement, and mental well-being: A follow-up study of return migrant children. *Journal of Child Psychology & Psychiatry & Allied Disciplines, 41,* 261–266.

Vygotsky, L. S. (1978). *Mind and society: The development of higher mental processes*. Cambridge, MA: Harvard University Press. (Original works published 1930, 1933, and 1935)

Waddington, C. H. (1957). *The strategy of the genes*. London: Allen.

Waddington, C. H. (1974). A catastrophe theory of evolution. *Annals of the New York Academy of Sciences, 231,* 32–41.

Waldrop, M., & Halverson, C. (1975). Intensive and extensive peer behavior: Longitudinal and cross-sectional analyses. *Child Development, 46,* 19–26.

Walker, E. (2002). Adolescent neurodevelopment and psychopathology. *Current Directions in Psychological Science, 11,* 24–28.

Walker, L. J. (1980). Cognitive and perspective-taking prerequisites for moral development. *Child Development, 51,* 131–139.

Walker, L. J. (1989). A longitudinal study of moral reasoning. *Child Development, 60,* 157–160.

Walker, L. J., de Vries, B., & Trevethan, S. D. (1987). Moral stages and moral orientations in real-life and hypothetical dilemmas. *Child Development, 58,* 842–858.

Walker-Andrews, A. S. (1997). Infants' perception of expressive behaviors: Differentiation of multimodal information. *Psychological Bulletin, 121,* 437–456.

Walker-Barnes, C., & Mason, C. (2004). Delinquency and substance use among gang-involved youth: The moderating role of parenting practices. *American Journal of Community Psychology, 34,* 235–250.

Wallerstein, J., & Lewis, J. (1998). The long-term impact of divorce on children: A first report from a 25-year study. *Family & Conciliation Courts Review, 36,* 368–383.

Wallien, M., & Cohen-Kettenis, P. (2008). Psychosexual outcome of gender-dysphoric children. *Journal of the American Academy of Child & Adolescent Psychiatry, 47,* 1413–1423.

Walters, G. (2011). Childhood temperament: Dimensions or types? *Personality and Individual Differences, 50,* 1168–1173.

Walters, R. H., & Brown, M. (1963). Studies of reinforcement of aggression: III. Transfer of responses to an interpersonal situation. *Child Development, 34,* 563–571.

Walusinski, O., Kurjak, A., Andonotopo, W., & Azumendi, G. (2005). Fetal yawning: A behavior's birth with 4D US revealed. *The Ultrasound Review of Obstetrics & Gynecology, 5,* 210–217.

Wang, Q. (2006a). Culture and the development of self-knowledge. *Current Directions in Psychological Science, 15,* 182–187.

Wang, Q. (2006b). Relations of maternal style and child self-concepts to autobiographical memories in Chinese, Chinese immigrant, and European American 3-year-olds. *Child Development, 77,* 1794–1809.

Wang, Y., & Lobstein, T. (2006). Worldwide trends in childhood over-weight and obesity. *International Journal of Pediatric Obesity, 1*, 11–25.

Ward, S. L., & Overton, W. F. (1990). Semantic familiarity, relevance, and the development of deductive reasoning. *Developmental Psychology, 26*, 488–493.

Wardle, J., Carnell, S., Haworth, C., & Plomin, R. (2008). Evidence for a strong genetic influence on childhood adiposity despite the force of the obesogenic environment. *American Journal of Clinical Nutrition, 87*, 398–404.

Warfield-Coppock, N. (1997). The balance and connection of manhood and womanhood training. *Journal of Prevention & Intervention in the Community, 16*, 121–145.

Warren, S., & Simmens, S. (2005). Predicting toddler anxiety/depressive symptoms: Effects of caregiver sensitivity on temperamentally vulnerable children. *Infant Mental Health Journal, 26*, 40–55.

Waseem, M. (2007). *Otitis media.* Retrieved March 18, 2008, from http://www.emedicine.com/ped/TOPIC1689.HTM

Waterman, A. S. (1985). Identity in the context of adolescent psychology. *New Directions for Child Development, 30*, 5–24.

Waterman, A. S. (1988). Identity status theory and Erikson's theory: Communalities and differences. *Developmental Review, 8*, 185–208.

Waters, H., & Waters, T. (2010). Bird experts: A study of child and adult knowledge utilization. In H. Waters & W. Schneider (Eds.), *Meta-cognition, strategy use, and instruction* (pp. 113–134). New York: Guilford Press.

Watson, A., Nixon, C., Wilson, A., & Capage, L. (1999). Social interaction skills and theory of mind in young children. *Developmental Psychology, 35*, 386–391.

Watson, J. B. (1913). Psychology as the behaviorist views it. *Psychological Review, 20*, 158–177.

Watson, J. B. (1928). *Psychological care of the infant and child.* New York: Norton.

Watson, J. B. (1930). *Behaviorism.* New York: Norton.

Watson, J. B., & Rayner, R. (1920). Conditioned emotional reactions. *Journal of Experimental Psychology, 3*, 1–14.

Watson, M. W., & Getz, K. (1990a). Developmental shifts in Oedipal behaviors related to family role understanding. *New Directions for Child Development, 48*, 29–48.

Watson, M. W., & Getz, K. (1990b). The relationship between Oedipal behaviors and children's family role concepts. *Merrill-Palmer Quarterly, 36*, 487–506.

Waxman, S. R., & Kosowski, T. D. (1990). Nouns mark category relations: Toddlers' and preschoolers' word-learning biases. *Child Development, 61*, 1461–1473.

Webb, R., Lubinski, D., & Benbow, C. (2002). Mathematically facile adolescents with math-science aspirations: New perspectives on their educational and vocational development. *Journal of Educational Psychology, 94*, 785–794.

Webster-Stratton, C., & Hammond, M. (1988). Maternal depression and its relationship to life stress, perceptions of child behavior problems, parenting behaviors and child conduct problems. *Journal of Abnormal Child Psychology, 16*, 299–315.

Webster-Stratton, C., & Reid, M. (2003). Treating conduct problems and strengthening social and emotional competence in young children: The dinosaur treatment program. *Journal of Emotional & Behavioral Disorders, 11*, 130–143.

Wechsler, D. (1974). *Manual for the Wechsler Intelligence Scale for Children–Revised.* New York: Psychological Corp.

Weimer, B., Kerns, K., & Oldenburg, C. (2004). Adolescents' interactions with a best friend: Associations with attachment style. *Journal of Experimental Psychology, 88*, 102–120.

Weinberg, R. A. (1989). Intelligence and IQ: Landmark issues and great debates. *American Psychologist, 44*, 98–104.

Weinfield, N., & Egeland, B. (2004). Continuity, discontinuity, and coherence in attachment from infancy to late adolescence: Sequelae of organization and disorganization. *Attachment & Human Development, 6*, 73–97.

Weisner, T. S. (1984). Ecocultural niches of middle childhood: A cross-cultural perspective. In W. A. Collins (Ed.), *Development during middle childhood: The years from six to twelve* (pp. 335–369). Washington, DC: National Academy Press.

Weiss, L. H., & Schwarz, J. C. (1996). The relationship between parenting types and older adolescents' personality, academic achievement, adjustment, and substance use. *Child Development, 67*, 2101–2114.

Welch-Ross, M. (1997). Mother-child participation in conversation about the past: Relationships to preschoolers' theory of mind. *Developmental Psychology, 33*, 618–629.

Wellman, H. M., & Hickling, A. K. (1994). The mind's "I": Children's conception of the mind as an active agent. *Child Development, 65*, 1564–1580.

Wentzel, K. R., (1997). Are effective teachers like good parents? Teaching styles and student adjustment in early adolescence. *Child Development, 73*, 287–301.

Wenz-Gross, M., Siperstein, G., Untch, A., & Widaman, K. (1997). Stress, social support, and adjustment of adolescents in middle school. *Journal of Early Adolescence, 17*, 129–151.

Werker, J. F., Maurer, D., & Yoshida, K. (2010). Perception. In M. Bornstein (Ed.), *Handbook of cultural developmental science* (pp. 89–125). New York: Psychology Press.

Werker, J. F., Pegg, J. E., & McLeod, P. J. (1994). A cross-language investigation of infant preference for infant-directed communication. *Infant Behavior and Development, 17*, 323–333.

Werker, J. F., Pons, F., Dietrich, C., Kajikawa, S., Fais, L., & Amano, S. (2007). Infant directed speech supports phonetic category learning in English and Japanese. *Cognition, 103*, 147–162.

Werker, J. F., & Tees, R. C. (2005). Speech perception as a window for understanding plasticity and commitment in language systems of the brain. *Developmental Psychobiology, 46*, 233–234.

Werner, E. E. (1986). A longitudinal study of perinatal risk. In D. C. Farran & J. D. McKinney (Eds.), *Risk in intellectual and psychosocial development* (pp. 3–28). Orlando, FL: Academic Press.

Werner, E. E. (1993). Risk, resilience, and recovery: Perspectives from the Kauai Longitudinal Study. *Development and Psychopathology, 5*, 503–515.

Werner, E. E. (1995). Resilience in development. *Current Directions in Psychological Science, 4*, 81–85.

Werner, E. E., & Smith, R. (2001). *Journeys from childhood to mid-life: Risk, resilience, and recovery.* Ithaca, NY: Cornell University Press.

Werner, L. A., & Gillenwater, J. M. (1990). Pure-tone sensitivity of 2- to 5-week-old infants. *Infant Behavior and Development, 13*, 355–375.

West, P., Sweeting, H., & Ecob, R. (1999). Family and friends' influences on the uptake of regular smoking from mid-adolescence to early adulthood. *Addiction, 97*, 1397–1411.

Wetzel, N., Widmann, A., Berti, S., & Schröger, E. (2006). The development of involuntary and voluntary attention from childhood to adulthood: A combined behavioral and event-related potential study. *Clinical Neurophysiology, 117*, 2191–2203.

White, J. (2006). Multiple invalidities. In J. Schaler (Ed.), *Howard Gardner under fire: The rebel psychologist faces his critics* (pp. 45–72). Chicago, IL: Open Court.

White, K. S., Bruce, S. E., Farrell, A. D., & Kliewer, W. L. (1997, April). *Impact of exposure to community violence on anxiety among urban adolescents: Family social support as a protective factor.* Paper presented at the biennial meetings of the Society for Research in Child Development, Washington, DC.

White-Traut, R., Nelson, M., Silvestri, J., Vasan, U., Littau, S., Meleedy-Rey, P., Gu, G., & Patel, M. (2002). Effect of auditory, tactile, visual, and vestibular intervention on length of stay, alertness, and feeding progression in preterm infants. *Developmental Medicine and Child Neurology, 44,* 91–97.

Wicks-Nelson, R., & Israel, A. (1997). *Behavior disorders of childhood.* Upper Saddle River, NJ: Prentice-Hall.

Wigfield, A., Eccles, J. S., MacIver, D., Reuman, D. A., & Midgley, C. (1991). Transitions during early adolescence: Changes in children's domain-specific self-perceptions and general self-esteem across the transition to junior high school. *Developmental Psychology, 27,* 552–565.

Wilen, J., & Mounts, K. (2006). Women with depression: You can't tell by looking. *Maternal and Child Health Journal, 10,* 183–187.

Williams, J. E., & Best, D. L. (1990). *Measuring sex stereotypes: A multi-nation study* (Rev. ed.). Newbury Park, CA: Sage.

Williams, J. E., & Best, D. L. (1994). Cross-cultural views of women and men. In W. Lonner & R. Malpass (Eds.), *Psychology and culture* (pp. 191–201). Boston: Allyn & Bacon.

Williams, W. (1998). Are we raising smarter children today? School and home related influences on IQ. In U. Neisser (Ed.), *The rising curve: Long-term gains in IQ and related measures* (pp. 125–154). Washington, DC: American Psychological Association.

Williams, W. M., & Ceci, S. J. (1997). Are Americans becoming more or less alike? Trends in race, class, and ability differences in intelligence. *American Psychologist, 52,* 1226–1235.

Willinger, M., Hoffman, H. J., & Hartford, R. B. (1994). Infant sleep position and risk for sudden infant death syndrome: Report of meeting held January 13 and 14, 1994, National Institutes of Health, Bethesda, MD. *Pediatrics, 93,* 814–819.

Wilson, M. N. (1986). The black extended family: An analytical consideration. *Developmental Psychology, 22,* 246–258.

Wilson, M. N. (1989). Child development in the context of the black extended family. *American Psychologist, 44,* 380–385.

Wilson, W. J. (1995). Jobless ghettos and the social outcome of youngsters. In P. Moen, G. H. Elder, Jr., & K. Lüscher (Eds.), *Examining lives in context: Perspectives on the ecology of human development* (pp. 527–543). Washington, DC: American Psychological Association.

Winfield, L. F. (1995). The knowledge base on resilience in African-American adolescents. In L. J. Crockett & A. C. Crouter (Eds.), *Pathways through adolescence* (pp. 87–118). Mahwah, NJ: Erlbaum.

Witt, E., Donnellan, M., & Trzesniewski, K. (2011). Self-esteem, narcissism, and Machiavellianism: Implications for understanding antisocial behavior in adolescents and young adults. In C. Barry, P. Kerig, K. Stellwagen, & T. Barry (Eds.), *Narcissism and Machiavellianism in youth: Implications for the development of adaptive and maladaptive behavior* (pp. 47–67). Washington, DC: American Psychological Association.

Witt, E., Massman, A., & Jackson, L. (2011). Trends in youth's video-game playing, overall computer use, and communication technology use: The impact of self-esteem and the big five personality factors. *Computers in Human Behavior, 27,* 763–769.

Wolpe, J. (1958). *Psychotherapy by reciprocal intuition.* Stanford, CA: Stanford University Press.

Wonderlich, S., Crosby, R., Mitchell, J., Thompson, K., Redlin, J., Demuth, G., Smith, J., & Haseltine, B. (2001). Eating disturbance and sexual trauma in childhood and adulthood. *International Journal of Eating Disorders, 30,* 401–412.

Wong, C., & Tang, C. (2004). Coming out experiences and psychological distress of Chinese homosexual men in Hong Kong. *Archives of Sexual Behavior, 33,* 149–157.

Wood, C., & Terrell, C. (1998). Pre-school phonological awareness and subsequent literacy development. *Educational Psychology, 18,* 253–274.

Wood, D. J., Bruner, J. S., & Ross, G. (1976). The role of tutoring in problem solving. *Journal of Child Psychology and Psychiatry, 17,* 89–100.

Woodhouse, S., Ramos-Marcuse, F., Ehrlich, K., Warner, S., & Cassidy, J. (2010). The role of adolescent attachment in moderating and mediating the links between parent and adolescent psychological symptoms. *Journal of Clinical Child & Adolescent Psychology, 39,* 51–63.

Woodward, A. L., & Markman, E. M. (1998). Early word learning. In W. Damon (Ed.), *Handbook of child psychology: Vol. 2. Cognition, perception, and language* (5th ed., pp. 371–420). New York: Wiley.

Woodward, S., McManis, M., Kagan, J., Deldin, P., Snidman, N., Lewis, M., & Kahn, V. (2001). Infant temperament and the brainstem auditory evoked response in later childhood. *Developmental Psychology, 37,* 533–538.

Woolley, M., & Grogan-Kaylor, A. (2006). Protective family factors in the context of neighborhood: Promoting positive school outcomes. *Family Relations, 55,* 93–104.

World Health Organization (WHO). (2010). *Maternal mortality.* Retrieved July 4, 2010, from http://www.who.int/making_pregnancy_safer/topics/maternal_mortality/en/index.html

van Wormer, K., & McKinney, R. (2003). What schools can do to help gay/lesbian/bisexual youth: A harm reduction approach. *Adolescence, 38,* 409–420.

Worrell, F. (1997). Predicting successful or non-successful at-risk status using demographic risk factors. *High School Journal, 81,* 46–53.

Wozniak, J., Biederman, J., Kwon, A., Mick, E., Faraone, S., Orlovsky, K., Schnare, L., Cargol, C., & van Grondelle, A. (2005). How cardinal are cardinal symptoms in pediatric bipolar disorder? An examination of clinical correlates. *Biological Psychiatry, 58,* 583–588.

Wright, B., Robertson, S., & Hadfield, L. (2011). Transitivity for height versus speed: To what extent do the under-7s really have a transitive capacity? *Thinking & Reasoning, 17,* 57–81.

Wright, J., Huston, A., Murphy, K., St. Peters, M., Pinon, M., Scantlin, R., & Kotler, J. (2001). The relations of early television viewing to school readiness and vocabulary of children from low-income families: The early window project. *Child Development, 72,* 1347–1366.

Wright, V., Schieve, L., Reynolds, M., & Jeng, G. (2005). Assisted reproductive technology surveillance—United States, 2002. *Morbidity & Mortality Weekly Report, 54,* 1–24.

Wu, P., Liu, X., & Fan, B. (2010). Factors associated with initiation of ecstasy use among adolescents: Findings from a national survey. *Drug and Alcohol Dependence, 106,* 193–198.

Wyatt, J., & Carlo, G. (2002). What will my parents think? Relations among adolescents' expected parental reactions, prosocial moral reasoning and prosocial and antisocial behaviors. *Journal of Adolescent Research, 17,* 646–666.

Xia, G., & Qian, M. (2001). The relationship of parenting style to self-reported mental health among two subcultures of Chinese. *Journal of Adolescence, 24,* 251–260.

Xie, H., Cairns, R., & Cairns, B. (1999). Social networks and configurations in inner-city schools: Aggression, popularity, and implications for students with EBD. *Journal of Emotional & Behavioral Disorders, 7,* 147–155.

Xu, J., Kochanek, M., Murphy, S., & Tejada-Vera, B. (2010). Deaths: Final data for 2007. *National Vital Statistics Reports, 58,* 1–73.

Yamada, A., & Singelis, T. (1999). Biculturalism and self-construal. *International Journal of Intercultural Relations, 23,* 697–709.

Yaman, A., Mesman, J., van IJzendoorn, M., & Bakermans-Kranenburg, M. (2010). Parenting and toddler aggression in second-generation immigrant families: The moderating role of child temperament. *Journal of Family Psychology, 24,* 208–211.

Yazzie-Mintz, E. (2010). *Charting the path from engagement to achievement: A report on the 2009 high school survey of student engagement.* Bloomington, IN: Center for Evaluation & Education Policy. Retrieved July 26, 2011, from http://www.indiana.edu/~ceep/hssse/images/HSSSE_2010_Report.pdf

Yirmiya, N., & Shulman, C. (1996). Seriation, conservation, and theory of mind abilities in individuals with autism, individuals with mental retardation, and normally developing children. *Child Development, 67,* 2045–2059.

Yonas, A. (1981). Infants' responses to optical information for collision. In R. Aslin, J. R. Alberts, & M. R. Peterson (Eds.), *Development of perception: Vol. 2. From perception to cognition* (pp. 80–122). Orlando, FL: Academic Press.

Yonkers, K., Wisner, K., Steart, D., Oberlander, T., Dell, D., Stotland, N., et al. (2009). The management of depression during pregnancy: A report from the American Psychiatric Association and the American College of Obstetricians and Gynecologists. *Obstetrics & Gynecology, 114,* 703–713.

Young, A. (1997). I think, therefore I'm motivated: The relations among cognitive strategy use, motivational orientation and classroom perceptions over time. *Learning & Individual Differences, 9,* 249–283.

Young, M., & Bradley, M. (1998). Social withdrawal: Self-efficacy, happiness, and popularity in introverted and extroverted adolescents. *Canadian Journal of School Psychology, 14,* 21–35.

Young, T., Turner, J., Denny, G., & Young, M. (2004). Examining external and internal poverty as antecedents of teen pregnancy. *American Journal of Health Behavior, 28,* 361–373.

Yu, C., & Ballard, D. (2007). A unified model of early word learning: Integrating statistical and social cues. *Neurocomputing: An International Journal, 70,* 2149–2165.

Yuji, H. (1996). Computer games and information-processing skills. *Perceptual & Motor Skills, 83,* 643–647.

Zahn-Waxler, C., & Radke-Yarrow, M. (1982). The development of altruism: Alternative research strategies. In N. Eisenberg (Ed.), *The development of prosocial behavior* (pp. 109–138). New York: Academic Press.

Zahn-Waxler, C., Radke-Yarrow, M., & King, R. (1979). Child rearing and children's prosocial initiations toward victims of distress. *Child Development, 50,* 319–330.

Zajonc, R., & Sulloway, F. (2007). The confluence model: Birth order as a within-family or between-family dynamic? *Personality and Social Psychology Bulletin, 33,* 1187–1194.

Zamboni, B. (2006). Therapeutic considerations in working with the family, friends, and partners of transgendered individuals. *The Family Journal, 14,* 174–179.

Zani, B. (1993). Dating and interpersonal relationships in adolescence. In S. Jackson & H. Rodrigues-Tomé (Eds.), *Adolescence and its social worlds* (pp. 95–119). Hove, England: Erlbaum.

Zaslow, M. J., & Hayes, C. D. (1986). Sex differences in children's responses to psychosocial stress: Toward a cross-context analysis. In M. E. Lamb, A. L. Brown, & B. Rogoff (Eds.), *Advances in developmental psychology* (Vol. 4, pp. 285–338). Hillsdale, NJ: Erlbaum.

Zeanah, C., & Fox, N. (2004). Temperament and attachment disorders. *Journal of Clinical Child & Adolescent Psychology, 33,* 32–41.

Zelazo, P. D., Helwig, C. C., & Lau, A. (1996). Intention, act, and outcome in behavioral prediction and moral judgment. *Child Development, 67,* 2478–2492.

Zelazo, P. R., Zelazo, N. A., & Kolb, S. (1972). "Walking" in the newborn. *Science, 176,* 314–315.

Zeldin, A., & Kao, A. (2010). *Mental retardation.* Retrieved July 27, 2011, from http://emedicine.medscape.com/article/1180709-overview#a0104

Zeskind, P. S., & Barr, R. G. (1997). Acoustic characteristics of naturally occurring cries of infants with "colic." *Child Development, 68,* 394–403.

Zeskind, P. S., & Ramey, C. T. (1981). Preventing intellectual and interactional sequelae of fetal malnutrition: A longitudinal, transactional, and synergistic approach to development. *Child Development, 52,* 213–218.

Zhai, F., Brooks-Gunn, J., & Waldfogel, J. (2011). Head Start and urban children's school readiness: A birth cohort study in 18 cities. *Developmental Psychology, 47,* 134–152.

Zhang, R., & Yu, Y. (2002). A study of children's coordinational ability for outcome and intention information. *Psychological Science (China), 25,* 527–530.

Zhao, Y., Montoro, R., Igartua, K., & Thombs, B. (2010). Suicidal ideation and attempt among adolescents reporting "unsure" sexual identity or heterosexual identity plus same-sex attraction or behavior: Forgotten groups? *Journal of the American Academy of Child & Adolescent Psychiatry, 49,* 104–113.

Zhou, Y., & Liu, X. (2010, August). *Self-esteem of students with learning disability: Not low but unstable.* Paper presented at the annual meeting of the American Psychological Association, San Diego, CA.

Zigler, E. (2010). Commentary: Are we promising too much for preschool education programs? In A. Reynolds, A. Rolnick, M. Englund, & J. Temple (Eds.), *Childhood programs and practices in the first decade of life: A human capital integration* (pp. 235–239). New York: Cambridge University Press.

Zigler, E., & Finn-Stevenson, M. (1993). *Children in a changing world: Developmental and social issues.* Pacific Grove, CA: Brooks/Cole.

Zigler, E. F., & Styfco, S. J. (1993). Using research and theory to justify and inform Head Start expansion. *Social Policy Report, Society for Research in Child Development, 7*(2), 1–21.

Zill, N., Moore, K. A., Smith, E. W., Stief, T., & Coiro, M. J. (1995). The life circumstances and development of children in welfare families: A profile based on national survey data. In P. L. Chase-Lansdale & J. Brooks-Gunn (Eds.), *Escape from poverty: What makes a difference for children?* (pp. 39–59). Cambridge, England: Cambridge University Press.

Zill, N., & Nord, C. W. (1994). *Running in place: How American families are faring in a changing economy and an individualistic society.* Washington, DC: Child Trends.

Zimmerman, F., Christakis, D., & Meltzoff, A. (2007). Television and DVD/video viewing in children younger than 2 years. *Archives of Pediatric & Adolescent Medicine, 161,* 473–479.

Zimmermann, P. (2004). Attachment representations and characteristics of friendship relations during adolescence. *Journal of Experimental Child Psychology, 88,* 83–101.

Zoccolillo, M. (1993). Gender and the development of conduct disorder. *Development and Psychopathology, 5,* 65–78.

Zoghbi, H. (2003). Postnatal neurodevelopmental disorders. *Science, 302,* 826–830.

Zola, S., & Squire, L. (2003). Genetics of childhood disorders: Learning and memory: Multiple memory systems. *Journal of the American Academy of Child & Adolescent Psychiatry, 42,* 504–506.

Zuloaga, D., Puts, D., Jordan, C., & Breedlove, S. (2008). The role of androgen receptors in the masculinization of brain and behavior: What we've learned from the testicular feminization mutation. *Hormones and Behavior, 53,* 613–626.

# CREDITS

## PHOTO CREDITS

### Chapter 1

p. 1 © dejanristovski/istockphoto, p. 3 © John Watson and infant, p. 4 © (left) Pablo Paul/Alamy, (right) © David Young-Wolff/PhotoEdit, p. 6 © David Young-Wolff/PhotoEdit, p. 9 © Getty Images, p. 10 © (left) National Geographic Image Collection/Alamy Limited, (right) auremar/ Shutterstock, p. 11: © AGE fotostock/SuperStock, p. 13 © Wayne Ford, p. 15 © Monkey Business Images/Shutterstock, p. 21 © Laura Dwight Photography, p. 25 © Jeremy Horner/Corbis.

### Chapter 2

p. 29 © moodboard/Alamy, p. 31 (top) © Lisa McClellan, (bottom) © SPL/ Photo Researchers, Inc., p. 36 (clockwise from top) © Nucleus Medical Art, Inc./Alamy, Dorling Kindersley, petit Format/Photo Researchers, Inc. SPL/Photo Researchers, Inc., Scanpix, p. 39 (top) © Dr. Olivier Walusinski (bottom) Reprinted from Applied Radiology, Vol. 33, No. 2, S.D. Brown et al., Fetal MRI, pages 9–25, Copyright 2004, with permission from Anderson Publishing Ltd., p. 45 moodboard/Alamy, p. 49 (left and right) © George Steinmetz Photography

### Chapter 3

p. 56 © Blend Images/Alamy, p. 57 AP Images, p. 58 (top) RIA Novosti/ Topham/The Image Works, (bottom left) David Young-Wolff/Alamy, (bottom right) Janine Wiedel Photolibrary/Alamy, p. 63 © Visual&Written SL/Alamy, p. 64 (top) © Elizabeth Crews/The Image Works (bottom) Cathy Melloan/PhotoEdit, p. 69 © Anna Jurkovska/Shutterstock, p. 71 (center left) © Eric Tormey/Alamy, (center right) Radius Images/Alamy, p. 72 © Flashon Studio, 2010/Shutterstock, p. 74 © Richard Meats/Getty

### Chapter 4

p. 81 © Kapu/Dreamstime LLC, p. 82 © Zena Holloway/Getty Images, p. 90 (left) © Skip Nall/Alamy, (center) Jack Hollingsworth/Getty Images, (right) Matka Wariatka/Shutterstock, p. 93 © Journal-Courier/Steve Warmowski/ The Image Works, p. 96 © Mike Kemp/Glow Images, p. 100 © Ed Quinn/ Corbis, p. 103 © A. Ramey/PhotoEdit, p. 106 © Ted Foxx/Alamy

### Chapter 5

p. 115 © Jose Luis Pelaez Inc /Blend Images/Alamy, p. 117 © Ellen Senisi/The Image Works, p. 119 © Michael Newman/PhotoEdit, p. 121 © Academic Press, p. 122 (top) © Picade LLC/Alamy, (bottom) Mark Richards/PhotoEdit, p. 126 (top) © Ariel Skelley/PhotoLibrary, (bottom) Szefei/Dreamstime LLC, p. 129 © JORGEN SCHYTTE/PhotoLibrary

### Chapter 6

p. 134 © Ian Shaw/Alamy, p. 135 Ellen B. Senisi/The Image Works, p. 140 © Elizabeth Crews/The Image Works, p. 142 © Ericka McConnell/Getty Images, p. 146 (top) © David Young-Wolff/PhotoEdit, (bottom) © Sean Sprague/The Image Works, p. 150 © Greenland | Dreamstime LLC, p. 153 © Bill Greenblatt/UPI/Newscom, p. 162 © Bob Daemmrich/The Image Works

### Chapter 7

p. 166 © Laura Dwight/PhotoEdit, p. 171 © Laura Dwight/PhotoEdit, p. 172 © Elizabeth Crews/PhotoEdit, p. 173 © Jim West/PhotoEdit, p. 176 © Laura Dwight/PhotoEdit, p. 178 © Paul Conklin/PhotoEdit, p. 183 © Cindy Charles/PhotoEdit.

### Chapter 8

p. 191 © Eye Ubiquitous/Alamy, p. 192 © PhotoEdit, p. 193 © Stuart Monk/Shutterstock, p. 196 © Apucizoli/Dreamstime LLC, p. 197 © David Young-Wolff/PhotoEdit, p. 201 © Explorer/Photo Researchers, Inc., p. 205 © Myrleen Ferguson Cate/PhotoEdit, p. 208 © Choi Changhee/ Age Fotostock, p. 209 © Richard G. Bingham II/Alamy, p. 213 © Michael Newman/PhotoEdit

## Chapter 9

p. 217 © Don Mason/Corbis, p. 220 © Wong Sze Yuen/Shutterstock, p. 221 © Laura Dwight/PhotoEdit, p. 224 © Joshua Zuckerman/ Workbook Stock/ Jupiter Images, p. 226 © Geri Engberg/The Image Works, p. 228 © IDAL/ Shutterstock, p. 229 © KidStock/Age Fotostock, p. 233 © Ellen B. Senisi/The Image Works, p. 235 © Eric Fowke/PhotoEdit

## Chapter 10

p. 241 © Frances Roberts/Alamy, p. 243 © Camille Tokerud/Stone/Getty Images, p. 245 © Ariel Skelley/Alamy, p. 247 © Jeff Greenberg/The Image Works, p. 250 (top) © Bananastock/Superstock, (bottom) © Blend Images/ Alamy, p. 251 © Mark Richards/PhotoEdit, p. 253 © Michael Newman/ PhotoEdit, p. 255 © Spencer Grant/PhotoEdit, p. 257 (top) © Helen Bee (bottom) © Bubbles Photolibrary/Alamy, p. 260 (top) © PhotoLibrary, (bottom) © AP Images/Paul Battaglia

## Chapter 11

p. 265 © Kablonk/PhotoLibrary, p. 267 © James Marshall/The Image Works, p. 268 © UpperCut Images/Alamy, p. 269 © Laura Dwight/Mira. com, p. 270 © Nick Greaves/Alamy, p. 271 © ACE Stock Limited/Alamy, p. 274 © wong sze yuen/Shutterstock, p. 276 © AGE fotostock/SuperStock, p. 278 © Ellen B. Senisi/The Image Works, p. 280 © i love images/ Alamy, p. 281 © Mark Hall/Getty Images, p. 284 (top) © Spencer Grant/ PhotoEdit (bottom) © Monkey Business Images/Shutterstock. p. 287 © Bob Daemmrich/The Image Works

## Chapter 12

p. 294 © Ilike/Shutterstock, p. 297 © David Young-Wolff/PhotoEdit, p. 300 © David Young-Wolff/PhotoEdit, p. 301 (left) © Tom Prettyman/PhotoEdit, (right) © Johner Images/Alamy, p. 307 © Kuttig - People - 2/Alamy, p. 309 © Kapoor Baldev/Sygma/Corbis, p. 313 © Steve Skjold/Alamy

## Chapter 13

p. 316 © Monkey Business/Fotolia, p. 318 © AP Images, p. 320 © Asia Images Group/PhotoLibrary, p. 323 © Bonnie Kamin/PhotoEdit, p. 328 © Szefei/Dreamstime LLC, p. 331 © Kayte Deioma/PhotoEdit, p. 332 (top) © Goodluz/Shutterstock (bottom) © GoGo Images Corporation/ Alamy. p. 334 (top) © Michael Newman/PhotoEdit (bottom) © Cindy Charles/PhotoEdit, p. 336 (left) © Blue Jean Images/Alamy (right) © Bob Daemmrich/The Image Works, p. 337 © Robert Nickelsberg/Getty Images

## Chapter 14

p. 339 © Sergio Azenha/Alamy. p. 341 © Dennis MacDonald/PhotoEdit, p. 349 © Michael Newman/PhotoEdit, p. 352 © Michael Newman/ PhotoEdit, p. 353 © Jim West/Alamy, p. 354 © Dennis MacDonald/ Alamy, p. 355 © Will Hart/PhotoEdit, p. 357 © Corbis/SuperStock, p. 359 © Bob Daemmrich/The Image Works, p. 363 © Mark Ludak/The Image Works, p. 364 © Chip East/Reuters/Landov, p. 365 (top) © Trish Tyson/ MCT/Landov (bottom) © Tony Freeman/PhotoEdit, p. 367 © Monkey Business Images/Shutterstock

## Chapter 15

p. 372 © Newscom, p. 374 © kondrytskyi/Shutterstock, p. 376 © David Young-Wolff/PhotoEdit, p. 379 © David Young-Wolff/PhotoEdit, p. 383 © Dave L. Ryan/Index Stock Imagery/Photolibrary, p. 384 © Jocelyn Lee, p. 386 © Keith Morris/Alamy, p. 392 © Ellen B. Senisi/The Image Works, p. 394 © Robin Nelson/PhotoEdit, p. 395 © Bubbles Photolibrary/Alamy

## Epilogue

p. 400 © Lisette Le Bon/Purestock/SuperStock, p. 402 © Laura Dwight Photography, p. 406 © Blend Images/Alamy, p. 408 © Jacky Chapman/ Alamy Limited, p. 412 © Spencer Grant/PhotoEdit, p. 414 © David Young-Wolff/PhotoEdit, p. 416 © Design Pics Inc./Alamy, p. 418 © Kablonk! RM/Golden Pixels LLC/Alamy, p. 419 © Bruce Robertson/Photo Researchers, Inc.

## Chapter 1

p. 3 Watson, J. B. (1930). *Behaviorism*. New York: Norton

## Chapter 4

p. 105 CDC, 2007

## Chapter 10

p. 246 Montemayor and Eisen (1977). pp. 317–18. The development of self conceptions from childhood to adolescence. *Developmental Psychology*, *13*, 314–319.  p. 247 Montemayor and Eisen (1977). pp. 318. The development of self conceptions from childhood to adolescence. *Developmental Psychology*,

## Chapter 12

p. 296, 297 Livesley,W. J., & Bromley, D. B. (1973). *Person perception in childhood and adolescence*. London: Wiley.  p. 299 Hoffman 1988,  pp. 509–510. Hoffman, M. L. (1988). Moral development. In M. H. Bornstein & M. E. Lamb (Eds.), *Developmental psychology: An advanced textbook Hillsdale,* NJ: Erlbaum.  p. 306 Kohlberg, L., & Elfenbein, D. (1975). The development of moral judgments concerning capital punishment. *American Journal of Orthopsychiatry*, *54*, 614–640.  p. 308 Snarey, 1985,  p. 221. Cross-cultural

## Epilogue

p. 414 Michael Rutter et al., 1997,  pp. 338, 339. Integrating nature and nurture: Implications of person environment correlations & interactions

## Chapter 3

p. 62 MacFarlane, 1977,  pp. 64–65. MacFarlane, A. (1977). *The psychology of child birth*. Cambridge, MA: Harvard University Press.

## Chapter 8

p. 200 de Villiers and de Villiers (1992). Language development. In M. H. Bornstein & M. E. Lamb (Eds.), *Developmental psychology: An advanced textbook* (3rd ed.,  pp. 337–418). Hillsdale, NJ: Erlbaum.

*13*,314–319. 97.  p. 250 Phinney & Rosenthal, 1992,  p. 160. Ethnic identity in adolescence: Process, context, and outcome. In G. R. Adams, T. P. Gullotta, & R. Montemayor (Eds.), *Adolescent identity formation* (pp. 145–172). Newbury Park, CA: Sage

universality of social-moral development: A critical review of Kohlbergian research. *Psychological Bulletin*, 97.  p. 308 Kohlberg, 1964,  p. 401. Kohlberg, L. (1964). Development of moral character. In M. L. Hoffman & L. W. Hoffman (Eds.), *Review of child development research*. NY: Russell Sage Foundation.  p. 309 Snarey, 1985,  p. 223, originally from Vasudev, 1983, Snarey, J. R. (1985). Cross-cultural universality of social-moral development. *Psychological Bulletin*, 97,  p. 7.

for developmental psychopathology. *Development & Psychopathology*, *9*, 335–364.

# NAME INDEX

McClure, J., 183
McCord, J., 322
McCrae, R. R., 221
McCredden, J., 152
McDonald, J., 75
McDonald, K., 280
McDonough, B., 65
McDougle, C., 393
McDowell, B., 65
McElhaney, K., 272, 280
McElwain, N., 330
McFarland, F., 272
McGee, B., 385
McGovern, C., 395
McGrath, M., 63
McGue, M., 175, 320
McGuffin, P., 53
McGuinn, M., 102
McGuire, S., 174, 286
McHale, S. M., 286
McIntire, D., 61
McIntosh, J., 335
McKeown, R., 377, 379
McKillop, D., 153
McLanahan, S. S., 331, 334
McLean-Heywood, D., 395
McLeod, P. J., 203
McLoyd, V. C., 361, 362
McManis, M., 224
McPherson, B., 259
McRae, C., 333
McRorie, M., 185
Mediascope Press, 358
Mednick, S., 84
Medwell, J., 158
Meece, D., 290
Mehler, J., 196
Mehta, P., 209
Mei, Z., 88
Meijer, A., 66
Meisinger, E., 158
Melby, J. N., 322
Melot, A., 146
Melson, G., 256
Meltzoff, A., 140, 213
Meltzoff, A. N., 142, 145
Menesini, E., 291
Meng, L., 395
Merrill, M. A., 167
Mervis, C. B., 197
Merz, E., 270
Merz, F., 350
Mescle, H., 158
Metallidou, P., 290
Meyer-Bahlburg, H. F. L., 101
Michiels, D., 271
Midgley, C., 351
Mikach, S., 332
Mikulincer, M., 277
Miles, J., 334, 335
Miller, A., 330
Miller, B., 99
Miller, C., 258

Miller, D., 250
Miller, P., 149, 301
Miller, P. H., 160
Milligan, K., 146
Mills, D., 86
Milne, E., 31
Milos, G., 385
Minzi, M., 276
Mio, J., 252
Mischel, W., 229, 259
Mishra, R. C., 138, 350
Misra, G., 176
Missmer, S., 31
Mitchell, K., 31, 313
Mitchell, P. R., 193
Mize, J., 290
Moffitt, T., 290, 383
Moffitt, T. E., 6, 104, 173, 229
Mohanty, A., 212
Mohay, H., 63
Mohsin, M., 49
Moilanen, B., 74
Moilanen, I., 213
Molander, B., 286
Molenaar, P., 83, 87
Molinari, L., 66, 67
Molnar, P., 142
Monga, M., 310
Montemayor, R., 246, 247, 262
Montgomery, M, 284
Montoro, R., 101
Moody, E., 311
Moon, J., 390
Mooney, K., 284
Moore, C., 46, 297, 377, 379
Moore, C. F., 313
Moore, D., 41, 389
Moore, E., 359
Moore, E. G. J., 131
Moore, K. A., 203, 362
Moore, K. L., 38, 59
Moore, L., 111
Moorman, E., 321
Morgan, C., 77
Morgan, J., 204
Mori, M., 185
Morison, K., 355
Morral, S., 147
Morris, T., 209
Morrison, F., 348
Morrison, F. J., 350
Morrissey, T., 336
Morrongiello, B. A., 120
Morrow, R., 340
Mortensen, E., 172
Mortimer, J., 353
Mory, M. S., 283
Moseley, K., 11
Moses, L., 130
Mosher, C., 333
Mostow, A., 324
Mott, J., 111
Mounts, N., 382

Mounts, N. S., 326
Mueller, U., 154
Muhuri, P. K., 75
Muir, J. E., 160
Mulder, C., 363
Mulder, E., 40
Müller, U., 143
Munakata, Y., 14
Munch, C., 158
Munir, K., 376
Munniksma, A., 290
Muraskas, J., 57
Muris, P., 272
Murphy, S., 387
Murphy, S. O., 286
Murray, A., 183
Murray, J., 152, 176, 357
Murray, V., 286
Musher-Eizenman, D., 358
Must, A., 169
Must, O., 168, 169
Myers, B., 358
Myers, S. J., 58


Nadel, L., 390
Nagy, E., 142
Nagy, G., 184
Nagy, W., 210
Naito, A., 388
Nakazawa, S., 83
Nanin, J., 285
Narang, S., 251
Narvaez, D., 311
National Association for the
    Education of Young
    Children (NAEYC), 346
National Center for Chronic
    Disease Prevention and
    Health Promotion
    (NCCDPHP), 105
National Center for Educational
    Statistics (NCES), 183, 212,
    213, 348, 354, 355, 356, 363,
    392, 396
National Center for Health Sta-
    tistics (NCHS), 78, 79, 106,
    107, 332, 333
National Center for Injury
    Prevention and Control
    (NCIPC), 387, 388
National Institute of Mental
    Health (NIMH), 386, 393
National Middle School Associa-
    tion (NMSA), 352
Naus, M., 301
Nedergard, N., 334
Nederhof, E., 411
Needlman, R. D., 65, 89
Neiderhiser, J., 224
Neisser, U., 179, 180
Nelson, C., 84, 85, 130
Nelson, K., 197, 204

Nelson, S., 303
Nemeroff, C., 376
Nemeth, R., 255
Netherlands Twin Register, 5
Netley, C., 45
Nettelbeck, T., 169, 186
Nettle, D., 286
Neubauer, A., 185
Neufeld, G., 279
Neulinger, K., 63
Neumann, C., 169
Neumark-Sztainer, D., 107
Neville, H., 86
Newcomb, A., 282
Newcomb, A. F., 278, 279,
    288–289
Newcomb, M., 388
Newcomb, P., 50
Newman, D., 125
Newman, M., 184
Newton, E., 304
New Zealand Ministry of
    Education, 355
Ni, Y., 183
NICHD Early Child Care
    Research Network, 342,
    343, 344
Nichikawa, S., 272
Nicholas, J., 125
Nicholas, P., 357
Nicholls, C., 388
Nicholls, M., 87
Nichols, P. L., 176
Nicklaus, S., 120
Niederhiser, J., 238
Nijhuis, J., 41
Niller, E., 222
Nilsson, A., 277
Nilsson, E., 385
Nilsson, L., 286
Nisan, M., 309
Nobile, C., 102
Noguchi, R., 279
Nomaguchis, K., 342
Nóra, S., 183
Norman, A. D., 311
Norton, A., 149
Norwood, M. K., 328
Notari, A., 346
Novak, E., 128
Novak, M., 128
Nugent, L. D., 157
Nunes, L. R. D., 142
Nunner-Winkler, G., 304
Nussbaum, A., 181


Obel, C., 334
Oberklaid, F., 225
O'Boyle, C., 259
O'Callaghan, F., 176
O'Callaghan, M., 63
O'Connell, B., 193

Raj, A., 42, 43
Rakhlin, N., 146
Ramey, C., 176
Ramey, C.T., 178, 179
Ramey, C. T, 7, 406
Ramey, C. T., 178
Ramey, S., 176
Ramey, S. L., 178, 406
Ramos-Marcuse, F., 277
Ramsay, D., 243
Ramsdell, C., 301
Ranson, K., 276
Raphael, B., 387
Rastam, M., 385
Ratcliffe, S., 282
Räty, H., 184
Rauch, J., 251
Rauch, S., 224
Raudik, V., 169
Rauer, A., 311
Rauscher, F., 24
Raviv, A., 102
Ray, B., 344, 356, 356–357
Rayner, R., 3
Reddy, R., 387
Redzepi, M., 120
Reene, K., 154
Rees, J. M., 62
Rees, S., 39
Reese, H. W., 121, 237
Rego, A., 210
Reichel, M., 226
Reid, J. B., 326
Reid, M., 290
Reijneveld, S., 335
Reimer, J., 309
Reimers, P., 162
Reiner, W., 242, 262
Reinisch, J., 172
Reiser, M., 245, 281
Reiss, D., 6, 224, 238
Reiss, N., 381
Reiter, S., 397
Remafedi, G., 100
Remer, H., 350
Rende, R., 179
Renk, K., 261
Renouf, A. G., 254
Resnick, M., 100, 101
Resnick, M. D., 272
Resnick, S., 276
Rest, J. R., 310
Retz, W., 223
Reuman, D., 348
Revelle, W., 100
Rey, J., 387
Reykowski, J., 312
Reynolds, A. J., 348, 349
Reynolds, C., 391
Reznick, J. S., 195, 199, 219
Rhee, S., 290
Rhodes, J., 387
Ribas, I., 48

Richards, H. C., 311
Richards, J., 140
Richards, M. H., 284
Richardson, D., 361
Richardson, J., 111
Richardson, L., 253
Richert, R., 203
Richters, J., 321
Ridderinkhof, K., 380
Rideout, V., 180, 222, 279, 281,
      357, 358, 359
Riegel, K. F., 401
Rieser-Danner, L. A., 124
Rietveld, M., 172
Rigby, C., 358
Rigg, J., 107, 108
Riggle, E., 101
Righetti, P., 42
Riisdijk, F., 53
Rijken, M., 91
Riksen-Walraven, J., 131, 274
Riley, B., 285
Rinderman, H., 185
Riordan, K., 276
Ripple, C., 177, 178
Risley, T. R., 175
Risser, A., 83
Ritter, J. M., 124
Ritter, P. L., 326
Rizzolatti, G., 323
Robb, M., 203
Roberts, D., 180, 222, 279, 281,
      357, 358, 359, 362, 365
Roberts, D. F., 326
Roberts, J., 86
Roberts, R., 96
Roberts, W., 301
Robertson, S., 152
Robins, R., 383
Robinson, N. M., 176
Robles, C., 222
Roche, A. F., 94
Rock, A., 125
Rodkin, P., 288
Rodrigo, M., 320
Rodriguez, G., 111
Roeser, R., 246, 282, 351
Rogers, J., 24, 179
Roggman, L. A., 124
Rogido, M., 62, 63
Rogoff, B., 350
Rogosch, F., 104, 304, 376
Rohner, R., 324
Rollins, K. B., 349
Romeo, R., 387
Rosario, M., 285
Rose, A. J., 83, 262, 302
Rose, K., 341
Rose, S., 118
Rose, S. A., 185, 224
Rosenberg, M., 102
Rosenblatt, J., 352
Rosenblatt, P., 365

Rosenfield, R., 94
Rosenkrantz, P. S., 258
Rosenkrantz, T., 49
Rosenthal, D. A., 250
Rosenthal, R., 246
Rosenthal, S., 92, 262
Rosicky, J., 130
Ross, D., 357
Ross, G., 13, 270
Ross, H., 286
Ross, M., 96, 286
Ross, R., 90
Ross, S., 357
Rossi, P. G, 85
Rossi, S., 281
Rossor, M., 65
Rostosky, S., 101
Roth, E., 162
Rothbart, M., 256
Rothbart, M. K., 218, 219,
      225, 376
Rothwell, H., 111
Rotter, J., 230
Rovee-Collier, C., 70, 141
Rovet, J., 45, 83
Rovine, M., 342
Rowan, K., 226
Rowe, D. C., 179
Rowe, I., 413
Rowe, M., 202
Roy, E., 87
Rubin, H., 178
Rubin, K., 224, 225
Rubin, K. H., 225, 226, 245, 279,
      280, 281, 286, 291, 295
Ruble, D., 255, 256, 257, 258,
      260, 261, 279
Ruble, D. N., 40, 255, 257
Rueter, M. A., 272
Ruggiero, G., 385
Ruhm, C., 340
Rushton, J., 173, 174, 179, 180
Russell, J. A., 131
Russo, M., 96
Rutter, D. R., 8, 201
Rutter, M., 4, 270, 394, 414, 417,
      418
Ruys, J. H., 91
Ryan, J., 111
Ryan, R., 358
Rydell, M., 181
Rydell, R., 181
Ryder, D., 153
Ryder, J., 211
Ryu, E., 383


Sabatier, C., 251
Sabatos-DeVito, M., 159
Sabbagh, M., 146, 146–147
Sackett, G., 118
Saddler, B., 210
Sadeh, A., 102

Saewyc, E., 101
Safford, P., 213
Safron, D., 353
Sagi, A., 207, 275
Sagi-Schwartz, A., 274, 275
Sai, F, 123
Saine, N., 209
Sak, U., 188
Saklofske, D., 289
Saksvik, L., 222
Salkeld, L., 388
Sallquist, J., 280, 299
Salovey, P., 298
Salpekar, J., 87
Sameroff, A., 276
Sampson, M., 277
Sampson, P., 49, 50
Sampson, R. J., 362
Sanchez, R., 380
Sanchez-Hucles, J., 362
Sandefur, G., 331, 334
Sanders, S., 172
Sandfort, T., 332
Sandler, I., 334, 335
Sandman, C., 41
Sangrador, J., 311
Sani, F., 257, 258
Sanson, A., 225
Santesso, D., 125
Sapienza, P., 262
Sarkar, P., 403
Sasher, T., 393
Sattler, J., 170, 172, 173
Saudino, K., 224
Saudino, K. J., 6, 224
Saults, J., 157
Savage, M., 97
Savage-Rumbaugh, E. S., 193
Savonlahti, E., 48
Sawaguchi, T., 347
Sawdon, J., 66
Sawyer, M., 387
Say, L., 47, 51
Sayer, A., 362
Saylor, C., 289
Scarr, S., 174, 175, 342, 343
Scerif, G., 65
Schaal, B., 42
Schank, R. C., 296
Schatschneider, C., 158, 209
Schechter, R., 395
Scheffer, R., 16, 386, 387, 393
Scher, L., 384
Scheres, A., 380
Schermerhorn, A., 267
Schiller, M., 276
Schlagmüller, M, 160
Schleiss, M., 47
Schlochtermeier, L., 380
Schlundt, B., 118
Schmidt, L., 125, 224
Schmitz, S., 245
Schneider, B., 183, 290

# SUBJECT INDEX

Family systems
    child within, 316–338
    individuals in, 320–322
    theory, 317–318
    understanding, 317–319
FAS. *See* Fetal alcohol syndrome
    (FAS)
Fast-mapping, 196
Fat, 89–90
Father-child bonds, 268
Feelings, reading others', 298–301
Feminine person, 261
Fetal alcohol syndrome (FAS), 49
Fetal assessment and treatment, 44
Fetal brain, 38–39
Fetal stage, 37–38
Figurative schemes, 136
First sentences, 198–199
First words, 192–196
Flynn effect, 169
Fontanels, 89
Foreclosure, 248
Formal operations stage, 138
Fraternal twins, 35
Freud's psychosexual stages,
    232–233
Friendships
    describing, 301–302
    reciprocal, 279–280
Full scale IQ score, 169

Games, video, 357–358
Gametes, 30
Gardner's multiple intelligences,
    187–188
Gay
    lesbian, and bisexual
        adolescents, 100–101
    and lesbian families, 332
Gender, 241–264
    concept, 255–256
    constancy, 256
    differences in temperament,
        256
    identity, 255
    stability, 255
Gender and sex roles, 254–263
    biological approaches,
        262–263
    developmental patterns,
        255–256
    sex-role concepts and stereo-
        types, 257–259
    sex-role development,
        259–262
Gender schema theory, 260–261
Gender schemas, individual,
    261–262
Gene-environment interactions, 6
Genes, 31, 32
    dominant and recessive, 33–34

Genetic and biological
    explanations of personality,
    223–227
Genetic disorders, 42–44
Genetic inheritance, patterns of,
    32–35
Genetics
    behavior, 5
    conception and, 30–35
Genomic imprinting, 34–35
Genotype, 32–33
Germinal stage, 35
Gestures
    early sounds and, 192–193
    sign language and, 194
Giftedness, 392–393
Gilligan's ethic of caring,
    313–314
Girls and boys, sequence of
    changes in, 93–95
Glands
    endocrine, 92
    master, 92
    pituitary, 92, 93
Glial cells, 39
Goal-corrected partnership, 271
Goals
    ability, 351
    tasks, 351
Gonadotrophic hormones, 92
Goodness-of-fit, 276
Grammar and pragmatics,
    development of, 198–202
Grammar explosion, 199–200
    adding inflections, 199
    negatives, 199–200
    overregulation, 200
    questions, 199–200
    vocabulary and grammar
        explosion, 199
Grammar learning, later, 200–201
Group differences
    in IQ or achievement test
        scores, 179
    in language development,
        206–208
Groups
    control, 23
    ethnic, 364
    experimental, 23
Growth, 88–89
Growth curves, 88
    and health, 103
Growth spurts, 82–84

Habituation, 70–71
Hand, repetitive strain injury
    (RSI) of, 106
Handedness, 87–88
Handwriting and brain
    development, 211

Health
    adolescent, 230
    care, 73, 74–75
    in childhood, 102–104
    growth curves and, 103
    poverty and children's, 107–109
Health and wellness, 102–111
    in early infancy, 73–79
Health information on Internet,
    cohort effects of, 11
Health-care needs, 102
Hearing and other senses, 119–121
Hedonistic reasoning, 312
Heroin, 50
Heterosexual relationships, 284
Heterozgous, 32
High-risk pregnancies, 48
Hippocampus, 85
Hispanic Americans, 365–366
History-graded changes,
    normative, 10
HIV/AIDS, 46
    and pregnancy across
        cultures, 47
Holophrases and first sentences,
    198–199
Homeschooling, 355–357
Homosexual teens, 285
Homozgous, 32
Horizontal decalage, 150–151
Hormones, 92–93
    gonadotrophic, 92
Hostile aggression, 288
Hostility, warmth versus, 322
Hypotheses, 20
Hypothesis, resource dilution, 286
Hypothetico-deductive
    reasoning, 154

Id, 12
Identical twins, 35
Identity
    achievement, 248
    diffusion, 248
    gender, 255
    play in virtual environments,
        249
    versus role confusion, 248
Identity crisis, Erikson's, 248
Identity development, sex roles
    and adolescent, 259
Identity in adolescence
    ethnic, 250–252
    self-concept and, 247–248
Identity statuses, Marcia's, 248
IDS. *See* infant-directed speech
    (IDS)
Illnesses
    and accidents, 103
    chronic, 47
    of infants, 75–76

Imitation, 142
Immunizations, 73, 74–75
Implants, cochlear, 125
Inborn biases, 5
Inclusive education, 395
Independent variable, 23
Indexes
    perceptual reasoning, 169
    processing speed, 169
    verbal comprehension, 169
    working memory, 169
Individual and group differences
    in language development,
    206–208
Individual differences, 10
Individual gender schemas,
    261–262
Individuals in family system,
    320–322
Individuation, 272
Inductive logic, 149
Infancy, 139–142
    behavior in early, 64–73
    birth and early, 56–80
    health and wellness in early,
        73–79
Infancy, challenges to Piaget's
    view of, 140–142
    imitation, 142
    memory, 140–142
Infancy and preschool years, peer
    relationships in, 278–279
Infant Development, Bayley
    Scales of, 170
Infant mortality, 76–79
    ethnic differences in, 78–79
Infant sleep patterns, cross-
    cultural differences in re-
    sponse to, 66–68
Infant-directed speech (IDS),
    203–204
Infants
    illnesses of, 75–76
    learning from television, 141
    preterm, 62
    responses to maternal
        depression, 130
    small-for-date, 62
    tests, 169–171
    variations in cries of, 68
Infants learning to suck, preterm,
    70
Infections
    ear, 76
    upper respiratory, 75–76
Information-processing skills,
    development of, 157–163
Information-processing theory,
    14, 185–186
Inheritance
    dominant/recessive pattern
        of, 33

mitochondrial, 34–35
multifactorial pattern of, 34
polygenic pattern of, 34
Insecure attachments, 273–275
Instrumental aggression, 288
Intellectual, atypical, 389–397
Intellectual power, measuring, 167–174
Intelligence. *See also* IQ
alternative view of, 185–187
analytic, 187
creative, 187
defined, 167
practical, 187
tests and creativity, 188
triarchic theory of, 186–187
Intelligences, Gardner's multiple, 187–188
Intentions, understanding rules and, 303
Interactive skill, development of, 267–268
Intermodal perception, 126
Internal models of experience, 6
Internal working model, 267
Internalizing problems, 374
Internet, cohort effects of health information on, 11
Invented spelling, 209
IQ (intelligence quotient), 168
IQ or achievement test scores, group differences in, 179
IQ score, full scale, 169
IQ scores
cultural differences across ethnic groups, 181–182
early interventions and, 177–179
interaction of heredity and environment, 179
prediction of, 173–174
IQ scores, explaining individual differences in, 174–184
family characteristics and IQ scores, 175–177
twin and adoption studies, 174–175
IQ scores, family characteristics and, 175–177
differences within families, 177
protective factors, 176–177
risk factors, 175–176
IQ tests
and ethnic differences, 180–182
first, 167–168
modern, 169–172
scores, sex differences and, 183–184

Kids. *See also* Children
Kids and parents, sleep for, 102

Kohlberg's levels and stages of moral development, 306–310
age and moral reasoning, 309
levels and stages, 306–309
moral reasoning stages across cultures, 310
sequence of stages, 309–310

Labor, stages of, 59
Labor and delivery, drugs during, 57–58
Language
development of, 191–216
expressive, 193
learning second, 211–214
receptive, 193
Language approach, whole, 210
Language development
differences in, 207–208
explaining, 202–204
individual and group differences in, 206–208
Language development, explaining constructivist theories, 204–206
environmental theories, 202–204
infant-directed speech (IDS), 203–204
linguistic environment, 202–203
nativist theories, 204
Language development, individual and group differences in cross-cultural universals, 207–208
differences in language development, 207–208
differences in rate, 206–207
Languages, how many? 213
Lateralization, 86–88
LBW. *See* Low birth weight (LBW)
LD. *See* Learning disabilities (LD
Learning, 69–71
explanations of personality, 227–230
to read and write, 209–214
second language, 211–214
and unlearning prejudice, 297
Learning disabilities (LD), 391–392
Learning theories, 15–17
Learning theory, social, 259–260
Left- and right-brain dominance, 86
Lesbian adolescents, 100–101
Lesbian families, gay and, 332
Libido, 11
Listening, 123–125

Literate in school, becoming, 210–211
Locations, detecting, 120
Logic, 154–155
deductive, 149
inductive, 149
Longitudinal design, 20–21
Looking, 121–123
Low birth weight (LBW), 62–63
causes of, 62
health status of infants, 62–63
long-term consequences of, 63

Macrosystem effects, 360–369
Major depressive disorder (MDD), 385
Marcia's identity statuses, 248
Marcia's theories, Erikson's and, 248–250
Marijuana, 50
Masculine person, 261
Master gland, 92
Maternal depression, infant responses to, 130
Maternal diseases, 45–48
Maturation, 4–5
MDD. *See* Major depressive disorder (MDD)
Mean length of utterance (MLU), 206
Media
entertainment, 357–360
impact of entertainment, 357–360
reports of research, 24
Medulla, 82
Memory, 140–142. *See also* Metamemory
children's, 157
Memory index, working, 169
Memory strategies, 158–161
Menarche, 93
Mental age, 168
Mental retardation, 389–391
Metacognition, 161–162
Metamemory, 161–162
Methods
descriptive, 22
experimental, 23–24
research designs and, 19
Microsystem with digital communications, 319
Midbrain, 82
Middle childhood, attachments in, 271
Mind, theories of, 145–146
Minority youth, sexual, 100–102
Mirror neurons, 323
Mitochondrial inheritance, 34–35

Model, internal working, 267
Moral behavior, 305
moral reasoning and, 311–312
Moral development, 304–314
dimensions of, 304–306
social-cognitive and, 294–315
Moral development, causes and consequences of, 310–312
moral reasoning and cognitive development, 310–311
moral reasoning and moral behavior, 311–312
Moral development, Kohlberg's levels and stages of, 306–310
age and moral reasoning, 309
levels and stages, 306–309
moral reasoning stages across cultures, 310
sequence of stages, 309–310
Moral dilemmas, alternative views, 312–314
Moral emotions, 304
Moral realism stage, 305
Moral reasoning, 305–306
age and, 309
and cognitive development, 310–311
and moral behavior, 311–312
Moral relativism stage, 305
Moral rules, 303
Morality
conventional, 308
postconventional, 308
preconventional, 306
principled, 308
Moratorium, 248
Moro reflexes, 64, 65
Mortality, 111
ethnic differences in infant, 78–79
infant, 76–79
Motherese, 203
Mother's age, 52
Motion, senses of touch and, 120
Motor, sensory, and perceptual abilities, 68–69
Motor development, 90, 91
cultural practices and, 69
Motor skills, 68–69
Multifactorial pattern of inheritance, 34
Multiple intelligences, 187–188
Multitasking, electronic, 359–360
Muscles, 89–90
Myelination, 85

Nativism, 116
arguments for, 117–118

Nativist theories, 204
Naturalistic observation, 22
Nature-nurture debate, 2–3
Needs-oriented reasoning, 312
Negative reinforcement, 16
Neglect, child abuse and, 104
Neglected children, 280
Neglecting style, 325
Neglecting type, 326
Neo-Piagetian theories, 147–148
Nervous system, 82–88
Neuronal migration, 38
Neuronal proliferation, 38
Neurons, 38
    mirror, 323
Neuroticism, 220
Neurotransmitters, 84
Newborn, first greeting of
    parents, 62
Newborn, assessing, 61–62
Nonnormative changes, 10
Nonparental care, 340–345
    before- and after-school care,
        344–345
    attachment, 342
    cognitive development, 342
    difficulties in studying,
        340–341
    effects on development,
        341–343
    personality, 342–343
Nonshared environments, 177
Normative age-graded changes, 10
Normative history-graded
    changes, 10
Norms, 3
Nutrition, 73, 74, 104

Obese, 105
    severely, 105
Object concept, 127–129
Object constancy, 127
Object perception, 127–128
Object permanence, 127, 129, 139
    and cultural practices, 129
    stages in development of, 129
Objective self, 242, 243
ODD. See Operational defiant
    disorder (ODD)
Oedipus conflict, 232
OM. See Otitis media (OM)
Openness/intellect, 220
Operant conditioning, 15–16, 70
Operation, 138
Operational defiant disorder
    (ODD), 381
Operational efficiency, 147
Operative schemes, 136
Organization, 136
Ossification, 89
Otitis media (OM), 76

Overextension, 196
Overregulation, 200
Over-the-counter drugs, 50–51
Overweight, 105
Ovum, 30


Parallel play, 278
Parent, child's attachment to,
    269–271
Parental employment, 335–336
Parent-child relationships in
    adolescence, 271–272
Parenting styles, 325–329
    culture, ethnicity,
        socioeconomic status
        (SES) and, 327–329
    and development, 326–327
    types of, 325–326
Parents
    attachment to, 272
    families headed by two
        biological, 329–330
    sleep for kids and, 102
    social support for, 336–337
Parents, relationships with, 266–272
    attachment theory, 266–267
    child's attachment to parent,
        269–271
    parent-child relationships in
        adolescence, 271–272
    parent's bond to child,
        267–268
Parent's bond to child, 267–268
Parent's characteristics, 321–322
Partnership, goal-corrected, 271
PDDs. See Pervasive develop-
    mental disorders (PDDs)
Pediatric bipolar disorder (BD),
    386
Peer relationships
    in adolescence, 281–284
    in infancy and preschool
        years, 278–279
    at school age, 279–280
Peers
    behavior with, 286–291
    relationship with, 278–284
Perception, 68
    intermodal, 126
    of social signals, 130–132
    spatial, 86–87
Perceptual abilities, sensory and, 69
Perceptual constancies, 126, 127
Perceptual information,
    ignoring, 126–127
Perceptual reasoning index, 169
Perceptual skills, 121–127
Performance, 171
Periods
    critical, 5
    sensitive, 5

Permissive style, 325
Permissive type, 325
Perpetual development, 115–133
Personality, defining, 218–223
Personality, genetic and biologi-
    cal explanations of, 223–227
    biological argument,
        223–226
    critique of biological
        theories, 226–227
Personality, learning explana-
    tions of, 227–230
    critique of learning models,
        228–230
Personality, psychoanalytic
    explanations of, 231–238
    critique of psychoanalytic
        theories, 236
    Erikson's psychosocial stages,
        233–235
    evidence and applications,
        235–236
    Freud's psychosexual stages,
        232–233
    possible synthesis, 237–238
    psychoanalytic argument,
        231–232
Personality development,
    alternate views of, 217–240
Personality traits, Big Five, 220–223
Perspective taking, 143–145
Pervasive developmental disor-
    ders (PDDs), 393–395
PFC. See Prefrontal cortex (PFC)
Phenotype, 32–33
Phonics, systematic and explicit,
    210
Phonological awareness, 209–210
Phonology, 192
Physical development, 81–114
Piaget's basic ideas, 136–139
    adaptation, 137–138
    causes of cognitive
        development, 138–139
    challenges to Piaget's view of
        infancy, 140–142
    infancy, 139–142
    schemes, 136
Piaget's view of concrete
    operations, 149–151
Piaget's view of early childhood,
    challenges to, 143–145
Piaget's view of preoperational
    stage, 142–143
Pituitary gland, 92, 93
Placenta, 37
Plasticity, 84
Play, parallel, 278
Polygenic pattern of inheritance,
    34
Popular children, 280
Positive reinforcement, 15

Postconventional morality, 308
Post-Piagetian work on adoles-
    cent thought, 155–156
Poverty, 53
    child, 360–361, 362–363
    and children's health,
        107–109
    of families, 361–362
Practical intelligence, 187
Pragmatics, 201–202
    development of grammar
        and, 198–202
Preconventional morality, 306
Prefrontal cortex (PFC), 83
Pregnancies, high-risk, 48
Pregnancy, teenage, 99–100
Pregnancy across cultures, HIV/
    AIDS and, 47
Prejudice, learning and
    unlearning, 297
Prelinguistic phase, 192–194
Prenatal behavior, 41–42
Prenatal development, 29–55
    conception and genetics,
        30–35
    development from concep-
        tion to birth, 35–42
    problems in, 42–53
    sex differences in, 40
    stages of, 35–39
Preoperational stage, 138
    Piaget's view of, 142–143
Preschool, explaining effects of,
    347–348
Preschool classroom, computers
    in, 346
Preschool years, 142–149
    challenges to Piaget's view
        of early childhood,
        143–145
    peer relationships in infancy
        and, 278–279
    Piaget's view of preopera-
        tional stage, 142–143
Prescription drugs, 50–51
Preterm infants, 62
    learning to suck, 70
Primary circular reactions, 139
Primitive reflexes, 64
Principle of contrast, 197
Principled morality, 308
Problems
    attention, 374, 377–383
    externalizing, 374, 377–383
    internalizing, 374, 383–389
    in prenatal development,
        42–53
Problem-solving, systematic,
    152–153
Processing speed index, 169
Production deficiency, 159
Prosocial behavior, 287–288

Social cognition, development of, 295–303
    describing friendships, 301–302
    describing other people, 296–298
    general principles and issues, 295–296
    reading others' feelings, 298–301
    understanding rules and intentions, 303
Social cognitive theory, Bandura's, 16–17
Social development, atypical intellectual and, 389–397
Social learning theory, 259–260
Social networking, suicide and, 388
Social referencing, 131
Social relationships, development of, 265–293
Social signals, perception of, 130–132
Social skills, 71–72
    emergence of emotional expression, 72
    taking turns, 72
Social status, 280–281
Social support for parents, 336–337
Social-cognitive and moral development, 294–315
Socio-cultural theory, Vygotsky's, 148–149
Socioeconomic status (SES), 108, 327–329
    and development, 360–364
Sounds and gestures, early, 192–193
Spanking, 324
Spatial cognition, 87
Spatial perception, 86–87
Speech, telegraphic, 198
Speech development, cochlear implants and, 125
Spelling, invented, 209
Sperm, 30
Stability, gender, 255
Stages
    embryonic, 37
    Erikson's psychosocial, 233–235
    fetal, 37–38
    Freud's psychosexual, 232–233
    germinal, 35
    moral realism, 305
    moral relativism, 305
    Piaget's view of preoperational, 142–143
    psychosexual, 12
    psychosocial, 12

Stamina, 90
Stanford Binet IQ test, 167
States of consciousness, 65
STDs. See Sexually transmitted diseases (STDs)
Stereotypes, sex-role, 257–258
Sternberg's triarchic theory of intelligence, 186–187
Strange situation, 273
Strategy training, 160–161
Stress, 52–53
    and protective factors, 363–364
Structural immersion, 212
STSS. See Short-term storage space (STSS)
Students
    achieving, 355
    disengaged, 353
Subjective self, 242–243
Submersion, 213
Suck, preterm infants learning to, 70
Sudden infant death syndrome (SIDS), 76–77
Suicide
    adolescent, 387–389
    and social networking, 388
Superego, 12
Synapses, 38
Synaptic development, 84
Synaptogenesis, 84
Syndrome, respiratory distress, 63
Syntax, 192
Systematic and explicit phonics, 210
Systematic problem-solving, 152–153

Task goals, 351
Tasting, 120
Teenage pregnancy, 99–100
Teenaged employment, 353
Teens. See also Adolescents
    homosexual, 285
    transgendered, 101–102
Telegraphic speech, 198
Television, 357–358
    infants learning from, 141
Temperament, 71–72, 218–220
    across cultures, 220
    and attachments, 275–276
    emerging consensus, 219–220
    gender differences in, 256
    three views of, 218–219
Temperamental surgency in toddler classroom, 219

Teratogens, 42, 45–50
    maternal factors and miscellaneous, 50
Tertiary circular reactions, 139
Test scores
    digital divide and cognitive, 180, 181
    group differences in IQ or achievement, 179
    stability of, 172–173
Tests
    achievement, 171–172
    infant, 169–171
Theories
    Bandura's social cognitive, 16–17
    cognitive-developmental, 13, 260
    comparing, 17–19
    constructivist, 204–206
    developmental, 11
    dynamic systems, 65
    Erikson's and Marcia's, 248–250
    family systems, 317–318
    gender schema, 260–261
    information-processing, 14, 185–186
    learning, 15–17
    of mind, 145–146
    nativist, 204
    neo-Piagetian, 147–148
    psychoanalytic, 11–13
    Siegler's wave, 151–152
    social, 259–260
    Vygotsky's socio-cultural, 148–149
Theory of intelligence, triarchic, 186–187
Therapy for children, cinema cinema cinema, 301
Thinking, divergence, 188
Thoughts, 145–146
    adolescent, 155–156
    approaches to concrete operational, 151–152
Toddler classroom, temperamental surgency in, 219
Touch and motion, senses of, 120
Tracking objects in visual field, 119
Trait aggression, 289–291
Transgendered teens, 101–102
Transitivity, 152
Triarchic theory of intelligence, 186–187
Trisomies, 45
Twins
    dizygotic, 35
    fraternal, 35
    identical, 35
    and siblings, 35

Umbilical cord, 37
Underextension, 196
Undifferentiated individuals, 261
Upper respiratory infections, 75–76
Uterus, 30
Utilization deficiency, 160

Validity, 173
Variables, dependent and independent, 23
Verbal comprehension index, 169
Very low birth weight (VLBW), 62
Viability, 38
Victims, bullies and, 290–291
Video games, 357–358
Violence, preventing, 299
Virtual environments, identity play in, 249
Vision, color, 119
Visual acuity, 119
Visual field, tracking objects in, 119
VLBW. See Very low birth weight (VLBW)
Vulnerability and resilience, 8–9
Vygotsky's socio-cultural theory, 148–149

Warmth
    versus hostility, 322
    and responsiveness, 322–323
Wave theory, Siegler's, 151–152
Weight gain, excessive, 104–107
Wellness
    in early infancy, 73–79
    health and, 102–111
Whole language approach, 210
WISC-IV (Wechsler Intelligence Scales for Children), 169
Word, before first, 192–194
Word learning
    constraints on, 197–198
    later, 196–197
Words, first, 194–196
Words and word meanings, learning, 194–198
Working memory index, 169
WPPSI-III (Wechsler Preschool and Primary Scale of Intelligence), 169
Write, learning to read and, 209–214

Youth, sexual minority, 100–102

Zone of proximal development, 13
Zygote, 30

# what's new in PSYCHOLOGY

## Abnormal Psychology

**Beidel, Bulik & Stanley**  ABNORMAL PSYCHOLOGY, 2/E
©2012    9780205205011 / 0205205011

**Oltmanns & Emery**  ABNORMAL PSYCHOLOGY, 7/E
©2012    9780205037438 / 0205037437

**Meyer & Chapman & Weaver**  CASE STUDIES IN
ABNORMAL BEHAVIOR, 9/E
©2012    9780205036998 / 0205036996

## Adjustment

**Duffy, Kirsh & Atwater**  PSYCHOLOGY FOR LIVING:
ADJUSTMENT, GROWTH AND BEHAVIOR, 10/E
©2011    9780205790364 / 0205790364

## Adolescent Development

**Arnett**  ADOLESCENCE AND EMERGING ADULTHOOD:
A CULTURAL APPROACH, 4/E
©2010    9780138144586 / 0138144583

**Dolgin**  THE ADOLESCENT, 13/E
©2011    9780205731367 / 0205731368

**Garrod, Smulyan, Powers & Kilkenny**  ADOLESCENT
PORTRAITS: IDENTITY, RELATIONSHIPS, AND
CHALLENGES, 7/E
©2012    9780205036233 / 0205036236

## Adulthood & Aging

**Bjorklund**  JOURNEY OF ADULTHOOD, 7/E
©2011    9780205018055 / 020501805X

**Mason**  ADULTHOOD AND AGING
©2011    9780205433513 / 0205433510

## Behavior Modification

**Martin & Pear**  BEHAVIOR MODIFICATION, 9/W
©2011    9780205792726 / 0205792723

## Biopsychology / Behavioral Neuroscience

**Pinel**  BIOPSYCHOLOGY, 8/E
©2011    9780205832569 / 0205832563

## Child Development (Chronological Approach)

**Feldman**  CHILD DEVELOPMENT, 6/E
©2012    9780205253548 / 0205253547

## Child Development (Topical Apprh)

**Kail**  CHILDREN AND THEIR DEVELOPMENT, 6/E
©2012    9780205034949 / 0205034942

**Boyd**  THE DEVELOPING CHILD, 13/E
©2012    9780205256020 / 0205256023

## Clinical Psychology

**Lilienfeld & O'Donohue**  GREAT READINGS IN
CLINICAL SCIENCE
©2012    9780205698035 / 0205698034

**Linden & Hewitt**  CLINICAL PSYCHOLOGY
©2012    9780132397278 / 0132397277

## Close Relationships / Interpersonal

**Erber & Erber**  INTIMATE RELATIONSHIPS: ISSUES,
THEORIES, AND RESEARCH, 2/E
©2011    9780205454464 / 0205454461

## Cognition

**Levitin**  FOUNDATIONS OF COGNITIVE PSYCHOLOGY:
CORE READINGS, 2/E
©2011    9780205711475 / 0205711472

**Robinson-Riegler**  COGNITIVE PSYCHOLOGY: APPLYING THE
SCIENCE OF THE MIND, 3/E
©2012    9780205033645 / 0205033644

## Cross-Cultural / Multicultural Psychology

**Parham, Ajamu & White**  PSYCHOLOGY OF BLACKS, 4/E
©2011    9780131827738 / 0131827731

## Drugs and Behavior

**Ettinger**  PSYCHOPHARMACOLOGY
©2011    9780136013068 / 0136013066

**Levinthal**  DRUGS, BEHAVIOR, AND MODERN SOCIETY, 7/E
©2012    9780205037261 / 0205037267

**Grilly**  DRUGS AND HUMAN BEHAVIOR, 6/E
©2012    9780205750528 / 0205750524

## Gender

**Helgeson**  PSYCHOLOGY OF GENDER, 4/E
©2012    9780205050185 / 0205050182

## Health Psychology

**Ragin**  HEALTH PSYCHOLOGY
©2011    9780131962972 / 0131962973

## Human Sexuality

**King**  HUMAN SEXUALITY TODAY, 7/E
©2012    9780205015672 / 0205015670

**Hock**  HUMAN SEXUALITY, 3/E
©2012    9780205225682 / 0205225683

## Infant Development

**Gross**  INFANCY: FROM BIRTH TO AGE 3, 2/E
©2011    9780205734191 / 0205734197

## Introductory Psychology

**Ciccarelli & White**  PSYCHOLOGY, 3/E
©2012    9780205832576 / 0205832571

**Wade & Tavris**  PSYCHOLOGY, 10/E
©2011    9780205711468 / 0205711464

**Zimbardo**  THE WORLD OF PSYCHOLOGY, 7/E
©2011    9780205215133 / 0205215130